ADDISON-WESLEY SECONDARY MATH

Focus on Geometry

AN INTEGRATED APPROACH

ALAN R. HOFFER
ROBERTA KOSS
Jerry D. Beckmann • Phillip E. Duren • Julia L. Hernandez
Beth M. Schlesinger • Catherine Wiehe

PROGRAM CONCEPTUALIZERS

Barbara Alcala
Randall I. Charles
John A. Dossey
Betty M. Foxx
Alan R. Hoffer
Roberta Koss
Sid Rachlin
Freddie L. Renfro
Cathy L. Seeley
Charles B. Vonder Embse

Scott Foresman
Addison Wesley

Editorial Offices: Menlo Park, California • Glenview, Illinois
Sales Offices: Reading, Massachusetts • Atlanta, Georgia •
Glenview, Illinois • Carrollton, Texas • Menlo Park, California

1-800-552-2259
http://www.sf.aw.com

Cover images

Front

Armillary (predecessor to the astrolabe) from the Vatican/ Black, Mary (Navajo/Paiute). Wedding Basket. 1989. Museum of Northern Arizona.

Back

Top left: Photo of financial district, Toronto, Ontario/ Klee, Paul. Castle and Sun. 1928. Private Collection, London, Great Britain. *Top right:* Kabotie, Michael (Hopi). Kachina Song Poetry. 1985. Acrylic on canvas/ Photo of circuit board. *Bottom left:* Armillary (predecessor to the astrolabe) from the Vatican/ Black, Mary (Navajo/Paiute). Wedding Basket. 1989. Museum of Northern Arizona. *Bottom right:* Italian ceramic tile/ Fractal from the Mandelbrot Set.

Printed in the United States of America.

ISBN 0-201-86970-5

1 2 3 4 5 6 7 8 9 10 – VH – 99 98 97

PROGRAM CONCEPTUALIZERS

Barbara Alcala
Whittier High School
Whittier, California

Randall I. Charles
San Jose State University
San Jose, California

John A. Dossey
Illinois State University
Normal, Illinois

Betty M. Foxx
Collins High School
Chicago, Illinois

Alan R. Hoffer
University of California
Irvine, California

Roberta Koss
Redwood High School
Larkspur, California

Sid Rachlin
East Carolina University
Greenville, North Carolina

Freddie L. Renfro
Goose Creek Independent
School District
Baytown, Texas

Cathy L. Seeley
(Formerly) Texas
Education Agency
Austin, Texas

Charles B. Vonder Embse
Central Michigan University
Mt. Pleasant, Michigan

FOCUS ON GEOMETRY AUTHORS

Alan R. Hoffer
Lead author
University of California
Irvine, California

Roberta Koss
Associate lead author
Redwood High School
Larkspur, California

Jerry D. Beckmann
East High School
Lincoln, Nebraska

Phillip E. Duren
California State University
Hayward, California

Julia L. Hernandez
Rosemead High School
Rosemead, California

Beth M. Schlesinger
San Diego High School
San Diego, California

Catherine Wiehe
San Jose High Academy
San Jose, California

OTHER SERIES AUTHORS

Barbara Alcala
Whittier High School
Whittier, California

Penelope P. Booth
Baltimore County Public Schools
Towson, Maryland

Randall I. Charles
San Jose State University
San Jose, California

James R. Choike
Oklahoma State University
Stillwater, Oklahoma

David S. Daniels
Longmeadow High School
Longmeadow, Massachusetts

John A. Dossey
Illinois State University
Normal, Illinois

Trudi Hammel Garland
The Head-Royce School
Oakland, California

Pamela Patton Giles
Jordan School District
Sandy, Utah

Virginia Gray
South Medford High School
Medford, Oregon

Howard C. Johnson
Syracuse University
Syracuse, New York

Stephen E. Moresh
City College of New York
(Formerly) Seward Park
High School
New York, New York

J. Irene Murphy
North Slope Borough
School District
Barrow, Alaska

Andy Reeves
Florida Department of Education
Tallahassee, Florida

Kathy A. Ross
(Formerly) Jefferson Parish
Public School System
Harvey, Louisiana

Cathy L. Seeley
(Formerly) Texas
Education Agency
Austin, Texas

Alba González Thompson
(In memoriam)

Charles B. Vonder Embse
Central Michigan University
Mt. Pleasant, Michigan

Sheryl M. Yamada
Beverly Hills High School
Beverly Hills, California

CONSULTANTS AND REVIEWERS

CONTENT REVIEWERS

Bridget Arvold
University of Georgia
Athens, Georgia

Paul G. Dillenberger
Franklin Middle School
Minneapolis, Minnesota

Catherine Y. Figuracion
San Pedro High School
San Pedro, California

Donald Hastings
Stratford Public Schools
Stratford, Connecticut

Melanie Hildreth
Walnut High School
Walnut, California

Jim Velo
West High School
Columbus, Ohio

Joanne Wainscott
Mission Bay High School
San Diego, California

Denise Walston
Maury High School
Norfolk, Virginia

Dr. Art W. Wilson
Abraham Lincoln High School
Denver, Colorado

MULTICULTURAL REVIEWERS

LaVerne Bitsie
Oklahoma State University
Stillwater, Oklahoma

Claudette Bradley
University of Alaska
Fairbanks, Alaska

Yolanda De La Cruz
Arizona State University West
Phoenix, Arizona

Genevieve Lau
Skyline College
San Bruno, California

William Tate
University of Wisconsin
Madison, Wisconsin

INDUSTRY CONSULTANTS

Joseph M. Cahalen
Xerox Corporation
Stamford, Connecticut

Clare DeYonker
AMATECH
Bingham Farms, Michigan

Harry Garland
Cannon Research Center
America, Inc.
Palo Alto, California

Timothy M. Schwalm, Sr.
Eastman Kodak Company
Rochester, New York

Diane Sotos
Maxim Integrated Products
Sunnyvale, California

Earl R. Westerlund
Eastman Kodak Company
Rochester, New York

Charles Young
General Electric Research and
Development Center
Schenectady, New York

John Zils
Skidmore, Owings & Merrill
Chicago, Illinois

Table of Contents

Getting Started: What Do YOU Think?			**i**
	Part A	Working Together	**ii**
	Part B	Solving Problems	**iv**
	Part C	Making Connections	**vi**
CHAPTER 1	**Visual Thinking and Mathematical Models**		**2**
	1-1	**Using Familiar Models**	**5**
	Part A	Geometric Models	**6**
	Part B	Algebraic Models	**11**
	Part C	Making Connections	**16**
	1-2	**Reasoning and Logic**	**19**
	Part A	Inductive Reasoning	**20**
	Part B	The Language of Logic	**25**
	Part C	Deductive Reasoning	**30**
	Part D	Making Connections	**36**
	1-3	**Measuring Figures**	**39**
	Part A	Measuring Segments	**40**
	Part B	Measuring Angles	**45**
	Part C	Congruence	**52**
	Part D	Making Connections	**58**
	1-4	**Symmetry and Reflections**	**61**
	Part A	Symmetry	**62**
	Part B	Reflections	**67**
	Part C	Properties of Reflections	**73**
	Part D	Making Connections	**77**
CHAPTER 1	**Review** *(Key Terms, Concepts and Applications, Concepts and Connections, Self-Evaluation)*		**80**
CHAPTER 1	**Assessment** *(Test, Performance Task)*		**82**
CHAPTER 2	**The Foundations of Geometry**		**84**
	2-1	**The Need for Precise Language**	**87**
	Part A	Conditional Statements	**88**
	Part B	Related Conditional Statements	**94**
	Part C	The Rules of Logic	**99**
	Part D	Making Connections	**104**

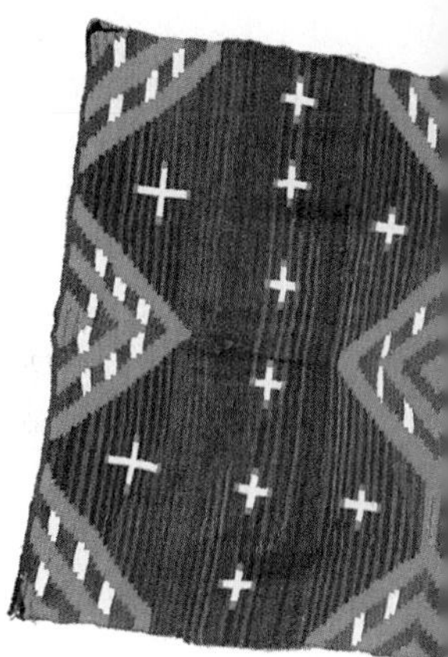

2-2	**Stating Our Assumptions**	**107**
Part A	Undefined Terms and Definitions	**108**
Part B	Postulates	**114**
Part C	Working in a Deductive System	**119**
Part D	Making Connections	**126**
2-3	**Drawing Techniques and Parallel Lines**	**129**
Part A	Perspective Drawing	**130**
Part B	Orthographic and Isometric Drawing	**135**
Part C	Parallel Lines and Planes	**141**
Part D	Making Connections	**146**
CHAPTER 2	**Review** *(Key Terms, Concepts and Applications, Concepts and Connections, Self-Evaluation)*	**149**
CHAPTER 2	**Assessment** *(Test, Performance Task)*	**150**

CHAPTER 3	**Angles and Parallel Lines**	**152**
3-1	**Angles and Navigation**	**155**
Part A	More About Rays and Angles	**156**
Part B	Bearings	**161**
Part C	Vectors	**165**
Part D	Translations	**171**
Part E	Making Connections	**176**
3-2	**Rotations**	**179**
Part A	Rotational Symmetry	**180**
Part B	Rotations	**185**
Part C	Making Connections	**189**
3-3	**Precise Thinking with Angles**	**191**
Part A	Postulates About Angles	**192**
Part B	Assumptions and Figures	**197**
Part C	Angle Pairs	**201**
Part D	Vertical Angles and Angle Bisectors	**207**
Part E	Making Connections	**212**
3-4	**Parallel Lines and Transversals**	**215**
Part A	Transversals and Angles	**216**
Part B	Parallel Lines, Transversals, and Angles	**221**
Part C	Proving Lines Parallel	**226**
Part D	Making Connections	**231**
CHAPTER 3	**Review** *(Key Terms, Concepts and Applications, Concepts and Connections, Self-Evaluation)*	**233**
CHAPTER 3	**Assessment** *(Test, Performance Task)*	**235**

CHAPTER 4 **Triangles** 238

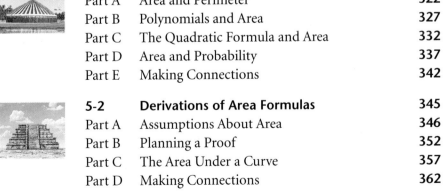

4-1 **Tessellations and Triangles** 241
Part A Angles Inside the Triangle 242
Part B Angles Outside the Triangle 247
Part C Making Connections 252

4-2 **Deductive Proof with Triangles** 255
Part A Correspondence and Congruence 256
Part B Congruent Triangles 260
Part C Organizing a Proof 266
Part D Corresponding Parts 274
Part E Making Connections 281

4-3 **Properties of Special Triangles** 285
Part A Isosceles Triangles 286
Part B Right Triangles 292
Part C Perpendiculars, Bisectors, and Locus 299
Part D Lines Associated with Triangles 304
Part E Making Connections 310

CHAPTER 4 **Review** *(Key Terms, Concepts and Applications, Concepts and Connections, Self-Evaluation)* 314

CHAPTER 4 **Assessment** *(Test, Performance Task)* 316

CHAPTER 5 **Area** 318

5-1 **Understanding and Applying Area** 321
Part A Area and Perimeter 322
Part B Polynomials and Area 327
Part C The Quadratic Formula and Area 332
Part D Area and Probability 337
Part E Making Connections 342

5-2 **Derivations of Area Formulas** 345
Part A Assumptions About Area 346
Part B Planning a Proof 352
Part C The Area Under a Curve 357
Part D Making Connections 362

5-3	**The Pythagorean Theorem**	**365**
Part A	The Pythagorean Theorem	366
Part B	Special Right Triangles	370
Part C	The Distance Formula Revisited	376
Part D	The Converse of the Pythagorean Theorem	380
Part E	Making Connections	385

CHAPTER 5 **Review** *(Key Terms, Concepts and Applications, Concepts and Connections, Self-Evaluation)* **388**

CHAPTER 5 **Assessment** *(Test, Performance Task)* **390**

CHAPTER 6 **Polygons and Polyhedrons** **392**

6-1	**Polygons and Polyhedrons**	**395**
Part A	Exploring Quadrilaterals	396
Part B	Exploring Polygons	402
Part C	Exploring Polyhedrons	409
Part D	Making Connections	414
6-2	**Deductive Proof with Quadrilaterals**	**417**
Part A	Proofs with Parallelograms	418
Part B	Proving Quadrilaterals Are Parallelograms	423
Part C	Proofs with Special Parallelograms	427
Part D	Quadrilaterals and Coordinate Proof	433
Part E	Making Connections	438
6-3	**Regular Polygons and Polyhedrons**	**441**
Part A	Regular Polygons	442
Part B	Regular Polyhedrons	448
Part C	Making Connections	452

CHAPTER 6 **Review** *(Key Terms, Concepts and Applications, Concepts and Connections, Self-Evaluation)* **455**

CHAPTER 6 **Assessment** *(Test, Performance Task)* **456**

CHAPTER 7 **Similarity** **458**

7-1 **Similar Figures** **461**
Part A Changing the Size of Figures **462**
Part B Similar Polygons **468**
Part C Areas and Perimeters of Similar Polygons **473**
Part D Golden Rectangles **478**
Part E Making Connections **482**

7-2 **Properties of Similar Figures** **485**
Part A Similar Triangles **486**
Part B SAS Similarity **491**
Part C Dilations **496**
Part D Triangle Midsegments **501**
Part E Making Connections **507**

7-3 **Trigonometry** **511**
Part A Trigonometric Ratios **512**
Part B Angles of Elevation and Depression **518**
Part C Vectors and Trigonometry **523**
Part D Making Connections **528**

CHAPTER 7 **Review** *(Key Terms, Concepts and Applications, Concepts and Connections, Self-Evaluation)* **531**

CHAPTER 7 **Assessment** *(Test, Performance Task)* **534**

CHAPTER 8 **Circles and Spheres** **536**

8-1 **Circles, Circumference, and Area** **539**
Part A Inscribed and Circumscribed Figures **540**
Part B Circles and Tangent Lines **544**
Part C The Circumference of a Circle **550**
Part D The Area of a Circle **555**
Part E Making Connections **560**

8-2	**Angles, Arcs, and Chords**	**563**
Part A	Arcs and Central Angles	**564**
Part B	Arc Length and Sectors	**570**
Part C	Radius-Chord Conjectures	**574**
Part D	Making Connections	**580**
8-3	**The Inscribed Angle Theorem**	**583**
Part A	Inscribed Angles	**584**
Part B	Angles Formed by Secants and Tangents	**588**
Part C	Making Connections	**594**

CHAPTER 8 **Review** *(Key Terms, Concepts and Applications, Concepts and Connections, Self-Evaluation)* **597**

CHAPTER 8 **Assessment** *(Test, Performance Task)* **599**

CHAPTER 9 **Surface Area and Volume** **600**

9-1	**Surface Area**	**603**
Part A	Surface Area of Prisms	**604**
Part B	Surface Area of Pyramids	**610**
Part C	Surface Area of Cylinders and Cones	**614**
Part D	Making Connections	**620**
9-2	**Volume**	**623**
Part A	Volume of Prisms	**624**
Part B	Volume of Pyramids	**630**
Part C	Volume of Cylinders and Cones	**635**
Part D	Surface Area and Volume of Spheres	**639**
Part E	Making Connections	**644**
9-3	**Similar Solids**	**647**
Part A	Surface Area of Similar Solids	**648**
Part B	Volume of Similar Solids	**653**
Part C	Making Connections	**657**

CHAPTER 9 **Review** *(Key Terms, Concepts and Applications, Concepts and Connections, Self-Evaluation)* **661**

CHAPTER 9 **Assessment** *(Test, Performance Task)* **663**

CHAPTER 10 Transformations and Patterns 664

10-1 Putting Transformations Together 667
Part A Isometries 668
Part B Compositions of Transformations 673
Part C Transformations of Algebraic Functions 679
Part D Making Connections 683

10-2 Classifying Patterns 687
Part A Frieze Patterns 688
Part B Wallpaper Patterns 694
Part C Making Connections 700

CHAPTER 10 Review *(Key Terms, Concepts and Applications, Concepts and Connections, Self-Evaluation)* 703

CHAPTER 10 Assessment *(Test, Performance Task)* 705

CHAPTER 11 Geometric Inequalities and Optimization 706

11-1 Indirect Reasoning and Inequalities 709
Part A Indirect Reasoning 710
Part B Inequalities in a Triangle 714
Part C The Triangle Inequality Theorem 720
Part D Making Connections 724

11-2 Optimization 727
Part A Optimizing Areas and Perimeters 728
Part B Optimizing Volumes and Surface Areas 734
Part C Making Connections 740

CHAPTER 11 Review *(Key Terms, Concepts and Applications, Concepts and Connections, Self-Evaluation)* 743

CHAPTER 11 Assessment *(Test, Performance Task)* 744

CHAPTER 12 Astronomy and Geometric Models 746

12-1 Using Geometry to Model the Earth 749
Part A Fractals 750
Part B Longitude and Latitude 756
Part C Measurement in Astronomy 762
Part D Making Connections 768

12-2 Euclidean and Non-Euclidean Geometries 771
Part A Euclidean Geometry 772
Part B Non-Euclidean Geometry 777
Part C Making Connections 782

CHAPTER 12 Review (*Key Terms, Concepts and Applications, Concepts and Connections, Self-Evaluation*) 786

CHAPTER 12 Assessment (*Test, Performance Task*) 788

REFERENCE CENTER

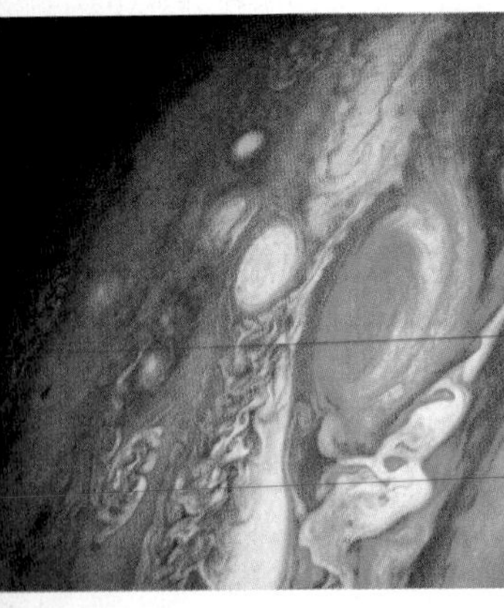

Additional Lessons
- Proof Skills and Strategies 789
- Graphing Linear Equations 796
- Three-Dimensional Coordinate System 798
- Overlapping Triangles 800
- Compound Loci 803
- Geometric Means and Right Triangles 805
- Segments of Chords, Tangents, and Secants 808
- Hinge Theorem 811

Spiral Review 813
Symbols 837
Formulas 838
Postulates and Theorems 839
Glossary 846
Selected Answers 856
Credits 881
Index 883

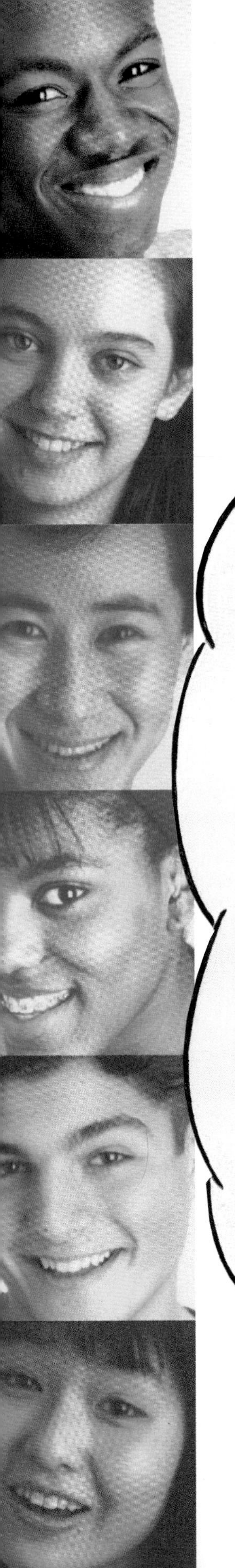

Getting Started

What Do YOU Think

In the twenty-first century, computers will do a lot of the work that people used to do. Even in today's workplace, there is little need for someone to add up daily invoices or compute sales tax. Engineers and scientists already use computer programs to do calculations and solve equations. By the twenty-first century, a whole new set of skills will be needed by almost everyone in the work force.

Some important skills for the twenty-first century will be the ability to think creatively about mathematics and to reason logically. It will also be important to work as a team member and to be able to explain your thinking. Although it will still be necessary to be able to do computations, it will become increasingly necessary to analyze problems and determine the most appropriate way to solve them. After all, what good is it to solve an equation if it is the wrong equation?

This course will help you to develop many of the skills you will need for the future. On the way, you will see the value of creative thinking. The students shown here will be sharing their ideas throughout this book. But the key question will always be "What do YOU think?"

1. Why do you need to take this math class?
2. In your last math class, what was the most interesting or useful thing you learned?
3. What are some job skills that you have (or can learn) that will make it difficult to replace you with a computer?

PART A Working Together

← CONNECT →

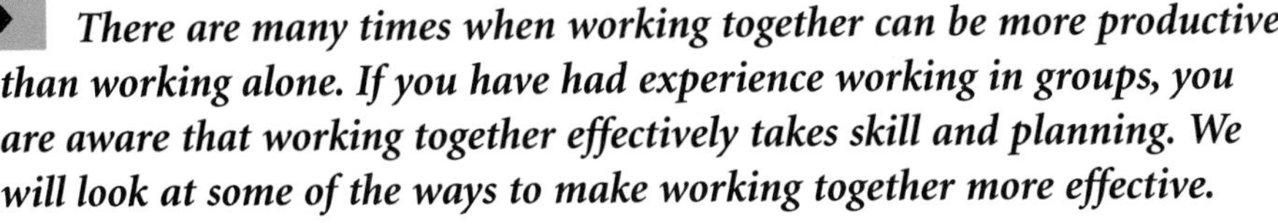

There are many times when working together can be more productive than working alone. If you have had experience working in groups, you are aware that working together effectively takes skill and planning. We will look at some of the ways to make working together more effective.

Working as a team member is an important skill in today's workplace. Many industries assign teams of employees to work on projects. Each employee brings a different skill to the team. Teamwork is also important in other situations. For example, in organizing a school fund-raiser, each person on the committee may have a specific role.

Working in a group can also make learning more productive and enjoyable. In order to work together, you must be able to communicate clearly with your group members.

1. **What does it mean to communicate?**
2. **How can everyone in a group be encouraged to participate?**
3. **When you're working in a group, when should you ask the teacher for help?**

In the following Explore, you will have a chance to work with your classmates. Be sure to pay attention to how well your group is working as a team!

EXPLORE: FIGURE IT OUT!

Figures such as the ones shown here are an important part of a geometry textbook.

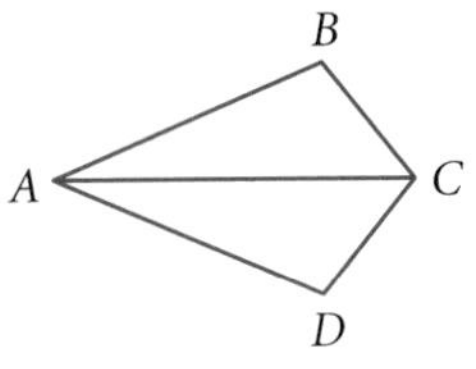

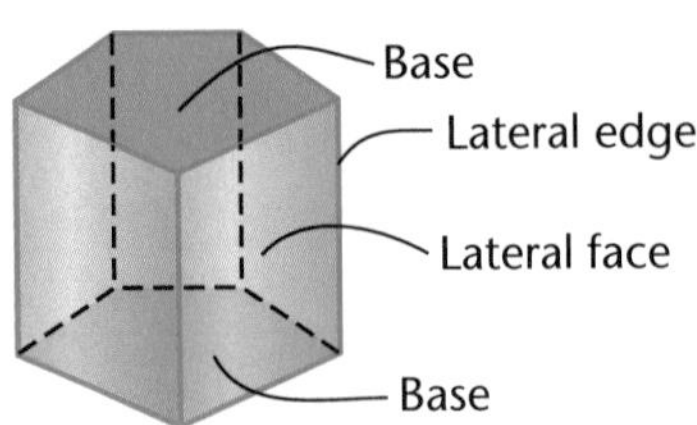

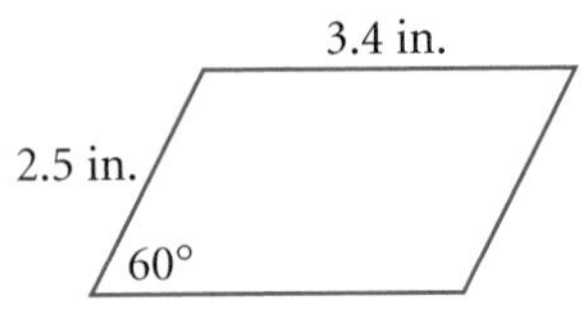

1. Work in a group to estimate how many such figures are contained in this book.
2. Does everyone in your group agree with the final estimate? Why or why not?
3. Compare your group's estimate with those of other groups. Were your estimates very different? Do you want to revise your estimate?

Working in a group can be an exciting way to learn mathematics. Throughout this course, you will have many opportunities to team up with your classmates.

REFLECT

1. Develop a list of at least five rules for successful cooperative groups. These rules should address any problems you may have had working in a group in the preceding Explore.
2. Describe some ways in which working in a group may be helpful to you throughout this course.

Exercises

1. Describe a situation in which you were part of a team (for example, a club or a sports team). What were the advantages and disadvantages of being part of this group? Were you able to do things with the group that you couldn't have done individually?

The following figures all occur elsewhere in this textbook. Using what you already know about geometry, describe each figure as best you can. (You will learn more about each figure later.)

2.

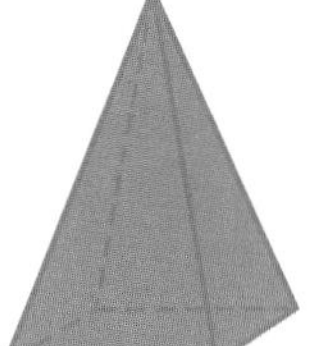

3.

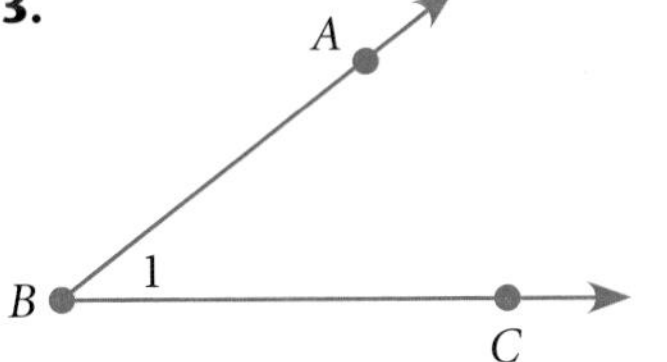

4.

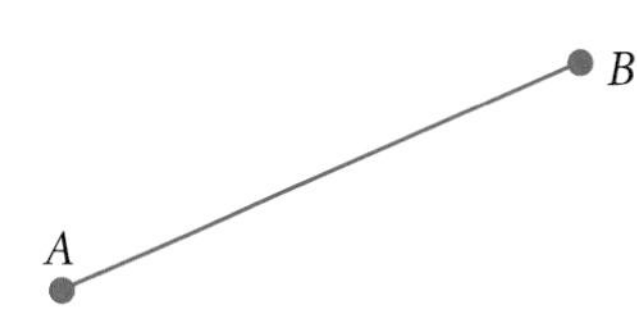

5.

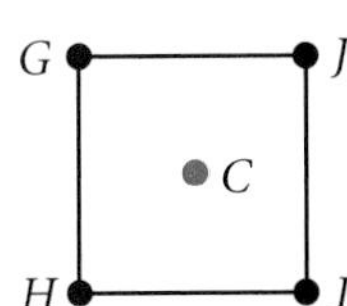

6.

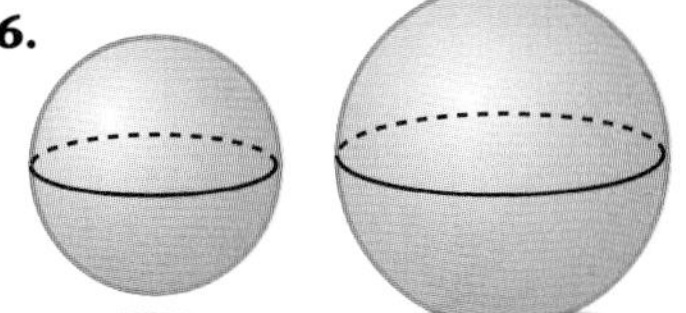

7.

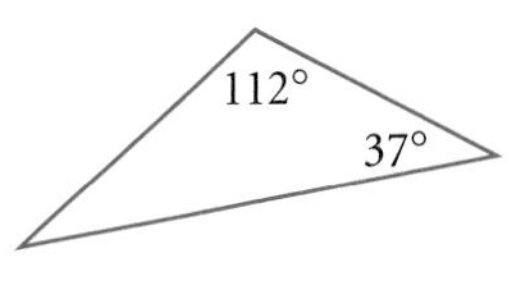

PART B Solving Problems

← CONNECT → ***You have solved many mathematical problems before taking this class, and you have probably already used some type of problem-solving guidelines and strategies. All of these strategies and techniques can be used in this class.***

Problem solving does not mean just finding the answer to a problem in a math book! All through our lives we are presented with new and challenging problems. Learning to think critically and creatively gives us the ability (mathematical and otherwise) to solve the problems we encounter.

1. **What are some different strategies you have used to solve problems?**
2. **If you do not immediately understand a problem, what are some things you can do to help get started?**

Whenever the solution to a problem is not immediately apparent, it may be helpful to follow some guidelines and questions for problem solving, such as the ones listed below.

PROBLEM-SOLVING GUIDELINES

Understand the Problem	**Develop a Plan**
What is the situation all about? What are you trying to find out? What are the key data/conditions? What are the assumptions?	Have you ever worked a similar problem before? Will you estimate or calculate? What strategies can you use?
Implement the Plan	**Look Back**
What is the solution? Did you interpret correctly? Did you calculate correctly? Did you answer the question?	Could you work the problem another way? Is there another solution? Is the answer reasonable?

EXPLORE: GETTING SQUARED AWAY

1. How many squares are contained in the figure at the right? (Be sure to consider squares of various sizes.)

Problem-Solving Tip

Make a table.

2. Describe the process you used to solve this problem. Is there anything you might have done differently? If so, what?

Have you ever had the feeling of a light bulb going on when you made a new discovery or solved a challenging problem? This book is dedicated to that rewarding "aha!" feeling. We hope many light bulbs will go on as you use this textbook.

REFLECT

1. You may have used the strategy of making a table in the preceding Explore. List some other common strategies for solving problems.
2. Can you think of anything to add to the Problem-Solving Guidelines on the preceding page? If so, describe a situation in which your suggestion might be useful.

Exercises

1. **a.** Farmer McDonald raises cows and ducks. He is standing in his field and sees 9 heads and 26 feet. How many ducks and how many cows does Farmer McDonald have?
   b. Describe the process you used to solve this problem.
2. The figure at the right shows the water level of a bathtub over time. Write a short paragraph to describe what might have occurred.

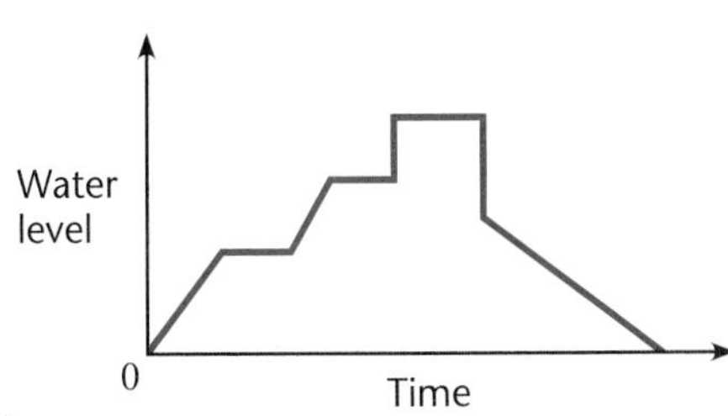

3. What is the maximum number of pieces into which a circular pizza can be cut with 4 straight cuts? (The pieces cannot be moved or stacked after cuts are made.)

PART C Making Connections

← CONNECT → ***You have seen how to use problem-solving guidelines to help you solve problems, and you have practiced working in a group. Now you will use these skills as we look at other important techniques.***

As you use this book, you will have many opportunities to work in groups (in Explore activities) and many opportunities to practice what you have learned (in Try It activities). You will also look at how the topics you learn are connected to each other, and you will see how mathematics is connected to other things.

Another important component of this book is a feature called What Do YOU Think? There is often more than one correct way to approach a problem. The students you have been introduced to on page *i* will be sharing their thinking throughout this book. You may find that you agree with their thinking, or you may have your own ideas.

WHAT DO YOU THINK?

Describe the connection between the equation on the left and the figure on the right.

$y = 3x + 2$

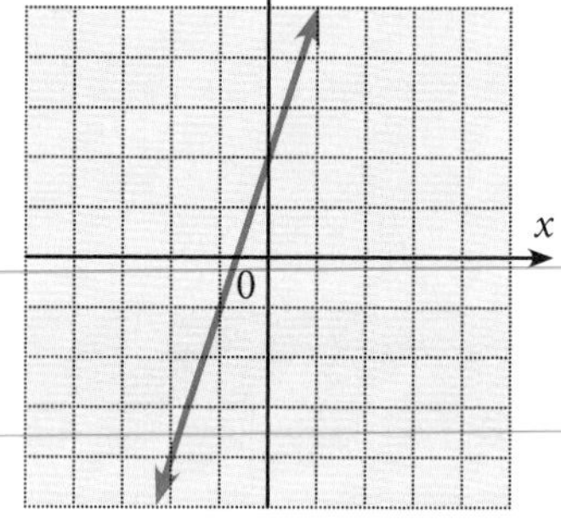

Henry Thinks . . .

I can make a table of values for the equation $y = 3x + 2$. If I plot these points, they will lie on a straight line. The line is the one shown in the graph.

x	*y*
−1	−1
0	2
1	5

Heather Thinks . . .

The equation is in the form $y = mx + b$. The value of m is 3, and this is the slope of the graph of the equation. The value of b is 2, and this means that the y-intercept of the graph is 2. If I put those two things together, I get the line in the figure.

1. Do you agree with Heather and Henry's thinking? Can you think of another way to describe the connection between the equation and the graph on the preceding page?

You will often be asked to explain your thinking. As you study geometry, you may find that *how* you communicate your thoughts is as important as getting the "right answer."

REFLECT

1. Describe two different methods for solving a problem that you studied in a previous course. Discuss the advantages or disadvantages of each method.
2. Why do you think it is important to understand the connections between mathematics and other disciplines?
3. Why do you think it is important to understand the connections between different subjects within mathematics?

Exercises

1. Describe the connection between the figure below left and the figure on the right.

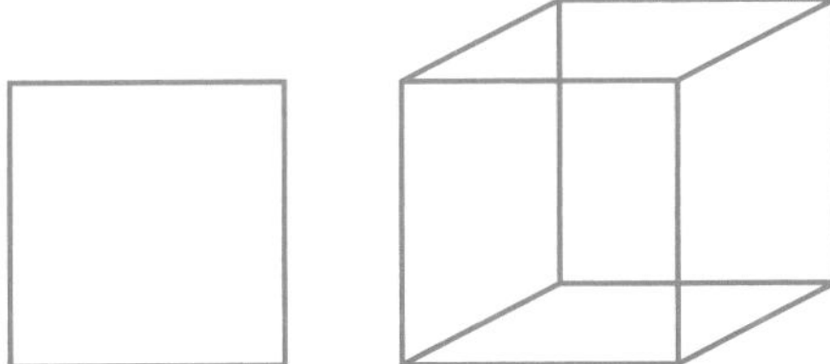

2. Write a short paragraph describing the optical illusion shown at the right.

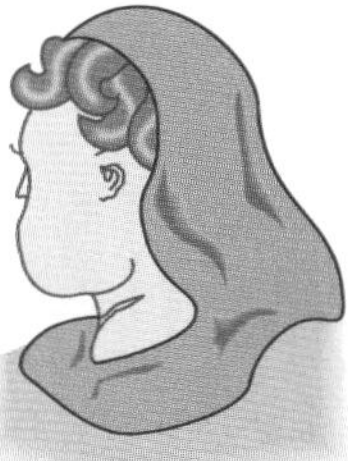

3. There is an important connection between geometry and language. Make a chart that illustrates basic geometric figures. For each figure, include a sketch as well as a brief written description of the figure. If you know the names of the figures, be sure to include them.

Chapter 1 Visual Thinking and Mathematical Models

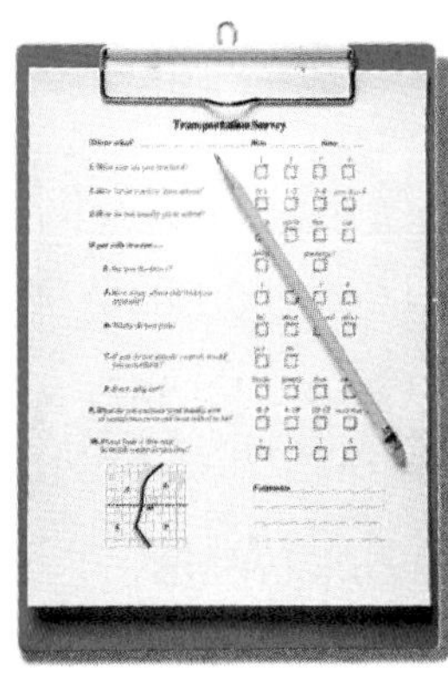

Project A
May I Have a Moment of Your Time?
Did you ever take part in a survey? Who decides what questions will be asked?

Project B
How Do You Get There From Here?
How are city maps made? How are they different from other maps?

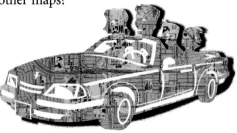

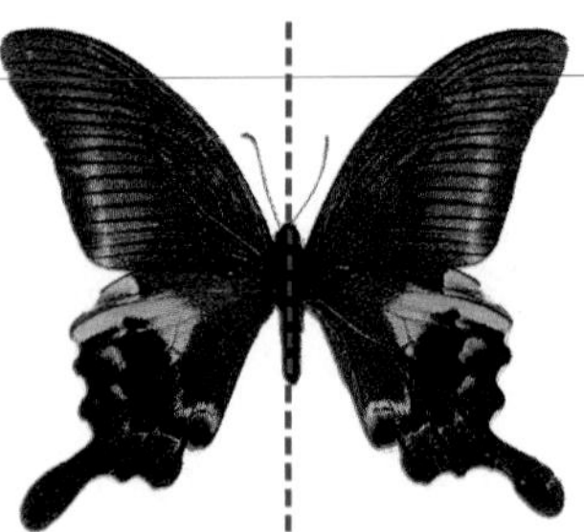

Project C
Let Nature Unfold
How does nature mirror itself? Why don't you have two left feet?

ANN GREENWAY

I was not good at math in high school, so I got very frustrated. I thought I would need math only for personal things, like paying bills.

Now I conduct surveys on drug use in schools. I organize the results using technology. I use the displays in teacher training programs. Our world demands increasing communication and technology. Math is critical in both of these areas.

Ann Greenway
Drug Free Schools and Communities Administrator
Louisiana State Department of Education
Baton Rouge, Louisiana

Ann Greenway

Chapter 1 Getting Ready

Visual Thinking and Mathematical Models

1-1 Geometric Models

In 1-1 you will create algebraic and geometric models. You will use the following skills from previous courses.

Name and describe each geometric shape. [Previous course]

1. **2.** **3.** **4.**

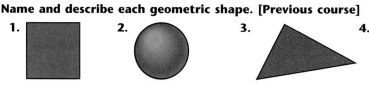

Graph these lines on a coordinate plane. [Previous course]

5. $y = 3x + 1$ **6.** $y = -2x + 4$ **7.** $y = 2 - x$ **8.** $5x + 3y = 6$

1-2 Reasoning and Logic

In 1-2 you will learn about inductive reasoning. You will need the following skills from previous courses.

Determine whether each statement is true or false. [Previous course]

9. If $3x = 4$, then $x = \frac{4}{3}$ **10.** If $x^2 = 9$, then $x = 3$

11. $(x + 2)^2 = x^2 + 4$

1-3 Measuring Figures

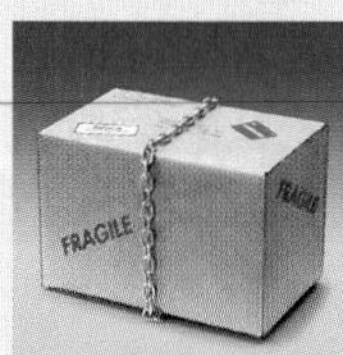

In 1-3 you will measure length by counting units or by using formulas. You will need the following skills from previous courses.

Solve. [Previous course]

12. $|5|$ **13.** $|-5 - 9|$ **14.** $\sqrt{25}$ **15.** $\sqrt{144}$

16. $\sqrt{3^2 + (-3)^2}$ **17.** $\sqrt{(5-2)^2 + (4-8)^2}$

18. $\sqrt{(10-5)^2 + (9-(-3))^2}$

1-4 Symmetry and Reflections

In 1-4 you will explore the patterns and balance of symmetrical figures. You will need the following skills from previous chapters and courses.

Copy and complete the mirror image of each figure. [Previous course]

19.

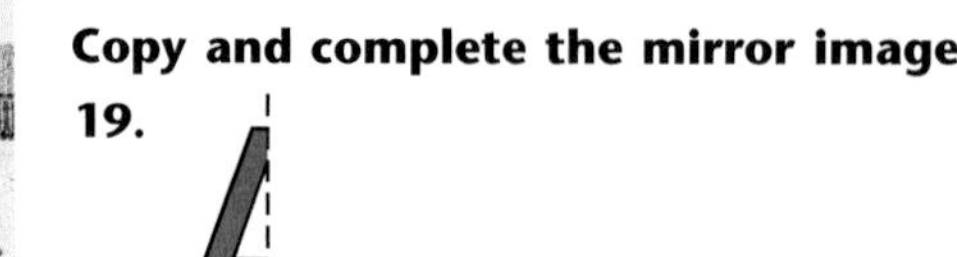

20.

1-1 Using Familiar Models

Do you recognize the globe above? It looks familiar, but we are used to seeing it in a different position. Maps and globes are usually shown with north at the top. When the position (or orientation) changes, it is difficult to recognize what region the map represents. You may need to orient yourself by finding familiar landmarks.

Maps and globes are models of the earth. One commonly used model is the Mercator projection. Mercator drew the earth as if it were a cylinder, not a sphere. The Mercator projection is useful for navigation, but it has problems with size distortion. The farther you move from the equator, the more distorted the map becomes! Canada is not twice the size of the United States, although it looks that way on Mercator's map.

In 1923, a "better" map was drawn by J. P. Goode at the University of Chicago. This earth model is not nearly as distorted as the Mercator projection. Goode's projection is like flattening an orange peel. Although Goode's projection shows accurate shapes, areas, and distances, people like their world without gaps. This "orange peel" projection has never been popular.

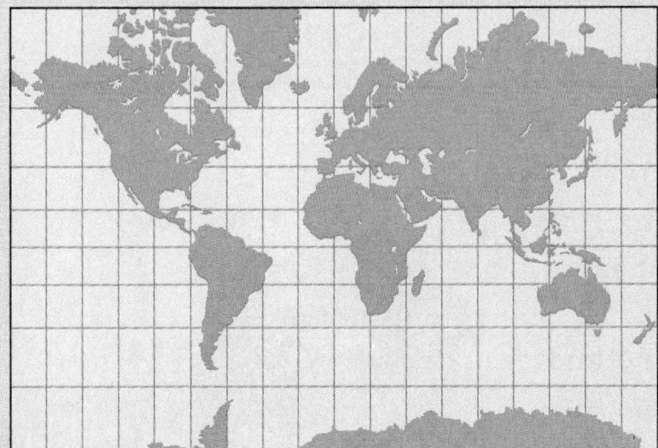

Mercator projection

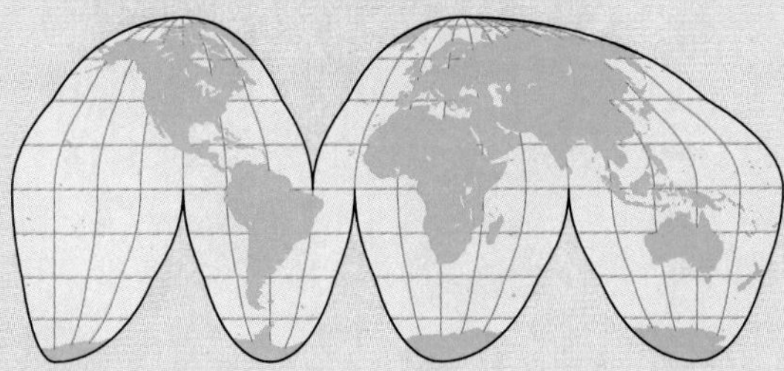

Goode's projection

1. **Why do you think it is difficult to represent the earth's surface on a flat map? How might this problem explain the distortions in Mercator's map?**
2. **A map and a globe are models of the earth. How do these models differ from the earth itself?**
3. **Which representation of the earth seems best — a map or a globe? Why?**

1-1 PART A Geometric Models

← CONNECT →

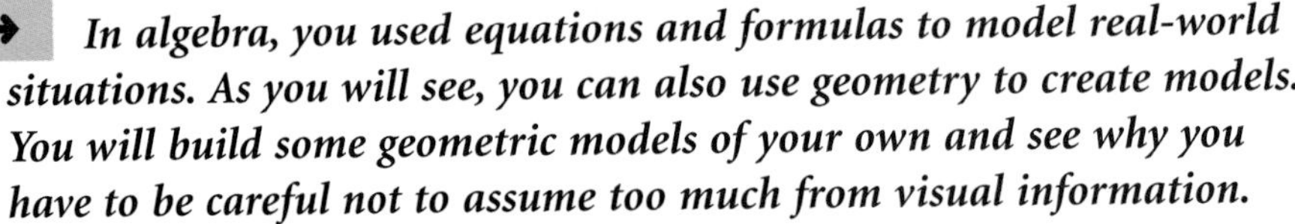

In algebra, you used equations and formulas to model real-world situations. As you will see, you can also use geometry to create models. You will build some geometric models of your own and see why you have to be careful not to assume too much from visual information.

Geometry involves the study of the properties of two-dimensional and three-dimensional figures. These figures can be used as mathematical models to help understand things as small as an atom or as large as a galaxy. Geometry also teaches methods of thinking that will help you to discover and justify the properties of these figures for yourself.

Geometry helps us to sort out visual information. In geometry, you must be careful not to assume too much from a picture or figure. Look at the photograph at the left. This San Francisco street has an unfamiliar orientation. The buildings look dangerously tilted. If one of them toppled, the domino effect could be devastating.

1. Why are the buildings in the photograph tilted?

When you see an optical illusion, your eyes seem to play tricks on your mind. Even your lifetime of experience doesn't help; in fact, it may sometimes confuse you. Optical illusions are fun, but they are also important reminders that we can't always trust our eyes.

M. C. Escher was an artist and mathematician who enjoyed creating optical illusions. In this lithograph titled *Ascending and Descending,* Escher created a building topped by a very interesting staircase.

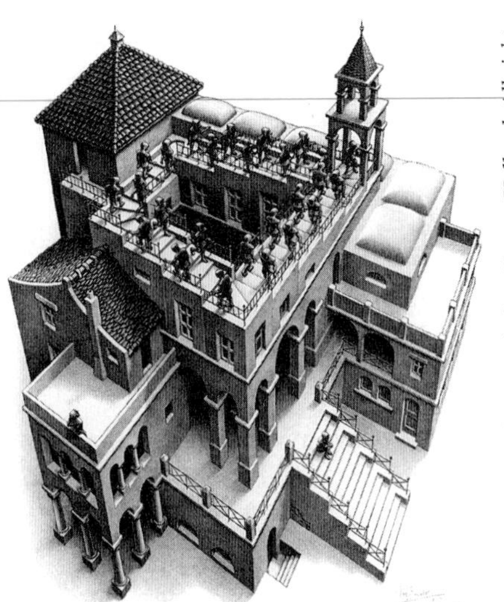

2. What is unusual about the staircase?
3. Is it possible to build a three-dimensional model of Escher's staircase? Explain your answer.

Models can give people a clearer understanding of a real-world object, idea, or phenomenon. A **mathematical model** uses geometry, algebra, or other mathematical tools to represent an idea or concept in the real world. These representations include figures, equations, graphs, and computer programs.

Some people spike volleyballs over nets. Mathematicians use nets to build and model geometric figures. A **net** is a pattern that can be cut out and folded into a three-dimensional figure (sometimes called a *solid*). In the following Explore, you'll investigate different nets for a familiar solid.

EXPLORE: SHAPE UP!

MATERIALS

Ruler, Paper, Scissors, Tape

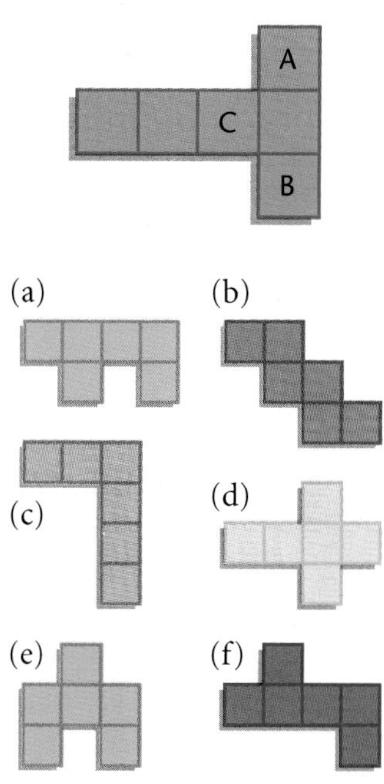

1. The T-shaped net at the right can be folded to create a solid. Carefully draw an enlarged version of the net.
   - Use a ruler to make sure that all sides are straight and the same length.
   - Use the corner of a rectangular sheet of paper to draw the corners.
   - Label squares A, B, and C.
   - Cut out your net. Fold up squares A and B. Fold up square C and tape it to A and B. Then fold up and tape the other squares. What figure do you get?
2. The T-shaped net is not the only one that folds into this figure. Which of the nets illustrated at the right can be used to create the same figure? Try to visualize the nets folded into this solid.
3. How many different nets are there for this solid? Sketch as many as you can. Discuss your results with your classmates.

Mathematical models come in many shapes and sizes. They can be flat (two-dimensional) or solid (three-dimensional). The common three-dimensional geometric figures below can be useful models. For example, the earth can be modeled by a sphere, a shoe box by a rectangular prism, and a juice can by a cylinder.

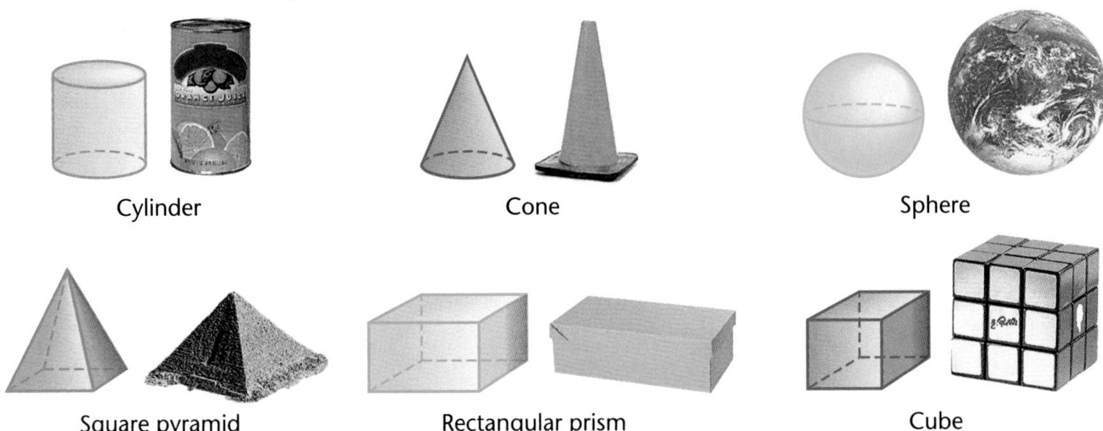

REFLECT

1. How many squares are needed in a net for a cube? How do you know?
2. Define *mathematical model* in your own words.
3. Geometry involves the study of figures like triangles, circles, pyramids, and cylinders. Describe something that could be modeled by one of those figures. Explain how understanding the figure might help you understand the real-world object.

Exercises

CORE

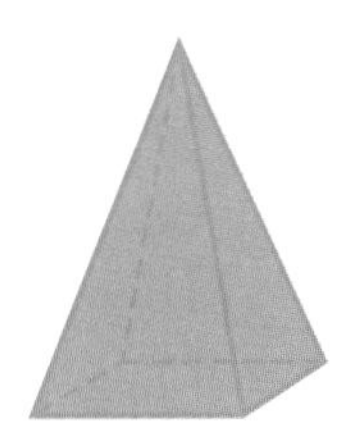

1. **Getting Started** Draw a net for a square pyramid as follows.
   a. Name all of the two-dimensional figures that are part of the net. How many of each are there?
   b. Sketch one of the figures as the "base" of your net.
   c. Identify the other figures that touch the base. Include these in your net, sketching them adjacent to the sides of the base.
   d. Check to see whether you are missing any of the figures listed in **1a**. (Sometimes the base of a three-dimensional figure will not touch all of the sides.) If any are missing, add them to the net.

2. Draw a net for the rectangular solid at the right.

3. How many vertices, edges, and faces does a cube have?

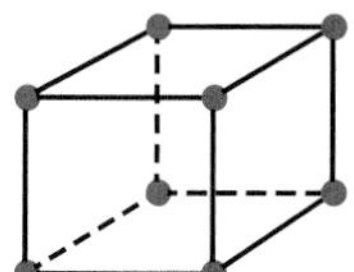

The corners of a cube are its *vertices.*

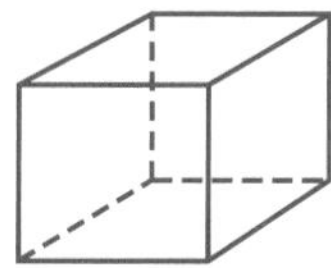

These are the *edges* of the cube.

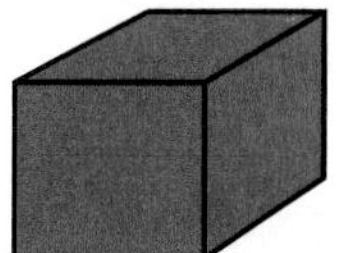

The sides of the cube are its *faces.*

4. Write the letter of the second pair that best matches the first pair.

Net: solid as (a) oak: tree, (b) wrapping: box, (c) cube: square, (d) coordinate: axis

5. Dot's Right Three different views of the same die are shown.

a. How many dots are opposite the one-dot side? the two-dot side? the three-dot side?

b. What is the sum of the dots on opposite sides of a die?

c. Sketch at least four differently shaped nets for a die. Include the dots. Be sure that the rule you found in **5b** applies when your nets are folded up.

d. What is the probability that a single roll of this die will give you a six? Explain.

6. Are the sides of the triangle straight or bent? What do you think causes this illusion?

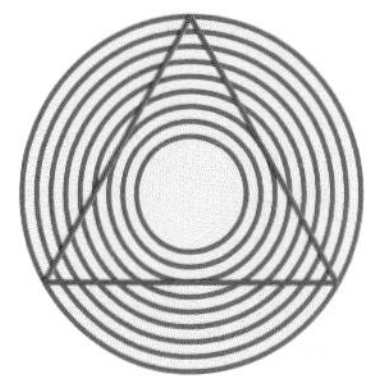

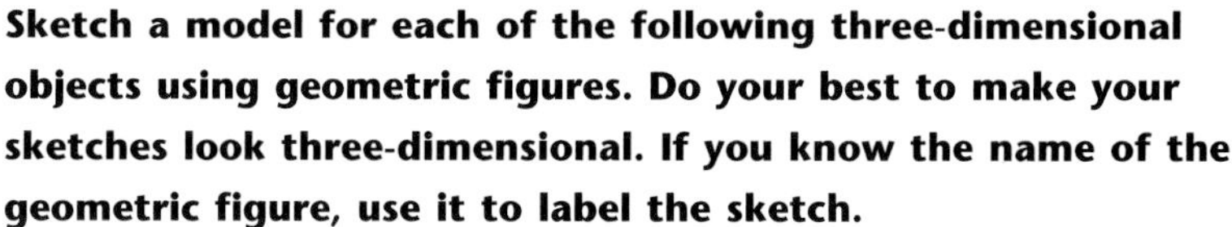

Sketch a model for each of the following three-dimensional objects using geometric figures. Do your best to make your sketches look three-dimensional. If you know the name of the geometric figure, use it to label the sketch.

7. a soup can **8.** a refrigerator **9.** a football

10. The perspective drawing at the right gives the illusion of depth and distance. Are the three penguins in the picture all the same size? Which one appears to be the tallest? Use a ruler to check. Why do you think this illusion consistently fools people?

11. Cone Crossing Three-dimensional shapes can be visualized in two dimensions in many ways. A cross section view of a solid is made by imagining a plane slicing through it. Sketch this cone and draw two other cross sections, each with a different shape. Describe the shape of each cross section.

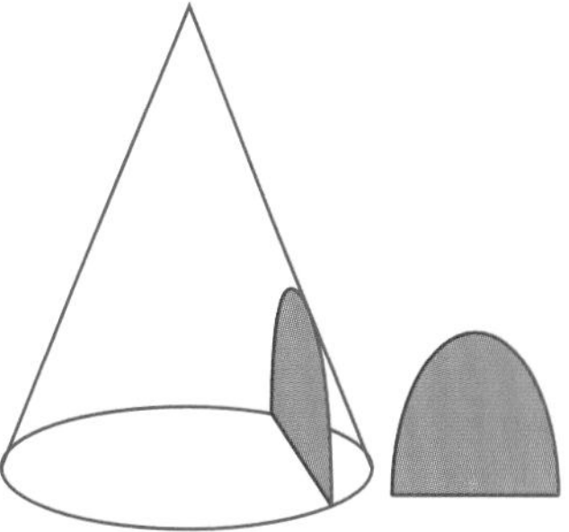

12. The pictures below are small sections of larger photographs. What do you think is shown in each photograph? Explain how you were able to predict the larger photographs from the small sections shown.

a.

b.

Social Science

13. Like a map of the world, a map of your neighborhood is also a flat model of a curved area. Why aren't there problems with size distortion in these neighborhood maps as there are in the Mercator projection? Or are there? Explain.

LOOK AHEAD

14. Plot each of the following on the same coordinate plane.

a. Plot the points (1, 4), (3, −2), and (−3, 0).

b. Plot a point on the y-axis. What is its ordered pair?

c. Plot a point with negative x- and y-coordinates. Which quadrant is it in?

15. Graph the line $x = 4$ on a coordinate plane. Describe the line.

16. Graph the line $y = -3$ on a coordinate plane. Describe the line.

17. Graph the line $y = x$ on a coordinate plane. Describe the line.

MORE PRACTICE

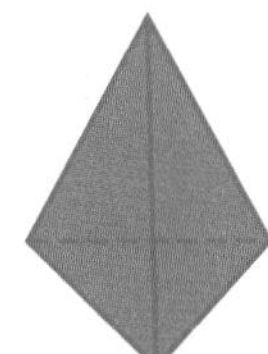

18. A tetrahedron is a pyramid with four triangular faces. Create a net for a tetrahedron. How many vertices, edges, and faces does a tetrahedron have?

19. Create a net for a cylinder.

Sketch a model for each of the following three-dimensional objects using geometric figures.

20. a brick **21.** a television set **22.** a drinking glass **23.** a hamburger

MORE MATH REASONING

24. Merging the 'Mids A tetrahedron is a pyramid with four triangular faces. A square pyramid is a pyramid with a square base and four triangular faces. The two pyramids shown at the right are special because all of the edges in both figures are the same length.

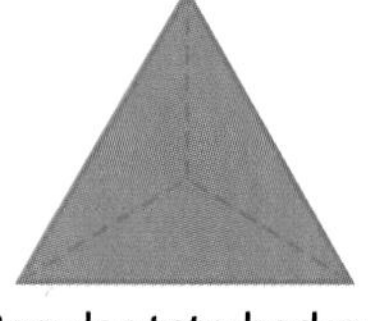

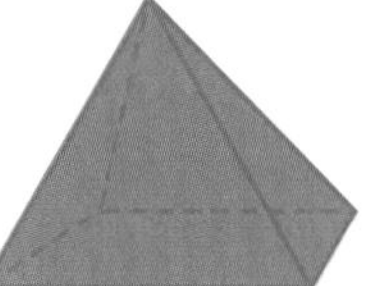

Regular tetrahedron   Square pyramid

(Due to perspective, lengths of some edges may appear unequal.)

If the tetrahedron and the square pyramid are joined together by joining two triangular faces so that they coincide (match exactly), how many faces will the resulting solid have? After you have made your best guess, create nets for the two pyramids similar to the nets shown. Build the pyramids. Join them together and count the number of faces. Was your prediction correct?

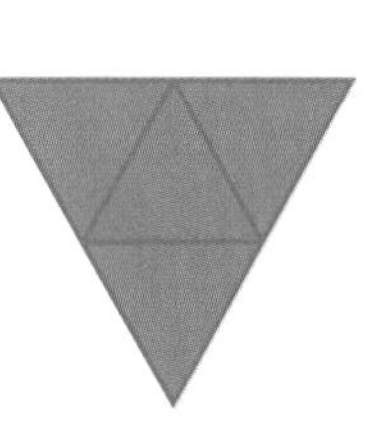

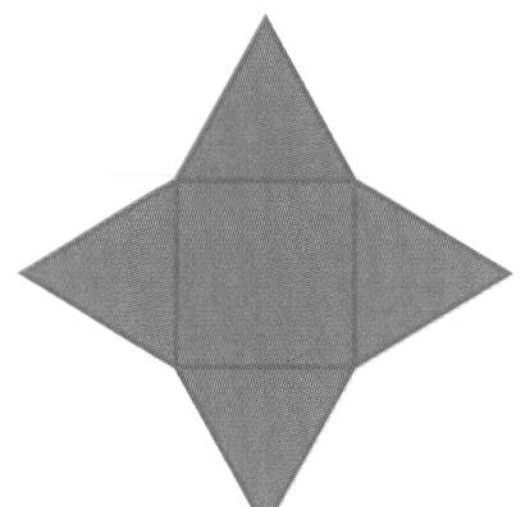

25. The Painted Cube The 6 outside surfaces of a cube are painted blue. The cube is then cut up into 27 small cubes ($3 \times 3 \times 3$). How many of the small cubes have no blue faces? 1 blue face? 2 blue faces? 3 blue faces? 4 blue faces? 5 blue faces? 6 blue faces?

1-1 PART B Algebraic Models

← CONNECT → ***You've used coordinate planes in algebra. The coordinate plane is one of the most frequently used models. Now you will see how coordinate planes are used to display data and in map making.***

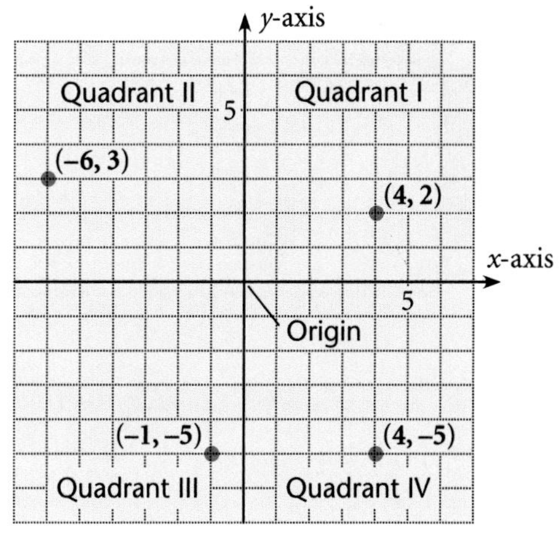

The figure points out some familiar features of the coordinate plane. It should help you refresh your memory about the four quadrants, the x- and y-axes, the origin, and ordered pairs.

TRY IT

Plot each point on a coordinate plane.

a. (3, 1) **b.** (2, −1) **c.** (0, −9) **d.** (−3, −4)

The map of the continental United States is shown on a coordinate plane.

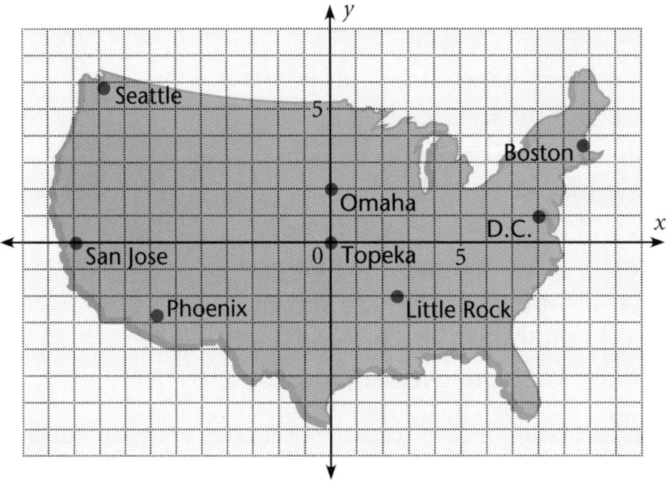

e. Which city is located at the origin?
f. Name a city or state in each quadrant.
g. Name a city on the x-axis and a city on the y-axis.
h. Give the ordered pair for each of the following.
(1) Seattle, Washington
(2) Washington, D.C.
(3) Little Rock, Arkansas

1. Using the preceding map, estimate the ordered pair for Anchorage, Alaska.

A coordinate plane can be used as a model to locate points on a map. Coordinate planes are also used as models in statistics. A graph showing a set of points based on paired data is a **scatter plot**. In the following Explore, you'll collect data and analyze it with the help of a scatter plot.

EXPLORE: HANDY-DANDY SURVEY

MATERIALS

Graph paper
Watch or clock

Are you right-handed or left-handed? Are you ambidextrous: that is, can you use both hands equally well? The following is a "handedness survey" that will help you find out how ambidextrous you are.

1. Which hand do you use most often and most easily? This is your dominant hand. Do you think your dominant hand is extremely, moderately, or only slightly dominant over the other hand?

2. Have one person be a timer. For 60 seconds, draw small Xs with your right hand in the squares on a sheet of graph paper as quickly as possible. Count the Xs. Repeat using your left hand.

3. Plot the data you collected on graph paper. Let the right-hand count be the x-coordinate and the left-hand count be the y-coordinate. (See the example at the right.) Gather data from other students and plot their ordered pairs on your graph.

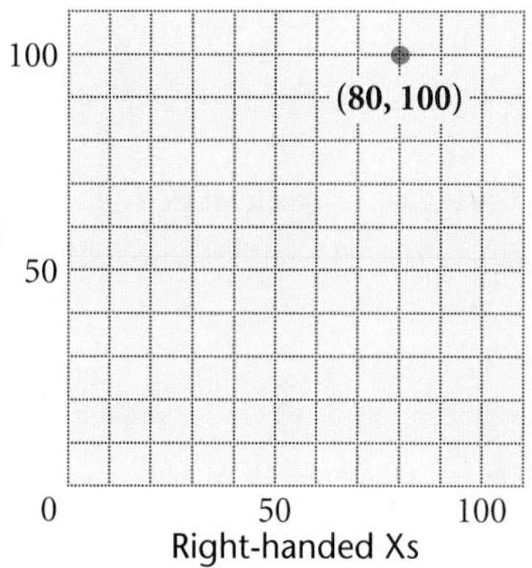

If you make 80 Xs with your right hand and 100 Xs with your left, plot the ordered pair (80, 100).

4. a. From the graph you made in **3,** determine which students are left-handed. Explain how you can tell. (It may help to draw the line $y = x$ on your graph. If you do this, explain how you might use this line.) What percentage of the class is left-handed?

b. Are any students ambidextrous? close to being ambidextrous? Explain your answer in terms of your scatter plot.

5. Suppose that a classmate makes 75 Xs with her right hand in one minute. Use the data you've gathered to predict how many Xs she could make with her left hand. Explain your method. How confident are you that your prediction is accurate?

REFLECT

1. What are some ways of displaying data besides using a scatter plot? If you have a lot of data to show, which method is the most practical? Why?

2. Name a way to use coordinates besides in maps and scatter plots. Explain why coordinates are helpful in this situation.

3. Write a brief definition of each of the following in your own words.

a. the x- and y-axes **b.** an ordered pair

c. the origin **d.** the four quadrants

Exercises

CORE

Getting Started **Plot the following points on a coordinate plane.**

1. $(3, -2)$ **2.** $(0, 0)$ **3.** $(-4, 2)$ **4.** $(-4, -1)$

5. $(0, -4)$ **6.** $(3, 1)$ **7.** $(5, -7.5)$

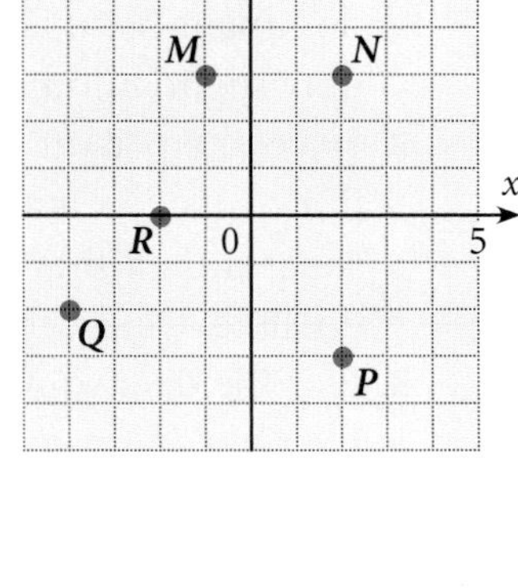

Give the coordinates for each point.

8. M **9.** N **10.** P

11. Q **12.** R

Draw four-sided figures (quadrilaterals) with the given vertices on a coordinate plane.

13. $(2, -3), (-5, -3), (-7, -6), (0, -6)$

14. $(0, 2), (4, 5), (1, 9), (-3, 6)$

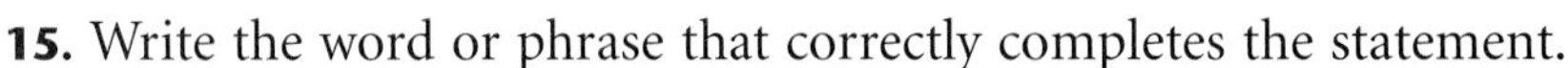

15. Write the word or phrase that correctly completes the statement.

A ____ is a graph showing a set of points based on paired data.

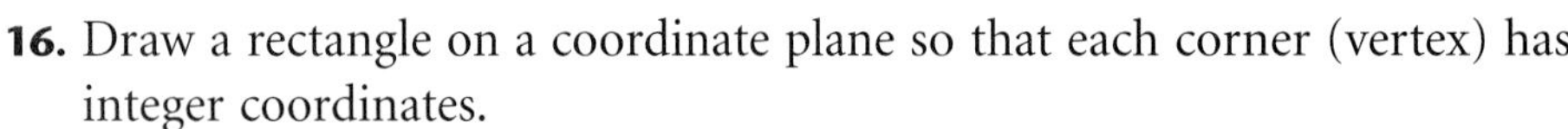

16. Draw a rectangle on a coordinate plane so that each corner (vertex) has integer coordinates.

a. What are the coordinates of the vertices you chose?

b. Is it possible to draw a rectangle whose vertices have integer coordinates so that no side is parallel to either the x-axis or the y-axis? If so, sketch such a rectangle on a coordinate plane.

17. Flipping Pages, Flipping Channels The hypothetical scatter plot below represents how many hours 10 people watch television and how many hours they read each week. The line $y = x$ is also shown on the graph.

a. What are the ordered pairs for each of the points on the scatter plot?

b. One point lies on the line $y = x$. What does this mean?

c. What can you conclude about the points above the line $y = x$?

d. Estimate the number of hours per week you spend watching TV. Estimate the number of hours per week you spend reading. Where does your point lie on the scatter plot? Explain.

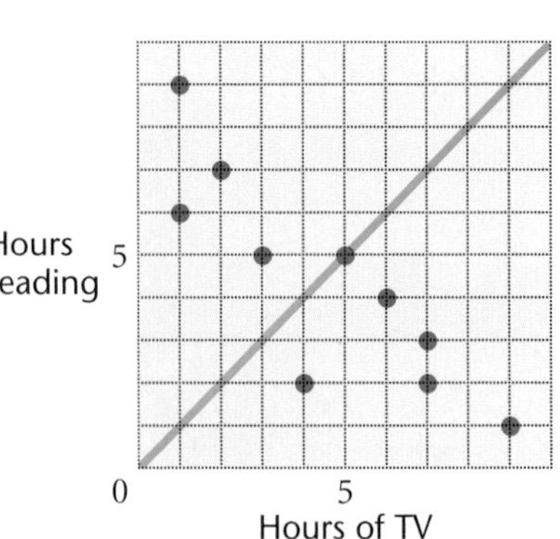

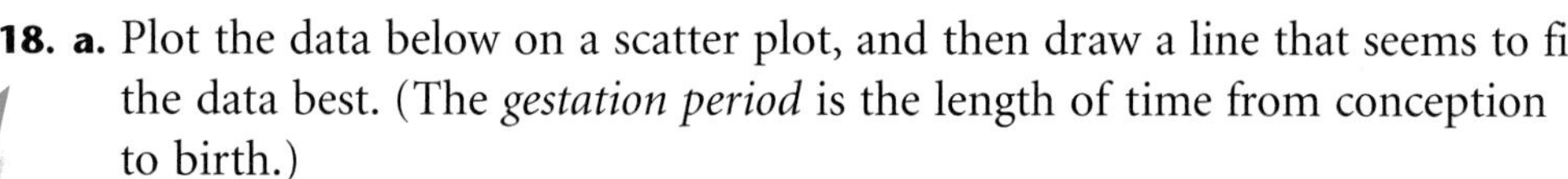

18. a. Plot the data below on a scatter plot, and then draw a line that seems to fit the data best. (The *gestation period* is the length of time from conception to birth.)

Animal	Cat	Fox	Hamster	Rabbit	Rat	Squirrel
Average Life Span (years)	12	7	2	5	3	10
Average Gestation Period (days)	63	52	16	31	21	44

b. The average life span of a chipmunk is 6 years. Use your scatter plot to predict the gestation period of a chipmunk.

LOOK BACK

Simplify each expression. [Previous course]

19. $2y + 7y - 6y$ **20.** $6(3 - 2x)$ **21.** $-2r + 3r(r - 4)$

Evaluate each expression for $x = 2$ and $y = -3$. [Previous course]

22. $5(x + 2)$ **23.** $5x^2 - 2y$ **24.** $2y^3$ **25.** $(2y)^3$

MORE PRACTICE

Plot the following points on a coordinate plane.

26. $(5, -2)$ **27.** $(0, -3)$ **28.** $(2, 0)$

29. $(-3, 1)$ **30.** $(-2, -4)$ **31.** $(1.5, 1)$

32. $(-2.5, 4)$ **33.** $\left(-1\frac{1}{2}, 2\frac{3}{4}\right)$

Give the coordinates for each point.

34. C **35.** D **36.** E

37. F **38.** G **39.** H

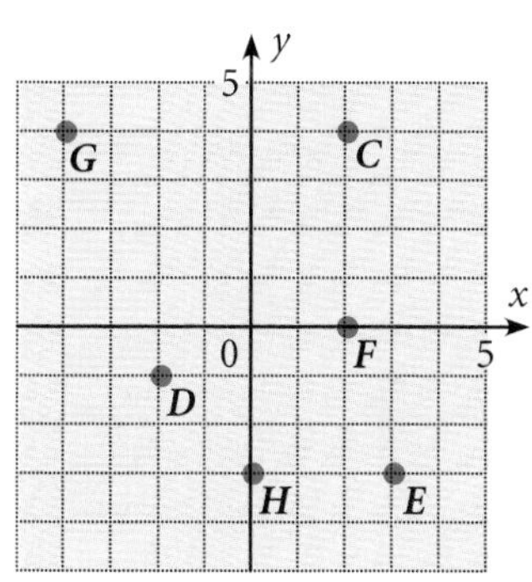

Draw triangles with the given vertices on a coordinate plane.

40. $(-8, 2), (5, 2), (1, -4)$

41. $(0, 0), (-4, 2), (-3, -3)$

42. The scatter plot at the right shows miles traveled and gallons of gas consumed for 15 automobiles.

a. Which car traveled the most miles?

b. Which car consumed the most gallons of gas?

MORE MATH REASONING

43. This exercise uses the same data as Exercise 42.

a. Which car had the best mileage (miles per gallon)?

b. Which car had the poorest mileage (miles per gallon)?

c. Use the scatter plot from Exercise 42 to predict the number of miles traveled by a car that consumed 25 gallons of gas. Explain how you made this prediction.

44. Cube Cutter What is the smallest number of cuts needed to cut the block of wood at the left into 9 small cubes? What is the smallest number needed to cut the block at the right into 27 small cubes?

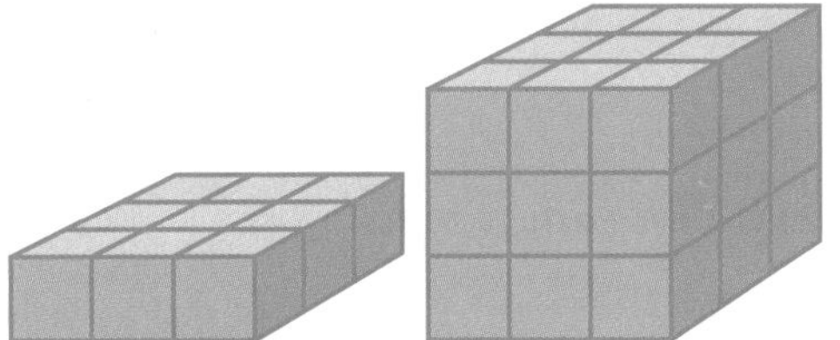

1-1 PART C Making Connections

← CONNECT → ***Models help people understand things that are too large, too small, or too complicated to study directly. Algebra showed you some ways to use mathematics to model real-world situations. Now you've learned how to recognize, visualize, and create models.***

Maps, geometric figures, coordinate planes, and scatter plots are different types of mathematical models. You are now more familiar with some of the uses of mathematical models and more aware of the dangers of assuming too much from limited or misleading information.

Vertical and horizontal lines form grids across most local maps. Many maps have letters spaced evenly along the horizontal axis and numbers placed along the vertical axis. One letter and one number can describe the approximate location of any landmark on a typical map.

EXPLORE: MAP MAKER, MAP MAKER, MAKE ME A MAP

MATERIALS

Graph paper
Ruler

As shown at the right, modern map makers use computers in their work; however, maps were once drawn by hand. You can make a hand-drawn map of your school on graph paper. Begin by setting up a coordinate system, selecting a convenient point for the origin, and drawing the coordinate axes. Label points of interest such as the main office, the cafeteria, and the library.

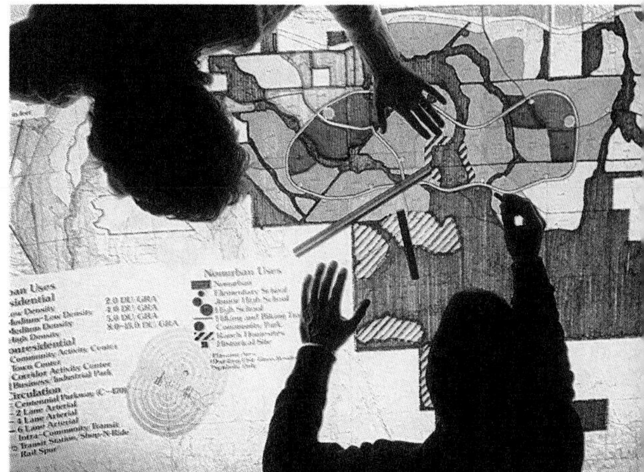

1. Describe the coordinate system you chose for your school map. Why did you choose this particular coordinate system?
2. Write a paragraph describing your daily route from class to class. Use the coordinate system you've devised to help describe locations.

REFLECT

1. Write a paragraph explaining how mathematical models can be helpful. Give some examples of useful mathematical models besides a map.
2. Describe some of the possible weaknesses of mathematical models.
3. Mathematical modeling has become much more powerful since the invention of computers. Explain why computers might improve mathematical models and make them easier to use.

Self-Assessment

1. Draw models of a bowl, a baseball, a textbook, and an ice cream cone.
2. Which of these nets will fold to make an open box?

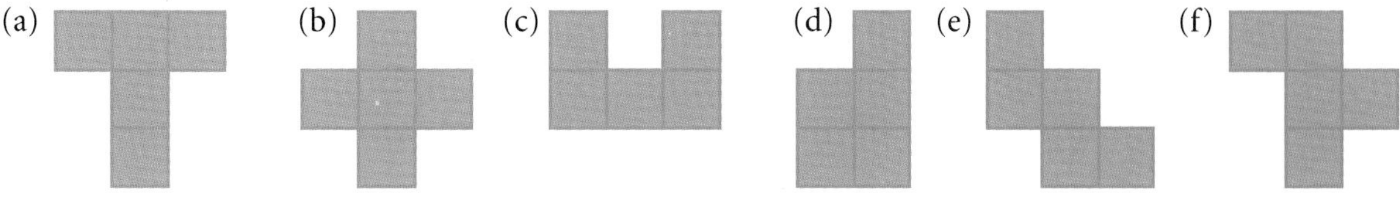

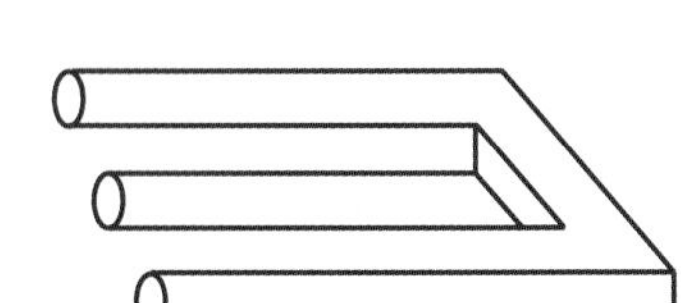

3. Sketch a net for the pyramid shown at the right.

4. Study the illusion shown.
   a. What do you see?
   b. Why are the left and right sides of the drawing inconsistent?
   c. Sketch an optical illusion of your own in which the top half and the bottom half are inconsistent.

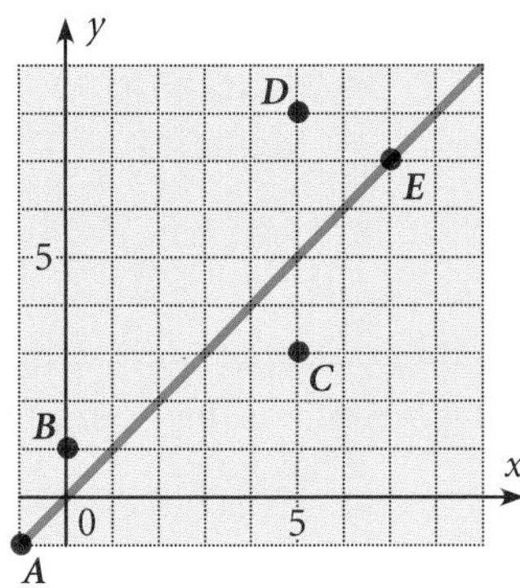

Simplify each expression. [Previous course]

5. $9x + 5x - 3x$ 6. $4(5 - 8z) + 11z$

Evaluate each expression for $x = 3$ and $y = -1$. [Previous course]

7. $4(y - 7) + 3x$ 8. $5x^2 - 4y$

9. The line $x = y$ is drawn in the graph at the right. If $r > s$, which of the points shown could have coordinates (r, s)?
(a) A (b) B (c) C (d) D (e) E

10. Find 10 different rectangular objects in your room. Measure the length and width of each, and plot the results on a scatter plot. Does the ratio of length to width of these objects vary widely, or can you identify a "typical" ratio? Explain.

11. **Testing, Testing** Engineers at NASA build models of spacecraft for simulations. Give at least three reasons for building models before an actual space flight.

12. The following pairs give the age and height, in inches, of 10 female elementary school students: (7, 49), (7, 46), (8, 50), (8, 52), (9, 51), (9, 55), (10, 57), (10, 56), (11, 57), (11, 59).
   a. Make a scatter plot of these data. Use your scatter plot to predict the height of a 6-year-old girl and a 13-year-old girl. How did you make these predictions?
   b. Use your scatter plot to predict the height of a 20-year-old woman. Does your result make sense? If not, explain.

13. For each team in the NFL's American Football Conference, the scatter plot at the right plots the length of the name of the home city versus the number of games it won during the 1991 season. What does the scatter plot tell you about the relationship between the length of the city's name and the number of wins? Do you think the number of letters in a city's name actually affects a team's performance?

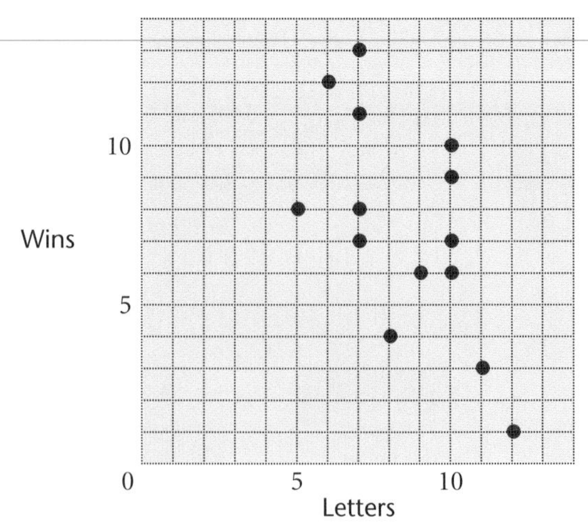

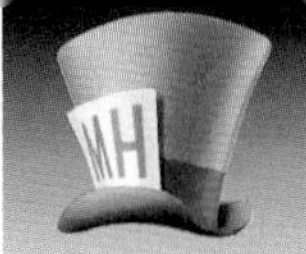

1-2 Reasoning and Logic

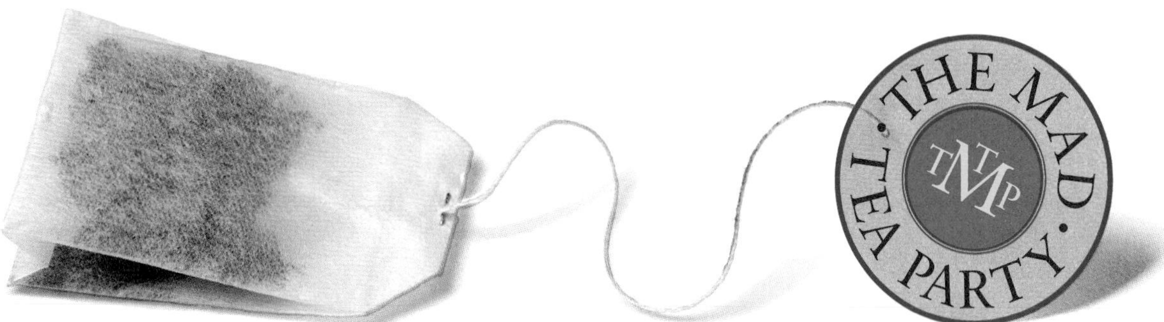

In the following excerpt from *Alice in Wonderland* by Lewis Carroll, Alice and several of the Wonderland characters attend a "Mad Tea Party."

The Hatter opened his eyes very wide... but all he said was, "Why is a raven like a writing-desk?"

"Come, we shall have some fun now!" thought Alice. "I'm glad they've begun asking riddles—I believe I can guess that," she added aloud.

"Do you mean that you think you can find out the answer to it?" said the March Hare.

"Exactly so," said Alice.

"Then you should say what you mean," the March Hare went on.

"I do," Alice hastily replied; "at least—at least I mean what I say—that's the same thing, you know."

"Not the same thing a bit!" said the Hatter. "Why, you might just as well say that 'I see what I eat' is the same thing as 'I eat what I see'!"

"You might just as well say," added the March Hare, "that 'I like what I get' is the same thing as 'I get what I like'!"

"You might just as well say," added the Dormouse, which seemed to be talking in its sleep, "that 'I breathe when I sleep' is the same thing as 'I sleep when I breathe'!"

"It is the same thing with you," said the Hatter, and here the conversation dropped, and the party sat silent for a minute, while Alice thought over all she could remember about ravens and writing-desks, which wasn't much.

1. Why do *you* think a raven is like a writing desk?
2. Why do you think using precise language is important in mathematics?
3. Give some examples of every-day situations where saying exactly what you mean is very important. Explain why precise language is necessary in each situation.

1-2 PART A Inductive Reasoning

← CONNECT → ***You've already been using reasoning skills to choose appropriate mathematical models. Now you will learn more about one particular type of reasoning.***

You will soon be investigating basic geometric figures. So that everyone can use the same vocabulary and notation, some of these figures are described below.

A **point** is a specific location. It has no size, but it can be modeled by a dot, such as a dot on a map or a computer screen. To illustrate a point, we use a dot labeled with a capital letter. Points *A*, *B*, and *C* are shown.

A **line** is a set of points. It is straight, and it continues forever in both directions. A line has no thickness, but it has infinite length. A line can be named by a single lowercase letter or by any two points on the line. This is line ℓ, $\overleftrightarrow{DE}$, or $\overleftrightarrow{ED}$.

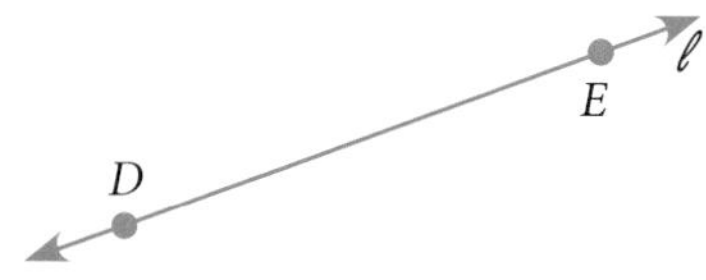

A **line segment** is a part of a line consisting of two **endpoints** and all the points between these points. Segments are named by their endpoints. This is segment $\overline{PQ}$ or $\overline{QP}$.

Note that when we refer to "two points" (lines, segments), we mean two *different* points (lines, segments).

When two geometric figures have points in common, we say that they **intersect**. $\overline{EF}$ intersects $\overleftrightarrow{HI}$ at *J*. (*J* is the **point of intersection** of $\overline{EF}$ and $\overleftrightarrow{HI}$.)

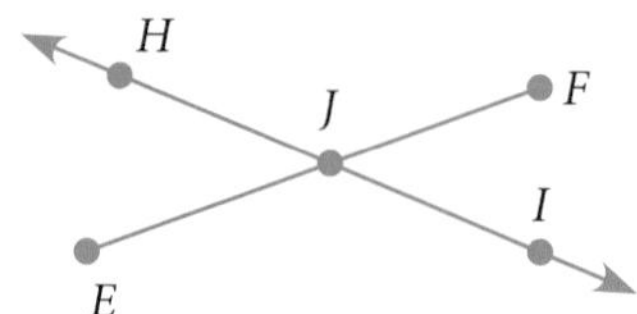

TRY IT

a. Draw a line $\overleftrightarrow{XY}$.

b. Add points M and N to your drawing so that M is on $\overleftrightarrow{XY}$ and N is not on $\overleftrightarrow{XY}$.

c. Name all of the segments that are determined by the labeled points on $\overleftrightarrow{XY}$.

In the following Explore, you'll be placing several points on the same line. Points on the same line are **collinear.**

EXPLORE: GET THE POINT

1. Draw a line. Draw points A and B on the line. How many different segments are determined by points A and B? Name the segment(s).

2. Draw another line. Draw points A, B, and C on the line. How many segments are determined by points A, B, and C? Name them.

3. Continue to draw lines, adding one point each time. Make a table showing the number of points and the number of segments they determine.

Problem-Solving Tip

Look for patterns in your data.

Continue the process until you are confident that you've found a pattern for the relationship between the number of points and the number of segments they determine.

4. If you draw 10 points on a line, how many segments do they determine?

5. If you draw n points on a line, how many segments do they determine? Can you find a formula? Compare your formula to those of your classmates. Discuss how you found these formulas.

In solving the problem in the Explore, you looked for a pattern in the data so you could make an educated guess about the formula. In mathematical terms, you used **inductive reasoning** to make a **conjecture.**

> A **conjecture** is a conclusion made from observing evidence. A conjecture may or may not be true.
>
> **Inductive reasoning** is the process of making a conjecture by looking at several specific examples and recognizing a pattern.

EXAMPLE

If you make c cuts in a rope, how many pieces will you end up with?

The following table shows the relationship between the number of cuts and the number of pieces. By using inductive reasoning, we make the conjecture that if you make c cuts, you end up with $c + 1$ pieces.

Cuts	0	1	2	3	4	...
Pieces	1	2	3	4	5	...

Inductive reasoning is a practical, though not foolproof, way to make conjectures. Inuits observe patterns in the sun, clouds, ocean, wind, and animals to predict the weather far in advance. A biologist uses inductive reasoning when she observes the behavior of one group of dolphins and then assumes that their behavior is typical of most dolphins. Scientists use inductive reasoning to help construct and check their current best guesses (*theories*) about how the world works.

Mathematics also frequently involves a search for patterns. When a mathematician first observes a pattern, she may make a conjecture about what it means. She might make hundreds or even thousands of observations before she believes her guess is true. For a mathematician, a conjecture is "true" only when she is certain that it is *always* true.

REFLECT

1. What is inductive reasoning? How are patterns used in inductive reasoning?
2. Describe three patterns that occur in nature.
3. Write three different number patterns. Explain the rule for each of your patterns.
4. Are conjectures made through inductive reasoning necessarily true? If not, give an example of a pattern that only holds in certain instances.

Exercises

CORE

1. Getting Started All sides of an equilateral triangle have the same length. Following the steps below, use inductive reasoning to find the perimeter (distance around the figure) when 100 equilateral triangles are pushed together as shown.

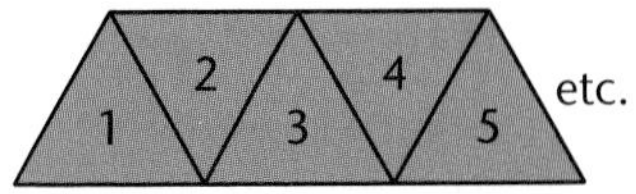

Problem-Solving Tip

Make a table to show your data.

a. One row of your table should show the number of triangles and the other the perimeter of the figure.

b. Sketch an equilateral triangle. Suppose the length of each side of the triangle is 1. Find the perimeter of the triangle, and record your results in the table.

c. Add a second triangle to your sketch. Find the perimeter of this figure and record your data.

d. Repeat **1c** for three and four triangles. Look for a pattern in your results.

e. Find a formula that relates n, the number of triangles, to p, the perimeter.

f. Check to see that your formula works. Then use it to predict the perimeter for 100 triangles pushed together.

Find the next number in each sequence. Explain the pattern.

2. 1, 4, 9, 16, 25, . . .

3. $0, \frac{1}{2}, \frac{3}{4}, \frac{7}{8}, \frac{15}{16}, \ldots$

4. 1, 2, 4, 8, 16, . . .

5. Name all the lines, points, and segments in the figure below.

6. List all sets of three collinear points in the figure.

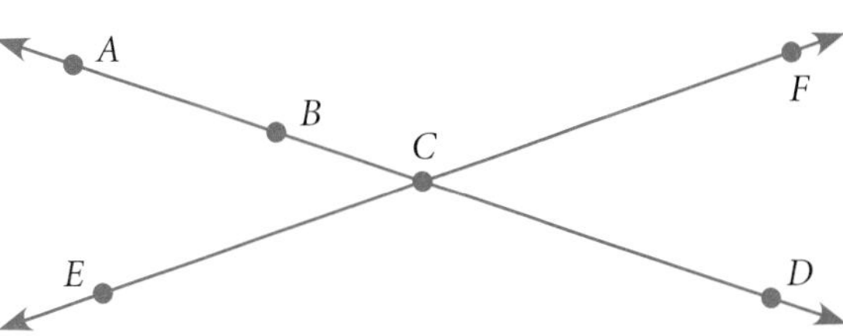

7. Draw a figure that shows the following:

- ℓ intersects m at G.
- $\overline{DO}$ is on m.
- K is not on ℓ or m.

Complete each statement with *point, line,* or *line segment*.

8. A ___ has no thickness, but it has infinite length.

9. A ___ has no thickness and has a finite length.

10. A ___ is a specific location.

11. A Tierful Pattern How many small, identical triangles does it take to build a larger triangle that is two tiers high? three tiers high? four tiers high? five tiers high? ten tiers high? n tiers high?

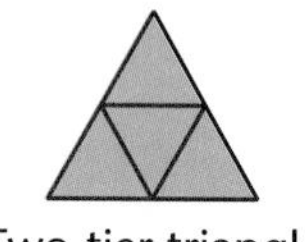
Two-tier triangle

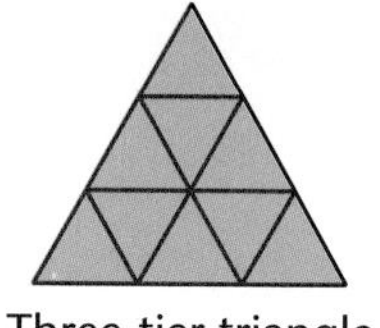
Three-tier triangle

12. Using graph paper, draw rectangles with integer side lengths that cover areas 2, 3, 4, 5, 6, 7, 8, 9, 10, 11, and 12. When there is more than one possible way to draw a rectangle, draw all possibilities. (A 1×3 rectangle and a 3×1 rectangle do not count as different rectangles.) Identify the areas that have only one rectangle. What is true about these areas? Make a connection to a type of number you studied in algebra.

13. Look at the number pattern at the right. Find the sums. Find a pattern. What is the sum of the first 10 odd numbers? the first 25 odd numbers? Make a conjecture about the sum of the first n odd numbers.

$1 =$
$1 + 3 =$
$1 + 3 + 5 =$
$1 + 3 + 5 + 7 =$
$1 + 3 + 5 + 7 + 9 =$
$1 + 3 + 5 + 7 + 9 + 11 =$
$1 + 3 + 5 + 7 + 9 + 11 + 13 =$

History

14. When he was 10 years old, the mathematician Karl F. Gauss was told to add all the numbers from 1 through 100. In a few minutes, Gauss gave the teacher the correct answer. How do you think he added these numbers so quickly without a calculator? What was his answer? (Hint: Find pairs of numbers in the line below that have the same sum.)

$1 + 2 + 3 + 4 + 5 + 6 + \ldots + 95 + 96 + 97 + 98 + 99 + 100 = ?$

LOOK AHEAD

Determine whether each statement below is true or false. Explain your reasoning.

15. All books have pages.
16. Some books have pages.
17. No birds are robins.
18. Some birds are eagles.
19. All birds are blue jays.
20. All orioles are birds.

MORE PRACTICE

Find the next number in each sequence. Explain the pattern.

21. 3, 9, 27, 81, . . .
22. 8, −4, 2, −1, . . .
23. 2, 4, 3, 9, 4, 16, 5, . . .

24. Name all the lines, points, and segments in the figure at the right.

25. Name a set of three collinear points in the figure.

H
G I J

26. Draw one figure that shows the following: $\overline{AB}$ intersects $\overline{CD}$ at E; Line n does not intersect $\overline{AB}$ or $\overline{CD}$; F is on n.

MORE MATH REASONING

27. Athena claimed that any two points are collinear. Do you agree or disagree? Why?

28. Patterns with Squares Each square shown is made of smaller unit squares. Some of the unit squares touch the shaded region on two sides, some on one side, and some do not touch it at all. Suppose an $n \times n$ square is drawn in the shaded region. How many unit squares will touch the shaded region on two sides? one side? zero sides?

29. Habits of Rabbits Rabbits have very consistent breeding habits. Suppose that, starting in the second month of their lives, a pair of adult rabbits produces an average of two offspring a month. Suppose you have a pair of baby bunnies, one male and one female. Assuming that each pair of babies consists of one male and one female and that no rabbits die, find the number of pairs of rabbits you would have each month for 12 months. Explain the pattern that these numbers follow.

Month	1st	2nd	3rd	4th	5th	. . .	12th
Pairs of Rabbits	bb	BB	BB bb	BB BB bb	BB BB BB bb bb	. . .	??

Note: bb denotes a pair of baby bunnies; BB denotes a pair of adult rabbits.

The problem about rabbits was first described in a math book by Leonardo Fibonacci of Pisa, Italy. The number pattern you've found is commonly known as the Fibonacci sequence.

1-2 PART B The Language of Logic

← CONNECT → ***You've seen that inductive reasoning is a practical form of reasoning. As you learn the language of logic, you will keep making conjectures and begin looking for counterexamples.***

When Alice in Wonderland claimed that "I mean what I say" is the same as "I say what I mean," the Mad Hatter, the March Hare, and the Dormouse each gave a counterexample of Alice's imperfect logic. A **counterexample** is an example that shows a statement to be false.

CONSIDER

Refer back to *The Mad Tea Party* on page 19 to answer the following questions.

1. What was Alice's false statement?
2. What counterexamples to Alice's logic were given by the Mad Hatter, the March Hare, and the Dormouse?
3. What is the difference between "I mean what I say" and "I say what I mean"?
4. If you had attended the tea party, what counter-example to Alice's logic could you have added to the conversation?

TRY IT

Give a counterexample that disproves each conjecture below.

a. All birds can fly.
b. All four-sided figures (quadrilaterals) are rectangles.

Notice that *one* counterexample proves that a conjecture is false!

When making a conjecture, you must be careful to say exactly what you mean. You need to use common terms like **all, some,** and **none** very carefully when making *logical statements.*

Here are some examples of how *all (every, each), some (at least one, one or more),* and *none (no, not any)* are used in mathematical and nonmathematical sentences.

All dogs in town need a license.	*All* squares are rectangles.
Some dogs have fleas.	*Some* quadrilaterals are squares.
No dogs say "meow."	*No* square is a circle.

Another way to represent these statements is by using **Venn diagrams.** Venn diagrams can help illustrate the relationships described by *all, some,* and *none.*

All whales are mammals.

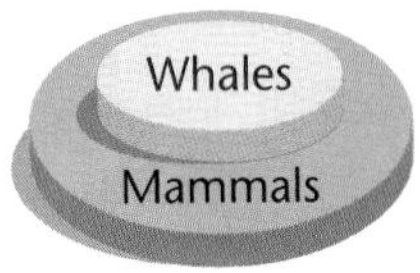

Some mammals can swim.

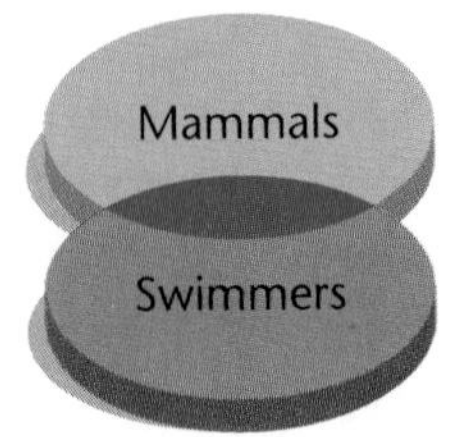

No whales can fly.

EXPLORE: SOME TRIANGLES ARE . . .

Consider the triangles at the right as you answer the following.

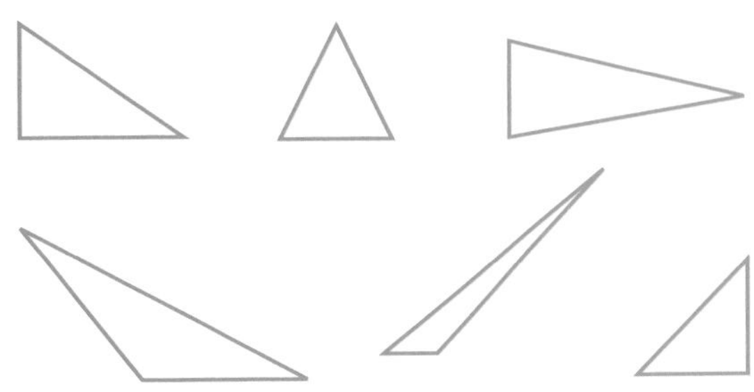

1. Write three statements beginning with the words *All triangles.*
2. Write three statements beginning with the words *Some triangles.*
3. Write three statements beginning with the words *No triangle.*
4. Does the statement "*Some triangles have three sides*" present an acceptable use of the word *some*? Discuss this with your classmates.

There are times when it is helpful to link two or more logical statements. The familiar words *and* and *or* give us an easy way to do this. Mathematicians are very particular about the meanings of these words. If you link two statements with *and,* both parts must be true for the combined statement to be true.

The word *or* is a little trickier. In daily life, a statement that uses *or* usually means that you are making a choice: you will do only one of two things. But in mathematics, a true statement with *or* can have one part true or both parts true.

EXAMPLES

Describe the conditions that make the following logical statements true and the conditions that make them false.

1. Seema will compete in the long jump, *and* she will run the 100 meters.

   This is true only if Seema does both.

   It is false under the following conditions:
   - She competes in the long jump but doesn't run the 100 meters.
   - She runs the 100 meters but doesn't compete in the long jump.
   - She does not compete in either event.

2. Juan is going to the store *or* he is going swimming.

This is true if either of the following is true:

- Juan goes to the store (whether he goes swimming or not).
- Juan goes swimming (whether he goes to the store or not).

It is false only if Juan neither goes to the store nor goes swimming.

REFLECT

1. Explain why just one counterexample to a conjecture proves that the conjecture is false.
2. Make a false statement about your school, using *all* or *none*. Give a counterexample that shows why the statement is false.
3. Suppose someone tells you, "You will clean your room, or you can't see your friends this weekend." Explain why you hope that they didn't learn about logic.

Exercises

CORE

1. **Getting Started** Give a counterexample that disproves the conjecture "All birds lay eggs."

Give a counterexample that disproves each conjecture below.

2. No triangles can have three equal sides.

3. For any real numbers a and b, $(a + b)^2 = a^2 + b^2$.

4. For any real number x, $x^2 \geq 1$.

Describe the conditions that make each of the following logical statements true and the conditions that make them false.

5. Steven will buy a newspaper, and he will eat lunch.

6. Tonya will visit her aunt or she will see a movie.

Draw a Venn diagram to illustrate each of the following statements.

7. All carrots are vegetables.

8. Some apples are green.

9. No apples are vegetables.

Determine whether each statement is true or false. If the statement is false, change the underlined word to make it true.

10. A <u>conjecture</u> disproves a rule.

11. A <u>line</u> has two endpoints.

12. Write three true statements about the United States using the terms *all, some,* and *none.* For example:

All states have governors.

Some states border Canada.

No states are larger than Alaska.

13. The following conjecture is false; it has only one counterexample. For any real number x, $x^2 > 0$.

a. Find the counterexample for this conjecture.

b. Give another conjecture that has only one counterexample.

14. a. Make a conjecture about the number of pieces of string into which the folded string is divided by n cuts.

b. Make a conjecture about the number of pieces of string into which the loop of string is divided by n cuts.

LOOK BACK

Solve each equation. [Previous course]

15. $18 = 4x + 2$

16. $5(x + 2) = 17 - 3x$

Graph each equation on a coordinate plane. [1-1]

17. $y = 3x - 5$

18. $y = -2x + 3$

19. $y = x^2 - 2$

20. Sketch a net for the pyramid at the right. [1-1]

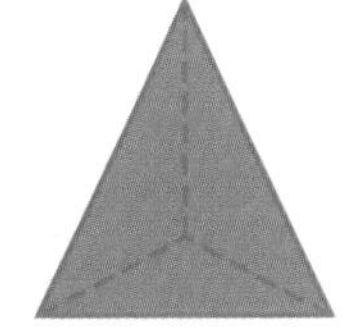

MORE PRACTICE

Give a counterexample that disproves each conjecture below.

21. No triangles have two sides of the same length.

22. All figures with four sides of equal length are squares.

23. No women have been elected U.S. senators.

24. Everyone who lives in Texas lives in Houston.

Describe the conditions that make each of the following logical statements true and the conditions that make them false.

25. I did my homework, and I cleaned my bedroom.

26. I'll borrow Janet's calculator, or I'll buy a calculator.

Write statements using *all, some,* and *none* to explain each Venn diagram.

27.

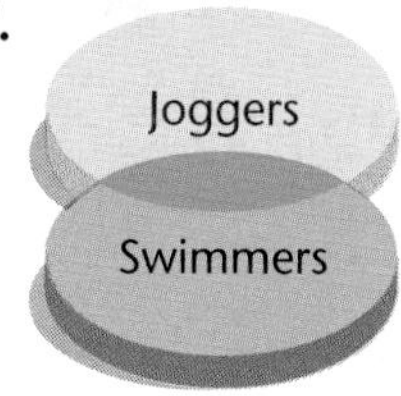

28.

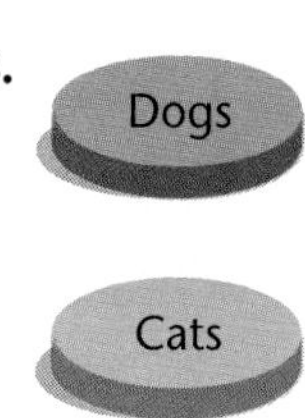

29.

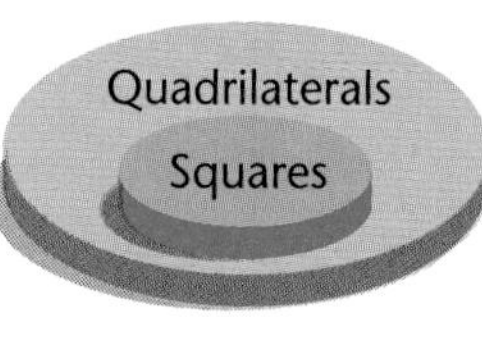

MORE MATH REASONING

30. Write three true statements about your school using the terms *all, some,* and *none.*

31. At Rosemead High School, 94 students take biology, 86 take ethnic studies, and 95 take geometry. Thirty-seven students take both biology and geometry, 43 take geometry and ethnic studies, and 42 take ethnic studies and biology. Twenty-eight students take all three subjects.

a. Draw a Venn diagram to illustrate this problem. How many students take geometry but not ethnic studies or biology?

b. What is the probability that a student chosen at random will be taking all three of the courses?

1-2 PART C Deductive Reasoning

← CONNECT → ***You've used inductive reasoning to make conjectures based on patterns and evidence. Now you will look at a different way to make conjectures—deductive reasoning.***

Raymond Smullyan, a professor of mathematical logic, based his book of brainteasers, *Alice in Puzzleland,* on the characters in the original *Alice in Wonderland.* The following Explore is based on one of the sets of puzzles in his book.

EXPLORE: DUM DEEDUCING

Tweedledum and Tweedledee are identical twins who usually have their names embroidered on their collars so people can tell them apart. Today, however, they have decided to entertain themselves by confusing Alice.

One of the brothers—of course, we don't know which—says, "In these puzzles, each of us will pick one of two cards, either an orange one or a blue one. The one with the orange card will always tell the truth. The one with the blue card will always lie."

1. The two brothers hide behind a wall, draw cards, and return with the cards hidden behind their backs.
   The one on the left says, "I have the blue card, and I am Tweedledee."
   The one on the right says, "You are not! *I* am Tweedledee!"
   "This is fun!" Alice says, and picks out Tweedledee immediately! Which one is it, and how did she (or you) figure it out?
2. "Not bad," one of the brothers says, and they walk behind the wall again, looking very determined. They return, having picked cards again.
   The one on the left says, "Tweedledum is now carrying a blue card."
   The one on the right just smiles!
   Alice looked confused for a moment, then thought as logically as she could and solved the puzzle. Who is Tweedledum? How can you tell? Explain your reasoning.
3. You are *not* using inductive reasoning as you solve these puzzles—there's no pattern! Explain how the type of reasoning you are using is different from inductive reasoning.

In this Explore, you used **deductive reasoning.**

Deductive reasoning is the process of drawing conclusions from given information by using rules of logic. In deductive reasoning, we must be able to justify any statement that we make.

When you solve algebraic equations step by step, you are using deductive reasoning. You can justify every step (for instance, adding 3 to each side) with one or more properties (the Addition Property of Equality).

WHAT DO YOU THINK?

Kevin and Maria are both trying to figure out how they did on yesterday's history quiz.

Maria thinks . . .

I was able to answer all four questions, so I have a chance to get all 20 points. After class, I checked three answers in the book, and all of them were right. So I should get at least 15 out of 20. Since 12 is a passing score, I'm sure that I passed the quiz.

Kevin thinks . . .

We've had five history quizzes this quarter, and I've passed all of them. Also, Leah and I almost always get similar scores, and she got a perfect score on hers. So, I'm sure that I passed the quiz.

1. **In the preceding situation, who is using inductive reasoning, Kevin or Maria? Who is using deductive reasoning?**
2. **In this case, which type of reasoning seems more convincing? Why?**

Deductive reasoning can be a powerful tool. Lawyers use it to prove things true beyond a reasonable doubt. Mathematicians have an even stronger use for deductive reasoning. They use it to prove that their conjectures *must* be true given certain assumptions. Euclid, a Greek mathematician, based his famous geometry book, *The Elements,* on a system of deductive reasoning.

TRY IT

Suppose that the statements at the top of page 33 are true. For each set of statements, use deductive reasoning to give another statement that must also be true.

a. All reptiles have scales. An iguana is a reptile.
b. No fish have toes. I have toes.

In our deductive system, most of the terms you will use, like *line segment,* are **defined terms.** They are defined precisely so that you know exactly what they mean. Before you can start writing definitions, however, you need to know the meanings of at least a few terms. *Point* and *line* are two of the **undefined terms** in geometry.

Geometric conjectures also fall into two categories. Many of them, called **theorems,** are possible to prove deductively. However, you cannot prove anything unless you start with a few basic assumptions, called **postulates.** Postulates are assumed to be true without proof.

You'll investigate these parts of a deductive system in Chapter 2. As you develop your thinking skills and geometric knowledge, you'll be able to write good definitions and prove theorems yourself.

REFLECT

1. Explain, in your own words, how deductive reasoning works.
2. How is deductive reasoning different from inductive reasoning? Is one more reliable than the other? Why?
3. Is it possible for a valid deductive argument to lead to a false conclusion? How?

Exercises

CORE

1. **Getting Started** Suppose that the statements "All cats have fur" and "Fluffy is a cat" are true. Use deductive reasoning to give another statement that must also be true.

Suppose that each statement below is true. Use deductive reasoning to give another statement that must also be true.

2. No one living in Wyoming has a house on the beach. Chao-Yee has a beach-front house.
3. The figure Kai drew is a parallelogram. All parallelograms have four sides.
4. No elementary school student is old enough to vote. Kendrick is old enough to vote.

5. Days Daze In Lewis Carroll's *Through the Looking-Glass,* Alice met a lion and a unicorn. Suppose that the lion lies on Monday, Tuesday, and Wednesday, and the unicorn lies on Thursday, Friday, and Saturday. At all other times both animals tell the truth. Alice has forgotten the day of the week during her travels through the Forest of Forgetfulness.

"Yesterday was one of my lying days," said the lion.

"Yesterday was one of my lying days, too," said the unicorn. Alice, who was very smart, was able to deduce the day.

What day of the week is it? Explain.

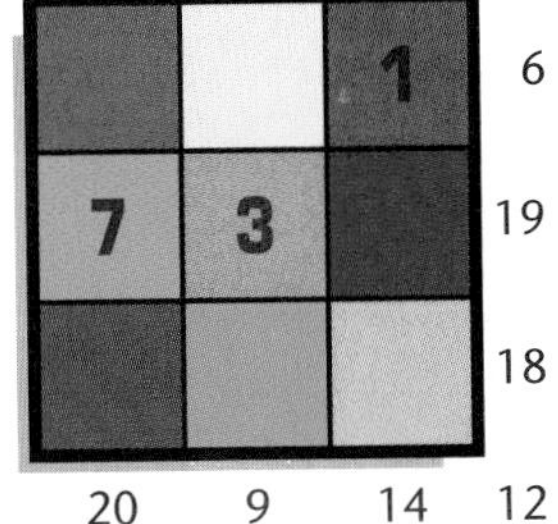

6. What are the missing numbers in the square at the right? Explain your answers. (The numbers outside the square show the sums of the numbers in the rows, columns, and diagonal.)

7. Make a conjecture about the following number trick.

a. Choose a number. **b.** Double it. **c.** Add 10.
d. Divide by 2. **e.** Add 7. **f.** Subtract the original number.

Conjecture: The result is always ___.

Now, use algebra to verify your conjecture.

> **Problem-Solving Tip**
>
> Use your skills in translating words into algebraic terms to write an expression to represent each step. (Hint: First, let *n* equal the number. Simplify each expression.)

8. Is the following statement true or false? Explain. *Some snakes are reptiles.*

9. Solve the following equation for x. Show each step, and explain why each step is valid.
$3x - 2(25 - 3x) = 40$

Did you use inductive or deductive reasoning to solve this equation?

10. One way to try to convince you that the sum of two even numbers is always even is to show you that this conjecture is true for several examples. This is an inductive argument. Describe another method that would convince you that this statement is true. Explain how it differs from inductive reasoning.

11. Population Explosion! The growth of the world's population in the 20th century is shown in the table below.

Social Science

Year	1900	1950	1980	1991
Population (billions)	1.6	2.6	4.5	5.4

a. Make a scatter plot of the population data.
b. Though you have limited data, use your scatter plot to predict the world's population in the year 2010. Did you use inductive or deductive reasoning? Explain.

LOOK AHEAD

Simplify each expression.

12. $3 - (-4)$ **13.** $-5 - 8$ **14.** $-7 - (-2)$ **15.** $6 - 11$

16. Plot points with coordinates -2, 3, $\frac{1}{3}$, and -4.5 on a number line.

17. Plot points with coordinates $(-1, 4)$, $(2, 5)$, and $(0, -3.5)$ on a coordinate plane.

MORE PRACTICE

Suppose that each statement below is true. Use deductive reasoning to give another statement that must also be true.

18. Every child needs attention. William is a child.

19. No one who lives in San Diego lives in Illinois. Tamika lives in Illinois.

20. No mathematicians are boring. Kenji is a mathematician.

21. Every square is also a rectangle. Every rectangle is also a parallelogram.

MORE MATH REASONING

22. Finding Your Marbles Three containers each contain two marbles. One container has two blue marbles, another has two white marbles, and the third has a blue and a white marble. The containers are labeled BB, WW, and BW, but, unfortunately, all of the labels are wrong! What is the least number of draws that you must make to determine the contents of the containers? Explain.

23. Examine these three-step sequences adapted from *Symbolic Logic* by Lewis Carroll. Are they logical or are they nonsense? Carroll liked to write both. Why do you think they are or are not valid?

a. All well-fed canaries sing loudly.
No canary is sad if it sings loudly.
Therefore, all well-fed canaries are not sad.

b. Every eagle can fly.
Some pigs cannot fly.
Therefore, some pigs are not eagles.

24. Illustrate the following with one Venn diagram. Your diagram should include real numbers, rational numbers, irrational numbers, and integers.

- All real numbers are either rational numbers or irrational numbers.
- No rational numbers are irrational numbers.
- All integers are rational numbers.
- All rational numbers and irrational numbers are real numbers.

1-2 PART D Making Connections

← CONNECT → ***Reasoning involves many skills, including the ability to recognize patterns and to justify conclusions by using accepted facts. You need these skills to be able to draw sound conclusions from known information. You've looked at some ways of reasoning. The two types of thinking you've explored are inductive and deductive reasoning.***

You've seen inductive and deductive reasoning used in Wonderland and in the real world. People—even fictional characters like the Mad Hatter—use both types of reasoning in mathematics, science, and everyday conversation. In the following Explore, you will use your reasoning skills to help make a convincing argument.

EXPLORE: DENSITY AND DOLLARS

The following tables show 1990 population densities and per-capita income for the eight most densely populated and least densely populated states. The data comes from *The 1993 Information Please Almanac.*

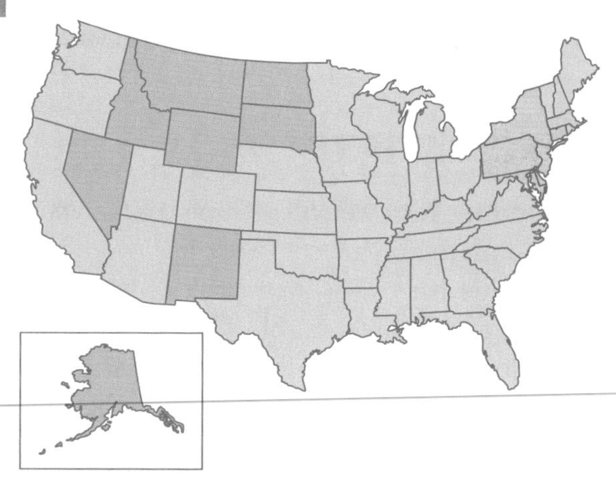

State	Population Density (people per square mile)	Per-capita Income (dollars per person)
New Jersey	1035.1	24,881
Rhode Island	951.1	18,809
Massachusetts	768.9	22,555
Connecticut	674.7	25,395
Maryland	486.0	21,857
New York	379.7	22,129
Delaware	344.8	20,095
Pennsylvania	264.7	18,679

State	Population Density (people per square mile)	Per-capita Income (dollars per person)
New Mexico	12.5	14,254
Idaho	12.2	15,250
Nevada	10.9	19,049
South Dakota	9.1	15,890
North Dakota	9.0	15,355
Montana	5.5	15,304
Wyoming	4.7	16,283
Alaska	1.0	21,646

1. In your group, create the *strongest argument that you can* to convince someone that states with a greater population density tend to have a higher per-capita income. You need not rely on the table alone; you may also use your own thinking to strengthen your argument.
2. Analyze how your argument uses inductive reasoning.
3. Analyze how your argument uses deductive reasoning.
4. Do the most convincing arguments rely on inductive reasoning, deductive reasoning, or both? Explain.

REFLECT

1. Is a scientist more likely to use inductive or deductive reasoning? Why?
2. Is a mathematician more likely to use inductive or deductive reasoning to show that a conjecture is true? Why?
3. When showing *that* something is true, do people tend to rely more on inductive or deductive reasoning? How about when they are showing *why* it is true? Explain your answer.

Self-Assessment

Indicate whether each of the following statements is more illustrative of inductive or deductive reasoning.

1. One counterexample proves that a conjecture is false.
2. Gathering many examples helps to verify the conjecture.
3. You give evidence that your conjecture is true.
4. You show why your conjecture makes sense.

Find the next number in each sequence. Explain the pattern.

5. 6, 11, 16, 21, . . .

6. 0, 3, 8, 15, 24, . . .

7. 1, 8, 27, 64, . . .

Solve each equation. [Previous course]

8. $12 = 5x - 3$

9. $7y + 2(y - 5) = 3y$

Graph each equation on a coordinate plane. [Previous course]

10. $y = 2x - 1$

11. $y = -\frac{3}{2}x + 3$

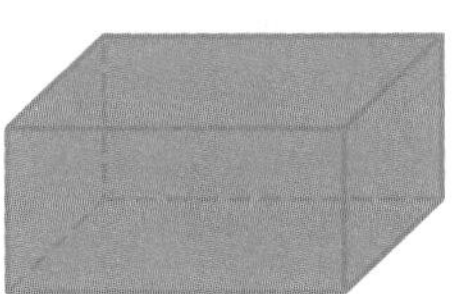

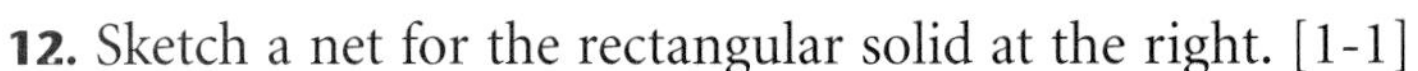

12. Sketch a net for the rectangular solid at the right. [1-1]

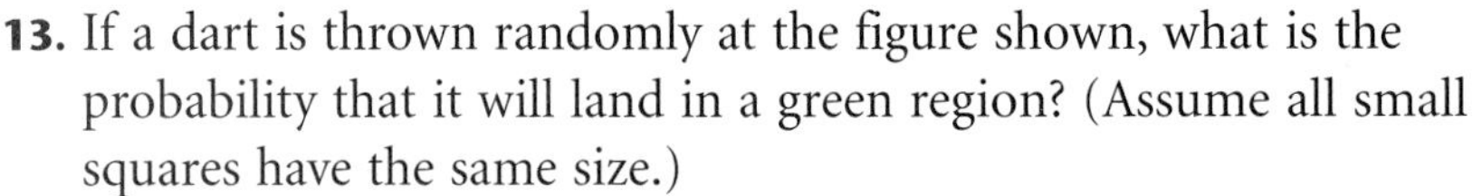

13. If a dart is thrown randomly at the figure shown, what is the probability that it will land in a green region? (Assume all small squares have the same size.)

(a) $\frac{3}{8}$ (b) $\frac{1}{2}$ (c) $\frac{9}{16}$ (d) $\frac{7}{16}$ (e) $\frac{1}{3}$

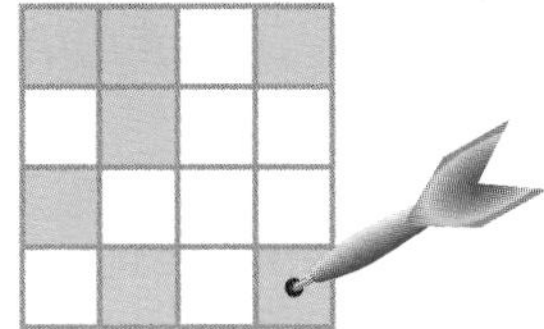

14. How many regions are formed in a circle by segments connecting points on the circle? The sequence is begun at the right.

a. Make a conjecture about the number of regions formed by connecting n points on a circle.

b. Test your conjecture by drawing 6 points on a circle and drawing segments to connect the points in all possible ways. Count the regions formed. Is your conjecture valid? Explain.

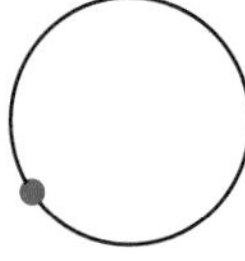

1 point
1 region

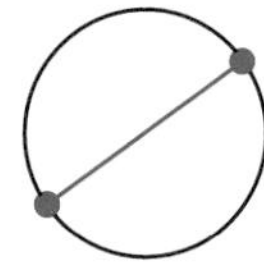

2 points
2 regions

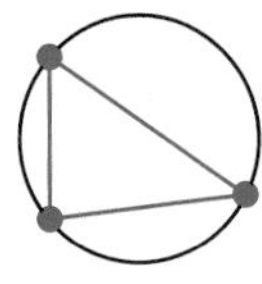

3 points
4 regions

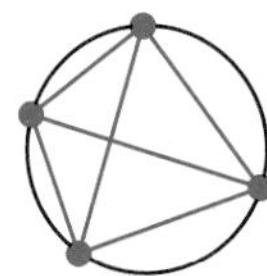

4 points
? regions

15. Step-by-Step Reasoning Find an expression for the number of small squares in a "staircase" that is n units high. Explain how you found your answer and whether you used inductive reasoning, deductive reasoning, or both.

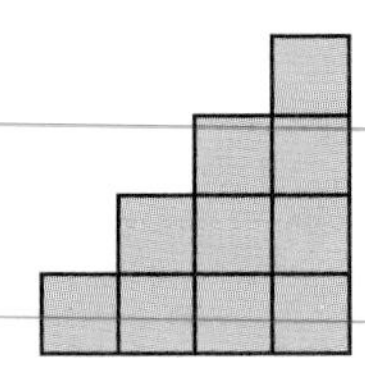

Literature

16. Glad to Meet You! During her adventures in Wonderland, Alice made many unusual acquaintances. Imagine that Alice held a tea party for 10 of her new acquaintances. As each guest arrived, he or she shook hands exactly once with every other person, including Alice. How many handshakes were there all together? Write a brief explanation of how you found your answer.

Problem-Solving Tip

It may help to draw a diagram to represent the problem.

1-3 Measuring Figures

PACKAGE WT: 36LB. SIZE:46 INCHES. CONTENTS: LOBSTERS - FRAGILE. ORIGIN: BOSTON. DEST: DINNER

United Parcel Service (**UPS**) usually transports packages, but when their aircraft are not filled to capacity, available space is used creatively to generate more revenue.

One flight took some passengers from Boston to a dinner party in Los Angeles. The plane landed safely and on schedule, but the passengers were just steaming after they arrived. Who were they? Nearly 200,000 pounds of live lobsters.

UPS drivers deliver millions of parcels each day. The parcels range in size from Letters to 150-pound packages. Prices for services within the United States and to many foreign countries are determined by measurement. The size and weight of the package and the distance that the package needs to travel are all factors in determining the cost.

Packages come in different sizes and shapes, with just a few limitations. The maximum weight per package is 150 pounds. The maximum size is 130 inches in length and girth combined, with a maximum length of 108 inches. Drivers have a 130-inch chain so they can find out quickly if a package exceeds the size limits.

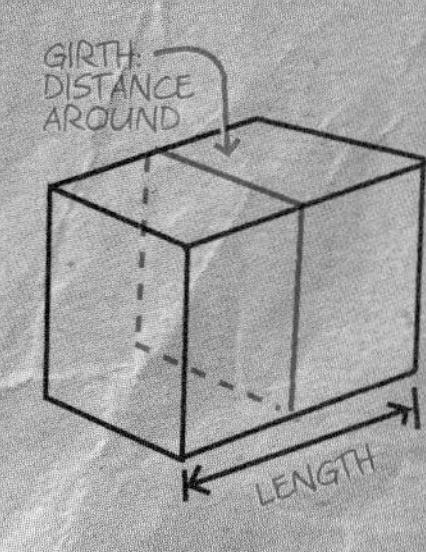

?

1. Describe how a UPS driver might use a 130-inch chain to see if a package exceeds the size limits.
2. Why do you think packages are not allowed to be longer than 108 inches?
3. How do you think drivers decide which dimension of a package is its "length"?

1-3 PART A Measuring Segments

← CONNECT →

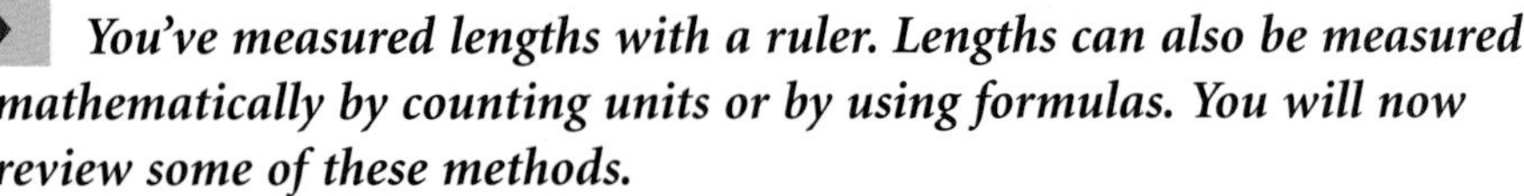

You've measured lengths with a ruler. Lengths can also be measured mathematically by counting units or by using formulas. You will now review some of these methods.

How long is an inch? If you had to show someone how long an inch is, you could probably cut a string to about the right length. Or you could bend your thumb. The distance from the tip of your thumb to the knuckle is about one inch.

Although people are not all the same size, some countries once based standard units on their kings or queens—on the person's height or the length of an arm, for example. When a new "ruler" came to power, the sizes of the units of measure changed. This was obviously inconvenient! It is said that the English yard was permanently established in the 1100s as the distance from the nose to the thumb of King Henry I. A line segment has a length, but the length of a segment is not the same thing as the segment itself. Some simple notation helps us know which we are talking about.

The **length** of segment $\overline{RS}$ is written RS (with no segment symbol above the letters). If the length of $\overline{RS}$ is 4 units, we write $RS = 4$. When we refer to RS, you know we mean a number, not a geometric figure.

R S
4

To find the length of a segment on a number line, find the distance between the coordinates of its endpoints.

EXAMPLE

Find the lengths of segments $\overline{AB}$, $\overline{AC}$, and $\overline{BC}$ on the number line below. (In other words, find AB, AC, and BC.)

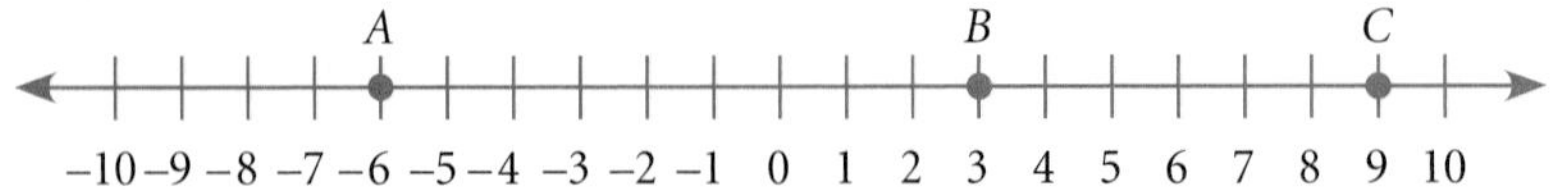

To find the length of a segment, first find the difference of the coordinates of its endpoints. Then, since distance is always positive, take the absolute value of the result, as shown on page 41.

$AB = |-6 - 3| = |-9| = 9$ or $AB = |3 - (-6)| = |9| = 9$

$BC = |3 - 9| = |-6| = 6$ or $BC = |9 - 3| = |6| = 6$

$AC = |-6 - 9| = |-15| = 15$ or $AC = |9 - (-6)| = |15| = 15$

In the Explore, you'll look at lengths and distances on a coordinate plane.

EXPLORE: FAR FROM IT

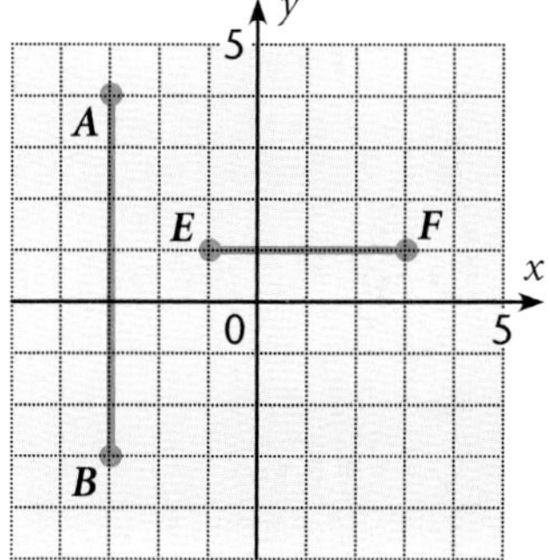

1. Look at the vertical segment $\overline{AB}$ on the coordinate plane. What is the ordered pair for point *A*? point *B*? What is *AB*?

2. What do you notice about the *x*-coordinates for the endpoints of $\overline{AB}$? their *y*-coordinates?

3. Explain how the method for finding the length of a segment on a number line can be applied to a vertical segment on a coordinate plane.

4. Now find the length of the horizontal segment $\overline{EF}$. Give a written explanation of how you found this length.

In algebra, you used the *distance formula* to find the distance between any two points, $A(x_1, y_1)$ and $B(x_2, y_2)$, on a coordinate plane.

$$D = \sqrt{(x_2 - x_1)^2 + (y_2 - y_1)^2}$$

(Later on, you will discover *why* this formula works.)

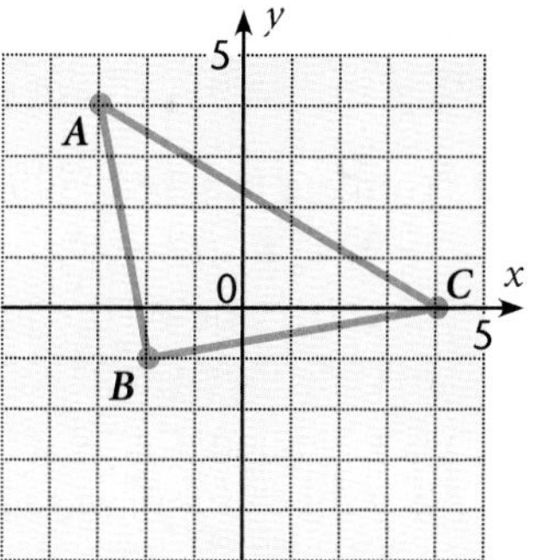

5. Record the length of each side of the triangle to the nearest tenth. Then find the perimeter of triangle *ABC*. (The perimeter of a figure is the sum of the lengths of its sides.)

The *distance between two points on a number line* with coordinates *a* and *b* is the absolute value of the difference of their coordinates.

$D = |a - b|$

The *distance between two points on a coordinate plane* whose coordinates are (x_1, y_1) and (x_2, y_2) is:

$D = \sqrt{(x_2 - x_1)^2 + (y_2 - y_1)^2}$

TRY IT

a. Find the lengths of $\overline{XY}$, $\overline{XZ}$, and $\overline{YZ}$ on a number line if the coordinate of X is -1.3, the coordinate of Y is -4, and the coordinate of Z is 2.7.

b. Find the lengths of $\overline{RS}$, $\overline{ST}$, and $\overline{TR}$ to the nearest tenth in the figure at the right.

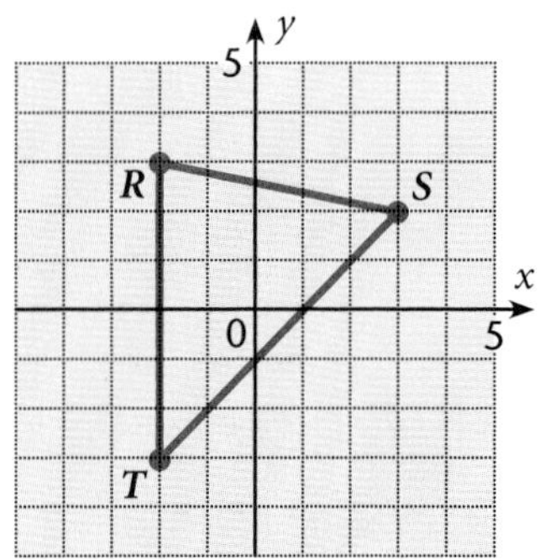

REFLECT

1. Segments on a coordinate plane can be measured by using a ruler or a formula. Which method gives you an exact answer? Explain.

2. How can you tell whether you'll have to use the distance formula to find the distance between two points on a coordinate plane or if you can use a simpler method?

Exercises

CORE

Where necessary, round your answers to the nearest tenth.

1. Getting Started Follow these steps to find the distance from $(-3, 4)$ to $(6, -4)$.

a. Label one of the points (x_1, y_1) and the other (x_2, y_2).

b. Calculate $(x_2 - x_1)$ and square the result.

c. Calculate $(y_2 - y_1)$ and square the result.

d. Add the squared values from **1b** and **1c**.

e. Take the square root of the result in Part **1d.**

Find the length of segment $\overline{AB}$ for each set of coordinates.

2. $a = 3, b = 6$

3. $a = -3, b = 6$

4. $a = 0.45, b = 2.23$

5. $a = -10, b = -4$

***R* and *S* are points on a coordinate plane. Find *RS* using the given coordinates.**

6. $R(2, 4), S(5, 4)$

7. $R(2, 4), S(2, -3)$

8. $R(-1, -3), S(-4, 4)$

9. $R(1.3, 2.8), S(5.1, 4.3)$

10. Explain the error in the following calculation of the distance from $(2, -5)$ to $(-6, 1)$.

$$D = \sqrt{(-6 - 2)^2 + (1 - (-5))^2}$$

$$D = \sqrt{(-8)^2 + 6^2}$$

$$D = \sqrt{64 + 36}$$

$$D = \sqrt{100}$$

$$D = 10 \text{ or } -10$$

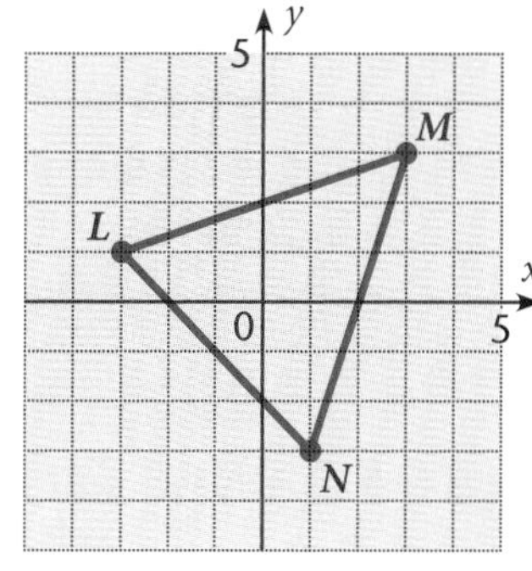

11. Find *LM*, *MN*, and *NL* in the figure at the right. Then find the perimeter of triangle *LMN*.

12. It may seem that the finer (more exact) a measurement is, the better it is. This is not always so. There are different units of measurement for different purposes. Choose the most appropriate unit of measure for each of the following. Explain your choice.

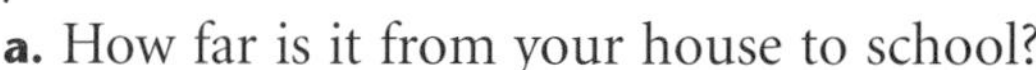

a. How far is it from your house to school?
b. How much milk is left in the refrigerator?
c. How far did the quarterback throw that pass?

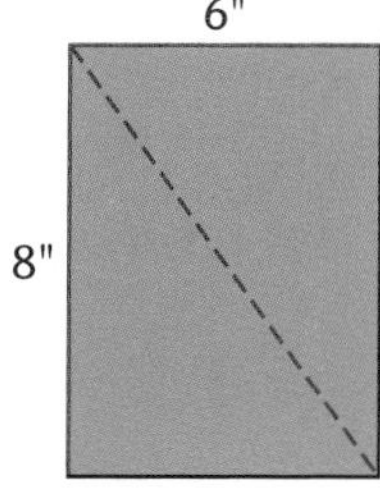

13. Paper Folding I How thick is a piece of paper? How thick will the paper be after 1 fold? after 2 folds? after 3 folds? How thick will the paper be after 50 folds? Give estimates, and explain your answers.

14. Paper Folding II A $6'' \times 8''$ paper rectangle is folded to create a diagonal. Find the length of the fold.

History

15. Printing on Paper A *pica* is a standard unit of measure in printing. (According to legend, movable type was invented by a Chinese woodcarver named Pi, and the term *pica* comes from his name.) A pica is approximately $\frac{1}{6}$ of an inch, and a point is $\frac{1}{12}$ of a pica.

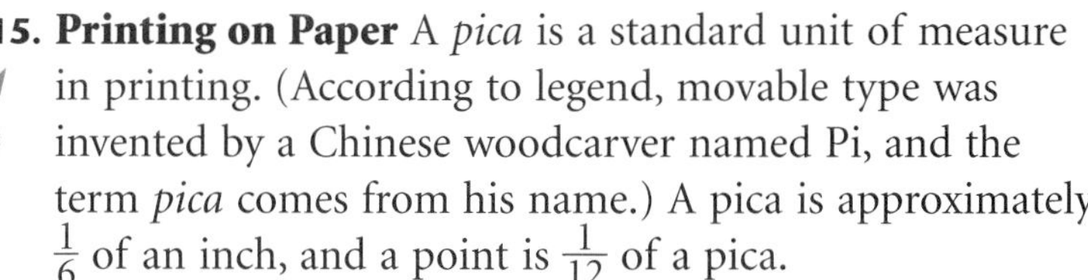

a. How many points are in one inch?

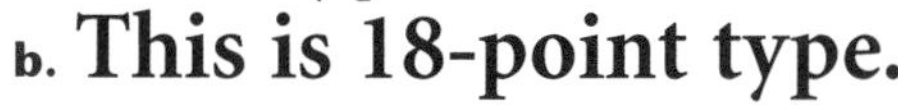

b. **This is 18-point type.**
How many picas are equal to 18 points?

16. Taking Aim This student is shooting a basketball. Describe several of the measurements that he is instinctively making.

LOOK BACK

17. Name all the points, lines, and segments in the figure. [1-1]

18. Name all the sets of three collinear points in the figure. [1-1]

19. List all the different names for line ℓ in the figure. [1-1]

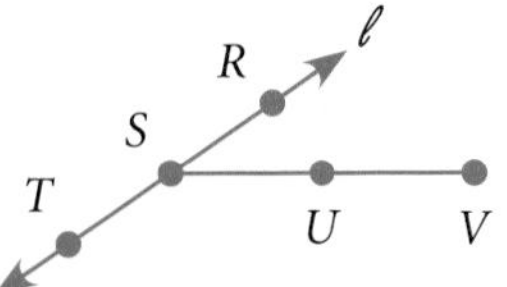

Find the next number in each sequence. Explain the pattern. [1-2]

20. 4.5, 6, 7.5, 9, . . .

21. $1, -\frac{1}{2}, \frac{1}{4}, -\frac{1}{8}, \ldots$

22. Gym Dandy Buff's Gym is open Monday through Saturday. Volleyball classes meet daily except Wednesdays. Tennis instruction is daily except Tuesdays and Saturdays. Swimming classes are held every other day starting on Mondays. Gymnastics instruction is available every day starting on Tuesdays. Which day has the most activities? Explain your reasoning. [1-2]

MORE PRACTICE

Find the length of segment $\overline{AB}$ for each set of coordinates.

23. $a = 4, b = 19$

24. $a = -4, b = 9$

25. $a = 0.21, b = 5.13$

26. $a = -41, b = -18$

***R* and *S* are points on a coordinate plane. Find *RS* using the given coordinates.**

27. $R(0, 4), S(3, 8)$

28. $R(-1, -4), S(-2, 4)$

29. $R(1.5, 3.8), S(3.4, 2.8)$

MORE MATH REASONING

30. The Lost City of Lead On an old map, Gold City is at (0, 0), and Silver Town is at (5, 2). The distance from Gold City to Lead Junction is 10, and the distance from Silver Town to Lead Junction is 5. The x-coordinate of Lead Junction is 8, but the y-coordinate has been lost. Where is Lead Junction?

31. Consider the 10×10 coordinate system at the right. Find the probability that a randomly selected point with integer coordinates will be more than 3 units away from the origin.

Problem-Solving Tip

Simplify the problem.

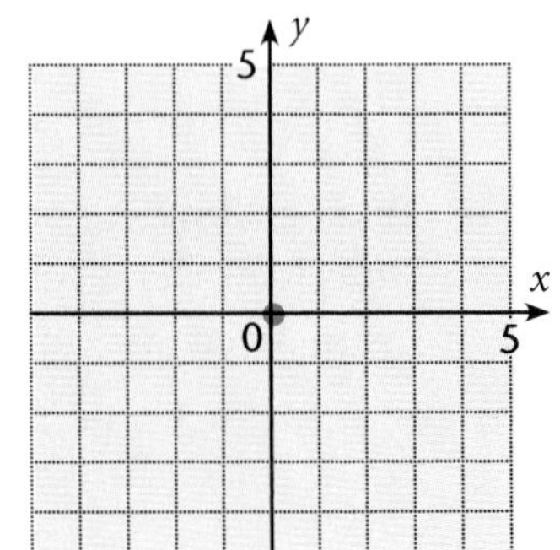

1-3 PART B Measuring Angles

← CONNECT → ***You've learned how to name and measure segments. Now you will see how to name and measure angles. You will also investigate the shortest distance from a point to a line.***

Before you name and measure angles, we need to introduce some vocabulary. You are probably familiar with many of these terms.

DEFINITION

A **ray** is a part of a line. It has one **endpoint** and extends infinitely in one direction.

A ray is named with its endpoint first, followed by another point on the ray. The ray shown above can be named $\overrightarrow{DB}$ or $\overrightarrow{DC}$.

TRY IT

a. Name the ray below in as many ways as you can.

An angle is made up of two rays.

DEFINITION

An **angle** is formed by two rays (that are not collinear) with a common endpoint, or **vertex.** The two rays are the **sides** of the angle.

The vertex of the angle shown is S, and its sides are $\overrightarrow{SR}$ and $\overrightarrow{ST}$.

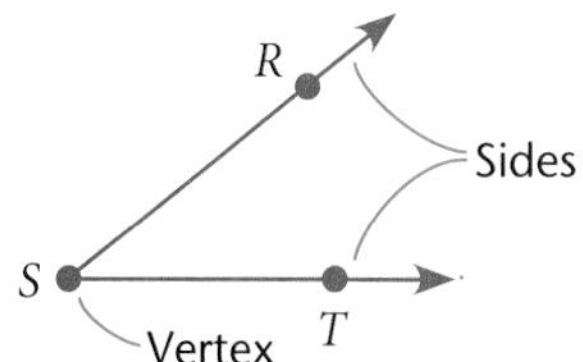

Angles can be named by using three different letters. The vertex is always written in the middle. The angle on page 45 can be called $\angle RST$ or $\angle TSR$. When no other angles share the same vertex point, an angle can be named by using just the vertex letter or a number.

EXAMPLE

Give four ways of naming the angle shown at the right.

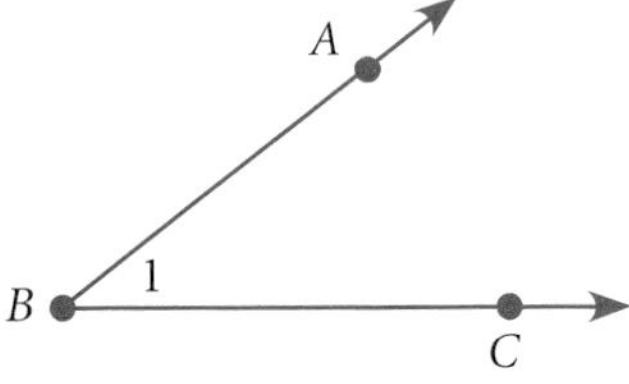

This is $\angle ABC$ or $\angle CBA$. Since there is no chance of confusion, it can also be named $\angle B$ or $\angle 1$.

Like segments, angles have different sizes. Angles are usually measured in **degrees.** The symbol for degree is °. A 1-degree angle looks like this:

Angles measure between 0° and 180°. (They cannot measure 0° or 180°.) As with segments, the size of an angle is not the same thing as the angle itself. The **measure** of angle $\angle XYZ$ is written $m\angle XYZ$. If $\angle XYZ$ is an 80° angle, we write $m\angle XYZ = 80°$.

We use a protractor to measure angles. The arc of a protractor measures 180°. The figure below shows protractors being used to measure $\angle ABC$ and $\angle CBD$.

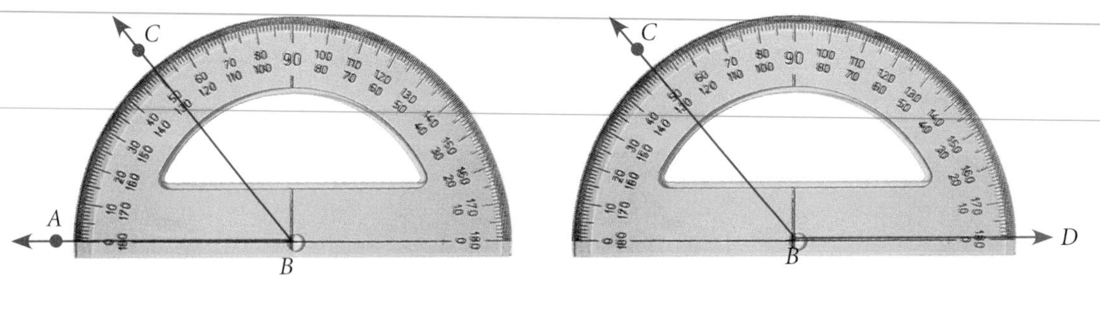

$m\angle ABC = 50°$ $m\angle CBD = 130°$

Notice that the small hole in the protractor is placed over the vertex of the angle.

TRY IT

Use your protractor to find the measure of each angle below.

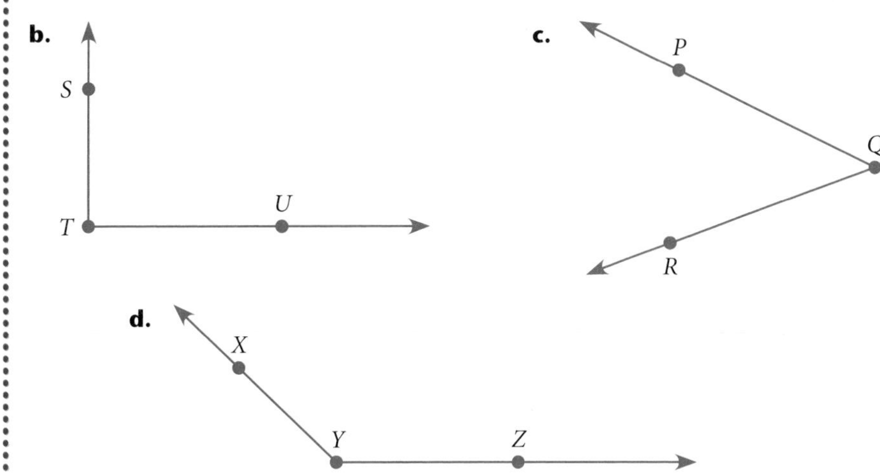

1. Describe how you know whether to use the outer number or the inner number on a protractor when measuring an angle.

Angles that measure 90° are particularly important in geometry. You see these angles everywhere: in buildings, on maps, and on basketball, volleyball, and tennis courts.

DEFINITIONS

A **right angle** is an angle that measures 90°.

Two lines that intersect at right angles are called **perpendicular lines.**

Right angles are sometimes marked with a small box at the vertex of the angle. The symbol for perpendicular is $\perp$. In the figure, $m \perp n$. Segments and rays that intersect lines or intersect each other at right angles are also considered perpendicular.

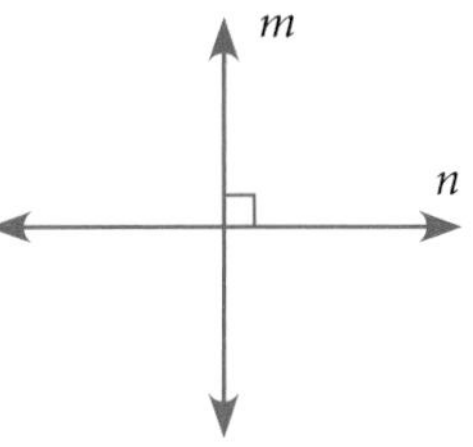

In the following Explore, you will use measuring tools to find the shortest segment from a point to a line.

EXPLORE: SHORT CUTS

MATERIALS

Ruler
Protractor
Geometry software (optional)

1. Sketch a line and a point not on the line. (It's best if the point is several inches away from the line.) Draw several segments from the point to the line, including the segment you think is the shortest one possible.
2. Using a ruler to measure the segments, identify the shortest segment from the point to the line.
3. Use a protractor to measure the angle formed by the line and the shortest segment.
4. Repeat **1, 2,** and **3** until you feel confident enough to make a conjecture about the shortest segment from a point to a line. Compare your conjecture with those of your classmates.

It is possible to prove the conjecture you made about the shortest segment from a point to a line, so we state it as a theorem (our first!).

THEOREM

The shortest segment from a point not on a line to the line is the perpendicular segment.

REFLECT

1. Why is 0° to 180° a convenient range of measurement for angles?
2. Suppose you're in a field next to a road. Describe the shortest path to the road from where you are. If you had a protractor, would it help you find the shortest path? Explain.
3. Name two things that can be modeled by a ray and two that can be modeled by an angle. Discuss the strengths and weaknesses of using a ray or angle as a model for each.

Exercises

CORE

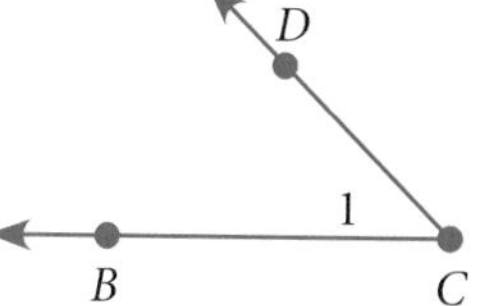

1. **Getting Started** Give four ways of naming the angle shown at the right.

2. Name all of the rays in the lower figure at the right.

3. Name all of the angles in the figure. How many angles are there?

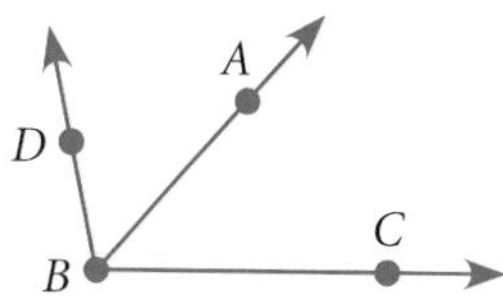

Estimate the measure of each angle below. Then use your protractor to find its measure.

4.

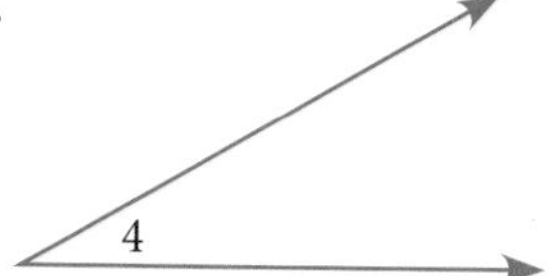

5.

Use your protractor to draw angles with the given measures. Include points so that the names of the angles are correct.

6. $m\angle ABC = 70°$
7. $m\angle FGH = 157°$
8. $m\angle LMN = 12°$

Make freehand sketches of angles that have approximately the following measures.

9. 45°
10. 90°
11. 150°

12. Write the letter of the second pair that best matches the first pair.

    Segment: length as (a) distance: road, (b) travel: distance, (c) number: figure, (d) angle: angle measure.

13. Explain why you can use AB to refer to the length of segment $\overline{AB}$ without confusion. How do you know it doesn't refer to the length of $\overrightarrow{AB}$ or $\overleftrightarrow{AB}$?

Estimate the angle formed by the hands of a clock at each of the following times.

14. 3:00
15. 11:00
16. 5:00
17. 8:20

18. An angle is a model for the hands of a clock. Describe several other objects that can be modeled by angles.

Find the measures of the following angles on a baseball diamond.

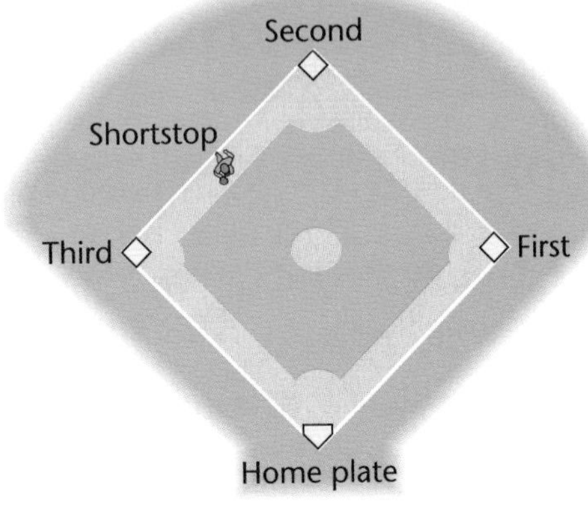

19. from home plate to first base to second base

20. from first base to home plate to second base

21. from the shortstop to home plate to first base (give an estimate)

22. When 1 ray is drawn inside an angle as shown at the right, 3 angles are formed. When 2 rays are drawn, 6 angles are formed. How many different angles are formed when 10 rays are drawn?

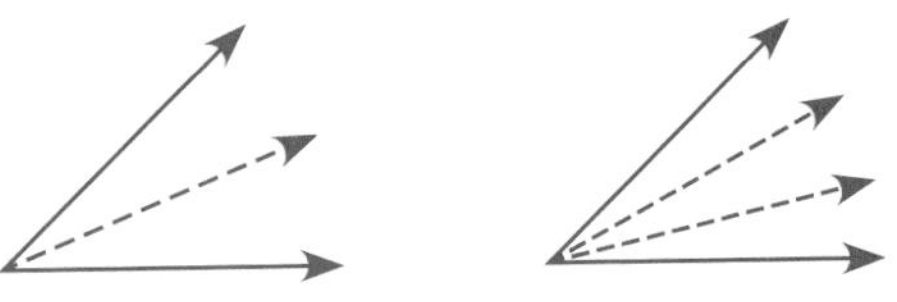

Problem-Solving Tip

Make a table and look for a pattern to help you make your prediction.

23. In the figure at the right, which segment is shorter, $\overline{LM}$ or $\overline{LN}$ ≃? Write a brief justification of your answer.

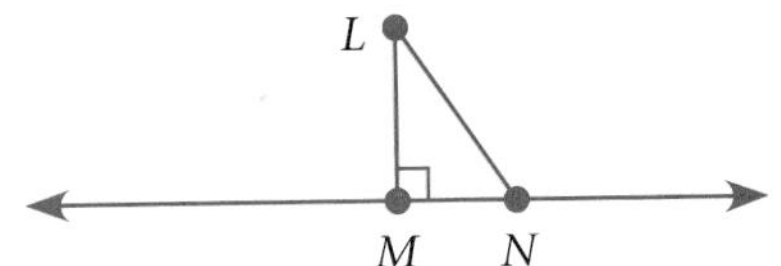

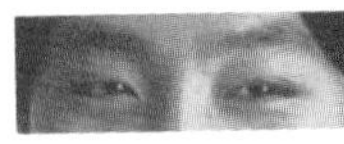

LOOK AHEAD

Points *A* and *B* have coordinates *a* and *b* on a number line. Find the coordinate of *C* so that *AB* = *BC*.

24. $a = 2, b = 4$

25. $a = -5, b = 3$

26. $a = -9, b = -12$

MORE PRACTICE

27. Name all of the rays in the figure.

28. Name all of the angles in the figure.

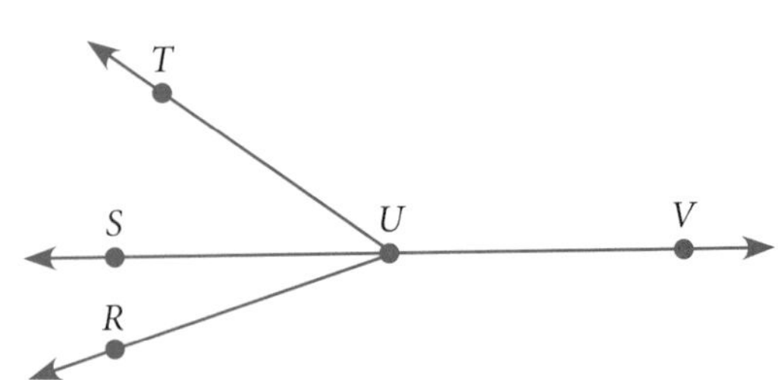

Estimate the measure of each angle below. Then use your protractor to find its measure.

29.

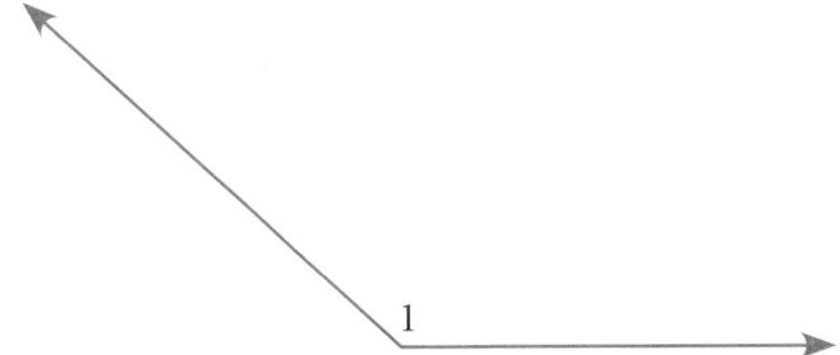

30.

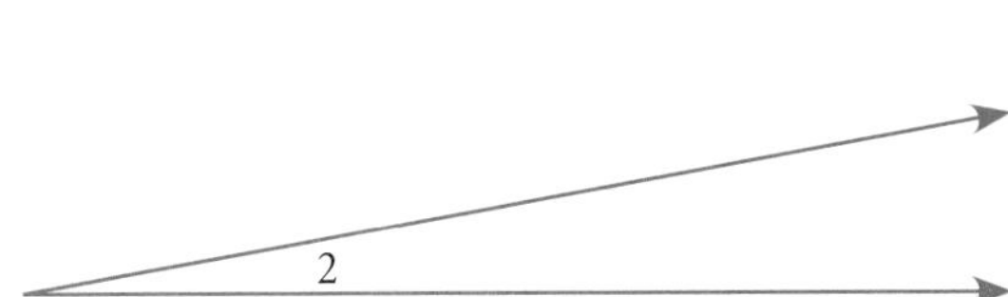

Use your protractor to draw angles with the given measures. Include points so that the names of the angles are correct.

31. $m\angle KLM = 60°$ **32.** $m\angle WXY = 98°$ **33.** $m\angle EFG = 22°$

MORE MATH REASONING

Science

34. Continental Drift As part of an international project that began in 1900, five observatories were set up to study changes in latitude caused by continental drift. The American observatories are located in Gaithersburg, Maryland, and Ukiah, California. Other observatories are on Sardinia, an island off the southwest coast of Italy, in Turkmenistan (the former Soviet Turkistan) in central Asia, and north of Tokyo on Honshu, the largest of the Japanese islands.

a. Why do you think these five locations were chosen for the project?

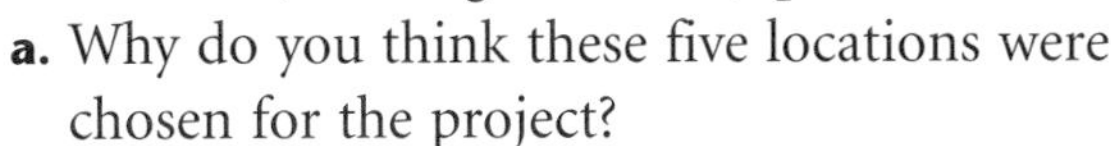

b. Each of the observatories makes nightly observations of 18 pairs of stars. How do you think scientists use these data to look for continental drift?

35. These statements can be used to show that $\overline{RS}$ is longer than both $\overline{ST}$ and $\overline{RT}$ in the triangle shown. Why is each statement true?

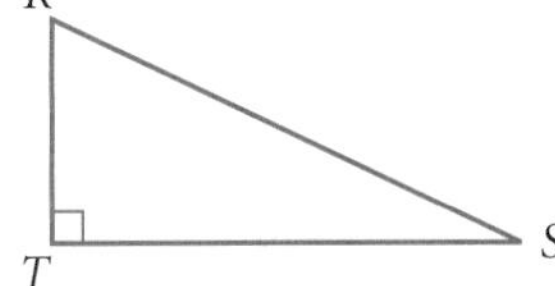

Statement	**Why?**
$\overline{ST} \perp \overline{RT}$	Given information
$\overline{RS} > \overline{RT}$	________________
$\overline{RS} > \overline{ST}$	________________

1-3 PART C Congruence

← CONNECT → *You've learned how to measure angles and segments. Now you will investigate angles and segments that have equal measures. You will also begin to use a compass and straightedge to do geometric constructions.*

In geometry, we often work with figures that are exactly the same size and shape. There is a special term for this relationship.

DEFINITION

Congruent figures have the same shape and size.

When two segments have the same length or two angles have the same measure, they are congruent. The symbol for congruence is ≅.

EXAMPLE

Is $\overline{PR} \cong \overline{RQ}$?

$PR = |1 - (-3)| = |4| = 4$

$RQ = |5 - 1| = 4$

Since $PR = RQ$, $\overline{PR} \cong \overline{RQ}$.

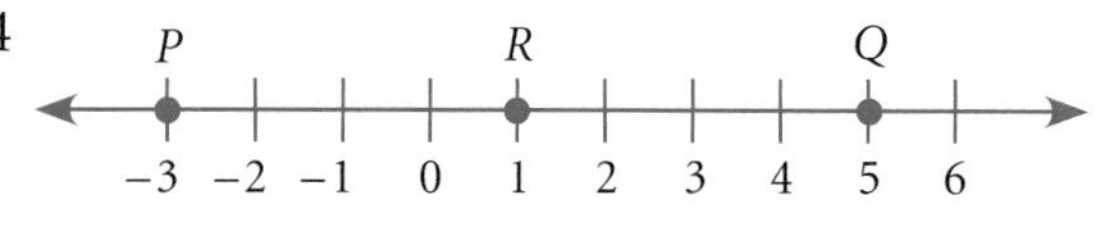

We show congruent segments by marking them with the same number of "tick marks." In the figure, $\overline{WX} \cong \overline{XY}$.

We show congruent angles by marking them with the same number of arcs near their vertices. In the figure, $\angle EIF \cong \angle FIG$.

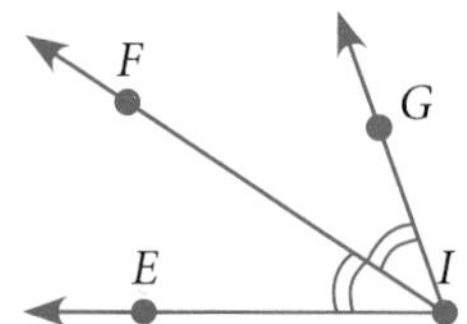

TRY IT

a. Draw and mark one figure that shows all of the following relationships. On line $\overleftrightarrow{AB}$, $\overline{AB} \cong \overline{BC}$. Also, $\angle ABD \cong \angle ABE$.

EXPLORE: COORDINATE CONGRUENCE

MATERIALS

Graph paper
Straightedge

You've used the distance formula $D = \sqrt{(x_2 - x_1)^2 + (y_2 - y_1)^2}$ to find the distance between two points $A(x_1, y_1)$ and $B(x_2, y_2)$ on a coordinate plane.

1. Name some line segments on the coordinate plane that *appear* to be congruent.
2. Use the distance formula to find the length of each line segment and determine which are *actually* congruent.
3. Draw a line segment congruent to $\overline{AB}$ on your graph paper. Explain how you know it is congruent.

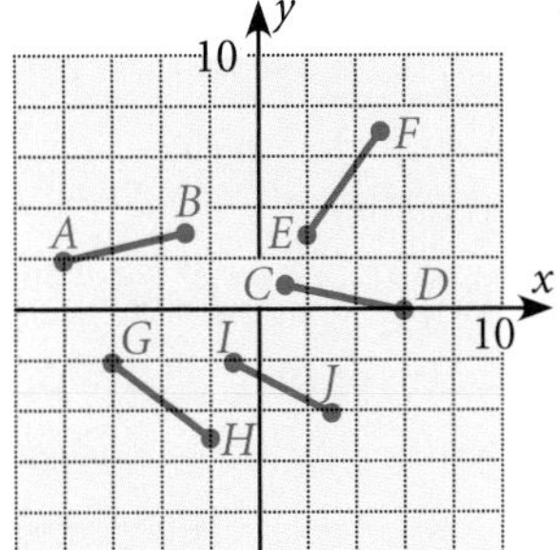

A geometric **construction** is a technique for drawing precise figures using only a straightedge and compass. The straightedge (a ruler with no markings) lets you draw straight line segments; the compass, when kept in one position, can be used to measure a consistent distance. When doing a construction, you are not allowed to do numerical measurement.

CONSTRUCTION: CONGRUENT SEGMENTS

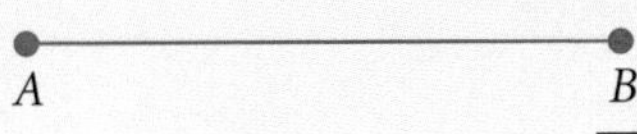

1. Begin by drawing a segment $\overline{AB}$ on your paper. This is the segment that you will copy in your construction.

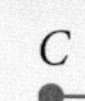

2. Draw a point *C*. Use a straightedge to draw a line segment starting at *C* that is longer than $\overline{AB}$. Point *C* corresponds to point *A* on the original segment.

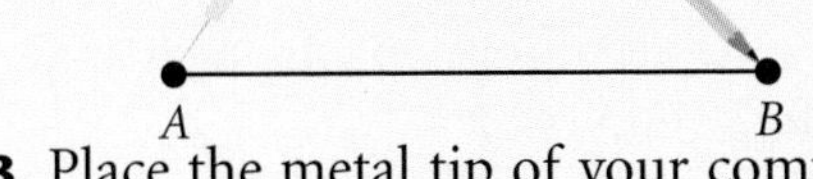

3. Place the metal tip of your compass at *A*, and open up your compass to the size of $\overline{AB}$ by moving the tip of the pencil to point *B*.

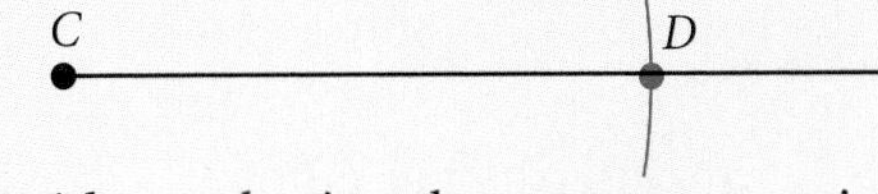

4. Without altering the compass opening, move the point of the compass to *C* and swing the pencil so that you make a mark on the line at distance *AB*. Place a point at this location, and label it *D*. $\overline{AB}$ and $\overline{CD}$ have the same length. We can write $\overline{AB} \cong \overline{CD}$.

You can also use a straightedge and compass to construct congruent angles.

CONSTRUCTION: CONGRUENT ANGLES

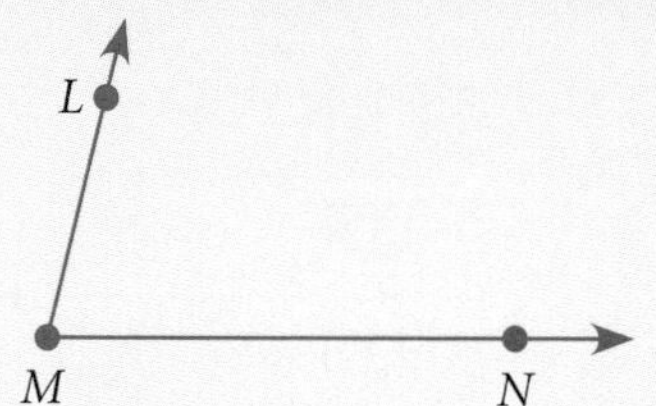

1. Begin by drawing angle $\angle LMN$ on your paper. This will be the angle that you copy in your construction.

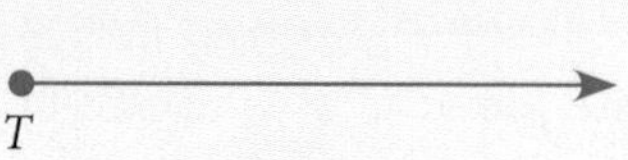

2. Use your straightedge to draw a ray. This will be one side of the copy. Label its endpoint *T*.

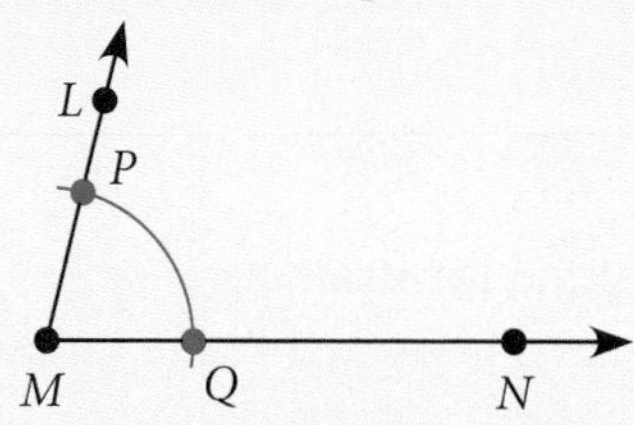

3. Place the compass tip on the vertex of $\angle LMN$. Draw an arc that intersects both rays of $\angle LMN$ as shown. Label the points of intersection of the angle and the arc *P* and *Q*.

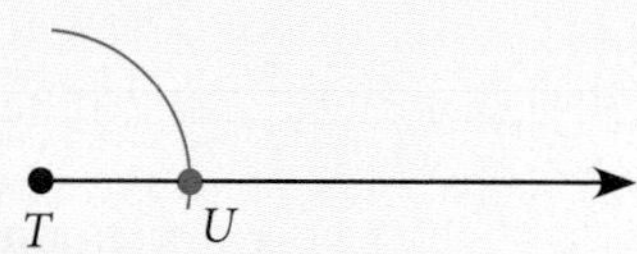

4. Without changing the compass opening, place the tip on the endpoint of the ray, *T*. Draw an arc about the same length as the arc on $\angle LMN$. Label the intersection of the arc and the ray point *U*, as shown.

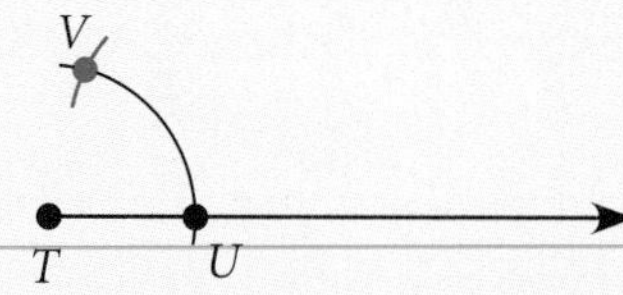

5. Use the compass to measure from point *P* to point *Q*. Without changing the compass opening, place the tip of the compass on point *U*. Make a small arc across the existing arc through *U*. Call the intersection point *V*.

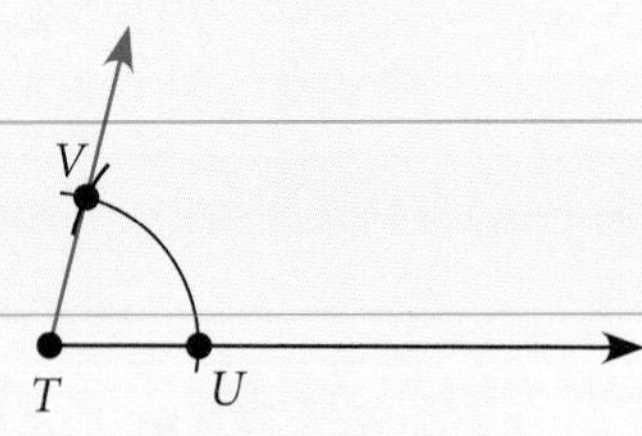

6. Draw the second ray of the new angle through point *V*. $\angle VTU \cong \angle LMN$.

1. **Explain how this construction technique guarantees that $\overline{MQ} \cong \overline{TU}$ and $\overline{UV} \cong \overline{PQ}$.**
2. **Why do you think this construction works? (We will be looking at this more closely in Chapter 8.)**

REFLECT

1. Explain how the statements below are related but different.
   - $EF = GH$
   - $\overline{EF} \cong \overline{GH}$
2. Many of the constructions you will do in this book were first developed in ancient Greece. Why do you think that making numerical measurements was not allowed in these techniques? Do some of the same concerns apply today?

Exercises

CORE

1. **Getting Started** Identify the pairs of figures that appear to be congruent from the six shown.

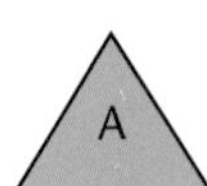

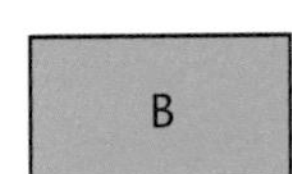

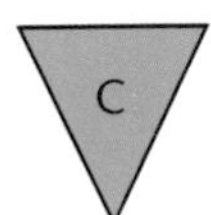

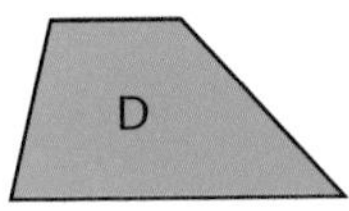

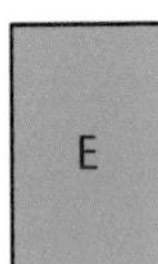

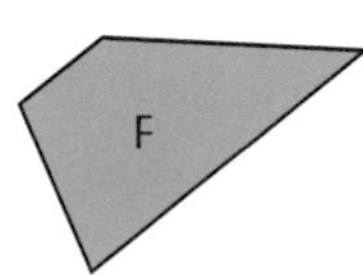

2. Is $\overline{XY} \cong \overline{YZ}$? Explain.

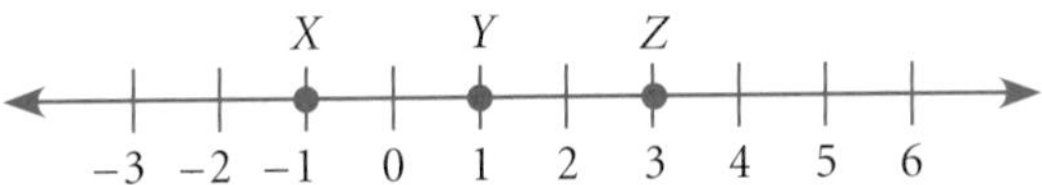

Copy the segments below. Then use a compass and straightedge to construct segments congruent to them.

3.

4.

Copy the angles below. Then use a compass and straightedge to construct angles congruent to them.

5.

6.

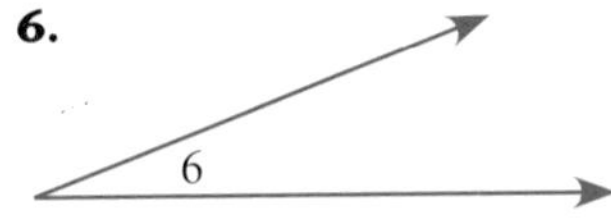

7. Construct a copy of the figure at the right. Make sure that the segments are the correct lengths.

8. Draw and mark one figure that shows all of the following relationships.

$\angle MNP \cong \angle MNQ$. Also, $\overline{NP} \cong \overline{NQ}$.

9. Suppose $\overline{GH} \cong \overline{HK}$. If all three points lie on a number line, and H has coordinate -4, and K has coordinate -12, find the coordinate of G.

10. Sketch $\angle ABC$ and $\angle ABD$ so that $\angle ABC \cong \angle ABD$. What is $m\angle ABC$ in terms of $m\angle CBD$? (Assume $m\angle ABC < 90°$.)

Suppose $\overline{RS} \cong \overline{MN}$. For each set of lengths, solve for x, and find the length of each segment.

11. $RS = 3x + 17, MN = 7x - 15$

12. $RS = \frac{x}{3} + 10, MN = \frac{2x}{3} + 4$

Write the letter of the second pair that best matches the first pair.

13. Congruent: equal as (a) similar: same, (b) length: distance, (c) segment: length, (d) construction: sketch.

14. Construction: sketch as (a) congruent: equal, (b) draft: book, (c) dog: puppy, (d) exact: approximate.

15. Use a straightedge to draw a triangle. Then use construction techniques to help you draw a second triangle that is congruent to the first. Explain how you made sure that the second triangle is congruent to the first. What do you think it means to say that two triangles are congruent?

16. Develop a method for constructing a segment four times as long as the one below. Show your construction and explain your method.

17. Light Exercise When a beam of light reflects off a mirror, the *angle of incidence* is congruent to the *angle of reflection*. If $m\angle ABC = 48°$, find $m\angle ABD$.

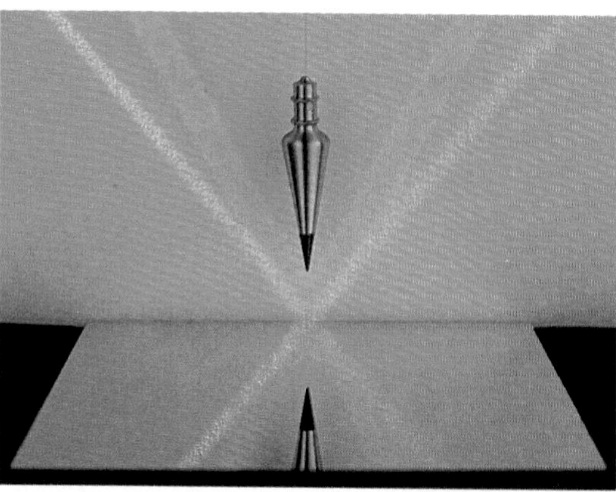

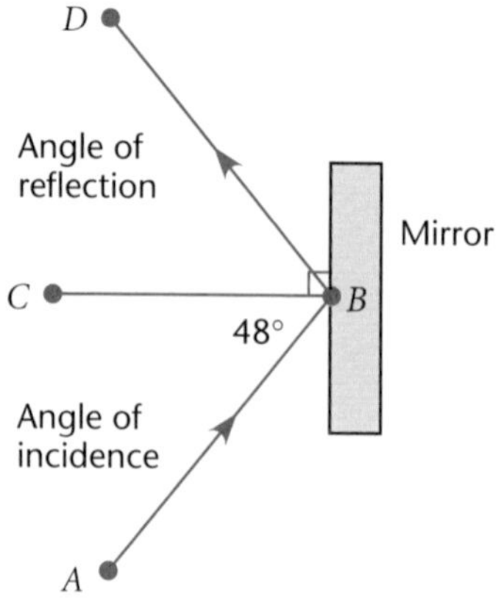

LOOK BACK

Graph each linear equation below. Give the slope and *y*-intercept of each line. [1-1]

18. $y = 4x - 2$

19. $y = -3x + 1$

20. $y = 3$

Find the slope of $\overleftrightarrow{AB}$ if *A* and *B* have the following coordinates. [1-1]

21. $A(3, 4), B(5, 8)$

22. $A(-2, 7), B(5, -2)$

23. $A(-4.2, 2.7), B(-4.2, -3.8)$

MORE PRACTICE

Construct segments congruent to the ones below.

24.

25.

Construct angles congruent to the ones below.

26.

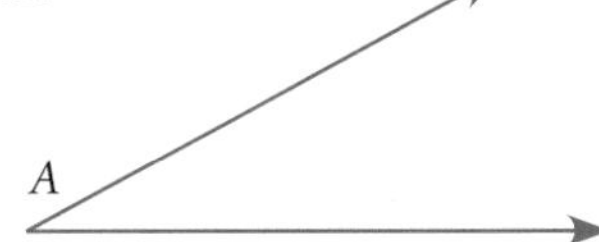

27.

$\angle DEF \cong \angle RST$. For each set of angle measures, solve for *x*, and find the measure of each angle.

28. $m\angle DEF = (x + 20)°$, $m\angle RST = (3x - 42)°$

29. $m\angle DEF = (5x + 18)°$, $m\angle RST = (6x - 5)°$

MORE MATH REASONING

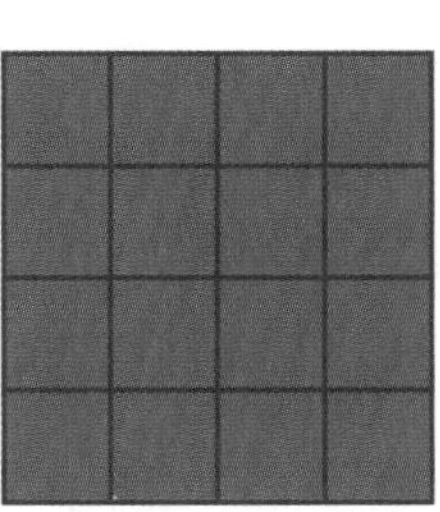

30. Square Counts How many congruent squares of various sizes are there on a 4-by-4 grid?

31. Suppose you use the congruent-angle construction to construct $\angle MNO \cong \angle PQR$. Then you use your protractor to measure each and find that $m\angle MNO = 76°$ and $m\angle PQR = 79°$. Give an explanation for what might have happened.

1-3 PART D Making Connections

← CONNECT → ***Measurement is used in many careers in many different ways. You've learned how to use the tools of geometric measurement—the ruler, compass, and protractor.***

You've seen that measurement is important in the shipping industry. It is also crucial in designing packages that the shipping industry can actually ship! The photo at the right shows shipping containers at the port of Los Angeles.

EXPLORE: NET-WORKING

MATERIALS

Scissors, Tape
Large sheets of paper
Compass, Ruler
Protractor

Design a net to make a small shipping package for UPS. It must meet the following standards.

- It must have a combined length and girth of no more than 36 in.
- To draw a side that is the same length as another side, you must use the congruent-segment construction. Show the construction marks on your paper.
- To make an angle that is the same measure as another angle, you must use the congruent-angle construction. Show the construction marks.
- All side and angle measures should be labeled on your net.
- When folded up, the package must have no open sides, gaps, or extra material.

Draw a net that you feel will meet these standards on one sheet of paper. Then make a copy of your net on a second piece of paper and check that it folds up properly. (You do not need to copy the construction marks.) Compare your design with those of your classmates.

REFLECT

1. Why are congruent sides and angles important in making a net that folds up into a good package?
2. How might measurement be used by an architect? an automobile mechanic? a baker? a softball player?
3. In your own words, explain how to find the length of a segment on the number line and how to find the length of a slanted segment on a coordinate plane.

Self-Assessment

For the coordinates listed, determine whether $\overline{AB} \cong \overline{BC}$.

Coordinates of A	Coordinates of B	Coordinates of C
1. (0, 3)	(0, 7)	(−4, 3)
2. (4, −2)	(−1, 1)	(−2, −3)
3. (3, 7)	(8, −5)	(−4, 0)

4. Does the order in which the letters are written matter when naming a segment? a ray? a line? an angle? Explain.

Explain what is wrong with each statement in Exercises 5–8.

5. $RS \cong YZ$ **6.** $\angle PQR = 55°$ **7.** $m\angle TRS = 216°$

8. For two angles to be congruent, their sides must be congruent.

9. A Slice of the Pie What is the angle measure of a pizza slice if the whole pizza is cut in the following ways?

a. five equal slices **b.** six equal slices
c. seven equal slices **d.** eight equal slices
e. nine equal slices **f.** ten equal slices
g. Suppose you are very hungry. Will you get more to eat if you have two slices of a five-slice pizza or four slices of a twelve-slice pizza? Compare the angle measures.

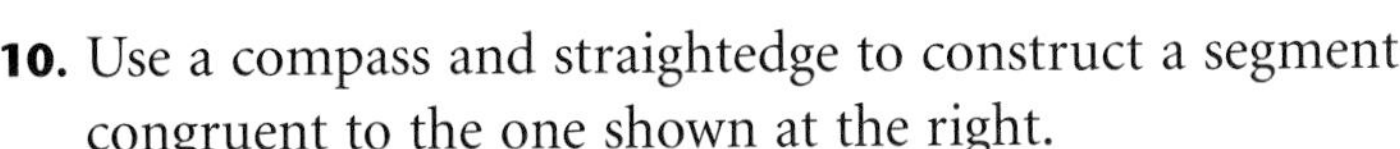

10. Use a compass and straightedge to construct a segment congruent to the one shown at the right.

11. Draw angle $\angle JKL$ using a straightedge. Then construct an angle congruent to $\angle JKL$.

12. Use a protractor to find the measures of these angles. Which angles appear to be congruent? (You may need to copy the figure and extend the lines to make measurement easier.)

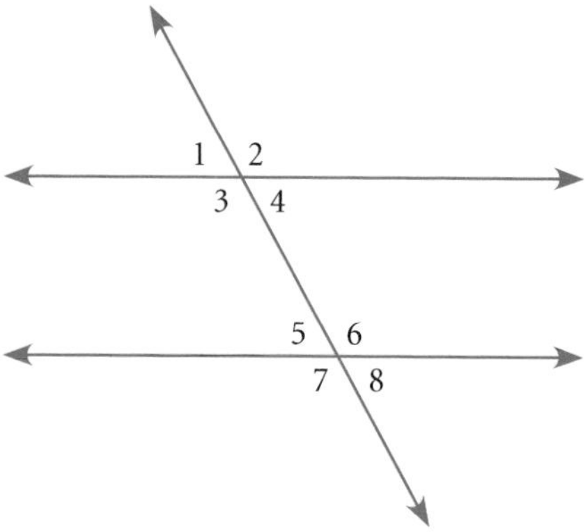

13. Suppose two points, Y and Z, are placed on m to the right of point X so that $XY = 2YZ$. What is $\frac{XZ}{YZ}$?

(a) 1 (b) $\frac{1}{2}$

(c) $\frac{3}{2}$ (d) 2

(e) Cannot be determined.

Find the next number in each sequence. Explain the pattern. [1-2]

14. 0, 1, 4, 9, . . .

15. 1, 3, 7, 15, 31 . . .

16. **Here's the Pitch** When an architect designs a home, the roof *pitch* (slope) must be carefully planned. According to Chiao Clerkin Architects, the climate, wind speed, and potential snow load are some of the factors used to determine the best roof pitch for any particular location.

Careers

a. Estimate the measure of the angle that the left side of each roof makes with a horizontal line.

b. Measure the rise and the run of a small section of the left side of each roof. Use these measurements to find their slopes. [Previous course]

c. Compare slope with angle measurement. As the slope gets larger, what happens to the angle measure?

d. Which roof pitch is appropriate for a very windy city? a town that experiences major blizzards? a dry desert climate? Explain your choices.

e. Which roof pitch do you find the most visually pleasing? Why?

17. Develop and describe a method for measuring angles that is different from the one you've used in this chapter.

18. Develop a way to construct an angle whose measure is twice the measure of the angle shown. Show your construction, and explain why it works.

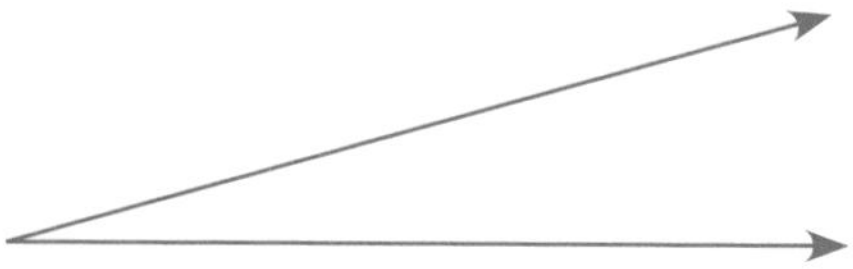

1-4 Symmetry and Reflections

ON THE OTHER HAND

The blankets of the Navajo people of the southwestern United States are renowned not only for their beauty, but for the balance (or symmetry) of their patterns. The Navajo learned the art of weaving from the Pueblo people around 1700. Over the next two centuries, the Navajo developed and refined different styles of blankets famous for their dazzling color and abstract design.

One of the most prized Navajo blanket styles is the finely-woven Chief Blanket. The designs of these blankets are classified into three phases. First-phase blanket designs feature stripes. Second-phase blankets have rectangular patterns as well as stripes. Third-phase blankets include diamond-shaped designs. All phases of Chief Blanket design show symmetry.

Most Navajo blankets are designed to be worn. When the blankets are draped over the head or wrapped around the body, the designs in the two halves of the blankets meet, giving the illusion of an unbroken pattern around the wearer.

?

1. Symmetry occurs in many natural and manufactured objects in our environment: Navajo blankets, spiders, and spider webs are some examples. What are some other examples of symmetry in the world around us?
2. Is the human face symmetrical or *asymmetrical* (not symmetrical)? Explain your answer.

1-4 PART A Symmetry

← CONNECT → ***You've already explored some patterns in geometry. Now you will explore the patterns and the balance of symmetrical figures.***

The word **symmetry** comes from Greek. The prefix *sym-* means "together," and *metry* means "measure." So *symmetry* means "measuring together."

If you fold a picture in half and both halves match each other perfectly, then the figure has **line symmetry** (*symmetry* for short). The fold is the **line of symmetry,** or **axis of symmetry.** A line of symmetry divides a figure into two mirror-image halves. All the Native American masks shown above have line symmetry.

EXAMPLES

Consider the alphabet shown below.

A B C D E F G H I J K L M N O P
Q R S T U V W X Y Z

1. Which letters have a vertical axis of symmetry?
A H I M O T U V W X Y

The vertical lines of symmetry for A and H are shown.

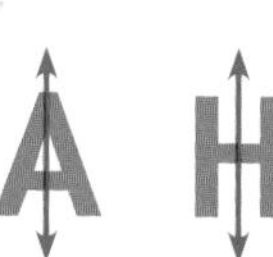

2. Which letters have a horizontal axis of symmetry?
C D E H I K O X

The horizontal lines of symmetry for E and C are shown.

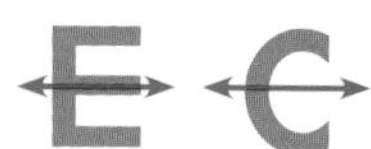

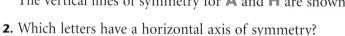

3. Which letters have two or more axes of symmetry?
H I O X

Both lines of symmetry are shown for H and X.

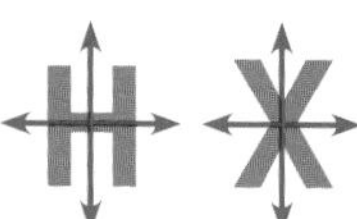

TRY IT

Copy the figures below and sketch all lines of symmetry for each.

a.

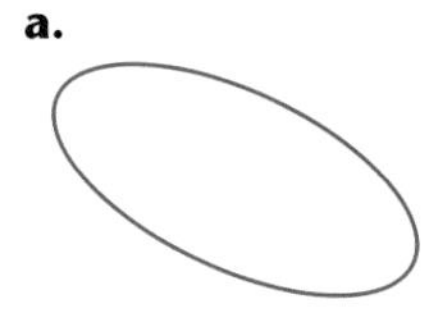

b.

c.

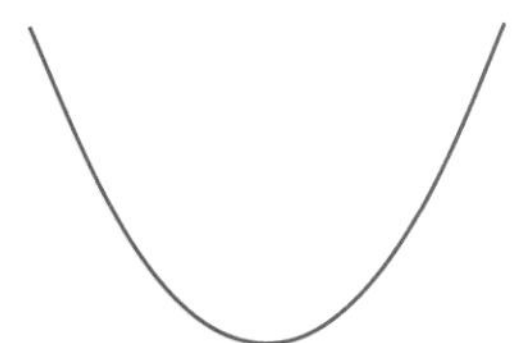

In the following Explore, you will investigate figures with different numbers of lines of symmetry.

EXPLORE: KEEPING IT SYMMETRIC

MATERIALS

Straightedge
Tracing paper
Protractor

1. Use a straightedge to draw a line on tracing paper. Then draw a curve from one point on the line to another point on the line, as shown at the right.
2. Fold the paper on the line so that you can copy the curve, and draw the other half of the pattern. Check to see if your finished design has symmetry.
3. Now draw two perpendicular lines of symmetry. (Use a protractor if necessary.) Draw a quarter of your figure from one of the lines to the next, as shown in the middle figure at the right.
4. Fold the tracing paper, and complete a symmetric design. How many times did you need to fold the paper?
5. Try four lines of symmetry, as shown in the drawing. (The angles between the lines measure 45°.) Again, report on how many folds you needed to make before your design was complete.
6. Make any conjectures you can relating lines of symmetry, folds, and the characteristics of your final figure.

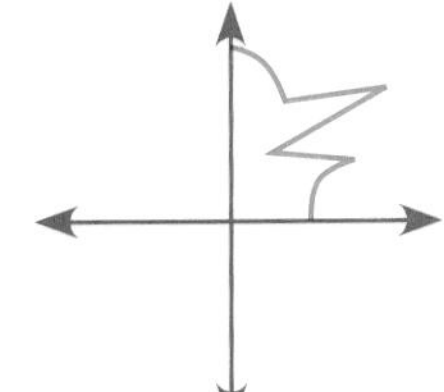

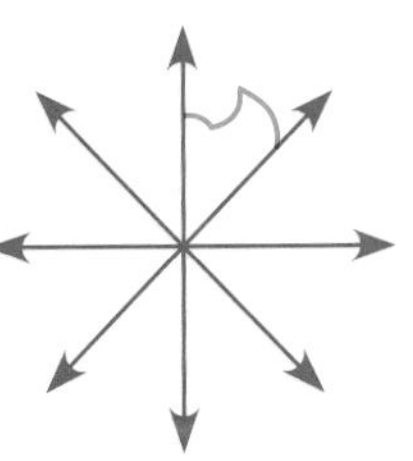

REFLECT

1. Explain how a mirror can help to illustrate line symmetry.
2. Define *symmetry* and *axis of symmetry* in your own words.
3. Can you draw triangles with the following characteristics?
   a. no lines of symmetry
   b. exactly one line of symmetry
   c. exactly two lines of symmetry
   d. exactly three lines of symmetry

Exercises

CORE

Getting Started Copy the figures below, and sketch all lines of symmetry for each. If there are no such lines, say so.

1. 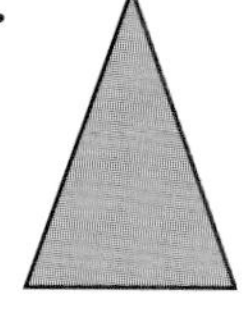

2. 

3. 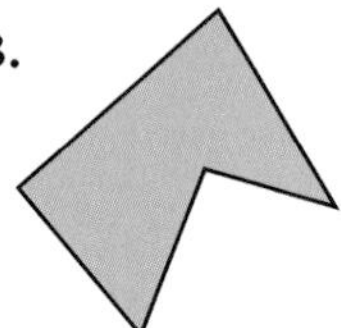

4. 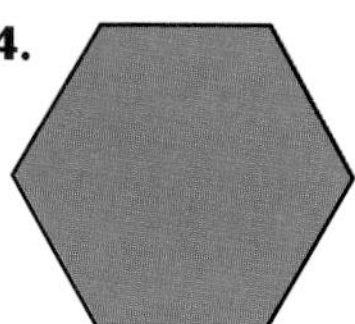

Is the red line in each figure a line of symmetry? Are there other lines of symmetry for any of the figures? If so, copy those figures, and draw the other lines of symmetry.

5. 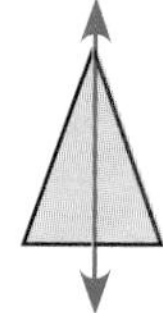

6. 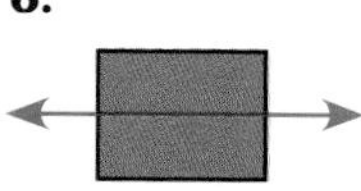

7. 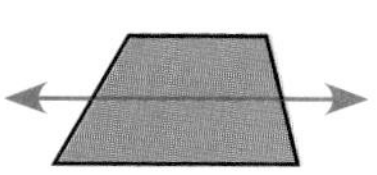

Copy each figure. Then draw the other half of each figure so that the red line is a line of symmetry.

8. 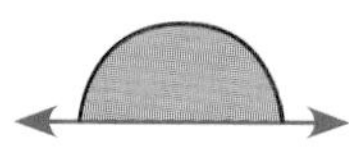

9. 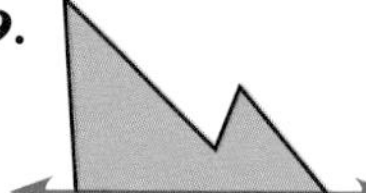

10. 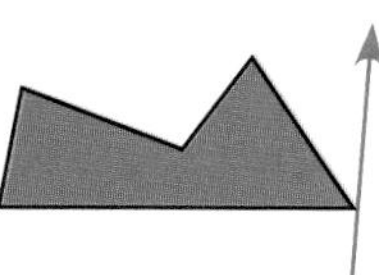

Give the number of lines of symmetry for each traffic sign. Then copy the signs, and draw the lines of symmetry.

11. 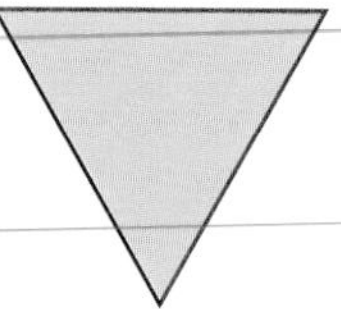

12. 

13. 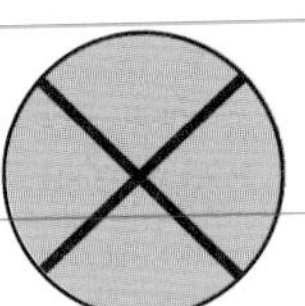

14. 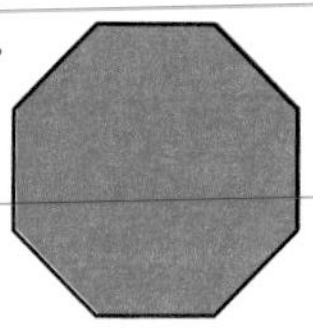

15. Write the word or phrase that correctly completes the statement.

If a line divides a figure into two mirror-image halves, it is a ____ for the figure.

16. A rectangle has two lines of symmetry.

a. How many lines of symmetry does a square have?

b. How many lines of symmetry does a circle have?

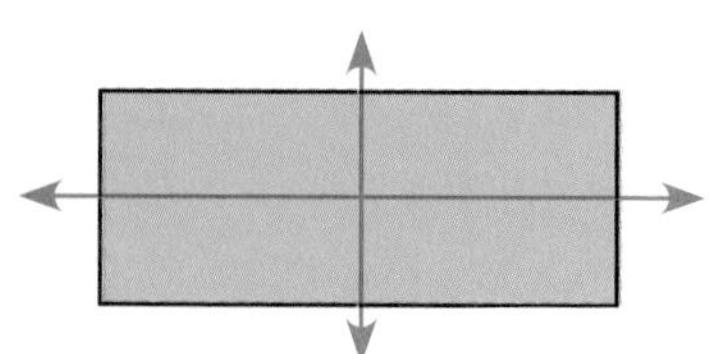

17. Draw a quadrilateral (four-sided figure) that has exactly four lines of symmetry.

18. Make a design that has two lines of symmetry. Show both lines of symmetry in your sketch.

Literature

19. **Symmetry in Poetry** The following passage is an excerpt from a poem written by William Blake (1757–1827).

Tiger! Tiger! burning bright
In the forests of the night,
What immortal hand or eye
Could frame thy fearful symmetry?

Describe or illustrate a line of symmetry for a tiger.

20. The word **"MOM"** has a vertical line of symmetry. Find at least three other words that have vertical lines of symmetry. Which capital letters of the alphabet can be used to create such words?

21. The word **"BOB"** has a horizontal line of symmetry. (Disregard the slight difference between the upper and lower halves of the letter "B".) Find at least three other words that have horizontal lines of symmetry. Which capital letters of the alphabet can be used to create such words?

22. **The Best "Bet"?** Which of the two alphabets below has more symmetrical letters? Do you feel that the more symmetrical alphabet is more appealing to look at? Explain.

A B C D E F G H I J K L M N O P Q R S T U V W X Y Z

A B C D E F G H I J K L M N O P Q R S T U V W X Y Z

23. A triangle with two vertices at G and H is to be completed by selecting one of the other points shown, A–F. What is the probability that the triangle will have line symmetry?

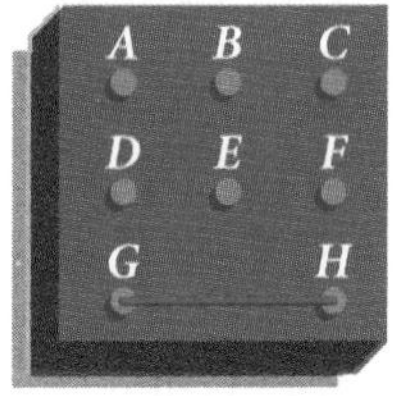

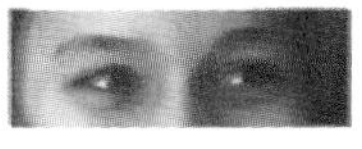

LOOK AHEAD

24. Finish the figure at the right so that it has line symmetry. Explain the method you used to complete the figure. Is there more than one way to complete the figure?

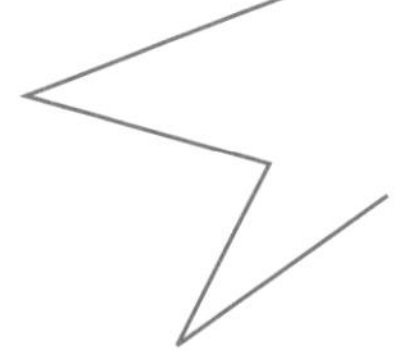

25. Explain how the reflected image of an object in a mirror is different from the object itself.

MORE PRACTICE

Copy the figures below and sketch all lines of symmetry for each. If there are no such lines, say so.

26. 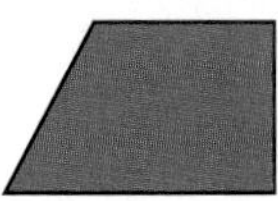

27. 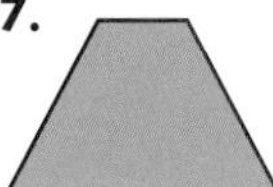

28. 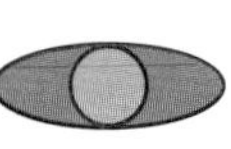

29. 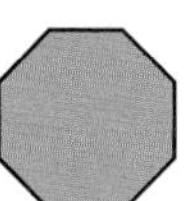

Copy each figure. Then draw the other half of each figure so that the red line is a line of symmetry.

30. 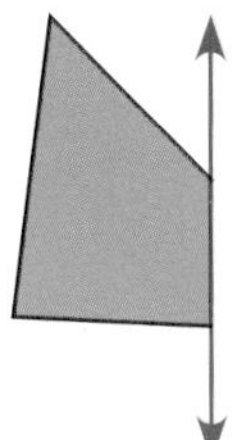

31. 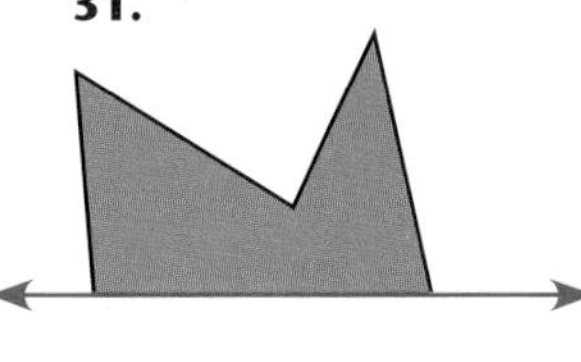

32. 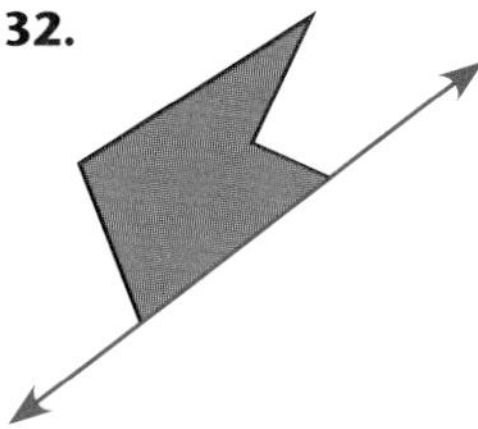

MORE MATH REASONING

Science

33. Snowflake Problem Snowflakes are examples of symmetry in nature.

a. How many lines of symmetry do these snowflakes have?

b. You can make a model of a snowflake by folding a round piece of paper and cutting out shapes along the fold lines. Explain how you can fold a piece of paper to get a model of the lines of symmetry for a snowflake.

Graph the following equations. Show the line of symmetry for each graph. Then write the equation of the line of symmetry.

34. $y = x^2$

35. $y = x^2 + 1$

36. $y = (x + 3)^2$

37. How is congruence related to symmetry? Write a brief paragraph explaining the connection.

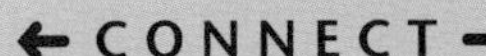

1-4 PART B Reflections

← CONNECT → ***You've explored figures that have lines of symmetry. Now you will reflect geometric figures over lines. Your measuring skills will help you understand the relationship between a figure and its reflection.***

Suppose you draw a geometric figure on a piece of paper. If you make a second drawing of a figure that looks exactly like the first but is shifted, flipped, enlarged, shrunken, or rotated, the second figure is called a **transformation** of the first.

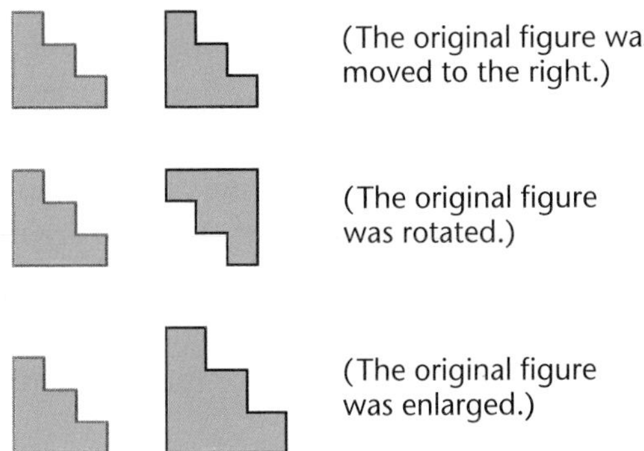

(The original figure was moved to the right.)
(The original figure was rotated.)
(The original figure was enlarged.)

A reflection is a special type of transformation. A **reflection** is a flipping of a figure over a line. This line is the **line of reflection.** Line ℓ below is a line of reflection. The original figure, called the **pre-image,** is shown in black. The **image,** after the transformation, is in blue.

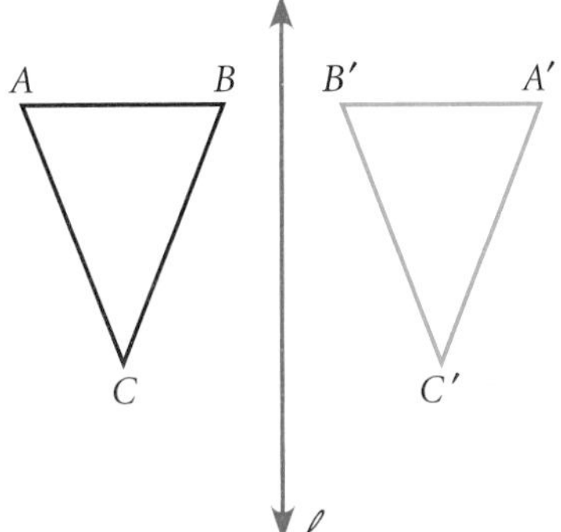

When a point on the pre-image is labeled, like A, B, or C in the figure, the matching (or corresponding) point on the image is often labeled with the same letter followed by a prime sign. So C' (C-prime) is the image of point C. The image of triangle ABC is triangle $A'B'C'$. (When naming images of figures, we list corresponding points in the same order.)

In the following Explore, you will investigate the relationship between measurement and reflection.

EXPLORE: REFLECTIVE DETECTIVE

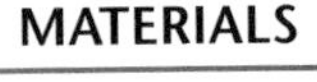

Paper, Ruler Protractor

1. Fold a rectangular sheet of paper in half. Poke the tip of a pencil through the folded paper at three points that are not collinear.
2. Open the paper and draw segments connecting the holes on each side of the fold. (You should have two triangles, with the fold as the line of reflection.) Label the vertices of the pre-image, and use prime notation to label the points of the image.
3. Draw segments connecting the points of the image with the corresponding points of the pre-image. Measure some of the segments that cross the fold. Then measure the distances from the points to the fold. Finally, measure the angles these segments make with the fold.

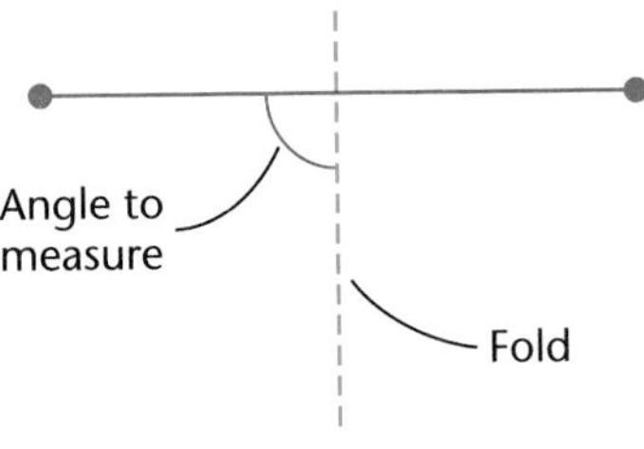

4. What do you notice about the distances? the angles? Make any conjectures you can about the angle and distance measurements involving a point and its reflection image. Discuss your conjectures with your classmates.

The following terms are useful in describing reflections.

The **distance from a point to a line** is the length of the perpendicular segment from the point to the line.

If two points are the same distance from another point (or segment, line, or other element), they are **equidistant** from it.

A figure is **bisected** by another figure when it is cut into two congruent halves. So a **perpendicular bisector** of a segment is a line (or segment) that divides the segment into two congruent segments and is perpendicular to it.

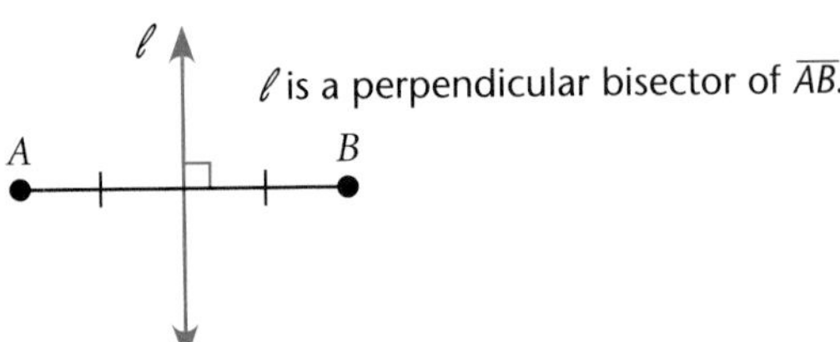

Using a compass and straightedge, you can construct a perpendicular to a line from a given point, as shown on page 69.

CONSTRUCTION: PERPENDICULAR TO A LINE

1. Begin by sketching line ℓ and point P, not on ℓ. You will construct the line that goes through P and is perpendicular to ℓ.

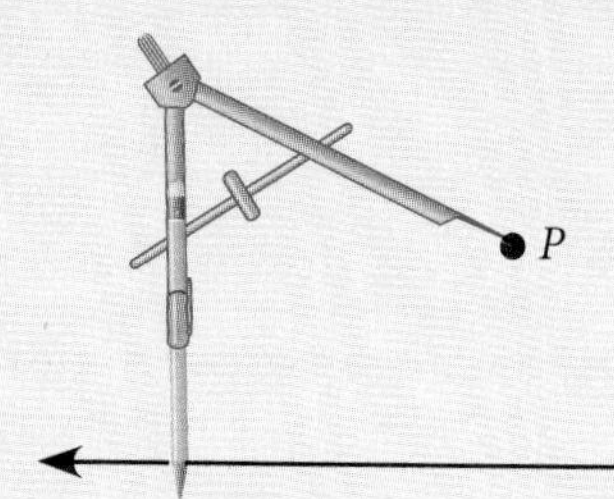

2. Open your compass to a measure greater than the distance from P to line ℓ. Place the point of the compass on P.

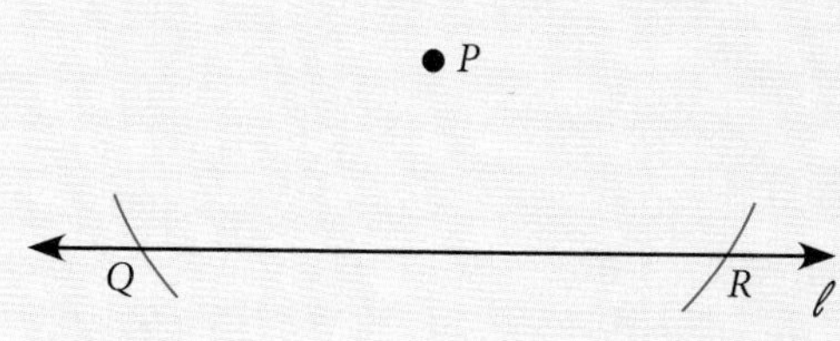

3. Keeping the setting of the compass consistent, make two arcs that intersect line ℓ. Label the intersection points of the arcs and the line Q and R.

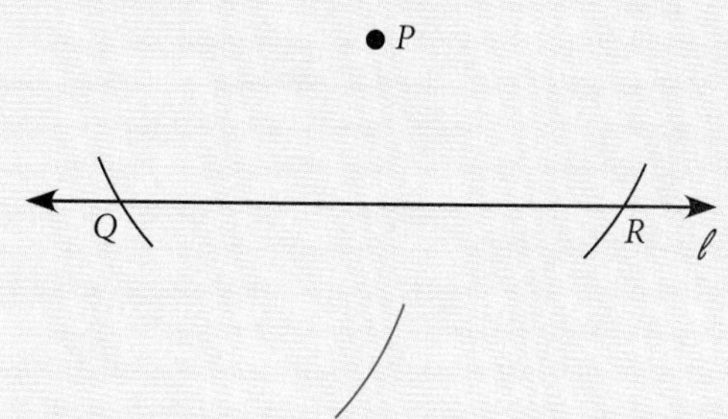

4. Now place the tip of the compass on point Q. Make an arc on the opposite side of the line from point P.

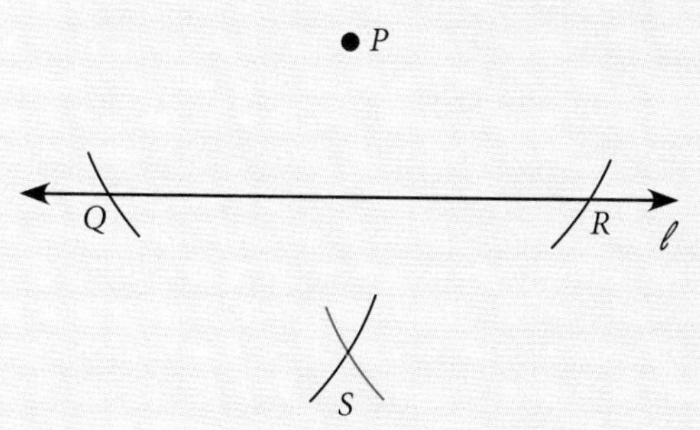

5. Leaving the compass opening the same size, move the tip of the compass to point R. Make an arc that intersects the arc you made in Step 4. Label the point where the arcs intersect S.

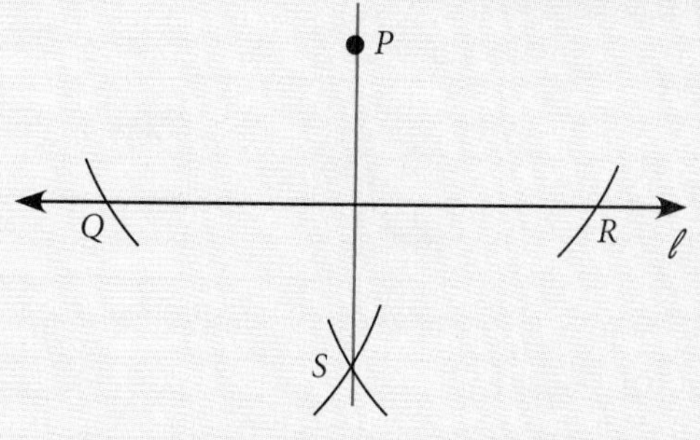

6. Draw the line through P and S. $\overleftrightarrow{PS}$ is perpendicular to line ℓ.

1. **How could you use the preceding construction to help you find the image of *P* after a reflection over line ℓ?**

We can now give a more formal definition of *reflection.*

DEFINITION

Point A' is the **reflection image over line ℓ** of point A if ℓ is the perpendicular bisector of $\overline{AA'}$.

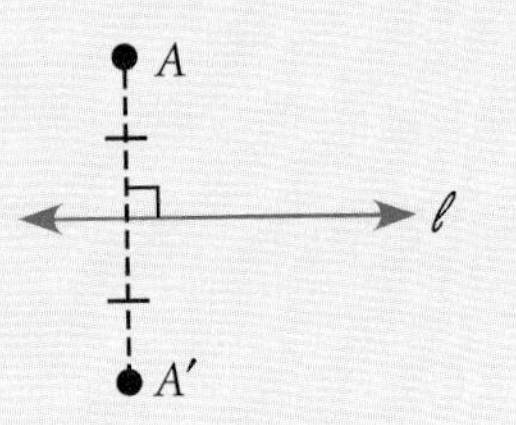

REFLECT

1. Describe how reflection is related to symmetry.
2. Suppose P' is the image of P after a reflection over line ℓ. Using the term *perpendicular bisector,* describe the relationship of ℓ to P and P'.
3. Suppose point A lies on line m. If point A is reflected over line m, what can you say about point A and its image?

Exercises

CORE

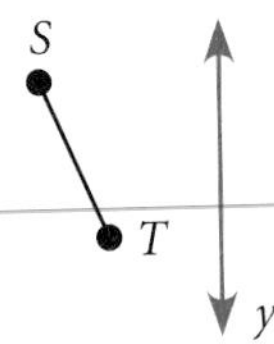

1. **Getting Started** Follow the steps below and at the top of page 71 to construct the reflection image of segment $\overline{ST}$ over line y.
   a. Sketch a figure with $\overline{ST}$ and line y similar to the one at the top right.
   b. Use your compass and straightedge to construct a line through S perpendicular to y. (The construction marks are not shown in the figure.)
   c. Use your compass to measure the perpendicular segment from S to y. Construct another segment congruent to it on the same line, but on the other side of y. You have located the reflection image of S. Label it S'.

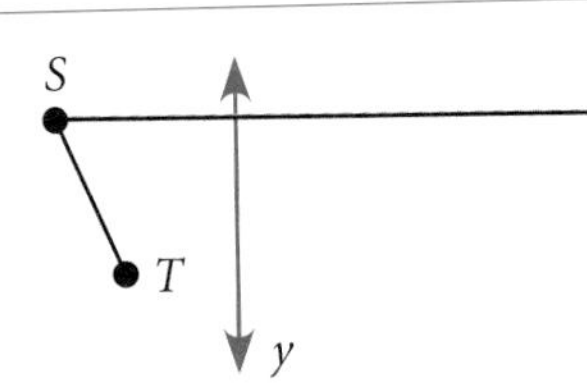

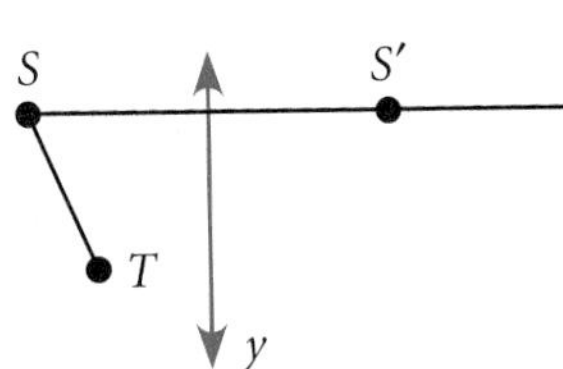

d. Repeat **1b** and **1c** to find the reflection image of T. Label it T'.

e. Use your straightedge to connect S' and T'. $\overline{S'T'}$ is the reflection image of $\overline{ST}$ over line y.

2. Draw a triangle with vertices F, G, and H. Add a line of reflection, ℓ. Then use a compass and straightedge to construct the reflection of the triangle over line ℓ.

Line ℓ is a line of reflection in the figure.

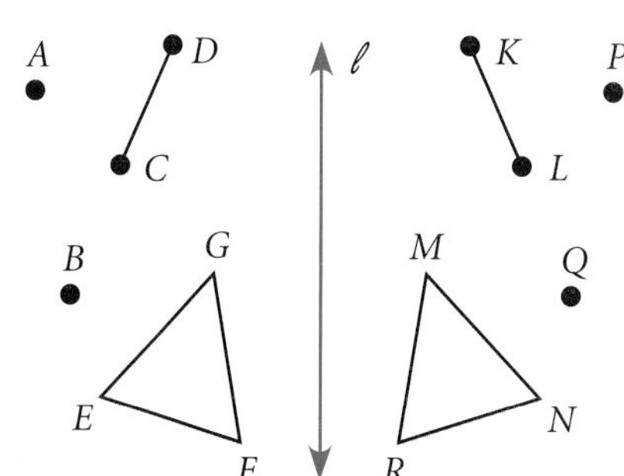

3. What is the reflection image of A?

4. What is the reflection image of B?

5. What is the reflection image of $\overline{CD}$?

6. What is the reflection image of triangle EFG?

In the figure, X' is the reflection image of X.

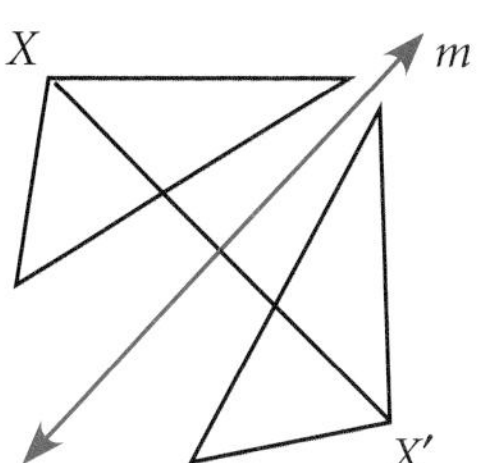

7. What is the measure of the angle formed by the line of reflection and the segment connecting points X and X'? Explain.

8. How is the distance from X to the line of reflection related to the distance from X to X'? How do you know?

Determine whether each statement is true or false. If the statement is false, change the underlined word to make it true.

9. Symmetry is a transformation.

10. A line of symmetry divides a figure into two halves that are mirror images.

11. The coordinate system is useful in analyzing reflections.

a. Point C has coordinates $(2, 3)$. Find the coordinates of the image of point C after a reflection over the x-axis.

b. Find the coordinates of the image of point C after a reflection over the y-axis.

c. What is the reflection image of (a, b) over the x-axis?

Problem-Solving Tip

Look for a pattern.

d. What is the reflection image of (a, b) over the y-axis?

Fine Arts

12. Blanket Symmetry Describe the lines of symmetry in this Navajo blanket. How are these related to reflections?

13. a. Find the distance from point G to line $\overleftrightarrow{HI}$ in the figure at the right. What is another name for the distance you found?
b. Find GI. How does this compare to the distance from G to $\overleftrightarrow{HI}$?
c. What property of segments from a point to a line does your work in **13a** and **13b** illustrate?

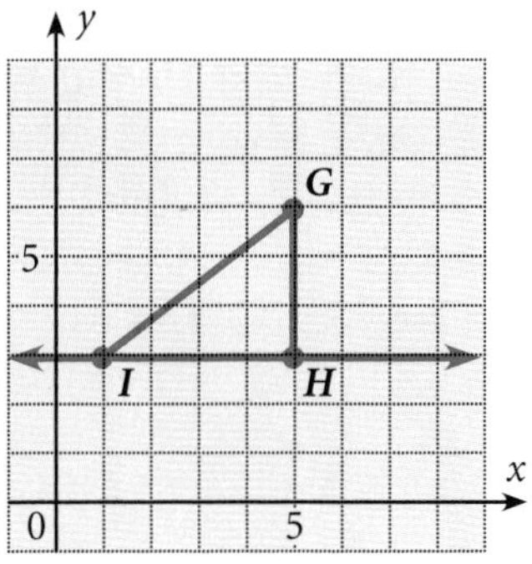

LOOK BACK

Draw a Venn diagram to illustrate each of the following. [1-2]

14. All horses are mammals.

15. No planets are cubes.

16. Some baseball players are catchers.

17. Every turtle is a reptile.

Find *AB* for each set of coordinates. Where necessary, round answers to the nearest tenth. [1-3]

18. $A(2, 5), B(5, 1)$

19. $A(-3, -11), B(2, -23)$

20. $A(2.2, 1.3), B(6.4, -2.7)$

MORE PRACTICE

21. Draw a rectangle and a line of reflection that is not parallel to any of the sides of the rectangle. Then construct the reflection of the rectangle.

Line ℓ is a line of reflection in the figure.

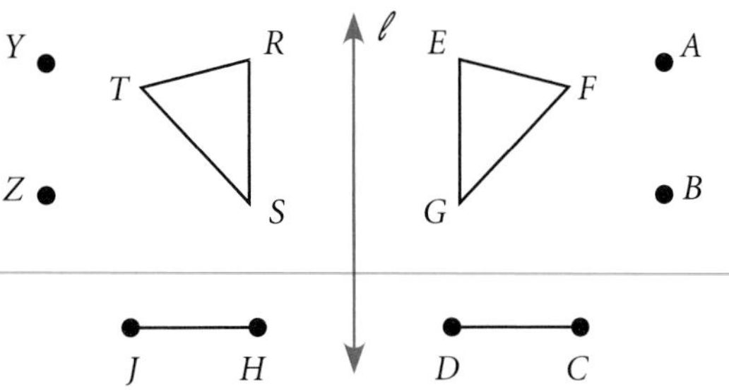

22. What is the reflection image of A?

23. What is the reflection image of B?

24. What is the reflection image of $\overline{CD}$?

25. What is the reflection image of triangle EFG?

MORE MATH REASONING

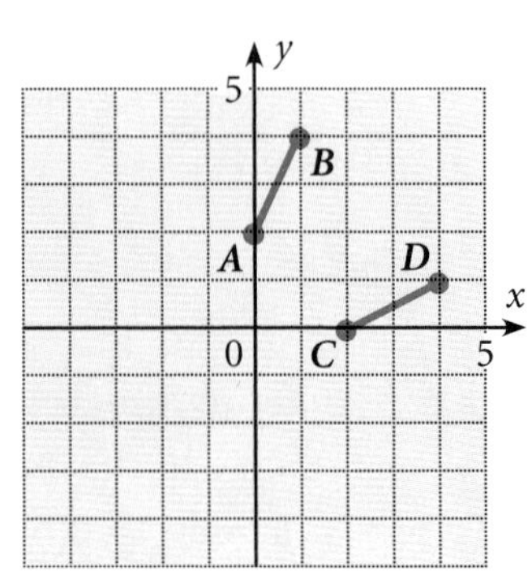

26. A segment and its reflection image are shown.
a. Name two pairs of corresponding points and their coordinates.
b. Copy the figure, and sketch the line of reflection. Write the equation for the line of reflection.
c. Make and justify a conjecture about the reflection of any point (a, b) over the line $y = x$.

27. Use a ruler and protractor for the following.
   a. Draw two segments, $\overline{ST}$ and $\overline{YZ}$, that are perpendicular bisectors of each other but are not congruent. Draw the segments $\overline{SY}$, $\overline{YT}$, $\overline{TZ}$, and $\overline{ZS}$. What do you notice?
   b. Repeat **27a**, but this time make $\overline{ST}$ congruent to $\overline{YZ}$. What do you notice?
   c. Make as many conjectures as you can about your results in **27a** and **27b.** (If you need to, make additional drawings to convince yourself of your conjectures.)

1-4 PART C Properties of Reflections

← CONNECT → ***You know how to reflect a geometric figure over a line. Now you will discover some of the properties of reflections.***

In our informal definition of transformations, we said that an image "looks exactly like" its pre-image. But the image *is* usually different from the pre-image in some ways. Exactly which characteristics of the pre-image are changed and which stay the same depends on the transformation. You will now investigate this for reflections.

EXPLORE: TO PRESERVE OR NOT TO PRESERVE

MATERIALS

Compass, Ruler Protractor

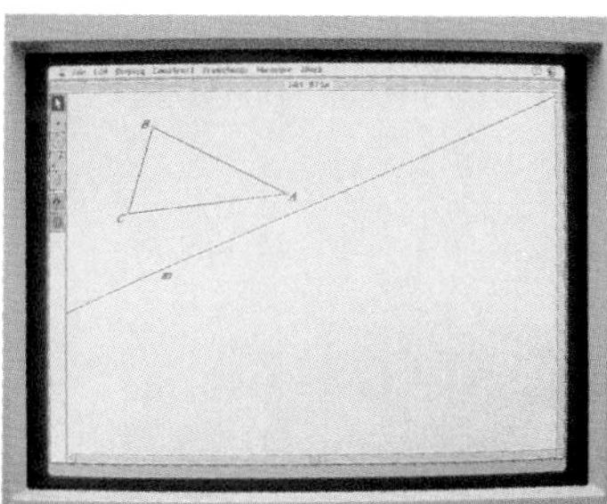

1. Draw a line, m, to divide your paper in half. On one side of the line, draw a scalene triangle. (Scalene triangles have no two sides the same length.) Label the vertices of the triangle ABC.
2. Use a compass and straightedge to construct the reflection of the triangle over line m. Label the reflection image $A'B'C'$.
3. Investigate the triangles using any methods and measuring tools you think are appropriate. Identify the characteristics of the image that are preserved (kept the same) by reflection and the characteristics that are not preserved. (For example, how does AB compare to $A'B'$?) Summarize your conclusions.

The **orientation** of a figure can be clockwise or counterclockwise, depending on how you look at it! Tracing this triangle from J to L to K shows a clockwise orientation. But tracing from J to K to L shows a counterclockwise orientation.

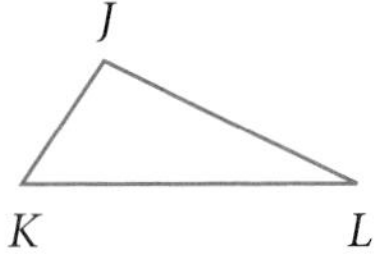

1. In the figure at the right, triangle $A'B'C'$ is the reflection image of triangle ABC over line m. Does reflection preserve the orientation of a figure? Explain.

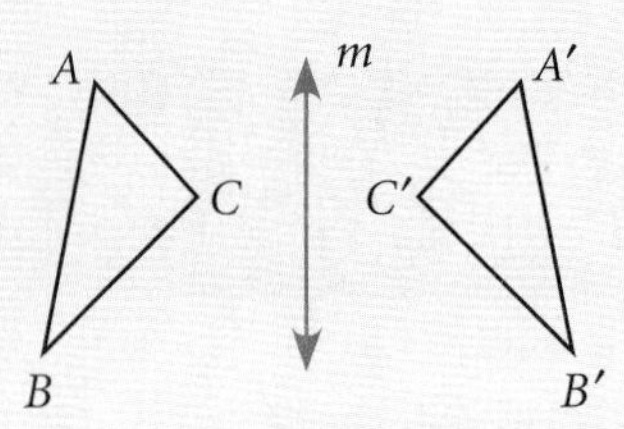

TRY IT

Suppose triangle $M'N'P'$ is the reflection image of triangle MNP. State any conclusions you can make if you know each of the following.

a. $MP = 8$
b. $m\angle P'M'N' = 75°$
c. As you move from M to P, you are going clockwise.
d. The perimeter of triangle $M'N'P'$ is 20.
e. The area of triangle MNP is 24.

The properties of reflections you've discovered are summarized below.

> Reflections preserve any property of a figure having to do with size. This includes lengths of sides, measures of angles, area, and perimeter. Reflections reverse the orientation of a figure.

REFLECT

1. Is a figure always congruent to its reflection image? Why or why not?
2. Describe at least one transformation that preserves the orientation of a figure.
3. Suppose you have the reflection pre-image and image of a figure. Can you tell which is which just by looking? Explain why or why not.

Exercises

CORE

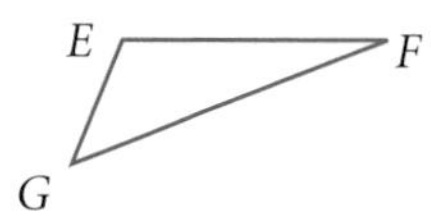

1. **Getting Started** Sketch triangle *JKL* congruent to triangle *EFG* so that *JKL* and *EFG* do not have the same orientation.

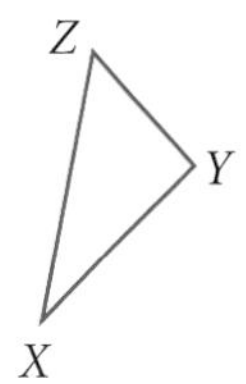

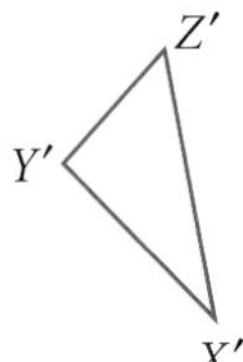

2. Mika knows that $m\angle X = 53°$, $YZ = 5$, and $X'Z' = 6$. She also knows that triangle $X'Y'Z'$ is a reflection of triangle XYZ. What else can Mika conclude about the two triangles?

Triangle *A′B′C′* is the reflection of triangle *ABC* over line *m*.

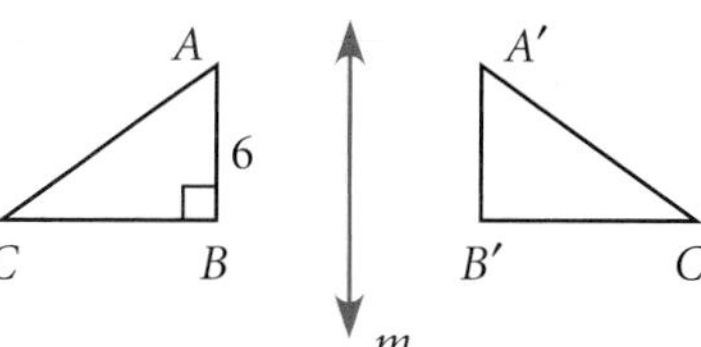

3. Find $m\angle A'B'C'$.
4. Find the length of $\overline{A'B'}$.
5. $\overline{D'E'}$ is the reflection image of $\overline{DE}$. The coordinates of D and E are $(-5, 4)$ and $(4, -8)$. Find $D'E'$.

Use each of the following words in a sentence that describes a property of reflection. (Write one sentence using each word.)

6. *equidistant* or *equal distance*
7. *perpendicular*
8. *orientation*
9. *preserves*

Careers

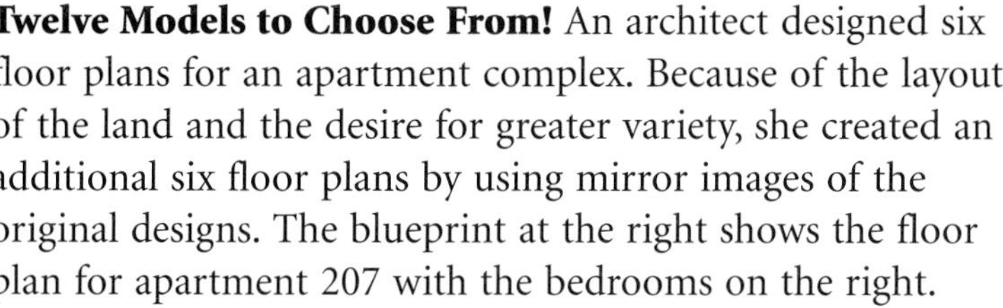

10. **Twelve Models to Choose From!** An architect designed six floor plans for an apartment complex. Because of the layout of the land and the desire for greater variety, she created an additional six floor plans by using mirror images of the original designs. The blueprint at the right shows the floor plan for apartment 207 with the bedrooms on the right.
    a. Draw the reflection of apartment 207 so that the bedrooms are on the left. (This is apartment 208.)

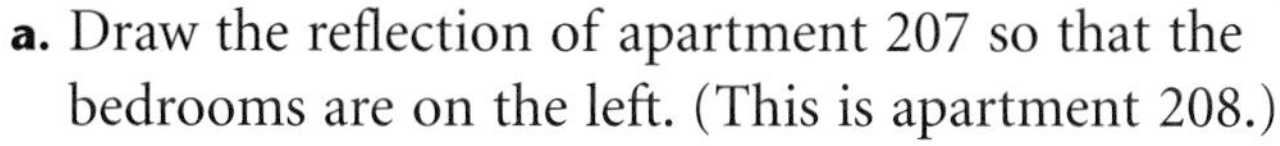

    b. If the distance from the kitchen door to one bedroom in apartment 207 is 8 ft, how far is it to the same bedroom in apartment 208?
    c. If the entry door is on the east side of apartment 208, where is it in apartment 207?

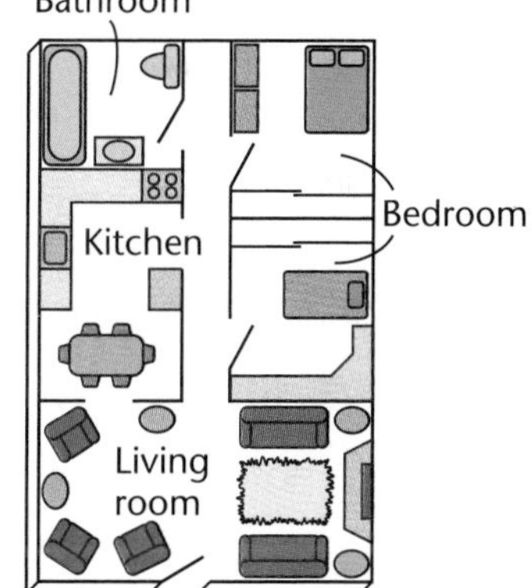

11. **A Pointed Question** Rglph is a glove maker on planet Pmrgk, where everyone has pointed fingers. One of her customers, Vwzxr, has lost his right glove. Using the left glove shown here, draw a pattern for the right glove. Explain why your process works.

12. Stereoisomers are molecules made of the same materials that are mirror images of each other. Even though they are made of the same materials, stereoisomers can have different chemical properties.

One of the possible arrangements of a molecule is shown at the right. Draw its stereoisomer using the given line of reflection.

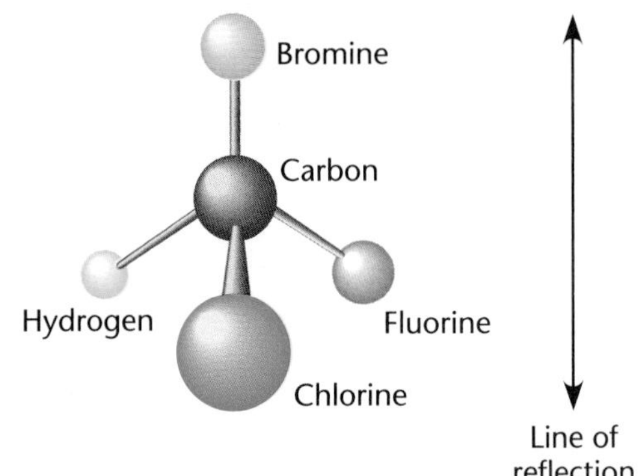

(Note: The fluorine, chlorine, bromine, and hydrogen atoms are arranged like the corners of a pyramid.)

LOOK AHEAD

The statement "Every student in the 10th grade is a sophomore" can be rewritten as: "If a student is in the 10th grade, then he or she is a sophomore." Rewrite each of the following statements in the form, "If . . . , then . . ."

13. Everyone who lives in San Francisco lives in California.

14. All birds have wings.

15. Kendrick can get a driver's license if he is 16.

MORE PRACTICE

16. Sabine knows that triangle $P'Q'R'$ is the reflection of triangle PQR. She also knows that $m\angle P = 65°$, $m\angle Q' = 70°$, and $RQ = 7$. What else can Sabine conclude about the two triangles?

17. $\overline{M'N'}$ is the reflection image of $\overline{MN}$. The coordinates of M and N are $(-3, 2)$ and $(-6, -5)$. Find $M'N'$.

Triangle *A′B′C′* is the reflection of triangle *ABC* over line *m*.

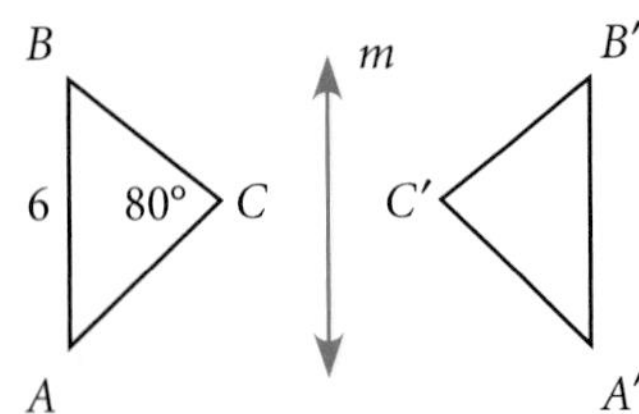

18. Find $m\angle A'C'B'$.

19. Find the length of $A'B'$.

MORE MATH REASONING

Complete each statement with *always, sometimes,* or *never.* Explain your answer.

20. A line of reflection is ___ the perpendicular bisector of the segment from a point to its reflection image.

21. A segment and its reflection image are ___ congruent.

22. A point and its reflection image are ___ equidistant from the line of reflection.

23. Reflections ___ preserve orientation.

24. On a coordinate plane, copy the triangle, and draw its reflection over the y-axis. Then draw its reflection over the x-axis.

a. Describe the orientation of each of the triangles.

b. Suppose you think of the y-axis reflection as a pre-image and the x-axis reflection as its image. How can you tell that this image is *not* a reflection of this pre-image?

c. Describe a transformation that gives you this image (the x-axis reflection) from this pre-image (the y-axis reflection). Do not use *reflection* in describing this new transformation.

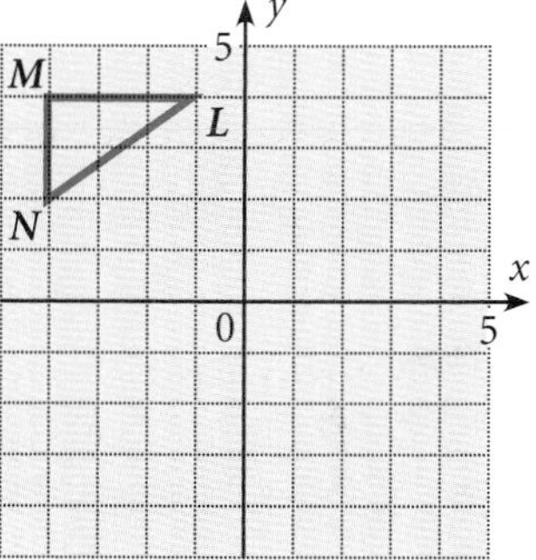

1-4 PART D Making Connections

← CONNECT → ***Reflections and symmetry are important in nature, architecture, and art. You've discovered symmetry in a variety of settings and learned how reflections and symmetry are related.***

You've seen examples of symmetry in math, art, architecture, and language. Part of the beauty of Navajo blankets is due to their symmetry. Blankets of other cultures, such as the *kilims* of the Middle East, also contain beautifully symmetrical patterns. The photo at the left shows symmetry in a plate by Maria Martinez of San Ildefonso Pueblo, New Mexico.

In the following Explore, you will use symmetry and reflections to create your own blanket design.

EXPLORE: DO-IT-YOURSELF SYMMETRY

Create a design for a blanket that uses reflection and symmetry. Follow the guidelines below.

1. Fold your paper in half. Create a design on one half of the paper. Be sure to use at least three different geometric figures that have line symmetry.
2. Draw the lines of symmetry in these figures.
3. Now use construction techniques and measurement to reflect the design over the fold. (You do not have to reflect the lines of symmetry.)

MATERIALS

Construction paper
Straightedge
Compass

REFLECT

1. Explain how the construction of a perpendicular from a point not on a line can be used to find the reflection of a point over a line.
2. Write a list of properties of reflections. Draw a picture to illustrate each property.
3. Describe a figure with infinitely many lines of symmetry. Sketch the figure. Can you think of another?

Self-Assessment

Line ℓ is a line of reflection in the figure shown. Name the image or pre-image of each figure.

1. the image of A
2. the pre-image of $\overleftrightarrow{QR}$
3. the image of $\overline{AB}$
4. the pre-image of Q
5. If $AC = 12$, find PR.
6. Does every angle have a line of symmetry? If so, describe it, and provide a figure.

Draw a Venn diagram to illustrate each of the following. [1-2]

7. Some pilots are women.
8. No Democrats are Republicans.
9. All segments have two endpoints.

Find *AB* for each set of coordinates below. Where necessary, round answers to the nearest tenth. [1-3]

10. $A(-2, 4)$, $B(4, 12)$

11. $A(1.5, 2.6)$, $B(-2, 5.8)$

12. Write a list of properties of reflections. Then draw a triangle, a line of reflection, and the reflection image of the triangle. Explain how your pre-image and image demonstrate each of the properties you listed.

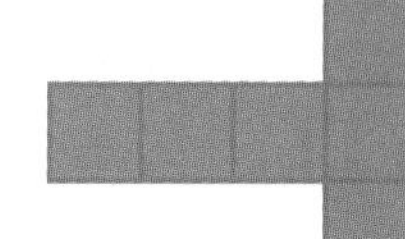

13. a. Is the figure at the right a net for a cube?

b. Sketch a reflection of the net. Is the reflection still a net for a cube?

14. If one illustration is selected randomly from those shown below, what is the probability that it will *not* have line symmetry?

(a) $\frac{1}{2}$ (b) 1 (c) $\frac{3}{4}$ (d) 0 (e) $\frac{1}{4}$

Butterfly

Star

Leaf

Yin-yang symbol

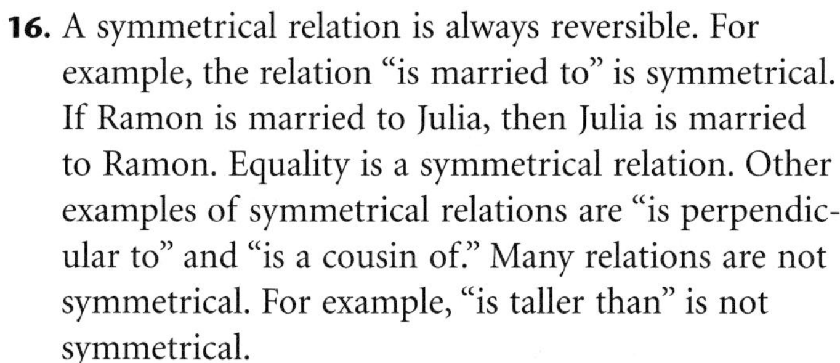

15. This alphabet, created by Scott Kim, is symmetrical. Or is it? Describe three different places where part of the design does not exactly match its reflection image.

16. A symmetrical relation is always reversible. For example, the relation "is married to" is symmetrical. If Ramon is married to Julia, then Julia is married to Ramon. Equality is a symmetrical relation. Other examples of symmetrical relations are "is perpendicular to" and "is a cousin of." Many relations are not symmetrical. For example, "is taller than" is not symmetrical.

a. Give two other examples of symmetrical relations.

b. Give two other examples of asymmetrical relations.

Two vertices of a rectangle and a line of symmetry for the rectangle are given. Find the other vertices of the rectangle.

17. (4, 1) and (4, 5); $x = 3$

18. (4, 1) and (9, 1); $y = 3$

Chapter 1 Review

In Chapter 1, you investigated mathematical models. You explored algebraic models (for example, scatter plots) and geometric models (for example, nets). Developing inductive and deductive reasoning skills and learning some basic geometric terms helped you to make better geometric models. These ideas are all useful in studying symmetry and reflections, our first transformation.

KEY TERMS

angle [1-3]
bisect [1-4]
collinear [1-2]
congruent [1-3]
conjecture [1-2]
construction [1-3]
counterexample [1-2]
deductive reasoning [1-2]
degree [1-3]
endpoint of a ray [1-3]
endpoints of a segment [1-2]
equidistant [1-4]
image [1-4]
inductive reasoning [1-2]
intersect [1-2]
length [1-3]
line of reflection [1-4]
line of symmetry [1-4]
line segment [1-2]
line [1-2]
mathematical model [1-1]
measure of an angle [1-3]
net [1-1]
orientation [1-4]
perpendicular bisector [1-4]
perpendicular lines [1-3]
point [1-2]
pre-image [1-4]
ray [1-3]
reflection image [1-4]
reflection [1-4]
right angle [1-3]
scatter plot [1-1]
sides of an angle [1-3]
symmetry [1-4]
transformation [1-4]
Venn diagram [1-2]
vertex [1-3]

Write the word or phrase that correctly completes each statement.

1. The process of making a conjecture by looking at specific examples and recognizing a pattern is ___ reasoning.
2. The two rays that form an angle have a common endpoint, called the ___ of the angle.
3. The figure that results after a transformation of a figure is the ___ of the original figure.
4. Two lines that intersect at ___ are perpendicular lines.

CONCEPTS AND APPLICATIONS

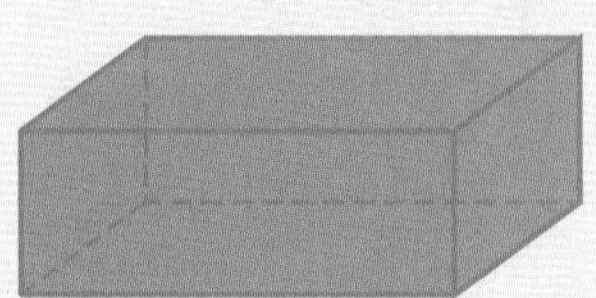

5. Draw a net for the solid at the right. [1-1]

The scatter plot shown represents how many hours eight students studied and the scores they received on a history test. Use this scatter plot for items 6–8. [1-2]

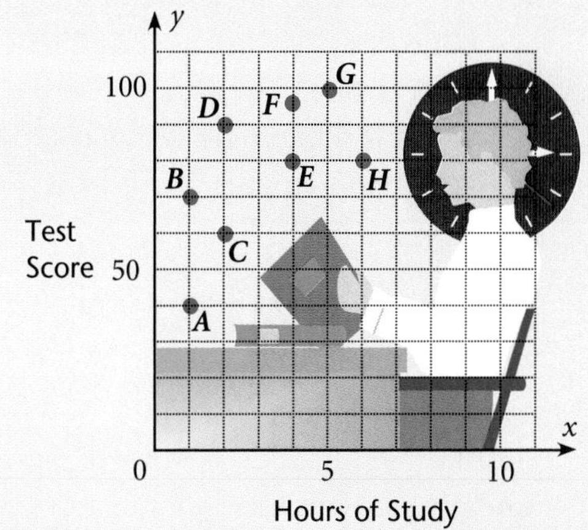

6. Give the ordered pairs for each point on the scatter plot.

7. Which student studied the longest? Did that student get the highest score?

8. Suppose a student not shown on the scatter plot told you he studied three hours for the test. What score would you predict he received? Why?

9. Solve $5x + 9 = 3(x - 1) + 4$. [Previous course]

10. A sequence of figures is made from small squares, as shown. [1-2]

a. How many small squares would it take to make the figure at Step 7?

b. How many small squares would it take to make the figure at Step *n*?

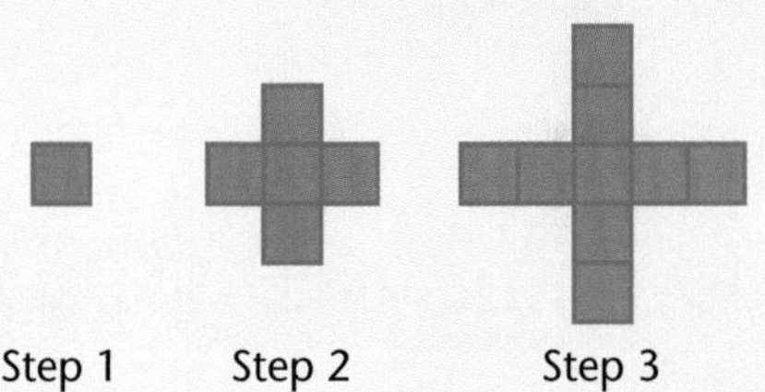

11. Write a brief paragraph describing what deductive reasoning is. Give specific examples of its use. [1-2]

Suppose that each statement below is true. Use deductive reasoning to give another statement that must also be true. [1-2]

12. Every freshman has attended orientation. Luis has never been to orientation.

13. No triangle has four sides. Marie drew a four-sided figure.

Find the length of $\overline{FG}$ using the given coordinates. [1-3]

14. $F(-2, 0)$, $G(3, 8)$

15. $F(5, -5)$, $G(-3, -6)$

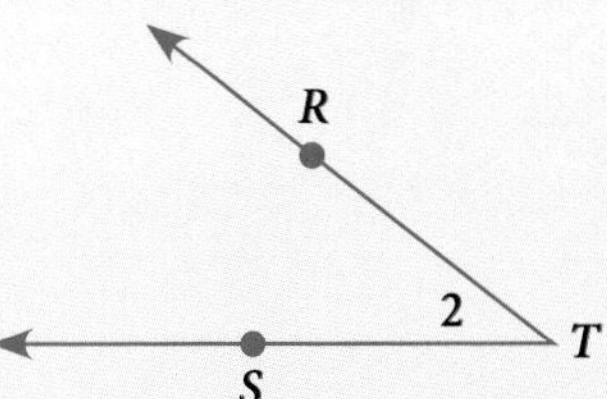

16. Name the angle at the right in as many ways as possible. [1-3]

17. Use a compass and straightedge to construct an angle congruent to the angle at the right. [1-3]

18. Draw a figure with exactly two lines of symmetry. [1-4]

Line *m* is a line of reflection in the figure at the right. [1-4]

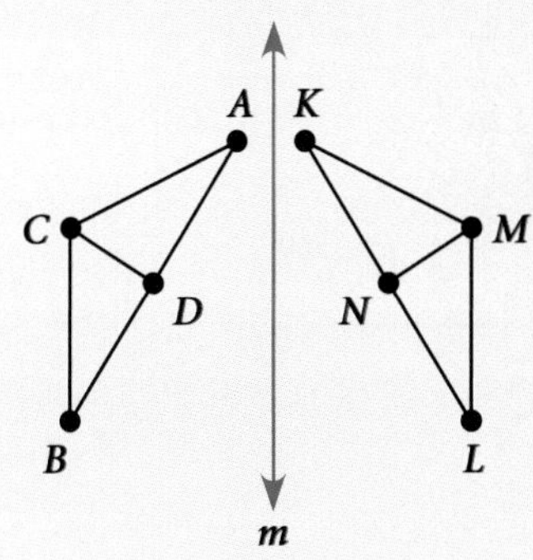

19. What is the reflection image of point *A*?

20. What is the reflection image of $\overline{CD}$?

21. What is the pre-image of triangle *KLM*?

CONCEPTS AND CONNECTIONS

22. Architecture As an architect, you've been asked to prepare a floor plan for a two-bedroom apartment. Your clients want you to make the apartment as symmetrical as possible. They would also like the apartment to contain at least one angle that is not a right angle. Draw a simple floor plan for such an apartment, marking congruent lengths, congruent angles, and right angles as appropriate.

SELF-EVALUATION

Write a paragraph describing how geometry can be used to model the world around you. Include in your paragraph the new ideas you learned in Chapter 1, and give specific examples of how you can use these ideas in modeling real-world situations. Be sure to include any topics that you found difficult, and describe your plans for studying those topics.

Chapter 1 Assessment

TEST

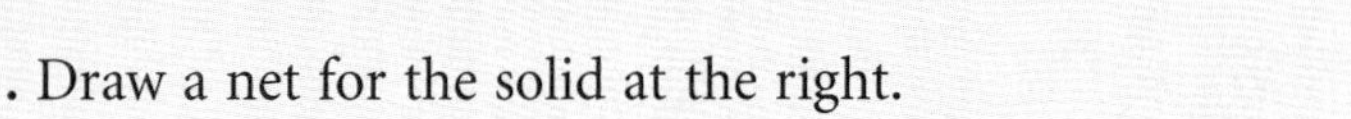

1. Draw a net for the solid at the right.

Determine whether each statement is true or false. If the statement is false, change the underlined word or words to make it true.

2. Two lines that intersect at right angles are <u>equidistant</u> lines.

3. <u>Deductive reasoning</u> is a process in which conclusions are drawn from given information by rules of logic.

Give a counterexample for each of the following conjectures.

4. All triangles have three sides of equal length.

5. No positive numbers are less than 1.

6. Consider the sequence of figures shown at the right.

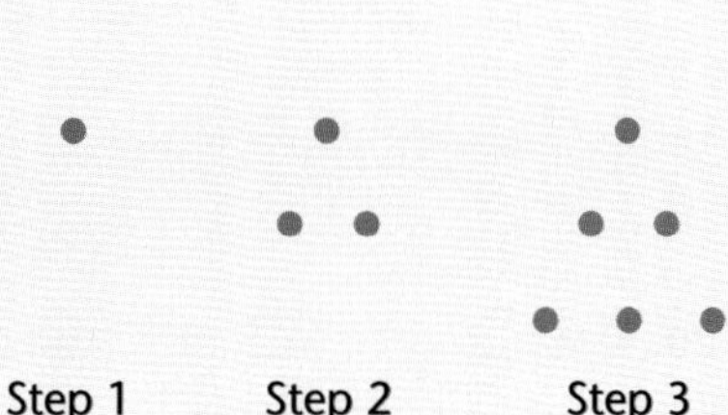

a. How many dots will be in the figure at Step 16?
b. How many dots will be in the figure at Step *n*?
c. What type of reasoning did you use to solve this problem? Write a brief description of how this type of reasoning works.

Find the length of $\overline{AB}$ using the given coordinates.

7. $A(4, -6)$, $B(6, -4)$

8. $A(-3, -2)$, $B(-1, 7)$

9. Find the slope of $\overleftrightarrow{RS}$ if R and S have coordinates $R(3, -9)$ and $S(-4, -2)$.

The scatter plot shows the literacy rate and the yearly per-capita income for 11 nations.

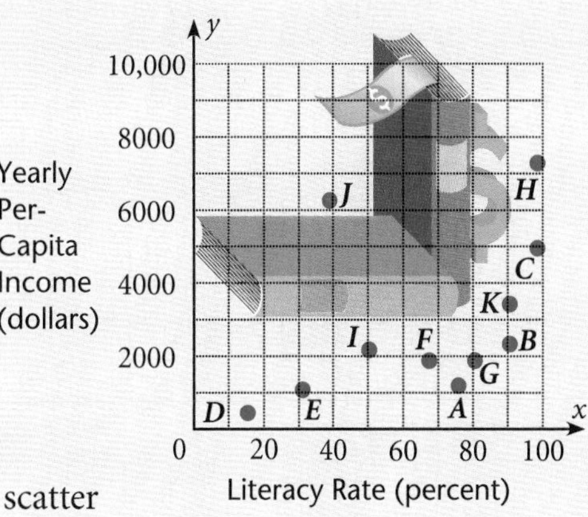

10. Which nation has the highest literacy rate? the lowest?

11. What conclusion can you draw from the scatter plot about the relationship between the literacy rate and per-capita income? Is there a nation that doesn't seem to fit this conclusion? Explain.

12. Suppose Country L has a literacy rate of 83%. Use the scatter plot to make a prediction of its yearly per-capita income.

13. Copy the figure at the right. Then use a compass and straightedge to construct a perpendicular from point P to line m.

P

m

Line *n* is a line of reflection in the figure at the right.

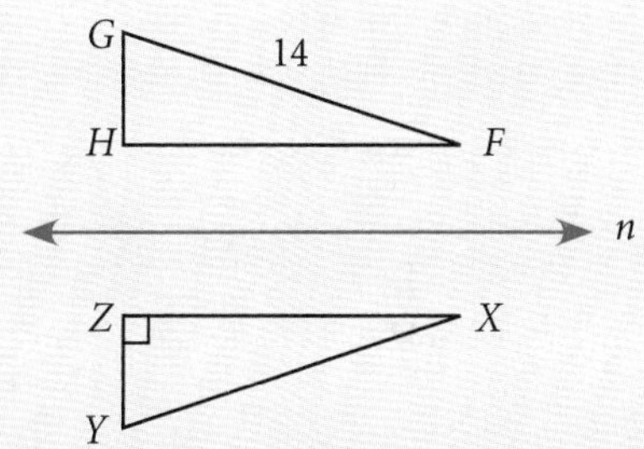

14. Name the pre-image of $\overline{XY}$.

15. Find $m\angle H$.

16. Find XY.

17. Write a list of as many properties as you can that are preserved by reflections. Then give at least one property that is not preserved by reflections. Include an illustration.

PERFORMANCE TASK

When three lines are drawn on a sheet of paper, they can intersect to form 0, 1, 2, or 3 points of intersection as shown below. Investigate the number of points of intersection that are possible when four lines are drawn on a sheet of paper. Prepare a figure for each possibility, and explain how you know your results are complete.

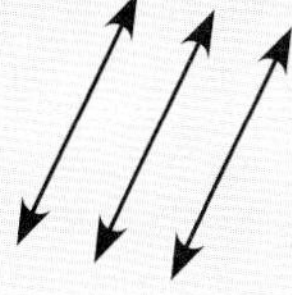

0 points

1 point

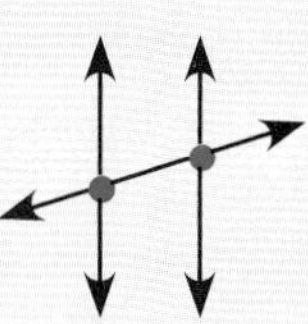

2 points

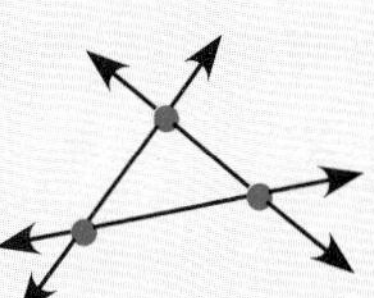

3 points

Chapter 2 The Foundations of Geometry

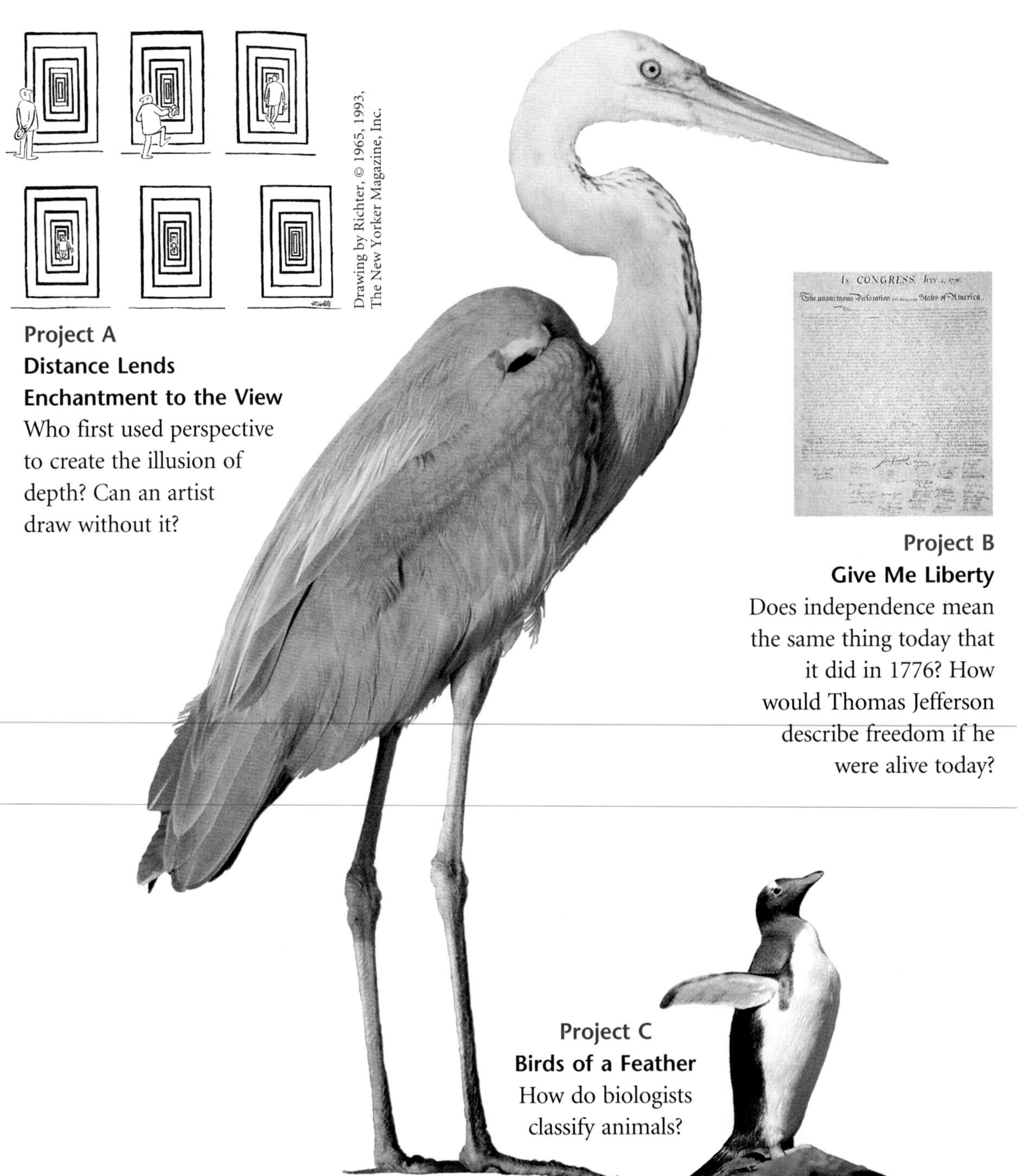

Drawing by Richter, © 1965, 1993, The New Yorker Magazine, Inc.

Project A

Distance Lends Enchantment to the View

Who first used perspective to create the illusion of depth? Can an artist draw without it?

Project B

Give Me Liberty

Does independence mean the same thing today that it did in 1776? How would Thomas Jefferson describe freedom if he were alive today?

Project C

Birds of a Feather

How do biologists classify animals?

REBECCA ANDERSON

I liked math in high school because it was methodical. It was satisfying to come up with a solution. I didn't know until my last year that I would be an engineer.

In college I enjoyed my classes in computer-assisted drafting (CAD). I learned 1-, 2-, and 3-point perspective, and isometric drawing. I use these to translate a two-dimensional drawing into three-dimensional, real space. As I read blueprints, I can see what is going on from one floor to the next. I think people in every field need a solid background in math.

Rebecca Anderson
Structural Engineer
Skidmore, Owings & Merrill, Inc.
Chicago, Illinois

Rebecca Anderson

Chapter 2 The Foundations of Geometry

GETTING READY

2-1 The Need for Precise Language

In 2-1 you will examine conditional (if..., then...) statements. You will use the following reasoning skills from previous chapters and courses.

True or false. If false, give an example. [Previous course]

1. All triangles have 3 sides.

2. All dogs have 4 legs.

3. No square has 6 sides.

4. Positive numbers are greater than 0.

5. -1000 is less than 0.0001.

6. $1 - x$ is less than 1.

Make this construction. [1-4]

7. Draw a line segment $\overline{AB}$. Construct a line segment $\overline{CD}$ that bisects $\overline{AB}$.

2-2 Stating Our Assumptions

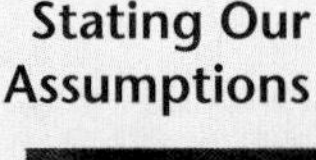

In 2-2 you will learn about postulates, undefined terms, defined terms, and theorems. You will use the following skills from previous courses.

Find the average. [Previous course]

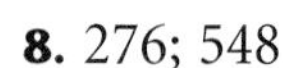

8. 276; 548 **9.** 75; 83 **10.** 42; 86; 99; 61 **11.** 147; 225; 178

Use the distributive property to simplify these expressions. [Previous course]

12. $4(3x - 7)$ **13.** $2(6x + 11)$ **14.** $5(2x^2 - 3x)$ **15.** $x(2x + 5y)$

2-3 Drawing Techniques and Parallel Lines

In 2-3 you will investigate different ways to visualize three-dimensional figures. You will use the following skills from previous chapters.

Copy each figure. Count the number of faces and vertices. [1-1]

16.

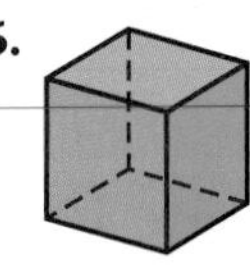

17.

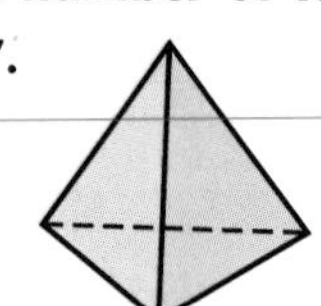

18.

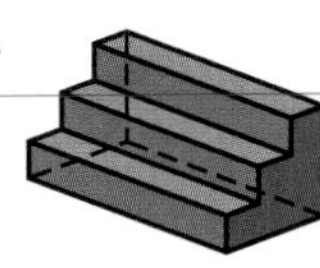

Solve each equation for $x = -10$, 0, and 10. [Previous course]

19. $y = x - 5$

20. $y = 2x + 2$

21. $y = -x + 1$

22. $y = \frac{1}{2}x$

23. $y = \frac{1}{10}x + 10$

24. $y = \frac{1}{100}x + 1$

2-1 The Need for Precise Language

TRUTH *IN* ADVERTISING

NEW!

"Is this true or is it an ad?" a child asked a parent. We learn at an early age that not every advertisement's claim is true. Yet companies spend billions of dollars in advertising research.

According to Goodrum and Dalrymple's book *Advertising in America*, one of the classic sayings in advertising is "We are certain that half the money we spend on advertising is wasted. The trouble is, we don't know which half."

Advertisers often use subtle "hidden assumptions" to call your attention to their product. They want to persuade you that their hidden assumption—the condition that the advertisement is based on—is true. In the 1903 advertisement shown, one of the hidden assumptions is that women want men to help with the wash. It is important for consumers to be able to determine whether an advertisement's conclusion is valid.

Cigarette and alcohol advertisements often show scenes of active, healthy people having fun. One of the hidden assumptions these advertisements want you to make is "If you use these products, then you will enjoy the good life." The work, health, and family problems that affect many people who use these products are never in the picture!

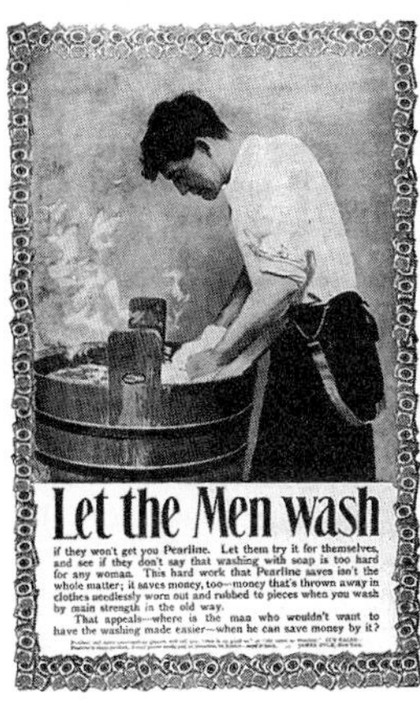

Let the Men wash
if they won't get you Pearline. Let them try it for themselves, and see if they don't say that washing with soap is too hard for any woman. This hard work that Pearline saves isn't the whole matter; it saves money, too—money that's thrown away in clothes needlessly worn out and rubbed to pieces when you wash by main strength in the old way.
That appeals—where is the man who wouldn't want to have the washing made easier—when he can save money by it?

?

1. Identify a hidden assumption in an advertisement you have recently seen.
2. Suppose that, for this particular advertisement only, the hidden assumption is true. Should you necessarily conclude that you ought to buy the product?
3. How might knowing the assumptions behind advertisements help you from being fooled by them?

BUY IT!

2-1 PART A Conditional Statements

← CONNECT → *You've already learned some of the language of logic. Now you will investigate a type of logical statement that is especially important: the conditional statement.*

Businesses hope that consumers will believe their advertising claims. These claims are often made indirectly, perhaps through pictures. Sometimes the claim *is* directly stated. In the advertisement from the late 1800s shown at the right, the claim is "If you use Carter's Little Liver Pills, then you will have no more sick headache."

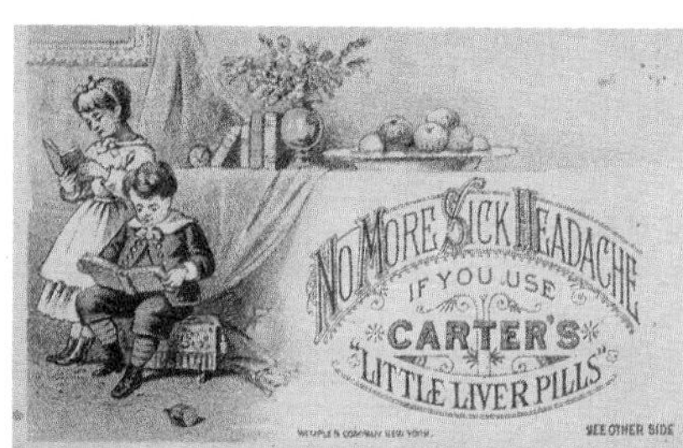

In mathematics, statements in if-then form are called **conditional statements.** The *if* part is the **hypothesis,** and the *then* part is the **conclusion.** The hypothesis and conclusion of a conditional statement are illustrated below.

If you use Mighty Mousse, then your hair will stay in place in a hurricane.

↑ Hypothesis (you use Mighty Mousse) — ↑ Conclusion (your hair will stay in place in a hurricane)

EXAMPLE

1. Identify the hypothesis and the conclusion of the statement "If you use Carter's Little Liver Pills, then you will have no more sick headache."

Hypothesis: You use Carter's Little Liver Pills.

Conclusion: You will have no more sick headache.

Notice that the words *if* and *then* are not part of the hypothesis or the conclusion.

TRY IT

Write a conditional statement from the given information.

a. Hypothesis: You talk on the telephone more than one hour per night.

Conclusion: Your grade will drop one letter.

Conditional statements aren't always in if-then form. However, any conditional statement can be rewritten in that form. When you put a statement in if-then form, it is much easier to identify its hypothesis and conclusion.

The 1902 advertisement at the right claims that eating Quaker Oats will keep you young. You could rewrite this claim as a conditional statement: "If you eat Quaker Oats, then you will put off old age."

It Puts Off Old Age

by nourishing the entire system. Quaker Oats makes your blood tingle; nerves strong and steady: brain clear and active; muscles powerful. It makes flesh rather than fat, but enough fat for reserve force. It builds children up symmetrically into brainy and robust men and women. You can work on Quaker Oats. It stays by you, At all grocers' in 2-lb. packages only.

TRY IT

Rewrite each conditional statement in if-then form.

b. Help save our forests by using recycled paper.
c. A whole number with three or more factors is not a prime number.

Both consumers and mathematicians must be able to determine when a statement is true. In the following Explore, you will discover when a conditional statement is true and when it is false.

EXPLORE: CHECK THE CONDITIONALS

1. Write a list of several conditional statements in if-then form that you believe are true. Then make a list of several that you feel are false.
2. Use your lists to decide how you can determine whether a conditional statement is true or false by experimenting with the "truth values" of the hypotheses and the conclusions of your statements. Write a short summary describing how you can tell whether a conditional is true or false. Compare your ideas with those of your classmates.

EXAMPLE

2. Determine whether the conditional statement below is true or false. Explain how you know.

If two numbers are both odd, then their sum is odd.

Suppose that two numbers are odd, for example, 3 and 5. Their sum, 8, is not odd. This counterexample shows that the conditional is false, because its conclusion is false even though its hypothesis is true.

The properties of true and false conditional statements are summarized below.

> For a conditional statement to be true, the conclusion must be true whenever the hypothesis is true. A conditional is false only if there is a case in which the hypothesis is true and the conclusion is false.

In formal logic, a conditional statement is considered true if the hypothesis is false. (In everyday situations, a conditional is usually considered *irrelevant* when the hypothesis is false.)

You can use a Venn diagram to illustrate conditional statements. The Venn diagram below illustrates the statement "If an animal is a collie, then it is a dog." Since all collies are dogs, this is a true conditional statement. Notice that in this true conditional, no part of the "if circle" lies outside the "then circle." You can also use the Venn diagram to show the following is true: If Shep is a collie, then Shep is a dog.

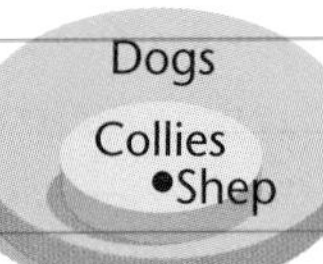

REFLECT

1. Why might companies choose not to put their advertisements in if-then form?

2. Should a conditional statement be considered true if the conclusion is *sometimes* true when the hypothesis is true? For instance, is "If it is cloudy, then it will rain" a true statement?

Exercises

CORE

Getting Started Identify the hypothesis and the conclusion of each conditional.

1. If you want to stay healthy, then you should eat fruits, grains, and vegetables.

2. If $a > b$, then $a + c > b + c$.

For each hypothesis and conclusion, write a conditional statement from the given information.

3. Hypothesis: It rains.

Conclusion: I won't go swimming.

4. Hypothesis: You eat too much spicy food.

Conclusion: You will want a glass of milk.

Rewrite each conditional statement in if-then form.

5. Cherry flavoring will make children love to take their medicine.

6. A burst of mint flavor brightens your mouth when you eat Sparkos!

7. Integers divisible by 4 are also divisible by 2.

8. Write the letter of the second pair that best matches the first pair.

Hypothesis: conclusion as (a) some: all, (b) fact: belief, (c) if: then, (d) rectangle: square

Refer to the Venn diagram at the right.

Math students

Geometry students

9. Use the Venn diagram to write a conditional that is true.

10. Use the Venn diagram to write a conditional that is false.

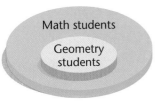

Determine whether each conditional is true or false. Explain how you know.

11. If you smoke cigarettes, then you increase your risk of heart disease or lung cancer.

12. If a figure is a rectangle, then it is a square.

Rectangle Square

13. If $3x - 4 = 17$, then $x = 7$.

14. Write a brief summary explaining how you decide whether a conditional statement is true or false.

15. A Future in Advertising Invent a conditional advertisement in if-then form for one of your favorite products.

16. Condition-All **a.** Sketch a Venn diagram to illustrate the statement "All dogs who eat Muscle Pup are healthy and strong!"

b. Write a conditional statement in if-then form that has the same meaning.

c. Can you always convert a statement that begins with *all (each, every)* into a conditional in if-then form? If so, explain how.

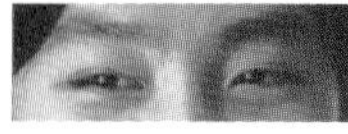

LOOK BACK

Write each number using scientific notation. [Previous course]

17. 1875

18. 0.234

19. 602,300,000,000,000,000,000,000

Write each number without using scientific notation. [Previous course]

20. 7×10^3

21. 1.4×10^{-6}

22. 7.02×10^8

23. Copy segment $\overline{AB}$. Then use a compass and straightedge to construct a segment congruent to $\overline{AB}$. [1-3]

A B

24. Sketch line m and point S not on m. Then use a compass and straightedge to construct the line through S that is perpendicular to m. [1-4]

MORE PRACTICE

Identify the hypothesis and the conclusion of each conditional.

25. If a student enrolls in Algebra II, then he will learn about logarithms.

26. If $|3x - 2| = 10$, then $x = 4$ or $x = -\frac{8}{3}$.

For each hypothesis and conclusion, write a conditional statement from the given information.

27. Hypothesis: A mosquito bites you.

Conclusion: You will get a bump on your arm.

28. Hypothesis: A person doesn't stop at a stop sign.

Conclusion: She may get a ticket.

Rewrite each conditional statement in if-then form.

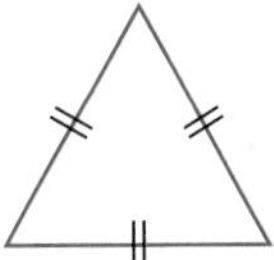

29. A triangle is equilateral if all of its sides have the same length.

30. The product of two negative numbers is positive.

Determine whether each conditional is true or false.

31. If it is raining, then there are clouds in the sky.

32. If there are clouds in the sky, then it is raining.

33. If $x^2 = 4$, then $x = 2$.

MORE MATH REASONING

34. Mail Order Randy received the letter shown at the right from the Buy-It-Today Corporation. Randy thought, "If I don't buy today, then I won't get the lowest price!" Is his thinking valid? If so, explain why. If not, explain why not, and give a possible reason why the company made this statement.

35. Computer Conditionals A computer program includes these statements:

100 Let $x = n + 1$

200 If $x < 3$, then go to 500

300 Print "I am the greatest."

400 Jump to 600

500 Print "Your wish is my command."

600 End

Predict the output of the program (the things that are printed) for the following values of n.

a. $n = 0$

b. $n = 3$

c. $n = 2$

d. Suppose you use an if-then statement in a computer program. Under what circumstances does the computer execute the *then* part?

2-1 PART B Related Conditional Statements

← CONNECT → ***You've explored conditional statements, and you know how to determine whether they are true or false. Now you will look at several ways to rearrange conditionals and see whether these rearrangements affect the truth of the conditionals.***

Every conditional has three related statements. These statements are the converse, inverse, and contrapositive of the conditional. Consider the map at the left as you read the following examples.

CONVERSE	
The **converse** of a conditional is formed by interchanging the hypothesis and the conclusion.	*Conditional:* (If p, then q.) If you live in Miami, then you live in Florida. *Converse:* (If q, then p.) If you live in Florida, then you live in Miami.
INVERSE	
The **inverse** of a conditional is formed by taking the *negations* of the hypothesis and the conclusion. (Negations state the opposite of the original phrase.)	*Conditional:* (If p, then q.) If you live in Miami, then you live in Florida. *Inverse:* (If not p, then not q.) If you do *not* live in Miami, then you do *not* live in Florida.
CONTRAPOSITIVE	
The **contrapositive** of a conditional is formed by taking the negation of the hypothesis and conclusion, then interchanging them.	*Conditional:* (If p, then q.) If you live in Miami, then you live in Florida. *Contrapositive:* (If not q, then not p.) If you do *not* live in Florida, then you do *not* live in Miami.

TRY IT

a. Write the inverse, the converse, and the contrapositive of the statement "If you are fifteen, then you are a teenager."

In the following Explore, you will investigate a conditional and its converse, inverse, and contrapositive.

EXPLORE: WHAT'S THE RELATIONSHIP?

1. Write a list of several true conditional statements. Use your list to investigate the following questions.
   a. If a conditional statement is true, is its converse always true?
   b. If a conditional statement is true, is its inverse always true?
   c. If a conditional statement is true, is its contrapositive always true?
2. What conclusion can you draw from your investigation in Step 1? Are there any pairs of statements that always have the same truth value for a given hypothesis and conclusion? Discuss your conclusion with your classmates.

Problem-Solving Tip

Make a generalization.

A Venn diagram can help you see the relationship between a statement and its inverse, converse, and contrapositive. Suppose you need to investigate the statement "If you are a surgeon, then you wear a mask." Using the Venn diagram below, we see that Person A is a surgeon, and he is also a mask-wearer. The statement is *true.*

Now, suppose you need to investigate the inverse of the statement: "If you are not a surgeon, then you do not wear a mask." According to the diagram, this could be Person B (perhaps a deep-sea diver?) or Person C. But Person B does wear a mask, so the inverse of the original statement is false.

The relationships between the truth values of a conditional and its inverse, converse, and contrapositive are summarized below.

- If a conditional statement is true, its contrapositive is true; if a conditional statement is false, its contrapositive is false.
- The truth value of a conditional statement does not tell you whether its converse or its inverse is true or false. You must analyze those statements separately.

REFLECT

1. Are the truth values of the inverse and converse of a statement related? If so, describe how and explain why.

2. Consuela says, "If I take the converse of the inverse of a conditional statement, I get the statement's contrapositive." Show whether she is right or wrong.

3. Write an advertisement with a conditional statement for a fictitious product. Would it benefit your company if people assumed that the inverse of your statement was also true? Explain.

Exercises

CORE

1. Getting Started The photo at the lower right shows the Katsura Imperial Villa in Kyoto. Write the inverse, converse, and contrapositive of the statement "If you live in Kyoto, then you live in Japan."

Write the inverse, converse, and contrapositive of each conditional. Then determine which statements are true and which are false.

2. If $x^2 = 4$, then $x = 2$.

3. If two angles are right angles, then they are congruent.

4. If you finish a triathlon, then you are in good shape.

5. If you are an elephant, then you do not know how to fly.

6. If you have a cold, then you are sick.

In Exercises 7 and 8, determine whether each statement is true or false. If the statement is false, change the underlined word to make it true.

7. To form the <u>converse</u> of a conditional statement, switch the hypothesis and the conclusion.

8. If a conditional statement is true, its contrapositive must be <u>false</u>.

9. Write a false conditional statement. Then write its inverse, converse, and contrapositive, and determine whether each statement is true or false.

Write a conditional statement with each of the following sets of characteristics.

10. The conditional is true, and its converse is false.

11. The conditional is false, and its inverse is true.

12. The conditional is true, and its inverse and converse are false.

13. The conditional and all of its related statements are true.

14. Take Your Vitamins! Mr. Perkins heard an advertisement that said, "If you take a multivitamin tablet each day, then you'll stay healthy." Mr. Perkins began to feel uneasy, thinking, "If I don't take a multivitamin tablet each day, then I won't stay healthy." Is his thinking valid? If so, explain why. If not, explain the error he is making.

15. On Cloud Nine Judy's mother received an advertisement that said, "If you are fashionable, then you wear Cloud Nine shoes." She said to Judy, "I wear Cloud Nine shoes; therefore, I must be fashionable."

a. If you use "if p, then q" to abbreviate the statement in the advertisement, how would you abbreviate the assumption that Judy's mother made?

b. Was her mother's reasoning logically correct? Explain why or why not.

LOOK AHEAD

When a conditional and its converse are both true, you can combine the two statements into one statement, called a *biconditional,* by using the phrase "if and only if." For example, the two statements "if tomorrow is Saturday, then today is Friday" and "if today is Friday, then tomorrow is Saturday" become "tomorrow is Saturday if and only if today is Friday." Use this information to help you with Exercises 16 and 17 on page 98.

Write the converse of each conditional. If both the original statement and its converse are true, then rewrite them as a single biconditional statement.

16. If an angle is a right angle, then it measures 90°.

17. If two angles are congruent, then they have the same measure.

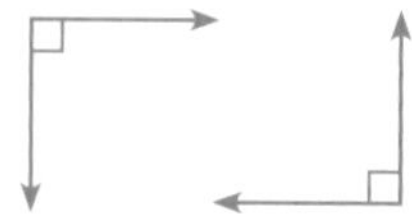

Suppose $m\angle A + m\angle B = 180°$. Find $m\angle A$ for each $m\angle B$ below.

18. $m\angle B = 120°$

19. $m\angle B = 45°$

20. $m\angle B = 90°$

21. Write an expression for $m\angle A$ in terms of $m\angle B$.

MORE PRACTICE

For Excercises 22–25, write the inverse, converse, and contrapositive of each conditional. Then determine which statements are true and which are false.

22. If it is raining, then the sidewalk is wet.

23. If $t^2 > 0$, then $t > 0$.

24. If a whole number has exactly two whole-number factors, then it is a prime.

25. If you are not over four feet tall, then you are not riding the RocketCoaster.

26. **a.** Assume the following statement is true, and illustrate it with a Venn diagram.

If you want to become a businessperson, then you will need to take math.

b. Write the converse of the statement. Is the converse true or false?

c. Write the inverse of the statement. Is the inverse true or false?

d. Write the contrapositive of the statement. Is the contrapositive true or false?

MORE MATH REASONING

27. Write a conditional statement in if-then form. Then write the inverse of the converse of its contrapositive. Explain why your statement turns out the way it does.

28. **Vase Case** Latasha is a lawyer. She wants to prove that her client, Chip, did not break an expensive vase in a gift shop. Obviously, if her client broke the vase, then he was in the gift shop. How can Latasha prove that Chip is innocent without ever saying that he did not break the vase? Why will this strategy work?

2-1 PART C The Rules of Logic

← CONNECT → ***You know the conditions that make a single conditional statement true. Now you will investigate rules of logic that allow you to link logical statements together to make a valid deductive argument.***

Advertisements often try to persuade you to buy a product by getting you to believe a conditional statement is true. Once the conditional statement is accepted, the advertisement tries to persuade you to buy the product (hypothesis) and benefit from the promise (conclusion).

There are some rules of logic that people frequently use without realizing it. In the following Explore, you will identify some of your intuitive rules of logic.

EXPLORE: LOGICAL LINKS

Assume that the statements below are true. Some of them fit together. Use them to write other statements that must be true. Then summarize any general rules of logic that you seemed to use consistently.

Frida Kahlo, *Self-Portrait with Monkey,* 1945. Fundacion Dolores Olmedo, Mexico City, Mexico.

If I get a better English grade, then I can go to college and become a famous scientist.

If I learn more about my culture, then I can share it better with other people.

If a self-portrait is by Frida Kahlo, then it was painted before 1955.

I'm proud of my heritage.

If my vision is blurry, then I will get glasses.

The self-portrait at the right is by Frida Kahlo.

If I see better, then I can read faster.

If I can read faster, then I'll get a better English grade.

If I'm proud of my heritage, then I will learn more about my culture.

If I get glasses, then I'll see better.

TRY IT

Assume that the following statements are true. Write another true statement if possible. If it is not possible, explain why.

a. If I clean my room, then I'll find my shoes. If I find my shoes, then I'll be able to go to the store.

b. If Fran gets an A in Spanish, then she will make the Honor Roll. Fran gets an A in Spanish.

One pattern you may have discovered is the **Law of Detachment.** If you are given a true conditional statement and you know the hypothesis is true, then the conclusion must also be true. The pattern is called the Law of Detachment because it detaches the conclusion from a conditional. The following summary of the Law of Detachment includes an example on the right.

LAW OF DETACHMENT	
Assumption: If p is true, then q is true.	If Chanelle is in 12th grade, then she is a senior.
Assumption: p is true.	Chanelle is in 12th grade.
Conclusion: q is true.	Chanelle is a senior.

Another rule of logic that you might have found is the **Chain Rule** (see the summary and example that follow). The Chain Rule links two true conditional statements. It can only be used if the hypothesis of one statement is the conclusion of the other.

CHAIN RULE	
Assumption: If p is true, then q is true.	If Chanelle is in 12th grade, then she is a senior.
Assumption: If q is true, then r is true.	If she is a senior, then she is in government class.
Conclusion: If p is true, then r is true.	If Chanelle is in 12th grade, then she is in government class.

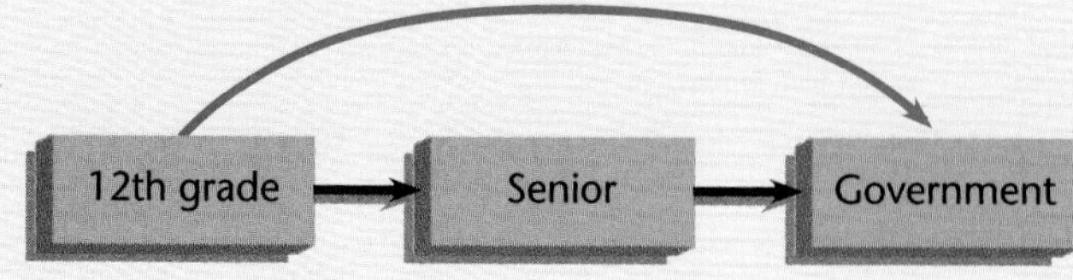

These laws of logic may seem obvious, but we need to agree on them so that we understand and believe each other's deductive arguments. These laws also help you to think about what you are doing when you work with mathematical statements instead of ordinary sentences.

REFLECT

1. In your own words, explain when you can make a valid deduction by the following rules of logic.

   a. the Law of Detachment
   b. the Chain Rule

2. Give your own examples of logical reasoning that illustrate the Law of Detachment and the Chain Rule.

Exercises

CORE

1. **Getting Started** Assume that the following statements are true. Use the Law of Detachment to write another true statement.

   If figure *EFGH* is a square, then $\overline{EG} \cong \overline{HF}$. Figure *EFGH* is a square.

Assume that the following statements are true. Use the Law of Detachment to write another true statement if possible. If it is not possible, explain why.

2. If two lines are perpendicular, then they intersect. Lines $\overleftrightarrow{AB}$ and $\overleftrightarrow{CD}$ intersect.

3. If a state has 9 members of the House of Representatives, then it has 11 electoral votes. In 1992, the state of Washington had 9 representatives.

Assume that the following statements are true. Use the Chain Rule to write another true statement if possible. If it is not possible, explain why.

4. If it is raining, the sky is cloudy. If the sky is cloudy, then you can't see the sun.

5. If the legal minimum wage is too high, then employers will hire fewer people. If the legal minimum wage is too low, then there will be a shortage of workers.

Rewrite the first statement in if-then form. Then make a deduction using the Law of Detachment.

6. The Secretary of Transportation is a member of the Cabinet. In 1993, Federico Peña became the Secretary of Transportation.

7. Baseball players wear spikes on natural-grass fields. Ken Griffey, Jr., is a baseball player.

Rewrite both statements in each pair in if-then form. Then make a deduction using the Chain Rule if possible.

8. Stag beetles are insects. All insects have six legs.

9. A rational number can be written as a fraction. Pi can be written as the fraction $\frac{\pi}{1}$.

Identify the law of logic used to reach each of the following conclusions.

10. If $\overrightarrow{BD}$ is perpendicular to $\overleftrightarrow{AC}$, then $\angle ABD$ and $\angle DBC$ are right angles. If $\angle ABD$ and $\angle DBC$ are right angles, then $\angle ABD$ and $\angle DBC$ measure 90°. Conclusion: If $\overrightarrow{BD}$ is perpendicular to $\overleftrightarrow{AC}$, then $\angle ABD$ and $\angle DBC$ measure 90°.

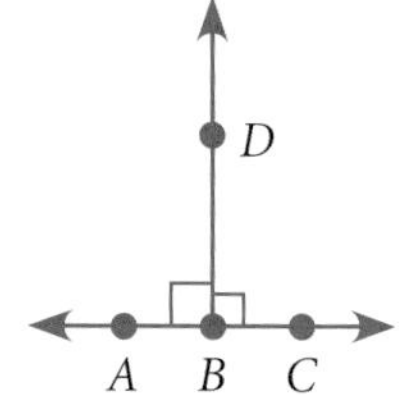

11. If I can't find my keys, then I'll have to stay home. I can't find my keys. Conclusion: I'll have to stay home.

Arrange some or all of the following conditionals into an order that allows you to make the given conclusions.

If *A*, then *B*. If *X*, then *R*. If *M*, then *Y*. If *R*, then *M*. If *Y*, then *A*.

12. If *X*, then *Y*.

13. If *X*, then *B*.

Science

14. **Do I Kneed Surgery?** A patient comes to a doctor with an injured knee. The doctor knows that if the patient has torn a ligament, he may need to have arthroscopic surgery. She also knows that if his knee is swollen, there may be ligament damage. An MRI (magnetic resonance imaging) scan can detect ligament damage. Her patient's knee is badly swollen, painful, and difficult to move. Given only this information, what do you think the doctor will recommend? Explain how you reached this conclusion, and describe how you used the Chain Rule and the Law of Detachment in your reasoning.

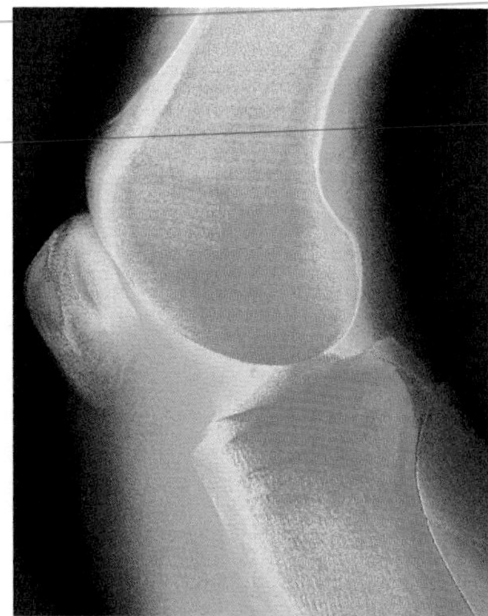

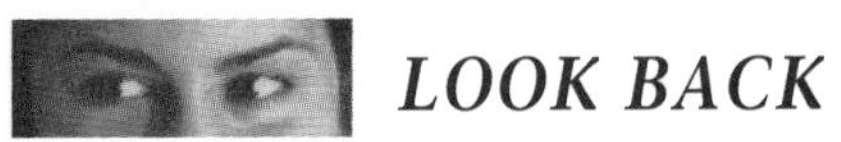

LOOK BACK

Factor each expression. [Previous course]

15. $x^2 - 6x + 9$ **16.** $y^2 + 11y + 28$ **17.** $3c^2 - 4c - 15$

Answer each of the following. Then state the type of reasoning you used to solve the problem. [1-2]

18. The first four numbers in a sequence are 1, 3, 6, and 10. Find the fifth and sixth numbers.

19. Harvey never tells the truth. Alex always tells the truth. Roger sometimes tells the truth. Who is the person in the middle?

MORE PRACTICE

Assume that the following statements are true. Use the Law of Detachment to write another true statement if possible. If it is not possible, explain why.

20. If an animal is a mammal, then it is warm-blooded. A seal is a mammal.

21. If a figure has four sides, then it is a quadrilateral. A rectangle has four sides.

Assume that the following statements are true. Use the Chain Rule to write another true statement if possible. If it is not possible, explain why.

22. If it rains, then we go to the movies. If we go to the movies, then we get popcorn.

23. If you reflect a segment across a line, the image has the same length as the pre-image. If two segments have the same length, then they are congruent.

MORE MATH REASONING

24. Write a chain of three conditional statements in if-then form that will allow you to conclude, "If you vote for me, then your taxes will be lower."

25. Grade Gossip Arthur, Beth, Carlos, and Diane were discussing their geometry grades. All of their statements were true.

Arthur said, "If I get an A, then Beth will get an A."

Beth said, "If I get an A, then Carlos will get an A."

Carlos said, "If I get an A, then Diane will get an A."

a. Only two of the students received an A. Which two?

b. How would the answer to **25a** change if Diane had said, "If I get an A, then Arthur will get an A"?

2-1 PART D Making Connections

← CONNECT → ***You've learned how to form and to use the most common type of logical statement in geometry—the conditional statement.***

The Law of Detachment and the Chain Rule are ways to build logical arguments from conditional statements. You will now use conditional statements and rules of logic to create your own advertisement.

EXPLORE: I'LL BUY THAT!

MATERIALS

Construction paper (optional)
Marking pens (optional)

1. Design your own 30-second TV advertisement for a product of your choice. You may use dialogue, visuals, or music, but your advertisement must have the following characteristics:

- the use of several conditional statements (they do not have to be in if-then form);
- the use of both rules of logic;
- the use of persuasion to convince your audience to buy your product.

What do you want the customer to believe after seeing your advertisement? Show the rules of logic, and explain the thought process you hope customers go through when they see your ad.

2. Present your advertisement to the class.

REFLECT

1. Describe some ways that advertisements use logical statements and rules of logic.
2. Explain how you can determine whether a conditional statement is true or false.
3. Write a letter to a friend who has not studied geometry explaining how you can use the Law of Detachment or the Chain Rule to prove a point. Use a real-life example from history, current events, or your own experience to help illustrate the rule.

Self-Assessment

In Exercises 1–3, rewrite each conditional statement in if-then form. Then identify its hypothesis and conclusion.

1. All squares are quadrilaterals.
2. You should buy Frumworts because they make you happy!
3. You waste gasoline when you drive too fast.
4. A student says, "If I don't have a lot of homework, then my book bag will not be heavy."
   a. Write the converse, inverse, and contrapositive of this conditional.
   b. Determine whether each of the four statements is true or false. Give a counterexample to justify a false value.
5. Draw a Venn diagram to show that the following argument is valid.

   If a family lives in Chicago, then they live in Illinois.

   The Dias family lives in Chicago.

   Therefore, the Dias family lives in Illinois.
6. **Broken Promise?** Jon told his younger brother, "If you don't clean up your mess in my room, then I won't take you to the game tonight." Jon's brother did clean up his mess in Jon's room, but Jon decided not to take his brother to the game. Jon's brother claims he broke his promise. Explain to Jon's brother why Jon didn't really break his promise.

Write each number using scientific notation. [Previous course]

7. 327
8. 0.003042
9. 186,282 (This is the number of miles light travels in 1 sec.)

10. The Pizza Puzzle Carol decided to make a mystery game for her birthday party. Can you deduce how the game ended? Which friend found the real pizza, what topping was on the pizza, and where was it hidden? [1-2]

- There were four pizzas, but only one was real. Four friends were looking for the real pizza. Each pizza had a different topping: pepperoni, sausage, ham, or extra cheese.
- Sara found the ham pizza behind the wall picture in the living room.
- The friend who found the pepperoni pizza did not find it under the kitchen sink.
- The real pizza was not found under the couch or in the freezer; two false pizzas were found there.
- Fumiko found a pizza under the kitchen sink.
- Michelle found the pizza with extra cheese, but it was a fake.
- Zuri did not find her pizza in the freezer.
- Sara did not find the real pizza.

11. Assume that each of the following statements is true.

If you are a dreet, then you are a drook.
If you are not a dran, then you are not a drook.
If you are a dran, then you are not a drilp.
You are a drook.

Which of the following statements must also be true?

(a) You are a drilp. (b) You are a dran.
(c) You are a dreet. (d) You are not a drilp.
(e) both (b) and (d) (f) both (a) and (c)

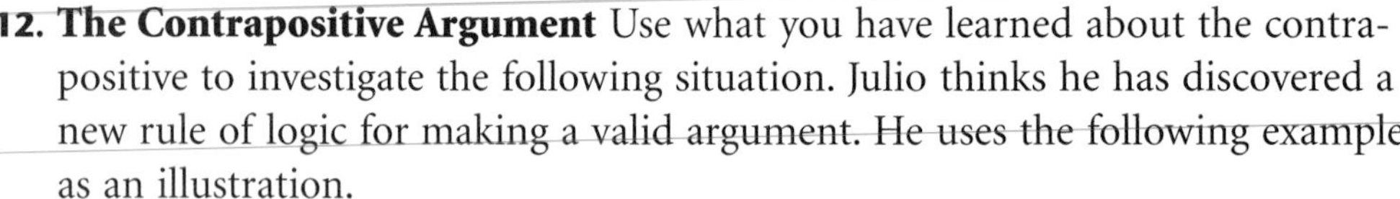

12. The Contrapositive Argument Use what you have learned about the contrapositive to investigate the following situation. Julio thinks he has discovered a new rule of logic for making a valid argument. He uses the following example as an illustration.

If a whale is a killer whale, then it has a dorsal fin.
This whale does not have a dorsal fin.
Therefore, this whale is not a killer whale.

a. Is Julio's conclusion logical?
b. In your own words, describe the rule he is using.
c. Investigate other conditionals using Julio's rule. Does this rule always work?

2-2 Stating Our Assumptions

On July 4, 1776, 56 representatives of the 13 colonies unanimously passed and signed the Declaration of Independence marking the beginning of the United States of America. The heart of the document is highlighted here. The colonists formed a new nation based on the assumptions stated in the Declaration. Any system of government has some basic assumptions that are taken to be true without proof. In the Declaration of Independence, assumptions are either words that are not defined or ideas that are taken for granted with no justification given.

We hold these truths to be *self-evident*, that all men are created equal, that they are endowed by their Creator with certain unalienable Rights, that among these are Life, Liberty and the pursuit of Happiness.—That to secure these *rights*, Governments are instituted among Men, deriving their just powers from the *consent* of the governed,—That whenever any Form of Government becomes destructive of these ends, it is the Right of the People to alter or to abolish it, and to institute new Government, laying its *foundation* on such principles and organizing its powers in such form, as to them shall seem most likely to effect their Safety and Happiness.

?

1. In this excerpt from the Declaration of Independence, which statements are assumptions made without any proof? Explain your choices.
2. Why do you think some assumptions in government and mathematics have to be made without proof?

Building a Foundation

2-2 PART A Undefined Terms and Definitions

← CONNECT → *You are familiar with some of the important logical statements and rules of logic in our deductive system. Now you'll see why undefined terms are needed, and you'll begin to write accurate definitions of other terms.*

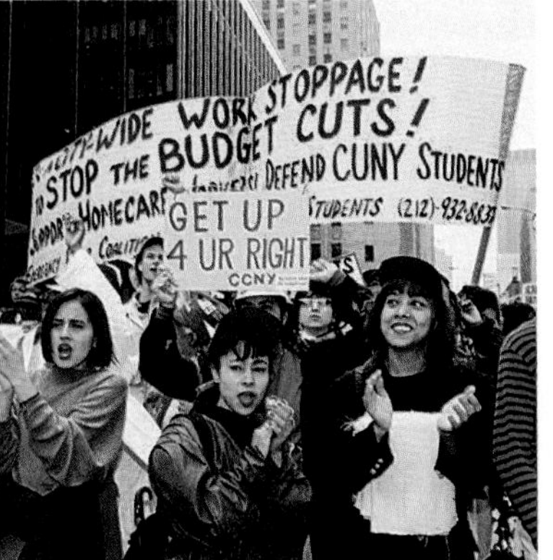

Over the years, we have needed to interpret key words and phrases from the Declaration of Independence. For example, did *liberty* mean freedom to vote, freedom of speech, or more? We must define key words precisely in a system of government and in a deductive system like geometry, so that everyone can use these words in the same way.

Dictionaries seem to define almost every word in a language, but you can't use a dictionary if you don't already know some of the words in it! Before you can begin to define words in geometry, you must know terms that are fundamental to the whole system.

1. Which of the geometry terms that you've learned do you think are the most basic? Explain why you selected these terms.

In geometry, we need some undefined terms—words that we simply "understand." You have already seen explanations (not definitions!) of two of these.

A **point** is a specific location that has no size.

A **line** is an infinite, straight set of points that continues forever in both directions. A line has no width or thickness, but it has infinite length.

A third undefined term in geometry is *plane*. A **plane** is a flat surface that extends infinitely. A plane has infinite length and width, but no thickness. A plane is named by a single capital letter.

This is plane $\mathcal{P}$.

We use these undefined terms to build definitions such as the following.

DEFINITION

Coplanar points are points that lie in the same plane.

A, *B*, *C*, and *D* are coplanar—they all lie in plane $\mathcal{P}$. But *A*, *B*, *C*, *D*, and *E* are **noncoplanar**—there is no flat surface that contains all of them.

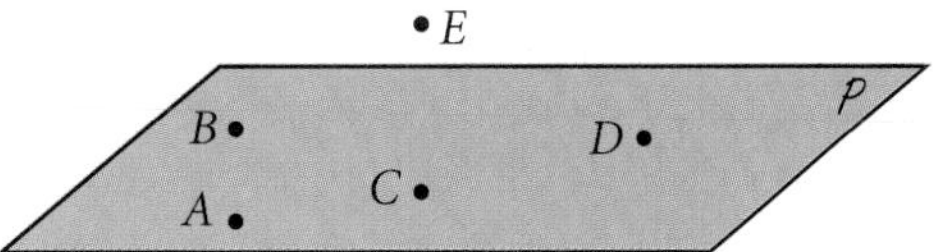

In mathematics, there are two important steps to making a good definition. The first step involves identifying the *critical attributes* of a concept. These are characteristics that are always true of the concept.

EXAMPLE

List the critical attributes of right angles.

These are right angles. These are not.

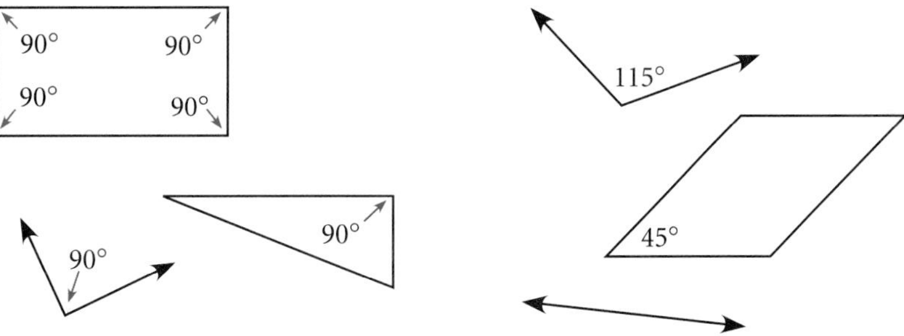

The critical attributes of a right angle are the characteristics that all right angles share.

<u>Critical Attributes</u>
It must be an angle.
It must measure 90°.

Other characteristics of an angle, like its position or the type of figure it's in, don't determine whether or not it's a right angle. Such characteristics are not critical attributes of right angles.

The second step in making a good definition is to put the critical attributes into a statement that defines the term precisely in as few words as possible. Keep these goals in mind as you write your own definition of *midpoint* in the following Explore.

EXPLORE: WHAT MAKES A MIDPOINT?

1. Examine the examples and nonexamples of midpoints. Identify the critical attributes of a midpoint.

These red points are *midpoints of a segment* whose endpoints are shown in black.

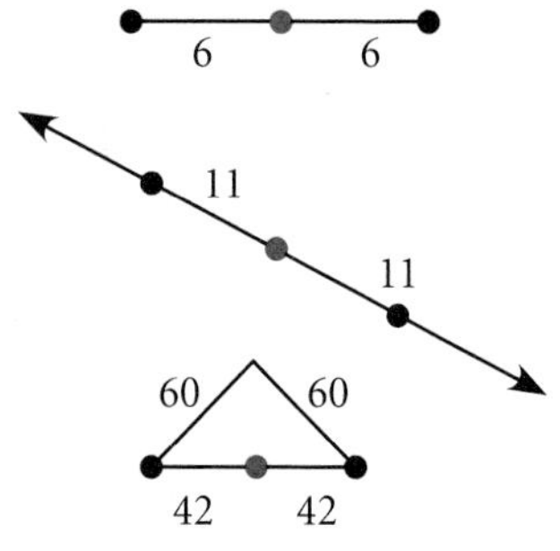

These red points are not.

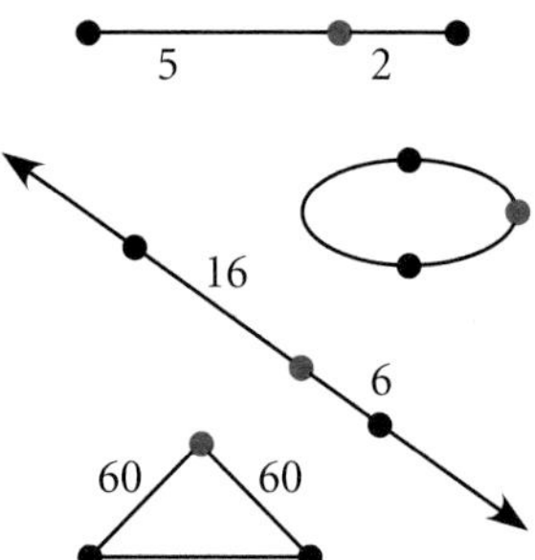

2. Using the critical attributes you found, write a definition of the midpoint of a segment.

When both a conditional and its converse are true, you can combine the two into one **biconditional** statement using the connector phrase "if and only if." Our formal definition of the midpoint of a segment, in biconditional form, is shown below.

DEFINITION

Point M is the **midpoint** of $\overline{AB}$ if and only if it divides $\overline{AB}$ into two congruent segments, $\overline{AM}$ and $\overline{MB}$.

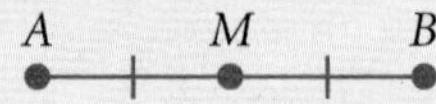

Compare this definition to the one you developed in the Explore.

Our definition of *midpoint* means that *both* of the following statements are true.

- If M is the midpoint of $\overline{AB}$, then it divides $\overline{AB}$ into two congruent segments.
- If a point M divides $\overline{AB}$ into two congruent segments, then it is the midpoint of $\overline{AB}$.

REFLECT

1. Suppose we propose the following definitions of *right angle* and *perpendicular.*
   - *Perpendicular* lines are lines that form right angles.
   - *Right angles* are the angles formed by perpendicular lines.

   Are these good definitions? Explain why or why not.
2. Obviously, all terms in a definition have to be understood before you can use the definition. Identify the geometric terms used in the formal definition of *midpoint.* Are all of them either undefined terms or previously defined terms? Explain.
3. What are the characteristics of a good definition?

Exercises

CORE

1. **Getting Started** Use the steps below to write a definition of *collinear* as a biconditional statement.
   a. Take the definition "Collinear points are points that lie on the same line," and write it in if-then form, starting with "If a set of points is collinear . . ."
   b. Write the converse of the conditional statement you wrote in **1a.** Check to see that both statements are true.
   c. If both the statement and its converse are true, write the biconditional by linking the hypothesis of either of the statements to its conclusion with the words "if and only if."

Write each definition as a biconditional statement.

2. Two lines that meet to form a right angle are **perpendicular.**

3. The **converse** of a conditional statement is formed by interchanging the hypothesis and conclusion.

Write each statement as two conditional statements in if-then form.

4. An angle is a right angle if and only if it measures 90°.

5. M is the midpoint of $\overline{AB}$ if and only if it divides $\overline{AB}$ into two congruent segments, $\overline{AM}$ and $\overline{MB}$.

6. You may run for the United States Senate if and only if you are at least 30 years old and have been a citizen of the United States for at least 9 years.

List the critical attributes of the following terms. Then write a definition for each word, using "if and only if."

7. These are **perpendicular bisectors.** These are not.

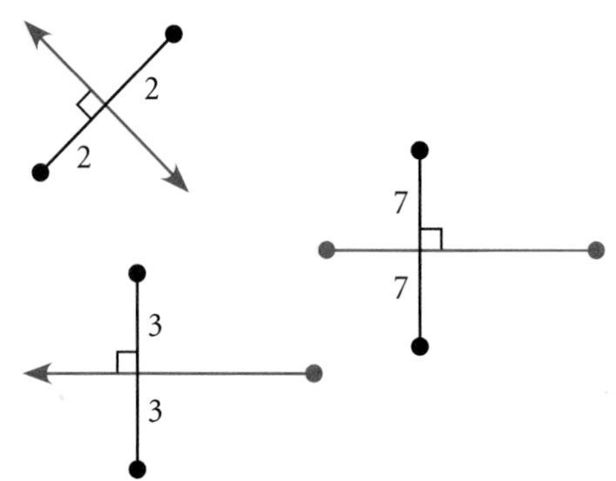

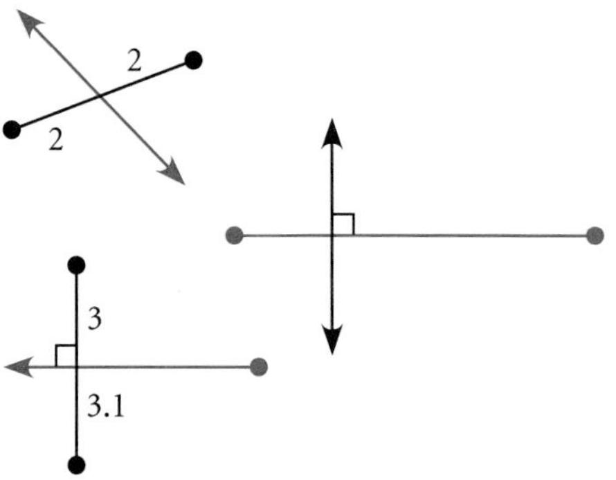

8. These are **coplanar points.** These are not.

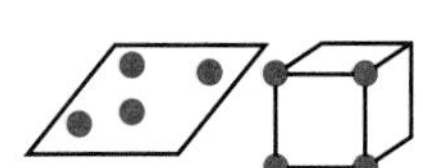

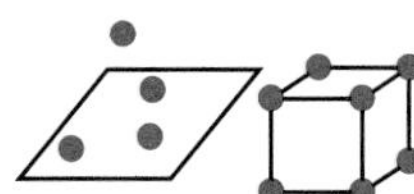

***M* is the midpoint of $\overline{JK}$. Find each missing length.**

9. $JM = 6$, $MK =$ _____, $JK =$ _____.

10. $JM =$ _____, $MK = 12.4$, $JK =$ _____.

11. $JM =$ _____, $MK =$ _____, $JK = 5$.

12. $JM =$ _____, $MK =$ _____, $JK = 8\frac{2}{3}$.

13. **Venn Is a Statement Biconditional?** Remember that you can illustrate a true conditional statement with a Venn diagram.
   a. Sketch a Venn diagram to illustrate the biconditional statement "An integer is even if and only if it is divisible by two." (Hint: It may be helpful to break it down into two conditional statements, one of which is the converse of the other.)
   b. What does your diagram look like? Do you think a diagram that shows a true biconditional statement will always look like this? Explain why or why not.
   c. Explain how this diagram demonstrates the idea that we should be able to express good definitions as biconditionals.

LOOK AHEAD

State whether you believe each of the following is true or false. Explain.

14. Two points may be contained in two different lines.

15. Whenever two planes intersect, their intersection is a single point.

16. Any three points can be contained by a single line.

MORE PRACTICE

List the critical attributes of the following terms. Then write a definition for each word, using "if and only if."

17. These are **line segments.**

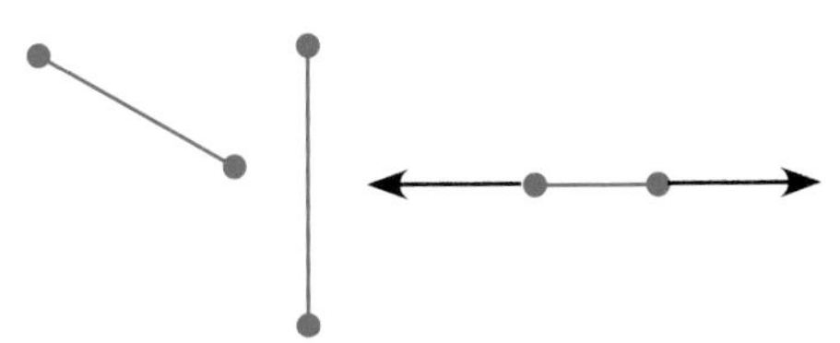

These are not.

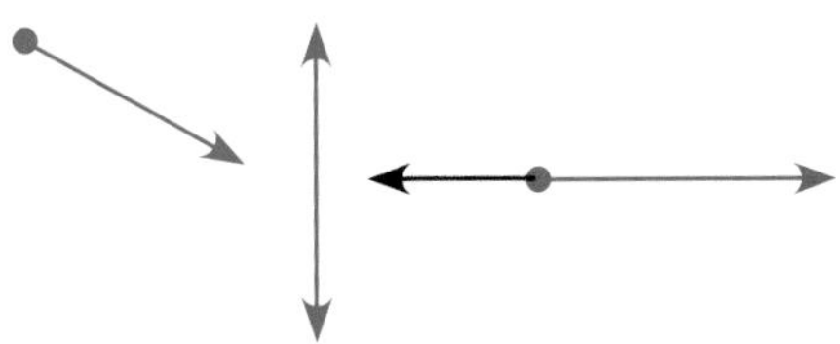

18. These are **collinear points.**

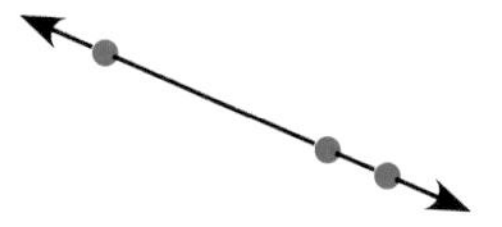

These are not.

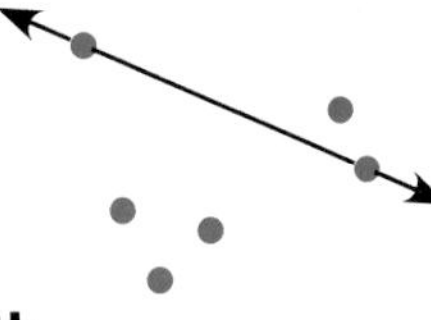

***M* is the midpoint of $\overline{FG}$. Find each missing length.**

19. $FM = 15$, $MG =$ _____ , $FG =$ _____ .

20. $FM =$ _____ , $MG = 11.7$, $FG =$ _____ .

21. $FM =$ _____ , $MG =$ _____ , $FG = 1\frac{4}{5}$.

MORE MATH REASONING

Determine whether each biconditional statement is true or false. If the statement is false, give a counterexample.

22. $x \times y = 0$ if and only if $x = 0$ or $y = 0$.

23. The contrapositive of a statement is true if and only if the statement is true.

24. Three points are coplanar if and only if they are collinear.

25. K is the midpoint of $\overline{LM}$. The coordinates of L and M are $(-3, -5)$ and $(4, -5)$, respectively. $\overline{KN} \perp \overline{LM}$ and $\overline{KN} \cong \overline{KL}$. Find all possible coordinates for N.

2-2 PART B

Postulates

← CONNECT → ***You've seen the need to accept some terms without definitions. Now you will investigate some facts that are accepted without proof.***

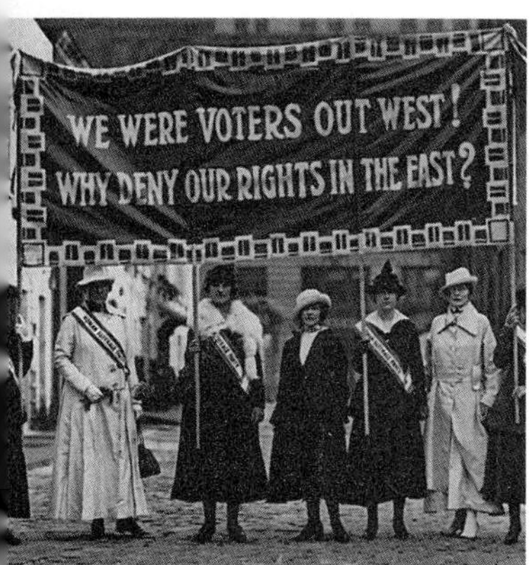

The Continental Congress used the assumptions stated in the Declaration of Independence in writing the original United States Constitution in 1787. Over time, 26 amendments have been added to give us our current Constitution. For example, in 1920 the nineteenth amendment gave women the right to vote.

Mathematical systems are also built on assumptions. You have seen some properties of numbers in algebra. These properties are assumptions about how numbers behave. Segment lengths and angle measures are numbers, so these assumptions are also important in geometry.

For all real numbers a, b, c, and d, the following are true.

PROPERTIES OF EQUALITY	
Reflexive Property	$a = a$
Symmetric Property	If $a = b$, then $b = a$.
Transitive Property	If $a = b$ and $b = c$, then $a = c$.
Addition Property	If $a = b$, then $a + c = b + c$.
Multiplication Property	If $a = b$, then $ac = bc$.
PROPERTIES OF ADDITION AND MULTIPLICATION	
Associative Properties	$a + (b + c) = (a + b) + c$; $a(bc) = (ab)c$
Commutative Properties	$a + b = b + a$; $ab = ba$
Distributive Property	$a(b + c) = ab + ac$

TRY IT

State the property of real numbers that justifies each statement.

a. $AB + CD = CD + AB$

b. If $x - 20 = 44$, then $x - 20 + 20 = 44 + 20$

We all make decisions based on unproved assumptions. The organizations that affect your life also operate on certain assumptions.

Each of the situations or organizations listed below has a set of rules. These rules are based on assumptions about how things "should" be done. See if you can identify some of the underlying assumptions behind the rules.

1. **your school's graduation requirements**
2. **driving a car or riding a bicycle**

The ancient Egyptians and Babylonians had many practical uses for mathematics. The Greeks expanded on their knowledge. Euclid, a Greek mathematician, wrote *The Elements* around the year 300 B.C. This work organized much of the geometry and other mathematics known at that time into a deductive system. Euclid called the basic assumptions of his system *self-evident truths.*

For most of this course, you will be investigating a geometry system based on Euclid's work. In the following Explore, you will discover some of the self-evident truths, or *postulates,* of our geometric system.

EXPLORE: POSSIBLE POSTULATES

Use everyday objects to help investigate each of the following. For each question, make a conjecture based on your observations. If possible, write your conjecture as a conditional statement in if-then form. After you finish, compare your conjectures with those of your classmates.

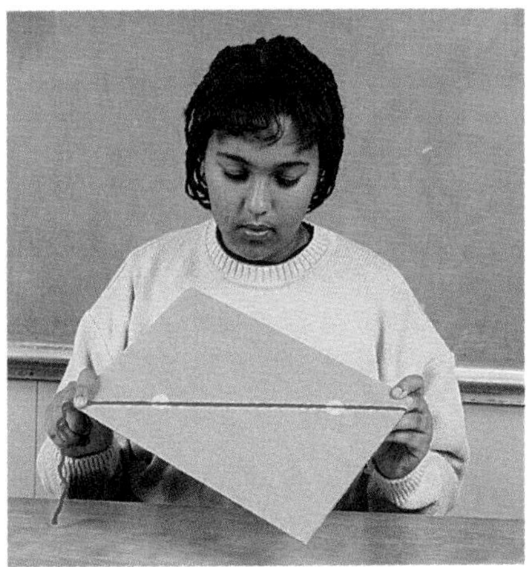

1. What is the smallest number of points through which only one line can be drawn?
2. Three points, A, B, and C, are not all on the same line. How many planes contain all three of the points?
3. What does the intersection of two planes look like?
4. If a plane contains two points of a line, must it contain the whole line?
5. What is the smallest number of points that cannot be contained in just one plane?

Compare the postulates you discovered to those stated below. Note how the first postulates involve undefined terms.

DEFINITION

Space is the set of all points.

POINTS-EXISTENCE POSTULATE

Space contains at least four noncoplanar points. Every plane contains at least three noncollinear points. Every line contains at least two points.

STRAIGHT-LINE POSTULATE

Two points are contained in one and only one line. (Two points determine a line.)

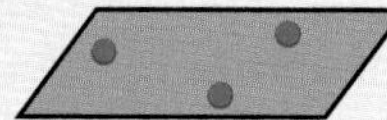

PLANE POSTULATE

Three noncollinear points are contained in one and only one plane. (Three noncollinear points determine a plane.)

FLAT-PLANE POSTULATE

If two points are in a plane, then the line containing the points is in the same plane.

PLANE-INTERSECTION POSTULATE

If two planes intersect, then their intersection is a line.

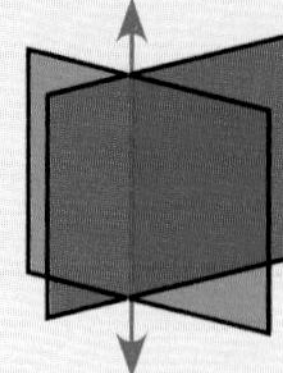

TRY IT

State the postulate or postulates that justify each statement.

c. If ℓ contains A and B, then there is no other line that contains these points.
d. If points H and K lie in plane $\mathcal{R}$, then $\overleftrightarrow{HK}$ lies in plane $\mathcal{R}$.
e. A plane contains at least one line.

REFLECT

1. Name some everyday situations that suggest each of the five postulates listed above.
2. Explain why it is necessary for a deductive system to start with some unproved assumptions.

Exercises

CORE

Getting Started Draw a figure to represent each situation described below, and name the postulate it illustrates.

1. Points R and S are in plane $\mathcal{A}$. $\overleftrightarrow{RS}$ is also in plane $\mathcal{A}$.

2. There is some point F that is not in the plane containing B, C, and D.

Determine whether each statement is true or false. If true, state the postulate or postulates that justify it. If false, state or sketch a counterexample.

3. P lies in plane $\mathcal{B}$. The line containing P and Q must lie in plane $\mathcal{B}$.

4. Planes $\mathcal{A}$ and $\mathcal{B}$ intersect. Their intersection is a line.

5. Points E and F determine a line.

6. $\overleftrightarrow{FE}$ and $\overleftrightarrow{NF}$ determine a plane.

Determine whether each conjecture is true or false. If true, state the postulate(s) that justify it. If false, state or sketch a counterexample.

7. If three points lie in a plane, then they are collinear.

8. If two lines do not intersect, then they are not in the same plane.

State the property of real numbers that justifies each statement.

9. $m\angle RST = m\angle UVW$. Therefore, $m\angle UVW = m\angle RST$.

10. $m\angle ABC + (m\angle DEF + m\angle GHI) = (m\angle ABC + m\angle DEF) + m\angle GHI$

11. $5(TM + JF) = 5TM + 5JF$

12. If $m\angle XYZ = m\angle TUV$, then $\frac{1}{2}m\angle XYZ = \frac{1}{2}m\angle TUV$.

13. If $JK = KL$, then $JK + 6 = KL + 6$.

14. How many planes contain the following numbers of points?
a. one point
b. two points
c. three noncollinear points

Use postulates to explain each situation.

15. Rocking Chair A carpenter knows that a four-legged chair will sometimes rock on a level floor, but a three-legged stool is always steady.

16. A surveyor (shown at the right) can always find a straight line from the point where he is to any other point that he can see.

17. When constructing a building, a contractor knows that the corner formed by two flat walls is a straight line.

LOOK BACK

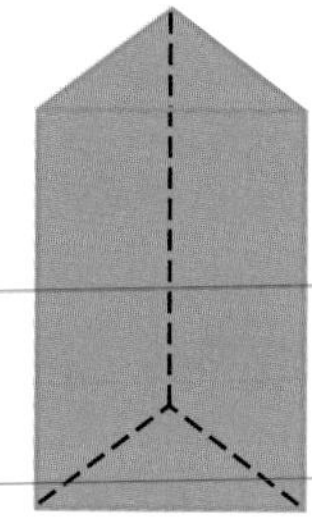

18. Draw a net for the figure at the right. [1-1]

19. Write the converse, inverse, and contrapositive of the following statement. Then determine whether each statement is true or false. [2-1]

If a number is evenly divisible by 3, then it is evenly divisible by 9.

MORE PRACTICE

Sketch figures for the situations described below, and name the postulate that each illustrates.

20. The noncollinear points *T*, *S*, and *R* are all contained in plane $\mathcal{M}$.

21. In plane $\mathcal{M}$, there is some point, *W*, that is not on the line containing *P* and *Q*.

Determine whether each statement is true or false. If true, state the postulate(s) that justify it. If false, state or sketch a counterexample.

22. Points A, B, and C determine a plane.

23. The line containing points F and G lies in exactly one plane.

Determine whether each conjecture is true or false. If true, state the postulate(s) that justify it. If false, state or sketch a counterexample.

24. Three points cannot be contained in two different planes.

25. If three lines intersect in the same point, then they are coplanar.

26. Three planes cannot intersect in just one point.

MORE MATH REASONING

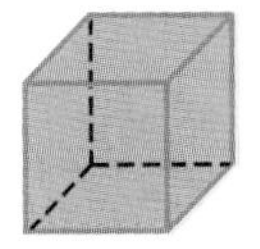

Cube

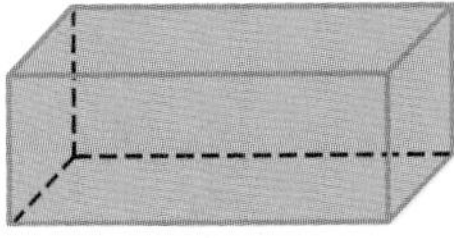

Rectangular prism

27. How many planes are determined by the vertices of a cube? Does this change if the cube is stretched in one direction to form a rectangular prism (box)?

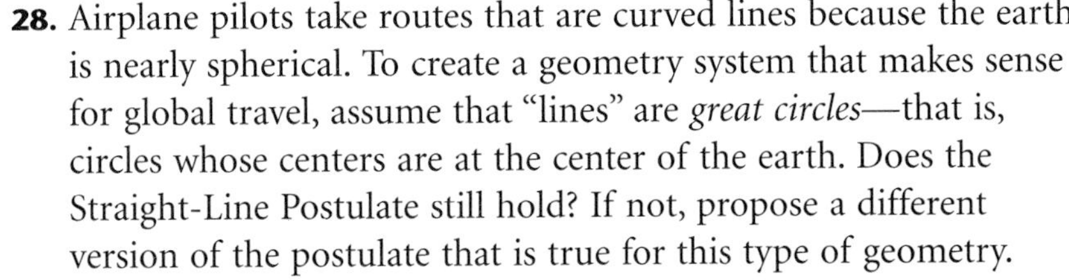

28. Airplane pilots take routes that are curved lines because the earth is nearly spherical. To create a geometry system that makes sense for global travel, assume that "lines" are *great circles*—that is, circles whose centers are at the center of the earth. Does the Straight-Line Postulate still hold? If not, propose a different version of the postulate that is true for this type of geometry.

2-2 PART C Working in a Deductive System

← CONNECT → ***You have worked with undefined terms, definitions, and postulates. Now you will begin to see how they fit together to form a system of geometry.***

In beginning to build a system of geometry, you have identified three undefined terms and five postulates. You have seen some defined terms, whose definitions use undefined terms and previously defined terms. And you've seen your first theorem, a statement whose truth can be proved using postulates, definitions, and previously proved theorems.

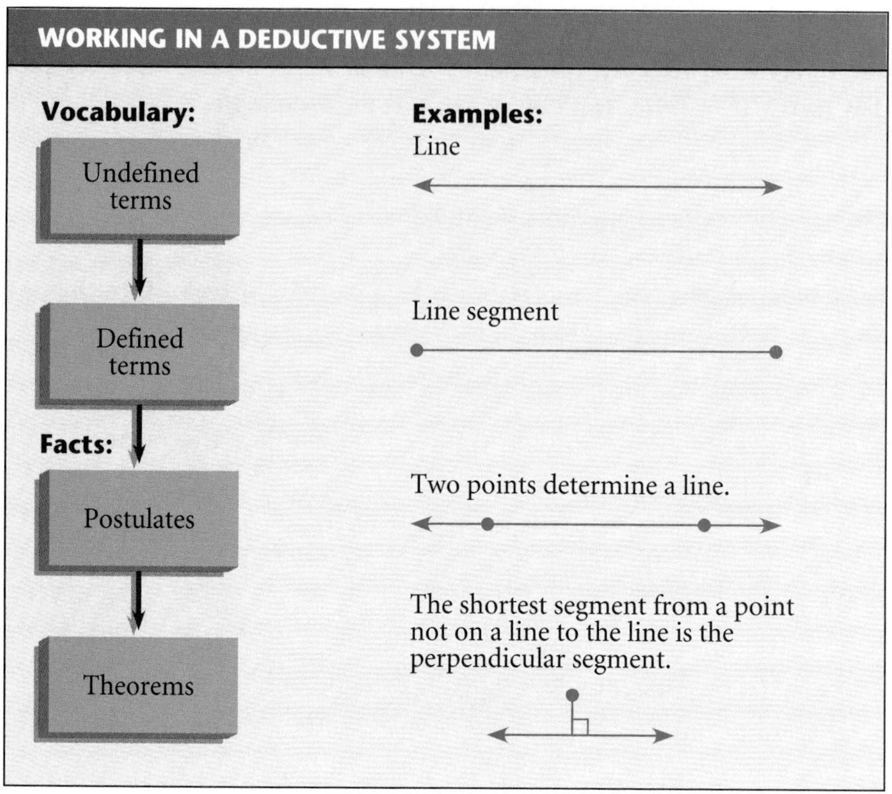

WORKING IN A DEDUCTIVE SYSTEM
Vocabulary:
Undefined terms
Defined terms
Facts:
Postulates
Theorems
Examples:
Line
Line segment
Two points determine a line.
The shortest segment from a point not on a line to the line is the perpendicular segment.

Because you are working in a deductive system, you must be able to justify everything you do, even measuring with a ruler! For example, the Ruler Postulate says that our method for finding distances between points on a number line is valid.

RULER POSTULATE

The points on a line can be paired with the real numbers so that the following statements are true.

- One of the points has coordinate 0, and another has coordinate 1.
- For any choice for coordinates 0 and 1 and for each real number x, there is exactly one point on the line with coordinate x.
- The distance between any two points with coordinates x and y is the absolute value of the difference of their coordinates, $|x - y|$.

In the following Explore, you will discover some properties of distances related to collinear points.

EXPLORE: IT ADDS UP

MATERIALS

Ruler

1. Identify the critical attributes of *betweenness.*

These red points are **between** the black points.

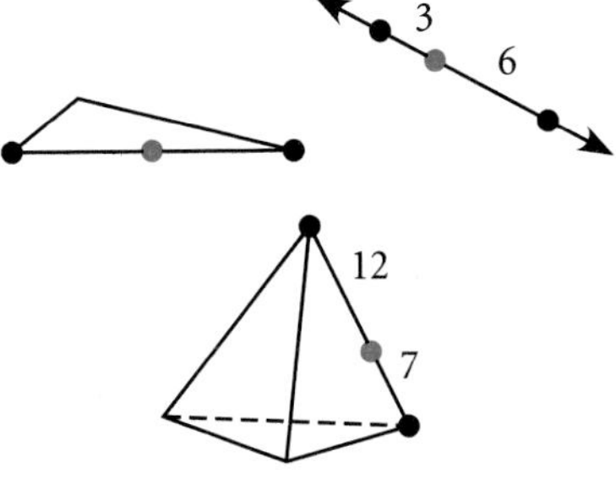

These red points are **not between** the black points.

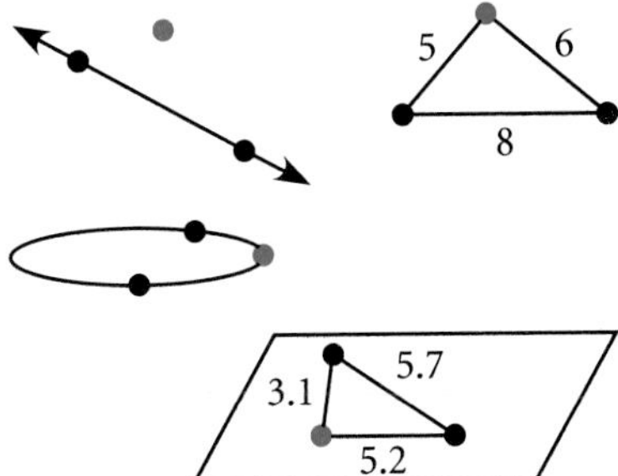

2. Mark three points, A, B, and C, on a line. Measure the distance between each pair of points (AB, BC, and AC). What is their relationship?
3. Reposition the three points on the line, keeping the same point between the other two. Measure AB, BC, and AC again. What changed and what stayed the same? Give a short written summary.

Problem-Solving Tip

Look for a pattern.

4. Suppose you know that R, S, and T are collinear points, with $RT = 8$, $ST = 6$, and $RS = 14$. Which point is between the other two? How do you know?
5. Write a generalization about the relationship of three collinear points, betweenness, and distance.

In geometry, you will need to be able to add the lengths of adjacent segments to find the length of longer segments.

SEGMENT-ADDITION POSTULATE

Point B is between points A and C if and only if A, B, and C are collinear and $AB + BC = AC$.

The midpoint of a segment is a special type of point that lies between two other points. We have already defined *midpoint* geometrically as the point that divides a segment into two congruent segments. Combining these ideas with some algebra gives us the following theorem.

THEOREM

If M is the midpoint of $\overline{AB}$, then $AM = \frac{1}{2}AB$.

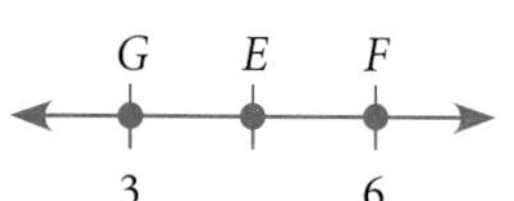

The coordinate of the midpoint of $\overline{AB}$ is $\frac{a+b}{2}$, where a and b are the coordinates of A and B on a number line. The preceding statement is a theorem because we can prove it. There is also a formula for the midpoint of a segment on a coordinate plane, which you will work with in Exercise 8.

TRY IT

a. E is the midpoint of $\overline{FG}$. Find FE and the coordinate of E.

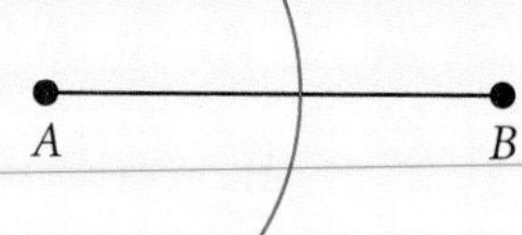

CONSTRUCTION: MIDPOINT OF A SEGMENT

1. Begin by drawing segment $\overline{AB}$. This will be the segment you bisect in your construction.

A B

2. Open your compass to more than half the length of $\overline{AB}$. Draw an arc from point A.

A B

3. Using the same compass setting, draw an arc from point B that intersects the previous arc at points C and D.

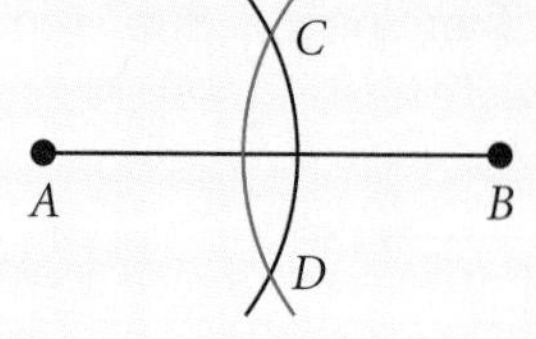

4. Draw the line connecting points C and D to intersect $\overline{AB}$ at E. E is the midpoint of $\overline{AB}$.

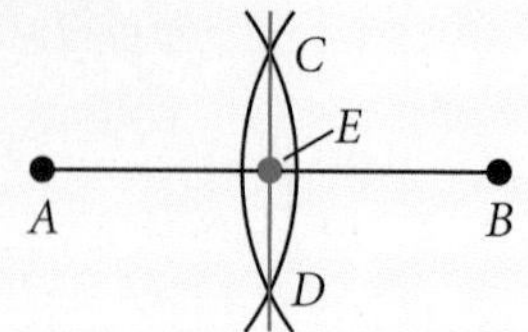

1. The preceding construction finds the midpoint of a segment. What other geometric figure do you construct when you find the midpoint?

You've now seen the components of a deductive system in action. Notice how combining a postulate (the Segment-Addition Postulate) with some algebra and a definition (the definition of midpoint) led to a theorem (if M is the midpoint of $\overline{AB}$, then $AM = \frac{1}{2}AB$).

REFLECT

1. What are the components of our deductive system? Which parts of the system form our geometry vocabulary? Which are our geometry "facts"?
2. Name two ideas from this lesson that are important to both algebra and geometry. How does this connection help you to understand the ideas?

Exercises

CORE

Getting Started Find the coordinate of the midpoint of $\overline{XY}$ if X and Y have coordinates x and y, respectively.

1. $x = 1, y = 7$ **2.** $x = -1, y = 7$ **3.** $x = -3\frac{1}{2}, y = 5\frac{3}{4}$

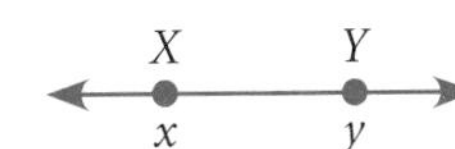

4. Use the figure to find the length of each segment.

a. $\overline{AF}$ **b.** $\overline{AE}$ **c.** $\overline{BF}$

d. What postulate or theorem justifies your answers to **4a, 4b,** and **4c**?

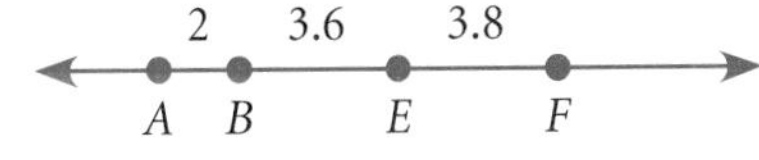

5. R, S, and T are three points on a line. The coordinates of R and S are -14.5 and 2.7, respectively. If S is the midpoint of $\overline{RT}$, what is the coordinate of T? Make a sketch that illustrates R, S, and T.

6. Draw a line segment, and label it $\overline{EF}$. Use a compass and straightedge to construct the midpoint of $\overline{EF}$, and label it G.

7. Write the letter of the second pair that best matches the first pair.

Postulate: theorem as (a) belief: fact, (b) hypothesis: conclusion, (c) proof: conjecture, (d) deductive: inductive

MIDPOINT FORMULA

On a coordinate plane, the midpoint of the segment with endpoints (x_1, y_1) and (x_2, y_2) has coordinates $\left(\frac{x_1 + x_2}{2}, \frac{y_1 + y_2}{2}\right)$.

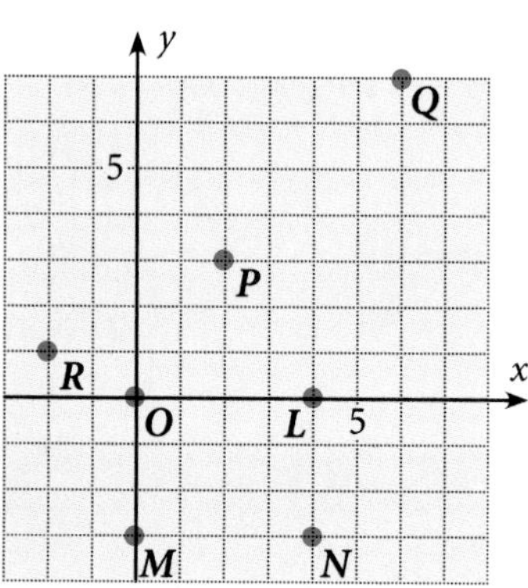

8. Use the formula above to find the coordinates of each midpoint.

a. midpoint of $\overline{OL}$ **b.** midpoint of $\overline{MN}$

c. midpoint of $\overline{PQ}$ **d.** midpoint of $\overline{PR}$

e. Explain why the midpoint formula works. (Hint: How do you find the number exactly halfway between two other numbers? What is that number called?)

9. I Want Proof! The following is part of a flow proof of the theorem "If *M* is the midpoint of $\overline{AB}$, then $AM = \frac{1}{2}AB$." Tell *why* each statement must be true. As justification, use a postulate or definition from the list below the diagram.

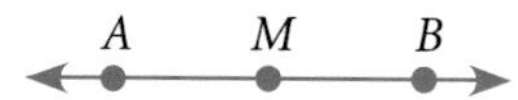

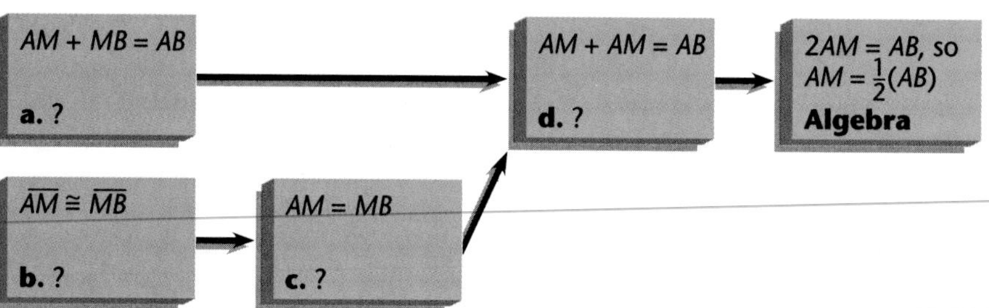

1. Straight-Line Postulate
2. Plane Postulate
3. Segment-Addition Postulate
4. Definition of Midpoint
5. Definition of Congruent
6. Substitution

10. D Tour Points *D, E, F,* and *G* represent four towns on a map. If you draw a line from *D* to *F*, it passes through *E*. If you draw a line from *E* to *G*, it passes through *F*. List all of the following statements that must be true. Provide a sketch to support your choice(s).

(a) *E* is between *D* and *F*.
(b) $\overline{DF}$ and $\overline{EG}$ are congruent.
(c) *D, E, F,* and *G* are collinear.
(d) *E* and *F* are between *D* and *G*.

LOOK AHEAD

Find the total number of cubes in each building. Assume that the visible cubes are resting on others, and that there are no hidden stacks of cubes.

11.

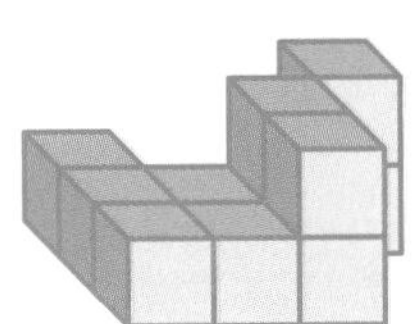

12.

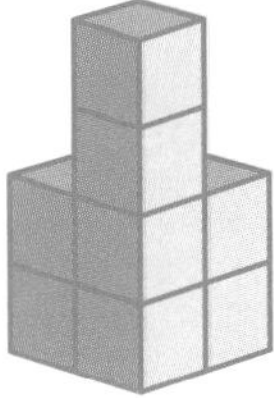

13.

14.

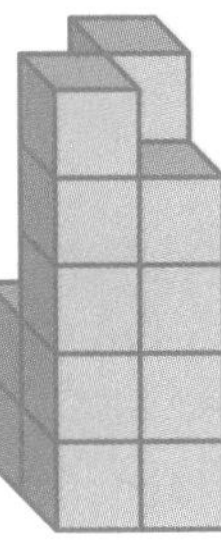

MORE PRACTICE

Find the coordinate of the midpoint of $\overline{XY}$ if X and Y have coordinates x and y, respectively.

15. $x = 4, y = 14$

16. $x = -3, y = -2.2$

17. $x = 1.6, y = 1.7$

X Y
x y

18. Use the figure to find the length of each segment.

a. $\overline{PS}$ **b.** $\overline{QS}$ **c.** $\overline{QT}$

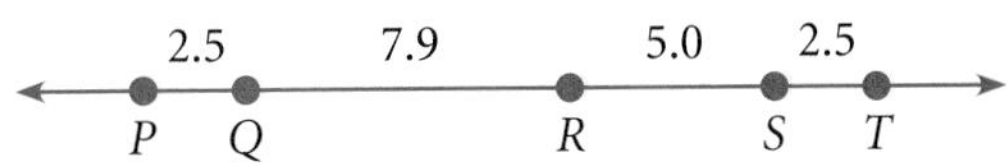

19. Draw a rectangle, and label its vertices. Construct the midpoint of each side. Can you find all four midpoints with only two constructions?

Find the coordinates of the midpoint of each segment.

20. $\overline{AO}$

21. $\overline{BF}$

22. $\overline{AD}$

23. $\overline{BC}$

24. $\overline{OF}$

25. $\overline{AF}$

26. $\overline{CD}$

27. $\overline{BD}$

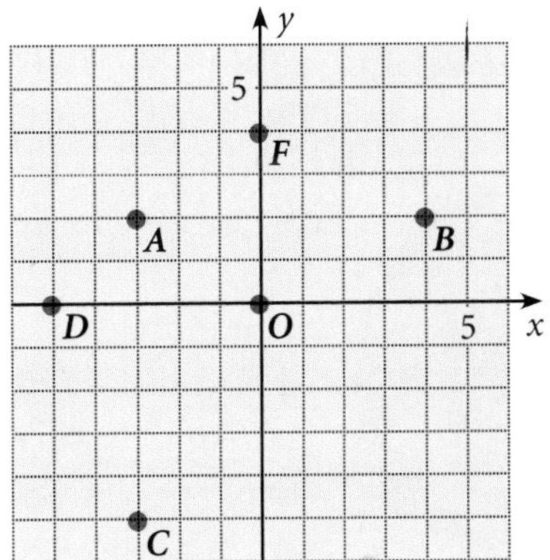

MORE MATH REASONING

28. Taxicab Geometry "It's eight blocks to the subway station from my office." "The Jacksons' house is four blocks from ours." These are the actual distances a person has to walk to get from one place to another. *Taxicab geometry* is based on these distances instead of the straight-line distance that is sometimes called "as the crow flies." In taxicab geometry, any point can be reached by traveling along vertical or horizontal lines.

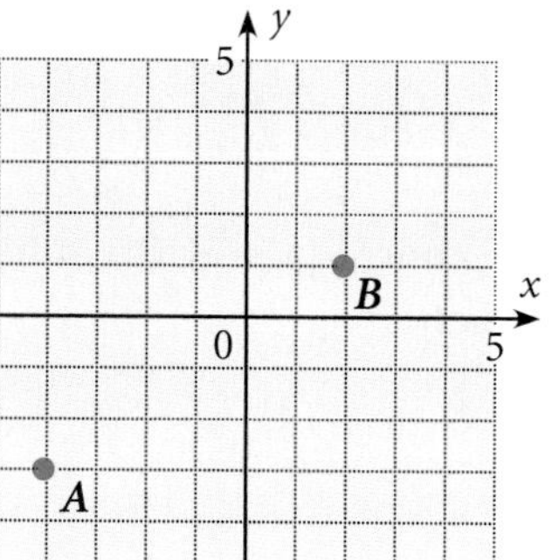

The grid at the right represents a map of a city. The center of town is at the origin. Think of the lines of the grid as streets.

a. What are the coordinates of A and B?

b. Plot P at $(-2, -1)$. What is the taxi distance from A to P?

c. Plot all the points you can find at a taxi distance of 4 from B. Connect these points. This figure is a *taxi circle.*

d. What is the shortest taxi distance from A to B? Is there only one shortest taxi path between them?

e. Plot C at $(-3, 1)$. What is the sum of the taxi distance from C to A plus the taxi distance from C to B?

f. Plot all the points that are an equal taxi distance from A and B.

2-2 PART D Making Connections

← CONNECT → ***Postulates, undefined terms, defined terms, and theorems are the components of our system of geometry. You've seen why some terms are undefined, and why postulates are assumed to be true. You've also learned how to develop definitions and theorems.***

THE EUCLIDEAN
CLUB
Rule #1: Two points determine a line.

The initial postulates, undefined terms, defined terms, and theorems that you have investigated form a modern version of a geometry system developed by Euclid over 2000 years ago. In the following Explore, you will use these ideas to develop a constitution for a club at your school.

EXPLORE: A STRONG CONSTITUTION

Develop a one-page written constitution for a new club for your school. Discuss the following questions with classmates to help formulate your constitution.

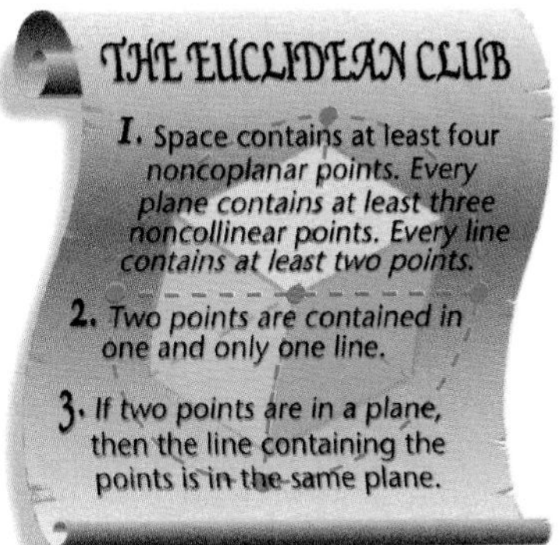

1. What assumptions (postulates) will you take as true without proof?
2. What key words will you leave undefined (for instance, *participation, freedom,* etc.)?
3. What words will you choose to define carefully? Give an example of one such word and provide your definition for it.
4. How will you provide for new laws (theorems) or amendments (postulates) to be added to your club's constitution?
5. Present a description of your club and its constitution to your class.

REFLECT

1. Why do you think Euclid chose the undefined terms that he did?
2. Write the five postulates on Page 116 in your own words. Draw figures where needed.
3. Why is it important to justify any new theorems by using postulates, previously defined terms, and previously proved theorems?

Self-Assessment

Determine whether each statement is true or false. Draw sketches to justify your answers. If the statement is true, state the postulate that it illustrates. If the statement is false, correct it so that it is true.

1. Three points determine three distinct lines.
2. Two lines ℓ and m intersect in points E and F.
3. Two lines determine a plane.
4. Planes $\mathcal{N}$ and $\mathcal{P}$ intersect. Their intersection is a line.

In each of the following, the first statement is true. State the postulate that allows you to conclude that the second statement is true.

5. Points E and F are in plane $\mathcal{P}$. Therefore, every point of $\overleftrightarrow{EF}$ is in plane $\mathcal{P}$.

6. Points C and D are both contained in planes $\mathcal{R}$ and $\mathcal{S}$. Therefore, $\overleftrightarrow{CD}$ is the intersection of $\mathcal{R}$ and $\mathcal{S}$.

Draw a conclusion from each of the following if possible. State postulates or definitions to justify your conclusion.

7. Point K is between L and M.

8. Planes $\mathcal{P}$ and $\mathcal{Q}$ have at least one point in common.

9. Points R, S, and T are collinear, and $\overline{RS} \cong \overline{ST}$.

10. Choose the best answer to complete the sentence below. [1-1]

    A mathematical model ____ .
    (a) is an attempt to simulate something real
    (b) can be an equation
    (c) is not exactly like the thing it models
    (d) has characteristics (a), (b), and (c)
    (e) has characteristics (a) and (b) only

In Exercises 11–12, write a conditional statement with each of the following sets of characteristics. [2-1]

11. The conditional is true, and its inverse is false.

12. The conditional and all of its related statements are false.

13. Carefully draw a square. Use a compass and straightedge to construct the midpoint of each side. Then connect the consecutive midpoints and make a conjecture about what you see.

14. **Coordinated Apartment Hunting** Amanda and Ricardo are looking for an apartment. Amanda manages a store at $(-3, 2)$. Ricardo works in an office at $(2, -5)$. They would like their apartment to be located the same distance from each of their jobs. They also want the sum of the distances that they must commute to work to be as small as possible. Prepare a graph to show where their apartment should be located. Give the coordinates of this location. Explain how you found your answer.

15. In *The Physiology of Common Life,* the English author George Henry Lewes (1817–1878) wrote, "We must never assume that which is incapable of proof." Is this statement true for geometry? Explain.

2-3 Drawing Techniques and Parallel Lines

PUTTING IT IN Perspective

Have you ever stood on a railroad track or a straight road and looked far down the track or road to the horizon? If you did, you probably noticed how the parallel sides appear to get closer together as they get farther from you. You also know that objects appear larger when they are near you and smaller when they are farther from you.

Perspective is a method of showing three-dimensional objects on a flat surface so that they appear real. People of all cultures have struggled with the problem of how to capture the reality of the three-dimensional world in a two-dimensional drawing or painting. For example, Japanese artists skillfully used landscapes to try to give an illusion of depth and space.

At the beginning of the Renaissance period (the early 1400s A.D.), Brunelleschi, an Italian architect, discovered a mathematical way to create perspective by using a *horizon line* and *vanishing points*.

***Left:** Canaletto (Giovanni Antonio Canal),* Piazza San Marco, *The Metropolitan Museum of Art, Purchase, Mrs. Charles Wrightman Gift, 1988 (1988.162)*

***Right:** Suzuki Harunobu,* The Evening Glow of the Ando *from the series* Eight Parlor Views. *© The Art Institute of Chicago, All Rights Reserved*

1. What do you think the terms *horizon line* and *vanishing point* mean?

2. Why do you suppose that many Renaissance artists like Raphael, Leonardo Da Vinci, and Michelangelo were engineers and architects who knew a great deal about mathematics?

2-3 PART A Perspective Drawing

← CONNECT → ***You have already sketched two- and three-dimensional figures informally. Now you will explore some ways to make your sketches more realistic.***

In attempting to sketch a solid object or scene on a flat piece of paper, we must deal with the fact that parallel lines seem to get closer together as they get farther away. One way to take this into account is to use a horizon line and one or more vanishing points. The **horizon line** is a horizontal line at the eye level of the artist. A **vanishing point** is a point on the horizon line where parallel lines appear to meet. In the photo at the left, the horizon line is shown in red and the vanishing point is shown in green.

1. Describe the locations of the vanishing point and the horizon line drawn in the picture above.

If converging parallel lines in a picture appear to come together at one vanishing point, the drawing is in **one-point perspective.** If there are two vanishing points, the drawing is in **two-point perspective.**

EXAMPLES

1. Draw a cube in one-point perspective.

Step 1
Start with a square. Choose a horizon line and a vanishing point.

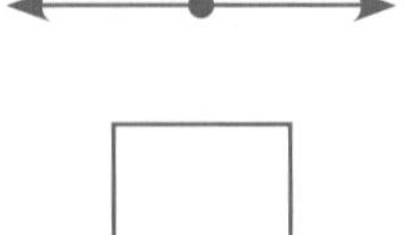

Step 2
Draw lines from the vertices to the vanishing point.

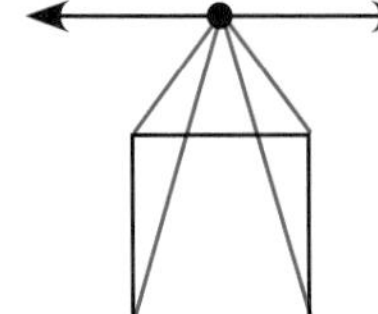

Step 3
Complete the figure by drawing lines parallel to the edges of the original figure.

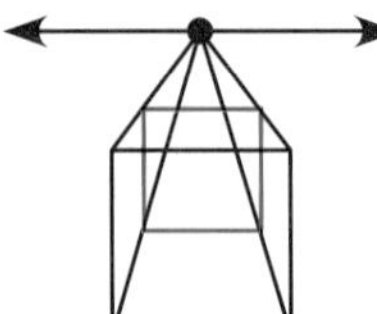

Step 4
Erase the lines to the vanishing point; make hidden lines in the figure dashed.

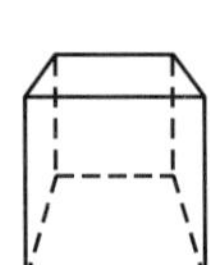

2. Draw a cube in two-point perspective.

Step 1
Start with a vertical segment. Choose a horizon line and vanishing points.

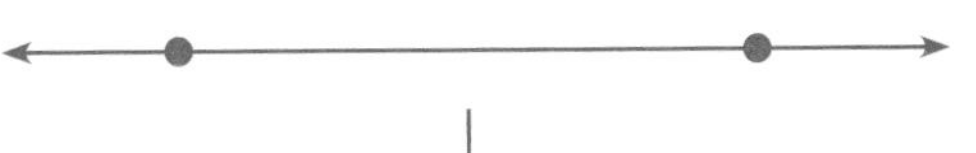

Step 2
Draw lines from the endpoints to the vanishing points. Add lines to complete the two front faces of the cube.

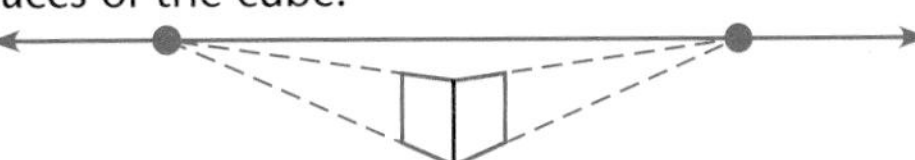

Step 3
Draw lines from the vertices of the front faces to the vanishing points. Use these lines to complete the cube.

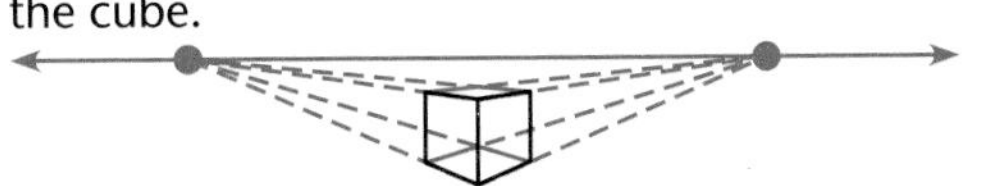

Step 4
Erase the lines to the vanishing points; make hidden lines in the figure dashed.

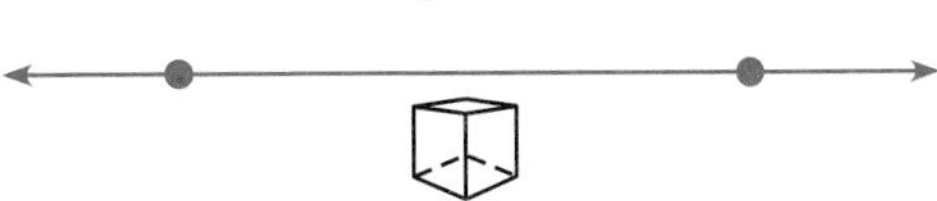

TRY IT

a. Draw a long rectangular box (prism) in one-point perspective.

Sometimes you need to draw figures to help you solve problems, but you may not want to take the time to use one- or two-point perspective. The following Explore will help you develop some rules of thumb for drawing figures.

EXPLORE: GETTING A NEW PERSPECTIVE

MATERIALS

5″× 8″ card or notebook paper

1. Draw a square, a circle, and a vertical line segment on the card or paper. Make them large enough to fill the card.

2. Hold the card about 1 ft in front of you. Slowly tilt the card away from you, and watch what happens to the three figures. Repeat by tilting to the right and left. Use your observations to answer the following questions.

   a. Describe what appears to happen to the square as it tilts directly away from you. What type of figure is it? What type of figure does the square appear to be when you tilt it to the right or left?

   b. Describe what the circle looks like when you tilt the card.

   c. Describe what seems to happen to the segment.

3. Explain how you would sketch a circle, a square, and a segment on a plane that tilts away from you.

If you need to draw a three-dimensional object, you can use what you have learned about sketching simpler figures.

EXAMPLES

Sketch each figure.

3. a triangular prism
(slice of pie or cake)

Step 1

Step 2

Step 3

4. a cylinder on its side
(can of soup)

Step 1 

Step 2 

Step 3 

Visible edges are solid lines, and edges that are hidden are dashed. The following chart summarizes the key rules of thumb for making a quick three-dimensional sketch.

RULES OF THUMB FOR THREE-DIMENSIONAL DRAWING

Represent a plane by a rectangle or parallelogram, depending on where it is with respect to your line of sight.

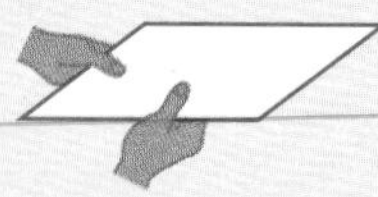

Represent a line by an oblique (slanted) segment if it extends away from you. Represent a circle by an oval if it extends away from you.

To draw a cube, show the front and back faces as squares. Then connect the corresponding vertices. Represent the hidden edges with dashed segments.

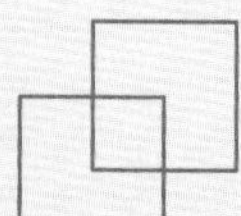
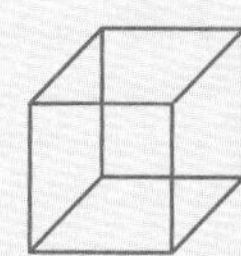
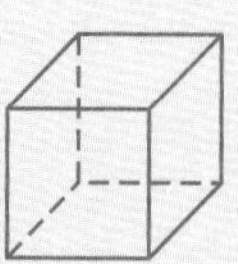

To draw other three-dimensional figures, draw lines, circles, and planes as already shown.

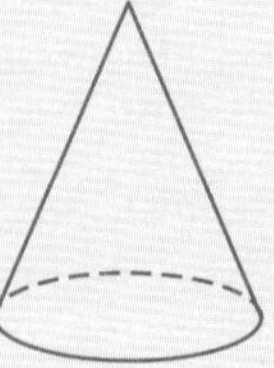

REFLECT

1. When you sketch a cube using the method in the rules of thumb, are you using one-point perspective, two-point perspective, or a different method? How does this sketch show perspective? In what ways does it fail to show perspective?
2. How can you use the position of the horizon line to help determine where an artist was when he made a perspective drawing?

Exercises

CORE

Arts

Getting Started How many vanishing points are there in each photograph or painting? Describe where the artist or photographer was in relation to the subject.

1.

2.

Gustave Caillebotte, *Paris Street; Rainy Day*. Photograph © The Art Institute of Chicago, All Rights Reserved.

Write the word or phrase that correctly completes each statement.

3. In a perspective drawing, the ____ is a horizontal line at the artist's eye level.
4. In a perspective drawing, a ____ is a point where parallel lines appear to meet.

Sketch each of the following.

5. a line in a plane that appears to be tilted away from you
6. a pyramid with a square bottom
7. a basketball court (shown at the right) viewed from one corner of the court

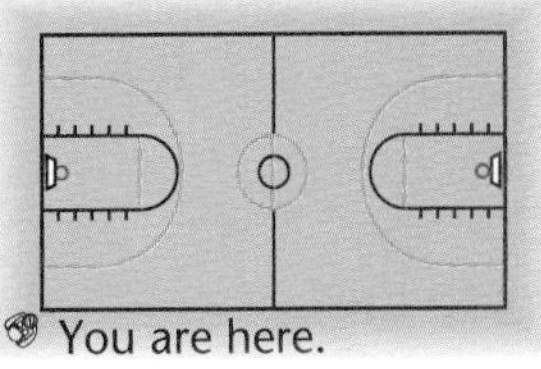

8. Use graph paper or dot paper and a straightedge to draw a two-point perspective sketch of a building. Assume you are standing opposite a corner of the building.

9. A Question of Perspective Designers often use one-point perspective when making a sketch of the interior of a room. Write a short paragraph explaining why they might choose to use one-point perspective instead of two-point perspective.

Careers

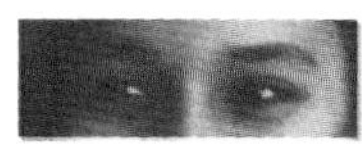

LOOK BACK

The figure at the right shows the reflection of triangle *XYZ* over line *v*. [1-4]

10. Name the image of Z.

11. Name the pre-image of $\overline{RS}$.

12. Give the length of $\overline{RS}$.

13. Find $m\angle YZX$.

14. Find the pre-image of triangle SRT.

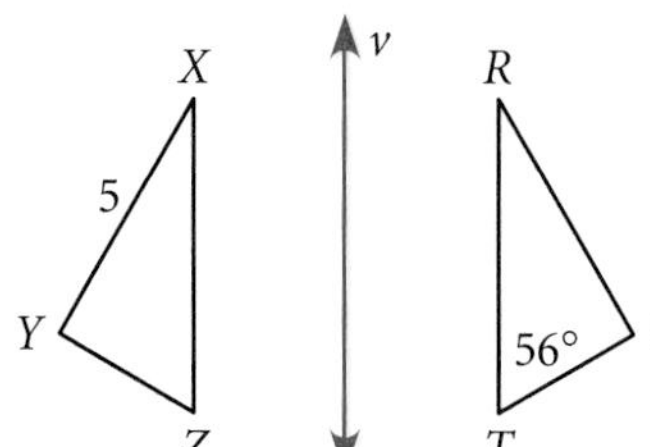

Determine whether each statement is true or false. If it is true, state the postulate or postulates that justify it. If false, explain why. [2-2]

15. Points S and T lie in plane $\mathcal{R}$. $\overleftrightarrow{ST}$ lies in $\mathcal{R}$.

16. Lines m and n intersect. Their intersection is $\overline{AB}$.

17. Plane $\mathcal{K}$ is the only plane that contains noncollinear points L, M, and N.

MORE PRACTICE

Draw each of the following.

18. a circle in a plane tilted away from you

19. a cone lying on its side

20. a flashlight resting at a slight angle away from you on a table

21. your geometry book lying on a desk top as you stand to the left of the desk

MORE MATH REASONING

22. The Road Ahead Imagine a straight road ahead of you for as far as you can see to the horizon (the place where the sky and level ground appear to meet). Draw the road in one-point perspective. Add a fence along one side of the road and a railroad track on the other side. Add other details in perspective.

23. Which Cube Looks More Cubic?

a. Make two different sketches of cubes using two-point perspective. Keep the position of the horizon line and the length of the front edge of the cube the same in each drawing, but have the vanishing points close together in the first and far apart in the second.

b. Which sketch looks more realistic?

c. Describe where the artist is located for each drawing. Explain how the distance of the artist from the cube affects the appearance of the cube.

2-3 PART B Orthographic and Isometric Drawing

← CONNECT → ***You have polished your perspective-drawing skills. Now you will explore another way to show a three-dimensional object—by showing two or more views of the object. This is especially important to architects, designers, and engineers who produce detailed plans for making new products.***

Drawings are important tools in many careers. Manufacturing companies employ engineers, designers, and draftspeople to prepare technical drawings of products. **Orthographic** (or **orthogonal**) views show an object's exact shape and dimensions. You see orthographic views when you look directly at an object's top, front, back, left side, or right side.

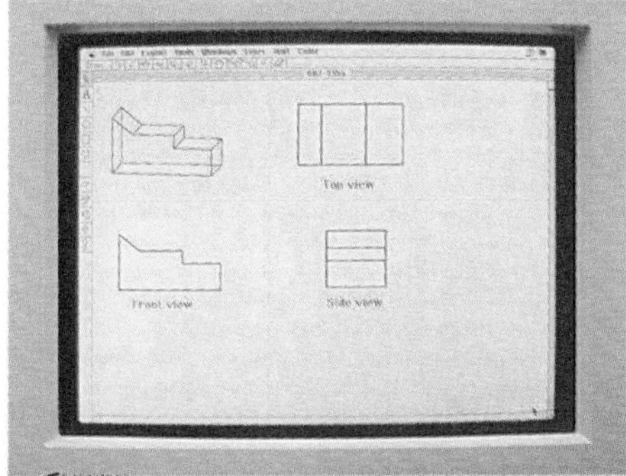

Alan Hoffer and Richard Koch, 3D Images, William K. Bradford Publishing Co.

The top orthographic view shows what the foundation (base) of an object or building looks like. If you build a building by stacking cubes, you can describe the heights of the stacks by writing the number of cubes on the columns shown in the top view.

In the figure at the right, a square with the number 3 means that the "building" is 3 cubes high at that point. When looking at a stack of cubes in this book, you may assume that all cubes are stacked on other cubes.

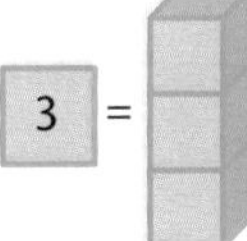

EXAMPLES

1. Draw the top view of the building shown at the left below. Assume that there are no unseen stacks of cubes, and that you are looking at the building from the left front corner.

The building has a 2-by-2 square foundation. The top view is shown at the right below.

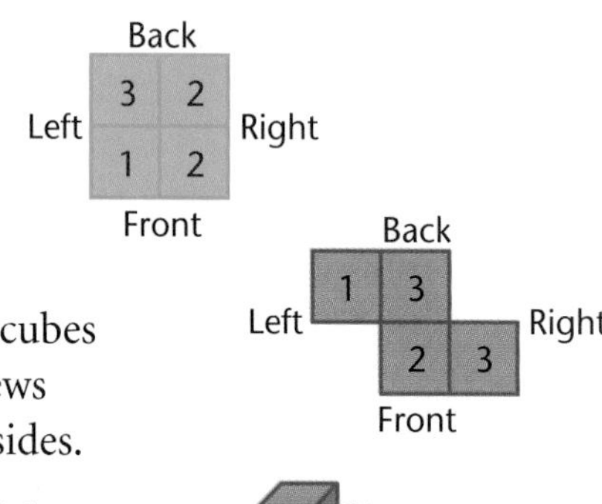

2. The top view of a building made of cubes is shown. Draw the orthographic views from the front, back, left, and right sides.

Remember that you are looking straight down at the building. Decide how many columns of cubes wide each view should be, and look for the largest number of cubes in each row to determine how high each stack should be. You could also visualize the building as shown in the first figure at the right, and then sketch the orthographic views.

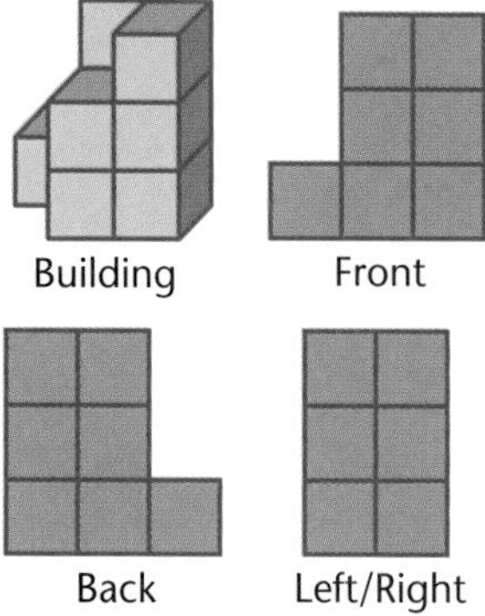

1. You may notice a familiar relationship between the front and back views of the building shown in Example 2. How are the views related? Do you think this is always true? Explain.

TRY IT

a. The top view of a building is shown at the right. Draw the front, back, and left orthographic views.

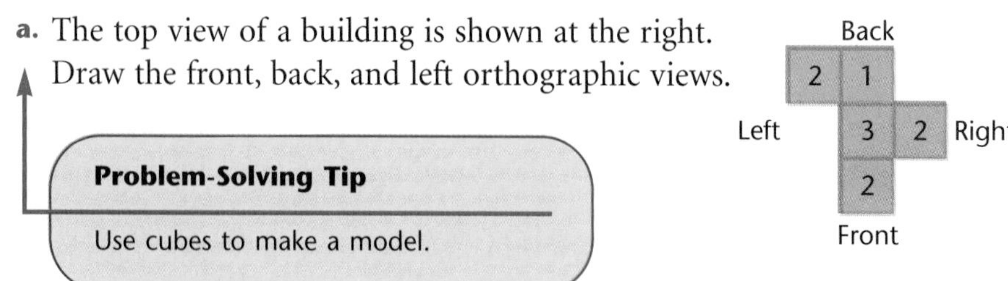

A special type of drawing, called **isometric drawing,** helps to show the connection between perspective and orthographic views. It is often faster to draw an isometric view rather than a two-point perspective sketch because the isometric drawing is done on isometric dot paper. You do not need to use a horizon line and vanishing points.

This is how you can use isometric paper to show a stack of two cubes. In the drawing, we have shaded the top and right sides of the cubes to give an illusion of depth.

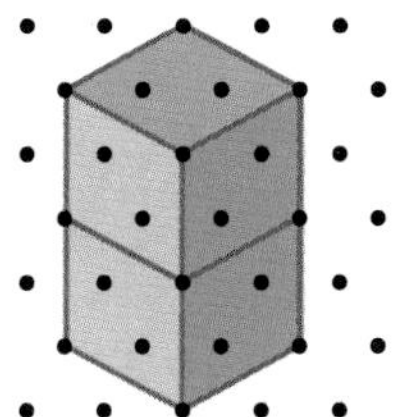

Isometric drawing is different from one-point or two-point perspective because parallel edges are actually parallel in the drawing. If you extend the edges of the cubes shown, they do not meet at a vanishing point.

In the following Explore, you will look at cube buildings from both orthographic and isometric views.

EXPLORE: ARCHITECTURE MADE EASY

MATERIALS

Cubes
Isometric dot paper

1. Make a building out of 10 cubes. To make the building interesting, have at least 3 stacks of cubes with different heights.
2. Sketch the orthographic top view of your building, giving the number of cubes in each stack.
3. Use isometric dot paper to sketch views of your building from two different corners.
4. Exchange your isometric sketches with those of another student. See if you can build his or her building correctly.

REFLECT

1. What characteristics of an object are better seen from an orthographic rather than an isometric view?
2. In isometric drawings of an object, two views, from opposite corners, are often shown. What is the purpose of showing these two views?

Exercises

CORE

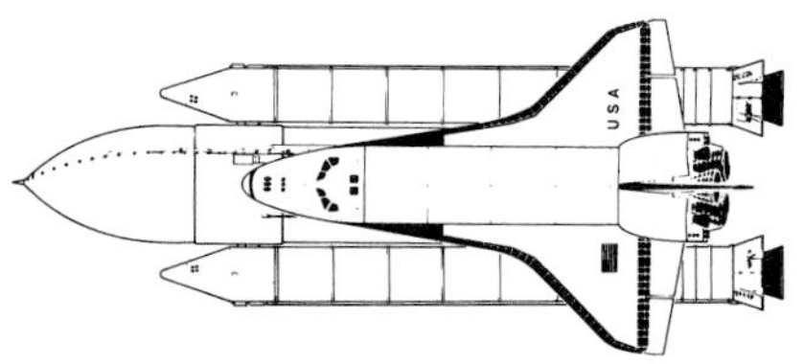

1. Getting Started Is the sketch of the space shuttle at the right an isometric or orthographic view? Why?

Draw the top view of each building. (Assume that no stacks of blocks are hidden.) Label the heights of the columns.

2.

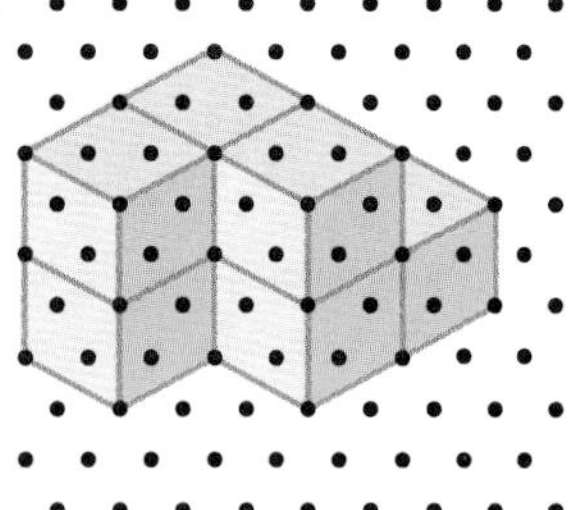

3.

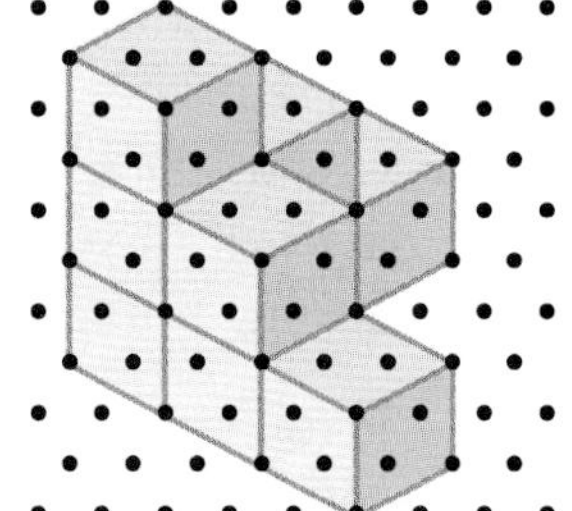

4. Match the letter of each corner view with the corresponding isometric drawing.

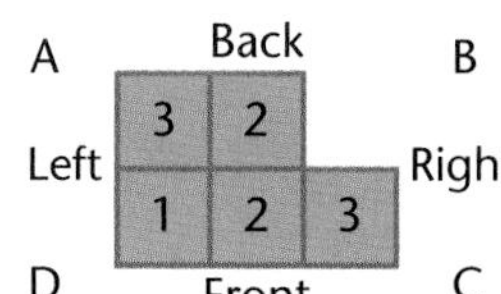

(a)

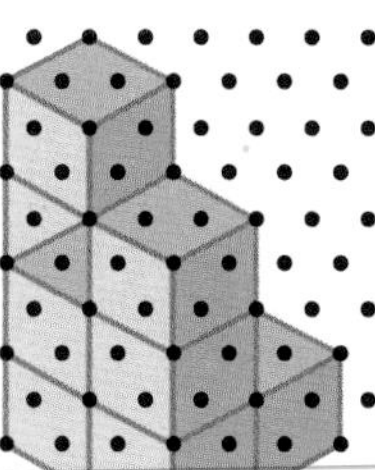

(b)

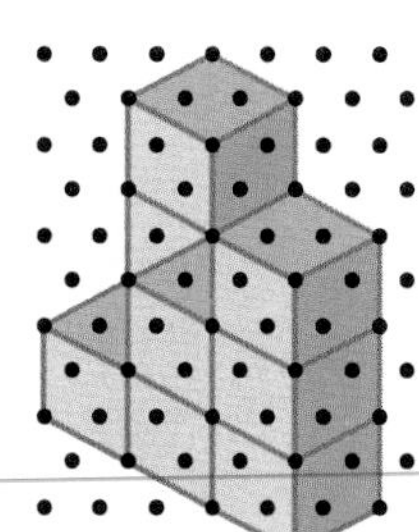

(c)

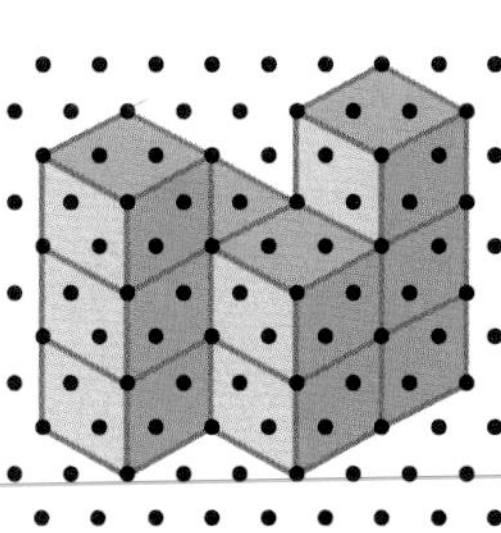

(d)

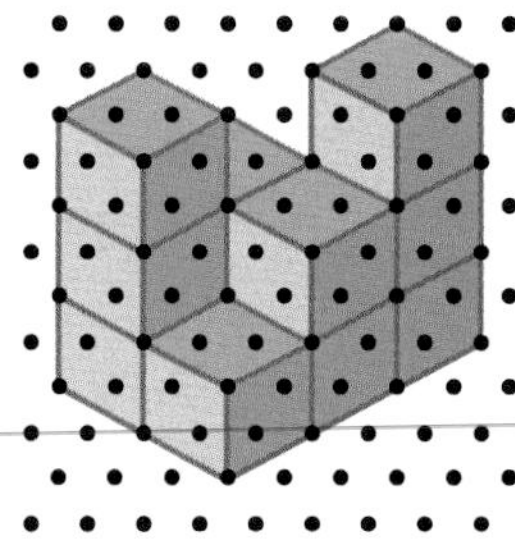

5. Write the word or phrase that correctly completes the statement below.

A view that shows only the front of a building is an ____ view.

6. The top view of a building is shown at the right.

a. Draw the front and left orthographic views. How are these related to the back and right views?

b. Suppose that an electrician is rewiring the offices in one of the cubes. What is the probability that she is working on the second floor of the building?

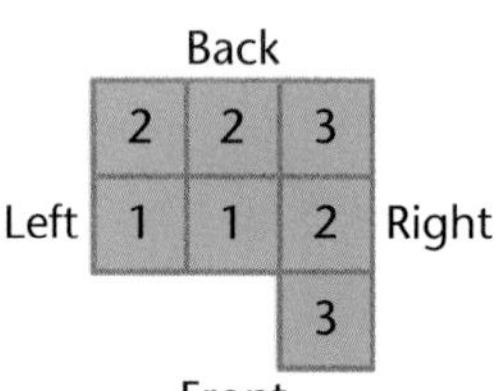

Match each isometric view with the correct orthographic views. In each case, the figure on top is a possible top view; the other views are front and right views.

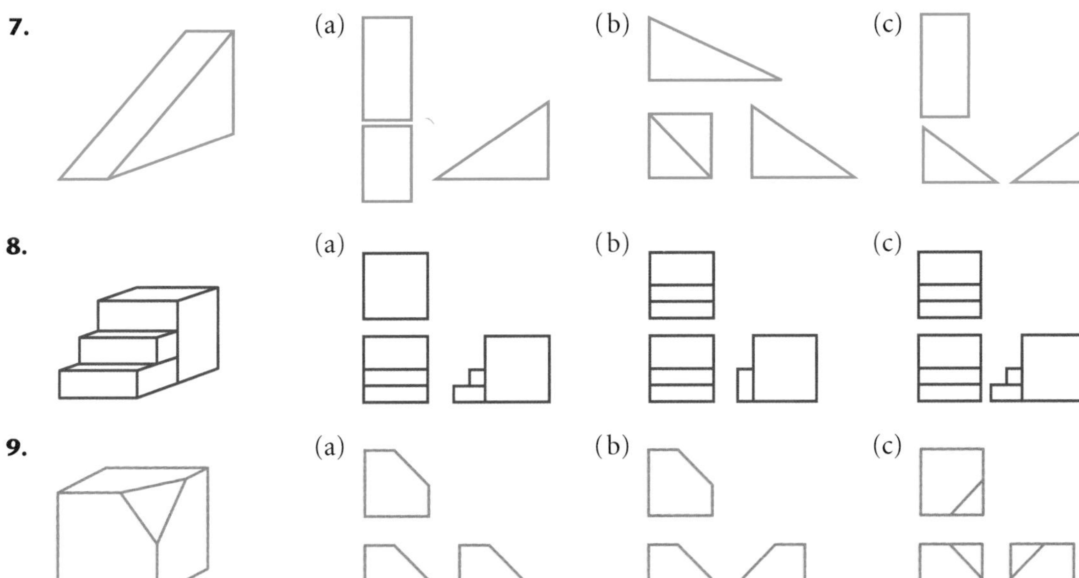

10. Summarize the advantages and disadvantages of orthographic and isometric views.

LOOK AHEAD

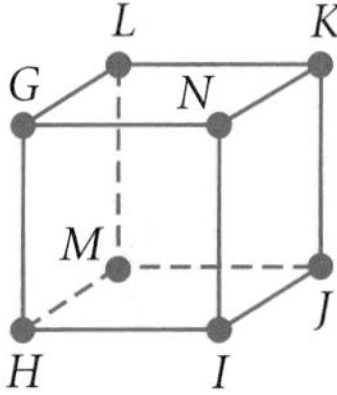

11. Use the cube at the right to give examples of

a. two coplanar lines that intersect

b. two coplanar lines that do not intersect

c. two noncoplanar lines

d. In which of the above would you say you found two *parallel* lines?

MORE PRACTICE

Draw the top view of each building. (Assume that no stacks of blocks are hidden.) Label the heights of the columns.

12.

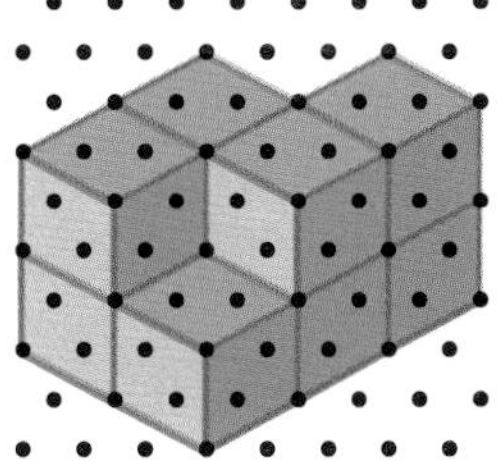

13.

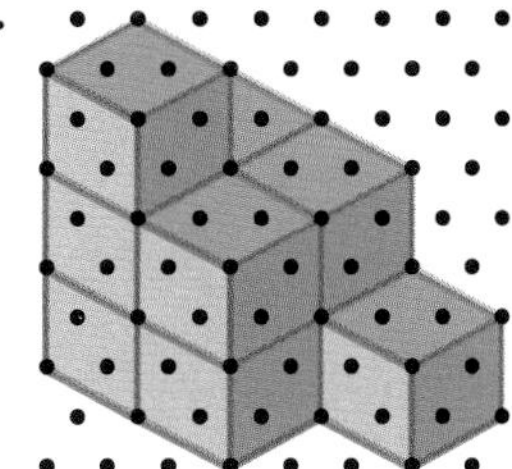

Match each isometric view with the correct orthographic views. In each case, the figure on top is a possible top view; the other views are front and right views.

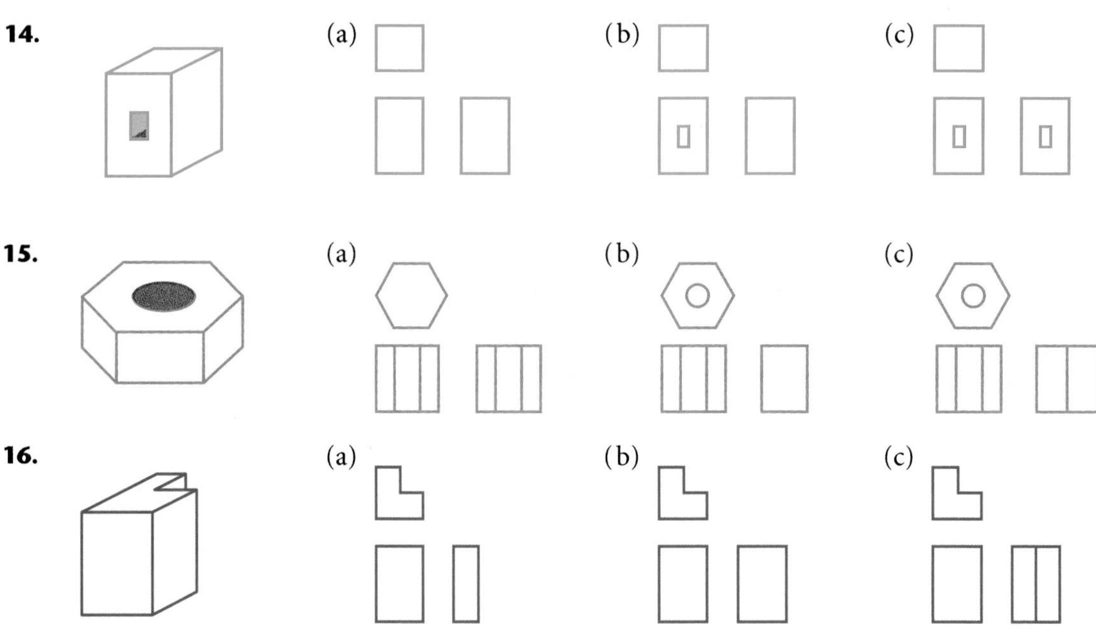

MORE MATH REASONING

17. Polycube Search Polycubes are formed by arranging cubes so that each cube has at least one face exactly matching a face of another cube.

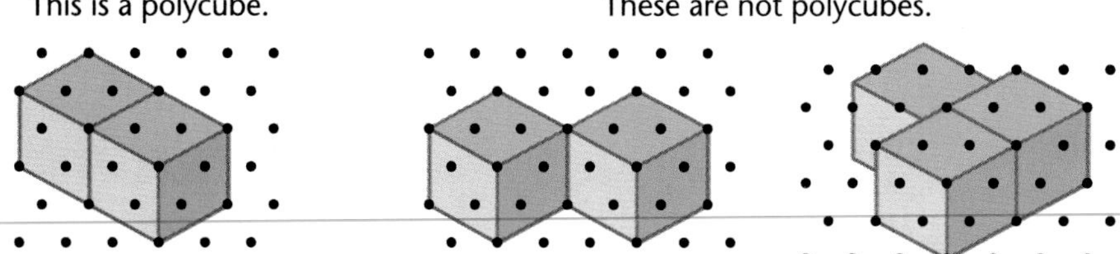

Find as many different shapes of four-cube polycubes (*quadracubes*) as you can. Draw each one on isometric dot paper.

18. Can You Top This? The front and right views of a building are shown. Draw three possible top views showing the number of cubes in each column. (Assume that the building is made of stacked cubes.)

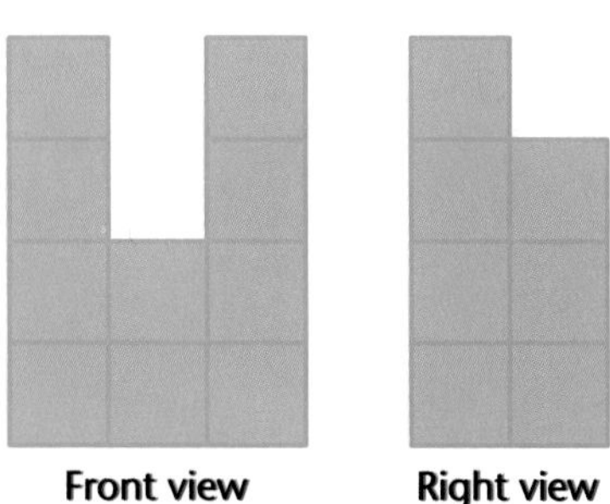

2-3 PART C Parallel Lines and Planes

← CONNECT → ***Parallel lines play an important role in the drawings you've been making. Now you will take a closer look at parallel lines. You will see a precise definition of parallel lines, make an important assumption about them, and investigate the relationship between parallel lines and slope.***

From your experience with parallel lines in algebra, you probably developed the idea that parallel lines do not meet. To write formal definitions, we need to refine our notion of parallel lines and planes.

> **DEFINITION**
>
> **Parallel lines** are coplanar lines that do not intersect.

Lines p and q in plane $\mathcal{S}$ are parallel. To show this, we use the symbol $\|$, and write $p \parallel q$.

To show that two lines in a figure are parallel, we can use arrows, as shown below.

In this figure a∥b and c∥d.

A line may be parallel to a plane, and planes may be parallel to each other.

> **DEFINITION**
>
> A line and a plane, or two planes, are **parallel** if and only if they do not intersect.

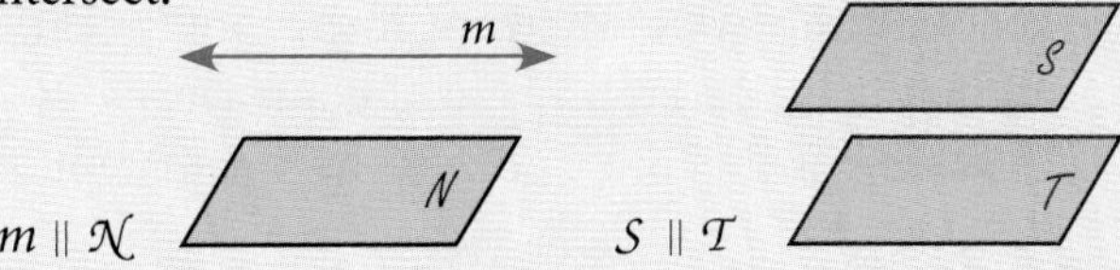

Noncoplanar lines cannot intersect.

DEFINITION

Skew lines are noncoplanar lines.

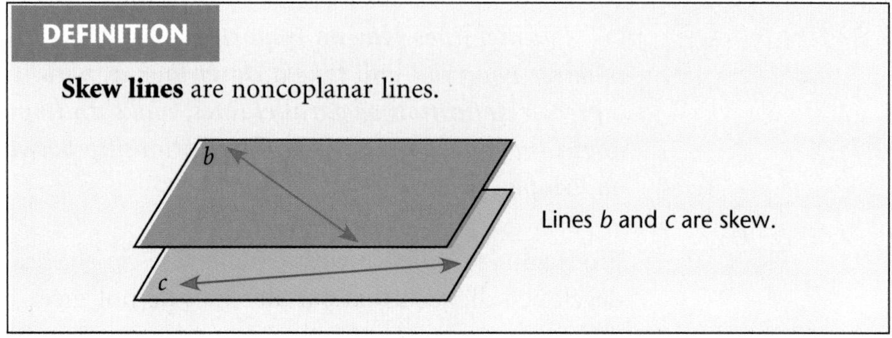

Lines *b* and *c* are skew.

TRY IT

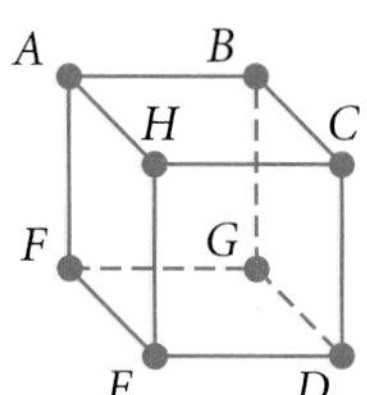

a. Name all the lines parallel to $\overleftrightarrow{AB}$ that contain edges of the cube at the right.

b. Name all of the lines that are skew to $\overleftrightarrow{EF}$ that contain edges of the cube.

The slopes of parallel and perpendicular lines have special relationships.

DEFINITION

Two nonvertical lines are parallel if and only if their slopes are equal. Two nonvertical lines are perpendicular if and only if the product of their slopes is –1.

How many lines can be drawn parallel to a given line through a point not on that line? The following Explore looks at this question.

EXPLORE: PARALLEL PROGRESSION

You have worked with the slope-intercept form for a linear equation. Recall that if the equation is in the form $y = mx + b$, m is the slope of the line, and b is the y-intercept.

MATERIALS

Graph paper
Graphing utility (optional)

1. Graph $y = 3x - 2$.
2. Find an equation of a line whose graph is parallel to $y = 3x - 2$.
3. How many other equations of lines parallel to $y = 3x - 2$ can you find? Explain why this is the case.
4. Write an equation of a line parallel to $y = 3x - 2$ that has a y-intercept of 5.
5. How many other equations of lines parallel to $y = 3x - 2$ with a y-intercept of 5 are there? Explain.
6. If you are given the equation of line ℓ and the coordinates of point P on the y-axis that is not on the line, describe how you can find an equation of a line that goes through P and is parallel to ℓ.

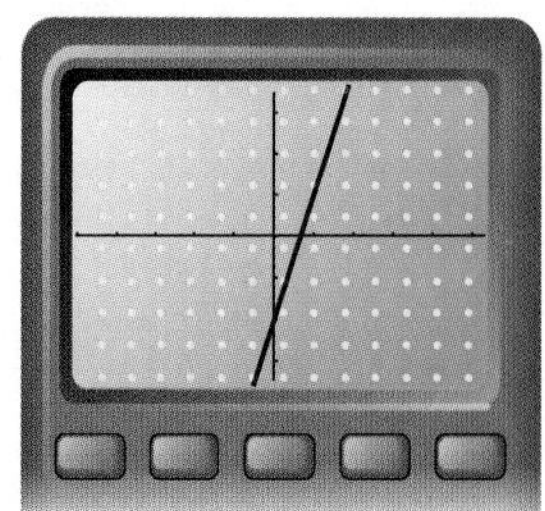

Your conclusions in the preceding Explore should make the following postulate seem reasonable.

PARALLEL POSTULATE

Through a given point, P, not on a line, ℓ, exactly one line may be drawn parallel to line ℓ.

This postulate was first stated by Euclid. For over 2000 years after Euclid, mathematicians doubted that this assumption was necessary. Many tried to prove the Parallel Postulate, but all failed. Instead, mathematicians found that by making different assumptions about parallel lines, they could create other, non-Euclidean systems of geometry. Nevertheless, we will use Euclid's Parallel Postulate. It most closely fits our ideas about geometric figures and their relationships in the world around us. We will look at non-Euclidean systems of geometry in Chapter 12.

REFLECT

1. Two noncoplanar lines cannot intersect. Why?
2. Can two planes ever be skew? Why or why not?
3. If a line is parallel to a plane, is it parallel to every line in the plane? Justify your answer with a sketch.

Exercises

CORE

Getting Started Refer to the cube at the right for Exercises 1–4.

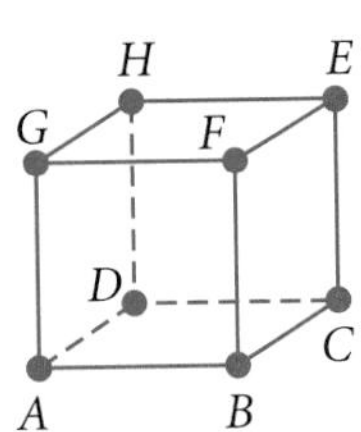

1. Name all of the lines parallel to $\overleftrightarrow{CE}$ that contain edges of the cube.

2. Name a line parallel to the plane containing points *F*, *B*, and *H*.

3. Identify a plane parallel to the plane containing *A*, *B*, and *C*.

4. Name a line through *F* that contains an edge of the cube and is skew to $\overleftrightarrow{AG}$.

Using the map of Washington, D.C., tell whether the streets given in Exercises 5–8 suggest parallel lines, intersecting lines, some of both, or neither.

5. streets passing through Dupont Circle

6. 15th St., 16th St., 17th St., and so on

7. O, P, and Q Streets

8. streets whose names are neither letters nor numbers

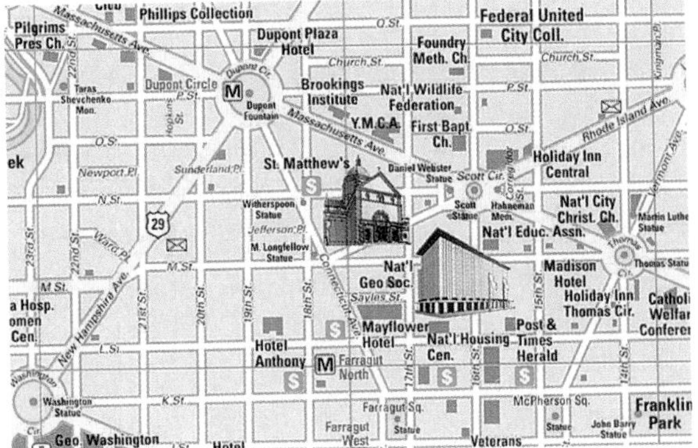

CityFlash Map ©1994 by Rand McNally R.L. 94-S-140

9. Write the letter of the second pair that best matches the first pair.

Skew: coplanar as (a) flat: plane, (b) points: collinear, (c) plane: line, (d) parallel: intersecting

10. Identify objects in your classroom that suggest parallel and skew lines.

Draw each figure if possible. If it is not possible, explain why.

11. Line $j \parallel k$; j and k lie on plane $\mathcal{L}$.

12. Planes $\mathcal{R}$ and $\mathcal{S}$ are parallel.

13. Line $p \parallel q$, lines p and r are skew, and lines q and r are skew.

14. In the figure at the right, a line is to be drawn that passes through two points chosen randomly from those labeled *A*–*F*.

a. What is the probability that the line will be parallel to *m*?

b. What is the probability that the line will be perpendicular to *m*?

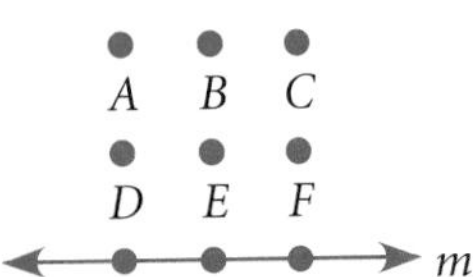

Write an equation of a line that meets the given requirements.

15. $\parallel$ to $y = -3x + 4$

16. through (0, 4) and $\parallel$ to $y = \frac{3}{5}x - \frac{1}{5}$

17. $\perp$ to $y = \frac{3}{4}x + 2$

18. through (0, 0) and $\parallel$ to $y = -6$

19. through (2, 3) and $\parallel$ to $y = -4$

20. through (0, −2) and $\perp$ to $y = \frac{4}{3}x + 5$

21. through (−4, −2) and $\parallel$ to $y = -\frac{3}{2}x + \frac{1}{3}$

22. through (2, 3) and $\perp$ to $y = -\frac{1}{4}x - 2$

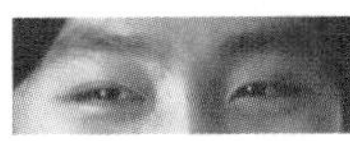

LOOK BACK

Use a protractor to draw angles with each of the following measures. [1-3]

23. 10°

24. 45°

25. 150°

Write each biconditional statement as two separate conditional statements in if-then form. [2-2]

26. Two lines are noncoplanar if and only if they are skew lines.

27. Two lines are parallel if and only if they are coplanar and do not intersect.

28. Point B is between points A and C if and only if $AB + BC = AC$.

MORE PRACTICE

Refer to the cube at the right for Exercises 29–31.

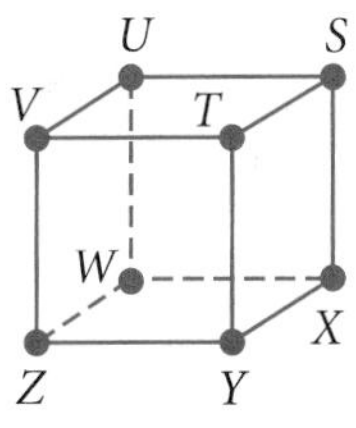

29. Name all of the lines skew to $\overleftrightarrow{XY}$ that contain an edge of the cube.

30. Identify a plane parallel to the plane containing U, V, and S.

31. Name three lines parallel to $\overleftrightarrow{WZ}$ that contain an edge of the cube.

Draw each figure if possible. If it is not possible, explain why.

32. Line p intersects line m, line $p \parallel$ line n, and line $m \parallel$ line n.

33. Line a intersects line b, line a intersects line c, and line b is skew to line c.

Write an equation of a line that meets the given requirements.

34. parallel to $y = \frac{3}{7}x + 1$

35. perpendicular to $y = \frac{3}{7}x + 1$

36. through (3, 2) and parallel to $y = -5x + \frac{4}{5}$

37. through (−2, 6) and perpendicular to $y = \frac{2}{3}x + 10$

MORE MATH REASONING

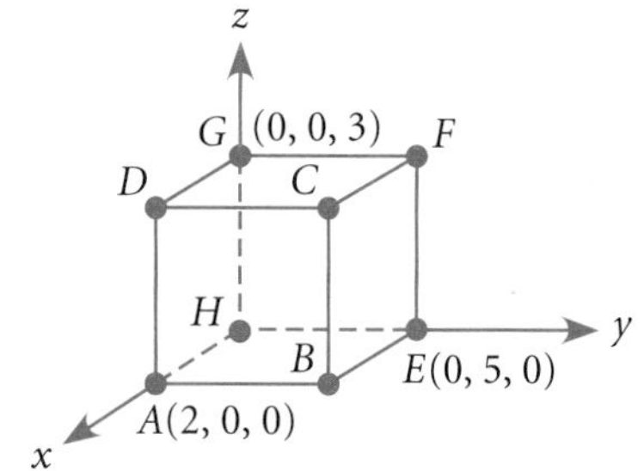

38. 3-D Coordinates By now you know how to set up an x-y coordinate system on a plane. To locate a point in three-dimensional space, we need to add a third axis. Any point in an x-y-z coordinate system can be named by three coordinates (x first, y second, z third). In the figure, the x-y-z coordinates of three vertices of a box (rectangular prism) are given.

a. Give the coordinates for each of the other vertices of the box.

b. Name three sets of parallel line segments.

Assume the following statements are true. Make a conjecture using each set of statements. Make a sketch to illustrate each conjecture.

39. Lines ℓ, p, and q are coplanar. Line $p \parallel q$, and ℓ intersects p.

40. Lines r, s, and t are coplanar. Line $r \parallel s$, and $t \perp r$.

41. Plane $\mathcal{P} \parallel \mathcal{Q}$. Plane $\mathcal{N}$ intersects $\mathcal{P}$.

2-3 PART D Making Connections

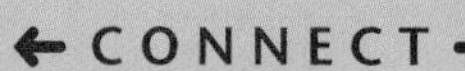

← CONNECT →

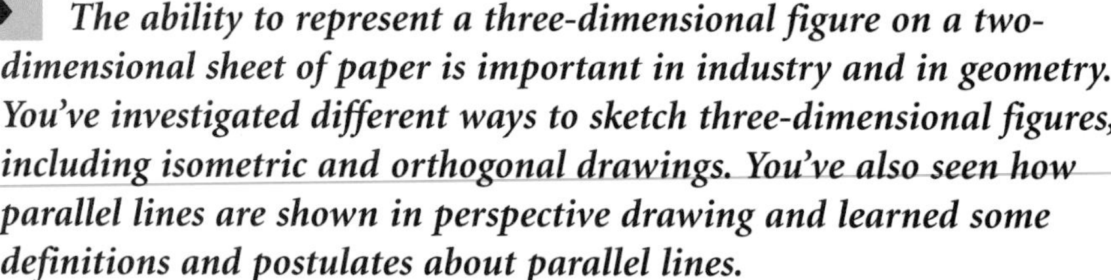

The ability to represent a three-dimensional figure on a two-dimensional sheet of paper is important in industry and in geometry. You've investigated different ways to sketch three-dimensional figures, including isometric and orthogonal drawings. You've also seen how parallel lines are shown in perspective drawing and learned some definitions and postulates about parallel lines.

Different cultures and professions have looked at and used parallel lines in many different ways. The photo at the left shows a track with lane markings that are indicated by parallel lines.

You have learned how to use parallel lines and planes to make more realistic-looking drawings of three-dimensional objects. In the following Explore, you will use these new skills to design a transit station.

EXPLORE: STATION DESIGNER

MATERIALS

Drawing materials

The photo at the right shows a commuter station in Washington, D.C. Your class has been asked to design a new commuter station for your home town. Since it is too big a task to do alone, you are to design one of the following aspects of the station.

- the front layout of the site
- the passenger building
- the docking terminal
- the parking area

Choose the type of drawing (one-point or two-point perspective, orthographic, or isometric) that will convey your idea best. Your drawing must include parallel lines and planes. When you have finished, your work should be suitable for a presentation to your class or the community.

REFLECT

1. What are the advantages and disadvantages of using perspective drawings instead of orthographic drawings to represent three-dimensional objects?
2. There are only three different relationships possible for two lines. Describe and illustrate all three relationships.

Self-Assessment

Determine whether each statement is true or false. Explain your answers.

1. Two lines that do not intersect are parallel.
2. A line and a plane that do not intersect are parallel.
3. In an isometric drawing of a cube, parallel edges will appear to meet at one point.
4. The right and left orthographic views of a building made of cubes are always reflections of one another.

5. The architectural drawing at the right is by Julia Morgan. Is it an isometric view, an orthographic view, in one-point perspective, or in two-point perspective? Explain how you decided.

6. Give the equations of three lines parallel to $y = \frac{3}{2}x - 3$.

7. Give an equation for a line through (0, 5) perpendicular to $y = \frac{3}{2}x - 3$.

8. The top view and an isometric view of a block building are shown. From which corner of the building was the isometric view drawn?
(a) right front (b) left front
(c) right rear (d) left rear

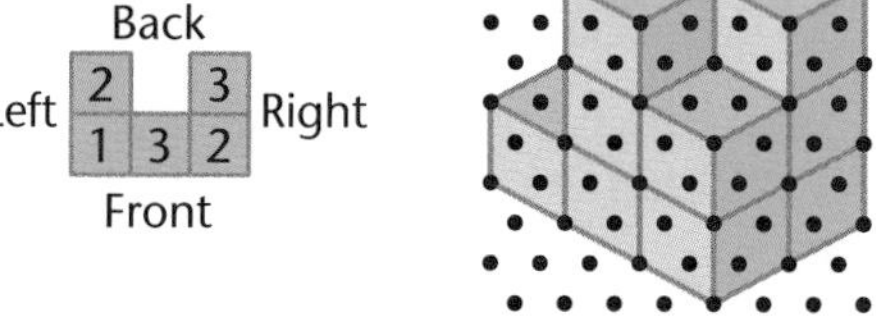

9. Copy the figure at the right. Sketch the reflection of the triangle *EFG* across line *m*. Label its image triangle *VWX*. Then do the following: [1-3, 1-4]
a. Use your protractor to find the measure of $\angle E$.
b. Without measuring, find the measure of $\angle V$. Explain your reasoning.

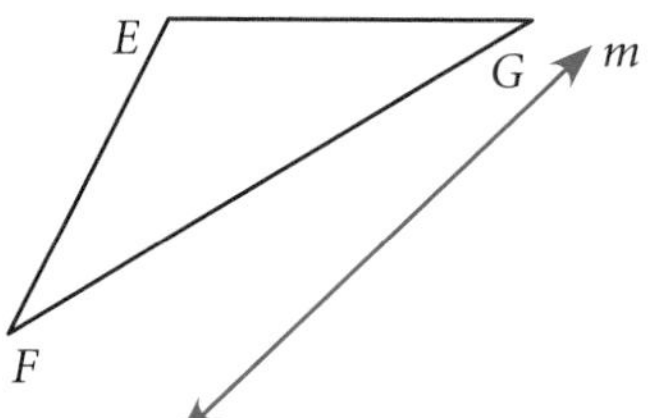

Determine whether each statement is true or false. If true, state the postulate or postulates that justify it. If false, explain why. [2-2]

10. Line $\overleftrightarrow{JK}$ is the only line containing *J* and *K*.

11. The intersection of planes $\mathcal{F}$ and $\mathcal{G}$ is point *H*.

12. The intersecting lines $\overleftrightarrow{AB}$ and $\overleftrightarrow{BC}$ must be coplanar.

13. The top view of a block building is shown at the right. Draw an orthogonal view from the front side and the right side of the building.

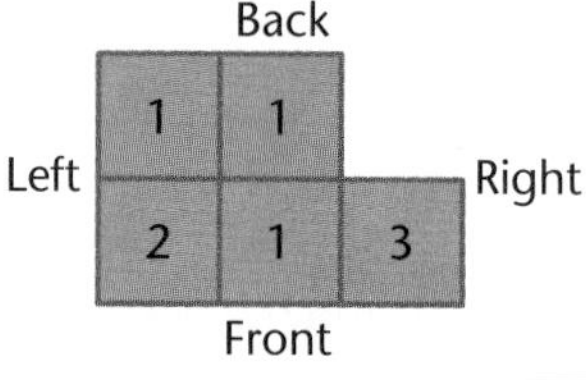

Determine whether each statement is true or false. For each false statement, give a counterexample.

14. If two lines have the same slope, then they are parallel.

15. Two lines with the same *y*-intercept are perpendicular.

16. If the product of the slopes of two lines is -1, then they are perpendicular.

17. If two lines are perpendicular, then the product of their slopes is -1.

18. You Be the Architect! Sketch a building of your own design, using one of the techniques you have learned in this chapter. Identify the technique you are using.

Chapter 2 Review

In Chapter 2, you investigated the rules and language of logic, including conditionals and their related statements. You learned how to write definitions of geometric terms, and how undefined terms, definitions, postulates, and theorems fit together to form our system of geometry. You also explored two-dimensional representations of three-dimensional objects and investigated parallel lines.

KEY TERMS

biconditional statement [2-2]
Chain Rule [2-1]
conclusion [2-1]
conditional statement [2-1]
contrapositive [2-1]
converse [2-1]
coplanar points [2-2]
horizon line [2-3]
hypothesis [2-1]
inverse [2-1]
isometric drawing [2-3]
Law of Detachment [2-1]
midpoint [2-2]
noncoplanar [2-2]
one-point perspective [2-3]
orthogonal view [2-3]
orthographic view [2-3]
parallel [2-3]
parallel lines [2-3]
plane [2-2]
skew lines [2-3]
space [2-2]
two-point perspective [2-3]
vanishing point [2-3]

Write the word or phrase that correctly completes each statement.

1. A statement containing a hypothesis and a conclusion is called a ____ statement.

2. A conjecture that is accepted without proof is called a ____ .

3. Coplanar lines that do not intersect are called ____ lines.

CONCEPTS AND APPLICATIONS

4. Write a false conditional statement that has a true inverse. [2-1]

5. Determine whether the following conditional statement is true. "If a number is divisible by 4, then it is divisible by 16." Write the inverse, converse, and contrapositive of the conditional, and determine whether each is true or false. [2-1]

Determine whether each statement is true or false. If true, state the postulate that it illustrates. If false, correct it so that it is true. [2-2]

6. Two planes intersect only in the point P.

7. If points A and B lie in a plane, then the midpoint of $\overline{AB}$ also lies in that plane.

8. Factor the expression $x^2 + 4x - 12$. [Previous course]

9. Find the coordinates of the midpoint of the segment with endpoints $(3, -8)$ and $(-1, 6)$. [2-2]

10. Give the equation of the line that is parallel to the line $y = 5x - 7$ that passes through $(0, 6)$. [2-3]

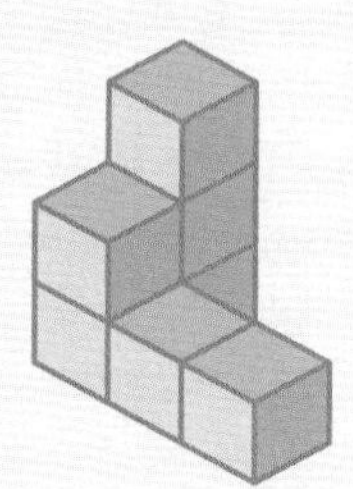

11. Draw the top view of the building shown. Label the heights of the columns. Assume that there are no unseen stacks of cubes. [2-3]

CONCEPTS AND CONNECTIONS

12. **Computer Games** You are designing pieces for a "three-dimensional" computer game in which players put together buildings made of small cubes. Design a set of three pieces that can be put together to form a $3 \times 3 \times 3$ cube. Draw your pieces using a different method of representation for each. Include one isometric drawing, one set of orthographic views, and one perspective drawing.

SELF-EVALUATION

Write a summary of what you have learned in this chapter. Include examples of how the new ideas you learned in Chapter 2 can be used to model real-world situations. Include topics that you found difficult, and describe your plans for reviewing them.

Chapter 2 Assessment

TEST

In items 1 and 2, determine whether each statement is true or false. If a statement is false, provide a counterexample to illustrate this.

1. If a conditional statement is true, then its contrapositive must be true.

2. If a conditional statement is false, then its inverse must be true.

3. Assume that the statements below are true. Some of them fit together. Use them to write at least two other statements that must be true. For each new statement, name the rule that you used.

   If there is fire, there is smoke. If I win the lottery, I will be rich. If I go to Hawaii, I will go surfing. If I get rich, I will go to Hawaii. There is fire.

4. Determine whether the following conditional statement is true or false. "If a number is odd, then its square is odd." Write the converse, and determine whether it is true or false. If both the original statement and its converse are true, rewrite them as a single biconditional statement.

Write each number using scientific notation.

5. 0.000206

6. 1800

7. 306,000,000

Points *R* and *S* are points on a coordinate plane. Find the midpoint of $\overline{RS}$ using the given coordinates.

8. $R(-2, 3), S(1, 8)$

9. $R(4, -3), S(10, -5)$

10. Use a straightedge to draw a line segment about 3 in. long. Then use your compass and straightedge to construct its midpoint.

11. Do you think it is possible to construct a system of geometry that does not include any undefined terms? Write a paragraph explaining why or why not.

12. Points *A*, *B*, *C*, and *D* are coplanar points. A line segment drawn from *A* to *B* passes through *C*. A line segment drawn from *C* to *B* passes through *D*. Determine which of the following must be true.
(a) $AC + CD = AB$
(b) $AD + CD = AC$
(c) Points *A*, *B*, *C*, and *D* are collinear.
(d) Point *C* is the midpoint of $\overline{AB}$.

13. Give the equation of the line parallel to $y = 6x - 2$ that passes through $(0, 1)$.

14. The top view of a building is shown. Sketch an isometric view of the building from the left front corner.

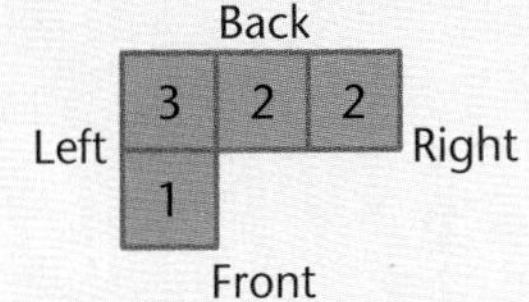

15. Draw a wide rectangular box (prism) in two-point perspective.

PERFORMANCE TASK

Given a conditional statement, how many possibilities are there for the truth values of the statement, its converse, its inverse, and its contrapositive? For example, one possibility is that the statement, its converse, its inverse, and its contrapositive are all true. What are the other possibilities? Show the other possibilities in a table like the one begun for you below. For each row in the table, give an example of a conditional statement with the specified truth values.

Conditional	**Converse**	**Inverse**	**Contrapositive**
True	True	True	True

Chapter 3 Angles and Parallel Lines

Project A
Can You Read My Writing?
How were books duplicated before the days of movable type?

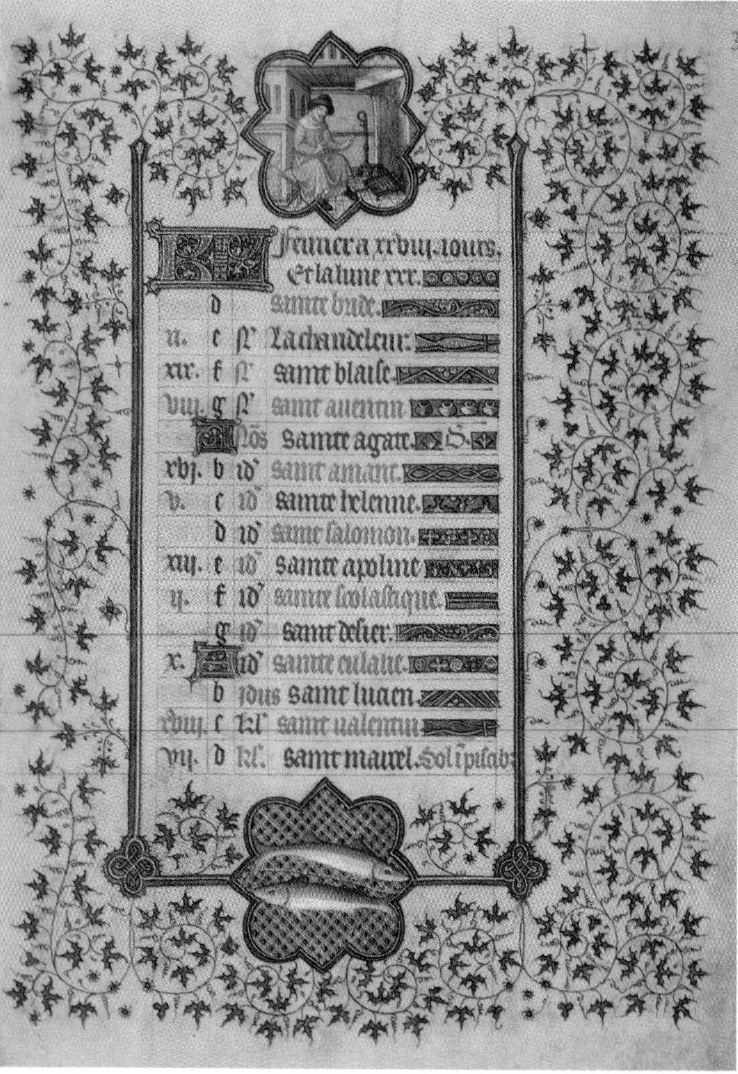

The Metropolitan Museum of Art, The Cloisters Collection, 1954.

Project B
Steer by the Stars
How did the early Polynesians find their way among the islands of the Pacific Ocean? Why was Columbus indebted to China?

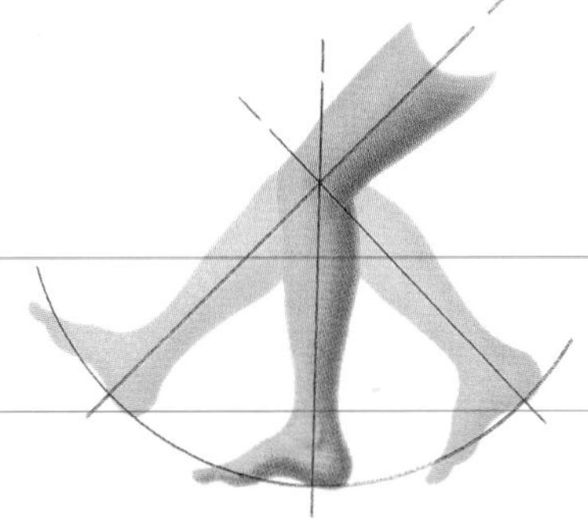

Project C
The Squeaky Hinge Gets the Oil
Why is arthritis painful? What is the normal range of motion for a knee or an elbow?

MARK LINANE

Biology was my favorite subject in high school, then math. I found math to be straightforward and tangible, and I thought I would just need it for my personal finances.

Every day I use angles and measurements as I treat patients. I measure their strength and their range of motion, and I help them improve their flexibility. After I've made these measurements, I adjust the equipment so that the workout will challenge the patient without causing injury.

Mark Linane
Physical Therapist
Caremark Orthopedic Services
Allen, Texas

Mark Linane P.T., M.S.

Chapter 3 Angles and Parallel Lines

GETTING READY

3-1
Angles and Navigation

In 3-1 you will solve problems using angles, bearings, and vectors. You will use the following skills from previous chapters.

M is the midpoint of segment LN. Find each missing length. [2-2]

1. $MN = 27$, $LN =$ ____, $LM =$ ____

2. $LM = 18.25$, $MN =$ ____, $LN =$ ____

3. $LM = 3x - 1$, $MN =$ ____, $LN =$ ____

4. $MN = 4\frac{1}{2}$, $LM =$ ____, $LN =$ ____

3-2
Rotations

In 3-2 you will learn about rotations and rotational symmetry. You will need the following skills from previous chapters and courses.

Graph the following equations. Show the line of symmetry for each graph. [Previous course]

5. $y = x^2$ **6.** $y = (x + 2)^2$ **7.** $x = \frac{1}{2}y^2$ **8.** $y = x^2 - 2$

3-3
Precise Thinking with Angles

In 3-3 you will investigate angle pairs and relationships. You will apply the following ideas from previous courses.

Measure the angles below. [Previous course]

9. **10.** **11.** **12.**

3-4
Parallel Lines and Transversals

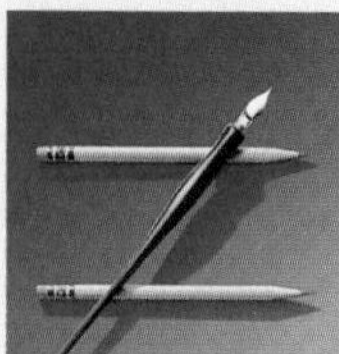

In 3-4 you will investigate parallel lines and the angles formed by a transversal line crossing parallel lines. You will apply the following ideas from previous chapters and courses.

Solve these equations. [Previous course]

13. $2x + 54 = 90$ **14.** $18 - 3x = 78 - 6x$ **15.** $45 - 3x = 100 - 8x$

Write the inverse, the converse, and the contrapositive. [2-1]

16. If $|x| = 5$, then $x = \pm 5$. **17.** If $\angle A$ is acute, then $m\angle A < 90°$.

3-1 Angles and Navigation

The Portuguese explorer Ferdinand Magellan began the first voyage around the world in 1519. Navigating by the stars with simple tools, Magellan and his crew sailed through one of the roughest stretches of the sea: just south of the tip of South America, where the Atlantic and Pacific oceans meet. Although Magellan died during the voyage, one of his five ships eventually circled the globe.

The following excerpt from *Magellan*, by Alan Villiers, appeared in *National Geographic*, June 1976.

As beautiful day followed beautiful day, and the Pacific trade winds wafted the small ships along, the same monotonous, empty horizon encircled what appeared to be the last three ships on earth. The crews, by then gaunt, wild-eyed men, fiercely hunted over their craft for something, anything to sustain life. As [a crew member] recorded, they not only pursued rats to make into stew, but they also cut down the leather chafing mats for food. This hard sunbaked stuff they soaked for days, then beat it as soft as possible with belaying pins, and boiled and boiled it. The soup tasted like old hides and provided little nourishment.

By chance of the route he took, [Magellan] sighted only two lonely islands of all the great South Pacific groups, and could not land on those. He saw none of the many isles where he might have found glorious fruits and fat fish. But had he sailed among them, he might have struck a hidden reef and been lost in mid-Pacific.

?

1. The line on the map shows Magellan's route. Describe this path in your own words.
2. Suppose you want to give directions to friends telling them how to travel from your school to your home. How would you describe a path for them to follow?
3. What are some ways that angles are used to describe directions?

3-1 PART A More About Rays and Angles

← CONNECT → ***You've learned about angles before. Now you will see how to identify different types of angles.***

An accurate description of a route for a ship or an airplane is essential for these crafts to get to the right place at the right time. Navigators depend on rays and angles to plan a course and ensure that they stay on it.

The figure below shows some vocabulary associated with angles.

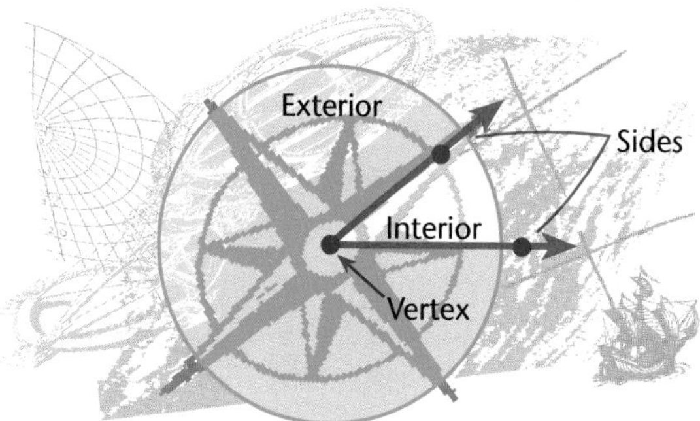

Angle measurement is important in describing directions. It is sometimes useful to talk about an angle's size in a more general way. We have already defined one of the terms below; you are probably familiar with all of them.

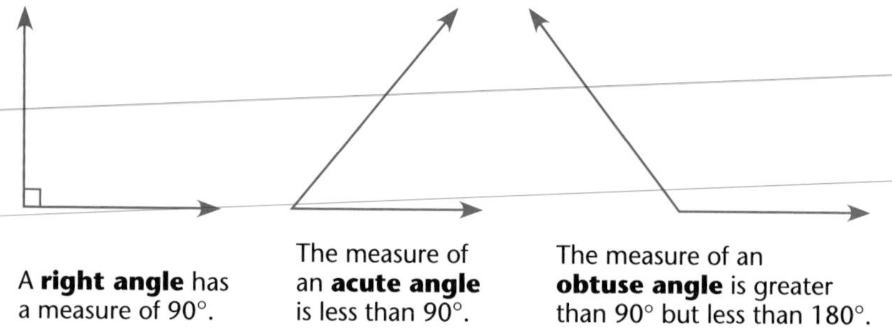

A **right angle** has a measure of 90°.

The measure of an **acute angle** is less than 90°.

The measure of an **obtuse angle** is greater than 90° but less than 180°.

These angle classifications are critical in the design and use of navigational tools. The navigational tool shown at the left is called a *sextant.*

As you know, angles are two noncollinear rays that have the same endpoint. There is also a special name for two collinear rays with the same endpoint that point in opposite directions.

DEFINITION

If point M is between X and Y on line $\overleftrightarrow{XY}$, the rays $\overrightarrow{MX}$ and $\overrightarrow{MY}$ are **opposite rays.**

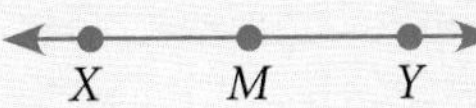

TRY IT

a. Name a pair of opposite rays in the figure at the right.

b. Name all the acute angles, right angles, and obtuse angles in the figure.

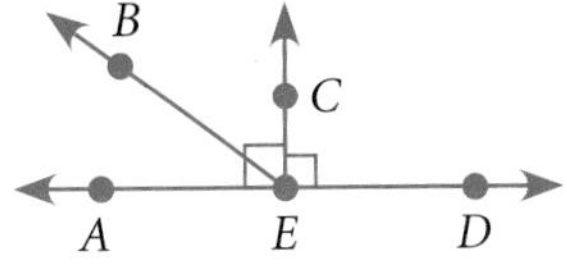

EXPLORE: AS THE EARTH TURNS

MATERIALS

Protractor

Reading and using maps are crucial skills in navigation. This map shows the earth viewed from the North Pole (P). The map also shows Tokyo (T), Rome (R), Lisbon (L), New York (N), and San Francisco (S).

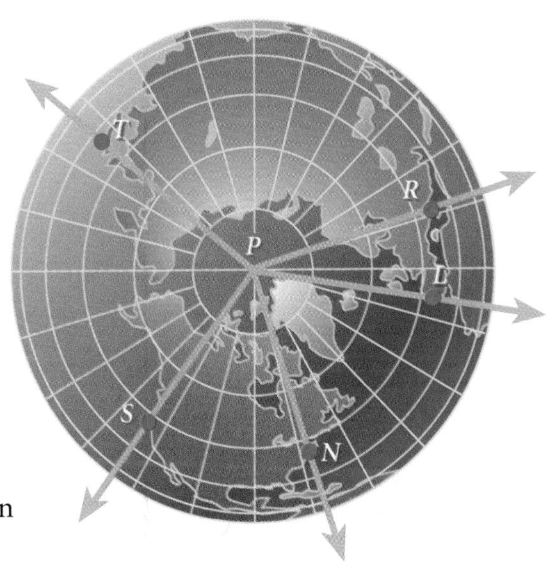

1. Name all of the rays shown on the map.
2. Name a city that lies in the interior of $\angle SPN$. Name a city that lies in the exterior of $\angle SPN$.
3. Name all of the angles in the diagram. Classify each as acute, right, or obtuse. If necessary, use your protractor to measure the angles.
4. Use your protractor to find the measure of the angle through which the earth rotates from
   a. San Francisco to New York
   b. Lisbon to Rome **c.** Rome to Tokyo
   d. Lisbon to Tokyo
5. When viewed from above, as in the map, the earth rotates counterclockwise. It takes the earth approximately 24 hr to make one complete rotation (360°). Use a proportion and your angle measurements to find out how long it should take for the earth to rotate from San Francisco to New York. Compare your result with those of your classmates.
6. Does your result in **5** above fit what you know about time zones? Explain.

REFLECT

1. Are rays $\overrightarrow{AB}$ and $\overrightarrow{BA}$ sometimes, always, or never opposite rays? Explain why or why not.
2. Write a summary that describes acute, right, and obtuse angles. Provide drawings of each.

Exercises

CORE

Getting Started Name each of the following, using the figure below.

1. two opposite rays
2. three different angles
3. two perpendicular rays
4. a point in the interior of $\angle JKN$
5. two points in the exterior of $\angle MKN$
6. the sides of $\angle MKN$

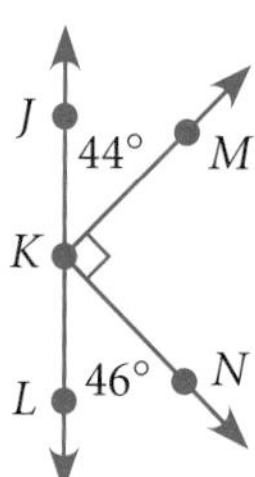

Determine whether each angle appears to be acute, obtuse, or right, and estimate its measure. Then use a protractor to measure the angle and check your estimate.

7.

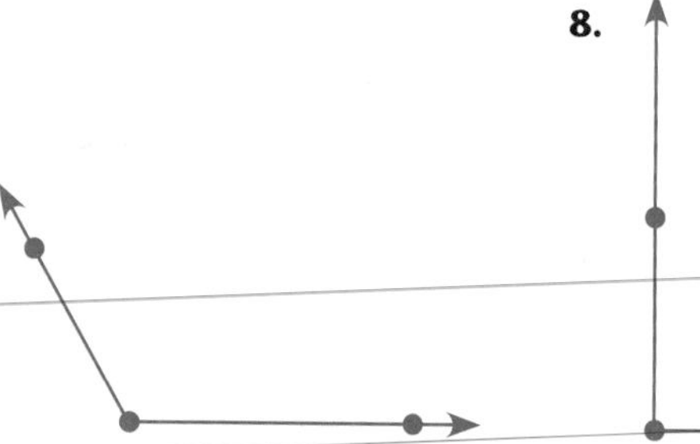

8.

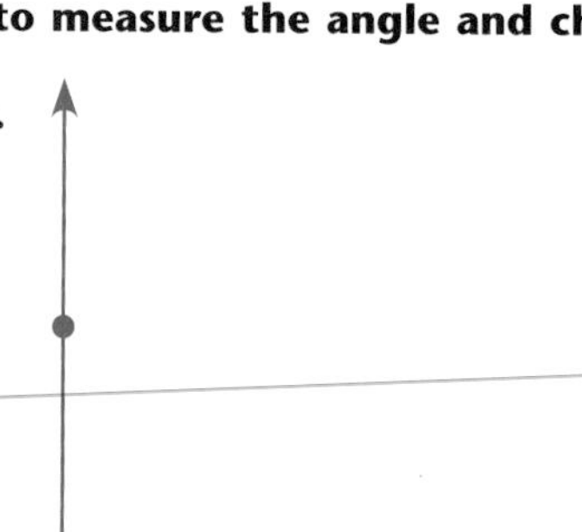

9.

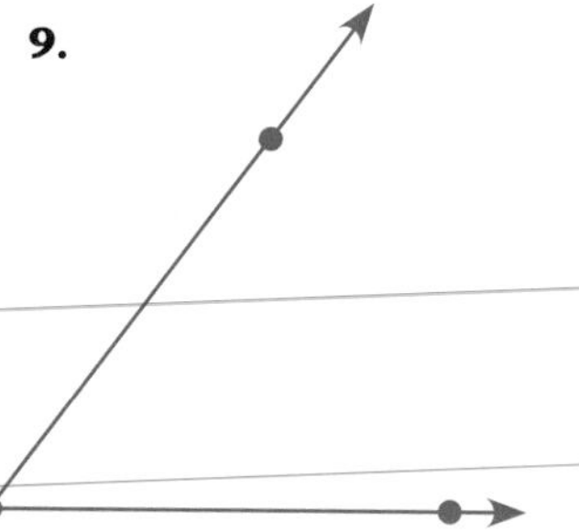

Write the word or phrase that correctly completes each statement.

10. The measure of a(n) ___ angle is greater than 90°.
11. The measure of a(n) ___ angle is less than 90°.
12. The measure of a(n) ___ angle is exactly 90°.
13. Draw one ray that could correctly be named $\overrightarrow{AB}$, $\overrightarrow{AC}$, or $\overrightarrow{AD}$.

14. Solve the inequality $3x + 7 \geq 19$, and graph the solution on a number line.

a. Is the graph a ray? Why or why not?

b. If the graph is a ray, what is the endpoint?

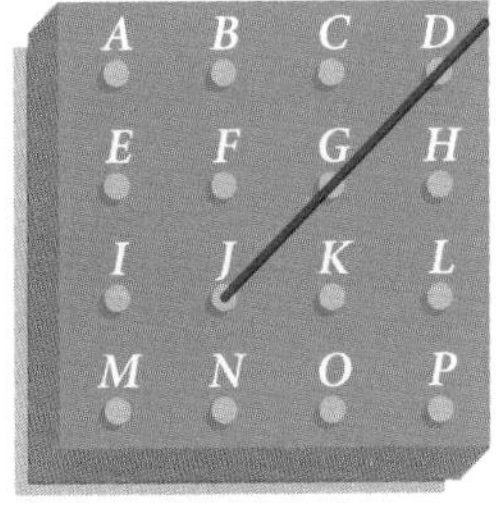

15. Use the points on the grid for each of the following.

a. How many different angles can be drawn with vertex J, side $\overrightarrow{JD}$, another side containing a grid point, and exactly one grid point in the interior? Name the angles.

b. What is the probability that a randomly drawn angle with vertex J, side $\overrightarrow{JD}$, and another side containing at least one grid point will have exactly one grid point in the interior?

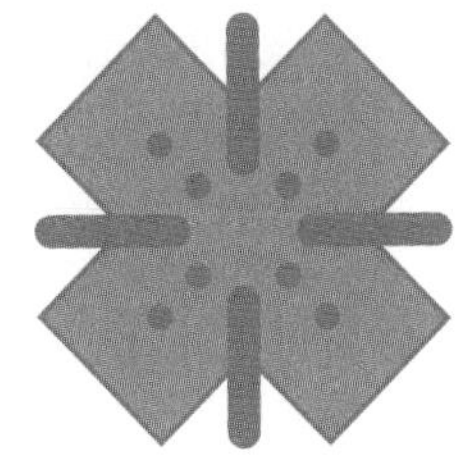

16. Copy the figure at the right. Then draw all lines of symmetry. How many right angles are formed by the lines of symmetry?

Science

17. A Good Reflection When a beam of light reflects off a mirror, the angle of incidence is congruent to the angle of reflection. What can you say about $\angle DBC$ in the figure below?

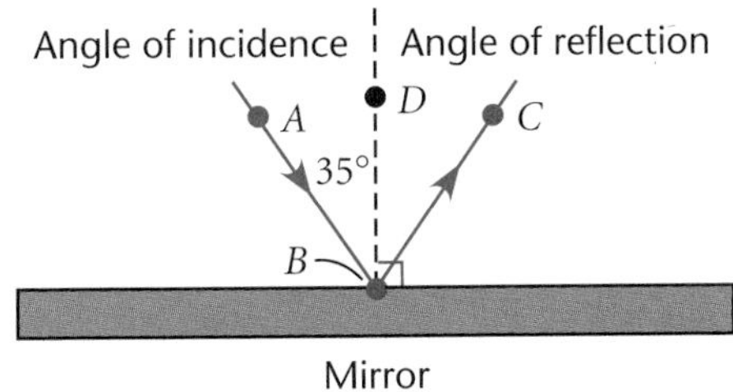

LOOK BACK

Give a counterexample for each conjecture. [1-2]

18. If two angles are acute, then they are congruent.

19. No mammals live in the ocean.

Determine whether each statement is true or false. If true, state one or more postulates that justify the statement. If false, state or sketch a counterexample. [2-2]

20. The line containing points G and H lies in exactly one plane.

21. Any four noncollinear points can be contained in one plane.

22. There is at least one point that is not on plane $\mathcal{P}$.

MORE PRACTICE

Name each of the following, using the figure at the right.

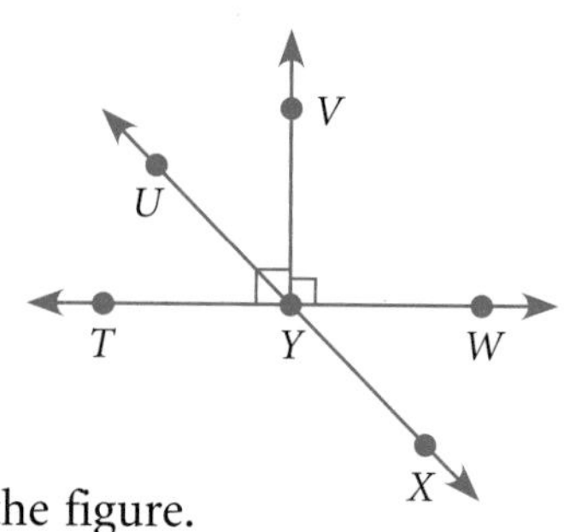

23. two opposite rays

24. three different angles

25. two perpendicular rays

26. the sides of $\angle TYX$

27. a point in the interior of $\angle VYT$

28. two points in the exterior of $\angle VYT$

29. Name all of the acute angles, right angles, and obtuse angles in the figure.

30. Solve the inequality $4y \leq 7y + 12$, and graph the solution on a number line. Name the endpoint of the ray you have drawn.

MORE MATH REASONING

31. How many different angles are formed when 10 distinct rays are drawn in the interior of an angle as shown at the right?

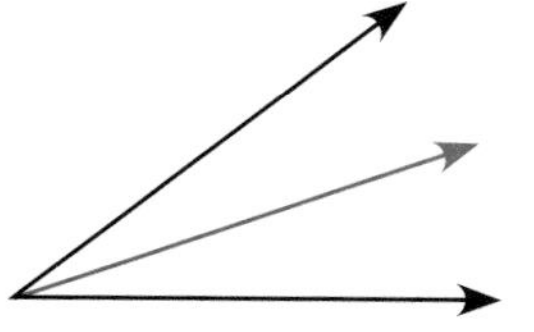

When one ray is drawn, three angles are formed.

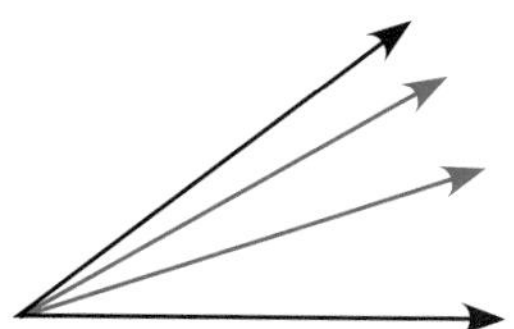

When two rays are drawn, six angles are formed.

Problem-Solving Tip

Make a table and look for a pattern to help predict the number of angles formed when 10 rays are drawn.

32. The Plane Truth Modern navigation relies heavily on radar. For example, air traffic controllers depend on radar to track and guide airplanes. Radar screens show the position of every plane within 50 mi of the airport. Use the screen shown to answer the following.

a. Estimate the number of degrees through which the radar must sweep to "see" the planes at points *A*, *B*, *C*, *D*, and *E*. (Assume that the radar sweep moves clockwise.)

b. Suppose it takes the radar 10 sec to make one full sweep of the screen. Approximately how long should it take to sweep past the 5 planes?

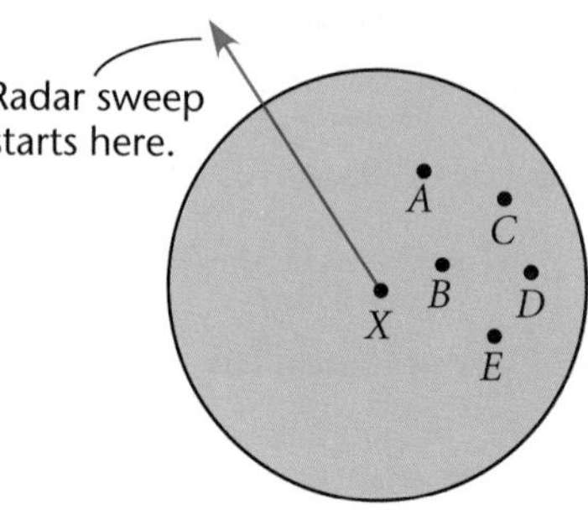

3-1 PART B Bearings

← CONNECT → ***You know how to measure and classify angles. Bearings, which are related to angles, are used in navigation to describe positions. Now you will discover how to use bearings.***

Bearings help describe positions. To find the bearing of an object, first locate north (N), which is toward the top of most maps. Then turn clockwise from north to point in the direction of the object, and measure the angle of the turn. Since there are 360° in a full turn, three digits are usually used to describe bearing. For example, a bearing of 075 means a 75°-clockwise turn is needed to point in the direction of the object.

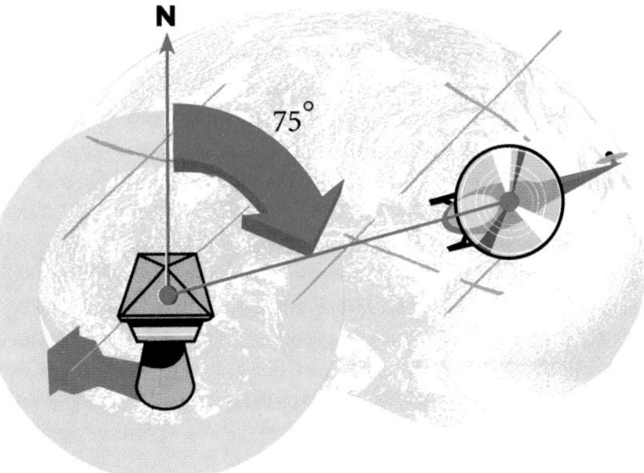

In the figure above, the bearing of the helicopter from the control tower is 075. In the following Explore, you will investigate bearings greater than 180.

EXPLORE: BEARING WITH IT

How might you measure the bearing of the airplane from the tower in the figure at the right? Describe a method for measuring bearings equal to or greater than 180. Compare your method with the ones your classmates develop. Then use a protractor to find the bearing of the airplane.

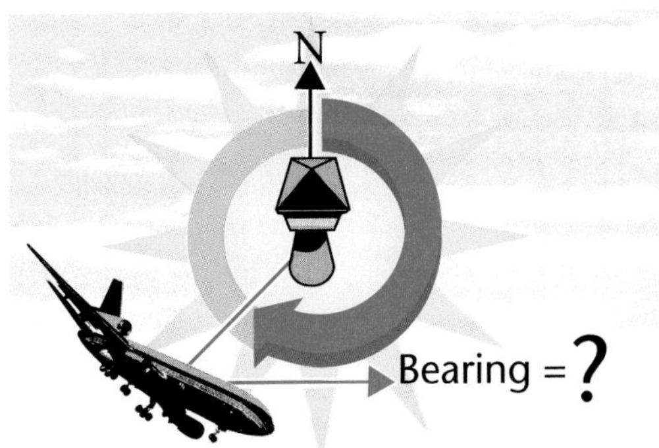

TRY IT

a. Use a protractor to measure each bearing in the figure below.

   i. the bearing of the fire from the observation tower

   ii. the bearing of the cabin from the observation tower

   iii. the bearing of the boat from the cabin

b. Estimate the bearing of the observation tower from the cabin in the figure below.

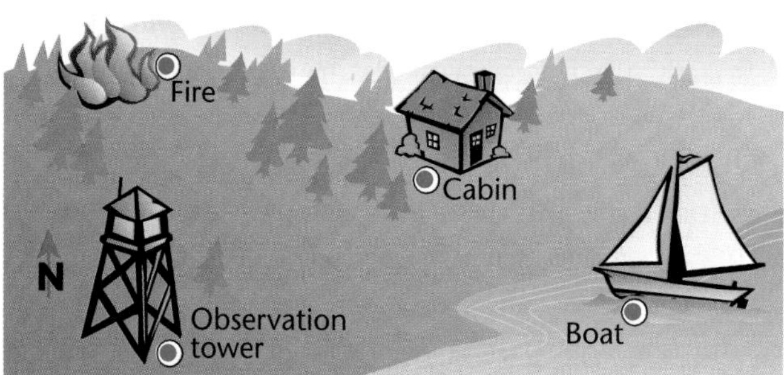

1. In the figure above, suppose you know that the angle formed by the fire, the observation tower (at the vertex), and a campsite is obtuse. What can you say about the campsite's bearing from the observation tower?

It is important to understand the differences and similarities between bearings and angles. For instance, angle measures are between 0° and 180°. However, since bearings measure rotations, we need a range of 000 to 360 to measure bearings. Although an angle cannot measure 200°, you can have a bearing of 200.

REFLECT

1. Look at the map of Magellan's route on page 155. How could you use bearings to describe his initial path as he left the coast of Spain? Give an estimate of Magellan's bearing at this stage of his journey.

2. Why do you think bearing measures are between 000 and 360 instead of between 000 and 180? Describe an alternate method for measuring bearings that only involves measures between 000 and 180.

Exercises

CORE

1. Getting Started Follow the steps below to find the bearing of the helicopter from the landing pad.

a. Copy the figure at the right. Sketch ray $\overrightarrow{LH}$ and a ray $\overrightarrow{LT}$ pointing due north.

b. Use your protractor to measure the angle formed by the rays you drew in **1a.**

c. If you placed your protractor on the right side of $\overrightarrow{LT}$ to measure the angle, the angle measure you found in **1b** is the bearing. If you placed the protractor on the left side of $\overrightarrow{LT}$, subtract the measure from 360° to find the bearing. Write your answer as a three-digit number, and remember that bearings are not expressed in degrees.

Use a protractor to measure each bearing.

2. the treasure from the ship
3. the giant squid from the treasure
4. the ship from the whirlpool
5. the whirlpool from the giant squid

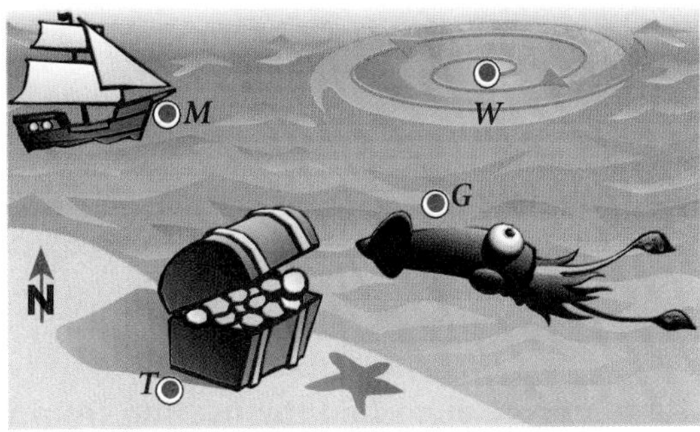

A forest ranger spots plumes of smoke having each of the following bearings. Give the compass direction to the fire.

6. 090 **7.** 180 **8.** 270 **9.** 225

10. Name all points on the grid with a bearing of 045 from point *M*.

11. Name all points on the grid whose bearing from point *C* is greater than 180.

12. Where There's Smoke . . . A forest fire has a bearing of 135 from point *E* (on the grid at the right) and 270 from point *P*. Where is the forest fire?

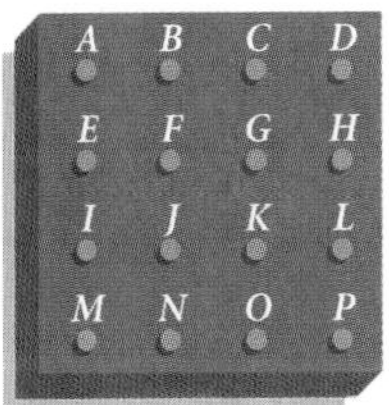

Complete each conditional statement.

13. If an object is at a bearing of 090 from you, then it is directly ___ of you.

14. If an object is directly south of you, then its bearing from you is ___.

15. If an object is at a bearing of 180 from you, then it is directly ___ of you.

16. Water, Water, Everywhere A city aquarium has a tank that surrounds a circular viewing platform. If you face due north, you can see the part of the tank up to 60° left or right of due north. You especially want to see the baby dolphin in the tank.

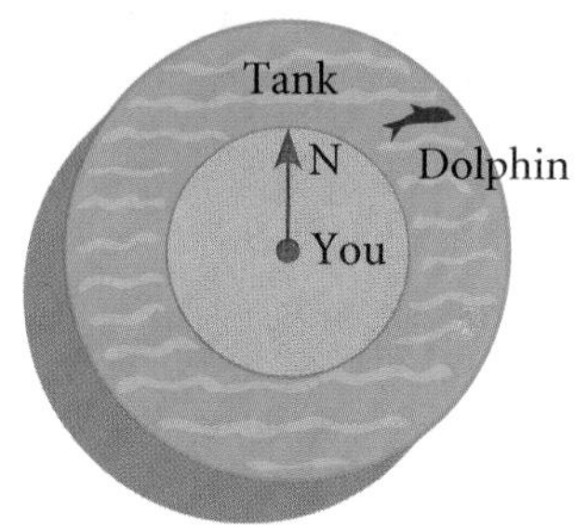

a. What is the range of bearings of the dolphin from you that will allow you to see it?

b. If the dolphin swims randomly around the tank, what is the probability that you will be able to see it at any particular time?

LOOK AHEAD

17. Suppose you take a trip in which you fly 400 mi due east and then 300 mi due north. Sketch this trip on graph paper. Then describe, as accurately as you can, how you could get to the same destination in one (straight) flight. Use any tools that you find helpful.

18. What do you think is the measure of $\angle PQR$? Explain your reasoning.

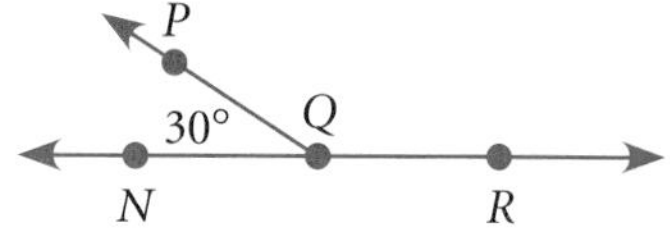

MORE PRACTICE

Use a protractor to find the bearing from the watchtower to each of the following.

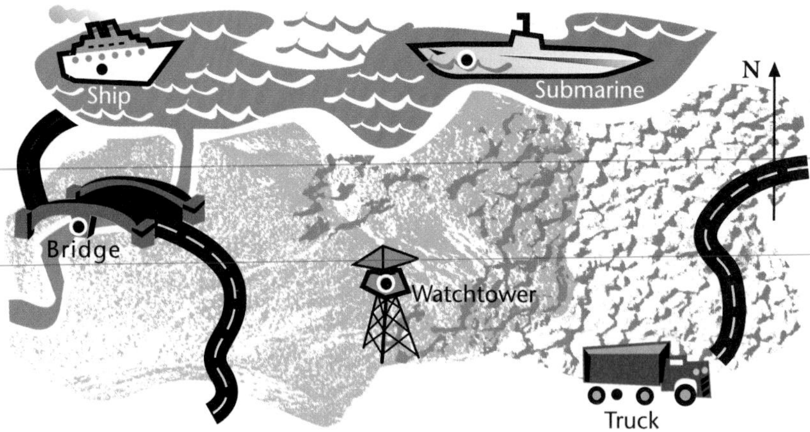

19. the ship **20.** the submarine **21.** the truck **22.** the bridge

23. Measure the bearing from the submarine to the truck.

24. Measure the bearing from the bridge to the truck.

MORE MATH REASONING

25. Is the bearing from one point enough to determine the exact position of an object? Why or why not? If not, what additional information do you need to determine the position?

26. Bear Mountain Suppose you are flying an airplane near a large mountain. You fly only in a straight-line path.

a. At noon, the bearing of the mountaintop (from you) is 000. Later, the bearing of the mountaintop is 180. In what direction are you flying?

b. A while later, you find that the bearing of *everything* from you is 180. Where are you?

3-1 PART C Vectors

← CONNECT → ***You've seen that a ray can be thought of as a figure that begins at a point and travels in one direction forever. Vectors also begin at a point and have a direction, but they do not go on forever. Now you will learn some properties of vectors and discover how vector addition works.***

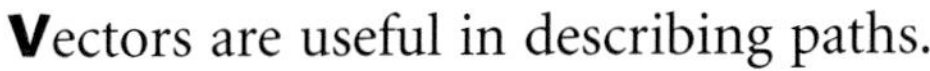

Vectors are useful in describing paths.

DEFINITION

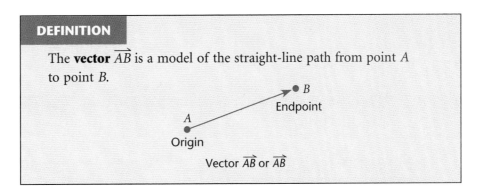

The **vector** $\overrightarrow{AB}$ is a model of the straight-line path from point A to point B.

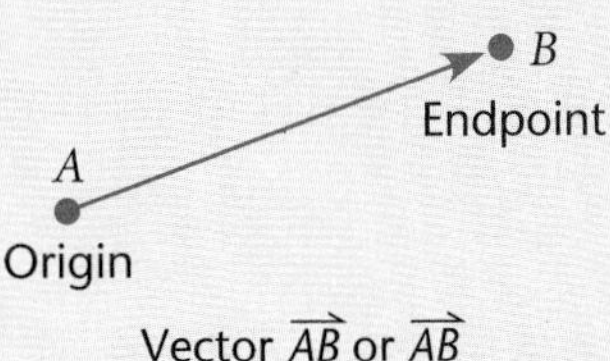

In other words, a vector is a "directed" line segment—we begin at point A and move in a straight line to point B. Point A is the *origin* and point B is the *endpoint* of vector $\overrightarrow{AB}$.

Beware—a vector is not a ray! Unlike a ray, a vector has both a *direction* and a *length*. For example, the statement "From the school entrance, I went three blocks north" describes a vector. The distance is three blocks; the direction is north.

The **length** of $\overrightarrow{AB}$ is the distance between A and B. The **direction** of a vector is measured counterclockwise from the horizontal (the positive x-axis). Two different vectors are **equal vectors** if they have the same direction and the same length.

EXAMPLE

Draw vector $\overrightarrow{YZ}$ with direction 45° and length 27 mm. Then draw a second vector, $\overrightarrow{EF}$, that is equal to $\overrightarrow{YZ}$.

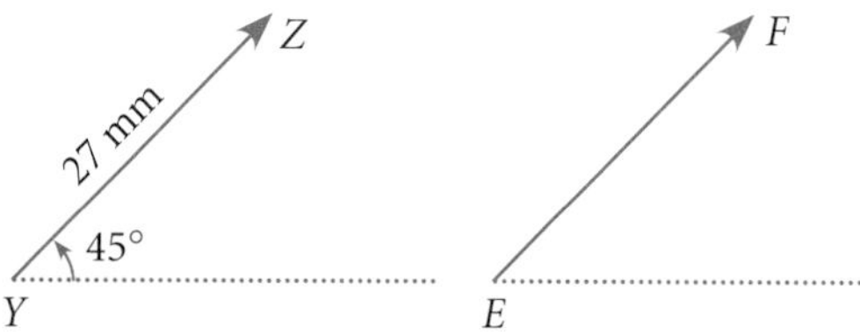

Draw a horizontal line. Then use a ruler and protractor to draw $\overrightarrow{YZ}$ with the correct length and direction. Repeat the process to draw $\overrightarrow{EF}$.

1. In the example above, vectors $\overrightarrow{YZ}$ and $\overrightarrow{EF}$ are equal. What else appears to be true about $\overrightarrow{YZ}$ and $\overrightarrow{EF}$?

TRY IT

a. Use your protractor and ruler to find the length and direction of $\overrightarrow{VW}$. Then draw vector $\overrightarrow{PQ}$, which is equal to $\overrightarrow{VW}$.

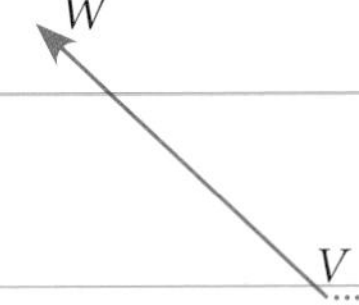

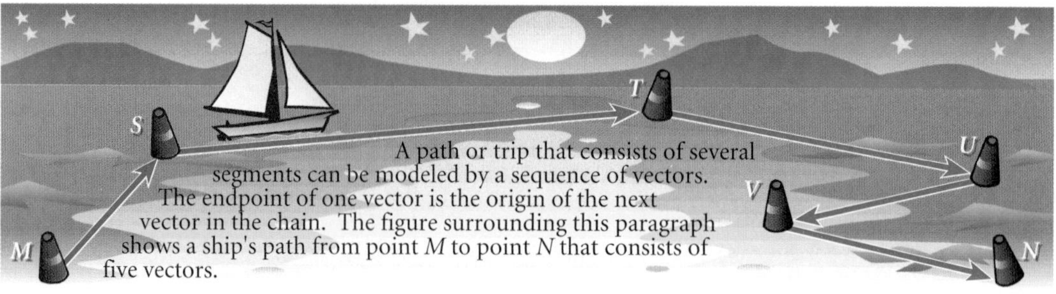

A path or trip that consists of several segments can be modeled by a sequence of vectors. The endpoint of one vector is the origin of the next vector in the chain. The figure surrounding this paragraph shows a ship's path from point M to point N that consists of five vectors.

EXPLORE: A MATH PATH

1. Draw two points, A and M, and a path from A to M consisting of any number of vectors. What is the *shortest* path from A to M?
2. A **vector sum,** $\overrightarrow{XY} + \overrightarrow{YZ}$, means the vector $\overrightarrow{XY}$ followed by the vector $\overrightarrow{YZ}$. (Note: Equal vector sums start and end in the same location, although the paths they use to get to that location may be different.) Write your trip in Step 1 as a vector sum. Then write a single vector that the sum is equal to. Your vector equation should be similar to the one shown.

   $\overrightarrow{AB} + \overrightarrow{BC} + \overrightarrow{CD} + \ldots = \underline{\quad}$

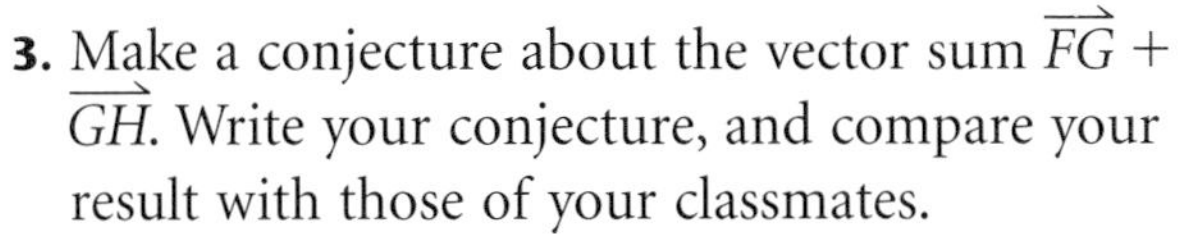

3. Make a conjecture about the vector sum $\overrightarrow{FG} + \overrightarrow{GH}$. Write your conjecture, and compare your result with those of your classmates.

An important property of vector addition is summarized below.

For vector sums, the following is true: $\overrightarrow{XY} + \overrightarrow{YZ} = \overrightarrow{XZ}$.

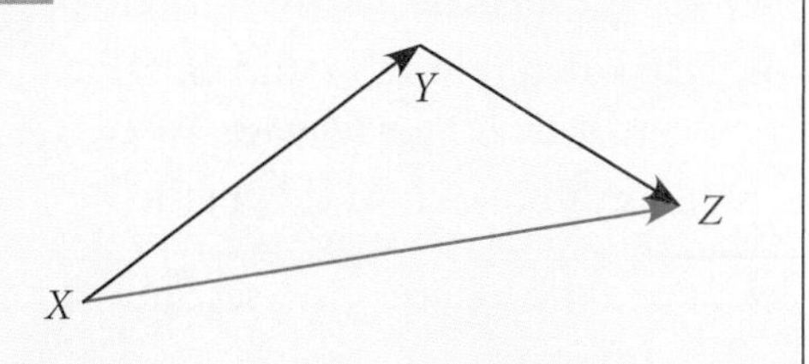

REFLECT

1. How is a vector similar to a ray? How is a vector different from a ray?
2. Consider a segment $\overline{AB}$. You can "direct" it as a vector in two ways, $\overrightarrow{AB}$ and $\overrightarrow{BA}$. If you take a trip that has the path $\overrightarrow{AB} + \overrightarrow{BA}$, where do you start the trip? Where do you end up? Can you describe the result with a single vector? Vectors $\overrightarrow{AB}$ and $\overrightarrow{BA}$ are called **opposite vectors.**
3. Write an explanation of the difference between how vectors are measured and how bearings are measured. Include symbols and drawings in your explanation.

Exercises

CORE

Getting Started Write the name of each vector. Then use a ruler and protractor to find its direction and length.

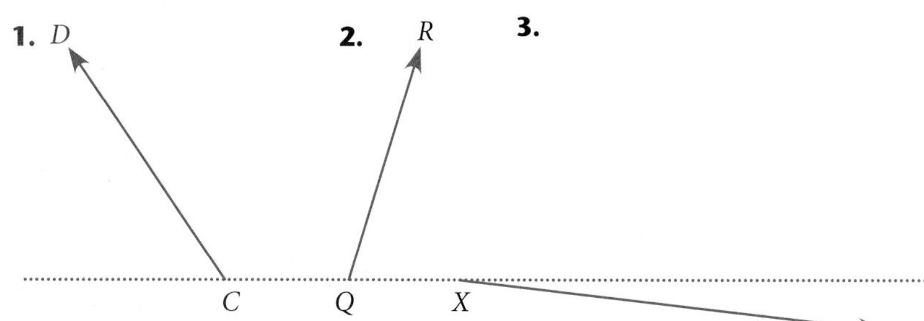

4. Draw vector $\overrightarrow{AB}$ with direction 80° and length 4 cm. Then draw a second vector, $\overrightarrow{EF}$, that is equal to $\overrightarrow{AB}$. Explain why the vectors are equal.

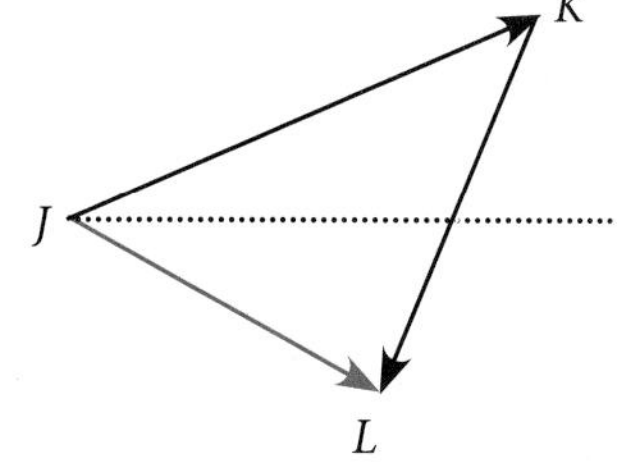

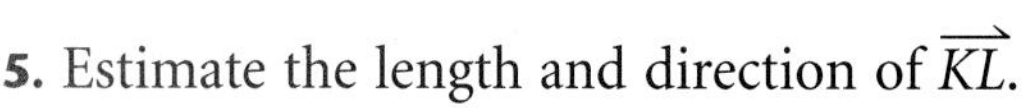

5. Estimate the length and direction of $\overrightarrow{KL}$.

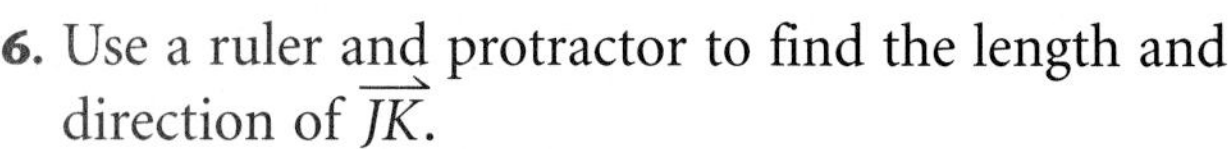

6. Use a ruler and protractor to find the length and direction of $\overrightarrow{JK}$.

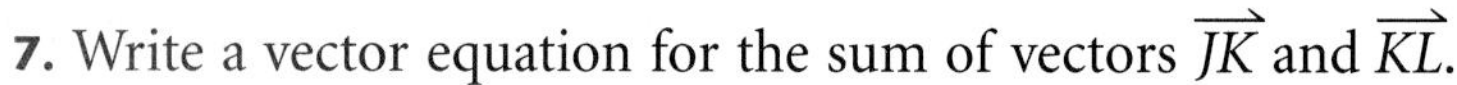

7. Write a vector equation for the sum of vectors $\overrightarrow{JK}$ and $\overrightarrow{KL}$.

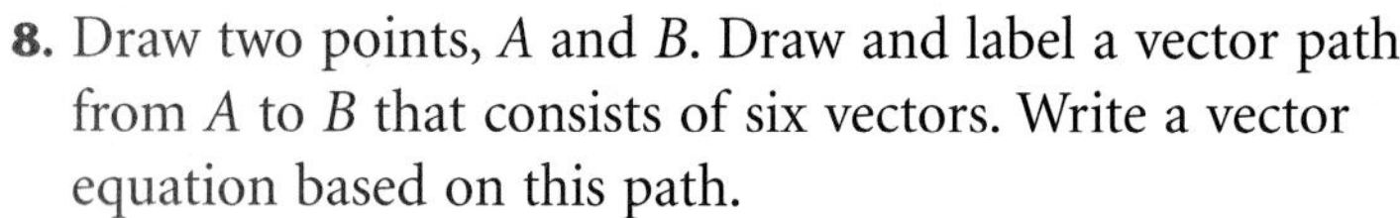

8. Draw two points, A and B. Draw and label a vector path from A to B that consists of six vectors. Write a vector equation based on this path.

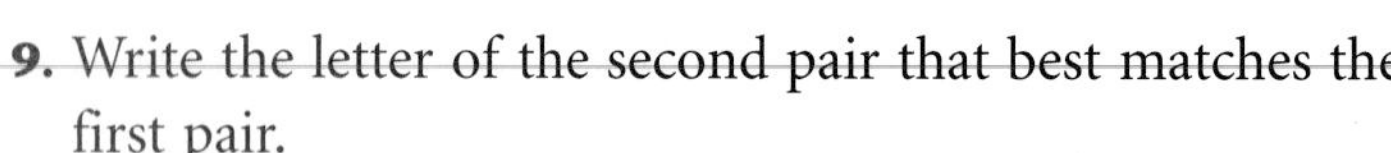

9. Write the letter of the second pair that best matches the first pair.

   Vector: ray as (a) direction: length, (b) segment: line, (c) segment: length, (d) angle: interior

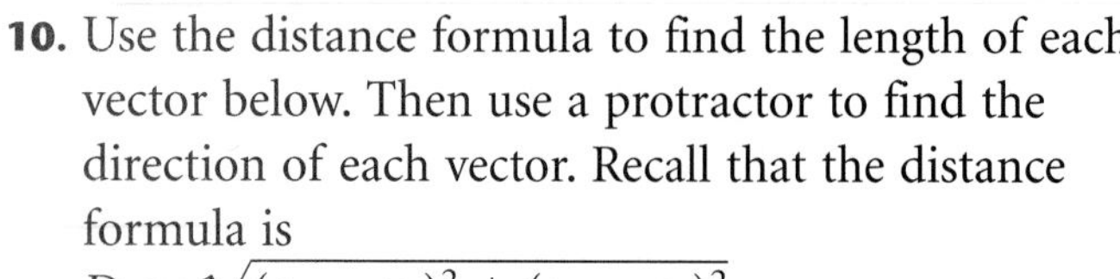

10. Use the distance formula to find the length of each vector below. Then use a protractor to find the direction of each vector. Recall that the distance formula is
    $D = \sqrt{(x_1 - x_2)^2 + (y_1 - y_2)^2}$.

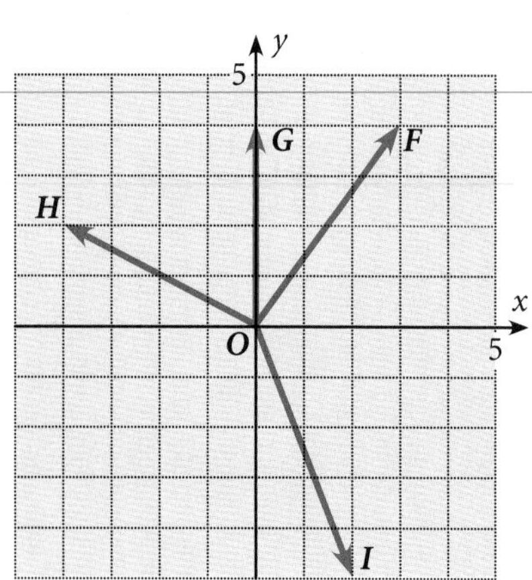

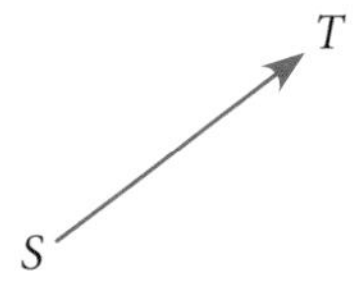

11. a. In the figure, vector $\overrightarrow{ST}$ has direction 30° and length 50 units. What is the length and direction of the vector $\overrightarrow{TS}$?

b. Vectors like $\overrightarrow{ST}$ and $\overrightarrow{TS}$ are **opposite vectors.** Make a generalization about opposite vectors based on **11a.** Write a short paragraph justifying your idea.

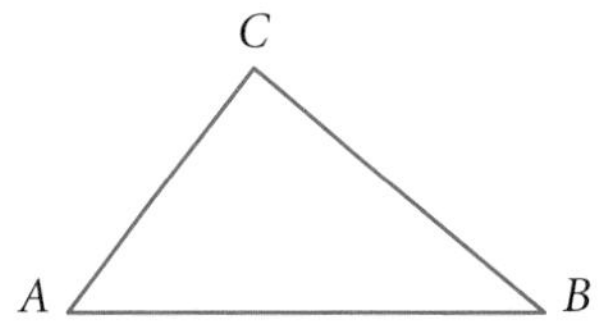

12. You can assign vectors to the sides of geometric figures. For example, in triangle *ABC*, use the sides $\overline{AB}$ and $\overline{BC}$ to form vectors $\overrightarrow{AB}$ and $\overrightarrow{BC}$. Draw the figure and label the vectors. What is another vector you can use to describe the path formed by the two vectors? (Hint: $\overrightarrow{AB} + \overrightarrow{BC} = ?$)

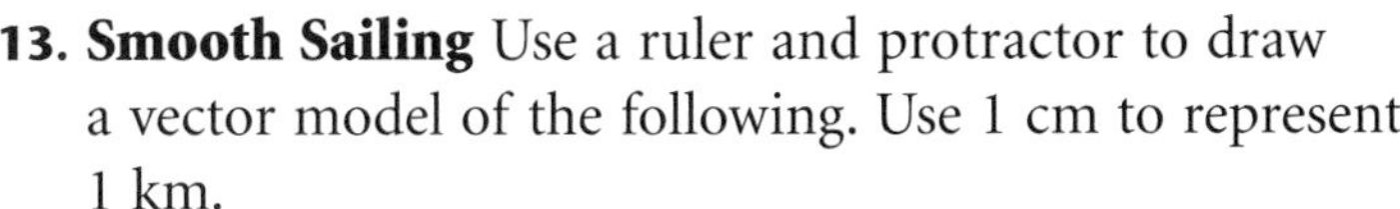

13. Smooth Sailing Use a ruler and protractor to draw a vector model of the following. Use 1 cm to represent 1 km.

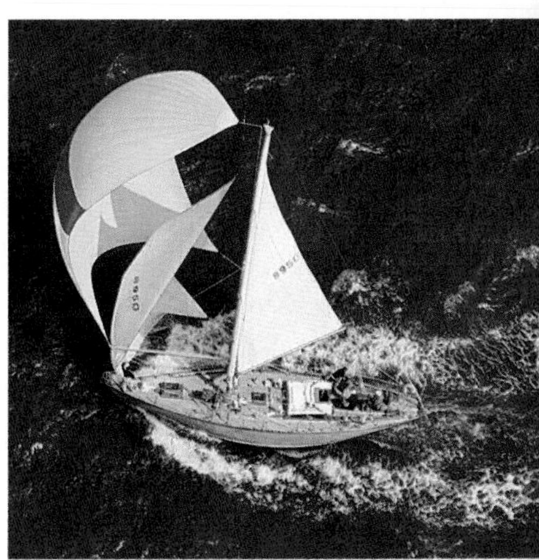

Akeli left the harbor at East Baytown (E) and sailed 3 km east to an island (I). She then sailed 6 km north to Rocky Point (R). She completed her trip by sailing 5 km northwest to Cape Thomas (T).

a. Write Akeli's trip as a sum of vectors.

b. What vector represents a trip in which Akeli sails directly from East Baytown to Cape Thomas?

c. Use your ruler to find the length of this vector. What is its direction?

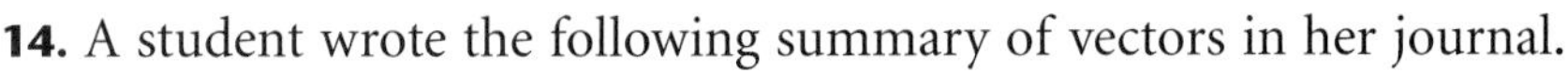

14. A student wrote the following summary of vectors in her journal.

A vector has direction and length. It doesn't matter where you draw it, as long as it has the right length and points in the right direction.

Evaluate the student's summary. Is there anything you would add or change? If so, write your own version of this journal entry.

LOOK BACK

15. Draw a four-sided figure with exactly one line of symmetry. Then draw a four-sided figure with two lines of symmetry. [1-4]

16. List the critical attributes of equal vectors. Then write a definition of equal vectors using "if and only if." [2-2]

MORE PRACTICE

Write the name of each vector. Then use a ruler and protractor to find its direction and length.

17. **18.** **19.**

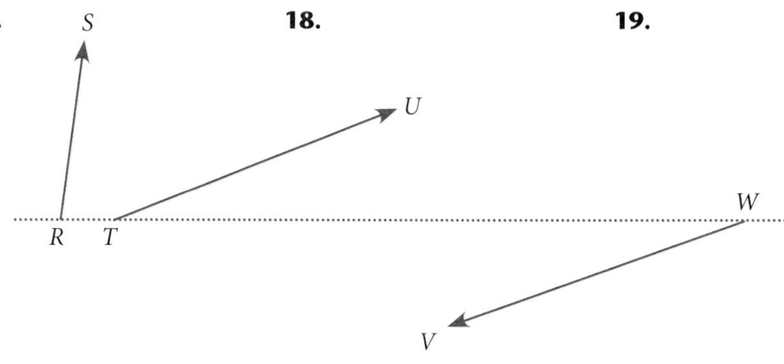

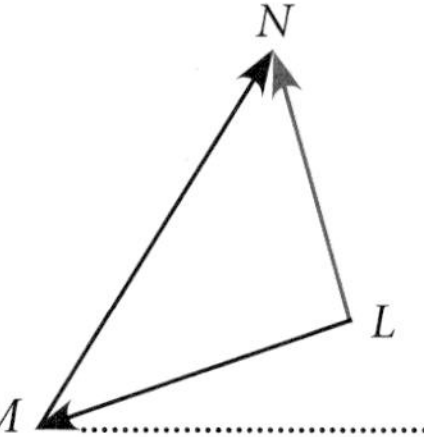

20. Estimate the length and direction of $\overrightarrow{LM}$.

21. Use a ruler and protractor to find the length and direction of $\overrightarrow{MN}$.

22. Write a vector equation for the sum of vectors $\overrightarrow{LM}$ and $\overrightarrow{MN}$.

MORE MATH REASONING

23. Is it true that vector directions add when you add vectors? For example, suppose $\overrightarrow{LM}$ has direction 30° and $\overrightarrow{MN}$ has direction 40°.

a. What vector represents the sum of $\overrightarrow{LM}$ and $\overrightarrow{MN}$?

b. Does this vector have direction 70°? Draw a picture to support your answer.

24. Vectors in Space In this exercise you will see how to use vectors to describe the edges of a cube.

a. Using point A as the origin for your vectors, what three vectors describe the edges that intersect at point A?

b. What vectors describe the other edges of the cube?

c. Name a set of four equal vectors. Is there another set?

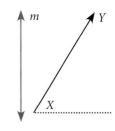

25. Copy the figure and draw the reflection image of $\overrightarrow{XY}$ across line m.

a. Use a ruler to find the length of $\overrightarrow{XY}$. How does the length of the image compare to the length of the pre-image?

b. Use a protractor to find the direction of $\overrightarrow{XY}$. How does the direction of the image compare to the direction of the pre-image?

c. State a generalization about the effect that a reflection across a vertical line has on a vector.

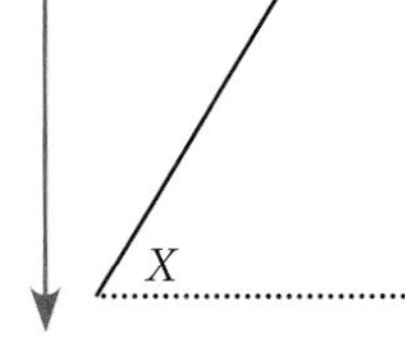

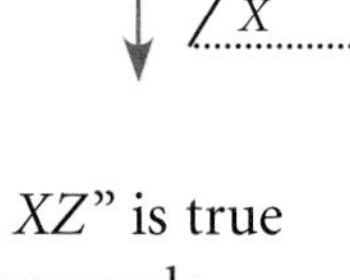

26. Determine whether the statement "If $\overrightarrow{XY} + \overrightarrow{YZ} = \overrightarrow{XZ}$, then $XY + YZ = XZ$" is true or false. If true, explain why. If false, explain why, and sketch a counterexample.

3-1 PART D Translations

← CONNECT → ***You have already explored reflections. Now you will investigate a transformation that is based on sliding a figure—translation. Translations can be described with vectors.***

In 1936, the Dutch artist M. C. Escher studied the tile patterns in the Alhambra, a palace in Granada, Spain. One of the patterns is shown at the left. The Islamic artists who created these patterns (1248–1354 A.D.) used their knowledge of geometry to express their philosophy. Escher sketched many of the patterns in the Alhambra and later created similar patterns of his own.

Transformations are useful in creating patterns. In mathematics, you can move figures any distance and in any direction. This transformation—sliding a figure a certain distance in a given direction—is a translation.

> **DEFINITION**
>
> A **translation** is a transformation that moves all the points in a plane a fixed distance in a given direction.

An arrow can be used to show the direction of a translation. The length of the arrow is the distance the figure is to be moved. Here are some translations of the letter F.

Pre-image and its translation image

F F

Pre-image and its translation image

Since vectors have a distance and a direction, they are often used to describe translations. The **translation vector** $\overrightarrow{GG'}$ illustrates the translation shown below. Its direction shows the direction of the translation, and its length gives the distance each point travels.

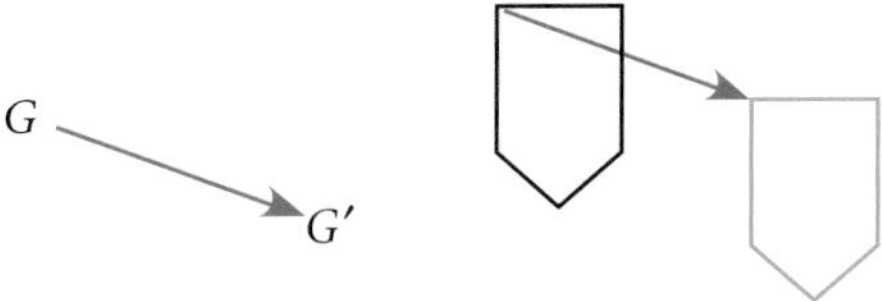

EXAMPLES

For the translation with vector $\overrightarrow{PQ}$, find the translation image of each of the following:

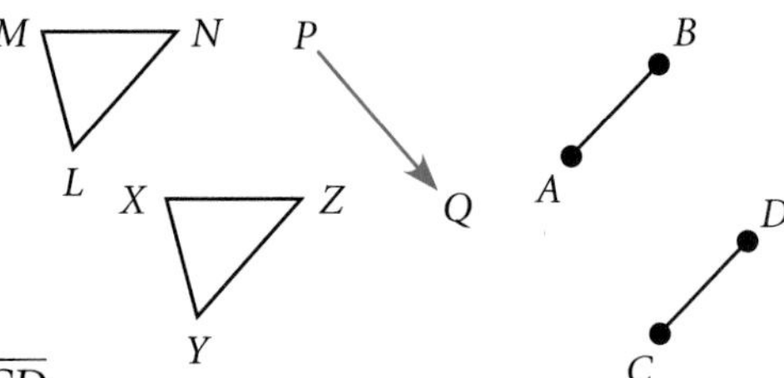

1. point L
2. segment $\overline{AB}$
3. segment $\overline{MN}$
4. triangle LMN
5. point B

1. point Y 2. segment $\overline{CD}$
3. segment $\overline{XZ}$ 4. triangle YXZ 5. point D

You can use a coordinate system to describe translations. In the following Explore, you will learn some notation for translation vectors and discover whether a translation changes the properties of a figure.

EXPLORE: ¡TRADÚZCALO! (TRANSLATE IT!)

MATERIALS

Ruler
Protractor
Graph paper

1. In the translation with vector $\overrightarrow{MN}$ shown at the right, N is the translation image of M.
   a. Copy the figure on graph paper.
   b. Find the coordinates of the image of point Q and the pre-image of P under this translation. Plot these points. Explain how you found the image and pre-image.
   c. Sketch the segments joining each pre-image to its image. What do you notice about these segments?
   d. Find the translation image of any point (x, y) under this translation.
   e. You can show the translation vector $\overrightarrow{MN}$ by writing <3, 6>. Explain how this notation works.

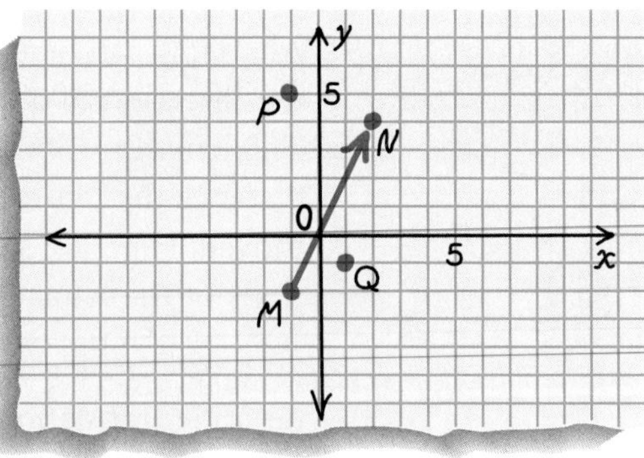

2. Draw a triangle on graph paper, and choose a translation. Then draw the image of the triangle. Use a ruler, protractor, or other measuring tool to determine which characteristics of the triangle (for example, side length or orientation) are or are not preserved by the translation. Make a conjecture about the properties of figures that translations do and do not preserve.

TRY IT

a. The translation image of $A(4, -2)$ is $B(5, 2)$. Give the translation vector and the coordinates of the image of $C(-1, 4)$.

The properties of a figure that translations do and do not preserve are summarized below.

> Translations **change** only the location of a figure.
>
> Translations **preserve** any property that has to do with the size of a figure, including
> - the lengths of its sides
> - the measures of its angles
> - the area and perimeter of the figure
>
> Translations also **preserve** the orientation of the figure.

REFLECT

1. Describe how translations and reflections are similar. How are they different?
2. Explain why vectors are useful for describing translations.

Exercises

CORE

Getting Started For each set of figures below, identify the figure on the right that can be obtained from the figure on the left by one translation.

1.  (a) 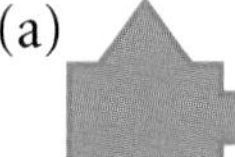 (b)  (c)  (d) 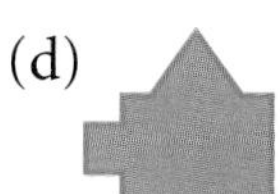

2.  (a) (b)  (c) 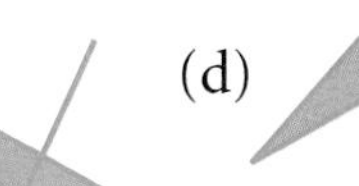 (d)

3.  (a) (b)  (c) 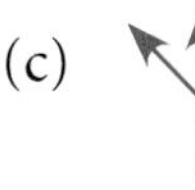 (d) 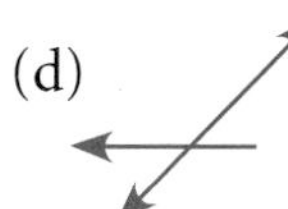

State whether each pair of figures below illustrates a reflection or a translation.

4. 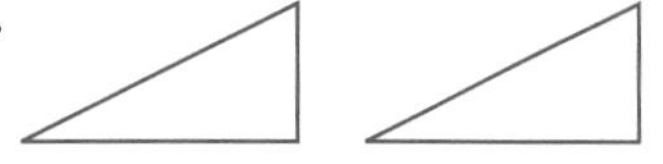

5. 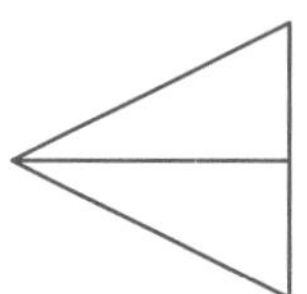

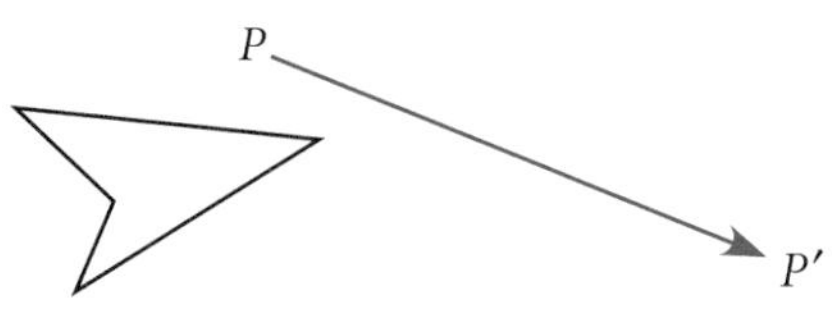

6. Copy the figure and the translation vector $\overrightarrow{PP'}$ onto your paper. Sketch the translation image of the figure.

For the translation with vector $\overrightarrow{UV}$, find the translation image of each of the following.

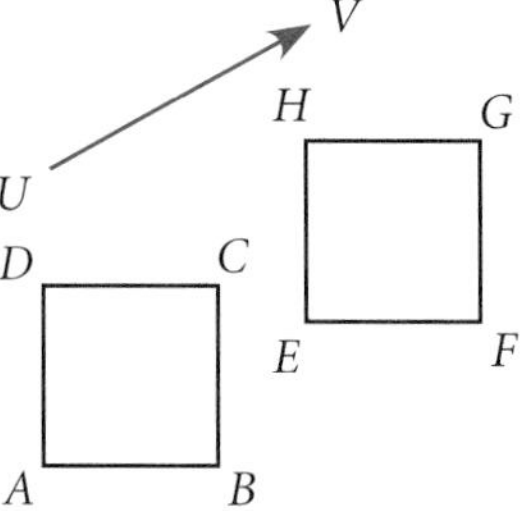

7. point B

8. segment $\overline{DC}$

9. point C

10. square $ABCD$

11. The translation image of $M(-4, 3)$ is $N(-5, -4)$. Give the translation vector and the coordinates of the image of $P(4, 5)$.

Suppose the points on the graph are translated using translation vector $\overrightarrow{WW'}$. Find the coordinates of the image of each point.

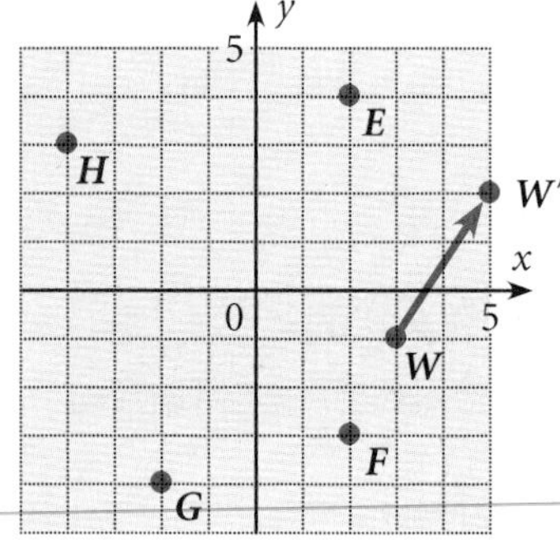

12. point E

13. point F

14. point G

15. point H

16. the point $(3, 1)$

17. the point $(4, -2)$

18. the point (x, y)

19. the segment with endpoints $(-2, 3)$ and $(2, -1)$

20. Suppose the line $y = \frac{3}{2}x - 3$ undergoes translation $<3, -1>$. What is the equation of its image?

21. When you create a pattern by doing a translation followed by a reflection, followed by a translation, followed by a reflection, and so on, you have made a **glide-reflection** pattern. Many artists have used glide reflections to create patterns. Footprints are an example of a glide-reflection pattern.

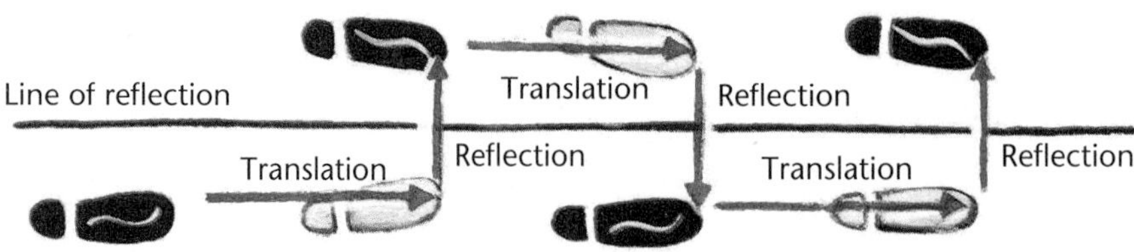

Copy the two figures at the right onto graph paper. As explained at the bottom of page 174, each figure is the glide-reflection image of the other. Sketch three more glide-reflection figures.

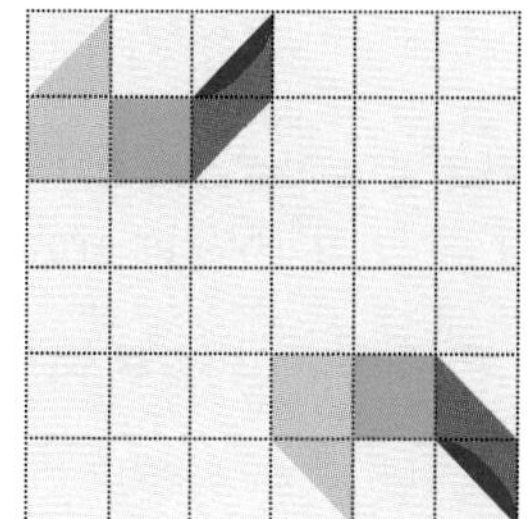

LOOK AHEAD

Using your protractor and a compass, draw angles $\angle ABA'$ with the given measures, so that $AB = BA'$.

22.

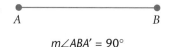

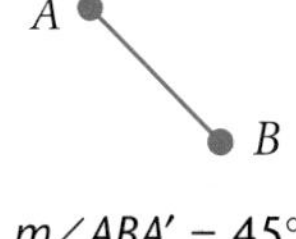

$m\angle ABA' = 45°$

23. A B

$m\angle ABA' = 90°$

24.

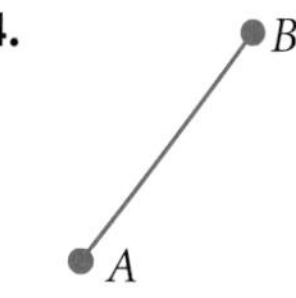

$m\angle ABA' = 60°$

25. If you spin so that you end up facing the opposite direction ($\frac{1}{2}$ of a complete turn), what would you say is the measure of your rotation? What if you make a full turn? $\frac{1}{4}$ of a turn?

MORE PRACTICE

For the translation with vector $\overrightarrow{XY}$, find the translation image of each of the following.

26. point O **27.** segment $\overline{MN}$ **28.** triangle NMO

29. The translation image of $F(1, -3)$ is $G(3, 2)$. Give the translation vector and the coordinates of the image of $H(-3, 0)$.

Y R Q X O P N M

Suppose the points on the graph are translated using translation vector $\overrightarrow{AA'}$. Find the coordinates of the image of each point.

30. point T **31.** point U **32.** point V

33. point W **34.** the point $(0, -5)$ **35.** the point (x, y)

36. the segment with endpoints $(1, 0)$ and $(4, -3)$

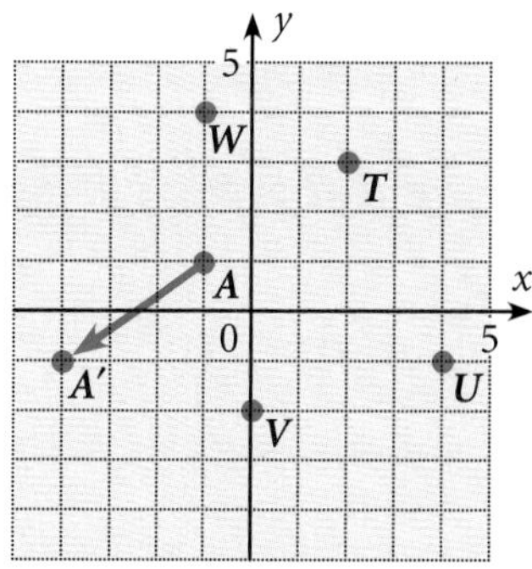

MORE MATH REASONING

37. On a coordinate plane, $\overrightarrow{PQ}$ is a translation vector, where P is (a, b), and Q is (t, u). What are the coordinates of the translation image of point $R(c, d)$?

38. Summing It Up Copy the figure below on graph paper.

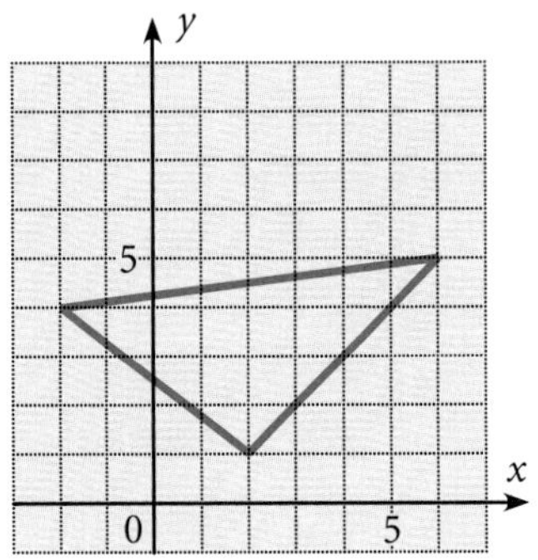

a. Locate the vertices of the image of the triangle after a translation with vector $<-6, -5>$ followed by a translation with vector $<14, 3>$. Create the translated image by connecting the vertices.

b. Give the vector for the single translation that is equivalent to the two translations above.

c. Make a conjecture: A translation with vector $\overrightarrow{AB}$ followed by a translation with vector $\overrightarrow{BC}$ is equivalent to ____.

d. Have you seen a property similar to the one you discovered in **38c**? If so, identify it, and explain why the connection makes sense.

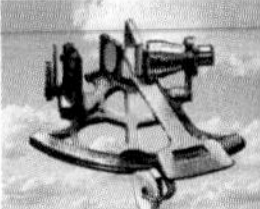

3-1 PART E Making Connections

← CONNECT → ***Angles, bearings, vectors, and translations are important for anyone who needs to describe positions. You have learned how to describe and measure each of these.***

The concepts of angles, bearings, vectors, and translations are useful in navigation because they are well suited to describing positions, directions, and paths. In the following Explore, you will use these concepts to discuss Magellan's route.

EXPLORE: TRAVELS WITH MAGELLAN

Revisit Magellan's route shown on the map on page 155.

1. Describe Magellan's route using the language of rays and angles.
2. Describe Magellan's route using the language of bearings.
3. Describe Magellan's route using the language of vectors and translations.
4. Which of the above do you think provides the best description of Magellan's route? Would it be helpful to use the vocabulary and ideas of **1–3** above in some combination? If so, how?

World Map by Battista Agnese. Courtesy of the John Carter Brown Library at Brown University.

REFLECT

1. Draw a visual summary of rays, angles, bearings, and vectors. Include any information you need to be able to tell them apart. Also include a verbal description of how they are measured.
2. Use the map of the Mediterranean to plot a ship's course from Athens to Rome. The course should use only straight segments and need not be the shortest one possible. Describe the course as accurately as possible, using rays, angles, bearings, vectors, or any other concepts.

Self-Assessment

Complete each statement with *always, sometimes,* or *never*. Explain your answers.

1. An angle is ___ formed by two rays.

2. Opposite rays ___ form a straight line.

3. An acute angle ___ measures 90°.

4. An angle with measure less than 100° is ___ acute.

5. The length of a vector is ___ a negative number.

6. A translation ___ preserves angle measures.

7. What range of values is possible for each of the following?
a. an angle's measure
b. a bearing

8. The measure of $\angle A$ is twice the measure of $\angle B$. If $\angle B$ is an acute angle, which of the following must be true of $\angle A$?
(a) It is obtuse. (b) It is acute. (c) It is a right angle. (d) Not here

Determine whether each statement is true or false. If it is true, state a postulate or postulates that justify the statement. If false, state or sketch a counterexample. [2-2]

9. If points X and Y are in plane $\mathcal{P}$, then $\overleftrightarrow{XY}$ is also in plane $\mathcal{P}$.

10. Planes $\mathcal{Q}$ and $\mathcal{R}$ intersect. The intersection of $\mathcal{Q}$ and $\mathcal{R}$ is a line.

11. Any three points can be contained in one line.

12. List the critical attributes of acute angles. Then write a definition of acute angles using "if and only if." [2-2]

13. Suppose you are given the pre-image and image for a transformation shown at the right. Explain how you can determine whether the transformation was a reflection or a translation.

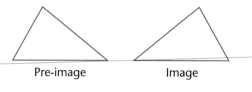

Pre-image Image

14. The graphs of two equations are shown at the right. (Recall from algebra that graphs like these are called *parabolas.*) Find the translation vector for the translation that maps the parabola on the left onto the parabola on the right.

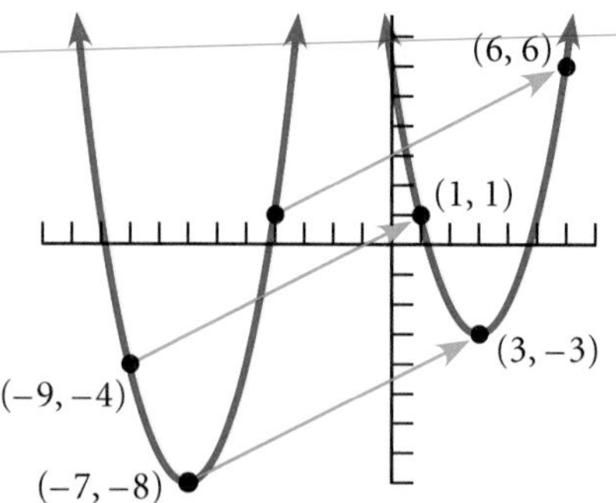

15. Sketch Artist Sketch a tower, airplane, and helicopter so that the following are true. The bearing of the airplane from the tower is 045. The bearing of the helicopter from the tower is 270. The helicopter is closer to the tower than the airplane is.

3-2 Rotations

GEARING UP... OR IS IT DOWN?

The following whimsical passage is an excerpt from *The Way Things Work* by David Macaulay.

ON EARLY MAMMOTH POWER

As far as I can ascertain, the first use of mammoths in industry was to provide power for the famous merry-go-round experiment. The equipment consisted of two wheels, one large and one small, placed edge to edge so that when the mammoths turned one wheel, the other would turn automatically. At first seats were hung from the small wheel which was driven by the large wheel. The result was a hair-raising ride. When the wheels were reversed, the ride was far too sedate. Eventually belts connected to drive wheels of different sizes operated two rides simultaneously, one fast and one gentle. Carrot consumption during the experiment was astronomical.

?

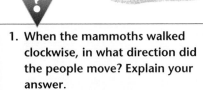

1. When the mammoths walked clockwise, in what direction did the people move? Explain your answer.
2. Why do you think the people were thrown from their seats when the mammoths were on the larger wheel?
3. Name some household items that use wheels or gears.

3-2 PART A Rotational Symmetry

← CONNECT → ***You've already seen figures that show line symmetry. Now you will learn about rotational symmetry.***

When you worked with bearings and vectors, you had to allow for measures greater than 180°. You will also need to do this whenever you are measuring rotations. You probably know that "a 360" is a complete rotation. The basketball player "doing a 360" at the left makes a complete turn in mid-air.

DEFINITIONS

A **rotation** is a transformation that turns a set of points about one point, the **center of rotation.** The pre-image and image of any point are the same distance from the center of rotation.

The **angle of rotation** measures how much a point is turned about the center. For example, if point P is rotated 45° clockwise about center of rotation Q, $m\angle PQP' = 45°$.

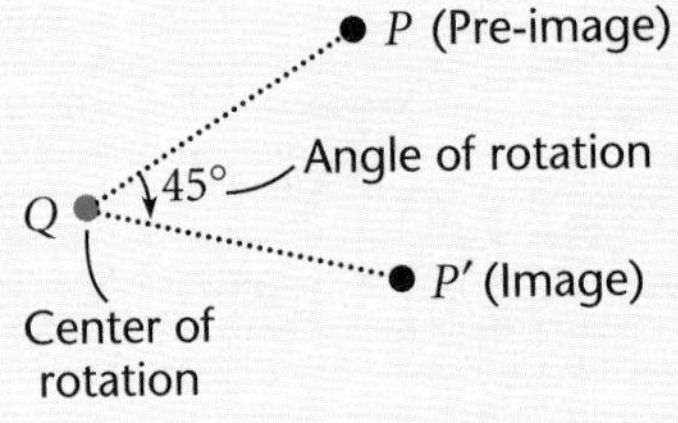

EXAMPLE

Rotate triangle RST 90° clockwise about point C. Label the images of points R, S, and T points X, Y, and Z, respectively.

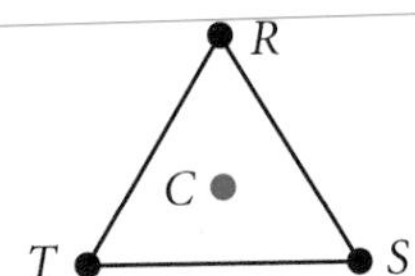

Draw $\overline{CR}$. Then use your protractor to draw a 90° clockwise angle, $\angle RCM$. Measure $\overline{CR}$, and place X on $\overline{CM}$ so that $CR = CX$. Repeat the process for points S and T to find points Y and Z.

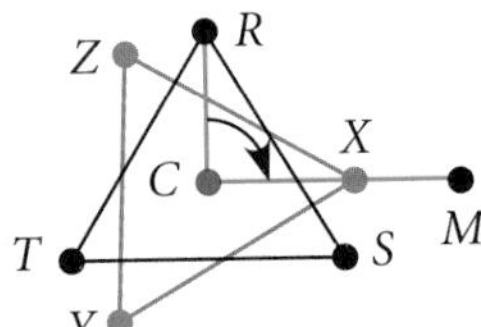

EXPLORE: SPIN IT

MATERIALS

Straightedge
Protractor
Geometry software (optional)

Use paper and pencil or geometry software to investigate rotations of the figure at the right.

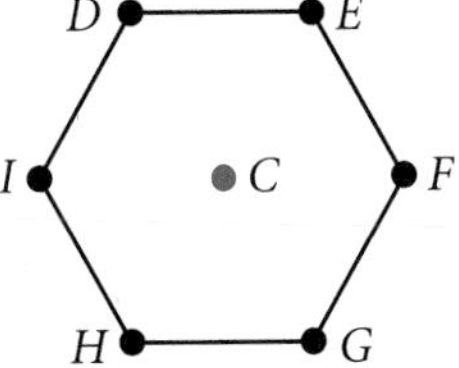

1. Copy the figure and the center of rotation *C*. Then make a rotation image of the figure for each rotation.
   a. 30° clockwise **b.** 60° clockwise
   c. 90° clockwise **d.** 120° clockwise
2. Which rotations gave you an image that exactly overlapped the pre-image? Find all clockwise and counterclockwise angles of rotation between 0° and 360° that have this property.
3. If a figure can be rotated onto itself with an angle of rotation between 0° and 360°, the figure has *rotational symmetry*. Sketch one figure that has rotational symmetry and one that does not. Show the center of rotation in your sketch.

TRY IT

Identify the figure(s) that have rotational symmetry and the clockwise angles of rotation between 0° and 360° that cause the image and pre-image to overlap.

a. 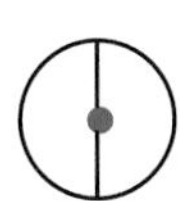 **b.** 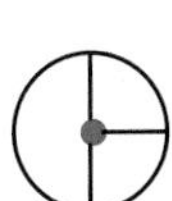 **c.**  **d.**  **e.** 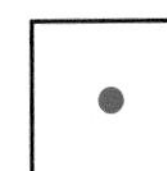

The definitions of rotational symmetry and some associated terms are given below.

DEFINITIONS

If a figure can be rotated about some point onto itself through a rotation of between 0° and 360°, then it has **rotational symmetry.**

A design with rotational symmetry is a **rosette.**

A figure that can be rotated onto itself through an angle of 180° has **point symmetry.**

A rotation of 180° is also known as a **half-turn.**

When a rectangle is given a half-turn about its center point, you can see that it has point symmetry.

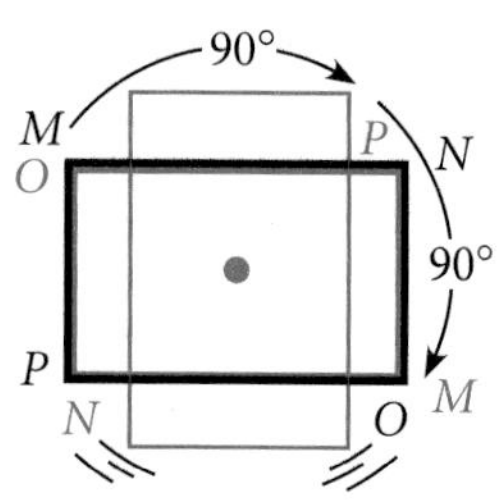

REFLECT

1. Describe the differences between point symmetry and line symmetry. Also describe any connections that you see between these two concepts.
2. Consider two clockwise rotations—one of 40° and one of 400°. How are they different? How are they alike?

Exercises

CORE

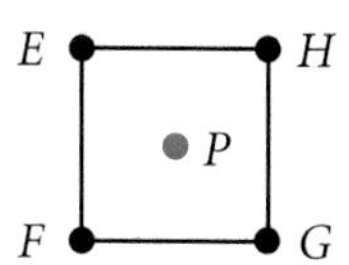

Getting Started When square *EFGH* is rotated 90° counterclockwise about point *P*, it is rotated onto itself. Find each image or pre-image.

1. the image of point E
2. the pre-image of point E
3. the image of segment $\overline{FG}$
4. Which capital letters of the alphabet shown below have point symmetry?

A B C D E F G H I J K L M N O P Q R S T U V W X Y Z

5. Pictures of diatoms, single-celled sea plants, are shown below. Which of them exhibit rotational symmetry? For those that do, what clockwise angles of rotation between 0° and 360° make the diatoms rotate onto themselves?

a.

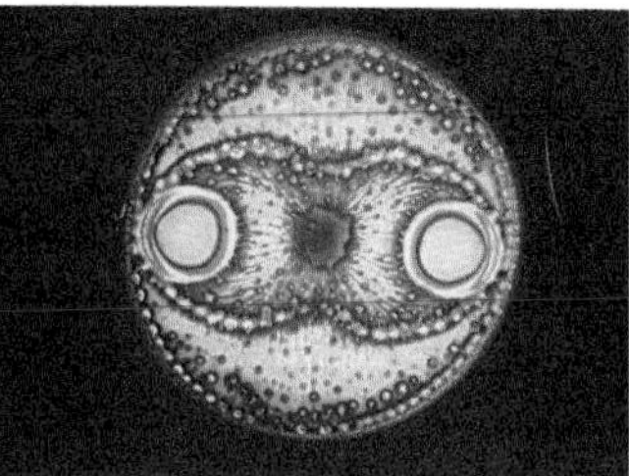

b.

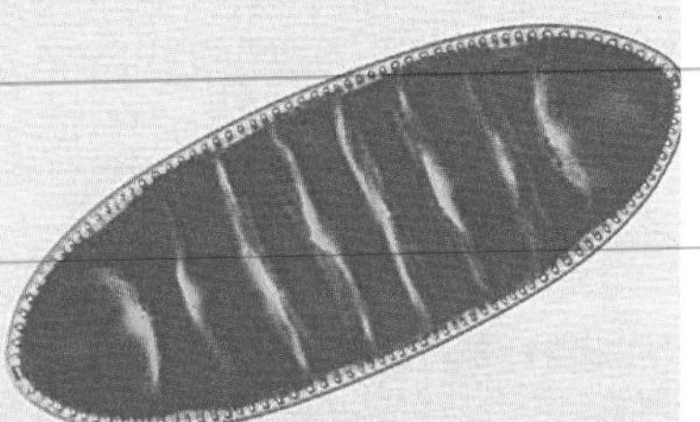

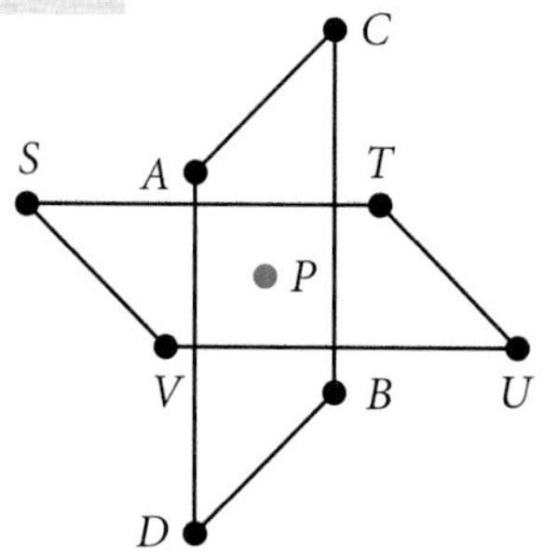

Parallelogram *STUV* is rotated 90° clockwise about point *P*. Find each image or pre-image.

6. the image of point S
7. the pre-image of point A
8. the image of $\overline{TU}$

9. Determine whether the following statement is true or false. If the statement is false, change the underlined word or phrase to make it true.

All rosettes have point symmetry.

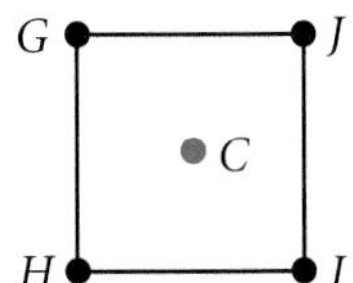

10. Copy square *GHIJ* and point *C*. Rotate square *GHIJ* 45° counterclockwise about *C*. Label the images of points *G*, *H*, *I*, and *J* points *M*, *N*, *O*, and *P*, respectively.

11. Determine if each figure below has rotational symmetry. If it does, give the number of degrees of all clockwise rotations less than 360° that map the figure onto itself.

a. 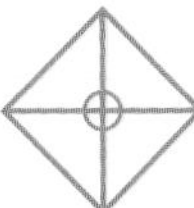

b. 

c. 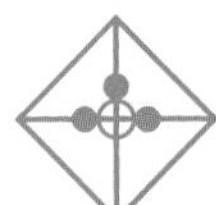

Determine which of these basic geometric figures have rotational symmetry.

12. line

13. segment

14. ray

15. Four cards from an ordinary deck of playing cards are shown below.

a. Which have point symmetry, and which do not?

b. If you choose one of these four cards at random, what is the probability that it will have point symmetry?

LOOK BACK

Sketch each of the following. [2-3]

16. a circle in a plane that is tilted away from you

17. a cereal box

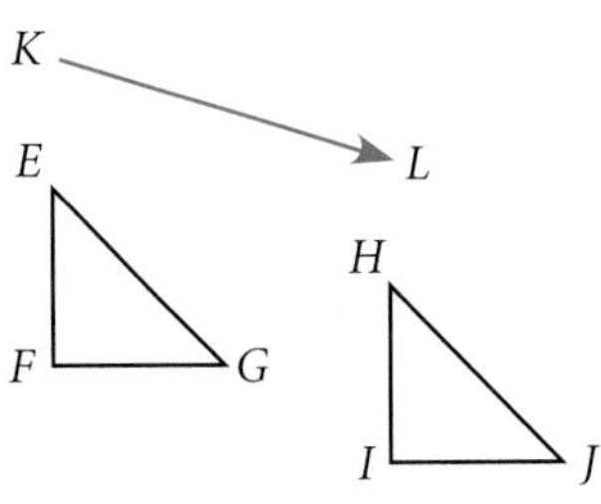

Use the translation vector $\overrightarrow{KL}$ to name the image of each of the following. [3-1]

18. point *E*

19. segment $\overline{FG}$

20. point *G*

21. triangle *EFG*

MORE PRACTICE

When square *ABCD* is rotated 180° clockwise about point *P*, it is rotated onto itself. Find each image or pre-image.

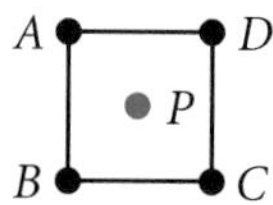

22. the image of point A

23. the pre-image of point A

24. the image of $\overline{BC}$

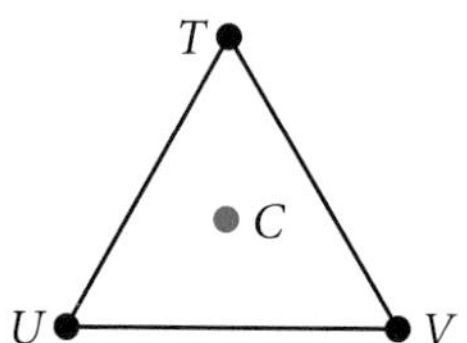

25. Copy triangle TUV and point C. Rotate TUV 90° clockwise about C. Label the images of points T, U, and V points W, X, and Y, respectively.

Determine which of these basic geometric figures have rotational symmetry. For those that do, sketch an example, and give the direction and number of degrees of the rotation.

26. a line **27.** a circle **28.** a 40° angle

MORE MATH REASONING

29. Describe two rotations that each have the same effect as the ones listed.

a. 40° counterclockwise **b.** 359° clockwise **c.** 90° clockwise

d. Make a conjecture about rotations that have the same effect. Explain your reasoning in making this conjecture.

30. Can a figure have rotational symmetry but not line symmetry? If so, draw an example. Can a figure have line symmetry but not rotational symmetry? If so, draw an example.

31. Tile in Style Use the tiles at the right for the following.

a. Give the number of degrees of all clockwise rotations of less than 360° that map one tile onto itself.

b. Sketch a design of your own that has the same rotational symmetries as those you found in **31a.** The design should fit in a square tile.

3-2 PART B Rotations

← CONNECT → ***You've seen that many two-dimensional figures have rotational symmetry. Now you will work with rotations of figures in a plane. You will investigate the properties of a figure that are and are not preserved by rotations.***

The rotations you've done so far have all had the center of rotation at the center of the rotated figure. It is also possible to rotate a figure about other points.

EXAMPLE

Draw the rotation image of triangle *FGH* about center of rotation *K* with a 120° counterclockwise angle of rotation.

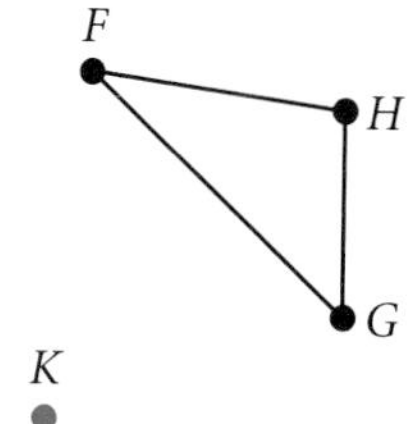

Use a protractor to draw a 120° angle, $\angle GKZ$, in the counterclockwise direction. Then place G' on $\overrightarrow{KZ}$ so that $KG' = KG$. Repeat the process for points *H* and *F*.

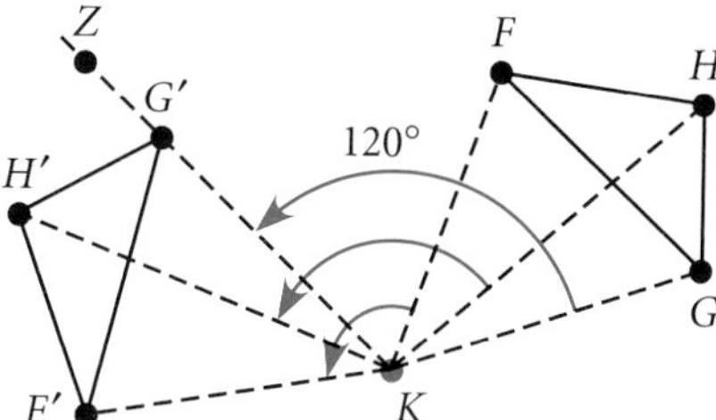

EXPLORE: RECTANGLE ROTATIONS

MATERIALS

Ruler, Protractor
Geometry software (optional)

1. Copy the rectangle *ABCD* and center of rotation *E*. Draw the rotation image of *ABCD* under a 60° counterclockwise rotation about *E*.
2. Use this rotation to help you determine the characteristics of a figure that are and are not preserved by a rotation.

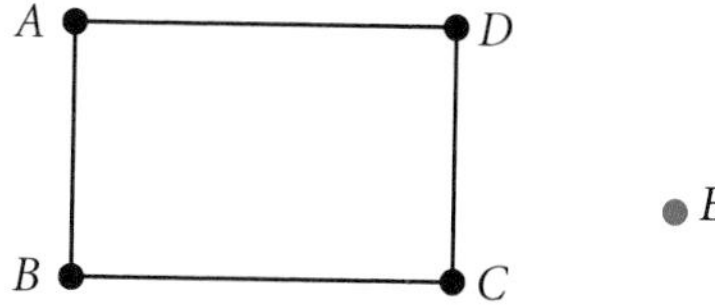

TRY IT

In the figure, $\angle STU$ has been rotated 180° about point V. Fill in each blank.

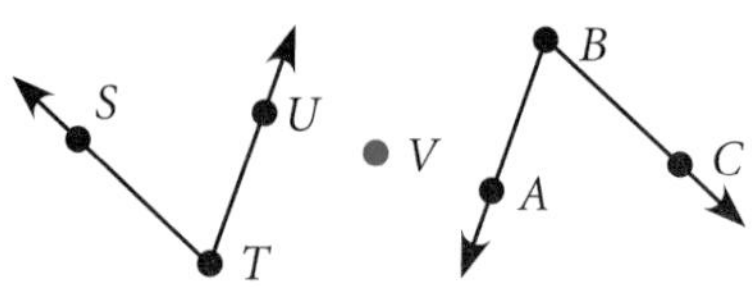

a. The image of $\overline{ST}$ is ____.

b. The pre-image of C is ____.

c. $AB =$ ____

d. $\angle STU \cong$ ____

e. $CV =$ ____

You've now investigated three transformations: reflection, rotation, and translation. Properties of rotations are summarized below.

> Rotations **preserve** any property that has to do with the size of a figure, including
>
> - the lengths of its sides
> - the measures of its angles
> - the area and perimeter of the figure
>
> Rotations also **preserve** the orientation of the figure.

In Chapter 7, you will explore a fourth transformation—the dilation. In Chapter 10, you will see how all of these transformations can be used together.

REFLECT

1. What can you say about a 30° clockwise rotation followed by a 40° clockwise rotation about the same point?
2. Describe two different rotations that each have the same effect as a 360° clockwise rotation. Are even more answers possible? Explain.

Exercises

CORE

1. **Getting Started** Follow the steps below to draw the rotation image of segment $\overline{AB}$ under a 90° counterclockwise rotation about C.
   a. Use a protractor to draw a 90° angle, $\angle ACZ$, in the counterclockwise direction.
   b. Use a compass or ruler to place A' on $\overrightarrow{CZ}$ so that $CA' = CA$.
   c. Repeat **1a** and **1b** for point B to find B'. Finally, draw $\overline{A'B'}$.

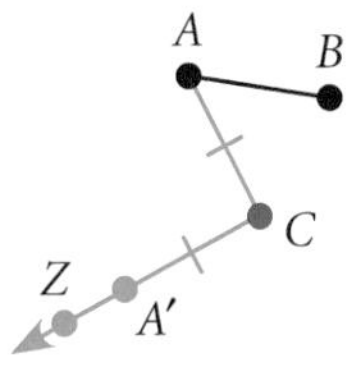

Steps a and b

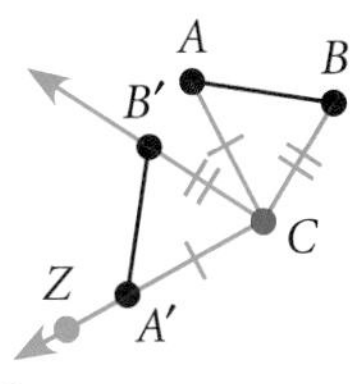

Step c

Rectangle *ZXWY* is the image of rectangle *OPMN* under a 90° counterclockwise rotation about point *C*.

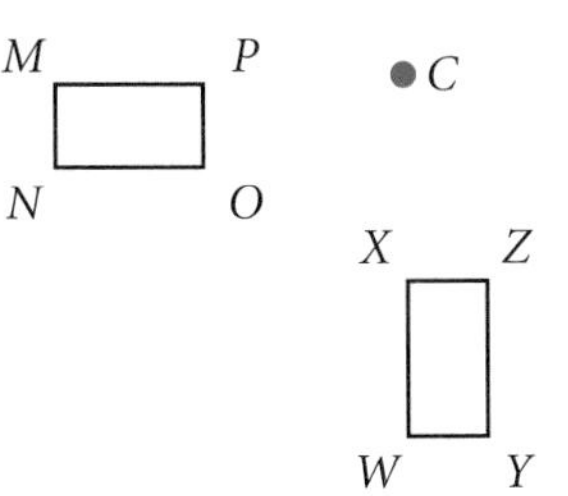

2. Find the image of point M.
3. Find the pre-image of point Z.
4. Find the image of $\angle NOP$.
5. Find the pre-image of $\angle XWY$.
6. Copy triangle QRS and point C. Draw the rotation image of triangle QRS about C with a 120° clockwise angle of rotation. Label the images of points Q, R, and S points T, U, and V, respectively.

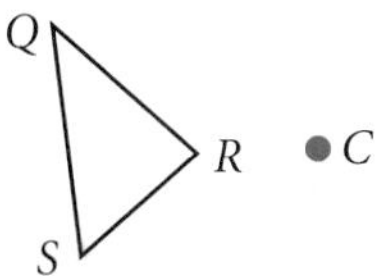

Plot points *C*(0, 4) and *D*(3, 4) on a coordinate plane. Then find the coordinates of the rotation images of *C* and *D* when they are rotated about the origin with each rotation angle below.

7. 90° clockwise
8. 180° clockwise
9. 270° clockwise

10. Make conjectures about the effects of clockwise rotations of 90°, 180°, and 270° on the coordinates of a point.
11. The minute hand of a clock is shown at the right.
    a. What are the center of rotation and the direction of the rotation of the minute hand?
    b. How long does it take the minute hand to rotate through an angle of
       i. 360°? **ii.** 90°? **iii.** 180°? **iv.** 36°?
    c. Through how many degrees does the minute hand rotate in
       i. 30 minutes? **ii.** 45 minutes? **iii.** 1 minute?

LOOK AHEAD

Draw a figure to illustrate each situation below. Include appropriate marks in your figures.

12. Lines *m* and *n* are parallel.

13. Lines *s* and *t* are perpendicular.

14. $\overleftrightarrow{DE} \perp \overleftrightarrow{EF}$. $\overleftrightarrow{DE} \parallel \overleftrightarrow{FG}$.

15. $\overline{YX}$ is the perpendicular bisector of $\overline{ST}$.

MORE PRACTICE

Square *IJLK* is the image of square *QRST* under a 180° clockwise rotation about point *Z*. Find each image or pre-image.

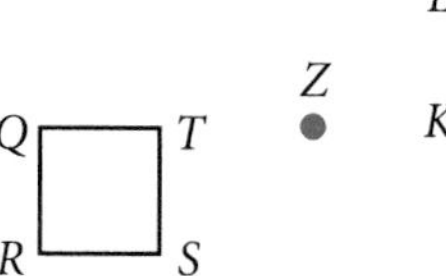

16. the image of point *S*

17. the pre-image of point *I*

18. the image of $\overline{RQ}$

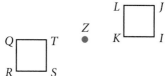

Point *T* has coordinates (−3, 1). Find the coordinates of the rotation image of *T* when it is rotated about the origin with each rotation angle below.

19. 90° clockwise

20. 180° clockwise

21. 270° clockwise

MORE MATH REASONING

22. Geometry Hardware To insert a screw with a screwdriver, do you turn the screwdriver clockwise or counterclockwise? Are there any other tools or household items that tighten or open when turned one way and loosen or close when turned the other? Collect data and make a table to show the effects of clockwise and counterclockwise turns on a few of these items. Make any generalizations that you can.

Item	Clockwise	Counterclockwise
Jar lid	?	?

23. Triangle Twists Suppose a triangle is rotated 180° about the midpoint of one of its sides. What figure is formed by union of the image and pre-image? Does your result hold for any triangle?

3-2 PART C Making Connections

← CONNECT → ***Rotating objects, such as gears and wheels, are critical parts in many machines. You have learned some basic facts about rotations and examined figures for rotational symmetry.***

Many of the ideas you've learned about rotations will be useful in understanding the problems with the mammoth merry-go-round from *The Way Things Work* described on page 179.

EXPLORE: A MAMMOTH RIDE

The figure at the right shows the large and small wheels in the mammoth merry-go-round and their circumferences. (The *circumference* is the distance around a circle.)

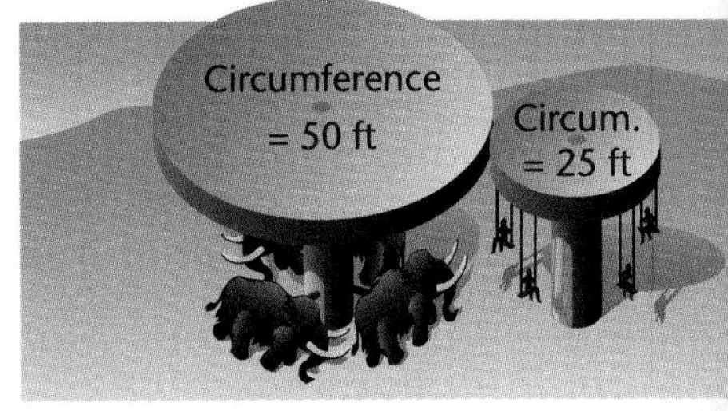

One wheel turns the other by friction: as one wheel turns, it "drags" the other along with it. When the edge of the drive wheel—the one that is powered by the mammoths—turns one foot, the edge of the other wheel also turns one foot.

1. Suppose that the mammoths are hitched to the larger wheel, and the children's seats are attached to the smaller wheel.
   a. If the larger wheel makes four complete revolutions (turns), how many revolutions will the smaller wheel make? How many revolutions will it make if the larger wheel makes one revolution?
   b. If the mammoths turn the wheel at eight revolutions per minute, at how many revolutions per minute will the children's wheel turn?
   c. If Elly (one of the mammoths) walks 60° counterclockwise, as shown at the right, what will be the direction and degree of rotation of Cathy (one of the children)?

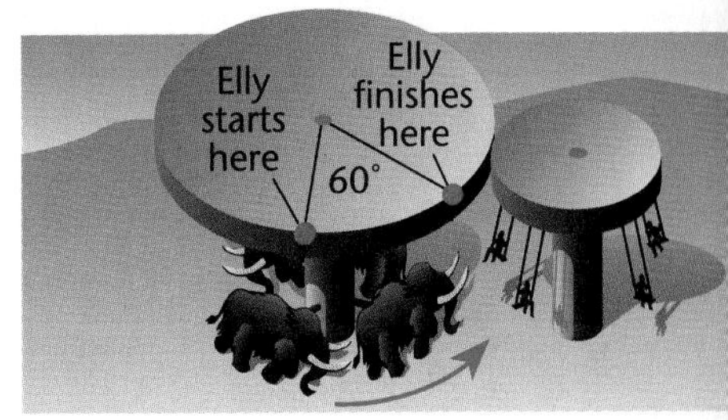

2. If the mammoths are hitched to the smaller wheel, and the children's chairs are on the larger wheel, what are the answers to the preceding questions?
3. Explain why the children were thrown from the wheel when they were on the smaller wheel, but were put to sleep when they rode on the larger one.

REFLECT

1. Describe some other rotations that have the same effect as a clockwise rotation of 30°.
2. Explain the differences between *rotation, rotational symmetry,* and *point symmetry.*
3. Compare the properties of a figure that are and are not preserved by reflections, rotations, and translations. Which properties are preserved by all three of these transformations?

Self-Assessment

1. In your own words, explain the similarities and differences between rotations, translations, and reflections.
2. Which of the following sets of letters form a rosette?
   (a) **TOT** (b) **NON** (c) **HAH** (d) **WOW**
3. Is it possible to draw a triangle that does not have rotational symmetry? If so, draw such a triangle.

Refer to the pentagon (five-sided figure) at the right. A rotation of the pentagon about point *C* maps the pentagon onto itself. Point *P* maps onto *Q*. Find each image or pre-image.

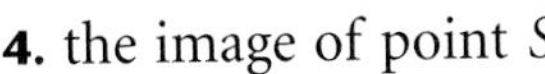

4. the image of point S
5. the pre-image of point S
6. the pre-image of segment $\overline{TP}$
7. the image of $\angle PQR$

Sketch each of the following. [2-3]

8. a pyramid with a square base
9. a can of soda

Use the translation vector <1, −3> to give the coordinates of the image of each of the following. [3-1]

10. point X
11. point Y
12. point Z
13. the origin

14. **A Missing Tooth** Gear 1 at the right has lost a tooth, as shown. Gear 2 slips each time the missing tooth moves to point *A*. If Gear 1 rotates 12° each second, how many times will Gear 2 slip in one minute? Explain.

HEAT WAVE

If you have ever spent a night in a city after a hot, humid day, you know that sundown may not bring much relief. In its Spring 1992 article, "Hot Times in the City," *Exploratorium Quarterly* magazine explains why cities sometimes become "heat islands."

"Temperature maps of most cities on a summer evening show an area of high temperatures over the urban center. The city center can be much hotter than its surroundings...Hot summer nights in New York make the national news as people seek relief from the city-augmented temperatures. In the city, nighttime temperatures remain over 99°F (37°C)—human body temperature. Across the river in rural New Jersey, temperatures drop below 85°F (30°C)."

One reason for sweltering summer nights is that narrow city streets and tall buildings trap and absorb the sun's heat during the day. "The canyons created by the vertical walls in the city absorb more solar energy than a flat or rolling landscape would absorb. The city simply has more surface to catch the light rays.

"When sunlight shines on flat land, some of the light scatters back into the sky. In the canyons of the city, however, light scattered by the ground or a building often hits another building. Instead of escaping, the heat is absorbed. At night... the city's masonry emits its stored thermal energy..."

?

1. Cities are also warmer than the surrounding countryside on winter nights. Aside from the reason discussed above, what might cause these warmer temperatures to occur?

2. Though a narrow street doesn't cool as quickly as a wide one, it also does not warm up as quickly. Explain why this might happen. (Hint: When will sunlight first reach a country road in the morning? a city street?)

3-3 PART A Postulates About Angles

← CONNECT → ***You've learned what an angle is and measured angles with a protractor. Now you will learn and use two postulates about angles.***

Although there are several ways to look at measuring angles, we will need to agree on one method for most purposes.

1. Reggie says $m\angle JFI = 50°$ because $160° - 110° = 50°$. Amy says $m\angle JFI = -50°$ because $110° - 160° = -50°$. Naoki says $m\angle JFI = 310°$ because $360° - 50° = 310°$. Who do you think is right? Why?

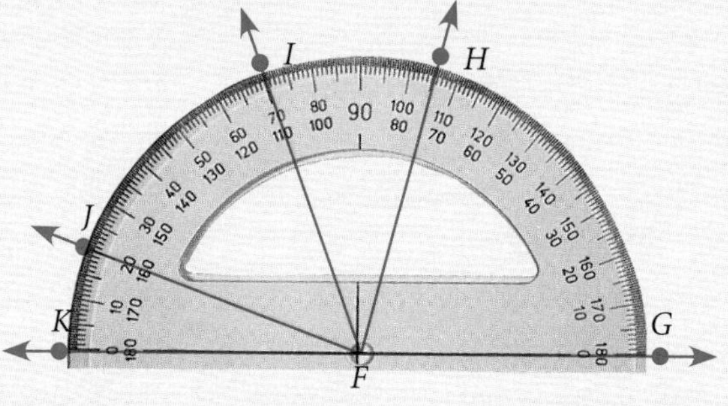

To avoid confusion, we adopt the following postulate.

PROTRACTOR POSTULATE

Given any line $\overleftrightarrow{AB}$ in a plane with point O between A and B; $\overrightarrow{OA}$, $\overrightarrow{OB}$, and all the rays from point O on one side of line $\overleftrightarrow{AB}$ can be matched one-to-one with the real numbers from 0 through 180 so that:

a. ray $\overrightarrow{OA}$ is matched with 0. **b.** ray $\overrightarrow{OB}$ is matched with 180.

c. if ray $\overrightarrow{OR}$ is matched with the number r and $\overrightarrow{OS}$ is matched with the number s, then $m\angle ROS = |r - s| = |s - r|$

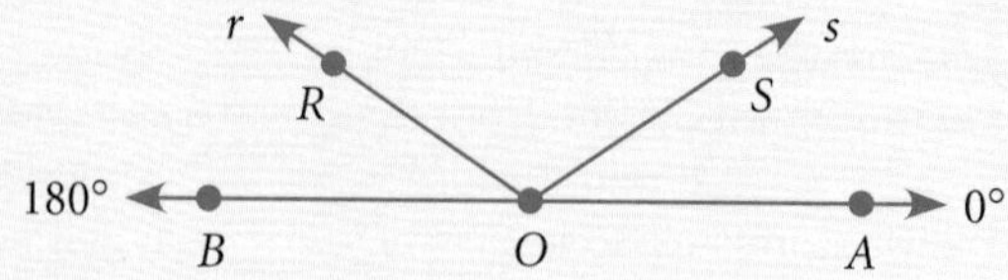

The Protractor Postulate does for angles what the Ruler Postulate does for segments. It guarantees that any angle has exactly one measure. Notice that the Protractor Postulate also ensures that all angle measures are less than 180°. (We will generally use this restriction; however, remember that measures for bearings, vectors, and rotations can be greater than or equal to 180°!)

TRY IT

a. Find the measure of each angle. What postulate assures you that each angle has a unique measure assigned to it?

i. $\angle SAQ$ **ii.** $\angle PAQ$

iii. $\angle VAT$ **iv.** $\angle WAT$

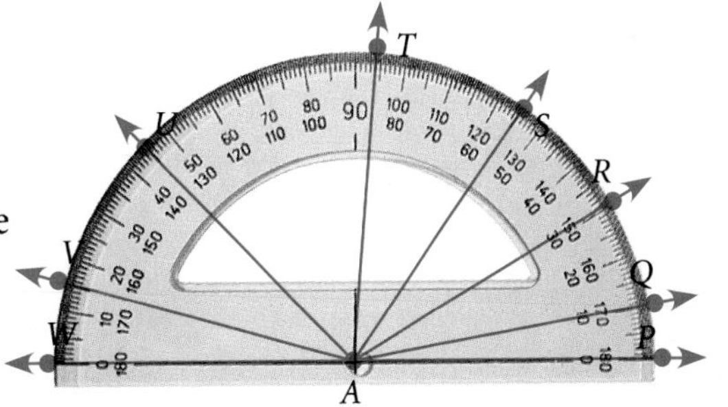

The following Explore will help you to discover another postulate about measuring angles.

EXPLORE: ANGLES, ANGLES, EVERYWHERE

1. Use the figure to find the measures of the angles listed below. (Don't use a protractor—use the measures shown!)

$m\angle AIC =$ ___ $m\angle BID =$ ___

$m\angle DIF =$ ___ $m\angle EIG =$ ___

$m\angle GID =$ ___ $m\angle FIH =$ ___

$m\angle AIG =$ ___

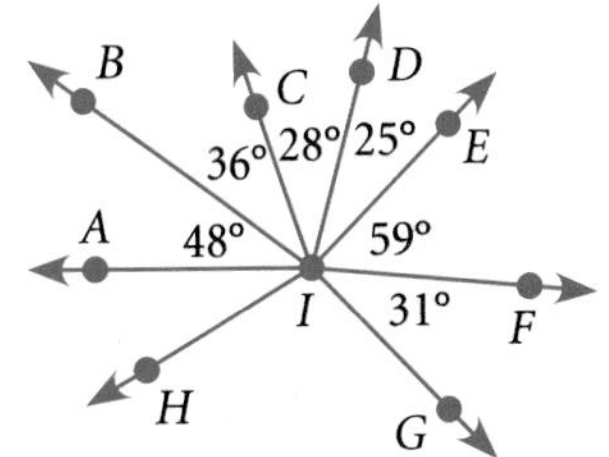

2. Explain how you found the measures of these angles. If there are any that you cannot find, explain why.

TRY IT

b. $m\angle QRP = 45°$, and $m\angle QRN = 132°$. Find $m\angle PRN$.

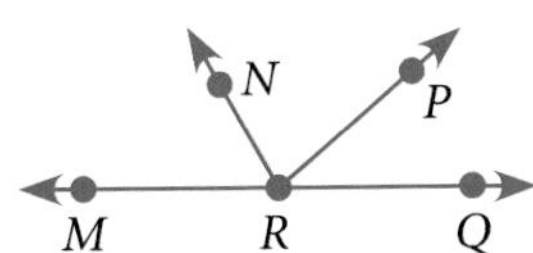

c. Suppose $m\angle BAC = 137°$. Find $m\angle BAD$ and $m\angle DAC$.

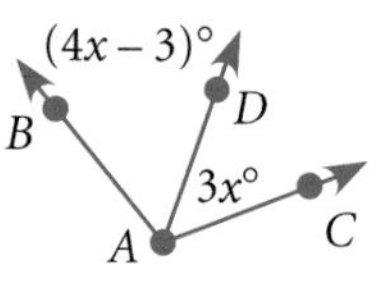

Problem-Solving Tip

Write an equation to represent the situation.

The method you have discovered for adding angle measures is formalized in the Angle-Addition Postulate.

ANGLE-ADDITION POSTULATE

If F is in the interior of $\angle EHG$, then $m\angle EHF + m\angle FHG = m\angle EHG$.

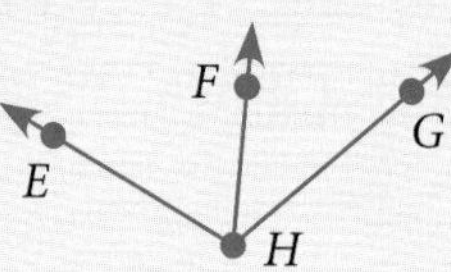

REFLECT

1. What postulate about segments is like the Angle-Addition Postulate? Explain the similarities and differences between the postulates.
2. Explain why the Angle-Addition Postulate begins with "If F is in the interior . . ." Use a sketch of $\angle EHG$ with a point, F, that is not in its interior to illustrate your answer. What requirement for adding segment lengths is similar to the requirement that F be in the interior of the angle?

Exercises

CORE

Getting Started **Find the measure of each angle.**

1. $\angle WXV$ **2.** $\angle VXU$ **3.** $\angle VXS$

4. $\angle UXT$ **5.** $\angle RXP$

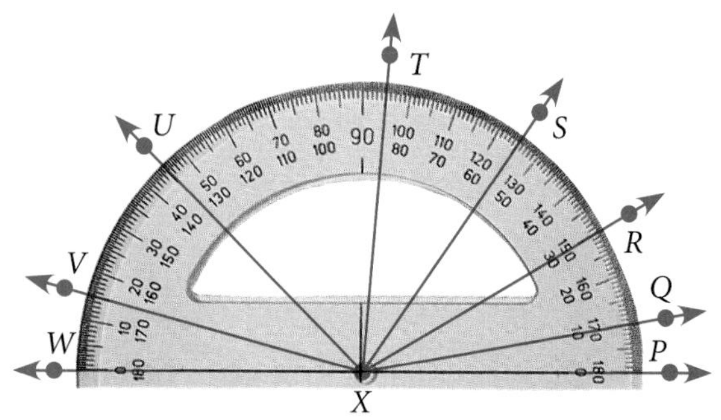

Write and solve an equation to find the measure of each angle.

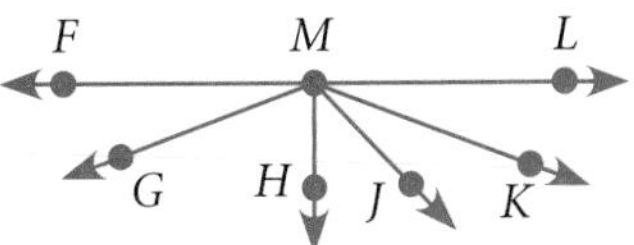

6. $m\angle BCE = 45°$ and $m\angle DCE = 26°$. Find $m\angle BCD$.

7. $m\angle BCE = 80°$ and $m\angle BCD = 37°$. Find $m\angle DCE$.

8. $m\angle BCE = 4x°$, $m\angle DCE = 2x°$, and $m\angle BCD = 24°$. Find $m\angle DCE$ and $m\angle BCE$.

9. $m\angle BCD = (2x + 7)°$, $m\angle DCE = (3x - 11)°$, and $m\angle BCE = 76°$. Find $m\angle BCD$ and $m\angle DCE$.

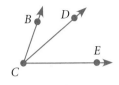

In the figure at the right, $\angle HML$ is a right angle, $m\angle KML = 20°$, $m\angle JMK = m\angle HMJ$, and $m\angle FMG = m\angle KML$. Find the measure of each angle.

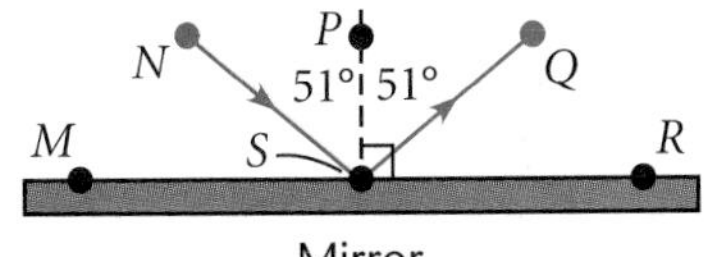

10. $\angle JMK$
11. $\angle HMK$
12. $\angle FMG$
13. $\angle GMH$
14. $\angle GMK$
15. $\angle GML$

A light ray reflects off a mirror as shown. Find the measure of each angle.

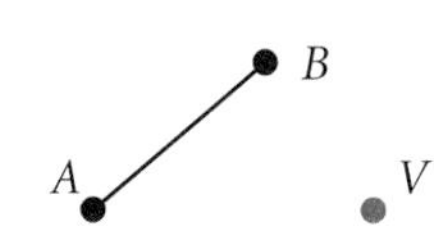

16. $\angle NSQ$
17. $\angle MSN$
18. $\angle NSR$

19. **Don't Scratch the Paint!** A car door is pushed open 35°. An additional push opens the door another 20°. What is the final angle of opening of the door? Which postulate justifies your answer?

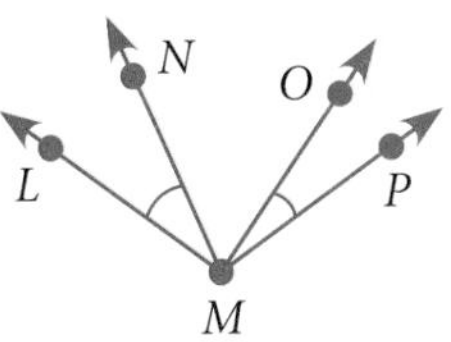

20. Copy segment $\overline{AB}$ and point V. Rotate $\overline{AB}$ 90° clockwise around V. Label the rotation image $\overline{CD}$. Then rotate $\overline{CD}$ 45° clockwise around V, and label its image $\overline{EF}$. What is the angle of rotation from $\overline{AB}$ to $\overline{EF}$? Explain your answer.

21. Using the figure at the right, justify the conjecture "If $\angle LMN \cong \angle OMP$, then $\angle LMO \cong \angle NMP$."

N
O
L
P
M

Sketch each figure.

22. two angles with equal measures that each have $\overrightarrow{AB}$ as a side

23. two angles in which the vertex of each is in the interior of the other

24. two angles that intersect in exactly one point

25. Two sides of a picture frame are glued together to form a corner.
    a. If each side is cut at a 45° angle, what is the angle measure of the corner of the frame? Which postulate or definition justifies your answer?
    b. You need to make a six-sided frame whose corners measure 120°. Explain how you would cut the sides of the frame.

LOOK BACK

Rewrite each statement or set of statements as a single conditional in if-then form. [2-1]

26. The midpoint of a segment must be between its endpoints.

27. All quadrilaterals have four sides.

28. "[Do you] love life? Then do not squander time. . . ." (Benjamin Franklin, *Poor Richard's Almanack*)

Determine whether each figure at the right has rotational symmetry. If it does, give the clockwise angles of rotation between 0° and 360° that cause the image and pre-image to coincide. [3-2]

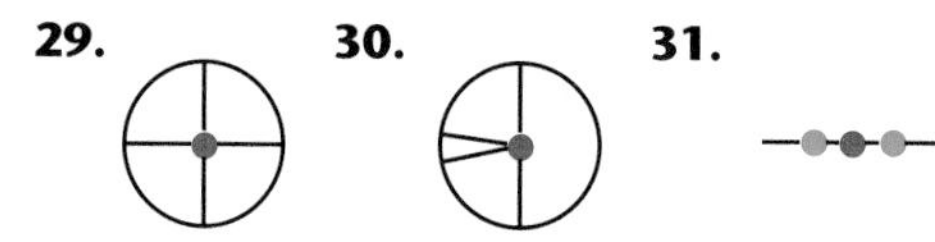

MORE PRACTICE

Find the measure of each angle.

32. $\angle SRT$ **33.** $\angle TRV$

34. $\angle URW$ **35.** $\angle TRX$

36. $\angle SRU$ **37.** $\angle VRX$

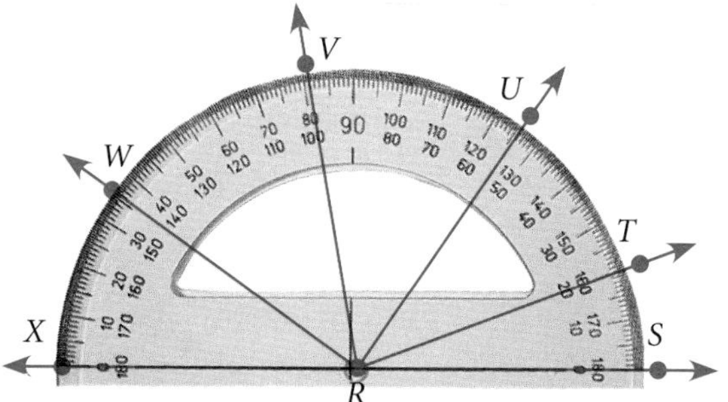

Write and solve an equation to find the measure of each angle.

38. $m\angle BCE = 131°$, and $m\angle DCE = 48°$. Find $m\angle BCD$.

39. $m\angle BCD = (4x + 20)°$, $m\angle DCE = (32 - 3x)°$, and $m\angle BCE = 62°$. Find $m\angle BCD$ and $m\angle DCE$.

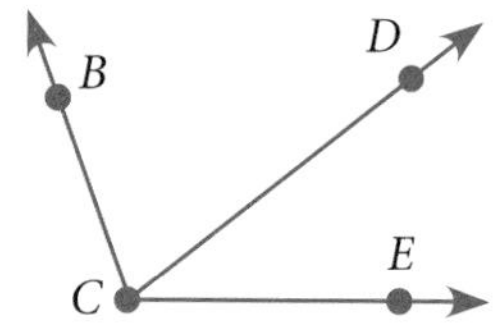

MORE MATH REASONING

40. Angle Time Find the exact measure of the angle made by the hands of a clock at each of the following times.
a. 8:00   **b.** 8:30   **c.** 8:25

41. Tonyetta wondered how many different figures could be formed by the intersection of a ray and an angle. Could they, for example, be drawn to intersect in a point? a segment? a ray? an angle? Try sketching each situation. Determine which are possible and which, if any, are not.

42. Sketch an "angle" that appears to be greater than 180°. What does the Protractor Postulate say about how to measure it?

3-3 PART B Assumptions and Figures

← CONNECT → ***You've seen how assuming too much from a picture can mislead you. Now you will discover the assumptions that you can and cannot make when you look at a geometric figure.***

The Angle-Addition Postulate makes sense, but you must be sure not to assume too much when you use it. For example, you can't say that $m\angle WXY + m\angle YXZ = m\angle WXZ$ unless you know something about the location of point Y.

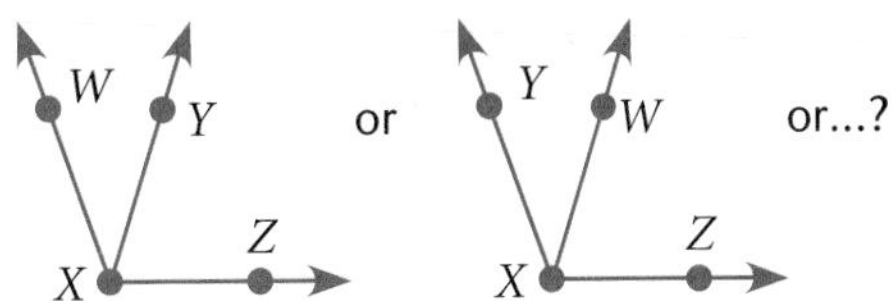

Unjustified assumptions can cause problems in geometry just as they can in everyday life. In a figure, what looks like a right angle might really measure 89.4°. Although this difference may seem unimportant, it is significant when you are placing a communications satellite in space or constructing a skyscraper.

Since you cannot always trust what you see, you must be careful of the assumptions you make when looking at a figure. In the following Explore, you will think about what can and cannot be assumed from a figure.

EXPLORE: TO ASSUME OR NOT TO ASSUME . . .

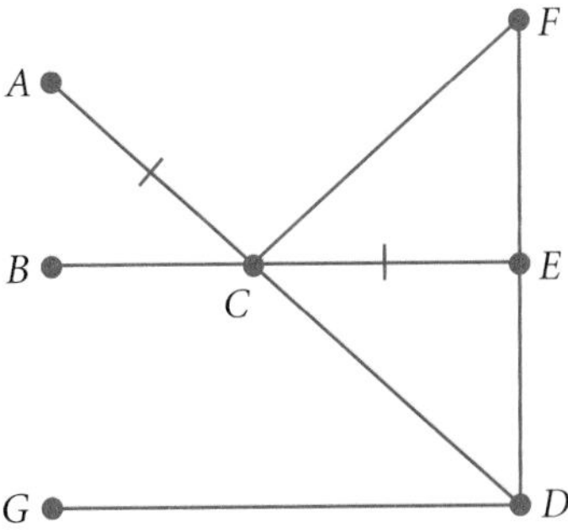

1. In the figure, do you think you would be justified in assuming that B, C, and E are collinear? that $\angle ACB \cong \angle FCE$? that $\overline{BE} \parallel \overline{GD}$? Make a list of things you think you can and cannot assume from this figure.
2. Make a list of rules about what you think you can and cannot assume. Compare your list with others. Then try to make a general statement about what you can and cannot assume from a figure.

The table below summarizes what can and cannot be assumed from a figure.

You *May* Assume:	**You *May Not* Assume (unless marked):**
• Things that look straight are straight.	• Exact measurements and relative sizes of figures.
• Points of intersection are shown accurately.	• Parallel or perpendicular lines.
• Points shown on a line are collinear. Unless planes are drawn, all points shown are coplanar.	• Congruence.
• Relative positions of points are accurate.	

EXAMPLES

Determine whether the following specific relationships can be assumed from the figure.

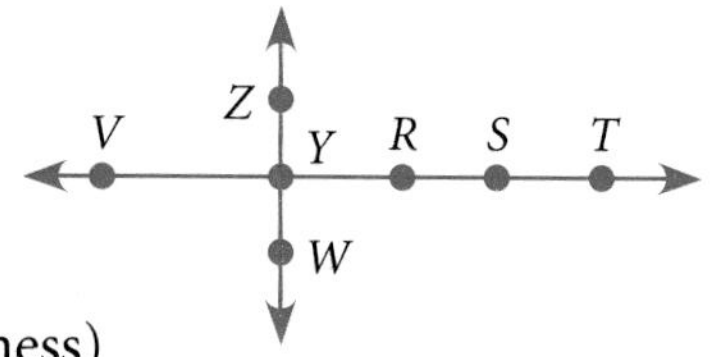

1. Point S is between R and T. (betweenness)
Yes; relative positions are accurate.

2. Points R, S, and T are collinear. (collinearity)
Yes; points shown on a line are collinear.

3. $\overline{RS} \cong \overline{ST}$ (congruence)
No; congruence cannot be assumed unless marked.

4. Point S is the midpoint of $\overline{RT}$. (midpoint)
No; you cannot assume that point S divides $\overline{RT}$ into two congruent segments.

5. $\overleftrightarrow{VR} \perp \overleftrightarrow{ZW}$ (perpendicularity)
No; perpendicularity cannot be assumed unless marked.

6. $\angle ZYV$ is a right angle. (angle size)
No; you cannot assume exact measurements.

7. $VY < TY$ (relative sizes of segments or angles)
No; you cannot assume that relative sizes of segments or angles are shown accurately.

You will soon draw and mark figures to illustrate deductive arguments. The following Try It will give you an opportunity to put together everything you know about figures.

TRY IT

a. Draw and mark one figure that shows all of the following relationships.

On line m, B is the midpoint of $\overline{AC}$.
Line $n \parallel m$
$\angle ABD \cong \angle ABE$

REFLECT

1. Identify the figures that allow you to conclude that $\overline{ST} \cong \overline{TU}$. Explain your choice(s).

(a) (b) (c)

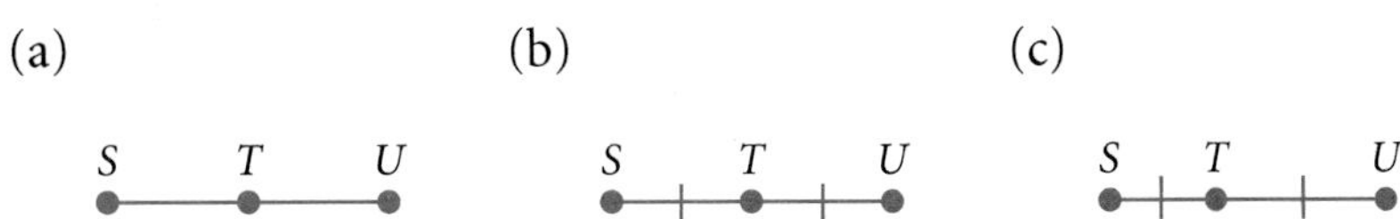

2. Do the guidelines for what you can and cannot assume from a figure make sense? If they do, explain why. If they do not, explain how you would change them and why you think they should be different.

Exercises

CORE

Getting Started In Exercises 1–4, determine whether the following specific relationships can be assumed from the figure at the right.

1. $\overrightarrow{GF}$ and $\overrightarrow{GI}$ are opposite rays.

2. $\angle HGF$ is a right angle.

3. $\overleftrightarrow{FI}$ is a straight line.

4. $\angle GFH$ and $\angle GHF$ are congruent.

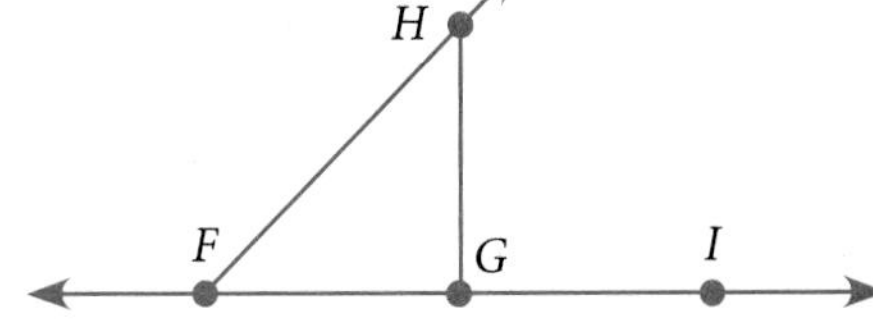

5. Make a sketch of your own that includes points, segments, and angles. Make up three true/false questions about what can and cannot be assumed in your figure, and give the answers for the questions.

Determine whether the following specific relationships can be assumed from the figure at the right. Explain.

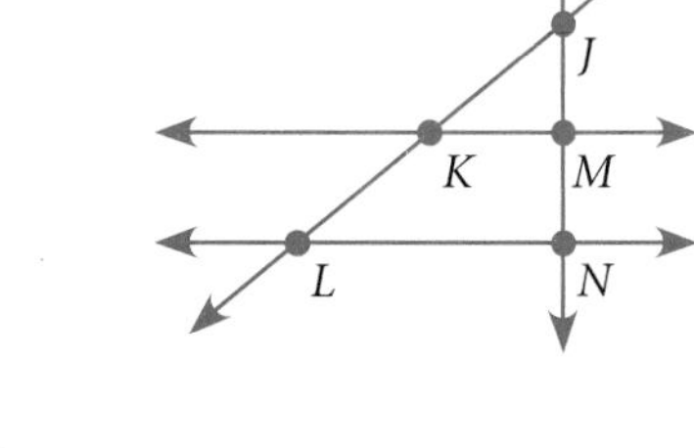

6. $\overline{JN} \perp \overline{LN}$

7. Points J, M, and N are collinear.

8. $\overline{JM} \cong \overline{KM}$

9. Point M is between J and N.

10. $\overleftrightarrow{JL}$ intersects $\overleftrightarrow{KM}$.

11. $\overleftrightarrow{KM} \parallel \overleftrightarrow{LN}$

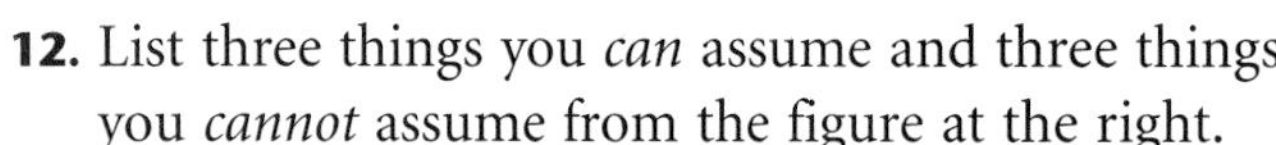

12. List three things you *can* assume and three things you *cannot* assume from the figure at the right.

B
A
C
D
E

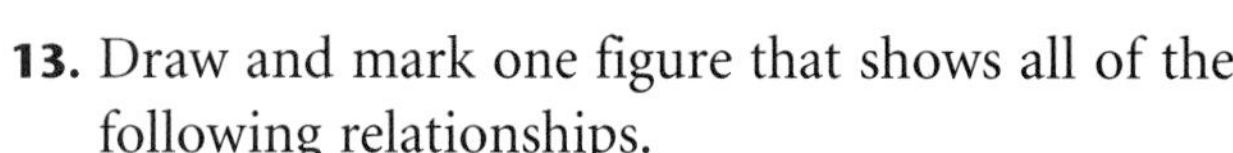

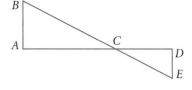

13. Draw and mark one figure that shows all of the following relationships.

    Point M is the midpoint of $\overline{NO}$. $\overrightarrow{MP} \perp \overline{NO}$. $\angle NMQ \cong \angle QMP$.

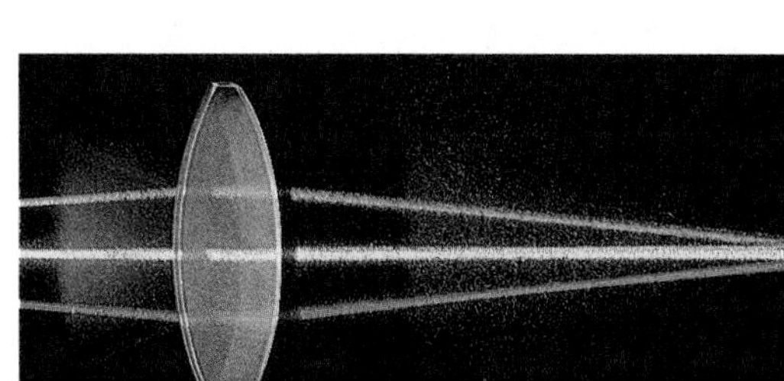

14. **Get Focused!** A convex lens focuses parallel light rays at a single point. Make a sketch based on the photograph, and add markings to show parallel light rays.

LOOK AHEAD

15. $m\angle ABC = 35°$. Determine the measures of angles $\angle FGH$ and $\angle PQR$ so that $m\angle ABC + m\angle FGH = 90°$, and $m\angle ABC + m\angle PQR = 180°$.

16. Suppose $m\angle JKL + m\angle STU = 90°$, and $m\angle JKL + m\angle XYZ = 90°$. What can you say about $\angle STU$ and $\angle XYZ$?

MORE PRACTICE

Determine whether the following specific relationships can be assumed from the figure at the right.

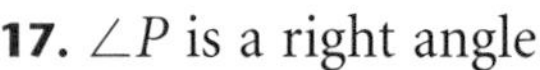

17. $\angle P$ is a right angle.

18. $\angle O$ is a right angle.

19. $\overline{MP} \cong \overline{NO}$

20. $MNOP$ is a rectangle.

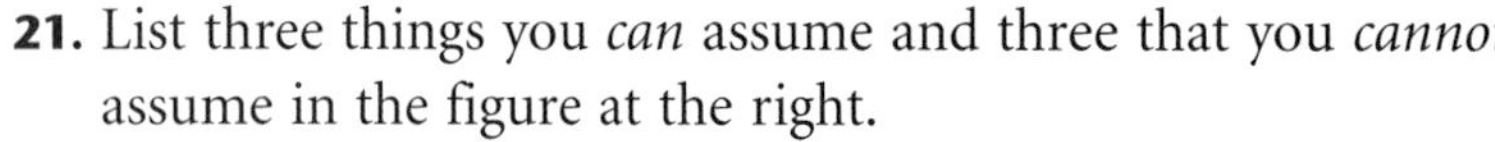

21. List three things you *can* assume and three that you *cannot* assume in the figure at the right.

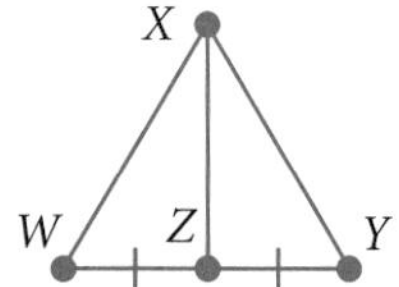

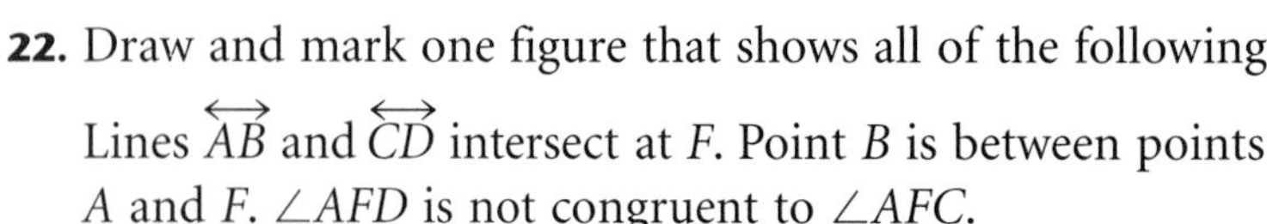

22. Draw and mark one figure that shows all of the following.

    Lines $\overleftrightarrow{AB}$ and $\overleftrightarrow{CD}$ intersect at F. Point B is between points A and F. $\angle AFD$ is not congruent to $\angle AFC$.

MORE MATH REASONING

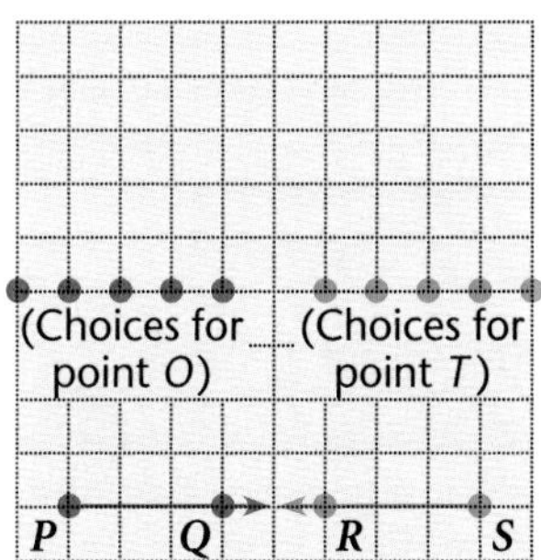

23. Angles $\angle OPQ$ and $\angle TSR$ are completed by randomly selecting points from the grid, as shown. What is the probability that the angles will be congruent? Explain.

24. A Matter of Degree Suppose that a person working on the construction of an office building assumed that the corner at the right measured exactly 90° when it actually measured 89°. After the wall is extended 5 ft, it is 1 in. out of alignment.

If the office building is 250 ft long, how far out of alignment will the end of the wall be? Explain your reasoning, and state any assumptions that you are making.

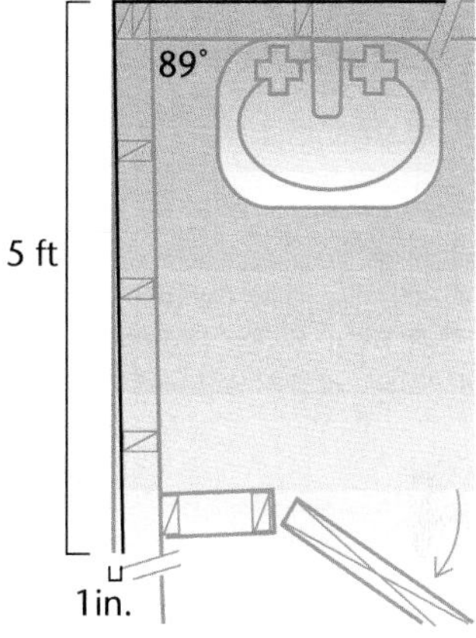

3-3 PART C Angle Pairs

← CONNECT → ***You know quite a bit about individual angles. Now you will develop some definitions and theorems about pairs of angles.***

You have seen how the Angle-Addition Postulate allows you to add the measures of angles under certain conditions. Now you will combine that postulate with some new angle classifications to make some new conjectures.

DEFINITIONS

Complementary angles are two angles whose measures add up to 90°.

Supplementary angles are two angles whose measures add up to 180°.

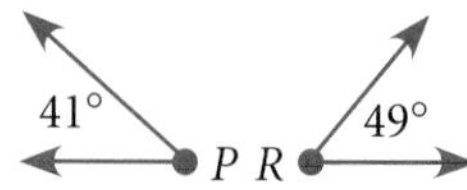

$\angle R$ is complementary to $\angle P$.
($\angle R$ is the *complement* of $\angle P$.)

$\angle S$ is supplementary to $\angle P$.
($\angle S$ is the *supplement* of $\angle P$.)

Angles can be complementary or supplementary regardless of their location. However, some angle pairs are determined by location.

DEFINITION

Two angles, $\angle ABD$ and $\angle DBC$, form a **linear pair** if and only if A, B, and C are collinear and D is not on $\overleftrightarrow{AC}$.

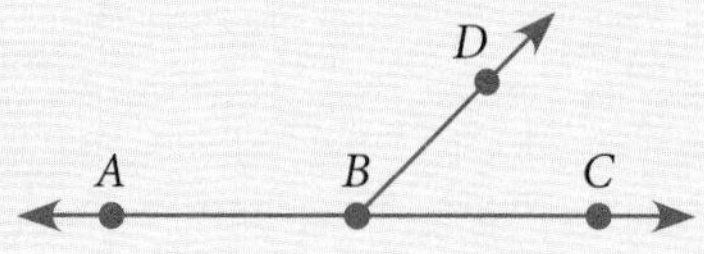

EXAMPLES

1. Name all linear pairs in the figure below.

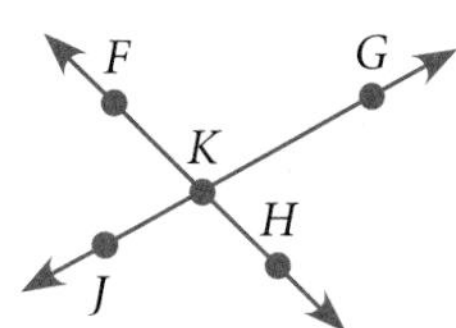

The four linear pairs are $\angle JKF$ and $\angle FKG$, $\angle FKG$ and $\angle GKH$, $\angle GKH$ and $\angle HKJ$, and $\angle HKJ$ and $\angle JKF$.

2. If $m\angle X = 64°$, find the measures of the angles that are complementary and supplementary to $\angle X$.
The measures of two complementary angles must add to 90°, so the measure of the complement of $\angle X$ is $90° - 64° = 26°$.
The measures of two supplementary angles must add to 180°, so the measure of the supplement of $\angle X$ is $180° - 64° = 116°$.

In the following Explore, you will make some conjectures about angles in a linear pair, complementary angles, and supplementary angles.

EXPLORE: ANGLING FOR THEOREMS

MATERIALS

Straightedge
Protractor

1. The photo shows linear pairs of angles in a leaf. Make as many conjectures about the angles in a linear pair as you can. Drawing one or more linear pairs and taking some measurements may help you.
2. Now you will investigate a relationship between angles and their supplements.
   a. Suppose an angle measures 50°. What is the measure of any angle that is supplementary to it?
   b. Suppose *two* angles each measure 50°. What is the measure of any angle supplementary to both of them?
   c. Make a conjecture about supplements of congruent angles. See if you can make a similar conjecture about any two angles that are supplementary to the same angle.
3. Using your conjectures from Step 2 as a guideline, make similar conjectures about complements of congruent angles and complements of the same angle.

TRY IT

a. List all pairs of congruent angles in the figure.

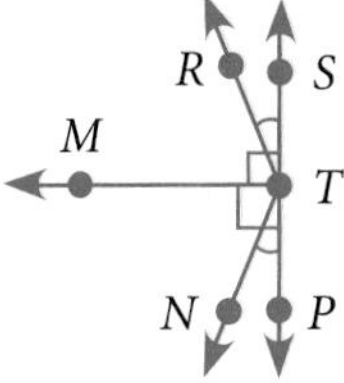

Find the measure of each of the following angles.

b. $\angle WZX$ **c.** $\angle WZY$ **d.** $\angle XZY$

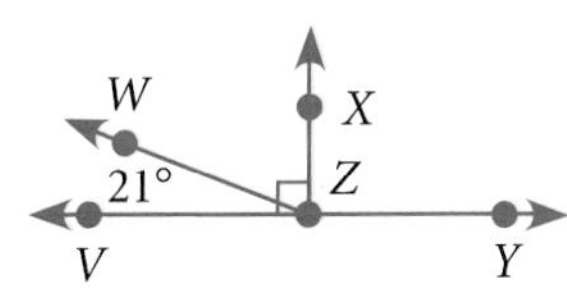

Some properties of angles and angle pairs are summarized below.

LINEAR-PAIR POSTULATE

The angles in a linear pair are supplementary.

THEOREMS

Supplements of congruent angles (or of the same angle) are congruent.

Complements of congruent angles (or of the same angle) are congruent.

REFLECT

1. Suppose that two angles that form a linear pair are congruent. What else can you say about them? Explain.
2. If the measure of an angle is $x°$, what are the measures of its complement and its supplement?

Exercises

CORE

Getting Started Use the figure at the right to name each of the following.

1. a pair of complementary angles
2. a pair of supplementary angles
3. a linear pair

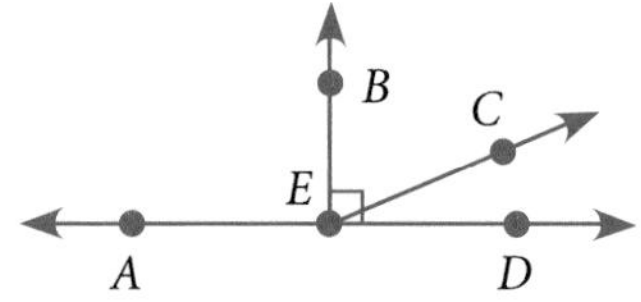

For each measure of $\angle 1$, find the measure of its complement and its supplement.

4. $m\angle 1 = 73°$
5. $m\angle 1 = 11.7°$
6. $m\angle 1 = 22\frac{1}{2}°$

Use the given information and the figure at the right to find each angle measure.

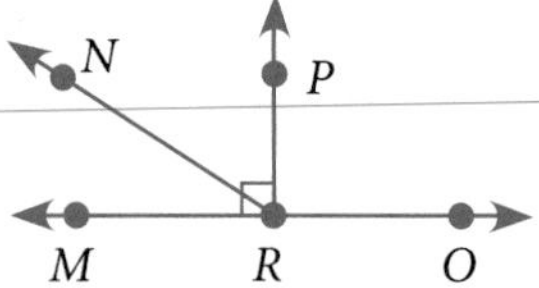

7. $m\angle MRN = 41°$. Find $m\angle NRP$ and $m\angle NRO$.
8. $m\angle NRP = 61°$. Find $m\angle MRN$.
9. $m\angle MRN = (45 - 3x)°$ and $m\angle NRP = (8x - 10)°$. Find $m\angle MRN$ and $m\angle NRP$.

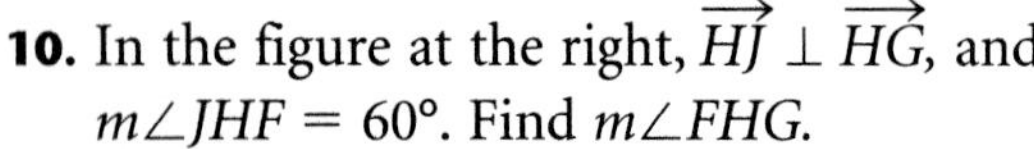

10. In the figure at the right, $\overrightarrow{HJ} \perp \overrightarrow{HG}$, and $m\angle JHF = 60°$. Find $m\angle FHG$.

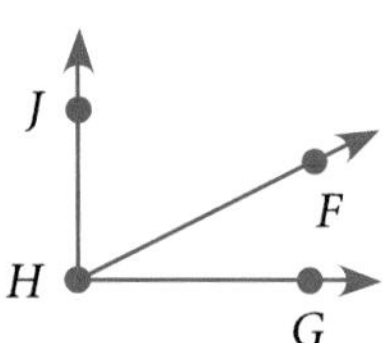

11. In the figure below, $\angle 2$ is five times as large as $\angle 1$. Find $m\angle 1$.

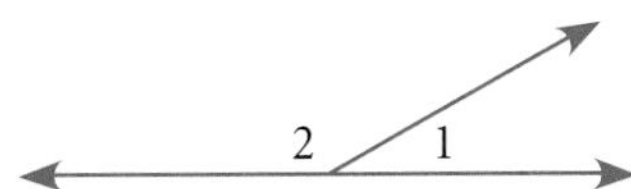

Determine whether each statement is true or false. If the statement is false, change the underlined word or phrase to make it true.

12. The sum of the measures of two <u>supplementary</u> angles is 180°.

13. If two congruent angles form a linear pair, then both of them must be <u>acute</u> angles.

14. Find the measure of an angle whose supplement is three times its complement.

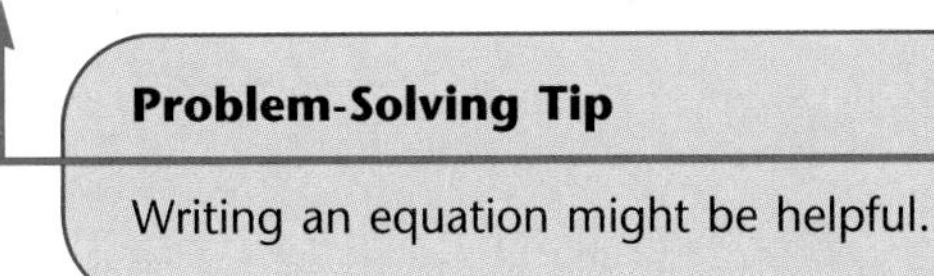

Problem-Solving Tip
Writing an equation might be helpful.

15. One of two supplementary angles is 104° more than the second. Find the measure of the larger angle.

Careers

16. Clearly Right When installing a window, a carpenter must be sure the vertical support forms a right angle with the window ledge. If she finds that $\angle 1$ is a right angle, must she also measure $\angle 2$? Write a brief justification of your decision.

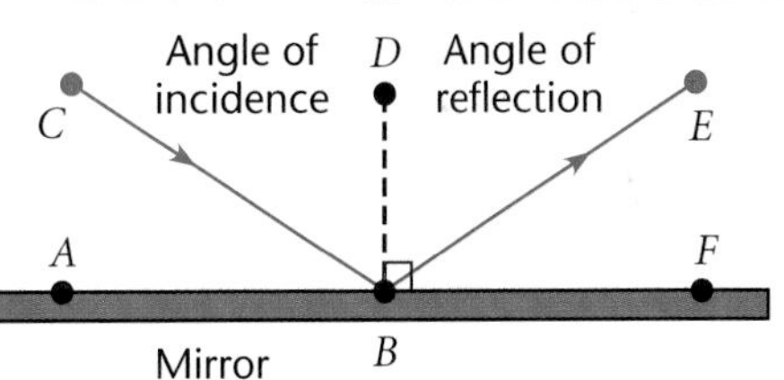

Science

17. When a beam of light reflects off a mirror, the angle of incidence is congruent to the angle of reflection. If the angle of incidence is 55°, find $m\angle EBF$.

18. If two angles have the same vertex, a common side, and lie on opposite sides of the common side, they are adjacent angles. Which two angles in the diagram are adjacent angles? Name two that are not adjacent.

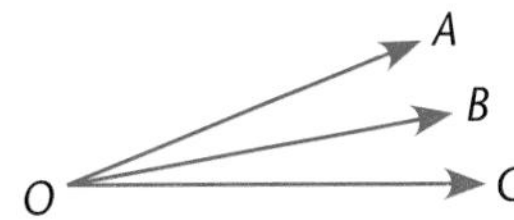

19. The following theorem is important, but it is not difficult to understand.

THEOREM

All right angles are congruent.

Give a deductive argument to justify this theorem.

LOOK BACK

Rewrite both statements in each pair below in if-then form. Then make a deduction using the Chain Rule, if possible. [2-1]

20. All natural numbers are positive. Positive numbers are greater than zero.

21. Artists who used geometric forms to represent real objects were called *cubists*. Cubists were not realists.

Triangle *XYZ* is the image of triangle *TUV* under a 90° clockwise rotation around point C. Find each image or pre-image. [3-2]

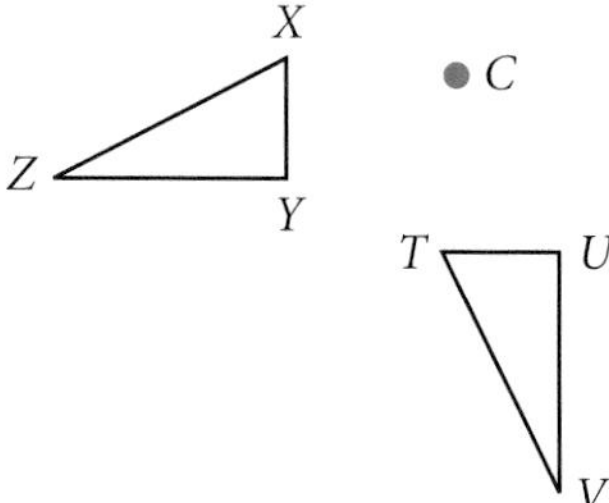

22. the image of point T **23.** the pre-image of point Y

24. the image of $\angle VTU$

MORE PRACTICE

For each measure of $\angle 1$, find the measure of its complement and its supplement.

25. $m\angle 1 = 20°$ **26.** $m\angle 1 = 49°$ **27.** $m\angle 1 = 55.5°$

MORE MATH REASONING

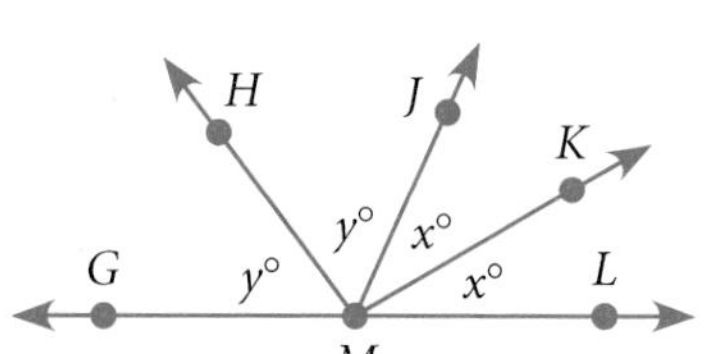

28. Explain why $\angle GMH$ is complementary to $\angle JMK$.

29. The measures of angles 1, 2, and 3 are in the ratio of 1:2:3 respectively. Find the measure of each angle.

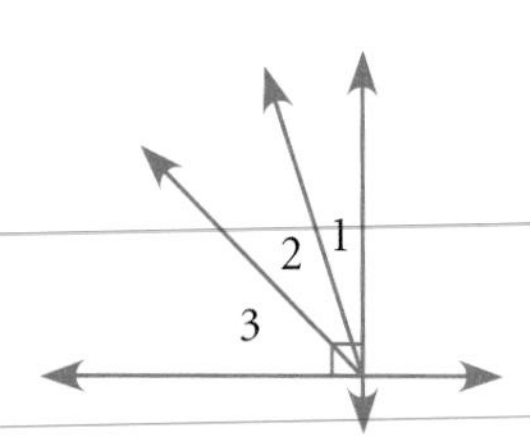

30. The flow proof shown below proves the following theorem.

If $\angle DEF$ is a right angle and point C is in the interior of $\angle DEF$, then $\angle DEC$ is complementary to $\angle CEF$.

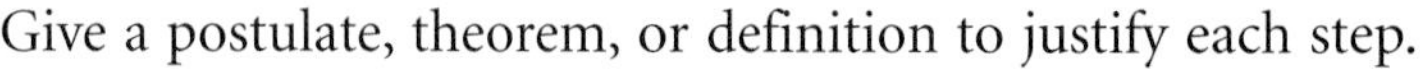

Give a postulate, theorem, or definition to justify each step.

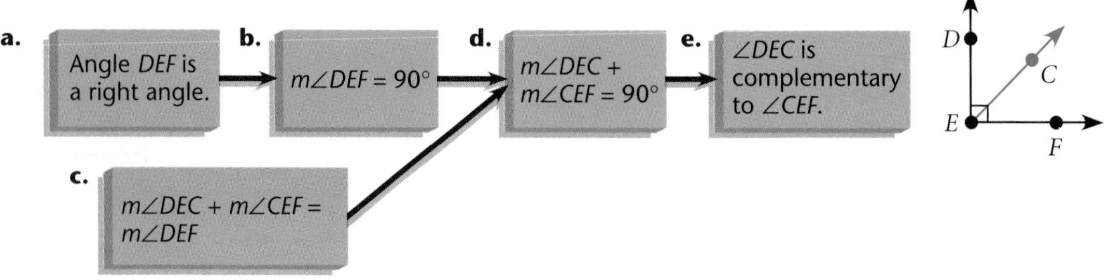

3-3 PART D Vertical Angles and Angle Bisectors

← CONNECT → ***You've explored several angle-pair relationships. Now you will discover and justify a theorem about a new angle pair and learn about angle bisectors.***

When two lines intersect, they form two pairs of *vertical angles.*

DEFINITION

Two angles are **vertical angles** if and only if their sides form two pairs of opposite rays.

In the figure at the right, ∠1 and ∠3 are vertical angles, and ∠2 and ∠4 are vertical angles.

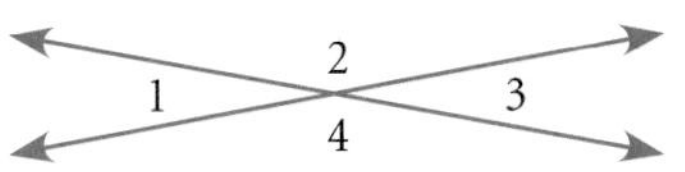

EXPLORE: "X" MARKS THE SPOT

MATERIALS

Straightedge, Protractor
Geometry software (optional)

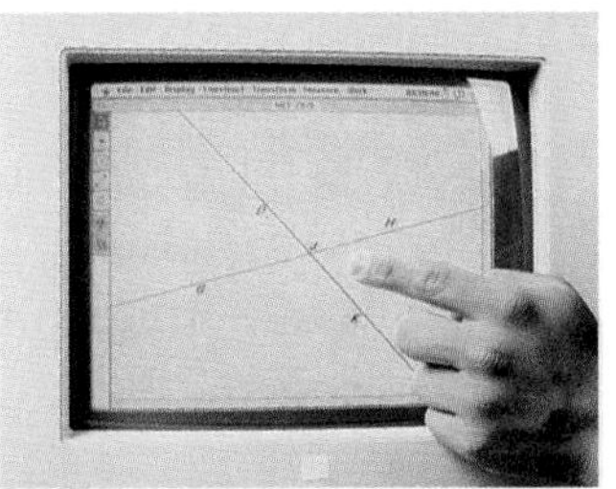

1. Use a straightedge or geometry software to draw a large X. Measure the four angles formed. Then draw a second X so that the angles are different sizes, and repeat your measurements. Make a conjecture about vertical angles.
2. Provide a deductive argument to support your conjecture. It may help to sketch and label two intersecting lines. However, you cannot assume that any of your angles has a specific measure. (Hint: Think about linear pairs of angles.)

TRY IT

a. Find the measures of ∠1, ∠2, and ∠3.

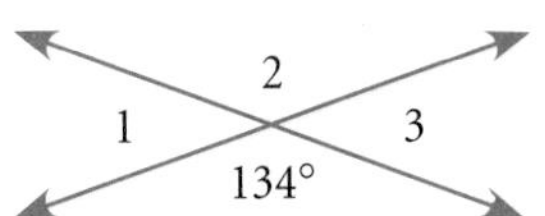

You've seen the term *bisect* before. You may be able to predict what an angle bisector is before reading the following definition.

DEFINITION

$\overrightarrow{LM}$ is the **angle bisector** of $\angle NLP$ if and only if M is in the interior of $\angle NLP$ and $\angle NLM \cong \angle MLP$.

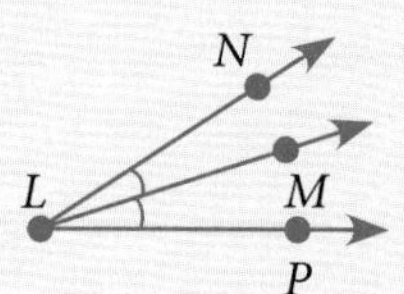

CONSTRUCTION: ANGLE BISECTOR

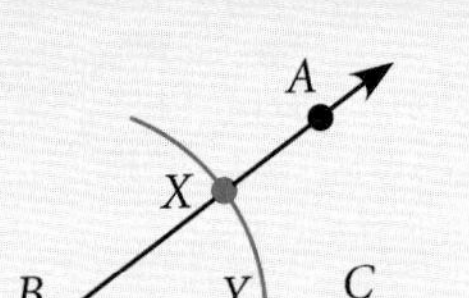

1. Begin by drawing angle $\angle ABC$. This will be the angle you bisect in your construction.

2. Using the vertex of the angle as the center, swing an arc through sides $\overrightarrow{BA}$ and $\overrightarrow{BC}$. Label the points where the arc intersects the sides X and Y.

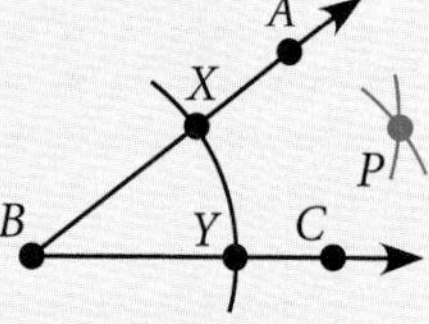

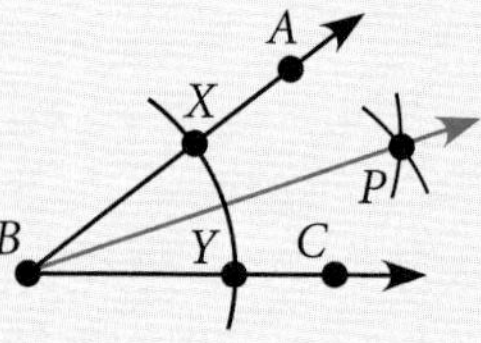

3. With the compass point at X, swing an arc in the interior of the angle. Using the same compass setting, make a similar arc from point Y. Label the intersection of the two arcs P.

4. Use a straightedge to draw $\overrightarrow{BP}$, the angle bisector of $\angle ABC$.

1. **Describe how you can *quadrisect* (divide into fourths) an angle using a straightedge and compass.**

Now you can begin to see how theorems are built up from undefined terms, definitions, postulates, and other theorems. To justify the vertical-angle conjecture that you made, you need to know definitions (linear pair, congruent), a postulate (the angles in a linear pair are supplementary), and a theorem (supplements of the same angle are congruent). So the first theorem below has quite a family tree!

The second theorem below can be proved by using the first. Exercise 30 gives you the opportunity to complete a plan for its proof.

THEOREMS

Vertical angles are congruent.

Two perpendicular lines form four right angles.

REFLECT

1. Suppose three coplanar lines intersect at one point. How many pairs of vertical angles are formed? Support your answer with a sketch.
2. Describe a method for constructing a 45° angle, using a compass and straightedge.
3. Give a real-world example of vertical angles.

Exercises

CORE

Getting Started Find the measures of ∠2, ∠3, and ∠4 for each value of $m\angle 1$.

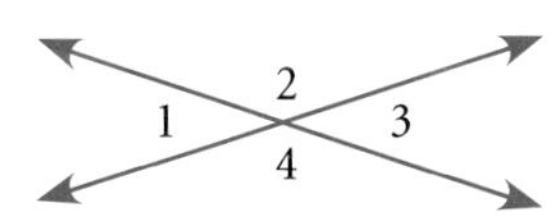

1. $m\angle 1 = 32°$
2. $m\angle 1 = 77°$
3. $m\angle 1 = 125°$
4. $m\angle 1 = 102.7°$

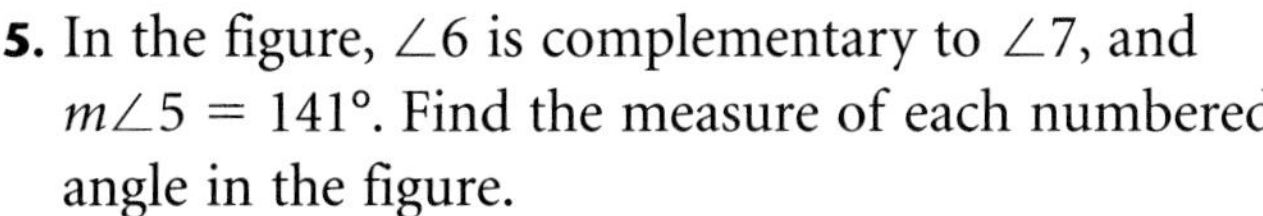

5. In the figure, ∠6 is complementary to ∠7, and $m\angle 5 = 141°$. Find the measure of each numbered angle in the figure.

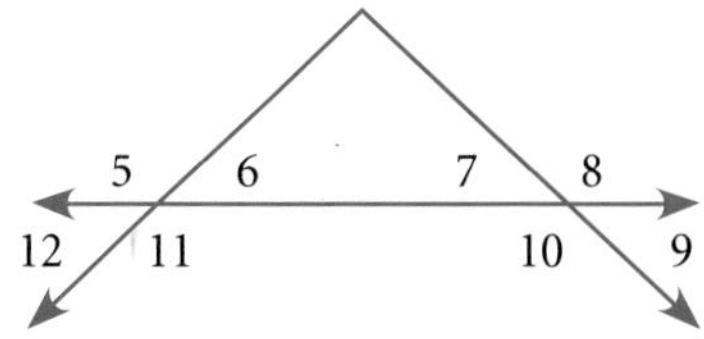

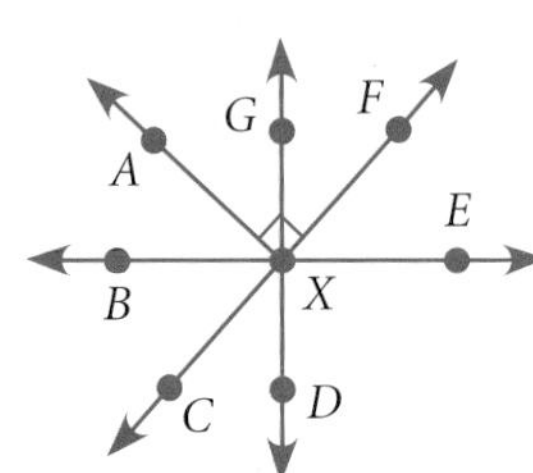

Find each of the following, assuming that $m\angle GXF = 53°$ and $m\angle FXE = 29°$.

6. $m\angle AXG$ **7.** $m\angle CXB$ **8.** $m\angle CXA$

9. $m\angle BXF$ **10.** $m\angle AXD$ **11.** $m\angle BXD$

Suppose that angles $\angle JKL$ and $\angle MKN$ are vertical angles. Find their measures if the following conditions apply.

12. $m\angle JKL = (5x - 30)°$, $m\angle MKN = (3x + 30)°$

13. $m\angle JKL = 4(y + 7)°$, $m\angle MKN = 3(2y - 12)°$

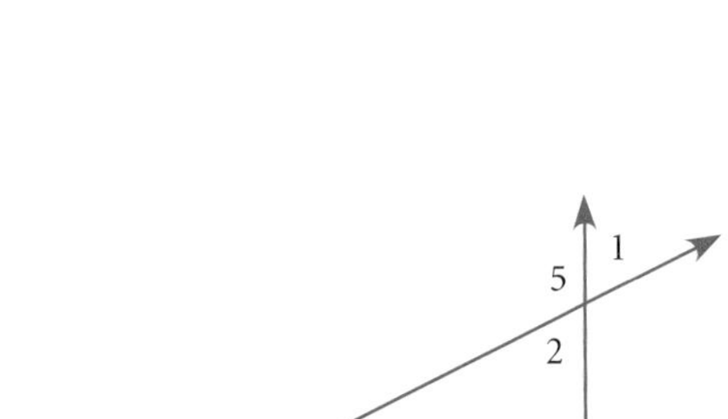

Give a reason (or reasons) to justify each statement.

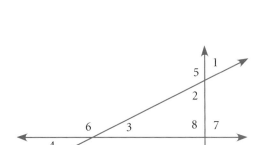

14. If $\angle 7$ and $\angle 8$ are right angles, then $\angle 7 \cong \angle 8$.

15. If $m\angle 2 + m\angle 3 = 90°$, then $\angle 2$ and $\angle 3$ are complementary.

16. $\angle 3 \cong \angle 4$

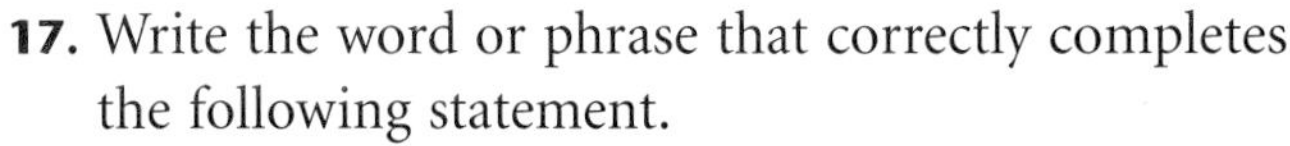

17. Write the word or phrase that correctly completes the following statement.

The point of intersection of two vertical angles is the ___ of each angle.

18. Rewrite the theorem "Vertical angles are congruent" in if-then form.

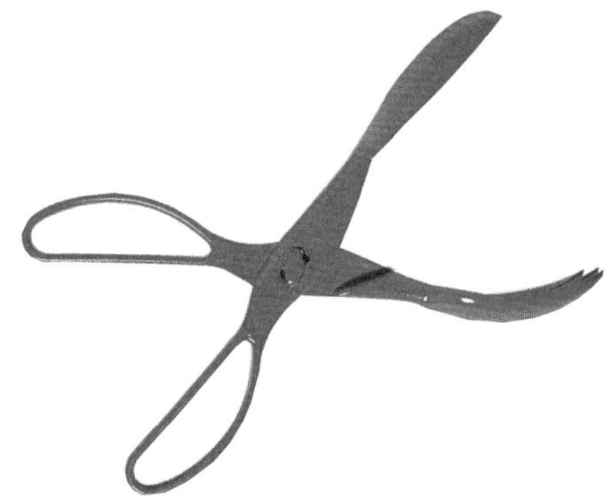

19. Tongs a Lot A pair of salad tongs is shown at the right. Use geometry to explain why closing the grips together allows you to pick up food.

20. Head for the Snow Olympic ski jumpers know that the angle of the ski jumper's body on take-off is critical for getting the maximum distance on a jump. If $m\angle 1 = 155°$, find $m\angle 2$.

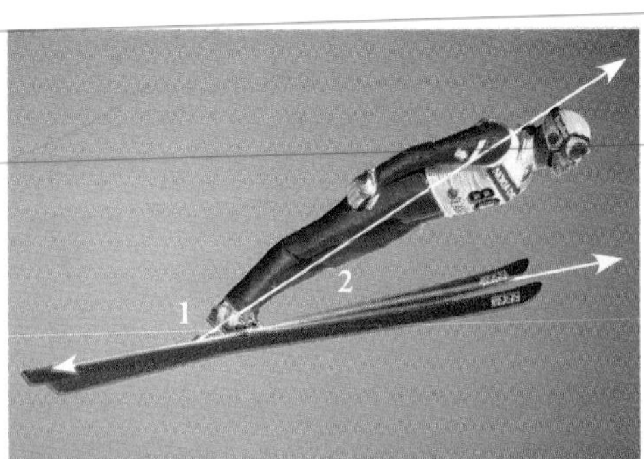

21. Draw an acute angle. Then use a compass and straightedge to construct its bisector.

LOOK AHEAD

22. Sketch two parallel lines. Then add a third line that intersects the two parallel lines. Label the angles formed, and list the pairs of vertical angles.

23. Draw a figure to illustrate the following statement.

Given: $\angle STU$ and $\angle UTV$ are a linear pair. $\angle STU \cong \angle UTV$.

What do you think you could *prove* about these angles?

MORE PRACTICE

In the figure at the right, $m\angle AEC = 42°$. Find each of the following.

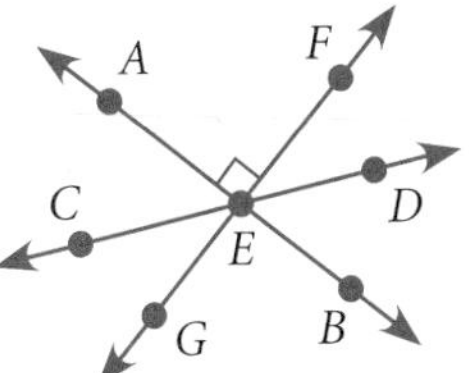

24. $m\angle DEB$ **25.** $m\angle CEG$ **26.** $m\angle FED$ **27.** $m\angle GEB$

Suppose that angles $\angle JKL$ and $\angle MKN$ are vertical angles. Find their measures under the following conditions.

28. $m\angle JKL = (2x + 40)°$, $m\angle MKN = (8x - 32)°$

29. $m\angle JKL = 3(y + 11)°$, $m\angle MKN = 2(10 + 2y)°$

MORE MATH REASONING

30. A Plan for Proof A plan for a deductive proof of the theorem "Two perpendicular lines form four right angles" is shown below. Fill in each blank to complete this plan for a proof.

Assume that $m \perp n$. Then m and n form at least one right angle because of the **a.** ____. This angle, $\angle 1$ in the figure, measures **b.** ____ because of the definition of a right angle. $\angle 3 \cong \angle 1$ because **c.** ____. Thus, $m\angle 3 = m\angle 1 = 90°$. Therefore, $\angle 3$ is a right angle, by the **d.** ____.

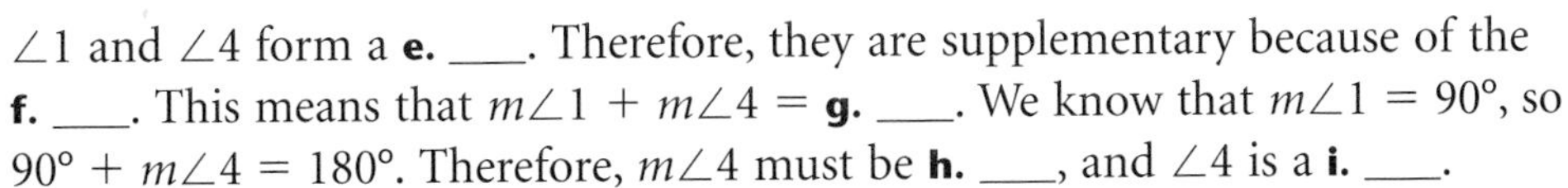

$\angle 1$ and $\angle 4$ form a **e.** ____. Therefore, they are supplementary because of the **f.** ____. This means that $m\angle 1 + m\angle 4 =$ **g.** ____. We know that $m\angle 1 = 90°$, so $90° + m\angle 4 = 180°$. Therefore, $m\angle 4$ must be **h.** ____, and $\angle 4$ is a **i.** ____.

The reasoning above can also be used to show that **j.** ____ is a right angle. Therefore, we can show that all four angles formed by two **k.** ____ must be **l.** ____.

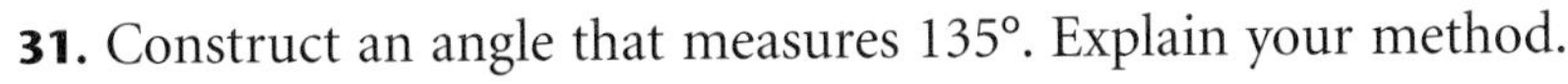

31. Construct an angle that measures 135°. Explain your method.

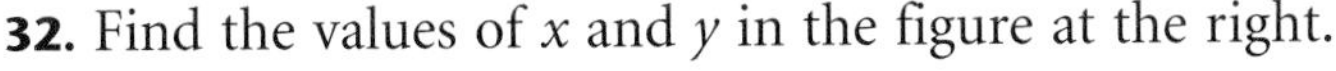

32. Find the values of x and y in the figure at the right.

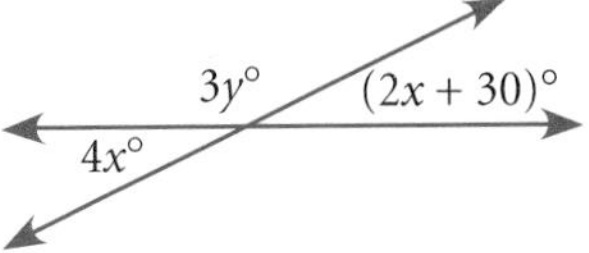

3-3 PART E Making Connections

← CONNECT → ***In geometry and in everyday life, you must be careful not to make assumptions that are not based on evidence. You've learned what you may and may not assume from a figure. You have also investigated different angle pairs and angle relationships.***

You've discovered relationships between several types of angles. In the Explore that follows, you will use these relationships to help analyze how the sun's heat gets trapped in city streets.

EXPLORE: CITY CANYONS

MATERIALS

Straightedge
Protractor

The figure on the left below shows the reflections of a ray of sunlight in a city street. As shown on page 191, the amount of heat absorbed by buildings on a street depends on the number of times the sun's rays are reflected.

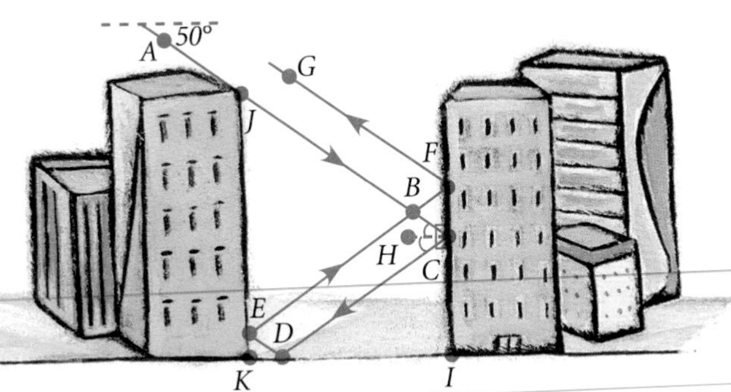

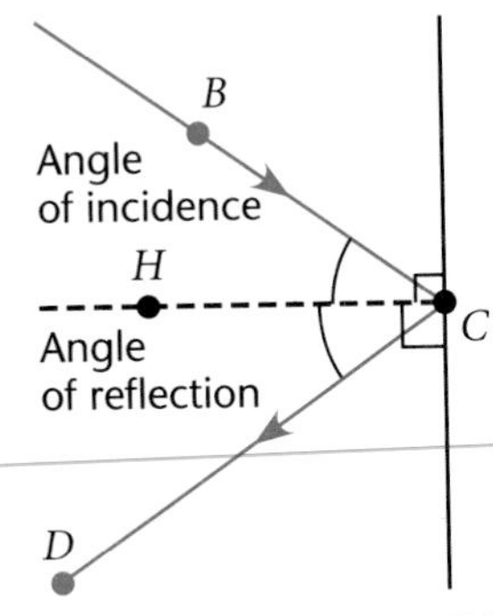

The figure on the right is an enlarged view of the first reflection at point C. In the following, it will help if you remember that when light rays are reflected, the *angle of incidence* is congruent to the *angle of reflection.*

1. Use the figure on the left above to find an example of each type of angle or angle pair.

a. a pair of vertical angles

b. a pair of complementary angles

c. a linear pair

d. a pair of supplementary angles

e. an angle bisector

2. Name a pair of angles in the figure on page 212 that are congruent because of each theorem.
   a. Vertical angles are congruent.
   b. Right angles are congruent.
   c. Complements of congruent angles are congruent.
   d. Supplements of congruent angles are congruent.
3. As a city planner, you might like to design a city street that does not become a heat island at night. Give one or more changes that you could make to the street in the figure that would help the problem. Explain the effect of each of your suggestions. Use a drawing like the preceding one on the left to illustrate your plan. Show what happens to a ray of sunlight that comes in just over the top of a building at the 50° angle shown.

REFLECT

1. Write a description of each term in your own words. Include a sketch with each definition.
   a. vertical angles
   b. linear pair
   c. complementary angles
   d. supplementary angles
   e. perpendicular lines
2. Describe an example of how making an unjustified mathematical assumption about a figure can cause a problem. When do you think an unjustified assumption might create a problem in a nonmathematical setting?

Self-Assessment

For each measure of $\angle A$, find the measure of its complement and its supplement.

1. $m\angle A = 65°$
2. $m\angle A = x$
3. $m\angle A = (20 - x)°$

In the following, assume that $m\angle TVU = 32°$. Find each measure.

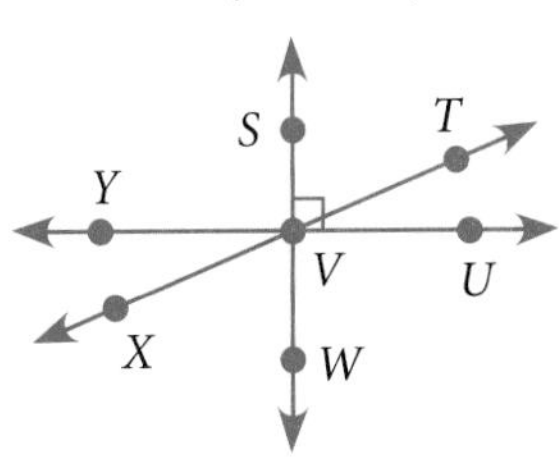

4. $m\angle SVT$
5. $m\angle YVX$
6. $m\angle UVX$
7. $m\angle SVX$

A billiard ball bounces off the sides of a billiard table at the same angle at which it arrives. Use the figure at the right to find an example of each type of angle pair.

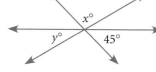

8. a pair of complementary angles

9. a linear pair

10. a pair of angles that are congruent because vertical angles are congruent

11. a pair of angles that are congruent because complements of congruent angles are congruent

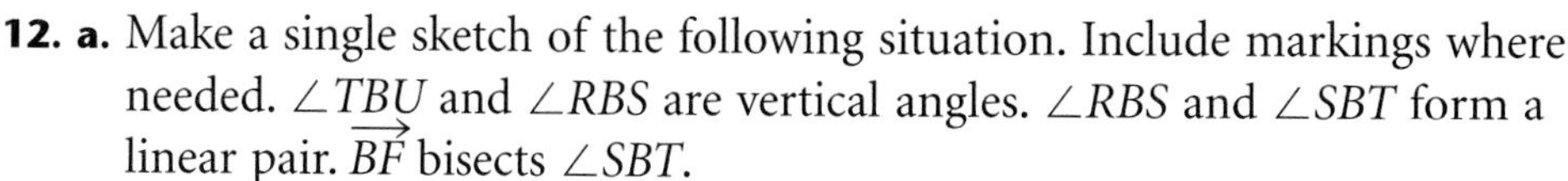

12. a. Make a single sketch of the following situation. Include markings where needed. $\angle TBU$ and $\angle RBS$ are vertical angles. $\angle RBS$ and $\angle SBT$ form a linear pair. $\overrightarrow{BF}$ bisects $\angle SBT$.

b. If the measure of $\angle FBS$ is 20°, find $m\angle TBU$, $m\angle RBS$, and $m\angle SBT$.

13. Explain what can and cannot be assumed from a geometric figure. Give specific examples of things that you may not assume from a figure unless they are marked.

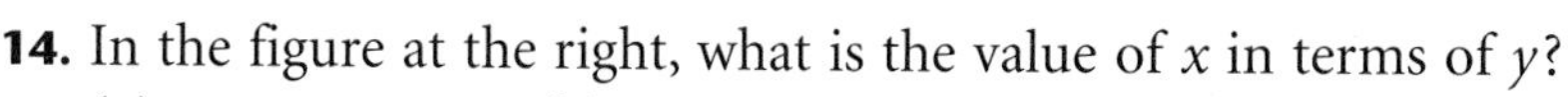

14. In the figure at the right, what is the value of x in terms of y?

(a) $135 + y$ (b) $315 - 2y$ (c) $180 - y$

(d) $45 + 2y$ (e) $135 - y$

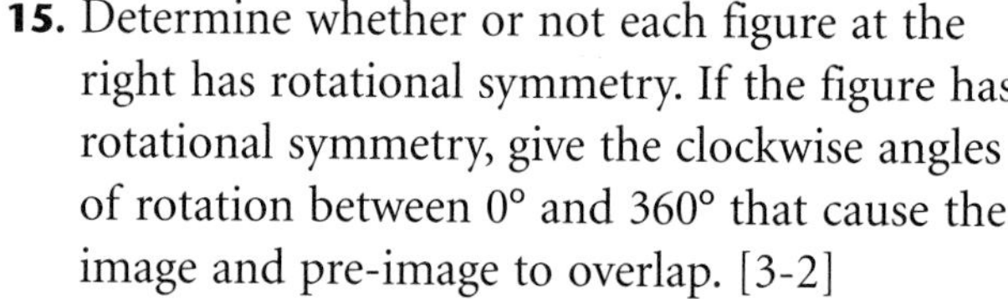

15. Determine whether or not each figure at the right has rotational symmetry. If the figure has rotational symmetry, give the clockwise angles of rotation between 0° and 360° that cause the image and pre-image to overlap. [3-2]

a. 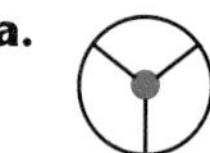 **b.**  **c.** 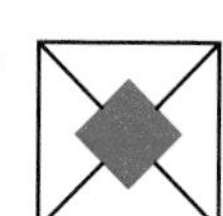

16. For any acute angle, what is the difference between its supplement and its complement? Make a generalization and use algebraic expressions to prove that the generalization is true.

Problem-Solving Tip

Try some examples with specific numbers.

17. Chemistry Lesson In an ethene molecule, two carbon atoms are bonded together, and each carbon atom is bonded to two hydrogen atoms. The centers of the six atoms in an ethene molecule lie in one plane. If all of the angles determined by the bonds shown are congruent, what is the measure of a hydrogen-carbon-hydrogen angle?

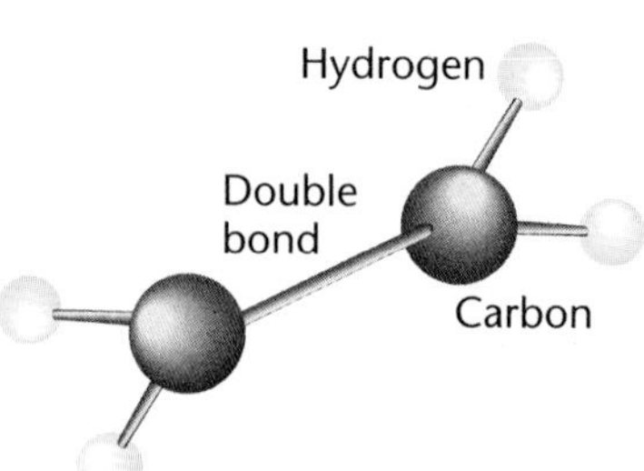

3-4 Parallel Lines and Transversals

THE WRITE STUFF

Calligraphy (kal-lig´-ra-fee), from the Greek *kalos* meaning beautiful and *grapho*, to write, is an art form with ancient roots. The developmental stages of writing took thousands of years. Calligraphy was stimulated, cultivated, and shaped from ancient times until the fifteenth century. At that time, calligraphy was used primarily in book production.

Scribes, skillful in the art of calligraphy (but having no access to a copy machine), copied the works of Cicero and other statesmen and orators by hand. There was also a great demand for multiple copies of the Bible. But with the invention of the printing press by Johann Gutenberg in about 1440, the demand for skilled calligraphers decreased.

The elegance of calligraphy has endured through time, from the days of scratching on the surface of a wax tablet with hollow reeds to today's use of precision pens and highly refined papers. Though it is no longer critical for communication, calligraphy is still important as an art form.

?

1. **What role do parallel lines play in calligraphy?**
2. **Describe any relationships you see between angles in the calligraphy samples shown.**
3. **Calligraphy fonts (type styles) are available for personal computers. Why might you still want to learn how to do calligraphy with pen and ink?**

3-4 PART A Transversals and Angles

← CONNECT → *You've seen how important it is to read and draw figures accurately. Now you will learn how to classify the angles formed when two lines are crossed by a third. You will also draw figures that illustrate conjectures.*

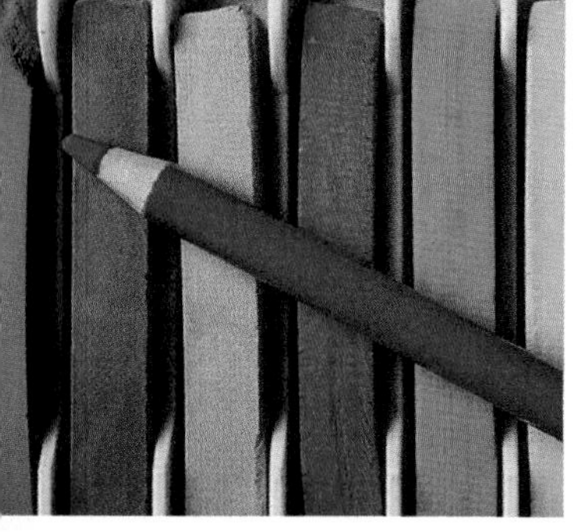

We have special names for angles formed when two coplanar lines are both intersected by a third.

DEFINITION

A **transversal** is a line that intersects two coplanar lines at two different points.

In the figure, transversal t intersects lines r and s. When a transversal crosses two lines, it forms eight angles. The relationships between these angles are important, so we have several names to identify the pairs of angles formed.

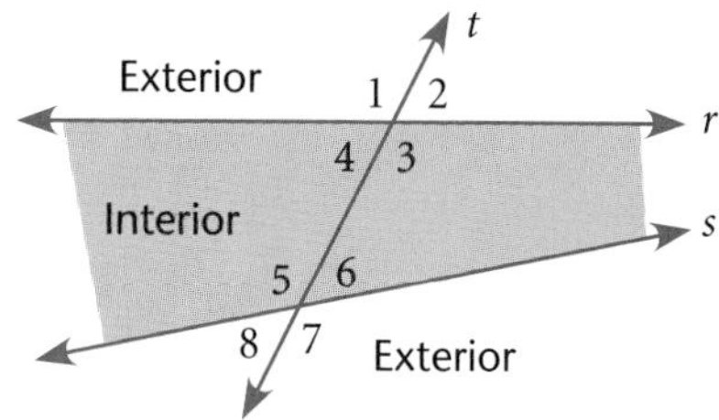

ANGLES FORMED BY TRANSVERSALS

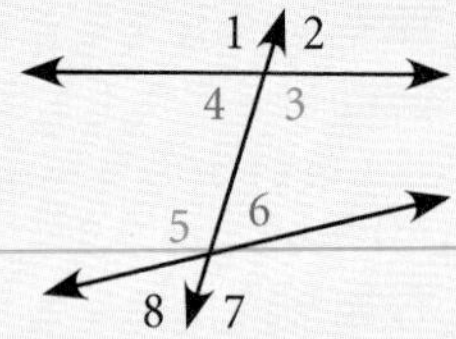

The pairs of **alternate interior angles** in the figure are ∠4 and ∠6, ∠3 and ∠5.

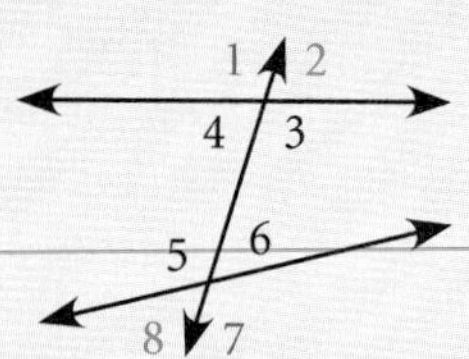

The pairs of **alternate exterior angles** are ∠1 and ∠7, ∠2 and ∠8.

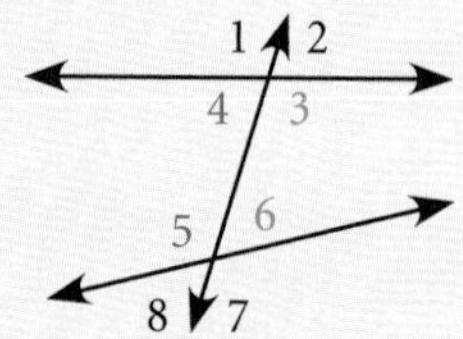

The pairs of **same-side interior angles** are ∠4 and ∠5, ∠3 and ∠6.

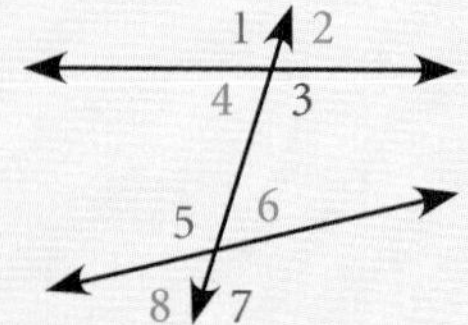

The pairs of **corresponding angles** are ∠1 and ∠5, ∠2 and ∠6, ∠3 and ∠7, and ∠4 and ∠8.

Although this seems like a lot to remember, it all makes sense. If you know the difference between *interior* and *exterior,* the difference between *same-side* and *alternate,* and what *corresponding* means, you can identify all of these pairs of angles easily.

TRY IT

Name each of the following in the figure at the right.

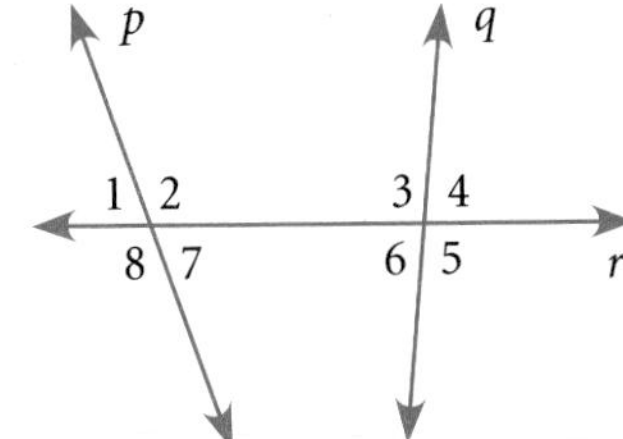

a. the transversal
b. two pairs of same-side interior angles
c. two pairs of alternate exterior angles
d. four pairs of corresponding angles
e. two pairs of alternate interior angles

You will soon make and prove some conjectures about the relationships between these angles when the lines that are cut by the transversal are parallel.

As you continue to develop your thinking skills, you will start to prove conjectures by deductive reasoning. The five-step process, outlined for you below, is one way to help you organize your thinking when proving a conjecture.

FIVE-STEP PROCESS FOR DEDUCTIVE PROOF

1. **Rewrite** the conjecture to be proved in if-then form.
2. **Draw** and label a figure to represent the given information.
3. **State** the statement to be proved in terms of the figure.
4. **Plan** the proof. (Find a logical sequence of steps that shows why the conjecture must be true. We'll look at this more closely in Chapter 5.)
5. **Demonstrate** the argument by translating your plan into writing. Every statement you make must be justified with a reason. (We'll look at this more closely in Chapter 6.)

Earlier, you learned how to *rewrite* a conjecture by writing it in if-then form. Now you will practice this step and the next two steps—the *draw* and *state* steps.

Draw means to illustrate and label the hypothesis of the statement you are trying to prove. *State* means to write the statement using the labels you put on your figure. The hypothesis becomes your *given* information, and the conclusion is what you are trying to *prove*.

EXAMPLE

Do the *rewrite, draw,* and *state* steps for the proof of the following theorem.

All vertical angles are congruent.

Rewrite: If two angles are vertical angles, then they are congruent.

Draw: Illustrate the hypothesis "Two angles are vertical angles."

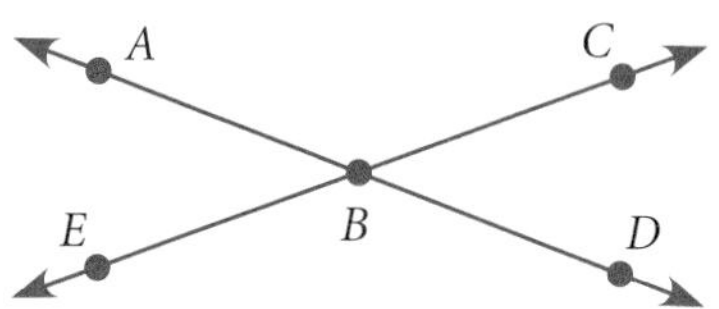

State: Write the hypothesis and conclusion of the statement using the labels in the figure.

Given: $\angle ABE$ and $\angle CBD$ are vertical angles.

Prove: $\angle ABE \cong \angle CBD$

EXPLORE: PROOF PREP

Do the *rewrite, draw,* and *state* steps for a proof of the following theorem.

Two coplanar lines that are perpendicular to the same line are parallel.

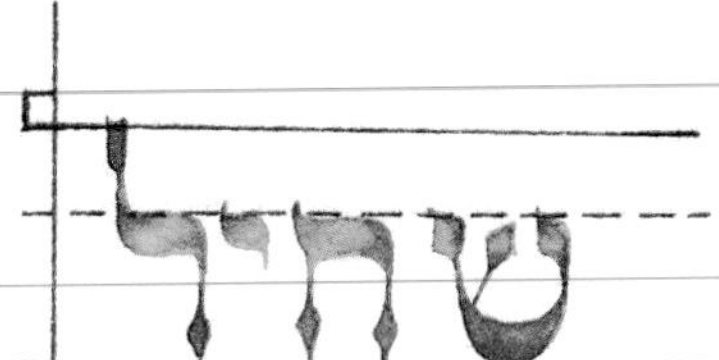

The calligraphy sample at the right, which shows Hebrew letters, may help you with the *draw* step. Don't worry about finishing the proof—you don't have quite enough information to complete it at this point. Compare your setup with those of other students, and decide which seems best.

REFLECT

1. In your own words, give a definition of *alternate exterior angles.*
2. Why is it important not to illustrate the conclusion when you are drawing a figure for use in a proof?
3. A transversal is a line that intersects two coplanar lines at two different points. What happens when a line intersects two coplanar lines at the *same* point? Sketch the situation. What type(s) of angles are formed?

Exercises

CORE

Getting Started Name each of the following in the figure at the right.

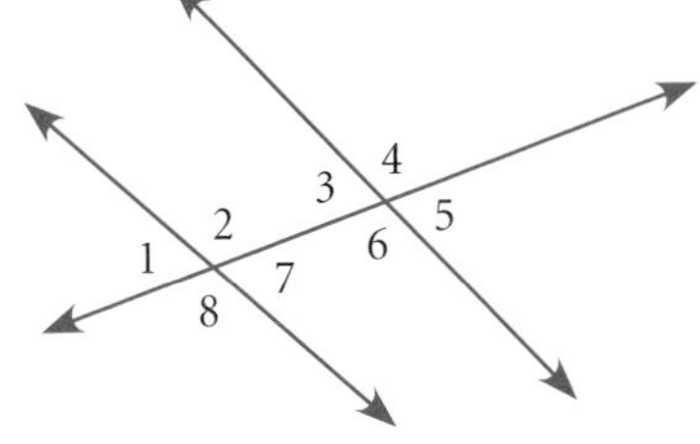

1. alternate interior angles
2. alternate exterior angles
3. same-side interior angles
4. corresponding angles
5. vertical angles
6. When two nonintersecting lines in a plane are intersected by a transversal, how many pairs of corresponding angles are formed? alternate interior angles? alternate exterior angles?
7. Think about the location of corresponding angles. How is this name descriptive of their location? Answer the same question for alternate interior and alternate exterior angles.

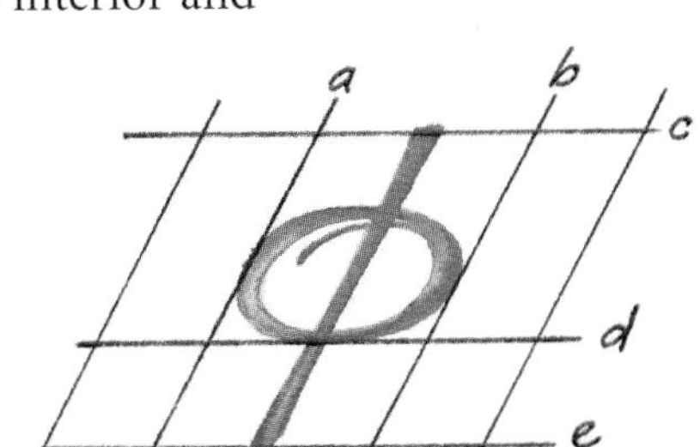

Fine Arts

8. Part of a calligraphy guidesheet is shown at the right. Name all transversals, and identify the pair(s) of lines for which they are transversals.
9. Choose the term in the group of terms below that does not belong, and explain why.

   alternate interior, corresponding, transversal, alternate exterior

Do the *rewrite, draw,* and *state* steps for the proof of each theorem.

10. Right angles are congruent.
11. If M is the midpoint of $\overline{AB}$, $AM = \frac{1}{2}AB$.

12. Graph each of the equations below on a coordinate plane. Then identify the equation of the line that is a transversal to the other two.

$y = 2x + 4$ $\qquad$ $y = -\frac{1}{2}x + 2$ $\qquad$ $y = 2x - 1$

13. Periscope Problem #1 In a periscope, a pair of mirrors are mounted parallel to each other, as shown. The path of the reflected light becomes a transversal. Name a pair of alternate interior angles.

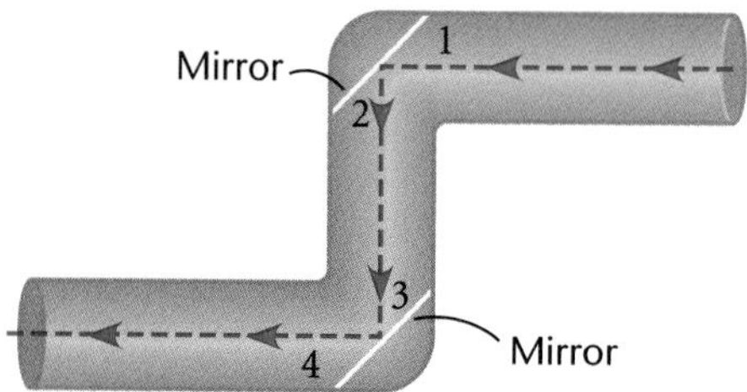

LOOK BACK

Write a conditional statement with each of the following sets of characteristics. [2-1]

14. The conditional is true, and its inverse is false.

15. The conditional and its inverse, converse, and contrapositive are all false.

For each measure of $\angle A$, give the measure of its complement and its supplement. [3-3]

16. $m\angle A = 42°$ $\qquad$ **17.** $m\angle A = 88°$ $\qquad$ **18.** $m\angle A = 32.4°$

MORE PRACTICE

Name each of the following in the figure at the right.

19. alternate interior angles

20. alternate exterior angles

21. same-side interior angles

22. corresponding angles

23. vertical angles

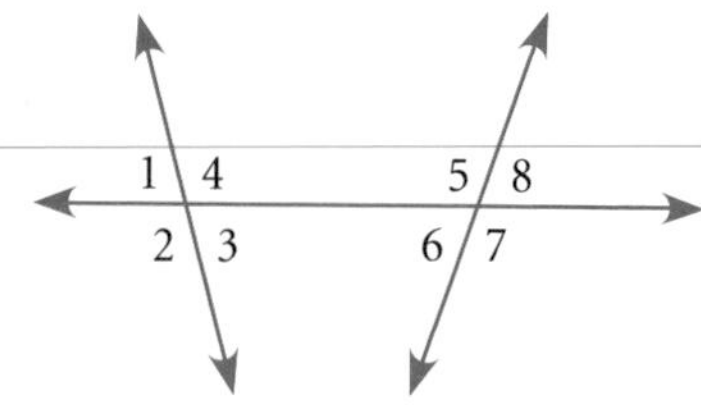

Do the *rewrite, draw,* and *state* steps for the proof of each theorem.

24. Two perpendicular lines form four right angles.

25. Two angles that are supplementary to the same angle are congruent.

MORE MATH REASONING

26. Suppose line m intersects lines n and p at two different points, but is *not* a transversal. Explain how this is possible.

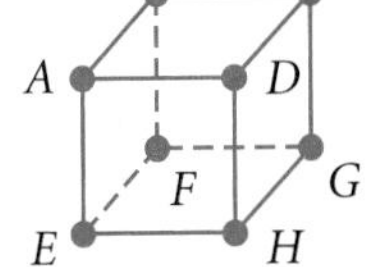

27. Crossing the Cube List all the pairs of lines through vertices of the cube for which $\overleftrightarrow{BH}$ is a transversal.

28. Do the *rewrite, draw,* and *state* steps for a proof of the following statement.

Angle congruence is transitive.

(Hint: The Transitive Property of Equality is: If $a = b$ and $b = c$, then $a = c$.)

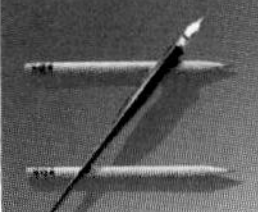

3-4 PART B Parallel Lines, Transversals, and Angles

← CONNECT → ***You've worked with parallel lines before. Now you will look at what happens when a transversal intersects two parallel lines.***

On calligraphy guidesheets, you see many parallel lines crossed by transversals. If you look closely at the angles formed by these lines, you may notice some consistent patterns. In the following Explore, you will check to see whether these relationships are always true.

EXPLORE: PARALLEL CROSSING

MATERIALS

Protractor, Straightedge
Geometry software (optional)

Use geometry software or the opposite edges of a straightedge to draw two parallel lines. Draw a transversal through the two lines.

Measure the various angles, and make as many conjectures as you can about the angles that are congruent and supplementary in your figure. (You may want to check to be sure that your conjectures hold for the calligraphy guidesheet at the right.)

TRY IT

a. If $p \parallel q$ and $m\angle 1 = 72°$, find the measures of all other angles in the figure.

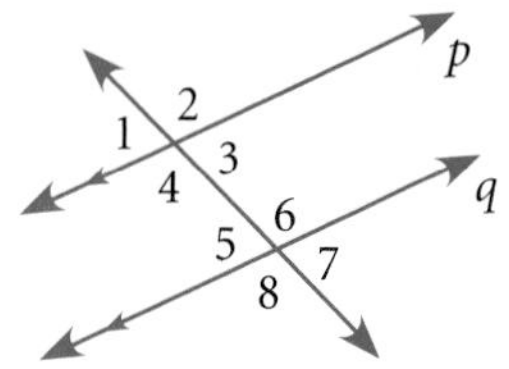

We can now summarize the angle relationships for parallel lines that are cut by a transversal. Notice that we have to assume that one of the conjectures is true. The others can be proved, but their proofs rely on the truth of the postulate.

POSTULATE

If parallel lines are cut by a transversal, then the alternate interior angles are congruent.

THEOREMS

If parallel lines are cut by a transversal, then the corresponding angles are congruent.

If parallel lines are cut by a transversal, then the alternate exterior angles are congruent.

If parallel lines are cut by a transversal, then the same-side interior angles are supplementary.

WHAT DO YOU THINK?

Kimiko and Mike's teacher asked the class to give evidence to support the theorem "If parallel lines are cut by a transversal, then the corresponding angles are congruent."

Mike thinks . . .

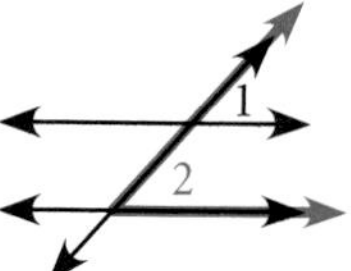

I'll draw a picture of two parallel lines with a transversal. If I trace $\angle 2$, and then translate it up along the transversal, I can see it's congruent to $\angle 1$. I can do the same thing for any pair of corresponding angles. SO I can use a translation to support this theorem.

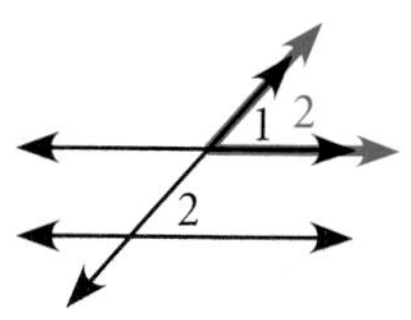

Kimiko thinks . . .

First, I'll draw a picture of two parallel lines with a transversal. I know that vertical angles are congruent, so $\angle 1 \cong \angle 3$. A postulate says that alternate interior angles of parallel lines are congruent, so $\angle 3 \cong \angle 2$. And if $\angle 1 \cong \angle 3$ and $\angle 3 \cong \angle 2$, then $\angle 1$ must be congruent to $\angle 2$. I can do the same thing for any pair of corresponding angles, so corresponding angles must be congruent.

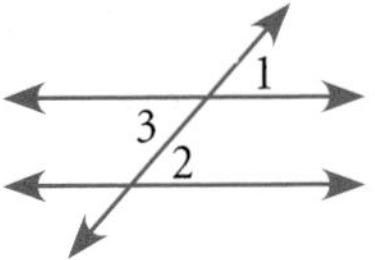

1. In the preceding situation, Mike used a translation to support the theorem about corresponding angles. Which transformation(s) could be used to support the theorem about alternate exterior angles?

REFLECT

1. Suppose two parallel lines are cut by a transversal that is not perpendicular to the lines. How many different measures are there among the angles formed? What is the relationship among these measures? Explain.
2. Justify the statement "If one of two parallel lines is perpendicular to a transversal, then so is the other."

Exercises

CORE

Getting Started Find the measures of all the numbered angles in the figure for each value of $m\angle 1$.

1. $m\angle 1 = 41°$ **2.** $m\angle 1 = 105°$

3. In the figure, $m\angle 1 = x°$. Find the measures of all other angles in terms of x. Then determine whether this statement is true or false: "If two parallel lines are cut by a transversal, the angles in any pair of angles formed are either congruent or supplementary." Explain.

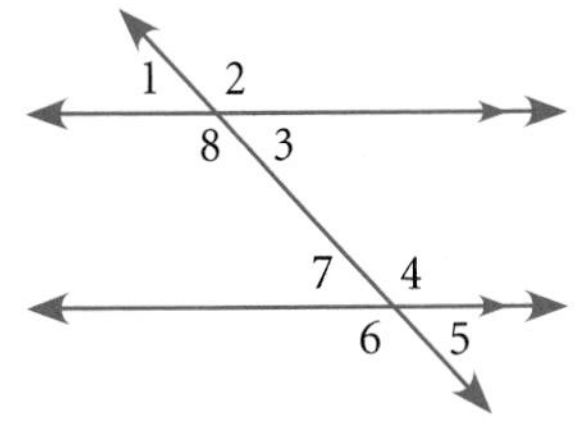

4. Explain how you could use a transformation to support the postulate that parallel lines have congruent alternate interior angles.

Do the *draw* and *state* steps for the proof of each theorem.

5. If parallel lines are cut by a transversal, then the alternate exterior angles are congruent.

6. If parallel lines are cut by a transversal, then the same-side interior angles are supplementary.

7. In the figure above, $r \parallel s$. Find the measure of $\angle X$. (Hint: Draw a line through the vertex of $\angle X$, parallel to lines r and s. Which postulate permits this?)

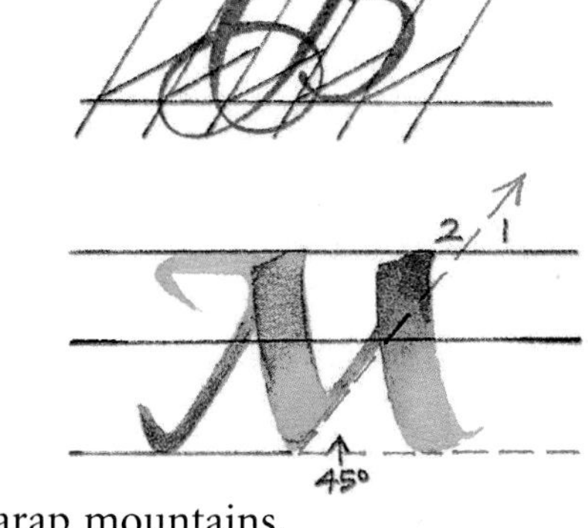

8. Describe the calligraphy worksheet at the right in terms of parallel lines and transversals.

9. The Calligraphy Angle When forming italic letters in calligraphy, the angle shown should be 45°.
a. Make a few italic letter *M*'s of your own.
b. Give the measure of the numbered angles.

10. Road Work While making a road through the remote Lellarap mountains, the construction team must put a turn of 100° in the road at point *A*. At what angle should the team put the turn at point *B* so that the road will head back in its original direction? Explain your answer.

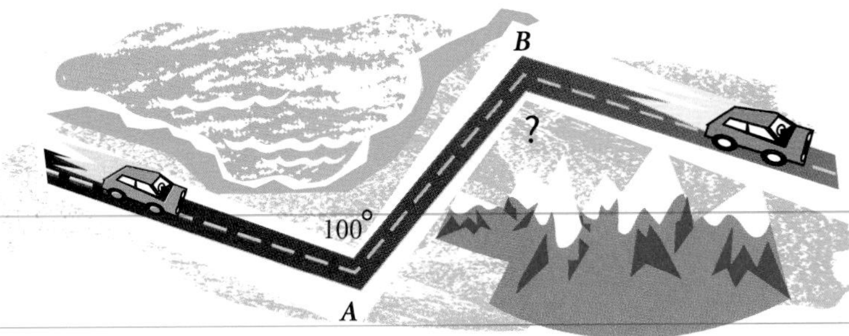

11. They Can't Miss Sue and Damaso are laying sections of pipe in trenches on opposite sides of Dartanian Street. Both are ready to start the section of pipe that will cross the street. Sue has placed her first section of pipe as shown. At what angle should Damaso place his first section so they will meet in a line? Explain. What are you assuming about the trenches?

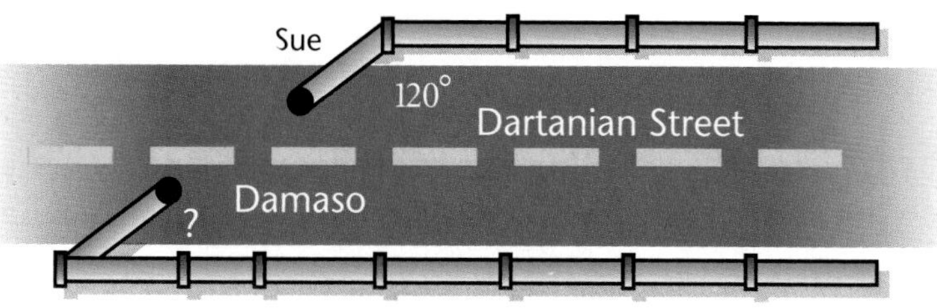

12. Justify statements **a, b,** and **c** in the flow proof with a reason from the list below.

If two parallel lines are cut by a transversal, then the alternate exterior angles are congruent.

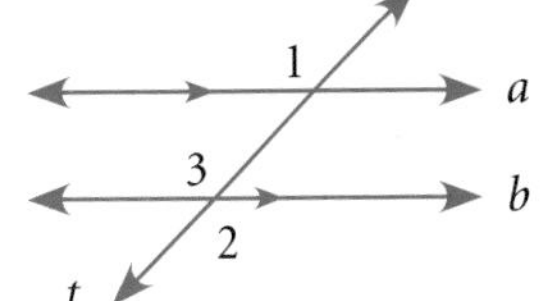

Given: Parallel lines a and b are cut by transversal t.

Prove: $\angle 1 \cong \angle 2$

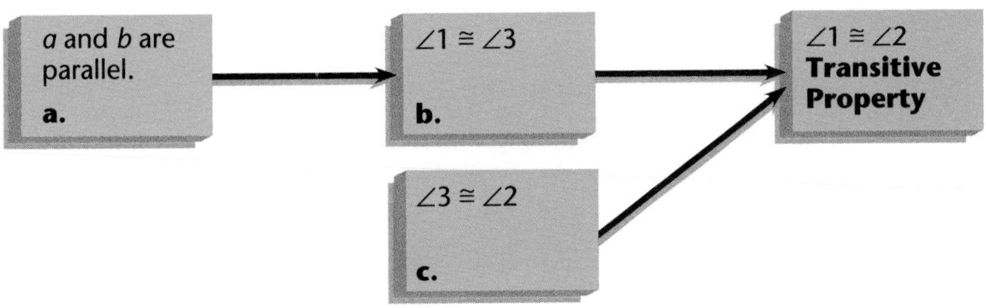

i. Vertical angles are congruent.
ii. If lines are parallel, their alternate interior angles are congruent.
iii. If lines are parallel, their corresponding angles are congruent.
iv. Given information

LOOK AHEAD

13. Write the inverse, converse, and contrapositive of the statement "If two angles are supplementary to the same angle, then they are congruent."

14. Draw an acute angle $\angle MNP$. Then use a compass and straightedge to construct $\angle JKL$ so that $\angle JKL \cong \angle MNP$.

MORE PRACTICE

Find the measures of all the numbered angles for each value of $m\angle 1$.

15. $m\angle 1 = 160°$

16. $m\angle 1 = 35°$

17. $m\angle 1 = 82.5°$

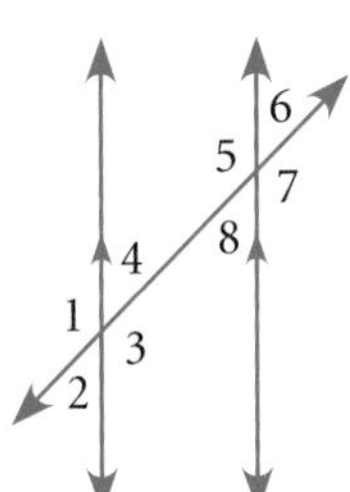

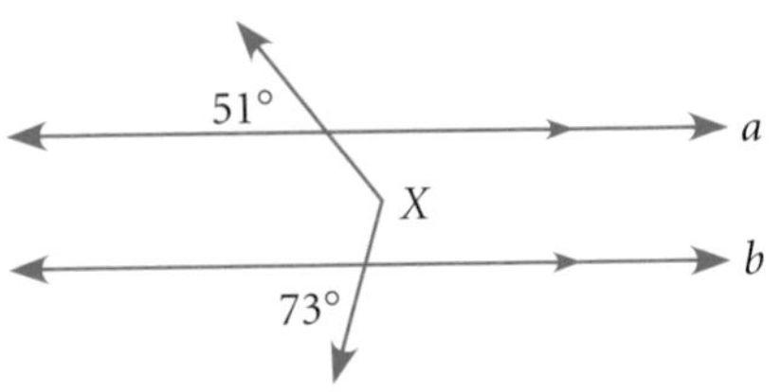

18. In the figure, $a \parallel b$. Find the measure of $\angle X$.

19. Do the *draw* and *state* steps for the proof of the following theorem.

If parallel lines are cut by a transversal, then the alternate interior angles are congruent.

MORE MATH REASONING

20. Lynn says, "If one of two parallel lines is perpendicular to a transversal, then the other one is too."
  a. Do the *draw* and *state* steps for a proof of this statement.
  b. Tell whether or not Lynn is correct, and why.

21. Consider the relation "is parallel to."
  a. Is a line parallel to itself? (In other words, is there a Reflexive Property for *parallel*?) Explain.
  b. If $m \parallel n$, is $n \parallel m$? (Is there a Symmetric Property for *parallel*?) Explain.
  c. If $m \parallel n$ and $n \parallel p$, is $m \parallel p$? (Is there a Transitive Property for *parallel*?) Explain.

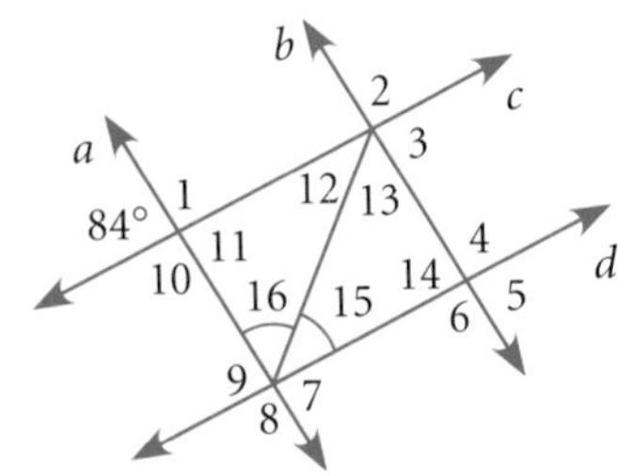

22. In the figure, $a \parallel b$, and $c \parallel d$. Calculate the measure of each numbered angle.

3-4 PART C Proving Lines Parallel

← CONNECT → ***You've explored properties of the angles formed when two parallel lines are cut by a transversal. Now you will investigate the converses of these properties to find ways to show that lines are parallel.***

You have discovered and used several of the relationships about angles formed by parallel lines and a transversal. But suppose you want to make a calligraphy worksheet. How can you be sure that your lines are parallel? In the following Explore, you will see if the converses of some of the statements about angles and parallel lines are true as well.

EXPLORE: CONVERSELY . . .

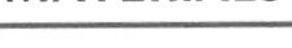

MATERIALS

Compass
Straightedge
Protractor

1. Use a straightedge to draw two intersecting lines, a and b. Label an angle at their intersection $\angle 1$. Select a point X on line a. Construct an alternate interior angle at X congruent to $\angle 1$, using a compass and straightedge. Extend the side of the new angle, and label it line c. What seems to be true about lines c and b?
2. Repeat the steps above, but this time construct a congruent corresponding angle. Are the lines parallel?
3. There are two other theorems about the angles formed by parallel lines.
   - If parallel lines are cut by a transversal, then the alternate exterior angles are congruent.
   - If parallel lines are cut by a transversal, then the same-side interior angles are supplementary.

   Investigate the converses of these theorems. Use a figure like the one in the photo to begin your investigations. You may use a protractor to draw the angles.
4. Write your conjectures in if-then form. Are all of them converses of the postulate and theorems about the angles formed by parallel lines?

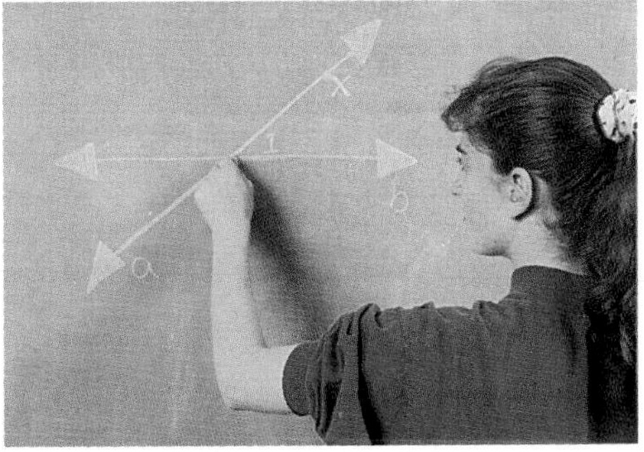

TRY IT

a. List the pairs of parallel lines in the figure at the right. Explain how you *know* the lines are parallel.

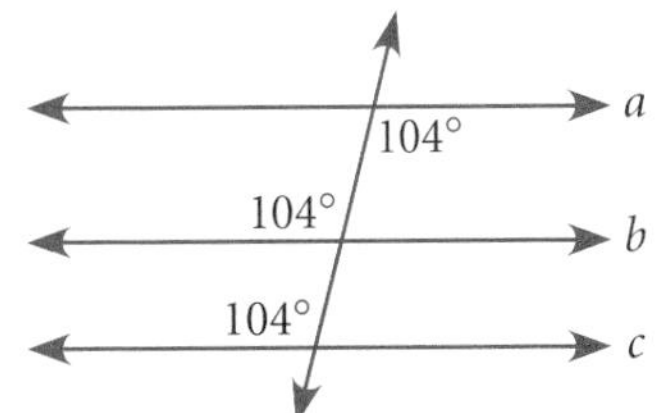

b. A contractor wants to guarantee that the new street she is marking off is parallel to Douglass Street. She finds that $m\angle 1 = 45°$. Give three different ways that she can use angles to be sure that the new street is parallel to Douglass Street.

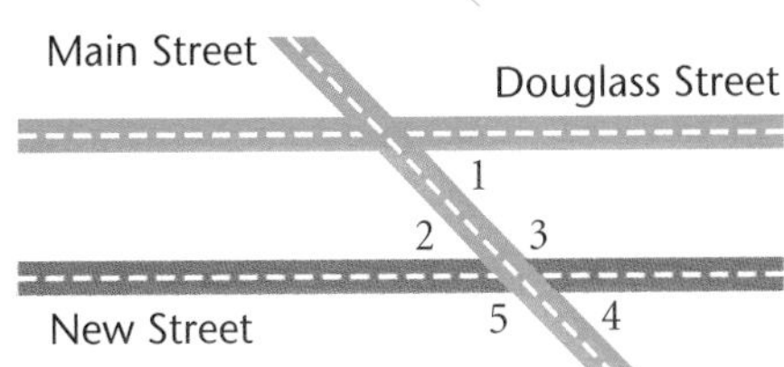

The following statements give ways to prove that lines are parallel. They are all converses of the statements that you learned about parallel lines.

POSTULATE

If two lines are cut by a transversal so that a pair of alternate interior angles are congruent, then the lines are parallel.

THEOREMS

If two lines are cut by a transversal so that a pair of corresponding angles are congruent, then the lines are parallel.

If two lines are cut by a transversal so that a pair of alternate exterior angles are congruent, then the lines are parallel.

If two lines are cut by a transversal so that a pair of same-side interior angles are supplementary, then the lines are parallel.

REFLECT

1. If two lines are cut by two transversals, what is the smallest number of angles that you need to measure to make sure the lines are parallel *and* the transversals are parallel?

2. Can you tell whether lines x and y are parallel from the given information? Why or why not?

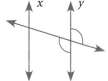

Exercises

CORE

Getting Started For each figure, give a reason why line ℓ is parallel to line m.

1.

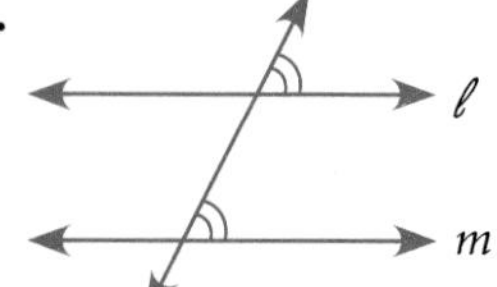

2.

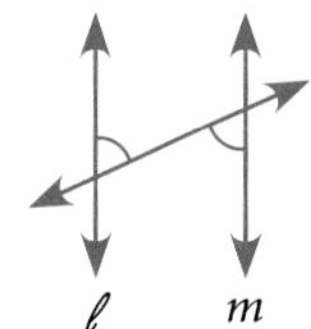

3.

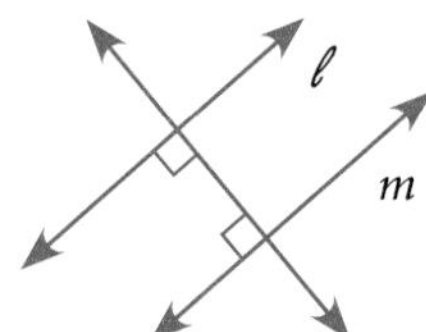

Use the given information to decide which lines are parallel. Justify your answers with a theorem or postulate.

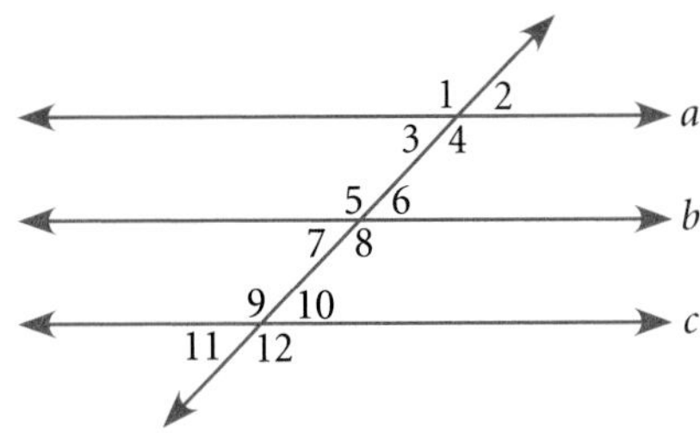

4. $\angle 1 \cong \angle 9$

5. $\angle 3 \cong \angle 6$

6. $m\angle 8 + m\angle 10 = 180°$

7. $\angle 4 \cong \angle 9$

8. $\angle 8 \cong \angle 12$

9. $\angle 1 \cong \angle 8$

Find the value of *x* for which $s \parallel t$.

10. $m\angle 2 = 2x°, m\angle 3 = 4x°$

11. $m\angle 1 = 2x°, m\angle 6 = 136°$

12. $m\angle 1 = 3x°, m\angle 5 = 60°$

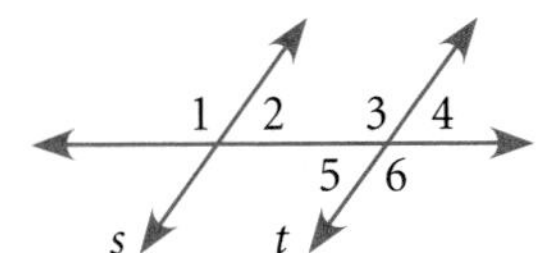

ience

13. Periscope Problem #2 The mirrors in a periscope are mounted parallel to each other, as shown. Because the angle of incidence of a light ray is congruent to the angle of reflection, $\angle 1 \cong \angle 2$.

Explain why the light entering the periscope is parallel to the light leaving the periscope. (Hint: What is the transversal for these light rays?)

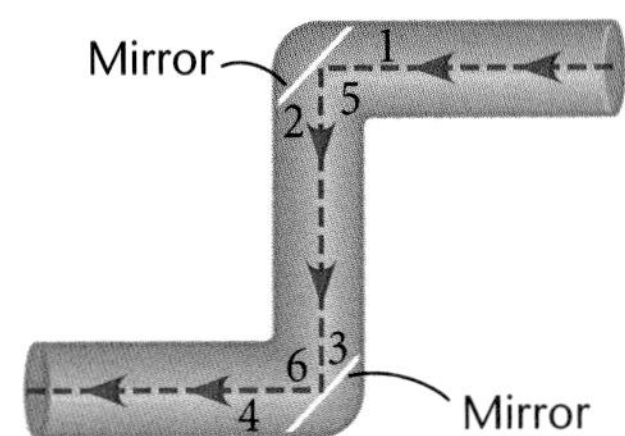

14. Geometry Training The rails of a railroad track must always be parallel. Assume that $\angle 8$ is a right angle. List all the possible ways to check that the rails are parallel by measuring one of the other numbered angles.

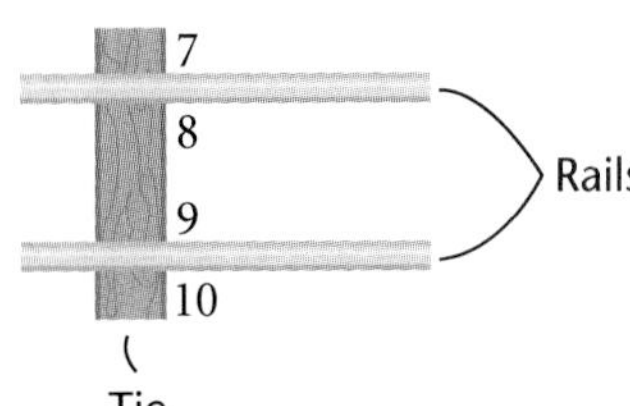

15. Do the *draw* and *state* steps for the proof of the following.

If two lines are cut by a transversal so that a pair of corresponding angles are congruent, then the lines are parallel.

16. Write a procedure for constructing a line parallel to a line ℓ through a point P not on line ℓ. Then copy the figure and show your construction.

LOOK BACK

In Exercises 17 and 18, write each biconditional as two conditional statements. [2-2]

17. An angle is acute if and only if it measures less than 90°.

ience

18. A chemical reaction is exothermic if and only if it releases heat.

19. Draw an obtuse angle, $\angle ABC$. Then use a compass and straightedge to construct $\overrightarrow{BD}$, the angle bisector of $\angle ABC$. [3-3]

MORE PRACTICE

Use the given information to decide which lines are parallel. Justify your answers with a theorem or postulate.

20.

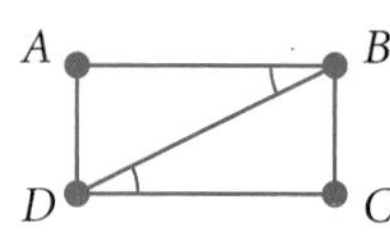

21.

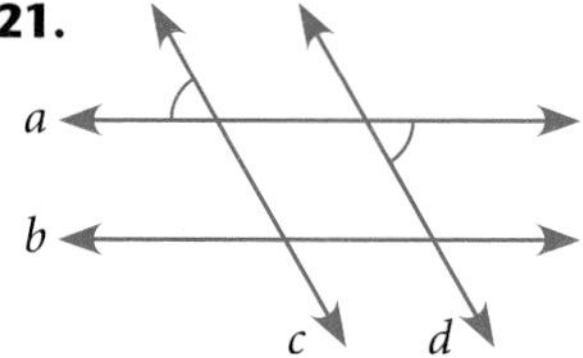

22.

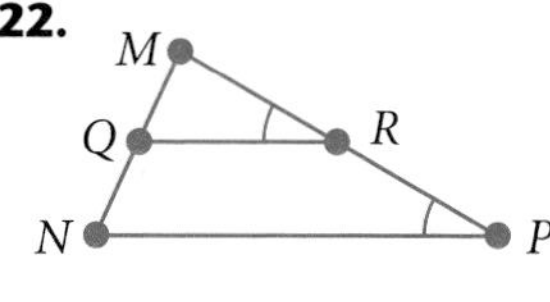

Find the values of *x* and *y* for which *m* || *n*.

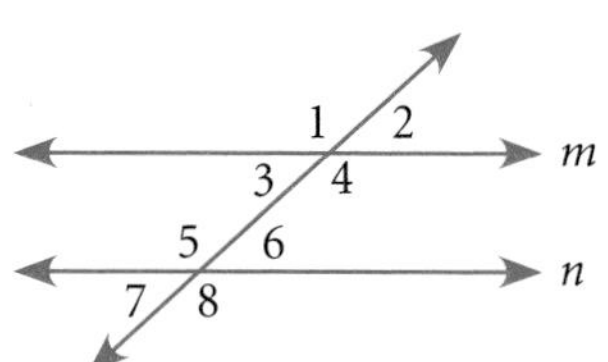

23. $m\angle 1 = (x + y)°$, $m\angle 4 = (x - y)°$, and $m\angle 8 = 118°$

24. $m\angle 3 = (2x - y)°$, $m\angle 6 = (x + 2y)°$, and $m\angle 7 = 75°$

25. $m\angle 2 = 63°$, $m\angle 3 = (x - 3y)°$, and $m\angle 6 = (7x - 2y + 2)°$

MORE MATH REASONING

26. Use a straightedge to draw two parallel lines and a transversal. Then use a protractor to bisect a pair of alternate exterior angles. Write a statement about these bisectors, and explain why the statement is true.

> **Problem-Solving Tip**
>
> Use deductive reasoning.

27. The proof below is shown in paragraph form. Fill in the blanks to complete the proof.

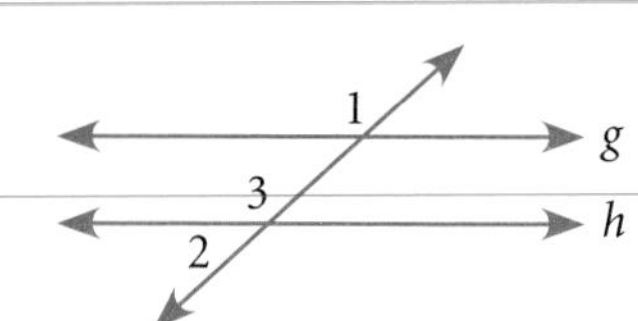

Given: $\angle 1$ is supplementary to $\angle 2$.

Prove: $g \parallel h$

Proof: We are given that $\angle 1$ and $\angle 2$ are supplementary. $\angle 2$ and $\angle 3$ are a linear pair, by the **a.** ____. This means that they are supplementary, by the **b.** ____. $\angle 1$ and $\angle 3$ are both **c.** ____ to $\angle 2$, and supplements of the same angle are **d.** ____. $\angle 1$ and $\angle 3$ are corresponding angles, by the definition of corresponding angles. Therefore, since a pair of corresponding angles are **e.** ____, we know $g \parallel h$.

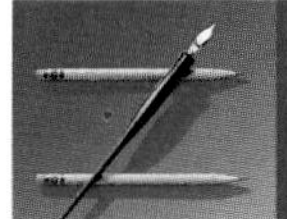

3-4 PART D Making Connections

← CONNECT → ***Examples of parallel lines are everywhere, both in nature and in manufactured objects. You've explored parallel lines and the angles formed when they are intersected by transversals.***

In the following Explore, you will see how our results about parallel lines, transversals, and angles can be used to create your own calligraphy worksheet.

EXPLORE: GETTING THE RIGHT ANGLE

MATERIALS

Protractor
Straightedge

In the calligraphy worksheet at the right, the measure of the alternate interior angles determines the slant of the letters created.

1. Create your own calligraphy worksheet by experimenting with different measures for the alternate interior angles. Find an angle that you think makes the best-looking letters. Set up a section of your worksheet using this angle, and use this section to write your name.
2. On this section of your worksheet, mark a set of parallel lines and a transversal. Label some points, so that you can list the pairs of corresponding angles, alternate interior angles, alternate exterior angles, and same-side interior angles. Give the measures of all the angles on your worksheet.

REFLECT

1. All of the facts you have learned about the angles formed by parallel lines and transversals have true converses. Give an example of a true statement about parallel lines that has a false converse.
2. Write a summary of the theorems and postulates about parallel lines and transversals. Illustrate each with a sketch.

Self-Assessment

Determine whether each statement is true or false. If a statement is false, explain why.

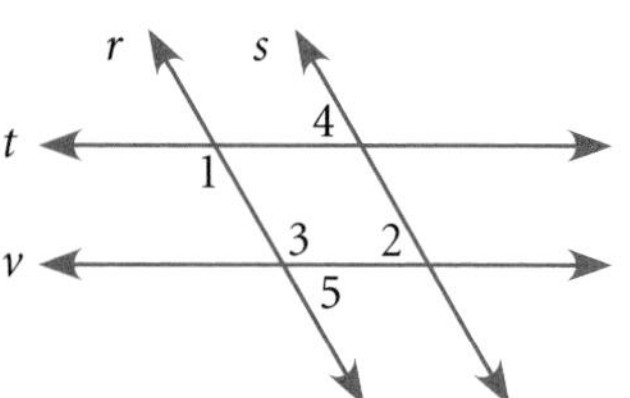

1. $\angle 1$ and $\angle 3$ are alternate interior angles.
2. If $t \parallel v$, then $m\angle 2 + m\angle 5 = 180°$.
3. If $\angle 2 \cong \angle 4$, then $t \parallel v$.
4. If $t \parallel v$, $r \parallel s$, and $m\angle 4 = 24°$, then $m\angle 3 = 24°$.

Use the given information to name the lines (if any) that are parallel.

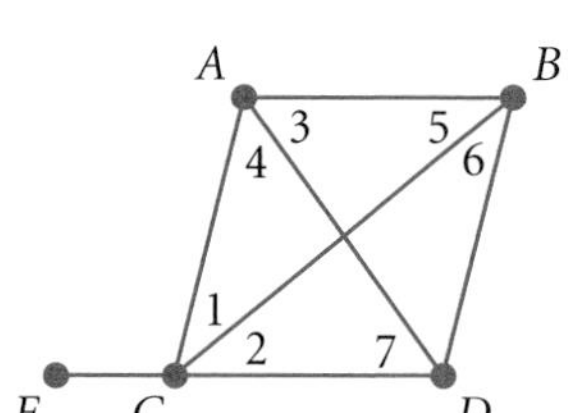

5. $\angle 3 \cong \angle 7$
6. $\angle 2 \cong \angle 6$
7. $\angle 2 \cong \angle 3$
8. $\angle ACE \cong \angle BDC$
9. $m\angle ACD + m\angle BDC = 180°$
10. Suppose $m\angle 2 = (3x + 10)°$ and $m\angle 5 = (x + 28)°$. Find the value for x for which $\overline{AB} \parallel \overline{CD}$.

Use the figure at the right to answer each question. [3-3]

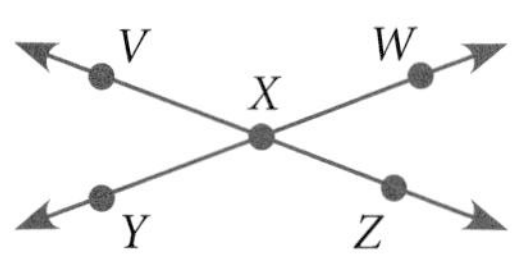

11. Name two pairs of congruent angles. Explain why they are congruent.

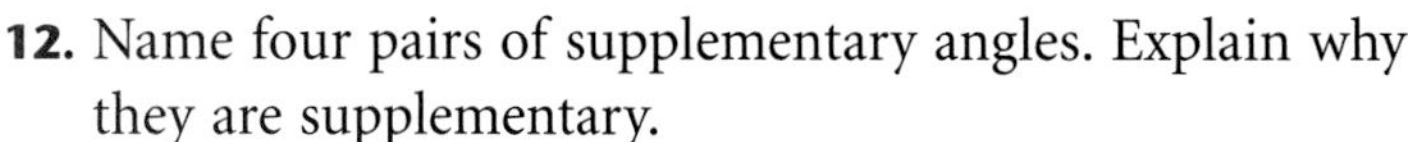

12. Name four pairs of supplementary angles. Explain why they are supplementary.

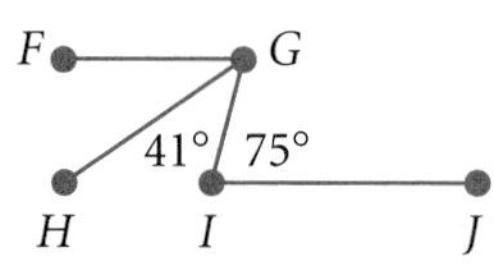

13. In the figure at the right, $\overline{FG} \parallel \overline{IJ}$. $m\angle FGH =$ ____.
    (a) 34° (b) 41° (c) 45° (d) 75° (e) 116°

14. **Refract Facts** Because light travels at different speeds in air and water, light rays are refracted (bent) when they go from one medium to the other. Light rays are bent by the same amount, so if they are parallel in the water, they are also parallel in the air. In the figure at the right, $m\angle 1 = 45°$ and $m\angle 2 = 122°$. Find the measures of all other numbered angles.

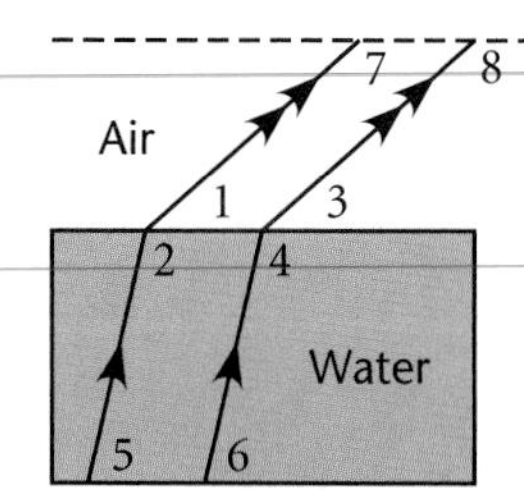

15. **Handwriting Analysis** Write a few words on your paper. Then measure the angle of inclination (angle to the right of vertical) of your handwriting. Get writing samples from two other people. What is the range of their angles of inclination? Do any of the samples have a "negative" angle of inclination? What is the average angle of inclination?

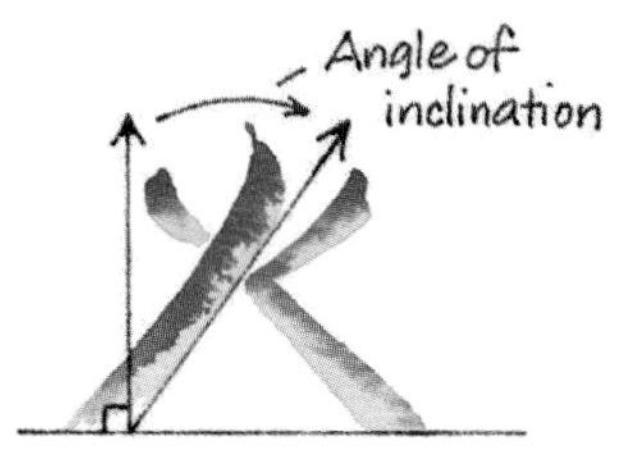

Chapter 3 Review

In Chapter 3, you learned about angles, bearings, translations, and vectors. You investigated rotations and rotational symmetry and explored the assumptions that may be made about angles and distances in a figure. You also explored the relationships between pairs of angles and between the angles formed by two parallel lines and a transversal.

KEY TERMS

acute angle [3-1]	half-turn [3-2]	same-side interior angles [3-4]
alternate exterior angles [3-4]	linear pair [3-3]	supplementary angles [3-3]
alternate interior angles [3-4]	obtuse angle [3-1]	translation [3-1]
angle bisector [3-3]	opposite rays [3-1]	translation vector [3-1]
bearing [3-1]	point symmetry [3-2]	transversal [3-4]
complementary angles [3-3]	right angle [3-1]	vector sum [3-1]
corresponding angles [3-4]	rotation [3-2]	vector [3-1]
equal vectors [3-1]	rotational symmetry [3-2]	vertical angles [3-3]

Determine whether each statement is true or false. If the statement is false, change the underlined word or phrase to make it true.

1. A vector is a directed line segment.

2. The measure of an acute angle is greater than 90° but less than 180°.

3. If a figure can be rotated onto itself through an angle of 180°, it has point symmetry.

4. Complementary angles are angles whose measures add up to 180°.

5. A transversal is a line that intersects two coplanar lines in two different points.

CONCEPTS AND APPLICATIONS

Name each of the following, using the figure at the right. [3-1]

6. two opposite rays

7. one acute angle, one obtuse angle, and one right angle

8. a point in the interior of $\angle DAC$

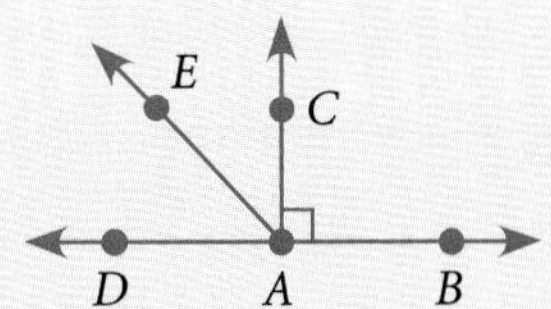

9. The bearing of a mountaintop from point P is 120°, and the bearing of a lake from point P is 270°. Given this information, is it possible to find the bearing of the mountaintop from the lake? If so, what is the bearing? If not, what additional information do you need? [3-1]

10. For each vector at the right, write the name of the vector, use the distance formula to find its length, and use your protractor to find its direction. [3-1]

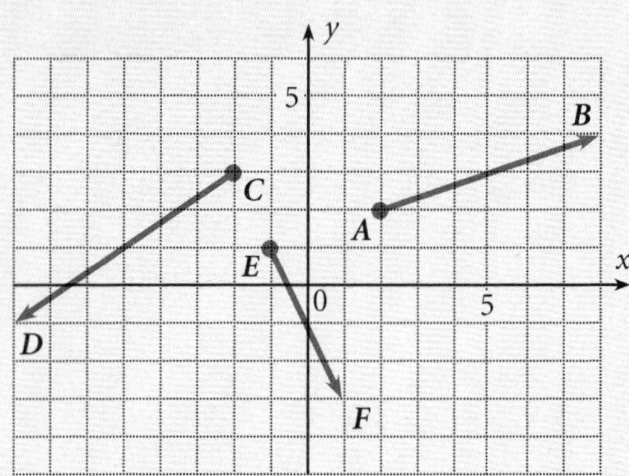

Determine which of the designs below have rotational symmetry. For those that have rotational symmetry, give the direction and number of degrees of all clockwise rotations of less than 360° that map the figure onto itself. [3-2]

11.

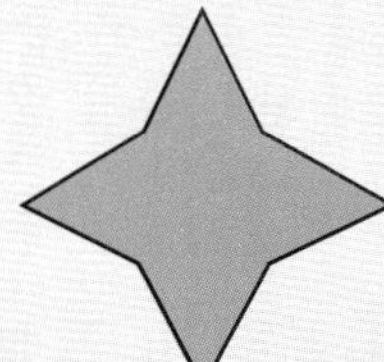

12.

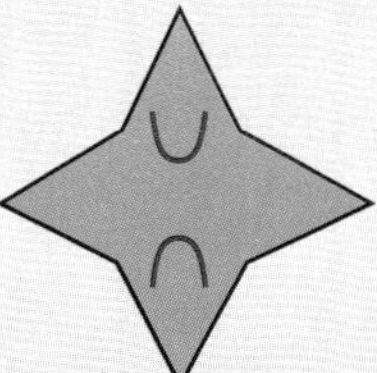

13.

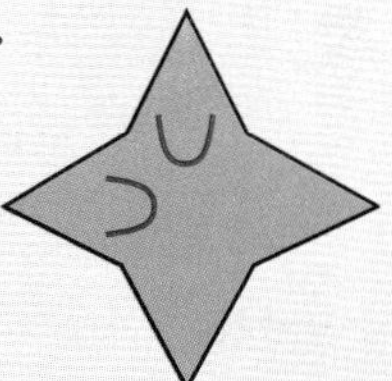

In each of the following, write and solve an equation to find the measures of ∠*AOB* and ∠*COD*. [3-3]

14. $m\angle AOB = m\angle COD$, $m\angle BOC = 40°$, and $m\angle AOD = 130°$.

15. $m\angle AOB = (x + 10)°$, $m\angle BOC = 40°$, and $m\angle COD = 2x°$, $m\angle AOD = 5x°$.

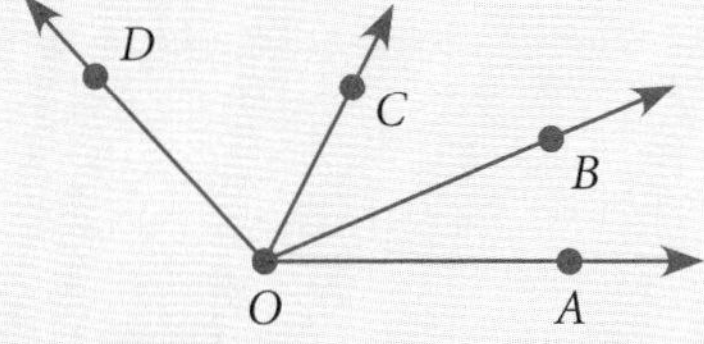

16. Find the measures of the numbered angles in the figure at the right. [3-3]

17. Write a summary of the relationships among the angles formed by a transversal that intersects two parallel lines. Sketch and mark a figure to illustrate each relationship.

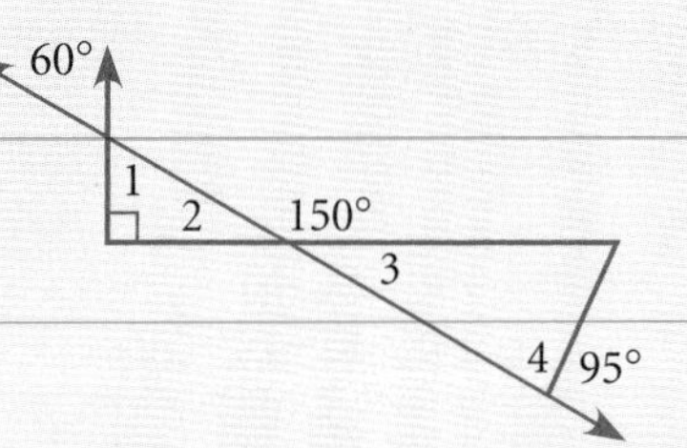

Determine whether each statement is true or false. If true, state the postulate that justifies it. [2-2]

18. The noncollinear points A, B, and C are contained in two different planes.

19. Space contains at least one point not in plane A.

In each figure, determine which, if any, of the lines must be parallel. Justify each answer with a theorem or postulate. [3-4]

20.

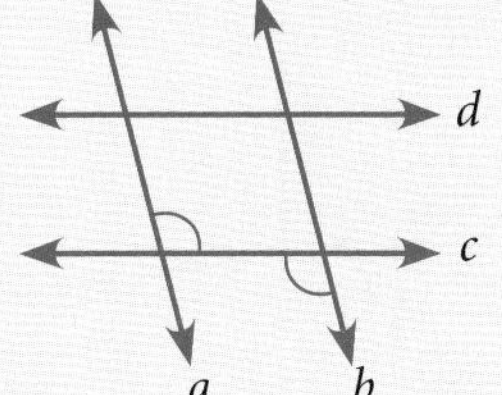

21.

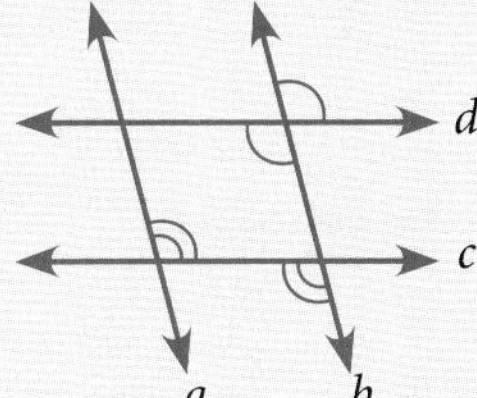

22.

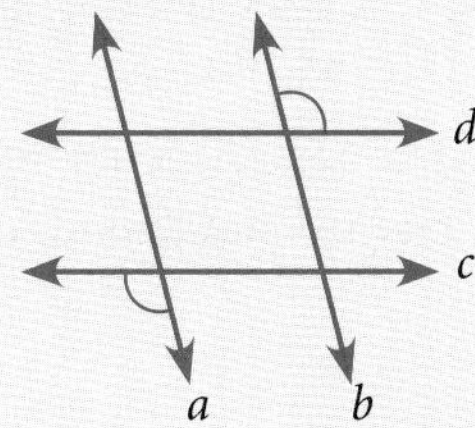

CONCEPTS AND CONNECTIONS

Science

23. Geography Choose two cities in the United States. Sketch a route between the two cities, using at least four straight segments. Each segment should join two large cities. Describe the route, using the language of translations and vectors. Name the translation vector for each segment, and estimate the length and direction of each vector. Then describe the route using the language of bearings; for each segment, estimate the bearing of the second city from the first.

SELF-EVALUATION

Write a paragraph summarizing the main facts about angles covered in Chapter 3. Be sure to include concepts related to bearings, vectors, rotations, angle pairs, and transversals. Describe any topics that you found difficult, and describe how you plan to review those topics.

Chapter 3 Assessment

TEST

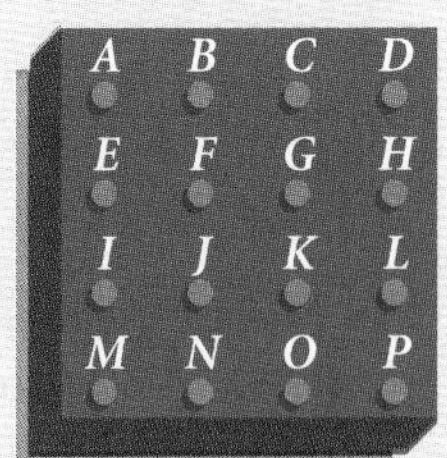

1. Which points on the grid at the right have a bearing greater than 090 and less than 180 from point *B*?

2. Which point on the grid has a bearing of 045 from *J* and 090 from *B*?

3. What is the image of the point (−2, 1) under the translation with vector <2, 5> followed by the translation with vector <−2, 3>? What is the vector for the single translation that is equivalent to the two translations given?

4. Is it true that vector lengths add when you add vectors? For example, if $\overrightarrow{RS} = \overrightarrow{RT} + \overrightarrow{TS}$, is $RS = RT + TS$? If it is not always true, is it sometimes true? What is true of vectors whose lengths add when they are added?

Using the vector $\overrightarrow{SS'}$ as a translation vector, find the coordinates of the translation image of each of the following.

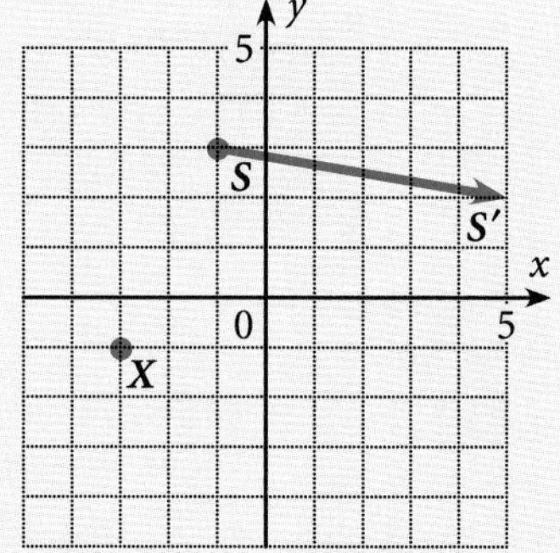

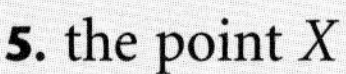

5. the point X

6. the point (u, v)

7. the segment with endpoints $(6, 3)$ and $(1, -2)$

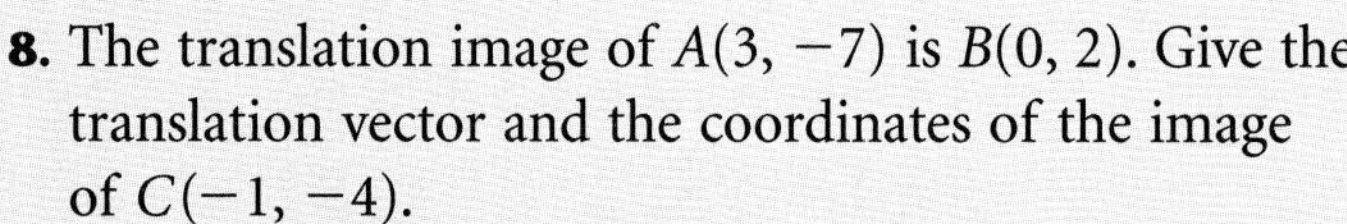

8. The translation image of $A(3, -7)$ is $B(0, 2)$. Give the translation vector and the coordinates of the image of $C(-1, -4)$.

9. Assume that the following conditional statement is true: "If it is raining, then it is cloudy." Write the inverse, converse, and contrapositive, and determine which of these, if any, are also true.

Determine whether each figure has rotational symmetry. For those that have rotational symmetry, give the number of degrees of all clockwise rotations of less than 360° that map the figure onto itself.

10. 

11. 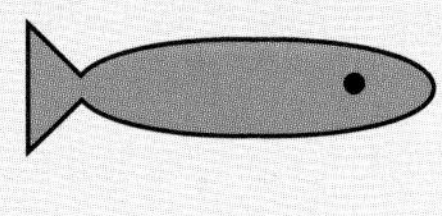

12. 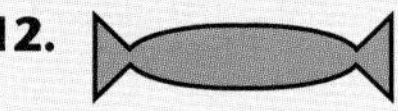

13. Find the measure of an angle whose supplement is four times its complement.

14. In the figure below, $m\angle AOB = (2x + 10)°$, $m\angle BOC = (4x - 20)°$, and $m\angle AOC = 110°$. Write and solve an equation to find $m\angle AOB$ and $m\angle BOC$.

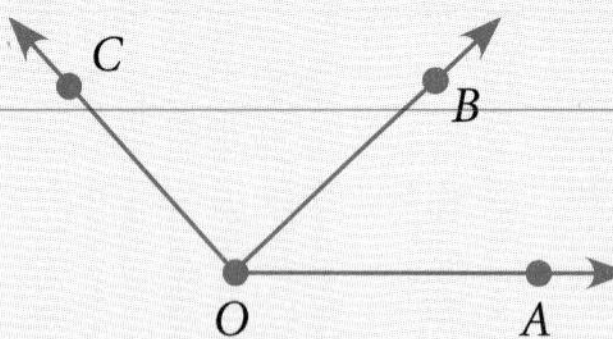

15. Suppose that $\angle A$ and $\angle B$ are complementary angles, $\angle B$ and $\angle C$ are vertical angles, $\angle C$ and $\angle D$ are supplementary angles, and $\angle D$ and $\angle E$ are vertical angles. Which of the following must be true?

a. $m\angle E + m\angle C = 180°$

b. $m\angle B + m\angle C = 90°$

c. $m\angle C + m\angle A = 90°$

d. $\angle B \cong \angle D$

Determine which of the following may be assumed from the figure at the right. Explain.

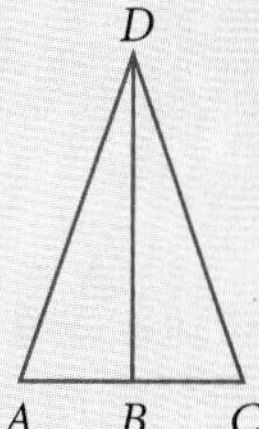

16. Point B is between points A and C.

17. $\angle DAC \cong \angle DCA$

18. $DA > CA$

19. Find the measure of each of the numbered angles in the figure below.

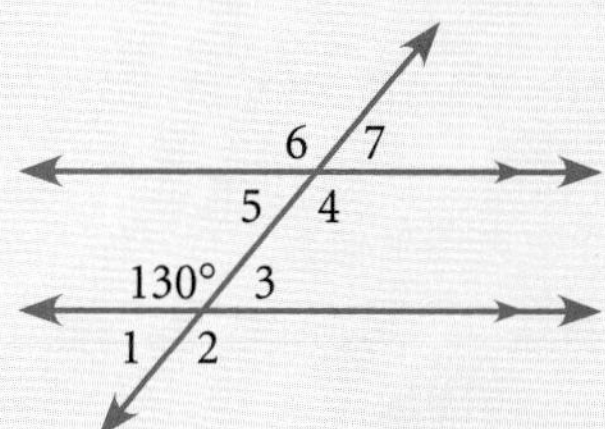

20. How many different measures are there among the angles in the figure below? Explain your answer.

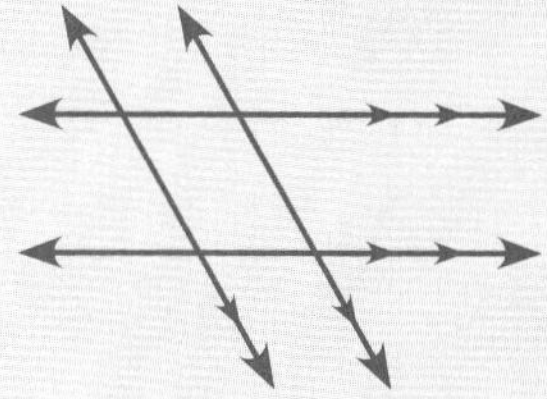

21. Eddie is standing on a trapeze. When the trapeze swings sideways, $\angle 1$ and $\angle 2$ are supplementary. Why does the bar on which Eddie stands remain horizontal? Justify your answer with a theorem or postulate.

22. Write a summary of ways to show that two lines intersected by a transversal are parallel. Sketch and mark a figure to illustrate each method.

PERFORMANCE TASK

Draw a large figure showing two parallel lines and a transversal that intersects them. Then use a compass and straightedge to construct the bisector of each alternate interior angle. Repeat the construction, beginning with a different transversal. Make a conjecture about the pairs of angle bisectors you constructed, and give a deductive argument that shows why your conjecture is true.

Chapter 4 Triangles

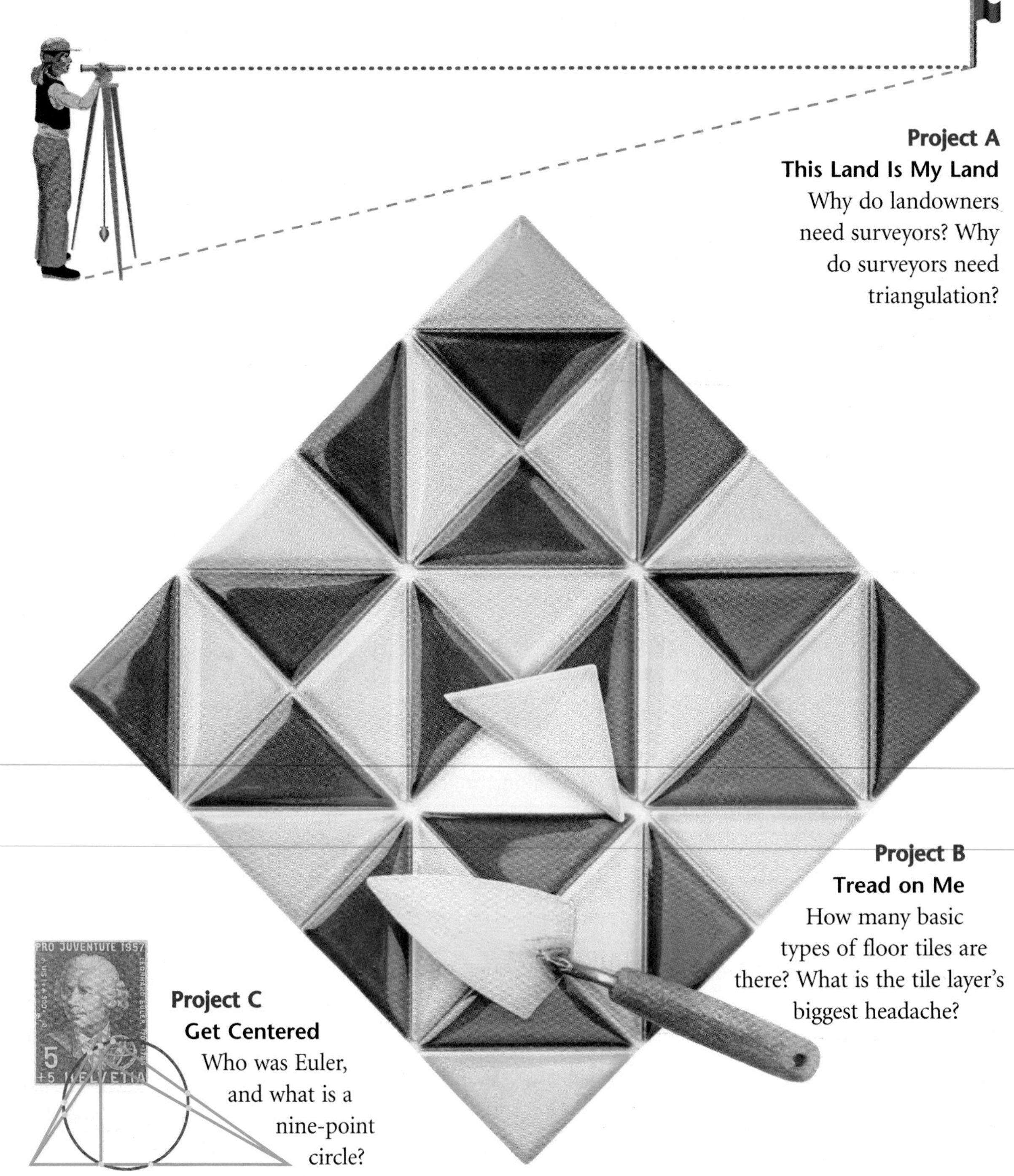

Project A
This Land Is My Land
Why do landowners need surveyors? Why do surveyors need triangulation?

Project B
Tread on Me
How many basic types of floor tiles are there? What is the tile layer's biggest headache?

Project C
Get Centered
Who was Euler, and what is a nine-point circle?

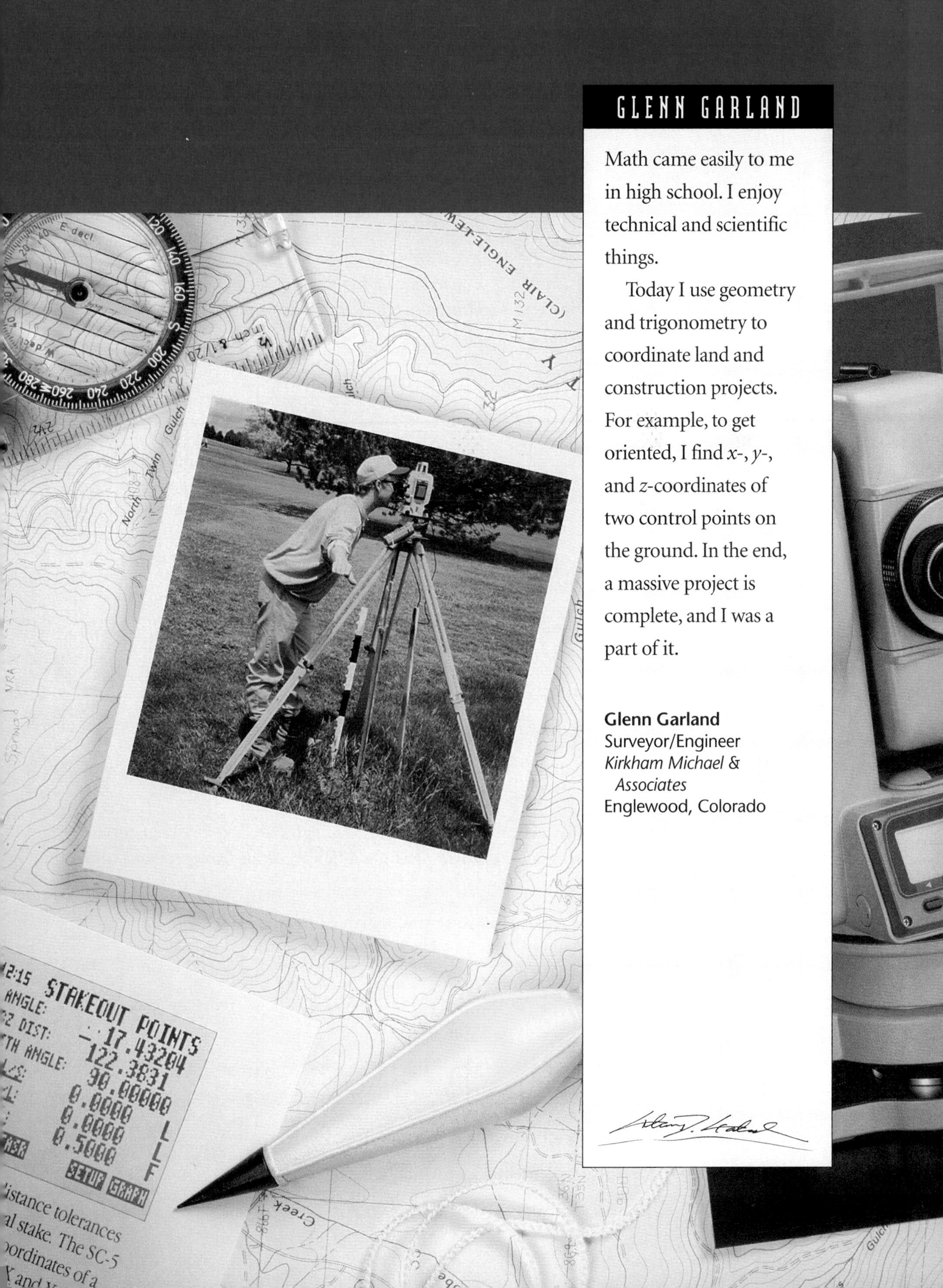

GLENN GARLAND

Math came easily to me in high school. I enjoy technical and scientific things.

Today I use geometry and trigonometry to coordinate land and construction projects. For example, to get oriented, I find *x*-, *y*-, and *z*-coordinates of two control points on the ground. In the end, a massive project is complete, and I was a part of it.

Glenn Garland
Surveyor/Engineer
Kirkham Michael & Associates
Englewood, Colorado

Chapter 4 Triangles

GETTING READY

4-1
Tessellations and Triangles

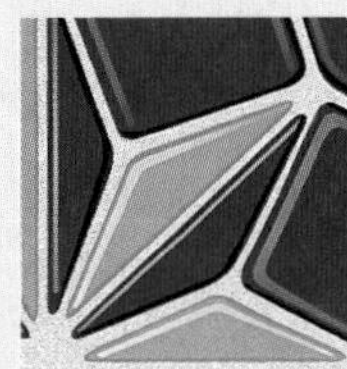

In 4-1 you will learn about properties of triangles and see how these properties relate to tessellations. You will use the following skills from previous chapters.

1. Complete the table. [3-3]

$m\angle ABC$	$m\angle BAC$	$m\angle ACB$	$m\angle BCD$
	75°		96°
59°	92°		
87°		27°	

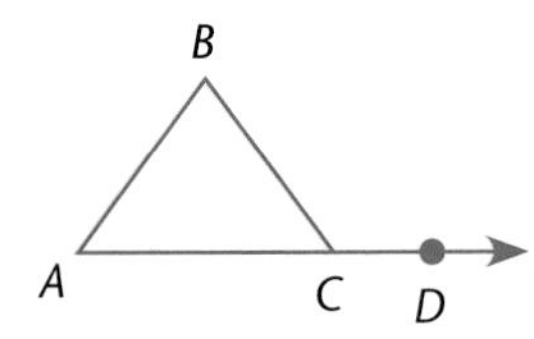

4-2
Deductive Proof with Triangles

In 4-2 you will explore more properties of triangles and develop skills for deductive proof. You will need the following skills from previous chapters.

Identify the hypothesis and conclusion of each statement. [2-1]

2. If $x = 3$, then $2x - 4 = 2$.

3. If $x = 2$, then $x^2 + 5x + 6 = 0$.

4. If $x < 0$, then $|x| = -x$.

5. If Kathy uses the Internet, then she has a computer.

6. If Tom is having a party, then it must be his birthday.

4-3
Properties of Special Triangles

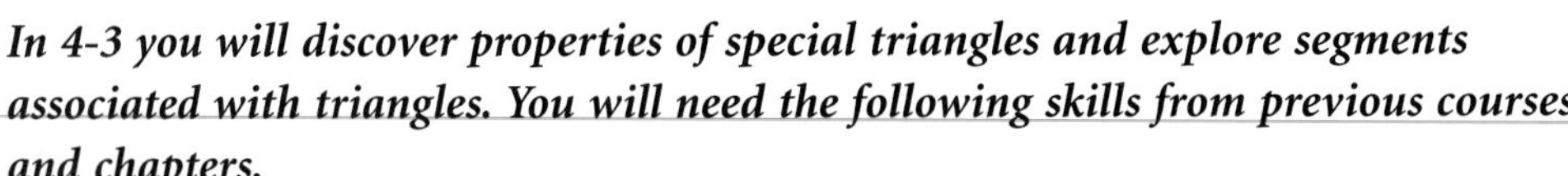

In 4-3 you will discover properties of special triangles and explore segments associated with triangles. You will need the following skills from previous courses and chapters.

Use the figure at right to answer the questions below. [3-4]

7. Complete the table.

$m\angle 1$	$m\angle 2$	$m\angle 3$	$m\angle 4$	$m\angle 5$	$m\angle 6$	$m\angle 7$	$m\angle 8$
87°							
		102°					
						149°	

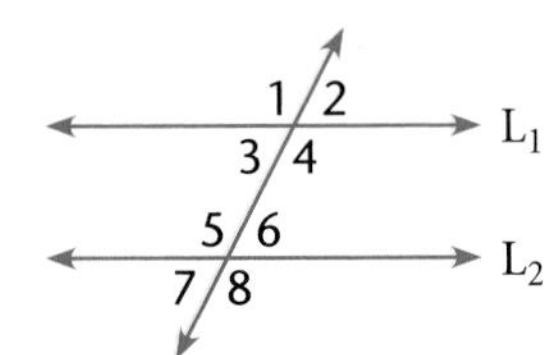

8. Which angles are congruent to angle 1?

9. Angle 3 is supplementary to which angles?

4-1 Tessellations and Triangles

Miles *of* Tiles

For centuries, geometric figures have been a part of art and architecture. Mosaics — designs composed of many small tiles set in clay or plaster — were used by the Sumerians in architectural surfaces as early as 4000 B.C. These tiles served not only as artistic decorations, but also as part of the structure.

The Persians showed that they were masters of tile decoration by covering buildings with mosaics. Construction on the Madrasah on Reghistan in Samarkand (in what is now Uzbekistan) began in 1420 A.D. Perhaps the most elaborate example of tiled architecture was created for a temple in Isfahan, the construction of which began in 1602.

Lutfallah Mosque, Isfahan, Iran

Masjia-E Shah, Isfahan, Iran

The Romans also used tiles, called *tesserae*, in buildings, floors, and roads. A fort called Vollubilis stood at the edge of the Roman Empire in what is now Morocco. Stunning mosaics cover the floor of the fort.

Artists from the areas around Egypt, Turkey, and Spain also used patterns of geometric figures as decorations. Even today, artists and architects use simple geometric figures, and the patterns created by fitting the figures together, in their design of modern structures.

?

1. **A *tessellation* is a repeating pattern that completely fills up a plane region. What Roman (Latin) word is the root word for tessellation?**
2. **Identify two tessellations in your classroom. What geometric figures are used in these tessellations?**
3. **Name some common geometric figures that can be used to tessellate (fill up) a region.**

4-1 PART A Angles Inside the Triangle

← CONNECT → ***You have worked with angles and triangles before. Now you will learn some ways to classify triangles. You will also discover a useful fact about the angles of a triangle.***

A tessellation is a repeating pattern of figures that completely covers a plane region without gaps or overlaps. The walls of the building at the left (located near Orlando, Florida) contain examples of tessellation patterns. You will soon investigate several geometric figures to see whether or not they can be used to tessellate a plane.

We will begin with triangles. Although you are already familiar with triangles, it is important for everyone to use the same terms.

DEFINITION

A **triangle** is a figure formed by three line segments that connect three noncollinear points.

The figure below illustrates some vocabulary commonly associated with triangles.

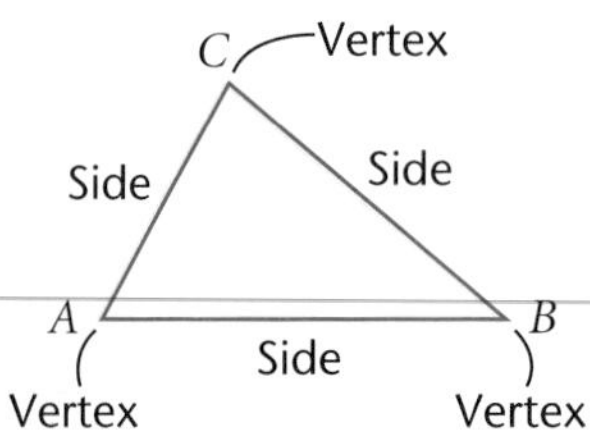

A triangle is named using its vertices and a $\triangle$ symbol. For example, the triangle shown can be named $\triangle ABC$.

In the following Explore, you will investigate an important property of the angles of a triangle.

EXPLORE: THE THIRD DEGREE!

MATERIALS

Straightedge
Scissors
Paper

1. Use a straightedge to draw a large triangle. Cut out your triangle. Label the angle that appears to have the largest measure $\angle 1$, and label the others $\angle 2$ and $\angle 3$. Label the angles on the front and the back of your triangle.
2. Fold $\angle 1$ so that its vertex touches the opposite side of the triangle; the fold should look parallel to that side. Then fold $\angle 2$ and $\angle 3$ inward so that they touch the vertex of $\angle 1$. Your triangle should now look something like an envelope.

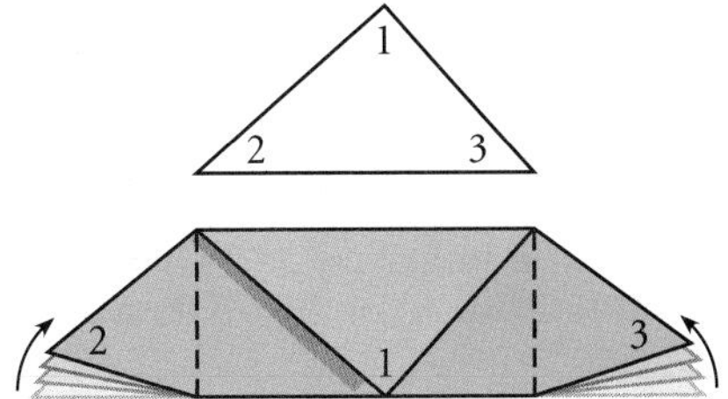

3. Make a conjecture about the sum of the measures of the angles in a triangle. Explain how folding the triangle illustrates your conjecture. Compare your conjecture with those made by your classmates. Does the sum depend on the size or shape of the triangle?
4. Does the tessellation at the right formed by congruent triangles support your conjecture about the angles of a triangle? If so, how?

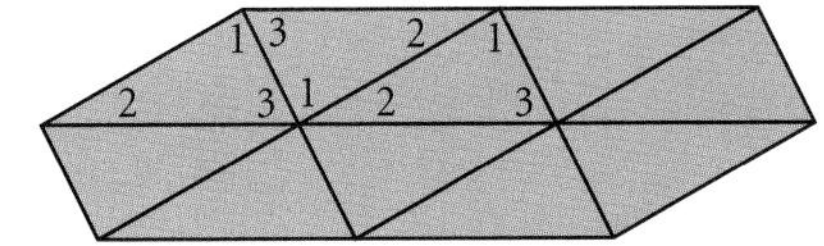

TRY IT

a. Two angles of a triangle measure 40° and 58°. What is the measure of the third angle?

Earlier you saw that an angle can be classified by its measure. Triangles can also be classified in several ways.

TRIANGLE CLASSIFICATION BY SIDES

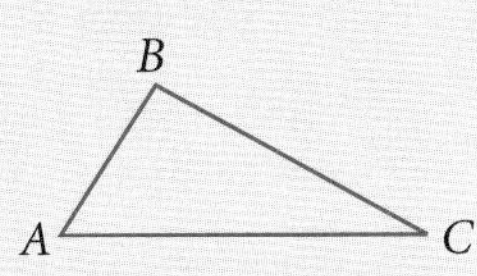

$\triangle ABC$ is a **scalene triangle.** No two of its sides are congruent.

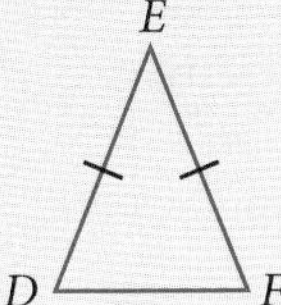

$\triangle DEF$ is an **isosceles triangle.** At least two of its sides are congruent.

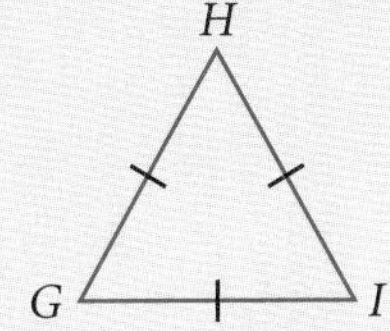

$\triangle GHI$ is an **equilateral triangle.** All of its sides are congruent.

The sides and angles of an isosceles triangle have special names, as shown at the right.

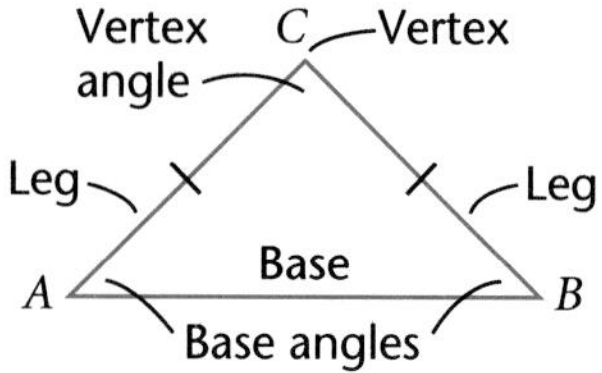

TRIANGLE CLASSIFICATION BY ANGLES

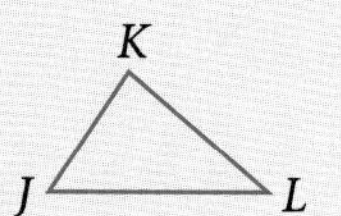

$\triangle JKL$ is an **acute triangle.** All of its angles are acute.

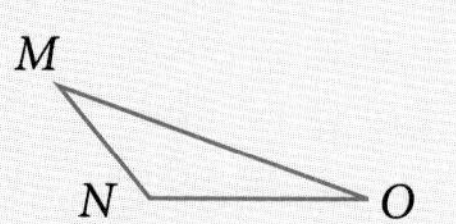

$\triangle MNO$ is an **obtuse triangle.** It has one obtuse angle.

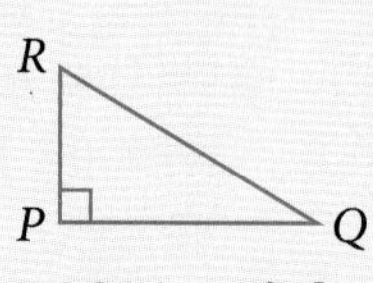

$\triangle PQR$ is a **right triangle.** It has one right angle.

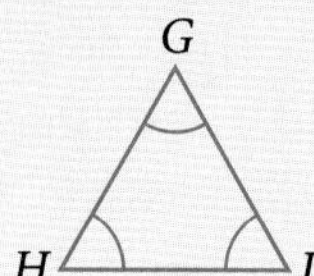

$\triangle GHI$ is an **equiangular triangle.** All of its angles have the same measure.

You may notice that $\triangle GHI$ also appears to be equilateral. The fact that a triangle is equilateral if and only if it is equiangular is important, and you will soon investigate this further.

The sides of a right triangle also have special names, as shown at the right.

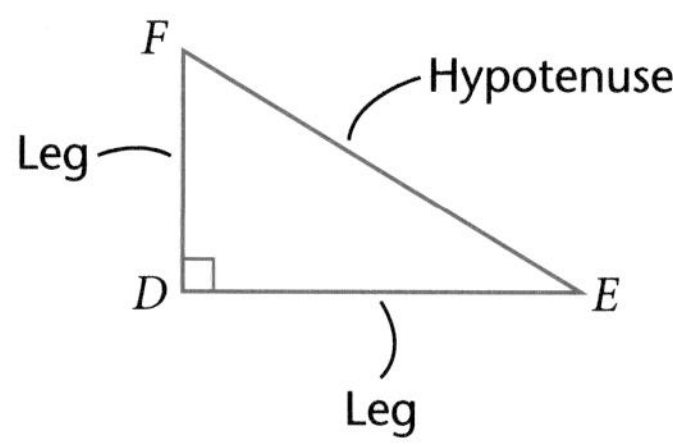

EXAMPLES

Classify each triangle using both angle and side classification.

1.

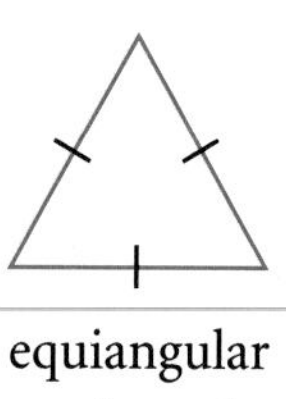

equiangular
equilateral

2.

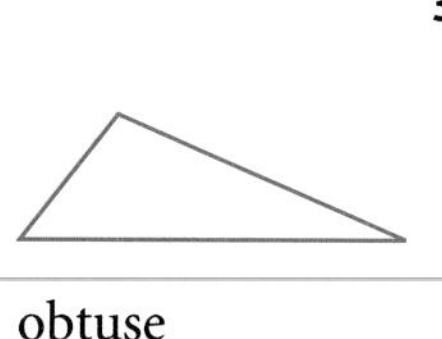

obtuse
scalene

3.

right
scalene

4.

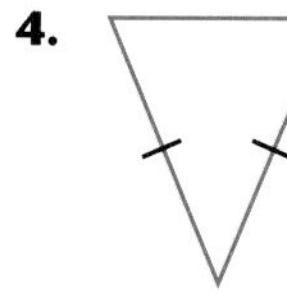

acute
isosceles

TRY IT

b. Draw an isosceles triangle, $\triangle PRS$, with base $\overline{PR}$. Name the legs and the vertex angle.

c. Draw a right triangle, $\triangle FGH$, with right angle $\angle F$. Name the hypotenuse and the legs.

The property you investigated in the Explore can be proved, so we state it as a theorem. You will be asked to justify this theorem in Exercise 18.

TRIANGLE ANGLE-SUM THEOREM

The sum of the measures of the angles of a triangle is 180°.

1. What does the Triangle Angle-Sum Theorem tell you about the measures of each angle in an equiangular triangle?

REFLECT

1. Is it possible for a triangle to have more than one obtuse angle? more than one right angle? more than one acute angle? Explain each of your answers.
2. Explain why an acute triangle cannot be an obtuse triangle.
3. Which angle in a right triangle has the largest measure? Why? What does this tell you about the other two angles?

Exercises

CORE

Getting Started Name and classify each triangle, using both angle and side classification.

1. 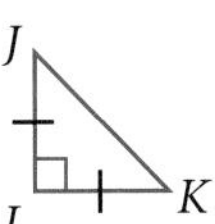

2. 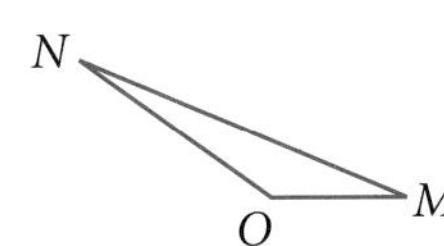

3. 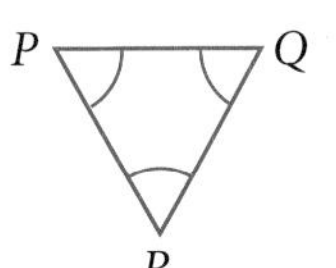

4. 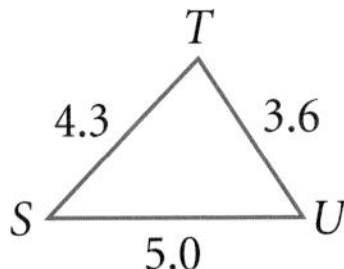

5. List all the possible names for the triangle at the right.

M

L

N

Is it possible for each of the following types of triangles to exist? If so, sketch an example. If not, explain why not.

6. obtuse isosceles

7. right equilateral

8. right scalene

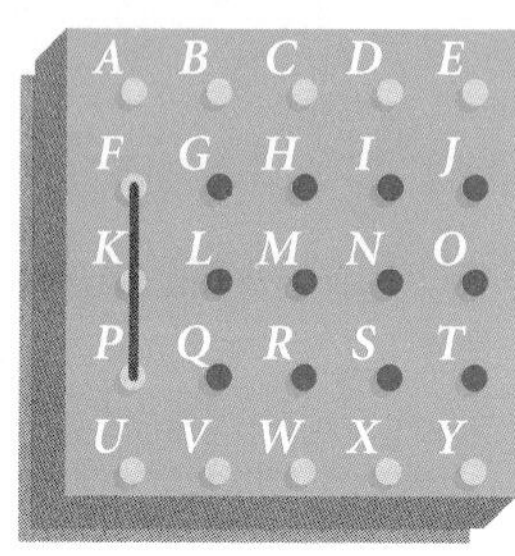

9. $\overline{FP}$ is one side of a triangle on the grid. List the possibilities for the third vertex if the triangle is of the following type.
   a. obtuse **b.** right **c.** isosceles
   d. Suppose the third vertex of the triangle is chosen randomly from the points shown in red. What is the probability that the triangle will be a right triangle?

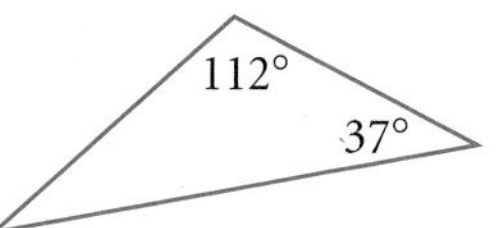

10. A surveyor measured two angles of a triangular lot as shown. What is the measure of the third angle? What theorem justifies your answer?

Find the measure of ∠1 in each figure.

11. 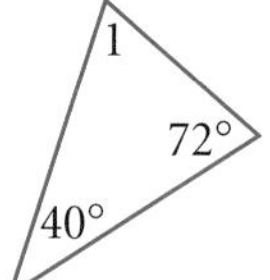

12. 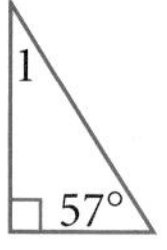

13. 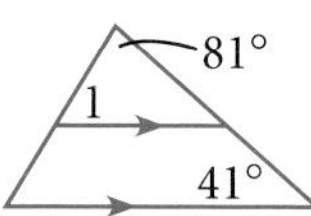

14. 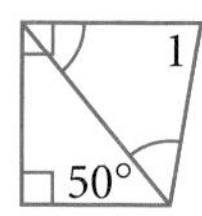

15. In $\triangle ABC$, $m\angle A = (x + 20)°$, $m\angle B = (2x - 42)°$, and $m\angle C = (3x + 4)°$. Find the measure of each angle.

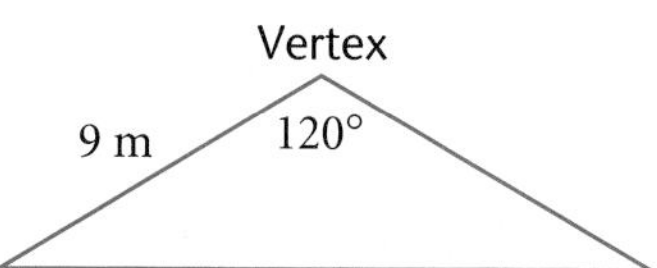

16. **Shingle Minded** A carpenter is building a roof frame. The cross section of the frame is an isosceles triangle, as shown. What is the length of the other leg of the roof frame? How do you know?

Careers

17. The measure of one of the acute angles in a right triangle depends on the measure of the other. Suppose ∠1 and ∠2 are the acute angles of a right triangle. Write an equation for $m\angle 1$ in terms of $m\angle 2$.

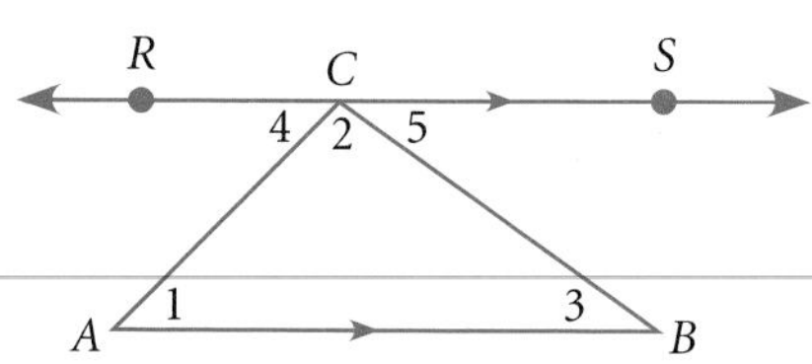

18. **Justify It** Explain how the properties of parallel lines can be used to justify the Triangle Angle-Sum Theorem. Assume $\overline{RS} \parallel \overline{AB}$.

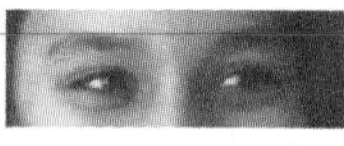

LOOK AHEAD

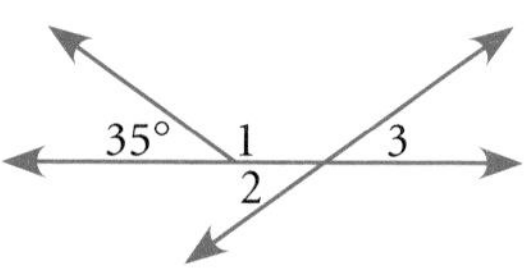

19. If ∠1 and ∠2 are supplementary, what is the measure of ∠3?

Use the figure at the right to find $m\angle 1$ in each of the following.

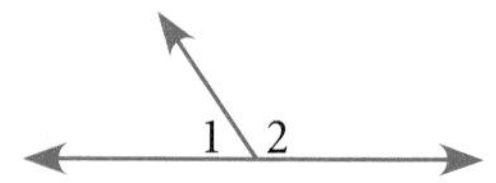

20. $m\angle 1 = (x - 20)°$, and $m\angle 2 = (4x + 20)°$.

21. The measure of ∠2 is 60° more than the measure of ∠1.

MORE PRACTICE

Is it possible for each of the following types of triangles to exist? If so, sketch an example. If not, explain why not.

22. acute scalene

23. isosceles equiangular

24. scalene right

Draw and classify each triangle.

25. $\triangle FGH$ with $FG \neq GH \neq FH$

26. $\triangle QPR$ with $m\angle P = 105°$ and $m\angle R = 28°$

Find the measure of $\angle 1$ in each figure.

27.

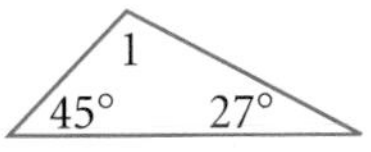

28.

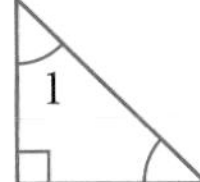

29.

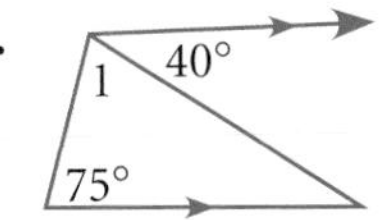

30.

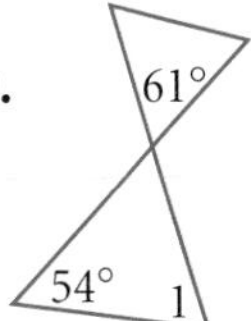

MORE MATH REASONING

31. The coordinates of the vertices of $\triangle ABC$ are $A(3, 3)$, $B(-1, 6)$, and $C(-4, 2)$.

a. Classify the triangle by its angles and by its sides.

b. How many points with integer coordinates lie in the interior of the triangle?

32. Roshawn wrote the following statement in her journal.

If two angles of one triangle are congruent to two angles in another triangle, then the third pair of angles also has to be congruent.

Do you agree? Explain.

4-1 PART B Angles Outside the Triangle

← CONNECT → ***You have learned about the sum of the measures of the angles inside a triangle. Now you will discover some relationships between angles inside and outside a triangle.***

You'll see that figures that tessellate a plane have particular measures for their interior and exterior angles. An **exterior angle** of a triangle is formed by extending one of the sides of the triangle.

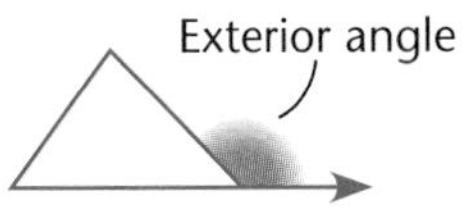

$\triangle ABC$ has each side extended to form the exterior angles $\angle 1$, $\angle 2$, and $\angle 3$. The interior angle in a linear pair with exterior $\angle 1$, $\angle CAB$, is called its **adjacent interior** angle. $\angle CBA$ and $\angle ACB$ are the **remote interior** angles of exterior $\angle 1$.

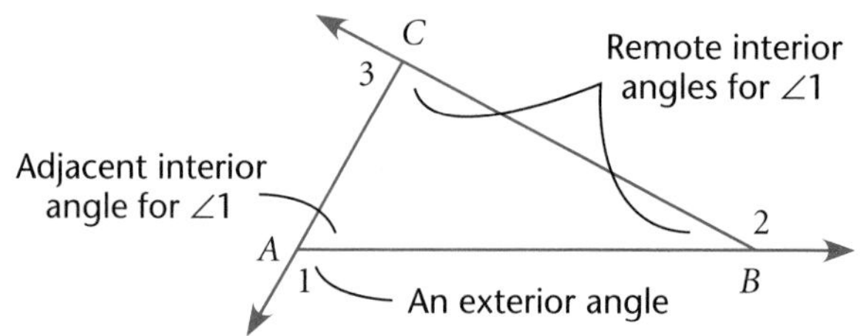

TRY IT

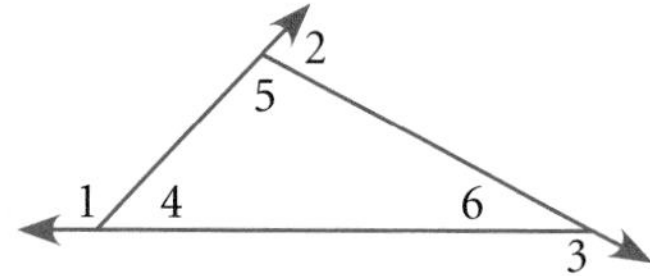

a. Name the exterior angles in the figure at the right.

b. Name the remote interior angles for $\angle 3$.

Earlier you found angle relationships formed by parallel lines and transversals. In this Explore, you will explore angle relationships in triangles.

EXPLORE: WHAT'S MY ANGLE?

MATERIALS

Ruler
Protractor
Geometry software (optional)

1. Use geometry software or a straightedge to draw an equilateral triangle. Draw an extension of one side. Measure the four angles formed by your figure.

2. Repeat Step 1 using an isosceles triangle, a right triangle, a scalene triangle, and an obtuse triangle.

Problem-Solving Tip

You may want to make a table to organize your data.

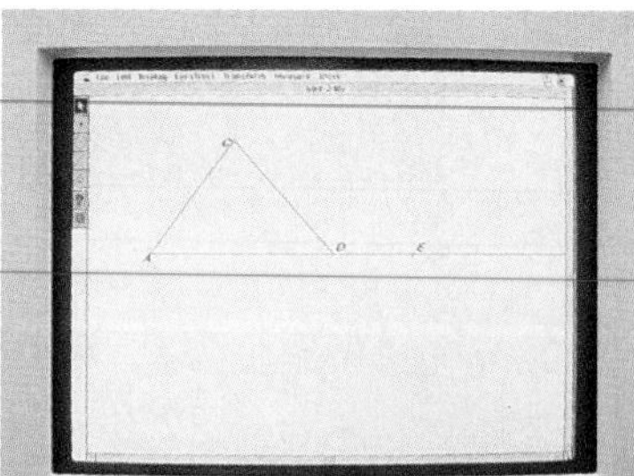

3. How does your data confirm the Triangle Angle-Sum Theorem? How does it show that equilateral triangles are also equiangular?

4. An important conclusion about triangles relates an exterior angle to its two remote interior angles. State this conclusion, and justify it deductively. (Hint: If you're stuck, try using the Triangle Angle-Sum Theorem.)

1. From the evidence you gathered in the Explore, what seems to be true about the acute angles of a right triangle? How does the Triangle Angle-Sum Theorem support this conjecture?

TRY IT

c. Complete the table for the triangle shown.

$m\angle 1$	$m\angle 2$	$m\angle 3$	$m\angle 4$
83°	40°		
	84°		148°
	71°	54°	

Some of the conjectures you may have made suggest the following theorems.

EXTERIOR ANGLE THEOREM

The measure of an exterior angle of a triangle is equal to the sum of the measures of its remote interior angles.

This theorem leads directly to another one. A theorem that follows immediately from another is called a **corollary** of the original theorem.

EXTERIOR ANGLE INEQUALITY THEOREM

The measure of an exterior angle of a triangle is greater than the measure of either of its remote interior angles.

THEOREMS ABOUT ANGLES IN SPECIAL TRIANGLES

Each angle of an equilateral triangle measures 60°.

The acute angles of a right triangle are complementary.

REFLECT

1. Explain why the Exterior Angle Inequality Theorem is a corollary of the Exterior Angle Theorem.
2. Can a triangle ever have more than one acute exterior angle? Explain why or why not.

Exercises

CORE

Getting Started In each figure, name the remote interior angles for ∠1.

1.

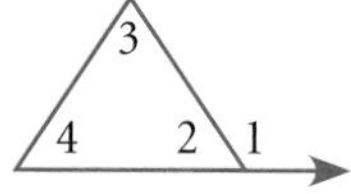

2.

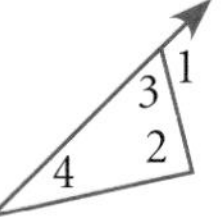

3.

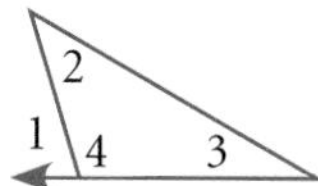

Complete the table for the triangle shown.

	$m\angle 5$	$m\angle 6$	$m\angle 7$	$m\angle 8$	
4.	104°		33°		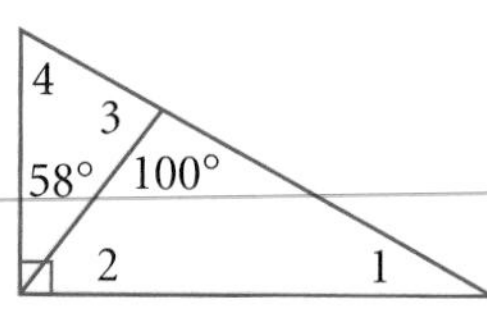
5.		72°		100°	
6.		43°	68°		
7.		$x°$	$(2x + 31)°$	$(4x - 19)°$	

8. Find the measures of ∠1, ∠2, ∠3, and ∠4 in the figure at the right.

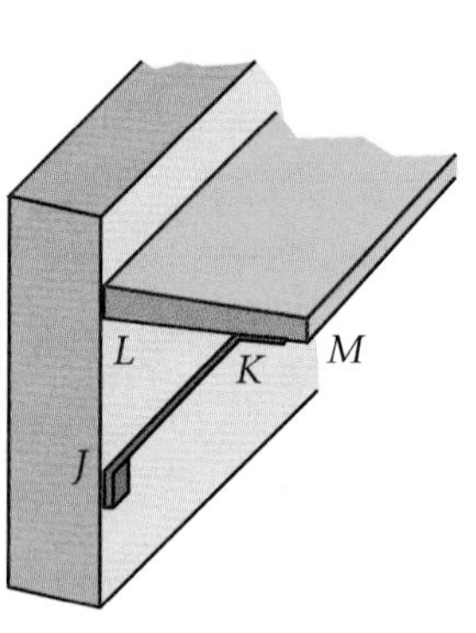

9. Determine whether the following statement is true or false. If it is false, change the underlined phrase to make it true.

The measure of an exterior angle of a triangle is equal to the sum of the measures of its <u>adjacent interior</u> angles.

10. Brace Your Shelf! The brace $\overline{JK}$ is fastened to the wall and the shelf shown at the right. Which angle has the greater measure, $\angle LJK$ or $\angle MKJ$? Justify your answer.

11. The measures of the acute angles of a right triangle are in the ratio 1:2. What is the measure of the smallest angle of the triangle?

12. If the measures of the exterior angles of the acute angles of a right triangle are $(6x + 23)°$ and $(4x + 17)°$, find the measures of the acute angles.

$\triangle BCD$ is a right triangle.

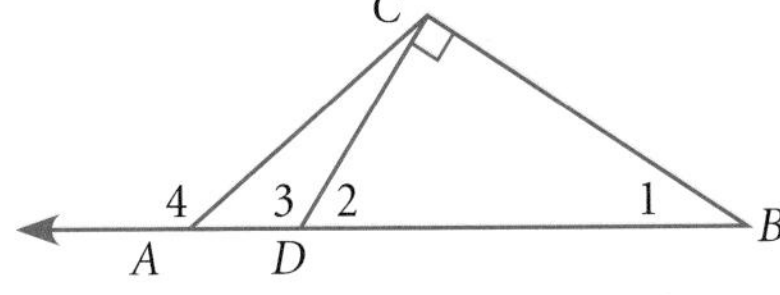

13. If $m\angle 1 = 18°$, find $m\angle 2$.

14. If $m\angle 4 = 150°$ and $m\angle 3 = 130°$, find $m\angle ACD$.

15. If $m\angle 1 = 20°$, find $m\angle 3$.

16. A Leaning Ladder A ladder is leaning against a wall. As the foot of the ladder (point B) slides on the ground away from the wall, the top slides down the wall. If $\overline{AB}$ represents the ladder, then the measures of $\angle 1$, $\angle 2$, $\angle 3$, and $\angle 4$ change as the ladder slides.

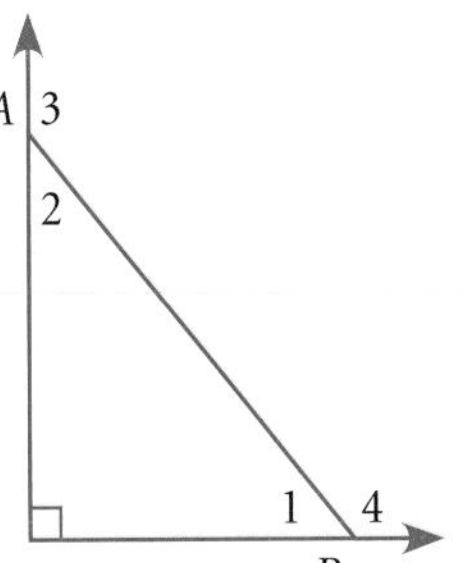

a. If $m\angle 1 = 45°$, what is $m\angle 4 + m\angle 3$?
b. If $m\angle 1 = 40°$, what is $m\angle 4 + m\angle 3$?
c. If $m\angle 1 = 35°$, what is $m\angle 4 + m\angle 3$?
d. Make a conjecture about $m\angle 4 + m\angle 3$. Write a statement explaining how you made your conjecture.

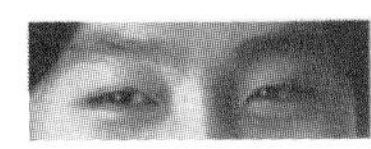

LOOK BACK

17. Do the *rewrite, draw,* and *state* steps for a proof of the Exterior Angle Theorem. [3-4]

Social Science

18. Find the mean, median, and mode of the unemployment rates in the data set given below. Where necessary, round answers to the nearest tenth. [Previous course]

Unemployment Rate in the Civilian Labor Force

Month	5/91	6/91	7/91	8/91	9/91	10/91	11/91	12/91	1/92	2/92	3/92	4/92
Rate (%)	6.8	6.9	6.8	6.8	6.8	6.9	6.9	7.1	7.1	7.3	7.3	7.2

MORE PRACTICE

19. Find the measure of $\angle ABC$.

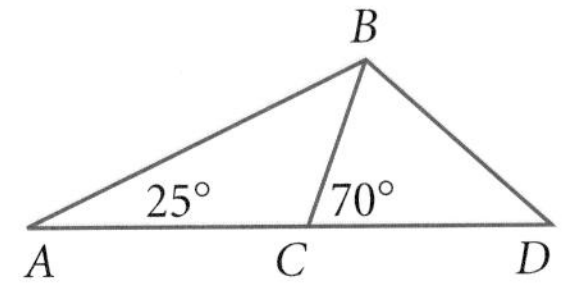

20. If $m\angle 1 = m\angle 2$, find $m\angle 3$.

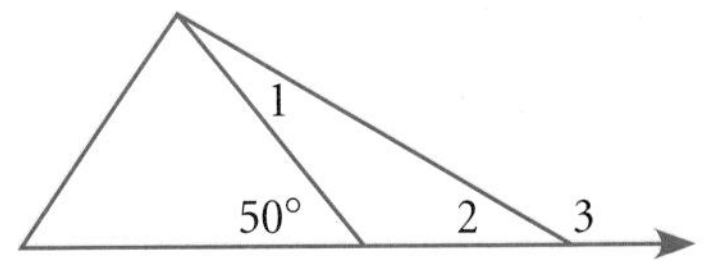

Complete the table for the triangle shown.

	$m\angle 1$	$m\angle 2$	$m\angle 3$	$m\angle 4$
21.	15°		44°	
22.		119°		39°
23.			37°	17°
24.	$(x - 20)°$		$(180 - 2x)°$	$(2x - 50)°$

MORE MATH REASONING

25. If $\overline{AC} \parallel \overline{BE}$, explain how the figure at the right shows that $m\angle 1 + m\angle 2 + m\angle 3 = 180°$.

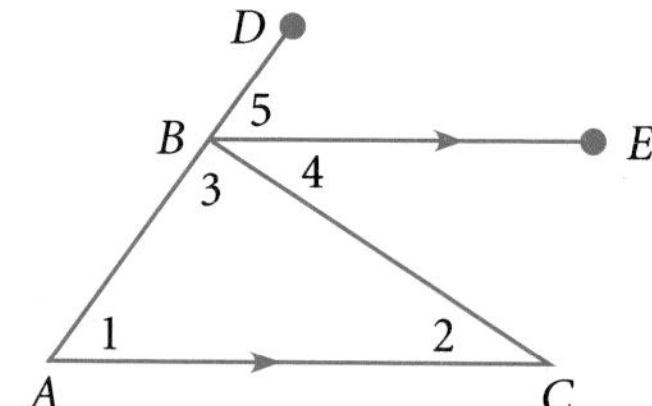

26. Stable Bearings A scout group hikes from camp (A) to a riding stable and then to a road—illustrated by $\triangle ABC$ in the figure below. An observation tower lies on the extension of segment $\overline{AC}$. What is the bearing of the riding stable from the observation tower?

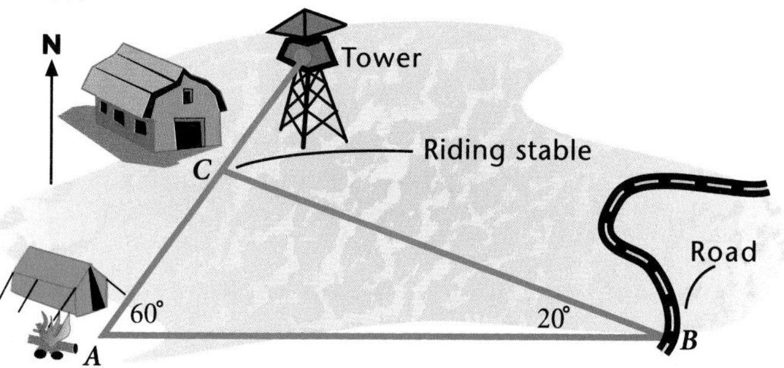

4-1 PART C Making Connections

← CONNECT → ***Triangles are important in the structures of buildings and in the art forms that decorate them. You have learned about some of the properties of triangles. Now you will explore how these properties relate to tessellations.***

The angle properties for triangles that you have become familiar with will help you in the following Explore when you investigate whether or not congruent triangles can tessellate a plane.

EXPLORE: TESSELLATION STATION

MATERIALS

Paper
Straightedge
Scissors
Protractor (optional)

1. Do you think *any* triangle can be used to tessellate a plane? Make an "educated guess" before continuing.

2. Fold a sheet of paper in half three times. Then use a straightedge to draw a scalene triangle on the folded paper. Cut out the triangle to make eight congruent copies. Now try to create a tessellation with the triangles.

3. Compare your tessellation with those of classmates. See if all of the different types of triangles you used formed tessellations.

4. A *tessellation vertex* is a point in a tessellation where several of the figures meet. Use your knowledge of rotations to determine what the sum of the angles at a tessellation vertex must be so that there are no gaps or overlaps in the pattern.

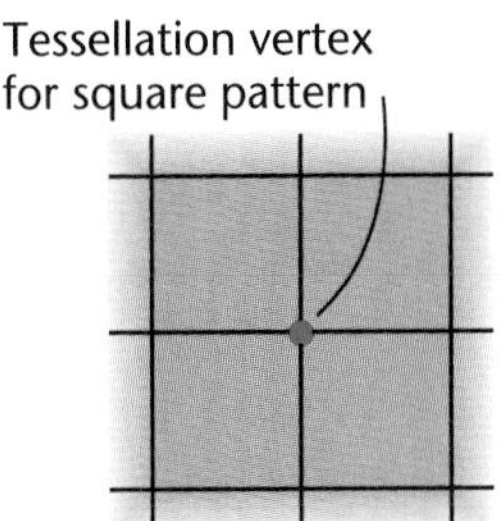

5. Look at a tessellation vertex in one of your triangle tessellations. Find the sum of all of the angles that meet at a vertex. (Hint: Label the angles of the triangles as shown at the right.)

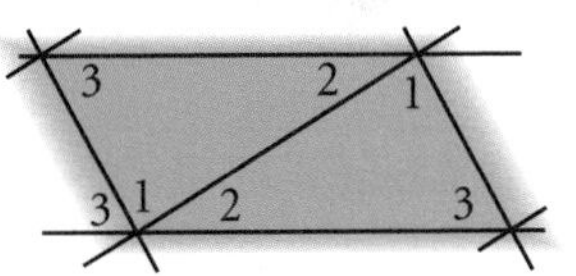

6. Can any triangle be used to tessellate a plane? Justify your answer.

REFLECT

1. Explain how triangle tessellation patterns illustrate the following two theorems.
  a. the Triangle Angle-Sum Theorem
  b. the Exterior Angle Theorem

2. Prepare a summary of the different types of triangles you have learned about. Draw and label each type.

Self-Assessment

Is it possible for each of the following types of triangles to exist? If so, sketch an example. If not, explain why not.

1. right isosceles **2.** right equilateral **3.** obtuse isosceles

Complete each statement with *always, sometimes,* or *never.* Give an explanation for each answer.

4. A triangle with two complementary acute angles is ____ a right triangle.

5. An isosceles triangle is ____ a right triangle.

6. A triangle with an obtuse angle is ____ a right triangle.

7. A triangle with two sides congruent is ____ equilateral.

8. In the figure at the right, $m\angle 1 + m\angle 2 + m\angle 3 - m\angle 4 =$
(a) $m\angle 1$ (b) $m\angle 2$
(c) $m\angle 3$ (d) $m\angle 4$
(e) 180°

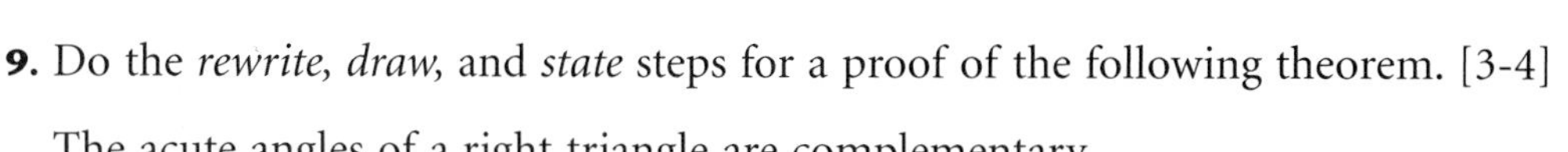

9. Do the *rewrite, draw,* and *state* steps for a proof of the following theorem. [3-4]

The acute angles of a right triangle are complementary.

10. Find the mean, median, and mode of the temperatures in the data set given below. Where necessary, round your answers to the nearest tenth. [Previous course]

Average High Temperature in April						
City	Quebec	Mexico City	Sydney	Hamilton (Bermuda)	Moscow	Cairo
Temp. (°F)	45	78	71	71	47	83

11. Can a triangle have angle measures of $(x + 40)°$, $(2x - 70)°$, and $(3x + 30)°$? If so, what is the value of x? If not, explain why not.

12. In the figure at the right, find $m\angle 1 + m\angle 3$. Justify your answer with a theorem.

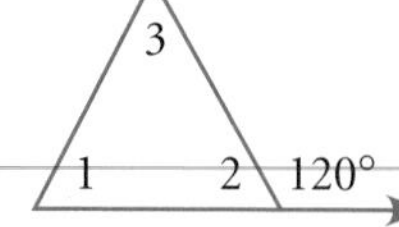

13. Find the measure of $\angle 2$. Justify your answer.

14. Find the measure of $\angle 3$ if possible. Write an explanation of your thinking.

15. Can an exterior angle of a triangle be congruent to a remote interior angle? Explain.

16. Explain how the triangular tessellation pattern at the right can be used to justify the Triangle Angle-Sum Theorem and the Exterior Angle Theorem. (Hint: The tessellation vertex shown will help in both explanations.)

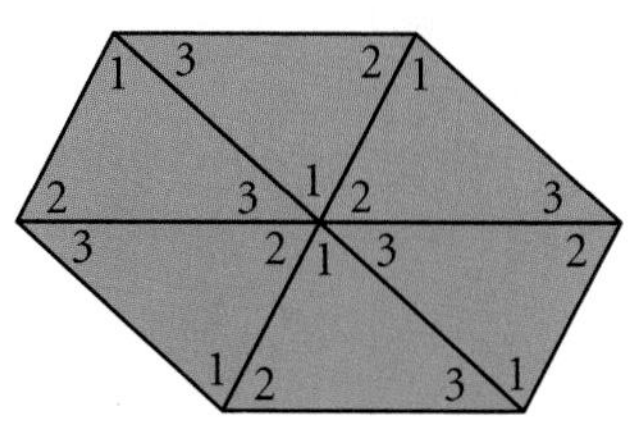

4-2 Deductive Proof with Triangles

Travels with Napoleon

Napoleon Bonaparte (1769–1821) ruled France from 1799 to 1815. During that period, his armies fought battles across Europe and North Africa. One of the most disastrous of these campaigns was Napoleon's invasion of Russia in the winter of 1812–1813. That winter was an especially harsh one in Europe. Although over 400,000 soldiers entered Russia as part of Napoleon's Grand Army, less than 10,000 made it back.

In 1862, a French engineer named Charles Minard created a graph to illustrate the terrible effect of the weather on Napoleon's troops. A simplified version of the graph is shown here.

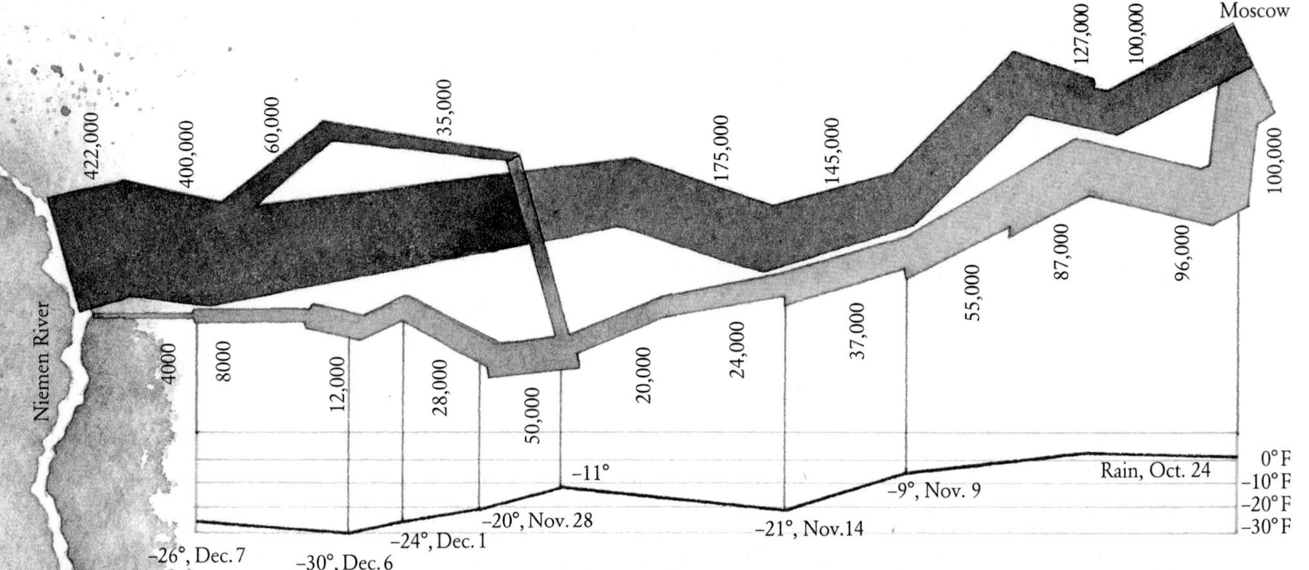

The wide band across the map of Europe shows the army moving toward Moscow; the width of the band is proportional to the number of soldiers in the army. The thinner band shows the return trip. Minard also added a line graph showing the sub-zero temperatures of the return trip. As the temperature plunges, the band representing the number of survivors becomes even thinner.

It is said that during one of Napoleon's campaigns, he needed to determine the distance across a river. One of his officers solved the problem using only a flagpole. As you learn more about congruent triangles, you will discover how his method worked.

?

1. Did Napoleon's army lose a greater number of soldiers on the way to Moscow or on the way back? In which direction did Napoleon's army lose a greater percentage of soldiers? Explain your ideas.

2. Describe some ways geometry can be used to find an unknown distance.

4-2 PART A Correspondence and Congruence

← CONNECT → ***You've discovered many facts about angles and sides in individual triangles. Now you will begin to investigate pairs of triangles.***

As you've seen when creating tessellations, it's helpful to be able to recognize congruent figures in different orientations.

1. Determine whether each pair of figures below is congruent. Explain your answers.

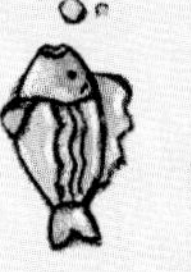

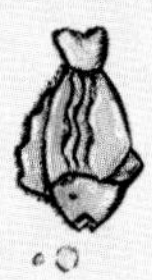

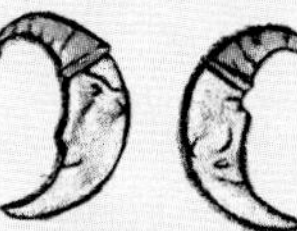

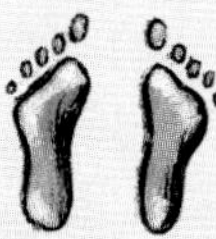

2. For the pairs of congruent figures, what transformation(s) is (are) necessary to move one figure so that it coincides with the other?

Congruent figures can be slid, flipped, and turned until they overlap exactly. It is important to match up parts correctly when you work with congruent triangles.

EXPLORE: FINDING THE RIGHT MATCH

MATERIALS

Ruler
Protractor

1. The two triangles below are congruent. Using whatever measurement tools you need, list all of the parts (angles and segments) of the triangles that are congruent. How many pairs of congruent parts do two congruent triangles have?

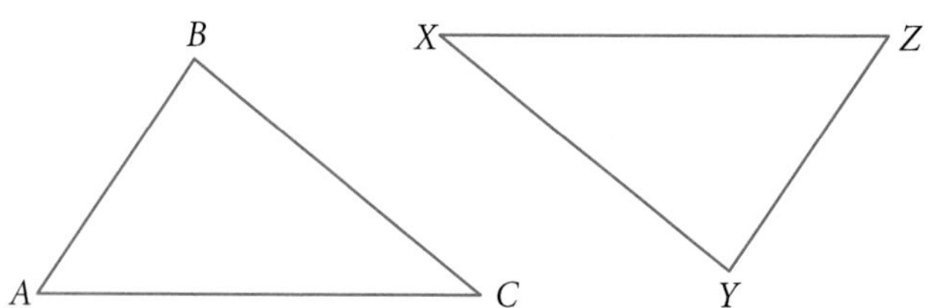

2. Using your list of congruent parts as a guide, identify the vertices of the two triangles that match up with one another.

3. Complete the following congruence statement in a way that shows the congruent parts of the triangles. $\triangle ABC \cong \triangle$____. What does the order of the letters tell you about the congruent parts of the triangles?

4. Suppose $\triangle JKL \cong \triangle PQR$. List all pairs of sides and angles that must be congruent.

TRY IT

a. Write a congruence statement for the triangles shown.

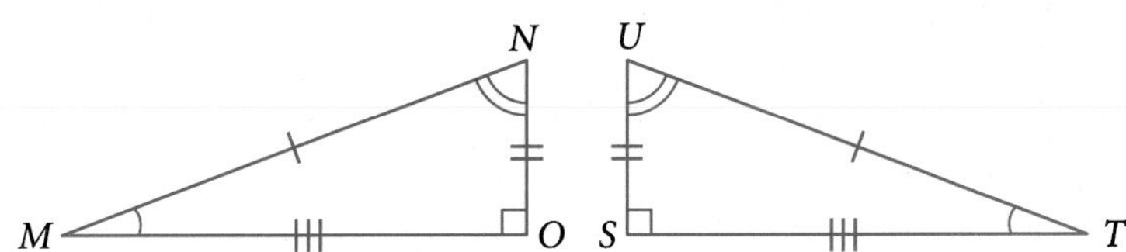

To write a useful congruence statement, you need to match up the vertices correctly to make a *correspondence.*

DEFINITIONS

A **correspondence** between two geometric figures is any way of pairing up their vertices. A **congruence correspondence** matches the vertices so that all pairs of corresponding parts are congruent.

The symbol for *corresponds to* is $\leftrightarrow$. One congruence correspondence between the two triangles below is $\triangle ABC \leftrightarrow \triangle RST$. The order of the letters in the correspondence statement specifies the corresponding sides and corresponding angles.

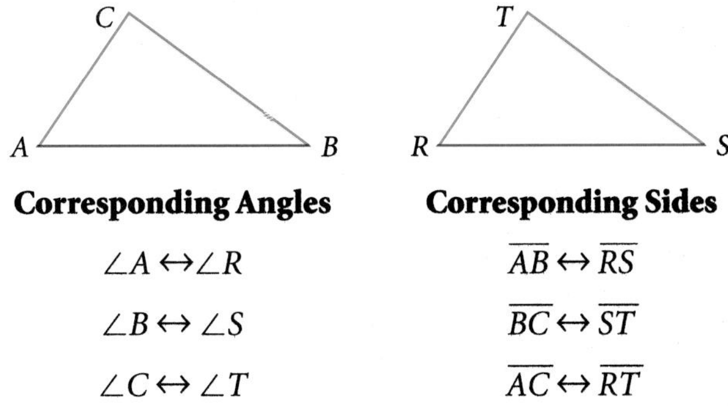

Corresponding Angles	**Corresponding Sides**
$\angle A \leftrightarrow \angle R$	$\overline{AB} \leftrightarrow \overline{RS}$
$\angle B \leftrightarrow \angle S$	$\overline{BC} \leftrightarrow \overline{ST}$
$\angle C \leftrightarrow \angle T$	$\overline{AC} \leftrightarrow \overline{RT}$

Up until now, we have simply stated that congruent triangles "have the same shape." Now we are ready to give a more useful definition.

DEFINITION

Two triangles are **congruent triangles** if and only if all of their corresponding parts are congruent.

REFLECT

1. Have you ever used the idea of correspondence to match up vertices of figures before? Explain. (Hint: Think about transformations.)
2. Explain the difference between congruence and correspondence.

Exercises

CORE

Getting Started Give a congruence correspondence for each figure. Use the symbol ≅ to write the congruence.

1.

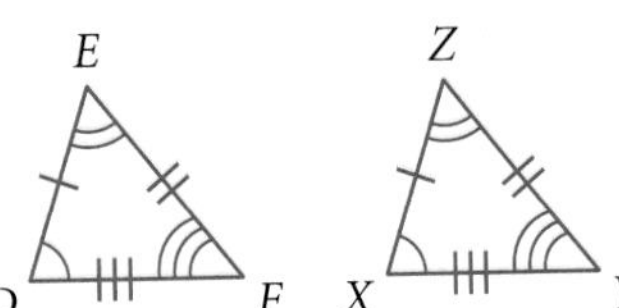

2.

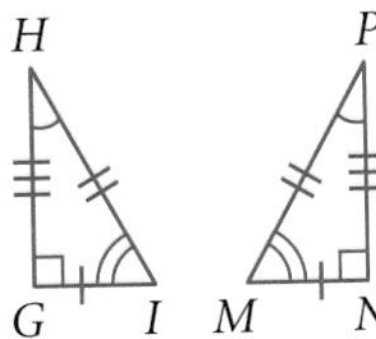

3. Draw $\triangle XYZ$ and $\triangle UVW$ so that $\triangle XYZ \cong \triangle UVW$. Mark the congruent parts. List the pairs of corresponding congruent parts.

4. Draw and mark triangles for the congruence $\triangle JKL \cong \triangle MNP$. Rewrite the congruence in five other ways.

Suppose $\triangle RST \cong \triangle LMO$. Complete each statement.

5. $m\angle R =$ ____

6. $\angle O \cong$ ____

7. $\overline{LM} \cong$ ____

8. Write congruence statements for the triangles in the figure that appear to be congruent.

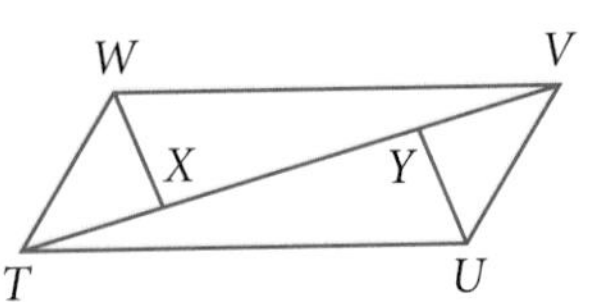

In the figure, $\triangle ABC \cong \triangle EDC$. Find each measure.

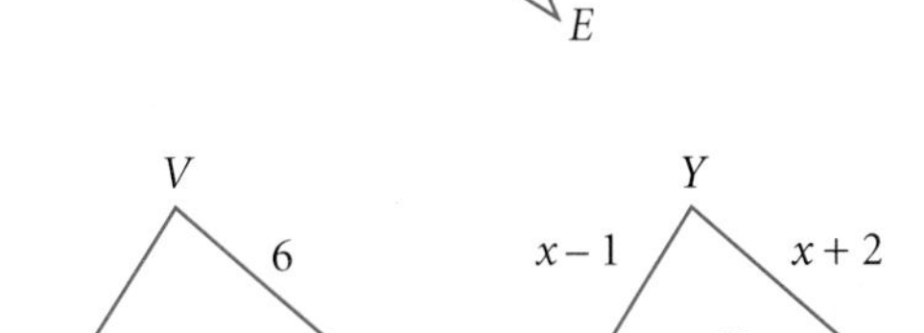

9. $m\angle D =$ ___ **10.** $CE =$ ___

11. $m\angle DCE =$ ___ **12.** $BC =$ ___

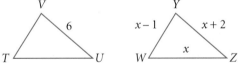

In the figure, $\triangle TUV \cong \triangle WZY$. Find each measure.

V
6
T
U
Y
$x - 1$
$x + 2$
x
W
Z

13. $YZ =$ ___ **14.** $WY =$ ___

15. $VT =$ ___ **16.** $TU =$ ___

17. The quilt shown at the right is made by sewing together triangular shapes. How many different noncongruent shapes are used?

18. Plot the points $M(2, 3)$, $N(6, 3)$, $P(8, 7)$, and draw $\triangle MNP$. Reflect $\triangle MNP$ across the y-axis, and label the image $\triangle RST$, so that $\triangle MNP \cong \triangle RST$. Give the coordinates of R, S, and T.

In the figure, $\triangle PQR \cong \triangle EFG$ and $EF = 7.4$. Find each measure.

R
G
95°
3.2
6.4
59°
P
E
Q
F

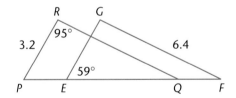

19. $m\angle P =$ ______ **20.** $RQ =$ ______

21. $FE =$ ______ **22.** $m\angle PQR =$ ______

LOOK BACK

23. Copy point P and line m. Use a compass and straightedge to construct a line through P that is parallel to m. [3-4]

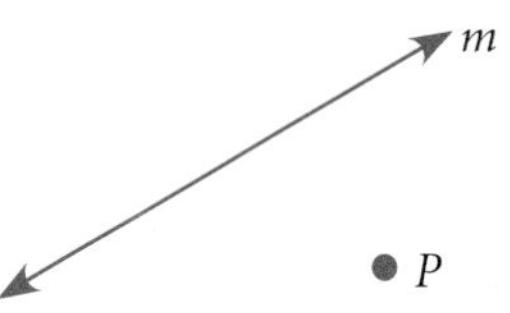

In each of the following, use the given information to find $m\angle C$. [4-1]

24. $m\angle A = 34°$, and $\angle A \cong \angle B$.

25. $\triangle ABC$ is equilateral.

26. $m\angle A = (x + 32)°$, $m\angle B = (2x - 11)°$, and $m\angle C = (3x + 21)°$.

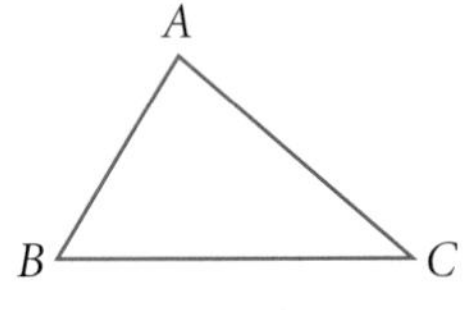

MORE PRACTICE

27. Draw a scalene triangle, $\triangle DEF$, congruent to $\triangle LMN$ ($\triangle DEF \cong \triangle LMN$).
- **a.** Is $\triangle DEF \cong \triangle LNM$? Why or why not?
- **b.** Is $\triangle FED \cong \triangle NML$? Why or why not?
- **c.** Is $\triangle EDF \cong \triangle MLN$? Why or why not?

$\triangle ABC \cong \triangle RST$. Complete each statement.

28. $\overline{AC} \cong$ ___ **29.** $m\angle ABC =$ ___ **30.** $m\angle TSR =$ ___

$\triangle ABC \cong \triangle FGB$. Find each measure.

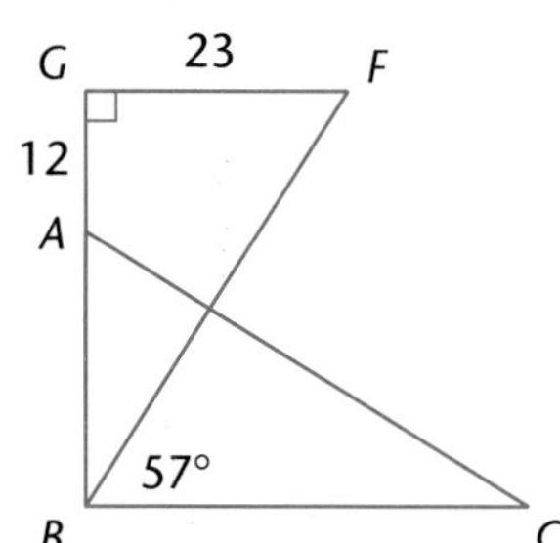

31. $AB =$ ______ **32.** $m\angle ABC =$ ______

33. $BC =$ ______ **34.** $m\angle C =$ ______

MORE MATH REASONING

35. If $\triangle ABC \cong \triangle CBA$, what type of triangle is $\triangle ABC$? Explain your answer.

36. Scalene triangle $\triangle PQR$ is congruent to a triangle with vertices S, T, and U, but the congruence correspondence is not necessarily in that order. If you complete the congruence statement $\triangle PQR \cong \triangle$___ by writing S, T, and U in a random order, what is the probability you will write a true congruence statement?

4-2 PART B Congruent Triangles

← CONNECT → *You've seen what is needed to establish congruence of triangles. Now you will investigate some shortcuts for proving triangles congruent.*

This textile pattern from Thailand contains many sets of congruent triangles. You know that two congruent triangles have six pairs of corresponding congruent parts: three pairs of sides and three pairs of angles.

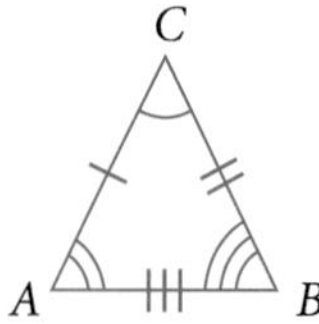

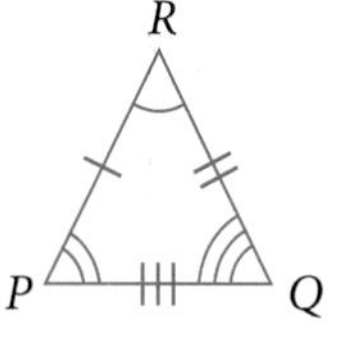

Do you really need to know *all six* of these congruences to conclude that two triangles are congruent? Are there some shortcuts? To help investigate this question in the following Explore, you will need to become familiar with some new terms.

You can describe the parts of a triangle by their relative position as follows.

$\angle R$ is *opposite* side $\overline{ST}$.

$\overline{RT}$ is *opposite* $\angle S$.

$\angle S$ is *included* between $\overline{RS}$ and $\overline{ST}$.

$\overline{RT}$ is *included* between $\angle R$ and $\angle T$.

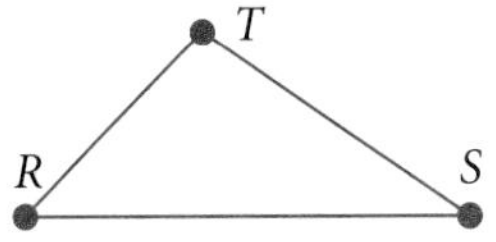

EXPLORE: WHAT DO YOU NEED TO KNOW?

MATERIALS

Ruler
Protractor
Compass (optional)

Work in pairs. In Steps 1–5, alternate roles so that each of you has a chance to draw the initial triangle.

1. Draw a triangle. Measure *two sides* and their *included angle*. Then tell your partner just those three measurements, and have him draw a triangle with those characteristics. Compare your triangles to see whether or not they are congruent.
2. Repeat the process with a new triangle, but this time tell your partner the measures of *two angles* and their *included side*. Compare your triangles for congruence.
3. This time, tell your partner the measures of all *three angles* of your triangle. Compare your triangles for congruence.
4. Now, tell your partner the measures of *two angles* and a *side opposite* one of the angles. Compare your triangles for congruence.
5. Tell your partner the measure of all *three sides* of your triangle. (Hint: Making this triangle might be a bit tougher; use the figure at the right as a hint.) Compare your triangles for congruence.
6. List any conditions you discovered that seem to guarantee congruent triangles.

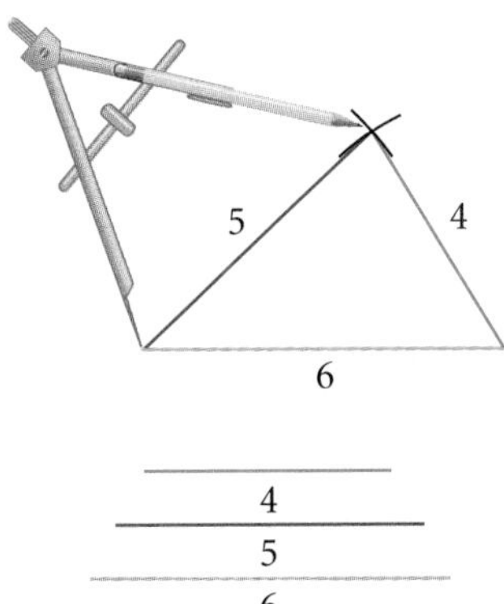

You have just explored four ways to show that triangles are congruent using only three pairs of corresponding congruent parts.

SIDE-SIDE-SIDE CONGRUENCE POSTULATE (SSS)

If each of the three sides of one triangle are congruent to the sides of another triangle, then the two triangles are congruent.

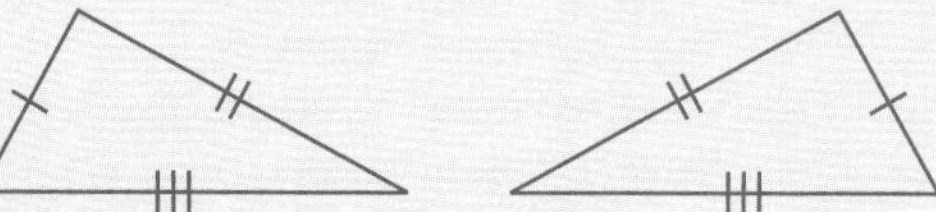

SIDE-ANGLE-SIDE CONGRUENCE POSTULATE (SAS)

If two sides and the included angle of one triangle are congruent to two sides and the included angle of another triangle, then the two triangles are congruent.

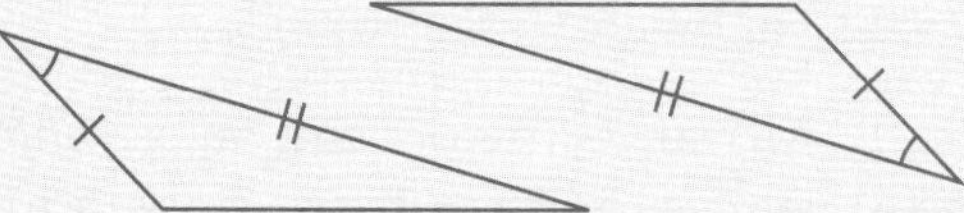

ANGLE-SIDE-ANGLE CONGRUENCE POSTULATE (ASA)

If two angles and the included side of one triangle are congruent to two angles and the included side of another triangle, then the two triangles are congruent.

SIDE-ANGLE-ANGLE CONGRUENCE POSTULATE (SAA)

If two angles and a side opposite one of them in one triangle are congruent to the corresponding parts of another triangle, then the two triangles are congruent.

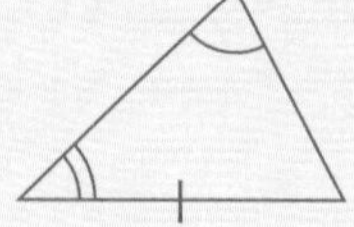

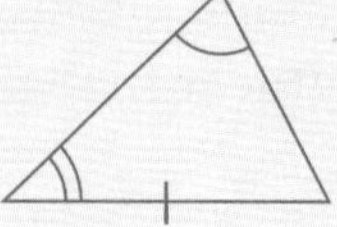

TRY IT

If possible, write a congruence statement for each pair of triangles. Then name the triangle-congruence postulate that applies. If the triangles are not congruent, say so.

a. 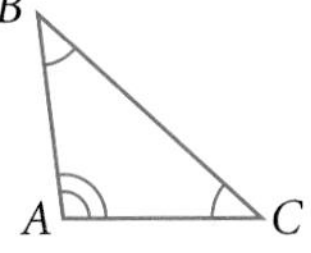

b. 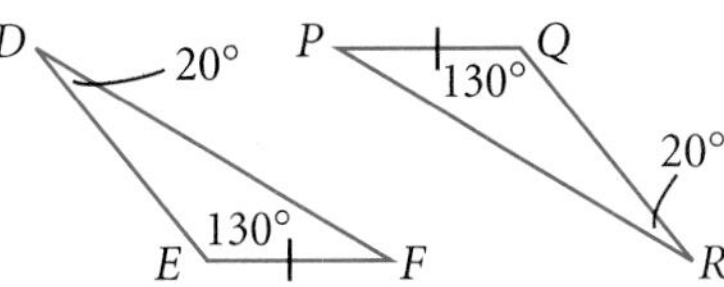

REFLECT

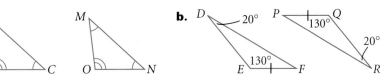

1. If you use the definition of congruent triangles to show that two triangles are congruent, how many pairs of corresponding congruent parts do you need to have? How many pairs do each of the postulates require?
2. A welder must make two congruent triangular steel frames. She does this without ever measuring an angle. How? Which postulate is she using?

Exercises

CORE

Getting Started In each of the following, name the required angle or side.

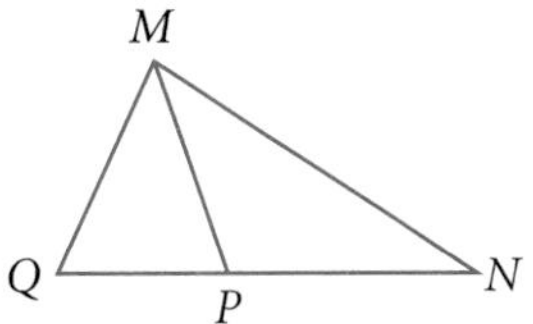

1. the side opposite $\angle MPN$
2. the angle opposite $\overline{QN}$
3. the included side for $\angle QMP$ and $\angle QPM$
4. the included angle for $\overline{QP}$ and $\overline{PM}$

If possible, write a congruence statement for each pair of triangles. Then name the triangle-congruence postulate that applies. If the triangles are not congruent, say so.

5. 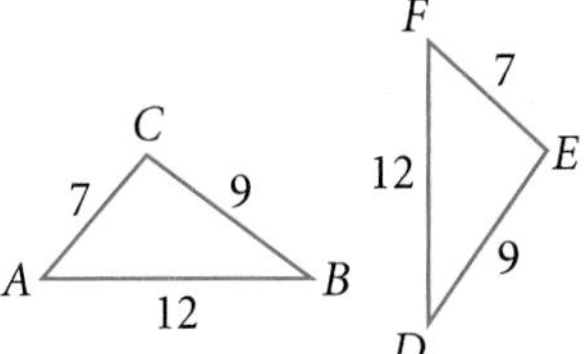

6. 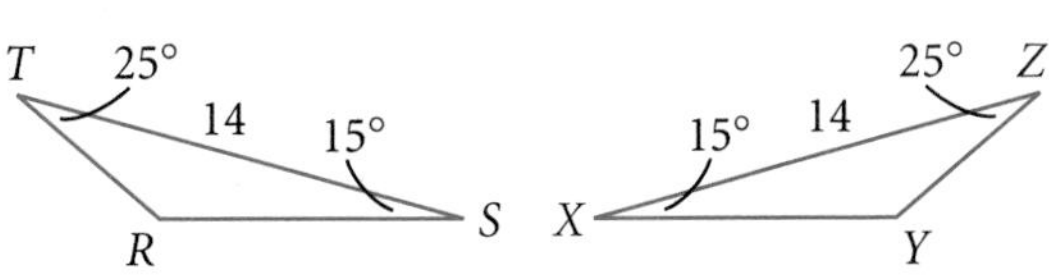

If possible, write a congruence statement for each pair of triangles. Then name the triangle-congruence postulate that applies. If the triangles are not congruent, say so.

7.

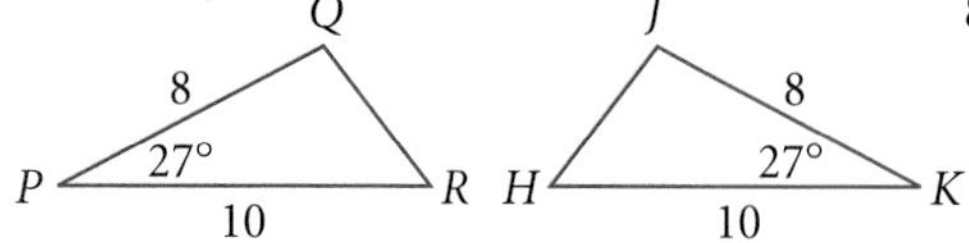

8.

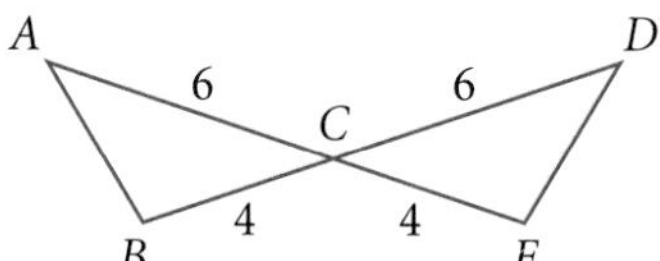

9.

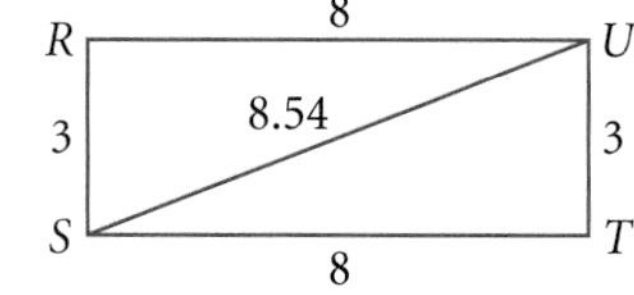

10. $\angle QPR \cong \angle MPN$, $\overline{MN} \cong \overline{QR}$, and $\angle QRP \cong \angle MNP$. Complete the statement and state the triangle-congruence postulate that supports your conclusion. $\triangle PQR \cong$ _____.

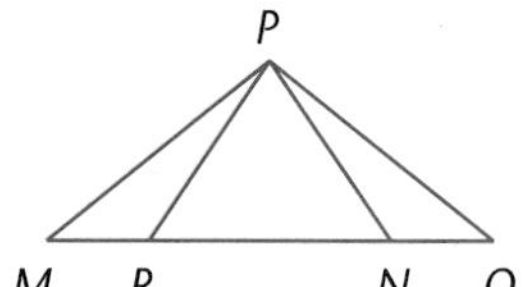

Under the conditions stated, are the triangles $\triangle GHJ$ and $\triangle MNO$ congruent? If so, write the congruence statement and name the congruence postulate that justifies it.

11. $\overline{GH} \cong \overline{MN}$, $\angle J \cong \angle O$

12. $\overline{GH} \cong \overline{MN}$, $\overline{HJ} \cong \overline{NO}$

13. $\angle G \cong \angle M$, $\overline{HJ} \cong \overline{NO}$

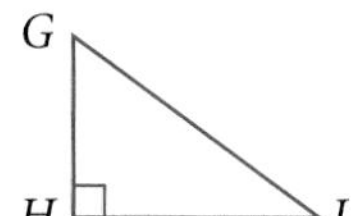

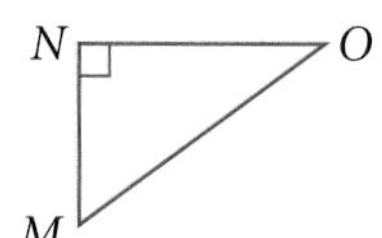

14. Show that there is no Angle-Angle-Angle (AAA) Postulate by drawing two noncongruent triangles with three pairs of congruent corresponding angles.

15. For the following statement, *draw* and label a figure to represent the hypothesis, and *state* what is given and what is to be proved.

If $\overline{CA} \cong \overline{AB}$, D is on $\overline{BC}$, and $\angle CAD \cong \angle DAB$, then D is the midpoint of $\overline{BC}$.

16. Peddle the Metal Ehlers Steel Co. needs to sell some of its 20-in.-long steel tubing. Wheelright Bicycle Manufacturers have a bicycle frame design featuring one equilateral triangle, and the triangles in all of their bicycle frames must be congruent. Ehlers's sales representative calls up Wheelright and says, "If you buy our tubing, we will guarantee that all of the triangles you make out of it will be equilateral and exactly the same size! You'll never have to measure another angle again!" Assuming that all of Ehlers's tubes are exactly 20 in. long, is their guarantee valid? Why?

LOOK AHEAD

17. *Draw* a figure and mark the given information.

Given: $\triangle ABC$ with $\overline{AB} \cong \overline{AC}$ and X the midpoint of $\overline{BC}$

Use the figure below to give a reason that justifies each statement.

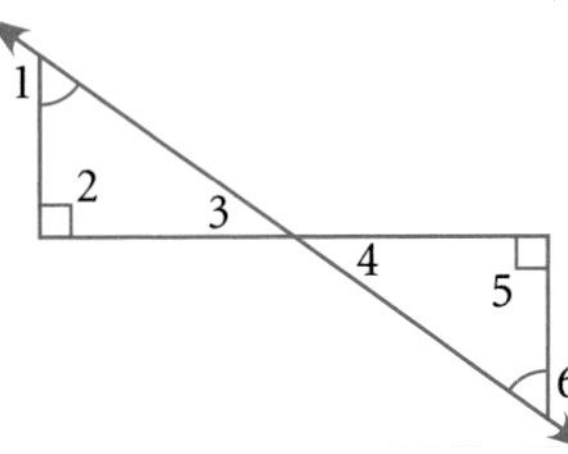

18. $\angle 2 \cong \angle 5$

19. $\angle 3 \cong \angle 4$

20. $\angle 1 \cong \angle 6$

MORE PRACTICE

If possible, write a congruence statement for each pair of triangles. Then name the triangle-congruence postulate that applies. If the triangles are not congruent, say so.

21.

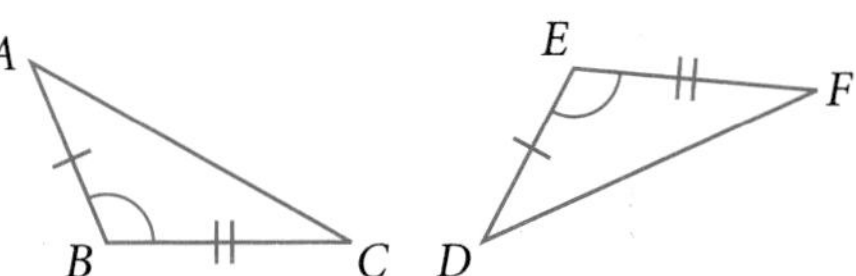

22.

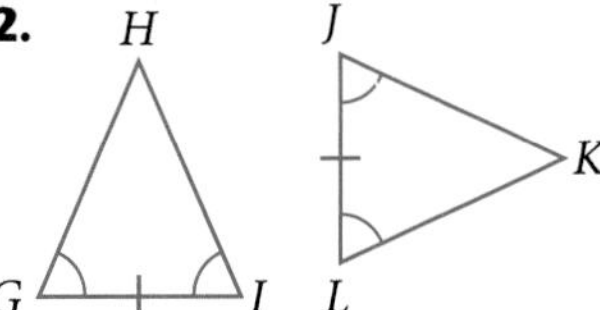

Under the conditions stated, are the triangles $\triangle ABC$ and $\triangle DEC$ congruent? If so, write the congruence statement, and name the congruence postulate that justifies it.

23. $\overline{AB} \cong \overline{DE}$, $\angle A \cong \angle D$

24. $\overline{AC} \cong \overline{DC}$, $\overline{BC} \cong \overline{EC}$

25. $\angle B \cong \angle E$, $\angle A \cong \angle D$

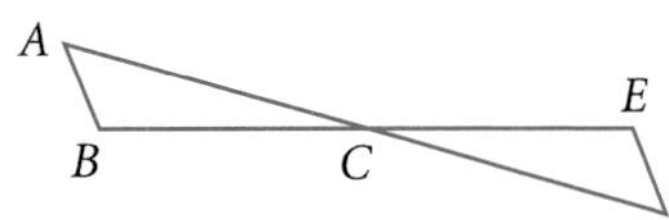

MORE MATH REASONING

26. Find all possible coordinates for point T so that $\triangle MNP \cong \triangle RST$ if the coordinates of the other points are $M(-2, 4)$, $N(1, 4)$, $P(1, 7)$, $R(5, 2)$, and $S(8, 2)$.

27. *Rewrite* the following statement, *draw* and label a figure that represents the statement, and *state* the Given and Prove.

Statement: The two diagonals on a face of a cube are congruent.

What triangle-congruence postulate justifies the conclusion to this statement?

28. Fill in the missing reasons in the flow chart to complete the following proof. Then rewrite as a two-column proof.

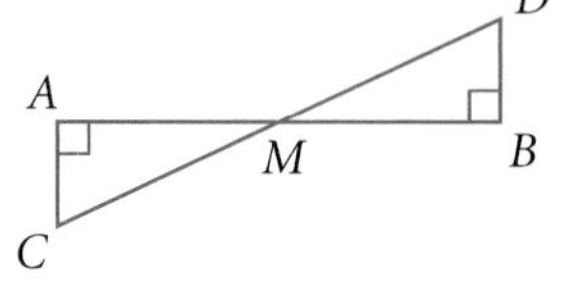

Given: M is the midpoint of $\overline{AB}$, $\angle A$ is a right angle, and $\angle B$ is a right angle.

Prove: $\triangle AMC \cong \triangle BMD$

Proof:

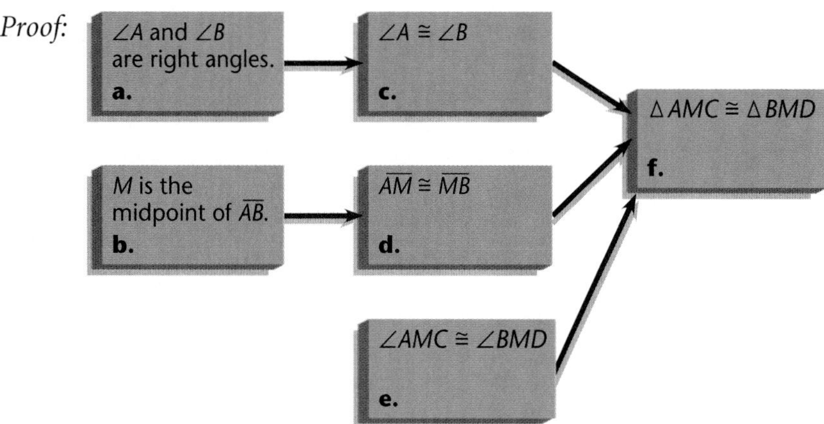

4-2 PART C Organizing a Proof

← CONNECT → ***You've seen many situations in which you need to organize facts to draw a correct conclusion. Now you will review our five-step process for deductive proof and learn about ways to write out a proof.***

A proof is a sequence of true facts (statements) placed in a logical order. To convince others that a proof is valid, we supply a reason to justify each statement. The reasons that can be used for justifying statements are the following:

- the hypothesis (given information) and information that can be assumed from a figure
- definitions
- postulates and algebraic properties
- theorems that have already been proved

You've already been introduced to five steps for preparing a proof: *rewrite, draw, state, plan,* and *demonstrate.* In Chapters 5 and 6, you will gradually become more familiar with the last two steps of this process. In the rest of this chapter, you will be completing proofs that have been started for you.

In the following example, we illustrate a complete proof so that you can become more familiar with how one looks.

EXAMPLE

Prove the following: If $\overline{AC}$ and $\overline{BD}$ bisect each other at M, then $\triangle AMB \cong \triangle CMD$.

Rewrite: (The statement is already in if-then form.)

Draw:

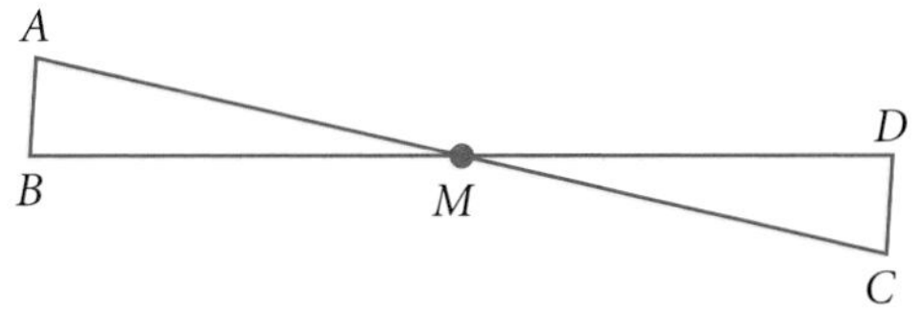

A D B M C

State: *Given:* $\overline{AC}$ and $\overline{BD}$ bisect each other at M.

Prove: $\triangle AMB \cong \triangle CMD$

Plan: Bisect means "cut in half," so we have two pairs of congruent segments crossing at M. Their included angles are vertical angles, so the angles are congruent. We can use the SAS Postulate to show that the triangles are congruent.

Proof: We are given that $\overline{AC}$ and $\overline{BD}$ bisect each other at M. Therefore, $\overline{AM} \cong \overline{MC}$, and $\overline{BM} \cong \overline{MD}$, by the definition of *bisect.* $\angle AMB \cong \angle CMD$ because vertical angles are congruent. Therefore, $\triangle AMB \cong \triangle CMD$ by the SAS Postulate.

You will become familiar with three different formats for demonstrating a deductive proof. In the example, we used paragraph form. This is one of the most common ways to write out a proof.

A two-column format can also be used to organize your thinking. In two-column format, statements appear in a column on the left and the reasons are in a column on the right. We can also write a proof in flow-proof format. In this format, statements and reasons are given in boxes and linked by arrows.

WHAT DO YOU THINK?

Write out the *demonstrate* step for the preceding proof, using the format you think is clearest.

Atiba thinks . . .

I like the flow-proof format. I think it's the best way to show where each step comes from.

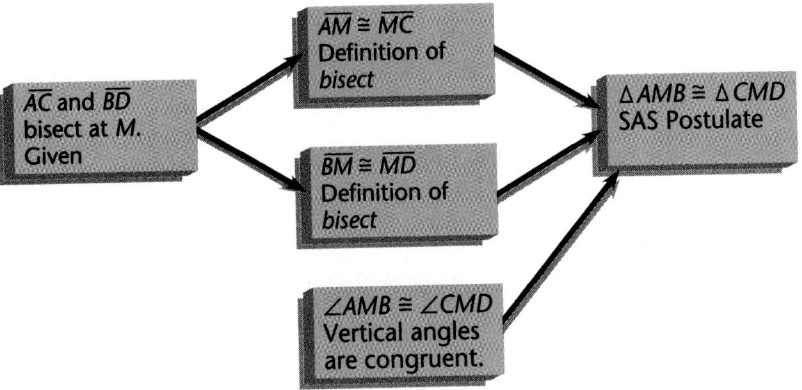

Heather thinks . . .

I'll use the two-column format since it's easy to read and clearly shows the reason for each statement.

Statements	**Reasons**
1. $\overline{AC}$ and $\overline{BD}$ bisect each other at M.	**1.** Given
2. $\overline{AM} \cong \overline{MC}$	**2.** Definition of *bisect*
3. $\overline{BM} \cong \overline{MD}$	**3.** Definition of *bisect*
4. $\angle AMB \cong \angle CMD$	**4.** Vertical angles are congruent.
5. $\triangle AMB \cong \triangle CMD$	**5.** SAS Postulate

1. Which of the three proof formats presented do you find the easiest to understand? Why?

EXPLORE: CONVINCE ME!

1. Copy the figure and mark the congruent parts. Then fill in the missing reasons to complete the paragraph proof below.

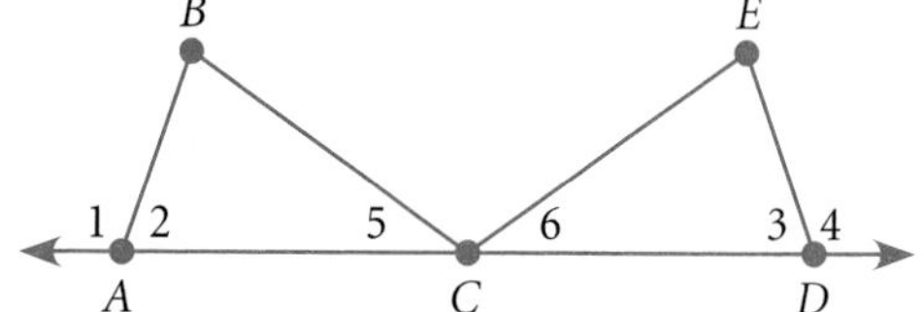

Given: $\angle 1 \cong \angle 4$

$\overline{AC} \cong \overline{CD}$

$\angle 5 \cong \angle 6$

Prove: $\triangle ABC \cong \triangle DEC$

Proof: $\angle 1$ and $\angle 2$ form a linear pair, as do $\angle 3$ and $\angle 4$. Thus, $\angle 1$ is supplementary to $\angle 2$, and $\angle 3$ is supplementary to $\angle 4$ because **a.** ____. The **b.** ____ tells us that $\angle 1 \cong \angle 4$. Therefore, $\angle 2 \cong \angle 3$ because **c.** ____. We also know that $\overline{AC} \cong \overline{CD}$, and $\angle 5 \cong \angle 6$ from **d.** ____. Therefore, we can conclude that $\triangle ABC \cong \triangle DEC$ by the **e.** ____ Postulate.

2. Put your paragraph proof into two-column form.

3. Show the same proof as a flow proof.

TRY IT

a. Complete the following two-column proof by choosing a reason for each statement from the Scrambled Reasons' list.

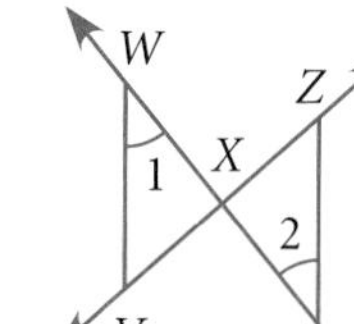

Given: X is the midpoint of $\overline{VZ}$.

$\angle 1 \cong \angle 2$

Prove: $\triangle VXW \cong \triangle ZXY$

Proof:

Statements	Reasons	Scrambled Reasons
1. X is the midpoint of $\overline{VZ}$.	**1.**	**a.** Supplements of congruent angles are congruent.
2. $\overline{VX} \cong \overline{XZ}$	**2.**	**b.** Given
3. $\angle WXV \cong \angle YXZ$	**3.**	**c.** SAA Postulate
4. $\angle 1 \cong \angle 2$	**4.**	**d.** Definition of *midpoint*
5. $\triangle VXW \cong \triangle ZXY$	**5.**	**e.** Vertical angles are congruent.
		f. Right angles are congruent.

REFLECT

1. What are some advantages and disadvantages of each of the three proof formats you have worked with?
2. Although most proofs written by mathematicians are in paragraph form, modern geometry books have primarily used the two-column format. Why do you think this has been the case?

Exercises

CORE

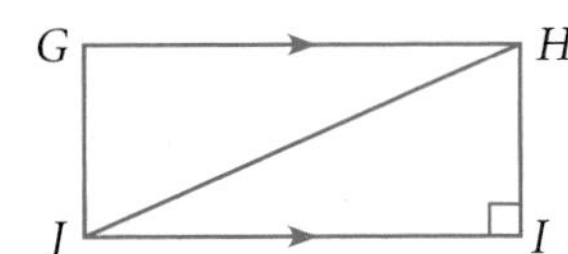

1. **Getting Started** Make a list of everything you know that must be true about the figure at the right.

2. Rewrite the following paragraph proof in two-column format.

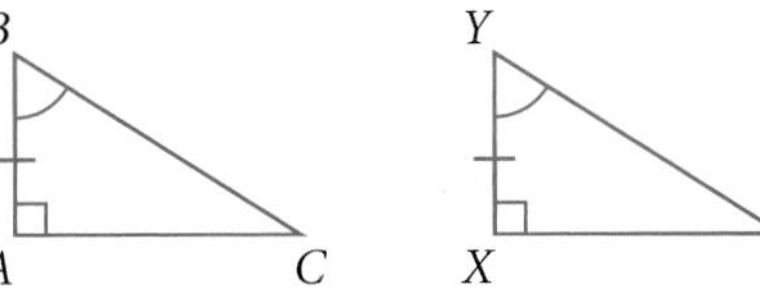

Given: $\triangle ABC$ and $\triangle XYZ$ are right triangles with right angles $\angle A$ and $\angle X$. $\overline{AB} \cong \overline{XY}$, and $\angle B \cong \angle Y$.

Prove: $\triangle ABC \cong \triangle XYZ$

Proof: The given information tells us that $\overline{AB} \cong \overline{XY}$ and that $\angle A$ and $\angle X$ are right angles. $\angle A \cong \angle X$ because all right angles are congruent. We are also given that $\angle B \cong \angle Y$. Therefore, $\triangle ABC \cong \triangle XYZ$ by the ASA Postulate.

3. **Brace Yourself** If a rectangle is made of wooden rods and hinges, it can collapse as shown.

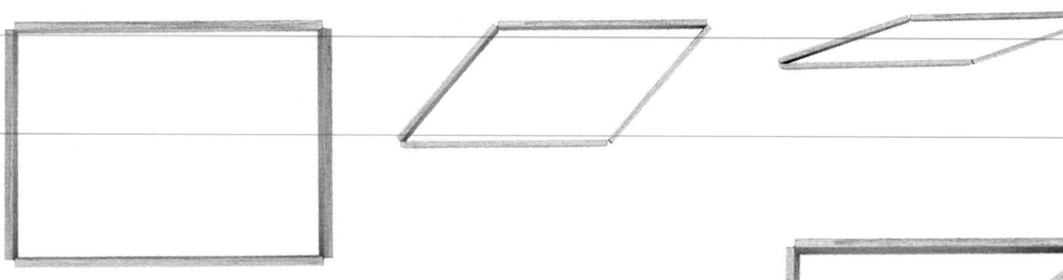

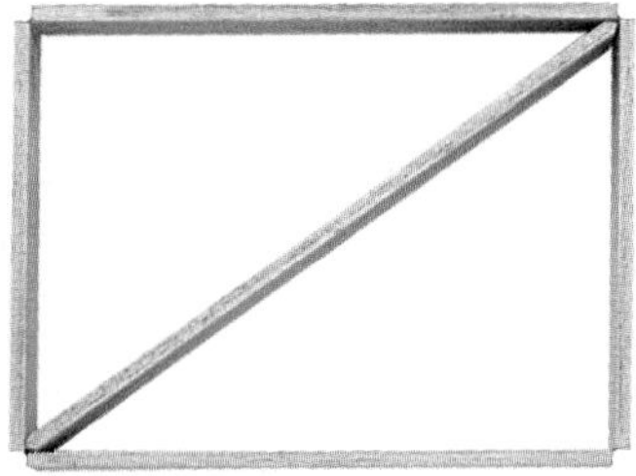

However, adding another wooden rod to form the diagonal of the figure makes the rectangle stable. What is true about the stability of triangles that is not true about figures with a greater number of sides? Why are triangular supports often seen in bridges, towers, and other large structures?

4. a. Complete the following proof by choosing a reason for each statement from the Scrambled Reasons' list.

Given: F is the midpoint of $\overline{DH}$ and $\overline{EG}$.

Prove: $\triangle DFE \cong \triangle HFG$

Proof:

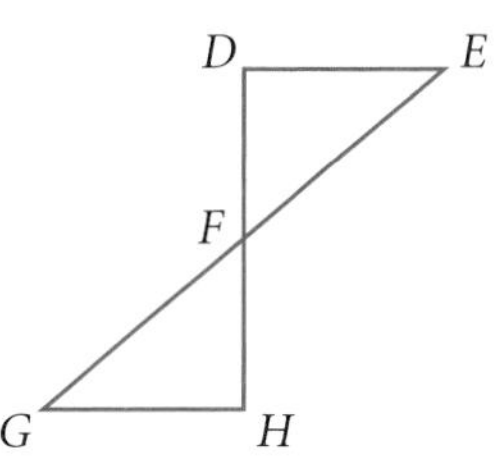

Statements	**Reasons**	**Scrambled Reasons**
1. F is the midpoint of $\overline{DH}$ and $\overline{EG}$.	**1.**	**a.** Vertical angles are congruent.
2. $\overline{DF} \cong \overline{HF}$	**2.**	**b.** Definition of *midpoint*
3. $\overline{EF} \cong \overline{GF}$	**3.**	**c.** Given
4. $\angle HFG \cong \angle DFE$	**4.**	**d.** SAS Postulate
5. $\triangle DFE \cong \triangle HFG$	**5.**	

b. Rewrite the proof in flow-proof format.

c. Which format do you think works better for this proof? Justify your choice.

5. Fill in the missing statements and reasons to complete the following two-column proof.

Given: $\overline{PQ} \parallel \overline{RS}$, $\overline{PQ} \cong \overline{RS}$

Prove: $\triangle PQS \cong \triangle RSQ$

Proof:

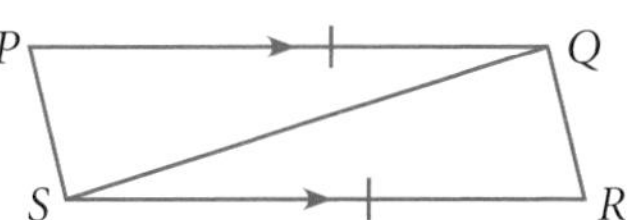

Statements	**Reasons**
1. $\overline{PQ} \cong \overline{RS}$	**1.**
2. $\overline{SQ} \cong \overline{SQ}$	**2.** Reflexive Property
3. $\overline{PQ} \parallel \overline{RS}$	**3.**
4.	**4.** If two parallel lines are cut by a transversal, the alternate interior angles are congruent.
5.	**5.** SAS Postulate

6. The vertices of triangles $\triangle ABC$ and $\triangle DEF$ are $A(2, 3)$, $B(5, 7)$, $C(8, -2)$, $D(-1, 3)$, $E(3, 6)$, and $F(-6, 9)$. Can you conclude that $\triangle ABC \cong \triangle DEF$? Justify your answer.

7. Fill in the missing statements and reasons to complete the following proof.

Given: $\overline{JK} \parallel \overline{LM}$
$\overline{JL} \parallel \overline{KM}$
$\overline{JL} \cong \overline{KM}$

Prove: $\triangle JLK \cong \triangle MKL$

Proof:

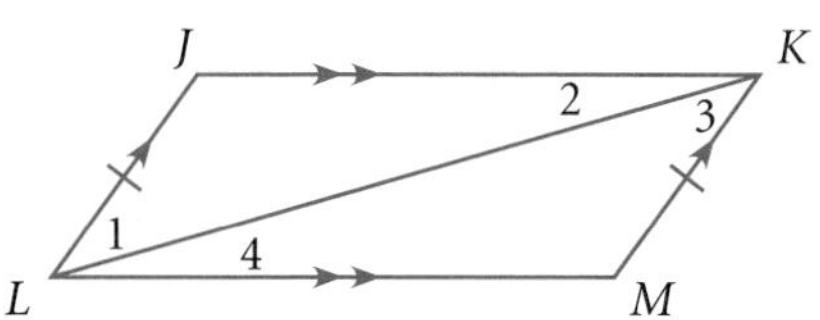

Statements	**Reasons**
1. $\overline{JK} \parallel \overline{LM}$	**1.**
2. $\angle 2 \cong \angle 4$	**2.**
3. $\overline{JL} \parallel \overline{KM}$	**3.**
4. $\angle 1 \cong \angle 3$	**4.**
5.	**5.** Given
6.	**6.**

LOOK BACK

8. Name all points on the grid with a bearing of 090 from point *I*. [3-1]

9. Name all points on the grid whose bearing from point *D* is greater than 180. [3-1]

10. What is the probability that a grid point randomly chosen from points *A* through *O* has a bearing greater than 315 from point *P*? [3-1]

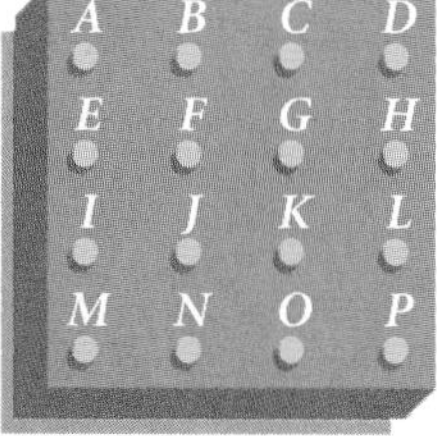

Complete the table for the triangle shown. [4-1]

	$m\angle 1$	$m\angle 2$	$m\angle 3$	
11.	146°		37°	
12.		81°	72°	
13.	161°	38°		

14. If $30° < m\angle 6 < 45°$, what measures are possible for $\angle 5$? [3-3]

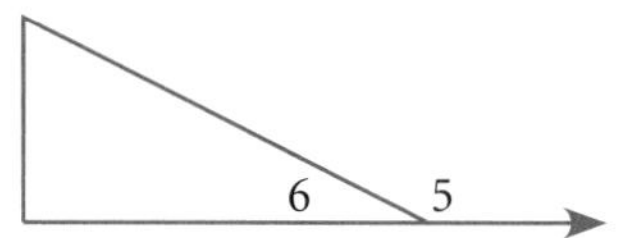

MORE PRACTICE

15. Fill in the missing reasons to complete the following proof.

Given: $\overline{AC} \cong \overline{ED}$
$\overline{AB} \cong \overline{EF}$
$\overline{BC} \cong \overline{FD}$

Prove: $\triangle ABC \cong \triangle EFD$

Proof:

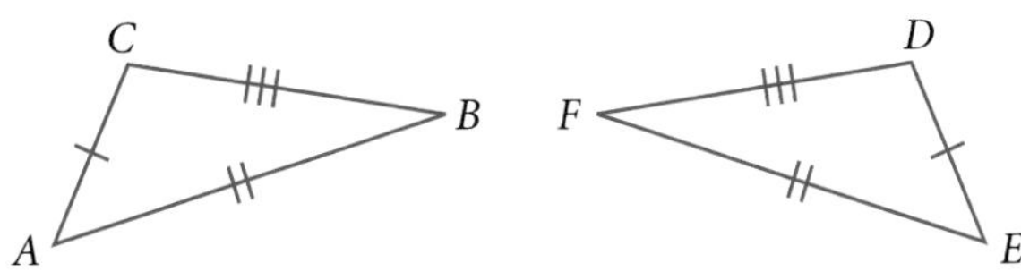

Statements	Reasons
1. $\overline{AC} \cong \overline{ED}$	**1.**
2. $\overline{AB} \cong \overline{EF}$	**2.**
3. $\overline{BC} \cong \overline{FD}$	**3.**
4. $\triangle ABC \cong \triangle EFD$	**4.**

16. Complete the following proof by choosing a reason for each statement from the Scrambled Reasons' list.

Given: J is the midpoint of $\overline{HL}$.
$\angle 1 \cong \angle 2$

Prove: $\triangle HIJ \cong \triangle LKJ$

Proof:

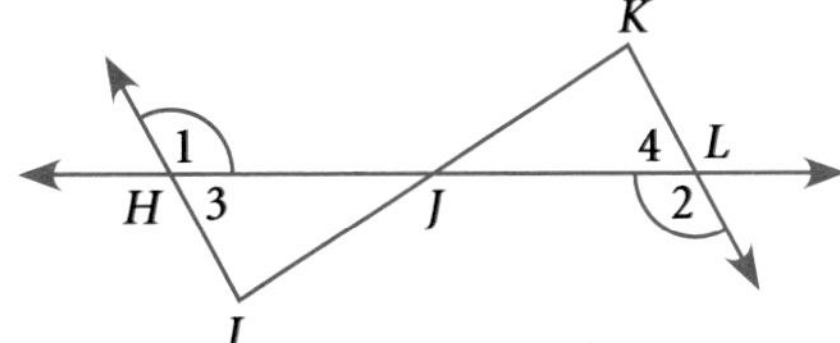

Statements	Reasons	Scrambled Reasons
1. J is the midpoint of $\overline{HL}$.	**1.**	**a.** ASA Postulate
2. $\overline{HJ} \cong \overline{JL}$	**2.**	**b.** Vertical angles are congruent.
3. $\angle 1$ and $\angle 3$ are supplementary. $\angle 2$ and $\angle 4$ are supplementary.	**3.**	**c.** Given **d.** Supplements of congruent angles are congruent.
4. $\angle 1 \cong \angle 2$	**4.**	**e.** Definition of *midpoint*
5. $\angle 3 \cong \angle 4$	**5.**	**f.** Linear pairs are supplementary.
6. $\angle HJI \cong \angle LJK$	**6.**	
7. $\triangle HIJ \cong \triangle LKJ$	**7.**	

MORE MATH REASONING

17. *Given:* G is the midpoint of $\overline{FH}$, and G is the midpoint of $\overline{EI}$. E is not on $\overleftrightarrow{FH}$.

Prove: $\triangle EFG \cong \triangle IHG$

a. *Draw* and label a figure for this proof.
b. Develop a *plan* for the proof. Then *demonstrate* the proof using any format.

18. Consider triangles $\triangle RST$ and $\triangle UVW$, where $\angle R \cong \angle U$, $m\angle R = (2x + 20)°$, $m\angle U = (x + 50)°$, $RS = 2x + 10$, $UV = 3x - 20$, $RT = x + 6$, and $UW = 2x - 24$.
a. Determine the value of x.
b. Determine the measures of the given sides and angles.
c. Explain why $\triangle RST$ is or is not congruent to $\triangle UVW$.

Use the figure at the right for Exercises 19 and 20.

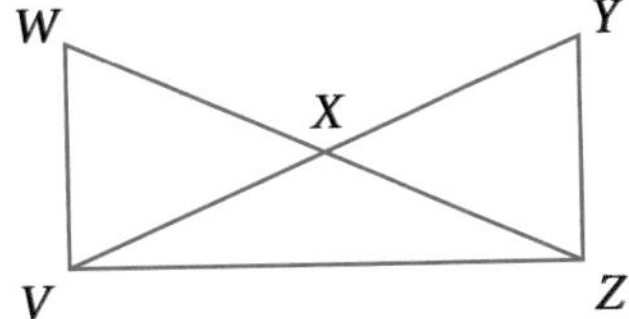

19. a. What additional information do you need to be able to prove $\triangle WXV \cong \triangle ZXY$?
b. Assuming this information, write a *plan* for the proof.

20. a. What additional information do you need to be able to prove $\triangle VZY \cong \triangle ZVW$?
b. Assuming this information, write a *plan* for the proof.

4-2 PART D Corresponding Parts

← CONNECT → ***You know that three pairs of congruent parts may be enough to prove two triangles congruent and that the triangles have six pairs of corresponding parts. Now you will connect these ideas to get "bonus information" when proving two triangles congruent.***

Congruent triangles can be found in everyday structures ranging from skyscrapers to fences. They are also useful in mathematics. In fact, proving that two triangles are congruent does not have to be the final step in a proof. As you will see, showing that triangles are congruent can be an important stepping stone to proving other things.

EXPLORE: ONE STEP BEYOND

1. Rearrange the statements for the following proof so that they form a logical sequence. Then write a reason to justify each statement.

Problem-Solving Tip

It may be helpful to work backwards.

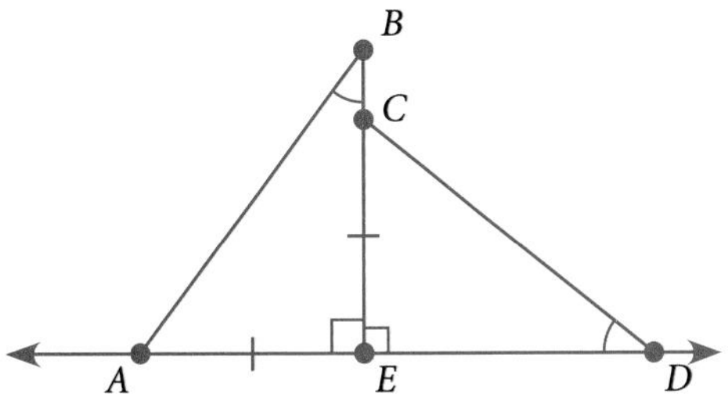

Given: $\overline{AE} \cong \overline{CE}$
$\angle ABE \cong \angle CDE$
$\angle AEB$ and $\angle CED$ are right angles.

Prove: $\overline{AB} \cong \overline{CD}$

Statements:

a. $\angle AEB \cong \angle CED$ **b.** $\overline{AE} \cong \overline{CE}$ **c.** $\angle AEB$ and $\angle CED$ are right angles.
d. $\angle ABE \cong \angle CDE$ **e.** $\overline{AB} \cong \overline{CD}$ **f.** $\triangle AEB \cong \triangle CED$

2. Explain how you used the next-to-last step of the proof to get to the last step. What reason justified the final step in the proof, and why did it work?
3. Compare your proof with that of a classmate. If there are differences, decide whether both versions of the proof are correct or whether you need to correct one or both of your proofs.

If you can prove that two triangles are congruent (usually by showing that three pairs of corresponding parts are congruent), you know from the definition of congruent triangles that all six pairs of corresponding sides and angles are congruent.

Corresponding **P**arts of **C**ongruent **T**riangles are **C**ongruent.

This fact is used so often that you may find it helpful to refer to it as CPCTC. Notice how CPCTC is used in the last step of the following flow proof.

EXAMPLE

Given: $\overline{XY} \cong \overline{ZW}$

$\overline{YZ} \cong \overline{WX}$

Prove: $\overleftrightarrow{WX} \parallel \overleftrightarrow{YZ}$

Proof:

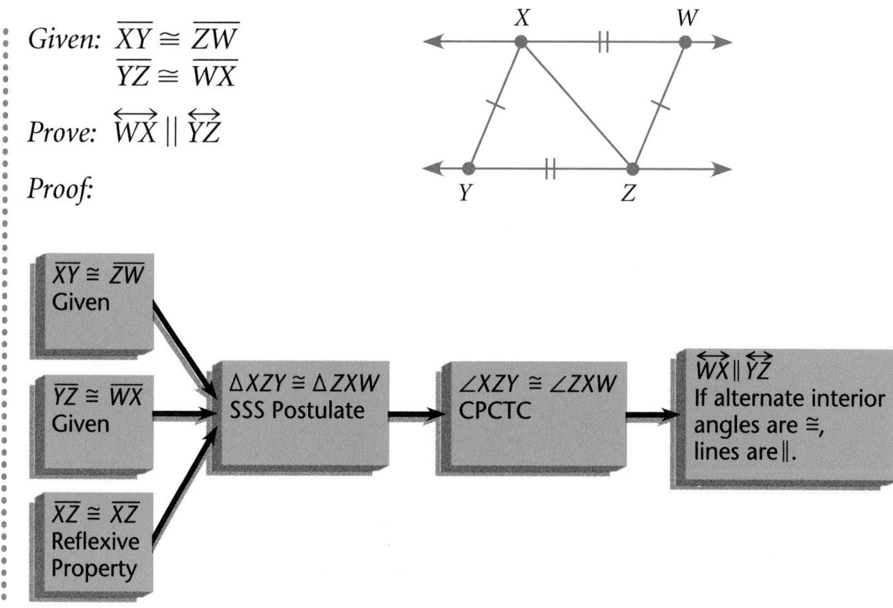

In this example, segment $\overline{XZ}$ is a part of both triangles that we want to prove congruent. To show that a side (or angle) shared by two triangles is congruent to itself, we use the Reflexive Property for congruence. This property, which is related to the Reflexive Property in algebra, says that a figure is congruent to itself. We can also use the Symmetric and Transitive Properties for congruence in proofs.

Properties of Congruence	**Examples**
• Reflexive Property	$\overline{AB} \cong \overline{AB}$
• Symmetric Property	If $\angle 1 \cong \angle 2$, then $\angle 2 \cong \angle 1$.
• Transitive Property	If $\overline{WX} \cong \overline{XY}$ and $\overline{XY} \cong \overline{YZ}$, then $\overline{WX} \cong \overline{YZ}$.

TRY IT

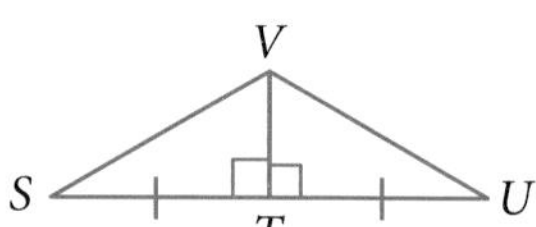

a. In the figure at the right, how can you prove that the triangles are congruent by using the SAS Postulate?

b. Which additional pairs of sides and angles could you then prove congruent by using CPCTC?

REFLECT

1. Do you think the definition of congruent triangles is often used to prove that two triangles are congruent? Why or why not?
2. Is $\triangle ABC \cong \triangle ABC$? Explain your reasoning.

Exercises

CORE

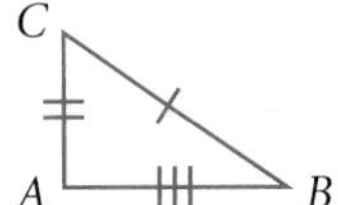

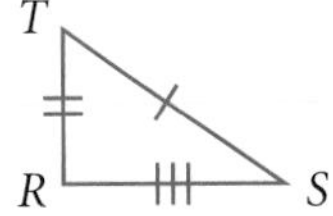

1. **Getting Started a.** Write a triangle-congruence statement for the triangles shown in the figure at the right.
   b. Which congruence postulate can be used to prove the triangles are congruent?
   c. Once you prove the triangles are congruent, how can you show that $\angle C \cong \angle T$?

Determine whether each statement is true or false. If the statement is false, change the underlined word or phrase to make it true.

2. The statement $\overline{RS} \cong \overline{RS}$ can be justified by the <u>Symmetric</u> Property.
3. If $\overline{VW} \cong \overline{XY}$, then $\overline{XY} \cong \overline{VW}$ by the <u>Transitive</u> Property.
4. Fill in the missing reasons to complete the following proof.

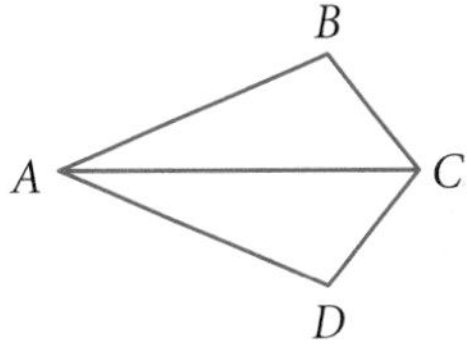

Given: $\overrightarrow{AC}$ bisects $\angle BAD$, and $\overrightarrow{CA}$ bisects $\angle BCD$.

Prove: $\overline{AD} \cong \overline{AB}$

Proof:

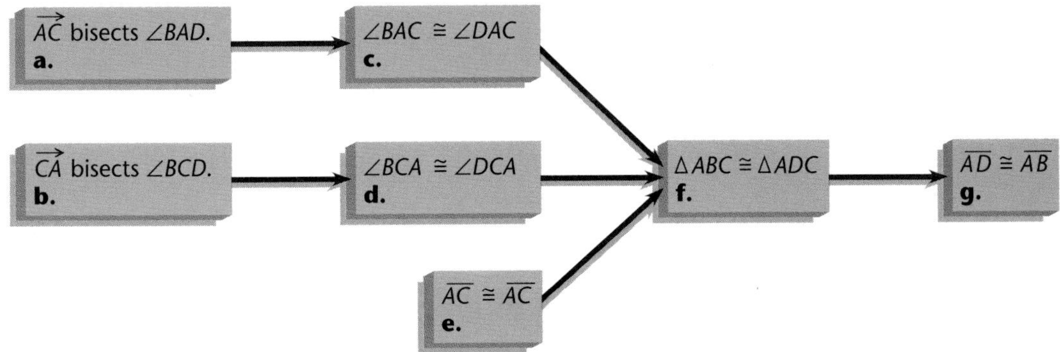

5. Arrange the scrambled statements for the following proof in a logical order. Then give a reason for each statement.

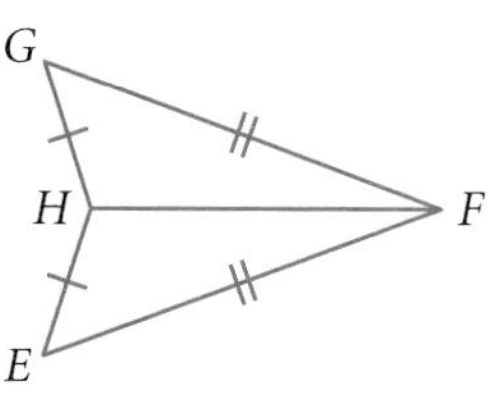

Given: $\overline{EH} \cong \overline{GH}, \overline{EF} \cong \overline{GF}$

Prove: $\angle GFH \cong \angle EFH$

Proof:

Statements	Reasons	Scrambled Statements
1.	**1.**	**a.** $\triangle GFH \cong \triangle EFH$
2.	**2.**	**b.** $\overline{EF} \cong \overline{GF}$
3.	**3.**	**c.** $\overline{HF} \cong \overline{HF}$
4.	**4.**	**d.** $\angle GFH \cong \angle EFH$
5.	**5.**	**e.** $\overline{EH} \cong \overline{GH}$

6. a. Fill in the missing statements and reasons to complete the following proof.

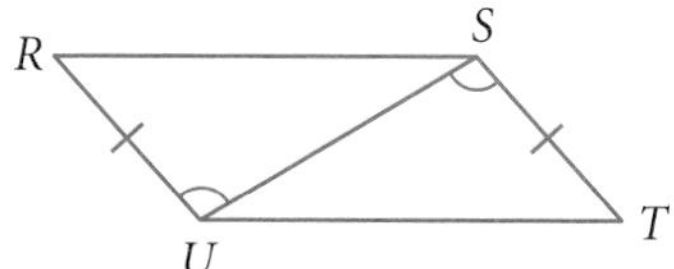

Given: $\overline{RU} \cong \overline{ST}$
$\angle RUS \cong \angle TSU$

Prove: $\overline{RS} \parallel \overline{UT}$

Proof:

Statements	Reasons
1. $\overline{RU} \cong \overline{ST}$	**1.**
2.	**2.** Reflexive Property
3.	**3.**
4. $\triangle RSU \cong \triangle TUS$	**4.**
5.	**5.**
6. $\overline{RS} \parallel \overline{UT}$	**6.**

b. Rewrite the completed proof in flow-proof format.

7. Copy and mark the figure. Then complete the following proof.

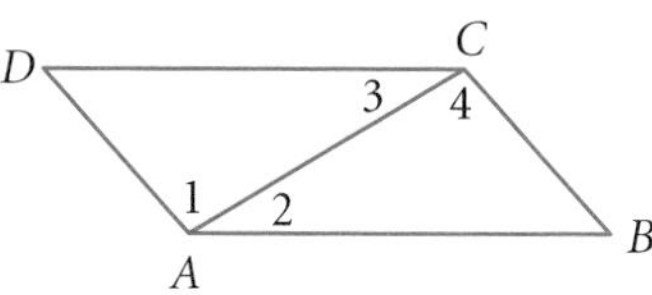

Given: $\overline{AD} \parallel \overline{BC}, \overline{AB} \parallel \overline{DC}$

Prove: $\overline{AD} \cong \overline{BC}$

Proof: Since it is given that $\overline{AD} \parallel \overline{BC}$ and $\overline{AB} \parallel \overline{DC}$, $\angle 3 \cong$ **a.** ____, and $\angle 4 \cong$ **b.** ____ because **c.** ____. $\overline{AC}$ is a shared side, and $\overline{AC} \cong \overline{AC}$ because of the **d.** ____. $\triangle ADC \cong \triangle$ **e.** ____ by **f.** ____. Finally, $\overline{AD} \cong \overline{BC}$ by **g.** ____.

8. A surveyor concludes that the fences shown are the same length. How can he make this conclusion?

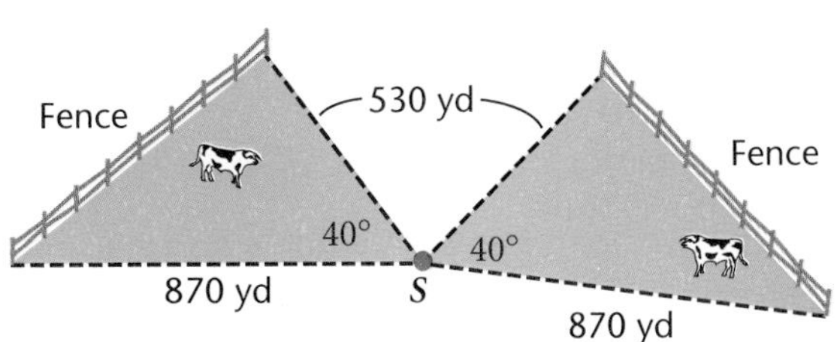

9. Street Repairs Helen's crew is doing some repairs, and they have dug up some asphalt on a street. The crew needs to cover the hole at night, but it is too wide to measure directly. Helen sets up two intersecting metal rods and then places a third rod across the other two as shown. How wide is the hole? Explain how Helen solved the problem.

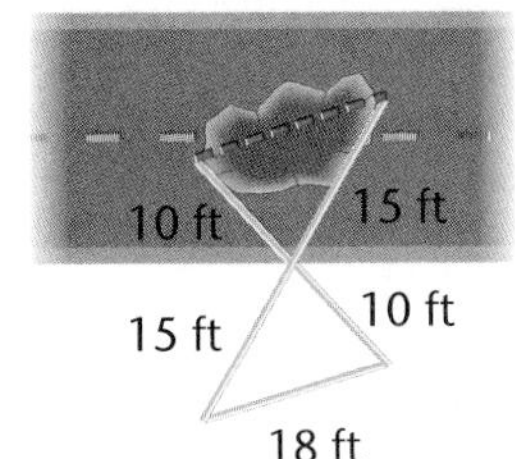

10. A New Construction The first two steps of the construction of a line perpendicular to a point on a given line are shown below.

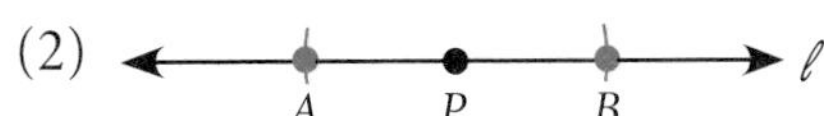

a. Explain how to complete the construction.

b. Draw line m and point K on m. Then use a compass and straightedge to construct line n perpendicular to m at K.

11. *Given:* $\overline{MP}$ and $\overline{NQ}$ bisect each other at O. Find the measure of $\angle N$. Explain your reasoning.

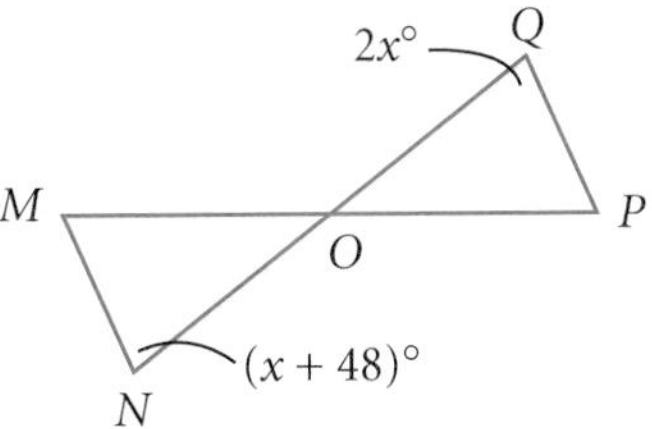

LOOK AHEAD

12. Name the hypotenuse of $\triangle ABD$.

13. Name the vertex angle of $\triangle ADC$.

14. Name the legs of $\triangle ADC$.

15. Name the legs of $\triangle ABD$.

16. Name the base angles of $\triangle ADC$.

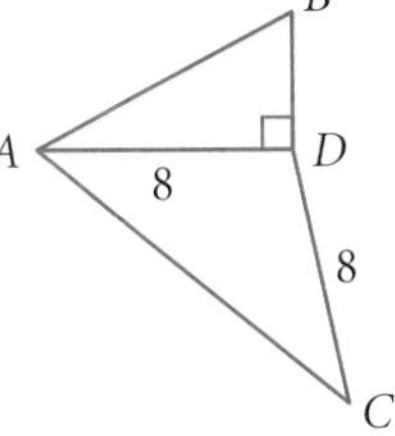

For each figure described, find the perimeter (distance around).

17. A rectangle with length 20 cm and width 11 cm.

18. An equilateral triangle with side length $3\frac{1}{6}$ in.

19. An isosceles triangle with base length 8.1 in. and leg length 6.5 in.

MORE PRACTICE

20. Fill in the missing statements and reasons to complete the following proof.

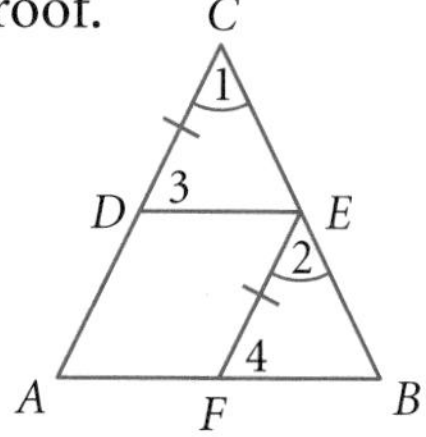

Given: E is the midpoint of $\overline{BC}$,
$\angle 1 \cong \angle 2$, and $\overline{CD} \cong \overline{EF}$.

Prove: $\angle 3 \cong \angle 4$

Proof:

Statements	**Reasons**
1. $\overline{CD} \cong \overline{EF}$	**1.**
2.	**2.** Given
3.	**3.** Given
4. $\overline{CE} \cong \overline{BE}$	**4.**
5.	**5.**
6. $\angle 3 \cong \angle 4$	**6.**

21. Copy and mark the figure. Then complete the following proof.

Given: $\angle 1 \cong \angle 4$, $\angle B \cong \angle D$

Prove: $\overline{AD} \cong \overline{BC}$

Proof: $\overline{AC}$ is congruent to itself by **a.** ____. $\angle 1 \cong \angle 4$ by the **b.** ____. $\angle B \cong \angle D$, also by the **c.** ____. Therefore, $\triangle$ **d.** ____ $\cong \triangle$ **e.** ____ by **f.** ____. Therefore, sides $\overline{AD}$ and $\overline{BC}$ are congruent by **g.** ____.

MORE MATH REASONING

22. Dig This! An archaeologist digging near the lost city of Ecneurgnoc discovers the ancient textbook page shown below. Translate the page into English as completely as you can.

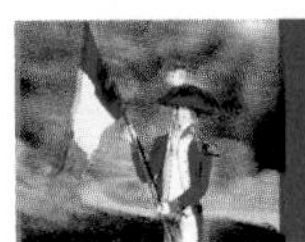

4-2 PART E Making Connections

← CONNECT → ***Most people use logical reasoning every day. You are asked to demonstrate such reasoning whenever someone says, "Is that so? Prove it!" You have explored more properties of triangles and continued to develop skills for deductive proof.***

The real test of understanding comes when you have to use your knowledge to solve a problem in a new situation. In the following Explore, you will look at a real problem that confronted Napoleon's troops.

EXPLORE: A CONGRUENT CROSSING

It is said that Napoleon once needed to find the distance across a river. One of his officers solved the problem by using geometry.

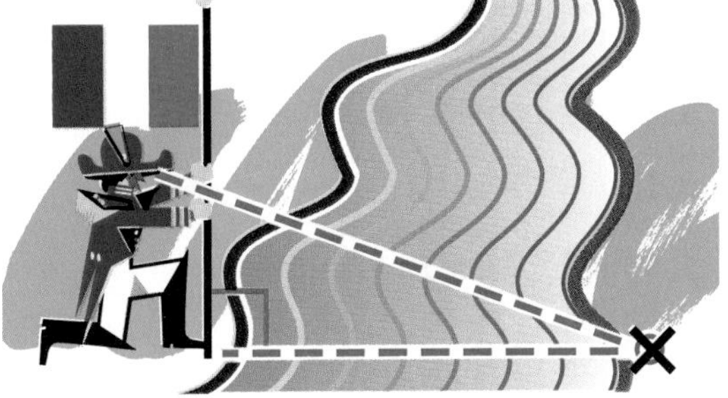

He placed a flagpole vertically at the edge of the riverbank and stood an arm's length away. He held the pole firmly with one hand while sliding the other hand to a position on the pole so that his line of sight with his hand was in line with the opposite riverbank.

Keeping the same angle of sight and his hands in the same position, he turned to sight a rock on his side of the riverbank.

1. *Draw* a figure that represents the problem. Label the figure. *State* the Given and Prove.
2. Name the corresponding sides and angles. Explain how you identified them.
3. Mark any parts that you know are congruent. Explain why each pair of parts is congruent.
4. How did Napoleon's officer determine the distance across the river? Write an explanation of the method he used.

REFLECT

1. Explain and illustrate each of the triangle-congruence postulates.
2. The definition of congruent triangles can be written as a biconditional statement.
   a. Write the definition in biconditional form.
   b. Break the definition into two conditional statements.
   c. One of the two conditionals is used much more frequently than the other. Identify the one that is rarely used, and explain why this is so.
3. Describe a situation in which triangle congruence can be used to find an unknown distance. Explain your method.

Self-Assessment

Complete each statement in Exercises 1–4 with *always, sometimes,* or *never.* Explain your answers.

1. Two triangles are ___ congruent if two sides and the included angle of one are congruent to two sides and the included angle of the other.
2. An equilateral triangle is ___ congruent to a right triangle.
3. If three angles of a triangle are congruent, then the triangle is ___ scalene.
4. If two triangles are congruent, the corresponding parts are ___ congruent.
5. Which of the following is *not* a triangle-congruence postulate?
   (a) SSS (b) SAS (c) AAA (d) SAA (e) ASA

Use each set of given information and the figures below to state a postulate or theorem that proves $\triangle ABC \cong \triangle RST$.

6. *Given:* $\angle A \cong \angle R$, $\overline{AB} \cong \overline{RS}$, $\angle B \cong \angle S$
7. *Given:* $\angle C$ and $\angle T$ are right angles, $\overline{AB} \cong \overline{RS}$, and $\angle A \cong \angle R$.

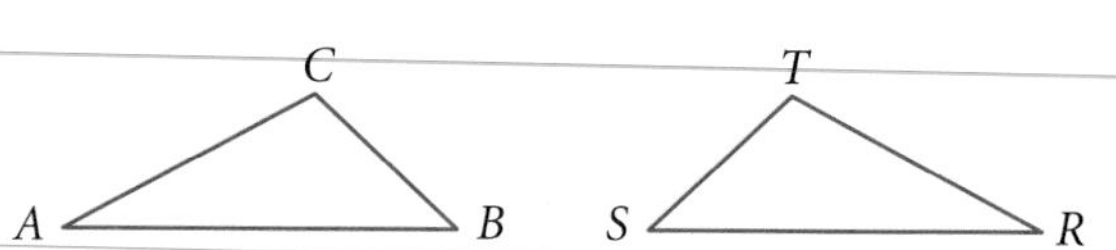

8. *Given:* $\angle C \cong \angle T$, $\overline{AC} \cong \overline{RT}$, $\overline{CB} \cong \overline{TS}$
9. **Bridging the Gap** Three bridges have been built to connect island M to cities S and T, and S and T to one another. Bridges parallel to these need to be built to connect S and T to island N. How long should bridges $\overline{NS}$ and $\overline{NT}$ be? Justify your answer.

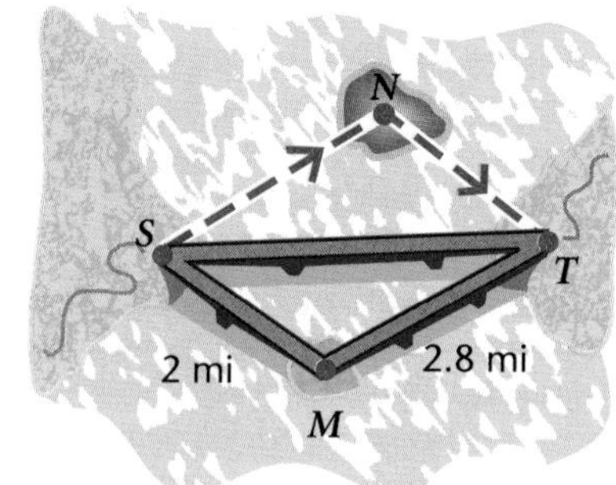

10. Write a description of how CPCTC is used to prove a pair of sides or angles congruent.

Use a protractor to find the bearing from the control tower to each of the following. [3-1]

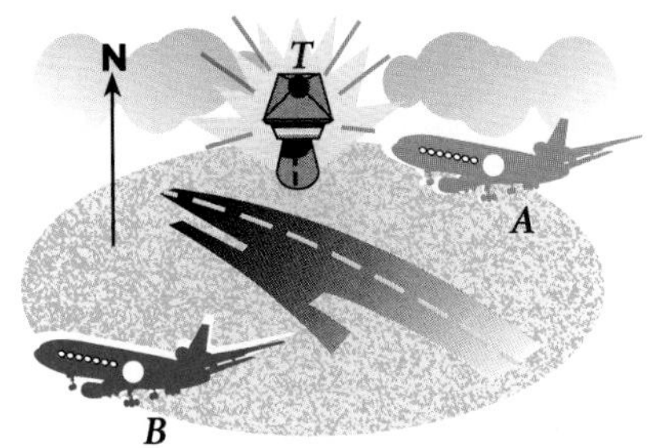

11. Airplane A

12. Airplane B

13. Find the bearing from Airplane A to Airplane B. How does this compare to the bearing from Airplane B to Airplane A? [3-1]

In each of the following, use the figure at the right and the given information to find $m\angle C$. [4-1]

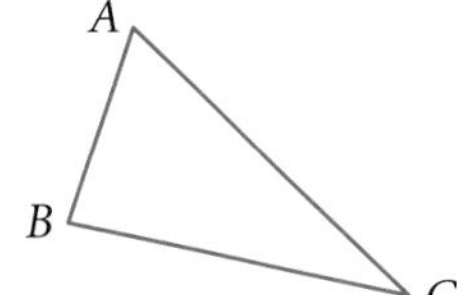

14. $m\angle A = 51°$, $m\angle B = 81°$

15. $m\angle A = 87°$, $\angle A \cong \angle B$

16. $m\angle A = (x + 54)°$, $m\angle B = (7x - 5)°$, $m\angle C = (51 - 3x)°$

17. Complete the following proof.

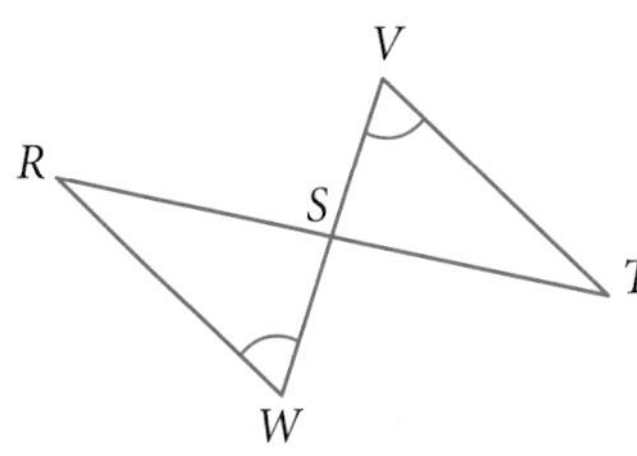

Given: $\angle W \cong \angle V$
S is the midpoint of $\overline{RT}$.

Prove: $\triangle WSR \cong \triangle VST$

Proof: S is the midpoint of $\overline{RT}$, so $\overline{RS} \cong \overline{ST}$ by the **a.** ____. Since **b.** ____, $\angle WSR \cong \angle VST$. $\angle W \cong \angle V$, from the **c.** ____. Therefore, we can conclude that $\triangle WSR \cong \triangle VST$ by the **d.** ____ Postulate.

18. *Given:* $\overline{AB} \cong \overline{CD}$
$\angle 1 \cong \angle 2$

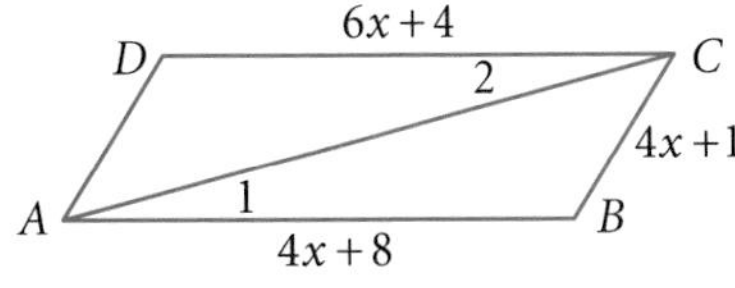

Find the length of $\overline{AD}$. Write a short paragraph to explain your reasoning.

19. *Given:* $\overline{EG} \perp \overline{FH}$, and G is the midpoint of $\overline{FH}$.

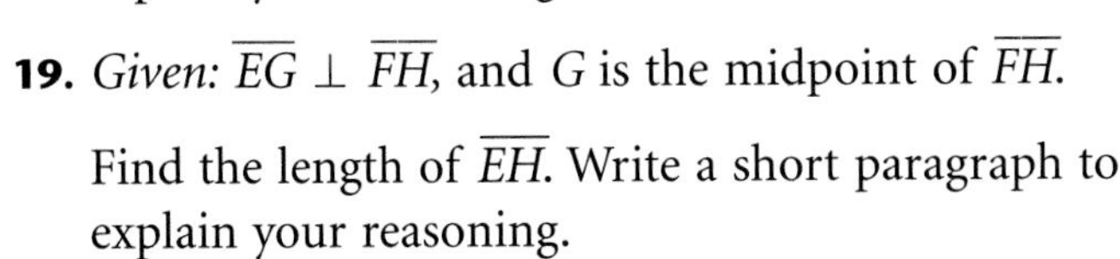

Find the length of $\overline{EH}$. Write a short paragraph to explain your reasoning.

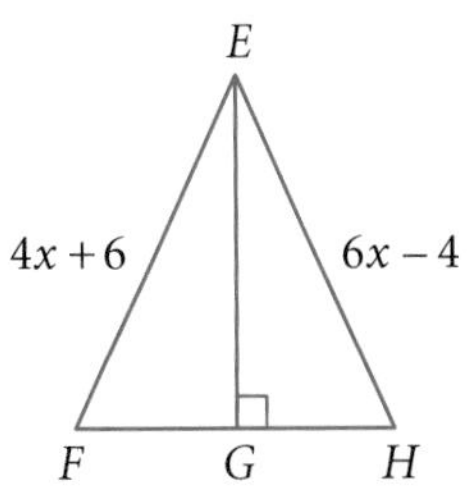

20. a. Complete the following proof.

Given: $\overline{RU} \parallel \overline{ST}$, $\angle S \cong \angle U$

Prove: $\overline{RS} \cong \overline{TU}$

Proof:

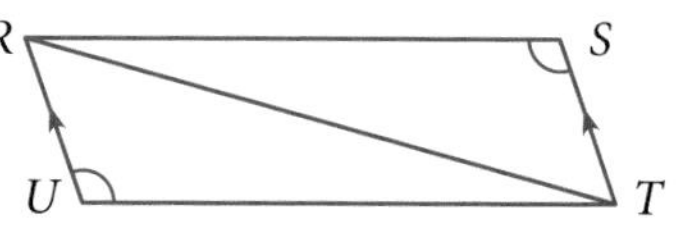

Statements	**Reasons**
1. $\overline{RU} \parallel \overline{ST}$	**1.**
2. $\angle URT \cong \angle STR$	**2.**
3.	**3.** Given
4.	**4.** Reflexive Property
5.	**5.**
6.	**6.**

b. Rewrite your proof in paragraph format.
c. Rewrite your proof in flow-proof format.

21. a. Draw line *s* and point *D* on *s*. Then construct line *t* perpendicular to *s* at *D*, using the construction technique you developed in Exercise 10 on page 279.
b. Mark the segments on your construction that must be congruent. Then explain why the construction works.

22. Supply reasons to complete the following proof.

Given: $\overline{AC}$ and $\overline{BD}$ bisect each other.

Prove: $\overline{AD} \parallel \overline{BC}$

Proof:

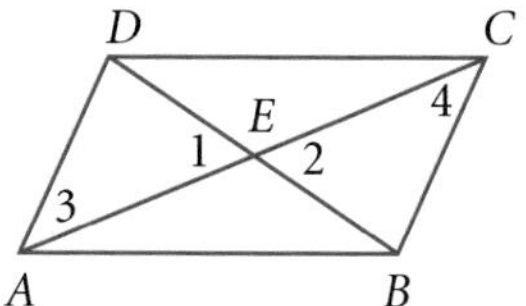

Statements	**Reasons**
1. $\overline{AC}$ and $\overline{BD}$ bisect each other.	**1.**
2. $\overline{AE} \cong \overline{CE}$, $\overline{DE} \cong \overline{BE}$	**2.**
3. $\angle 1 \cong \angle 2$	**3.**
4. $\triangle AED \cong \triangle CEB$	**4.**
5. $\angle 3 \cong \angle 4$	**5.**
6. $\overline{AD} \parallel \overline{BC}$	**6.**

4-3 Properties of Special Triangles

PEDALING THROUGH GEOMETRY

A Frenchman named de Sivrac invented the first bicycle around 1790. This bike, called the *célerifère*, had heavy, cart-like wheels. There was no way to steer it, and it had no pedals—the rider pushed it along with his or her feet.

In 1870, James Starley patented the first lightweight, all-metal bicycle. Its wire-spoked wheels were a great improvement over the heavy wheels used earlier. To increase the speed of the bicycle, the pedals were attached to a large front wheel. These "penny farthings" became the most popular type of bicycle, despite the difficulties of getting on, staying on, and figuring out how to get off at the end of the ride.

Today's bicycles have come a long way from these early designs. The most important part of a modern bicycle is the frame. Two popular frames are shown here.

The measurements of the tube lengths, seat angle, and head (or steering post) angle are referred to as the *frame geometry*. In addition to the seat and head angle, there is another important angle that can be called the *human angle*.

The properties of the frame geometry determine the bicycle's responsiveness, traction, and shock absorption.

Penny farthing

Racing bike

Mountain bike

?

1. Why do you think early bicycles with wagon-type wheels were called "boneshakers"?
2. Why did the large front wheel of a penny farthing increase the speed of the bicycle?
3. Why do you think triangles are used in bicycle frames?

4-3 PART A Isosceles Triangles

← CONNECT →

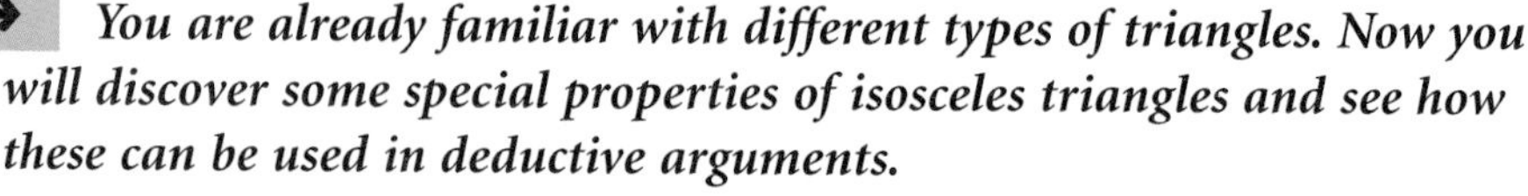

You are already familiar with different types of triangles. Now you will discover some special properties of isosceles triangles and see how these can be used in deductive arguments.

There are many types of bicycles. However, some of them have distinguishing features. For example, as shown in the illustrations on the previous page, the nonhorizontal top tube is characteristic of a mountain bike.

Some triangles also have "special features." For example, an equilateral triangle has three congruent sides, and an isosceles triangle (shown at the right) has at least two congruent sides. You will investigate some special characteristics of these triangles in the following Explore.

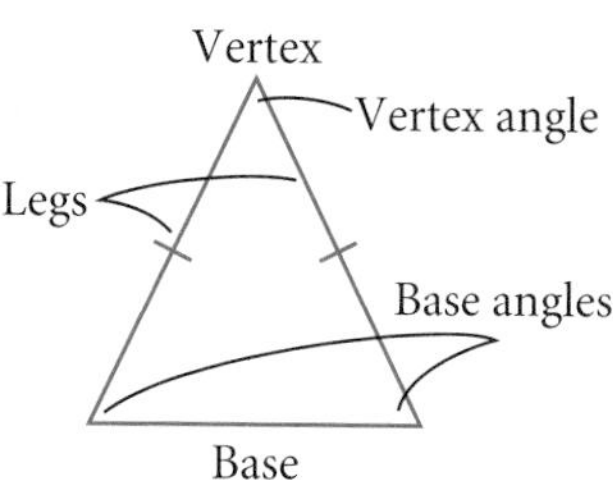

EXPLORE: THE ISOSCELES HAVE IT!

MATERIALS

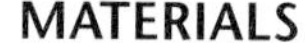

Paper
Ruler
Scissors
Protractor

1. Draw an isosceles triangle on a sheet of paper. Then cut out your triangle and fold it so that the two legs match up. What can you say about the base angles of the triangle? Write a conjecture in if-then form.
2. State the converse of your conjecture from Step 1. See whether the converse is true by cutting and folding triangles with the appropriate characteristics.
3. Look at the folds made in your cutout triangles. What transformation do these folds suggest? Make as many conjectures as you can about the segment determined by the fold. Compare your conjectures with those of your classmates.

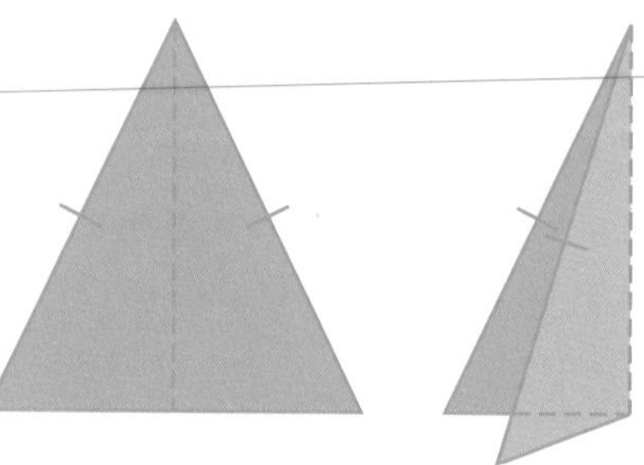

The properties of isosceles triangles that you have discovered are useful in finding unknown side lengths and angle measures.

TRY IT

a. In isosceles triangle $\triangle ABC$, $\overline{AB} \cong \overline{BC}$. What else must be true?

b. In $\triangle MNO$, $\angle M \cong \angle N$. Find the lengths of sides $\overline{MO}$ and $\overline{NO}$. (Hint: What do you know about these sides?)

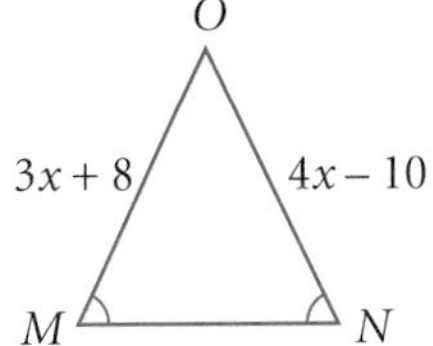

You have explored an important theorem about isosceles triangles and have seen that its converse is also true. We now state these theorems and a second pair of theorems that will be important in upcoming proofs.

ISOSCELES TRIANGLE THEOREM

If two sides of a triangle are congruent, then the angles opposite those sides are congruent.

CONVERSE OF THE ISOSCELES TRIANGLE THEOREM

If two angles of a triangle are congruent, then the sides opposite those angles are congruent.

UNIQUE BISECTOR THEOREMS

Every segment has a unique midpoint.

Every angle has a unique ray that bisects it.

1. State the Isosceles Triangle Theorem and its converse as a single biconditional statement.

2. Is the contrapositive of the Isosceles Triangle Theorem true? If so, state the contrapositive.

If a conjecture is called a *theorem,* we must be able to prove it. Watch for the "trick" in the following proof of the Isosceles Triangle Theorem. It is a technique that will be useful in many proofs.

EXAMPLE

Prove: If two sides of a triangle are congruent, then the angles opposite those sides are congruent.

Given: In $\triangle XYZ$, $\overline{XZ} \cong \overline{YZ}$.

Prove: $\angle X \cong \angle Y$

Plan: Add an *auxiliary segment* $\overline{ZM}$ from Z to M, the midpoint of $\overline{XY}$. Then prove that the two triangles formed are congruent by the SSS Congruence Postulate, and use CPCTC to show that the base angles are congruent.

Proof:

Statements	Reasons
1. Draw M, the midpoint of $\overline{XY}$.	**1.** Every segment has a unique midpoint.
2. Draw $\overline{ZM}$.	**2.** Two points determine a line.
3. $\overline{XM} \cong \overline{MY}$	**3.** Definition of *midpoint*
4. $\overline{ZM} \cong \overline{ZM}$	**4.** Reflexive Property
5. $\overline{XZ} \cong \overline{YZ}$	**5.** Given
6. $\triangle XMZ \cong \triangle YMZ$	**6.** SSS Postulate
7. $\angle X \cong \angle Y$	**7.** CPCTC

An **auxiliary line** is a line (or part of a line) added to a figure. You can add lines and points to a figure as long as you can show that they actually exist. Notice how this was done in Steps 1 and 2 of the proof in the preceding example.

2. How did the addition of an auxiliary line help prove the Isosceles Triangle Theorem?

3. Does the auxiliary line in the proof, shown in the example, remind you of something you saw in the Explore? Explain.

You will be asked to prove the converse of the Isosceles Triangle Theorem in Exercise 16.

REFLECT

1. Use the Isosceles Triangle Theorem to explain why an equilateral triangle must be equiangular.
2. a. You cannot assume that the angle bisector of an angle of a triangle intersects the opposite side at its midpoint. Why not?
   b. Does the angle bisector of the vertex angle of an isosceles triangle intersect the base at its midpoint? Explain.
3. Maritza says, "If an isosceles triangle is obtuse, the vertex angle has to be the obtuse angle." Is she right? If so, justify her statement. If not, provide a counterexample.

Exercises

CORE

Getting Started Give a reason to justify each statement.

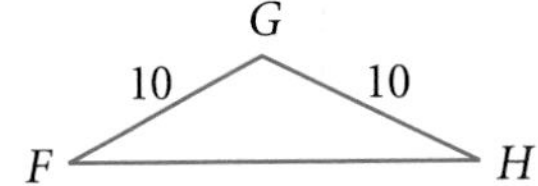

1. $\overline{FG} \cong \overline{GH}$
2. $\angle F \cong \angle H$
3. $\triangle FGH$ is isosceles.

Use the information in the figures to find the following.

4. $m\angle A$

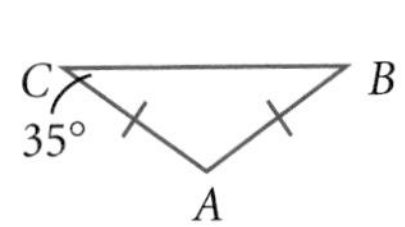

5. $m\angle D$

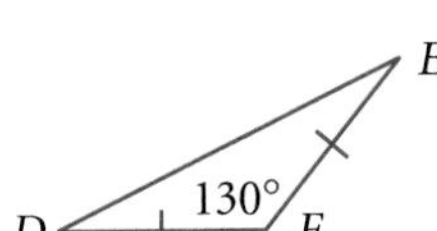

6. $m\angle G$

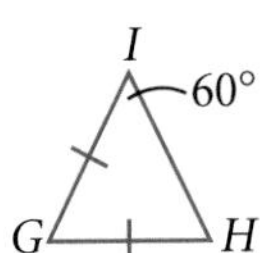

7. YZ

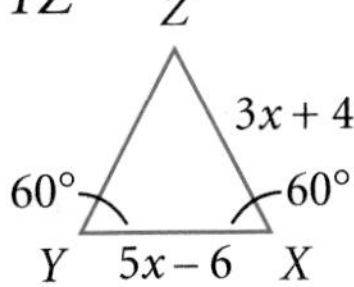

Use the figure at the right in Exercises 8–10.

8. *Given:* $\triangle ABC$ is isosceles, with base $\overline{AB}$.
   a. Name the congruent sides.
   b. Name the congruent angles.
   c. What theorem guarantees that the angles are congruent?
9. *Given:* $\angle CDE \cong \angle CED$
   a. Name the congruent sides in $\triangle DEC$.
   b. What theorem guarantees that the sides are congruent?
10. If $\triangle ABC$ is isosceles with base $\overline{AB}$, and $\overline{AD} \cong \overline{BE}$, is $\triangle DCE$ isosceles? Explain.
11. $\triangle RST$ is isosceles with base $\overline{RS}$. Draw $\triangle RST$, and mark the congruent sides. If $RT = 5x - 4$, $ST = 3x + 4$, and $RS = 2x + 9$, find the lengths of the sides of the triangle.

12. Steep Thinking A surveyor is curious about the height of a tall building. Using an ordinary protractor, he finds that the top of the building and the ground make a 45° angle when the protractor is 48 ft away from the base of the building. How tall is the building? Explain the reasoning you used to solve this problem.

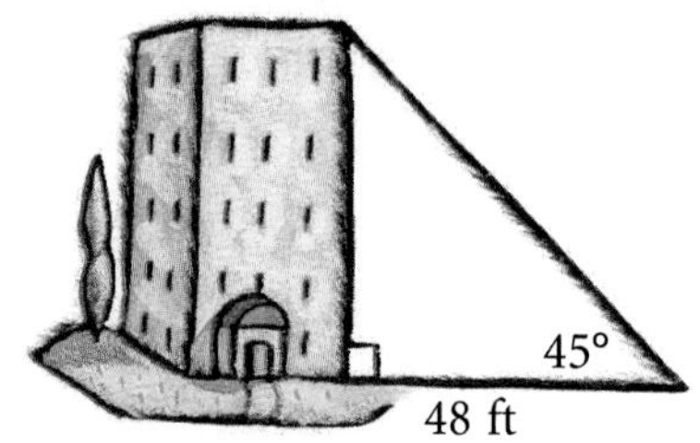

13. Write the Given and Prove for the following proof. Then arrange the statements in a logical order, and give a reason for each statement.

If $\angle 2 \cong \angle 4$, then $\triangle XYZ$ is isosceles.

Given: ___

Prove: ___

Proof:

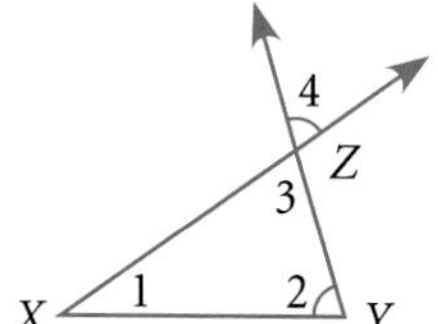

Statements	Reasons	Scrambled Statements
1.	1.	**a.** $\angle 2 \cong \angle 3$
2.	2.	**b.** $\angle 2 \cong \angle 4$
3.	3.	**c.** $\triangle XYZ$ is isosceles.
4.	4.	**d.** $\overline{XY} \cong \overline{XZ}$
5.	5.	**e.** $\angle 4 \cong \angle 3$

14. Draw three different isosceles triangles. For each, illustrate all the lines of symmetry that reflect the triangle onto itself. How many lines of symmetry does an isosceles triangle have?

History

15. Napoleon's Conjecture Napoleon is said to have made a conjecture about triangles suggested by the steps below. See if you can discover the conjecture he made.

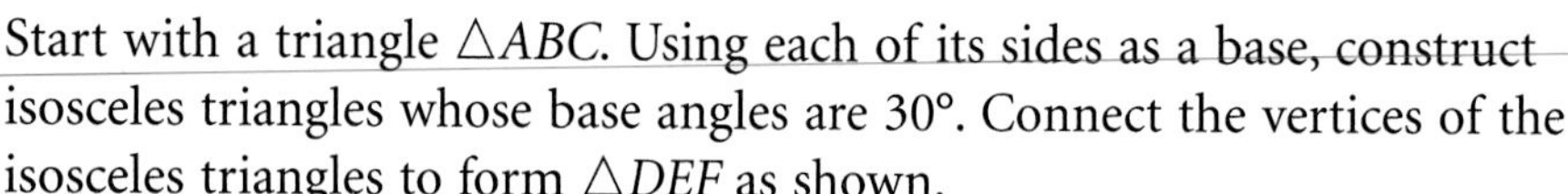

Start with a triangle $\triangle ABC$. Using each of its sides as a base, construct isosceles triangles whose base angles are 30°. Connect the vertices of the isosceles triangles to form $\triangle DEF$ as shown.

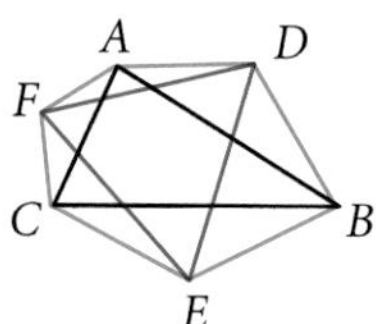

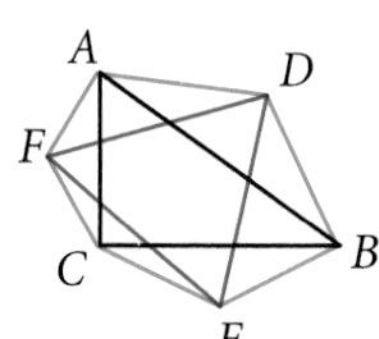

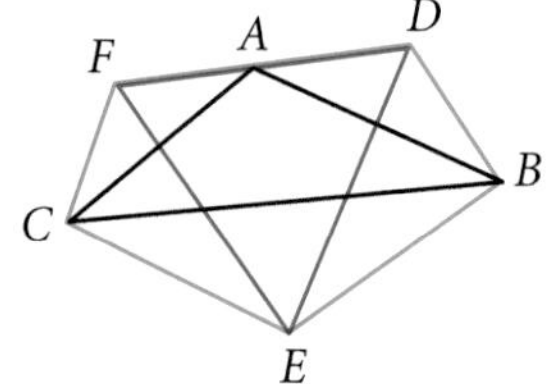

16. Proving the Converse *Draw* a figure to represent the Given information. Then add the auxiliary line discussed in the *plan,* and finally, rewrite the proof as a flow-proof.

Prove: If two angles of a triangle are congruent, then the sides opposite the angles are congruent.

Given: $\triangle ABC$ with $\angle A \cong \angle B$ *Prove:* $\overline{AC} \cong \overline{BC}$

Plan: Draw an auxiliary ray that bisects $\angle C$. Prove that the two triangles formed are congruent, and then use CPCTC.

Proof:

Statements	**Reasons**
1. Draw $\overrightarrow{CD}$, the angle bisector of $\angle C$ that intersects $\overline{AB}$ at D.	**1.** Every angle has a unique ray that bisects it.
2. $\angle ACD \cong \angle BCD$	**2.**
3.	**3.** Reflexive Property
4.	**4.** Given
5.	**5.**
6. $\overline{AC} \cong \overline{BC}$	**6.**

LOOK AHEAD

Name the triangle-congruence condition that could be used to show $\triangle ABC \cong \triangle RST$.

17. $\overline{BC} \cong \overline{ST}$, $\overline{AB} \perp \overline{BC}$, $\overline{RS} \perp \overline{ST}$, and $\overline{AB} \cong \overline{RS}$.

18. $\overline{AC} \cong \overline{RT}$, $\angle C \cong \angle T$, $m\angle B = 90°$, and $m\angle S = 90°$.

19. $\overline{AB} \cong \overline{RS}$, $\overline{AB} \perp \overline{BC}$, $\overline{RS} \perp \overline{ST}$, and $\angle A \cong \angle R$.

20. $\overline{AB} \cong \overline{RS}$, $\angle C \cong \angle T$, $m\angle B = 90°$, and $m\angle S = 90°$.

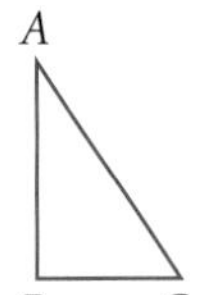

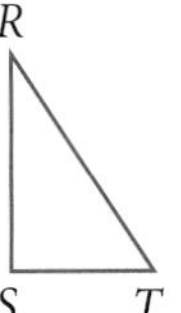

MORE PRACTICE

Use the information in the figures to find the following.

21. $m\angle A$

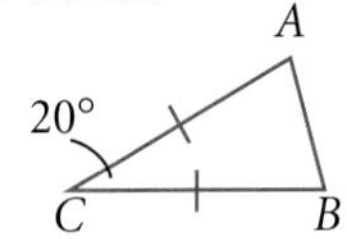

22. $m\angle D$

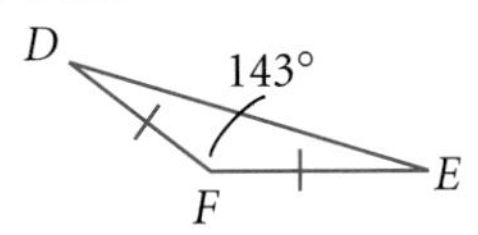

23. $m\angle H$

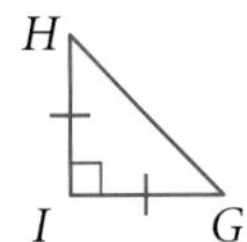

24. XZ

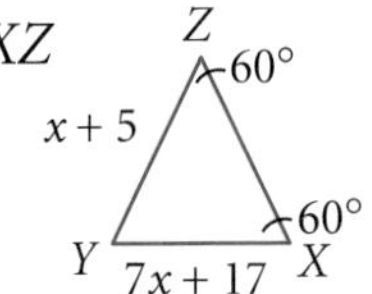

MORE MATH REASONING

25. Construct an equilateral triangle with a compass and straightedge. Explain the method that you used, and explain why it works.

26. In $\triangle ABC$, $AB = 9 - 2x$, $AC = 4x$, and $BC = x + 3$. Find all values of x that make $\triangle ABC$ isosceles.

27. A Futuristic Bike Karl tells a friend that he can use the gadgets on his new bike to find out how far away from the road a satellite tracking station is located. Karl explains that the bike's angle locator and odometer (the device that measures the distance traveled) will help him determine the distance to the tracking station.

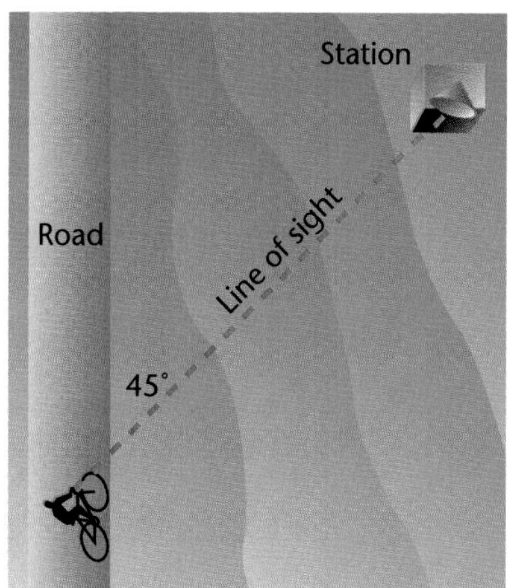

Karl says, "I'll keep checking the angle between the road and my line of sight to the station until I get a 45° angle. Then, I'll set the odometer to zero and ride down the road until the angle between the road and the line of sight to the station is a right angle. The odometer reading at that time will be the distance to the station."

Is Karl right? Explain.

4-3 PART B Right Triangles

← CONNECT → ***You've seen right triangles before, and you're familiar with several ways to prove triangles congruent. Now you will explore special congruence properties for right triangles and investigate whether or not there is a Side-Side-Angle congruence postulate.***

If you need to prove that two right triangles are congruent, you can use any of the triangle-congruence postulates that you've seen so far. However, there are some additional methods that apply only to right triangles. You will see that most of these are simply special cases of the postulates you already know.

LEG-LEG CONGRUENCE THEOREM (LL)

If the legs of a right triangle are congruent to the legs of another right triangle, then the two triangles are congruent.

Right triangles $\triangle ABC$ and $\triangle FGH$ are congruent by LL.

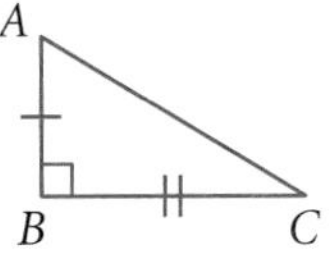

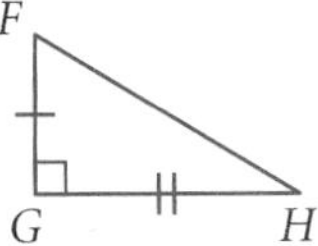

HYPOTENUSE-ACUTE-ANGLE CONGRUENCE THEOREM (HA)

If the hypotenuse and an acute angle of one right triangle are congruent to the hypotenuse and an acute angle of another right triangle, then the two triangles are congruent.

Right triangles $\triangle HIJ$ and $\triangle RST$ are congruent by HA.

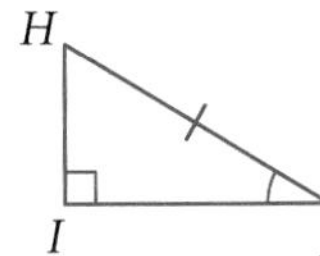

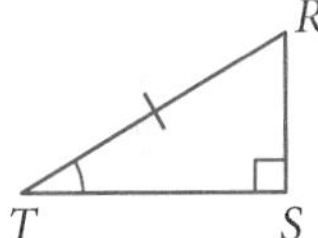

LEG-ACUTE-ANGLE CONGRUENCE THEOREM (LA)

If one leg and one acute angle of a right triangle are congruent to the corresponding leg and acute angle of another right triangle, then the two triangles are congruent.

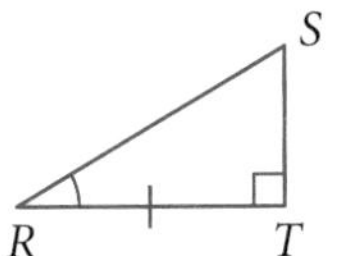

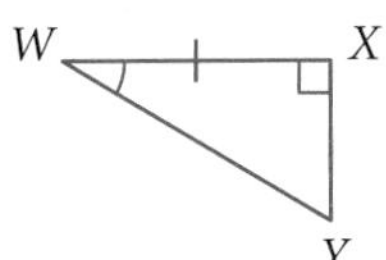

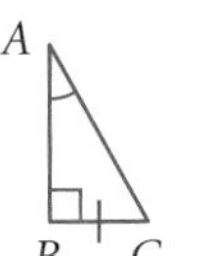

Right triangles $\triangle RTS$ and $\triangle WXY$ are congruent by LA. $\triangle ABC$ and $\triangle DEF$ are also congruent by LA.

CONSIDER

1. Which congruence theorem that applies to all triangles can be used instead of HA? Illustrate your answer.

You're familiar with the SAS Congruence Postulate, which uses two sides and an included angle. In the following Explore, you will investigate whether or not there is a Side-Side-Angle (SSA) Congruence Postulate, where the known angle is not the included angle.

EXPLORE: THE CASE OF THE AMBIGUOUS TRIANGLE

MATERIALS

Ruler
Protractor
Compass

1. Draw $\angle A$ with measure 30°. Along one side of $\angle A$, locate point B, 5 in. from A. Now complete $\triangle ABC$ with a segment $\overline{BC}$ that is $3\frac{1}{2}$ in. long. Compare your triangle with those made by your classmates. Are they all congruent? Do you think there is an SSA congruence postulate?
2. Repeat Step 1, but this time complete $\triangle ABC$ with a segment $\overline{BC}$ that is 2 in. long. Explain what this tells you about triangles with a 30° angle, a 5-in. side, and a 2-in. side opposite the angle.
3. Explore what is happening by experimenting with different lengths for $\overline{BC}$. Are there different ways the arc can intersect the side? Find all the possibilities, and draw a sketch of each. Make any conjectures you can.
4. In what case does SSA "work"—that is, when did you get just one triangle? Make a conjecture that describes this situation.

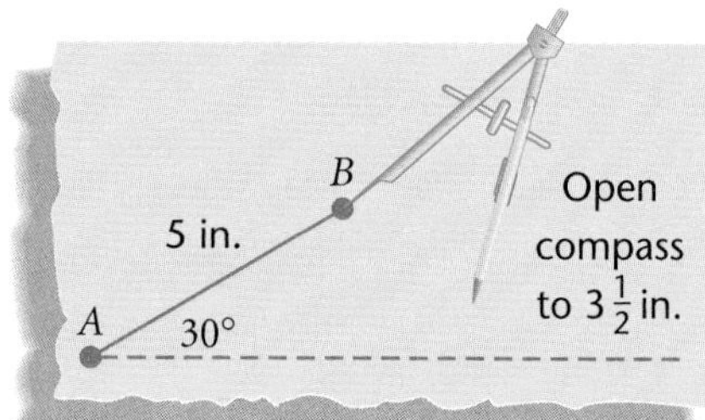

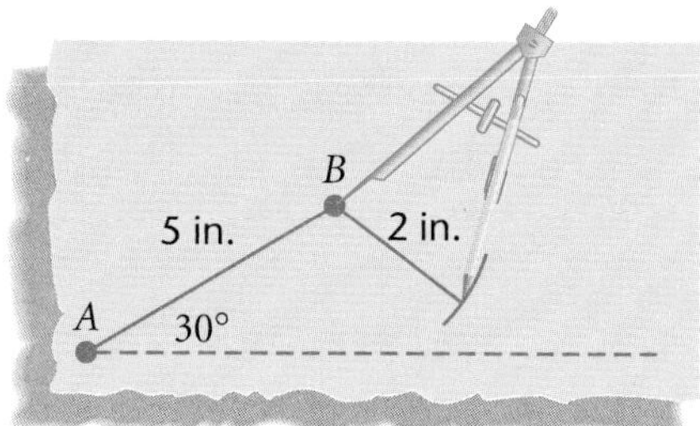

Although SSA does not work for triangles in general, the right-triangle version does work. This is the HL Congruence Theorem for right triangles.

HYPOTENUSE-LEG CONGRUENCE THEOREM (HL)

If the hypotenuse and a leg of one right triangle are congruent to the hypotenuse and a leg of another right triangle, then the two triangles are congruent.

EXAMPLE

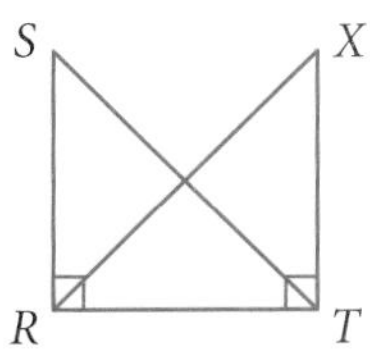

Given: $\overline{SR} \perp \overline{RT}$, $\overline{XT} \perp \overline{TR}$, $\overline{ST} \cong \overline{XR}$

Prove: $\triangle RST \cong \triangle TXR$

We can separate the overlapping triangles from the figure and mark the congruent parts.

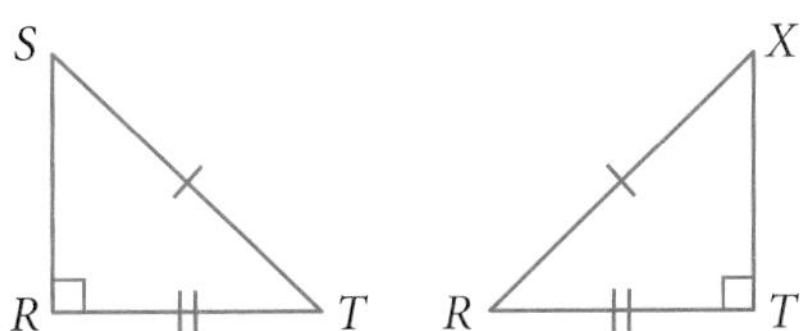

Proof: Since the given information tells us that $\overline{SR} \perp \overline{RT}$, and $\overline{XT} \perp \overline{TR}$, then $\angle SRT$ and $\angle XTR$ are right angles because perpendicular lines form right angles. $\triangle RST$ and $\triangle TXR$ are right triangles by the definition of *right triangle*. We are given that the triangles have congruent hypotenuses, $\overline{ST}$ and $\overline{XR}$, and the shared leg $\overline{RT}$ is congruent to itself by the Reflexive Property. It follows from the HL Theorem that $\triangle RST \cong \triangle TXR$.

REFLECT

1. What must you know before you use LL, LA, HA, or HL to prove triangles congruent?
2. Why is there no Side-Side-Angle congruence condition for triangles?

Exercises

CORE

Getting Started Name the right-triangle congruence theorem that shows why the triangles in each pair are congruent. If the triangles are not necessarily congruent, explain why.

1. 

2. 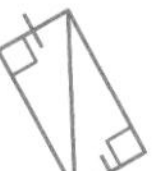

3. 

4. 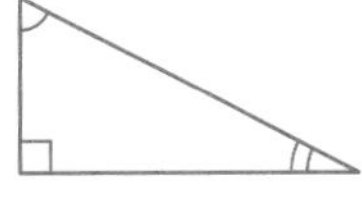 

Given that $\angle X$ and $\angle Y$ are right angles, state the pairs of corresponding parts that are needed to establish that $\triangle WXZ \cong \triangle ZYW$ by the given method. List all possible pairs of corresponding parts for each.

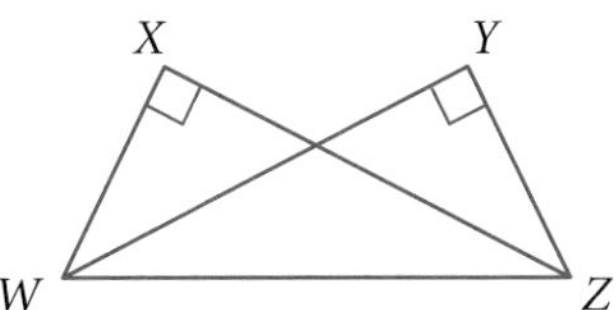

5. HL **6.** LL or SAS **7.** LA or ASA

8. Complete the following proof.

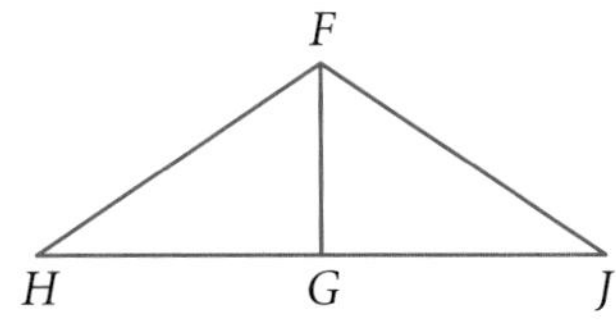

Given: $\overline{FG} \perp \overline{HJ}$
G is the midpoint of $\overline{HJ}$.

Prove: $\triangle HFJ$ is isosceles.

Proof: The **a.** ____ tells us that $\overline{FG} \perp \overline{HJ}$. Therefore, $\angle FGH$ and $\angle FGJ$ are right angles by the **b.** ____, and $\triangle FGH$ and $\triangle FGJ$ are right triangles by the **c.** ____. G is the midpoint of $\overline{HJ}$ from the **d.** ____, so $\overline{HG} \cong \overline{JG}$ by the **e.** ____. $\overline{FG} \cong \overline{FG}$ because of the **f.** ____. Therefore, $\triangle FGH \cong \triangle FGJ$ by the **g.** ____ Theorem. Since the triangles are congruent, $\overline{FH} \cong \overline{FJ}$ by **h.** ____. Finally, $\triangle HFJ$ is isosceles by the **i.** ____.

9. Complete the following proof.

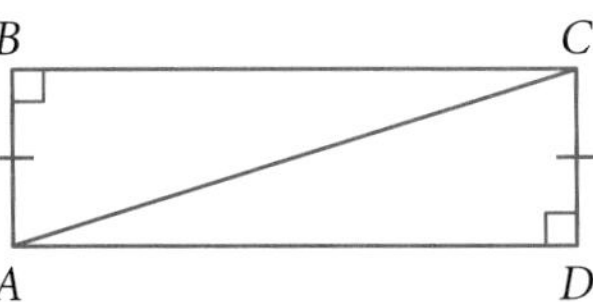

Given: $\angle B$ and $\angle D$ are right angles, and $\overline{AB} \cong \overline{CD}$.

Prove: $\triangle ABC \cong \triangle CDA$

Proof:

Statements	**Reasons**
1. $\angle B$ and $\angle D$ are right angles.	**1.**
2. $\triangle ABC$ is a right triangle. $\triangle CDA$ is a right triangle.	**2.**
3.	**3.** Given
4.	**4.**
5. $\triangle ABC \cong \triangle CDA$	**5.**

10. Looking for Planets Because Venus is nearer to the sun than the earth is, it always appears just above the horizon. The best time to see this planet is in the morning or evening when it is at a *maximum elongation,* as shown. At these positions, Venus is at its greatest distance from the horizon.

If we assume that Venus's orbit is perfectly circular, $\overline{SV_1} \cong \overline{SV_2}$. Explain why $\triangle SV_1E \cong \triangle SV_2E$.

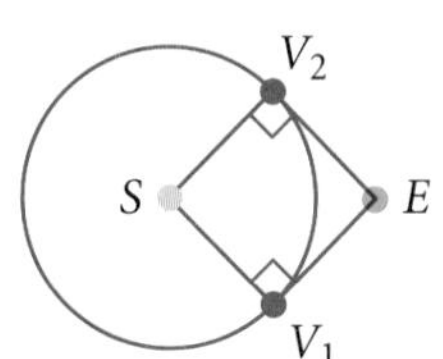

At V_1, Venus is at maximum eastern elongation.
At V_2, Venus is at maximum western elongation.

11. King-Post Truss One method of supporting the rafters of a roof is called a *king-post truss.* Assume rafter $\overline{AB} \cong$ rafter $\overline{CB}$, brace $\overline{DH}$ is placed at the midpoint of $\overline{AB}$, brace $\overline{HF}$ is placed at the midpoint of $\overline{BC}$, E is the midpoint of $\overline{AH}$, G is the midpoint of $\overline{CH}$, $\overline{DE} \perp \overline{AH}$, $\overline{BH} \perp \overline{AC}$, and $\overline{FG} \perp \overline{HC}$.

Industry

a. State congruences for three pairs of right triangles.

b. Support each congruence with a congruence theorem.

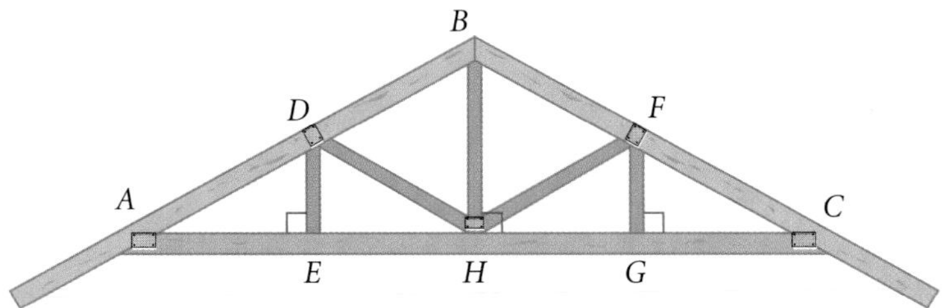

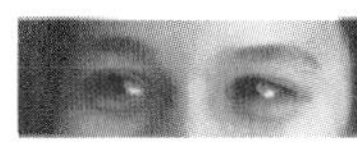

LOOK BACK

For each of the following transformations, copy $\triangle ABC$, and draw the image $\triangle A'B'C'$.

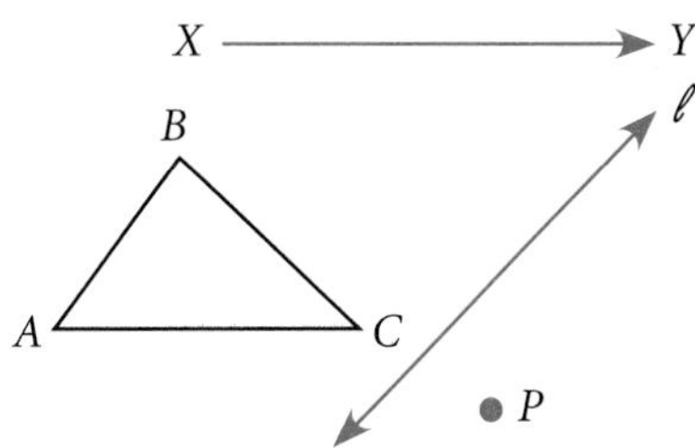

12. a 45° clockwise rotation around point P [3-2]

13. a reflection over line ℓ [1-4]

14. a translation with translation vector $\overrightarrow{XY}$ [3-1]

15. Complete the following proof. [3-4, 4-2]

Given: $\overline{VW} \cong \overline{ZY}$, $\overline{VW} \parallel \overline{ZY}$

Prove: $\triangle XVW \cong \triangle XZY$

Proof:

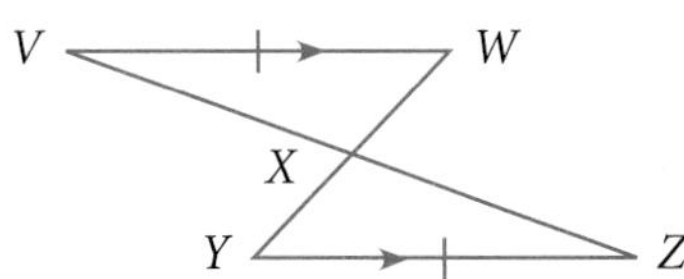

Statements	Reasons
1. $\overline{VW} \cong \overline{ZY}$	**1.**
2.	**2.** Vertical angles are congruent.
3. $\overline{VW} \parallel \overline{ZY}$	**3.**
4. $\angle WVX \cong \angle YZX$	**4.**
5.	**5.**

Now rewrite the proof as a flow-proof.

MORE PRACTICE

In each of the following, name the right-triangle congruence theorem that shows that $\triangle SQR \cong \triangle TQP$. If the triangles are not necessarily congruent, explain why.

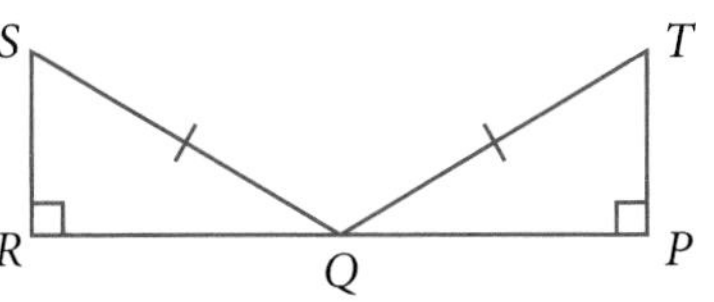

16. Q is the midpoint of $\overline{RP}$.

17. $\overline{RS} \cong \overline{TP}$

18. $\angle S \cong \angle T$

19. Complete the following proof.

Given: $\overline{DC} \cong \overline{FE}$
$\angle EDF$ and $\angle CFD$ are right angles.

Prove: $\overline{DE} \cong \overline{FC}$

Proof:

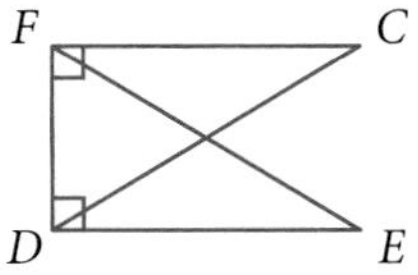

Statements	**Reasons**
1.	**1.**
2. $\triangle CFD$ is a right triangle. $\triangle EDF$ is a right triangle.	**2.**
3. $\overline{DC} \cong \overline{FE}$	**3.**
4.	**4.** Reflexive Property
5. $\triangle DFC \cong \triangle FDE$	**5.**
6.	**6.**

MORE MATH REASONING

20. The figure at the right shows an isosceles right triangle. Make a conjecture about the acute angles of an isosceles right triangle. Explain your reasoning.

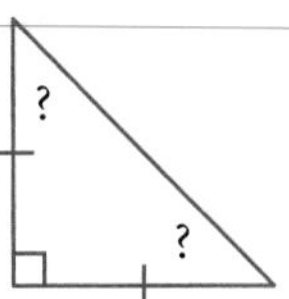

21. Explain why the word *corresponding* is important in the LA congruence theorem.

22. All four angles in a rectangle are right angles. Prove that the diagonals of a rectangle are congruent.

4-3 PART C Perpendiculars, Bisectors, and Locus

← CONNECT → *You're already familiar with angle bisectors and segment bisectors. Now you will investigate their special properties and see how they are related to the idea of locus.*

Many geometry problems can be solved by finding the set of points that satisfy certain conditions.

DEFINITION

A **locus** is the set of all the points that satisfy a given condition.

EXAMPLE

Determine the locus of points in a plane 2 in. from a given point Q.

Step 1: Plot point Q and several other points that are 2 in. from Q (points A–H).

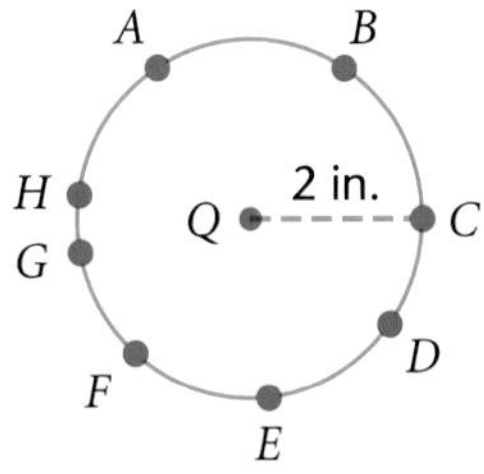

Step 2: Draw a figure that contains these points. The figure is a circle with radius 2 in.

Step 3: Check: Does every point on the figure satisfy the given condition? *(Yes)* Are there any points that satisfy the condition that are not on the figure? *(No)*

Therefore, the locus of all points in a plane 2 in. from a given point Q is a circle with radius 2 in. and center at point Q.

TRY IT

a. Describe the locus of points *in space* that are 2 in. from a given point C.

EXPLORE: BUILD IT THERE!

MATERIALS

Paper
Ruler
Protractor

A contractor has been commissioned to set up a transmitting tower. The tower must be equidistant from two towns, Wilbur and Clay Center, and must also be equidistant from two highways, Hwy 6 and Hwy 81.

After you complete Steps 1–3, you will be able to help the contractor identify the location for the tower.

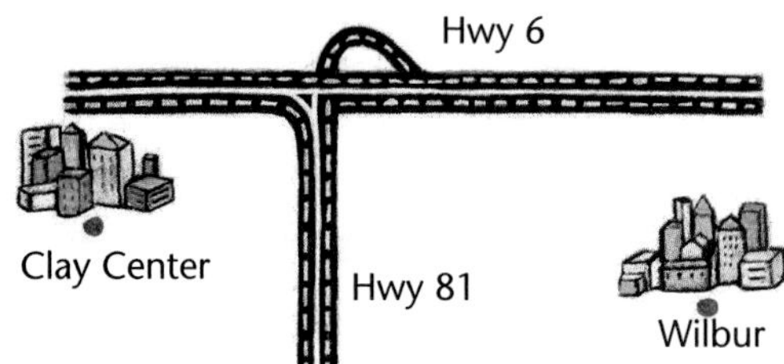

1. Draw points A and B on a sheet of paper. Fold the paper so that one point is reflected onto the other. What is the relationship of any point on the fold to these two points?
2. Use your straightedge to draw segment $\overline{AB}$. Make a conjecture about the relationship between the segment and the fold. Use measuring tools to confirm your ideas. What is the locus of points in a plane equidistant from two given points?
3. Draw an angle on a sheet of paper, and fold the paper so that one side of the angle is reflected onto the other. Make a conjecture about how the fold divides the angle. Then investigate the distances of the points on the fold from the two sides. Make a conjecture about the locus of points equidistant from the sides of an angle.
4. Find the location where the contractor should build the tower.

In the Explore, you used the perpendicular bisector of a segment. Although you have seen this term before, a quick reminder of its definition may be helpful.

A **perpendicular bisector** of a segment is a line, ray, segment, or plane that is perpendicular to the segment and divides it into two congruent segments. In the figure at the right, line m is the perpendicular bisector of $\overline{AB}$.

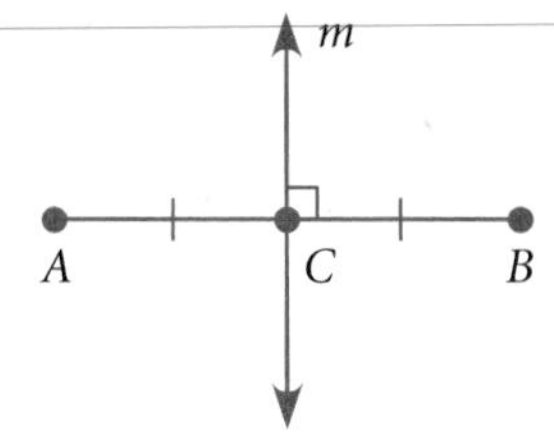

The next theorem states the relationship between any point on a perpendicular bisector and any point equidistant from two given points.

THEOREM

A point is on the perpendicular bisector of a segment if and only if it is equidistant from the endpoints of the segment.

A similar theorem describes the relationship between points on an angle bisector and the sides of the angle.

THEOREM

A point is on the angle bisector of an angle if and only if it is equidistant from the sides of the angle.

REFLECT

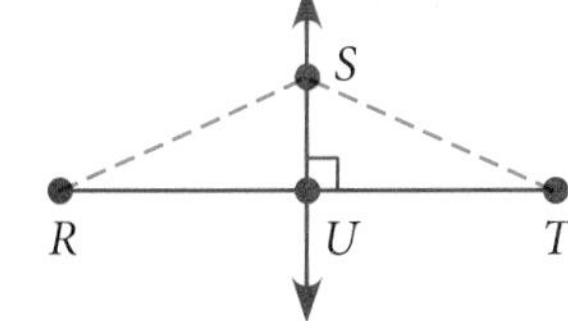

1. Explain why point S on the perpendicular bisector of $\overline{RT}$ must be equidistant from points R and T.
2. Suppose $m\angle NMP = 148°$, and point L is equidistant from rays $\overrightarrow{MN}$ and $\overrightarrow{MP}$. Find $m\angle NML$. Explain your reasoning.
3. Describe and illustrate the difference between a bisector of a segment and a perpendicular bisector of a segment.

Exercises

CORE

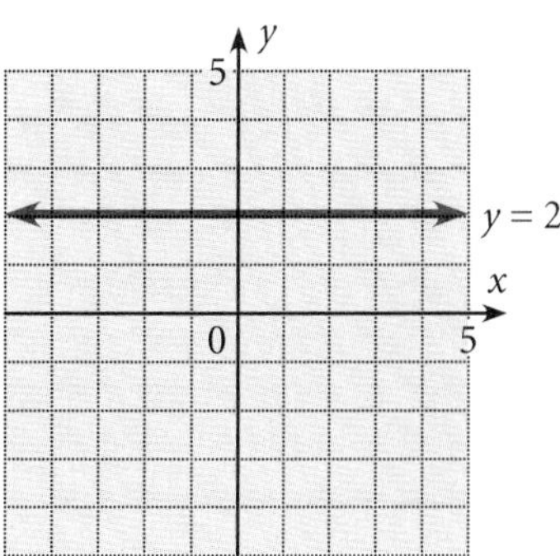

1. **Getting Started** Follow the steps below to find the locus of all the points on a coordinate plane that are 3 units from the line $y = 2$.
   - **a.** Choose any point on the line $y = 2$. Plot the point 3 units above this point and the point 3 units below it.
   - **b.** Repeat **1a** at different points along the line until you recognize the solution.
   - **c.** Complete the sketch of the locus.
   - **d.** Use equations to describe the locus.

Describe each locus of points in a plane. Give a sketch to illustrate each answer.

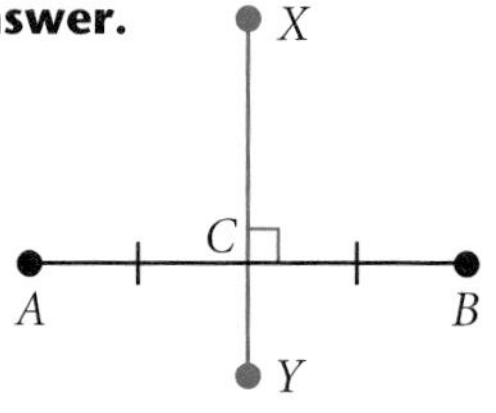

2. the locus of points 3 in. from point A
3. the locus of points 8 cm from line m
4. the locus of points 1 in. from segment $\overline{XY}$
5. In the figure at the right, $\overline{XY}$ is a perpendicular bisector of $\overline{AB}$. If $AX = 10x - 4$ and $BX = 4x + 8$, find x.
6. If $\angle 1 \cong \angle 2$, $EF = 2x + 8$, and $ED = 6x - 8$, find x.

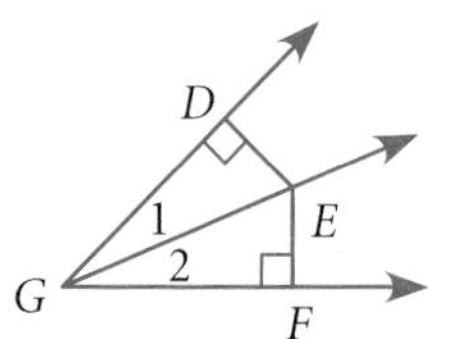

Write the word or phrase that correctly completes each statement.

7. The locus of points equidistant from the sides of an angle is ____.
8. The locus of points equidistant from the endpoints of a segment is ____.
9. Describe the locus of points in a plane that satisfies the equation $y = x$.
10. Sketch the locus of points in a plane equidistant from the sides of the angle determined by the positive x-axis and the line $y = 4x$ in the first quadrant.
11. Sketch the locus of points in a plane equidistant from the lines $y = 8$ and $y = 2$.
12. Fill in the missing statements and reasons to complete the proof of the following.

    If a point is on the perpendicular bisector of a line segment, then it is equidistant from the endpoints of the segment.

    Given: $\overline{TS}$ is a perpendicular bisector of $\overline{AB}$, and R lies on $\overline{TS}$.

    Prove: $\overline{RA} \cong \overline{RB}$

    Proof:

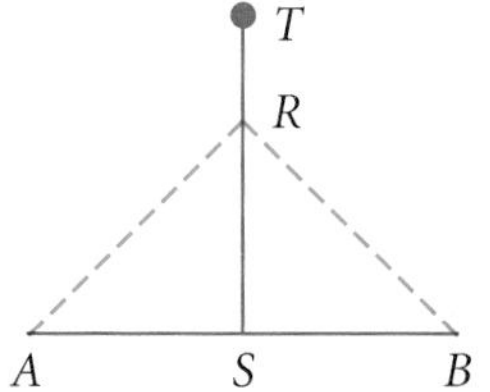

Statements	**Reasons**
1. $\overline{TS}$ is a perpendicular bisector of $\overline{AB}$; R lies on $\overline{TS}$.	**1.**
2. Draw $\overline{AR}$ and $\overline{BR}$.	**2.** Two points determine a line.
3. $\overline{AS} \cong \overline{SB}$	**3.**
4. $\overline{TS} \perp \overline{AB}$	**4.**
5. $\angle RSA$ and $\angle RSB$ are right angles.	**5.**
6.	**6.** Definition of *right triangle*
7. $\overline{RS} \cong \overline{RS}$	**7.**
8. $\triangle RSA \cong \triangle RSB$	**8.**
9. $\overline{RA} \cong \overline{RB}$	**9.**

13. A power substation is to be located along a power line and must be equidistant from the two cities shown.

Where should the substation be located? Make a sketch to show your answer. Explain the reasoning you used to find the location.

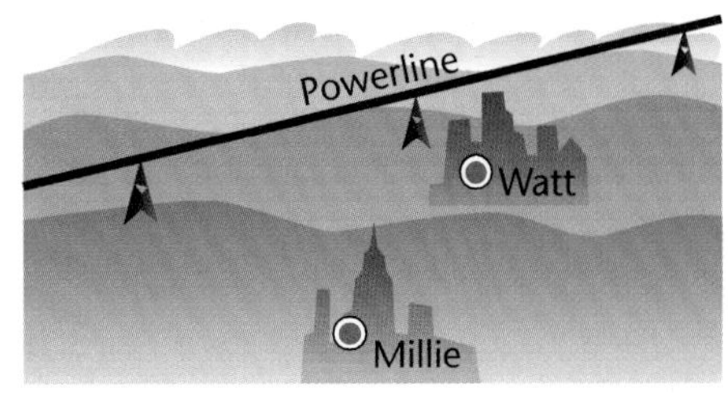

14. **Buried Treasure** The figure on the right is a partial map of "Treasure Island." A buried treasure is equidistant from the two straight shorelines, $\overline{FG}$ and $\overline{FH}$, and equidistant from two trees, J and K. Make a sketch of the map and locate the treasure. Write a note explaining your method.

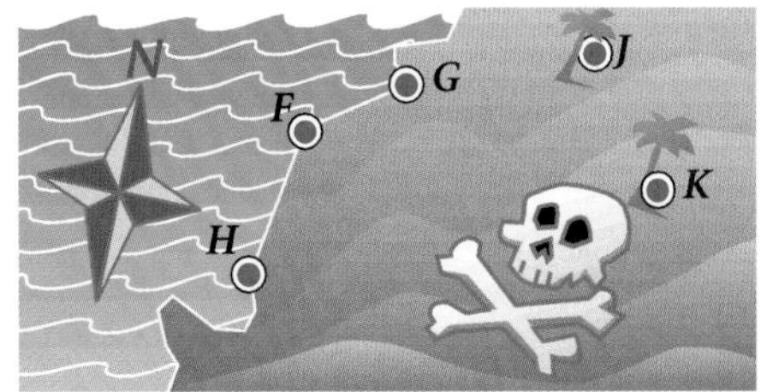

LOOK AHEAD

Name each of the following in the figure at the right.

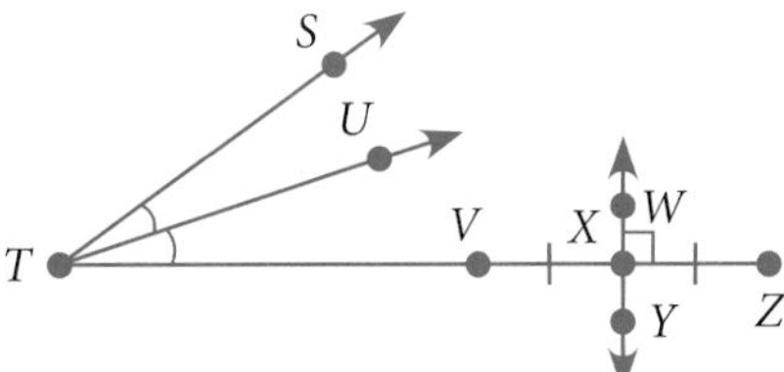

15. an angle bisector

16. a perpendicular bisector

17. perpendicular lines

18. a midpoint

19. Draw a large triangle, $\triangle ABC$. Then construct the midpoint of each side of $\triangle ABC$, using a compass and straightedge.

MORE PRACTICE

Describe each locus of points. Give a sketch to illustrate each answer.

20. the locus of points in a plane 2 cm from point X

21. the locus of points in space 3 in. from point K

22. the locus of points in space 1 m from line s

Find the missing value in each statement. Assume that $\overline{DF} \perp \overline{BC}$, $\overline{DE} \cong \overline{EF}$, and $\overline{AE} \cong \overline{BE}$.

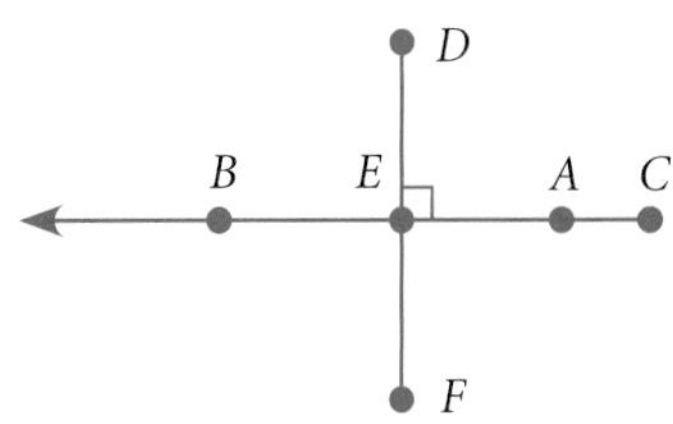

23. If $AD = 10$, then $BF =$ ____.

24. If $DC = 12x - 3$ and $FC = 21$, then $x =$ ____.

25. If $BD = 5x$ and $AD = 7x - 8$, then $AD =$ ____.

MORE MATH REASONING

26. A Key Question A group of campers was playing a game that gave clues to the location of various objects. The clues for finding a key were as follows.

- The key is equidistant from the segments joining cabin A to pine tree P and cabin B to oak tree O.
- The key is on the segment connecting cabin A and cabin B.

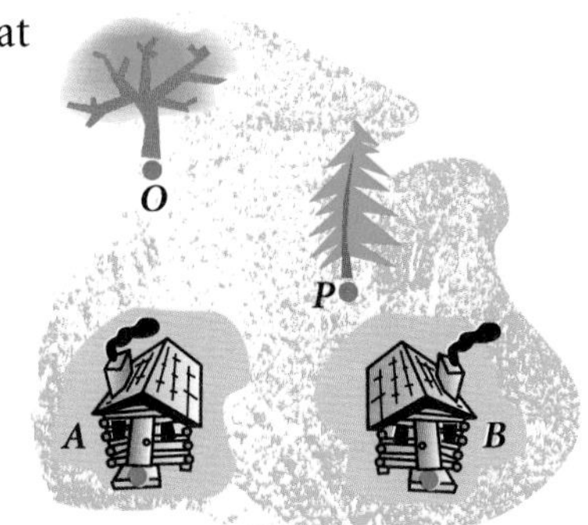

To win the game, you must give a written description of the precise location of the key. Describe the method you will use to find the key, and explain why the method works.

27. Prove the following statement.

If a point is on the angle bisector of an angle, then it is equidistant from the sides of the angle.

4-3 PART D Lines Associated with Triangles

← CONNECT → ***You've already learned about bisectors and perpendiculars. Now you will explore properties of bisectors and perpendiculars when they are contained in triangles.***

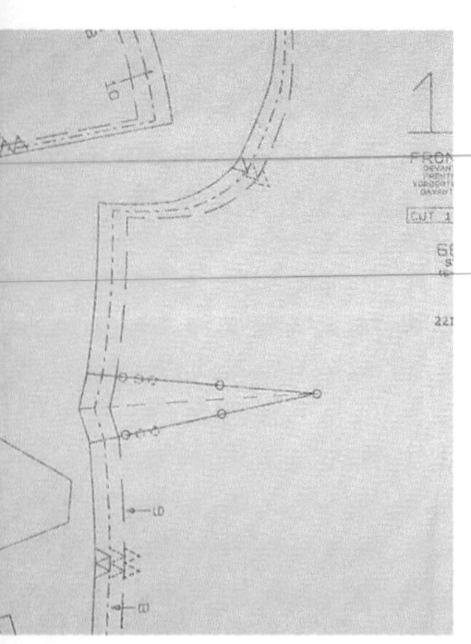

Segments that bisect sides and angles in triangles have some important properties. They are also useful choices for auxiliary lines in proofs.

The fabric pattern at the left illustrates an angle bisector. The bisector of an angle is a ray. However, when an angle bisector is used in a triangle, we restrict the ray to a segment. One endpoint of the segment is a vertex and the other endpoint is on the side opposite the bisected angle.

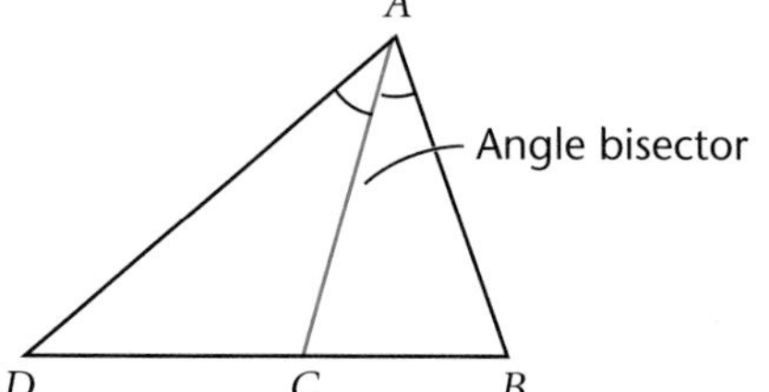

$\overline{AC}$ is an angle bisector of $\triangle ABD$ from vertex A to side $\overline{DB}$.

A **median** of a triangle is a segment whose endpoints are a vertex and the midpoint of the opposite side.

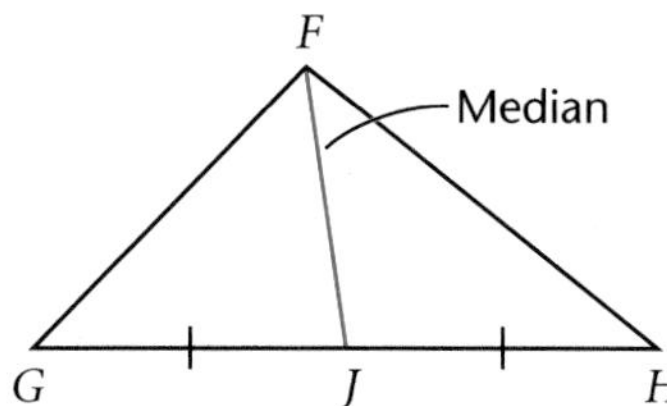

$\overline{FJ}$ is a median of $\triangle FGH$ from vertex F to side $\overline{GH}$.

An **altitude** of a triangle is a perpendicular segment drawn from a vertex to the line that contains the opposite side.

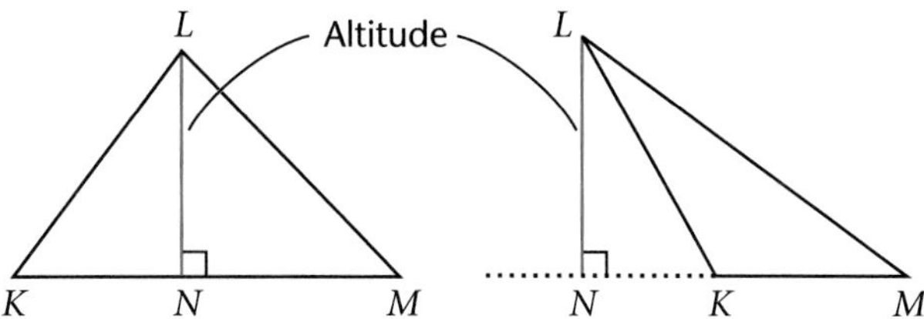

In the two triangles, $\overline{LN}$ is an altitude of $\triangle KLM$ from vertex L.

As seen in the figure on the right above, an altitude may lie outside the triangle. It may also be a side of the triangle.

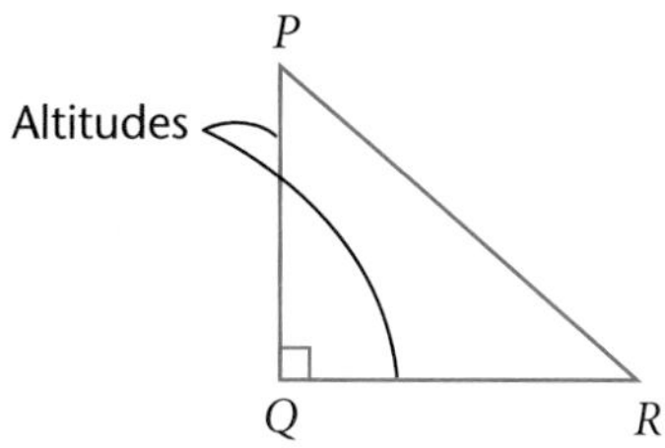

In $\triangle PQR$, $\overline{PQ}$ is the altitude from vertex P, and $\overline{RQ}$ is the altitude from vertex R.

A **perpendicular bisector** of a side of a triangle is a line perpendicular to a side through the midpoint of the side.

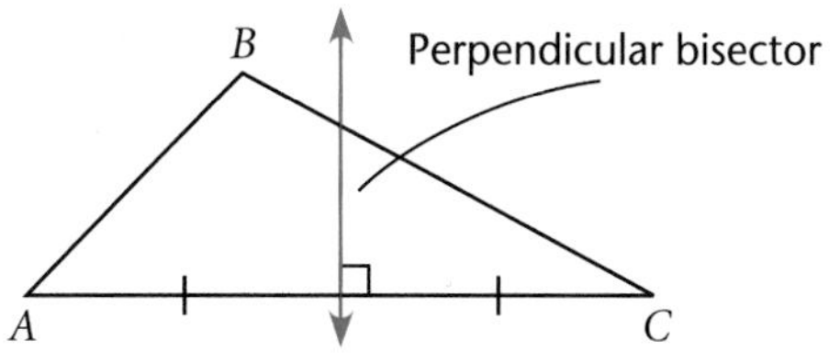

A perpendicular bisector of $\overline{AC}$ in $\triangle ABC$ is shown.

TRY IT

a. Draw an obtuse triangle $\triangle XYZ$ with obtuse angle $\angle Z$. Draw the median, angle bisector, and altitude from $\angle X$.

b. Draw an isosceles triangle $\triangle FGH$ with vertex angle $\angle G$. Draw the median, angle bisector, and altitude from $\angle G$.

In the following Explore, you will investigate some special properties of the medians of a triangle.

EXPLORE: BALANCING ACT

MATERIALS

Cardboard
Scissors
Ruler
Pencil

1. Cut a triangle out of cardboard. Then find the "center of balance" of the triangle by balancing it on the eraser of a pencil. Mark the center of balance. This point is the *centroid* of the triangle.
2. Using a ruler to help you find the midpoints of the sides, draw all three medians of your triangle. Mark the point of intersection of the medians. What is the relationship between this point and the centroid?
3. Repeat the process with a different triangle. Do all three medians still meet at one point? Is this point the centroid of the triangle?
4. The point of intersection of the three medians divides each median into two segments. Measure the two segments of each median in both of your triangles. Make a conjecture about your results.

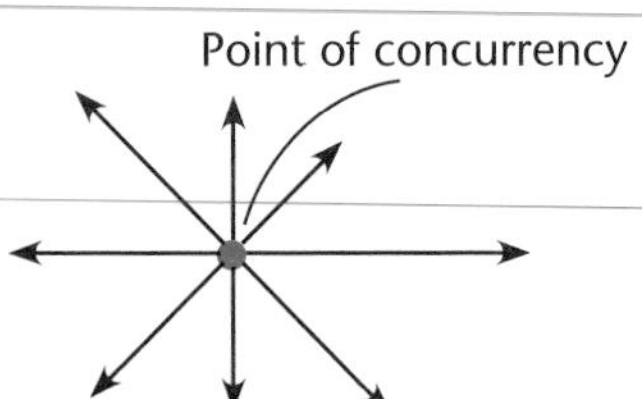

If three or more coplanar lines intersect at the same point, they are **concurrent lines.** The point of intersection is the **point of concurrency.**

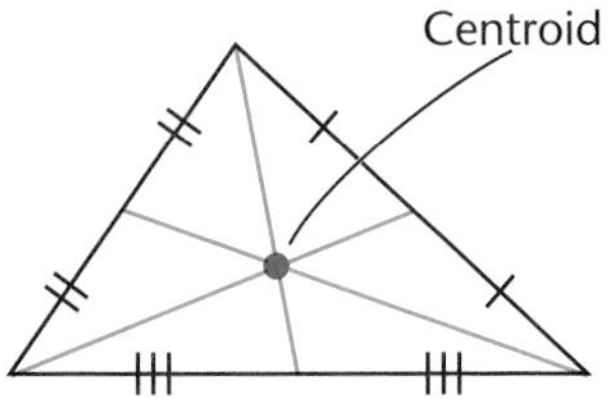

The point of concurrency of the medians of any triangle is called the **centroid.** The centroid is important because it is the *center of balance* (or *center of gravity*) of the triangle. You may also have discovered the following fact about centroids.

THEOREM

The centroid of a triangle is located two-thirds of the distance from each vertex to the midpoint of the opposite side.

REFLECT

1. Use the figures below and the idea of a center of balance to explain why the centroid of a triangle is farther from the vertex than it is from the opposite side.

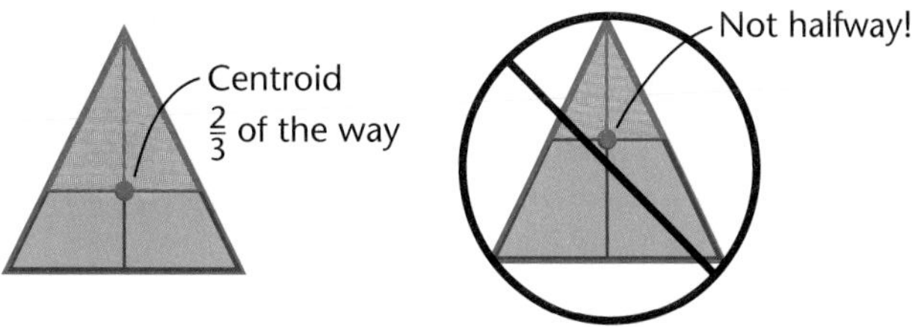

2. Is it possible for a segment to be both a median and an altitude of a triangle? Explain your answer with a sketch.
3. When is an altitude in the exterior of a triangle? a side of a triangle? Illustrate your answers.

Exercises

CORE

Getting Started Use the figure at the right for Exercises 1–4.

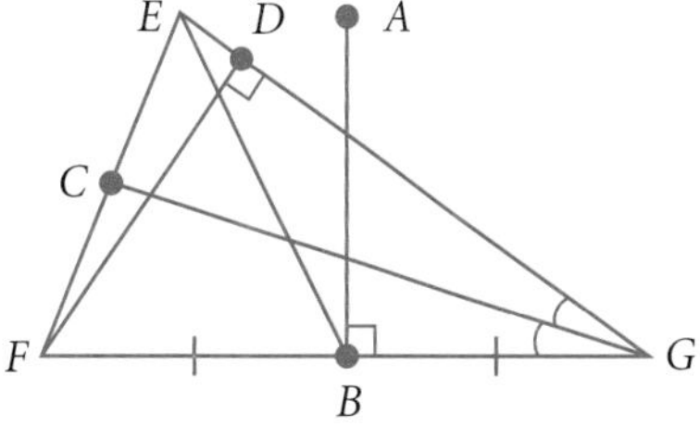

1. Name an angle bisector in $\triangle EFG$.
2. Name a median in $\triangle EFG$.
3. Name a perpendicular bisector in $\triangle EFG$.
4. Name an altitude in $\triangle EFG$.
5. Carefully draw an isosceles triangle. Then draw the altitude, the median, and the angle bisector from the vertex to the base. Make any conjectures that you can. Explain why your conjectures must be true.

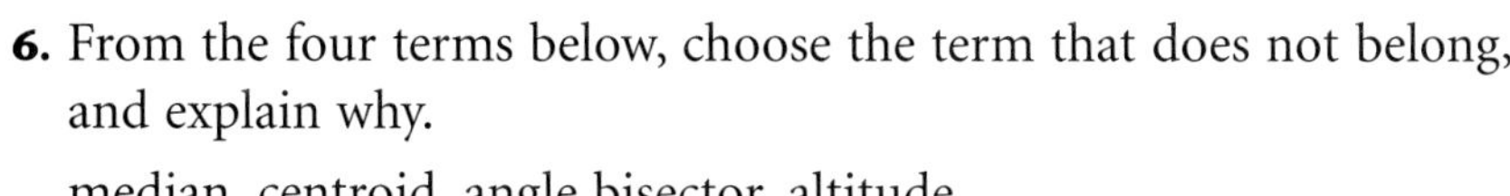

6. From the four terms below, choose the term that does not belong, and explain why.

   median, centroid, angle bisector, altitude

In $\triangle TUV$, $\overline{UX}$ and $\overline{TW}$ are medians, $TY > YW$, and $UY > YX$.

7. If $TY = 48$, find YW.

8. If $YX = 3.5$, find UX.

9. If $TY = 8x - 12$ and $YW = 2x$, find the following.

a. x **b.** YW **c.** TY **d.** TW

10. Explain why the point of concurrency of the angle bisectors of the sides of a triangle is equidistant from all the sides of the triangle.

11. Explain why the point of concurrency of the perpendicular bisectors of the sides of a triangle is equidistant from all the vertices of the triangle.

12. Fill in the missing statements and reasons in the proof to prove that the median from the vertex to the base of an isosceles triangle is also the angle bisector.

Given: Isosceles $\triangle ABC$ with $\overline{AB} \cong \overline{BC}$
$\overline{BD}$ is a median from the vertex B to base $\overline{AC}$.

Prove: $\angle 1 \cong \angle 2$

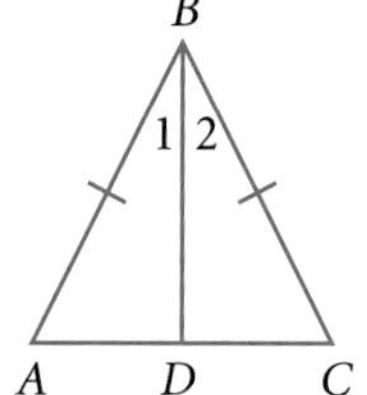

Proof:

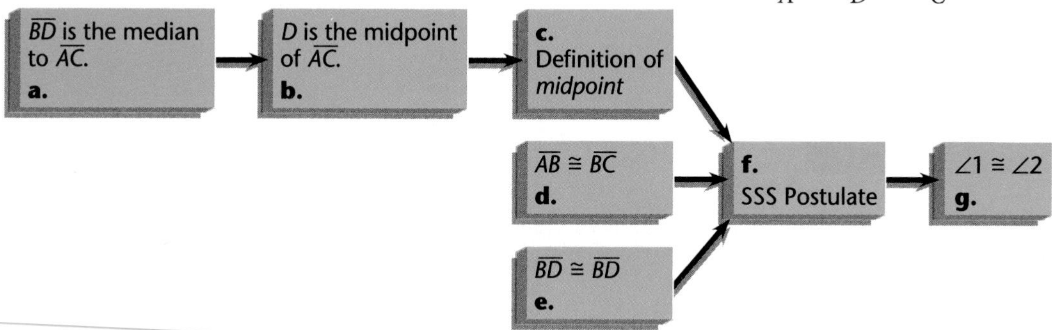

History

13. Do Your Level Best In carpentry and other trades, it is often important to make sure that something is exactly horizontal. The leveling instrument shown is similar to some Egyptian artifacts. An instrument like this may have been used in the building of the pyramids.

$\triangle ABC$ is isosceles, and the midpoint of $\overline{BC}$ is marked. A string with a weight is attached to the vertex. The string meets the base $\overline{BC}$ at point D.

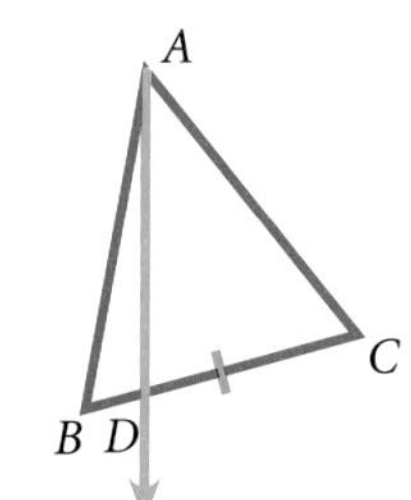

a. If the surface on which $\overline{BC}$ rests is perfectly horizontal, where will the weight hang? Why?

b. When $\overline{BC}$ is horizontal, what is true about $\triangle ADB$ and $\triangle ADC$? Justify your answer.

14. Cart Capers A cart manufacturer is interested in making a cart whose body is a triangular prism. Side views of two designs are shown at the right.

Science

a. Copy each figure and find the center of gravity of each of their triangular cross sections.

b. The lower the center of gravity, the more stable a cart is. Which design seems to be more stable? List other advantages and disadvantages of each design.

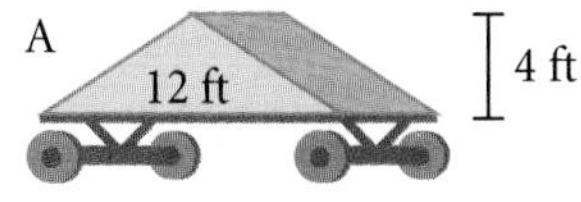

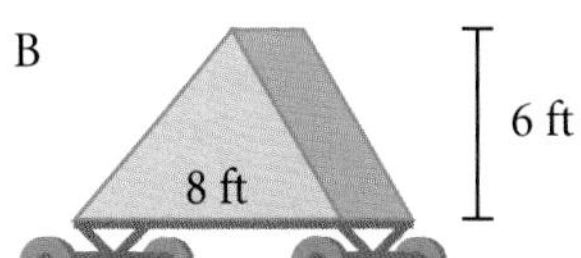

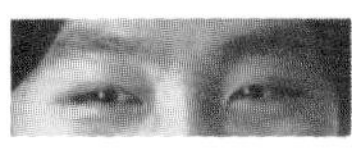

LOOK BACK

15. In the figure at the right, $m \parallel n$ and $s \parallel t$. Find the measures of the numbered angles. [3-4]

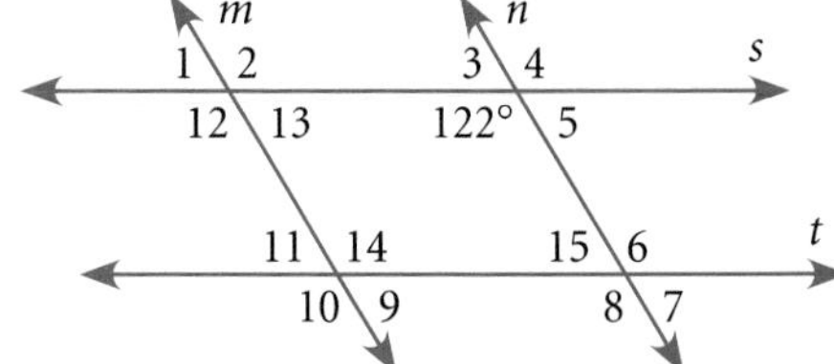

16. Complete the following proof. [3-4, 4-2]

Given: $\angle SVT \cong \angle UTV$

$\overline{SV} \cong \overline{UT}$

Prove: $\overleftrightarrow{ST} \parallel \overleftrightarrow{UV}$

Proof:

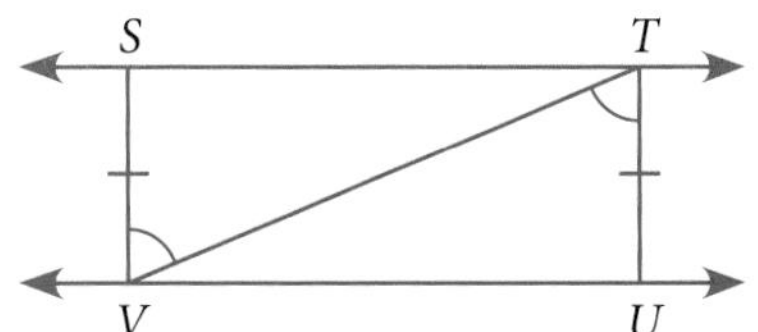

Statements	Reasons
1. $\angle SVT \cong \angle UTV$	**1.**
2.	**2.** Given
3.	**3.** Reflexive Property
4. $\triangle SVT \cong \triangle UTV$	**4.**
5.	**5.** CPCTC
6. $\overleftrightarrow{ST} \parallel \overleftrightarrow{UV}$	**6.**

MORE PRACTICE

17. Name an angle bisector in $\triangle MHI$.

18. Name a median in $\triangle MHI$.

19. Name a perpendicular bisector in $\triangle MHI$.

20. Name an altitude in $\triangle MHI$.

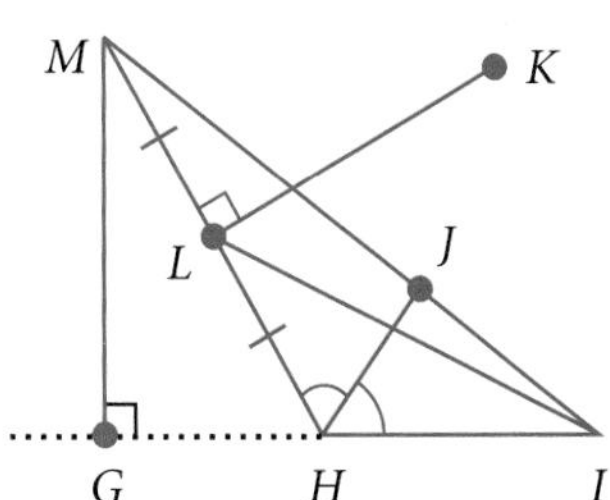

In $\triangle PQR$, $\overline{PS}$ and $\overline{RT}$ are medians. $UR > UT$, and $UP > US$.

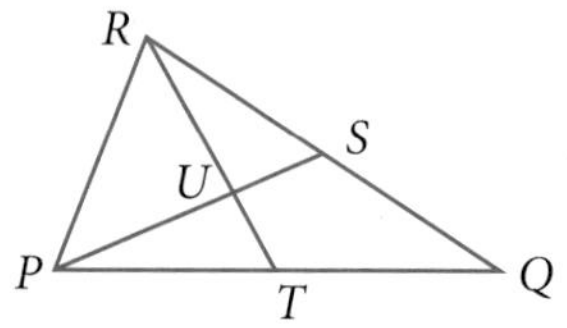

21. If $RT = 24$, find RU. **22.** If $US = 15$, find UP.

MORE MATH REASONING

23. There is a type of triangle in which every angle bisector is also a median, an altitude, and a perpendicular bisector. What type of triangle is it? Explain.

24. The Euler Line Draw a large acute scalene triangle and construct the point of concurrency of the medians. Then construct the points of concurrency of the altitudes, angle bisectors, and perpendicular bisectors.

a. Which three of these points are collinear?

b. The line that contains the three collinear points is called the Euler line. Make a conjecture about how the three points of concurrency divide the Euler line.

4-3 PART E Making Connections

← CONNECT → ***Special triangles and the lines associated with them are important in industries that need structural stability in their products. You've discovered some properties of special triangles and explored some special segments associated with triangles.***

This bicycle was built for paratroopers in World War II. It features a folding frame. In the following Explore, you will see how the properties of triangles and the lines associated with them can be used to investigate the structure of a bicycle frame.

EXPLORE: FRAME IT!

MATERIALS

Ruler
Geometry software (optional)

A bicycle frame contains the two triangles shown in the figure. (Note: The tip of the triangle at point B is actually cut off, but you may assume that the triangle is complete.)

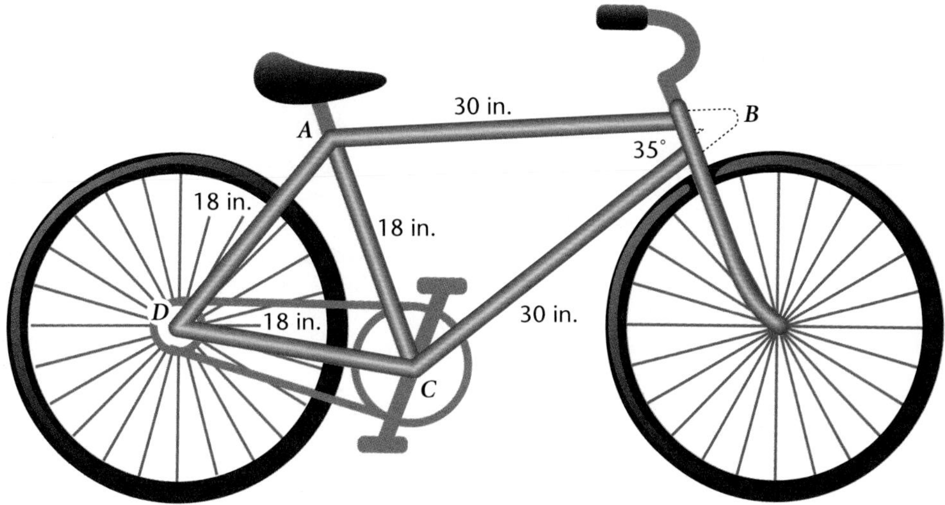

1. Find the measures of all angles in the two triangles. Explain your reasoning.
2. Copy the figure, using pencil and paper or geometry software. Find the center of gravity of each of the two triangles.
3. Estimate the center of gravity of the entire frame. Explain your method.
4. Suppose you want the bicycle to have a lower center of gravity. Describe one way you might modify the bicycle frame to achieve a lower center of gravity. Try your new design by sketching it or using geometry software to see whether or not it actually lowers the center of gravity.

REFLECT

1. The HL, LL, LA, and HA triangle-congruence theorems only require two pairs of congruent parts instead of the three needed in ASA, SAS, SSS, and SAA. Explain why.
2. List as many properties of isosceles triangles as you can. Provide a sketch for each property.
3. Is it possible for an altitude of a triangle to be on a side of the triangle? in the interior of the triangle? in the exterior of the triangle? Support your answers with drawings. What are the possibilities for the medians of a triangle? Explain.

Self-Assessment

State a congruence postulate or theorem that justifies each of the following.

1. $\triangle WZY \cong \triangle YXW$

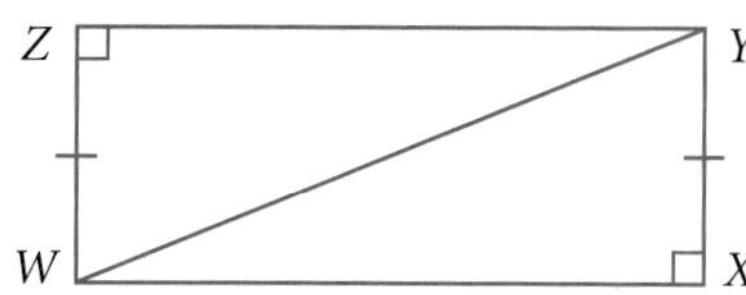

2. $\triangle STV \cong \triangle UTV$

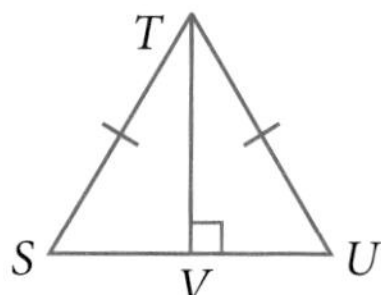

3. $\triangle LMN \cong \triangle NPL$

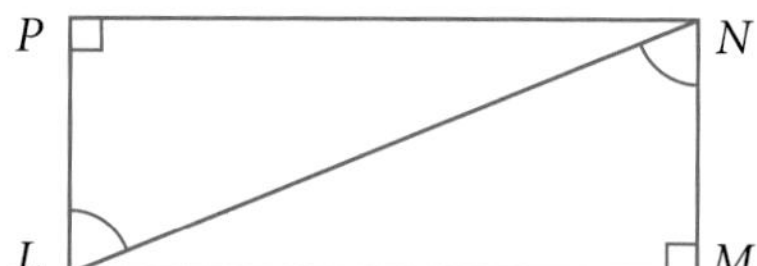

4. $\triangle GHK \cong \triangle JHI$

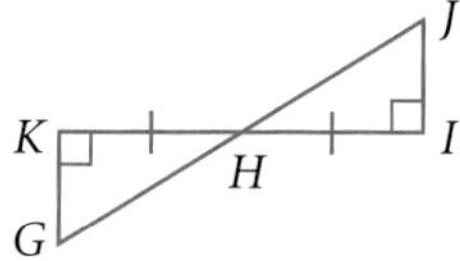

5. In $\triangle XYZ$, $m\angle Y = (4x - 10)°$, and $m\angle Z = (53 - 3x)°$. If $\triangle XYZ$ is isosceles with base $\overline{YZ}$, find $m\angle X$.

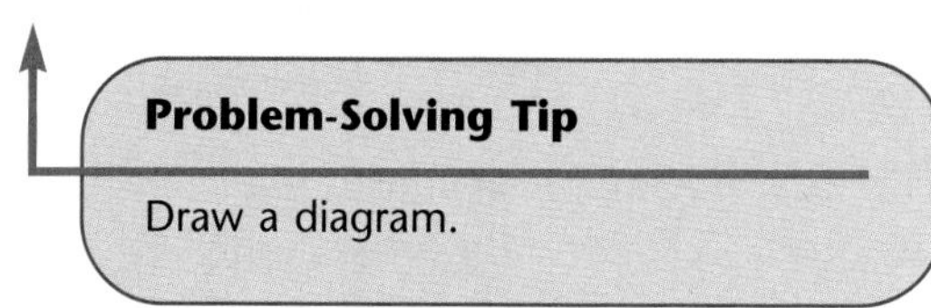

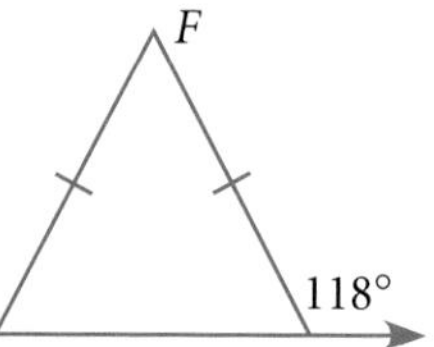

6. Which of the following is $m\angle F$?

(a) 56° (b) 59° (c) 62° (d) 118°

Describe and draw the locus of points in a plane that satisfies the given condition.

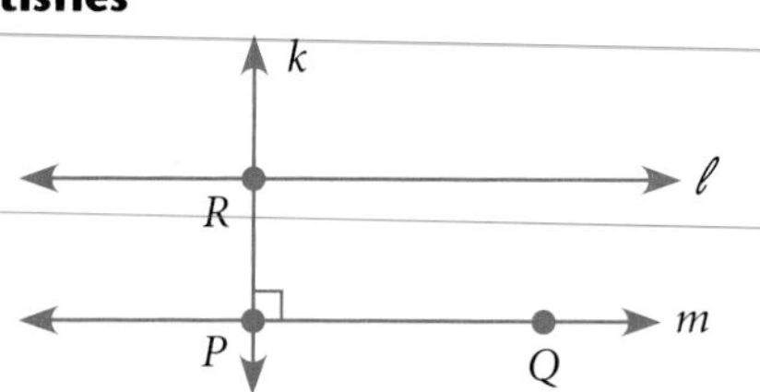

7. equidistant from lines ℓ and m

8. equidistant from P and Q

9. equidistant from the sides of $\angle RPQ$

Name the translation image of each figure for the given transformation. [1-4, 3-1, 3-2]

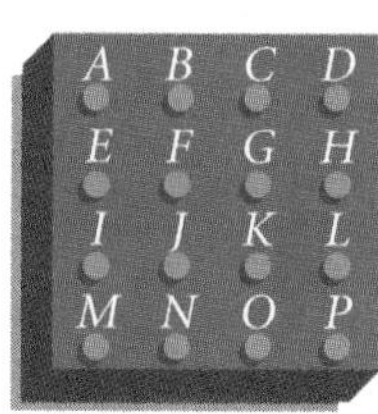

10. the image of point A under a translation with vector $\overrightarrow{EG}$

11. the image of segment $\overline{BC}$ under a reflection over line $\overleftrightarrow{EH}$

12. the image of $\triangle EFJ$ after a 180° clockwise rotation about point J

13. Complete the following proof.

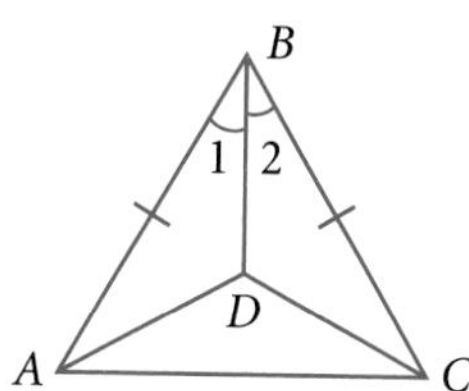

Given: $\triangle ABC$ is isosceles, $\overline{AB} \cong \overline{BC}$, $\angle 1 \cong \angle 2$.

Prove: $\angle DAC \cong \angle DCA$

Proof:

Statements	**Reasons**
1. $\overline{AB} \cong \overline{BC}$	**1.**
2.	**2.** Given
3.	**3.** Reflexive Property
4. $\triangle ADB \cong \triangle CDB$	**4.**
5. $\overline{AD} \cong \overline{CD}$	**5.**
6.	**6.**

14. Complete the following proof. [4-2]

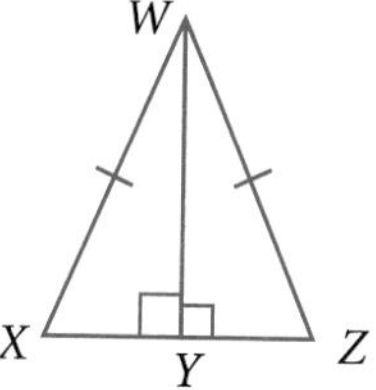

Given: $\angle WYX$ and $\angle WYZ$ are right angles.
$\overline{XW} \cong \overline{ZW}$

Prove: Y is the midpoint of $\overline{XZ}$.

Proof: The **a.** ___ tells us that $\angle WYX$ and $\angle WYZ$ are right angles. Therefore, $\triangle WYX$ and $\triangle WYZ$ are right triangles by the **b.** ___. $\overline{WY} \cong \overline{WY}$ because of the **c.** ___. **d.** ___ from the given information. Therefore, **e.** ___ by the HL congruence theorem. Since the triangles are congruent, $\overline{XY} \cong \overline{YZ}$ by **f.** ___. Finally, **g.** ___ by the definition of midpoint.

15. Name the right-triangle congruence theorem that is a "special case" of each of the following. Explain your answers with an illustration. In some cases, there may be more than one right-triangle theorem; in others, there may not be any.

a. SAS **b.** ASA **c.** SSS **d.** SAA

16. Just Resting A rest shelter is to be built along a bike trail equidistant from the city park and the post office. Copy the figure, and find the location for the shelter. Write a description of the method you used to solve the problem.

Chapter 4 Review

Triangles are important building blocks in geometry. In Chapter 4, you learned how to classify triangles, and you explored properties of different types of triangles. You also took a closer look at the idea of congruence and how it relates to triangles. By investigating congruent triangles, you were also able to further develop your proof skills.

KEY TERMS

acute triangle [4-1]
adjacent interior angle [4-1]
altitude [4-3]
auxiliary line [4-3]
base angle [4-1]
centroid [4-3]
concurrent lines [4-3]
congruence correspondence [4-2]
congruent triangles [4-2]
corollary [4-1]
correspondence [4-2]
equiangular triangle [4-1]
equilateral triangle [4-1]
exterior angle [4-1]
hypotenuse [4-1]
isosceles triangle [4-1]
leg [4-1]
locus [4-3]
median [4-3]
obtuse triangle [4-1]
perpendicular bisector [4-3]
point of concurrency [4-3]
remote interior angle [4-1]
right triangle [4-1]
scalene triangle [4-1]
tessellation [4-1]
triangle [4-1]
vertex angle [4-1]

Write the word or phrase that correctly completes each statement.

1. The side opposite the right angle of a right triangle is the ___.
2. The point of concurrency of the ___ of a triangle is the centroid.
3. A ___ triangle is one in which two sides are congruent.
4. A ___ is the set of points satisfying a given condition.

CONCEPTS AND APPLICATIONS

Find the measure of ∠1 in each figure. [4-1]

5.

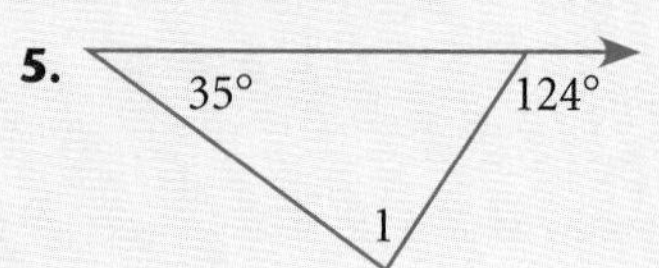

6.

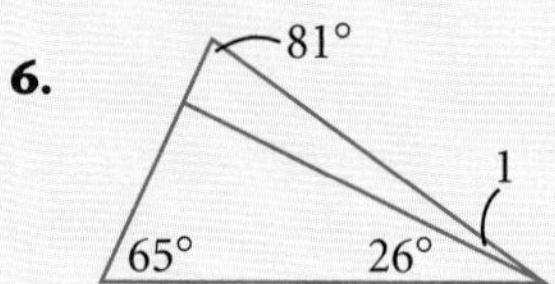

7. A triangle has angles that measure $(4x + 50)°$, $2x°$, and $(x + 39)°$. Find the measures of the angles of the triangle. [4-1]

8. If the bearing from a lighthouse to a ship is 062, what is the bearing from the ship to the lighthouse? Provide a sketch to illustrate your answer. [3-1]

If possible, write a congruence statement for each pair of triangles. Then name the congruence postulate that applies. If the triangles are not congruent, say so. [4-2]

9.

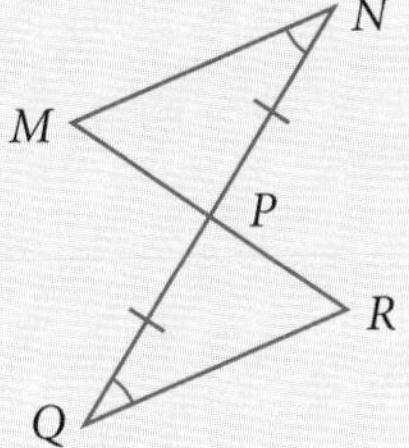

10.

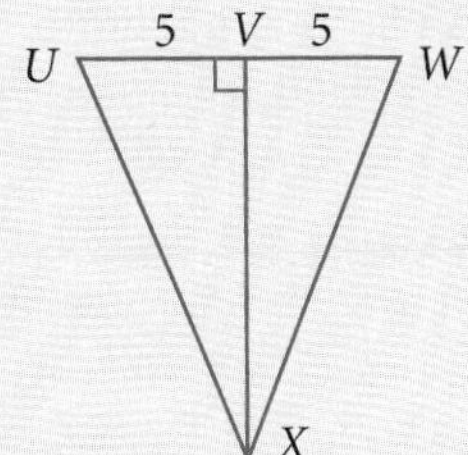

11. Write a summary describing how the LL, HA, and LA theorems for proving right triangles congruent are just special cases of the congruence postulates for all triangles. Provide a sketch to illustrate each case. [4-3]

12. Complete the following proof. [4-2]

Given: $\angle 1 \cong \angle 2$, and $\overline{DB}$ is perpendicular to $\overline{AC}$.

Prove: $\triangle ABD \cong \triangle CBD$

Statements	**Reasons**
1. $\angle 1 \cong \angle 2$	**1.**
2. $\angle DAB$ is supplementary to $\angle 1$, and $\angle DCB$ is supplementary to $\angle 2$.	**2.**
3. $\angle DAB \cong \angle DCB$	**3.**
4.	**4.** Reflexive Property
5. $\angle ABD$ and $\angle CBD$ are right angles.	**5.**
6. $\angle ABD \cong \angle CBD$	**6.**
7.	**7.**

13. A water tower is to be built equidistant from Highway 381 and Interstate 50. The tower must also be equidistant from the towns of Carterville and Ely. Copy the figure at the right, and indicate where the water tower should be built. Explain why your location for the tower works. [4-3]

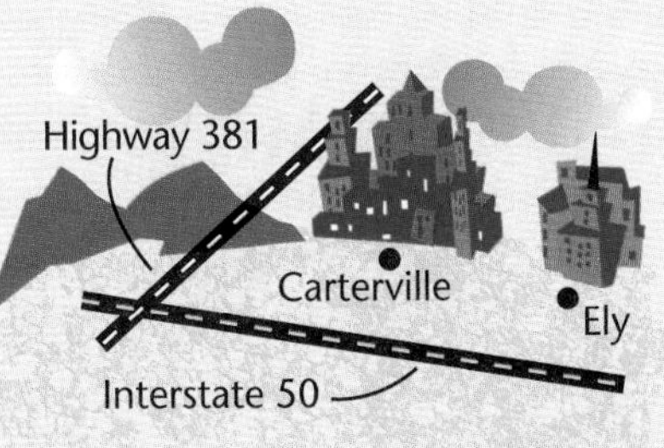

14. $\angle ABC$ is the vertex of isosceles triangle $\triangle ABC$. $\overline{AP}$, $\overline{BR}$, and $\overline{CN}$ are medians of $\triangle ABC$. Find BN and BQ. [4-3]

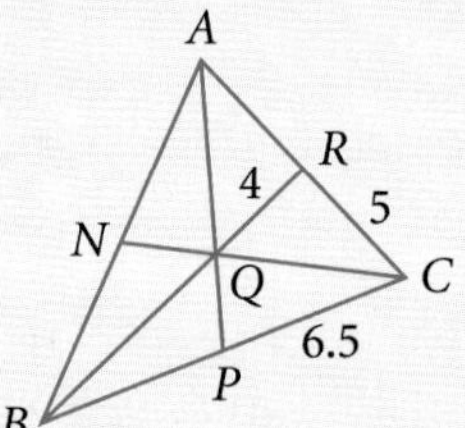

CONCEPTS AND CONNECTIONS

Fine Arts

15. Art Tessellations are found in the art of many cultures. Some of the most beautiful tessellations are those that contain more than one geometric figure. Create a tessellation using congruent copies of *two different* triangles. Use color or shading to distinguish the triangles from each other. Based on your work, do you think it is possible to create a tessellation from *any* two given triangles? Why or why not?

SELF-EVALUATION

Write a summary of the most important facts about triangles that you learned in Chapter 4. Include in your summary all of the methods you have learned for showing that two triangles are congruent. Provide a sketch to illustrate each postulate or theorem.

Chapter 4 Assessment

TEST

1. Find $m\angle WZY$ and $m\angle WYX$.

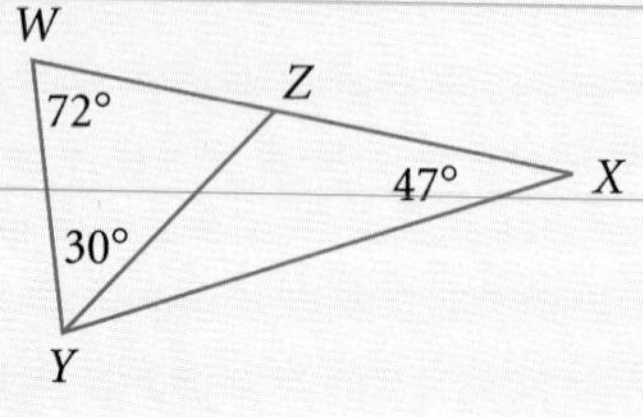

2. Find AB and ED.

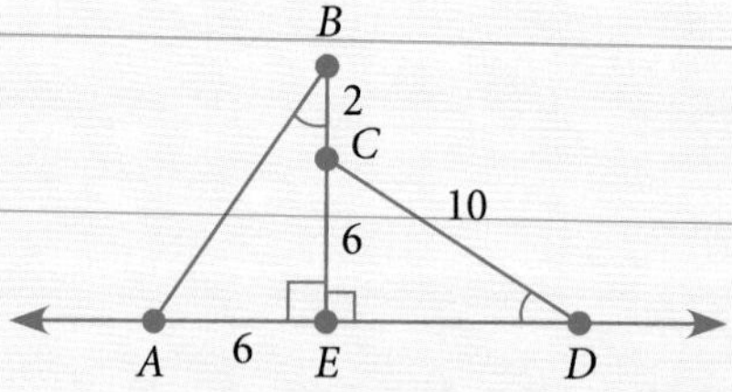

Careers

3. An architect is designing a park for a large apartment complex. The park includes a straight bike path. It is required that a pay phone be located equidistant from the endpoints of the bike path. The architect would also like the pay phone to be equidistant from Buildings A and B. Where should the phone be located? Explain.

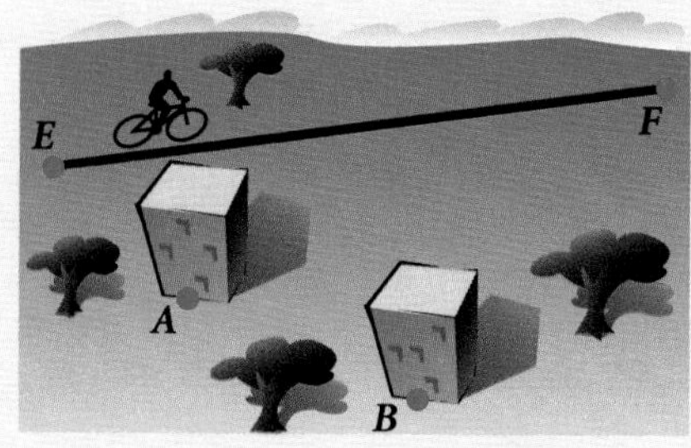

How many lines of symmetry do each of the following types of triangles have? Provide a sketch with each answer.

4. scalene triangle **5.** isosceles right triangle **6.** equilateral triangle

7. Complete the following proof.

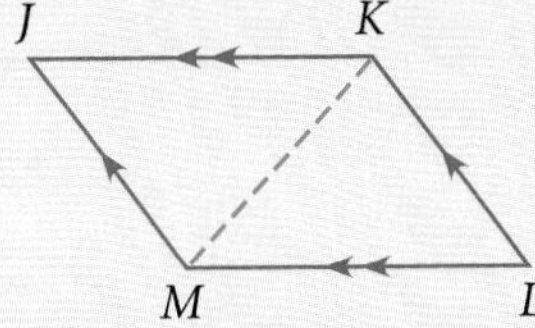

Given: In the figure, $\overline{JK} \parallel \overline{LM}$ and $\overline{JM} \parallel \overline{KL}$

Prove: $\angle J \cong \angle L$

Statements	**Reasons**
1. $\overline{JK} \parallel \overline{LM}$ and $\overline{JM} \parallel \overline{KL}$	**1.** Given
2. Draw $\overline{KM}$.	**2.**
3. $\angle KML \cong \angle JKM$ $\angle LKM \cong \angle JMK$	**3.**
4.	**4.** Reflexive Property
5. $\triangle JMK \cong \triangle LKM$	**5.**
6.	**6.** CPCTC

8. Write a brief explanation of why there is no SSA postulate for triangle congruence. Use a figure to illustrate your explanation.

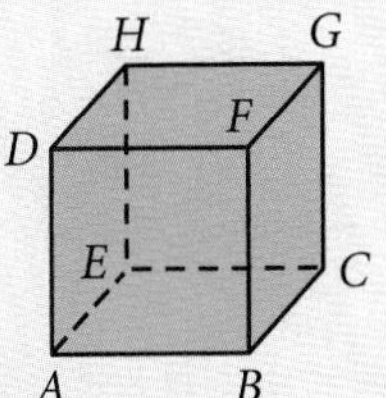

9. Suppose you form right triangles using the vertices of the cube at the right as vertices of the triangles. How many such triangles can be formed that lie on the faces of the cube?

10. Describe the locus of points in a plane 4 cm from line *t*.

11. Line *m* is parallel to line *n*. What are the measures of $\angle 1$ and $\angle 2$?

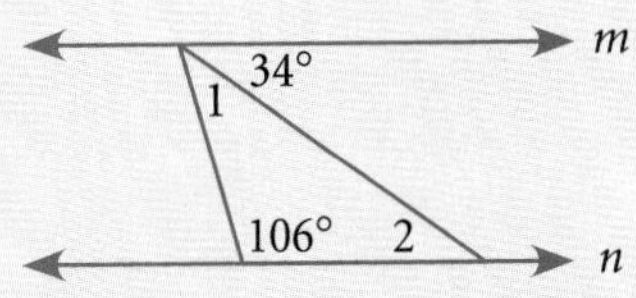

PERFORMANCE TASK

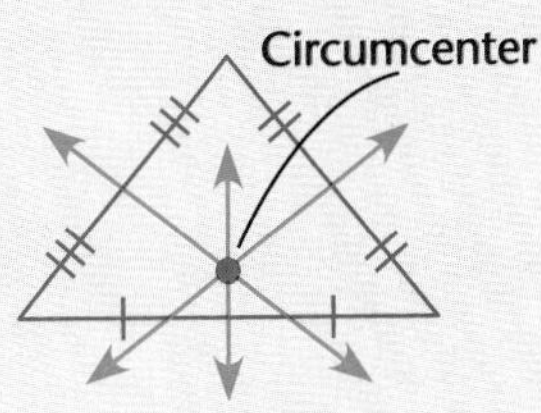

The *circumcenter* of a triangle is the point of concurrency of the perpendicular bisectors of the sides of the triangle. For what type of triangle does the circumcenter lie in the interior of the triangle? in the exterior of the triangle? on the triangle? Investigate these questions by drawing several different triangles. Use a compass and straightedge to find the circumcenter of each. After investigating various possibilities, use your results to make a conjecture.

Chapter 5 Area

Project A
How Dry I Am
How much water does a garden need? Are you ready to grow your own food?

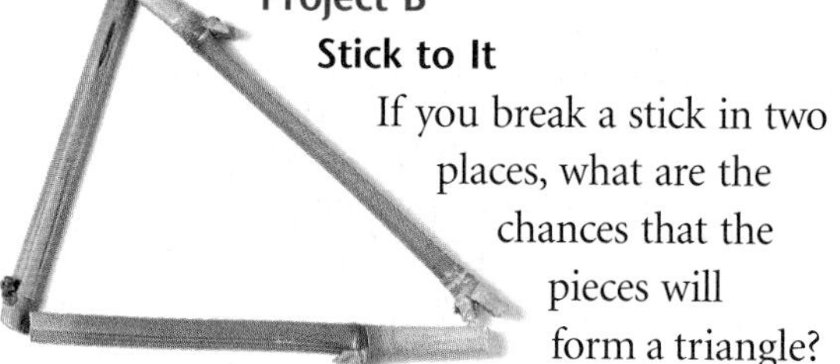

Project B
Stick to It
If you break a stick in two places, what are the chances that the pieces will form a triangle?

Project C
The Dots Have It
How are the paintings of Georges Seurat like a four-color printing process?

GEORGE TIGER

I liked math in high school because it seemed like solving a puzzle. I used it in woodworking (my hobby at the time), which took a lot of measuring.

Now I work with plants, and teach people how to care for them. I started a master gardener program here in southern Oregon. I have to schedule irrigation and know the water capacity of soils, which are some of the most difficult things gardeners have to deal with.

George Tiger
Horticulturist
Oregon State University Extension
Medford, Oregon

George Tiger

Chapter 5 Area

GETTING READY

5-1 Understanding and Applying Area

In 5-1 you will calculate area and perimeter, and see how area is related to algebra and probability. You will use the following skills from previous courses.

Factor each trinomial. [Previous course]

1. $2x^2 + 13x + 11$

2. $x^2 - 8x - 48$

3. $x^2 - 9x + 8$

4. $2x^2 + 2x - 12$

Find the products. [Previous course]

5. $(x + 8)(x - 5)$

6. $(2x - 7)(3x + 9)$

7. $(4 - x)(4 + x)$

8. $(x + 9)^2$

5-2 Derivations of Area Formulas

In 5-2 you will see where area formulas come from, and why they work. You will need the following algebra skills from previous courses.

Solve for the unknown. [Previous course]

9. $rt = d$, $r = 60$, $d = 300$

10. $V = \frac{1}{3}\pi r^2 h$, $r = 3$, $h = 5$

11. $mv = p$, $m = 10$, $v = 2$

5-3 The Pythagorean Theorem

In 5-3 you will learn about the Pythagorean Theorem. You will also see why the theorem is true. You will need the following skills from previous courses and chapters.

Find the distance between each pair of points. [1-3]

12. $(0, 3), (4, 0)$

13. $(5, 2), (-3, 6)$

14. $(8, 0), (7, 2)$

15. $(-6, -10), (-8, -5)$

Write each radical in simplest form. [Previous course]

16. $x^2\sqrt{y^8}$

17. $\sqrt{25x^2y^3}$

18. $\sqrt{16x^6y^5} - 4xy^2(x^4y)$

19. $\sqrt{8x^5y^7z}$

Solve these proportions. [Previous course]

20. $\frac{3}{2} = \frac{5}{x}$

21. $\frac{5}{8} = \frac{x}{20}$

22. $\frac{7}{\sqrt{2}} = \frac{7\sqrt{2}}{x}$

23. $\frac{1}{\sqrt{2}} = \frac{x}{\sqrt{8}}$

5-1 Understanding and Applying Area

HURRY, HURRY, STEP RIGHT UP!

"Ladies and gentlemen, children of all ages! Join me on a thrilling adventure under the big top, a journey to a world like no other." This ringmaster's announcement signals the start of the Ringling Brothers and Barnum & Bailey Circus. This circus presents two shows a day, and travels to 52 cities and towns across the country. It had its origins over a century ago.

In the late 1800s and early 1900s, circuses captivated audiences across America. People looked forward to the thrilling and exotic circus acts and the games of chance. In 1909, there were 98 touring circuses in the United States.

In the 1940s, circus attendance was at an all-time high. But the circus was competing with the phonograph, movies, radio, and later, television for people's entertainment time and money. The circus suffered a steady decline in attendance. Today there are only about half a dozen circuses still traveling the country and performing under canvas tents.

?

1. **Besides competing forms of entertainment, what other factors may have contributed to the decline of the circus?**
2. **The words *circus* and *circle* both have their origins in the Greek word *kirkos,* meaning *ring.* Explain the relationship between the words *circus* and *circle.***
3. **How might calculations of area and perimeter be important to a circus?**

5-1 PART A Area and Perimeter

← CONNECT → ***You already know how to find the area and perimeter of some geometric figures. Now you will explore some familiar formulas and begin to extend the ideas of area and perimeter to more complicated figures.***

The figure below shows that the **area** of a rectangle can be found by counting unit squares, or—more quickly—by multiplying the length of the rectangle by its width.

	1	4	7	10	13
3	2	5	8	11	14
	3	6	9	12	15
			5		

Since there are 3 rows of 5 squares, $A = \ell w = 3 \times 5 = 15$ square units.

Because a square is a rectangle whose length and width are equal, the area of a square is equal to the square of the length of one of its sides.

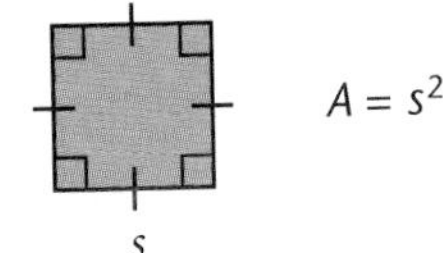

The area formula for a triangle may also be familiar to you. The area of a triangle is one-half the product of the length of the base and the height.

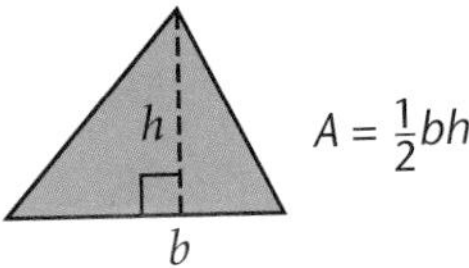

In 5-2, we will bring area formulas into our deductive system. You will see why these and other area formulas work. For now, we'll assume that a few basic formulas are valid, so that we can explore some connections between area, perimeter, algebra, and probability.

The following definition and postulates provide a foundation for studying area. Most of the figures you will be working with are **polygons.** As you'll see, a polygon is a many-sided plane figure whose sides are line segments.

DEFINITION

A **polygonal region** consists of a polygon and its interior.

A polygonal region can always be divided into nonoverlapping triangular regions as shown.

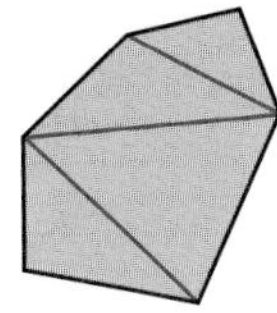

AREA POSTULATES

For every polygonal region, there is a unique positive number called the *area* of the region.

If two polygonal regions are congruent, then they have equal areas.

AREA-ADDITION POSTULATE

The area of a polygonal region is the sum of the areas of all of its nonoverlapping parts.

The Area-Addition Postulate helps you calculate the areas of complicated regions. You can find the area of a polygonal region by dividing it into convenient triangles and rectangles and adding their areas.

EXAMPLE

Find the area of the figure at the right.

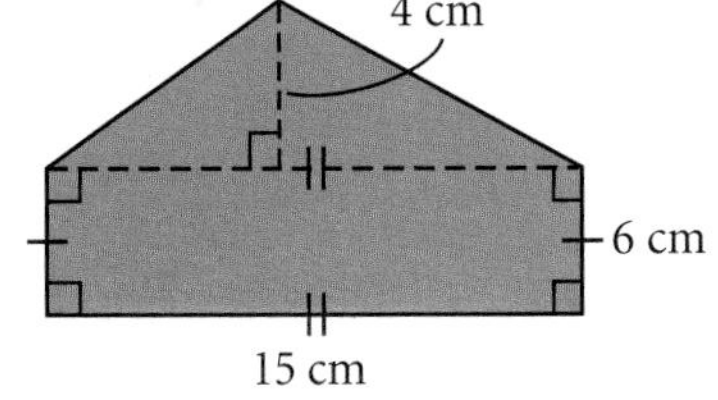

To find the area of the figure, add the area of the rectangle to the area of the triangle.

area of figure = area of rectangle + area of triangle

$= 6 \cdot 15 + \frac{1}{2} \cdot 15 \cdot 4$

$= 90 + 30$

$= 120 \text{ cm}^2$

Another measure of a figure is its **perimeter**—the distance around the figure. Remember that perimeter and area measure different things. Perimeter is a distance, so it is measured in linear units (for example, inches or centimeters). Area is measured in square units (for example, square feet or square meters).

EXPLORE: PERIMETER vs. AREA

MATERIALS

Graph paper
Geometry software (optional)

1. Use geometry software or graph paper to draw three noncongruent rectangles with the same area. Find their perimeters, and record your data.
2. Draw three different rectangles with the same perimeter. Find their areas, and record your data.
3. What type of rectangle has the largest area for any given perimeter? What type has the smallest area for any given perimeter (assuming the side lengths are whole numbers)? Make conjectures and compare your results with those of your classmates.
4. Does the area of a figure depend on its perimeter? Does the perimeter of a figure depend on its area? Explain.

TRY IT

Find the perimeter and area of each figure.

a.

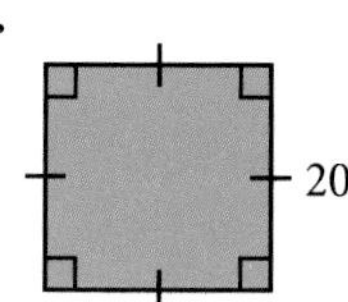

b.

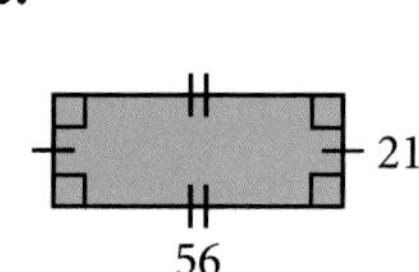

c.

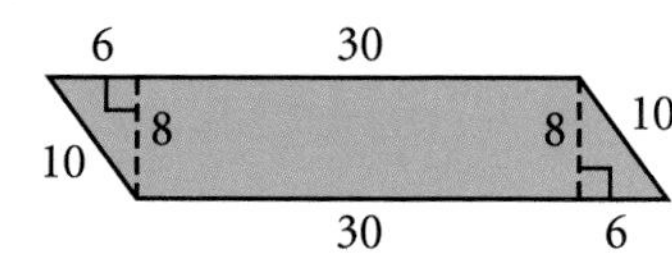

REFLECT

1. Explain the difference between perimeter and area.

Describe a way to find the area of each figure. Assume that you can measure any lengths that you wish.

2.

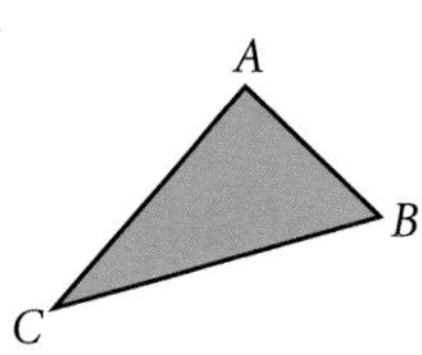

3.

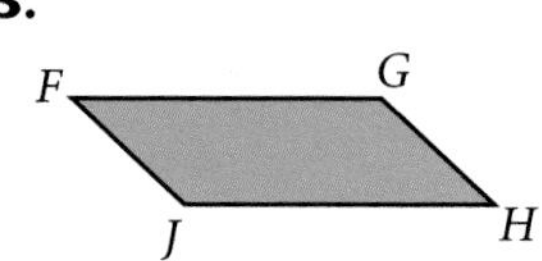

4.

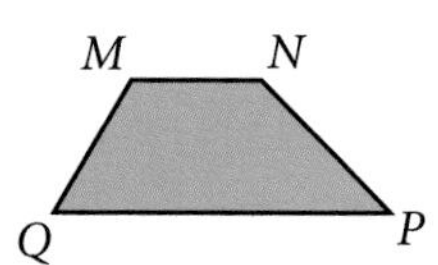

5. Soraya says, "If I have a ruler and a protractor, I know I can find the area of any polygonal region." Is this true? If so, how can Soraya justify her claim? If not, explain why not.

Exercises

CORE

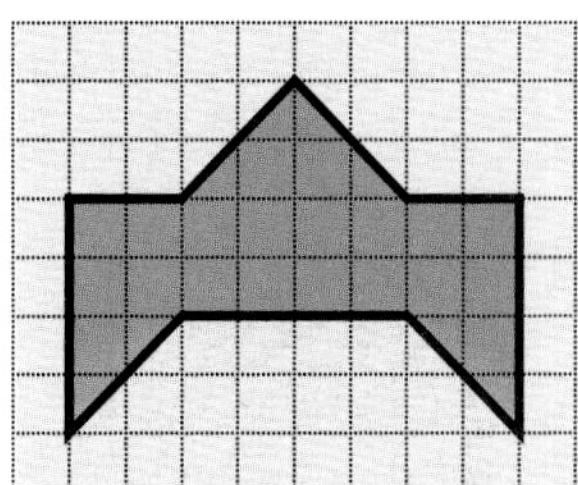

1. **Getting Started** Find the area of the figure. Each square on the grid has an area of 1 square unit.

Find the perimeter and area of each figure.

2.

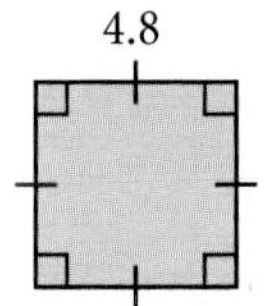

3.

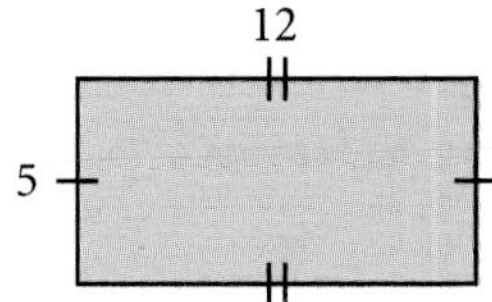

4.

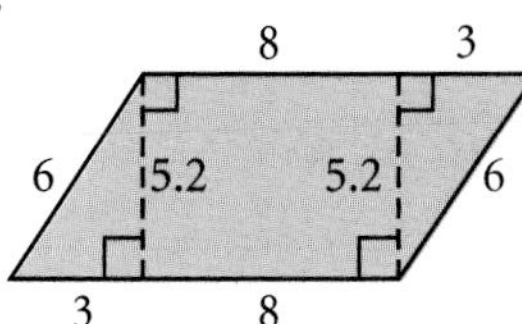

5.

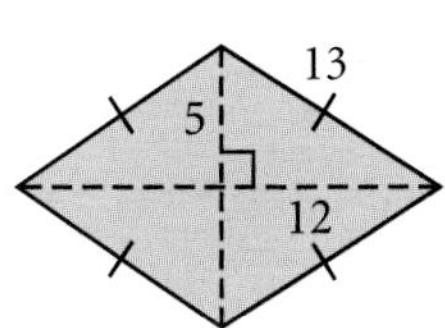

6.

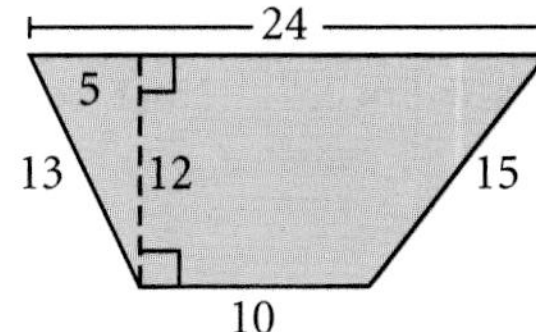

The area of Figure A is 28 square units, the area of Figure B is 32 square units, the area of Figure C is 19 square units, and the area of Figure D is 25 square units. Find the following areas. (Hint: Recall that ∪ means the union of two sets.)

7. the area of Figure A ∪ Figure C

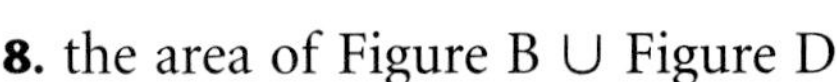

8. the area of Figure B ∪ Figure D

9. the area of Figure A ∪ Figure D

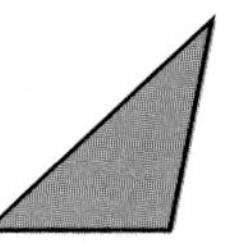

B

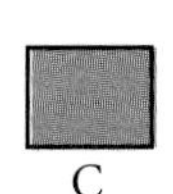

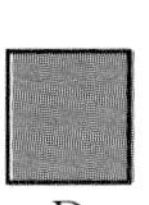

10. What postulate are you using in calculating the areas in Exercises 7–9?

11. What is the difference between 100 cm and 100 cm^2? Illustrate your answer.

12. Write the word or phrase that correctly completes the following statement.

    A polygonal region can be divided into nonoverlapping ____ regions.

13. Find formulas for the perimeter of a rectangle and the perimeter of a square.

14. **Remodeling the Kitchen** A rectangular kitchen measures 120 ft^2. The floor is to be covered with square tiles measuring 6 in. by 6 in. How many tiles will it take to cover the floor? Assume only whole tiles are used. Give a short, written description of how you solved this problem.

15. Find the area of a figure on the coordinate plane that is bounded by the x-axis, the line $y = 2x$, and the line $x = 7$.

16. **Okay, Corral It!** A horse rancher has to divide this parcel of land into four rectangular fenced regions. Corral fencing costs $8.00 per foot. Sketch a way to divide the land, and include the dimensions in your sketch. How much does the fencing cost?

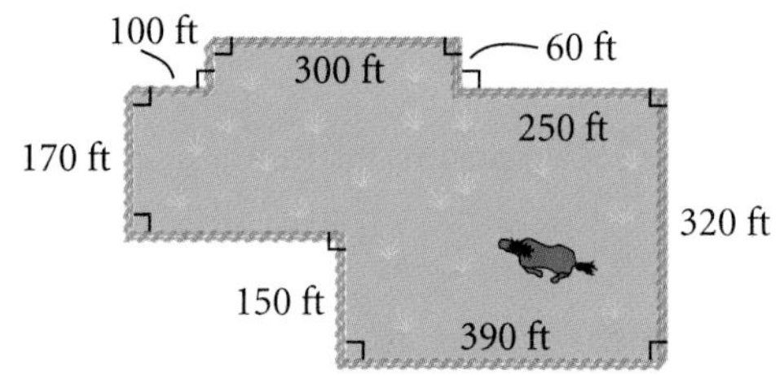

17. A stained-glass window has a central orange diamond with four triangles on its sides. Find the area of the orange region and the area of each of the triangles. Explain how you found the areas.

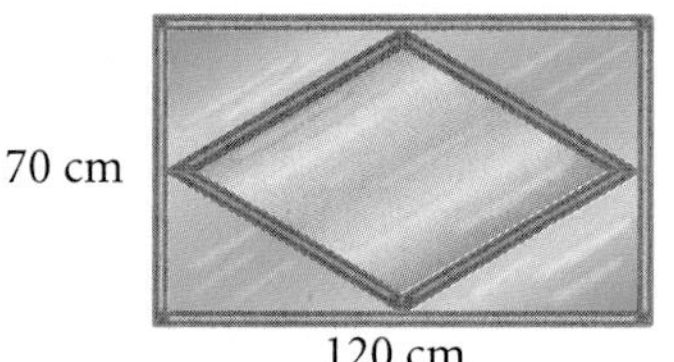

LOOK AHEAD

Identify each of these polynomials as a monomial (one term), a binomial (two terms), or a trinomial (three terms).

18. $3x^2$ **19.** $4y + 7$ **20.** $2x^3y^2z^4$ **21.** $x^2 + y^2 + z^2$

MORE PRACTICE

Find the area of each figure.

22.

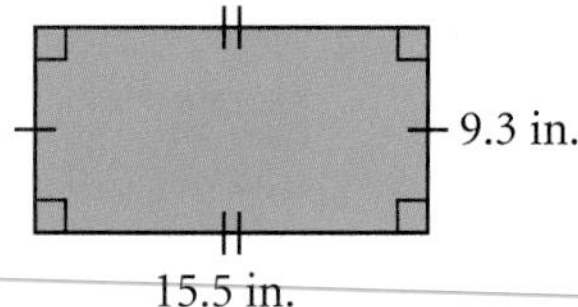

23.

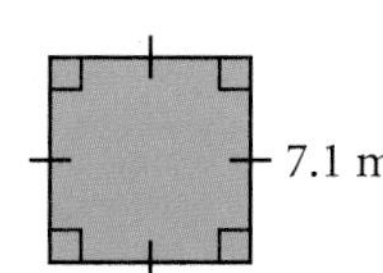

24.

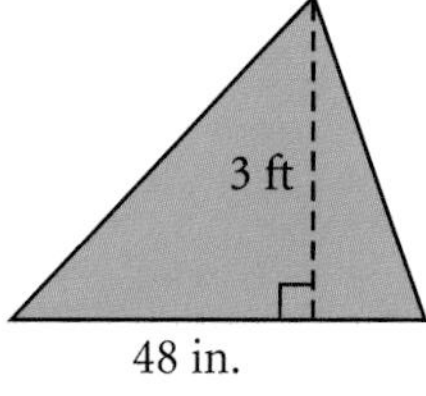

25.

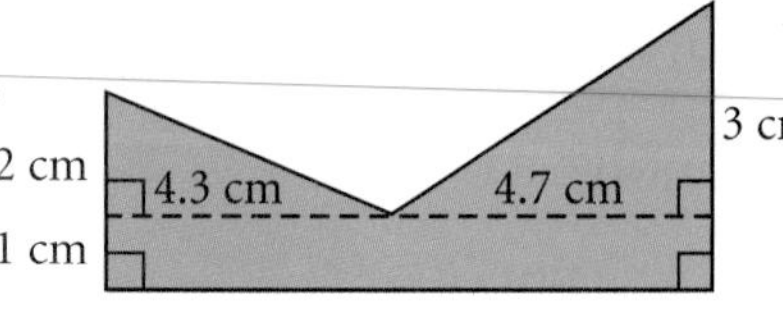

26.

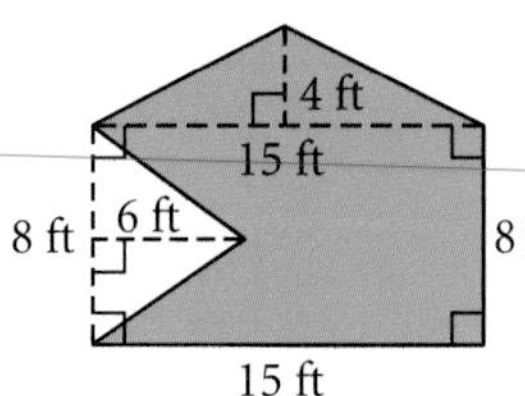

27.

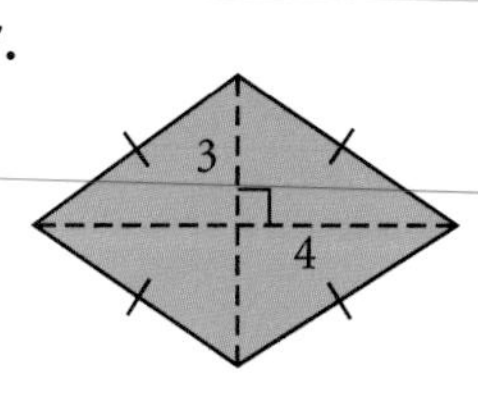

MORE MATH REASONING

28. Suppose that Figure A and Figure B are overlapping polygons.
  a. Describe a method for finding the area of A ∪ B.
  b. Write a formula for finding the area of A ∪ B. (Hint: The intersection of A and B is written A ∩ B.)

29. Triangular "checkerboards" of different sizes are shown below. Notice that the ratio of the blue area to the white area seems to decrease as the number of triangles on the board increases.

a. Identify a pattern in the numbers of blue and white triangles. Do these patterns continue?

b. Find the ratios for the next few checkerboards.

c. Write a formula for the number of blue triangles on a board that has n triangles on a side.

d. Does the ratio of blue to white triangles seem to approach a particular value? If so, what is this value? (Note: A value that a sequence or graph approaches is called a *limit.*)

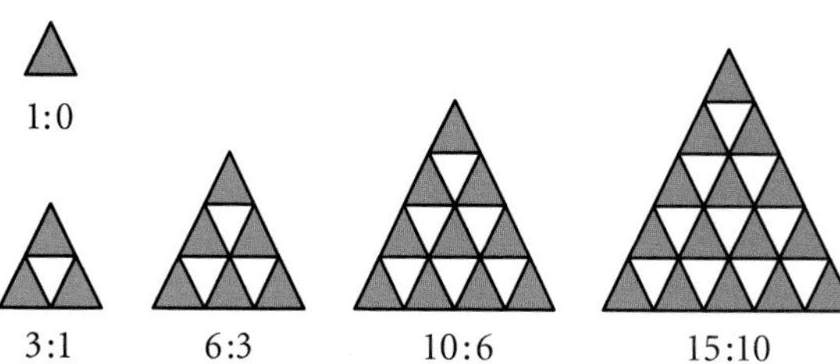

Polynomials and Area

← CONNECT → ***You have learned about polynomials in previous math courses. Now you will connect algebra and geometry by looking at polynomials and area.***

There are connections between mathematics and art, science, business, and nature. There are also connections between different areas of mathematics. Connections between numbers, equations, graphs, and geometric figures show the relationship between algebra and geometry.

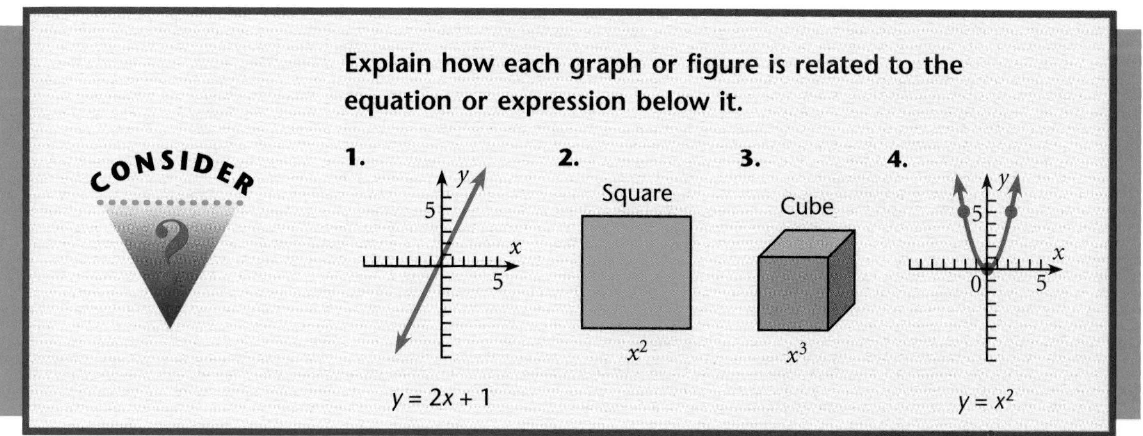

CONSIDER
?
Explain how each graph or figure is related to the equation or expression below it.
1.
y
5
x
5
y = 2x + 1
2.
Square
x2
3.
Cube
x3
4.
y
5
x
0
5
y = x2

We can multiply two binomials, like $(x + 3)$ and $(x + 5)$, geometrically. The process we will use is related to finding the area of a rectangle.

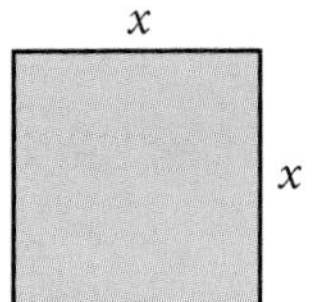

In this method, squares and rectangles model algebraic expressions.

The area of this large square is x^2, so a square of this size "equals" x^2.

This rectangle has length x and width 1, so it has an area of x.

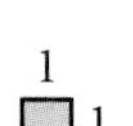

This small square has area 1. It is called the *unit square.*

EXAMPLES

Use squares and rectangles to represent each algebraic expression.

1. $x + 3$

Use an x rectangle and three unit squares.

2. $(x + 3)(x + 5)$

Start by measuring a horizontal segment of length $(x + 3)$. Use tick marks to mark lengths.

x 3

Add a vertical segment of length $(x + 5)$, as shown below on the left. Then extend the tick marks vertically and horizontally to complete the figure.

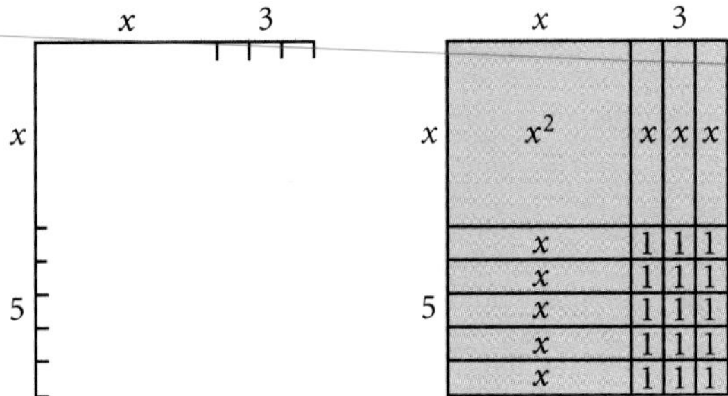

You can count squares and rectangles to see that the area of the large rectangle is $x^2 + 8x + 15$.

In the following Explore, you will investigate the connection between multiplying binomials geometrically and factoring trinomials.

EXPLORE: THE TILE FACTOR

MATERIALS

Algebra tiles (or graph paper and scissors)

1. Use squares and rectangles to represent $(x + 4)(x + 1)$. What is the area of the overall rectangle? Explain why this area is the product of $(x + 4)$ and $(x + 1)$.

2. What is the area of the large rectangle shown at the right? What product does it represent?

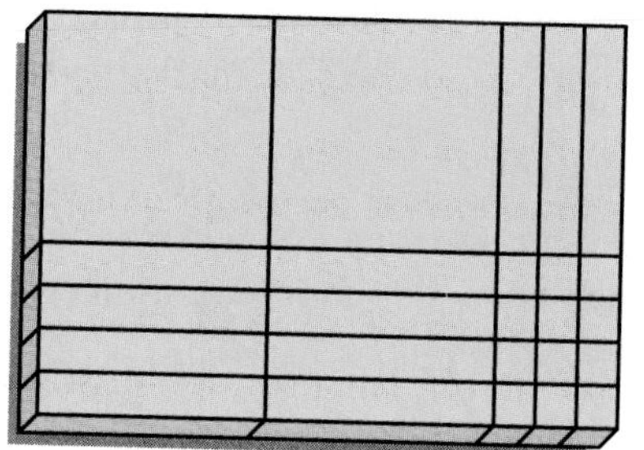

3. Suppose you want to use squares and rectangles to factor instead of multiply. Use algebra tiles to represent (or cut out graph paper to make) one x^2 square, eight x rectangles, and twelve unit squares. Arrange these into a rectangle to represent the expression $x^2 + 8x + 12$. Sketch your rectangle, and explain how it shows the factorization of $x^2 + 8x + 12$.

4. Write a paragraph explaining how to use squares and rectangles to factor trinomials.

TRY IT

a. Use squares and rectangles to multiply the binomials $(x + 4)$ and $(x + 2)$.

b. Use squares and rectangles to factor $x^2 + 7x + 10$.

REFLECT

1. Explain why finding the area of a rectangle that is $(x + 2)$ units by $(x + 6)$ units also finds the product of $(x + 2)$ and $(x + 6)$.

2. When using squares and rectangles to multiply or factor, does it matter what length you use to represent x? Why or why not?

3. Use squares and rectangles to explain why $(x + 2)^2 \neq x^2 + 4$. Provide a sketch with your explanation.

Exercises

CORE

1. **Getting Started** By following these steps, use squares and rectangles to represent the product $(x + 2)(x + 3)$.
   a. Draw a horizontal segment of length $(x + 2)$. Use tick marks to mark the lengths of the x rectangle and the unit squares.
   b. Add a vertical segment of length $(x + 3)$ perpendicular to the horizontal segment, using tick marks to mark off the lengths. Be sure to be consistent with the lengths you used in **1a.**
   c. Extend the tick marks vertically and horizontally to complete the figure.

Use squares and rectangles to represent each expression.

2. $x + 4$
3. $x + 6$
4. $x^2 + 2x$
5. $x^2 + 6x + 5$

6. Write out the product illustrated by the squares and rectangles at the right.

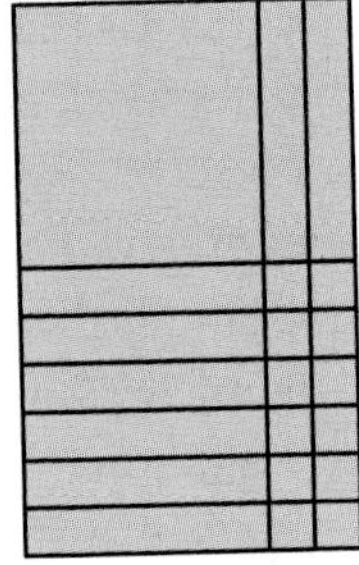

Use squares and rectangles to represent each product, and then write the product algebraically.

7. $(x + 1)(x + 3)$
8. $(x + 3)(2x + 1)$
9. $(2x)(3x + 5)$

Factor each trinomial, using squares and rectangles. Provide a sketch, and give an algebraic answer.

10. $x^2 + 4x + 3$
11. $x^2 + 8x + 15$
12. $2x^2 + 7x + 6$

13. **Is This Right?** A student answered a test question as shown.

    Question: Factor $x^2 + 16$. Answer: $\underline{(x + 4)(x + 4)}$

    Use squares and rectangles to show whether or not this is the correct answer. If it is not, give your response to the question, and explain why the student may have made this error.

14. Suppose that a rectangle has an area of $x^2 + 6x + 8$. If its length is $x + 4$, what is its width?

15. A rectangular field is two kilometers longer than it is wide.
    a. Use squares and rectangles to find the area of the field in terms of w, its width.
    b. If the field has an area of fifteen square kilometers, find its length and its width.

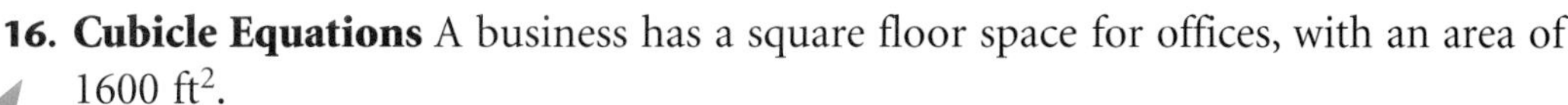

16. **Cubicle Equations** A business has a square floor space for offices, with an area of 1600 ft^2.

Careers

a. What are the dimensions of the office space?

b. If the average worker has a 50-ft^2 office, how many workers are there?

c. Heidi and Cristina, two industrial engineers, come up with a new design for the building space that increases the width of the available office space by 5 ft and the length by 10 ft. What are the dimensions of the new office space?

d. If the average space per worker stays the same, how many workers can use the new space? Explain how you found your answer.

LOOK BACK

Use the given information to determine which lines are parallel. Justify your answers with a theorem or postulate. [3-4]

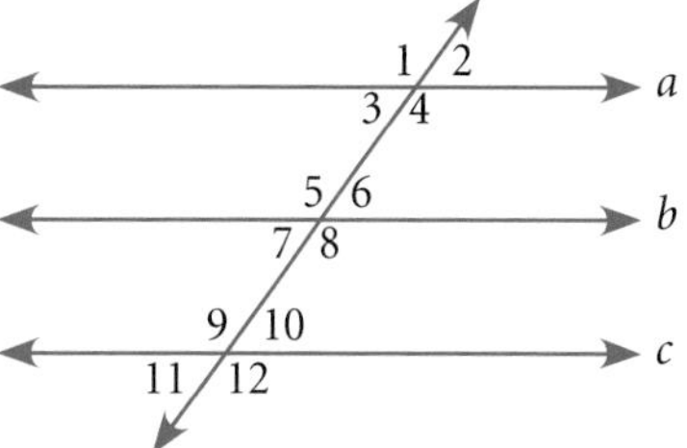

17. $\angle 1 \cong \angle 10$

18. $\angle 4 \cong \angle 8$

19. $m\angle 3 + m\angle 9 = 180°$

20. $\angle 5 \cong \angle 9$

21. $\angle 1 \cong \angle 8$

Write the congruence correspondence for each pair of triangles. Give the postulate or theorem that proves each pair of triangles congruent. [4-2]

22.

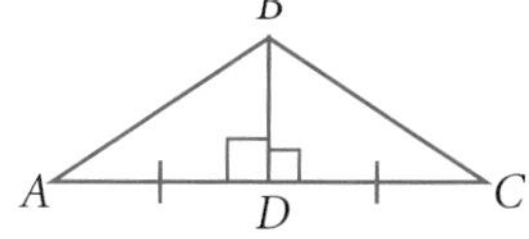

23.

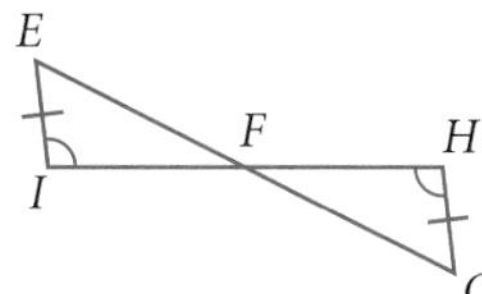

24.

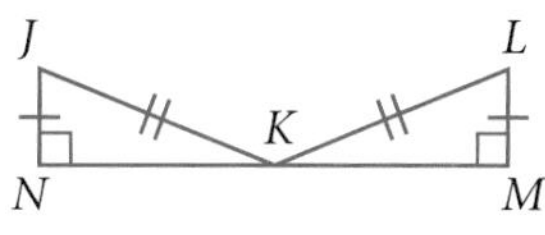

MORE PRACTICE

Use squares and rectangles to represent each expression.

25. $2x + 7$

26. $x^2 + 5$

27. $x^2 + 5x + 3$

Use squares and rectangles to represent each product, and then write the product algebraically.

28. $(x + 2)(x + 5)$

29. $(3x + 2)(x + 1)$

30. $(5)(2x + 3)$

Factor each trinomial by using squares and rectangles. Provide a sketch, and give an algebraic answer.

31. $x^2 + 4x + 3$

32. $x^2 + 8x + 15$

33. $2x^2 + 11x + 5$

MORE MATH REASONING

34. Suppose you want to apply our geometric multiplication technique to algebraic expressions that have x^3 terms. You'll need three-dimensional figures! Use solids to illustrate each of the following expressions.

a. x^3 **b.** x^2 **c.** x **d.** 1

e. Can you easily multiply $(x + 1)(x + 2)(x + 3)$ using the figures you have developed? Why or why not?

35. Count the dots in each dot-triangle. Describe any patterns that you see.

What happens if you add two consecutive numbers from the triangle sequence? Why do you think this is true?

5-1 PART C The Quadratic Formula and Area

← CONNECT → ***You've solved quadratic equations before. Now you will use the quadratic formula to solve problems involving area.***

Any equation that can be put into the form $ax^2 + bx + c = 0$ is a **quadratic equation.**

You may be able to solve a quadratic equation quickly by factoring, as in the following example.

Solve: $x^2 + 3x - 10 = 0$

$(x + 5)(x - 2) = 0$	Factor the trinomial.
$x + 5 = 0$ *or* $x - 2 = 0$	If the product of two quantities is zero, one of them must be zero.
$x = -5$ *or* $x = 2$	Solve the two equations.

Most quadratics cannot easily be solved by factoring. Fortunately, there is a formula that can always be used to find the solutions to a quadratic equation, if any exist.

THE QUADRATIC FORMULA

The solutions to the equation $ax^2 + bx + c = 0$ (where $a \neq 0$) are given by the following.

$$x = \frac{-b \pm \sqrt{b^2 - 4ac}}{2a}$$

EXAMPLE

Solve: $2x^2 - 4x - 5 = 0$. Round answers to the nearest hundredth.

Use the quadratic formula with $a = 2$, $b = -4$, and $c = -5$.

$$x = \frac{-(-4) \pm \sqrt{(-4)^2 - 4(2)(-5)}}{2(2)}$$

$$x = \frac{4 \pm \sqrt{16 + 40}}{4}$$

$$x = \frac{4 \pm \sqrt{56}}{4} = \frac{4 \pm 2\sqrt{14}}{4} = \frac{2 \pm \sqrt{14}}{2}$$

A calculator gives approximate solutions of $x = \frac{2 + \sqrt{14}}{2} \approx 2.87$, and $x = \frac{2 - \sqrt{14}}{2} \approx -0.87$.

TRY IT

a. Solve $x^2 + 2x = 10$. Round answers to the nearest hundredth. (Hint: Be sure to get one side of the equation equal to zero before applying the quadratic formula!)

1. Iliana used the quadratic formula to find the dimensions of a rectangle. When she solved for its length, she came up with two solutions, one positive and one negative. Why did this happen, and what should she do next?

In the following Explore, you will see how the quadratic formula can be used in a problem-solving situation.

EXPLORE: CIRCUS GIGANTICUS

Circus Giganticus is producing posters for its next tour. The posters must have an area of 1200 in^2. The designers have planned for a square image surrounded by a border 3 in. wide on the left and right and 2 in. wide on the top and bottom.

1. Use x to represent the side length of the square photograph. Write expressions for the length and width of the poster in terms of x.
2. What should the dimensions of the poster be? What should the area of the photograph be? Round your answers to the nearest tenth.

Problem-Solving Tip

Write an equation that represents the real-world situation.

3. Compare your methods and your results with those of your classmates.

The quadratic formula is an important algebraic tool because it finds all possible solutions for any quadratic equation. It requires some computation and simplification, however, so it may take more time than solving by factoring. You should be familiar with both methods so that you can choose the most appropriate one.

REFLECT

1. Describe the advantages and disadvantages of using the quadratic formula to solve a quadratic equation.
2. In general, how many solutions are there to a quadratic equation?

Exercises

CORE

1. **Getting Started** Follow these steps to solve $x^2 + 4x = 7$.
   a. Write the equation in the form $ax^2 + bx + c = 0$.
   b. Find the a, b, and c values. Substitute these values into the quadratic formula.
   c. If possible, simplify the square root.
   d. If possible, simplify the fraction. You now have exact solutions to the equation.
   e. Use your calculator to write the approximate solutions to the nearest hundredth.

Solve each equation. Round answers to the nearest hundredth.

2. $x^2 + 4x - 6 = 0$
3. $x^2 - 3x = 4$
4. $2x^2 - 9x + 7 = 0$
5. $-3x^2 + 5x + 1 = 0$
6. $1.3x^2 = -2.7x + 11.1$
7. $x^2 + 2x - 5 = 0$

8. Determine whether the following statement is true or false. If the statement is false, change the underlined words to make it true.

   You can use the quadratic equation to solve a quadratic formula.

9. **Carnival Canopy** The carnival at a circus operates under a tent with a rectangular base that is 18 ft longer than it is wide. If the total area under the tent is 7663 ft^2, what are the length and width of the tent?

10. The first mathematical work published in the Americas was the *Sumario Compendioso* (1556), by Juan Diez. It featured the following problem.

    A man takes passage on a ship and asks the ship's master what he has to pay. [T]he master replies: "[The price] will be the number of pesos which, multiplied by itself and added to the number, gives 1260."
    a. This problem can be represented by the quadratic equation $x^2 + x = 1260$. Explain why this equation represents the problem.
    b. How many pesos does the man pay for the trip?

11. The length of a rectangular basketball court is 6 ft shorter than twice its width.
    a. Find the length of the court in terms of w, its width.
    b. Find its area in terms of its width.
    c. If the area of the court is 4700 ft^2, find its length and width.

12. Quadratic-Sized Pool A rectangular swimming pool is 50 ft long and 25 ft wide. There is a walkway x ft wide surrounding the pool.

a. Find the length and width of the pool with the walkway in terms of x.

b. Find the area of the pool with the walkway in terms of x. Explain how you found this expression.

c. If the total area of the pool and the walkway is 2294 ft^2, what is the width of the walkway?

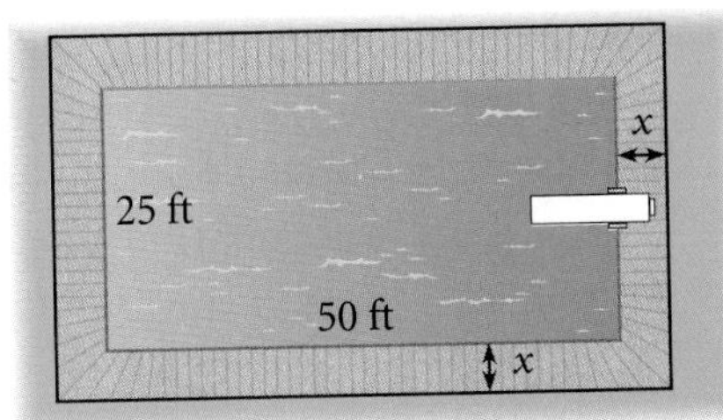

LOOK AHEAD

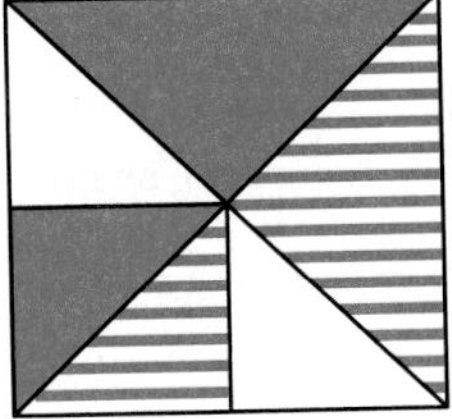

13. What fractional part of the interior of the square shown is colored as follows?

a. solid red

b. solid white

c. striped

d. solid red or solid white

Express each fraction in lowest terms. Then convert the fraction to an equivalent decimal and percentage. When necessary, round decimals to the nearest hundredth and percentages to the nearest one percent.

14. $\frac{3}{5}$ **15.** $\frac{8}{12}$ **16.** $\frac{26}{56}$ **17.** $\frac{36}{90}$

MORE PRACTICE

Solve each equation. Round answers to the nearest hundredth.

18. $x^2 + 6x + 5 = 0$

19. $3x^2 - 10x + 2 = 0$

20. $-2.3x^2 + 3.4 = 0.8x$

21. $4.4x^2 = 16.7$

MORE MATH REASONING

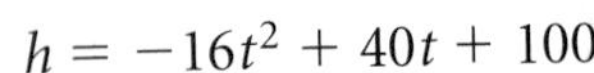

22. What Goes Up . . . If you throw a ball upward off a 100-ft building at 40 ft/sec, the equation below gives its approximate height t seconds after it is thrown.

Science

$h = -16t^2 + 40t + 100$

When will the ball hit the ground? Explain how you found your answer. (Assume the ball does not hit the building on the way down.)

23. Quest for Profit Elisa, the owner of a game store, finds that the total monthly profit generated by *Space Quest* depends on the price she charges for the game. She finds that a graph of profit (y) as a function of price (x) approximately follows the equation below.

$$y = -4x^2 + 145x - 750$$

a. Find the maximum and minimum prices that Elisa can charge so that *Space Quest* will make a (positive) profit.

b. Is this function a reasonable model for a real-world situation? Investigate the graph of the function. What happens when the price is low? high? How might this happen in a real situation?

5-1 PART D Area and Probability

← CONNECT → ***You may have studied probability using coins, dice, or random numbers. Now you will see how geometry and probability are related.***

The probability of an event measures how likely it is to happen. If we conduct an experiment with n equally likely outcomes, and m of those are "successful" outcomes, then the probability of a success is $\frac{m}{n}$. For example, if there are 6 green marbles in a bag with a total of 24 marbles, the probability that you will shake a green marble into your hand is $\frac{6}{24} = \frac{1}{4} = 0.25$, or 25%.

Notice that a probability may be expressed as a fraction, a decimal, or a percent.

TRY IT

a. What is the probability of throwing a one or a six on one toss of a die? Express your answer as a fraction.

b. A hotel has 14 rooms on the first floor, 12 on the second, and 15 on the third. If you are assigned a hotel room at random, what is the probability that it will be on the third floor? Express your answer in decimal form.

In **geometric probability,** the probability of an event is determined by comparing the areas (or perimeters, angle measures, or other measures) of the "successful" regions to the total area of the figure. (When working with geometric probability, assume that figures that appear congruent are congruent.)

EXAMPLE

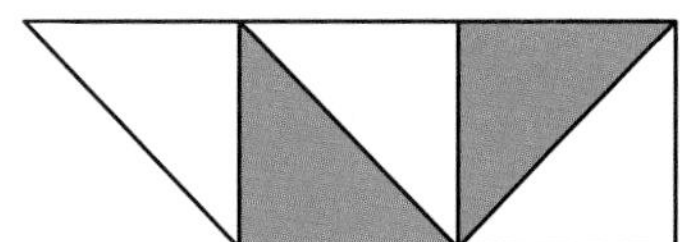

Find the probability that a randomly chosen point inside the figure shown will lie in a blue region.

The figure is divided into five regions of equal area. Two of the regions are blue, so the probability that a randomly selected point will be in a blue region is $\frac{2}{5} = 0.4 = 40\%$.

TRY IT

c. In an air hockey game, you score a goal when the puck goes into an opening at your opponent's end of the table.

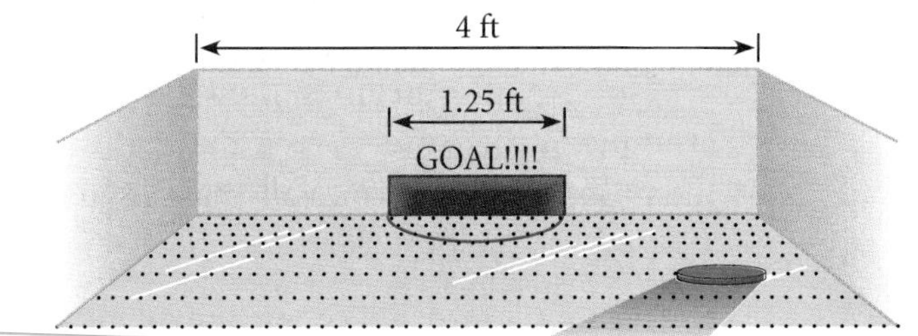

If you shoot the puck randomly and your opponent doesn't stop it, what's the probability that you will score a goal? (Don't consider the size of the puck.)

d. Your baby sister throws your favorite cassette toward the wall with the open window, as shown. Assuming she throws the tape randomly, what is the probability that it will go out the window?

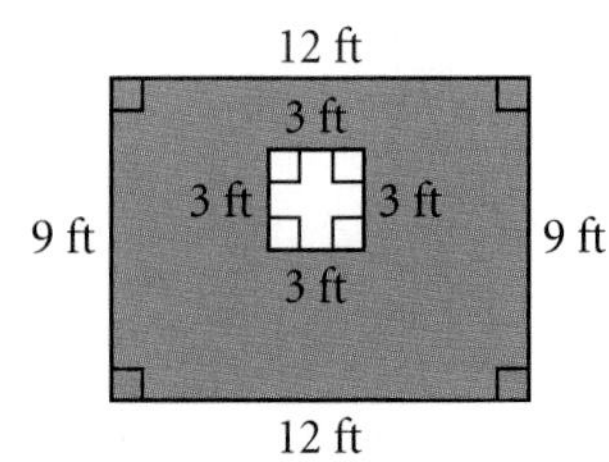

You now know how to calculate geometric probabilities for figures that are given. In the following Explore, you'll reverse this process and design figures that result in a specific geometric probability.

EXPLORE: TARGETING PROBABILITY

The targets at the right are used in a carnival dart-throwing contest. A contestant wins a stuffed dog if his dart hits the shaded region. Although the contestants hit the target every time, the darts are old and difficult to aim, so you may assume that the game is random. For the carnival to make a profit, the owner wants the probability of winning the game to be $\frac{1}{4}$.

1. Give dimensions for the shaded regions in each target so that the probability of winning is $\frac{1}{4}$.
2. Suppose a person plays the game twice in a row. What is the probability that he or she will win both times? Explain your reasoning.

a.

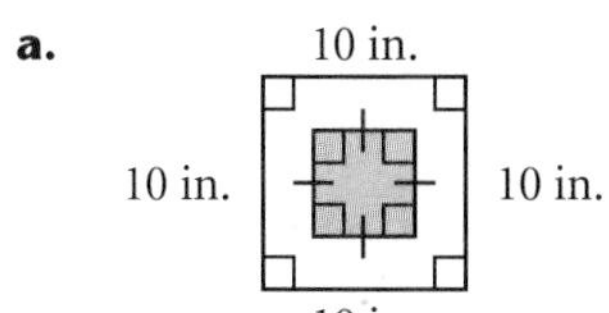

b.

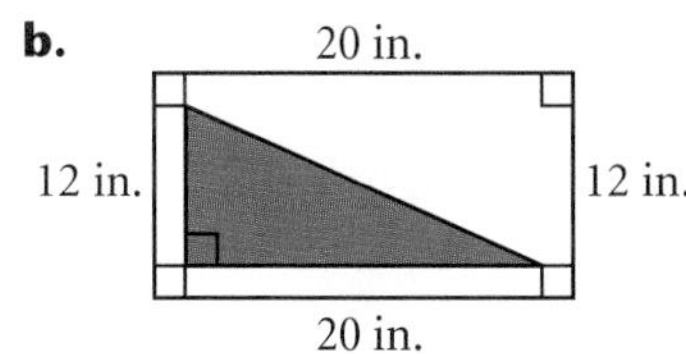

c.

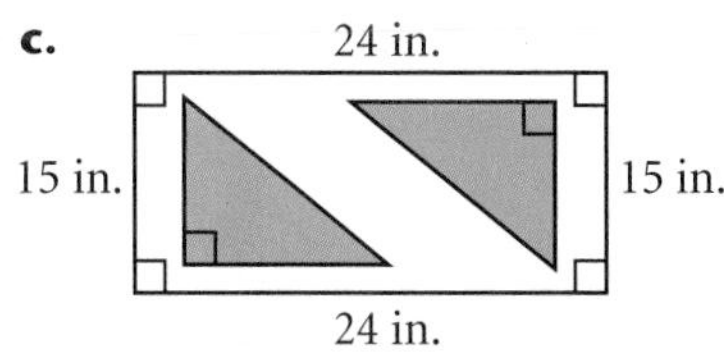

REFLECT

1. If a rectangle is divided into six congruent regions and three of them are shaded, what is the probability that you will randomly pick a point in the shaded area? Does it matter which three regions are shaded?
2. Describe one underlying assumption you make when using geometric probability. When is it inappropriate to use geometric probability in a situation involving areas?

Exercises

CORE

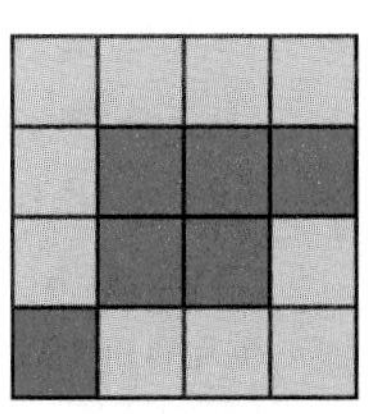

1. **Getting Started** Find the probability that a randomly chosen point inside the figure shown will lie in a red region. Express your answer as a fraction.

2. You are designing a new target that is a square inside a $16' \times 9'$ rectangle. What size should the square be if you want the following probabilities of winning the game?

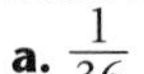

a. $\frac{1}{36}$ **b.** $\frac{1}{16}$ **c.** 0.25

3. What is the probability that you will get a star when you spin the spinner at the right? Express your answer as a fraction.

In a carnival game, you must hit the shaded area on a target with a dart to win a prize. Assume that all of your darts hit the target randomly. What is the probability that you will hit the shaded area for each of the regions? Express your answer as a decimal rounded to the nearest hundredth.

4.

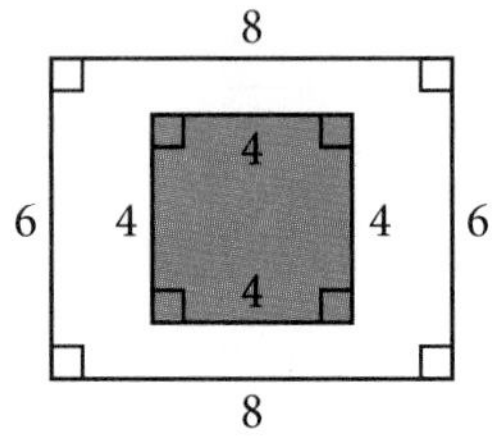

5.

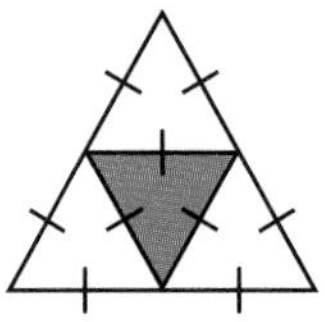

6.

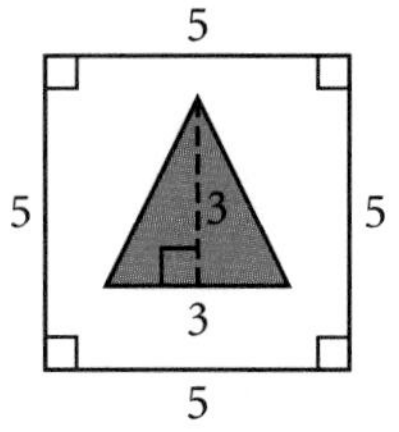

7.

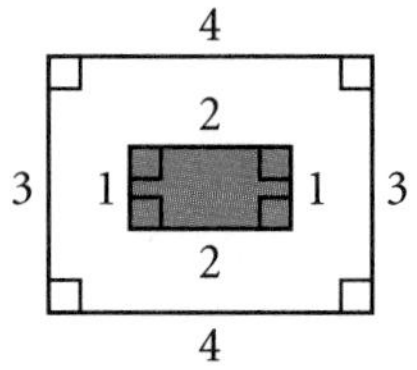

8. Which of the targets in Exercises 4–7 would you choose to throw at? Why?

9. Right on Target A skydiver is trying to land on the cross-shaped target. Assume that the diver is certain to land at a random point somewhere in the surrounding 10-m × 10-m square.

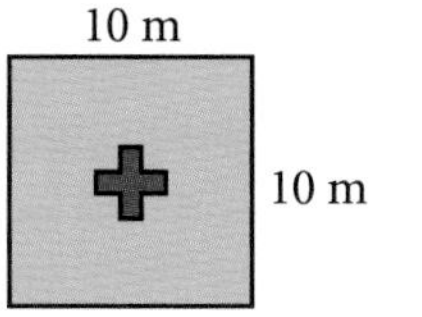

All edges of the target are 1 m long. All angles are right angles.

a. Find the probability that the diver will hit the target. Express your answer as a decimal rounded to the nearest hundredth.

b. If the skydiver is a professional who has made this jump hundreds of times, do you think his actual probability will be higher or lower than this? Explain your reasoning.

10. Lost Dogie A rancher realizes that a calf has been left behind in the round-up. She goes to look for the calf, which is somewhere in the fenced square area shown. She can only search the green area before sundown. What is the probability that she will find the calf before sundown? Express your answer as a fraction in lowest terms.

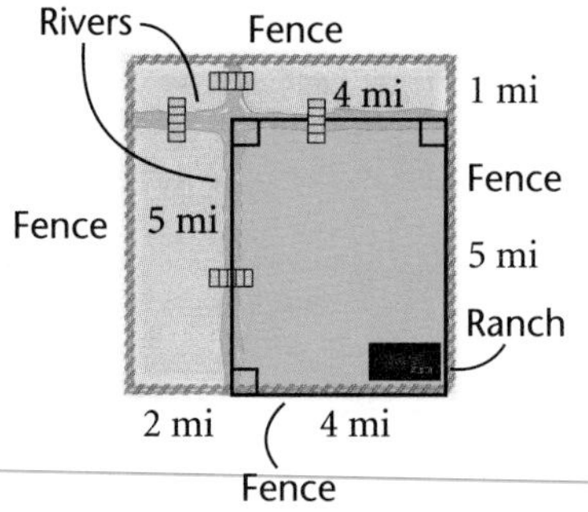

11. Water Bottle A child on a boat sealed a message inside a corked bottle and set it afloat in the center of Lake Michigan. The states around Lake Michigan and the approximate lengths of their shorelines are shown.

Social Science

Assume that the bottle lands randomly on the shoreline of Lake Michigan. What is the probability that it will land in each state? Express your answer as a decimal rounded to the nearest hundredth.

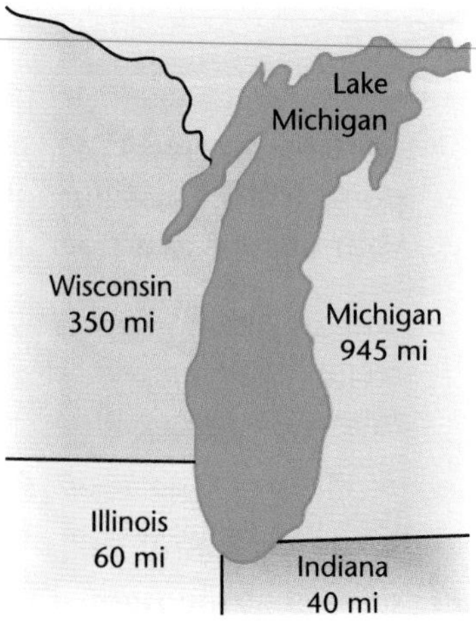

LOOK BACK

For each measure of $\angle 1$, find the measure of its complement and its supplement. [3-3]

12. $m\angle 1 = 21°$ **13.** $m\angle 1 = 84°$ **14.** $m\angle 1 = 33.5°$ **15.** $m\angle 1 = 48\frac{2}{3}°$

MORE PRACTICE

In a carnival game, you must toss a penny into the hole in a target to win a prize. Assuming that you toss the penny onto the target randomly, what is the probability that you will win a prize for each of the following targets? Express your answers in decimal form rounded to the nearest hundredth.

16.

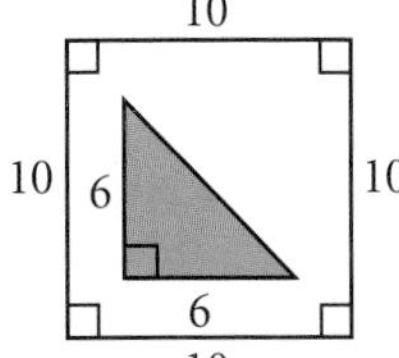

17.

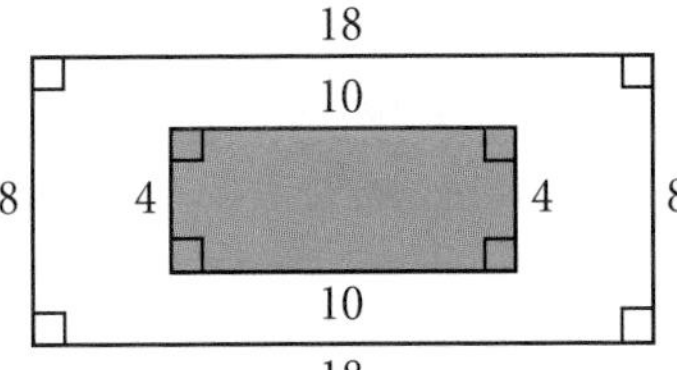

18.

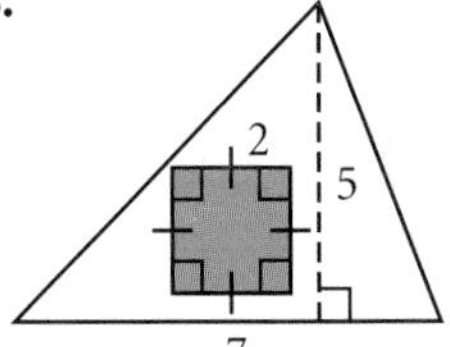

MORE MATH REASONING

19. Suppose you arrange seven tangram pieces into a perfect square as shown. If a fly lands on your tangram, what is the probability that it will land on each of the following pieces? (Hint: Trace and cut out the figure, or use an actual tangram to see the relationships of the various pieces.)

a. the parallelogram

b. the medium-sized triangle

c. one of the large triangles

d. Does it make a difference in your answers if you arrange your tangram pieces differently? Explain why the arrangement of the pieces does or does not make a difference.

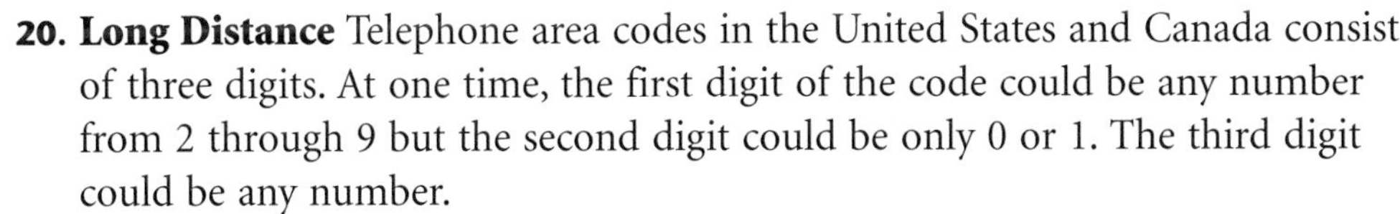

20. Long Distance Telephone area codes in the United States and Canada consist of three digits. At one time, the first digit of the code could be any number from 2 through 9 but the second digit could be only 0 or 1. The third digit could be any number.

If an area code was selected randomly from all of the possible codes, what was the probability of each of the following? Express your answers in decimal form rounded to the nearest hundredth.

a. the first digit of the area code is 3

b. the third digit is 4 or 5

c. the first two digits are 3–0

d. How many different area codes could be made using this system? Explain how you found your answer.

5-1 PART E Making Connections

← CONNECT → ***The areas and perimeters of simple geometric figures have important applications in everyday situations and in algebra. You've calculated areas and perimeters, and seen how areas are related to algebra, probability, and problem solving.***

In the following Explore, you will see how the ideas of area and geometric probability can be helpful in designing a carnival game of chance. You will also see how probability can be useful in making some related business decisions.

EXPLORE: CARNIVAL CALCULATIONS

In a carnival game, ping-pong balls are tossed onto a large, horizontal, square area. There are ten congruent triangular holes. A person who tosses a ball so that it falls into a hole wins a prize. (He does not win if the ball bounces into the target.)

1. If the ping-pong balls are thrown randomly, there should be a 20% probability of throwing a ball into a hole. Make a sketch of your design of the game. Include the dimensions of the figures in your sketch. Compare your design with those of your classmates.

2. Suppose you charge 50 cents to play your game (one toss). How much should the prizes be worth if you want to expect to break even at the end of the day? How much should the prizes be worth if you want to expect to have a profit at the end of the day? Why?

REFLECT

1. Explain how to find the probability of randomly hitting the shaded portion of a target.

2. Use sketches and words to show how the product of two binomials is connected to the idea of area.

3. What is the difference between yards and square yards? Explain when it is appropriate to use each unit.

Self-Assessment

Find the area of each figure.

1. 8

2.

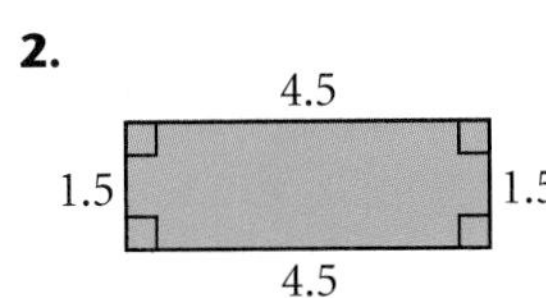

3.

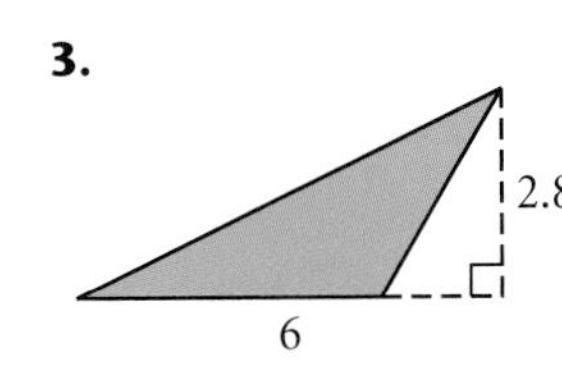

4.

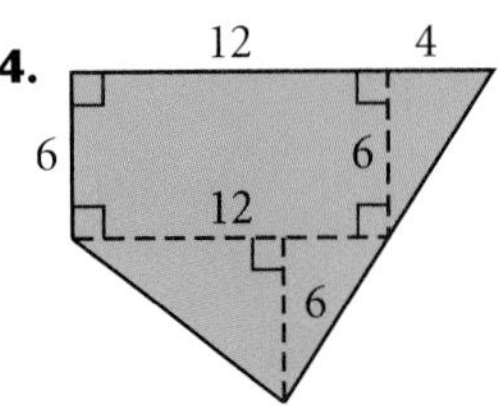

Find the perimeter of each figure.

5.

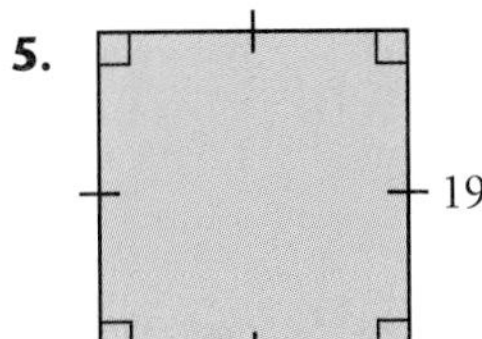

6.

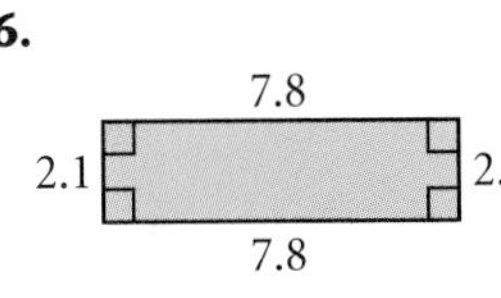

7.

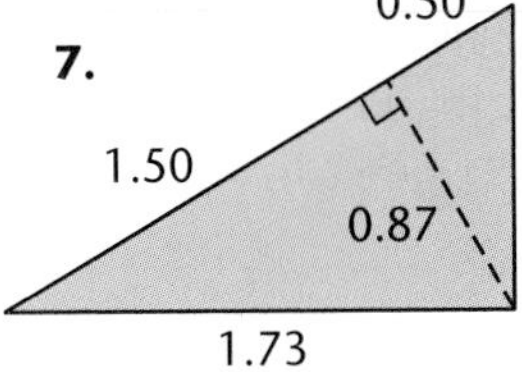

8.

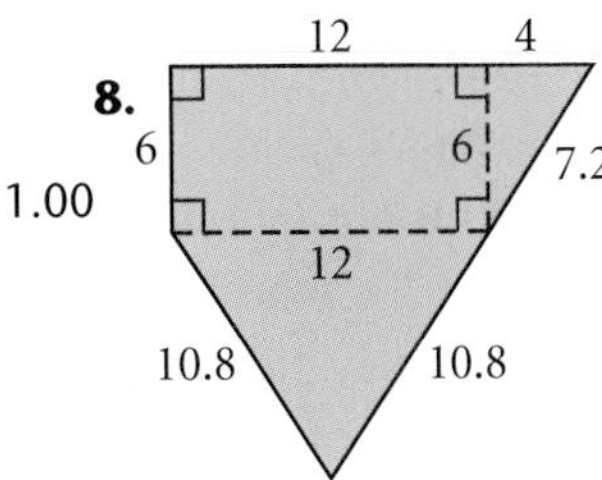

Use squares and rectangles for Exercises 9 and 10.

9. Multiply $(x + 2)$ and $(x + 3)$.

10. Factor $x^2 + 6x + 8$.

11. Solve $x^2 + 3x - 2 = 0$ using the quadratic formula.

12. Complete the following proof. [4-2]

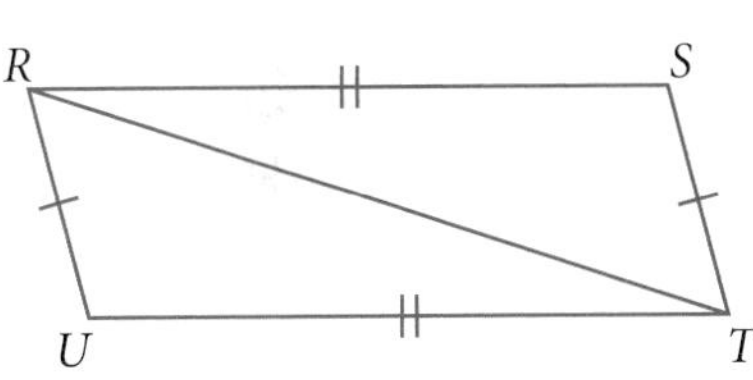

Given: $\overline{RU} \cong \overline{TS}$, $\overline{RS} \cong \overline{TU}$

Prove: $\overline{RS} \parallel \overline{TU}$

Proof:

Statement	**Reason**
1. $\overline{RU} \cong \overline{TS}$	**1.**
2. $\overline{RS} \cong \overline{TU}$	**2.**
3.	**3.** Reflexive Property
4.	**4.**
5. $\angle UTR \cong \angle SRT$	**5.**
6.	**6.**

Find the measures of all of the numbered angles for each measure of ∠1. [3-4]

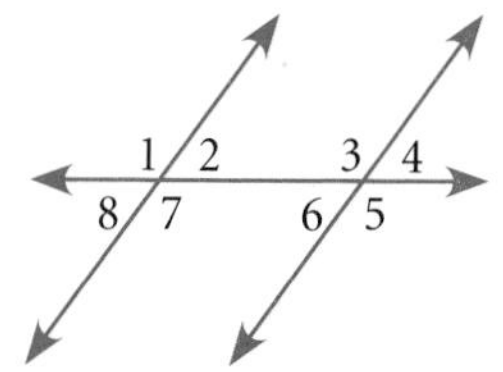

13. $m\angle 1 = 95°$

14. $m\angle 1 = 49°$

15. $m\angle 1 = 99.2°$

16. What is the probability of a randomly thrown dart hitting the triangular target on the rectangular background?

(a) $\frac{1}{2}$ (b) $\frac{1}{3}$ (c) $\frac{1}{4}$ (d) $\frac{1}{8}$ (e) $\frac{1}{10}$

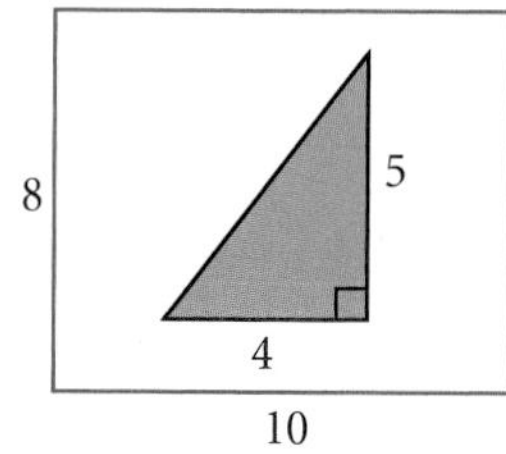

Social Science

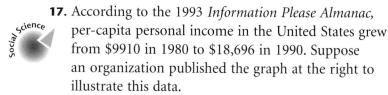

17. According to the 1993 *Information Please Almanac,* per-capita personal income in the United States grew from \$9910 in 1980 to \$18,696 in 1990. Suppose an organization published the graph at the right to illustrate this data.

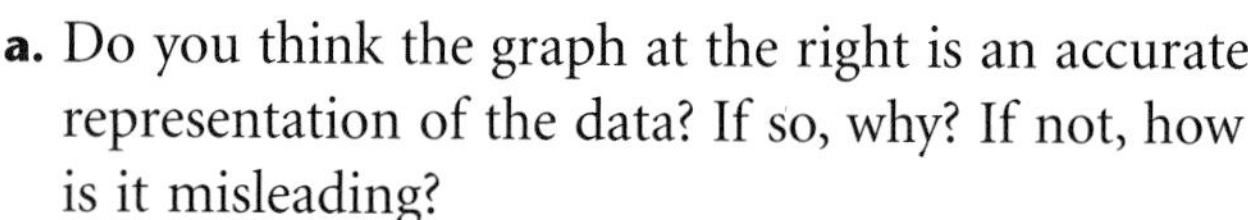

a. Do you think the graph at the right is an accurate representation of the data? If so, why? If not, how is it misleading?

b. Explain how this graph was made. If you feel the graph is misleading, explain how it should be drawn to represent the data accurately.

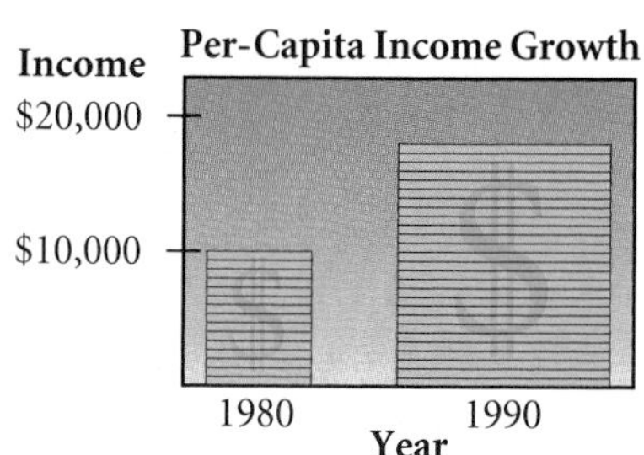

18. Free Game! At the end of a miniature golf game, you hit your golf ball up a ramp and into an 8-ft square target. If you hit the rectangular target, you win one free game. If you hit the triangular target, you win two free games. Assuming that the golf ball hits the target randomly and that the size of the ball doesn't affect the outcome, find each probability. Express your answers in decimal form rounded to the nearest hundredth.

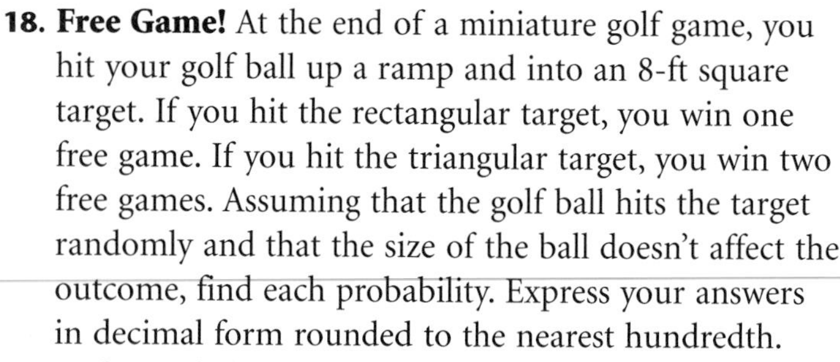

a. the probability that you win one free game

b. the probability that you win two free games

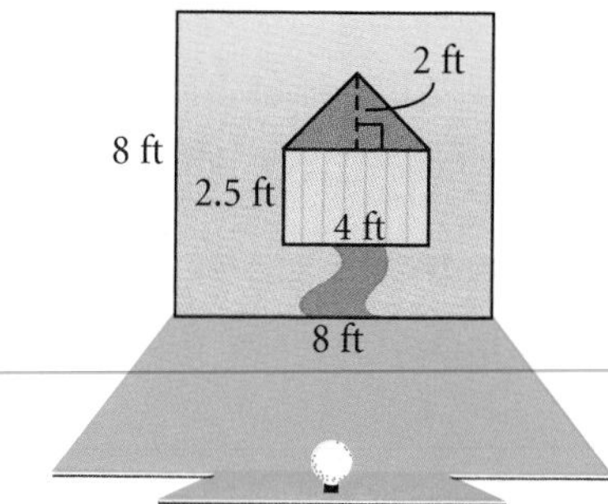

19. Mathematical Darts At a convention of Math Lovers Unite!, Keisha set up a carnival game. She used squares and rectangles to represent $(x + 5)(x + 4)$. A contestant who threw a dart and hit one of the x-sized rectangles won a prize. This was an interesting game, because the probability of winning depended on the value of x. Find the probability of winning in terms of x. Write a brief explanation of the method you used to solve the problem.

5-2 Derivations of Area Formulas

AZTEC AREA

Tenochtitlán, on the site of present-day Mexico City, was the capital of the Aztec civilization. This spectacular city featured huge pyramids and magnificent palaces. Two aqueducts brought in fresh water, and three drawbridges connected the island city to the mainland. In the 1400s, the population of Tenochtitlán may have been as large as 300,000—greater than that of any European city at the time.

This civilization had many "modern" features. For example, Aztec landowners paid property taxes. These taxes were based on records that gave the property's boundaries, area, and market value. Aztec farms usually had irregular shapes. Although these areas were not simple to calculate, Aztec measurements were very accurate.

In the Aztec civilization, length was measured in *quahuitls*, which were about 2.5 m long. Area was measured in square *quahuitls*. Aztec officials measured and recorded the dimensions of the property and may have sketched small scale drawings.

A recent comparison of Aztec land records to those made later by the Spanish showed that the Aztec records were more accurate. One reason for this might have been the Aztec expertise in planning cities and building pyramids—tasks that require very precise measurements.

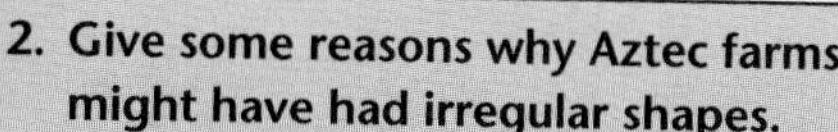

1. Why does it make sense for the property tax on a farm to be based on its area, not its perimeter?
2. Give some reasons why Aztec farms might have had irregular shapes.
3. Why might the Aztecs have needed precise measurements to build their pyramids?

5-2 PART A Assumptions About Area

← CONNECT →

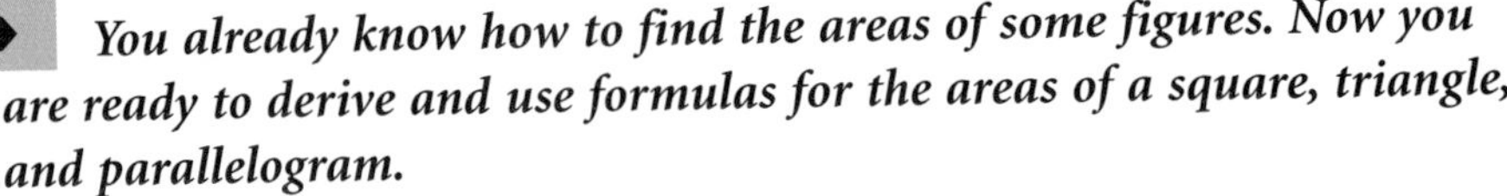

You already know how to find the areas of some figures. Now you are ready to derive and use formulas for the areas of a square, triangle, and parallelogram.

The photo at the left shows the present-day site of an Aztec ruin. You will see how the Aztecs may have used area formulas and will see how we can incorporate these formulas into our deductive system.

The figures below are familiar, but we need to give some formal definitions before looking at their areas.

DEFINITIONS

A **quadrilateral** is a polygon with four sides.

A **parallelogram** is a quadrilateral with two pairs of parallel sides.

A **rectangle** is a quadrilateral with four right angles.

A **square** is a quadrilateral with four right angles and four congruent sides.

You may know that squares and rectangles are parallelograms. The opposite sides of all parallelograms (including squares and rectangles) are congruent. You will justify properties of parallelograms deductively in Chapter 6.

The idea that the area of a rectangle is its length times its width makes sense when you see a rectangle on a grid.

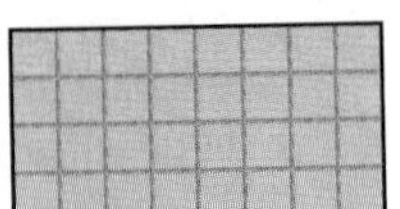

8 units × 4 units = 32 square units

When you accept the area result for a rectangle ($A = \ell w$), you can use it to find the areas of other figures. The "area suitcase" will fill up as you discover how to calculate the areas of more figures. Once you have derived a formula, you can use it to develop others. (Remember our deductive system!)

1. **Assuming that the area of a rectangle is ℓw, what is the area of a square of side s? Justify your answer.**
2. **Do you think that the area formula for a rectangle is a postulate or a theorem? What about your result for a square? Explain.**

In the following Explore, you will discover how to find the areas of a parallelogram and a triangle.

EXPLORE: IN THE AREA

MATERIALS

Paper, Scissors

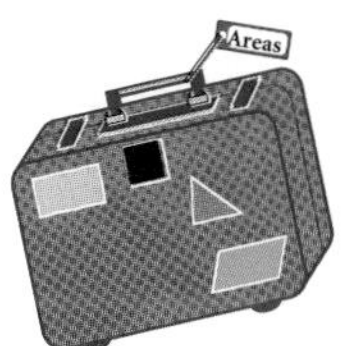

1. Cut out a paper parallelogram, and label a base and height as shown on the left below. By cutting and rearranging pieces, use the area formula for a rectangle to help find the area formula for a parallelogram in terms of the length of the base and the height. Give an illustrated explanation of your result.

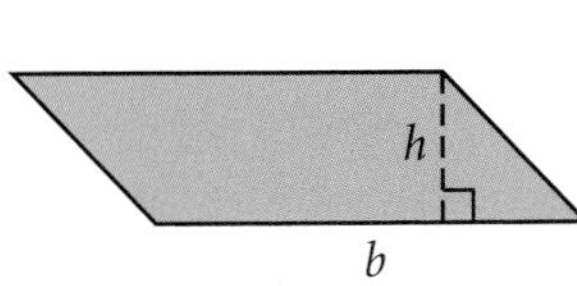

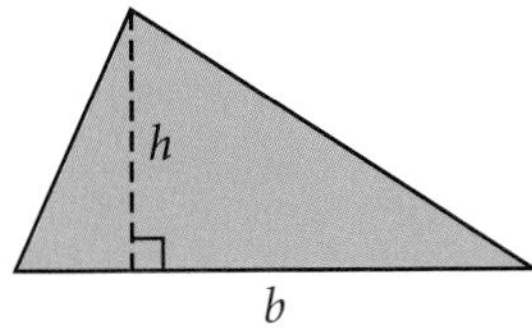

2. Now show why the area formula for a triangle works. Cut out or sketch a triangle as shown on the right above. Then look for a way to apply the area formula for a parallelogram or rectangle, so that you can find the triangle's area formula in terms of the length of the base and the height. Be creative!

TRY IT

Find the area of each figure.

a. (square with sides 7 and 7)

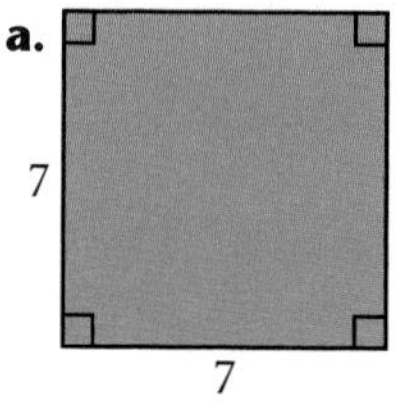

b.

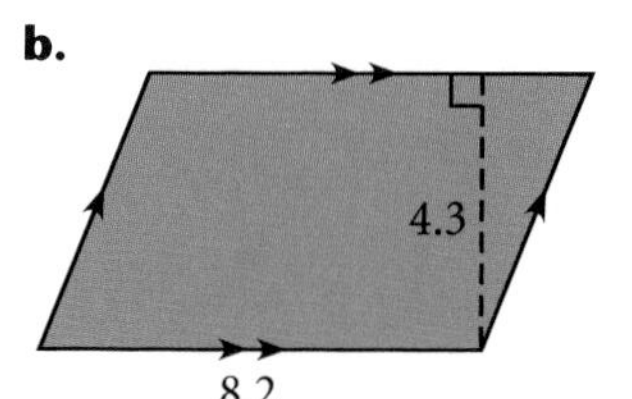

c.

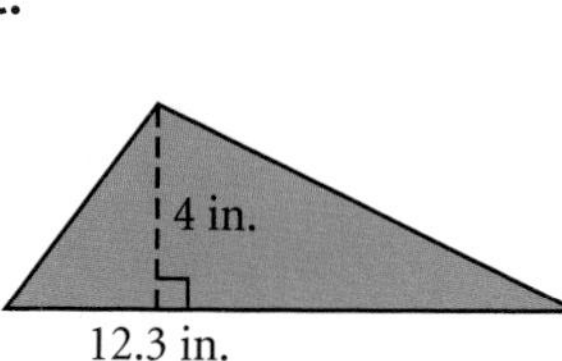

The area results that you investigated in the preceding Explore are summarized in the following list.

POSTULATE

The area of a rectangle is the product of its length (ℓ) and width (w).

$A = \ell w$

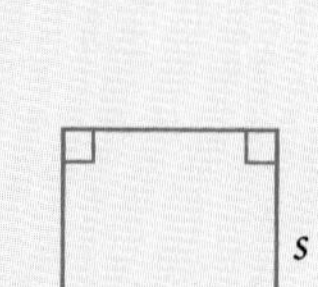

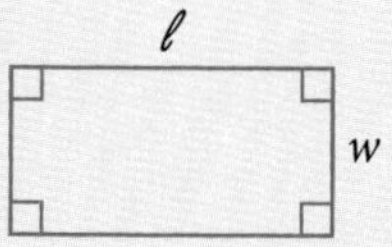

THEOREMS

The area of a square is the square of its side length (s).

$A = s^2$

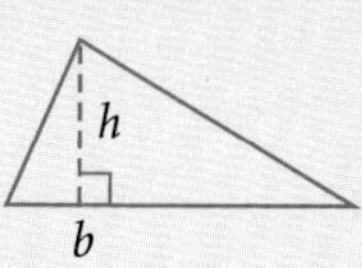

The area of a triangle is half the product of its base length (b) and corresponding height (h).

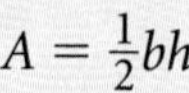

$A = \frac{1}{2}bh$

The area of a parallelogram is the product of its base length (b) and height (h).

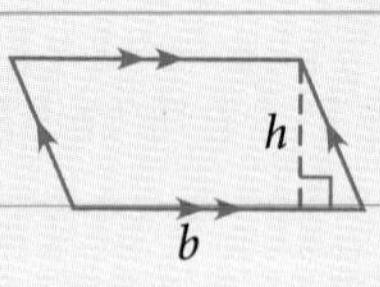

$A = bh$

REFLECT

1. Describe a way to justify that the area of a triangle is $\frac{1}{2}bh$ by using the following.

a. the area formula for a rectangle

b. the area formula for a parallelogram

2. State the information necessary to find the area of each figure.

a. a square **b.** a rectangle **c.** a triangle

Exercises

CORE

Getting Started Find the area of each figure.

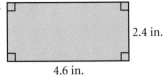

1. 2.4 in. 4.6 in.

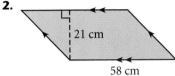

2. 21 cm 58 cm

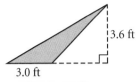

3. 3.6 ft 3.0 ft

Suppose the figures shown represent irregularly shaped Aztec farms. Find the area of each farm.

4.

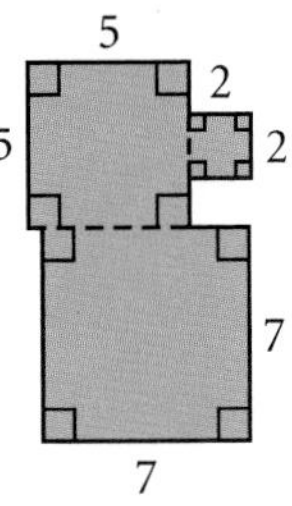

5.

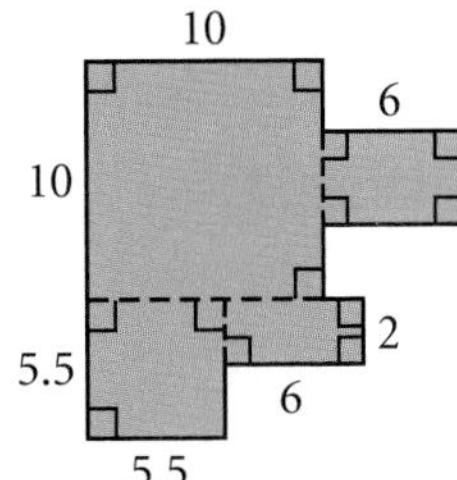

6.

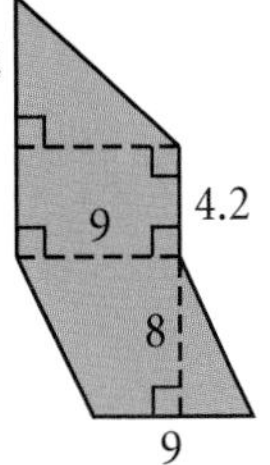

Find each of the following.

7. the area of a right triangle with legs of length 1.8 m and 3.2 m

8. the base length of a parallelogram with $A = 5.4$ in.^{2} and $h = 1.5$ in.

9. the length of a side of a square with $A = 2.89$ cm^2

10. Poetry Reading In an early reading of his poem, *The Thorn,* William Wordsworth (1770–1850) included these lines about a pond.

Literature

I've measured it from side to side:
'Tis three feet long, and two feet wide.

If the pond's surface is rectangular, what is its area?

From each group of terms, choose the term that does not belong, and explain why. Can you think of more than one possible answer?

11. quadrilateral, parallelogram, rectangle, square

12. right triangle, obtuse triangle, rectangle, square

13. If a quart of varnish covers 125 ft^2, how many quarts must you buy to apply two coats to a rectangular floor that is 12 ft by 14 ft? Explain.

Problem-Solving Tip

Check to see if your answer makes sense.

14. The photo at the right shows an Aztec bowl. Aztec agriculture supported a population of 1,000,000 to 1,500,000 people at a population density of 500 people/mi^2. Find minimum and maximum values for the area these people lived in.

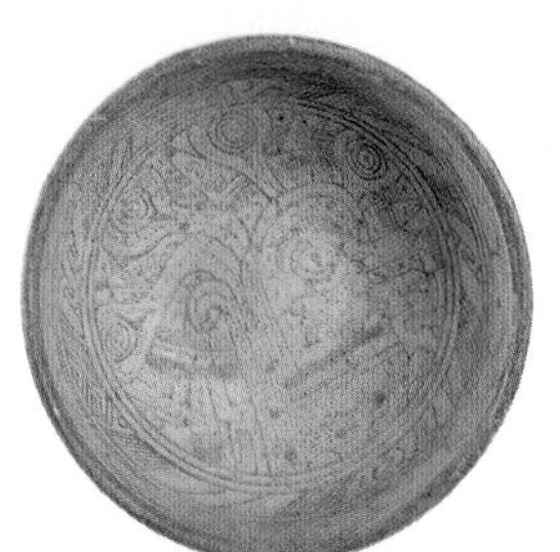

What is the probability that a randomly chosen point in each figure will lie in the shaded region? Express your answers as decimals rounded to the nearest hundredth.

15.

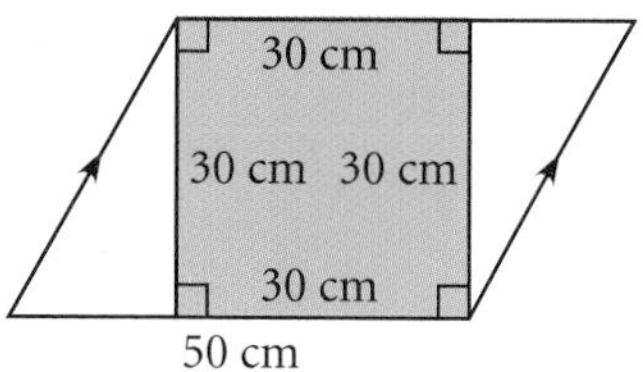

16.

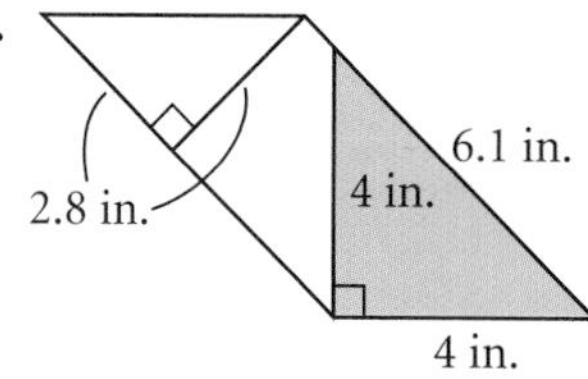

17.

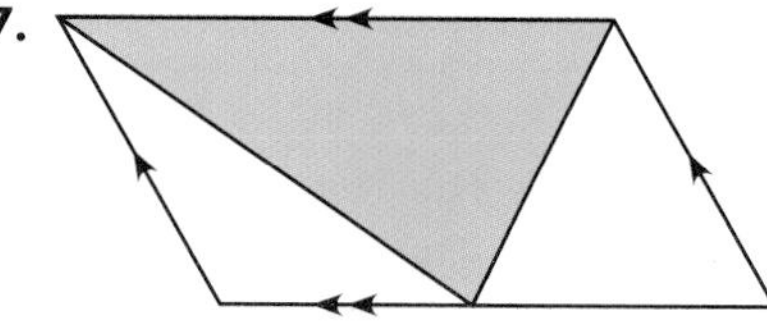

18. Skylight The glass ceiling of a building has metal supports that divide it into parallelogram-shaped regions. What is the area of each of the regions?

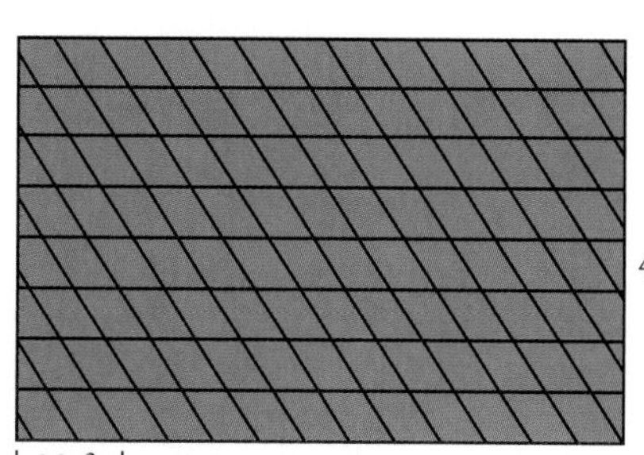

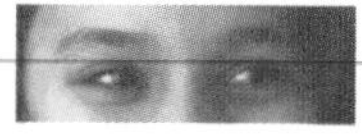

LOOK BACK

19. Fill in the missing reasons to complete this paragraph proof.

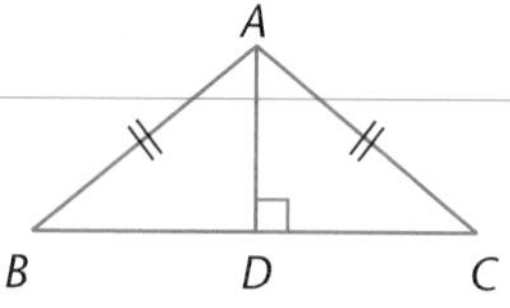

Given: $\overline{AB} \cong \overline{AC}$ and $\overline{AD} \perp \overline{BC}$

Prove: D is the midpoint of $\overline{BC}$

Proof: It is given that $\overline{AB} \cong \overline{AC}$ and $\overline{AD} \perp \overline{BC}$. $\angle ADB$ and $\angle ADC$ are right angles because **a.** ______, so $\triangle ADB$ and $\triangle ADC$ are right triangles by **b.** ______. $\triangle ADB \cong \triangle ADC$ by **c.** ______. $\overline{BD} \cong \overline{CD}$ by **d.** ______, so D is the midpoint of $\overline{BC}$ by **e.** ______.

Factor each trinomial, using squares and rectangles. Provide a sketch, and give an algebraic answer. [5-1]

20. $x^2 + 5x + 6$

21. $x^2 + 7x + 10$

22. $x^2 + 6x + 8$

MORE PRACTICE

Find the area of each figure.

23.

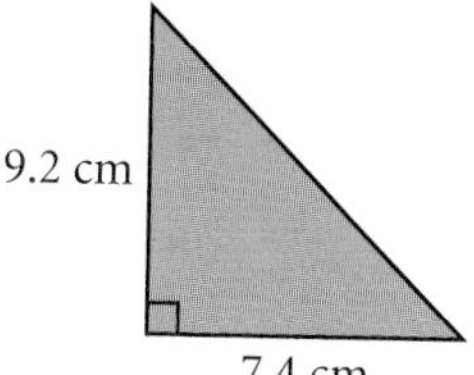

24.

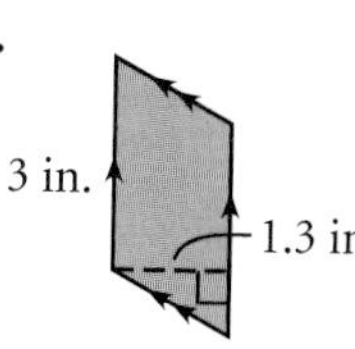

25.

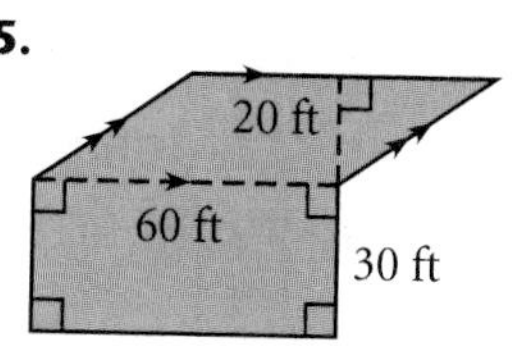

26.

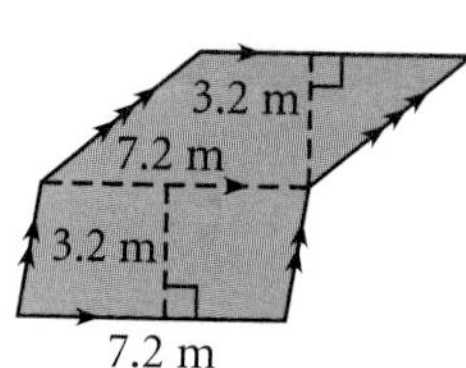

Find each of the following.

27. the height of a parallelogram whose area is 62 cm^2 and whose base length is 11.2 cm

28. the length of a side of a square whose area is 84.64 ft^2

29. the height of a triangle whose base length is 4 in. and whose area is 23 $in.^2$

30. the base length of a parallelogram whose area is 48 m^2 and whose height is half its base length

MORE MATH REASONING

31. Some of the earliest human artists traced their hands with paint on cave walls. The photograph at the right shows aboriginal art from a cave in Australia.

Trace your hand on graph paper and estimate its area.

32. Pick's Theorem Use a geoboard or dot paper and the following steps to discover Pick's Theorem.

a. Draw three different triangles and three different rectangles on a geoboard or dot paper. (Vertices should be at grid points.)

b. Find *X*, the number of grid points inside each figure.

c. Find *Y*, the number of grid points on the perimeter of each figure.

d. Make a table to record your results. Label the columns of your table *X*, *Y*, $\frac{1}{2}X$, $\frac{1}{2}Y$, and Area of Polygon.

e. Use area formulas to calculate the areas of the polygons, and record the results of your calculations.

f. Use your table to discover a formula to calculate areas of figures on a grid. (Hint: The sum of the values from two of the columns will get you very close!) This formula is known as Pick's Theorem.

5-2 PART B Planning a Proof

← CONNECT → ***You already know several area formulas. Now you will learn how to find the areas of trapezoids and rhombuses. You will also begin to write your own plans for deductive proofs.***

The definitions of two important types of quadrilaterals are given below.

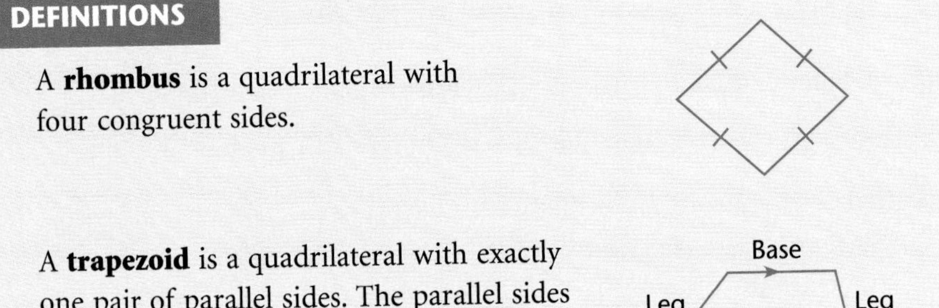

DEFINITIONS

A **rhombus** is a quadrilateral with four congruent sides.

A **trapezoid** is a quadrilateral with exactly one pair of parallel sides. The parallel sides are the *bases* of the trapezoid, and the nonparallel sides are its *legs*.

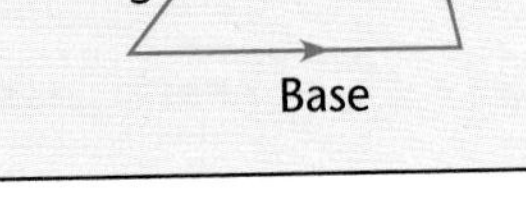

Like rectangles and squares, all rhombuses are parallelograms.

TRY IT

Classify each quadrilateral as a square, rectangle, rhombus, parallelogram, or trapezoid. Some figures may be classified in more than one way.

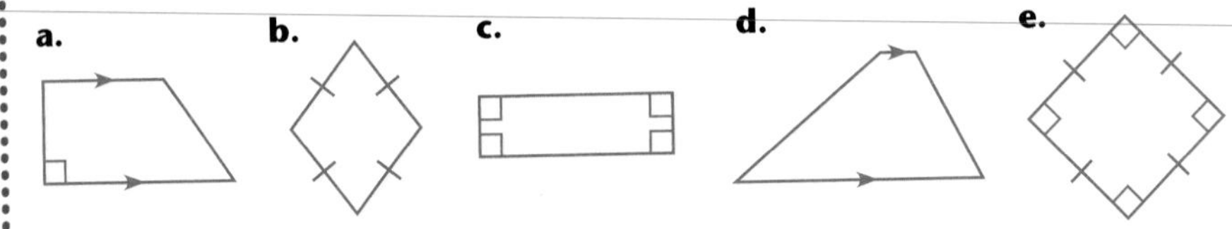

Making a *plan* is the fourth step in our five-step process for deductive proof. In the *plan* illustrated in the following example, notice the importance of adding an auxiliary line to the figure.

EXAMPLE

Write a *plan* for proving that all rhombuses are parallelograms.

Rewrite: If a quadrilateral is a rhombus, then it is a parallelogram.

Draw:

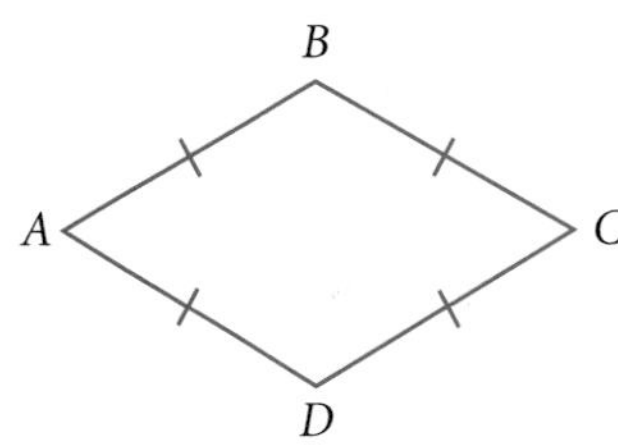

State: *Given:* Quadrilateral $ABCD$ is a rhombus.

Prove: $ABCD$ is a parallelogram.

Plan: To show that the rhombus is a parallelogram, we must show that $\overline{AB} \parallel \overline{CD}$ and $\overline{AD} \parallel \overline{BC}$. Adding diagonal $\overline{AC}$ provides a transversal to help prove lines parallel.

B

A C

D

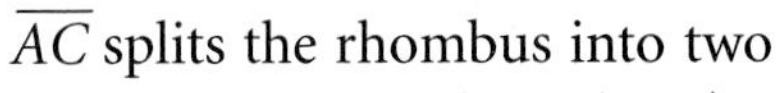

$\overline{AC}$ splits the rhombus into two triangles. We can show that $\triangle ABC \cong \triangle CDA$ by SSS.

$\angle BAC \cong \angle DCA$, and $\overline{AB} \parallel \overline{CD}$ since alternate interior angles are congruent. Also, $\angle BCA \cong \angle DAC$, so $\overline{AD} \parallel \overline{BC}$, and $ABCD$ is a parallelogram.

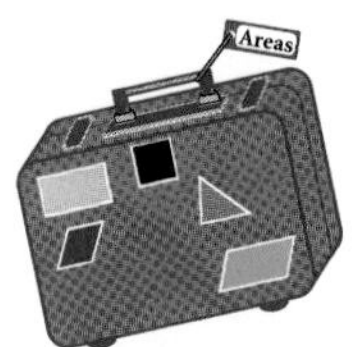

Since every rhombus is a parallelogram, you can find the area of a rhombus by using $A = bh$.

In the following Explore, you'll see how to calculate the area of a trapezoid. You will also write a *plan* to justify your result.

EXPLORE: FROM TRIANGLES TO TRAPEZOIDS

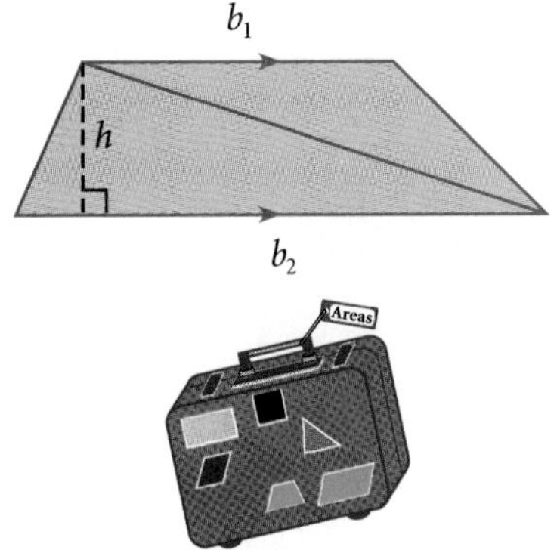

1. The area of a trapezoid with base lengths b_1 and b_2 and height h can be found by using what you have learned about the area of a triangle. Use the figure at the right to help find the formula for the area of a trapezoid.

2. Write a *plan* describing how you might prove your result from Step 1. Compare your *plan* with those developed by your classmates.

TRY IT

Find the area of each trapezoid.

f.

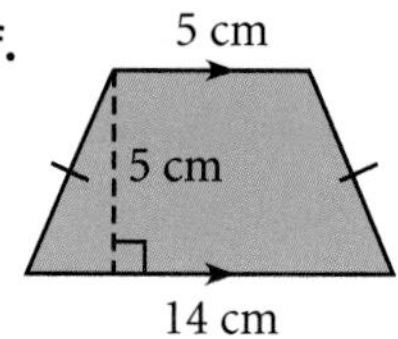

g.

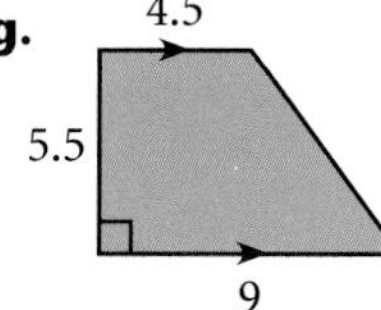

h.

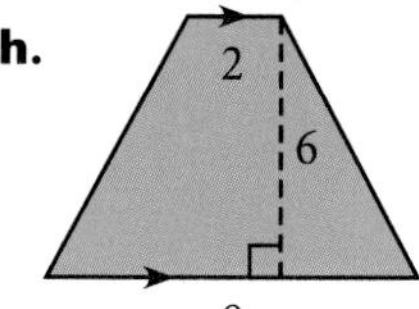

THEOREM

The area of a trapezoid is the product of half the sum of the bases (b_1 and b_2) and the height (h). $A = \frac{b_1 + b_2}{2}h$

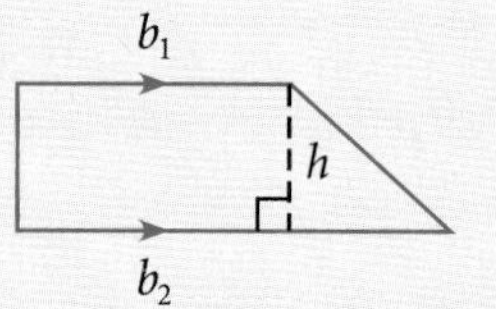

REFLECT

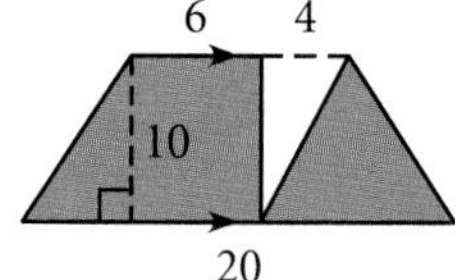

1. Can a trapezoid be a parallelogram? Explain.

2. How might the *rewrite, draw,* and *state* steps be helpful in planning a proof?

3. Write a *plan* for finding the area of the shaded region. Then calculate the area.

Exercises

CORE

Getting Started **Find the area of each figure.**

1.

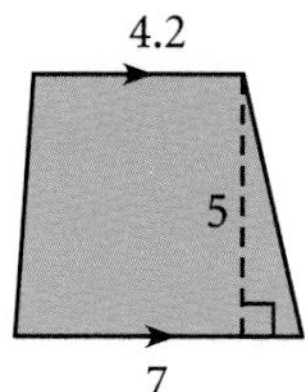

2.

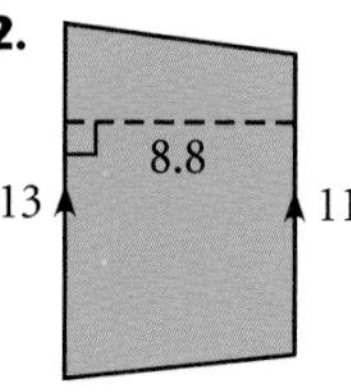

3.

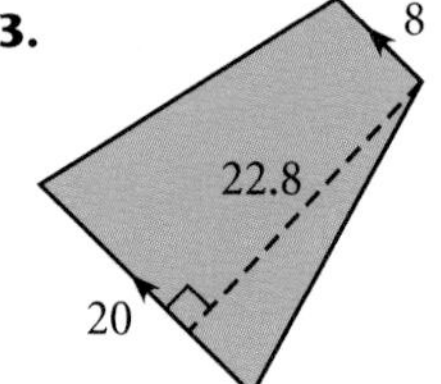

4.

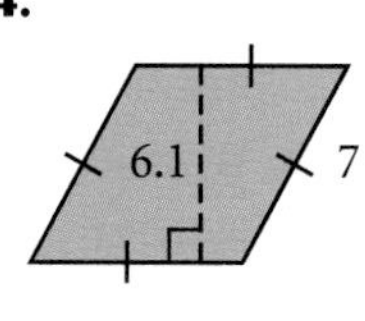

Find the area of each trapezoid.

5. base lengths = 10 in. and 12 in., height = 5 in.

6. base lengths = 6 ft and 10 ft, height = 7 ft

7. The area of a trapezoid is 84 square units. The length of one base is 8 units, and the length of the other base is 16 units. Find the height of the trapezoid.

8. The area of a trapezoid is 45 square units. The height is 5 units, and one of the bases is 8 units. Find the length of the other base.

Write the word or phrase that correctly completes each statement.

9. A ___ is a quadrilateral with four congruent sides.

10. If exactly two sides of a quadrilateral are parallel, then the quadrilateral is a ___.

11. Find two pairs of triangles that have equal areas in the figure at right. For each pair, *plan* a proof to show that their areas are equal.

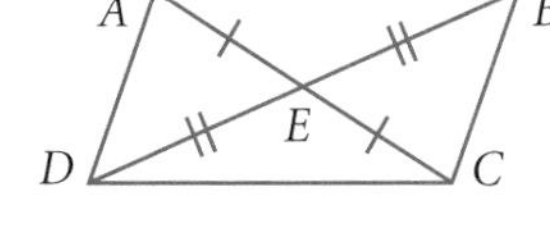

12. **Go Measure a Kite** A **kite** is a quadrilateral with two distinct pairs of adjacent, congruent sides. What is the area of a kite with diagonals of lengths a and b? *Plan* a logical argument to justify your area formula.

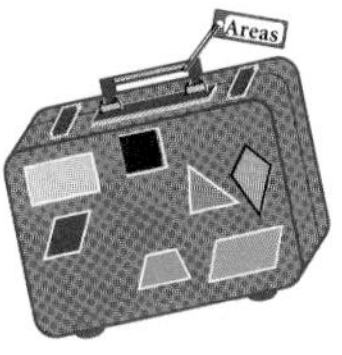

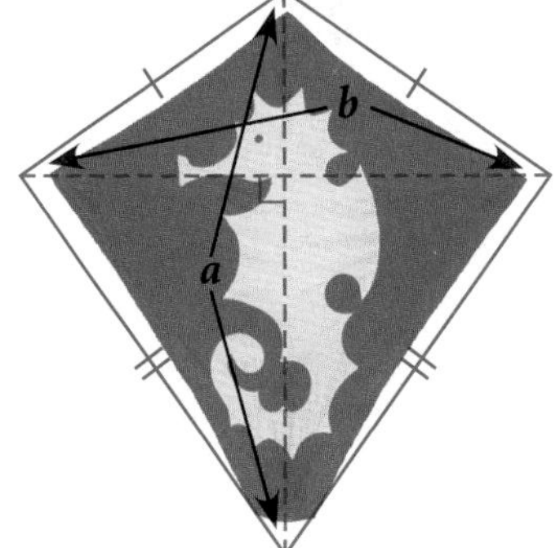

13. **Heron's Formula** Heron was a first-century Greek mathematician who discovered a formula for the area of a triangle by using only the lengths of its three sides. The area of any triangle with side lengths a, b, and c, is

$$A = \sqrt{s(s - a)(s - b)(s - c)}$$

where s is the semiperimeter (half the perimeter) of the triangle.

A surveyor needs to measure the area of the plot of land at the right.

a. Find the area of the plot of land by using Heron's Formula.

b. Why might it be good to have two different ways to find the area of a triangle? (Hint: Suppose the surveyor can only measure lengths by using ropes.)

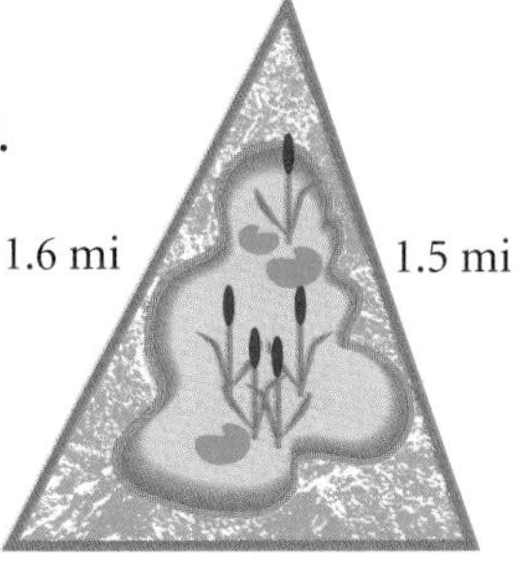

14. *Plan* a logical argument to show that congruent triangles have equal areas.

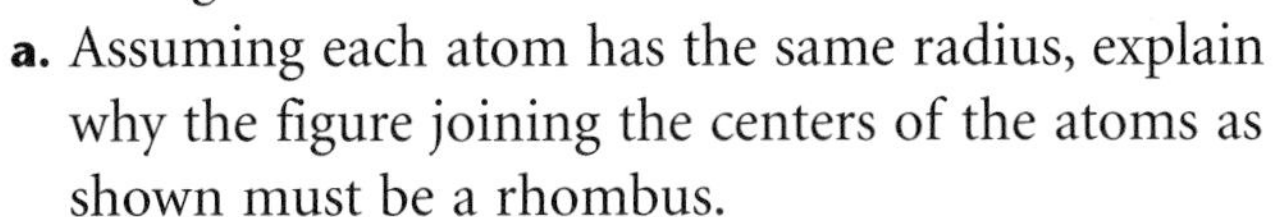

15. **Metallic Rhombuses** When bonded in metallic form, magnesium atoms form close-packed planes of atoms, as shown. The radius of a magnesium atom is 1.6×10^{-7} mm.

a. Assuming each atom has the same radius, explain why the figure joining the centers of the atoms as shown must be a rhombus.

b. Using the value of h given, find the area of the rhombus.

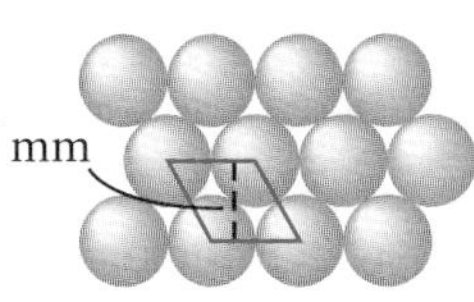

LOOK AHEAD

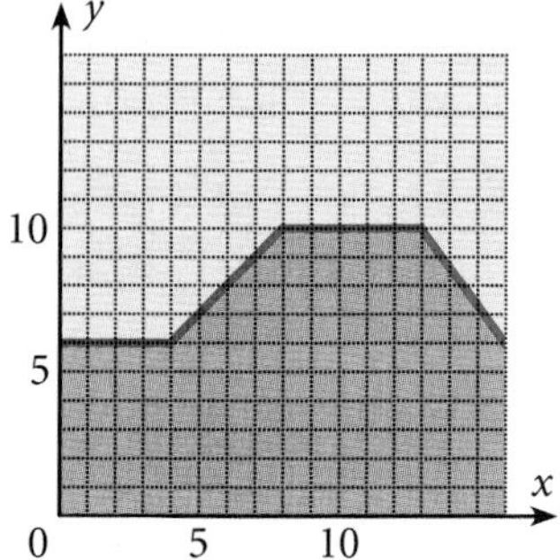

16. Find the area of the shaded region at the right. Explain your method.

MORE PRACTICE

Find the area of each figure.

17.

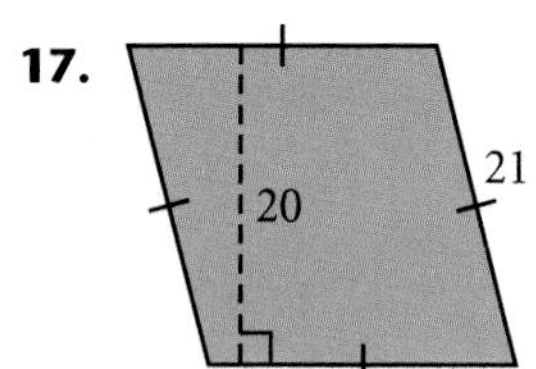

18.

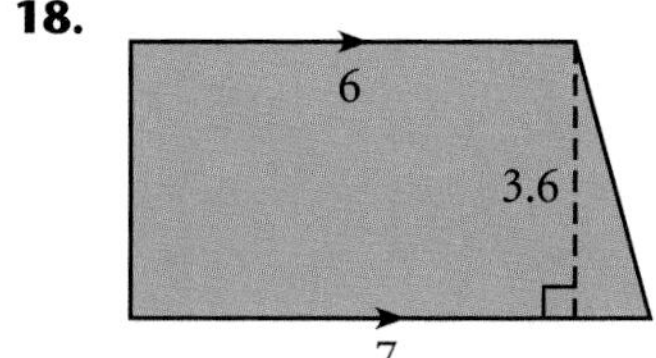

19.

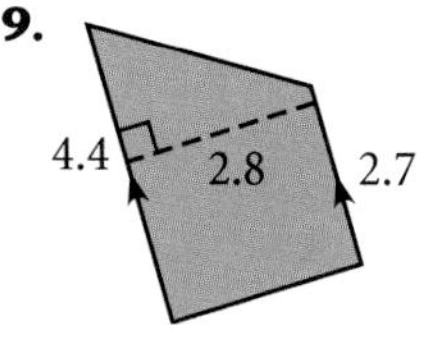

Find the area of each trapezoid.

20. base lengths = 6 in. and 8 in., height = 4 in.

21. base lengths = 11 m and 16 m, height = 5 m

22. base lengths = 5.4 cm and 8.8 cm, height = 12.1 cm

23. The area of a trapezoid is 25 m^2. The height is 4 m, and one of the base lengths is 3 m. Find the length of the other base.

MORE MATH REASONING

24. Darrell says, "The area of a trapezoid is equal to the average of its base lengths times its height." Is he correct? Why?

25. Algebra Trapezoid The area of a trapezoid is 66 square units. The length of its longer base is 4 units longer than the length of its shorter base, and its height is 7 units longer than the length of its shorter base. Find the length of each base and the height of the trapezoid.

26. A quadrilateral is divided into four triangles as shown. For each type of quadrilateral, which of the four triangles, if any, must be of equal area? Give a convincing argument in each case.

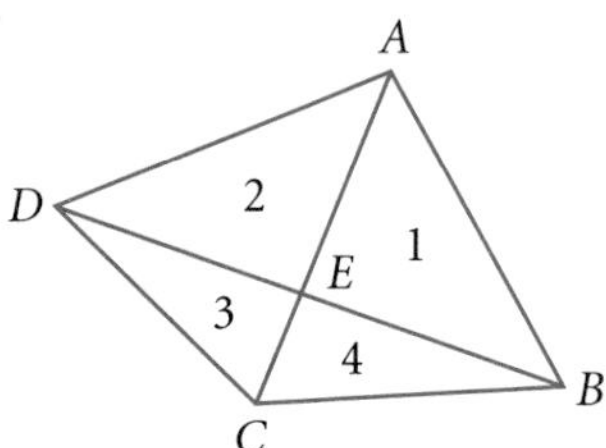

a. square
b. parallelogram
c. trapezoid

5-2 PART C The Area Under a Curve

← CONNECT → ***Scientists and engineers often need to calculate the areas of figures with irregular or curved surfaces. Now that you know how to find the areas of many geometric figures, you will expand your study of area to more complex figures.***

Finding the area under a curve is important in higher mathematics, and the technique has many practical applications. For example, the amount of glass needed for the front of the supermarket shown is approximately equal to the area under the curved roof.

The shaded regions below show the areas between the curve and the x-axis for graphs that are related to two useful mathematical equations.

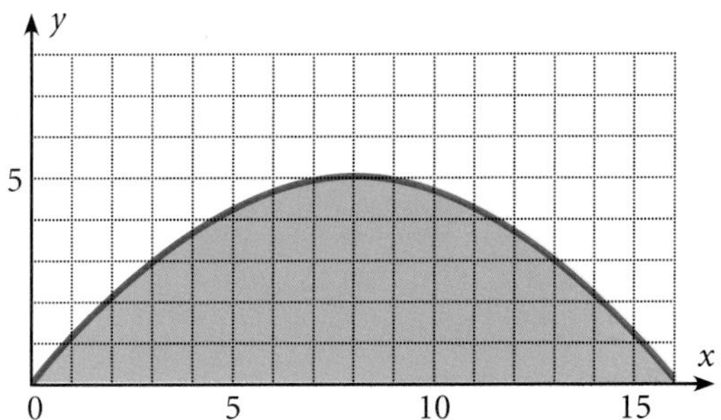

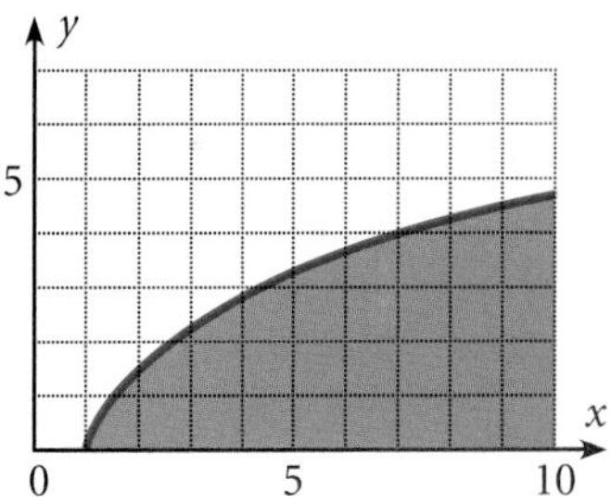

1. Using what you already know, how could you find an approximation for the area of the shaded regions above?

In the following Explore, you will find a way to approximate the area under $y = x^2$ between $x = 0$ and $x = 6$. You will also begin to look for ways to generalize your method.

EXPLORE: THE AREA UNDERNEATH

MATERIALS

Graph paper

1. Draw the graph of $y = x^2$ on a sheet of graph paper. Start at $x = 0$, and end at $x = 6$. Draw a vertical line down to the x-axis from your last point. Lightly shade the region under the curve.
2. Devise a method for finding the approximate area under this curve. Write an explanation of your method, and give your approximation for the area.
3. If you needed to use your method to find a more accurate answer, could you do it? How?
4. Compare your approximation and your method with classmates. Discuss whether some methods are more efficient or accurate than others. Which method would you use to find the area under this curve from $x = 0$ to $x = 60$? Explain your choice.

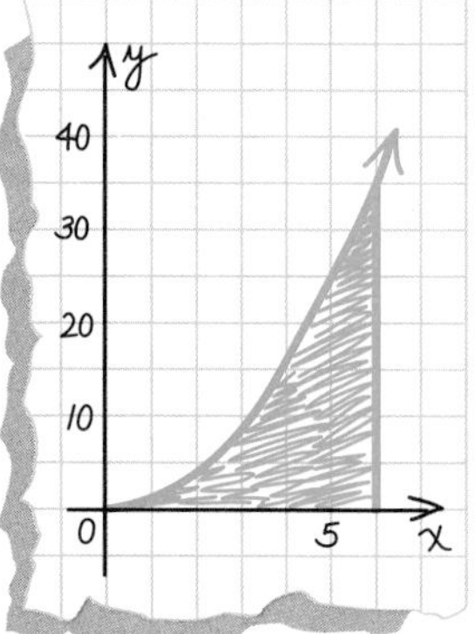

Although many methods give good approximations for the area under a curve, mathematicians have a method that is especially powerful.

To use this method, we pretend the region is a polygon and then break it down into pieces we can deal with. The pieces we'll use are trapezoids with vertical bases and equal heights along the x-axis.

The slanted line of the trapezoid follows the curve as well as it can, but doesn't exactly match it, so our answer is only an approximation.

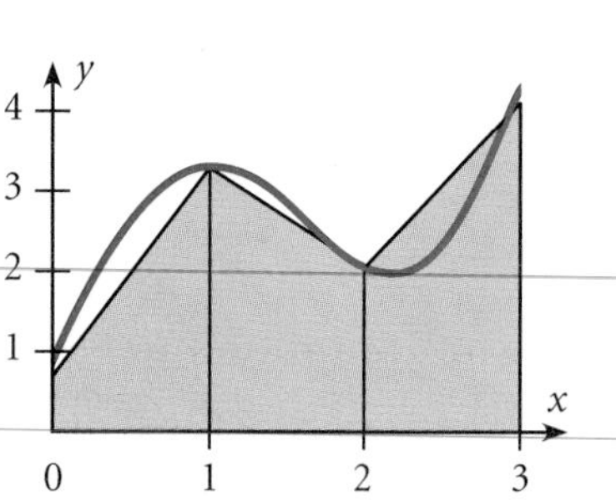

EXAMPLE

Find the approximate area between the positive x-axis and the graph of $y = 2\sqrt{x}$ from $x = 0$ to $x = 3$.

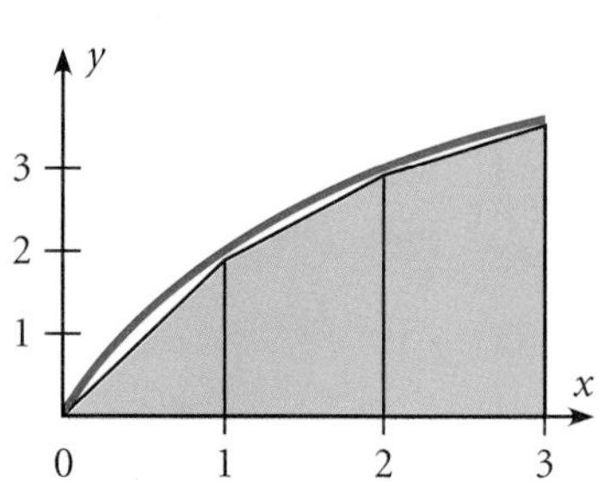

- Sketch a graph of the curve (see page 358).
- Choose a convenient height for the trapezoids. In this example, we will choose 1 unit. Remember that these trapezoids have their heights along the x-axis.
- Find the two bases of each trapezoid by substituting the x-values at the two ends of the trapezoid into the equation $y = 2\sqrt{x}$. The y-values give the bases of the trapezoids. Results are shown in the table.

First trapezoid	$x = 0$ $x = 1$	$y = 2\sqrt{0} = 0$ (left base) $y = 2\sqrt{1} = 2$ (right base)
Second trapezoid	$x = 1$ $x = 2$	$y = 2\sqrt{1} = 2$ (left base) $y = 2\sqrt{2} \approx 2.8$ (right base)
Third trapezoid	$x = 2$ $x = 3$	$y = 2\sqrt{2} \approx 2.8$ (left base) $y = 2\sqrt{3} \approx 3.5$ (right base)

- Now calculate the areas of the trapezoids, and add them.

Area under the curve $\approx \frac{0+2}{2}(1) + \frac{2+2.8}{2}(1) + \frac{2.8+3.5}{2}(1) =$

$1 + 2.4 + 3.15 = 6.55$

2. How could you use the trapezoid method to get a better estimate for the area under the curve in the example?

REFLECT

1. Could you choose a geometric figure other than a trapezoid to find the approximate area under a curve? If so, which figure? What are the advantages and disadvantages of using this figure?
2. Describe how you could find the area between the two curves shown in the figure at the right.

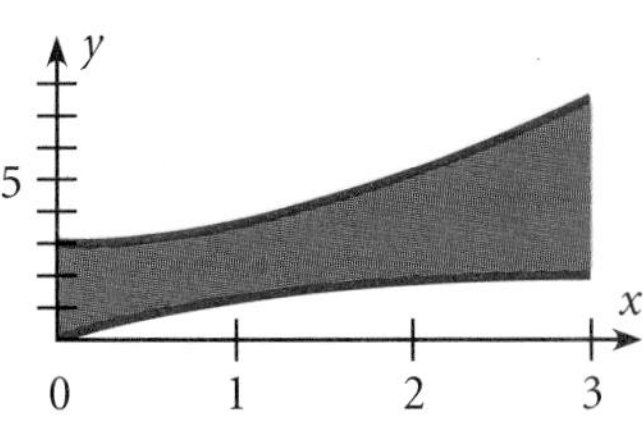

Exercises

CORE

1. **Getting Started** Follow these steps to find the approximate area between the positive x-axis and the graph of $y = \frac{1}{2}x^2$ from 0 to 4.
   - **a.** Make a table of ordered pairs, using the x-values 0, 1, 2, 3, and 4.
   - **b.** Use the table to sketch the graph on graph paper.
   - **c.** Divide the graph into trapezoids of height 1.
   - **d.** Find the lengths of the left and right bases for each trapezoid. (Hint: You should already have calculated these!)
   - **e.** Calculate the area of each trapezoid.
   - **f.** Find the approximate total area by finding the sum of the areas of the trapezoids.

2. Repeat Exercise 1, but now approximate the area between the positive x-axis and the graph of $y = \frac{1}{2}x^2$ from 0 to 4 by using trapezoids of height 2. Which approximation do you think is closer to the actual area? Explain why you feel this method is more accurate.

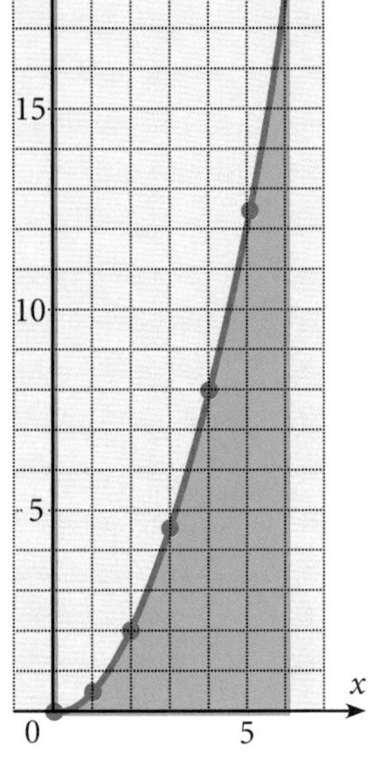

3. **a.** Find the approximate area of the shaded region between the x-axis and the curve shown from $x = 0$ to $x = 6$. Use trapezoids of height 1.
   - **b.** Suppose a point is selected randomly from the rectangular region outlined in blue. What is the approximate probability that the point will lie in the shaded region?

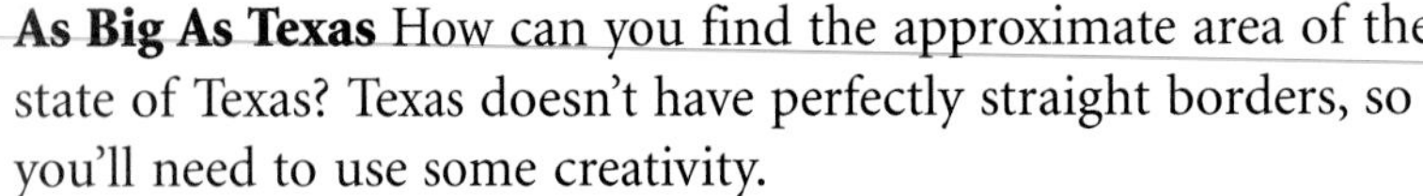

Social Science

4. **As Big As Texas** How can you find the approximate area of the state of Texas? Texas doesn't have perfectly straight borders, so you'll need to use some creativity.
   - **a.** Copy or trace the map of Texas. Draw and measure adjacent trapezoids that "fill" the interior. Estimate the area of Texas by finding the sum of the areas of the trapezoids.
   - **b.** How could you get a more accurate approximation of the area? Explain.
   - **c.** Alaska's area is about 2.18 times larger than the area of Texas. Approximate the area of Alaska.

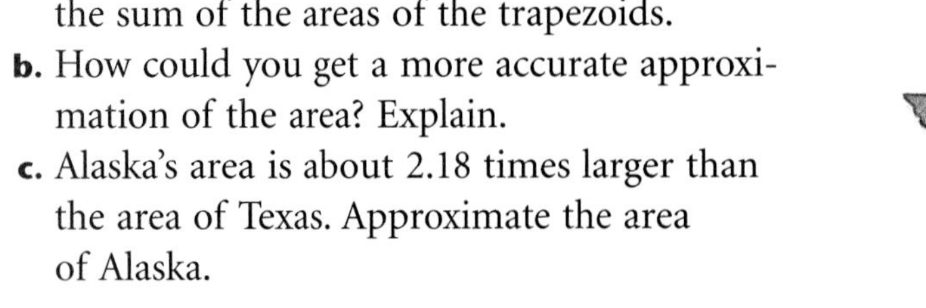

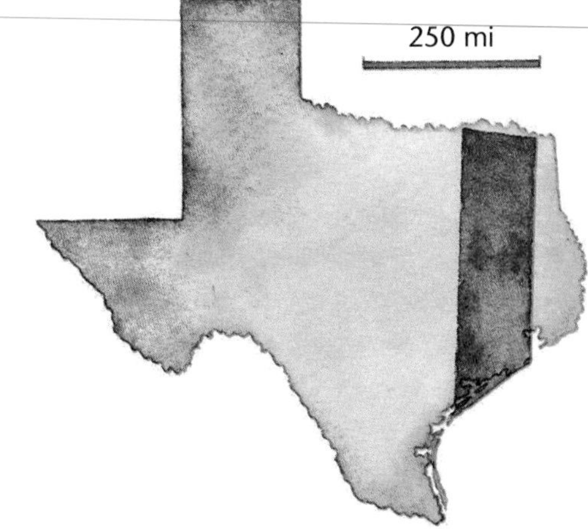

LOOK BACK

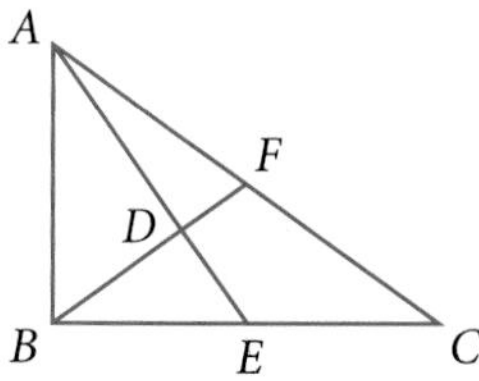

In $\triangle ABC$, $\overline{BF}$ and $\overline{AE}$ are medians. $BD > DF$, and $AD > DE$. [4-3]

5. If $BD = 38$, find DF.

6. If $DE = 11$, find AE.

7. If $AD = 6x - 16$ and $DE = 2x$, find the following.

a. x **b.** AD **c.** DE **d.** AE

Solve each equation. Give answers to the nearest hundredth. [5-1]

8. $x^2 + 2x - 5 = 0$

9. $x^2 - 4x = 3$

10. $2x^2 - 6x + 3 = 0$

MORE PRACTICE

11. Find the approximate area between the positive x-axis and the graph of the equation $y = \frac{1}{4}x^3$ from 0 to 3, using the trapezoid method. Use trapezoids of height 1.

12. Find the approximate area between the positive x-axis and the graph of the equation $y = 4\sqrt{x}$ from 0 to 4, using the trapezoid method. Use trapezoids of height 2.

MORE MATH REASONING

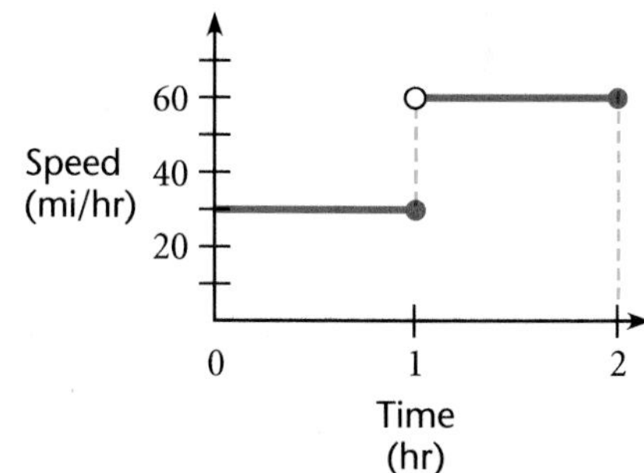

Science

13. Explain what the area under this graph tells you about the trip it represents. (Hint: Find the area under the graph. Then think about the two parts of the trip.)

14. The Koch Snowflake The Koch Snowflake begins with an equilateral triangle. Then, in the middle third of each segment, a new equilateral triangle is built. Each successive figure is made in the same way. The Koch Snowflake results when this process is repeated forever.

a. Each stage of the snowflake can be contained in the same circle. What does this tell you about the area of the Koch Snowflake?

b. What is the change in the perimeter of the snowflake each time a new set of triangles is added?

c. Write a brief paragraph about the Koch Snowflake using the words *finite* and *infinite* to describe its area and perimeter.

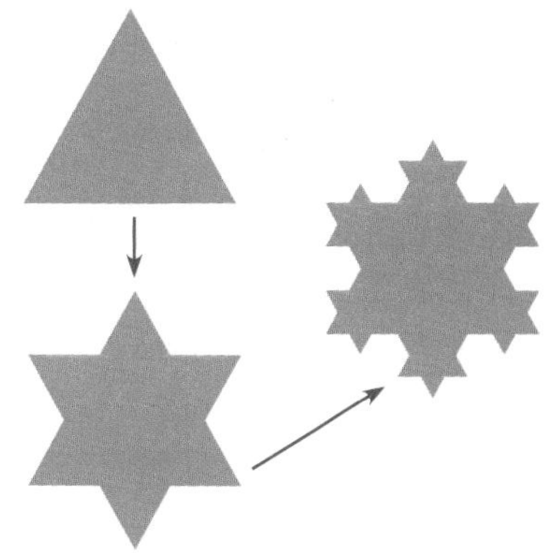

5-2 PART D Making Connections

← CONNECT → ***The ability to calculate areas accurately has been important for hundreds of years. You have examined area formulas and why they work. You've also planned logical arguments using area.***

There are several ways to find the area of a region, from counting squares to using the trapezoidal method. The Aztecs made accurate area calculations over 500 years ago. The photo at the left shows a piece of Aztec pottery.

In the following Explore, you will make scale drawings and calculate the areas of some irregularly shaped farms like those seen in Aztec records.

EXPLORE: AZTEC AGRICULTURE

MATERIALS

Graph paper
Compass

The Aztec fields on the left below have been drawn to scale, and measurements are shown in *quahuitls.* (A *quahuitl* was about 2.5 m long.)

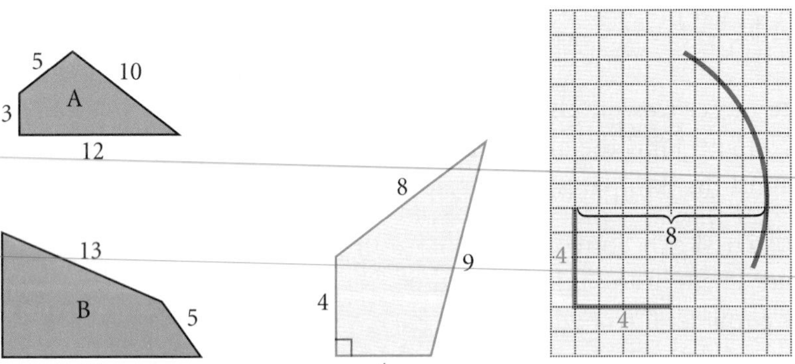

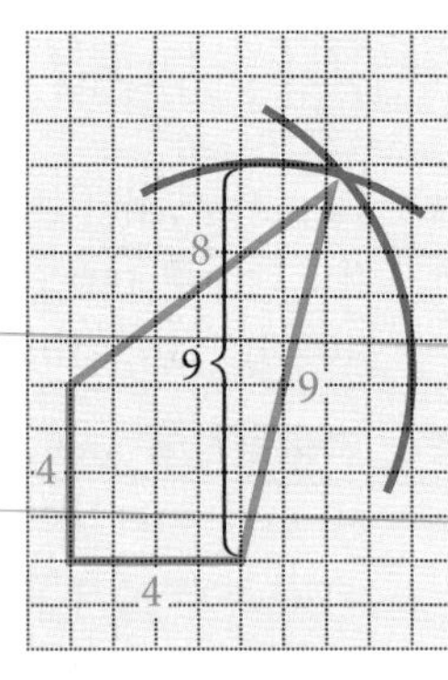

1. Make a careful drawing of Fields A and B on graph paper. Use one square of the paper to represent one square *quahuitl.* You may need to use a compass to locate the intersections of some sides, as shown by the series of figures above on the right.
2. Estimate the area of each field. Write a brief explanation of how you arrived at your estimates.
3. Find the exact area of each field. Write a brief explanation of how you found these.

REFLECT

1. Summarize the area formulas you have learned. Draw a sketch to illustrate each.
2. How many of the area formulas do you really need to memorize? Show how you can deduce area formulas from the rectangle formula.
3. When can you use area formulas to find the exact area of a region? When is it impossible to use the formulas to find the exact area?
4. Describe some different ways to find the areas of irregular figures. Give a brief summary of each method, and explain how it works.

Self-Assessment

Find the area of each figure.

1.

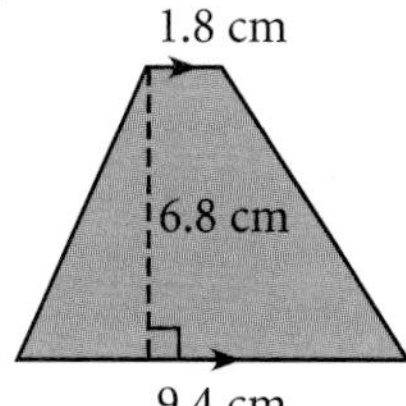

2.

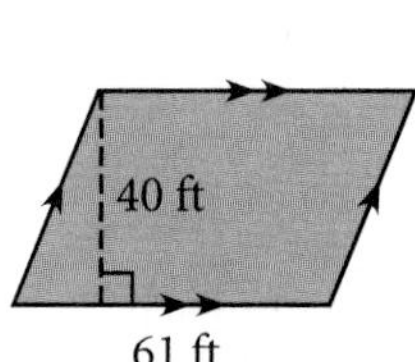

3.

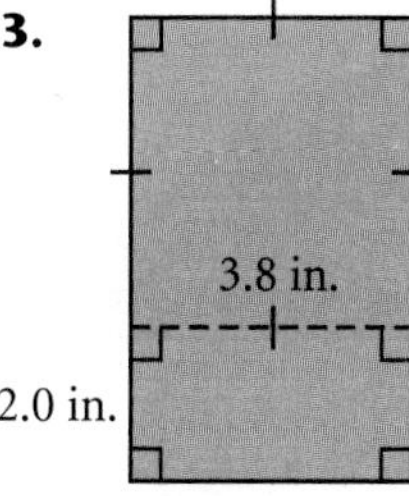

4.

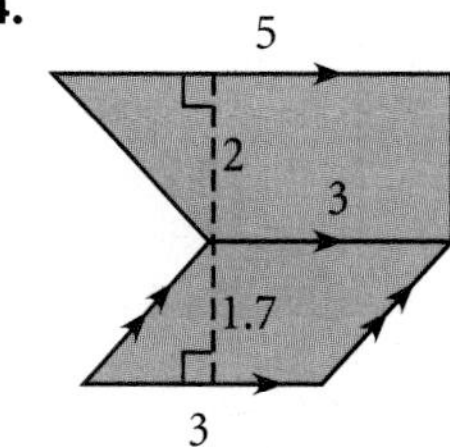

In Exercises 5–7, suppose *C* is the centroid of $\triangle MNP$. Point *C* is 4 cm from *M* and 6 cm from *N*. [4-3]

5. If *R* is the midpoint of $\overline{NP}$, find *RC*. Explain how you found your answer.
6. If *S* is the midpoint of $\overline{MP}$, find *NS*. Again, explain your solution method.
7. Use a ruler to draw $\triangle MNP$ that has these characteristics.
8. History **Aztec Pyramid** The central pyramid in Tenochtitlán has a square base that is 97 m on a side. Find the area of the base of the pyramid. (A similar pyramid in Chichen Itza is shown at the right.)

9. Science The length of Colorado, a rectangular state, is approximately 100 mi greater than its width. Colorado's area is 103,730 mi². Find the approximate length and width of Colorado. Round your answers to the nearest mile. If you used algebra to help solve this problem, explain how you used it. [5-1]

10. In the figure at the right, the area of trapezoid $ABCD$ is 16 square units. Rectangle $ABCE$ and $\triangle AED$ have equal areas. $DC =$

(a) 2 (b) 3 (c) 4

(d) 6 (e) 8

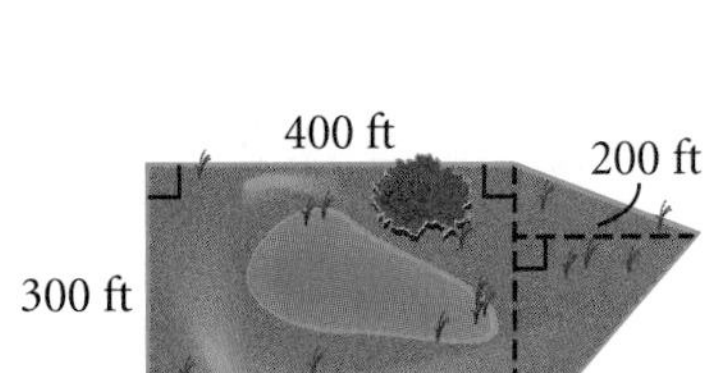

11. *Plan* a logical argument to show that the diagonals of a square are congruent.

12. Fields of Green A bag of fertilizer covers 5000 ft^2. A bag of grass seed covers 3000 ft^2. How many bags of each are needed to cover this plot of land?

300 ft

400 ft

200 ft

13. Find the approximate area between the x-axis and the curve shown, from $x = 0$ to $x = 16$. Use trapezoids of height 4.

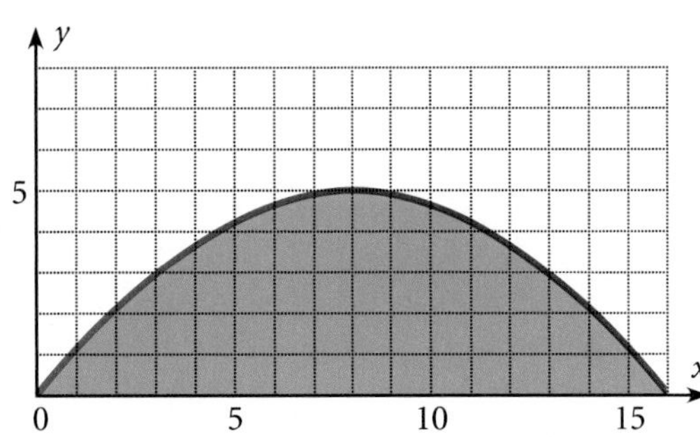

Draw a quadrilateral whose vertices have the following coordinates. Then find the area of the quadrilateral.

14. (0, 0), (4, 5), (4, 10), (0, 5)

15. (−4, 3), (6, 3), (10, 8), (0, 8)

16. Does Not Compute The computer screen shows two parallel lines. Points A and B do not move. Point C moves along its line from the left side of the screen to the right. What will happen to the numbers showing the area and perimeter of triangle $\triangle ABC$? Explain your reasoning.

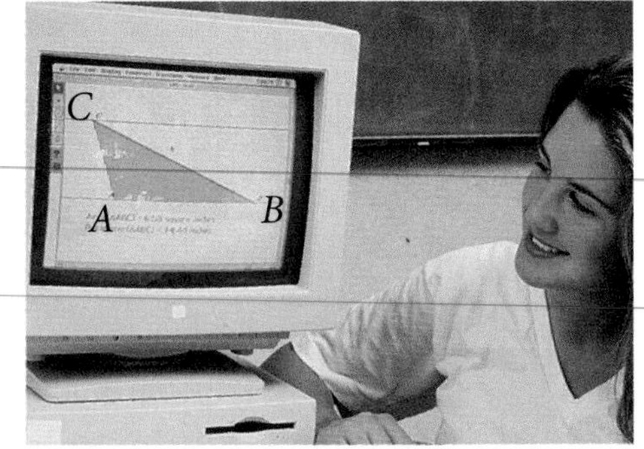

17. Suppose the trapezoid and parallelogram shown are cultivated fields on a rectangular plot of land. A raindrop falls randomly on the plot of land. What is the probability that it will land on one of the cultivated fields? Express your answer in decimal form rounded to the nearest hundredth.

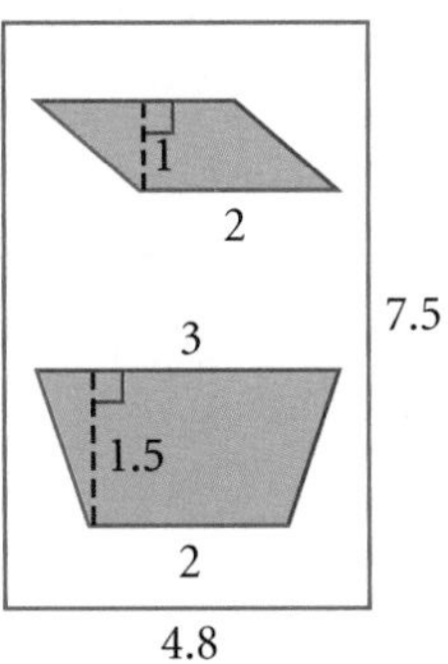

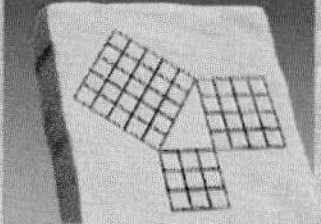

5-3 The Pythagorean Theorem

IT'S ALL BABYLONIAN TO ME

Four thousand years ago, the Babylonian civilization thrived in the Middle East area bounded by the Tigris and Euphrates Rivers. Using clay tablets and a pointed tool called a stylus to do their calculations, Babylonian students learned the same right-triangle theorem we study today. But they didn't call their theorem the "Pythagorean Theorem" because Pythagoras was not born for another thousand years. The theorem was probably so named because he was the first to prove it. He was certainly not the first to use it!

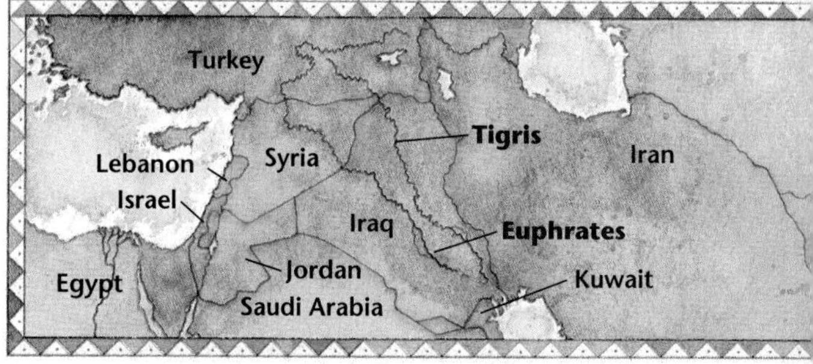

In modern times, a remarkable Babylonian tablet, called Plimpton 322, was discovered. It had survived undamaged underground for 4000 years. Ironically, someone dropped it and a piece broke off. Nobody knows the whereabouts of the missing piece, but the remaining portion lists columns of numbers showing the Babylonians' knowledge of relationships in right triangles. This tablet is now on display at Columbia University in New York.

?

1. The Babylonians based some of their mathematics on the number 60. Describe a current system of measurement in which the number 60 is important.
2. How do you think the Babylonians might have discovered the right-triangle theorem now known as the Pythagorean Theorem?

5-3 PART A The Pythagorean Theorem

← CONNECT → ***Your knowledge of area gives you the background needed to prove the Pythagorean Theorem. You will investigate one proof of the theorem and use it to calculate side lengths in a right triangle.***

Yale Babylonian Collection

The photograph at the left shows a portion of a Babylonian tablet. The marks on the tablet suggest that the Babylonians studied properties of right triangles.

The Pythagorean Theorem describes a special relationship between the lengths of the sides of a right triangle. It can be used to calculate the length of any side of a right triangle when the lengths of the other two sides are known.

PYTHAGOREAN THEOREM

In a right triangle, the square of the length of the hypotenuse is equal to the sum of the squares of the lengths of the legs.

$$a^2 + b^2 = c^2$$

EXAMPLES

The lengths of two sides of right triangle $\triangle STU$ are given. Find the length of the third side.

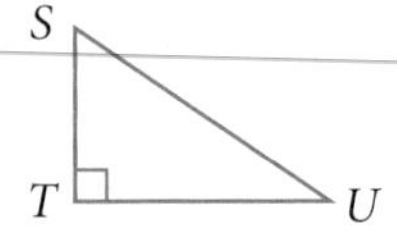

1. $ST = 3, TU = 4$

$$ST^2 + TU^2 = SU^2$$
$$3^2 + 4^2 = SU^2$$
$$25 = SU^2$$
$$5 = SU$$

2. $ST = 7, SU = 10$

$$ST^2 + TU^2 = SU^2$$
$$7^2 + TU^2 = 10^2$$
$$49 + TU^2 = 100$$
$$TU^2 = 51$$
$$TU = \sqrt{51} \approx 7.14$$

There are more than 370 known proofs of the Pythagorean Theorem. One of the most famous proofs is based on a cleverly drawn figure. The proof is attributed to Bhaskara, a Hindu mathematician of the twelfth century, who accompanied the proof with a single word—"Behold!"

EXPLORE: BEHOLD! THE BHASKARA PROOF

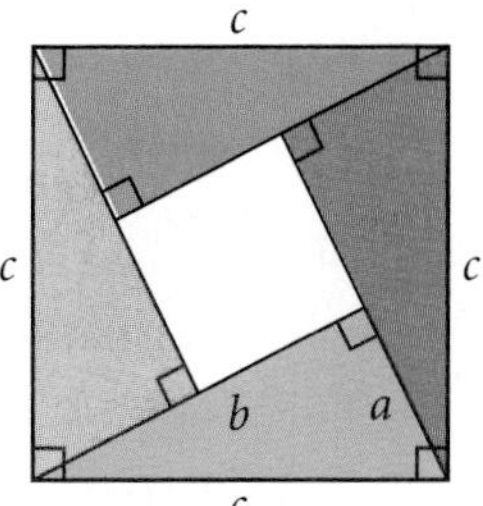

1. What is the area of the large square?
2. What is the area of each of the right triangles?
3. What figure remains in the interior of the figure? What is its area? (Hint: What is the length of one of its sides in terms of a and b?)
4. Use the Area-Addition Postulate, and then simplify your equation to "behold" the Pythagorean Theorem.
5. Write out a *plan* for the Bhaskara proof.

There are some special sets of positive integers that "work" in the Pythagorean Theorem. For instance, as you saw in Example 1, if the lengths of the legs of a right triangle are 3 and 4, the length of its hypotenuse is 5. The set of numbers 3, 4, 5 is a **Pythagorean triple.** It is useful to recognize sets of numbers that are Pythagorean triples.

TRY IT

Find the length of the missing side in each triangle. Then identify the corresponding Pythagorean triple.

a.

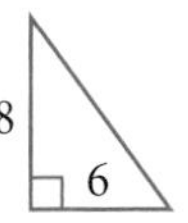

b.

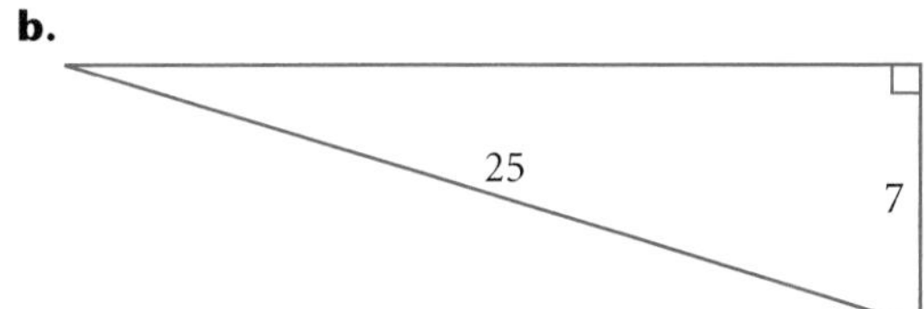

c.

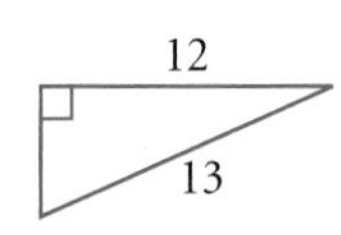

REFLECT

1. People had been using the Pythagorean Theorem long before Pythagoras proved it. Why is the proof of any theorem important?
2. Describe how the areas of the three large squares are related. How is this figure related to the Pythagorean Theorem?

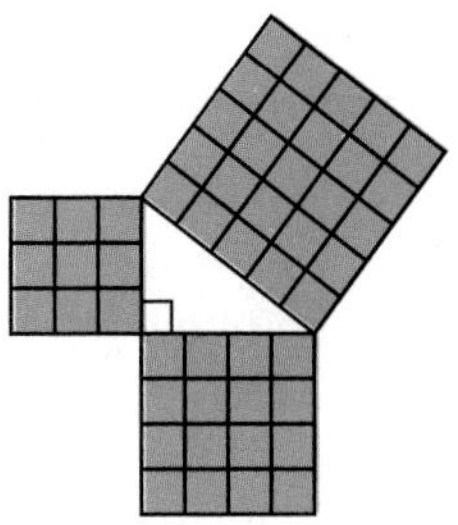

Exercises

CORE

1. Getting Started Follow these steps to find the length of $\overline{AB}$. Express your answer as a radical in simplest form and as a decimal approximation rounded to the nearest hundredth.

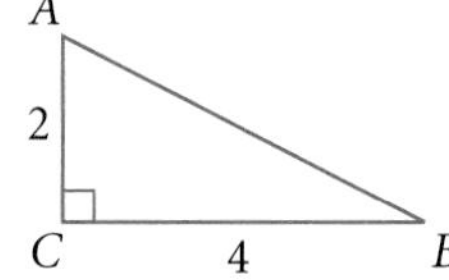

a. What are the lengths of the legs?
b. Square the lengths of the legs, and find the sum.
c. To find AB, take the positive square root of your answer, and simplify.
d. Use a calculator to find the decimal equivalent. Round to the nearest hundredth.

Find the length of the missing side in each triangle. Express it as a radical in simplest form (if possible) and as a decimal approximation rounded to the nearest hundredth.

2.
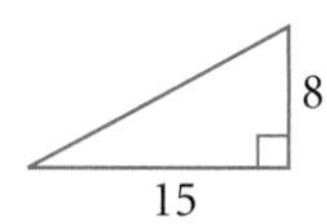

3.
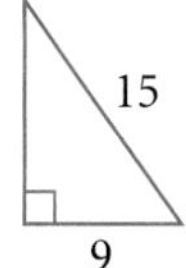

4.
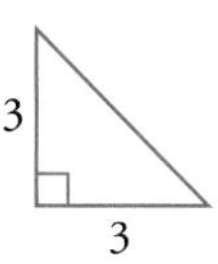

5.
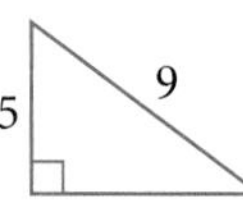

Use the figure at the right to complete the following.

6. $p = 7$, $q = 24$, $r =$ _____ **7.** $p = 15$, $r = 25$, $q =$ _____

8. $p = 2\sqrt{3}$, $r = 6$, $q =$ _____ **9.** $p = \sqrt{3}$, $q = \sqrt{2}$, $r =$ _____

10. $r = 6.7$, $q = 3.9$, $p =$ _____

11. History Write a *plan* for a proof of the Pythagorean Theorem that uses the figure at the right. (This figure is similar to one seen in the *Chóu-peï*, an ancient Chinese text. The author and date are unknown, but the book probably records ideas from about 1100 B.C.)

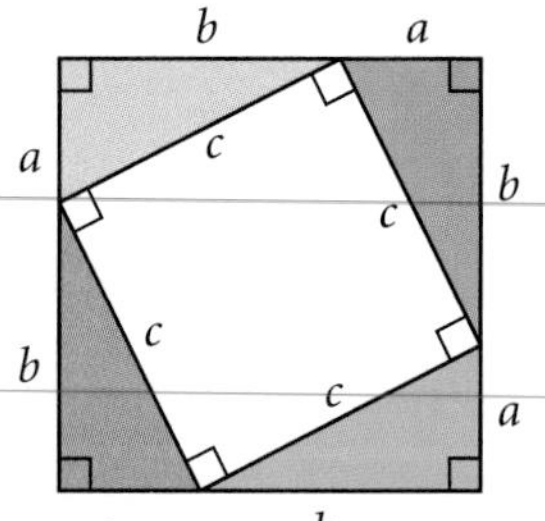

12. History A passage from the *Chóu-peï* reads, "Break the line and make the breadth 3, the length 4; then the distance between the corners is 5." Explain the meaning of this excerpt. Illustrate your answer with a sketch.

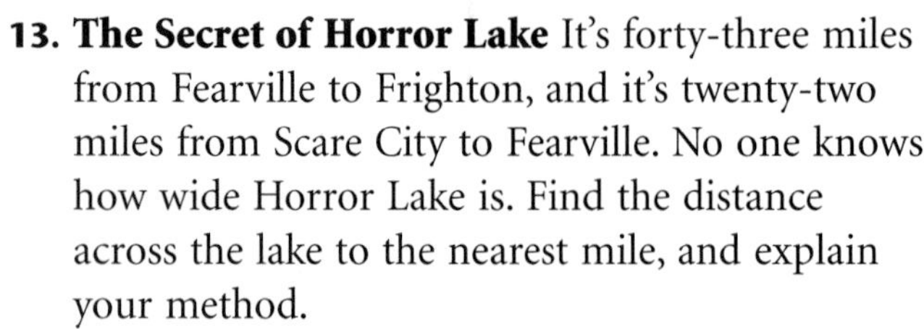

13. The Secret of Horror Lake It's forty-three miles from Fearville to Frighton, and it's twenty-two miles from Scare City to Fearville. No one knows how wide Horror Lake is. Find the distance across the lake to the nearest mile, and explain your method.

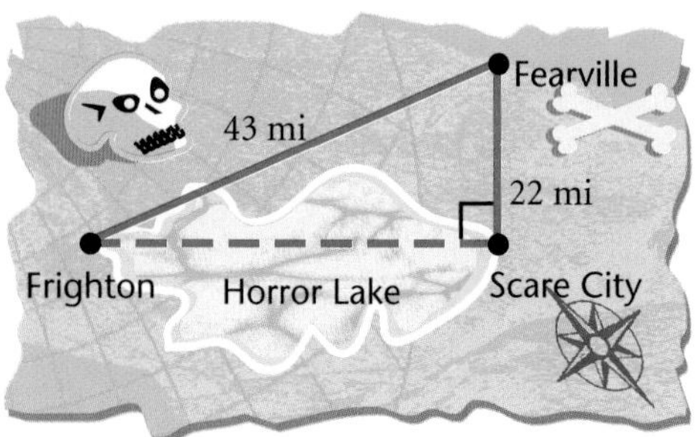

14. Find the length of the longest segment that can be drawn on an $8\frac{1}{2}'' \times 11''$ sheet of paper.

15. Window Washing The base of a 16-ft ladder is placed 6 ft from a wall. How far up the wall will the ladder reach? Round your answer to the nearest tenth of a foot.

16. Write the word or phrase that correctly completes the following statement.

If the sum of the squares of two positive integers is equal to the square of a third positive integer, then the three integers are a(n) ____.

17. A farmer can choose to fence off some of his land as a parallelogram or a rectangle, as shown.

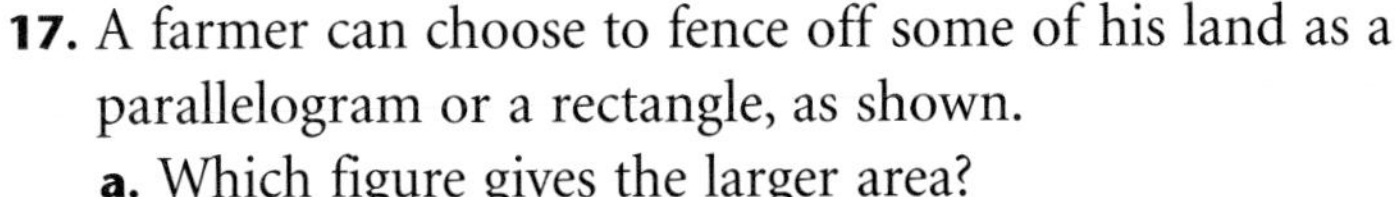

a. Which figure gives the larger area?
b. Which figure costs more to fence?
c. If you were the farmer, which figure would you choose for the field? Explain your decision.

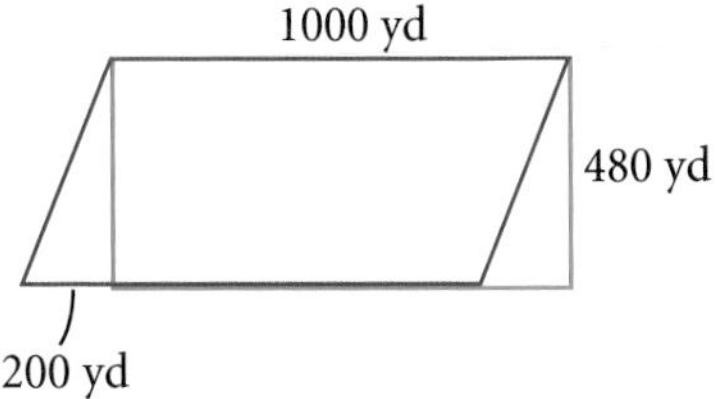

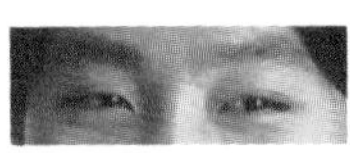

LOOK AHEAD

Write each radical in simplest form. Then express the radical as a decimal. Round answers to the nearest hundredth.

18. $\sqrt{25}$ **19.** $\sqrt{20}$ **20.** $\frac{7}{\sqrt{3}}$

Find the length of the diagonal of a square with each of the following side lengths.

21. 3 **22.** 8 **23.** $2\sqrt{5}$

MORE PRACTICE

Find the length of the unknown side in each triangle. Express it as a radical in simplest form (if possible) and as a decimal approximation rounded to the nearest hundredth.

24.

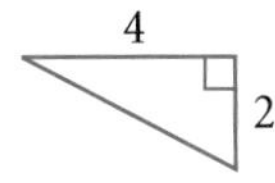

25.

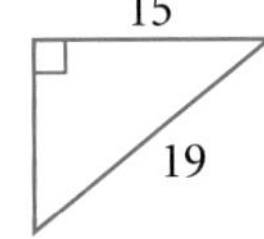

26.

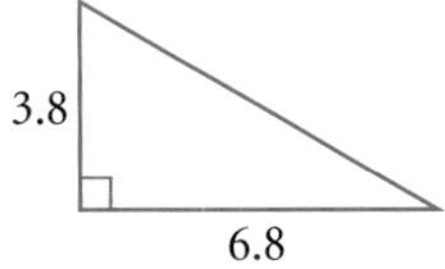

Use the figure at the right to complete the following.

27. $x = 6, y = 8, z =$ ____ **28.** $y = 5\sqrt{5}, z = 15, x =$ ____

29. $x = \sqrt{10}, z = \sqrt{15}, y =$ ____ **30.** $x = 4.4, y = 6.2, z =$ ____

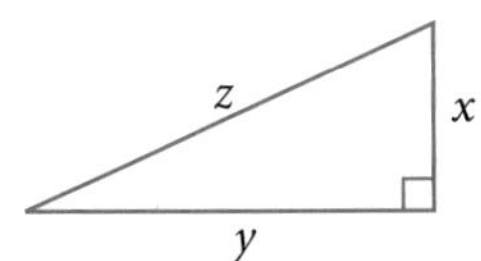

MORE MATH REASONING

31. Given a segment of length 1, describe how to construct a segment with length $\sqrt{2}$ by using a compass and straightedge. Then describe how to construct a segment with length $\sqrt{3}$ by using a compass and straightedge.

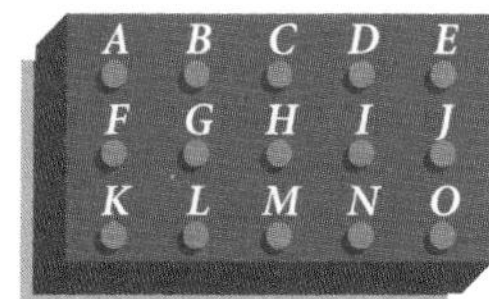

32. Assume the distance from A to B is one unit. If possible, find segments on the grid with one endpoint at A that have lengths $\sqrt{2}$, $\sqrt{3}$, $\sqrt{4}$, $\sqrt{5}$, $\sqrt{6}$, $\sqrt{7}$, $\sqrt{8}$, $\sqrt{9}$, and $\sqrt{10}$. (Hint: Three of these are not possible.)

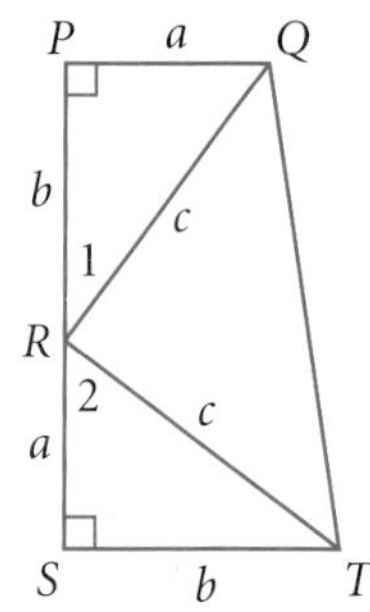

33. A Presidential Proof James A. Garfield, the 20th president of the United States, is also known for his original proof of the Pythagorean Theorem. Using his drawing (shown at the right) and your knowledge of area, reproduce his proof of the Pythagorean Theorem. (Hint: Write the area of trapezoid $PQTS$ two different ways.)

5-3 PART B Special Right Triangles

← CONNECT → ***You have justified the Pythagorean Theorem. Now you will use it to identify patterns in the side lengths of special right triangles.***

There are two types of right triangles that occur so often that they deserve special attention.

The first type of special triangle is an isosceles right triangle. One way to make an isosceles right triangle is to cut a square in half.

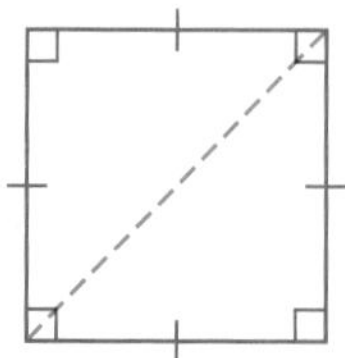
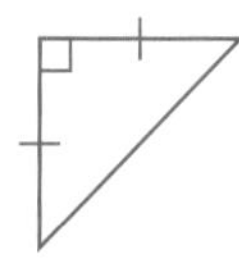
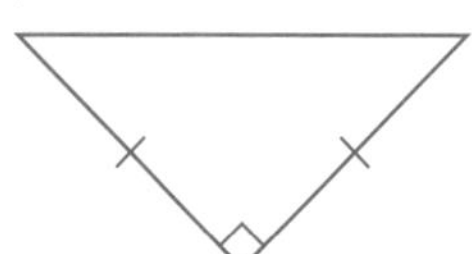
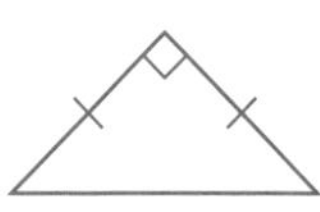

The three triangles on the right in the above figure are isosceles right triangles.

You can make the second type of special right triangle by cutting an equilateral triangle in half.

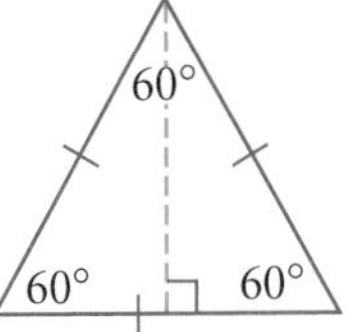

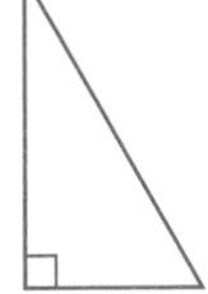
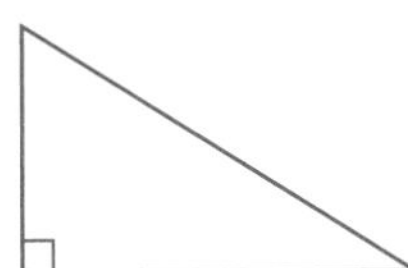
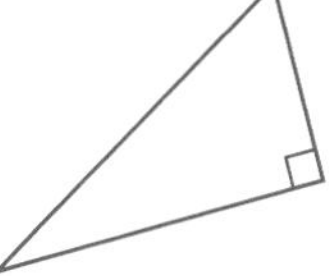

1. An isosceles right triangle is called a 45°-45°-90° triangle. Why?

2. What are the measures of the angles of half an equilateral triangle (as shown above)? Name this type of triangle, using the measures of the three angles.

Since the Pythagorean Theorem applies to all right triangles, it also applies to these special right triangles.

EXPLORE: RIGHT RATIOS

For this Explore, leave all measurements in simplest radical form.

1. Sketch a 45°-45°-90° triangle, and choose a whole number for the lengths of its legs (a sample triangle is shown). Then use the Pythagorean Theorem to find the length of its hypotenuse. Simplify your result. Repeat this process for several different triangles, and make a conjecture about the sides of 45°-45°-90° triangles.

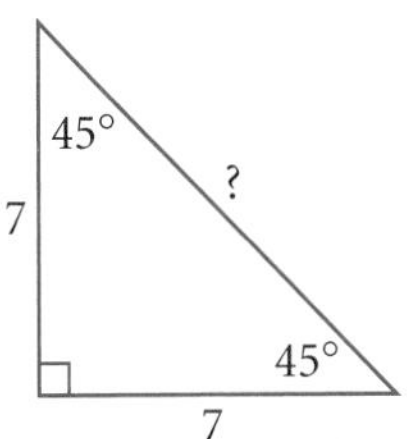

Problem-Solving Tip

Make a table, and look for a pattern in your results.

2. Sketch an equilateral triangle, and choose a whole number for the lengths of its sides. Make a 30°-60°-90° triangle by dividing the triangle in half (a sample triangle is shown). Find the length of the unknown leg by using the Pythagorean Theorem, and simplify your result. Repeat this process for several different triangles, and make a conjecture about the sides of 30°-60°-90° triangles.

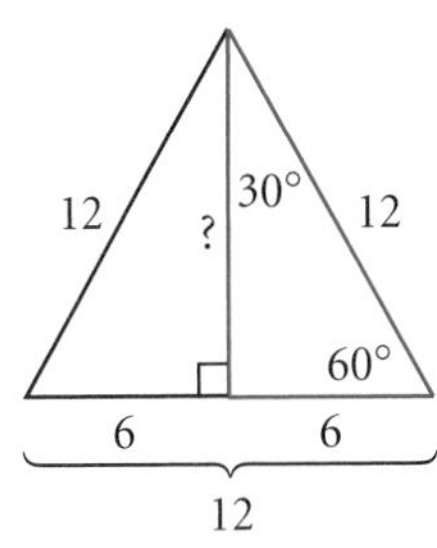

EXAMPLES

Find the lengths of the unknown sides in each triangle. Express each as a radical in simplest form (if possible) and as a decimal approximation rounded to the nearest hundredth.

1. $a = 10\sqrt{2} \approx 14.14$

2. $r = s = 4$

3. $x = y = \dfrac{9}{\sqrt{2}} \approx 6.36$

In Example 3, we had the expression $\frac{9}{\sqrt{2}}$. To put this expression in simplest form, we must clear the radicals from the denominator as follows.

$$\frac{9}{\sqrt{2}} \times \frac{\sqrt{2}}{\sqrt{2}} = \frac{9\sqrt{2}}{2}$$

Notice there are no radicals in the denominator of the simplified expression.

TRY IT

Find the length of the unknown sides in each triangle. Express each as a radical in simplest form (if possible) and as a decimal approximation rounded to the nearest hundredth.

	x	y	z
a.	4	___	___
b.	___	___	20
c.	___	$5\sqrt{3}$	___
d.	___	4.8	___

The results you have discovered about special right triangles are summarized below.

45°-45°-90° TRIANGLE THEOREM

In a 45°-45°-90° triangle, the hypotenuse is $\sqrt{2}$ times as long as either leg. The ratios of the side lengths can be written ℓ-ℓ-$\ell\sqrt{2}$.

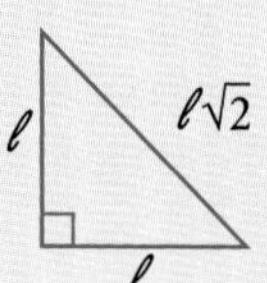

30°-60°-90° TRIANGLE THEOREM

In a 30°-60°-90° triangle, the hypotenuse is twice as long as the shorter leg (the leg opposite the 30° angle), and the longer leg (opposite the 60° angle) is $\sqrt{3}$ times as long as the shorter leg. The ratios of the side lengths can be written ℓ-$\ell\sqrt{3}$-2ℓ.

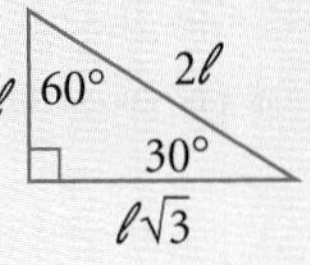

REFLECT

1. Why do 45°-45°-90° triangles have two sides with the same length? Be sure to support your answer with a theorem.
2. Explain why the length of the shorter leg of a 30°-60°-90° triangle is half the length of the hypotenuse.
3. If a square has sides that are *s* units long, what are the lengths of its diagonals? Why?

Exercises

CORE

Getting Started The length of one side of each triangle is given. Find the lengths of the other two sides in simplest radical form.

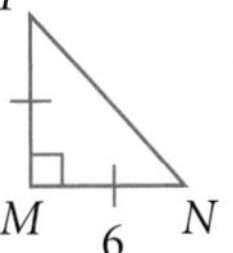

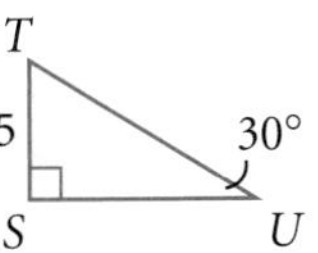

1. $MN = 6$

2. $ST = 5$

Find the lengths of the unknown sides in each triangle. Express each as a radical in simplest form (if possible) and as a decimal approximation rounded to the nearest hundredth.

	a	*b*	*c*	
3.	3	___	___	a, b, c; 45°, 45°
4.	___	___	$6\sqrt{2}$	
5.	___	4.6	___	
6.	___	___	5	

Find the lengths of the unknown sides in each triangle. Express each as a radical in simplest form (if possible) and as a decimal approximation rounded to the nearest hundredth.

	f	*g*	*h*
7.	7	___	___
8.	___	___	10
9.	___	$4\sqrt{3}$	___
10.	___	7.2	___

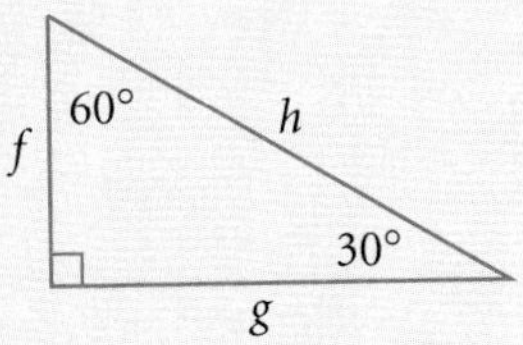

11. You're Out! A baseball diamond is a square with consecutive bases 90 ft apart. About how far does a catcher have to throw the baseball to catch a runner trying to steal second base? Explain how you solved this problem.

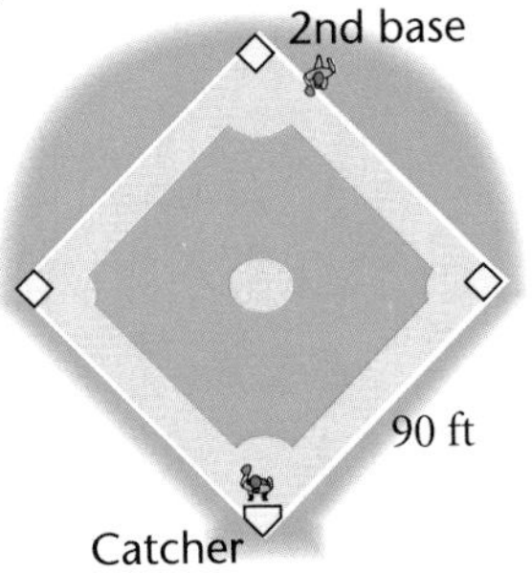

Find the area of each figure.

12.

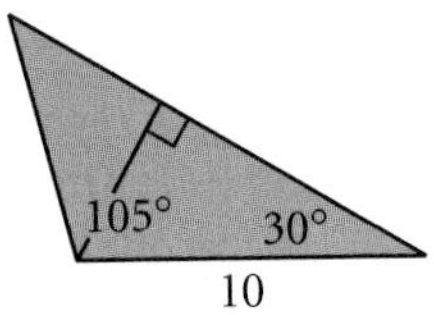

13.

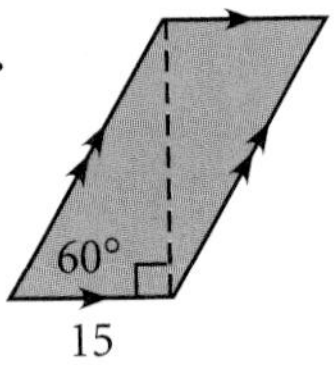

14.

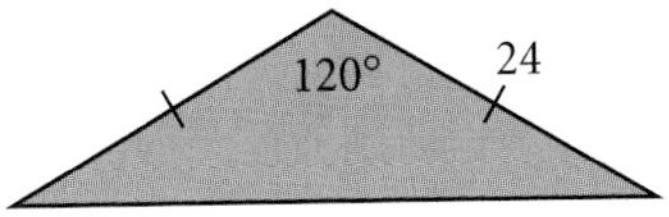

Find the lengths of the diagonals of a square with the following side lengths. Express your answers in simplest radical form.

15. 10 **16.** $8\sqrt{2}$ **17.** $22\sqrt{6}$

Science

18. Suppose that parallel rays of light pass through the center and the tip of the lens shown. After they are bent by the lens, the rays cross at focal point *F*. Find *FL* to the nearest tenth of a centimeter.

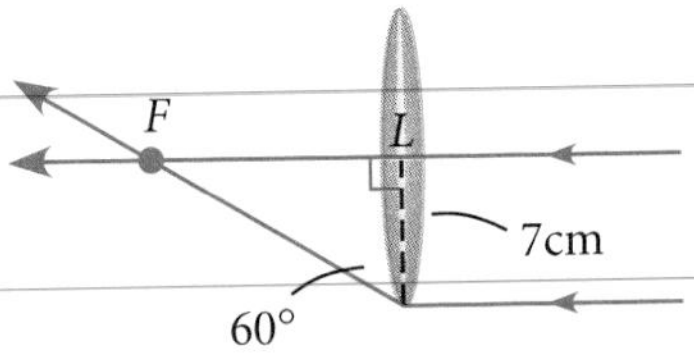

Careers

19. Parallel Parking As a city planner, you are designing parking for a downtown area. You are considering the two designs shown. In each design, the distance between the lines is 8 ft.

a. Which design allows more cars to be parked along a 200-ft block? Explain.

b. What advantages might the other design have?

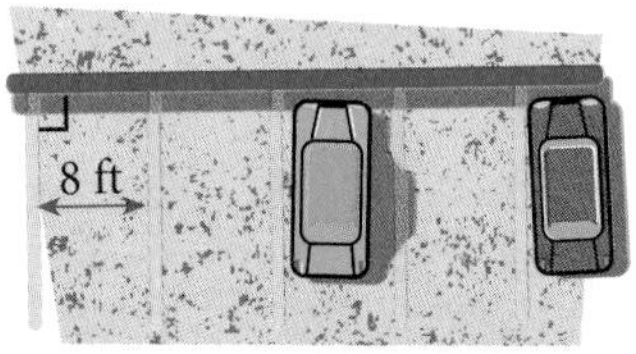

Perpendicular parking

Angle parking

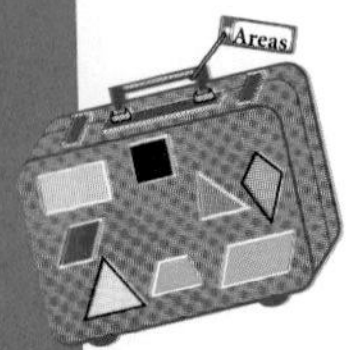

20. Use a compass and straightedge to construct an isosceles right triangle and a 30°-60°-90° triangle.

21. Find a formula for the area of an equilateral triangle in terms of *s*, the length of a side of the triangle.

LOOK AHEAD

Find the distance between each pair of points.

22. (0, 3) and (3, 7)

23. (2, 3) and (1, −7)

24. (−5, −3) and (−1, 4)

25. (2.2, −1.3) and (−4.7, −2.5)

MORE PRACTICE

Find the lengths of the unknown sides in each triangle. Express each as a radical in simplest form and as a decimal approximation rounded to the nearest hundredth.

	f	g	h
26.	7	___	___
27.	___	___	$11\sqrt{2}$
28.	___	___	18

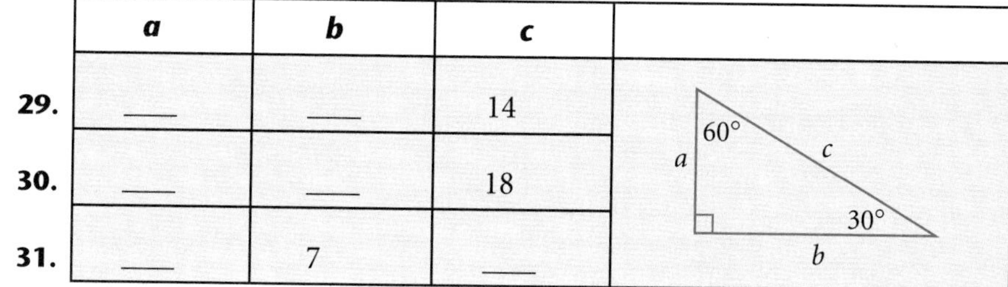

	a	b	c
29.	___	___	14
30.	___	___	18
31.	___	7	___

MORE MATH REASONING

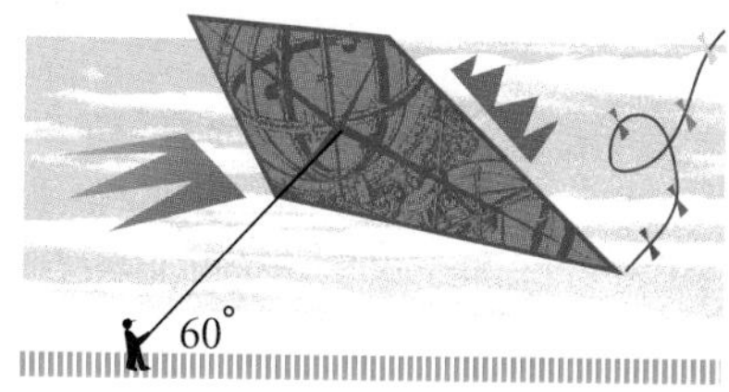

32. A kite string is 200 ft long, and the angle the string makes with the ground is 60°. How high is the kite?

Find the coordinates of point *P* on each circle. The radius of each circle is 1.

33.

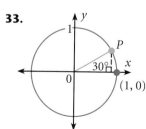

34.

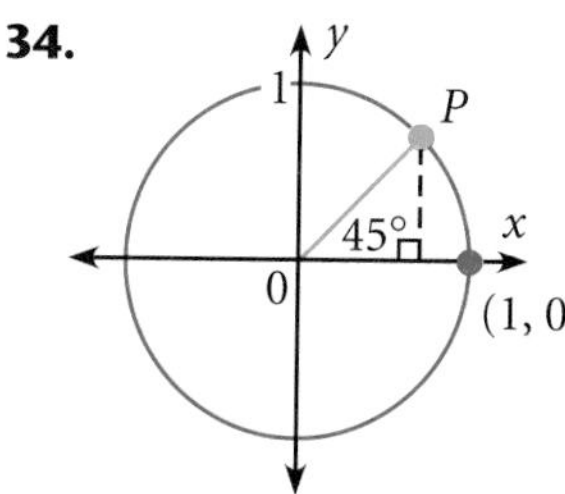

35.

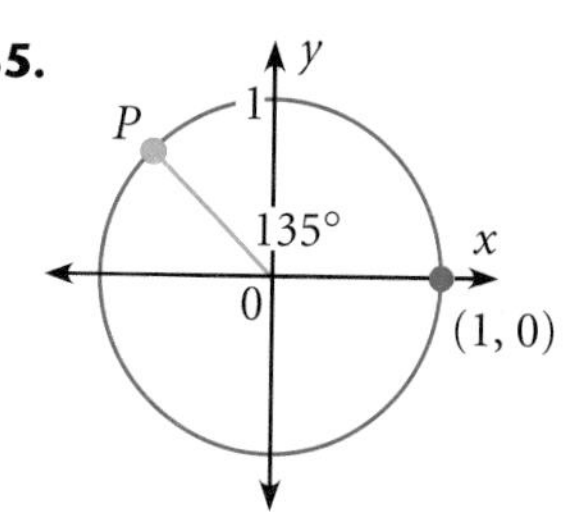

5-3 PART C

The Distance Formula Revisited

← CONNECT → ***You've already used the distance formula, but now you can justify why it works. You will also investigate the standard form for the equation of a circle.***

The formula for the distance between two points in a plane and the Pythagorean Theorem are the same thing written in two different ways. You will investigate this in the following Explore.

EXPLORE: GOING THE DISTANCE

Use the figure at the right and the Pythagorean Theorem to explain why the distance formula works. Use your explanation to write a *plan* for a proof of the distance formula.

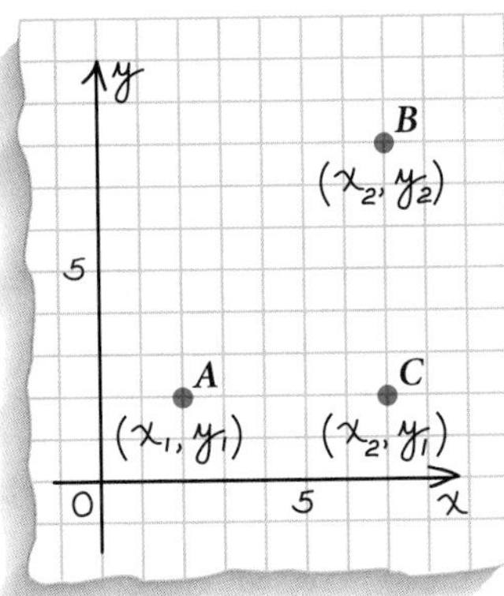

TRY IT

Find the distance between each pair of points.

a. (22, 4) and (2, 1)
b. (26, 0) and (6, 5)

A circle is the locus of points in a plane that are equidistant from a given point. Let's see what happens when we use the distance formula to help attach numbers to those characteristics.

One way to draw a circle with a radius of r is to use a string and a pencil. Since the string is r units long, all points on the circle are r units away from the center.

Let's put a coordinate system on this circle. The most convenient place for the center is (0, 0). Any point whose (x, y) coordinates are on the circle must be r units away from (0, 0).

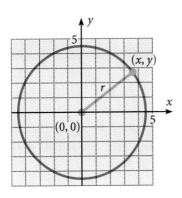

The distance from (x, y) to (0, 0) is r, so we have the following.

$$\sqrt{(x-0)^2 + (y-0)^2} = r$$

Simplifying gives $\sqrt{x^2 + y^2} = r$.

Finally, we square both sides to get the result shown below.

EQUATION OF A CIRCLE

The circle with radius r and center (0, 0) has the equation $x^2 + y^2 = r^2$.

TRY IT

What is the radius of each of the following circles?

c. $x^2 + y^2 = 9$ **d.** $x^2 + y^2 = 121$ **e.** $x^2 + y^2 = 21$

EXAMPLE

Sketch a graph of the circle whose equation is $x^2 + y^2 = 16$.

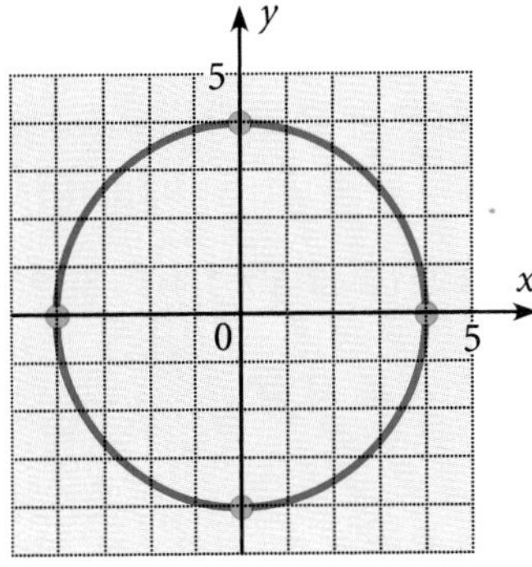

The center of the circle is (0, 0). Since $r^2 = 16$, the radius of the circle is 4. The points that are directly above, below, left, and right of the center are (0, 4), (0, −4), (−4, 0), and (4, 0). We can draw a smooth curve that connects these points.

REFLECT

1. Explain the connection between the distance formula and the Pythagorean Theorem.
2. Why do the points that satisfy the equation $x^2 + y^2 = 25$ form a circle whose center is at the origin and whose radius is 5?

Exercises

CORE

Getting Started Find the distance between each pair of points. Express your answers as decimal approximations rounded to the nearest hundredth.

1. $(-4, 9)$ and $(-4, -12)$

2. $(4, -3)$ and $(2, 7)$

3. $(-3, -2)$ and $(1, -6)$

4. $(17.2, 27.5)$ and $(27.2, 22.4)$

Find the distance between each pair of points.

5. (c, d) and (d, c), where $d > c$

6. (q, q) and $(-q, -q)$, where $q > 0$

Write an equation for a circle with center at (0, 0) and the given radius. Then sketch a graph of the circle.

7. $r = 1$

8. $r = 3$

9. Give an equation for the locus of points in the coordinate plane 10 units from (0, 0).

10. Going Swimming Alicia can swim one hundred and fifty yards in two minutes. She begins her swim at (0, 0).

a. A raft is located at the point (62, 77). Can she reach the raft in two minutes? Explain.

b. Write an equation for the locus of points one hundred and fifty yards from her starting point.

11. When the rotor of a helicopter spins very quickly, it looks like a disk. Explain why this happens.

History

12. Big Babylon Around the year 600 B.C., Babylon, the capital of Babylonia, was the largest city in the world. It covered an area of 2500 acres. If one acre is approximately equivalent to 1.56×10^{-3} mi^2, find the area of Babylon in square miles.

Science

13. The earth's orbit around the sun is nearly circular. The radius of the orbit is approximately 9.3×10^7 mi. Assuming the center of the sun is located at (0, 0) in the figure at the right, write an equation for the orbit of the earth around the sun.

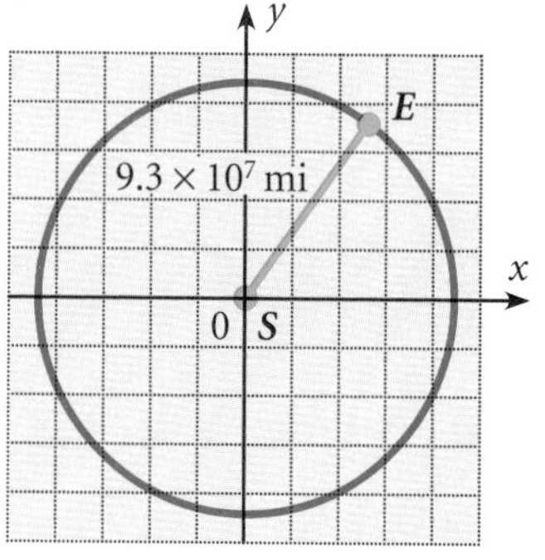

14. *Plan* a proof to show that the points $(-x, 0)$ and $(x, 0)$ are equidistant from $(0, y)$.

LOOK BACK

15. Fill in the missing reasons to complete the proof. [4-2, 4-3]

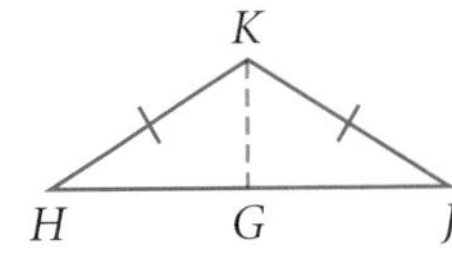

Given: $\triangle KHJ$ is isosceles, with $\overline{KH} \cong \overline{KJ}$.
$\overline{KG}$ is the median from K to $\overline{HJ}$.

Prove: $\overline{KG}$ is the angle bisector of $\angle HKJ$.

Proof: The **a.** ___ tells us that $\overline{KH} \cong \overline{KJ}$. We know that $\overline{KG} \cong \overline{KG}$ by the **b.** ___. We also know that $\overline{KG}$ is the median from K to $\overline{HJ}$ from the **c.** ___, so G is the midpoint of $\overline{HJ}$ by the **d.** ___. Therefore, $\overline{HG} \cong \overline{GJ}$ by the **e.** ___. $\triangle KGH \cong \triangle KGJ$ by the **f.** ___, and $\angle HKG \cong \angle JKG$ by **g.** ___. Therefore, $\overline{KG}$ is the angle bisector of $\angle HKJ$ by the **h.** ___.

Find the probability that a point selected at random will lie in each shaded area. [5-1, 5-2]

16.

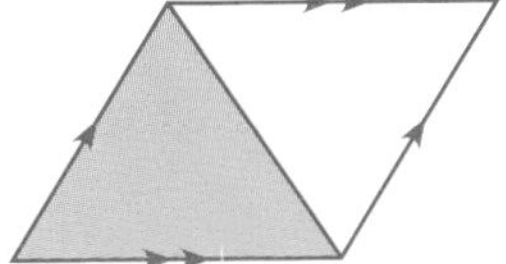

17.

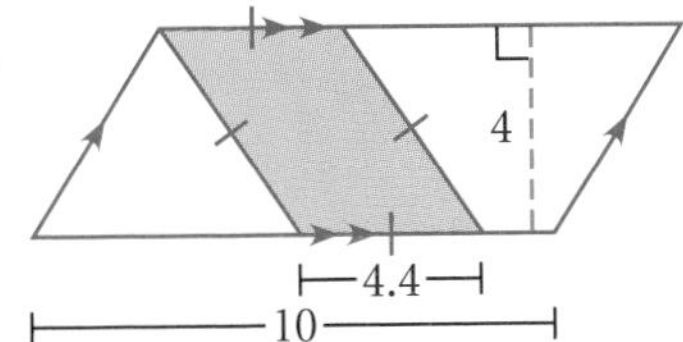

MORE PRACTICE

Find the distance between each pair of points. Express your answers as decimal approximations rounded to the nearest hundredth.

18. $(-7, 14)$; $(12, 14)$

19. $(19.3, 9.1)$; $(9.7, 19.9)$

20. $(5.2, 10.1)$; $(-5.2, -10.1)$

Write an equation for a circle with center at (0, 0) and the given radius.

21. $r = 7$

22. $r = \sqrt{21}$

23. $r = 2$

MORE MATH REASONING

24. Write an inequality to describe the locus of points that are no more than 5 units from $(0, 0)$. Graph the inequality.

25. In Exercise 13, you wrote an equation for the orbit of the earth around the sun. Find the possible y-values for the position of the earth when its x-value is 5.0×10^7 mi.

26. Graph the triangle with vertices $A(4, 3)$, $B(8, 2)$, and $C(1, 1)$. Find the image of $\triangle ABC$ under a 180° clockwise rotation around $(0, 0)$. Show that each point and its image are equidistant from $(0, 0)$.

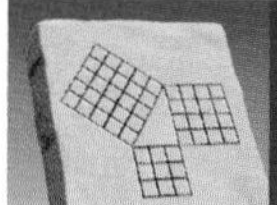

5-3 PART D The Converse of the Pythagorean Theorem

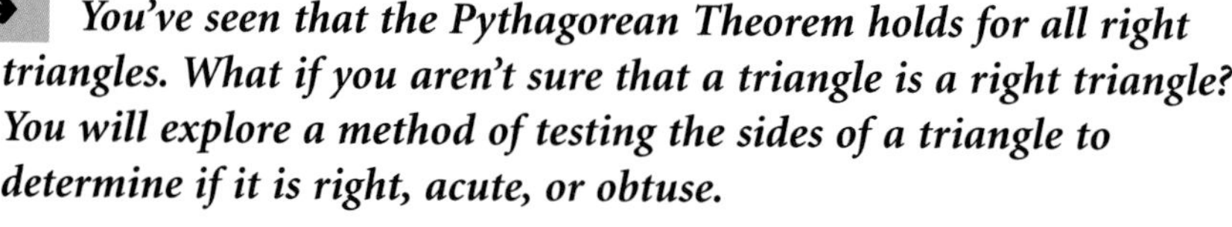

← CONNECT → ***You've seen that the Pythagorean Theorem holds for all right triangles. What if you aren't sure that a triangle is a right triangle? You will explore a method of testing the sides of a triangle to determine if it is right, acute, or obtuse.***

Like the Babylonians, the ancient Egyptians knew about properties of right triangles. The painting at the left shows Egyptian "rope stretchers" using what we now know as the converse of the Pythagorean Theorem. (You will take a closer look at this in Exercise 14.)

In the following Explore, you will investigate the converse of the Pythagorean Theorem.

EXPLORE: CONVERSELY . . . (AND MORE!)

MATERIALS

Paper, Ruler, Scissors
Geometry software (optional)

1. The table gives three different values for a and b. For each set of values, find three c values—one where $a^2 + b^2 = c^2$, one where $a^2 + b^2 < c^2$, and one where $a^2 + b^2 > c^2$. Be sure that c is greater than both a and b, but less than $a + b$.

	a	b	c
$a^2 + b^2 = c^2$	6	8	
$a^2 + b^2 < c^2$	6	8	
$a^2 + b^2 > c^2$	6	8	
$a^2 + b^2 = c^2$	5	12	
$a^2 + b^2 < c^2$	5	12	
$a^2 + b^2 > c^2$	5	12	
$a^2 + b^2 = c^2$	9	12	
$a^2 + b^2 < c^2$	9	12	
$a^2 + b^2 > c^2$	9	12	

2. Construct the triangles in your table using geometry software or by cutting strips of paper to the lengths of the sides. Are all of them right triangles? Explain.
3. Make a conjecture about the type of triangle that results for each of the following possibilities. (If you are using software, you may want to try a few more cases before making a conjecture.)
   a. $a^2 + b^2 = c^2$
   b. $a^2 + b^2 < c^2$
   c. $a^2 + b^2 > c^2$

Problem-Solving Tip

Look for a pattern before making a conjecture. Then check to see if your conjecture holds for the triangles in the table.

TRY IT

a. Is a triangle with sides 8, 15, and 17 a right triangle? If not, what type of triangle is it?
b. Is a triangle with sides 5, 6, and 8 a right triangle? If not, what type of triangle is it?
c. Is a triangle with sides 4, 5, and 6 a right triangle? If not, what type of triangle is it?

Based on your investigations in the preceding Explore, you may have made the following conjecture.

CONVERSE OF THE PYTHAGOREAN THEOREM

If the sum of the squares of the lengths of two sides of a triangle equals the square of the length of the third side, then the triangle is a right triangle and the longest side is the hypotenuse.

The inductive evidence shows that the converse of the Pythagorean Theorem seems to be true. Now we will prove it. Notice how we use the SSS Postulate in the proof.

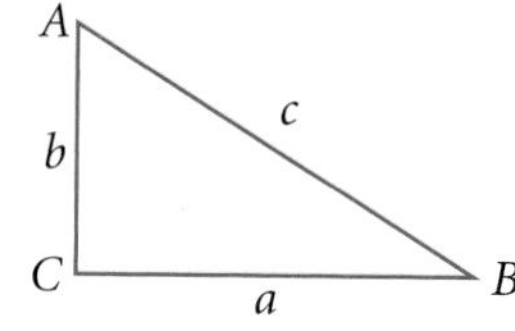

Given: $\triangle ABC$ with $a^2 + b^2 = c^2$

Prove: $\triangle ABC$ is a right triangle with hypotenuse c.

Plan: Show that any triangle whose side lengths satisfy the equation $a^2 + b^2 = c^2$ is congruent to a right triangle and is therefore a right triangle.

Proof: Draw a second triangle, $\triangle FGH$—a right triangle with legs a and b and hypotenuse h.

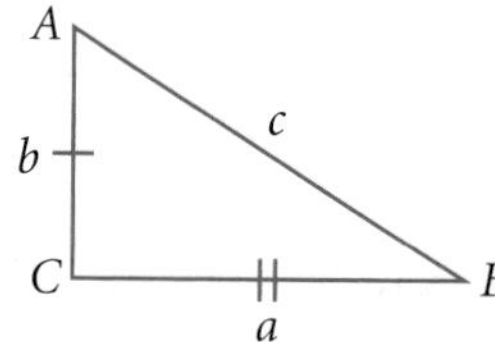

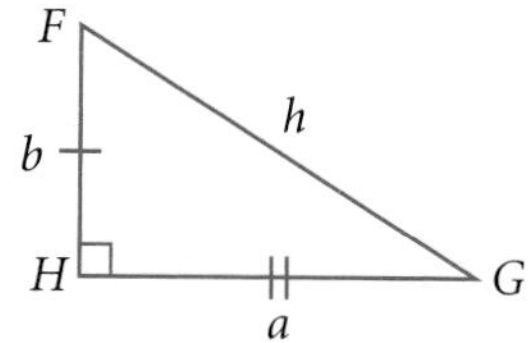

By the Pythagorean Theorem, $a^2 + b^2 = h^2$. We are given that $a^2 + b^2 = c^2$, so we can show by substitution that $h^2 = c^2$. Since both h and c are positive, $h = c$, and $\triangle ABC \cong \triangle FGH$ by SSS. Therefore, $\angle C \cong \angle H$ by CPCTC. $\angle H$ is a right angle, so it measures 90°. $\angle C$ must also measure 90°, by the definition of congruent angles, so $\angle C$ is also a right angle by the definition of right angles. Therefore, $\triangle ABC$ is a right triangle by the definition of right triangle, and c is its hypotenuse since it is opposite the right angle.

We summarize the inequalities related to the Pythagorean Theorem below.

PYTHAGOREAN INEQUALITY THEOREMS

If the sum of the squares of the lengths of the shorter two sides of a triangle is greater than the square of the length of the longest side, then the triangle is acute.

If the sum of the squares of the lengths of the shorter two sides of a triangle is less than the square of the length of the longest side, then the triangle is obtuse.

REFLECT

1. If you know the side lengths of a triangle, how can you determine if it is a right triangle, an acute triangle, or an obtuse triangle?
2. State the Pythagorean Theorem and its converse as a biconditional.

Exercises

CORE

1. **Getting Started** Follow the steps to determine whether a triangle with side lengths 4, 5, and 7 is acute, obtuse, or right.
   a. Find the sum of the squares of the smaller side lengths.
   b. Find the square of the largest side length.
   c. Is the square of the largest side length less than the sum of the squares of the other sides? If so, the triangle is acute. If it is greater than the sum of the other squares, the triangle is obtuse. If it is equal to the sum of the other squares, the triangle is a right triangle.

Given the following side lengths, classify each triangle as acute, obtuse, or right.

2. 3, 4, 5 **3.** 10, 12, 15 **4.** 11, 11, 15

5. $4, 4\sqrt{3}, 8$ **6.** 2, 2, 3 **7.** $\frac{5}{12}, 1, 1\frac{1}{12}$

Find the values of *x* that will make each triangle an acute triangle.

8. 4, *x*, 7 **9.** 3, 6, *x*

10. Charles knows that a triangle with sides measuring 3, 4, and 5 units is a right triangle. He says that if you multiply all three side lengths by the same number, you will still have a right triangle. Do you agree with him? Explain why or why not.

11. An Able Cable You are raising a twenty-foot telephone pole with a cable. The cable hoist is fifteen feet from the pole. How can you ensure that the pole will be vertical? Explain.

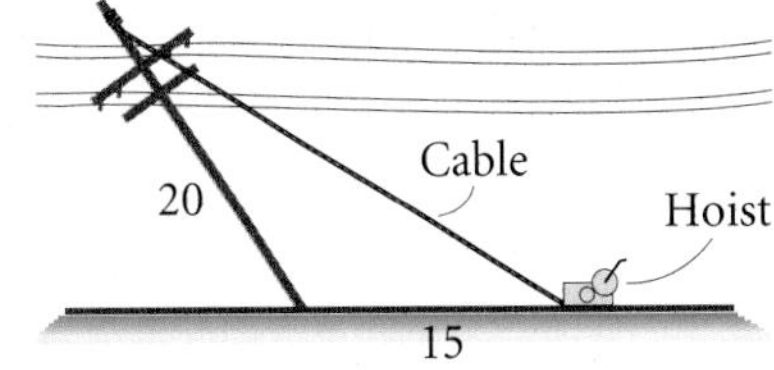

12. *Plan* a proof of the following statement: "If the side lengths of a triangle are 3, 3, and $3\sqrt{2}$, then the triangle is an isosceles right triangle."

13. Suppose you have computer software that draws straight line segments of any length and you can position the segments wherever you like. How can you use this software to draw a right angle?

14. Knot a Bad Idea Paintings in ancient Egyptian tombs depict people carrying ropes with equally spaced knots. These ropes may have been used by surveyors to make right angles and right triangles. Explain how a rope with 13 equally-spaced knots could be used to make a right triangle.

LOOK AHEAD

15. *ABCD* is a parallelogram. Copy *ABCD*, and draw diagonal $\overline{AC}$. Then list any pairs of angles that you know are congruent, and explain why they are congruent.

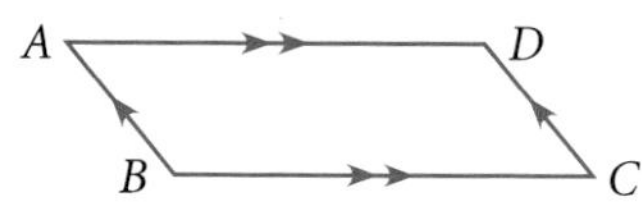

Define each of the following quadrilaterals in your own words.

16. parallelogram

17. square

18. rectangle

19. rhombus

20. trapezoid

MORE PRACTICE

Given the following side lengths, classify each triangle as acute, obtuse, or right.

21. 20, 21, 29

22. 9, 12, 15

23. 9, 9, 13

24. 18, 18, $18\sqrt{2}$

25. $\frac{1}{3}, \frac{1}{4}, \frac{1}{5}$

26. 4.3, 6.8, 10.1

MORE MATH REASONING

27. Malika claims that there are an infinite number of Pythagorean triples. Is she correct? Explain why you agree or disagree with her.

28. **Triple Play!** There is a simple way to create a long list of Pythagorean triples (a computer or programmable calculator can make it even easier). Choose any two positive integers *m* and *n*, with $m > n$. A Pythagorean triple (*a*, *b*, and *c*) will be given by the following equations:

$a = m^2 - n^2$

$b = 2mn$

$c = m^2 + n^2$

a. Generate a list of at least five Pythagorean triples using these formulas.
b. Why do these formulas work for generating Pythagorean triples?

29. Count the dots in each dot-square. Describe any patterns that you see.

5-3 PART E Making Connections

← CONNECT → ***The Pythagorean Theorem enables you to find an unknown side length in a right triangle. This is useful in architecture and other fields. You've learned about the history and applications of the Pythagorean Theorem and seen why the theorem is true.***

In the following Explore, you will investigate the Babylonian tablet known as Plimpton 322. You will do some archaeological detective work to find out what its numbers mean.

EXPLORE: TABLET TABULATIONS

Plimpton 322 contains columns of numbers written in base 60. Translated into base 10, the numbers are as follows.

119	169
3367	4825
4601	6649
65	97
319	481
2291	3541
799	1249
481	769
4961	8161
45	75

1. What is the significance of these numbers? What is their connection to the Pythagorean Theorem?
2. Add a third column to the table, and explain how you found the missing numbers.
3. If you were a scribe in ancient Babylonia, what other rows of numbers could you add to this list? (Give at least three more rows.)

REFLECT

1. If you know the lengths of all three sides of a triangle, what can you learn about the angles? Explain and illustrate your answer.
2. Use figures to show the ratios of the side lengths for special right triangles. Then explain why those ratios must be true for each type of triangle.
3. Explain how the figure at the right shows the relationship of the Pythagorean Theorem to the equation of a circle.

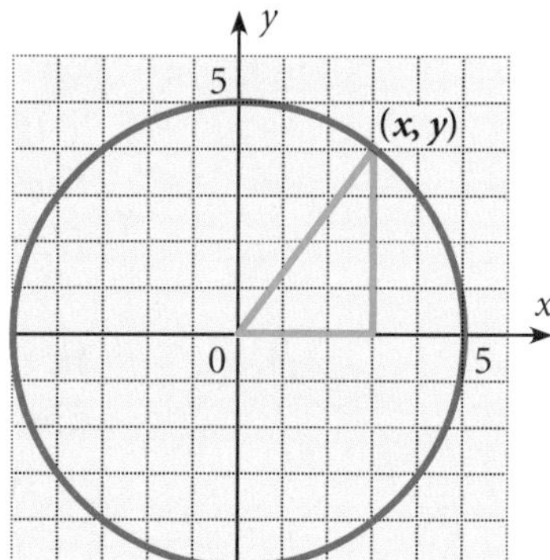

Self-Assessment

The shorter sides of a triangle are 6 cm and 8 cm long. Find a length for the longest side so that the triangle is

1. a right triangle
2. an acute triangle
3. an obtuse triangle

4. If you hike 2 mi north, 5 mi east, 4 mi north, 7 mi east, then 1 mi south, what is the distance from your final location to the starting point?
(a) $\sqrt{29}$ mi (b) 13 mi (c) 19 mi (d) $\sqrt{150}$ mi (e) not here

Find the probability that a point selected at random will be in the shaded area of each figure. [5-1, 5-2]

5.

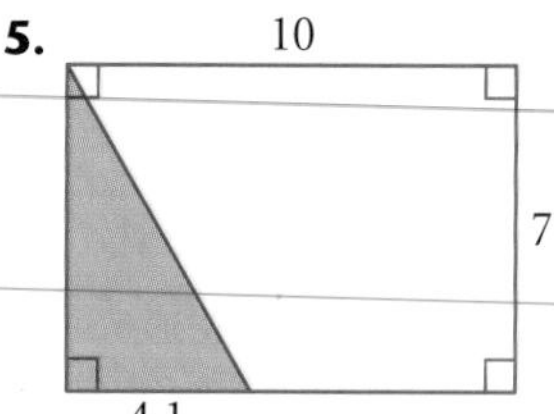

6.

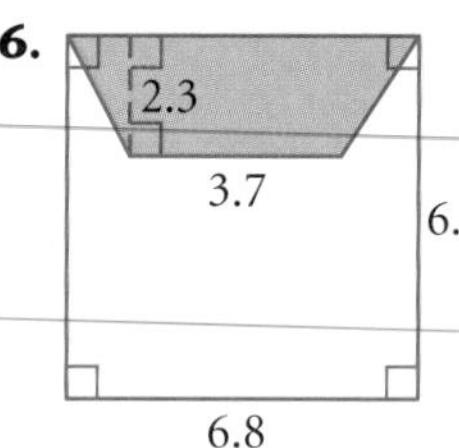

7. **A Stable Shed** Leilani is building a rectangular frame for a wall of a shed. She knows that rectangles are unstable, so she wants to add a diagonal support to the frame. To the nearest centimeter, how long should the support be? Explain your answer.

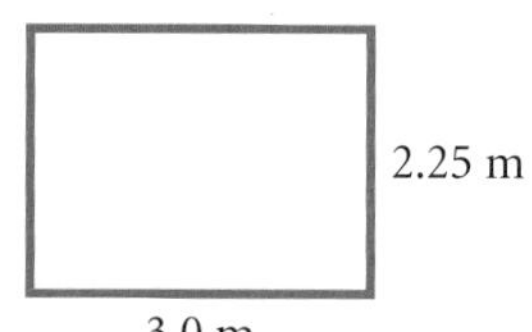

8. The point $(6, -8)$ is on a circle with center $(0, 0)$. Find the radius of the circle, and then write the equation of the circle.

9. **"A" Home** Find the height of the A-frame home shown at the right. Round your answer to the nearest tenth of a foot.

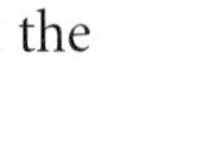

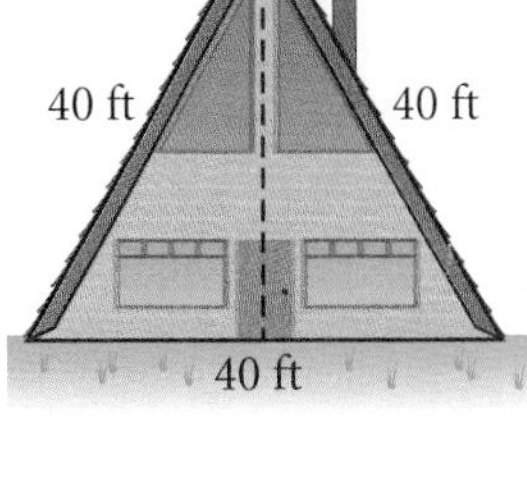

10. Complete the following proof. [4-2, 4-3]

Given: Quadrilateral $ABCD$ with $\overline{AB} \cong \overline{CD}$ and $\overline{BC} \cong \overline{AD}$

Prove: $\angle BAC \cong \angle DCA$

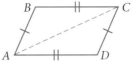

B C A D

Proof:

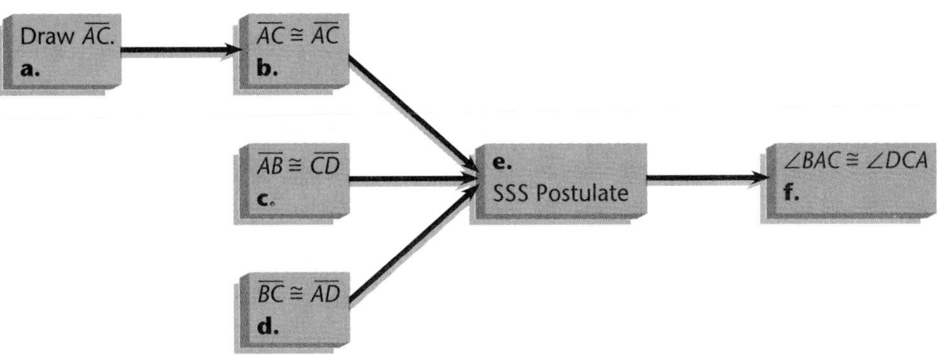

11. Find all possible lengths of segments whose endpoints are points on the 4×4 grid shown. (Assume the distance between adjacent vertical and horizontal points is 1.)

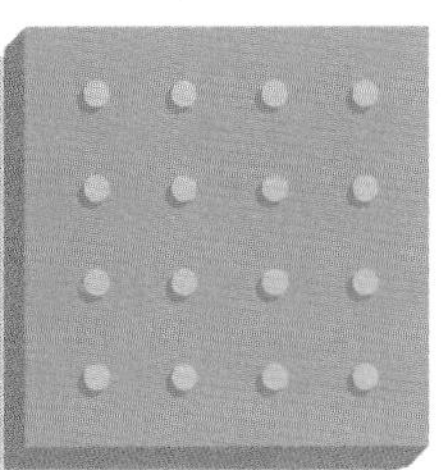

12. In the sequence of right triangles shown below, the original triangle (at the far right) is an isosceles right triangle with legs of length 1. Each additional right triangle is built with one leg on the hypotenuse of the preceding triangle and the other leg of length 1.

a. Find x.

b. If a dart is thrown randomly at this "target," what is the probability that it will hit the largest triangle? Express your answer as a decimal rounded to the nearest hundredth.

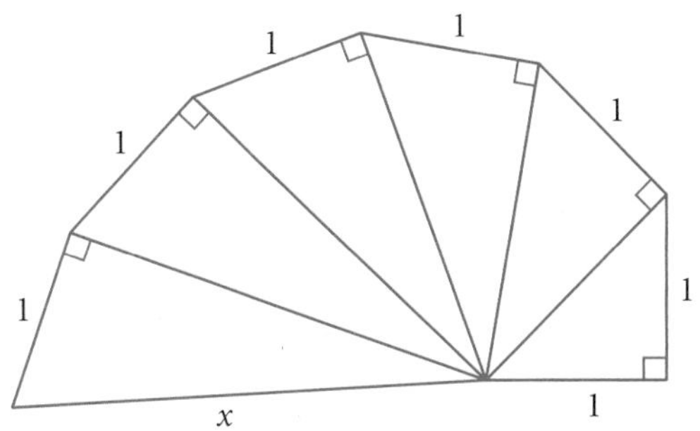

Chapter 5 Review

The measurement of area is among the oldest and most common applications of mathematics. In Chapter 5, you learned how to determine and use areas of various polygonal regions. You also learned how to apply the concept of area to quadratic equations, geometric probability, and the proof of the Pythagorean Theorem.

KEY TERMS

area [5-1]	polygonal region [5-1]	rectangle [5-2]
geometric probability [5-1]	Pythagorean triple [5-3]	rhombus [5-2]
parallelogram [5-2]	quadratic equation [5-1]	square [5-2]
perimeter [5-1]	quadrilateral [5-2]	trapezoid [5-2]
polygon [5-1]		

Determine whether each statement is true or false. If the statement is false, change the underlined word or phrase to make it true.

1. The area of a polygonal region is the sum of the areas of all of its overlapping parts.

2. A quadratic formula is of the form $ax^2 + bx + c = 0$.

3. A parallelogram is a quadrilateral with two pairs of parallel sides.

4. A quadrilateral with four right angles is a square.

CONCEPTS AND APPLICATIONS

Find the area of each figure. [5-1]

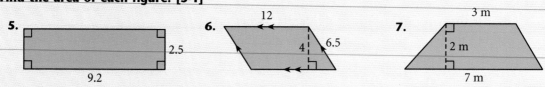

5.

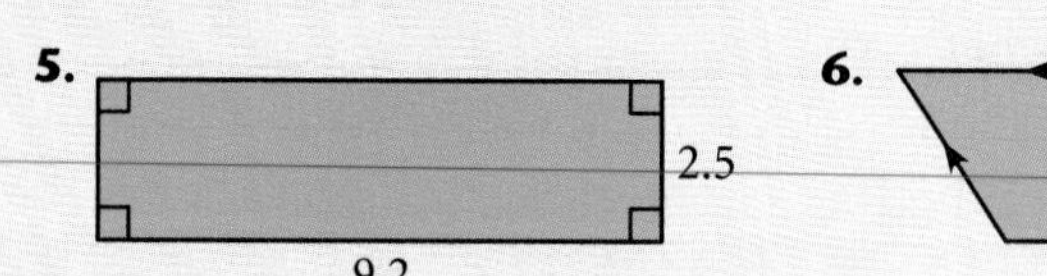

6.

12
4
6.5

7.

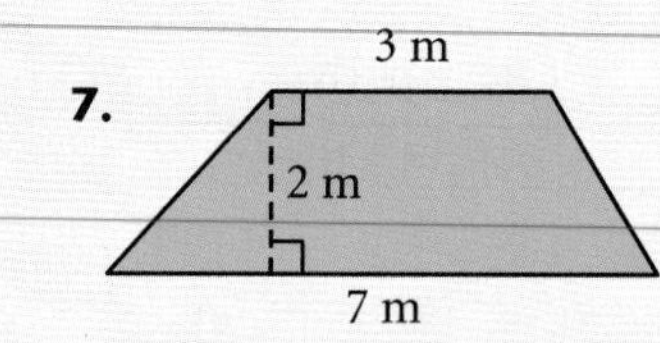

Find the perimeter of each figure. [5-1, 5-2, 5-3]

8. Rhombus $XYZW$

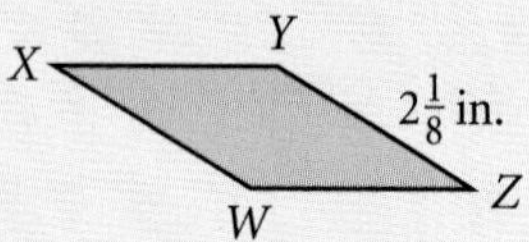

9.

5 cm
45°

10. Square $RSTU$

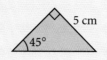

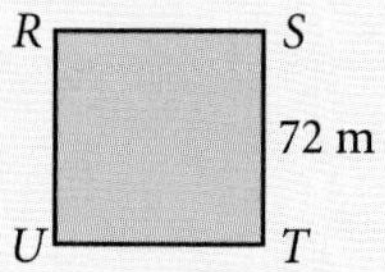

Represent each of the following, using squares and rectangles. Provide a sketch, and give an algebraic answer. [5-1]

11. Multiply $(x + 5)$ and $(x + 3)$.

12. Factor $x^2 + 12x + 20$.

13. A hockey player's slap shot from 20 ft away from the goal will hit randomly within the outer rectangle. The identical shaded regions are that part of the open goal that the goalie cannot defend. [5-1]

a. What is the total area of the shaded regions?

b. To the nearest hundredth, what is the probability that the shot will hit in the shaded regions, resulting in a score?

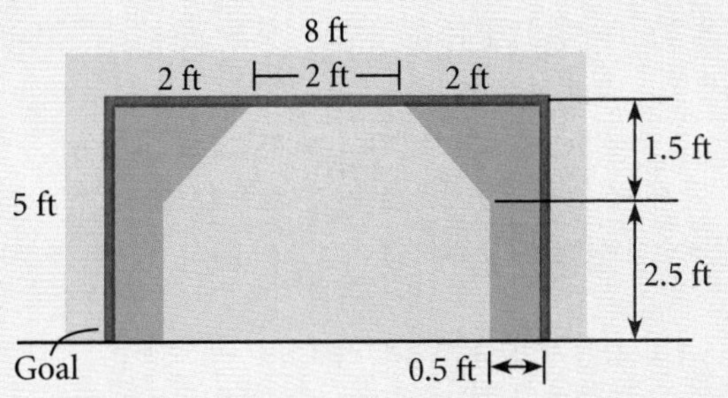

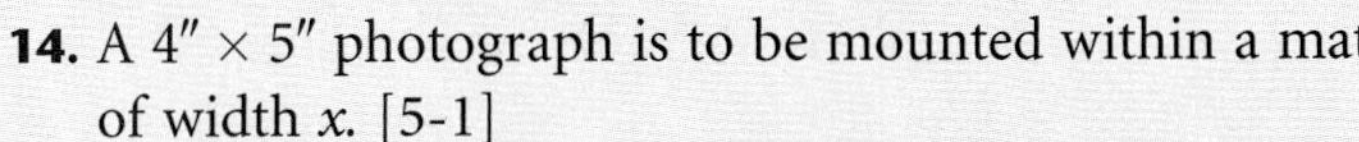

14. A 4″ × 5″ photograph is to be mounted within a mat of width x. [5-1]

a. What is the total area of the photograph and the mat in terms of x?

b. If the total area is 40 in.^{2}, what is the width of the mat to the nearest tenth of an inch?

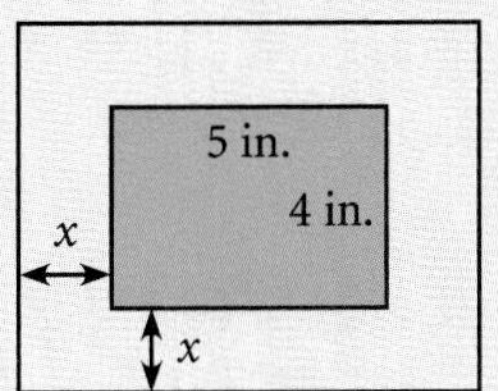

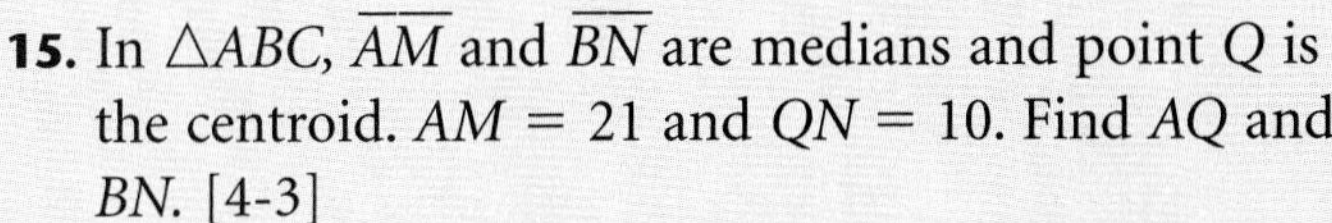

15. In $\triangle ABC$, $\overline{AM}$ and $\overline{BN}$ are medians and point Q is the centroid. $AM = 21$ and $QN = 10$. Find AQ and BN. [4-3]

16. The diagonals of quadrilateral $JKLM$ bisect each other. *Plan* a logical argument to show that $JKLM$ is a parallelogram. [5-2]

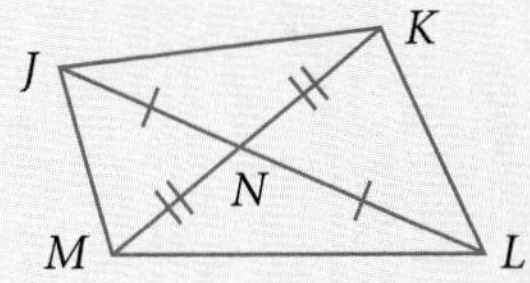

17. Find the approximate area between the x-axis and the graph of the equation $y = \sqrt{x}$ from $x = 0$ to 9, using the trapezoid method. Use trapezoids of height 3. [5-2]

18. What is the length of the cut where the sides of the picture frame are joined? [5-3]

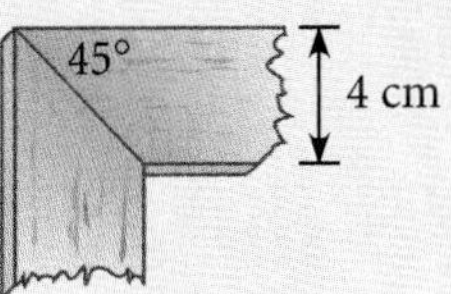

19. Find the length of the diagonal across a rectangular 20″ × 25″ television screen. [5-3]

20. Write a summary of the relationships among the equation of a circle, the distance formula, and the Pythagorean Theorem. [5-3]

CONCEPTS AND CONNECTIONS

21. Construction A farmer has 100 m of fencing to section off a corner of land for a new crop. One possible placement of the fence is shown. Make three other proposals for the placement of the fence. For each proposal, provide a sketch of the fence, showing as many dimensions as possible, and include information on the area of the fenced-off region. Which of your proposals do you think would be most appealing to the farmer? Why?

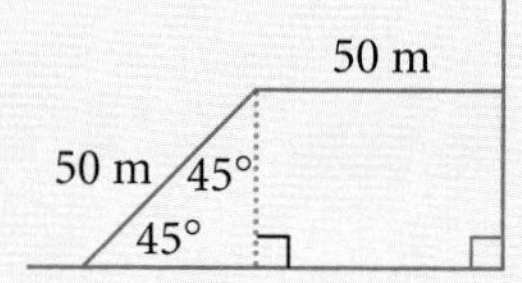

SELF-EVALUATION

Write a summary of the most important facts that you have learned from Chapter 5. Include facts about various quadrilaterals and right triangles as well as key formulas for determining areas and side lengths. Provide a sketch to illustrate each fact.

Chapter 5 Assessment

TEST

Find the area of each figure.

1. $8\frac{1}{2}$ in.

11 in.

2.

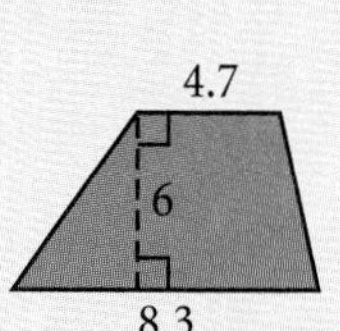

3.

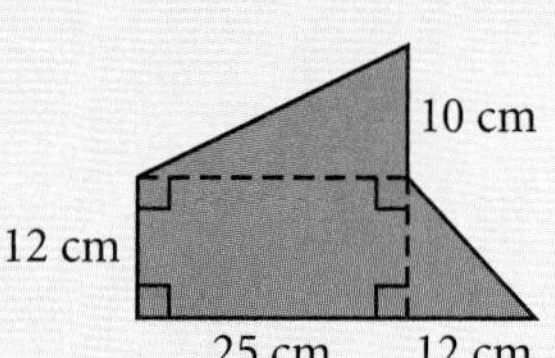

4.

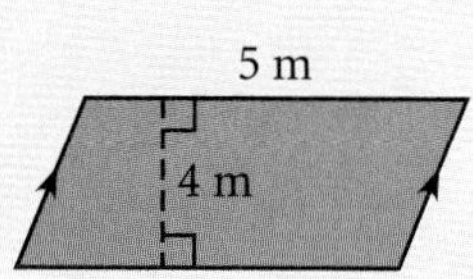

Find the length of each cable in the figure. Explain your method.

5. Cable 1

6. Cable 2

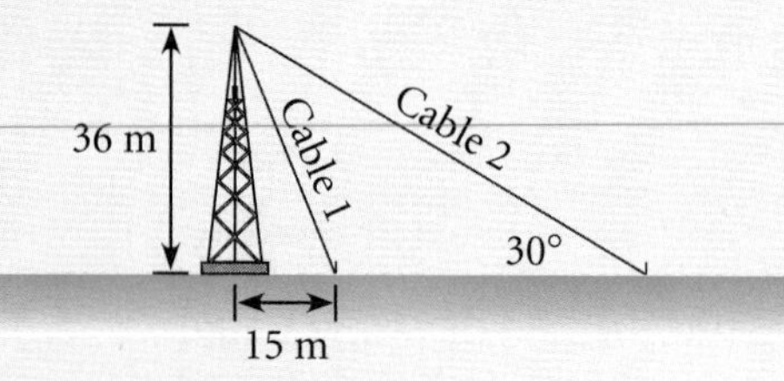

Represent each of the following using squares and rectangles. Provide a sketch, and give an algebraic answer.

7. Multiply $(x + 4)$ and $(x + 3)$.

8. Factor $x^2 + 7x + 6$.

9. For what value of x will the area of the larger rectangle be three times that of the smaller one?

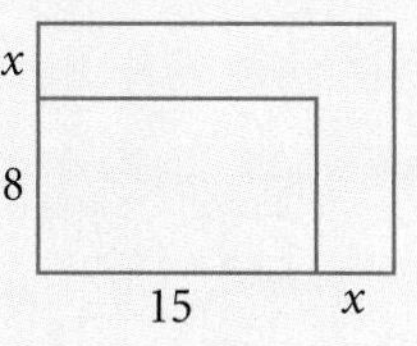

10. *Plan* a logical argument to show that a diagonal of a parallelogram divides it into two congruent triangles.

11. A slow-pitch softball pitcher with good control will always land her pitch within the outer rectangle in the figure. If the pitch lands within the shaded region, it is a strike.

a. What is the area of the shaded region?

b. To the nearest hundredth, what is the probability that the pitch will be a strike?

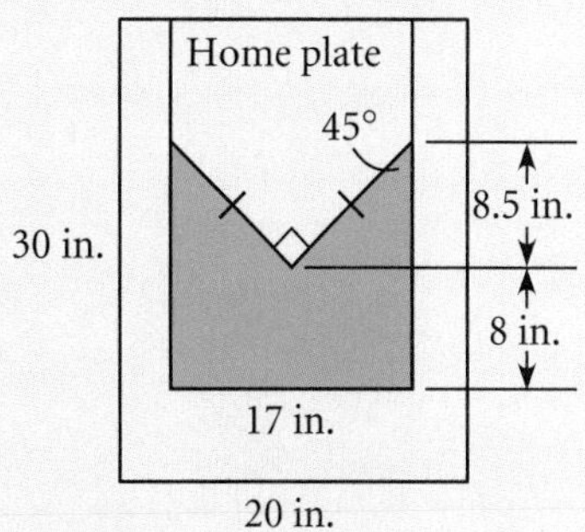

12. Find the approximate area between the x-axis and the graph of the equation $y = x^2$ from $x = 0$ to 3, using the trapezoid method. Use trapezoids of height 1.

Find the perimeter of each figure.

13. Rhombus *GHIJ*

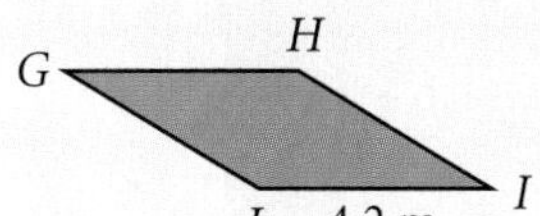

14.

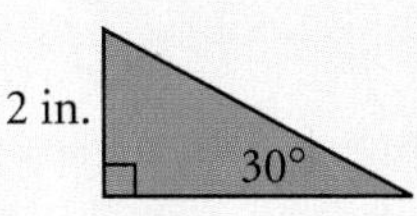

15.

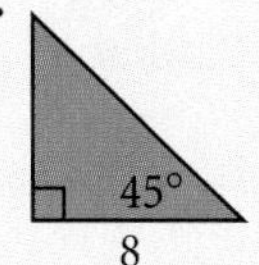

16. Write a summary of the methods for determining whether a triangle is right, acute, or obtuse when the lengths of its sides are known. Include sketches to illustrate the methods.

17. In $\triangle KLM$, $\overline{KW}$ and $\overline{LZ}$ are medians, $KW = 40$, and $LC = 12$. Find KC and LZ.

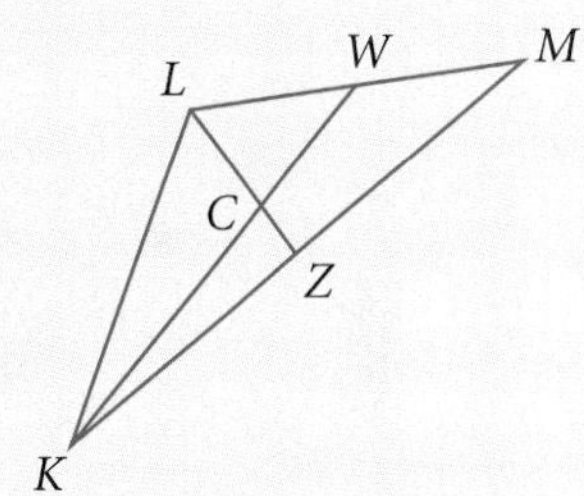

PERFORMANCE TASK

RSTU is a parallelogram, and V is any point in the interior of the parallelogram. Investigate how the area of the shaded region is related to the area of the parallelogram. Make a conjecture, and write a *plan* to justify your conjecture deductively.

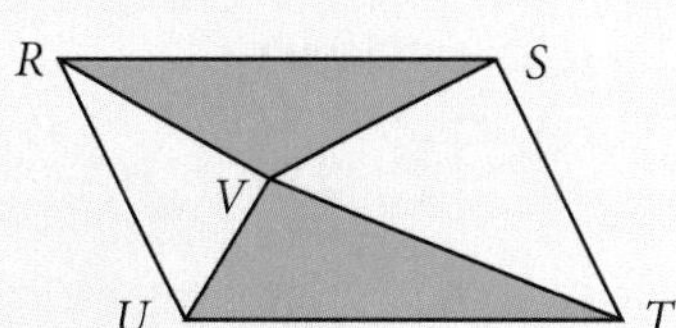

Chapter 6 Polygons and Polyhedrons

Project A
Model a Molecule
What are crystals, and how are they formed?

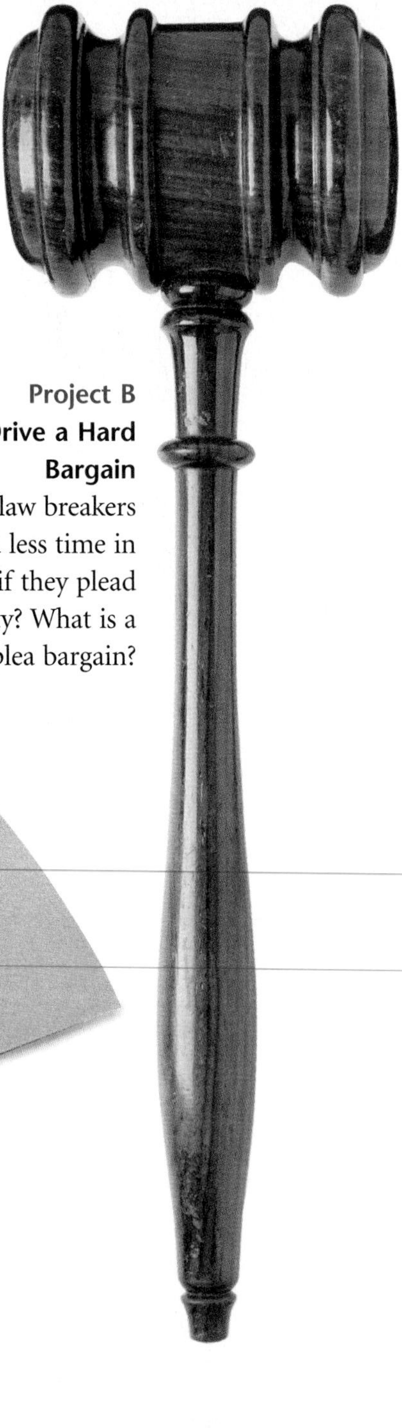

Project B
Drive a Hard Bargain
Do law breakers spend less time in jail if they plead guilty? What is a plea bargain?

Project C
Transcend the Triangle
How many convex solids can you build from equilateral triangles?

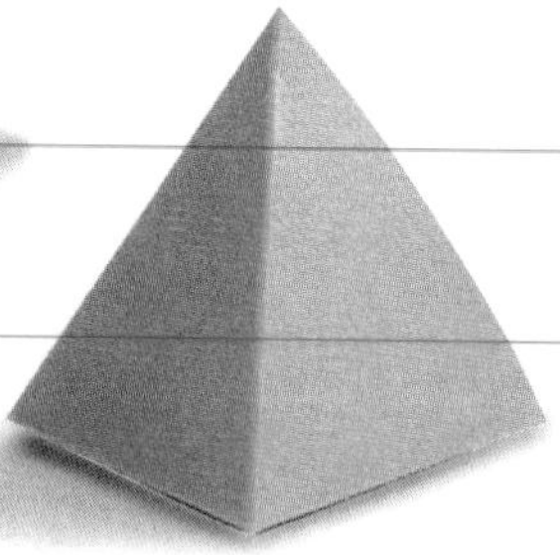

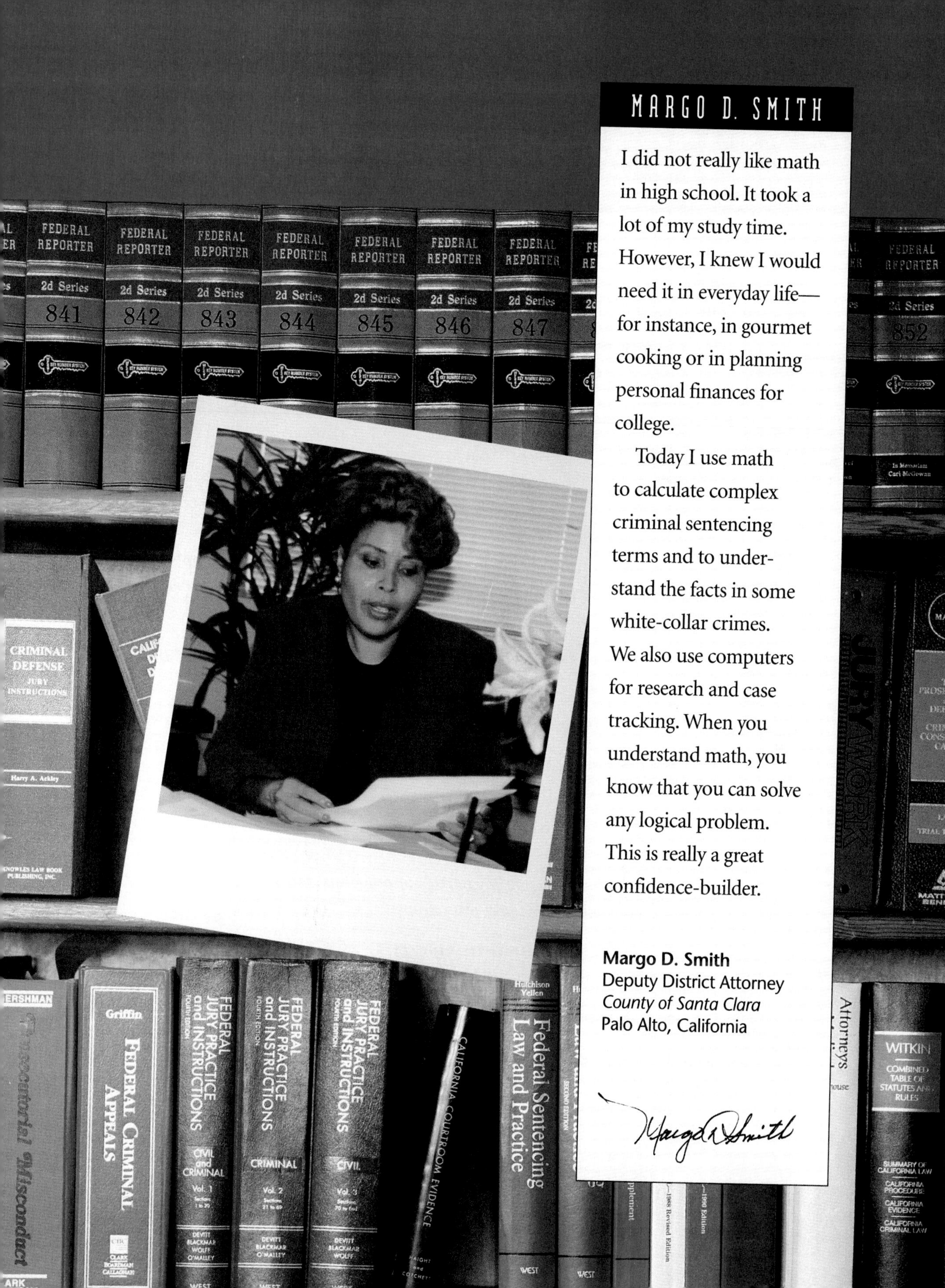

MARGO D. SMITH

I did not really like math in high school. It took a lot of my study time. However, I knew I would need it in everyday life—for instance, in gourmet cooking or in planning personal finances for college.

Today I use math to calculate complex criminal sentencing terms and to understand the facts in some white-collar crimes. We also use computers for research and case tracking. When you understand math, you know that you can solve any logical problem. This is really a great confidence-builder.

Margo D. Smith
Deputy District Attorney
County of Santa Clara
Palo Alto, California

Chapter 6 Polygons and Polyhedrons

GETTING READY

6-1 Polygons and Polyhedrons

In 6-1 you will explore properties of polygons and polyhedrons. You will use the following skills from previous chapters.

Find the missing lengths. [5-1]

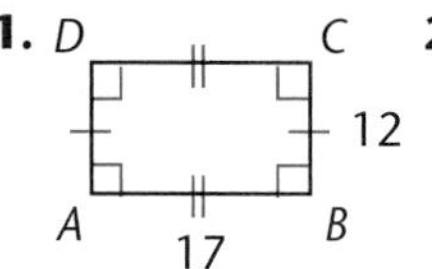

3. $14\sqrt{7}$ S R P Q

4. W x X 10 Z $2x$ Y

1. $AB =$ ____ $BC =$ ____

2. $GH =$ ____

3. $QR =$ ____ $PQ =$ ____

4. $x = 13$ $WX =$ ____

6-2 Deductive Proof with Quadrilaterals

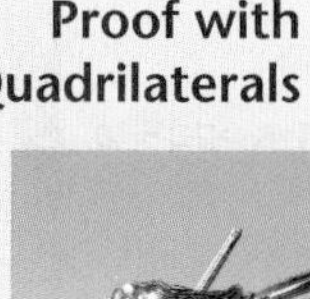

In 6-2 you will investigate properties of quadrilaterals and develop skills in writing deductive proof. You will need the following skills from previous courses and chapters.

Find the slope of the line through each pair of points. [Previous course]

5. $(1, 4), (0, 7)$

6. $(9, 6), (-8, -4)$

7. $(-8, -5), (6, -5)$

8. $(-9, 3), (2, -1)$

Find the midpoint of the segments with these endpoints. [2-2]

9. $(5, 9), (6, 13)$

10. $(4, 3), (8, -9)$

11. $(-4, 15), (-12, 8)$

12. $(-2, 5), (-6, -8)$

6-3 Regular Polygons and Polyhedrons

In 6-3 you will investigate properties of polygons and polyhedrons. You will need the following skills from previous chapters.

Find the area of each right triangle. [5-1]

13. base $= 10$, altitude $= 10$

14. legs $= 1$ and $\sqrt{3}$

15. leg $= 4$, hypotenuse $= 5$

Find the missing side of each triangle. [5-3]

16. Two angles are 30° and 60°. The shortest side is 10. What is the length of the longest side?

17. Two angles are 45° and 90°. The longest side is $10\sqrt{2}$. What are the lengths of the other sides?

6-1 Polygons and Polyhedrons

GEOMETRIC CONSTRUCTION ZONE

Ieoh Ming Pei, a Chinese-born American architect, is noted for his beautifully-designed urban buildings and complexes. Pei's innovative East Building of the National Gallery of Art, in Washington, D.C., is an elegant triangular composition that is recognized as one of his finest achievements.

Pei created urban projects, such as the Mile High Center in Denver, the Hyde Park Redevelopment in Chicago, and the Place Ville-Marie in Montreal. As the winner of a 1960 competition, Pei was chosen to design the airline terminal at John F. Kennedy International Airport. He also designed the New York City Convention Center, the John Hancock Tower in Boston, the Gateway office complex in Singapore, the Beijing Fragrant Hill Hotel, the Dallas Municipal Center, and the controversial glass pyramid for a courtyard at the Louvre Museum in Paris. Pei is noted for his bold, skillful arrangements of geometric figures. The pyramids, prisms, and tetrahedrons seen in his designs are all types of polyhedrons.

?

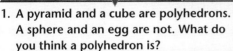

1. A pyramid and a cube are polyhedrons. A sphere and an egg are not. What do you think a polyhedron is?
2. Identify the two- and three-dimensional figures shown here in Pei's buildings.

6-1 PART A Exploring Quadrilaterals

← CONNECT → *You've worked with the area of some special four-sided figures. Now you will investigate properties that hold for every quadrilateral.*

The surface of the pine cone at the left contains quadrilaterals. You know that a quadrilateral is a polygon with four sides. Some familiar quadrilaterals include squares, rectangles, parallelograms, and rhombuses.

We name a quadrilateral by listing its vertices in order. The quadrilateral at the right can be named *WXYZ*, *XWZY*, *YZWX*, or in several other ways. A **diagonal** of a quadrilateral is a line segment whose endpoints are opposite vertices.

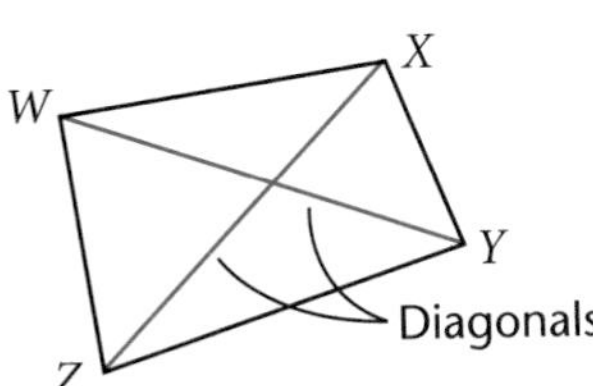

TRY IT

a. Name quadrilateral *ABCD* in three other ways.

b. Name the diagonals of *ABCD*.

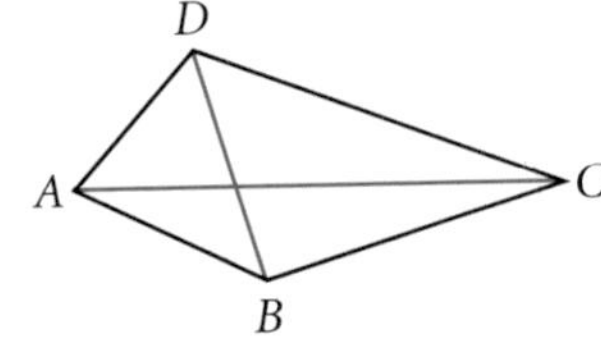

You already know about many special types of quadrilaterals. The definitions of some familiar ones are reviewed below.

DEFINITIONS

A **parallelogram** is a quadrilateral with two pairs of parallel sides.

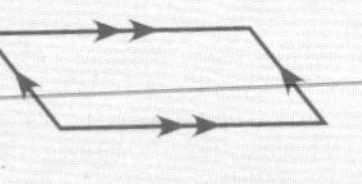

A **rectangle** is a quadrilateral with four right angles.

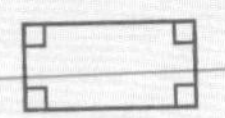

A **rhombus** is a quadrilateral with four congruent sides.

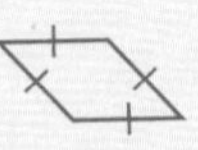

A **square** is a quadrilateral with four right angles and four congruent sides.

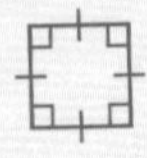

A **trapezoid** is a quadrilateral with exactly one pair of parallel sides.

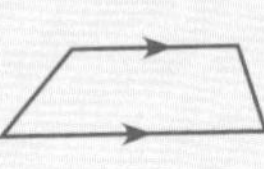

The diagram below shows the relationships among these quadrilaterals. Each figure inherits all of the characteristics of the figure(s) above it that are connected to it.

A Quadrilateral Family Tree

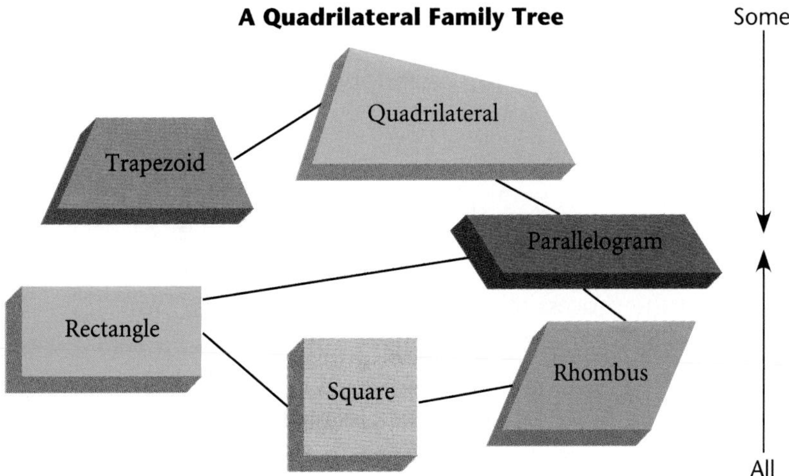

When you read the diagram downward, use the word *some* to note that "Some quadrilaterals are trapezoids," or "Some rhombuses are squares." When you read it upward, use the word *all* to note that "All squares are rectangles," or "All rhombuses are parallelograms." These properties can be proved, so you may use them as reasons in a deductive proof.

TRY IT

c. Classify the quadrilateral at the right.

d. Use the quadrilateral family tree to write three true statements about this type of quadrilateral.

1. Explain why *square* is linked to both *rhombus* and *rectangle* in the quadrilateral family tree.

You have seen that there is an Angle-Sum Theorem for triangles. In the following Explore, you will investigate a similar theorem for quadrilaterals.

EXPLORE: QUAD ANGLES

MATERIALS

Protractor, Straightedge
Geometry software (optional)

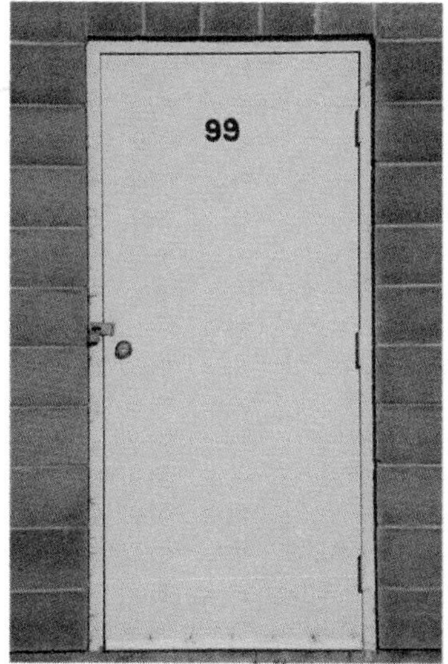

1. Use a straightedge or geometry software to draw a quadrilateral. Use your protractor to measure each of the interior angles. Find the sum of the measures of the angles.
2. Repeat the process with different quadrilaterals. (You may wish to use the photograph at the right as one of these.) Use your results to state a conjecture. Compare your results with those of your classmates.
3. Can you find a quadrilateral for which your conjecture doesn't hold? Illustrate and explain.

EXAMPLE

Find the measures of the angles of the quadrilateral.

$x + (x + 40) + 2x + (x + 10) = 360$

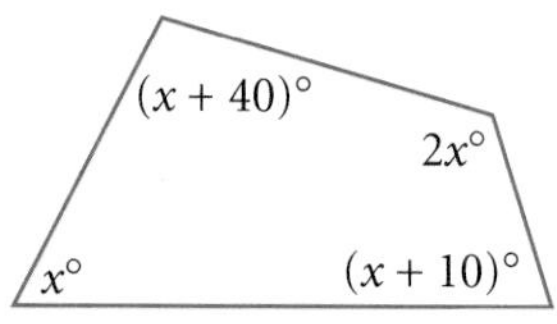

$5x + 50 = 360$

$5x = 310$

$x = 62$

Substituting gives angle measures of 62°, 102°, 124°, and 72°.

The quadrilaterals that you will study are convex quadrilaterals. A quadrilateral is **convex** if each diagonal (excluding the endpoints) lies in the interior of the quadrilateral. It is **concave** if any diagonal lies in the exterior of the figure.

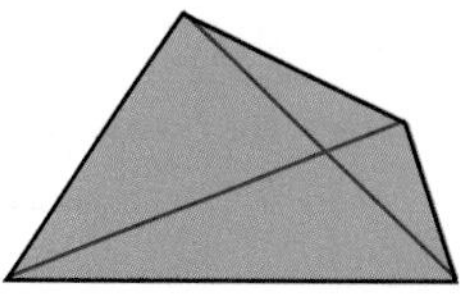

Convex quadrilateral

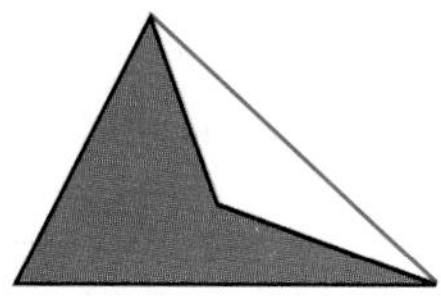

Concave quadrilateral

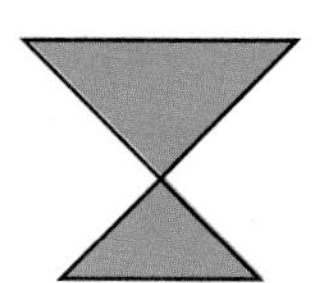

Not a quadrilateral

> **ANGLE-SUM THEOREM FOR QUADRILATERALS**
>
> The sum of the measures of the interior angles of a convex quadrilateral is 360°.

REFLECT

1. What types of quadrilaterals have parallel sides?
2. Describe some properties that rectangles and squares have in common.
3. It is possible to define a rectangle as a quadrilateral with four congruent angles. Explain why this definition is equivalent to the one we are using.

Exercises

CORE

Getting Started Use the figure at the right for Exercises 1 and 2.

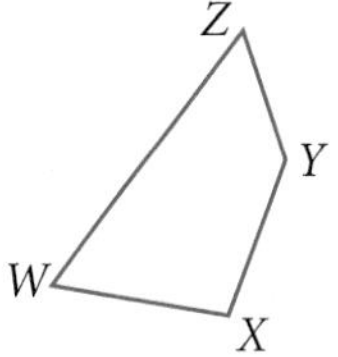

1. Name quadrilateral *WXYZ* in three other ways.

2. Name the diagonals of *WXYZ*.

Draw and classify the following quadrilaterals.

3. a quadrilateral *ABCD* with $\overline{AB} \cong \overline{BC}$

4. a quadrilateral with all sides congruent that is not a square

5. a quadrilateral *QRST* with $\overline{QR} \parallel \overline{ST}$, and $\overline{QT}$ not parallel to $\overline{RS}$

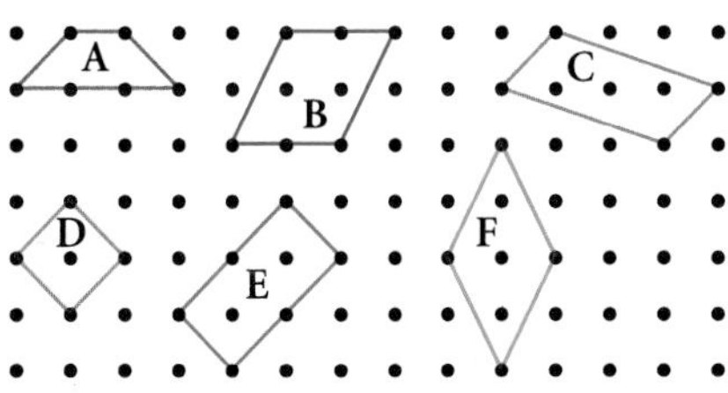

6. Give all possible classifications for each quadrilateral shown on the grid.

7. Determine whether the following statement is true or false. If the statement is false, change the underlined word to make it true.

   If $\overline{AC}$ passes through the exterior of quadrilateral *ABCD*, then *ABCD* is a <u>concave</u> quadrilateral.

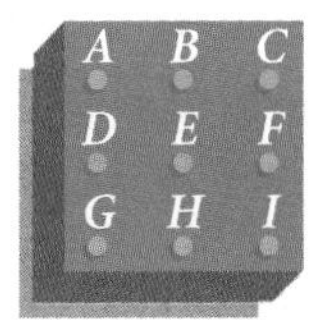

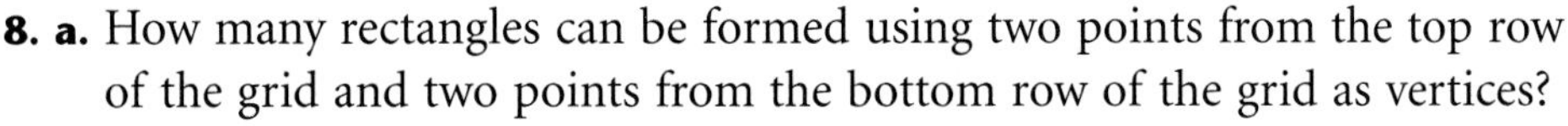

8. **a.** How many rectangles can be formed using two points from the top row of the grid and two points from the bottom row of the grid as vertices?
   b. How many trapezoids can be formed in the same way?

9. Room for Quadrilaterals Part of an excavation of Anasazi buildings at Mesa Verde is illustrated at the right. Estimate the measures of $\angle 1$, $\angle 2$, $\angle 3$, and $\angle 4$. Is the sum of your estimated measures what it should be? Explain.

If a quadrilateral is randomly selected from a set of five distinct quadrilaterals {square, rectangle, parallelogram, rhombus, trapezoid}, find the probability of the following.

10. None of the quadrilateral's sides are parallel.

11. The quadrilateral is a parallelogram.

12. All of the quadrilateral's sides are congruent.

13. Find x and measure the angles of quadrilateral $EFGH$.

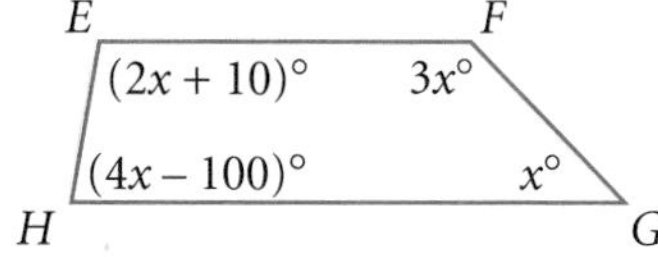

Find the measures of the angles of each quadrilateral.

14.

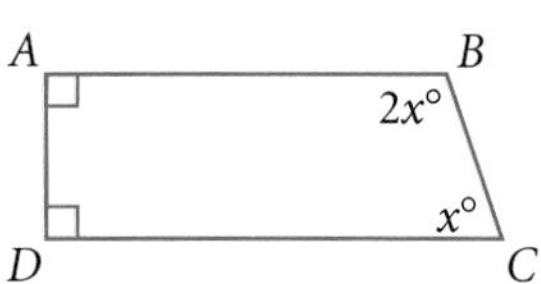

15.

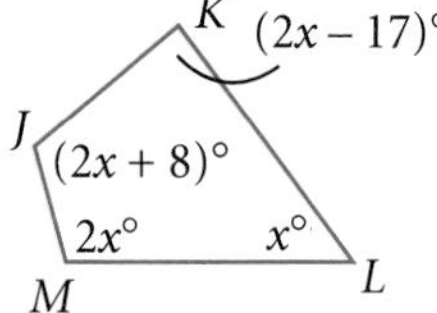

16.

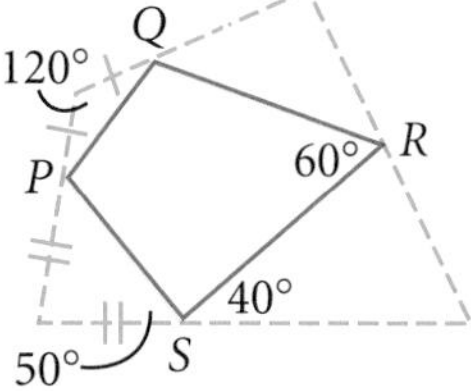

A **cross section** of a solid is the intersection of the solid and a plane. For example, the cross section produced by passing a plane through a cube as shown is a triangle.

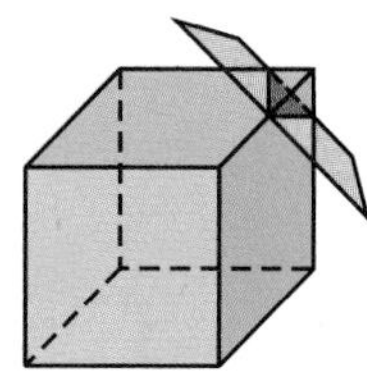

Draw and classify the cross section of the solid shown at the right when it is cut by the following planes.

17. a plane parallel to $\triangle EFG$

18. the plane through F and I perpendicular to $\overline{EG}$

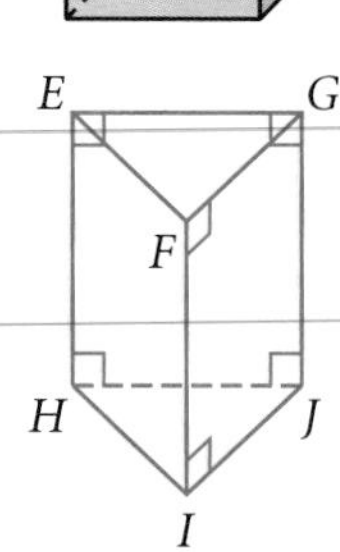

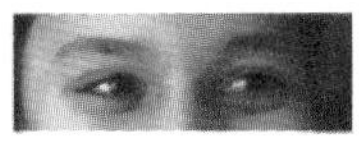

LOOK AHEAD

Sketch a polygon with the following number of sides.

19. 5 sides **20.** 6 sides **21.** 8 sides

22. Find the measure of the exterior angle and the measure of each interior angle in the figure.

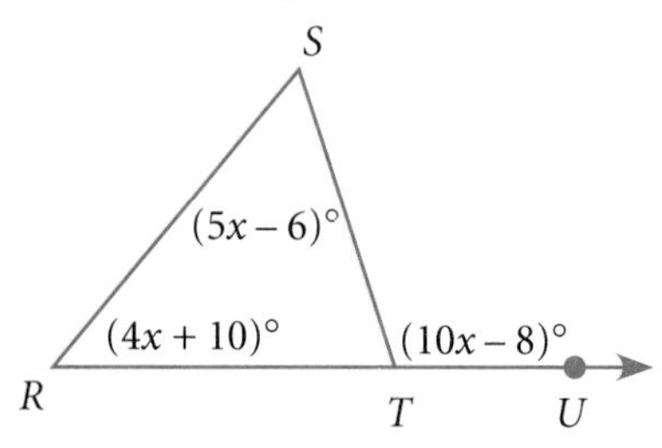

MORE PRACTICE

Draw and classify the following quadrilaterals.

23. a quadrilateral with exactly two consecutive right angles

24. a quadrilateral *PQRS* with four right angles

Suppose a quadrilateral with the given vertices is drawn on the grid. Classify the quadrilateral.

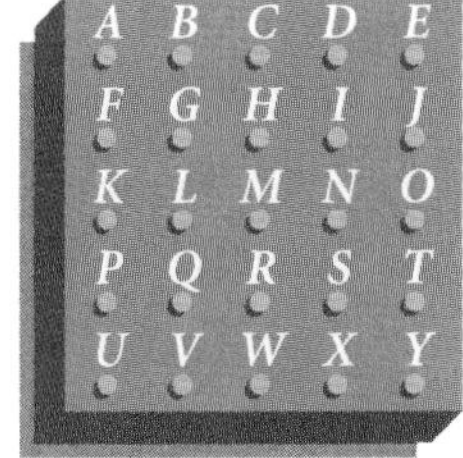

25. *A, K, N,* and *D*

26. *B, G, T,* and *E*

27. *U, L, O,* and *X*

28. *O, W, K,* and *C*

Find the measures of the angles of each quadrilateral.

29.

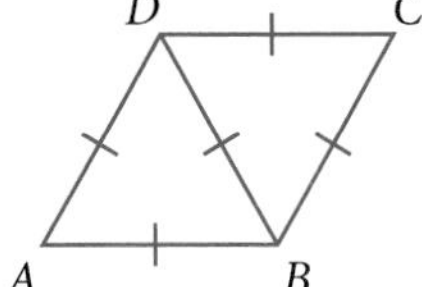

30.

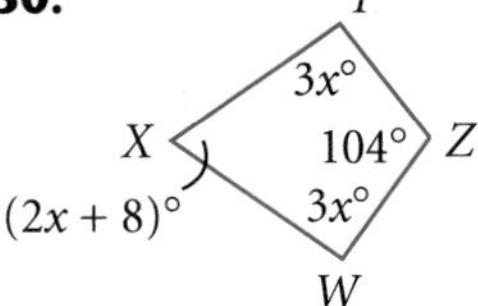

31.

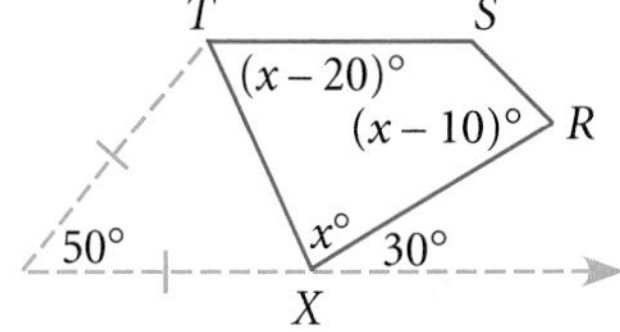

MORE MATH REASONING

32. Complete the following proof that all rectangles are parallelograms.

Given: *ABCD* is a rectangle.

Prove: *ABCD* is a parallelogram.

Proof:

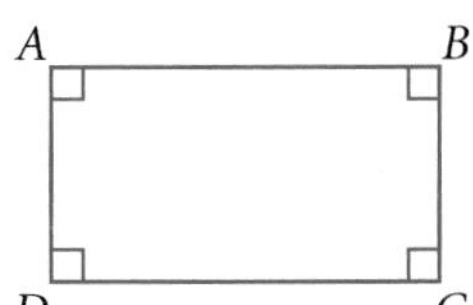

Statements	**Reasons**
1.	**1.** Given
2. $\angle A$, $\angle B$, $\angle C$, and $\angle D$ are right angles.	**2.**
3. $m\angle A = m\angle B = m\angle C = m\angle D = 90°$	**3.**
4. $\angle A$ and $\angle B$ are supplementary.	**4.**
5.	**5.** If two lines are cut by a transversal and the same-side interior angles are supplementary, then the lines are parallel.
6.	**6.** Definition of *supplementary*
7. $\overline{AB} \parallel \overline{DC}$	**7.**
8.	**8.**

33. Quad Odds If you randomly select a quadrilateral, replace it, and then select a second quadrilateral from a set of five distinct quadrilaterals {square, rectangle, rhombus, parallelogram, trapezoid}, what is the probability that both

a. will not have a pair of parallel sides?

b. will have at least three right angles?

c. will be parallelograms?

d. Explain how you calculated these probabilities. Would they be different if you did not replace the first quadrilateral?

34. Suppose a trapezoid was defined as a quadrilateral with at least one pair of parallel sides. How would this change affect the quadrilateral family tree? Explain your answer.

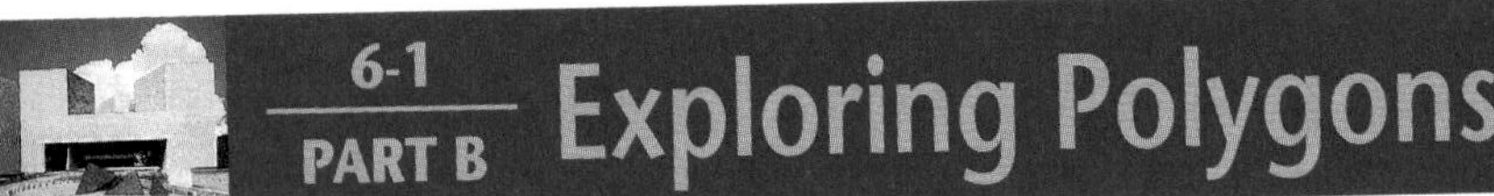

6-1 PART B Exploring Polygons

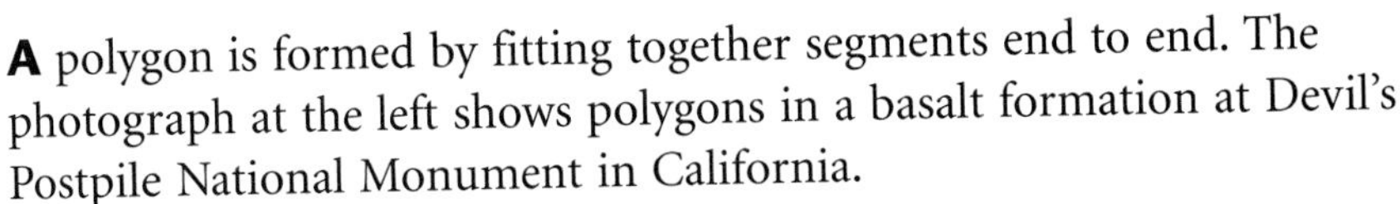

← CONNECT → ***You've discovered some of the properties of four-sided polygons. Now you will investigate polygons that have more than four sides.***

A polygon is formed by fitting together segments end to end. The photograph at the left shows polygons in a basalt formation at Devil's Postpile National Monument in California.

We've already defined the term *polygon* informally. As you begin to study polygons in more detail, you will need the more complete definitions below.

DEFINITIONS

A **polygon** is a plane figure whose sides are three or more coplanar segments that intersect only at their endpoints (the vertices). Consecutive sides cannot be collinear, and no more than two sides can meet at any one vertex.

A **diagonal of a polygon** is a line segment whose endpoints are any two nonconsecutive vertices of the polygon.

A **convex polygon** is one in which each diagonal (except its endpoints) is in the interior of the polygon.

Examples of figures that are and are not polygons are shown below. We will focus our investigations on convex polygons.

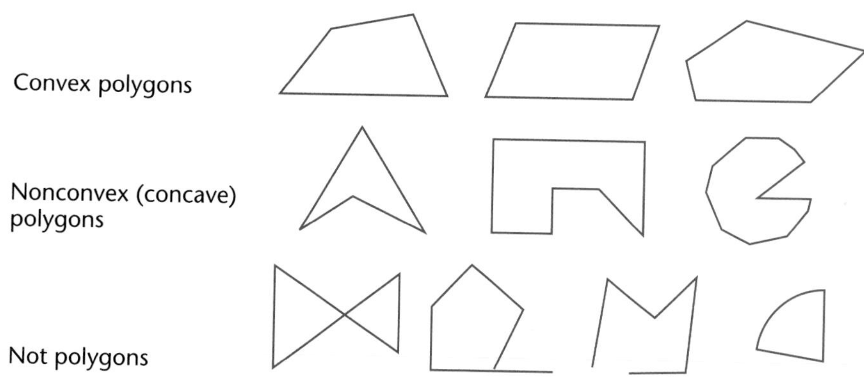

As with other figures, polygons are named using consecutive vertices. We classify a polygon by the number of sides it has. The following chart shows examples of some common polygons.

Classification of Polygons

Number of Sides	Polygon	Example	Number of Sides	Polygon	Example
3	Triangle (*tri* = three)		8	Octagon (*oct* = eight)	
4	Quadrilateral (*quadr* = four)		9	Nonagon (*non* = nine)	
5	Pentagon (*pent* = five)		10	Decagon (*dec* = ten)	
6	Hexagon (*hex* = six)		...	...	...
7	Heptagon (*hept* = seven)		n	n-gon	

TRY IT

a. Name the polygon at the right.
b. Classify the polygon.
c. How many diagonals can be drawn from vertex A?
d. Is the polygon concave or convex?

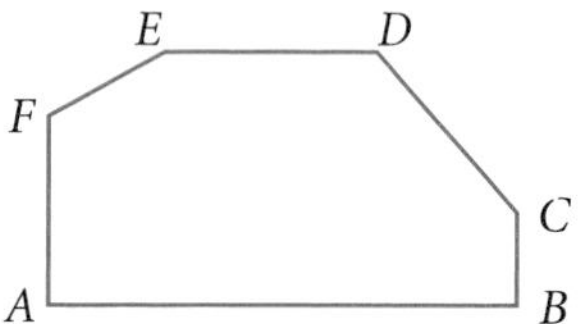

You have already found the sum of the measures of the interior angles for triangles and quadrilaterals. Now you will investigate the sum of the interior angles and the sum of the exterior angles of polygons.

EXPLORE: DIVIDE AND CONJECTURE

MATERIALS

Straightedge
Geometry software (optional)

1. Draw several convex polygons with different numbers of sides using a straightedge or geometry software. Draw all the diagonals from one vertex of each polygon.
2. In each case, how many triangles are formed? Find a relationship between the number of triangles and the number of sides. How many triangles are in an n-gon?
3. Use the triangles to help find the sum of the measures of the interior angles of each of your polygons.
4. What is the sum of the measures of the interior angles of an n-gon? Express your result as a function that gives S, the sum of the angle measures, in terms of n.
5. An exterior angle of a polygon is defined in the same way as an exterior angle for a triangle. The following sequence shows a “shrinking” heptagon with one exterior angle drawn at each vertex. As shown in the photograph, this is similar to how the aperture of a camera works.

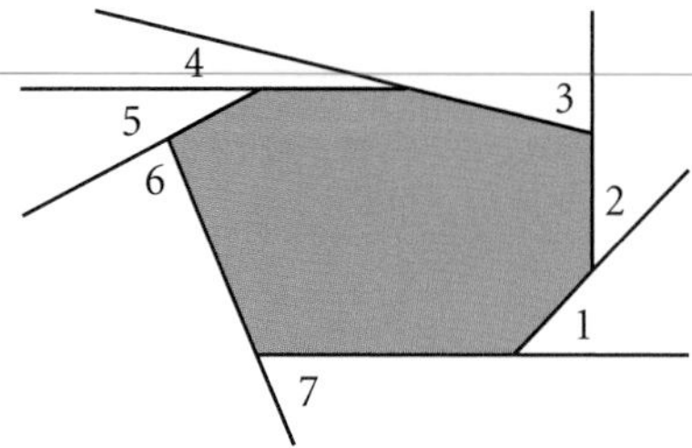

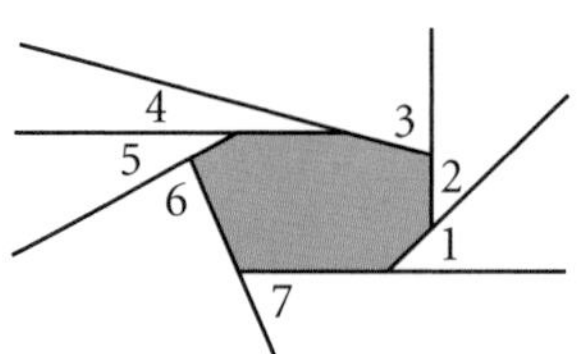

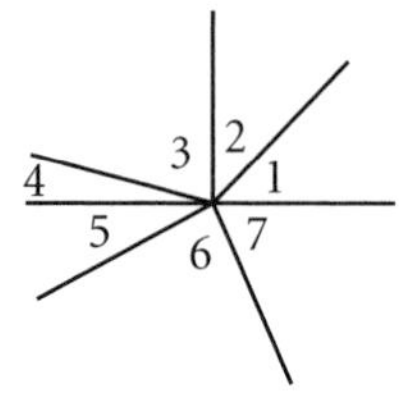

What does this sequence suggest about the sum of the measures of the exterior angles (one at each vertex) of a convex polygon? State a conjecture, and explain your reasoning.

EXAMPLES

Find the sum of the measures of the interior angles and exterior angles (one at each vertex) for each convex polygon.

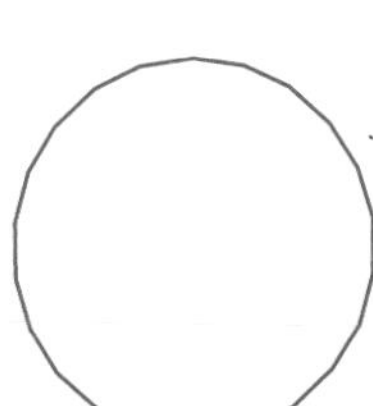

1. a heptagon

$$\begin{aligned}\text{interior angle sum} &= (n - 2)180^\circ \\ &= (7 - 2)180^\circ \\ &= 900^\circ\end{aligned}$$

2. a 22-gon

$$\begin{aligned}\text{interior angle sum} &= (n - 2)180^\circ \\ &= (22 - 2)180^\circ \\ &= 3600^\circ\end{aligned}$$

In both cases, the sum of the measures of the exterior angles is 360°.

Our results about the interior and exterior angles of a convex polygon are summarized below.

> **ANGLE-SUM THEOREM FOR POLYGONS**
>
> The sum of the measures of the interior angles of a convex polygon with n sides is given by $S = (n - 2)180^\circ$.
>
> **EXTERIOR ANGLE THEOREM FOR POLYGONS**
>
> The sum of the measures of the exterior angles of a convex polygon (one at each vertex) is 360°.

REFLECT

1. How does the Angle-Sum Theorem for polygons compare with the Angle-Sum Theorem for quadrilaterals? Explain.

2. Janine said, "The Angle-Sum Theorem for polygons also applies to triangles, so we don't need the Triangle Angle-Sum Theorem any longer." Tien said, "That's true, but we couldn't have figured out the Angle-Sum Theorem for polygons without it!" Are the students' statements correct? Explain why or why not.

Exercises

CORE

Getting Started Use the figures at the right for Exercises 1 and 2.

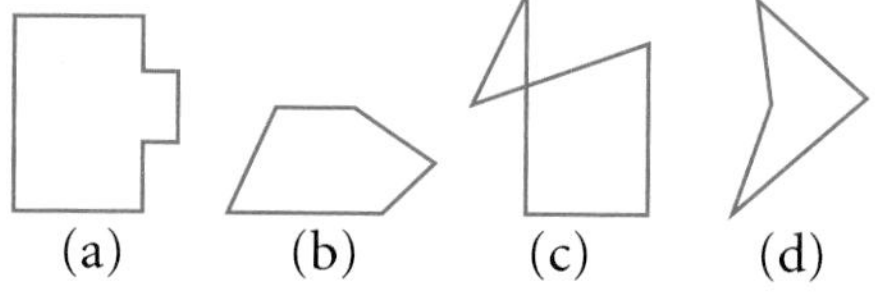

1. Which of the figures at the right are polygons? Classify each polygon.

2. Which are convex polygons? Why?

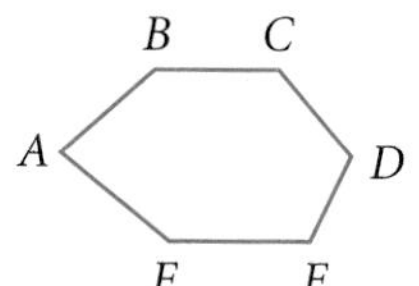

3. Name the polygon at the right in three different ways. Then classify the polygon.

4. Draw an equilateral hexagon that is not equiangular.

5. Identify and define common words that begin with the prefixes *quadr* and *oct*.

Write the word or phrase that correctly completes each statement.

6. A ___ has seven sides.

7. An octagon is a polygon with ___ sides.

8. If a polygon has ___ sides, then it is a pentagon.

9. The figure illustrates the facets cut on a stone. It is a view of the "crown" of the gem.
   a. Identify all the different types of polygons that appear on the gem crown. How many of each type are there?
   b. What is the sum of the measures of the interior angles for each type of polygon on the crown?
   c. How many pairs of polygons appear to be congruent?

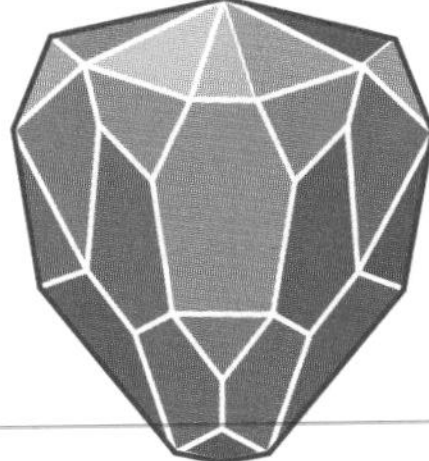

Find the sum of the measures of the interior and exterior angles (one at each vertex) for each convex polygon.

10. a pentagon

11. a 14-gon

12. an $(x + 2)$-gon

13. Science The electron microscope photograph at the right shows a magnification of aspirin. Find the sum of the measures of the angles for the outlined polygon.

The sum of the measures of the interior angles of a convex polygon is given. Find the number of sides of the polygon.

14. 720° **15.** 1800° **16.** $(x - 1)360°$

17. The John Hancock building in Boston (at the right) was designed by I. M. Pei. Identify the different types of polygons used in its design.

Careers

18. School Crossing A school-crossing sign is shown below. It has three right angles, and the other two angles are congruent. Find the measure of one of the non-right angles. Explain your method.

19. When using a public highway, vehicles that travel 25 mi/hr or less, such as farm equipment, must display a special sign. This sign is shown at the right. To form the polygonal sign, small equilateral triangles have been cut off each vertex of a larger equilateral triangle.

a. What is the sum of the measures of the interior angles of the sign? How do you know?

b. What is the measure of each interior angle of the sign?

LOOK BACK

Find the area of each figure. [5-2, 5-3]

20.

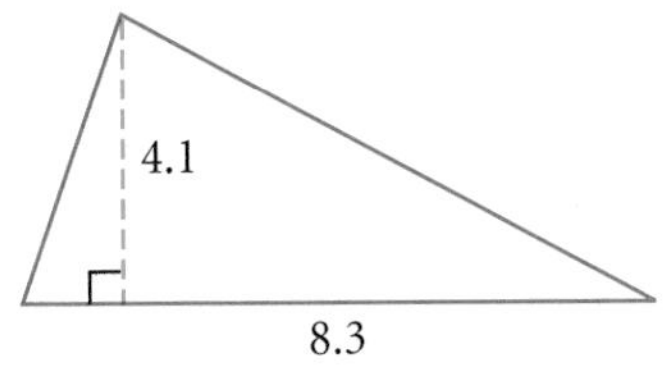

21.

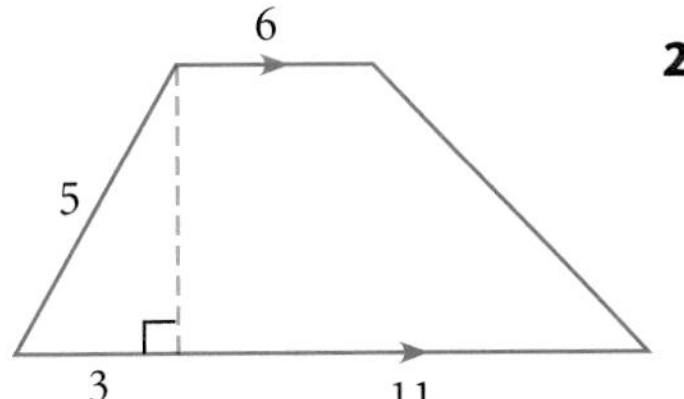

22.

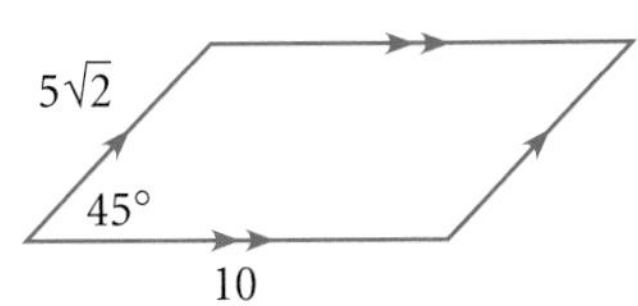

23. In the sequence of figures shown, how many cubes are needed to make a building with 10 steps? n steps? [1-2]

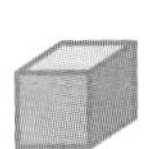

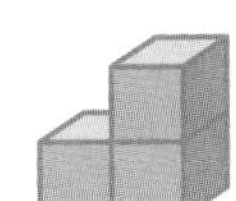

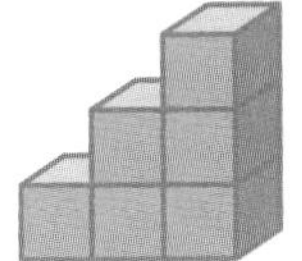

24. Complete the following proof. [4-3]

Given: $\overline{AB} \perp \overline{CD}$, and D is the midpoint of $\overline{AB}$.

Prove: $\overline{AC} \cong \overline{CB}$

Proof:

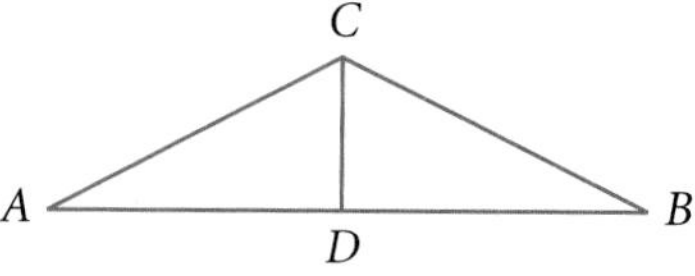

Statements	**Reasons**
1. $\overline{AB} \perp \overline{CD}$	**1.**
2. $\angle ADC$ and $\angle BDC$ are right angles.	**2.**
3. $\triangle ADC$ and $\triangle BDC$ are right triangles.	**3.**
4.	**4.** Given
5.	**5.** Definition of *midpoint*
6.	**6.** Reflexive Property
7.	**7.** LL Theorem
8.	**8.**

MORE PRACTICE

25. Which of the figures at the right are polygons? Classify each polygon.

26. Which figures at the right are convex polygons? Why?

(a) (b) (c)

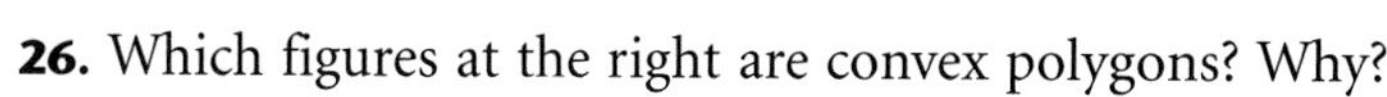

27. Draw an equiangular hexagon that is not equilateral.

28. Draw an equilateral pentagon that is not equiangular.

29. Draw a concave heptagon.

30. Draw an equilateral, concave hexagon.

Find the sum of the measures of the interior and exterior angles (one at each vertex) for each convex polygon.

31. a nonagon **32.** an 18-gon **33.** a $(2x - 2)$-gon

The sum of the measures of the interior angles of a convex polygon is given. Find the number of sides of the polygon.

34. 540° **35.** 1260° **36.** $(x + 4)180°$

MORE MATH REASONING

37. The sum of the measures of the interior angles of a polygon is three times the sum of the measures of its exterior angles (one at each vertex). Classify the polygon.

38. A Diagonal Table Find the number of diagonals of an n-gon.

a. Copy the table shown. Draw each polygon and complete the table.

Polygon	Number of Vertices	Number of Diagonals from One Vertex	Total Number of Diagonals
Quadrilateral			
Pentagon			
Hexagon			
Heptagon			
Octagon			
n-gon			

b. Look for a relationship between the number of vertices and the number of diagonals from one vertex. What is this relationship for the n-gon?

c. Look for a relationship between the data in the first two columns and the total number of diagonals. Write the formula as $D =$ ____.

d. How many diagonals are in a 40-gon?

6-1 PART C Exploring Polyhedrons

← CONNECT → *You've drawn and made nets for many three-dimensional figures. Three-dimensional figures whose faces are polygons are polyhedrons. Now you will begin to investigate some properties of polyhedrons.*

As shown at the left, I. M. Pei's design of the East Building of the National Gallery of Art features a tetrahedron near the fountain. The gallery buildings themselves are prisms.

These three-dimensional figures, whose faces are triangles, rectangles, and other polygons, are examples of **polyhedrons**.

DEFINITION

A **polyhedron** is a solid whose faces are polygons.

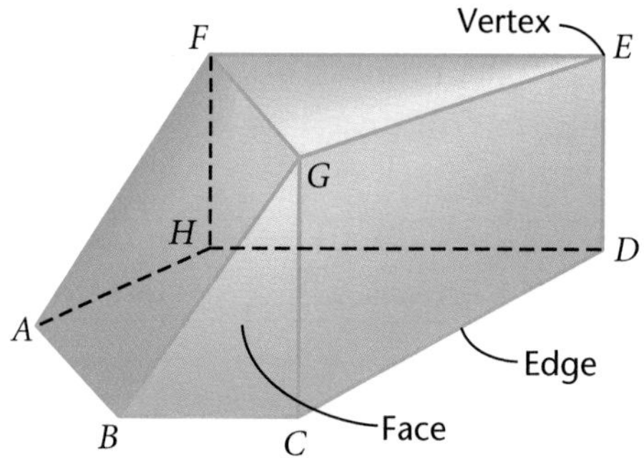

Faces are named in the same way as polygons. In the above figure, *ABCDH* is a pentagonal face.

TRY IT

The polyhedron shown is a cube with a corner cut off.

a. Name the triangular face of the polyhedron.
b. Name the face that includes *L, M,* and *Q* as vertices.
c. Find the number of faces, vertices, and edges of this polyhedron.

Polygons are classified by the number of sides they have. Similarly, polyhedrons are classified by the number of faces they have.

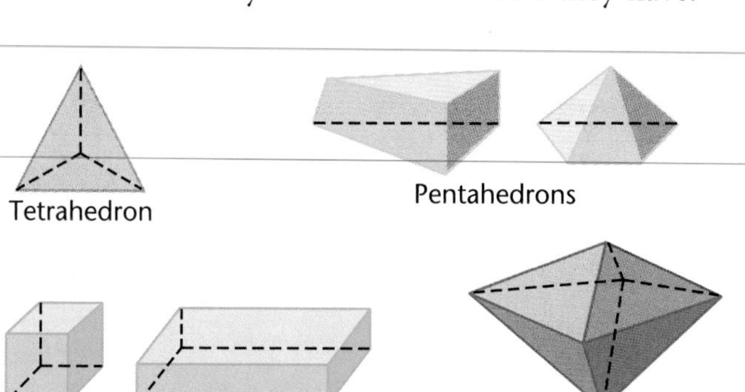

Other common polyhedrons include dodecahedrons, which have twelve faces, and icosahedrons, which have twenty.

In the following Explore, you will discover a relationship among the number of faces, edges, and vertices of a polyhedron.

EXPLORE: FACE FACTS

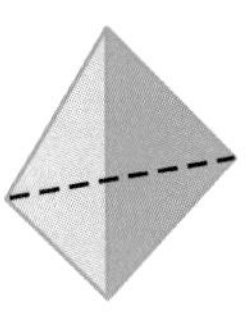
a.

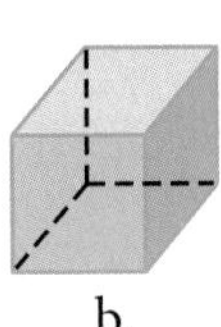
b.

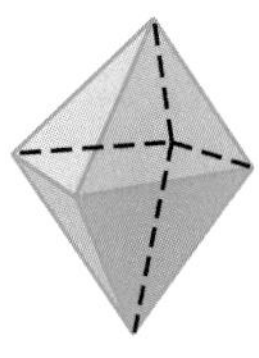
c.

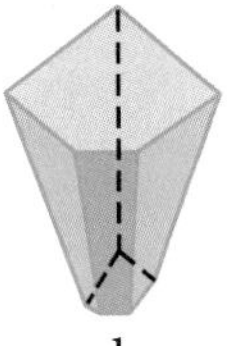
d.

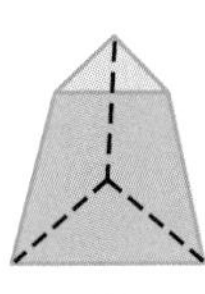
e.

1. Find the number of faces (F), vertices (V), and edges (E) of the polyhedrons shown above. Organize your data in a table.
2. There is a relationship among V, F, and E. Make a conjecture about this relationship, and write a formula to express your conjecture.
3. Check to see whether your conjecture holds for other polyhedrons illustrated elsewhere in this book.

1. Is there a relationship between the number of vertices and the number of sides of a polygon? If so, what is the relationship?

Leonhard Euler (1707–1783) was a Swiss mathematician who proved the formula you investigated in the Explore. This result is therefore known as Euler's Formula.

EULER'S FORMULA

For any polyhedron, the relationship among the number of faces (F), vertices (V), and edges (E) is $F + V - E = 2$.

You will have additional opportunities to work with Euler's Formula in the Exercises and in later chapters.

REFLECT

1. Give examples of polyhedrons in your classroom. Classify each one by the number of faces.
2. It's helpful to remember prefixes when classifying polygons and polyhedrons. Give some examples of everyday words that begin with the same prefixes we use to classify polygons and polyhedrons.

Exercises

CORE

Getting Started Use the figure at the right for Exercises 1–4.

1. Name the faces of the polyhedron.
2. Classify the polyhedron.
3. Find the number of faces, vertices, and edges of the polyhedron.
4. Verify that Euler's Formula holds for the polyhedron.

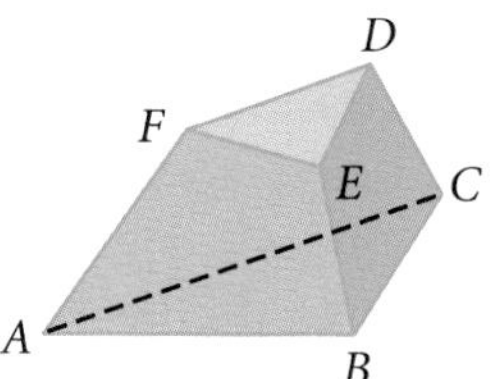

The polyhedron shown is a cube with each corner cut off. Use this polyhedron for Exercises 5–8.

5. Classify faces 1 and 2.
6. Name the vertices of face 1.
7. Name the sides of face 2.
8. How many faces, vertices, and edges does this polyhedron have? Does Euler's Formula hold?

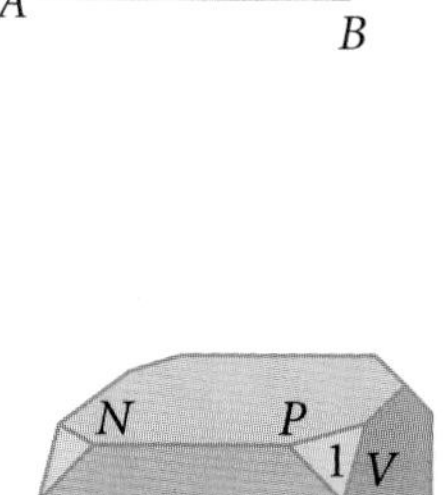

9. What is the smallest number of faces a polyhedron can have? Why?
10. What is the smallest number of vertices a polyhedron can have? Why?

In Exercises 11 and 12, determine whether each statement is true or false. If the statement is false, change the underlined word or phrase to make it true.

11. A <u>tetrahedron</u> is a polyhedron with four faces.
12. An octahedron has <u>six</u> faces.
13. Sketch a net for the octahedron shown at the right.

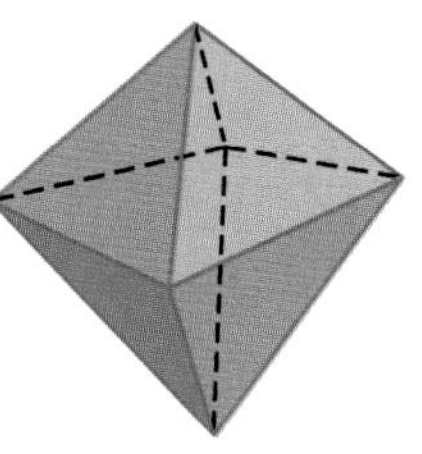

14. An *obelisk* is a monument with a square base that tapers to a square pyramid at the top. A 3500-year-old Egyptian obelisk at Karnak is 80 ft tall and 6 ft long on each side of its base. Classify the obelisk, and calculate the area of its base.

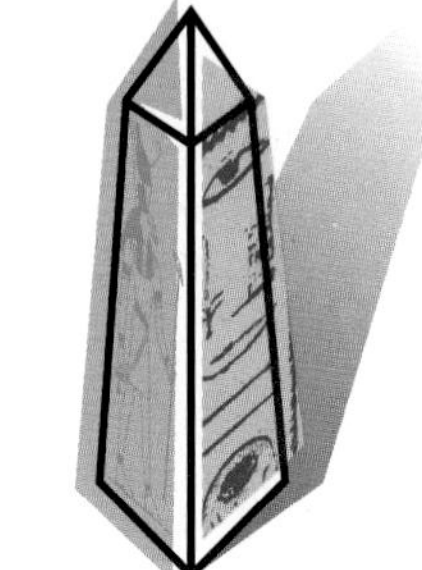
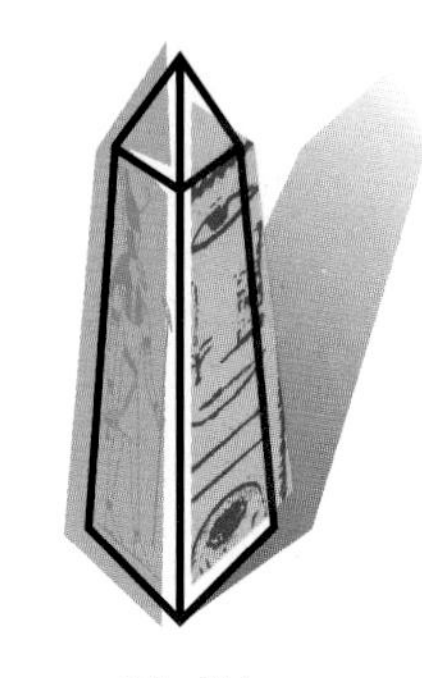
Obelisk

15. Polyhedron Chemistry A methane molecule has a carbon atom in the center and four hydrogen atoms around it, as shown in the perspective drawing at the right.

a. If you connect the hydrogen atoms, what polyhedron results? Sketch the polyhedron, and show the locations of the carbon and hydrogen atoms.

b. The hydrogen atoms in this molecule repel each other. Use this information to explain why a methane model has the shape it does.

Describe a horizontal cross section of each polyhedron.

16.

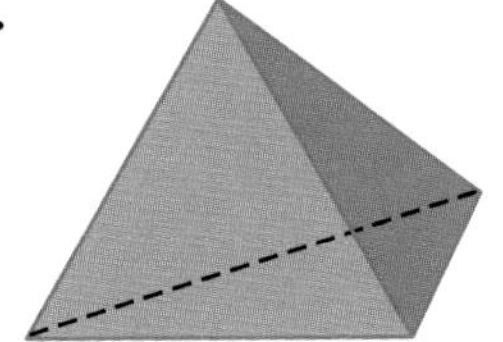
Tetrahedron

17.

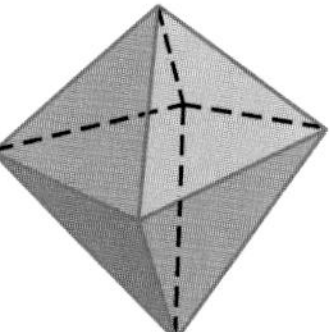
Octahedron

18.

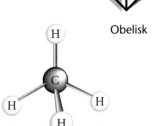

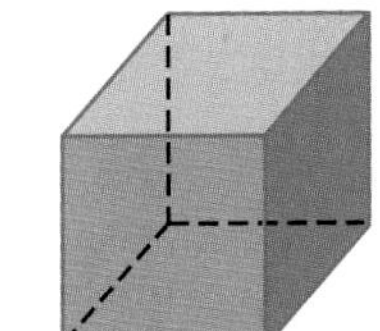
Hexahedron (cube)

19. Animal, Vegetable, or Zircon? Geologists are often asked to identify minerals found in geological explorations. The geometry of a mineral crystal is one way of identifying it. Draw your own simplified sketch of the zircon crystal shown in the photograph at the right. Then show that Euler's Formula holds for this crystal.

LOOK AHEAD

For each measure of $\angle A$, find the measures of the other angles of parallelogram *ABCD*. Justify each answer with a theorem or postulate.

20. $m\angle A = 107°$

21. $m\angle A = 64°$

22. $m\angle A = 138°$

MORE PRACTICE

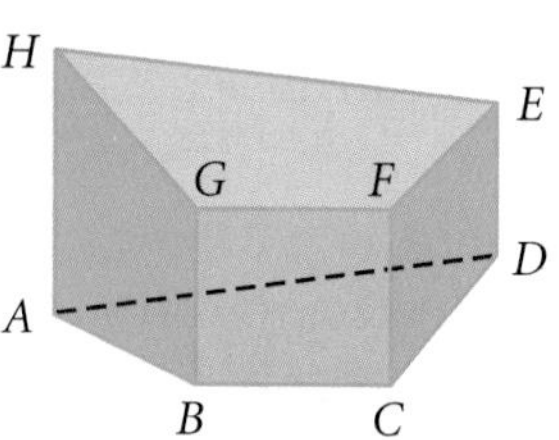

23. Name the faces of the polyhedron at the right.

24. Classify the polyhedron.

25. Verify that Euler's Formula holds for this polyhedron.

26. Sketch a net for the polyhedron.

27. Describe a horizontal cross section of the hexahedron shown at the right.

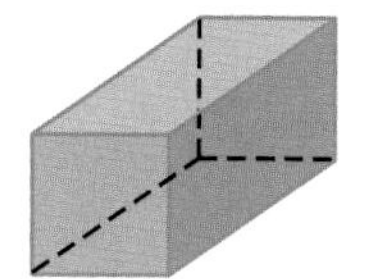

MORE MATH REASONING

Draw a sketch to show how a plane can intersect a cube in each of the following cross sections.

28. a square

29. a rectangle

30. an isosceles triangle

31. an equilateral triangle

32. Suppose a tetrahedron has all of its vertices cut off as shown.

a. What type of polyhedron is each piece that is cut off?

b. How many additional vertices and edges does cutting off the corners produce? Explain.

c. Show that Euler's Formula still holds for this truncated (cut-off) tetrahedron.

d. Sketch a net for the figure.

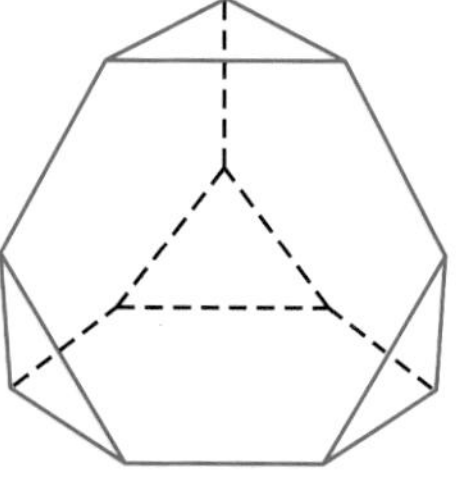

6-1 PART D Making Connections

← CONNECT → *Polyhedrons are present in manufactured and natural objects. You have discovered properties of polygons and learned how polygons are related to polyhedrons. You've also explored characteristics of polyhedrons.*

As shown in the photo on page 415, I. M. Pei used tessellations in designing the glass pyramid at the Louvre Museum in Paris. In many of his other buildings, the faces of his polyhedrons contain triangle and square tessellations. Could Pei have used other figures? You will investigate this possibility in the following Explore.

EXPLORE: PLANE OLD TESSELLATIONS

MATERIALS

Paper
Straightedge
Scissors

1. First, investigate whether any quadrilateral can tessellate a plane. Begin by folding a sheet of paper in half three times, drawing a quadrilateral on the paper, and cutting the folded sheet to make congruent quadrilaterals. Arrange the quadrilaterals to see if they tessellate the plane. Repeat the process with a different quadrilateral. Discuss your results with your classmates.
2. Make a conjecture about the quadrilaterals that will tessellate a plane. Explain why they tessellate.
3. You know that any triangle will tessellate a plane, and you have just investigated this possibility for quadrilaterals. Are there any other types of polygons that *always* tessellate a plane? Investigate pentagons, hexagons, and other polygons, and make a conjecture.

REFLECT

1. How are polygons and polyhedrons related? Give specific examples to support your ideas.
2. Explain how the classifications of polygons and polyhedrons are related. Give specific examples.
3. Explain why the sum of the measures of the interior angles of a polygon with n sides is $(n - 2)180°$. Use a sketch to illustrate your explanation.

Self-Assessment

1. Find x in the figure at the right. Then find the measure of each angle of $WXYZ$.

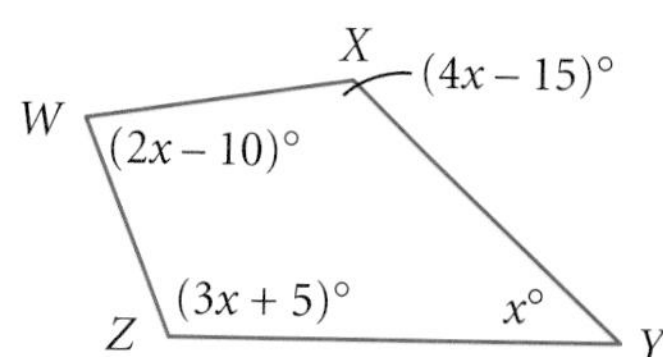

Find the sum of the measures of the interior and exterior angles (one at each vertex) for each polygon.

2. an octagon

3. a 15-gon

The figure shows the top view of the facets on the crown of a gem.

4. Identify all of the different types of polygons that appear on the gem crown. How many of each type are there?

5. What is the sum of the measures of the interior angles for each type of polygon on the crown of the gem?

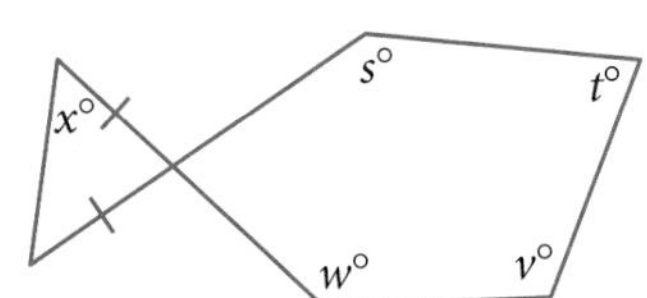

6. In the figure, $s + t + v + w = 470$. Therefore, $x =$
   (a) 35 (b) 45 (c) 55 (d) 60 (e) 75

Find the area of each figure. [5-2]

7.

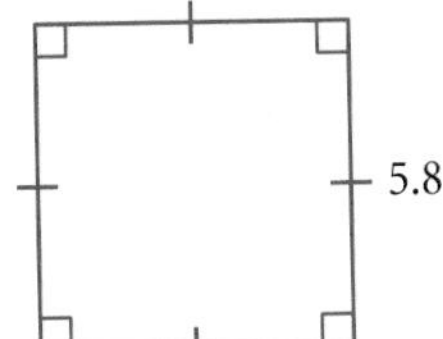

8.

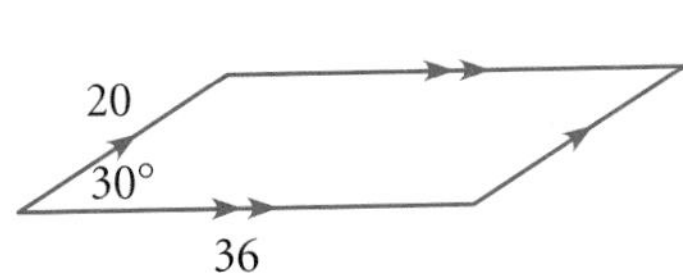

9.

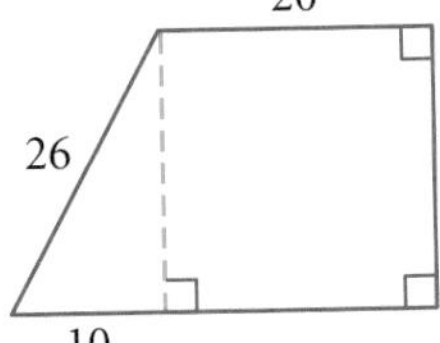

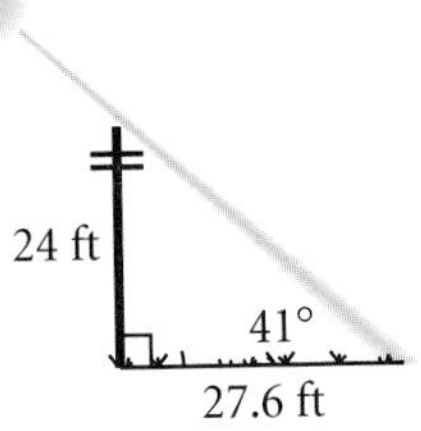

10. **Sun Day** When the sun is at a 41° angle as shown, a 24-ft-tall telephone pole casts a 27.6-ft-long shadow. The shadow of a nearby pole has the same length. Are the two poles the same height? Justify your answer. [4-3]

A pyramid with a square base is attached to a cube. The base of the pyramid is congruent to a face of the cube.

11. Compare the new polyhedron (cube + pyramid) to the cube. How many new faces, vertices, and edges were added by adding the pyramid?

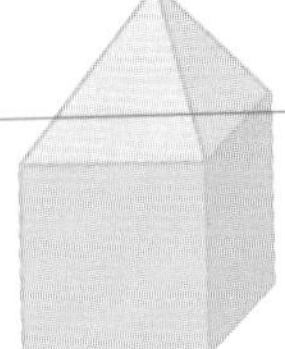

12. Show that Euler's Formula applies to the new polyhedron.

13. Classify the new polyhedron.

Sketch each of the following, if possible. If it is not possible, say so.

14. a concave quadrilateral

15. an equiangular pentagon that is not equilateral

16. a tetrahedron with six vertices

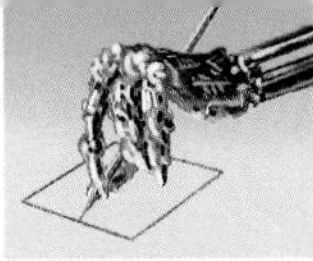

TEcHno PRooFs

Researchers in the field of artificial intelligence (AI) explore ways to make computers simulate human thought. The following excerpt is from *AI: The Tumultuous History of the Search for Artificial Intelligence,* by Daniel Crevier. It describes a computer program developed in the 1950s by Herbert Gelernter to prove high school geometry theorems.

The Geometry Theorem Prover worked backward. One first described to it the theorem to prove. Much as a human being does, the program then started to build a chain of intermediate results leading back to known theorems or axioms....[T]o figure out what steps might [work], the program looked at a drawing....Gelernter had to enter a representational figure as a series of point coordinates....Using these coordinates, the program was able to extract the same kind of information a human does...: Which sides are equal or parallel to each other? Are there any right angles? Are some angles equal to each other?

The figure shows a proof found by the Geometry Theorem Prover.

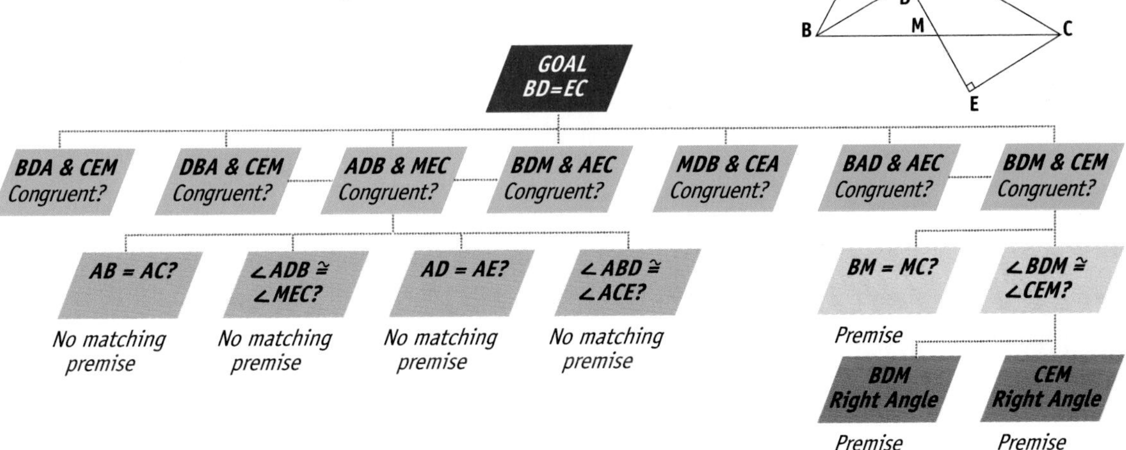

1. **What strategies for proof did the Geometry Theorem Prover use that might be helpful to people when doing a proof?**
2. **The Geometry Theorem Prover could only prove theorems requiring ten steps or less. Why might this be true? Do you think computers could do longer proofs today?**

6-2 PART A Proofs with Parallelograms

← CONNECT → ***You've already investigated some properties of quadrilaterals. Now you will focus on the properties of one member of the family of quadrilaterals—the parallelogram.***

The fact that the opposite sides of a parallelogram are parallel gives it some special properties. In the following Explore, you will investigate the properties of the angles, sides, and diagonals of a parallelogram.

EXPLORE: PARALLELOGRAM PROBE

MATERIALS

Ruler, Protractor
Geometry software (optional)

1. Use geometry software or a ruler and protractor to draw several different parallelograms. Draw the diagonals of each parallelogram.
2. Measure the various parts of each parallelogram and its diagonals. Develop as many conjectures as you can about the angles, sides, and diagonals of parallelograms. Compare your results with those of your classmates.

Problem-Solving Tip

Check each of your conjectures by testing them on a new figure.

TRY IT

Find each of the following in parallelogram *MNOP*.

a. $m\angle PMN$
b. $m\angle MNO$
c. $m\angle OPM$
d. MP
e. OP
f. MQ
g. NQ

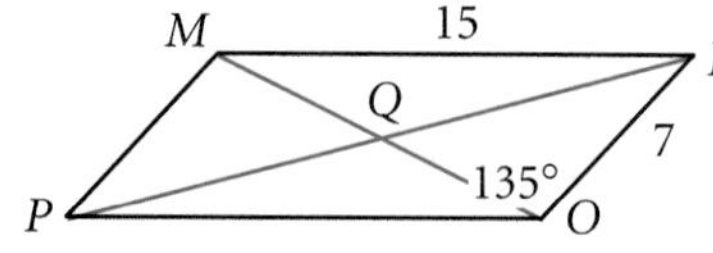

$NP = 21$
$MO = 11$

While you've been exploring geometry facts, you've also been developing your ability to justify those facts with deductive proof. Remember the five-step process introduced on page 217. Now you will be doing all five steps on your own. The following example shows a complete proof of one of the conjectures you may have made in the preceding Explore.

EXAMPLE

Prove: The opposite angles of a parallelogram are congruent.

Rewrite: If a quadrilateral is a parallelogram, then its opposite angles are congruent.

Draw:

State:

Given: $ABCD$ is a parallelogram.

Prove: $\angle ABC \cong \angle CDA$ and $\angle DAB \cong \angle BCD$

Plan: Draw an auxiliary line segment, diagonal $\overline{AC}$. Show $\triangle ABC \cong \triangle CDA$ by ASA. Use CPCTC to show $\angle ABC \cong \angle CDA$. To prove that $\angle DAB \cong \angle BCD$, repeat the process, using diagonal $\overline{BD}$.

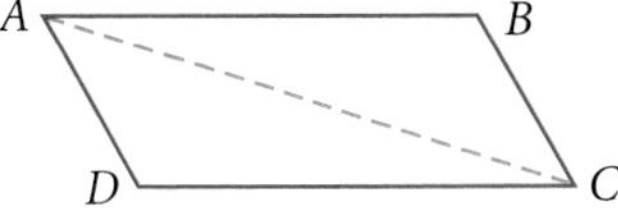

Demonstrate:

Statements	**Reasons**
1. Draw $\overline{AC}$.	**1.** Two points determine a line.
2. $ABCD$ is a parallelogram.	**2.** Given
3. $\overline{AB} \parallel \overline{DC}$ and $\overline{AD} \parallel \overline{BC}$	**3.** Definition of *parallelogram*
4. $\angle ACD \cong \angle CAB$ and $\angle DAC \cong \angle BCA$	**4.** If parallel lines are cut by a transversal, alternate interior angles are congruent.
5. $\overline{AC} \cong \overline{AC}$	**5.** Reflexive Property
6. $\triangle ABC \cong \triangle CDA$	**6.** ASA Postulate
7. $\angle ABC \cong \angle CDA$	**7.** CPCTC

To complete the proof, repeat Steps 1–6 using diagonal $\overline{BD}$ and the two triangles it forms to show that $\angle DAB \cong \angle BCD$.

Properties of parallelograms, including those properties you may have discovered in the preceding Explore, are summarized below. We proved one of the theorems in the example; you will have an opportunity to prove the others in the exercises.

PROPERTIES OF PARALLELOGRAMS

The opposite sides of a parallelogram are parallel (from the definition of a parallelogram).

The opposite angles of a parallelogram are congruent.

The opposite sides of a parallelogram are congruent.

The consecutive angles of a parallelogram are supplementary.

The diagonals of a parallelogram bisect each other.

REFLECT

1. Which special types of quadrilaterals also have the properties of parallelograms?
2. Draw a parallelogram and its diagonals. Mark all of the sides and angles that you know are congruent. (For clarity, you may want to draw more than one parallelogram.)
3. Why is drawing the diagonals of a parallelogram helpful in proving many of the parallelogram's properties?

Exercises

CORE

1. **Getting Started** Using parallelogram *ABCD*, list all pairs of
   a. parallel sides
   b. congruent sides
   c. congruent angles
   d. supplementary angles

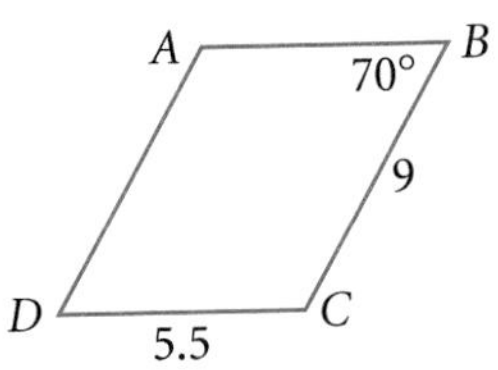

2. Find the measures of all angles and the lengths of all sides of parallelogram *ABCD*.

***EFGH* is a parallelogram. State a theorem that justifies each conclusion.**

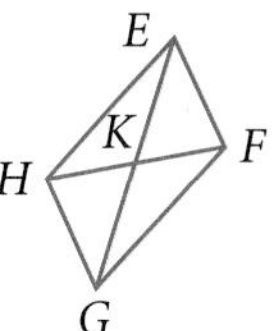

3. $\angle EHG \cong \angle EFG$

4. $\overline{EH} \cong \overline{FG}$

5. $\overline{HK} \cong \overline{KF}$

6. $\angle EHG$ is supplementary to $\angle HGF$.

***WXYZ* is a parallelogram. Complete each statement.**

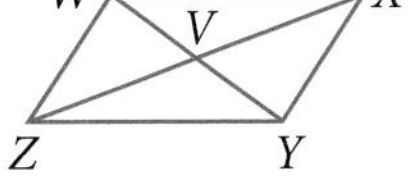

7. If $WX = 10$, $YZ =$ ____.

8. If $WY = 16$, $WV =$ ____.

9. If $m\angle XWZ = 102°$, $m\angle WZY =$ ____.

10. If $m\angle XWZ = 87°$, $m\angle XYZ =$ ____.

11. If $m\angle WZY = (2x + 12)°$ and $m\angle WXY = (5x - 36)°$, find $m\angle WXY$.

12. If $WY = 4x - 14$ and $VY = x + 8$, find WV.

13. The coordinates of three vertices of a parallelogram are (0, 0), (5, 0), and (4, 2). What are the possible coordinates for the fourth vertex?

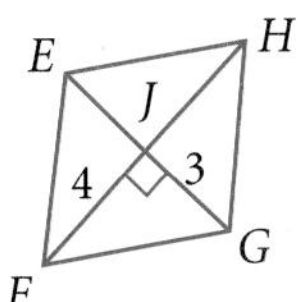

14. Quadrilateral *EFGH* is a parallelogram. Find the lengths of all segments in the figure.

15. Shelf Size A carpenter needs to make a shelf so that its opposite sides have the same length. He finds a long board whose sides are parallel, and then makes two parallel cuts with his saw to make the shelf. Explain why this ensures that the opposite sides of the shelf have the same length.

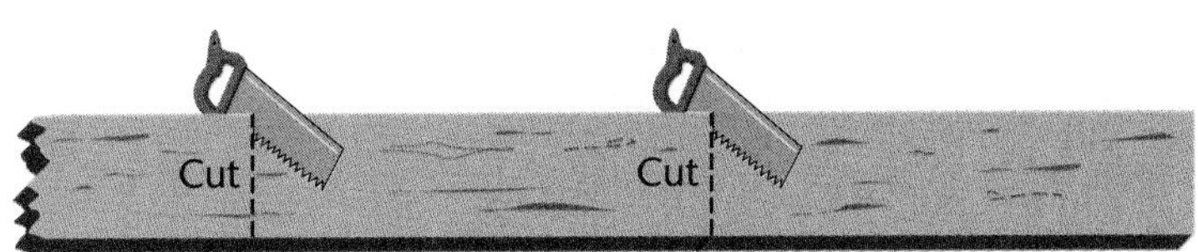

16. Prove that the opposite sides of a parallelogram are congruent.

Given: *ABCD* is a parallelogram.

Prove: $\overline{AB} \cong \overline{CD}$, $\overline{BC} \cong \overline{AD}$

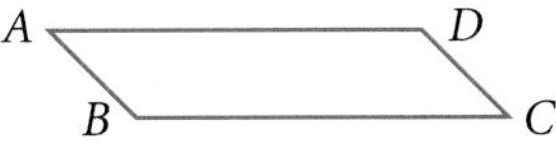

(Hint: Draw a diagonal.)

17. Prove that consecutive angles of a parallelogram are supplementary.

18. Prove that the diagonals of a parallelogram bisect each other.

19. An **isosceles trapezoid** is a trapezoid with congruent legs.

Given: *HIJK* is an isosceles trapezoid with legs $\overline{HK} \cong \overline{IJ}$.

Prove: $\angle K \cong \angle J$

(Hint: Add segment $\overline{IL}$ parallel to $\overline{HK}$.)

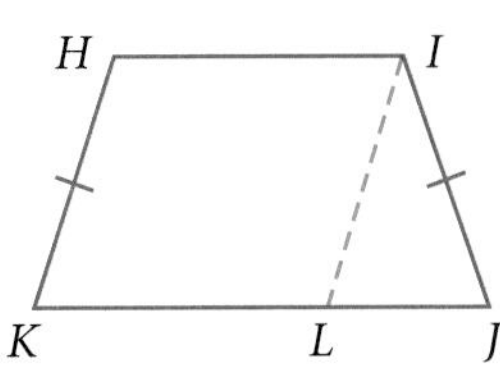

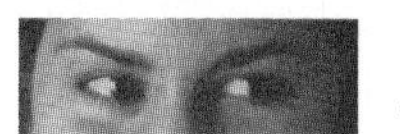

LOOK AHEAD

Write a congruence statement for each pair of triangles. Then name the postulate or theorem that allows you to conclude that they are congruent.

20.

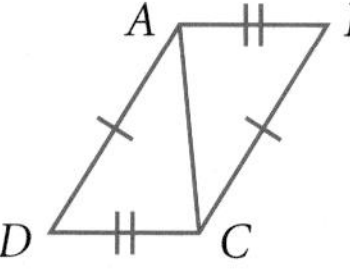

21.

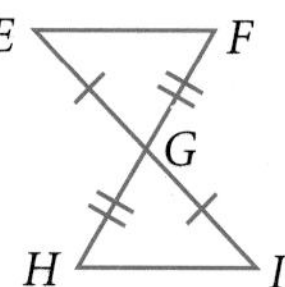

22.

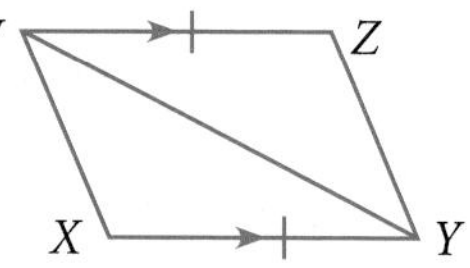

23. Find the length of an altitude of an equilateral triangle with a side length of 8 in.

MORE PRACTICE

24. Using parallelogram *QRST*, list all pairs of
a. parallel sides **b.** congruent sides **c.** congruent angles **d.** supplementary angles

Complete each statement for parallelogram *QRST*.

25. If $m\angle SRP = 28°$, $m\angle T =$ ____ .

26. If $QT = 14$, $SR =$ ____ .

27. If $m\angle TQR = 42°$, $m\angle TSR =$ ____ .

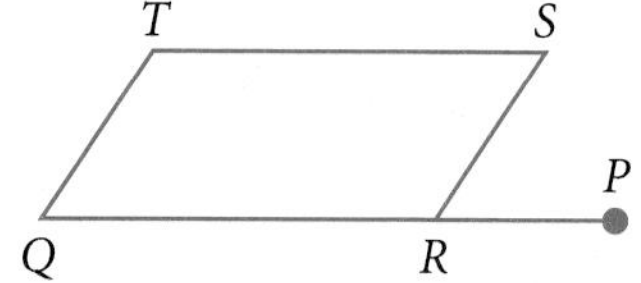

MORE MATH REASONING

28. Draw a parallelogram that is neither a rectangle nor a rhombus.
a. Draw and describe any lines of symmetry of the parallelogram.
b. Does the parallelogram have rotational symmetry? If so, locate the center of the rotation; then list all clockwise rotations of less than 360° that will rotate the parallelogram onto itself.

29. Electromotive Reasoning The figure and first "step" of the computer proof on page 417 are shown below. Explain the strategy the computer is using.

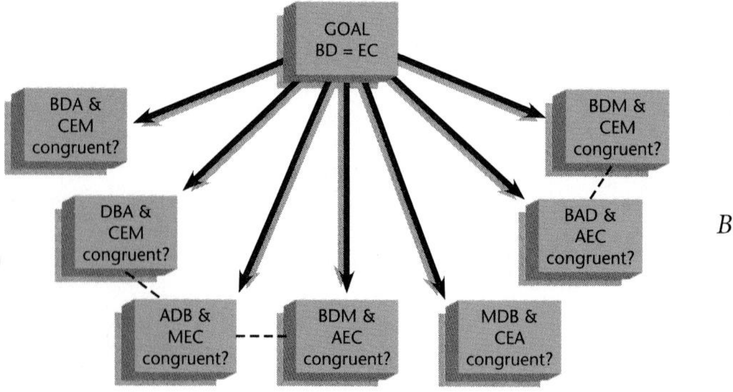

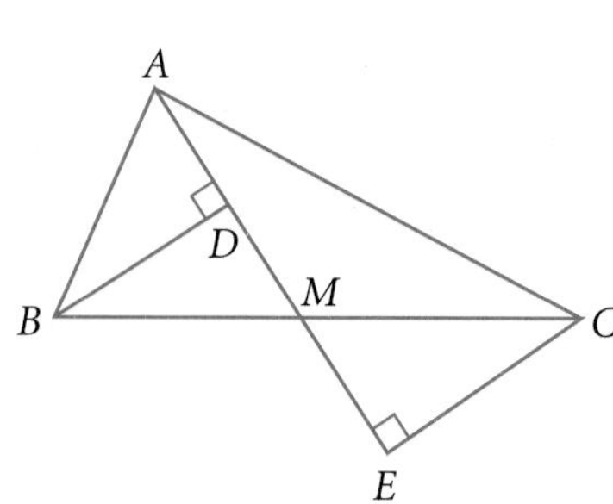

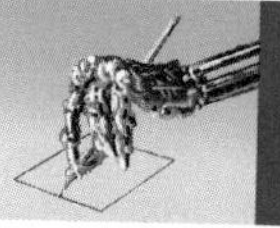

6-2 PART B Proving Quadrilaterals Are Parallelograms

← CONNECT → ***You now know about many properties of parallelograms. Next you will investigate several ways to show that a quadrilateral is a parallelogram.***

You can be sure that a quadrilateral is a parallelogram if both pairs of opposite sides are parallel.

1. Why does showing that the opposite sides of a quadrilateral are parallel prove that the quadrilateral is a parallelogram?

In the following Explore, you will look for other characteristics that assure you that a quadrilateral is a parallelogram. These characteristics will be useful in subsequent proofs.

EXPLORE: AM I A PARALLELOGRAM?

MATERIALS

Ruler, Protractor
Graph paper (optional)
Straws or sticks (optional)
Geometry software (optional)

1. State the converse of each of the four theorems about the properties of a parallelogram.
2. Investigate the converse of each theorem. You can draw and/or construct figures on graph paper, use straws or sticks to make models (as shown in the photograph at the right), or use geometry software.
3. Determine whether the converse of each theorem is true or false, and explain how you investigated it.
4. List all the ways that you know to show that a quadrilateral is a parallelogram. Compare your list with those of your classmates.

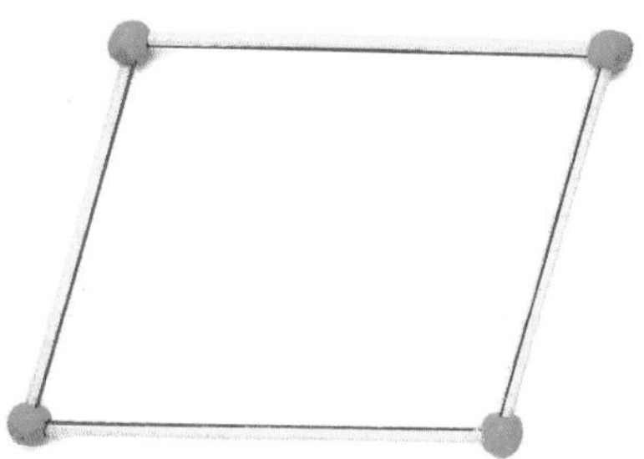

TRY IT

Determine whether each quadrilateral must be a parallelogram. Justify your answers.

a. 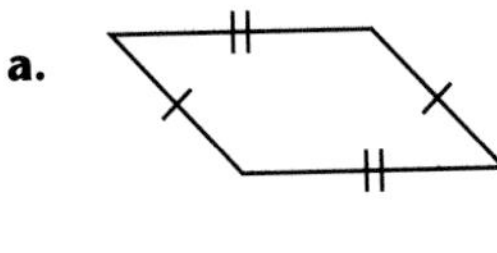

b. 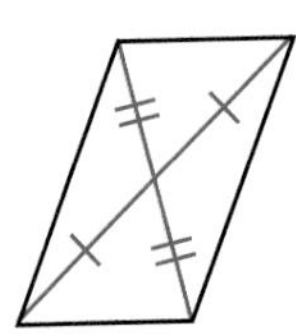

c. 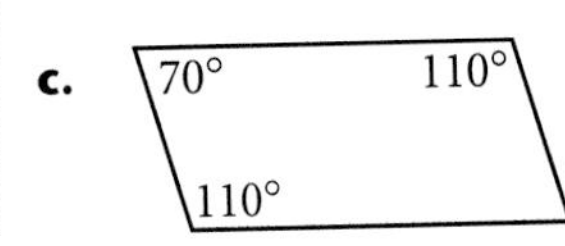

d. 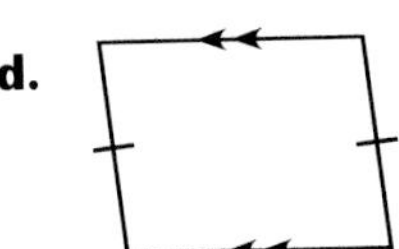

Although inductive investigations like the ones you did in the preceding Explore are important, we also want to be able to prove that what *usually* seems to work really *does* work under all circumstances. In the following Example, we will look at a proof of one of the conjectures you may have made in the Explore.

EXAMPLE

Prove: If the consecutive angles of a quadrilateral are supplementary, then the quadrilateral is a parallelogram.

Given: $\angle A$ and $\angle B$ are supplementary.
$\angle B$ and $\angle C$ are supplementary.
$\angle C$ and $\angle D$ are supplementary.
$\angle D$ and $\angle A$ are supplementary.

Prove: $ABCD$ is a parallelogram.

Proof: $\angle A$ and $\angle B$ are same-side interior angles for $\overline{AD}$ and $\overline{BC}$. They are supplementary (from the given information). Therefore, $\overline{AD}$ and $\overline{BC}$ are parallel, because lines cut by a transversal are parallel if their same-side interior angles are supplementary. In the same way, $\overline{AB}$ and $\overline{DC}$ are parallel. Because $\overline{AD} \parallel \overline{BC}$ and $\overline{AB} \parallel \overline{DC}$, $ABCD$ is, by definition, a parallelogram.

You may have discovered that all of the converses of the parallelogram properties listed on page 420 are true. These methods of showing that a quadrilateral is a parallelogram are summarized below. One of these theorems was proved in the Example. You will have a chance to prove the others in the Exercises.

CONDITIONS FOR A PARALLELOGRAM

A quadrilateral is a parallelogram if both pairs of opposite sides are parallel (definition).

If both pairs of opposite angles of a quadrilateral are congruent, then the quadrilateral is a parallelogram.

If both pairs of opposite sides of a quadrilateral are congruent, then the quadrilateral is a parallelogram.

If the consecutive angles of a quadrilateral are supplementary, then the quadrilateral is a parallelogram.

If the diagonals of a quadrilateral bisect each other, then the quadrilateral is a parallelogram.

REFLECT

1. Can you conclude that a quadrilateral with one pair of congruent sides is a parallelogram? Explain or give a counterexample.
2. State the theorems about the properties of parallelograms and the conditions for parallelograms as biconditionals.

Exercises

CORE

Getting Started Determine whether each quadrilateral must be a parallelogram. Justify your answers.

1. 95° 85° 85° 95°

2. 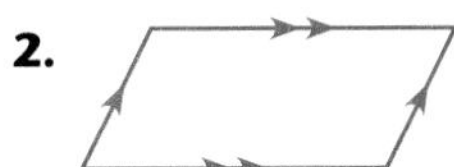

3. 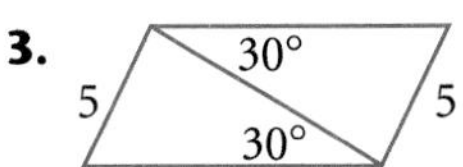

Given the following, determine whether quadrilateral *ABCD* must be a parallelogram. Justify your answers.

4. $\overline{AE} \cong \overline{EC}, \overline{DE} \cong \overline{EB}$

5. $\angle ADC \cong \angle ABC$

6. $\overline{AB} \cong \overline{CD}, \overline{AD} \cong \overline{BC}$

7. $\overline{AB} \parallel \overline{CD}, \overline{AD} \parallel \overline{BC}$

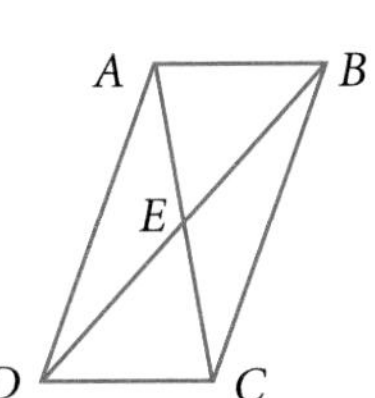

What information do you need in order to prove that *QRST* is a parallelogram using

8. all four of its sides?

9. consecutive angles?

What values of *x* and *y* guarantee that each quadrilateral is a parallelogram? Justify your answers.

10.

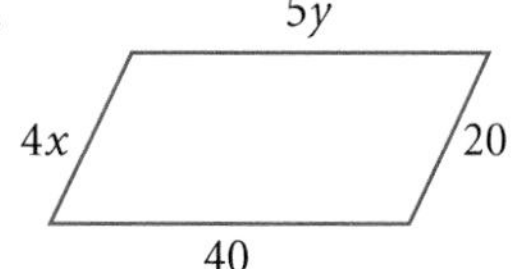

11.

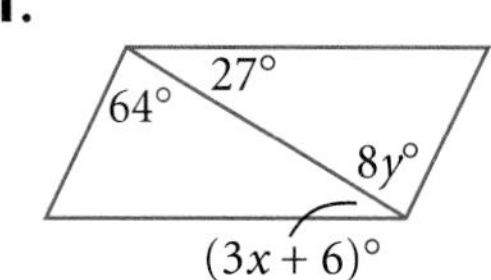

12. (5x + y)° (4x − y)° 125°

13. The Harmony of the Grids The three red points are vertices of a quadrilateral. If the fourth vertex is selected at random from the remaining grid points, what is the probability that the figure will be a parallelogram?

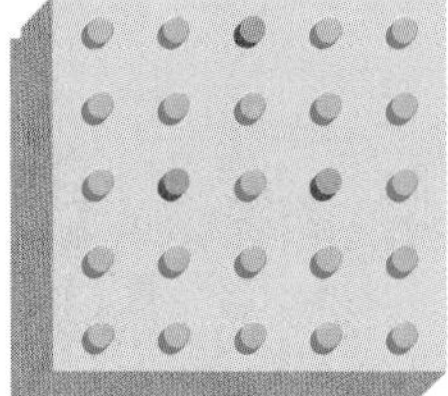

14. The seat of this director's chair is always parallel to the floor. Explain why this is the case.

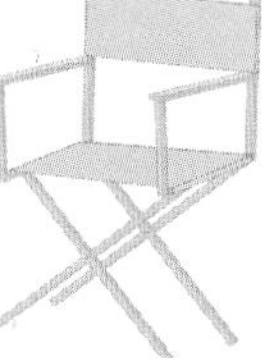

15. *Given:* $m \parallel n$, $\angle 1 \cong \angle 2$
Prove: $p \parallel q$

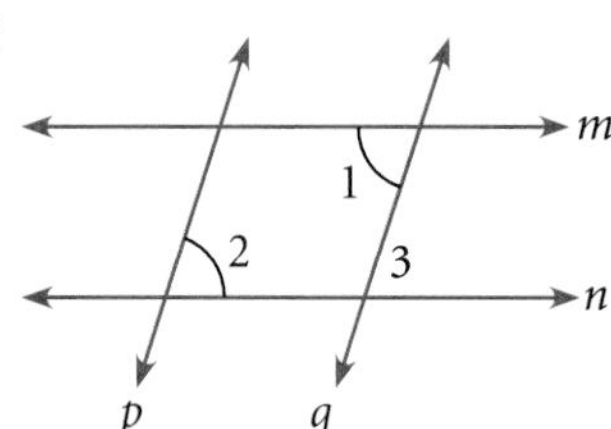

16. Prove: If both pairs of opposite sides of a quadrilateral are congruent, then the quadrilateral is a parallelogram.

17. Prove: If both pairs of opposite angles of a quadrilateral are congruent, then the quadrilateral is a parallelogram.

LOOK BACK

Find the length of the unknown side in each triangle. Express it as a radical in simplest form (if possible) and as a decimal approximation rounded to the nearest hundredth. [5-3]

18. $s = 9$, $t = 12$, $v =$ ____

19. $s = 8$, $t =$ ____, $v = 19$

20. $s = 3\sqrt{2}$, $t = 7$, $v =$ ____

21. $s =$ ____, $t = 14.2$, $v = 27.5$

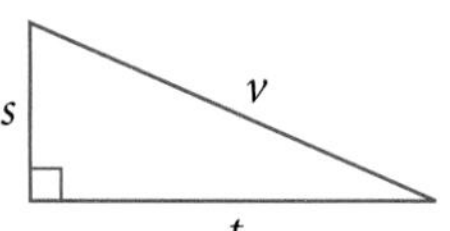

Give the sum of the measures of the interior and exterior angles (one at each vertex) for each polygon. [6-1]

22. a heptagon

23. a 16-gon

24. an $(x + 5)$-gon

MORE PRACTICE

Given the following, determine whether quadrilateral *JKLM* must be a parallelogram. Justify your answers.

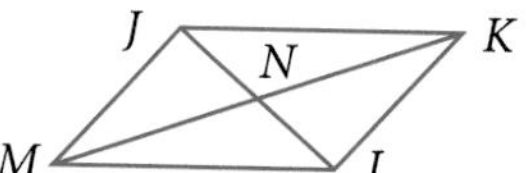

25. $\overline{JK} \cong \overline{LM}, \overline{JM} \cong \overline{LK}$

26. $\angle MJK \cong \angle MLK, \angle JML \cong \angle JKL$

27. $\overline{JN} \cong \overline{NL}, \overline{MN} \cong \overline{NK}$

28. $\overline{JK} \parallel \overline{LM}, \overline{JM} \cong \overline{LK}$

MORE MATH REASONING

29. Prove the following theorem: If the diagonals of a quadrilateral bisect each other, then the quadrilateral is a parallelogram.

30. Prove that the diagonals of an isosceles trapezoid (a trapezoid with congruent legs) are congruent. (Hint: See Exercise 19, page 421.)

31. Draw an isosceles triangle, $\triangle ABC$, and mark any point, P, on the base. Draw line segments from P to the other sides of the triangle that are parallel to the legs. Prove that these segments form a parallelogram.

32. Prove: If a quadrilateral is a parallelogram, then a diagonal divides it into two congruent triangles. Then prove the converse of this statement or disprove it by showing a counterexample.

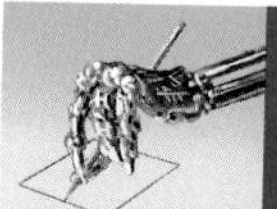

6-2 PART C Proofs with Special Parallelograms

← CONNECT → ***Quadrilaterals whose diagonals bisect each other are parallelograms. Now you will explore diagonal properties for special parallelograms.***

Since rhombuses, rectangles, and squares are special parallelograms, their diagonals have some unique characteristics. As you discover these, you will also see that these properties suggest ways to prove that a parallelogram *is* a rhombus, rectangle, or square.

Use the terms *parallelograms, rhombuses,* and *rectangles* to complete each statement. List all the terms that make the statement true.

1. All squares are ____. **2. All rhombuses are ____.**

3. All rectangles are ____.

In the following Explore, you will discover relationships between diagonals and special parallelograms.

EXPLORE: DRAW STRAWS

MATERIALS

Straws
Scissors
Thumbtacks
Ruler

1. You will need three straws—two that are the same length and one of a different length. Mark their midpoints.

2. Take two straws of different lengths. Cross them so that they bisect each other, and fasten them with a thumbtack. Place the straws on a sheet of paper, mark dots at the endpoints, and then use a straightedge to connect these points. What type of quadrilateral do you get?

3. Use the straws to find the type of quadrilateral that results for each combination below. In each case, be sure that the diagonals bisect each other.

a. Diagonals are not perpendicular and not congruent.
b. Diagonals are not perpendicular but are congruent.
c. Diagonals are perpendicular but are not congruent.
d. Diagonals are congruent and perpendicular.

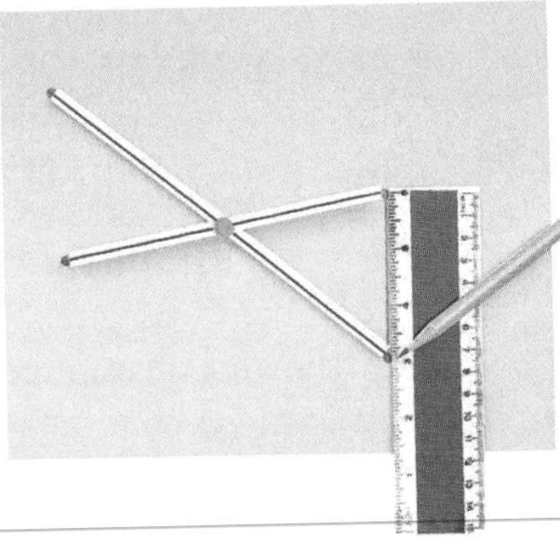

Write conditional statements to summarize your results.

4. State the converses of the theorems you discovered in the preceding Explore. Do you think the converses are true? Why or why not?

TRY IT

Classify quadrilateral $VWXY$ using the given information.

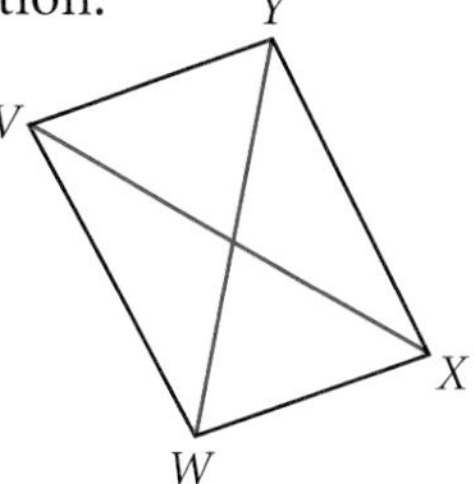

a. $\overline{VX}$ and $\overline{WY}$ bisect each other.
b. $\overline{VX}$ and $\overline{WY}$ bisect each other, and $\overline{VX} \perp \overline{WY}$.
c. $\overline{VX}$ and $\overline{WY}$ bisect each other, and $\overline{VX} \cong \overline{WY}$.
d. $\overline{VX}$ and $\overline{WY}$ bisect each other, $\overline{VX} \perp \overline{WY}$, and $\overline{VX} \cong \overline{WY}$.

EXAMPLE

Prove: If a parallelogram is a rectangle, then its diagonals are congruent.

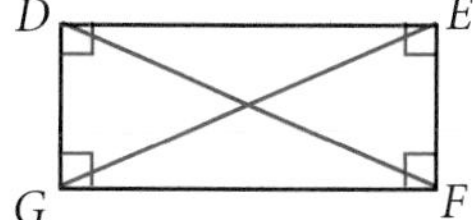

Given: Parallelogram $DEFG$ is a rectangle with diagonals $\overline{DF}$ and $\overline{GE}$.

Prove: $\overline{DF} \cong \overline{GE}$

Proof:

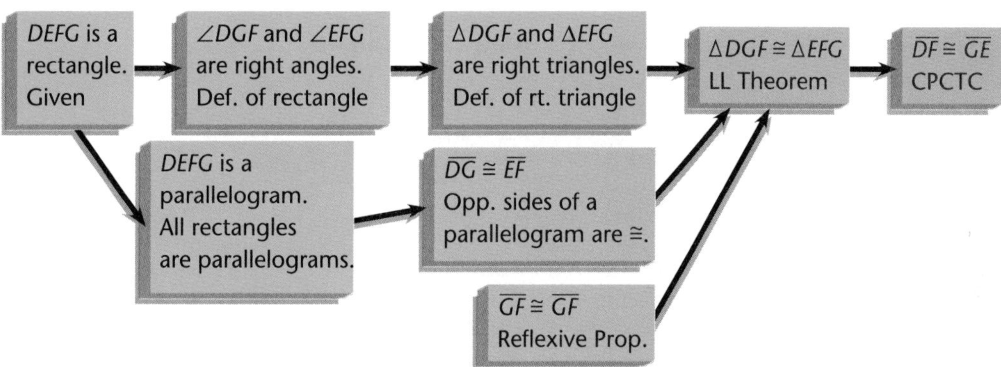

Your results from the Explore and their converses can be combined into the biconditional statements below.

THEOREMS ABOUT DIAGONALS OF SPECIAL PARALLELOGRAMS

A parallelogram is a rhombus if and only if its diagonals are perpendicular.

A parallelogram is a rectangle if and only if its diagonals are congruent.

A parallelogram is a square if and only if its diagonals are both perpendicular and congruent.

REFLECT

1. A square is also a rhombus, a rectangle, and a parallelogram. What diagonal properties does the square inherit from each?
2. State two properties of a rhombus that do not hold true for all parallelograms.
3. Summarize the theorems about the diagonals of a parallelogram by filling in the Venn diagram with the names of the different types of quadrilaterals.

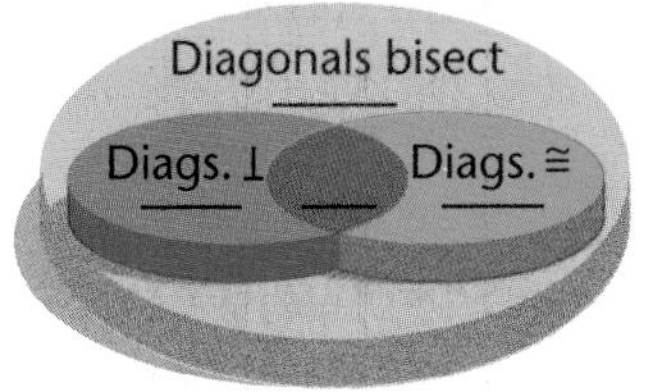

Exercises

CORE

Getting Started Classify quadrilateral *ABCD* using the given information.

1. $\overline{AC}$ and $\overline{BD}$ bisect each other.
2. $\overline{AC}$ and $\overline{BD}$ bisect each other, and $\overline{AC} \cong \overline{BD}$.
3. $\overline{AC}$ and $\overline{BD}$ bisect each other, and $\overline{AC} \perp \overline{BD}$.
4. $\overline{AC}$ and $\overline{BD}$ bisect each other, $\overline{AC} \perp \overline{BD}$, and $\overline{AC} \cong \overline{BD}$.

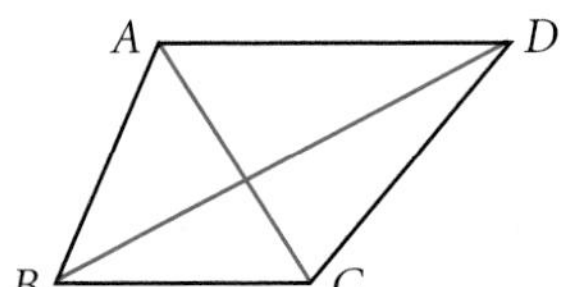

Copy the chart, and indicate with an X the quadrilaterals that have each property.

	Property	Parallelogram	Rectangle	Rhombus	Square
5.	Opposite sides are parallel.				
6.	Opposite sides are congruent.				
7.	Opposite angles are congruent.				
8.	Diagonals bisect each other.				
9.	Diagonals are congruent.				
10.	Diagonals are perpendicular.				
11.	All angles are right angles.				
12.	All sides are congruent.				

Find the values of x and/or y for each quadrilateral. Justify your answers.

13.

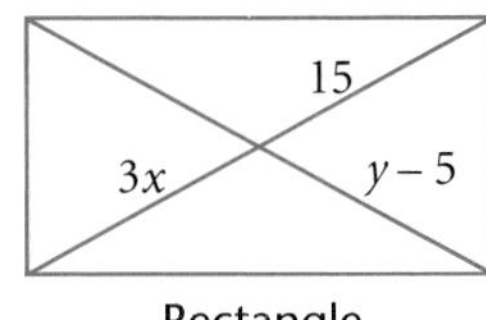

Rectangle

14.

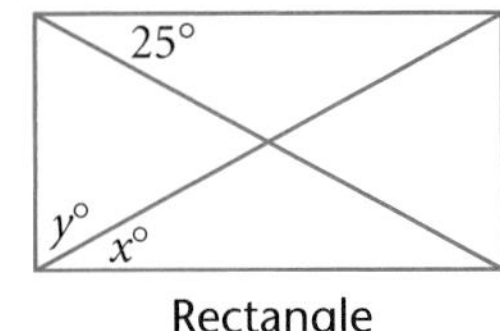

Rectangle

15.

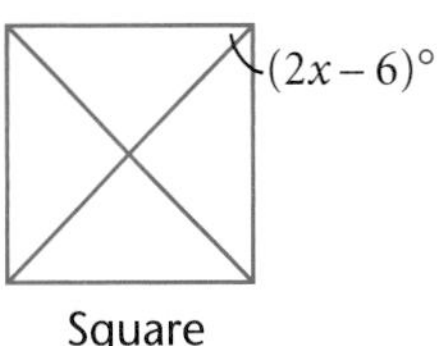

Square

Draw a parallelogram that satisfies each set of conditions or write *not possible.*

16. The diagonals are congruent, but the parallelogram has no right angles.

17. The diagonals are perpendicular but not congruent.

18. Two opposite angles are right angles, but the parallelogram is not a rectangle.

19. Elm Street and Sixth Street are the diagonals of Quad City. They intersect at their midpoints. Assuming that Quad City is a parallelogram, determine its shape under each of the following conditions. Explain each of your answers.
- **a.** Sixth Street is the same length as Elm Street, and they meet at a 45° angle.
- **b.** Sixth Street is longer than Elm Street, and they meet at a right angle.
- **c.** Sixth Street is the same length as Elm Street, and they meet at a right angle.

20. Support Your Case! Nora is assembling a bookcase with diagonal supports. How can she use a tape measure to check that the sides are perpendicular to the shelves? Justify your answer.

21. Suppose the diagonals of a quadrilateral are perpendicular, but they do not bisect each other. Sketch and describe a quadrilateral with these characteristics.

Sketch each figure and its line(s) of symmetry.

22. a rectangle

23. a rhombus

24. a square

25. Describe how to use reflections to generate a rhombus from a single right triangle.

26. Prove the following theorem: If the diagonals of a parallelogram are congruent, then the parallelogram is a rectangle.

27. Prove: If a parallelogram is a rhombus, then its diagonals are perpendicular.

LOOK AHEAD

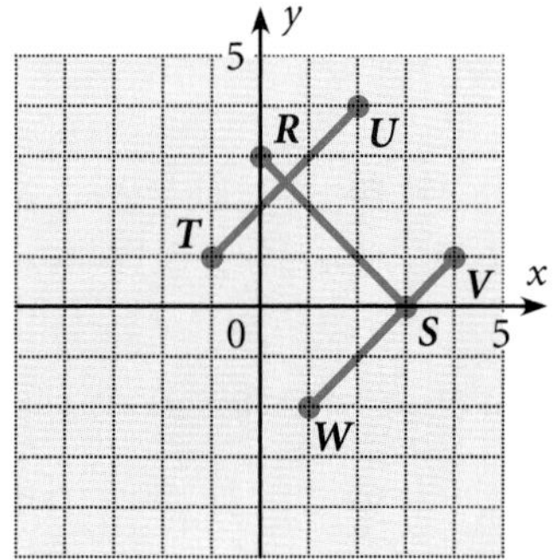

28. Find the length of $\overline{TU}$.

29. Find the slopes of $\overline{TU}$, $\overline{WV}$, and $\overline{RS}$.

30. Are $\overline{TU}$ and $\overline{WV}$ parallel? Explain.

31. Are $\overline{TU}$ and $\overline{RS}$ perpendicular? Explain.

32. Is *TUVW* a parallelogram? Explain.

MORE PRACTICE

What diagonal properties are true for quadrilateral *PQRS* if

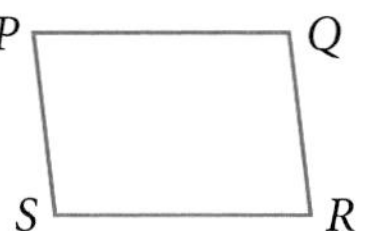

33. *PQRS* is a rectangle?

34. *PQRS* is a rhombus?

35. *PQRS* is a square?

Find the values of *x* and *y* for each quadrilateral. Justify your answers.

36.

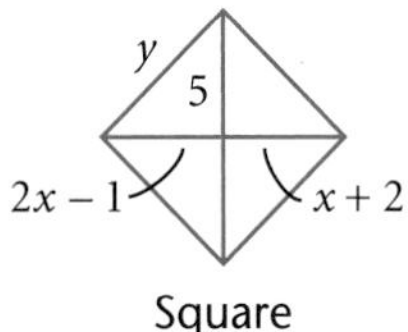

Square

37.

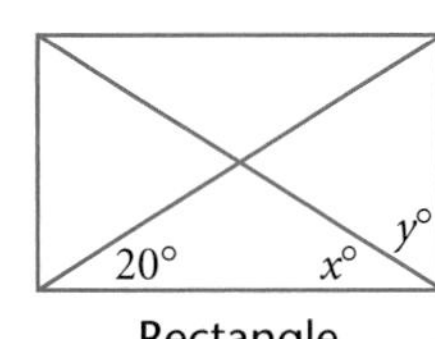

Rectangle

38.

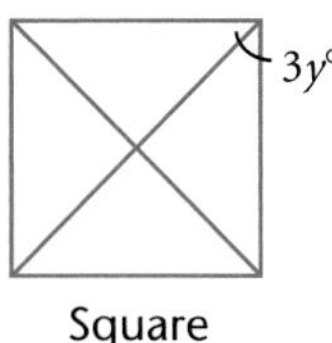

Square

MORE MATH REASONING

39. Prove: If the diagonals of a parallelogram are perpendicular and congruent, then the parallelogram is a square.

40. Prove: If a diagonal of a parallelogram bisects an angle of the parallelogram, then the parallelogram is a rhombus.

41. A kite is a quadrilateral with two distinct pairs of adjacent, congruent sides.

Prove: If exactly one diagonal of a quadrilateral bisects the other diagonal and the diagonals are perpendicular, then the quadrilateral is a kite.

Careers

42. Contractor Corner A contractor needs to mark the corners of the foundation of a new house. She has stakes to mark the corners, but the only other equipment she has are two long pieces of rope and a tape measure. Explain how she can mark the corners for a square foundation if she has no way to cut the rope or to measure angles.

6-2 PART D Quadrilaterals and Coordinate Proof

← CONNECT → ***You've already used the coordinate system to see the relationship between algebra and geometry. Now you will use algebra to help you in geometric proofs.***

Algebra and geometry do not lead separate lives. You've used algebra to find distances, midpoints, slopes of lines, and equations of lines and circles. When you assign coordinates to geometric figures, you are using *coordinate geometry.*

Many proofs can be made easier using coordinate geometry. To use this method, we first place the figure on a coordinate plane. Then we name the vertices and assign coordinates to them. An example is shown below for quadrilateral *WXYZ.*

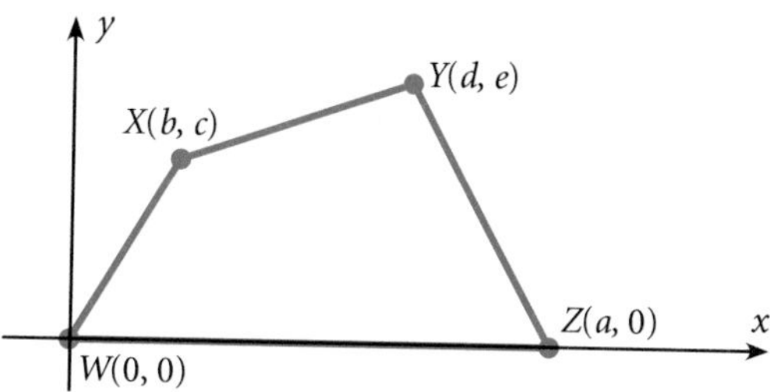

It's usually helpful to place the figure so that one vertex is at the origin and one side is on an axis. An easy problem can turn into a hard one if you don't choose a convenient placement.

EXAMPLE

Place a parallelogram on the coordinate plane. Whenever possible, place vertices on the axes. Let two vertices be the origin and $(a, 0)$. Place a vertex at (b, c). The last vertex insures that opposite sides have the same slope. Choose $(a + b, c)$ to make another horizontal side and a second side of slope $\frac{c}{b}$.

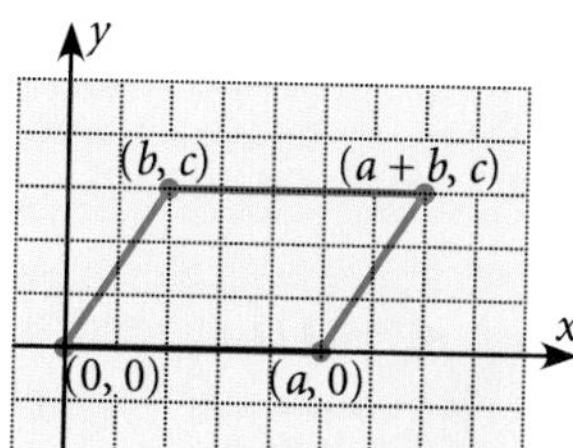

WHAT DO YOU THINK?

Henry and Janice were assigned the following proof for homework.

Prove: If a parallelogram is a rectangle, then its diagonals are congruent.

Given: Parallelogram $DEFG$ is a rectangle with diagonals $\overline{DF}$ and $\overline{EG}$.

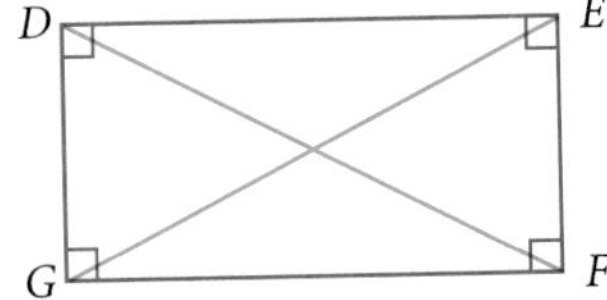

Prove: $\overline{DF} \cong \overline{EG}$

Henry thinks . . .

I'll see if I can prove that two of the triangles formed by the diagonals are congruent, and use CPCTC.

Proof: We are given that $DEFG$ is a rectangle, so $\angle DGF$ and $\angle EFG$ are right angles, by the definition of a rectangle. $\triangle DGF$ and $\triangle EFG$ are right triangles by definition. Both share $\overline{GF}$, which is congruent to itself by the Reflexive Property. Since a rectangle is a parallelogram, its opposite sides are congruent, so $\overline{DG} \cong \overline{EF}$. $\triangle DGF \cong \triangle EFG$ by the LL Theorem, and $\overline{DF} \cong \overline{EG}$ by CPCTC.

Janice thinks . . .

I'll put $DEFG$ on a coordinate plane and use the distance formula. If G is at $(0, 0)$, I can have F on the x-axis at $(a, 0)$ and D above G at $(0, b)$. $\overline{GF}$ is a units long, and opposite sides of $DEFG$ are congruent, so E is a units across from D at (a, b).

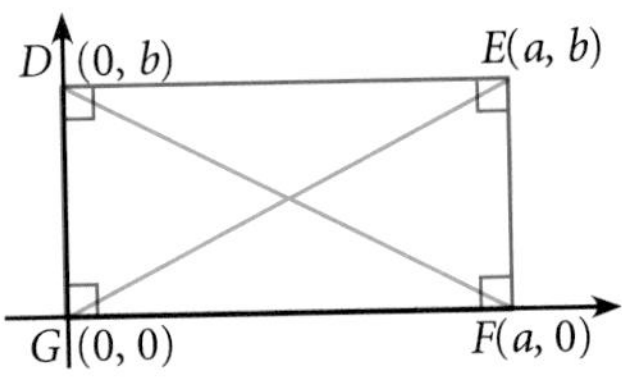

Proof: Using the distance formula, $EG = \sqrt{(a-0)^2 + (b-0)^2} = \sqrt{a^2 + b^2}$. Also, $DF = \sqrt{(0-a)^2 + (b-0)^2} = \sqrt{a^2 + b^2}$. Since their lengths are equal, the diagonals are congruent by the definition of congruent segments.

1. Explain the advantages and disadvantages of the methods Henry and Janice used. Are both methods correct?

In the following Explore, you will get some practice with coordinate proof.

EXPLORE: A WELL COORDINATED PROOF

MATERIALS

Graph paper

Prove that the diagonals of a square are perpendicular.

1. First, place square *ABCD*, with side length *a*, on a coordinate plane. Label the vertices, and give their coordinates. Explain how and why you chose this placement.
2. Use the slope formula to find the slopes of the diagonals $\overline{AC}$ and $\overline{BD}$.
3. Use your results from Step 2 to show that $\overline{AC}$ and $\overline{BD}$ are perpendicular. Explain your thinking.
4. Compare your results with those of your classmates. If you chose different placements for the square, discuss how your choices affected your proofs.

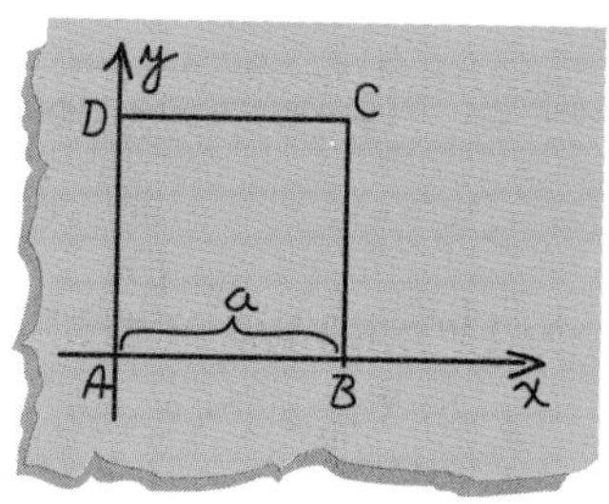

REFLECT

1. What properties can be used to show that lines are parallel or perpendicular when doing a coordinate proof?
2. Why is the use of coordinates a helpful strategy in some proofs?
3. In trapezoid *MNPQ*, you could give point *P* the coordinates (c, d). However, there is a better choice for them. Give coordinates for *P*, and explain why your choice is better than (c, d).

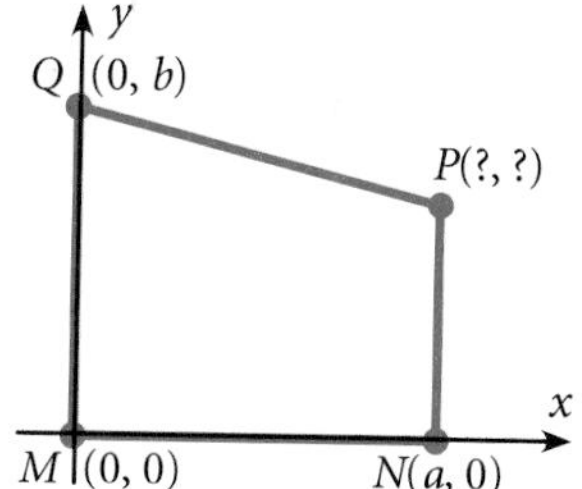

Exercises

CORE

1. **Getting Started** The figure shown at the right is an isosceles trapezoid. What are the coordinates of vertex *C*? (Hint: You will have to introduce one new variable. Remember that the bases are parallel.) What are the coordinates of vertex *D*?

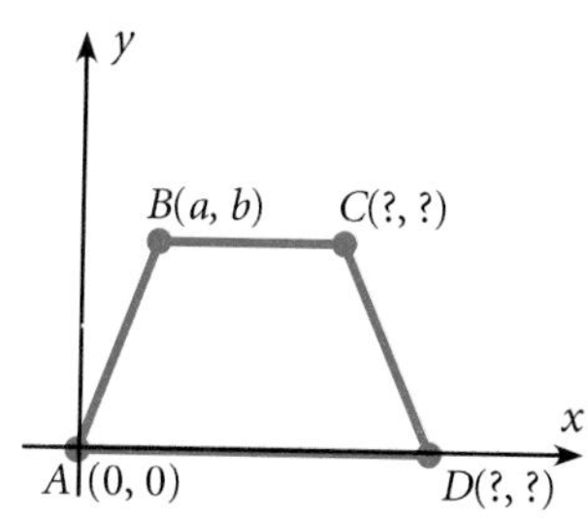

For each figure in Exercises 2–4, assign coordinates to the vertices. Do not introduce any new variables.

2. *ABCD* is a rectangle.

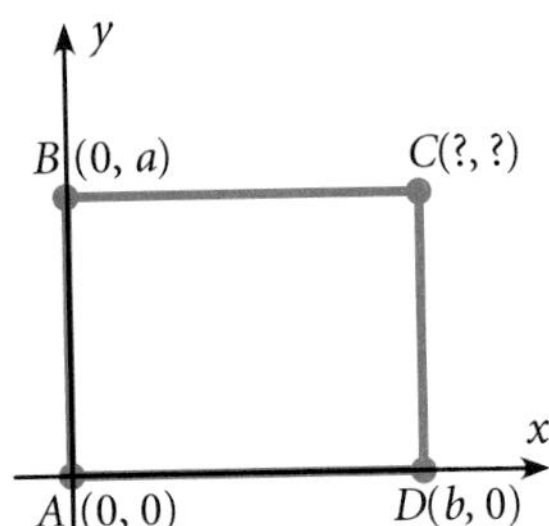

3. *DEFG* is a parallelogram.

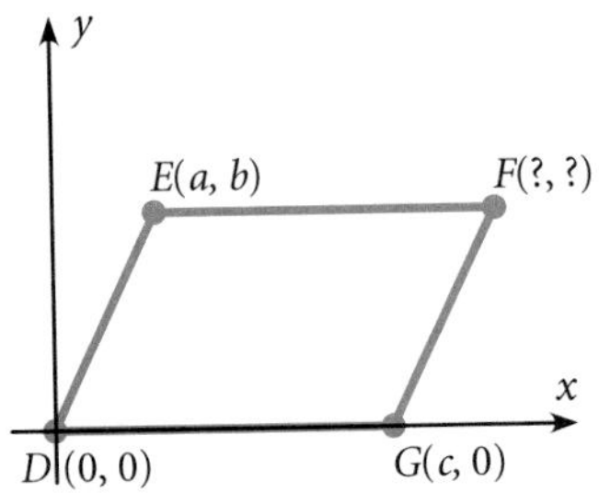

4. $\triangle HIJ$ is equilateral.

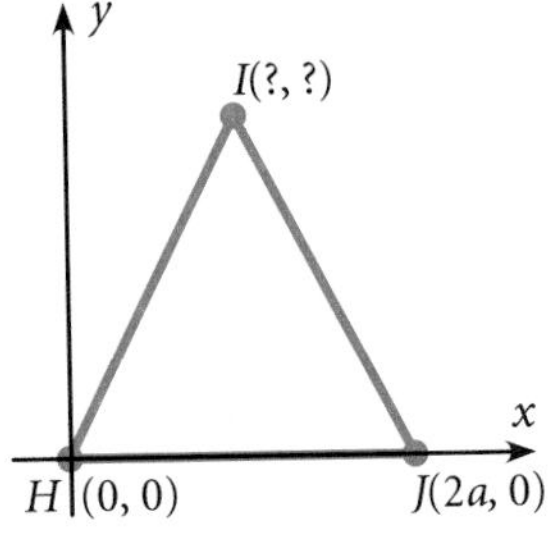

Use the figure at the right to verify each statement.

5. The opposite sides of *FGHJ* are parallel.

6. The opposite sides of *FGHJ* are congruent.

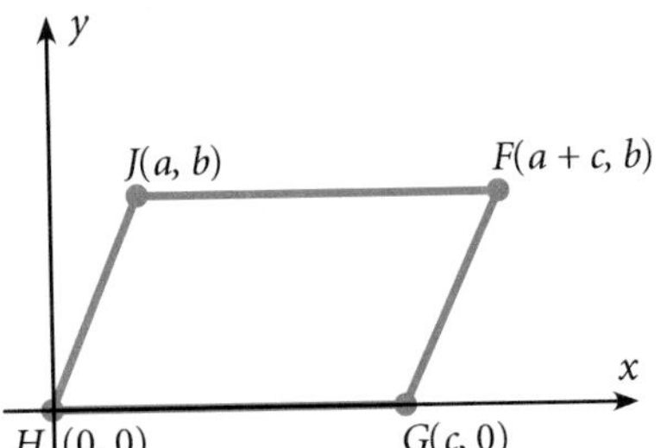

History

7. MariTime The ancient city-state of Mari, in what is now Syria, flourished around 2000 B.C. The main palace had 250 rooms. Suppose that archaeologists studying the palace set up a coordinate system to identify and record the location of artifacts. As shown below, (0, 0) is at the lower left corner of the palace, and each unit represents 20 meters.

a. What type of quadrilateral is the base of the palace? Explain how you know.

b. Prove that your answer in **7a** is correct.

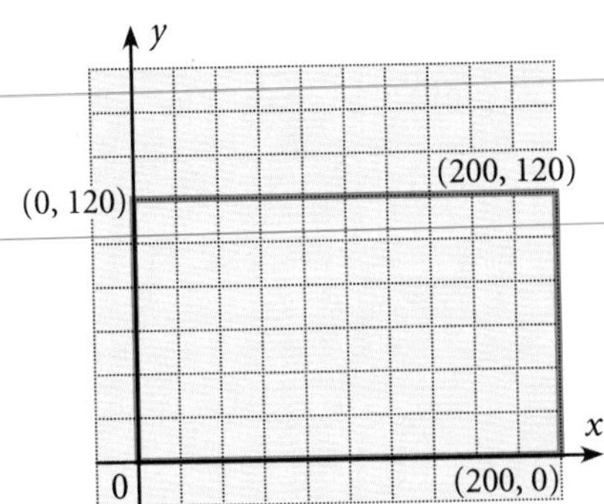

8. Use a coordinate proof to prove the following: If a quadrilateral is a square, then its diagonals are congruent.

9. Use a coordinate proof to prove the following: If a quadrilateral is a parallelogram, then its diagonals bisect each other. (Hint: Find the midpoints of the diagonals.)

10. *Given:* $WXYZ$ is a rhombus.
Prove: $\overline{WY} \perp \overline{XZ}$

a. Find the coordinates of points Y and Z.
b. Find the slopes of $\overline{WY}$ and $\overline{XZ}$. If the segments are perpendicular, what should be true about their slopes?
c. Give a written proof in paragraph form.

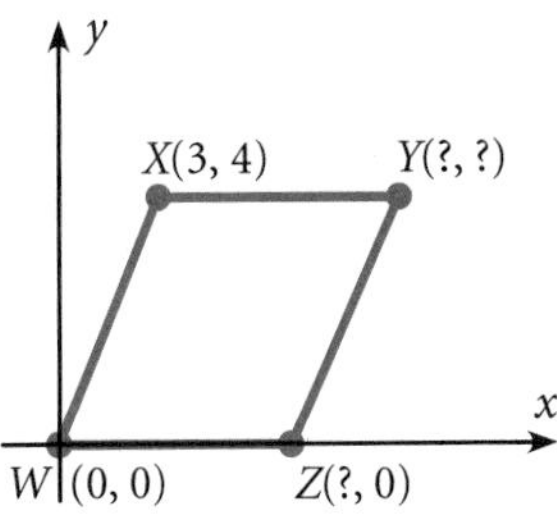

LOOK BACK

Given the following side lengths, classify each triangle as acute, obtuse, or right. [5-3]

11. 9, 12, 14

12. 3, 3, $3\sqrt{2}$

13. 12.3, 13.1, 24

14. 14, 48, 50

15. Draw a net for the polyhedron at the right. What figures form its faces? [1-1, 6-1]

16. Classify the polyhedron. [6-1]

17. Verify that Euler's Formula holds for the polyhedron. [6-1]

MORE PRACTICE

For each figure in Exercises 18–19, assign coordinates to the vertices. Do not introduce any new variables.

18. $ABCD$ is a square.

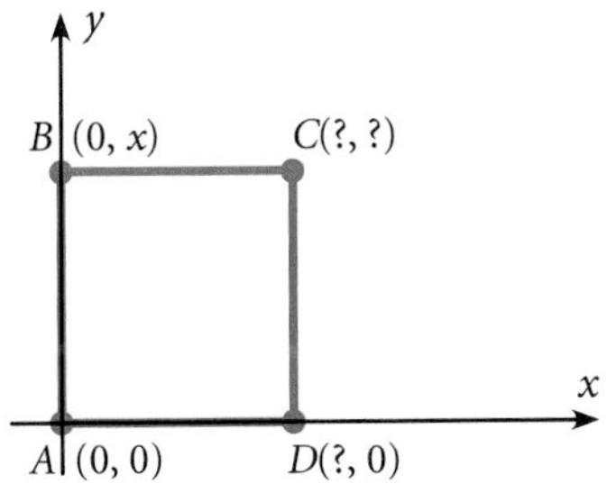

19. $DEFG$ is a rectangle.

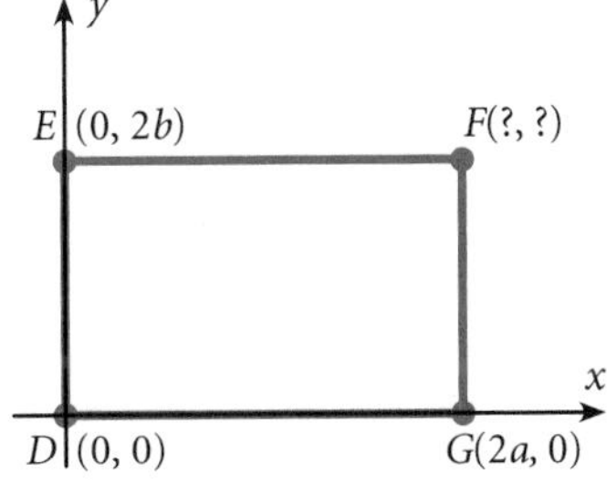

20. Use the figure to prove that the diagonals of square $WXYZ$ are perpendicular.

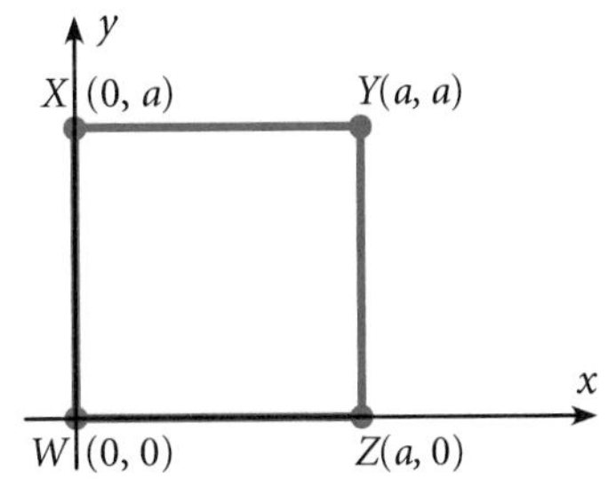

MORE MATH REASONING

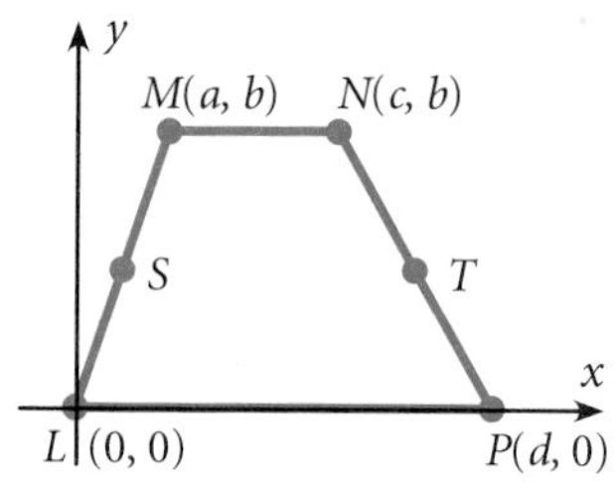

21. The **midsegment** of a trapezoid is the segment that joins the midpoints of its legs. Use a coordinate proof to prove the following: The midsegment of a trapezoid is parallel to the bases, and its length is the average of the lengths of the bases. (Hint: See the figure at the right.)

22. A kite is a quadrilateral with two distinct pairs of adjacent, congruent sides. Prove: If a quadrilateral is a kite, then its diagonals are perpendicular.

23. Who's the Human? The photo below shows humans interacting with a computer of the 1940s. The following excerpt of a "conversation" is from *Computer Power and Human Reason,* by Joseph Weizenbaum. It is an example of a communication between a human and a computer. (Some punctuation has been added.)

A: Do you think coming here will help you not to be unhappy?
B: I need some help, that much seems certain.
A: What would it mean to you if you got some help?
B: Perhaps I could learn to get along with my mother.
A: Tell me more about your family.
B: My mother takes care of me.
A: Who else in your family takes care of you?
B: My father.
A: Your father.
B: You are like my father in some ways.

a. Identify whether A or B is the computer. Explain.

b. What rules do you think the computer is following to model human conversation?

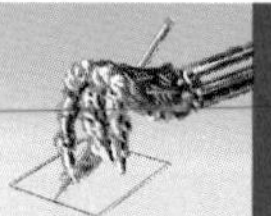

6-2 PART E

Making Connections

← CONNECT → ***You've investigated the properties of specific types of quadrilaterals. These properties are important in many professions, including carpentry and product design. You've also developed skills in writing and demonstrating a deductive proof.***

In the following Explore, you will use what you know to investigate a property of quadrilaterals that may surprise you.

EXPLORE: MIDPOINT SURPRISE

MATERIALS

Ruler
Protractor
Geometry software (optional)

1. Use geometry software or a ruler to draw any quadrilateral, and mark the midpoint of each of its sides, as shown on the left below. Connect the midpoints of adjacent sides. What type of quadrilateral seems to result? Draw several quadrilaterals, and join their midpoints until you feel confident enough to make a conjecture.

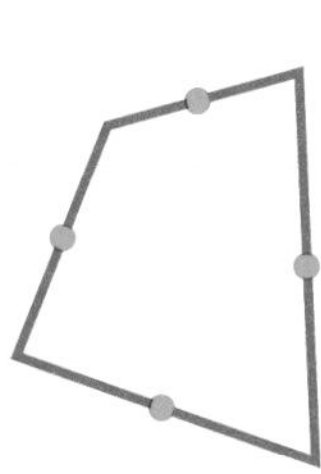

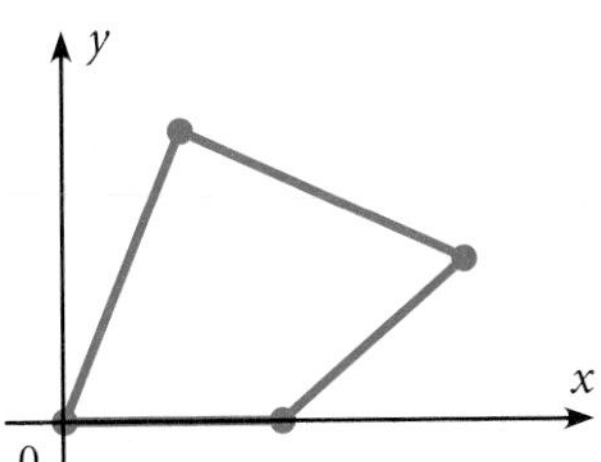

2. Now prove your conjecture with a coordinate proof. (Hint: Use the figure on the right above. When finding the coordinates of the vertices, remember that this quadrilateral is not necessarily a parallelogram. Once you have coordinates for the vertices, you can use the midpoint formula to find the coordinates of the midpoint of each side.)

REFLECT

1. Prepare a Venn diagram that shows how quadrilaterals are related. Explain how to read your diagram, and give all of the properties of each quadrilateral that you list.
2. Is coordinate proof an appropriate method for all proofs? Summarize the advantages and disadvantages of coordinate proofs, and give examples of things that might be difficult to prove with them.

Self-Assessment

Complete each statement with *always, sometimes,* or *never.* Explain each answer.

1. A rectangle ____ has perpendicular diagonals.
2. The diagonals of a rhombus ____ bisect each other.
3. The diagonals of a trapezoid ____ bisect each other.

List the types of quadrilaterals that have each property.

4. Diagonals are perpendicular and bisect each other.

5. Diagonals are congruent and bisect each other.

6. Diagonals are perpendicular, congruent, and bisect each other.

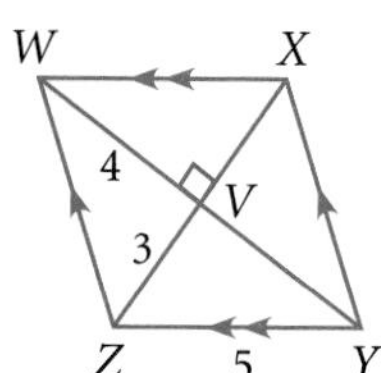

7. In the figure at the right, $WXYZ$ is a

(a) rectangle (b) trapezoid (c) rhombus
(d) square (e) rhombus and square

***ABCD* is a parallelogram.**

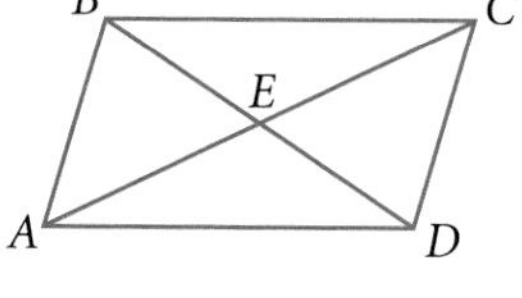

8. If $m\angle DAB = 65°$, find $m\angle ABC$.

9. If $AC = 6$, find CE.

10. If $m\angle CAB = 28°$, find $m\angle DCA$.

11. If $AD = 4y - 6$ and $BC = y + 6$, find AD.

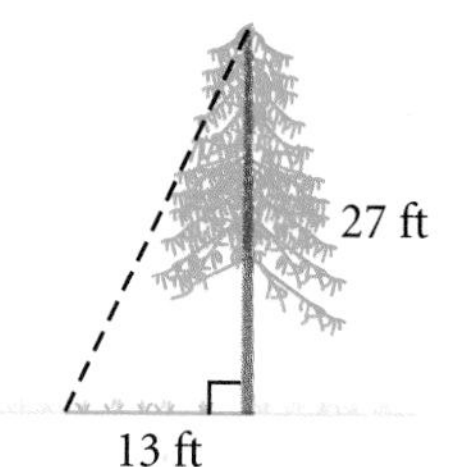

12. A bird lays an egg in a nest at the top of a twenty-seven-foot tree. A conservation worker is trying to retrieve the eggs so that they can be safely hatched. If she places the base of the ladder thirteen feet from the tree, how long is the ladder? Round your answer to the nearest tenth of a foot. [5-3]

Suppose the measures of all of the angles in each polygon are equal. Find the measure of one angle of each of the polygons. [6-1]

13. a quadrilateral **14.** a hexagon **15.** a decagon

16. Geometry Glide A children's glider swing hangs from a horizontal bar as shown below. The hangers are identical metal bars that are attached to the horizontal bar and to the swing so that they pivot freely at points A, B, C, and D. $AB = CD$. Explain why the swing is always parallel to the ground.

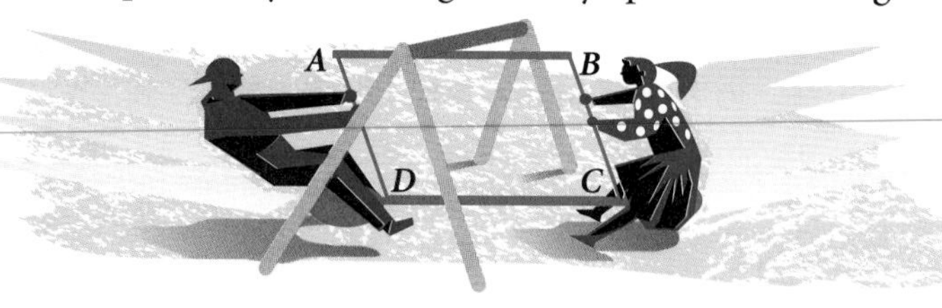

17. Use a coordinate proof to prove the following: If a quadrilateral is a rectangle, then its diagonals are congruent.

18. Summarize the advantages and disadvantages of using a coordinate proof instead of the proofs you worked with earlier (called *synthetic* proofs). Give examples of some of the relationships between segments that can be demonstrated using coordinate methods.

BEAUTY

AND THE BEES

The honeybee is one of nature's greatest architects. The home of the honeybee is called a comb. A comb is made up of hexagonal cells where the bees raise their young and store their food supply.

The comb itself is one of the marvels of animal architecture. It consists of a regular back-to-back pattern of hexagonal cells. There are two types of cells. The larger cells—worker cells—may be used for raising worker bees or for storing honey or pollen. The smaller cells—drone cells—are usually used for raising drone bees or for storing honey.

Hexagonal cells are common among cell-building insects, and there are good reasons for using this shape. Round, octagonal, or pentagonal cell arrangements leave empty spaces between cells, and triangles or squares have a greater perimeter than hexagons with the same area.

Unlike most other social insects, honeybees build their cells horizontally rather than hanging them vertically. However, the cells are angled up at about 13° from base to opening to prevent honey from running out.

1. Describe some advantages of using hexagonal cells instead of other shapes.
2. Why do you think it is important not to have empty spaces between cells?

6-3 PART A Regular Polygons

← CONNECT → ***You have learned some of the properties that hold true for all convex polygons. Now you will look at a special type of polygon—the regular polygon.***

Many natural objects and manufactured products are regular polygons. A **regular polygon** is both equilateral and equiangular. Some traffic signs are regular polygons, such as the Australian sign shown at the right.

TRY IT

Classify each polygon as equilateral, equiangular, and/or regular.

a.

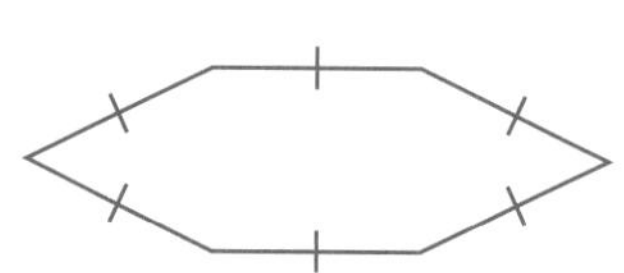

b.

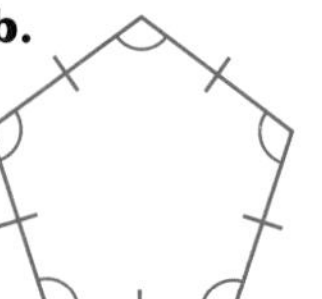

c.

1. Using what you know about the sum of the measures of the interior and exterior angles of polygons, find the measure of each interior and exterior angle of a regular hexagon. Explain your method.

The **center** of a regular polygon is the point of intersection of the perpendicular bisectors of the sides. The segment (or length of the segment) from a vertex to the center is the **radius.**

The perpendicular segment (or length of the segment) from the center to a side is an **apothem** (AP uh THEM).

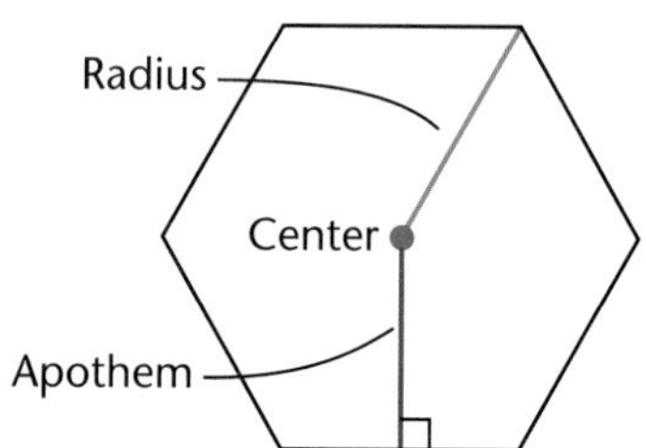

All of the radii of a regular polygon are congruent. Any regular polygon can be divided into congruent isosceles triangles by drawing all of its radii.

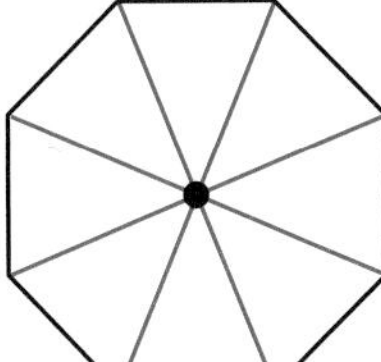

Regular octagon: eight congruent isosceles triangles

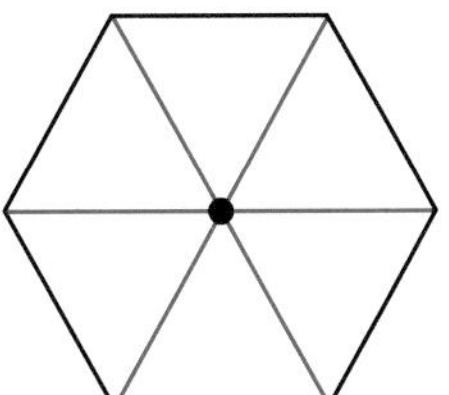

Regular hexagon: six congruent equilateral triangles

To find the area of a regular polygon, you could add the areas of all of these triangles. In the following Explore, you will investigate a faster way to find the area of a regular polygon.

EXPLORE: YOU'RE IN THE AREA

1. Answer the following questions for each regular polygon shown below.

a. How many sides does the polygon have?

b. Into how many triangles is it divided by the radii?

c. What is the area of each of these triangles in terms of a and s?

d. What is the area of the polygon in terms of a and s?

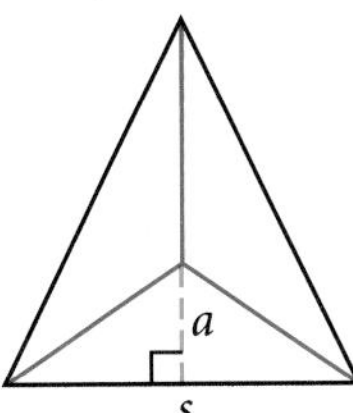

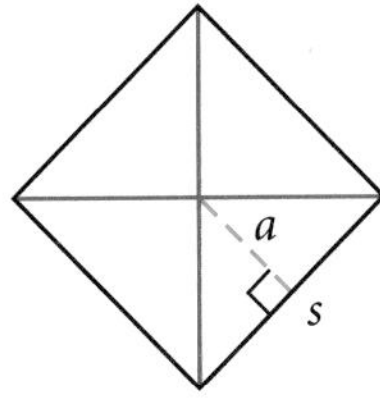

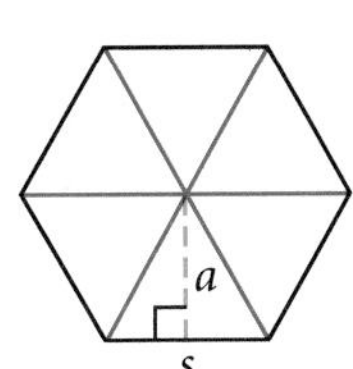

2. Write a formula for the area of a regular n-gon in terms of n, a, and s.

3. If a regular n-gon has apothem a and perimeter p, write a formula for its area in terms of a and p.

Problem-Solving Tip

See if your formula makes sense by testing it with specific three- and four-sided figures.

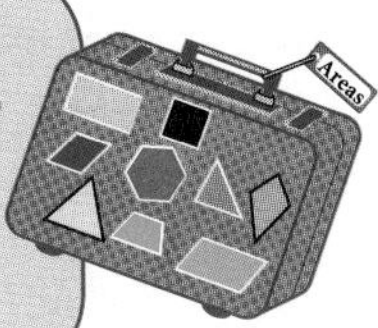

EXAMPLE

Find the area of the regular pentagon.

Since a regular pentagon has five congruent sides, the perimeter of this pentagon is $5 \times 10 = 50$.

10 in.

$a = 6.9$ in.

$$\text{Area} = \frac{1}{2}ap = \frac{1}{2}(6.9)(50)$$

$$= 172.5 \text{ in.}^2$$

TRY IT

d. Find the area of the regular octagon.

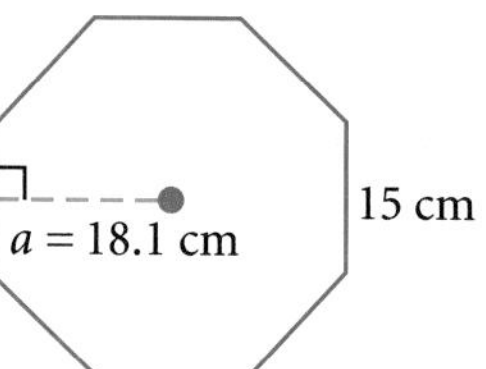

We can summarize the results about the area and angles of regular polygons as follows.

THEOREMS ABOUT REGULAR POLYGONS

The area of a regular polygon is one-half the product of its perimeter and its apothem. $A = \frac{1}{2}ap$

Each angle of a regular n-gon measures $\frac{(n-2)180°}{n}$.

Each exterior angle of a regular n-gon measures $\frac{360°}{n}$.

REFLECT

1. Explain why the radii of any regular polygon divide it into congruent isosceles triangles.

2. Why do the radii of a regular hexagon divide it into six congruent equilateral triangles?

3. Describe a method for constructing the center of a regular polygon with a compass and straightedge. Is there an easy method for finding the center of some regular polygons that doesn't work for others? Explain.

Exercises

CORE

Getting Started Classify each polygon as equilateral, equiangular, and/or regular.

1. 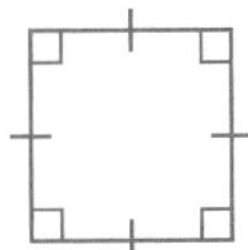

2. 

3. 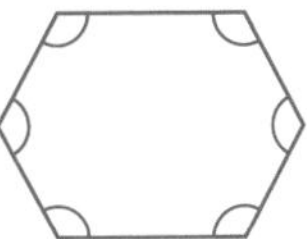

Find the measure of one interior angle and one exterior angle of each polygon.

4. regular heptagon **5.** regular octagon **6.** regular decagon

ience

7. The Measure of Angle Bee Find the measure of one interior angle and one exterior angle for a regular hexagonal beehive cell.

8. One angle of a regular polygon measures 160°. How many sides does the polygon have?

9. Is it possible for a regular polygon to have an interior angle of 156°? Explain.

10. As the number of sides of a regular polygon increases, what happens to the size of each interior angle of the polygon? Explain.

Write the word or phrase that correctly completes each statement.

11. The perpendicular bisectors of the sides of a regular polygon meet at its ____.

12. The distance from the center of a regular polygon to one of its sides is the ____ of the polygon.

13. The distance from the center of a regular polygon to one of its vertices is the ____ of the polygon.

14. An interior decorator is tiling a floor with the pattern of octagons and squares shown. Explain why this pattern tessellates a plane.

In Exercises 15–19, find the area of each regular polygon.

15. 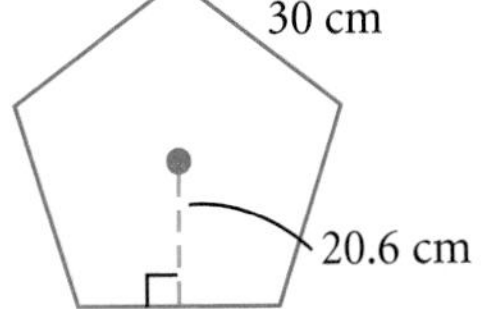

16. 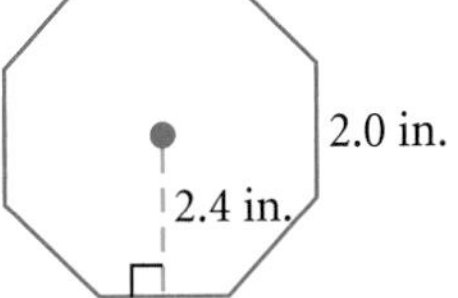

17. 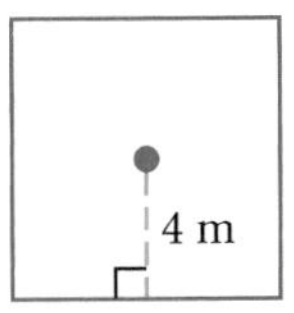

18. a regular decagon with apothem 6.8 m and side length 4.4 m

19. a regular octagon with apothem 14.5 in. and side length 12 in.

Find the apothem and radius of each regular polygon. Then find its area.

20.

12

a *r*

21.

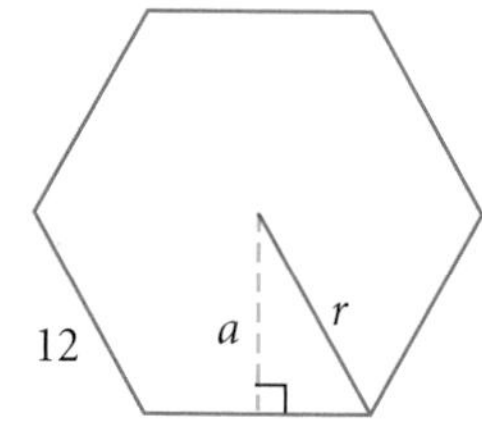

22.

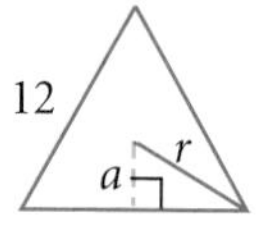

23. Stop Everything! The stop sign at the right was cut from a 30-in.-square piece of metal.

a. What type of regular polygon is the stop sign?

b. What is the measure of each interior angle of the sign?

c. How could you locate the center of the polygon?

d. Find the length of the apothem.

e. If the polygon's side length is 12.4 in., find the area of the stop sign.

f. Describe how to make this sign from a square piece of metal.

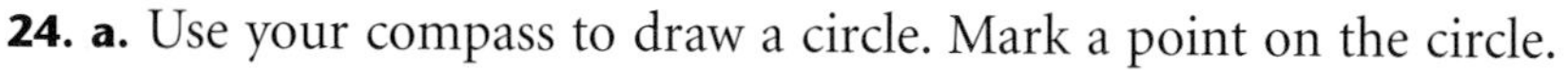

24. a. Use your compass to draw a circle. Mark a point on the circle.

b. Without changing the setting, move the tip of the compass to the point you marked on the circle. Draw an arc that intersects the circle as shown.

c. Move the tip of your compass to the intersection of the arc and the circle, and make another arc that intersects the circle. Repeat until you come back to the place you started. Draw segments that join the consecutive points on the circle.

d. What type of figure did you construct? Explain why this construction works. (Hint: Consider equilateral triangles.)

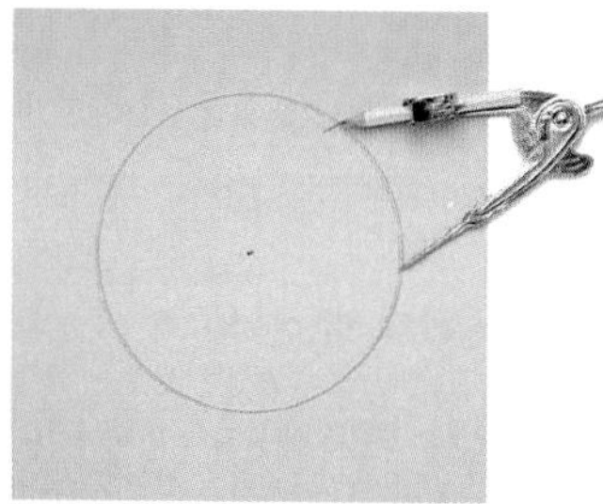

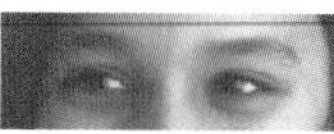

LOOK BACK

List all of the characteristics that you can for the diagonals of each figure. [6-2]

25. rhombus

26. square

27. rectangle

28. *Given:* $\overline{JK} \parallel \overline{HL}$ and $\angle H \cong \angle K$

Prove: $\triangle HJL \cong \triangle KLJ$

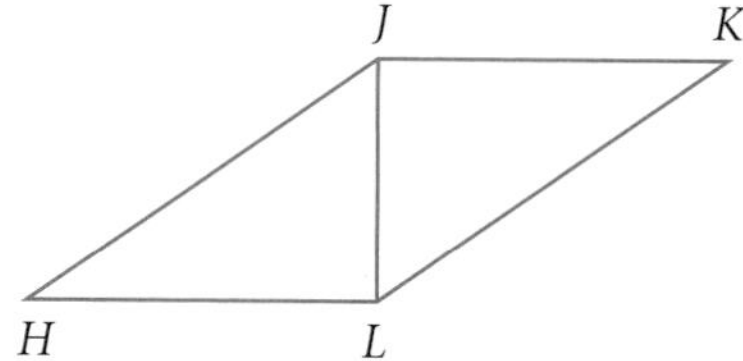

Solve each quadratic equation. [5-1]

29. $x^2 + 7x + 3 = 0$

30. $x^2 - 10x + 21 = 0$

31. $3x^2 - 4x = 10$

MORE PRACTICE

Find the measure of one interior angle and one exterior angle of each polygon.

32. regular pentagon

33. regular 12-gon

34. regular 18-gon

Find the area of each regular polygon.

35. a regular pentagon with apothem 2.2 ft and side length 3.2 ft

36. a regular octagon with apothem 12.1 cm and side length 10 cm

Find the apothem and radius of each regular polygon. Then find its area.

37.

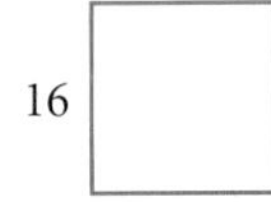

38.

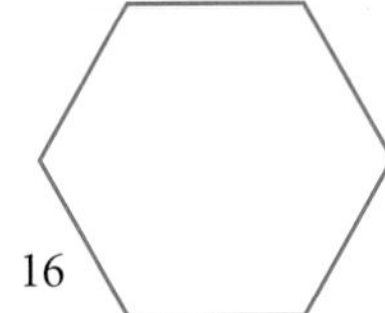

39.

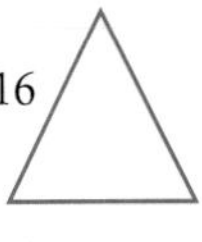

MORE MATH REASONING

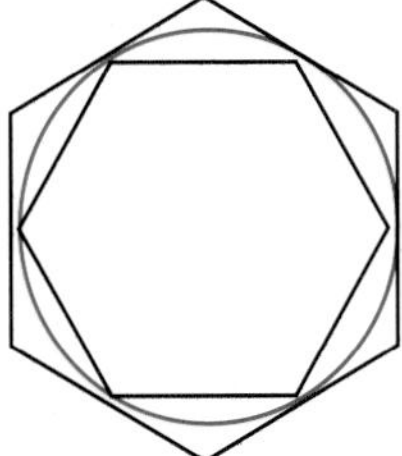

40. The circle in the figure at the right has a radius of 12 in. Find the ratio of the areas of the two regular hexagons.

41. Sign In, Please The diamond-shaped sign shown is a warning that you are coming to a stop sign. Most square warning signs are made with 30-in. sides. The actual stop sign is an octagon. It was cut from a 30-in. piece of metal, and each side of the octagon is 12.4 in. long.

a. What is the area of the octagon on the warning sign if its dimensions are one-half those of the actual stop sign?

b. Excluding the octagon, how many square inches need to be painted on the front of the warning sign?

c. How many times greater is the area of the actual stop sign than the area of the octagon on the warning sign?

6-3 PART B

Regular Polyhedrons

← CONNECT → ***You've investigated some properties of polyhedrons. Now you will see how regular polygons can be used to form special polyhedrons.***

A regular polyhedron has:

- congruent edges and faces;
- faces that are regular polygons;
- an equal number of edges meeting at each vertex.

A *convex* regular polyhedron is one with no "dents."

Although there are an infinite number of convex regular *polygons* (just keep adding sides!), there are only five convex regular *polyhedrons.* These polyhedrons were discovered over two thousand years ago and are named the **Platonic solids,** in honor of the Greek philosopher Plato.

In the following Explore, you will look for some of the Platonic solids and investigate a few of their properties.

EXPLORE: PURELY PLATONIC

MATERIALS

Segments
Connectors
(for example, toothpicks and gumdrops)

Two of the Platonic solids are shown below.

Regular icosahedron
(20 triangular faces)

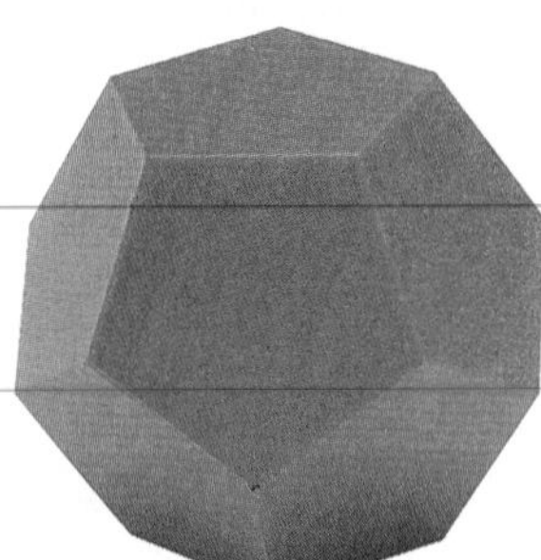

Regular dodecahedron
(12 pentagonal faces)

Use whatever segments and connectors you have available to find the rest of the Platonic solids. There are only three others, and they all have fewer faces than the two shown. Make a sketch of each, and complete the table on page 449. (If you need help remembering the names of polyhedrons, see page 410.)

Name	Type of Face	No. of Faces	No. of Vertices	No. of Edges
	Triangle			
	Square			
	Triangle			
Regular dodecahedron	Pentagon	12	20	30
Regular icosahedron	Triangle	20	12	30

TRY IT

Name the convex regular polyhedron that has the given set of characteristics.

a. five equilateral triangular faces meet at each vertex
b. square faces
c. three equilateral triangular faces meet at each vertex

The Platonic solids occur in nature in many ways. Sodium sulphantimonate molecules are tetrahedrons, chrome alum molecules are octahedrons, and salt crystals are cubes (hexahedrons). The photograph at the right shows the hexahedral structure of salt crystals.

Although there are only five Platonic solids, there are other regular polyhedrons. Two were discovered in the sixteenth century and two more in the nineteenth century. These *concave* regular polyhedrons are shown below.

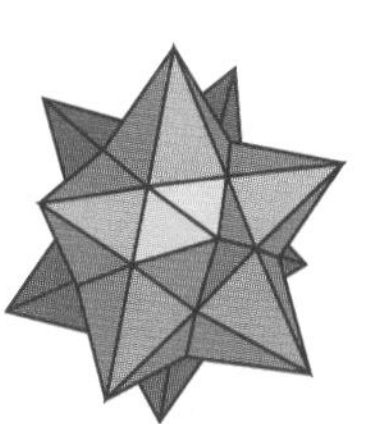

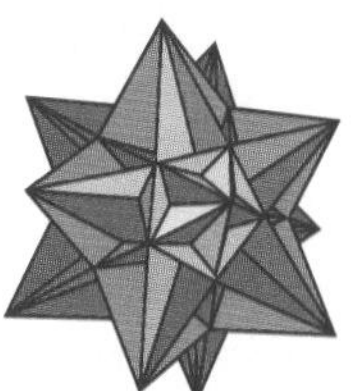

REFLECT

1. Give examples of Platonic solids in your classroom or in other everyday situations. Classify each by the number of faces.
2. What can you say about the faces of any Platonic solid? Explain.

Exercises

CORE

Getting Started Classify each regular polyhedron shown.

1. 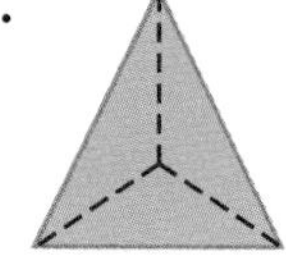

2. 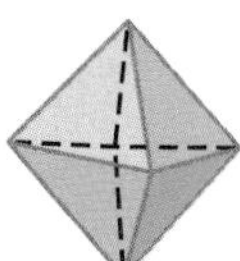

3. 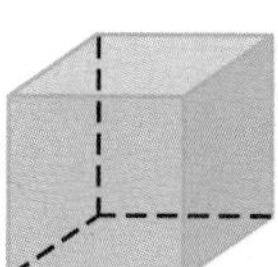

4. 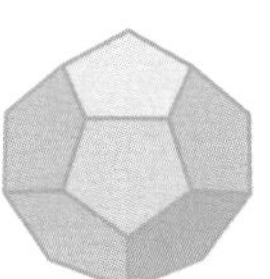

5. 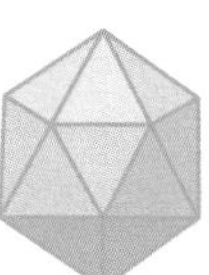

Name the convex regular polyhedron that has the given set of characteristics.

6. Four equilateral triangular faces meet at each vertex.

7. pentagonal faces

Sketch each Platonic solid.

8. a regular tetrahedron (4 faces)

9. a regular hexahedron (6 faces)

10. a regular octahedron (8 faces)

11. Name a Platonic solid that tessellates space.

12. If a Platonic solid is randomly selected from the five possibilities, what is the probability that the solid will have
a. triangular faces?
b. square faces?
c. pentagonal faces?

Science

13. As shown in the photo at the right, a sodium chloride (salt) crystal has a hexahedral shape.
a. What is another name for a convex regular hexahedron?
b. Verify that Euler's Formula holds for a hexahedral salt crystal.

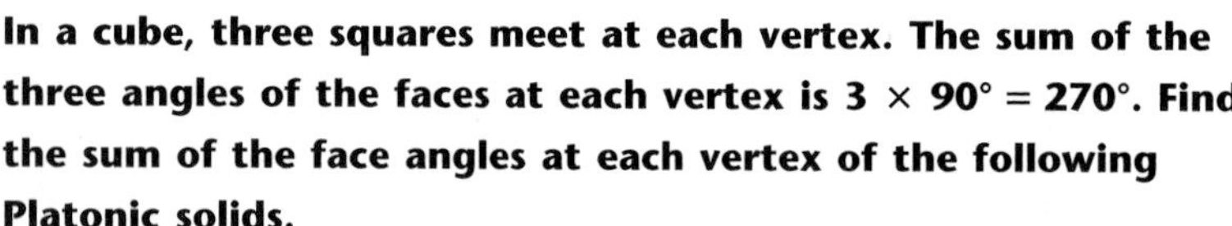

In a cube, three squares meet at each vertex. The sum of the three angles of the faces at each vertex is 3 × 90° = 270°. Find the sum of the face angles at each vertex of the following Platonic solids.

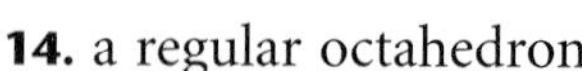

14. a regular octahedron

15. a regular dodecahedron

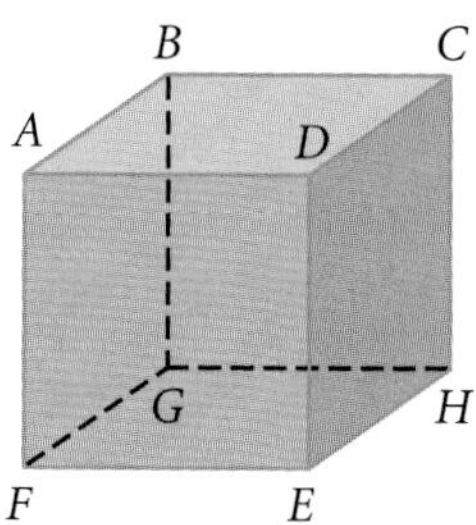

16. In the regular hexahedron at the right, $\overrightarrow{AB} = \overrightarrow{DC}$. Find at least three additional pairs of equal vectors, using the vertices of the hexahedron.

17. Crawling Out for Dinner Sparky the spider is located at point S on the wall of a regular hexahedral room. Sparky is 1 ft from the top of the room and 1 ft from the back. Sparky sees Frankie the fly at point F on the opposite wall, 1 ft from the bottom and 1 ft from the front. Sparky only takes trips that are the shortest possible distance.

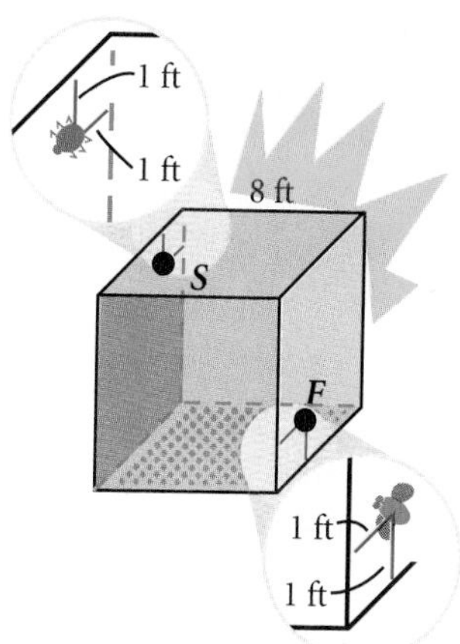

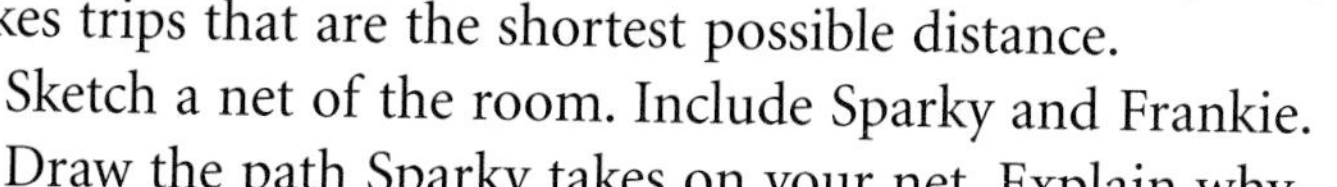

a. Sketch a net of the room. Include Sparky and Frankie.

b. Draw the path Sparky takes on your net. Explain why you think this is the shortest path.

c. What is the shortest distance along the walls from Sparky to Frankie?

LOOK AHEAD

Solve each proportion.

18. $\frac{x}{12} = \frac{6}{9}$ **19.** $\frac{3}{5} = \frac{8}{z}$ **20.** $\frac{AB}{8} = \frac{9}{12}$

In Exercises 21 and 22, a 90-m long rope is cut into two pieces.

21. One piece of rope has a length of 70 m. What is the ratio of the longer piece to the shorter piece?

22. Suppose the two pieces have a length ratio of 13:5. How long is each piece?

MORE PRACTICE

23. Which Platonic solids have the same number of vertices as faces?

24. Which Platonic solids have the same number of vertices as edges?

Find the sum of the face angles at each vertex of the following Platonic solids.

25. a regular tetrahedron **26.** a regular icosahedron

MORE MATH REASONING

27. On a Roll Suppose you create a game in which you want an equal chance of any of *four* numbers coming up on a roll of a die. Design a die for your game. Explain your design.

28. Face the Sum Find a formula for the sum of the angles of all faces of a Platonic solid in terms of n, the number of vertices.

6-3 PART C Making Connections

← CONNECT → ***Honeybees, gem cutters, and even Plato have found regular polygons and polyhedrons useful. You've investigated the properties of these figures.***

The photograph at the left shows honeybees at work in a hive. In the following Explore, you will become more familiar with the ingenuity of the honeybee and learn more about why it makes the architectural choices it does.

EXPLORE: BACK TO THE BEES

MATERIALS

Straightedge
Paper
Scissors

Is there a reason honeybees make hexagonal cells? Why not pentagons? octagons? 54-gons?

1. Make several copies of each figure. Check to see if they will tessellate a plane.

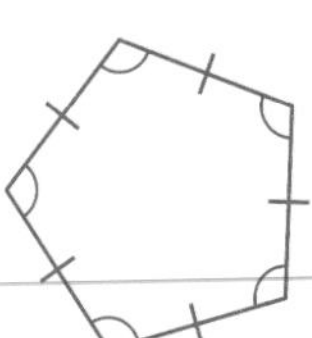

Regular pentagon

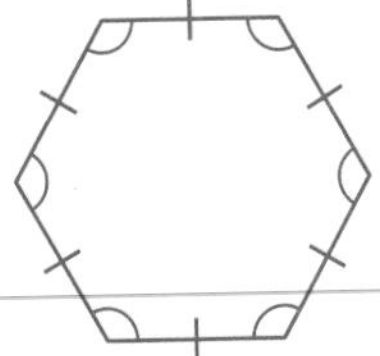

Regular hexagon

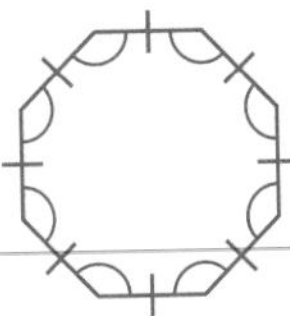

Regular octagon

2. Name three types of regular polygons that tessellate a plane, and explain why they tessellate. Are there other regular polygons that tessellate? Why or why not?
3. Explain why bees might want to have cell openings that tessellate.
4. Why do you think bees make hexagonal cells instead of using another regular polygon that tessellates? (We will investigate this in more detail in Chapter 11.)
5. Are beehive cells regular polyhedrons? Support your answer.

REFLECT

1. Write a short paragraph comparing and contrasting regular polygons and regular polyhedrons.
2. There are only five convex regular polyhedrons. List them and give the number and type of faces for each.
3. How can you make a regular hexagon by reflecting an equilateral triangle? Is there another way to use transformations to make a hexagon from an equilateral triangle? Explain your methods.

Self-Assessment

1. Explain the relationship between regular polygons and regular polyhedrons.

2. **Hive Society** As shown in the figure, there are approximately five worker-bee cells for each 25 mm in a comb.

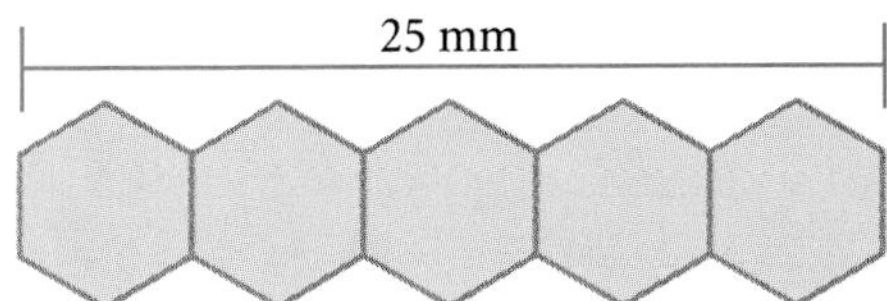

   a. What is the measure of one interior angle of each cell?
   b. What is the measure of one exterior angle of each cell?
   c. Find the apothem, radius, and area of one of the cells.
   d. How many cells take up an area of 100 mm^2?

3. The measure of an exterior angle of a regular n-gon is equal to

   (a) 360° (b) $\frac{360°}{n}$ (c) 180° (d) $\frac{(n-2)180°}{n}$ (e) $\frac{1}{2}ap$

In Exercises 4–6, sketch the following regular polygons, showing the lines of symmetry of each figure.

4. an equilateral triangle
5. a square
6. a regular hexagon
7. How many lines of symmetry are there in a regular n-gon?
8. Prove: If the diagonals of a parallelogram are perpendicular, then it is a rhombus. [6-2]
9. What quadrilateral is determined by the cross section of the cube containing A, B, G, and H? Why?

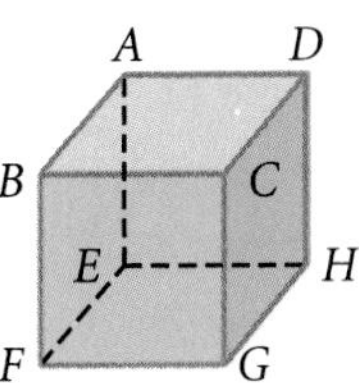

10. Mayan Palace The floor plan of the Palacio (shown at the right), a building in the ancient Mayan city of Palenque, is 48 ft longer than it is wide. The area of the base of the Palacio is 41,040 ft^2. Find the length and the width of the Palacio to the nearest tenth of a foot. Explain your method. [5-1]

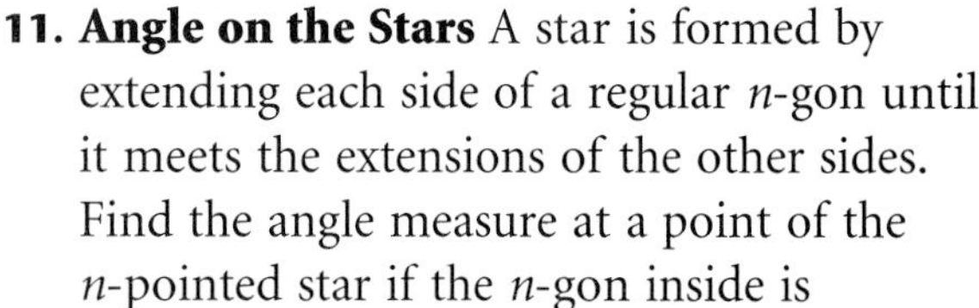

11. Angle on the Stars A star is formed by extending each side of a regular n-gon until it meets the extensions of the other sides. Find the angle measure at a point of the n-pointed star if the n-gon inside is

a. a pentagon

b. a hexagon

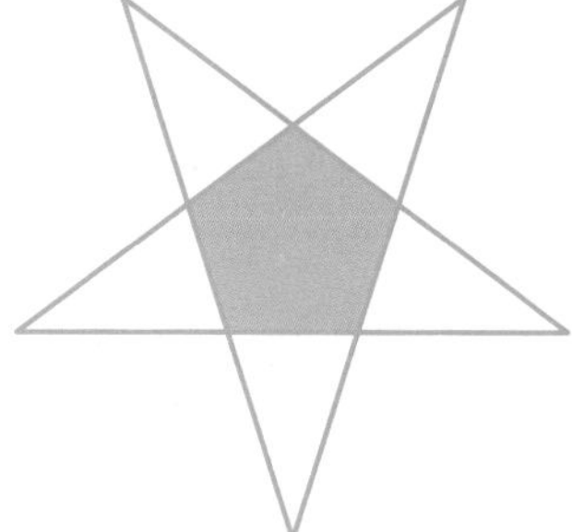

12. A deltahedron is a convex polyhedron whose faces are all triangles. Which of the five Platonic solids are deltahedrons?

13. Archimedean Solids Another set of polyhedrons is referred to as the Archimedean solids. There are thirteen of these solids. Five of them are shown below.

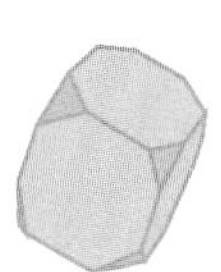
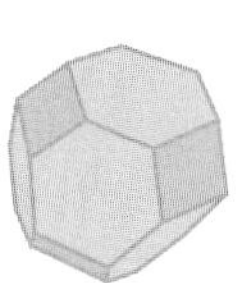

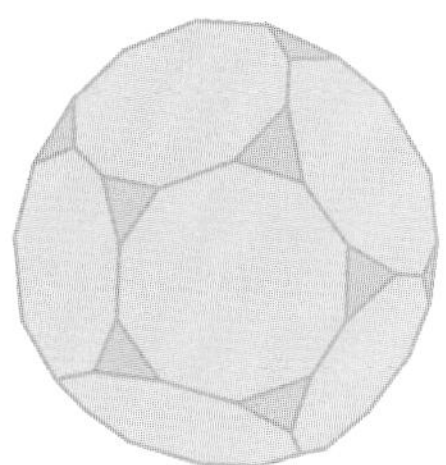

These five solids are truncated Platonic solids. This means that the vertices of a Platonic solid have been cut off to produce each solid. Describe how this was done to create the solids shown here.

14. Grace Chisholm Young (1868–1944) was an English mathematician. The net shown at the right is adapted from a net in her *First Book of Geometry,* published in 1905. When folded, the triangle labeled 1a coincides with the triangle labeled 1, and so on. What regular polyhedron results from folding up this net?

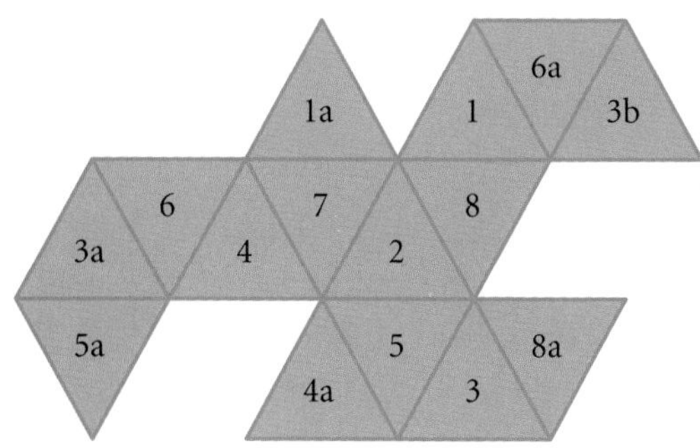

Chapter 6 Review

In Chapter 6, you explored polygons and polyhedrons, including properties of quadrilaterals, applications of regular polygons, and connections to coordinate proof.

KEY TERMS

apothem [6-3]
center of a regular polygon [6-3]
concave polygon [6-1]
convex polygon [6-1]
diagonal [6-1]
Platonic solids [6-3]
polyhedron [6-1]
radius of a regular polygon [6-3]
regular polygon [6-3]
regular polyhedron [6-3]

From each group of terms, choose the term that does not belong and explain why.

1. Convex, concave, regular, apothem

2. Center, altitude, radius, apothem

CONCEPTS AND APPLICATIONS

3. Find the sums of the measures of the interior angles and exterior angles (one at each vertex) for a pentagon. [6-1]

Sketch each of the following, if possible. If it is not possible, say so.

4. a concave hexagon [6-1]

5. a regular polygon whose interior angles measure 135° each [6-3]

6. A polyhedron has twelve edges and six vertices. How many faces does the polyhedron have? Name the polyhedron by its number of faces. [6-1]

Determine whether each quadrilateral must be a parallelogram. Explain. [6-2]

7.

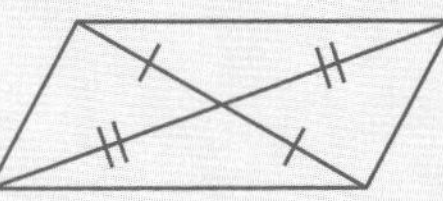

8.

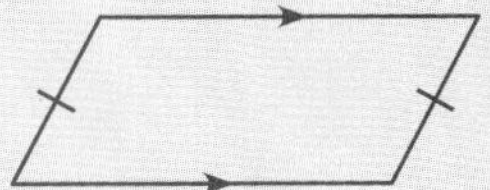

9.

10. Points M, N, O, and P are the midpoints of the sides of quadrilateral $XYZW$. Prove that $MNOP$ is a parallelogram. [6-2]

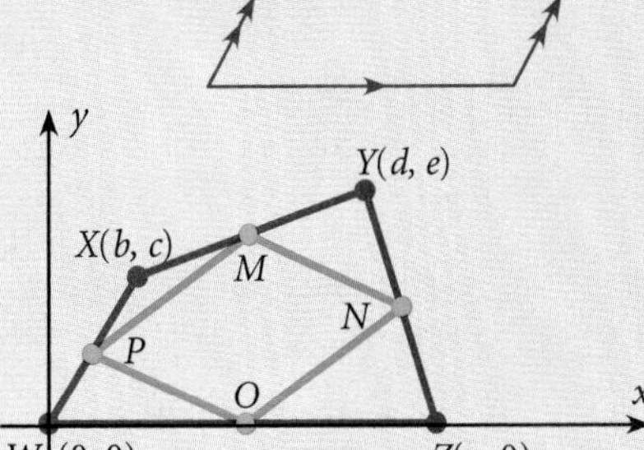

11. What is the measure of each interior angle of a regular 10-gon? [6-3]

12. A children's game uses a regular dodecahedron as a die. Explain how to assign the digits 1, 2, 3, 4, and 5 to the 12 pentagonal faces so that the probabilities of rolling 1, 2, 3, or 4 are the same and the probability of rolling a 5 is twice the probability of rolling a 1. [6-3]

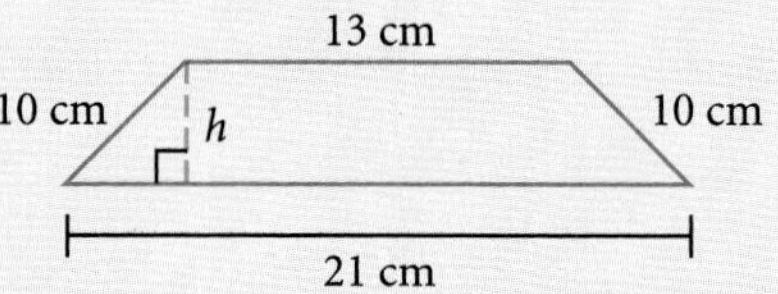

13. Find the apothem, radius, and area of an equilateral triangle with side length 6 in. [6-3]

14. Find the altitude, *h*, and area of this trapezoid. [5-2, 5-3]

15. Write a summary of formulas related to the angles of convex polygons.

CONCEPTS AND CONNECTIONS

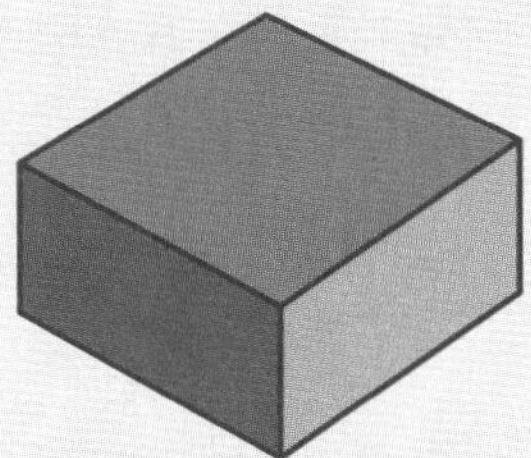

16. Technical Drawing An isometric view of a square-topped box is shown at the right. Draw orthogonal views of the box, as well as one-point and two-point perspective drawings. Describe the polygon that is used to represent the square top in each drawing. For each polygon, describe how the interior angles and any diagonal relationships differ from those of the square.

SELF-EVALUATION

Write a summary of the most important ideas in Chapter 6. Include in your summary the special properties of quadrilaterals, properties of regular polygons and polyhedrons, and important formulas. Mention concepts that gave you trouble.

Chapter 6 Assessment

TEST

1. Sketch a concave quadrilateral, if possible. If it is not possible, say so.

Determine whether each quadrilateral must be a parallelogram. Justify your answers.

2.

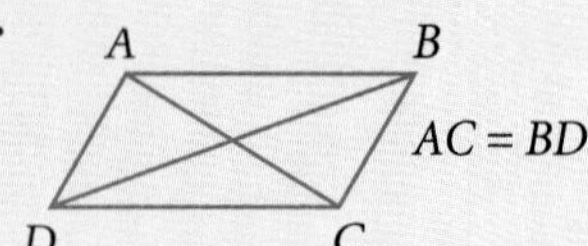

3.

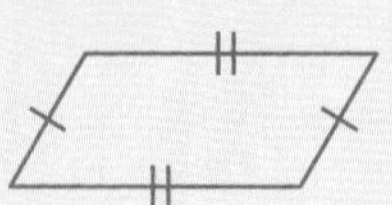

4.

5. Find the apothem and area of a regular hexagon with side length 5 m.

6. An n-gon is partitioned into triangles by drawing all of the diagonals from one vertex as shown. Explain what property of the n-gon is given by the expression $(n - 2)180°$ and explain how it is derived from this partitioning.

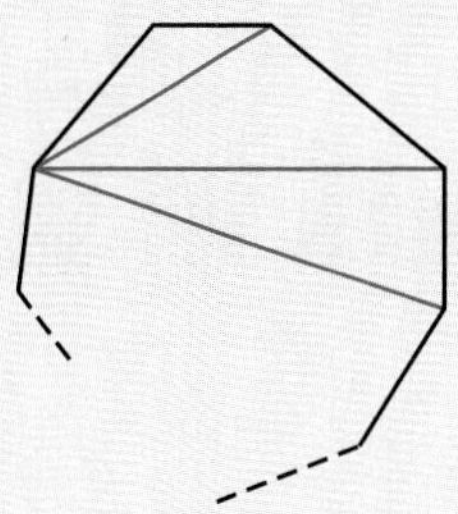

7. What is the sum of the measures of the exterior angles (one at each vertex) of a regular pentagon? What is the measure of each of its interior angles?

8. A triangle has sides of lengths 12, 17, and 27. Determine whether the triangle is acute, obtuse, or right. Explain.

9. A designer of a board game has asked you to design a die. The probability of rolling a 3 must be twice the probability of rolling a 1; the probability of rolling a 2 must be three times the probability of rolling a 1. Choose one of the Platonic solids, and explain how to assign numbers to its faces to satisfy the designer's criteria.

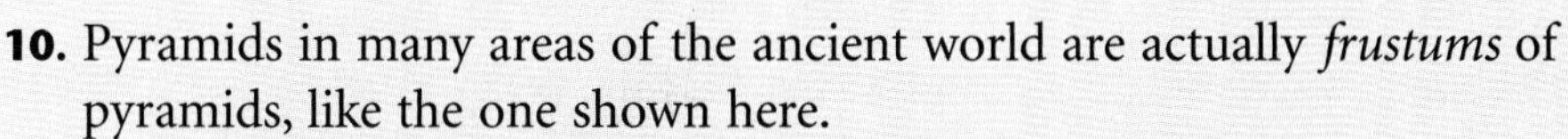

10. Pyramids in many areas of the ancient world are actually *frustums* of pyramids, like the one shown here.

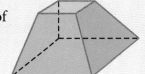

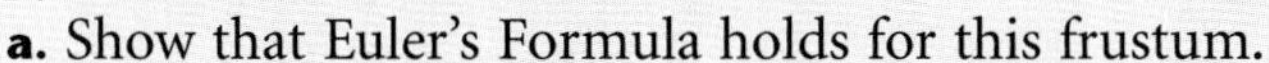

a. Show that Euler's Formula holds for this frustum.

b. Describe a vertical cross section of the frustum that contains the center of its base.

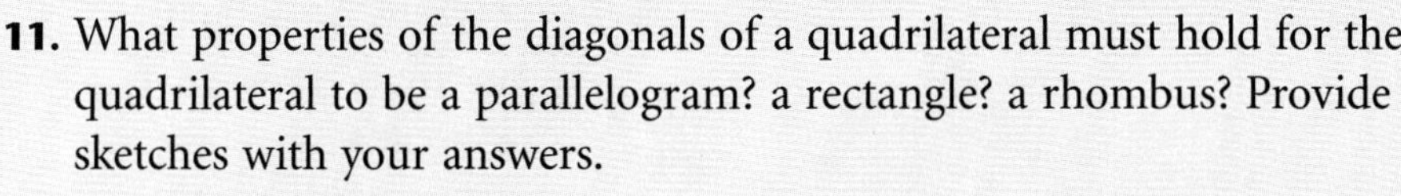

11. What properties of the diagonals of a quadrilateral must hold for the quadrilateral to be a parallelogram? a rectangle? a rhombus? Provide sketches with your answers.

12. Prove the following.

Given: $\overline{AB} \cong \overline{CD}$, $\overline{AB} \parallel \overline{CD}$

Prove: $ABCD$ is a parallelogram.

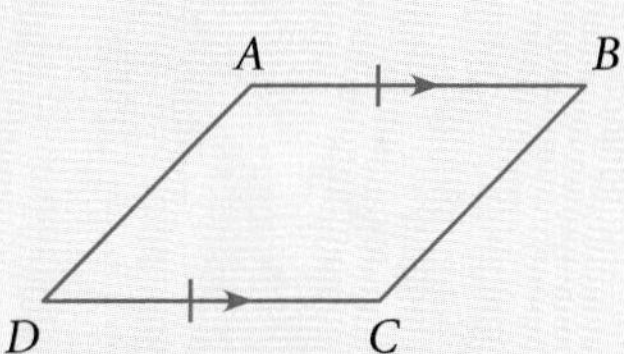

PERFORMANCE TASK

Carefully draw several right triangles and the median to the hypotenuse of each. Measure the median and hypotenuse in each triangle. Then state a conjecture relating the length of the hypotenuse and the length of the median to the hypotenuse.

Use the figure to help prove your conjecture. (Hint: Begin by locating a point P on $\overrightarrow{CM}$ so that $ACBP$ is a parallelogram. The other key step to the proof is showing that $ACBP$ is a rectangle.)

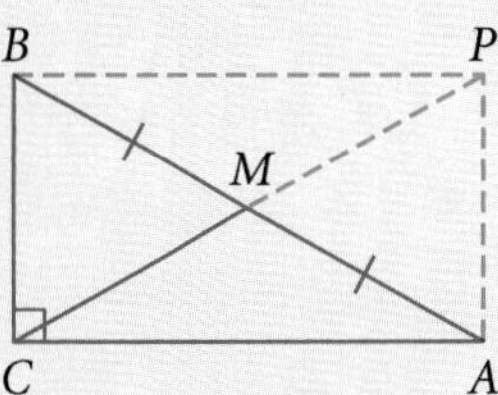

Chapter 7 Similarity

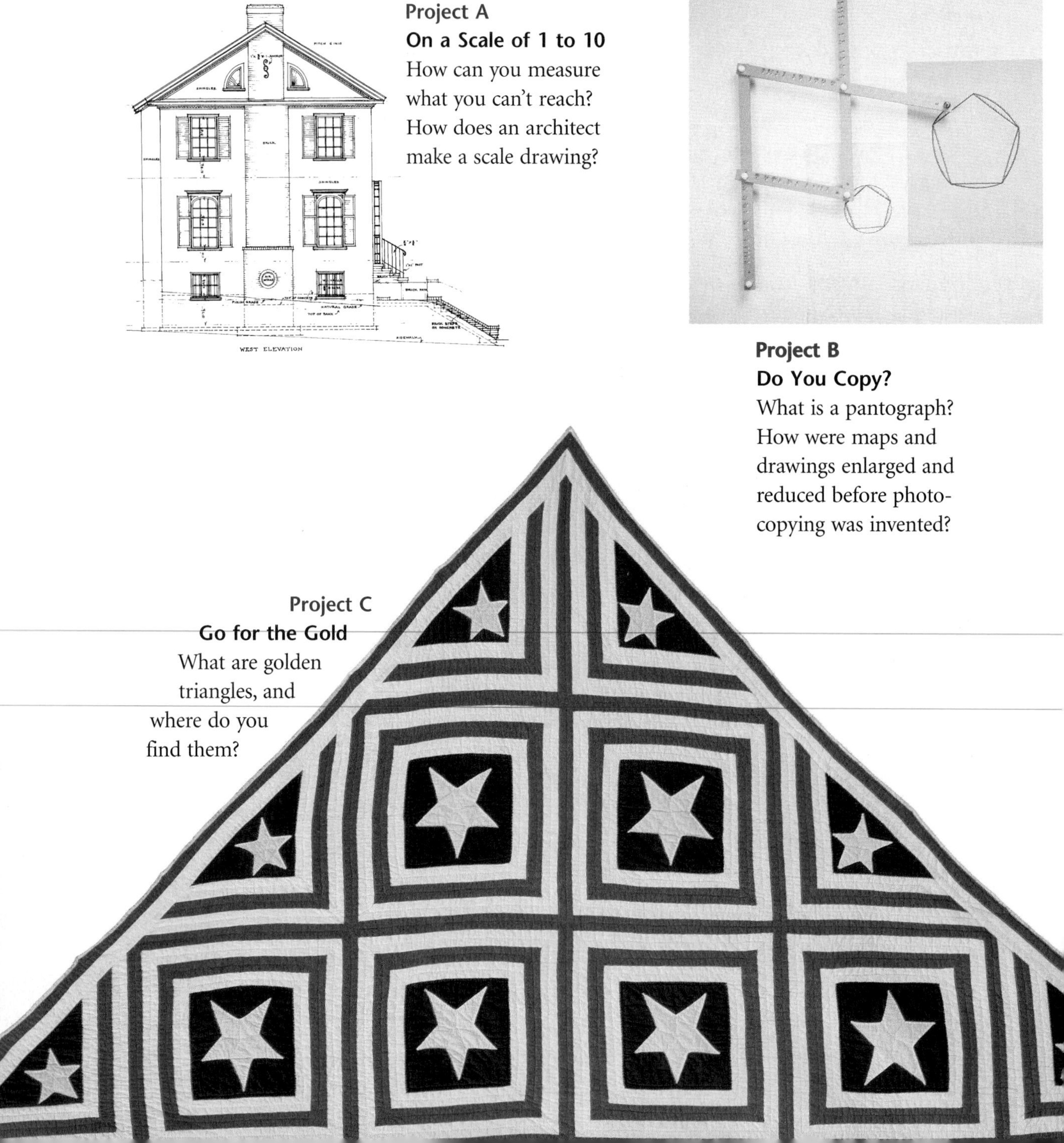

Project A

On a Scale of 1 to 10

How can you measure what you can't reach? How does an architect make a scale drawing?

Project B

Do You Copy?

What is a pantograph? How were maps and drawings enlarged and reduced before photocopying was invented?

Project C

Go for the Gold

What are golden triangles, and where do you find them?

SUSAN HELMAN-BRADFORD

I enjoyed algebra and trig in high school, but advanced math and physics were hard for me.

I was interested in art and engineering, and found both in architecture. I didn't realize the extent to which math is used in this field. I use math every day to calculate square footage, estimate structural loads, create detailed drawings for construction, and develop construction estimates. Math will always be a standard part of life, no matter what your work or lifestyle.

Susan Helman-Bradford
Designer and Computer Drafter
Helman/Bradford
Napa, CA

SEHBradford

Chapter 7 Similarity

GETTING READY

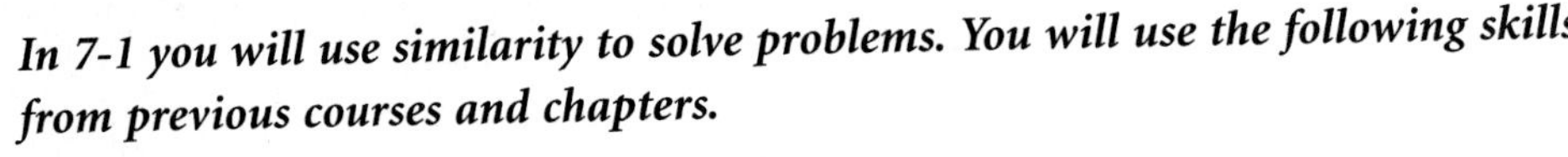

7-1 Similar Figures

In 7-1 you will use similarity to solve problems. You will use the following skills from previous courses and chapters.

Write a congruence statement for each pair of triangles. Then name the postulate or theorem that justifies the congruence statement. [4-2]

1.  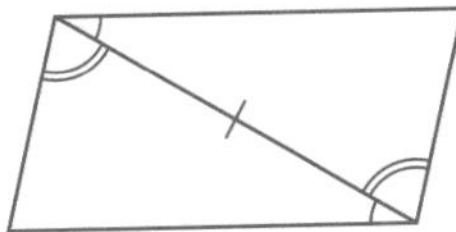

2. 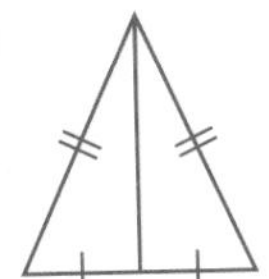

3. 

4. 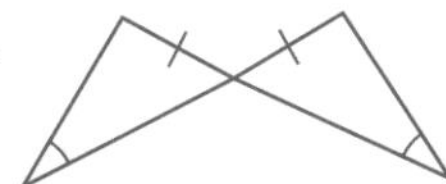

Solve each proportion. [Previous course]

5. $\frac{38}{57} = \frac{x}{15}$ **6.** $\frac{6}{15} = \frac{x}{9}$ **7.** $\frac{x}{20} = \frac{\pi}{24}$ **8.** $\frac{9}{x} = \frac{x}{4}$

9. $\frac{18}{x} = \frac{12}{30}$ **10.** $\frac{4.5}{7.2} = \frac{x}{12}$ **11.** $\frac{6}{80} = \frac{40}{x}$ **12.** $\frac{x}{\sqrt{2}} = \frac{\sqrt{8}}{3}$

7–2 Properties of Similar Figures

In 7-2 you will investigate ways to show triangles are similar. You will also investigate a new transformation, the dilation. You will need the following skills from previous courses.

Convert these fractions to decimals, accurate to the nearest hundredth. [Previous course]

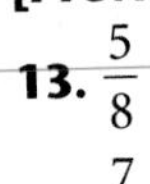

13. $\frac{5}{8}$ **14.** $\frac{14}{17}$ **15.** $\frac{\sqrt{3}}{2}$

16. $\frac{7}{9}$ **17.** $\frac{\pi}{3}$ **18.** $\frac{12\sqrt{2}}{8}$

7-3 Trigonometry

In 7-3 you will use trigonometry to find side lengths and angle measures in right triangles. You will need the following skills from previous courses.

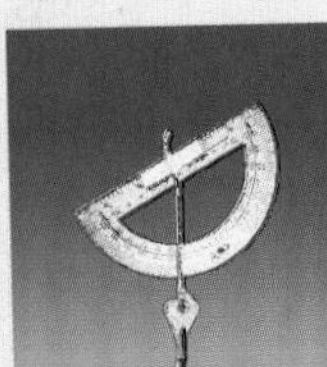

Solve for *x*. Give answers to the nearest hundredth. [Previous course]

19. $\frac{1}{x+1} = \frac{3}{5}$ **20.** $\frac{3.5}{7.5} = \frac{4.8}{x}$ **21.** $\frac{3}{x+2} = \frac{5}{x-2}$ **22.** $\frac{1.1x}{1.32} = \frac{3.3}{2.42}$

7-1 Similar Figures

FROM SILVER SCREEN TO GOLDEN RATIO

Advertisements for the 1933 film *King Kong* claimed that the movie "out-thrilled the wildest thrills!" The film was one of the first in which small models were used to give the illusion of an enormous monster. Marcel Delgado, an animator who worked on the film, wrote about his work in *King Kong and Me*.

"I made the two full-body models used in *King Kong*. Both models were 18 inches high, which is $\frac{3}{4}$ inch to the foot ...The skeletons of the limbs were made in the studio machine shops and I covered them with muscles and fur. The full-sized arm and hand had to be large enough to hold Fay Wray..."

Actress Fay Wray, best known for struggling in King Kong's hand as he stood on top of the Empire State Building, described her experiences in *The New York Times*.

"Then I saw the figure of Kong. He was in a miniature jungle habitat, and was less than 2 feet tall! It was only the great furry paw, in which I would spend much of the next ten months, that was absolutely enormous...the hand and arm in which my close-up scenes were made was about 8 feet in length."

?

1. **Name three other films in which small models might have been used to represent large creatures or objects.**
2. **What do you think Marcel Delgado meant when he described his model as $\frac{3}{4}$ inch to the foot?**
3. **Describe a situation for which you might need to make a model of something that is very large or very small. What advantages would the model have over the actual object?**

7-1 PART A Changing the Size of Figures

← CONNECT → ***You've seen maps as scaled-down models of cities and countries. Now you will see what happens to the sides and angles of figures when you enlarge or shrink them.***

In everyday conversation, we say two things are *similar* when we mean they are alike in some way. In mathematics, **similar** figures have the same shape but not necessarily the same size. Photographs, dollhouse furniture, and building plans are all mathematically similar versions of real objects.

These pairs of figures are similar. They have the same shape but not the same size.

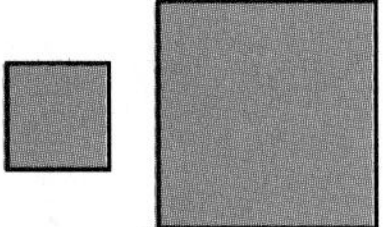
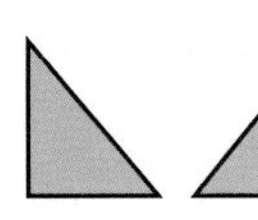
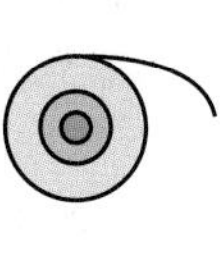
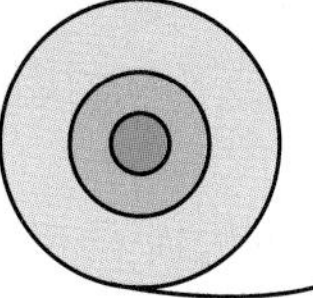

These pairs of figures are not similar. None of the paired figures have the same shape.

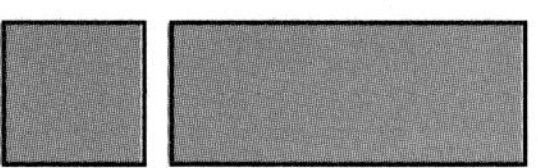
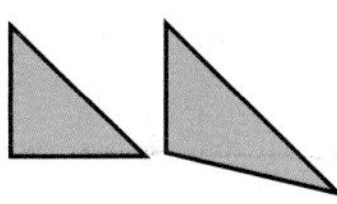
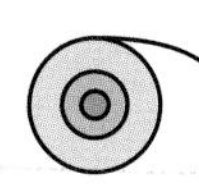
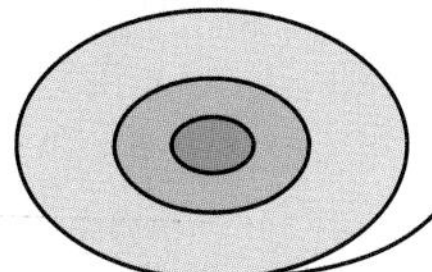

You may have noticed that similar figures are enlargements or reductions of each other. When two figures are similar, the amount of enlargement or reduction needed to get one figure from the other is called the **scale factor.** To find the dimensions of the enlarged or reduced figure, you multiply the dimensions of the original figure by the scale factor.

If the scale factor (s) is greater than 1, the similar figure is an **enlargement;** if the scale factor is less than 1, it is a **reduction.**

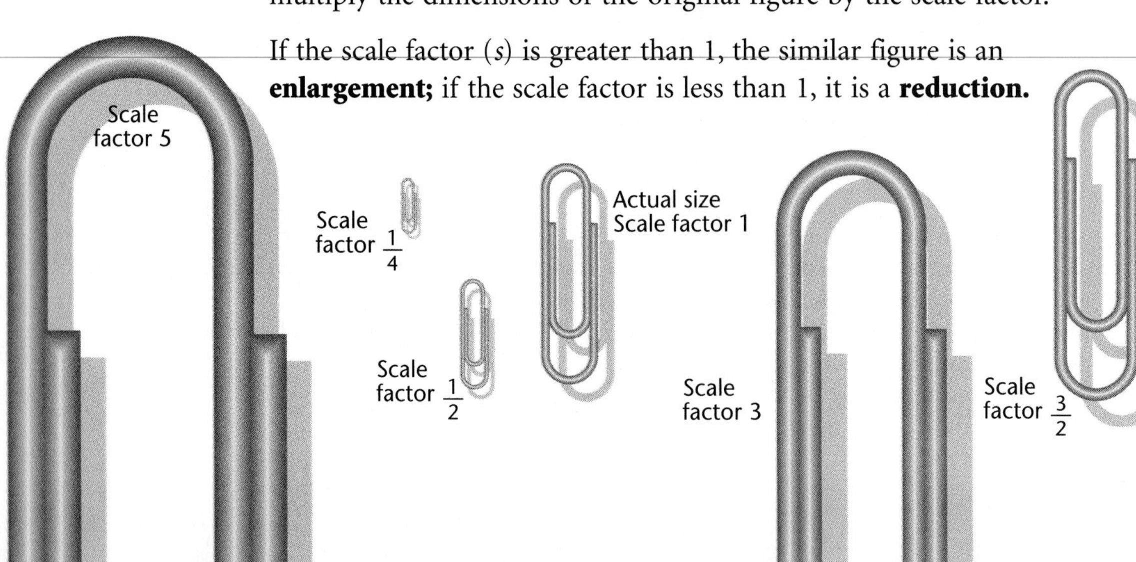

EXPLORE: HUMAN PHOTOCOPY MACHINE

MATERIALS

Graph paper

Use graph paper to enlarge or reduce each figure to create a similar figure.

1. Enlarge side lengths by a factor of 3.

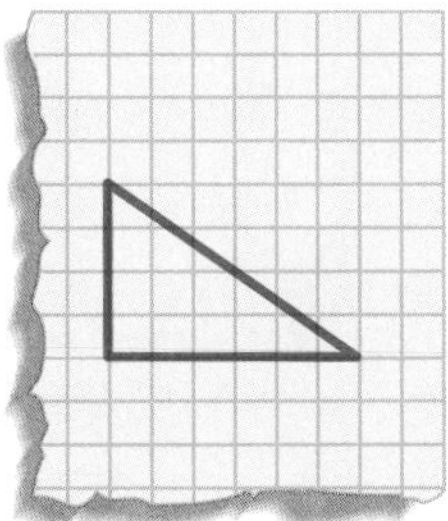

2. Reduce side lengths by a factor of $\frac{1}{2}$.

3. Choose a side in one of the original figures, and identify the corresponding side in your enlarged or reduced version. Find the ratio of the lengths of the sides. Is this ratio the same for any two corresponding sides of the figures?

4. Find pairs of corresponding angles and measure them. How do the corresponding angles compare?

5. Write a definition of similar figures based on your observations. Compare your definition with those of your classmates.

The ratio of the lengths of two corresponding sides of similar figures is the **similarity ratio.**

EXAMPLES

$\triangle ABC$ is similar to $\triangle XYZ$.

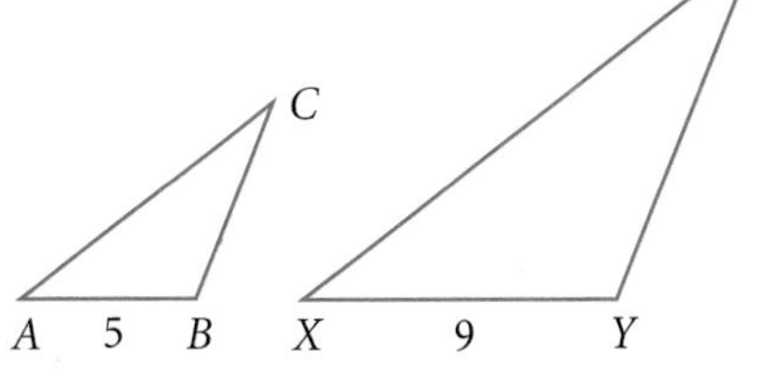

1. Find the similarity ratio of $\triangle ABC$ to $\triangle XYZ$.
The similarity ratio of $\triangle ABC$ to $\triangle XYZ = \frac{AB}{XY} = \frac{5}{9}$.

2. Find the similarity ratio of $\triangle XYZ$ to $\triangle ABC$.
The similarity ratio of $\triangle XYZ$ to $\triangle ABC = \frac{XY}{AB} = \frac{9}{5}$.

TRY IT

State whether or not each pair of figures is similar. For each pair of similar figures, find the similarity ratio of the figure on the left to the figure on the right.

a.

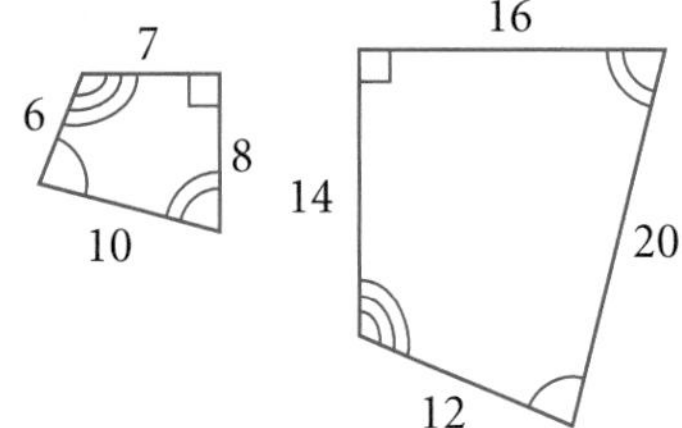

b.

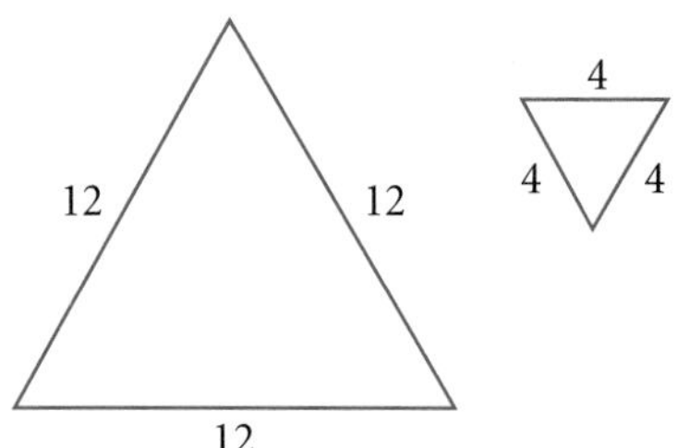

c.

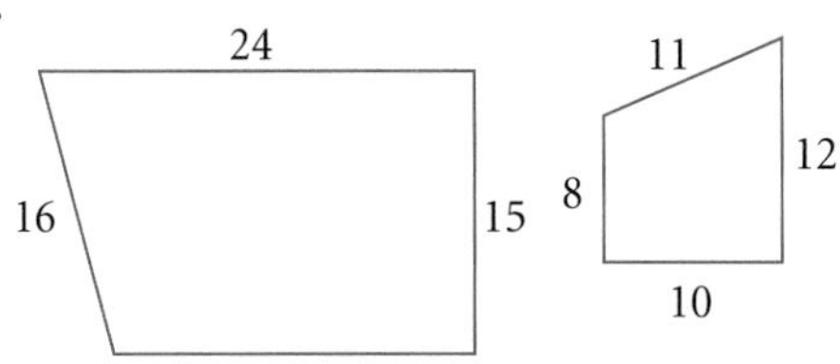

d.

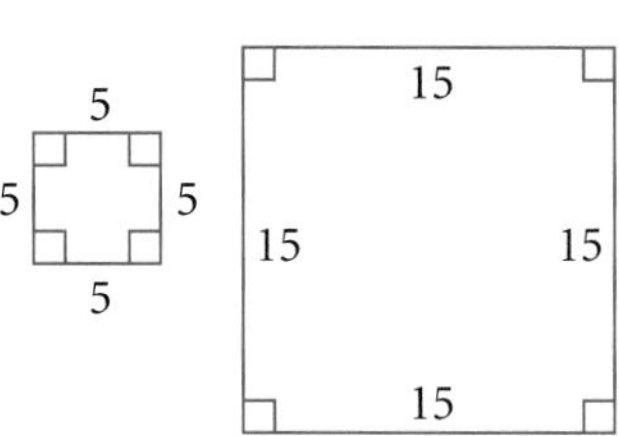

1. **Suppose you enlarge Figure A by a scale factor of s to create Figure B. What is the similarity ratio of Figure A to Figure B?**
2. **Explain the difference between *similarity ratio* and *scale factor.***

The properties of similar figures that you've investigated are summarized in the following definition.

DEFINITION

Two polygons are **similar** if and only if (1) their corresponding angles are congruent and (2) their corresponding side lengths are proportional.

REFLECT

1. Suppose you enlarge or reduce a figure to make a similar figure.
   a. What happens to the measure of each of the angles?
   b. What happens to the length of each line segment?
2. If Figure X is similar to Figure Y, how is the similarity ratio from X to Y related to the similarity ratio from Y to X?

Exercises

CORE

1. **Getting Started** Estimate the scale factor of the photograph on the left to the photograph on the right.

Sketch each figure on graph paper. Then draw a similar figure, using the given scale factor.

2. scale factor of 3

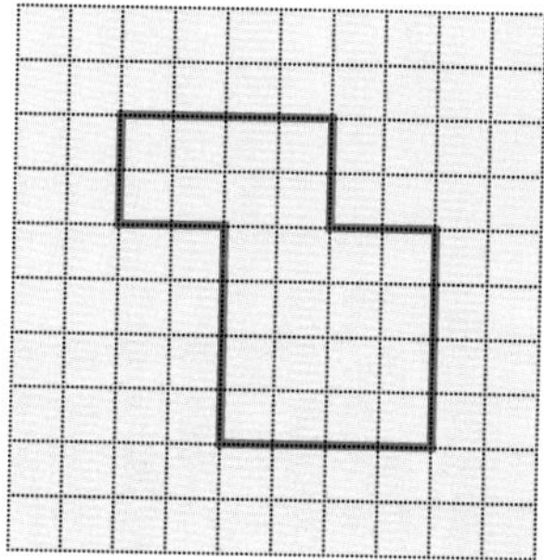

3. scale factor of $\frac{1}{2}$

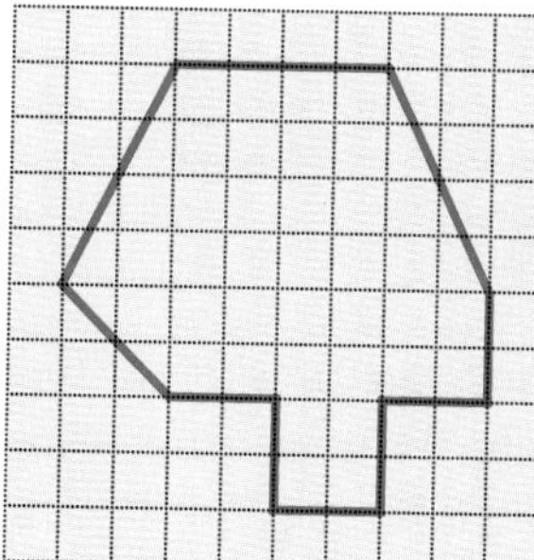

4. If you reduce a 15-cm × 20-cm rectangle by using a scale factor of $\frac{3}{5}$, what will the dimensions of the reduced rectangle be?

5. If you enlarge a 9-in. × 12-in. drawing by using a scale factor of 2.5, what will its new dimensions be?

Determine whether each statement is true or false. Give reasons to support your answers.

6. Any two squares are similar.

7. Any two rectangles are similar.

8. Any two rhombuses are similar.

9. Any two equilateral triangles are similar.

Suppose a copy machine can make an image whose dimensions are 65% to 140% of the size of the original picture.

10. If you have a 4-cm × 6-cm picture, what are the smallest and largest dimensions of a copy that you can make on one run through the machine?

11. How could you use this machine to create a reduction whose dimensions are approximately 20% of the original?

Each pair of figures is similar, and the lengths of corresponding sides are shown. Find the similarity ratio of Figure A to B and of Figure B to A.

12.

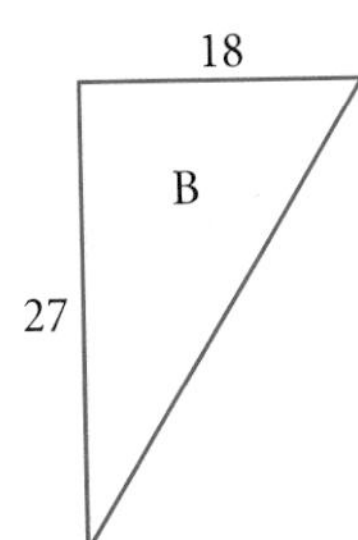

13.

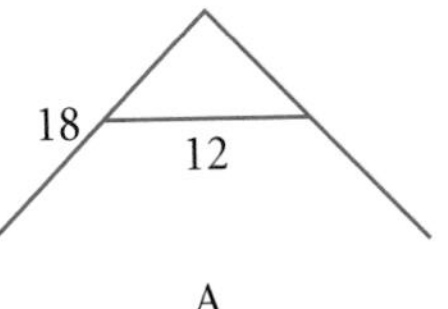

State whether or not each pair of figures is similar. If the figures are similar, find the similarity ratio of the figure on the left to the figure on the right. If the figures are not similar, explain why they are not similar.

14.

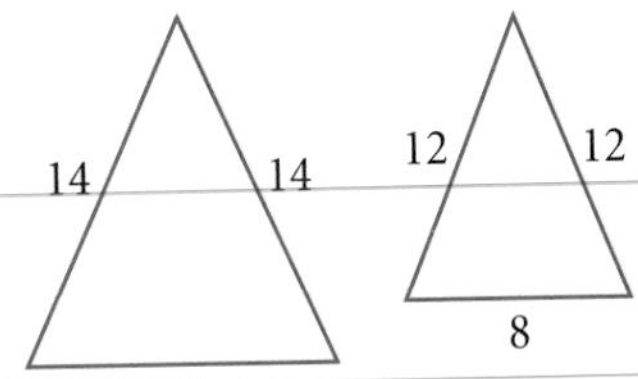

15.

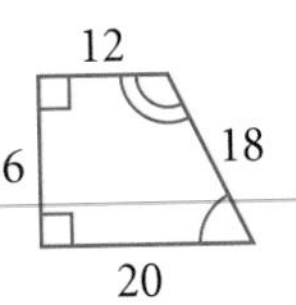

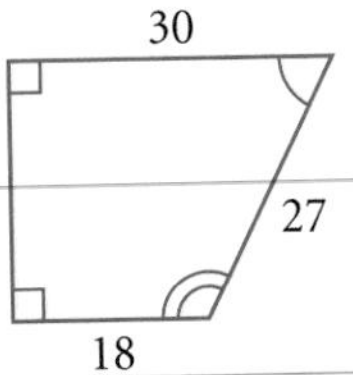

16. **Say Cheese** School pictures are offered in sizes of $2\frac{1}{2}$ in. × $3\frac{1}{2}$ in., $3\frac{1}{2}$ in. × 5 in., 4 in. × 6 in., 5 in. × 7 in., and 8 in. × 10 in. Which sizes are similar?

17. Amoeba Attacks Airport! Yvette is drawing scenes from a movie she is writing *(The Amoeba That Ate Altabula)*. She must show both an amoeba and the Altabula Airport on one $8\frac{1}{2}'' \times 11''$ sheet of paper. The actual airport is 2 mi wide and 3 mi long; an amoeba is 0.005 in. wide and 0.0075 in. long. What scale factors should she use for each so that sketches of both will fit on the paper and appear to have approximately the same size?

LOOK AHEAD

Solve each proportion.

18. $\frac{x}{8} = \frac{10}{16}$ **19.** $\frac{8}{12} = \frac{6}{y}$ **20.** $\frac{CD}{12} = \frac{7}{28}$ **21.** $\frac{2}{EF} = \frac{5}{6}$

22. A recipe that serves four people calls for two and one-half cups of flour. If you need to serve dinner to six people, how many cups of flour should you use in the adjusted recipe?

MORE PRACTICE

Sketch each figure on graph paper. Then draw a similar figure, using the given scale factor.

23. scale factor of 2

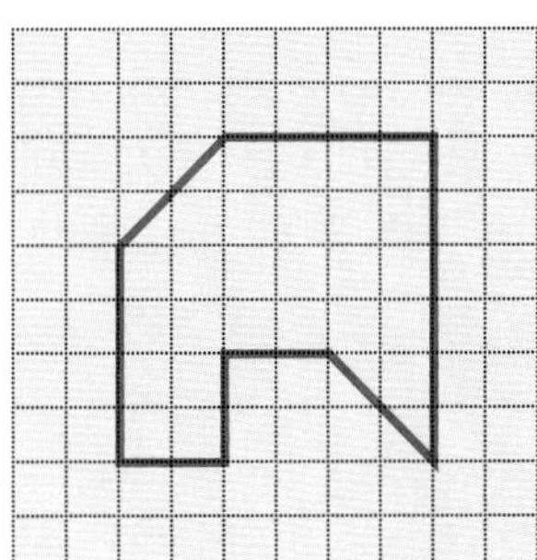

24. scale factor of $\frac{1}{3}$

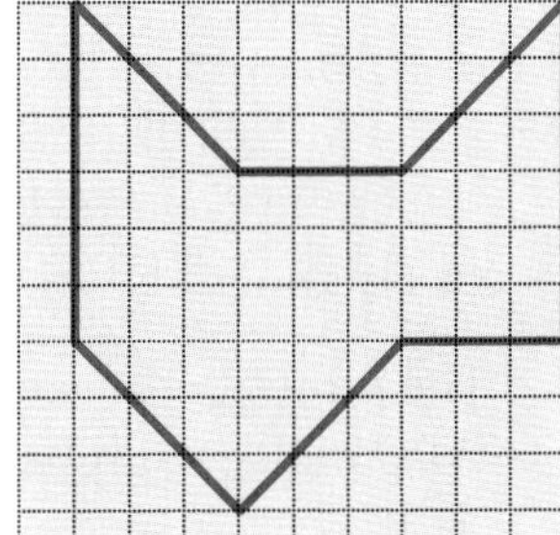

State whether or not each pair of figures is similar. If the figures are similar, find the similarity ratio of the figure on the left to the figure on the right. If the figures are not similar, explain why they are not similar.

25.

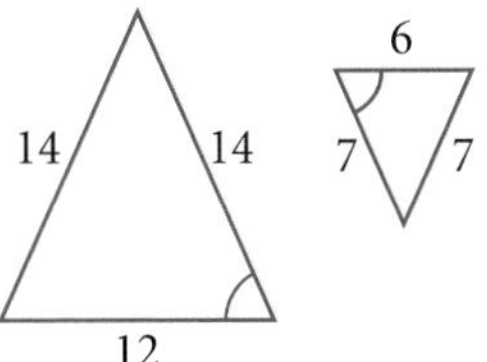

26.

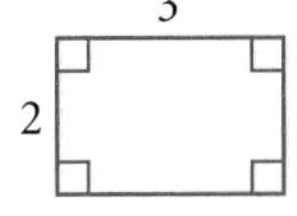

27. A newspaper asked the P.T.A. to reduce its 12-cm × 18-cm advertisement by a scale factor of $\frac{2}{3}$. What are the dimensions of the reduced ad?

MORE MATH REASONING

28. There are seven different sizes of triangles that are similar to $\triangle FPL$ with vertices at grid points, not including triangles congruent to $\triangle FPL$. For each size, name one triangle of that size, and give the lengths of its sides. (Use $AB = 1$ unit.)

29. Reduce to Fit An advertiser purchased a half-page ad (eleven inches by seventeen inches) in a school newspaper. They sent a fifteen-inch by twenty-inch poster and asked to have it reduced to fit the half-page. The newspaper ad must be similar to the poster. What are the dimensions of the ad that will take up the largest possible space on the half-page?

7-1 PART B Similar Polygons

← CONNECT → ***You know how to work with proportions algebraically, and you've seen that the lengths of the corresponding sides of similar polygons are proportional. Now you will use proportions to work with similar polygons.***

If the makers of this souvenir had not used the concept of similarity, they would have had to place a snow-filled dome over the Guggenheim Museum in New York. Similarity and proportionality allow people to cut buildings and movie monsters down to size.

The symbol ~ means "is similar to." If pentagons *ABCDE* and *MNOPQ* are similar, we write *ABCDE* ~ *MNOPQ*. The order of the letters in the similarity correspondence indicates the corresponding parts.

EXAMPLE

ABCDE ~ *MNOPQ*. Name all pairs of congruent corresponding angles, and write proportions using the pairs of corresponding sides.

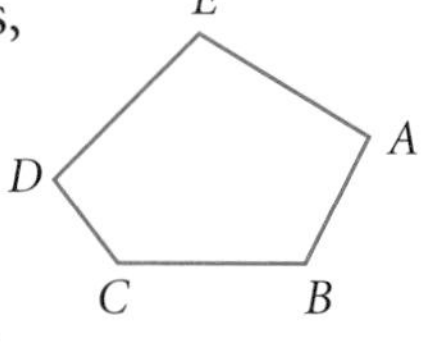

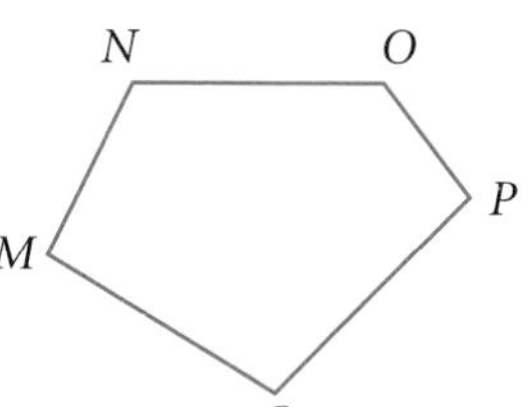

Angles: $\angle A \cong \angle M$, $\angle B \cong \angle N$, $\angle C \cong \angle O$, $\angle D \cong \angle P$, $\angle E \cong \angle Q$

Side lengths: $\frac{AB}{MN} = \frac{BC}{NO} = \frac{CD}{OP} = \frac{DE}{PQ} = \frac{EA}{QM}$

TRY IT

Write the similarity correspondence between each pair of figures. Name all pairs of congruent corresponding angles and write proportions using the pairs of corresponding sides.

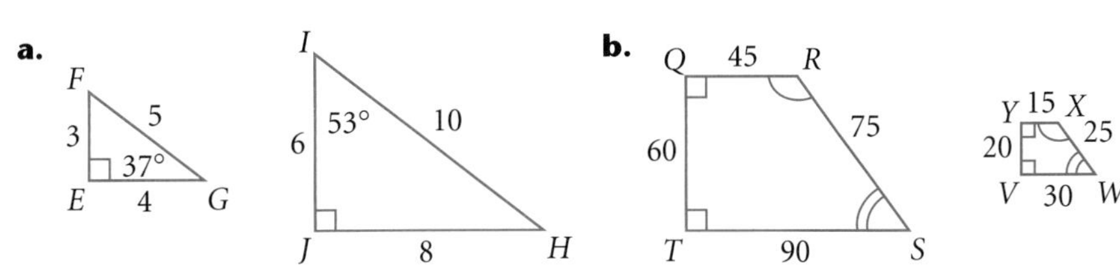

The scale on a map relates the size of an object on the map to its actual size. You can interpret the scale as a ratio and use algebra to find unknown lengths.

EXPLORE: MAPPING THE CAPITAL

MATERIALS

Ruler

This map shows the ruins of Angkor (the capital city) in Cambodia, built by the Khmer people from the 9th through the 12th centuries A.D.

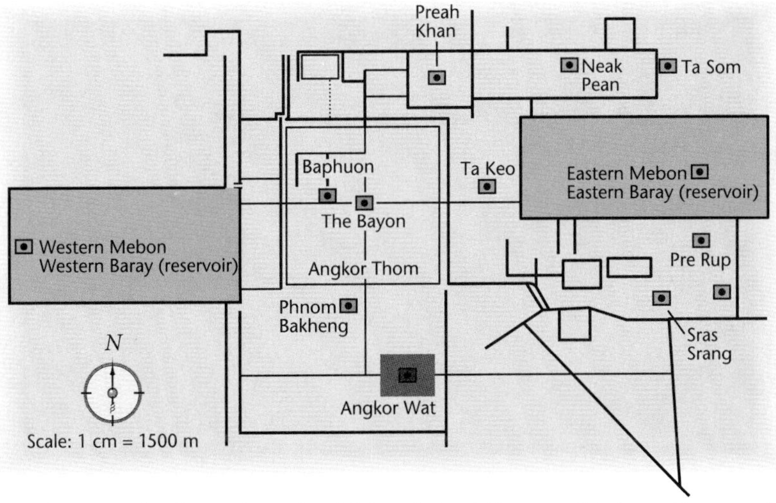

1. Measure the length and width of the Western Mebon Reservoir on the map. Then find the actual dimensions of the reservoir.
2. Find the shortest distance between Angkor Wat and Preah Kan.
3. Find the actual dimensions of Angkor Wat.
4. Explain how you can use scale drawings to find the actual dimensions of objects. Why does this method work?

You can use the definition of similar polygons to find unknown angle measures and side lengths in similar polygons. Proportional reasoning is also helpful in finding unknown side lengths.

WHAT DO YOU THINK?

Anne and Roberto were given the following problem to solve.

Given: $FGHJ \sim WXYZ$.
Find YZ.

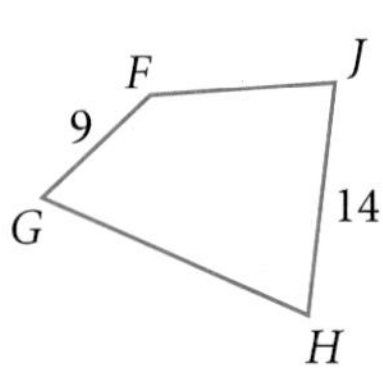

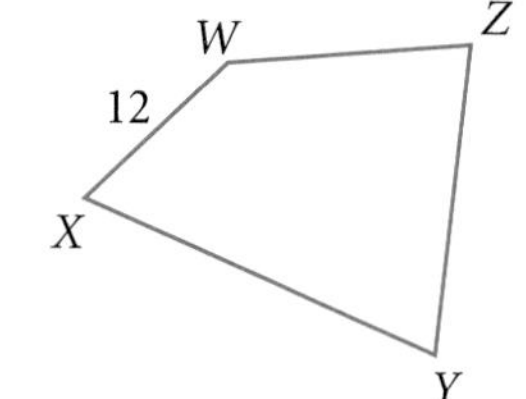

Anne thinks . . .

The similarity ratio is the ratio of the lengths of any two corresponding sides, so I can use $\frac{WX}{FG}$ to find it. The similarity ratio of $WXYZ$ to $FGHJ$ is $\frac{WX}{FG} = \frac{12}{9} = \frac{4}{3}$. YZ is HJ times the similarity ratio. $14 \times \frac{4}{3} = \frac{56}{3} = 18\frac{2}{3}$, so $YZ = 18\frac{2}{3}$.

Roberto thinks . . .

Since the lengths of the corresponding sides of similar figures are proportional, $\frac{FG}{WX} = \frac{HJ}{YZ}$.

Therefore, $\frac{9}{12} = \frac{14}{YZ}$.

$9 \times YZ = 14 \times 12$

$YZ = \frac{14 \times 12}{9}$

$YZ = 18\frac{2}{3}$

TRY IT

$EFGH \sim KNML$.

c. Find the measures of $\angle E$, $\angle G$, and $\angle N$.

d. Find x, y, and z.

e. What is the similarity ratio of $KNML$ to $EFGH$?

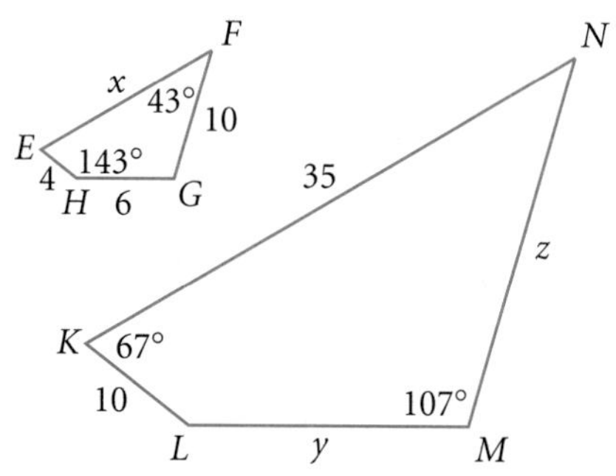

REFLECT

1. If you know all of the side lengths of one polygon, what other data do you need to solve for the side lengths of a similar polygon?
2. Write an explanation of how the scale of a map is related to the idea of a scale factor.

Exercises

CORE

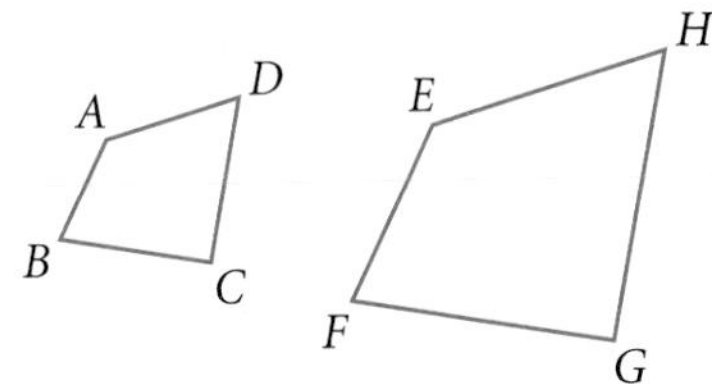

1. **Getting Started** *ABCD* ~ *EFGH*. Name all pairs of congruent corresponding angles and write proportions using the pairs of corresponding sides.

***IJKL* ~ *MNOP*. Find the following.**

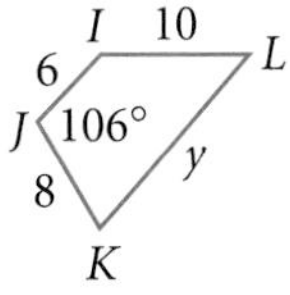

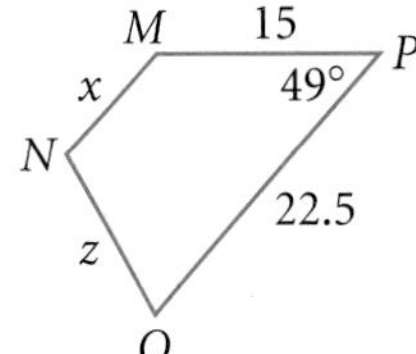

2. $m\angle N$
3. $m\angle L$
4. x
5. y
6. z
7. the similarity ratio of *IJKL* to *MNOP*
8. the similarity ratio of *MNOP* to *IJKL*
9. Ratios and proportions are important in many areas of mathematics. Describe how ratios and proportions are used in the following.
   a. identifying similar figures
   b. finding a probability
   c. calculating the slope of a line
10. **Working for the Government** In 1970, the population of the United States was about 203.3 million people, and 12.5 million people were employed by federal, state, and local governments. In 1990, the population had grown to 248.7 million.
    a. Estimate the number of people employed by federal, state, and local governments in 1990. Explain how you made your estimate.
    b. The actual number of government employees in 1990 was 18.3 million. Which grew at a faster rate from 1970 to 1990, the U.S. population or the number of government employees? Explain.

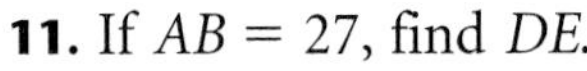

$\triangle ABC \sim \triangle DEF$. The similarity ratio of $\triangle ABC$ to $\triangle DEF$ is $\frac{7}{3}$.

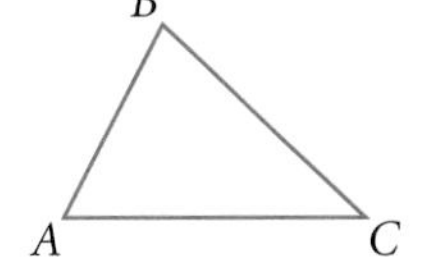

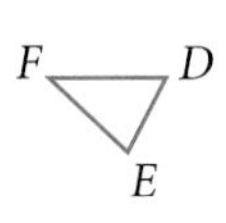

11. If $AB = 27$, find DE.
12. If $EF = 14$, find BC.
13. Find $\frac{DF}{AC}$.

The coordinates of rectangle *WXYZ* are *W*(1, 1), *X*(5, 1), *Y*(5, 4), and *Z*(1, 4). Rectangle *STUV* with lower left-hand vertex *S*(2, 7) is similar to *WXYZ*, and its sides are parallel to the corresponding sides of *WXYZ*. Find the coordinates of *T*, *U*, and *Z* for each similarity ratio.

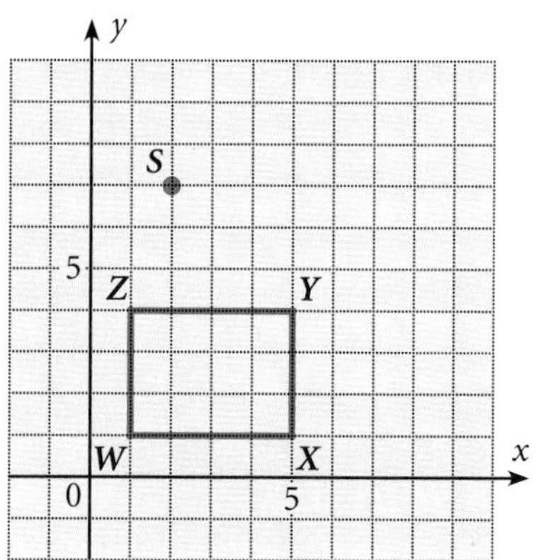

14. $\frac{ST}{WX} = 4$

15. $\frac{ST}{WX} = 1$

16. $\frac{ST}{WX} = \frac{1}{2}$

The following questions refer to a map of the United States on which 1 in. equals 156 mi.

17. If Boston and Houston are $10\frac{1}{4}$ in. apart on the map, what is the actual distance between the cities?

18. If Los Angeles and New York are actually 2451 mi apart, how far apart are they on the map?

19. Scaling Down Your Expectations The building plans for the new Washington High School gymnasium were drawn on a scale of 2.5 cm to the meter. The measurements on the original plans were 93.0 cm by 158.4 cm. However, due to budget cuts, the dimensions on the plans for the gym were reduced by $\frac{1}{6}$. What are the actual dimensions of the gym under the revised plan? Explain.

Problem-Solving Tip

Check to make sure that your answer makes sense.

LOOK BACK

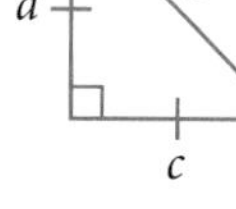

Find the lengths of the unknown sides in each triangle. Express them as decimal approximations rounded to the nearest hundredth. [5-3]

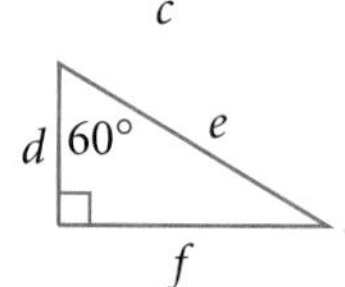

20. $a = 15$. Find b and c.

21. $b = 220$. Find a and c.

22. $e = 44$. Find d and f.

23. $f = 5237$. Find d and e.

Find the measure of one interior and one exterior angle of each polygon. [6-3]

24. regular pentagon

25. regular nonagon

26. regular 14-gon

MORE PRACTICE

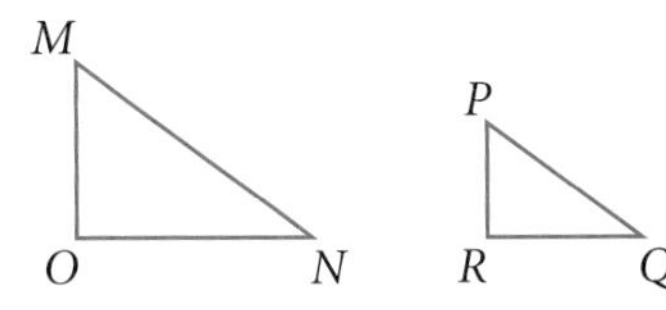

27. $\triangle MNO \sim \triangle PQR$. Name all pairs of congruent corresponding angles and write proportions using the pairs of corresponding sides.

***DEFGH* ~ *STUVW*. Find the following.**

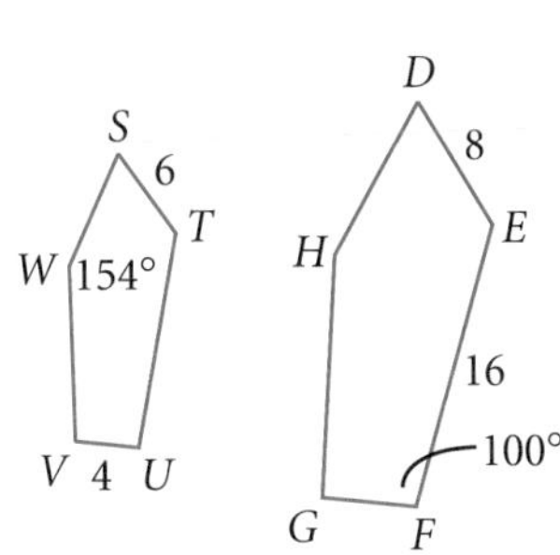

28. $m\angle H$ **29.** $m\angle U$ **30.** FG **31.** TU

32. the similarity ratio of *STUVW* to *DEFGH*

33. the similarity ratio of *DEFGH* to *STUVW*

MORE MATH REASONING

34. Is it possible for two triangles that are not similar to have two pairs of sides whose lengths are proportional? If yes, give an example. If not, explain why not.

35. Prove: Any two regular polygons with the same number of sides are similar.

7-1 PART C Areas and Perimeters of Similar Polygons

← CONNECT → ***You've seen that the lengths of corresponding sides of similar figures are proportional. Now you will discover how the ratios of the areas and perimeters of similar figures are related to the similarity ratio.***

The photograph at the right shows a King Kong poster from the 1930s. Not surprisingly, the area and perimeter of this photograph are related to the area and perimeter of the actual poster.

If you enlarge a figure, the area and the perimeter of the enlargement must be greater than the area and perimeter of the original. But can you tell how much greater they will be? The following Explore will help you answer this.

EXPLORE: SIMILARITY, PERIMETER, AND AREA

MATERIALS

Ruler

1. Draw a rectangle and measure its dimensions. Label the rectangle A.
2. Draw Rectangle B that is similar to Rectangle A. What similarity ratio did you use?
3. Investigate the ratios of the perimeters and areas of the two rectangles. Draw and investigate more pairs of similar rectangles. How do the similarity ratios of the rectangles relate to the ratios of their areas and perimeters? Make any conjectures that you can, and compare your conjectures to those made by your classmates.

TRY IT

ABCDE ~ *GHIJK*. The similarity ratio of *ABCDE* to *GHIJK* is 2.

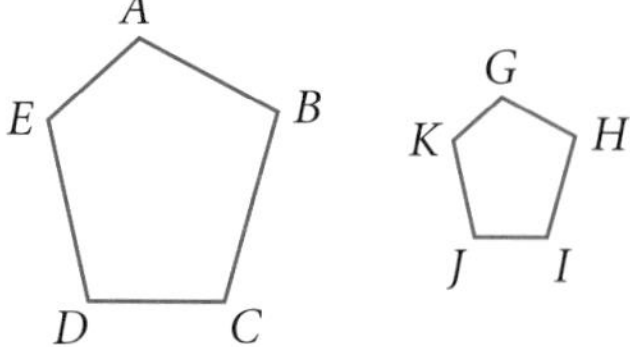

a. If the area of *ABCDE* is 24 cm^2, what is the area of *GHIJK*?

b. If the perimeter of *GHIJK* is 10 cm, what is the perimeter of *ABCDE*?

You can use the similarity ratio to find the ratios of the areas of similar figures. It's also possible to use the area ratio to find the similarity ratio.

EXAMPLES

The children's entrance to a toy store is similar to the adults' (big kids') entrance, but its area is $\frac{4}{9}$ as large.

1. Find the similarity ratio of the children's entrance to the adults' entrance.

The similarity ratio is the square root of the ratio of the areas: $\sqrt{\frac{4}{9}} = \frac{2}{3}$.

2. What is the ratio of the perimeter of the children's doorway to the perimeter of the adults' doorway?

The ratio of the perimeters is equal to the similarity ratio, so it is $\frac{2}{3}$.

3. If the adults' doorway is 210 cm tall and 120 cm wide, what are the dimensions of the children's doorway?
Height $= 210 \times \frac{2}{3} = 140$ cm; width $= 120 \times \frac{2}{3} = 80$ cm

The relationships between the similarity ratio and the ratios of the areas and perimeters of similar polygons are summarized below.

THEOREMS

The ratio of the perimeters of two similar polygons is equal to their similarity ratio.

The ratio of the areas of two similar polygons is equal to the square of their similarity ratio.

REFLECT

1. Use graph paper to help explain why doubling the length and width of a rectangle quadruples its area.
2. When a salesperson showed Glenn a rug, Glenn said, "I need one that's the same shape, but twice as big." The salesperson returned with two rugs and said, "I wasn't sure what you meant." How do you think the two rugs compared to the original? Explain why you need to be specific when you say one thing is "twice as big" as another.

Exercises

CORE

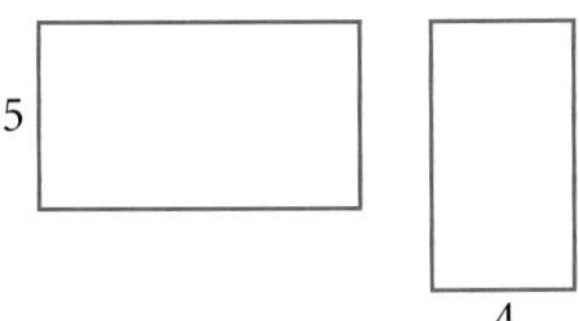

1. **Getting Started** The two figures shown are similar, and the lengths of a pair of corresponding sides are given.
   a. Find the similarity ratio of the figure on the left to the figure on the right. What is the ratio of the perimeter of the figure on the left to the perimeter of the figure on the right?
   b. The ratio of the areas of the figures is equal to the square of their similarity ratio. Find the ratio of the area of the figure on the left to the area of the figure on the right.

Find the ratio of the area of the figure on the left to the area of the figure on the right. Then find the ratio of the perimeter of the figure on the left to the perimeter of the figure on the right.

2.

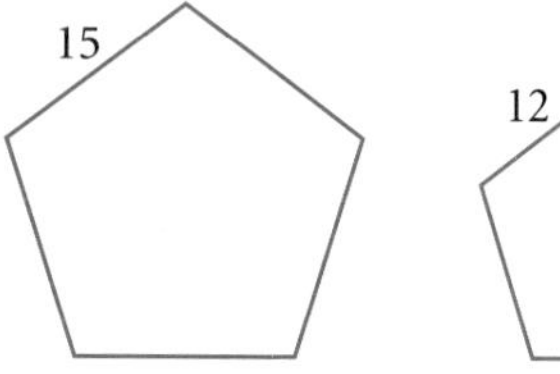

Regular pentagons

3.

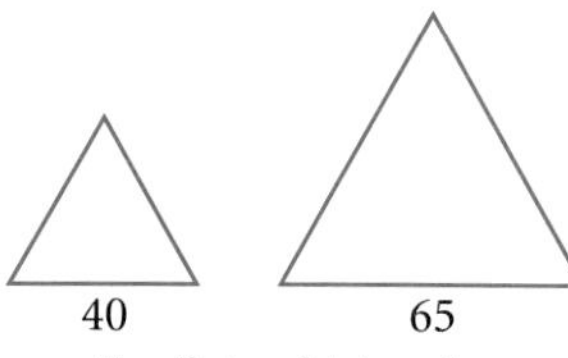

Equilateral triangles

$\triangle ABC \sim \triangle DEF$. Find each ratio.

4. $\dfrac{AB}{DE}$

5. $\dfrac{\text{perimeter } \triangle ABC}{\text{perimeter } \triangle DEF}$

6. $\dfrac{\text{area } \triangle ABC}{\text{area } \triangle DEF}$

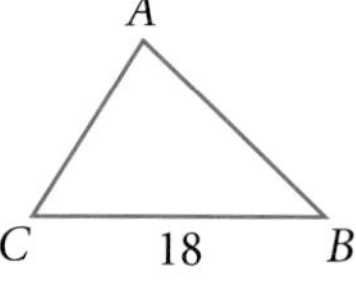

D
F 12 E

7. The ratio of the areas of two similar quadrilaterals is $\frac{25}{16}$. What is the ratio of the lengths of a pair of corresponding sides?

8. Rooting in the Garden A triangular garden has an area of 10 m^2. A similar garden has an area of 20 m^2. By what factor should you multiply the length of each side of the first garden to find the lengths of the sides of the second?

9. Prove that changing the side length (s) of a square by a scale factor of k changes its area by a factor of k^2.

10. If two similar polygons have the same area, must they be congruent? Explain your answer.

11. Anchovy Area Pauline's Proportional Pizza Parlor serves circular pizzas in two sizes. The small eight-inch-diameter pizza feeds two people. The large pizza has a sixteen-inch diameter. How many people do you think it serves? Explain your answer.

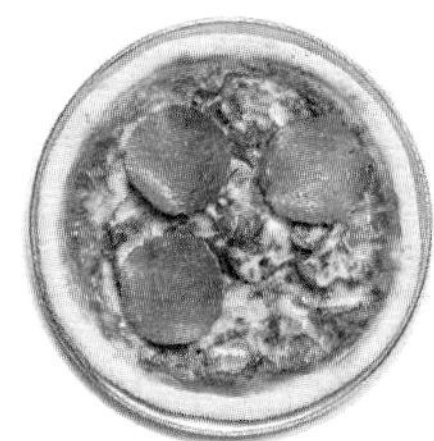

12. Joan wanted to run a 12-in.^{2} advertisement in a newspaper. The ad salesperson told her that a 12-in.^{2} ad costs \$180. The salesperson also told Joan that they had enough space available on the page to enlarge her ad by a scale factor of $\frac{5}{3}$. If the cost per square inch stays the same, how much does the larger ad cost? Do you think larger newspaper ads actually cost the same per square inch as smaller ones? Write a short paragraph explaining why or why not.

13. Twice the Price? Cecelia needed linoleum for the bathroom and kitchen in her house. Although she told the salesperson that the kitchen was twice the size of the bathroom, the linoleum for the kitchen cost her four times as much as the linoleum for the bathroom. Was Cecelia overcharged? Explain.

LOOK AHEAD

14. Measure three rectangular objects from the following list: a playing card, a window, a postcard, a paperback book, a rectangular picture frame.

a. Calculate the ratio of length to width for each object. Are the ratios close?

b. Find the mean (average) of the ratios.

15. If two rectangles have the same length-to-width ratio, are they similar? Explain.

MORE PRACTICE

Each pair of figures shown is similar. Find the ratio of the area of the figure on the left to the area of the figure on the right. Then find the ratio of the perimeter of the figure on the left to the perimeter of the figure on the right.

16.

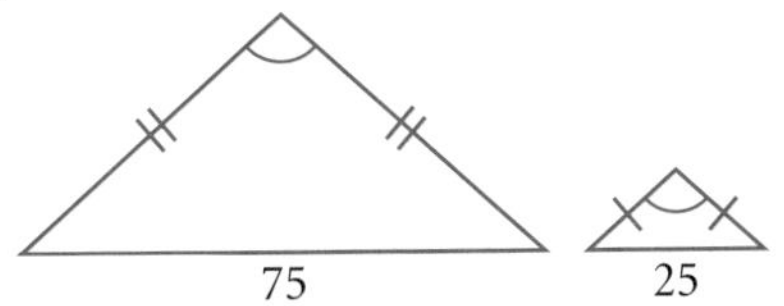

17.

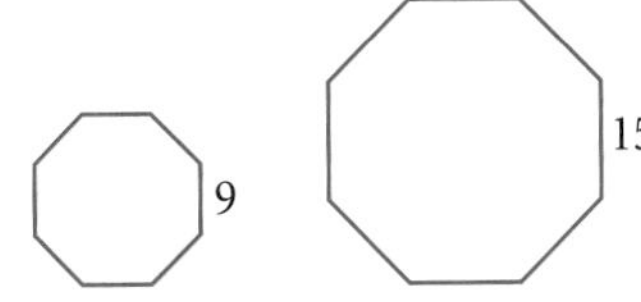

Both figures are regular octagons.

$\triangle MNO \sim \triangle JKL$. Find each ratio.

18. $\dfrac{MO}{JL}$

19. $\dfrac{\text{perimeter } \triangle MNO}{\text{perimeter } \triangle JKL}$

20. $\dfrac{\text{area } \triangle MNO}{\text{area } \triangle JKL}$

M
J
N 60 O K 45 L

MORE MATH REASONING

21. Crop Circles Suppose a crop circle with a radius of $\frac{1}{4}$ mi is planted in a 1-mile-square field as shown.

a. To the nearest hundredth, what is the probability that a raindrop that falls on the field will land on the crops? (Recall that the area of a circle is given by $A = \pi r^2$.)

b. The farmer increases the radius of the crop circle by a scale factor of 2. What is the new probability that a raindrop will land on the crops? How does this probability relate to the one you found in **21a**?

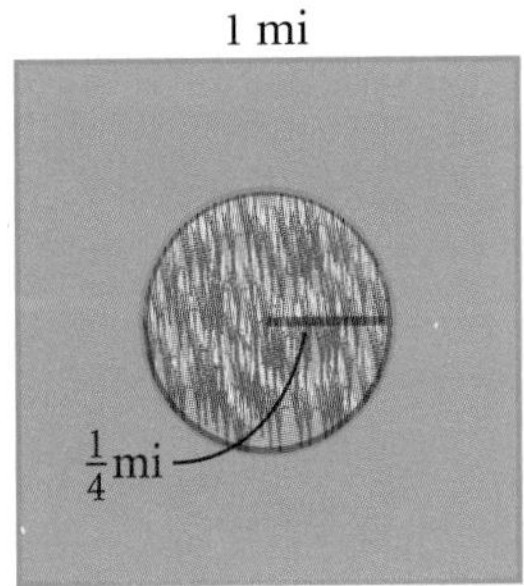

22. Carefully draw a rectangle. Then use a compass and straightedge to construct a rectangle similar to it whose area is four times as large. Explain how your construction works. Include sketches to illustrate your explanation.

7-1 PART D Golden Rectangles

← CONNECT → ***You've seen many types of similar polygons. Now you will investigate a family of similar rectangles that has been important to many cultures for thousands of years.***

People throughout history have felt that a certain type of rectangle "looks right" and has the "right" proportions. This type of rectangle is called a **golden rectangle**.

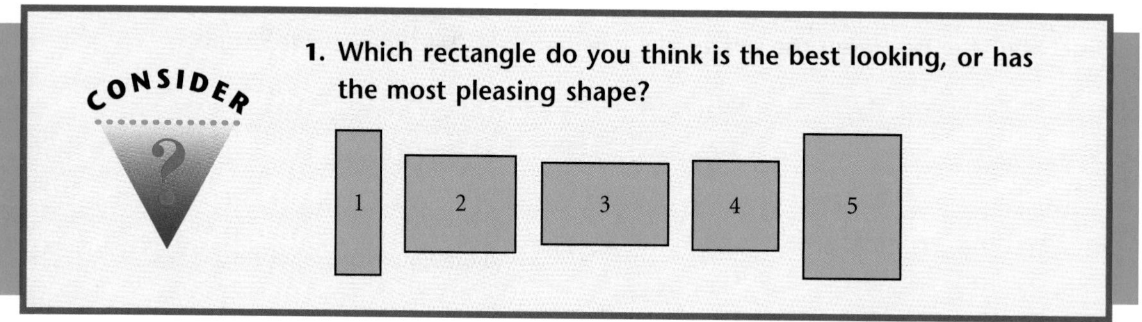

1. Which rectangle do you think is the best looking, or has the most pleasing shape?

Rectangles similar to number 3 above have been preferred in art and architecture by the ancient Egyptians, Greeks, and Persians, and by many modern cultures. These golden rectangles are found in advertisements, movie screens, credit cards, windows, and buildings.

DEFINITION

Rectangle *ACDF* is a **golden rectangle** if and only if square *ABEF* with side lengths *w* makes rectangle *CDEB* similar to rectangle *ACDF*.

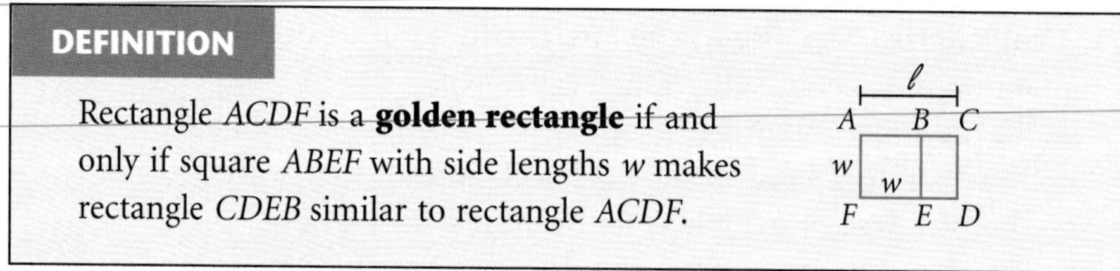

The definition above means that if you cut a golden rectangle into a square and a small rectangle, the small rectangle is also a golden rectangle. All golden rectangles are similar. The ratio of the length to the width is a constant called the **golden ratio.**

EXPLORE: SEARCHING FOR GOLD

MATERIALS

Ruler

1. Measure the length and width of the golden rectangles shown. Calculate the length-to-width ratio for each. How do the three ratios compare? Are the rectangles similar?

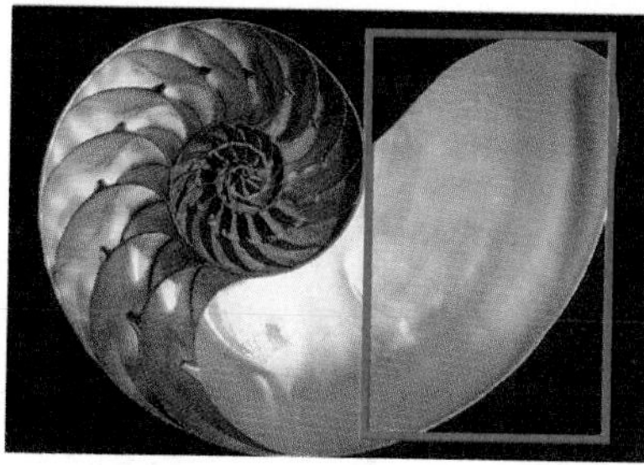

Seurat—*Invitation to the Sideshow (La Parade)*, The Metropolitan Museum of Art, Bequest of Stephen C. Clark, 1960 (61.101.17)

2. Discuss your findings with classmates and come up with an agreement on an approximate value for the golden ratio.

3. Now you can use the definition of a golden rectangle and some algebra to calculate the exact value of $\frac{\ell}{w}$, the golden ratio. (To simplify your work, use $w = 1$.) The definition of a golden rectangle tells you that $ACDF \sim CDEB$. Use the definition of similarity to complete the proportion $\frac{AC}{CD} = \frac{CD}{?}$. By substitution, this means $\frac{\ell}{1} = \frac{1}{?}$.

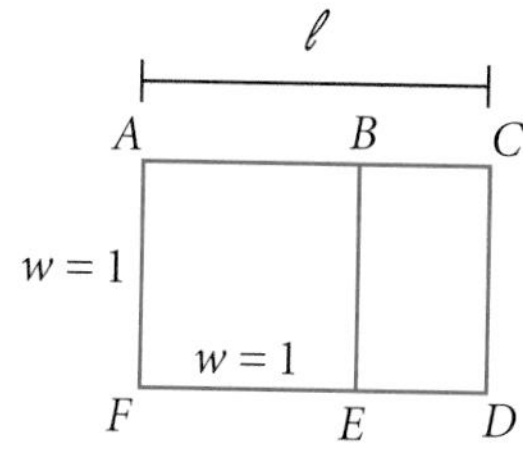

4. Use this proportion to write a quadratic equation for ℓ. Then use the quadratic formula to solve for ℓ. Give your answer in exact (square root) form.

5. Find a decimal approximation for your answer to the nearest thousandth. Is this close to the result you found in Step 2?

TRY IT

HIJK is a golden rectangle. Use an approximation for the golden ratio to find each length to the nearest tenth.

a. If $IJ = 25$, find JK.

b. If $HI = 10$, find HK.

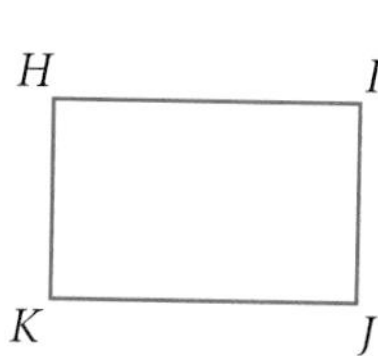

By using the definition of a golden rectangle, you calculated an exact value for the golden ratio. This is close to the length-to-width ratio for many rectangles seen in art, architecture, and everyday objects.

THE GOLDEN RATIO

In a golden rectangle, the ratio of the length, ℓ, to the width, w, is the golden ratio, $\frac{1 + \sqrt{5}}{2}$ (≈ 1.618).

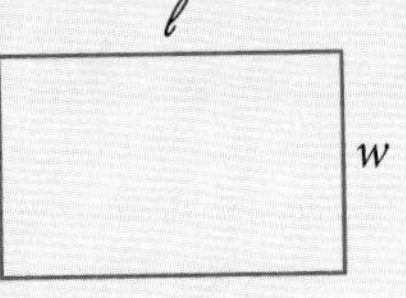

REFLECT

1. Identify some everyday objects that seem to be golden rectangles.
2. Explain why the value of the golden ratio does not depend on the size of the golden rectangle you are looking at.

Exercises

CORE

1. Getting Started Identify the golden rectangle from the figures below.

(a) (b) (c) (d)

GHIJ is a golden rectangle. Find each ratio.

G H J I

2. $\frac{GH}{HI}$ **3.** $\frac{GJ}{JI}$

4. If $GH = 25$, find HI to the nearest hundredth.

5. If $GJ = 100$, find JI to the nearest hundredth.

6. Find the reciprocal of the golden ratio. Round your answer to the nearest thousandth. Then subtract the reciprocal from the golden ratio itself. What do you find?

7. Find the area of a golden rectangle whose width is 20. Then find the length and width of a golden rectangle that has twice that area. Explain how you solved this problem.

8. Write the phrases that correctly complete the following statement.
If you divide the length of a ____ by its width, the number that you get is the ____.

9. Yellow Gold, White Gold Copy the lines in the painting by Piet Mondrian shown at the right. Identify three different golden rectangles in the painting.

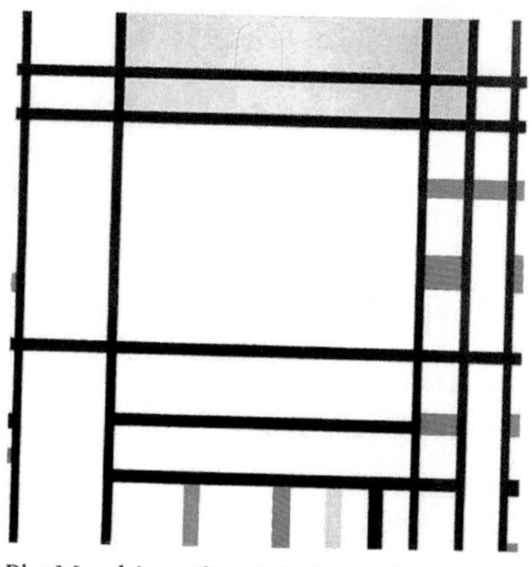

Piet Mondrian, *Place de la Concorde*, Dallas Museum of Art, Foundation for the Arts Collection, Gift of James H. and Lillian Clark Foundation

10. The Fibonacci numbers, 1, 1, 2, 3, 5, 8, 13, 21, 34, . . . , occur frequently in nature. Each number in the sequence is the sum of the two preceding numbers ($21 + 34 = \underline{55}$ and $34 + 55 = \underline{89}$ are the next two numbers in the sequence).

Find decimal approximations (to the nearest thousandth) for the following quotients of consecutive Fibonacci numbers.

a. $\frac{13}{8}$ **b.** $\frac{21}{13}$ **c.** $\frac{34}{21}$ **d.** $\frac{89}{55}$ **e.** $\frac{4181}{2584}$

f. Make a conjecture about the ratio of two consecutive Fibonacci numbers as the Fibonacci numbers get larger.

LOOK BACK

Find the area of each figure. [5-2, 5-3]

11.

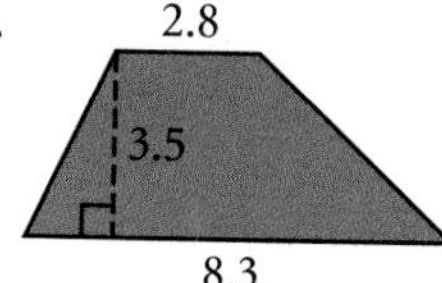

12.

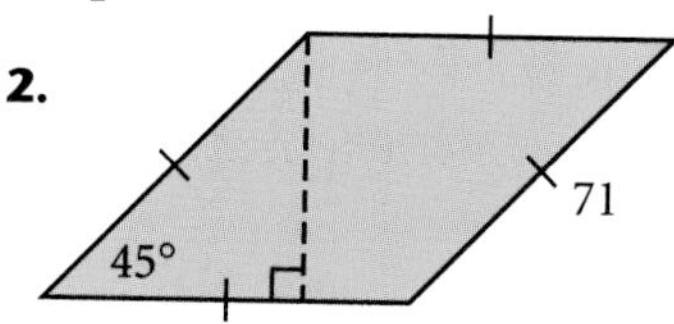

13.

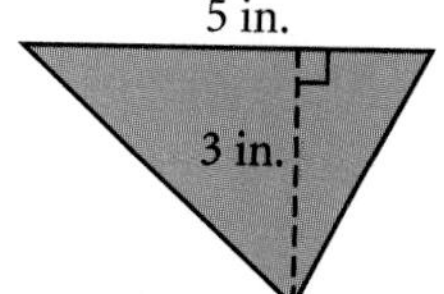

What values of *x* and *y* guarantee that each quadrilateral is a parallelogram? Justify your answers. [6-2]

14.

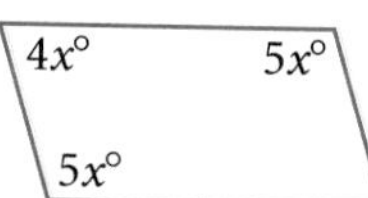

15.

16.

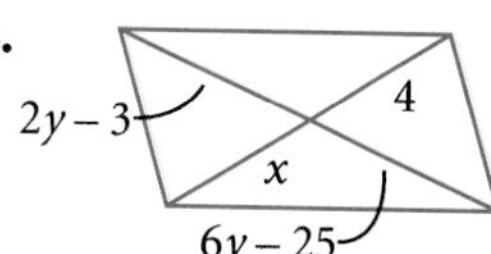

MORE PRACTICE

***PQRS* is a golden rectangle. Find each ratio.**

17. $\frac{PQ}{QR}$ **18.** $\frac{SP}{PQ}$

19. If $PQ = 30$, find PS to the nearest hundredth.

20. If $QR = 75$, find SR to the nearest hundredth.

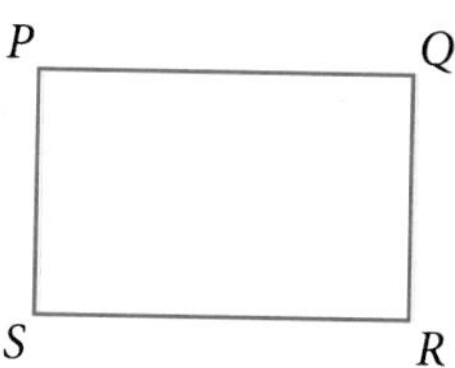

MORE MATH REASONING

21. Cutting a Golden Rectangle From which side of an $8\frac{1}{2}$-in. × 11-in. sheet of paper should you cut a strip so that the remaining rectangle is a golden rectangle? How wide should the strip be?

22. Show that if the difference between a positive number and its reciprocal is 1, then the number is the golden ratio.

23. Sketch the following on a piece of dot paper or graph paper.

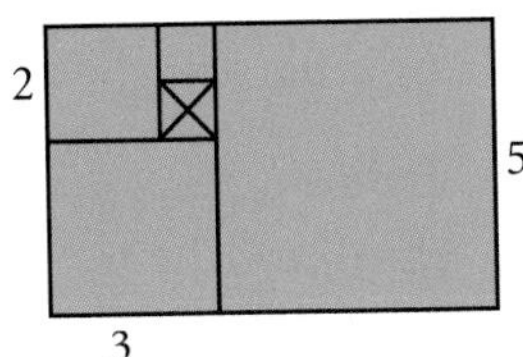

- Draw a square with sides 1 unit long. Mark an X inside the square.
- Attach a second 1-unit square to a side of the first as shown.
- Attach a 2-unit square.
- Attach a 3-unit square.
- Continue the pattern, attaching squares whose sides are 5, 8, 13, 21, and 34 units long.

a. Are the rectangles formed above golden rectangles? Why or why not?

b. Do you think that continuing this pattern will ever form a golden rectangle? Explain.

c. Beginning with the 1-unit square above the X, draw a quarter-circle in each square as shown. Can you think of anything in nature that has this type of spiral? If so, describe it.

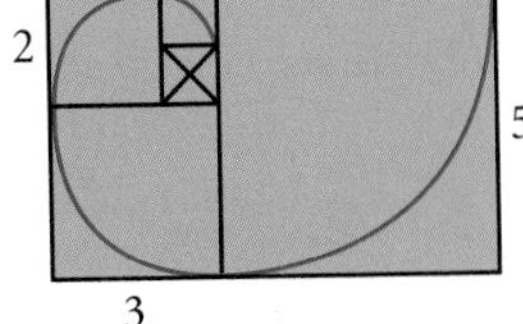

7-1 PART E Making Connections

← CONNECT → ***Models like the 18-in. version of King Kong are related to the mathematical idea of similarity. You've developed a precise definition of similarity and used this concept to solve problems.***

Movie directors often have designers build models of giant monsters, tall buildings, and futuristic spacecraft. Scale models are often used when the real object is too large, too expensive, or impossible to build.

In the following Explore, you will investigate the model used in the film *King Kong*.

EXPLORE: MODELING FOR MOVIES

MATERIALS

Tape measure

Recall that the model of King Kong was built on the scale of $\frac{3}{4}$ inch to the foot.

1. If the King Kong model was 18 in. tall, how tall would King Kong have been?
2. With a partner, use a tape measure to find the length of your arm and your height. How long would your arm be if you were as tall as King Kong? Compare this result to your partner's.
3. Fay Wray said that the "full-sized" arm of King Kong was 8 ft long. Does the 8-ft arm make sense for King Kong according to your results from Step 2? If not, how long should King Kong's arm have been?
4. Are there any problems in using your proportions to estimate the length of King Kong's arm? Explain.

REFLECT

1. Write definitions of *similar polygons, similarity ratio,* and *scale factor* in your own words. Explain the relationship among the three terms.
2. Describe how the concept of similarity might be used in a career of your choice.

Self-Assessment

Determine whether each statement is *always, sometimes,* or *never* true. Explain your answers.

1. Squares *ABCD* and *EFGH* are similar.
2. Isosceles triangles $\triangle PQR$ and $\triangle STU$ are similar.
3. An equilateral triangle, $\triangle GHJ$, and an equiangular triangle, $\triangle KLM$, are similar.

Find the measure of one interior and one exterior angle of each polygon. [6-3]

4. regular hexagon
5. regular 12-gon
6. regular 16-gon

The scale for a drawing of a room is 1 to 50. Use this information in Exercises 7–9.

7. The dimensions of the drawing are ten centimeters by eight centimeters. What are the dimensions of the room?

8. A table in the room is 145 cm long and 55 cm wide. Find its dimensions in the drawing.

9. A desk top in the drawing of the room is 1.5 cm by 2.0 cm. How long is the desk top? How wide is the desk top?

10. Gorilla in the Smog In the final scene of the movie, King Kong climbs the Empire State Building. If the building is 1250 ft tall and the scale of the model is $\frac{3}{4}$ in. = 1 ft, how tall should a model of the building have been?

$\triangle HJK \sim \triangle LMN$. Find the following.

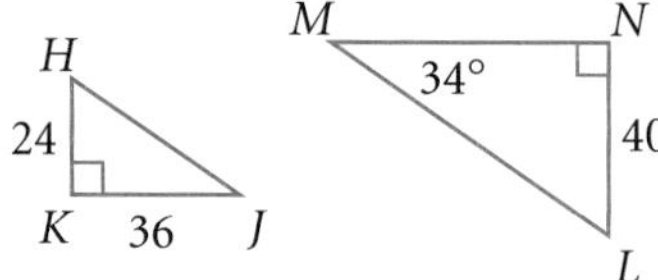

11. $m\angle N$ **12.** $m\angle H$ **13.** MN

14. the similarity ratio of $\triangle HJK$ to $\triangle LMN$

15. the similarity ratio of $\triangle LMN$ to $\triangle HJK$

Solve for *w*, *x*, *y*, and *z*.

16. $RSTU \sim DEFG$

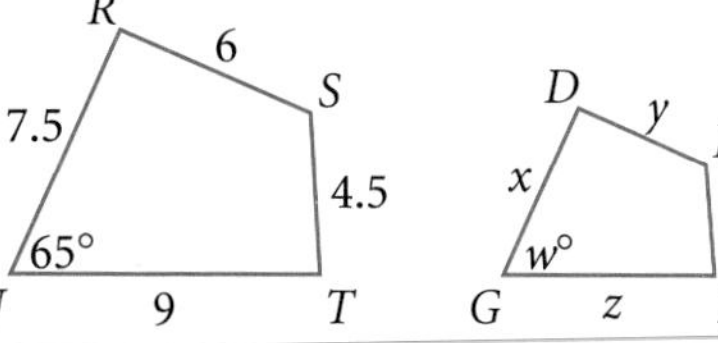

17. $\triangle JKL \sim \triangle JMN$

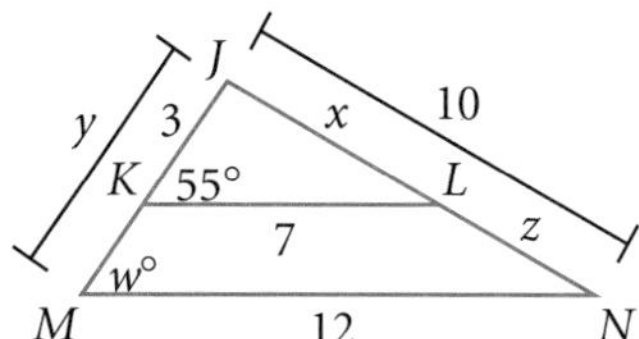

18. The two triangles shown are similar, and the lengths of two corresponding sides are given. The ratio of the area of the larger triangle to the area of the smaller is

(a) $\frac{12}{3}$ (b) $\frac{4}{1}$ (c) $\frac{2}{1}$ (d) $\frac{16}{1}$

19. Golden Screen Awards a. The owner of Comfy Cinema, a small movie theater, has a screen that is a golden rectangle. If it is eighteen feet long, how wide is it?

b. The owner of Tremendo Theater also has a screen that is a golden rectangle. In her advertisements, she claims, "Our screens have four times the area of Comfy Cinema's!" If this is true, what are the dimensions of Tremendo Theater's screen? Explain how you found your answer.

7-2 Properties of Similar Figures

San Francisco Chronicle

★★★★★ APRIL 14, 1993 50 CENTS

Building on Similarity

A story from the *San Francisco Chronicle* by Bill Workman on April 14, 1993, described plans for the construction of the world's tallest building in Tokyo, Japan. The following are excerpts from the article.

The Tokyo building will be 1,830 feet tall— or 376 feet taller than Chicago's Sears Tower, which is currently the world's tallest...The Shimizu office-retail skyscraper will have a daytime population of 50,000 and include two shopping malls and a major hotel in its upper floors, along with three stories of penthouse executive offices.

Seismic studies suggest that the Shimizu skyscraper's tapered, reinforced lightweight steel construction should be able to withstand a temblor of an unprecedented 8.4 magnitude and winds greater than 102 miles per hour...

Makato Watabe, senior managing director of the Shimizu Corporation, is one of many architects and structural engineers who have worked on the design of the project. To be able to design buildings of this size, people like Mr. Watabe coordinate aspects of perspective drawing, mathematics, structural engineering, and environmental control. As the project leader, he blends his technical knowledge with artistry and an understanding of the community's needs.

A model of the Shimizu skyscraper

1. Before any large building is constructed, a miniature model is made. How does the model help in the design of the building?

2. Describe how similarity might be used to construct the model.

3. What are some possible problems in using a model for a building of this size?

7-2 PART A Similar Triangles

← CONNECT → ***Polygons are similar if their corresponding angles are congruent and the lengths of their corresponding sides are proportional. Now you will see whether you can conclude that triangles are similar with less information.***

Shortcuts like ASA and SSS let you prove triangles congruent without knowing about every pair of corresponding parts. You might wonder if there are any postulates or theorems like these for similarity.

In the following Explore, you will investigate whether two triangles are similar if two angles of one triangle are congruent to two angles of the other. In other words, is there an Angle-Angle (AA) similarity shortcut?

EXPLORE: CHECKING UP ON THE ARCHITECTS

MATERIALS

Ruler, Protractor
Geometry software (optional)

1. Draw two triangles of different sizes with two pairs of corresponding angles congruent on your paper or computer screen. Are the remaining angles congruent? Are the side lengths proportional? Write down any conjectures that you can about the triangles.

2. After the Shimizu skyscraper is completed, Kyra visits Tokyo. She wants to check whether the building is actually 1830 ft tall. She places a mirror at her feet and walks back so that she can see the top of the building in the mirror.
Why is $\angle LMK \cong \angle SMT$? Does your conjecture from Step 1 apply to the triangles in the figure? Why or why not?

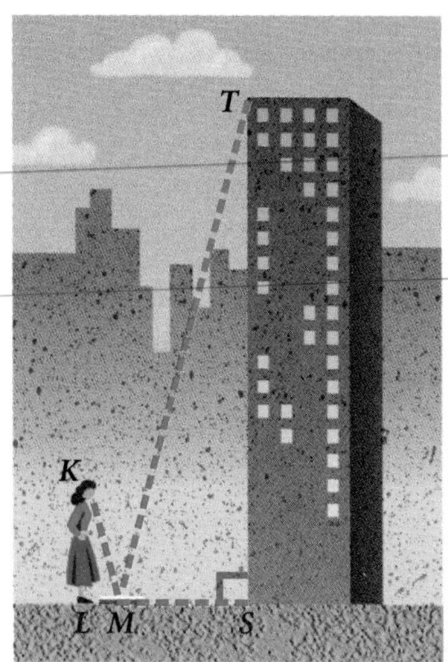

3. Kyra is 5′5″ tall, so she estimates that her eyes are 5 ft above the ground. The distance to the mirror, LM, is 1 ft. What other distance(s) does she need to measure before she can find TS, the height of the building?

4. Assume that the distance she needs to find in Step 3 is 366 ft. Is the building actually 1830 ft tall?

TRY IT

Give a similarity correspondence for each pair of triangles, and explain why the triangles are similar.

a.

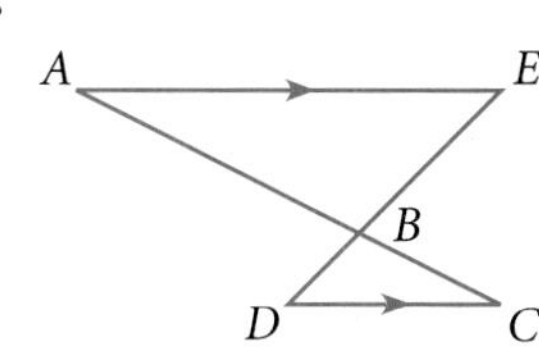

b.

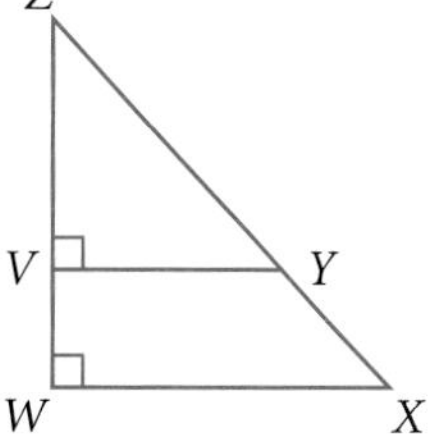

EXAMPLE

Solve for x in the figure at the right.

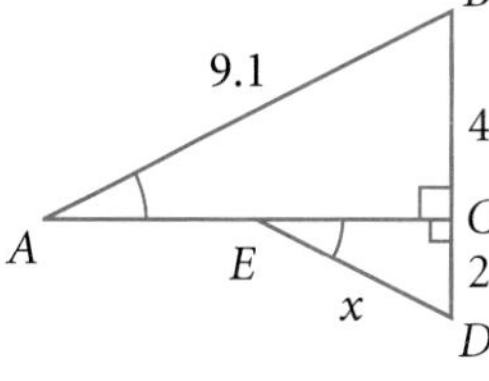

$\angle A \cong \angle DEC$, and $\angle DCE \cong \angle BCA$ because right angles are congruent. Therefore, $\triangle ACB \sim \triangle ECD$. Corresponding side lengths are proportional, so $\frac{x}{9.1} = \frac{2}{4}$.

Therefore, $4x = 18.2$, and $x = 4.55$.

You've seen a shortcut for showing that two triangles are similar—the AA Similarity Postulate.

AA SIMILARITY POSTULATE

If two angles of one triangle are congruent to two angles of another triangle, then the triangles are similar.

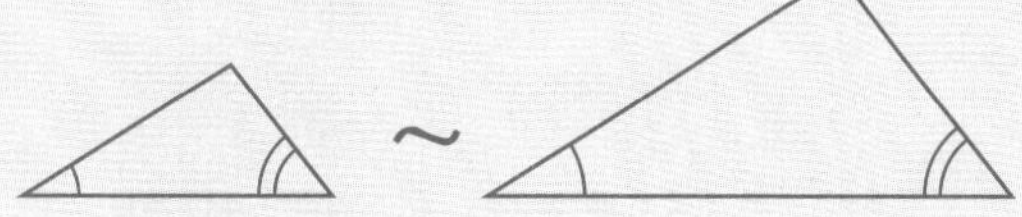

REFLECT

For a pair of triangles of each type, what additional information (if any) must be given about their angles for you to conclude that the triangles are similar?

1. right $\triangle$s **2.** isosceles $\triangle$s **3.** equilateral $\triangle$s

4. Suppose you draw $\triangle ABC$. Describe a way to construct $\triangle DEF$ so that $\triangle ABC \sim \triangle DEF$, and the similarity ratio of $\triangle ABC$ to $\triangle DEF$ is $\frac{1}{2}$.

Exercises

CORE

Getting Started Find the measure of ∠*A* that makes each pair of triangles similar.

1.

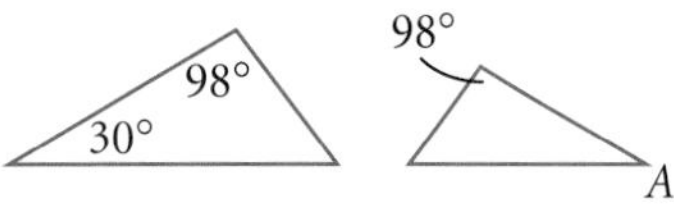

2.

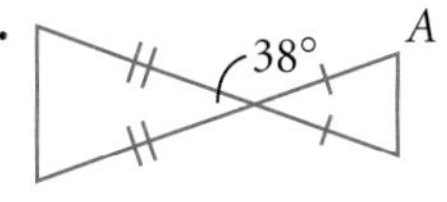

3.

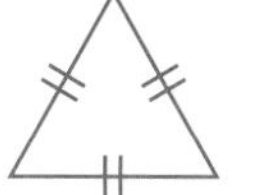

Determine whether each pair of triangles is similar. Explain your reasoning.

4. △*PQO* and △*NML*

5. △*NML* and △*TSR*

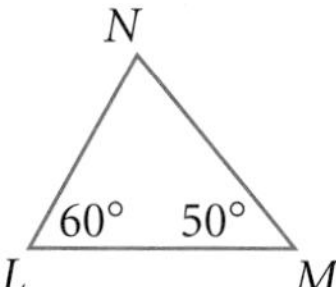

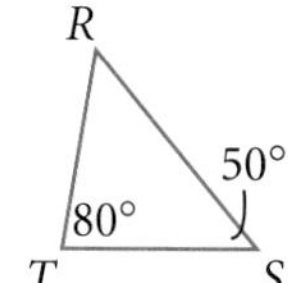

Give the similarity correspondence for each pair of triangles, and explain why the triangles are similar. Then solve for *x* and *y*.

6.

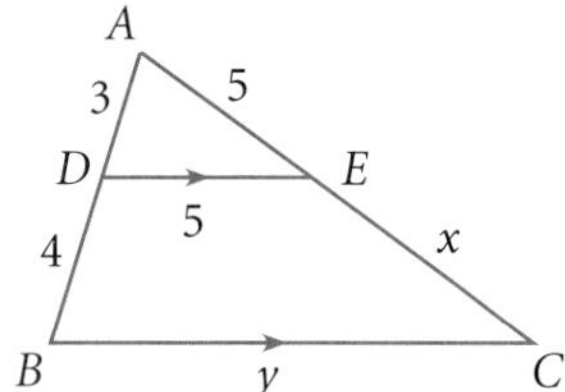

7.

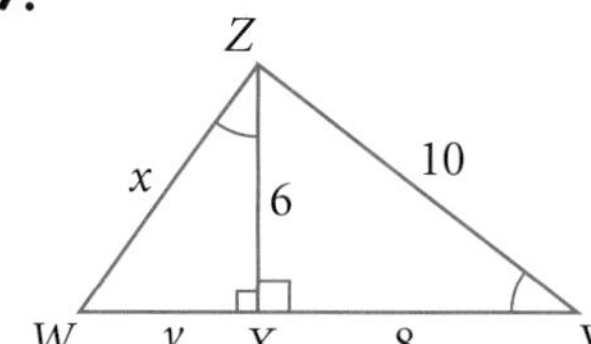

8.

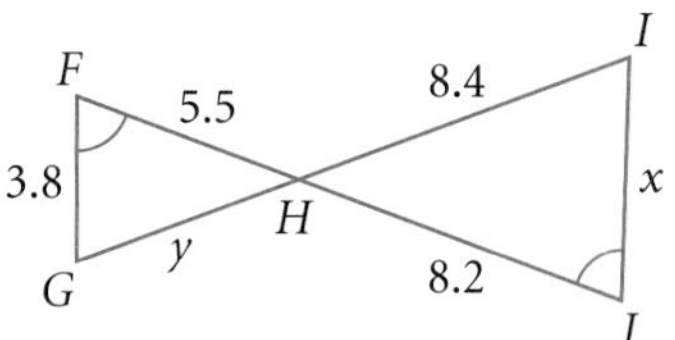

9. Tall Buildings in a Single Calculation From point *A*, a line segment includes the top of the head (*E*) of a person 6 ft tall and the top of a building (*D*). The distance *AB* is 8 ft, and the distance *BC* is 42 ft. What is the height of the building?

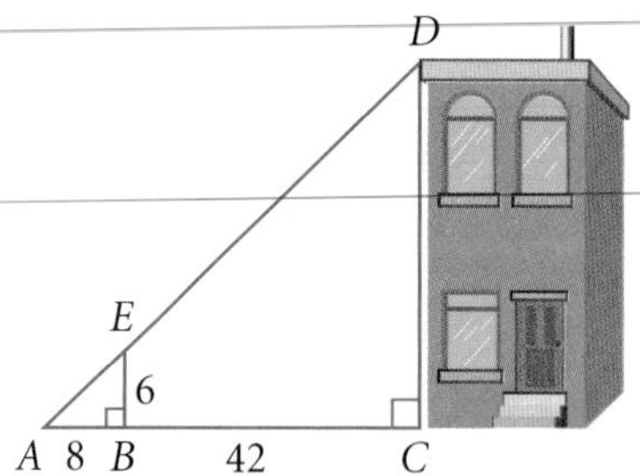

10. When an upright meter stick casts a shadow 0.8 m long, the shadow of a nearby tree is 10 m long. How tall is the tree? Draw an appropriate diagram and explain your reasoning.

11. *Given:* $\overline{VW} \parallel \overline{YZ}$

Prove: $\dfrac{VW}{YZ} = \dfrac{WX}{XY}$

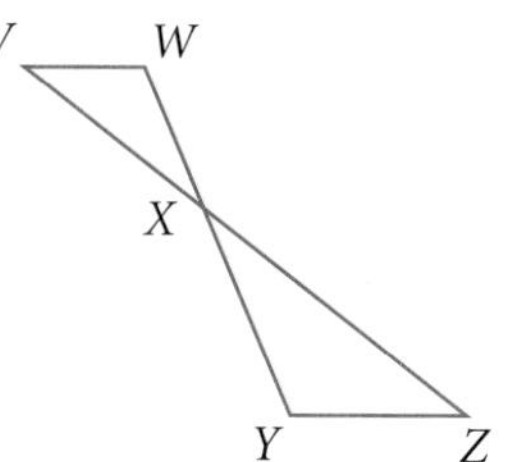

12. Spike It! Marta hits a volleyball so that it strikes the ground fifteen feet away from her.

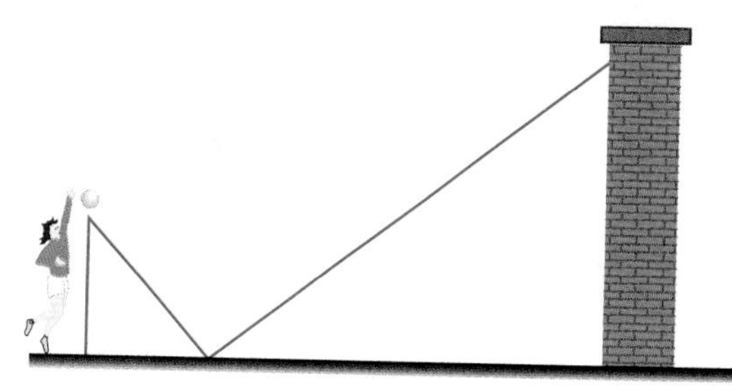

a. If her hand was nine feet off the ground when she hit the ball and the wall is fifty-four feet from where the ball hit the ground, use similar triangles to find how high up on the wall the ball will hit. Explain why the triangles you worked with are similar.

b. Do you think your answer in **12a** tells you exactly where the ball will hit, is a good approximation for where the ball will hit, or is a poor approximation for where the ball will hit? If it is an approximation, do you think it is an overestimate or an underestimate? Explain.

13. We say x is the **geometric mean** between a and b if $\frac{a}{x} = \frac{x}{b}$ and a, b, and x are positive. For example, 4 is the geometric mean between 2 and 8, since $\frac{2}{4} = \frac{4}{8}$. Use the figure to give examples of each of the following statements.

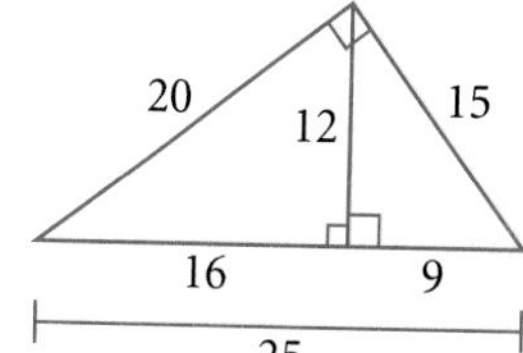

a. The length of the altitude to the hypotenuse of a right triangle is the geometric mean between the lengths of the two segments on the hypotenuse.

b. In a right triangle with an altitude to the hypotenuse, the length of each leg is the geometric mean between the length of the segment of the hypotenuse adjacent to the leg and the length of the whole hypotenuse.

14. *Given:* $\angle 1 \cong \angle 2$, $\overline{XY} \perp \overline{WZ}$

Prove: $\frac{WZ}{WY} = \frac{XZ}{YZ}$

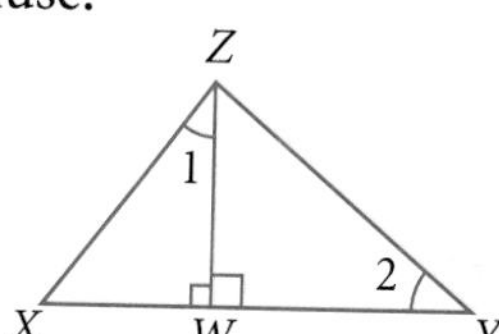

LOOK BACK

***ABCD* is a parallelogram. Complete each statement. [6-2]**

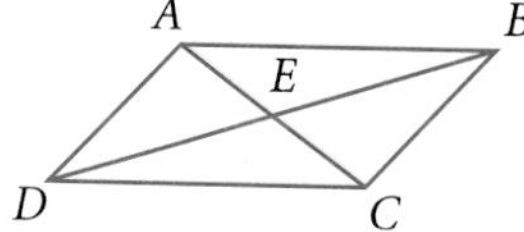

15. If $AD = 16$, $BC =$ ____.

16. If $AE = 12$, $AC =$ ____.

17. If $m\angle ADC = 52°$, $m\angle BAD =$ ____.

18. If $m\angle ADC = (2x + 24)°$ and $m\angle ABC = (5x - 57)°$, find $m\angle ABC$.

Trapezoid *HJKL* ~ trapezoid *MNOP*. Find each ratio. [7-1]

19. $\frac{HJ}{MN}$ **20.** $\frac{\text{perimeter } HJKL}{\text{perimeter } MNOP}$ **21.** $\frac{\text{area } HJKL}{\text{area } MNOP}$

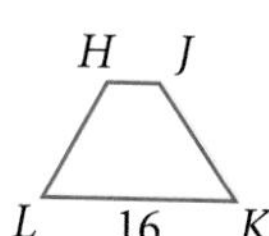

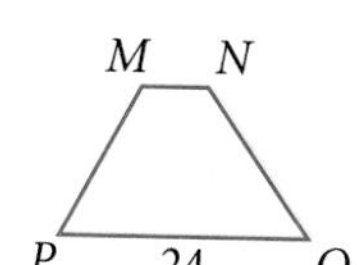

MORE PRACTICE

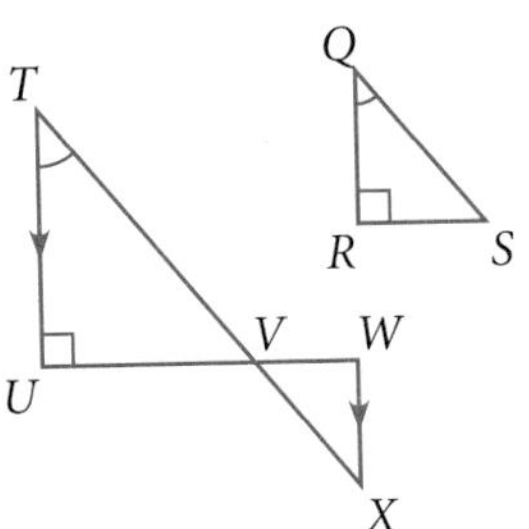

Determine whether each pair of triangles is similar. Explain your reasoning.

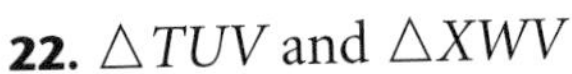

22. $\triangle TUV$ and $\triangle XWV$

23. $\triangle TUV$ and $\triangle QRS$

Give a similarity correspondence for each pair of triangles, and explain why the triangles are similar. Then solve for *x* and *y*.

24.

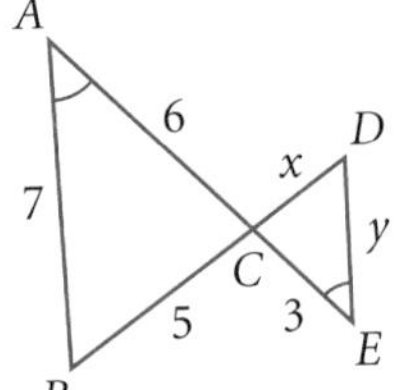

25.

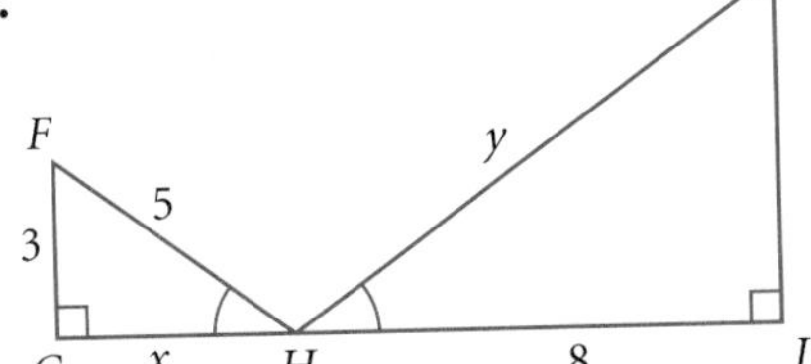

26.

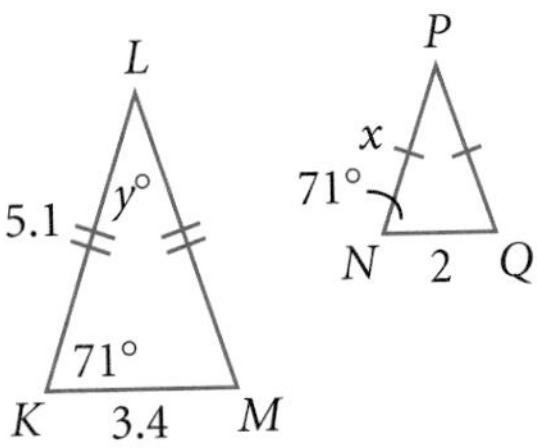

MORE MATH REASONING

27. The Inside Scoop The figure below shows a camera with a film width *XY* that is 35 mm and a focal length of 50 mm. The width of the scene is *AB*.

Science

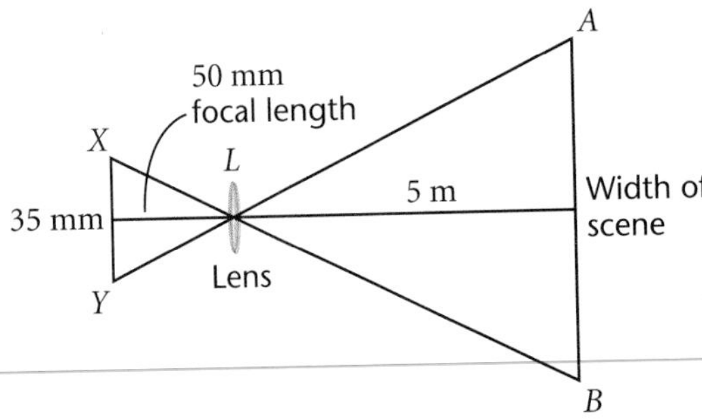

a. What assumptions could you make about this figure that allow you to conclude that $\triangle ALB \sim \triangle YLX$?

b. What is the width of the scene?

c. If the lens of the camera has a focal length of 70 mm, what is the width of the scene?

28. The Diagonal Test Rectangle *ABCD* overlaps rectangle *AEFG* so that $\overline{AE}$ lies on $\overline{AB}$ and $\overline{AG}$ lies on $\overline{AD}$. Show that the rectangles are similar if the diagonal from point *A* to point *C* passes through point *F*.

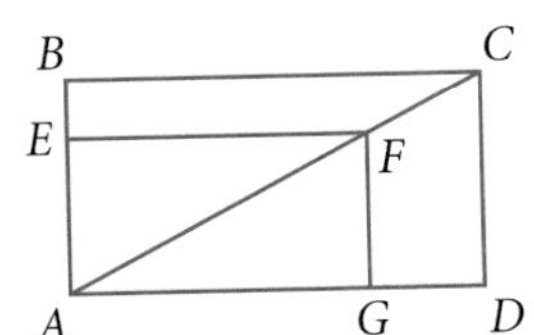

7-2 PART B

SAS Similarity

← CONNECT → ***You know one shortcut for showing that triangles are similar. Now you will investigate another way to prove triangle similarity.***

The congruence postulates and theorems for triangles all require that you have at least one pair of congruent sides. Of course, similar triangles have proportional side lengths. In the following Explore, you will see whether information about proportional side lengths can help you prove that two triangles are similar.

EXPLORE: USE SIMILAR REASONING

MATERIALS

Protractor, Ruler
Geometry software (optional)

1. An SAS similarity postulate or theorem would let you prove that two triangles are similar if two pairs of sides have proportional lengths and their included angles are congruent. Does SAS similarity work? To explore this, use geometry software or a protractor and ruler to draw two triangles with the SAS similarity characteristics. Are the triangles similar? Write a conjecture about SAS similarity.

2. Use similarity to make a plan for solving the following problem. Then create hypothetical values for any measurements you need, and solve the problem. Before making plans for a bridge from North Lake to Shore View, you need to know its approximate length. You can measure short distances using a tape measure and longer ones using the odometer on your truck. You can mark off straight lines, but you have no way to measure angles. How can you find the bridge's length?

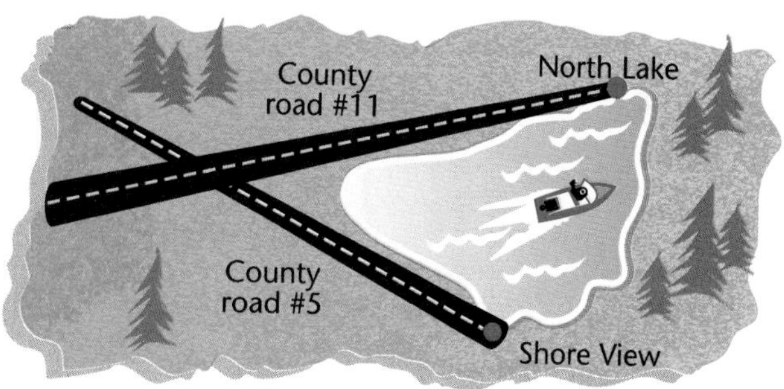

The following Example shows one way you can use SAS similarity.

EXAMPLE

Find a value of x that makes $\triangle ABC \sim \triangle EBD$.

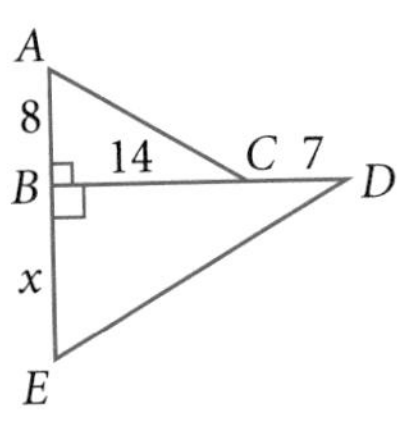

The right angles shown are congruent. Therefore, if $\frac{EB}{AB} = \frac{BD}{BC}$ or $\frac{x}{8} = \frac{21}{14}$, the triangles are similar.

$\frac{x}{8} = \frac{21}{14} = \frac{3}{2}$

$2x = 24$

Therefore, if $x = 12$, $\triangle ABC \sim \triangle EBD$.

TRY IT

Give a similarity correspondence for each pair of triangles, and explain why the triangles are similar. Then solve for x.

a.

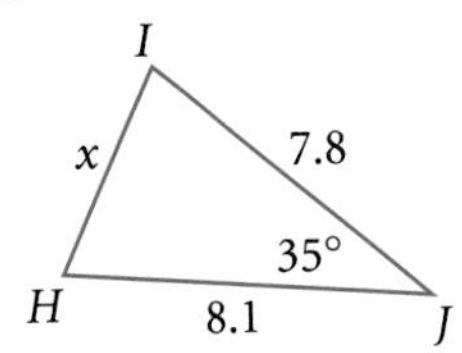

b.

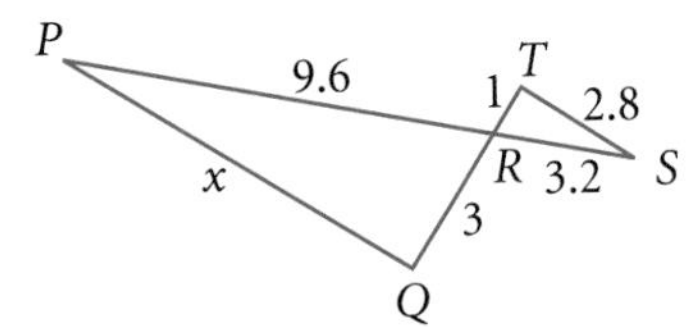

SAS similarity can be proved from the AA Similarity Postulate, so this result is stated as a theorem.

SAS SIMILARITY THEOREM

If an angle of one triangle is congruent to an angle of another triangle and the lengths of the sides that include the angles are proportional, then the triangles are similar.

REFLECT

1. Explain why there is no SA Similarity Theorem.
2. Why do you think it is often more convenient to use similar triangles than congruent triangles to solve real-world problems?

There is a third way to prove that triangles are similar. The SSS Similarity Theorem lets you conclude that two triangles are similar if all of the corresponding sides have proportional lengths.

SSS SIMILARITY THEOREM

If the lengths of three sides of one triangle are proportional to the lengths of three sides of another triangle, then the triangles are similar.

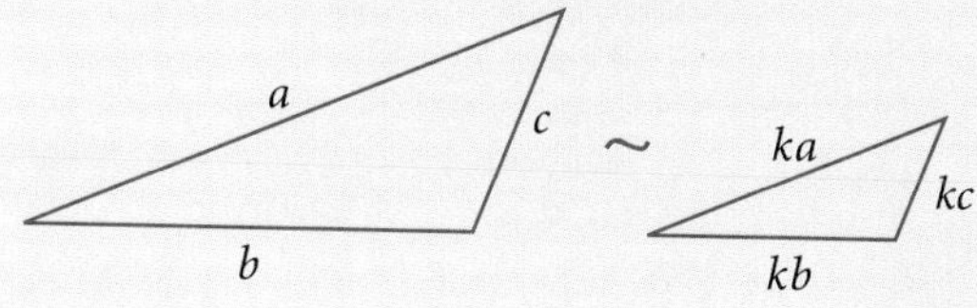

Exercises

CORE

Getting Started For each of the following, write a similarity statement, and give a reason that the triangles are similar.

1. F 20 E 10 D A 20 B 40 C

2. G H K I J

3. K 38 39 N L 26 M 57 P

Give a similarity correspondence for each pair of triangles, and explain why the triangles are similar. Then solve for *x* and *y*. Give exact values for *x* and *y*.

4.

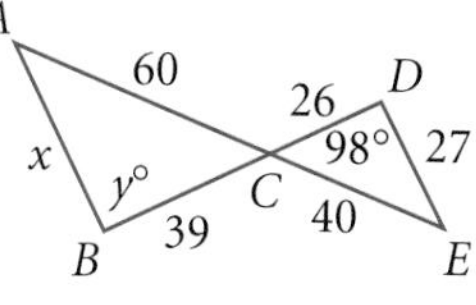

5.

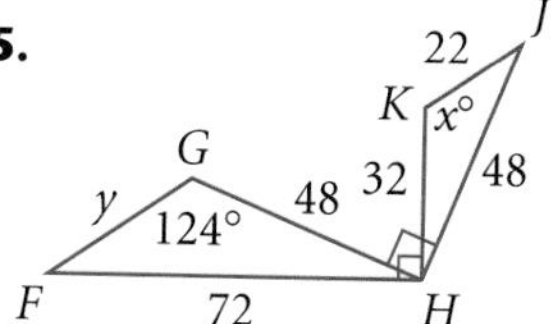

6. *Given:* $LN = 2NP$, $MN = 2NQ$

Prove: $\overline{LM} \parallel \overline{PQ}$

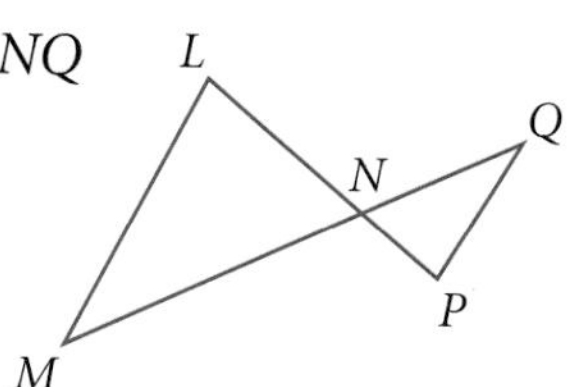

7. Off Course A golfer wanted to hit her ball 180 yd to the hole shown. She did hit the ball 180 yd, but, unfortunately, she sliced it in the wrong direction. She then put two 2-in. tees on the ground so that one lined up with her ball and one lined up with the hole. The ends of the tees were $\frac{1}{2}$ in. apart. How far is her ball from the hole? Explain your reasoning.

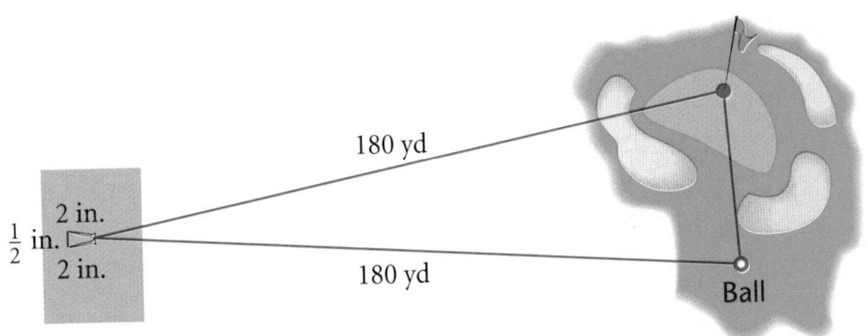

8. Do you think there is an SAS Similarity Theorem for parallelograms? Carefully draw several parallelograms to explore this possibility. Then state an SAS Similarity Theorem for parallelograms or provide a counterexample to show why it does not work.

Find a value of *x* that makes each pair of triangles similar. State the theorem or postulate that justifies your answer.

9.

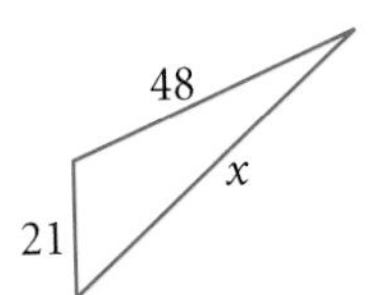

10.

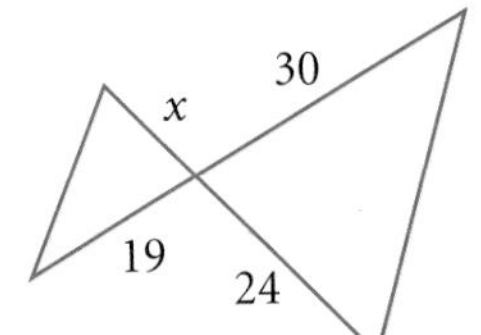

11.

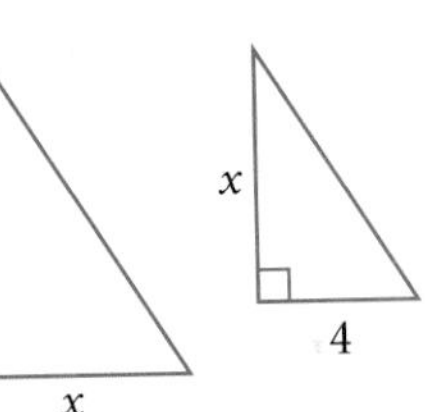

12. Could you make a scale model of the tower at the right without measuring any angles and be certain that it is similar to the actual tower? Write a short paragraph to explain your method.

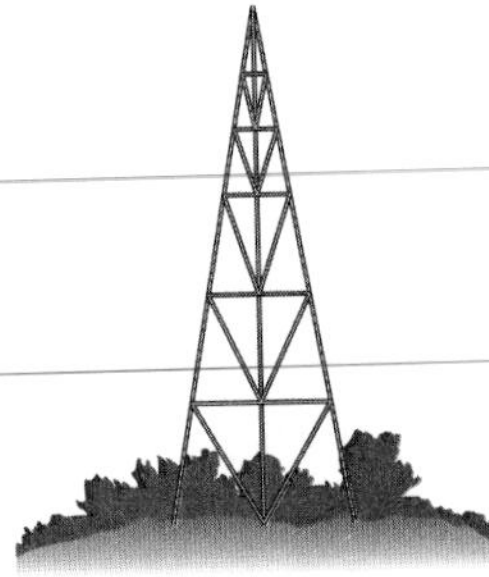

13. Prove: If two triangles are equilateral, then they are similar.

14. Do you think there is an SSA similarity shortcut? Why or why not?

15. A Shady Calculation It is said that Thales, a teacher of Pythagoras, found the height of the Egyptian pyramids by using similar triangles. He began by placing his staff at the tip of a pyramid's shadow, as shown below. Explain how he found the height of the pyramid.

History

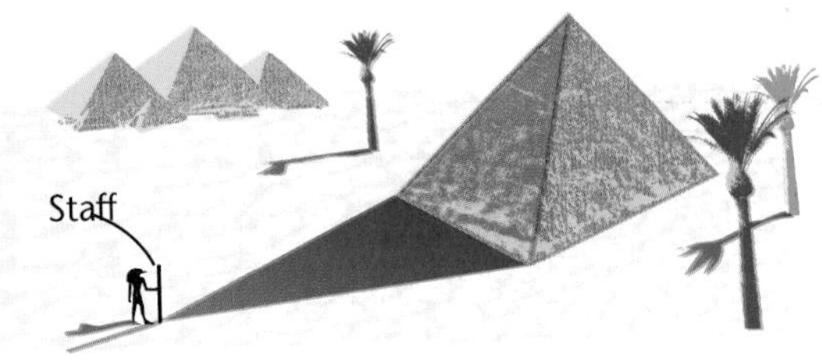

LOOK AHEAD

16. In your own words, define the scale factor of an enlargement or a reduction.

17. Draw triangle *RST*. Then use a compass and straightedge to construct triangle *RVW* similar to $\triangle RST$ so that

- *R*, *S*, and *V* are collinear
- *R*, *T*, and *W* are collinear
- $\frac{RV}{RS} = 2$

Explain how you drew $\triangle RVW$. What similarity postulate or theorem ensures that the triangles are similar?

MORE PRACTICE

Give a similarity correspondence for each pair of triangles, and explain why the triangles are similar. Then solve for *x* and *y*. Give exact values for *x* and *y*.

18.

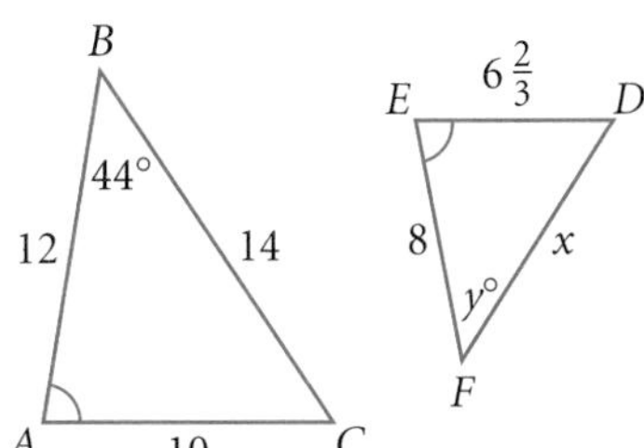

19.

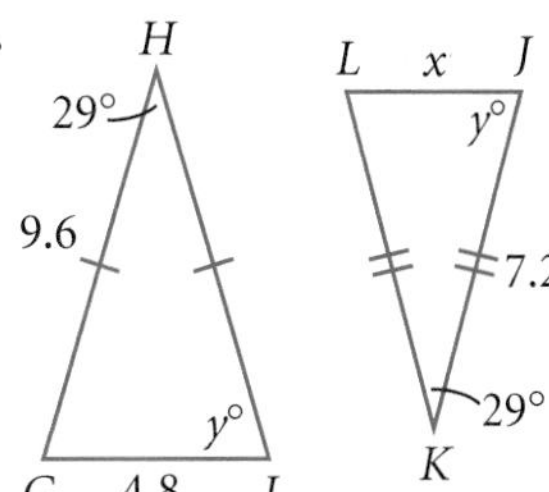

Find a value of *x* that makes each pair of triangles similar. State the theorem or postulate that justifies your answer.

20.

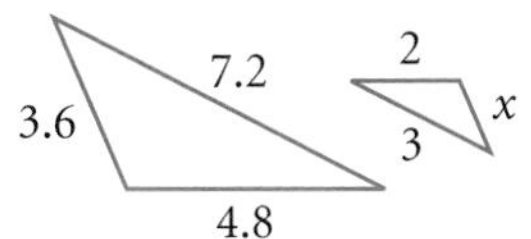

21.

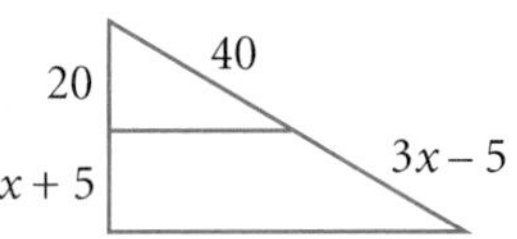

22.

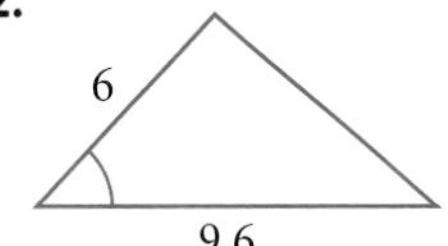

MORE MATH REASONING

Write a *plan* for each proof.

23. Prove that the lengths of corresponding medians of two similar triangles are in the same ratio as the lengths of two corresponding sides.

24. Prove that the lengths of corresponding altitudes of two similar triangles are in the same ratio as the lengths of two corresponding sides.

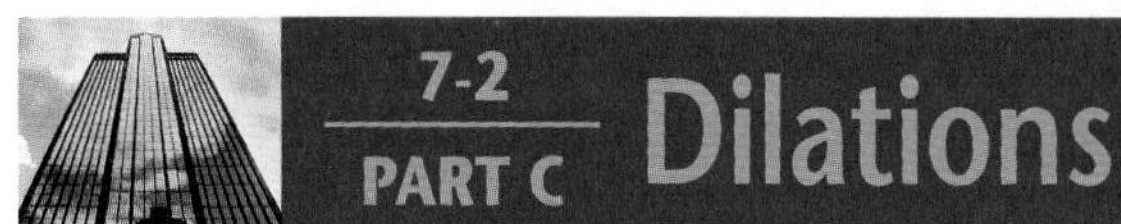

7-2 PART C Dilations

← CONNECT → ***You've seen enlargements and reductions of everyday objects and geometric figures. Now you will use your knowledge of similarity to discover how a transformation can enlarge or reduce a figure.***

In the following Explore, we'll investigate a way to draw similar triangles. This method will introduce a new transformation—the **dilation.**

EXPLORE: A "DILATE-FUL" TRANSFORMATION

MATERIALS

Protractor, Ruler
Geometry software (optional)

1. Reproduce the steps shown at the bottom of this page on your paper or computer screen.
2. $\triangle A'B'C'$ is the **dilation image** of $\triangle ABC$. Make any measurements necessary to check whether $\triangle ABC \sim \triangle A'B'C'$. If you find that the triangles are similar, give your reason and the supporting data.
3. Draw another triangle and its dilation image. Make measurements, and give data to show whether or not the triangles are similar.
4. Use your data and any other measurements you need to identify the properties of the original triangles that are preserved by a dilation. Which properties are not preserved?
5. When you dilate a figure, is its image always similar to its pre-image? Explain.

CREATING A DILATION

P, A, B, C	P, A, B, C	P, A, B, C, A′, B′, C′
Draw any triangle, $\triangle ABC$. Draw a point P outside the triangle. P will be the **center of dilation.**	Draw $\overrightarrow{PA}$, $\overrightarrow{PB}$, and $\overrightarrow{PC}$. (Make the rays more than three times as long as $\overline{PA}$, $\overline{PB}$, and $\overline{PC}$.)	Draw points A', B', and C' so that $PA' = 3PA$, $PB' = 3PB$, and $PC' = 3PC$. Draw $\triangle A'B'C'$.

Like reflections, rotations, and translations, dilations are transformations. Every dilation of a polygon produces a figure similar to the pre-image.

DEFINITION

A **dilation** with **center of dilation** C and **scale factor** $k > 0$ is a transformation of a plane that keeps point C where it is and maps every other point P to a point P' on $\overrightarrow{CP}$ so that $CP' = k(CP)$.

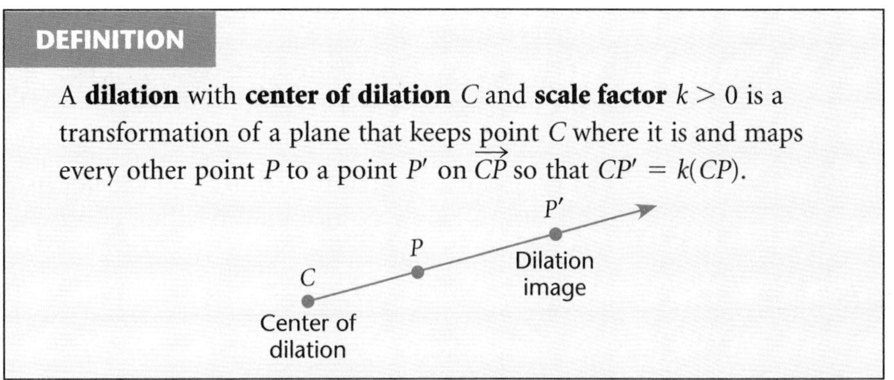

You use dilations of the coordinate plane when you use the *Zoom In* or *Zoom Out* features of a graphing utility.

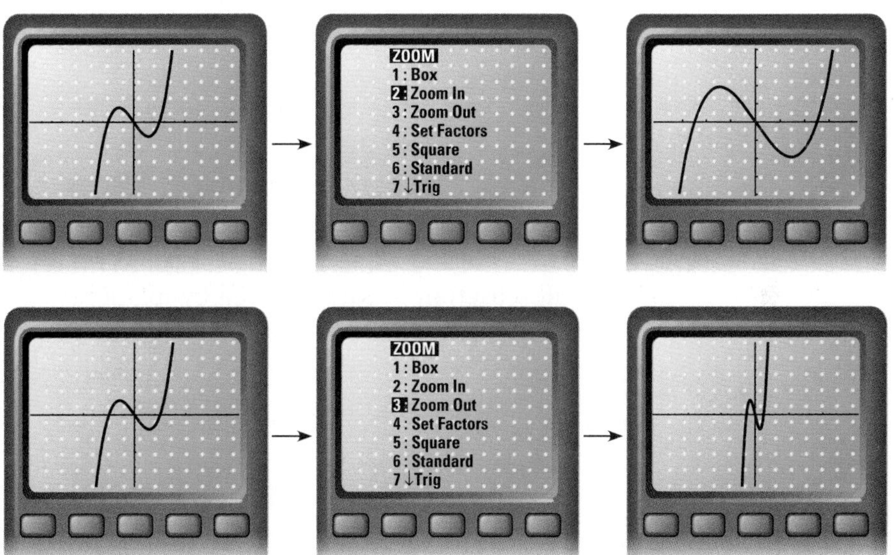

(The scale on the last window has been changed to make the graph visible.)

1. What point of the calculator screen appears to be the center of the dilation for the *Zoom In* and *Zoom Out* shown above?

TRY IT

Answer each of the following for dilations with center P.

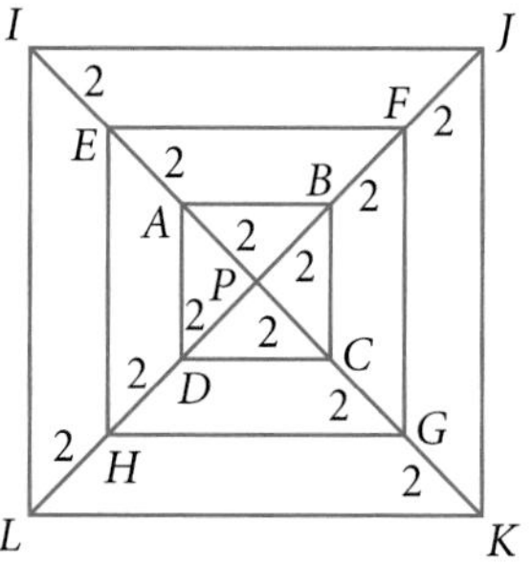

a. If $k = 3$, what is the image of $ABCD$? What is the pre-image of K?
b. If the image of F is J, find the scale factor k.
c. If the image of $EFGH$ is $ABCD$, find k.

The properties of a figure that are and are not preserved by a dilation are summarized below. Notice that these are consistent with the properties of similar polygons.

Dilations **change:**	Dilations **preserve:**
• the size of a figure (unless $k = 1$)	• the measures of the angles in a figure • the orientation of a figure • the shape of a figure

REFLECT

1. If the scale factor of a dilation is n, what is the ratio of the area of the image to the area of the pre-image?
2. What property of a figure that is preserved by translation, rotation, and reflection is not preserved by dilation?
3. If you dilate a triangle, then the dilation image is similar to the pre-image. Given two similar triangles, is it always possible to map one onto the other with just a dilation? Why?

Exercises

CORE

1. Getting Started A regular octagon with sides 2 cm long undergoes a dilation with a scale factor of 3.5.

a. How long is each side of the image?
b. What is the measure of each angle of the image?

In Exercises 2–4, answer each of the following for dilations with center *P*.

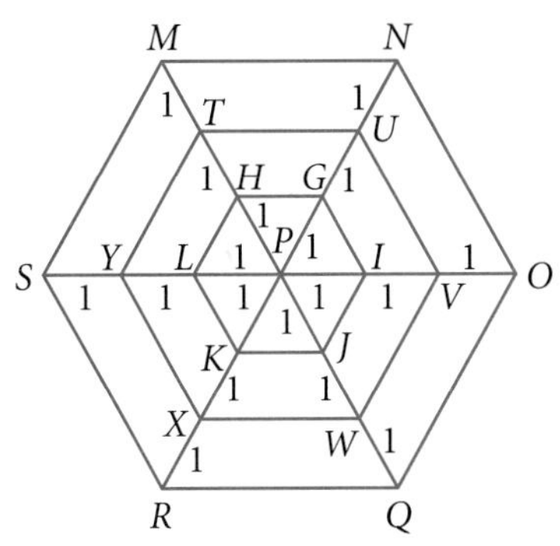

2. If $k = 2$, what is the image of *HGIJKL*? What is the pre-image of *T*?

3. If the image of *Q* is *J*, find the scale factor *k*.

4. If the image of *MNOQRS* is *TUVWXY*, find *k*.

Write the word or phrase that correctly completes each statement.

5. The ratio of the length of a side of a dilation image to the length of the corresponding side in the pre-image is called the ____.

6. A dilation image is always ____ to its pre-image.

7. **Scale the Building** A sketch of a plan for a new office is shown at the right. Copy the figure and then sketch its dilation image, using center *R* and scale factor 2.5.

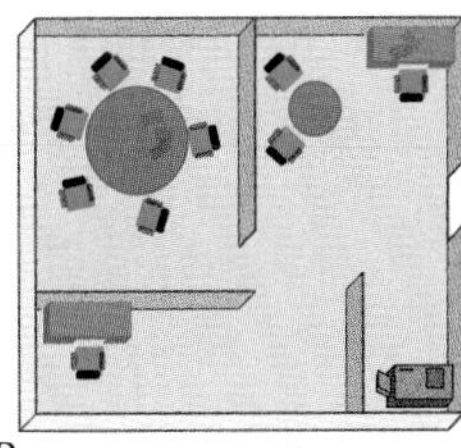

Copy each figure on graph paper. If the red figure is a dilation image of the black figure, is the dilation an enlargement or a reduction? Find the scale factor and the center of the dilation. Explain how you found the center of each dilation.

8.

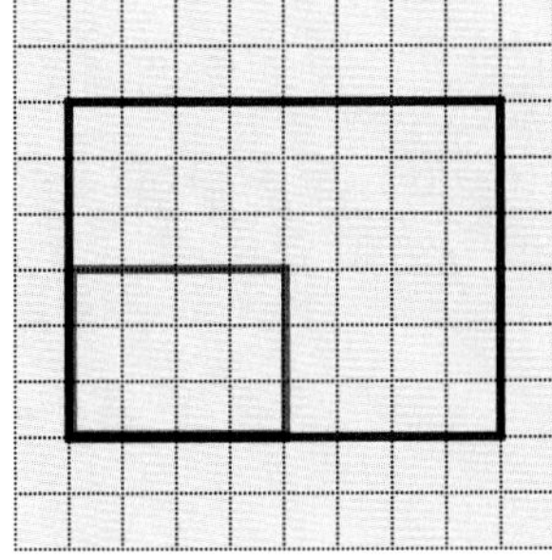

9.

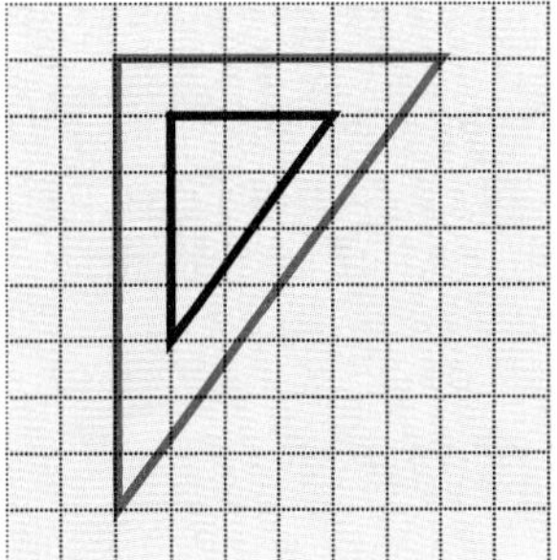

Find the coordinates of the images of points *A*, *B*, and *C* under a dilation with center *O* and the given scale factor.

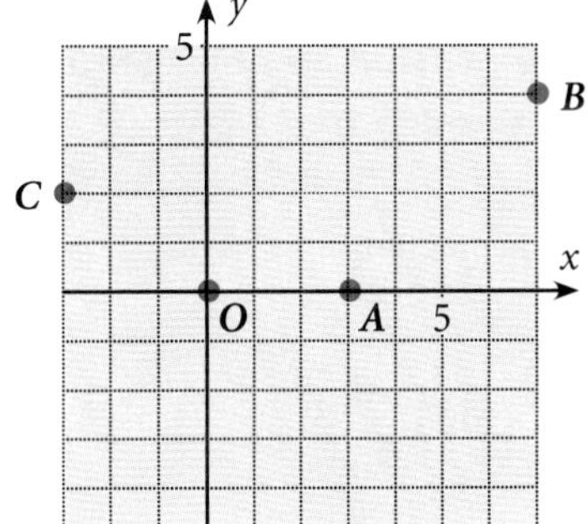

10. $k = 2$

11. $k = \frac{1}{2}$

12. $k = \frac{1}{3}$

13. Palace Plans The plan of the palace of the Deji of Akure (Nigeria) can be thought of as a dilation of the actual palace.

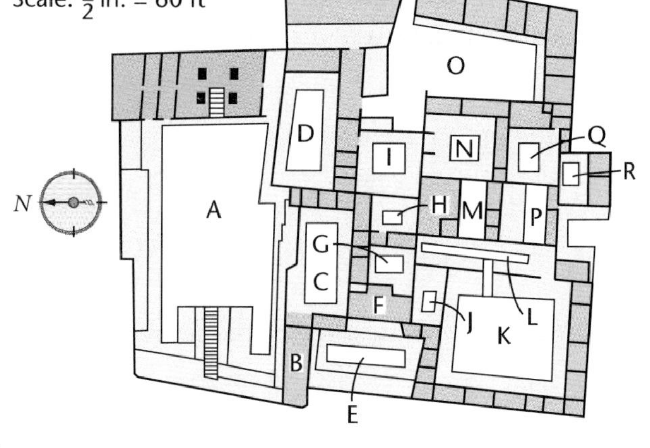

a. Find the scale factor of the dilation. How did you find this?

b. Find the approximate area of the actual courtyard K. Explain your method.

c. What is the ratio of the actual area of courtyard K to its area on the plan? Justify your answer.

14. Make a chart to show the properties of a figure that are and are not preserved by the four transformations you've studied. These properties should include location, size, angle measure, and orientation.

LOOK BACK

Quadrilateral *ABCD* has diagonals $\overline{AC}$ and $\overline{BD}$. What is true about $\overline{AC}$ and $\overline{BD}$ if the following is true? [6-2]

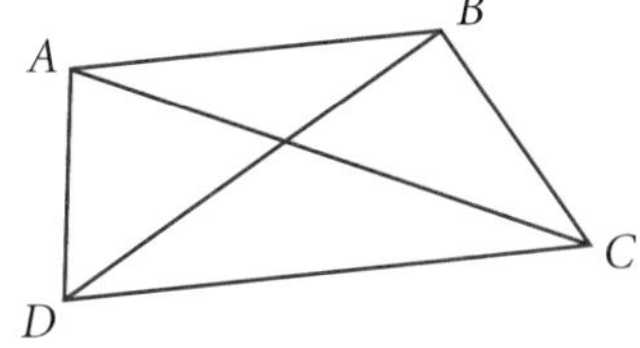

15. *ABCD* is a parallelogram. **16.** *ABCD* is a rhombus.

17. *ABCD* is a rectangle. **18.** *ABCD* is a square.

19. Carmen is drawing up blueprints for a new office building. On the blueprint, the reception area measures 5 in. by $3\frac{1}{2}$ in. If the scale used for the drawing is $\frac{1}{2}$ in. = 1 ft, what will the dimensions of the actual reception area be? [7-1]

MORE PRACTICE

Copy each figure on graph paper. If the red figure is a dilation image of the black figure, is the dilation an enlargement or a reduction? Find the scale factor and the center of the dilation.

20.

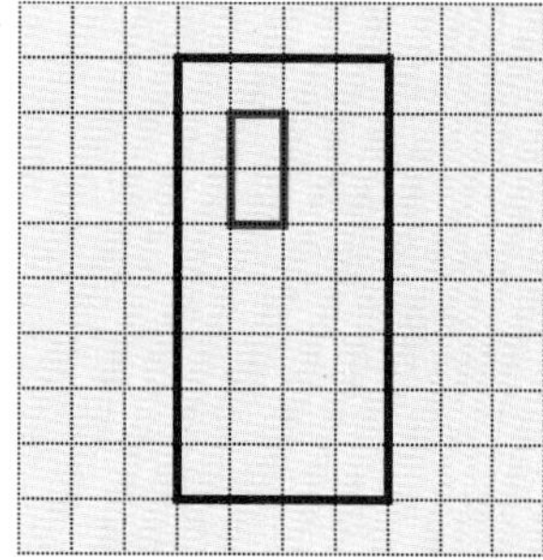

21.

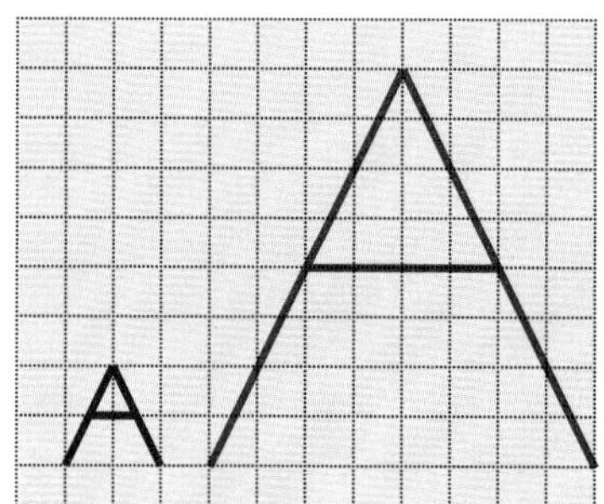

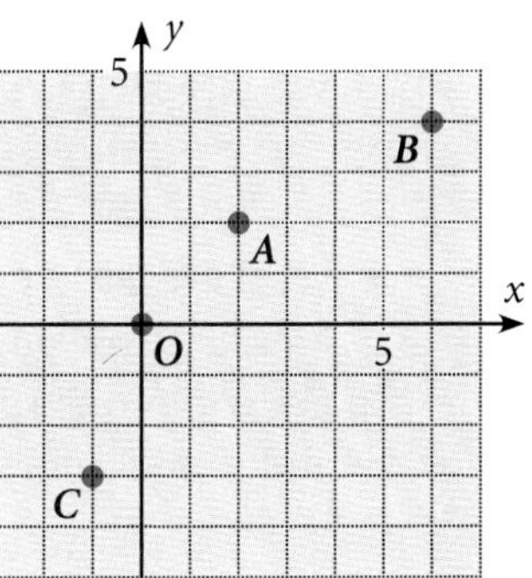

Find the coordinates of the images of points *A, B,* and *C* under a dilation with center *O* and the given scale factor.

22. $k = \frac{3}{2}$ **23.** $k = 3$ **24.** $k = 0.25$

Copy rectangle *MNPQ* on graph paper. Then draw each dilation image, using the given scale factors and center.

25. scale factor 3, center O

26. scale factor 0.75, center Q

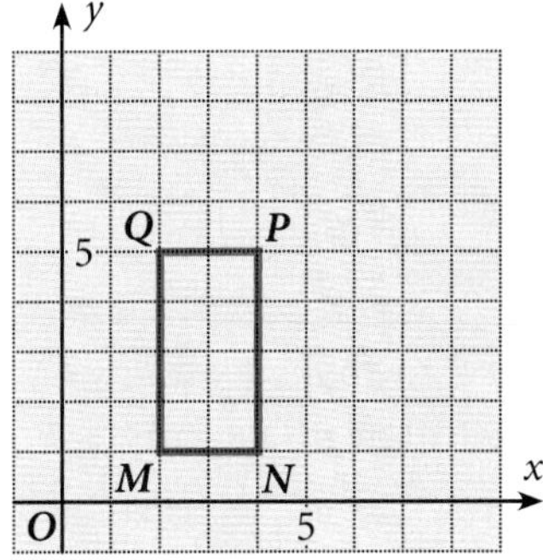

MORE MATH REASONING

27. Explain why a triangle is similar to its dilation image.

28. Line t contains the points (1, 5) and (3, 2). Line t' is the image of line t under a dilation with center (0, 0) and scale factor 2.

a. Calculate the slopes of t and t'. Do you notice a relationship between the slopes?

b. Do your slopes depend on the points of t chosen or do other points lead to the same result? Explain.

c. Suppose line p has the equation $y = mx$. What is the equation of the image of p under this dilation?

7-2 PART D Triangle Midsegments

← CONNECT → ***You've seen that parallel lines and transversals create special angle relationships. This knowledge will help you understand the connection between similarity and a special segment of a triangle.***

A segment whose endpoints are the midpoints of two of its sides is a **midsegment** of a triangle. You will investigate relationships involving a midsegment of a triangle, similar triangles, and parallel lines.

EXPLORE: MEASURING THE MIDSEGMENTS

MATERIALS

Protractor, Ruler
Compass (optional)
Geometry software (optional)

1. Use software or a straightedge to draw a large triangle. Measure the lengths of its sides.
2. Draw or construct the midpoints of two of the sides. Then add a midsegment of the triangle. Measure sides and angles.

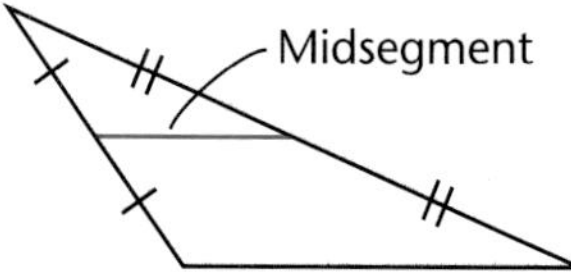

3. Repeat the process as needed to make as many conjectures as you can about the midsegment of a triangle.

TRY IT

Solve for x in each figure.

a.

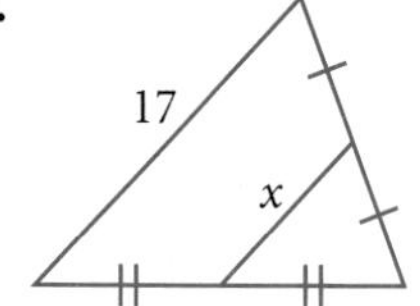

b.

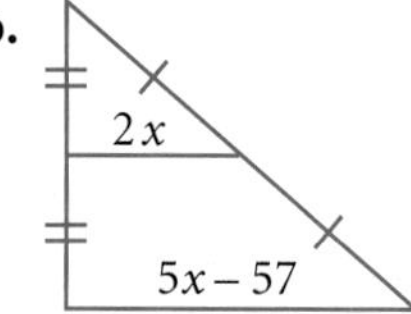

c.

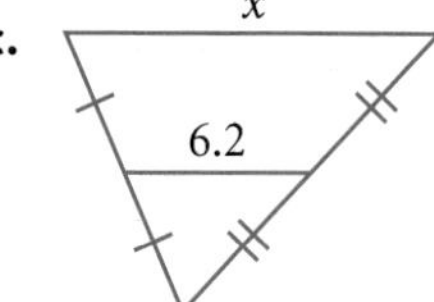

We can summarize the properties of triangle midsegments as follows.

MIDSEGMENT THEOREM FOR TRIANGLES

A segment whose endpoints are the midpoints of two sides of a triangle is parallel to the third side and half its length.

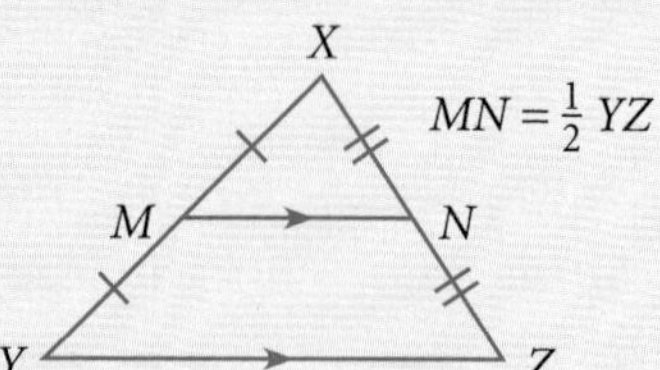

WHAT DO YOU THINK?

Adam and Hulleah are planning justifications of the Midsegment Theorem to present to their geometry class.

Adam thinks . . .

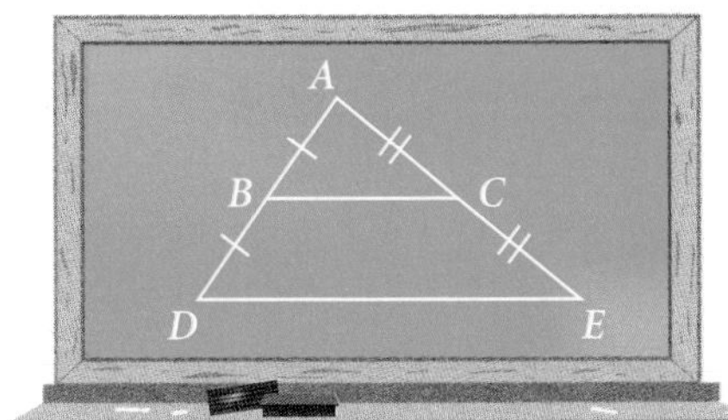

I'll use similar triangles. Since B and C are midpoints, $\frac{AB}{AD} = \frac{1}{2}$, and $\frac{AC}{AE} = \frac{1}{2}$. $\triangle ABC$ and $\triangle ADE$ also share $\angle A$, so they are similar. Then $\frac{BC}{DE} = \frac{1}{2}$, so the midsegment is half the length of the third side. Since the triangles are similar, $\angle ABC \cong \angle ADE$. Therefore, $\overline{BC} \parallel \overline{DE}$, because $\angle ABC$ and $\angle ADE$ are congruent corresponding angles for $\overline{BC}$ and $\overline{DE}$.

Hulleah thinks . . .

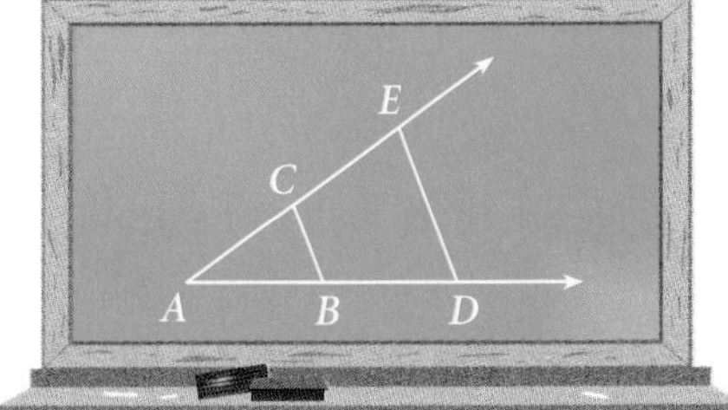

I'll sketch a figure to illustrate the theorem and show that the larger triangle is a dilation of the smaller one. If A is the center of a dilation with scale factor 2, $\triangle ADE$ is the image of $\triangle ABC$. Since the scale factor is 2, $\overline{BC}$ is half as long as $\overline{DE}$.

To show that $\overline{BC} \parallel \overline{DE}$, I can use corresponding angles. $\angle ACB$ and $\angle AED$ have to be congruent, so $\overline{BC} \parallel \overline{DE}$.

1. How did Adam know that $\triangle ABC \sim \triangle ADE$?

2. How did Hulleah know that $\angle ACB \cong \angle AED$?

Triangle midsegments are useful in perspective drawings. You will see an example of this in Exercise 9.

REFLECT

In the figure, the second triangle's base is a midsegment of the first triangle, the third triangle's base is a midsegment of the second, and so on.

1. If the length of $\overline{AB}$ is 8, what is the length of $\overline{GH}$?
2. How could you find the length of the base of the nth triangle?
3. What is true about the bases of all of the triangles?

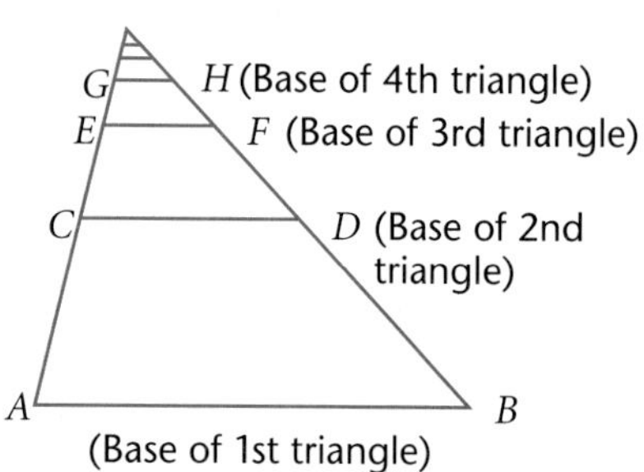

Exercises

CORE

Getting Started **In the figure, *S*, *W*, and *U* are midpoints of the sides of $\triangle RTV$. $RT = 60$, $RV = 80$, and $TV = 100$.**

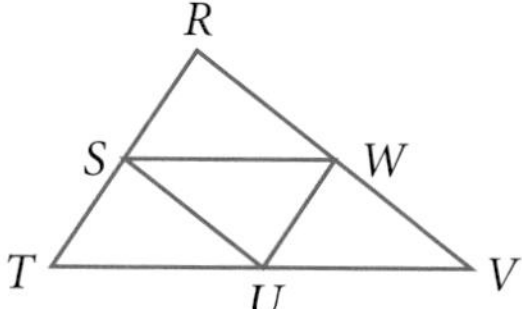

1. Find SW, WU, and US.

2. Name three pairs of parallel segments.

***B* is the midpoint of $\overline{AC}$ and *E* is the midpoint of $\overline{AD}$.**

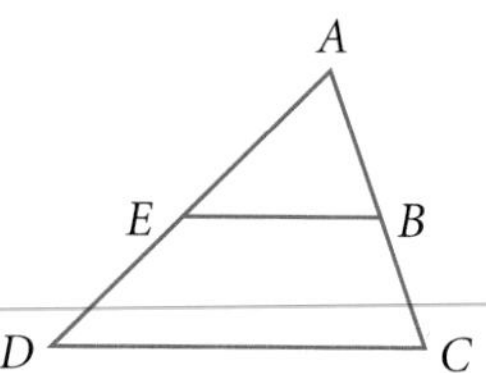

3. $AB = 10$, and $CD = 18$. Find AC, BC, and BE.

4. $m\angle AEB = 41°$, and $BE = 22.7$. Find $m\angle ADC$ and CD.

5. $DC = 17$, $CA = 17$, and $m\angle C = 71°$. Find $m\angle A$ and BE.

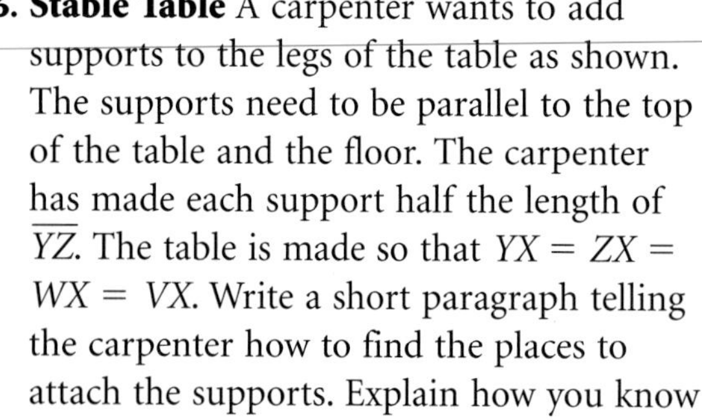

6. **Stable Table** A carpenter wants to add supports to the legs of the table as shown. The supports need to be parallel to the top of the table and the floor. The carpenter has made each support half the length of $\overline{YZ}$. The table is made so that $YX = ZX = WX = VX$. Write a short paragraph telling the carpenter how to find the places to attach the supports. Explain how you know your method works.

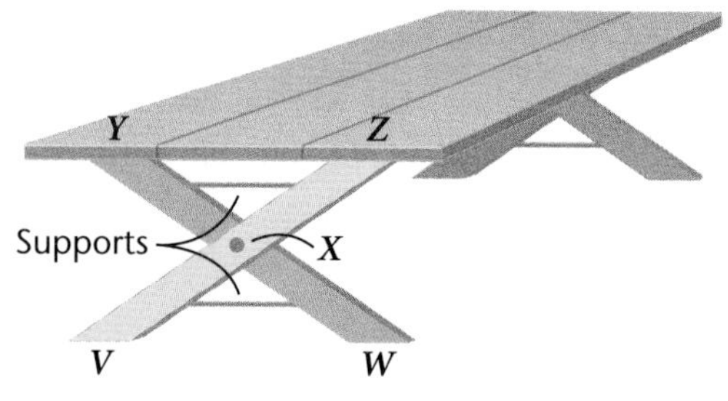

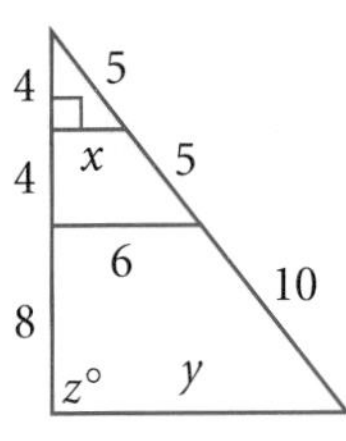

7. Solve for x, y, and z in the figure at the right.

8. Draw a triangle, $\triangle JKL$. Use a compass and straightedge to construct the midsegment of $\triangle JKL$ that intersects $\overline{JK}$ and $\overline{JL}$. Explain your construction.

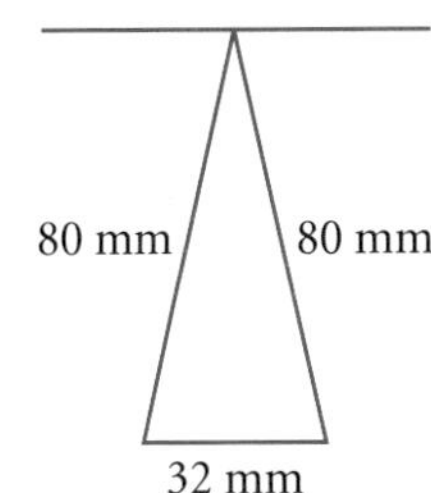

9. Art Training Kate is drawing a cartoon with railroad tracks disappearing into the distance as shown. To show perspective, she wants to add more ties (horizontal segments), with the first tie halfway to the horizon, the second tie half the remaining distance, and so on.

a. How long will the first tie be?

b. How long will the second tie be? Where should it be located?

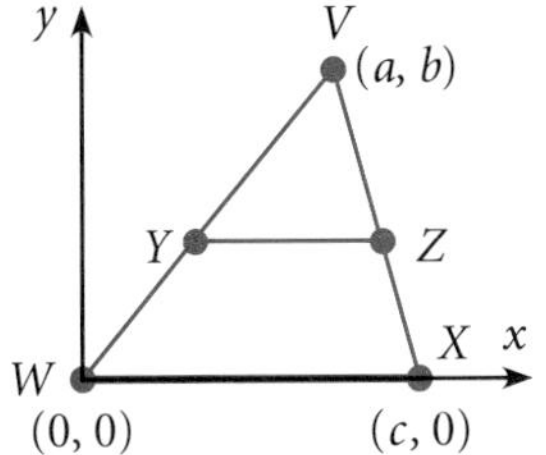

10. Prove the midsegment theorem using a coordinate proof.

Given: Y is the midpoint of $\overline{VW}$.
Z is the midpoint of $\overline{VX}$.

Prove: $\overline{YZ} \parallel \overline{WX}$
$YZ = \frac{1}{2}WX$

Before starting your proof, copy the figure at the right. Give the coordinates of Y and Z. (Hint: Use the Midpoint Formula.)

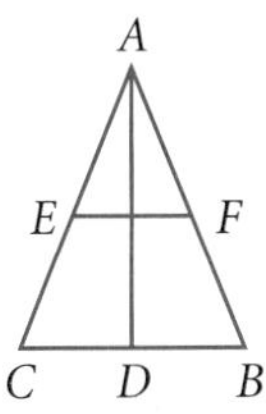

11. $\triangle ABC$ is isosceles, and $\overline{AD}$ is an altitude to base $\overline{BC}$. Does midsegment $\overline{EF}$ bisect $\overline{AD}$? Justify your answer.

LOOK AHEAD

12. Are all 45°-45°-90° triangles similar? Explain.

13. Are all 30°-60°-90° triangles similar? Explain.

14. Find each ratio.

a. the ratio of the length of a leg in a 45°-45°-90° triangle to the length of the hypotenuse

b. the ratio of the length of the shorter leg in a 30°-60°-90° triangle to the length of the hypotenuse

c. the ratio of the length of the longer leg in a 30°-60°-90° triangle to the length of the hypotenuse

d. Did any of your answers in **14a–c** depend on the size of the triangle?

MORE PRACTICE

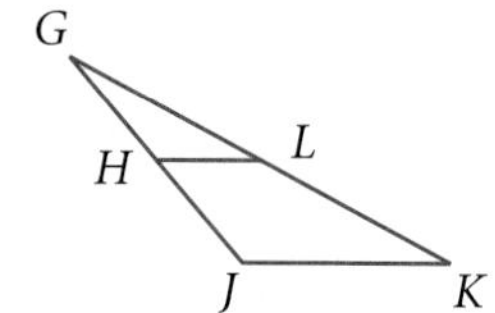

***H* is the midpoint of $\overline{GJ}$, and *L* is the midpoint of $\overline{GK}$.**

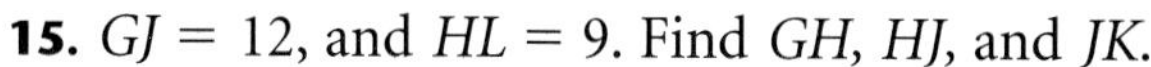

15. $GJ = 12$, and $HL = 9$. Find GH, HJ, and JK.

16. $m\angle GLH = 28°$, and $JK = 37.4$. Find $m\angle K$ and HL.

17. $GH = 7$, $HL = 7$, and $m\angle G = 21°$. Find $m\angle J$ and JK.

18. Solve for w, x, y, and z in the figure at the right.

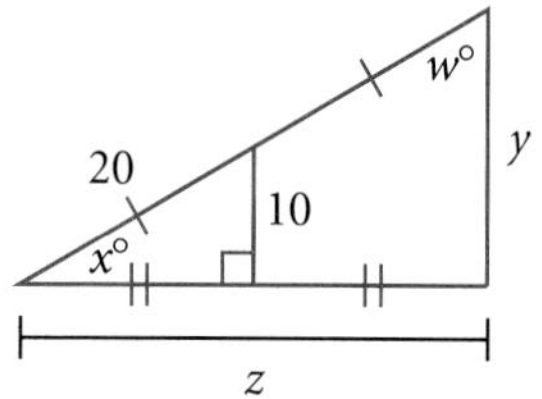

MORE MATH REASONING

Parallel lines can divide the sides of a triangle in a special way.

SIDE-SPLITTING THEOREM

If a line parallel to a side of a triangle intersects the other two sides, then it divides those sides proportionally.

19. Fill in the reasons to complete the proof of the Side-Splitting Theorem.

Given: $\overleftrightarrow{YZ} \parallel \overline{WX}$

Prove: $\frac{WY}{YV} = \frac{XZ}{ZV}$

Proof:

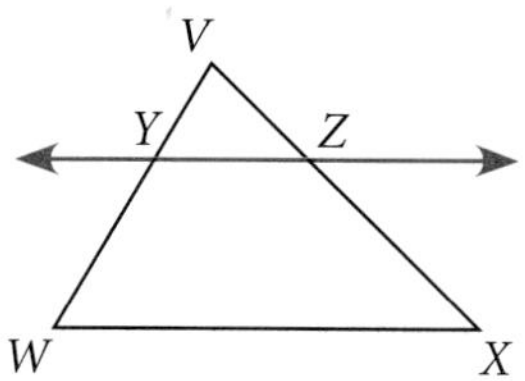

Statements	Reasons
1. $\overleftrightarrow{YZ} \parallel \overline{WX}$	**1.**
2. $\angle W \cong \angle VYZ$, and $\angle X \cong \angle VZY$.	**2.**
3. $\triangle WVX \sim \triangle YVZ$	**3.**
4. $\frac{WV}{YV} = \frac{XV}{ZV}$	**4.**
5. $WY + YV = WV$, and $XZ + ZV = XV$	**5.**
6. $\frac{WY + YV}{YV} = \frac{XZ + ZV}{ZV}$	**6.**
7. $\frac{WY}{YV} + \frac{YV}{YV} = \frac{XZ}{ZV} + \frac{ZV}{ZV}$	**7.** Algebra (Distributive Property)
8. $\frac{WY}{YV} = \frac{XZ}{ZV}$	**8.** Algebra (Addition Property of Equality)

Cross section $\triangle BCD$ of tetrahedron *AEFG* is parallel to the base.

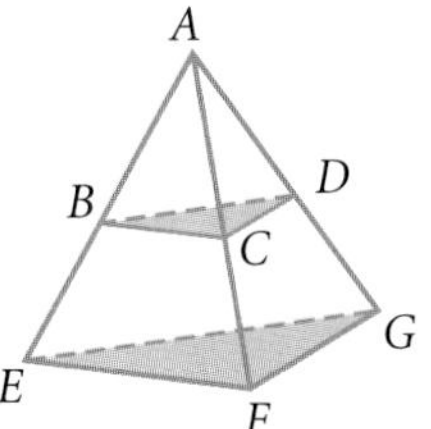

20. If $AB = 18$, $BE = 20$, and $AC = 15$, find AF.

21. If $AB = 10$, $BE = 14$, and $AG = 36$, find DG.

22. If $AB = 16$, $BE = 20$, and $BD = 22$, find EG.

23. Find the perimeter of $\triangle BCD$ if $AB = 14$, $AE = 35$, $EF = 27$, $FG = 21$, and $EG = 30$.

7-2 PART E Making Connections

← CONNECT → ***The characteristics of similar figures are important in architecture, computer-related design, and other industries. You've investigated ways to show that triangles are similar. You've also investigated dilations and seen how they are related to similarity.***

How can you find the height of a tall building like the Shimizu skyscraper described on page 485? In the following Explore, you will use similarity to measure some objects that are difficult to measure directly.

EXPLORE: THE HIP HYPSOMETER

MATERIALS

3 × 5 card, Scissors
Ruler or meter stick, Tape

To do this Explore, you will first need to construct a hypsometer. A hypsometer is used to measure an object or a distance by using similar triangles.

Take a 3 × 5 card, stand it on the 3-in. end, and cut a horizontal slit the width of a ruler from the bottom. Fold the card vertically as shown (the flap should make a right angle with the rest of the card). Use your ruler to mark off $\frac{1}{2}$-in. lengths along the edge of the fold (1-cm lengths if you are using a meter stick).

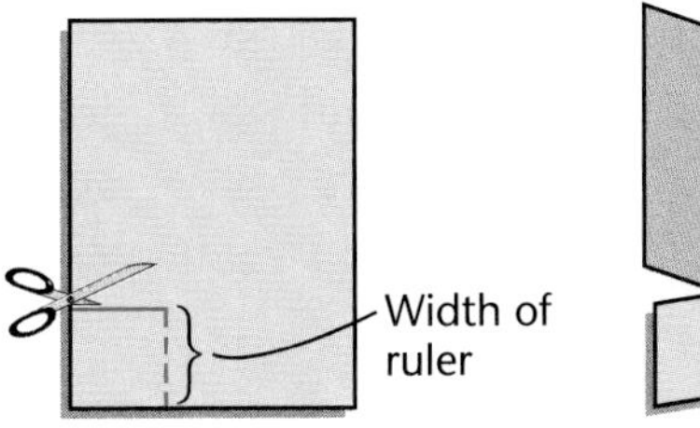

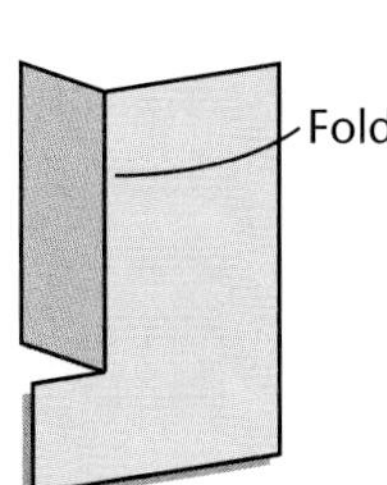

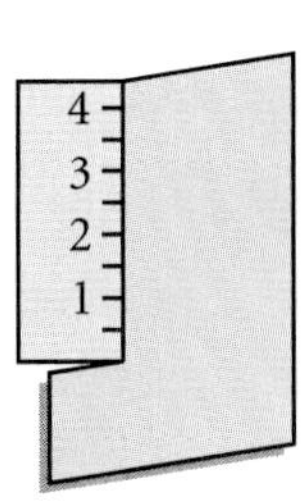

Tape the 3 × 5 card to the ruler as shown so that the fold is exactly at the 6-in. mark (or 50-cm mark if you are using a meter stick).

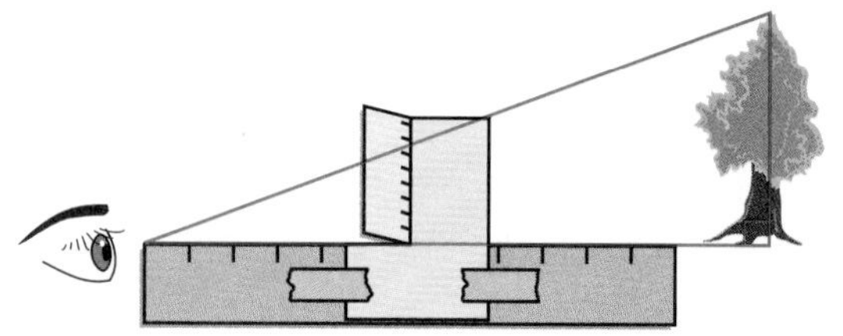

To use the hypsometer, hold it so that the bottom of the object is sighted along the ruler. Then read the length on the index card that corresponds to the top of the object. If you know the distance to the object, you can find its height and vice-versa.

1. Explain how the hypsometer works. What similar triangles does it use, and why are these triangles similar to each other?
2. Use the hypsometer to measure the height of your classroom. Record your readings, and sketch the similar triangles used to calculate the height. (Hint: Remember your own height when giving your final answer.)
3. If you can see a large object out of the window of your classroom, estimate how far you are from the object and calculate its height. You may need to break the object up into pieces, as shown. Record your readings, and sketch the similar triangles you used.
4. Compare your results with those of classmates. What might cause differences in your measurements?

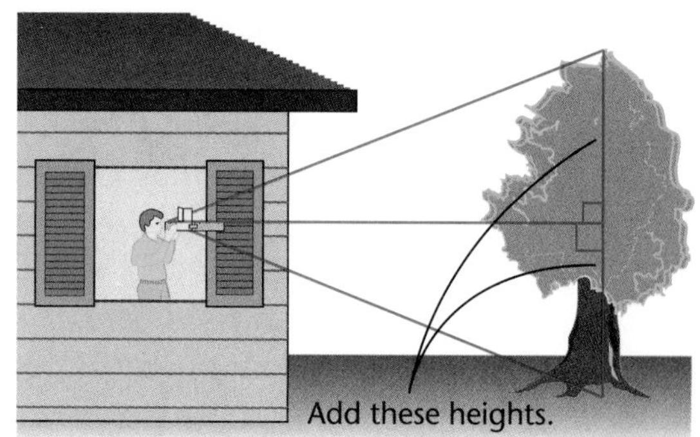

You will explore another device for indirect measurement in 7-3 Part D.

REFLECT

1. Using sketches, summarize the methods you know to show that two triangles are similar.
2. Explain how architects designing and building skyscrapers might use similarity concepts to help them in their planning.
3. What are the similarities and differences between dilations and the other transformations (reflections, rotations, and translations)?
4. Draw and label a figure to illustrate the Triangle Midsegment Theorem. Be sure to mark congruent angles and segments.

Self-Assessment

Find a value for x that makes the triangles similar. State the theorem or postulate that justifies your answer.

1.

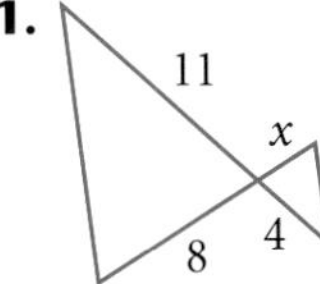

2.

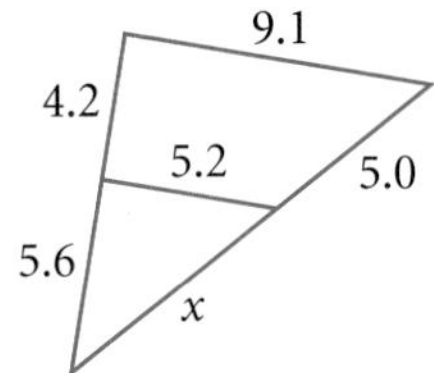

3.

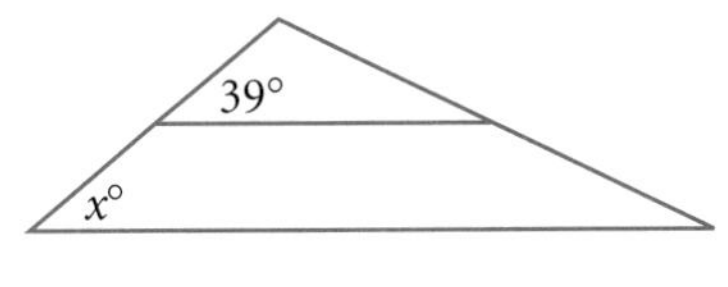

Give the similarity correspondence for each pair of triangles, and explain why the triangles are similar. Then solve for x and y.

4.

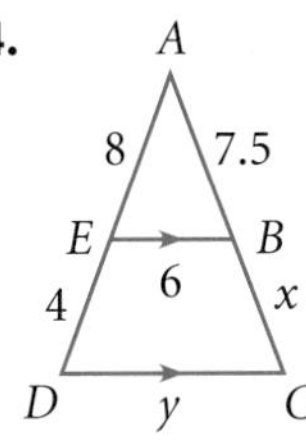

5.

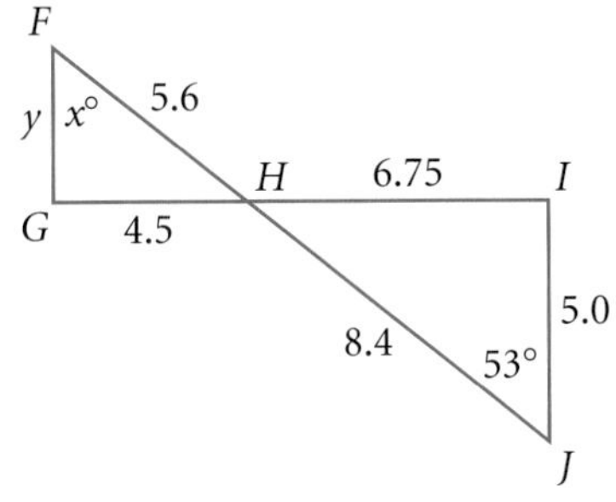

6.

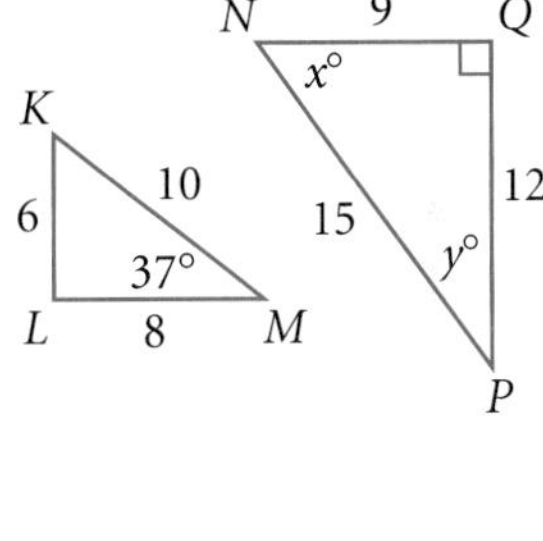

7. **Thinking Deeply** A hiker at the base of the Grand Canyon is curious about the actual depth of the canyon. She places a mirror on the ground and walks back until she sees the top of the canyon in the mirror. The hiker is 5′10″ tall, so she estimates that her eyes are 5.5 ft above the ground. The distance to the mirror, IJ, is 1 ft. If the distance from J to K is 841.8 ft, how deep is this part of the Grand Canyon?

Social Science

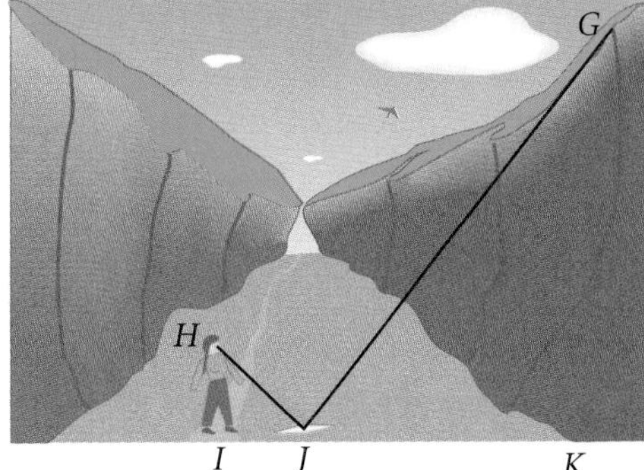

8. Use the figure at the right for the following.

Given: $\overline{TU}$ is a midsegment of $\triangle SVW$.

Prove: $\triangle STU \sim \triangle SVW$

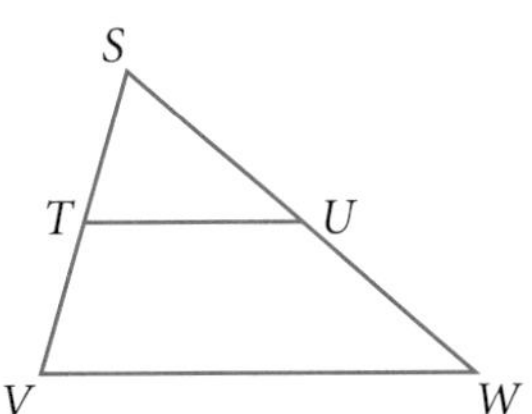

9. $\triangle XYZ$ is the image of $\triangle ABC$ under a dilation with scale factor 4. How is the area of $\triangle ABC$ related to the area of $\triangle XYZ$?

Find the values of x and y for each of the following quadrilaterals. Justify your answers. [6-2]

10.

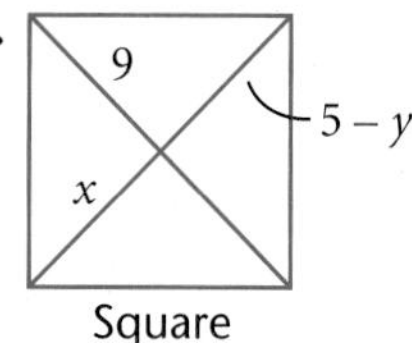

Square

11.

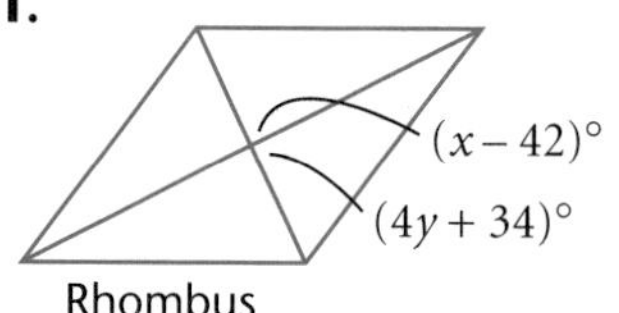

Rhombus

12.

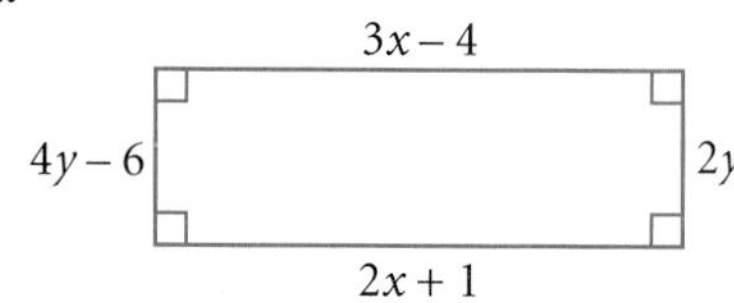

13. A Corny Problem Two cornfields have similar shapes, but the area of the larger one is twice the area of the smaller. [7-1]

a. Suppose the larger field produces b bushels of corn. How many bushels of corn would you expect the smaller one to produce? Explain your reasoning.

b. Suppose it costs f dollars to put a fence around the smaller cornfield. About how much would it cost to fence the larger one? Explain your reasoning.

Use the figure at the right for the following. Copy $\triangle RST$ on graph paper. Then draw each dilation image using the given scale factor and center. Also, give the ratios of the perimeters and the areas of the pre-images to the images.

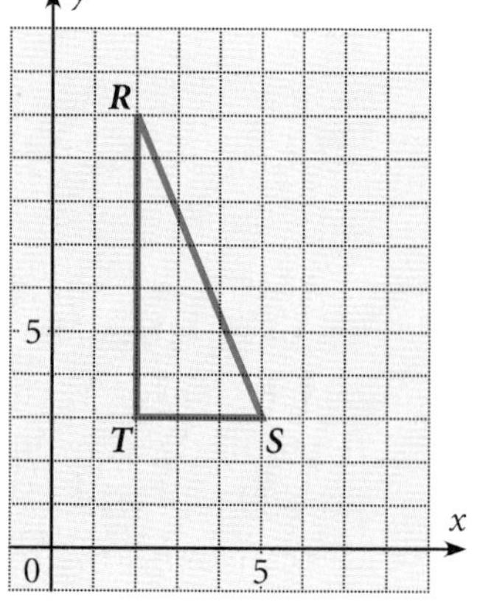

14. scale factor 2, center O

15. scale factor $\frac{2}{3}$, center T

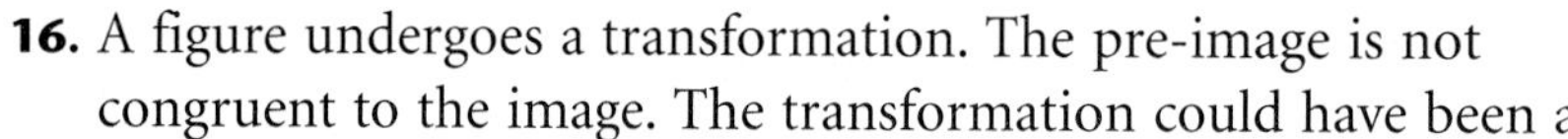

16. A figure undergoes a transformation. The pre-image is not congruent to the image. The transformation could have been a

(a) dilation (b) reflection
(c) rotation (d) translation

17. Write a brief paragraph to explain in your own words how dilations and similarity are related.

18. What are the coordinates of the dilation image of any point (x, y) under a dilation with center (a, b) and scale factor k?

19. You are designing tools for astronauts to use on a trip to an unexplored planet. Because of the planet's high atmospheric pressure, the space suits will need to be so rigid that the astronauts cannot bend over to measure small objects. You claim that you can design something that will allow them to do this using just two metal rods fastened at a pivot point and a ruler fastened to one of the handles. Draw a sketch of the tool, and give written instructions to the astronauts describing its use.

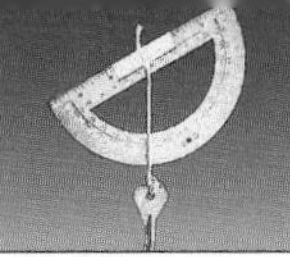

7-3 Trigonometry

From Stars to City Planning

In the early days of the United States, an African-American named Benjamin Banneker was a well known mathematician and astronomer. Banneker played an important part in planning Washington, D.C., in 1790–1791. As the astronomer for the surveying team, Banneker helped determine the borders of the District of Columbia. When the head of the planning committee suddenly resigned, taking the plans with him, it is said that Banneker reproduced the entire city plan from memory.

The Banneker U.S. Postal Service stamp.

The almanacs published by Banneker from 1792–1804 are his greatest scientific achievement. Using borrowed astronomy books and instruments, Banneker taught himself how to calculate the positions of the planets and predict the dates of lunar and solar eclipses. His almanacs gave the rising and setting times of the sun and moon and the positions of the planets for each day of the year. The almanacs were distributed

internationally by the anti-slavery movement and Banneker's achievements were described as, "proof that the powers of the mind are disconnected with the colour of the skin."

1. **Banneker taught himself astronomy. Describe how you can learn about a subject on your own.**
2. **Some of the streets of Washington, D.C., go out from a center point like spokes of a wheel rather than running north-south or east-west. Why do you think the city planners did this? What do you think might be located at the major "hubs"?**

7-3 PART A Trigonometric Ratios

← CONNECT → ***You've seen that similar triangles have proportional side lengths. Now you will investigate these ratios in right triangles and see how to use them to find unknown side lengths.***

The study of the special relationships between the angle measures and side lengths of right triangles is **trigonometry** (Greek for "triangle measuring"). All of the similarity properties for triangles apply to right triangles. In fact, with right triangles you can shortcut the shortcuts.

The two triangles below are similar. Therefore, their side lengths are proportional; for example, $\frac{AB}{DE} = \frac{BC}{EF}$.

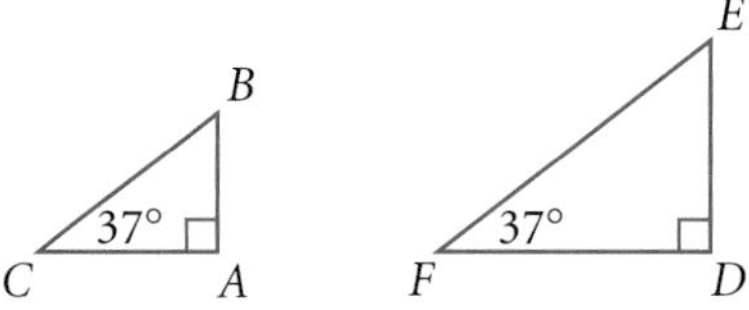

By applying algebra, we see that $\frac{AB}{BC} = \frac{DE}{EF}$; that is, the ratio of the length of the leg opposite the 37° angle to the length of the hypotenuse is the same in both triangles. No matter what size a right triangle with this acute angle measure is, the ratios of its side lengths are always the same. The trigonometry ratios you'll use are based on this fact.

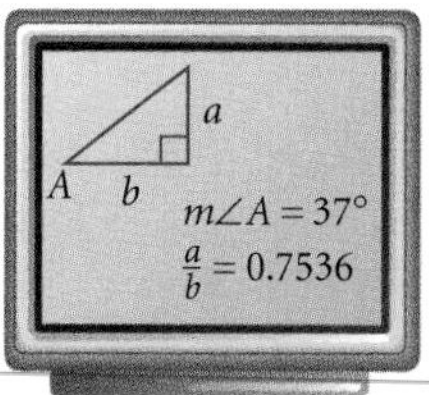

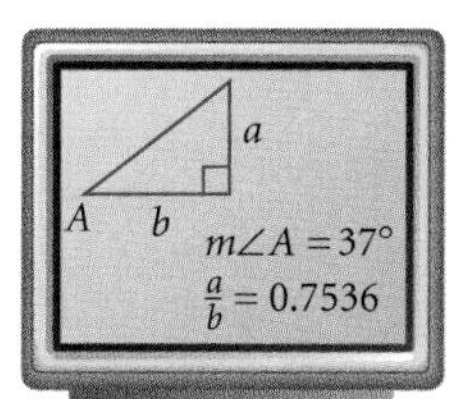

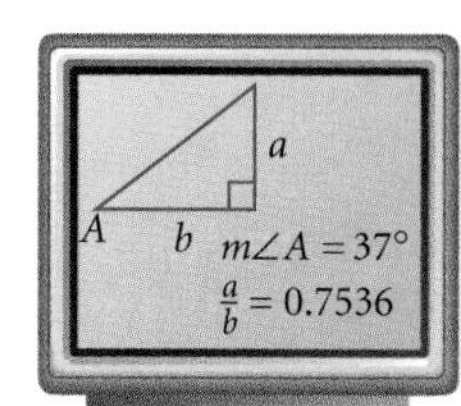

Trigonometric ratios are ratios of side lengths in right triangles. You've probably worked with the sine, cosine, and tangent ratios before.

B

Hypotenuse c

Opposite leg for ∠A a

A b C

Adjacent leg for ∠A

sine of $\angle A = \frac{\text{length of leg opposite } \angle A}{\text{length of hypotenuse}} = \frac{BC}{AB} = \frac{a}{c}$

cosine of $\angle A = \frac{\text{length of leg adjacent to } \angle A}{\text{length of hypotenuse}} = \frac{AC}{AB} = \frac{b}{c}$

tangent of $\angle A = \frac{\text{length of leg opposite } \angle A}{\text{length of leg adjacent to } \angle A} = \frac{BC}{AC} = \frac{a}{b}$

The ratios and their definitions are often abbreviated as follows.

$$\sin A = \frac{\text{opposite}}{\text{hypotenuse}} = \frac{a}{c}$$

$$\cos A = \frac{\text{adjacent}}{\text{hypotenuse}} = \frac{b}{c}$$

$$\tan A = \frac{\text{opposite}}{\text{adjacent}} = \frac{a}{b}$$

TRY IT

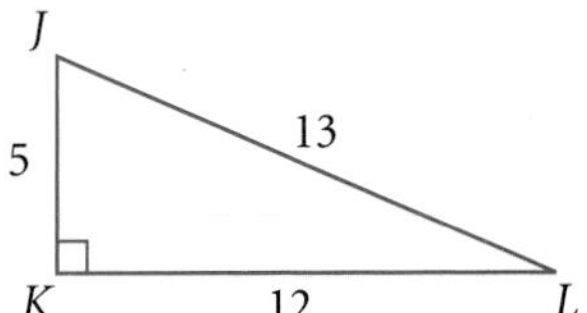

Express each trigonometric ratio as a fraction.

a. sin L **b.** sin J

c. cos L **d.** tan J

You can use a scientific calculator to find the value of a trigonometric ratio for an angle. To find the cosine of 58°, first make sure that the calculator is in "degree mode." Then enter the keystrokes shown.

EXAMPLE

Find the values of x and y.

To find x, use the definition of *cosine.*

Cos $42° = \frac{x}{15}$; therefore, $x = 15 \cos 42°$.

Enter 15 [×] 42 [COS] [=] to get $11.14717238 \approx 11.15$.

To find y, use the definition of *sine.*

Sin $42° = \frac{y}{15}$, so $y = 15 \sin 42° \approx 10.04$.

(You can also find y using the Pythagorean Theorem, since you know the length of the hypotenuse and x.)

Trigonometric ratios are useful for solving problems involving side lengths of right triangles.

EXPLORE: CLIMBING TO NEW HEIGHTS

House painters know that if you lean a ladder against a wall so that the angle it makes with the ground is too small, you risk having the bottom of the ladder slide out from under you. If the angle of the ladder is too great, the ladder may tip over backwards.

Suppose that the safe range of angles for a ladder is between 50° and 75°. Find the heights of the lowest and highest windows you can safely reach with a 20-ft ladder.

REFLECT

1. Daniel said, "If I know the measure of one side and one acute angle in a right triangle, I can find the measures of every other side and angle." Is he right? If so, explain how this can be done. If not, explain why not.
2. Is there an angle whose sine and cosine are equal? If so, what is it, and why are these ratios equal?
3. Which of the three ratios, sin A, cos A, or tan A, is equal to the slope of line m? Explain your answer.

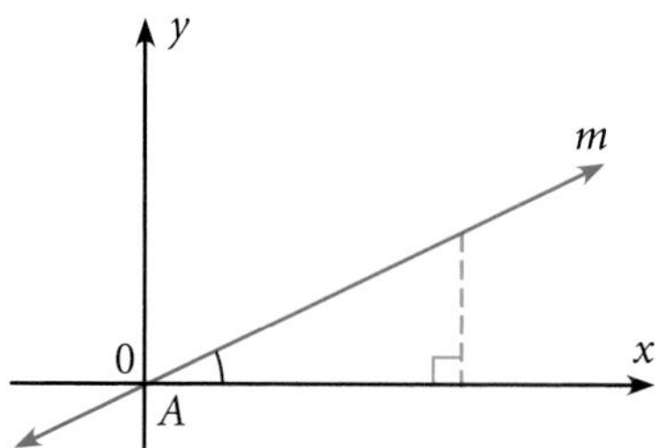

Exercises

CORE

1. **Getting Started** Follow these steps to solve for a in the right triangle.
   a. Which acute angle measure do you know?
   b. Which trigonometric ratio should you use? (Hint: Which side length do you know? Which side length do you need?)
   c. Use the definition of the trigonometric ratio you identified in **1b** to write an equation.
   d. Solve the equation for a.

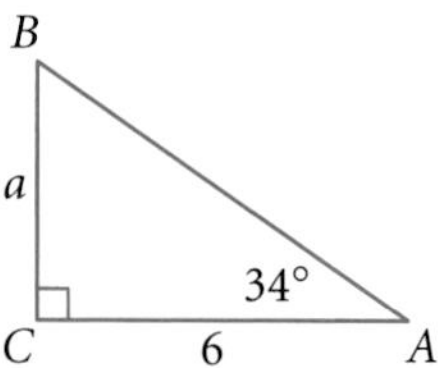

Express each trigonometric ratio as a fraction and as a decimal rounded to the hundredths place.

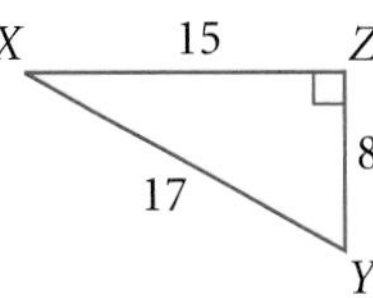

2. $\sin X$ **3.** $\cos X$ **4.** $\tan X$

5. $\sin Y$ **6.** $\cos Y$ **7.** $\tan Y$

Write the word or phrase that correctly completes each statement.

8. The ____ of an angle is the ratio of the length of the adjacent leg to the length of the hypotenuse.

9. The ____ of an angle is the ratio of the length of the opposite leg to the length of the hypotenuse.

Find the sine, cosine, and tangent of each angle. Round your answers to the nearest hundredth.

10. 8° **11.** 72° **12.** 25°

Find *x* and *y*.

13.

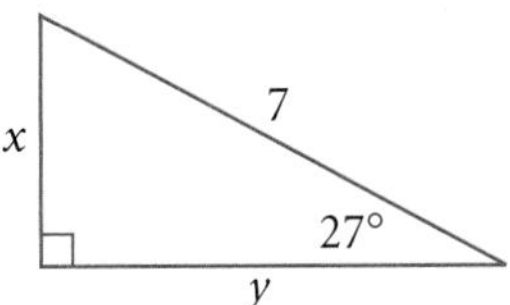

14.

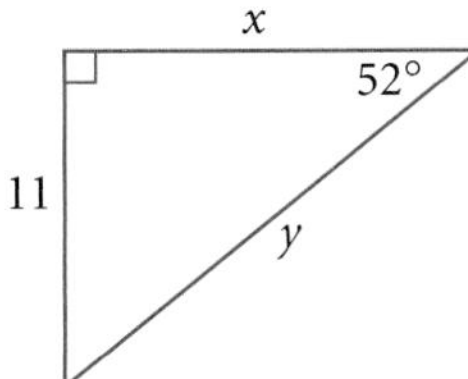

15.

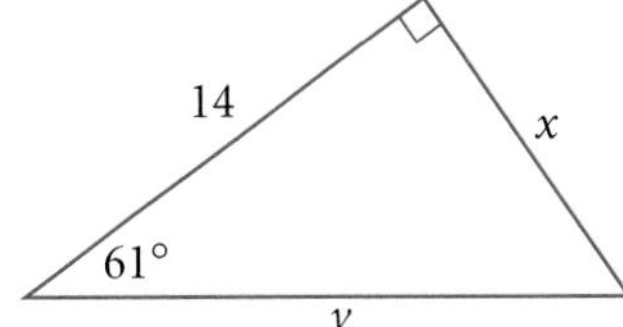

16. Pet Trig A firefighter is rescuing a cat in a tree. If the branch that the cat is on is fifteen feet above the ground and the ladder makes an angle of sixty-three degrees with the ground, how long is the ladder? Briefly describe the steps you used to solve this problem.

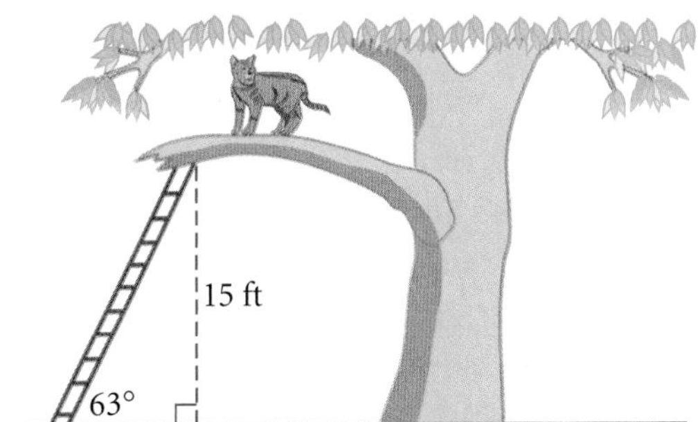

17. Cable Television A cable is used to support a 245-m television tower.

a. If the angle the cable makes with the ground is 78°, how long is the cable?

b. If the tower represents the y-axis of the coordinate plane and this part of the earth's surface represents the x-axis, what is the equation for the cable?

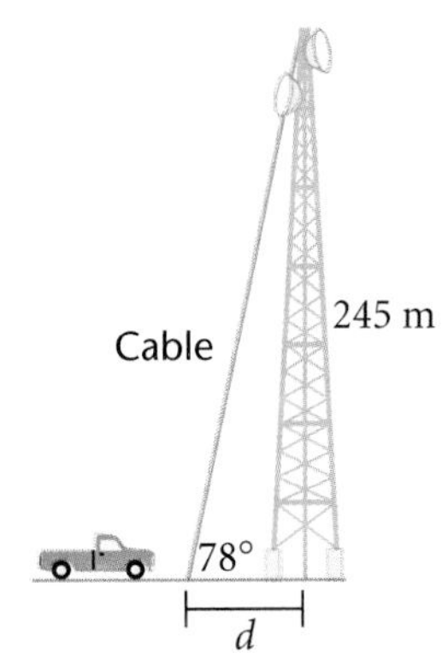

18. A surveyor needs to find out how far away she is from a 3000-ft cliff. If the angle shown is 22°, how far is she from the cliff?

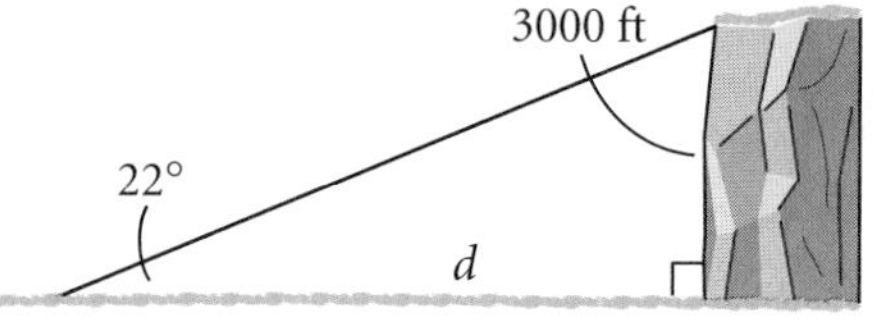

19. The boundaries of Washington, D.C., were intended to be 10 miles square. The accuracy of the measurements made by Benjamin Banneker's team were remarkable (the percent error for each side length is half of 1% or less), but exact measurements of long distances on the earth's curved surface were nearly impossible in 1790. The lengths of two of the sides of the "square" are shown.

History

a. Assuming $\angle A$ is a right angle, what is the tangent of $\angle ABD$ to the nearest thousandth?

b. If Washington, D.C., were a perfect square, what would you expect the measure of $\angle ABD$ to be? What would you expect its tangent to be?

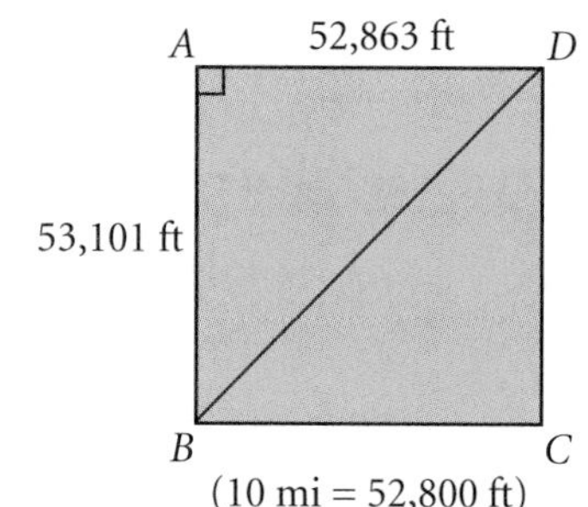

20. **Towering Tilt** The Leaning Tower of Pisa is 179 ft tall. It makes an angle of approximately 85° with the ground. About how far over does the tower lean?

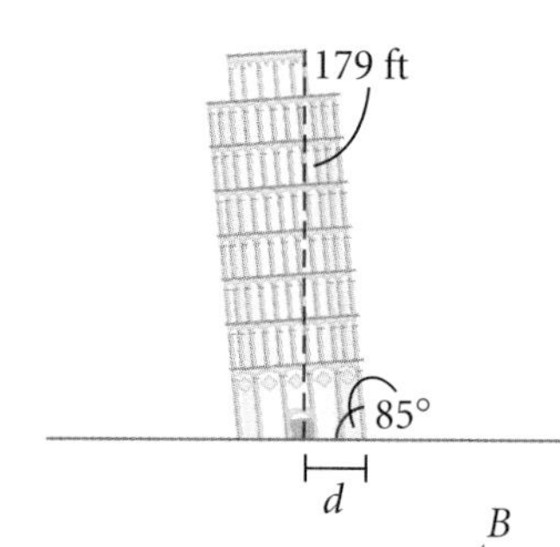

21. Use your calculator to find the sine of angle A and the cosine of the complement of the angle. Repeat, using angle B. What do you notice? Make a conjecture. Explain why your conjecture makes sense.

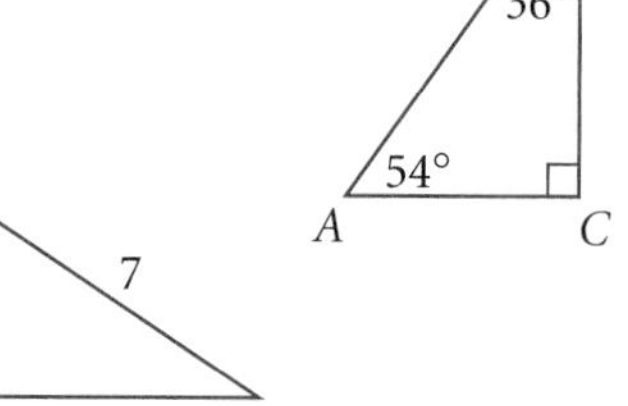

22. Explain what is wrong with the following.

$\tan M = \frac{7}{10}$

23. Only one of the three trigonometric ratios you have studied can have a value larger than 1. Identify the ratio, and explain why the values of the other two can never be greater than 1.

LOOK BACK

24. Sketch a regular tetrahedron. Find the number of vertices, edges, and faces of the tetrahedron. Finally, sketch a net of the tetrahedron. [6-3]

25. In $\triangle STV$, $\overline{TW}$ is an altitude. Prove $\triangle STV \sim \triangle TWV$. [7-2]

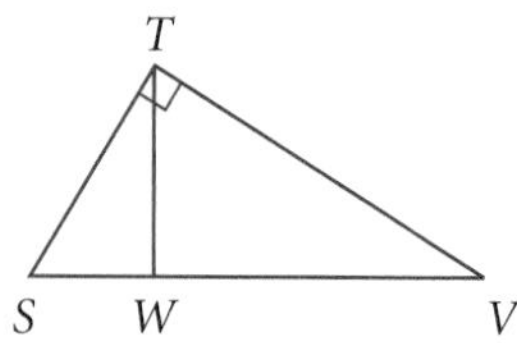

MORE PRACTICE

Express each trigonometric ratio as a fraction and as a decimal rounded to the hundredths place.

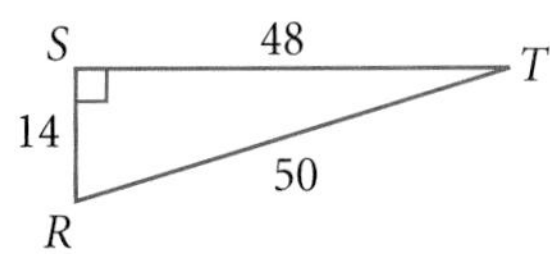

26. sin T

27. tan R

28. cos T

Find the sine, cosine, and tangent of each angle. Round your answers to the nearest hundredth.

29. 18°

30. 59°

31. 89°

Find x and y.

32.

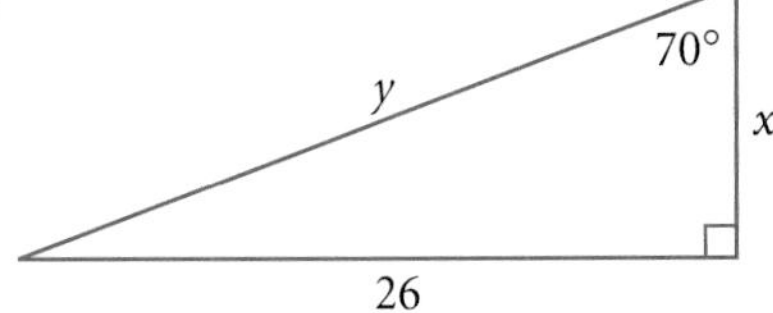

33.

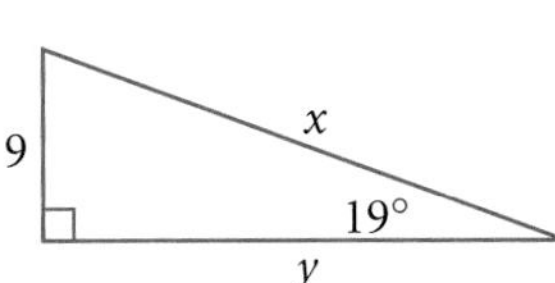

34.

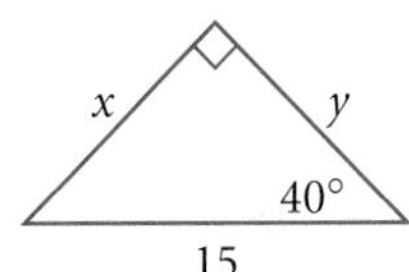

35. Kite Height A kite string is 100 m long. Find the height of the kite if the string makes an angle of 38° with the ground. (Assume the kite string does not sag.)

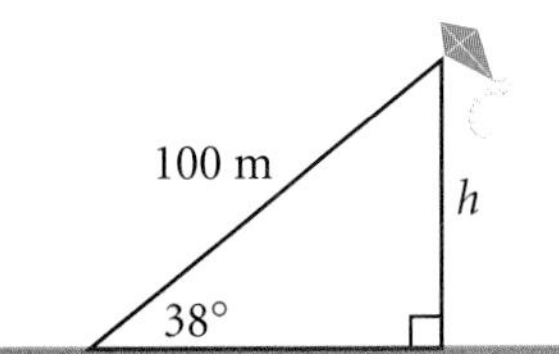

MORE MATH REASONING

36. It is often helpful to know the exact values of the trigonometric ratios for 30°, 45°, and 60° angles. Use what you know about the side lengths of special right triangles to prepare a table showing the sine, cosine, and tangent of 30°, 45°, and 60° angles. Express your results in simplified radical form.

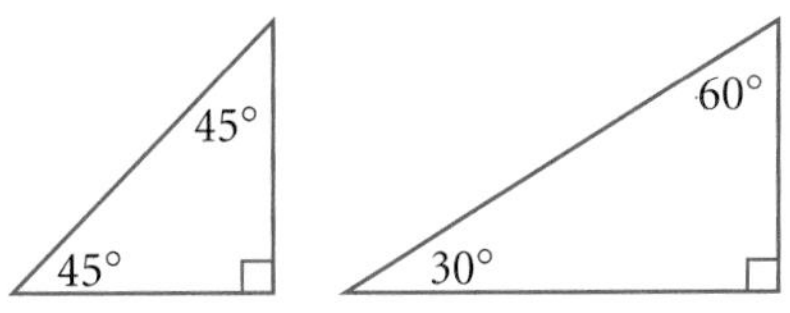

37. Find x in each of the following.

a. $x = (\sin 30°)^2 + (\cos 30°)^2$

b. $x = (\sin 60°)^2 + (\cos 60°)^2$

c. $x = (\sin 45°)^2 + (\cos 45°)^2$

d. Make a conjecture about $(\sin A)^2 + (\cos A)^2$.

Science

38. Face Reality The area of a square base of an Egyptian pyramid is 52,900 m^2. The faces of the pyramid make an angle of about 52° with the base. What is the shortest distance you would have to climb up a face to reach the top?

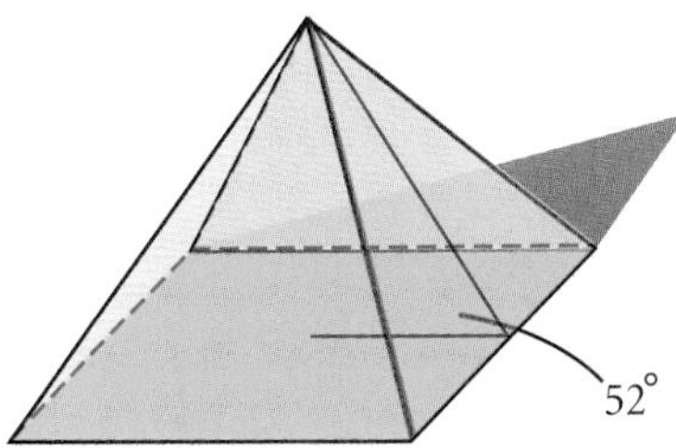

7-3 PART B Angles of Elevation and Depression

← CONNECT → ***Now that you know how to use the trigonometric ratios to find side lengths in right triangles, you will use those ratios to find the measures of angles.***

We use special terminology to describe angles in some situations. As shown, an **angle of elevation** and an **angle of depression** are formed by the line of sight and a horizontal line. The vertex of such an angle is the eye of the person looking at the object.

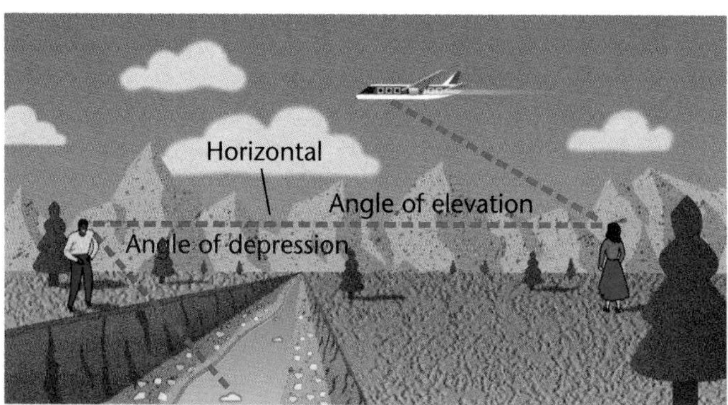

TRY IT

A person standing on a cliff looks up to see a hot air balloon and then looks down to see a sailboat.

a. Find the angle of elevation to the balloon.

b. Find the angle of depression to the sailboat.

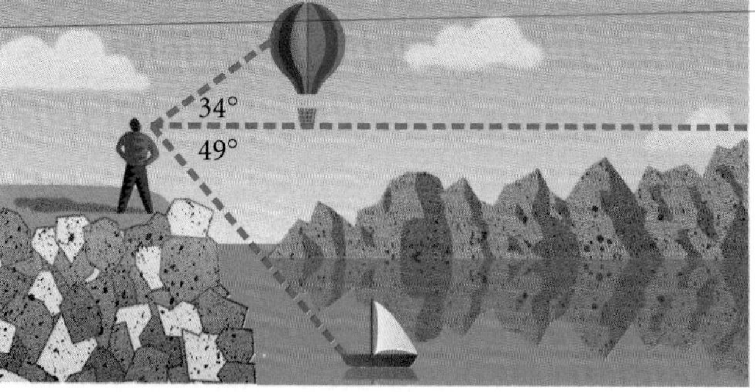

Sometimes you can use the angle of depression to find the angle of elevation or vice-versa.

EXAMPLE

An observer in an airplane at a height of 500 m sees a car at an angle of depression of 31°. If the plane is over a barn, how far is the car from the barn?

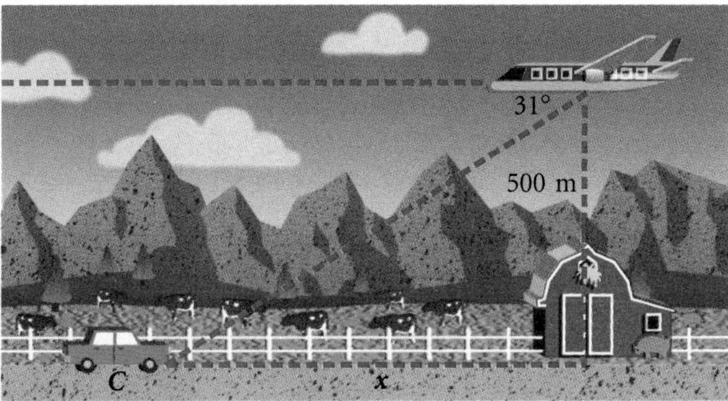

Alternate interior angles are congruent, so $m\angle C = 31°$. Therefore, $\tan 31° = \frac{500}{x}$, and $x = \frac{500}{\tan 31°} \approx 832.1$ m.

In the following Explore, you will find a way to use your calculator to solve for unknown angle measures.

EXPLORE: AN ANGLE IN THE SKY

A ground observer, 5 km from the space shuttle launch pad, watches the shuttle climb into the sky. The space shuttle's instruments report that it is 2 km above the ground. What is the shuttle's angle of elevation from the observer at that moment?

1. Draw a sketch of the problem. Write an equation in which one side length is the ratio of the two known distances and the other is a trigonometric ratio of the angle of elevation. Find the value of that ratio in decimal form.
2. Use your calculator to find the angle of elevation. (You may need to experiment with different keys on your calculator!) Write a brief explanation of how you used your calculator to solve for the angle. Compare results and methods with classmates.

TRY IT

c. Solve for $m\angle 1$ and $m\angle 2$ to the nearest degree.

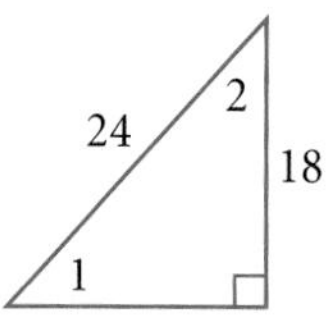

Problem-Solving Tip

Check to make sure that your answer makes sense.

REFLECT

1. What happens to the angle of elevation to the top of a flagpole as you move farther away from its base? Explain.
2. What is the difference between the two equations below? How can you use your calculator to solve each of them?

$\sin A = \frac{87}{100}$ $\qquad\qquad$ $\sin 87° = \frac{x}{10}$

Exercises

CORE

1. **Getting Started** From a scenic overlook, you can look up to see the top of a mountain and down to see a bridge on a river.
   a. Find the angle of elevation to the top of the mountain.
   b. If you know the height of the overlook, h, as well as the horizontal distance d to the bridge, what trigonometric ratio can you use to find the angle of depression?

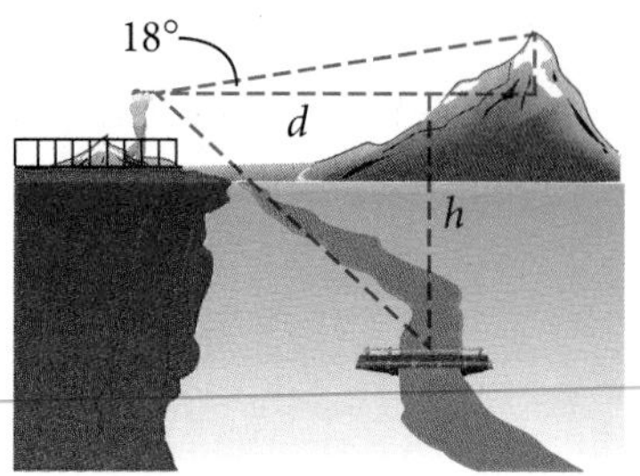

2. What forms the two sides of any angle of elevation or depression? Where is the vertex of the angle?

Find the measure of $\angle L$.

3. $\sin L = 0.6691$ 4. $\cos L = 0.2588$ 5. $\tan L = 1.2799$ 6. $\tan L = 1$

Solve for each indicated angle measure.

7. 4.4, 8.3, $x°$

8. 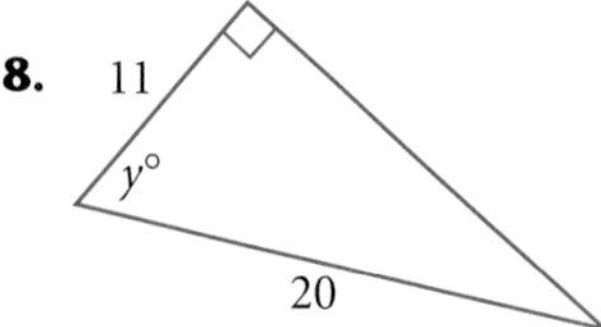

9. 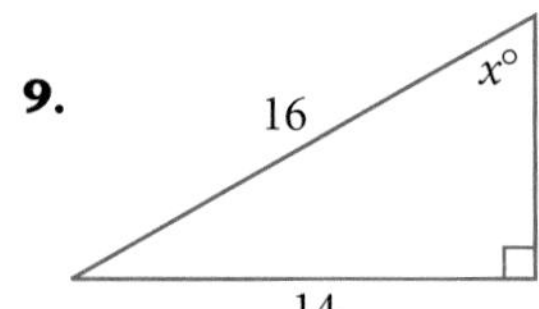

10. From a point 340 m from the base of Hoover Dam, the angle of elevation to the top of the dam is 33°. Find the height of the dam to the nearest meter.

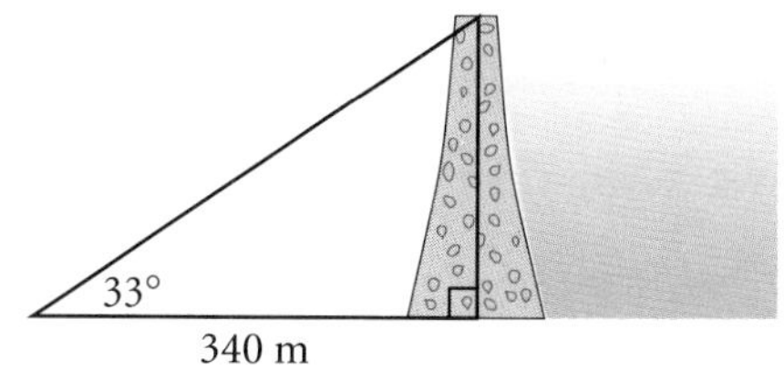

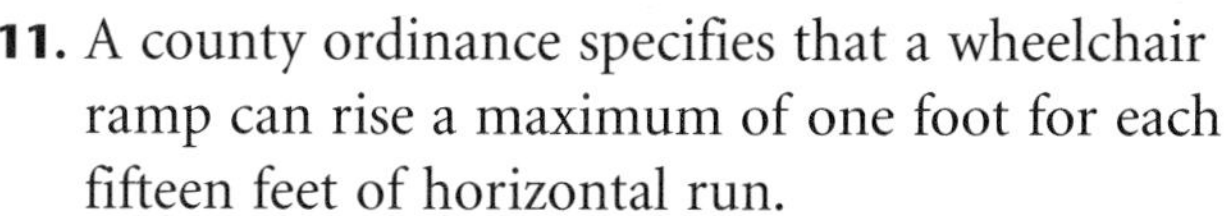

11. A county ordinance specifies that a wheelchair ramp can rise a maximum of one foot for each fifteen feet of horizontal run.

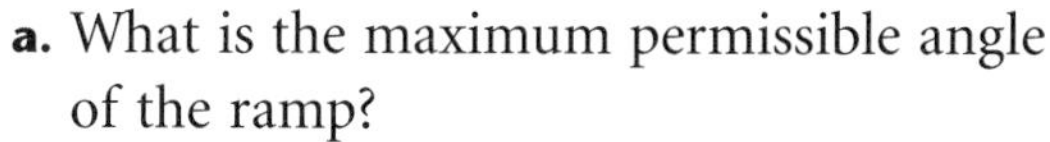

a. What is the maximum permissible angle of the ramp?

b. Write a short paragraph explaining why specifications like this are needed.

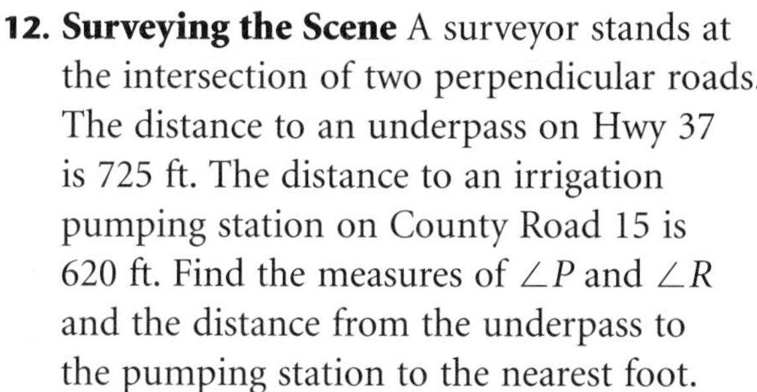

12. Surveying the Scene A surveyor stands at the intersection of two perpendicular roads. The distance to an underpass on Hwy 37 is 725 ft. The distance to an irrigation pumping station on County Road 15 is 620 ft. Find the measures of $\angle P$ and $\angle R$ and the distance from the underpass to the pumping station to the nearest foot.

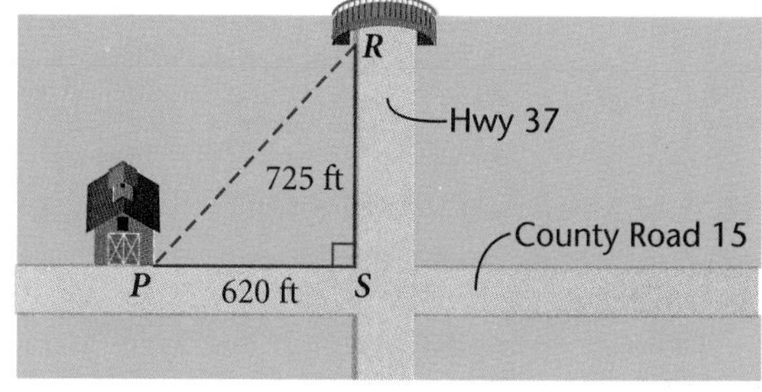

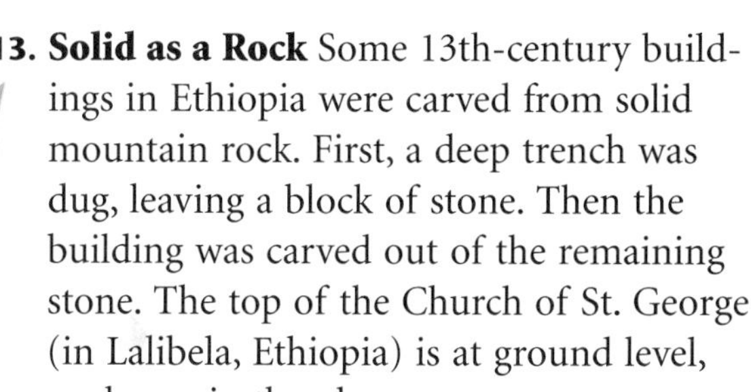

History

13. Solid as a Rock Some 13th-century buildings in Ethiopia were carved from solid mountain rock. First, a deep trench was dug, leaving a block of stone. Then the building was carved out of the remaining stone. The top of the Church of St. George (in Lalibela, Ethiopia) is at ground level, as shown in the photo.

Suppose an observer is at ground level. His eyes are 5.5 ft above the ground, and his horizontal distance from the church is 25 ft. If the angle of depression to the base of the church is 61.2°, how tall is the church?

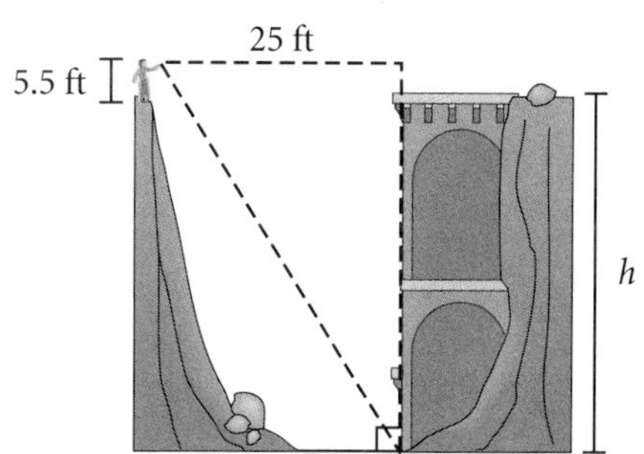

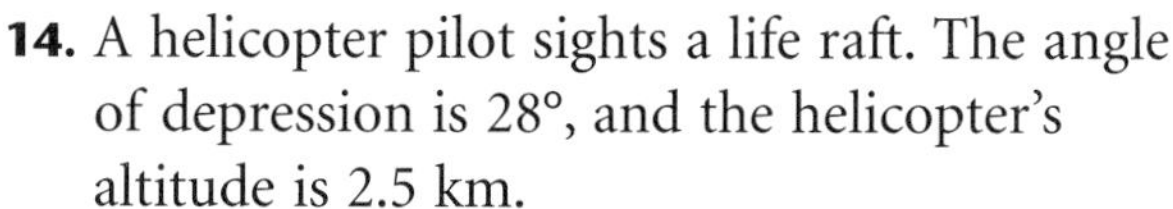

14. A helicopter pilot sights a life raft. The angle of depression is 28°, and the helicopter's altitude is 2.5 km.

a. Draw a figure to represent the situation.

b. What is the horizontal distance from the helicopter to the raft?

c. If the helicopter flies at a constant speed of 200 km/hr, how long will it be before it is directly above the raft? Assume that the altitude of the helicopter does not change.

LOOK AHEAD

15. Write the names for the vectors shown below. Use a ruler and protractor to find their directions and lengths.

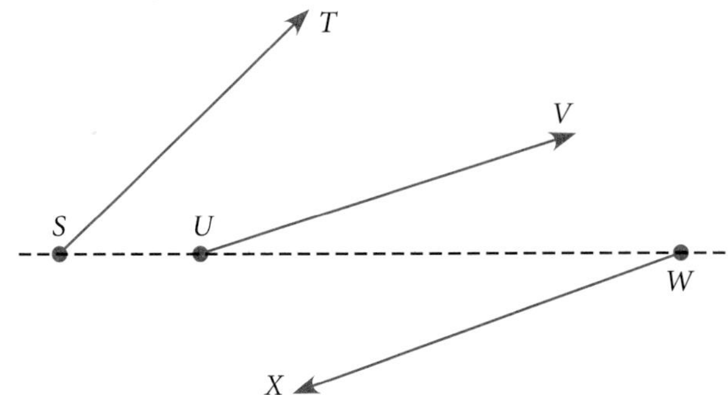

16. Use a ruler and protractor to draw a vector model of the following situation. Use a scale of 3 cm to 1 km.

Rina bicycled from her house (H) two kilometers east to the shopping mall (M). After doing some shopping, she rode three kilometers south to a restaurant (R). She then bicycled home.

a. Write Rina's ride as a sum of vectors.

b. Find the length of $\overrightarrow{RH}$. Explain how you found this length.

MORE PRACTICE

Find the measure of ∠*W*.

17. $\tan W = 0.0349$ **18.** $\sin W = \frac{1}{2}$ **19.** $\cos W = 0.4695$

Solve for each indicated angle measure.

20.

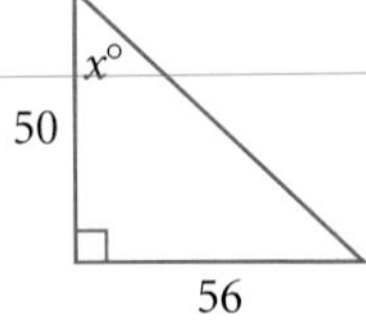

21.

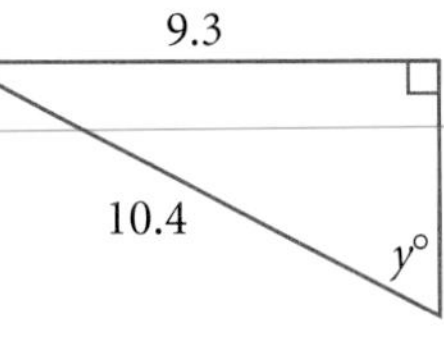

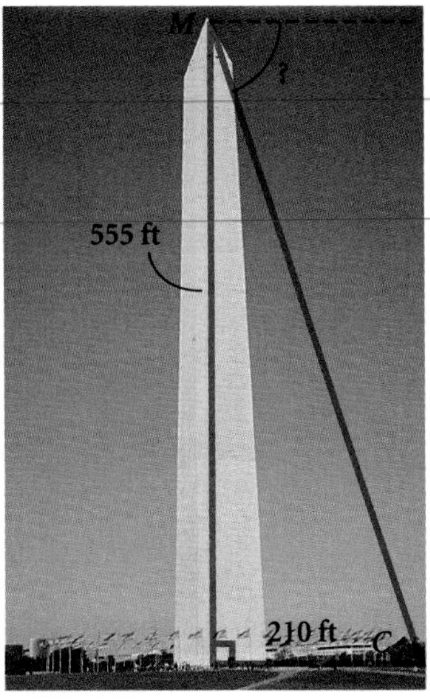

22. On a tour of Washington, D.C., Martha goes to the top of the 555-ft-tall Washington Monument. She spots her friend Chris 210 ft from the base of the monument. Find the angle of depression shown to the nearest degree. Then find the line-of-sight distance MC.

MORE MATH REASONING

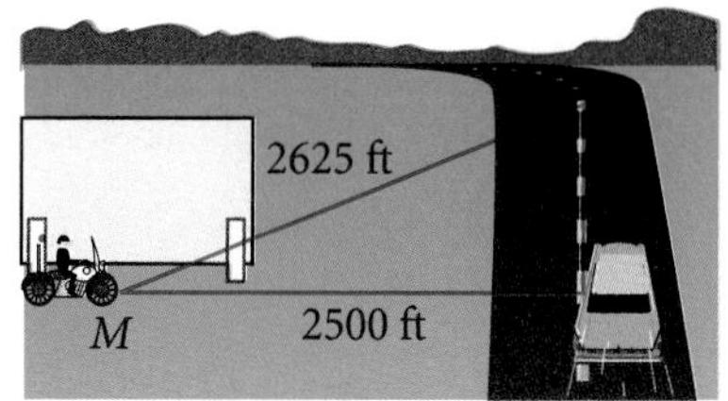

23. **Speed Trap** A car is passing by a police motorcyclist. At its closest point, it is 2500 ft from the motorcycle. Ten seconds later, the car is 2625 ft away.
    a. What is the measure of $\angle M$?
    b. How far did the car travel along the highway during this time?
    c. If the speed limit is 55 mi/hr, is the car speeding?

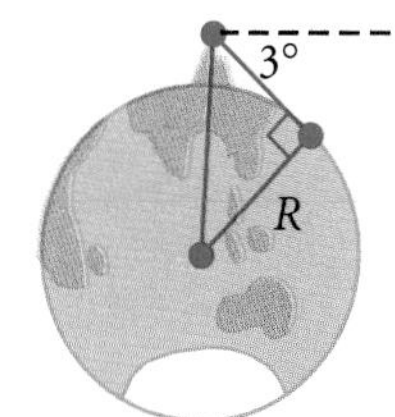

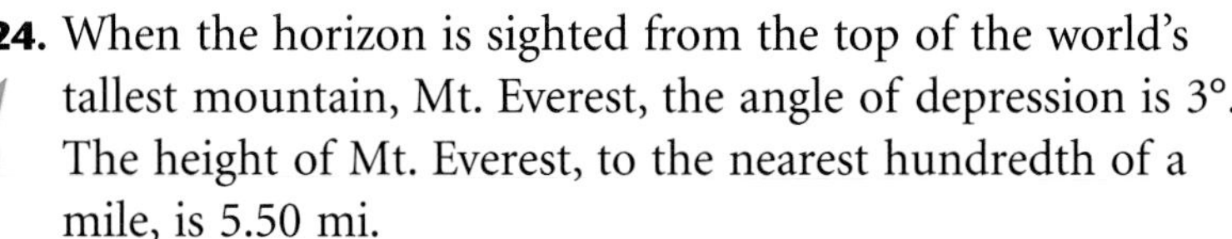

24. When the horizon is sighted from the top of the world's tallest mountain, Mt. Everest, the angle of depression is 3°. The height of Mt. Everest, to the nearest hundredth of a mile, is 5.50 mi.
    a. How can you use this information to find the distance, R, from the center of the earth to the earth's surface? Find R.
    b. Investigate how an error in measuring the angle of depression or the height of the mountain might affect the value of R. Explain your findings.

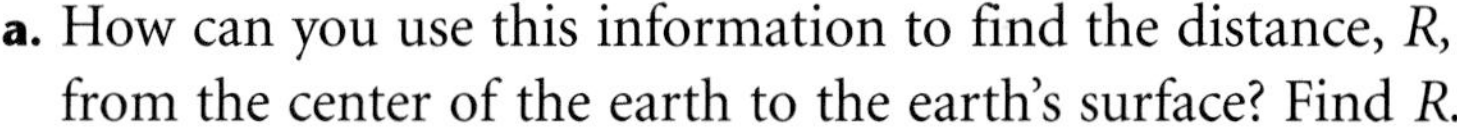

7-3 PART C Vectors and Trigonometry

← CONNECT → ***You are already familiar with vectors and vector addition. Now you will use trigonometric ratios to find the direction and length of the sum of two perpendicular vectors.***

Vectors have both a length and a direction. This makes them ideal for modeling forces and velocities. You need to know both the size and the direction of a force or velocity to completely understand what is happening—driving north at 30 mi/hr gets you to a very different place than driving south at the same speed!

1. Why do you think vectors are used to represent things like forces and velocities but not things like lengths and areas?

The velocity of a car traveling west at 50 mi/hr can be represented by a vector whose length is 50 and whose direction is 180°.

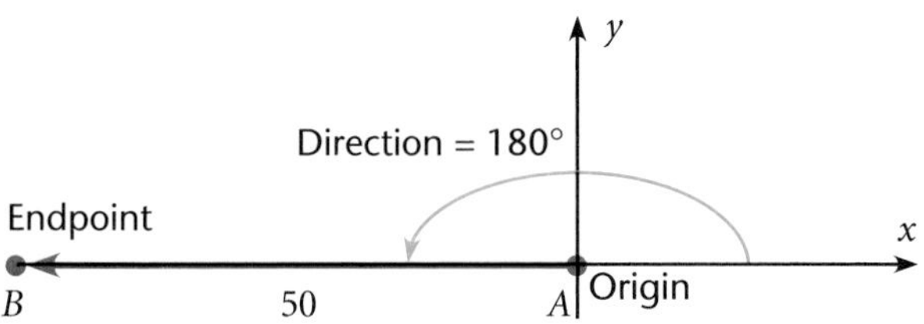

EXAMPLE

Find the direction and length of $\overrightarrow{MN}$.

Length $= \sqrt{(7-0)^2 + (3-0)^2} = \sqrt{58}$

We can use trigonometry to find the direction of $\overrightarrow{MN}$. By drawing the triangle shown, $\tan \angle LMN = \frac{3}{7} \approx 0.4286$. To find the angle when we know the value of its tangent, use the inverse tangent keys on your calculator. This gives a result of 23.19. . . °. Therefore, $m\angle LMN \approx 23°$.

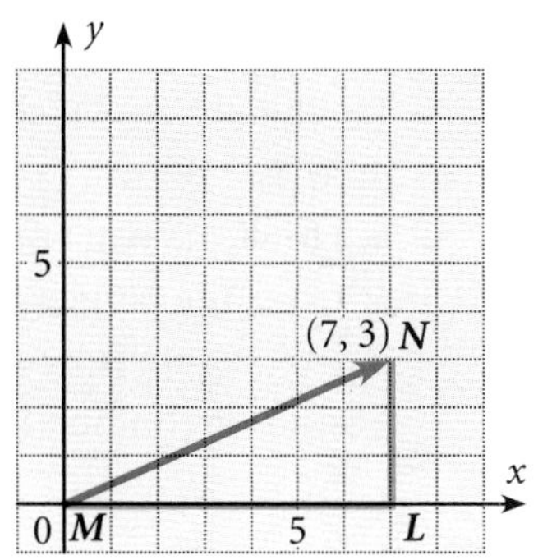

Recall that to find the sum of two vectors, you position the origin of the second vector at the endpoint of the first. In the figure, $\overrightarrow{XZ}$ is the vector sum of $\overrightarrow{XY}$ and $\overrightarrow{YZ}$.

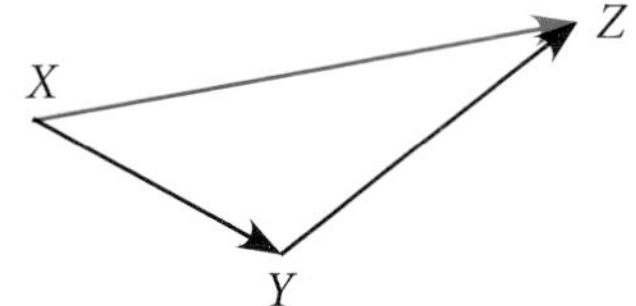

When a plane moves with or against a wind, its actual speed is just the sum or difference of the plane's speed and the wind's speed. However, this is only true when the velocities have the same or opposite directions.

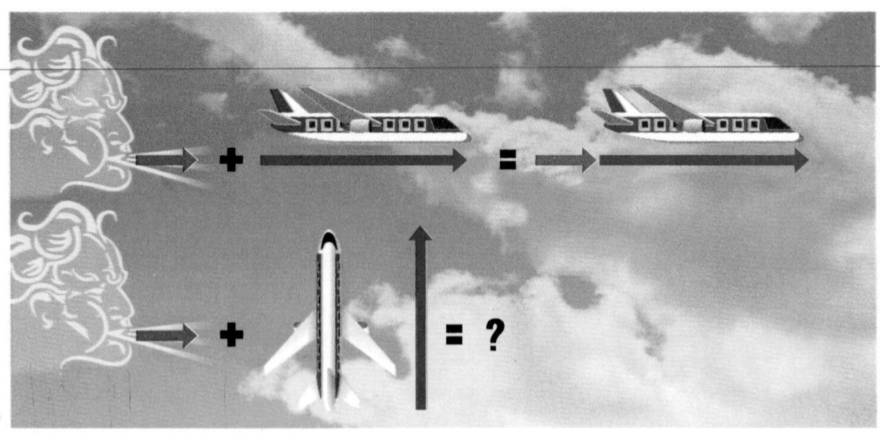

With vectors and trigonometry, you can investigate what happens when velocities are perpendicular to one another. You will take a closer look at this in the following Explore.

EXPLORE: JUST PLANE VECTORS

1. Crumple up a small piece of paper. Roll it across your desk while blowing gently at a right angle to the path of the paper. Make a sketch to illustrate what happens to the paper. Vary the speed of the paper and the force with which you blow and see how this changes the paper's path.
2. A passenger jet is heading due east. Without wind, the speed of the jet is 500 mi/hr. A strong 80 mi/hr wind is blowing. What will the actual speed and direction of the jet be
   a. if the wind is a tailwind?
   b. if the wind is a headwind?
   Make a sketch using vectors to show what happens in each case.

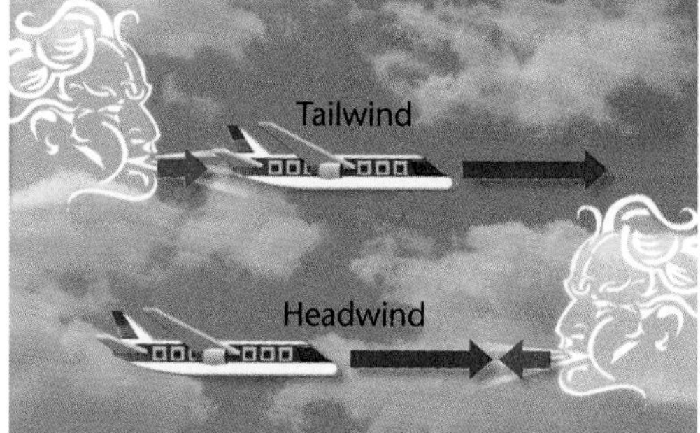

3. Now, suppose the wind in Step 2 is blowing due north at 80 mi/hr.
   a. Guess the approximate direction and speed of the plane in this wind.
   b. Draw vectors that represent the velocities of the plane and the wind. (Be sure the origin of the second vector is at the endpoint of the first.) Then draw the vector that shows the actual velocity of the airplane.
   c. Find the speed of the plane in the wind. How does this compare to the speeds you found in **2a** and **2b**? Does this make sense? Explain.
   d. Use a trigonometric ratio to find the direction of the plane. Does this answer seem reasonable? Why?

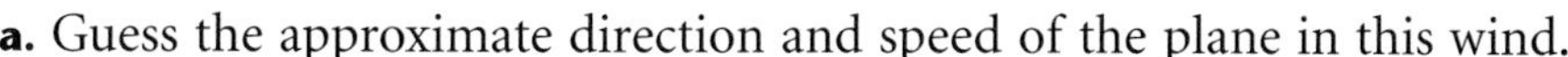

REFLECT

1. If you add two vectors that are perpendicular, is the length of their vector sum always greater than the length of either vector? Explain why or why not.
2. Suppose a boat sailing due east at 10 mi/hr suddenly meets a 10 mi/hr current that is moving due north. Find the speed and direction of the actual path of the boat without using trigonometry. Explain your method.

Exercises

CORE

Getting Started In Exercises 1–3, an airplane is flying due north with a speed (in still air) of 250 mi/hr.

1. Find the plane's actual speed and direction if there is a 45 mi/hr headwind.

2. Find the plane's actual speed and direction if there is a 45 mi/hr tailwind.

250 mi/hr

3. Suppose the wind blows due east at 45 mi/hr.
   a. Sketch a vector to represent the plane's velocity. Starting at the endpoint of the plane's velocity vector, sketch a vector to represent the wind's velocity.
   b. Sketch the vector sum that represents the actual path of the plane. The origin of this vector should be at the origin of the vector you drew in **3a**.
   c. Use the Pythagorean Theorem to find the length of the actual velocity vector.

Draw each vector on graph paper. Find its length, and use trigonometry to find its direction.

4. $\overrightarrow{AB}$ for $A(0, 0)$ and $B(5, 3)$
5. $\overrightarrow{EF}$ for $E(0, 0)$ and $F(7, 2)$
6. $\overrightarrow{JK}$ for $J(0, 0)$ and $K(4, 5)$

Sketch each pair of vectors on graph paper. Then sketch the vector sum of the two vectors. Write a vector equation that uses vector addition to describe your sketch.

7. $\overrightarrow{LM}$ has length 5 and direction 0°; $\overrightarrow{MN}$ has length 8 and direction 90°.

8. $\overrightarrow{RS}$ has length 7 and direction 90°; $\overrightarrow{ST}$ has length 3 and direction 180°.

9. **Off Course** Sean is paddling his kayak due east. In still water, his speed would be 15 km/hr. There is a 9 km/hr current going from north to south. Draw a sketch to illustrate this situation. Then find the actual speed of the kayak and the measure of the angle between its actual direction and its intended direction. Explain how you solved this problem.

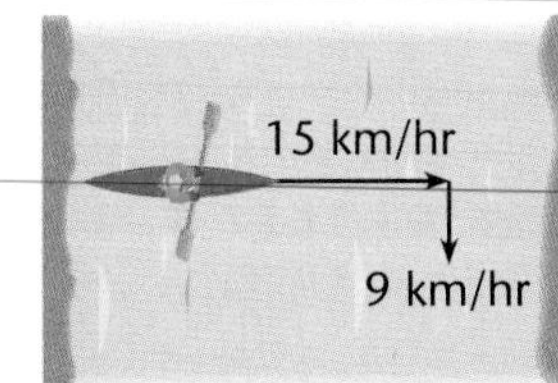

10. **Parrot Path** Ozzie the parrot is flying 20 mi/hr due east. There is an 11 mi/hr wind blowing due north. Find Ozzie's actual speed and the measure of the angle his actual path makes with his intended path.

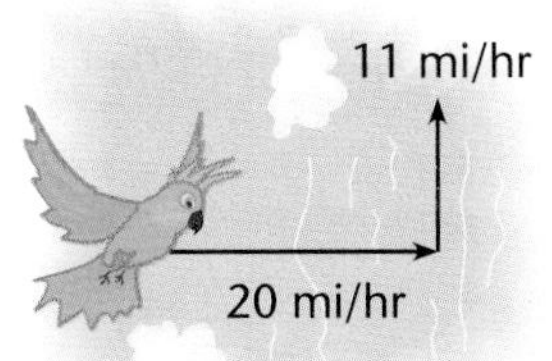

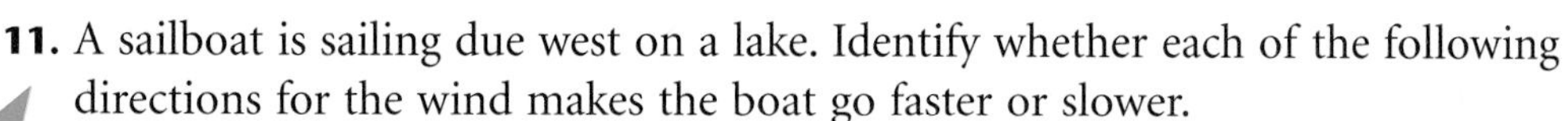

11. A sailboat is sailing due west on a lake. Identify whether each of the following directions for the wind makes the boat go faster or slower.

Science

a. due north **b.** due east **c.** due south **d.** due west

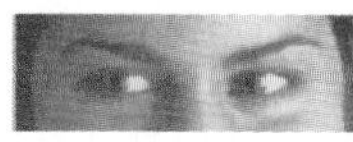

LOOK BACK

Find the area of each figure. Express your answer as a decimal rounded to the nearest hundredth. [6-3]

12. an equilateral triangle with radius 4.1 cm

13. a regular hexagon with side length 8 in.

***Z* is the midpoint of $\overline{VY}$, and *W* is the midpoint of $\overline{VX}$. [7-2]**

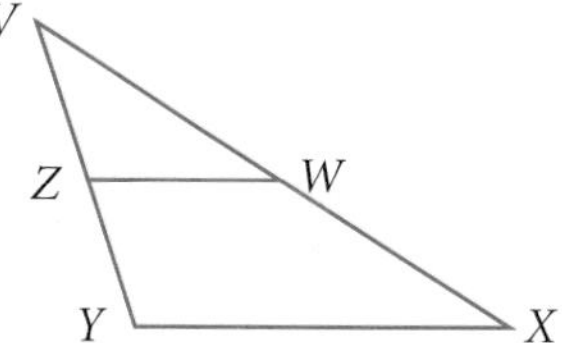

14. $VZ = 6$, and $XY = 13$. Find VY, WZ, and ZY.

15. $m\angle VWZ = 38°$, and $WZ = 34.4$. Find $m\angle VXY$ and XY.

16. $XY = 12$, $VX = 17$, and $m\angle Y = 84°$. Find $m\angle VZW$, VW, and WZ.

MORE PRACTICE

Draw each vector on graph paper. Find its length, and use trigonometry to find its direction.

17. $\overrightarrow{AB}$ for $A(0, 0)$ and $B(2, 6)$

18. $\overrightarrow{EF}$ for $E(0, 0)$ and $F(4, 7)$

Sketch each pair of vectors on graph paper. Then sketch the vector sum of the two vectors. Write a vector equation that uses vector addition to describe your sketch.

19. $\overrightarrow{GH}$ has length 6 and direction 180°; $\overrightarrow{HI}$ has length 7 and direction 90°.

20. $\overrightarrow{JK}$ has length 8 and direction 0°; $\overrightarrow{KL}$ has length 4 and direction 270°.

MORE MATH REASONING

Science

21. A plane is flying in a strong wind. The wind is blowing due west at 100 mi/hr. The plane's actual speed is 340 mi/hr, and its actual direction is due north. Find the speed and direction it would be flying if there were no wind.

22. Do you think you can use trigonometry to find the sum of two vectors that are not perpendicular? If so, write an explanation of your method. If not, explain how you could find the length and direction of the sum of two such vectors.

7-3 PART D Making Connections

← CONNECT → ***The relationships between the sides and angles of similar right triangles are useful in many fields, including astronomy, surveying, and engineering. You've used trigonometry to solve for unknown side lengths and angle measures in right triangles.***

Benjamin Banneker was a self-taught surveyor who helped draw up the original plans for Washington, D.C. One of the jobs of a surveyor is to determine the heights of hills, trees, and other objects on a piece of property. You can use trigonometry to recreate some of the things Banneker's surveying team may have done.

EXPLORE: ANGLE SIGHTING

MATERIALS

Protractor, String Tape, Weight

For this Explore, you will need to turn your protractor into a *clinometer*.

Hold your protractor with the straight edge up. Securely tape a string at the origin of the protractor. Tie a weight (like a key or a small washer) to the other end of the string.

To use the clinometer to measure angles, hold it up to your eye and look along its edge to sight an object. A partner can then read the angle the string is resting on. Using this angle, you can find the measure of the angle of elevation or depression. To find the height of the object, the only other information you need is the distance to the object.

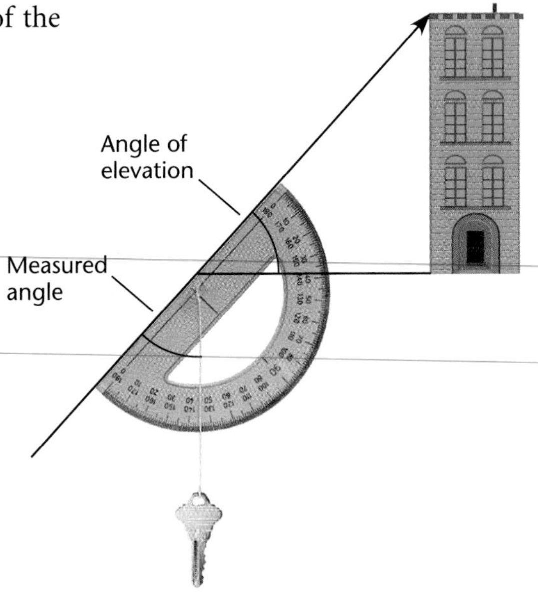

Explain how you can use the clinometer to find the height of a building or a tall tree. Choose an object that you know the distance to (or can find the distance to) and find its height. Record your readings and sketch the similar triangles you used.

REFLECT

1. Assume that you know the length of one side of a right triangle and the measure of an acute angle. Which trigonometric ratio do you use to find an unknown side length in the triangle? Explain.
2. You want to find the height of a tall tree. Draw a sketch showing how you can use trigonometry to find its height. Draw another sketch showing how you can use similar triangles. What are the advantages of each method?
3. What can you find out about the sum of two perpendicular vectors without using trigonometry? When do you need to use trigonometry?

Self-Assessment

Express each trigonometric ratio as a fraction and as a decimal rounded to the hundredths place.

1. $\sin J$ **2.** $\cos J$ **3.** $\tan J$

4. $\sin K$ **5.** $\cos K$ **6.** $\tan K$

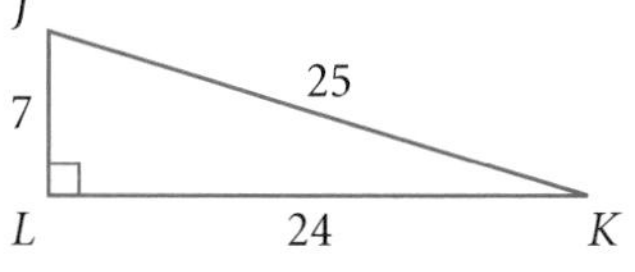

Find each indicated angle measure to the nearest degree or side length to the nearest hundredth.

7.

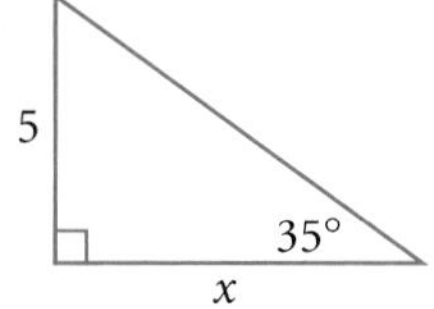

8.

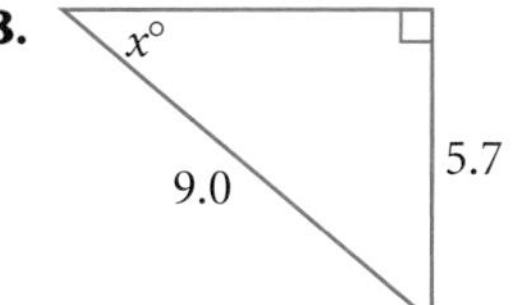

9.

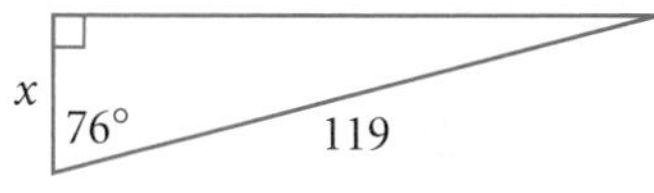

10. Angle Falls From a spot 383 ft from the base of Kaloba Falls in Zaire, the angle of elevation to the top of the falls is approximately 71°. Find the height of the waterfall to the nearest foot. (Allow 5 ft for the height of the viewer's eyes above the ground.)

Science

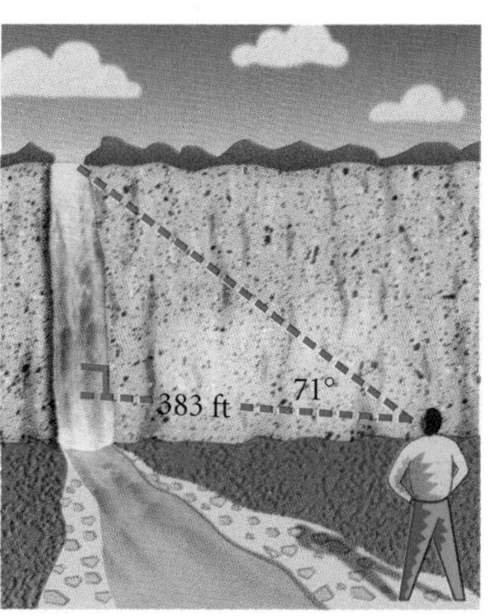

Find the area of each figure. Express your answer as a decimal rounded to the nearest hundredth. [6-3]

11. an equilateral triangle with radius 4 cm

12. a square with radius 4 cm

13. a regular hexagon with radius 4 cm

Find the value for x that makes the triangles similar. State the theorem or postulate that justifies your answer. [7-2]

14.

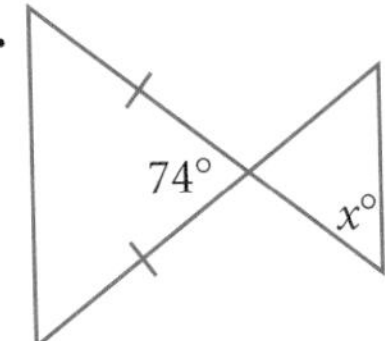

15.

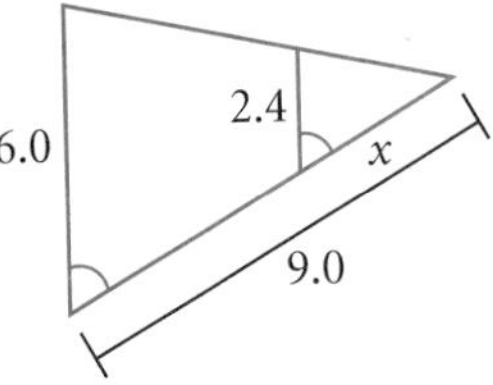

16.

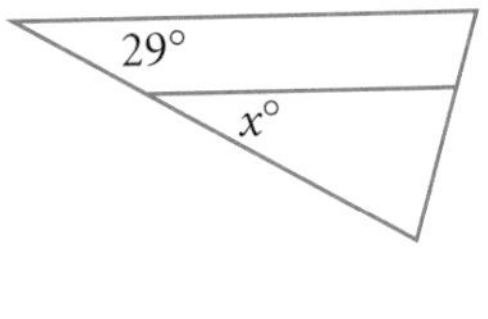

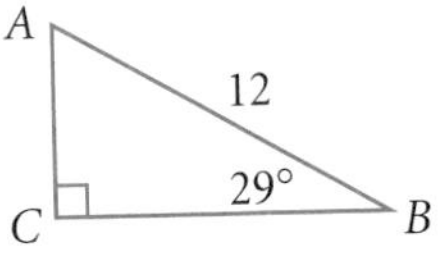

17. Which trigonometric ratio could be used to solve directly for AC?
(a) sin (b) cos (c) tan
(d) You cannot use trigonometry to solve for AC.

18. If the 622-ft-tall Tower of the Americas in San Antonio casts a 260-ft shadow, what is the angle of elevation of the sun, to the nearest degree? Explain how you solved this problem. If you used a sketch to help you, include it with your solution.

19. Both Boats An observer at the top of a 50-m lighthouse (with its base at sea level) sees two boats approaching, one behind the other. The angles to the boats are 39° and 25°, as shown. Find the distance between the boats to the nearest meter.

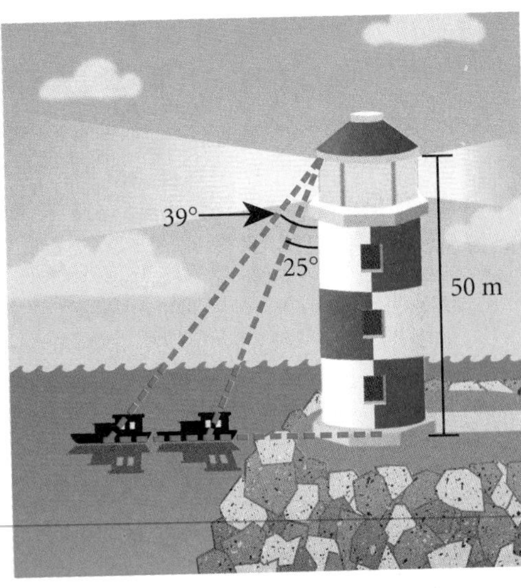

20. A plane is heading due east at 150 mi/hr, and the wind is blowing due north at 45 mi/hr. Sketch vectors to represent the plane's velocity in still air, the wind's velocity, and the actual velocity of the plane. Find the actual speed of the plane to the nearest tenth and the measure of the angle its actual path makes with due east to the nearest degree.

Complete each of the following statements with *always, sometimes,* or *never.* Explain each of your answers.

21. The tangent of an angle is ____ less than 1.

22. The angle of elevation from your eye to the top of a twenty-foot flagpole ____ gets smaller as you walk towards the flagpole.

23. Given the measure of an acute angle in a right triangle and the length of one of the triangle's legs, you can ____ use trigonometry to find the length of the hypotenuse.

Chapter 7 Review

In Chapter 7, you looked at applications of similarity. These included enlargements and reductions, the golden rectangle, dilations, and trigonometry. You also explored various ways to show that two triangles are similar. All of these ideas are useful to artists, surveyors, and mapmakers.

KEY TERMS

angle of depression [7-3]
angle of elevation [7-3]
center of dilation [7-2]
cosine [7-3]
dilation [7-2]
enlargement [7-1]
golden ratio [7-1]
golden rectangle [7-1]
midsegment [7-2]
reduction [7-1]
scale factor [7-1]
similar [7-1]
similarity ratio [7-1]
sine [7-3]
tangent [7-3]
trigonometry [7-3]

Write the word or phrase that correctly completes each statement.

1. An enlargement and a reduction are both examples of a ___.

2. A midsegment of a triangle is the segment joining ___.

3. A pilot considering the angle formed by the horizontal and his line of sight to an airport below is estimating an angle of ___.

4. The scale factor of an enlargement is ___ than 1.

CONCEPTS AND APPLICATIONS

Determine whether each statement is true or false. If it is true, explain why. If it is false, provide a counterexample. [7-1]

5. Any equilateral triangle is similar to any equiangular triangle.

6. All isosceles triangles are similar.

$\triangle MNO \sim \triangle RST$. Find the following. [7-1]

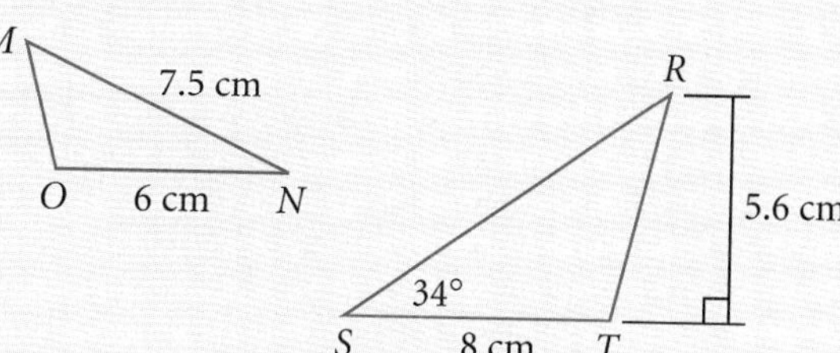

7. the similarity ratio of $\triangle MNO$ to $\triangle RST$

8. $m\angle N$

9. RS

10. area of $\triangle MNO$

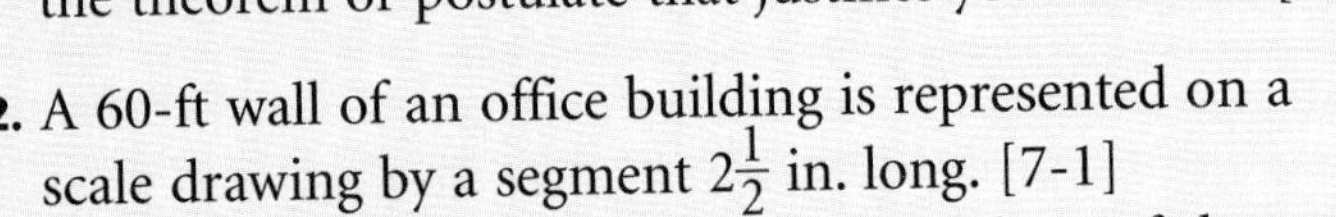

11. Find a value for x that makes the triangles similar. State the theorem or postulate that justifies your answer. [7-1]

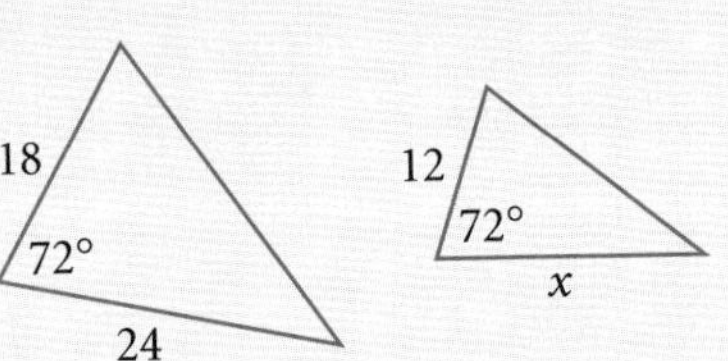

12. A 60-ft wall of an office building is represented on a scale drawing by a segment $2\frac{1}{2}$ in. long. [7-1]

a. On the drawing, what is the length of a 15-ft-long deck of the building?

b. If a planter box is a 1-in. × $1\frac{1}{4}$-in. rectangle on the drawing, what are its actual dimensions?

13. Write a summary of facts about golden rectangles and the golden ratio. Include illustrations with your summary. [7-1]

14. $\overline{UV}$ is a midsegment of $\triangle RST$ in the figure at the right. What is the ratio of the area of $\triangle RUV$ to the area of trapezoid $UVTS$? Explain how you know. [7-2]

15. You are planning to draw a smaller version of this boat by using a dilation with the center at the origin and a scale factor of $\frac{1}{2}$. [7-2]

a. What will be the length of the image of the deck, $\overline{AB}$?

b. Give the coordinates of the image of point C, the top of the mast.

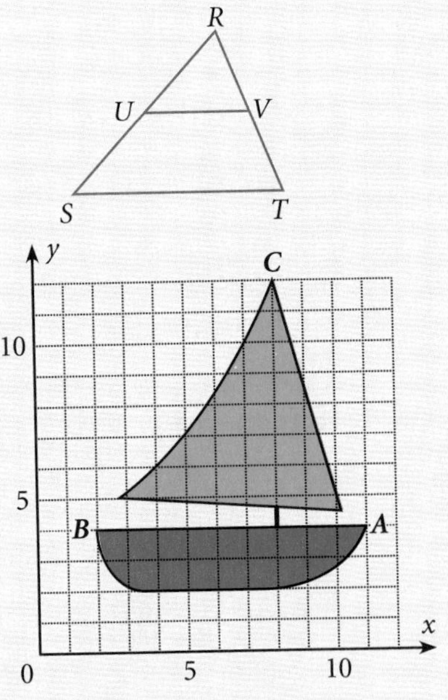

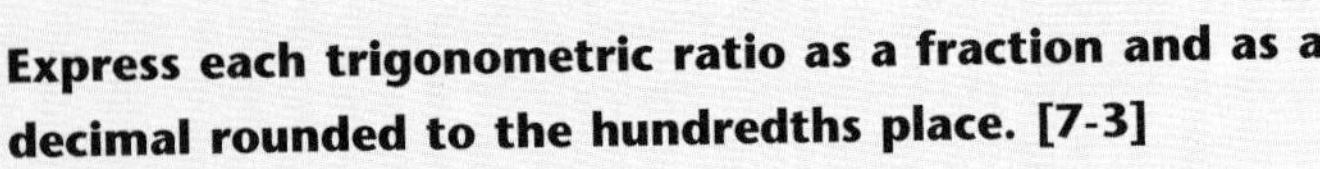

Express each trigonometric ratio as a fraction and as a decimal rounded to the hundredths place. [7-3]

16. cos R

17. sin R

18. tan P

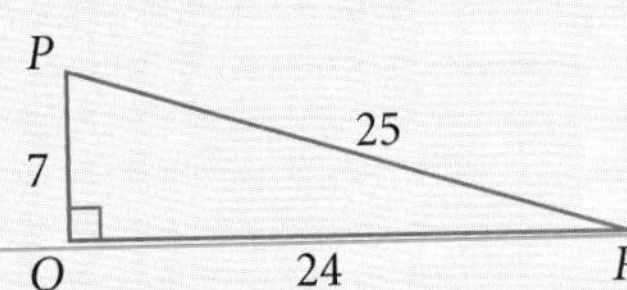

Find each indicated angle measure to the nearest degree or side length to the nearest hundredth. [7-3]

19.

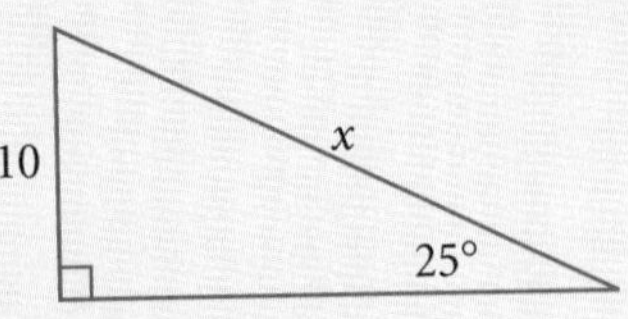

20.

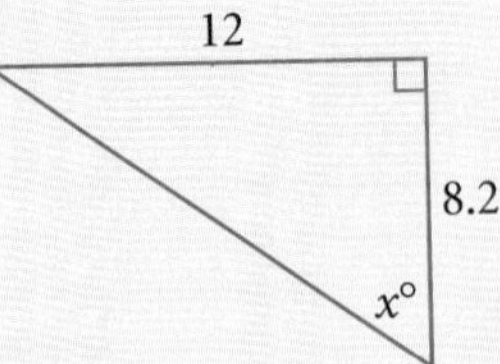

21.

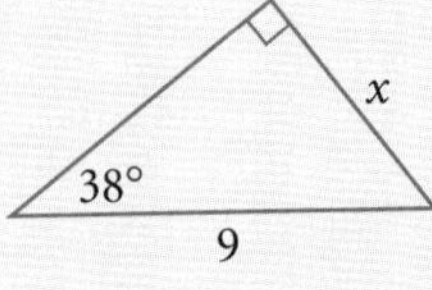

22. Find the perimeter and area of parallelogram $ABCE$. [5-2, 5-3]

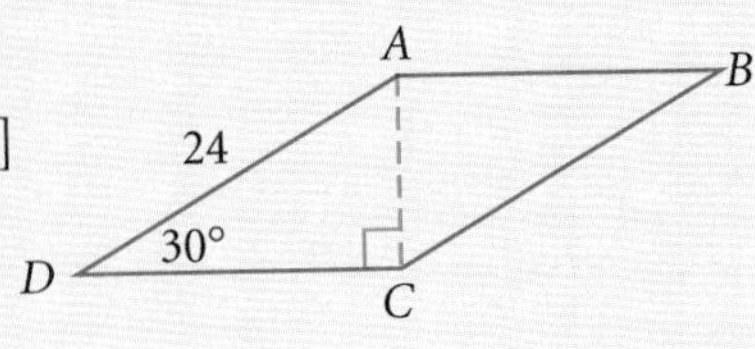

23. The Pyramid of the Sun (ca. 150 A.D.) in the ancient Mexican city of Teotihuacán was unearthed from 1904–1910. From a point on the ground 300 ft from the center of its square base, the angle of elevation to its top would have been 31°. [7-3]

History

a. What was the height of the pyramid?

b. If one story of a modern building is about 10 ft tall, about how many stories tall was this pyramid?

CONCEPTS AND CONNECTIONS

24. **History** In Oronce Fine's *De Re & Praxi Geometrica*, published in 1556, the method of measuring with a *baculum* is described. As shown in the lower figure at the right, the staff was marked off in intervals that were each as long as the crosspiece. First, the crosspiece was set at one of the interval marks. The user sighted along the staff to the approximate midpoint of the segment to be measured, $\overline{FG}$, standing at a distance chosen so that the crosspiece was parallel to the segment and barely covered its view. The crosspiece was then set one interval closer to the user and the process was repeated at a nearer position. The distance between the two observation positions, AK in the figure, equaled the desired length, FG. In terms of similar triangles, explain why this method worked.

History

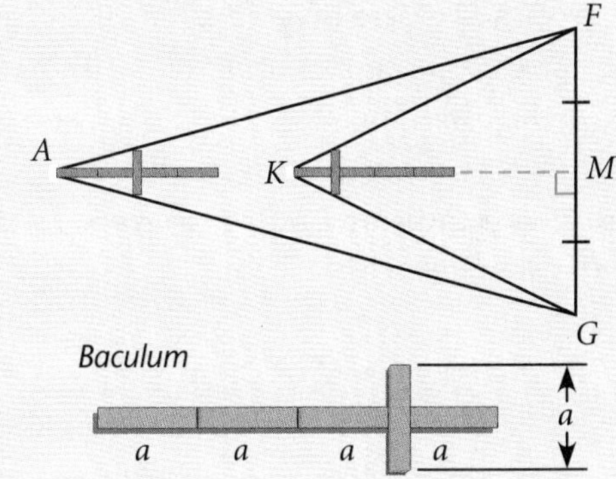

SELF-EVALUATION

Write a summary of what you know about similarity. Include as many methods as possible for concluding that two figures are similar. Also, include examples of how similarity can be applied to various careers. Be sure to discuss areas in which you had trouble, and describe your plans for studying these topics.

Chapter 7 Assessment

TEST

Give a similarity correspondence for each pair of triangles, and explain why the triangles are similar.

1. 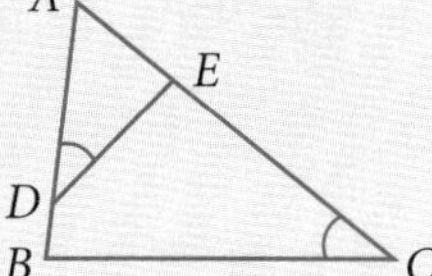

2. 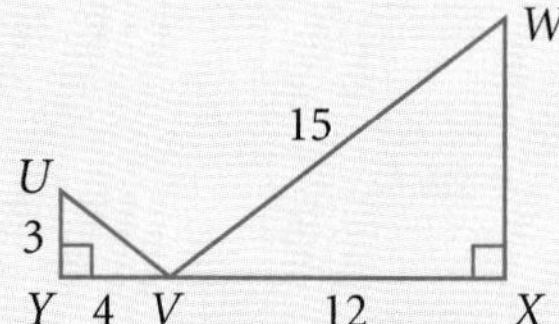

Use the figure at the right for items 3–5.

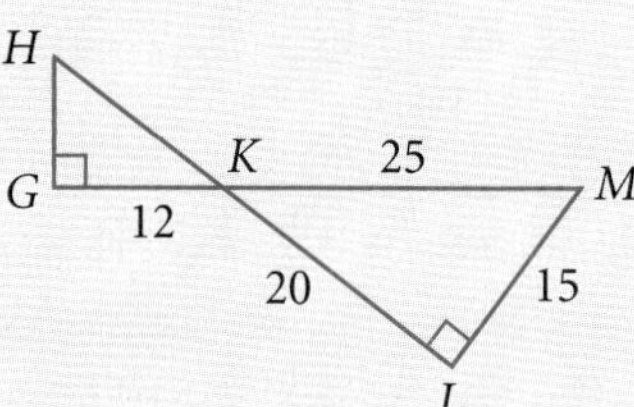

3. State a postulate or theorem that can be used to show $\triangle GHK \sim \triangle LMK$.

4. What is the similarity ratio of $\triangle GHK$ to $\triangle LMK$?

5. Find HG in the figure at the right.

6. The similarity ratio between two polygons is $\frac{2}{5}$. The perimeter of the larger polygon is 85 m, and its area is 320 m^2. What are the perimeter and area of the smaller polygon? Explain your thinking.

Find each indicated angle measure to the nearest degree or side length to the nearest hundredth.

7. 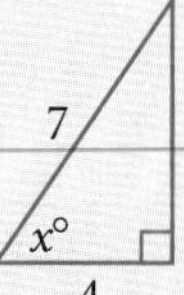

8. 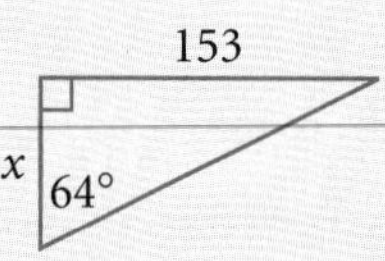

9. 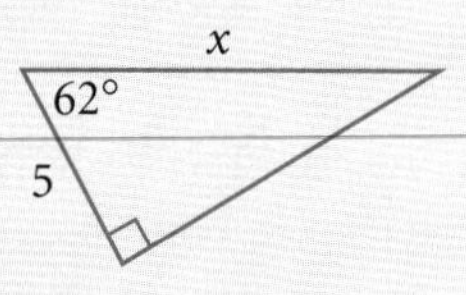

In $\triangle GHJ$, $GJ = 4$ and $\overline{KL}$ is a midsegment.

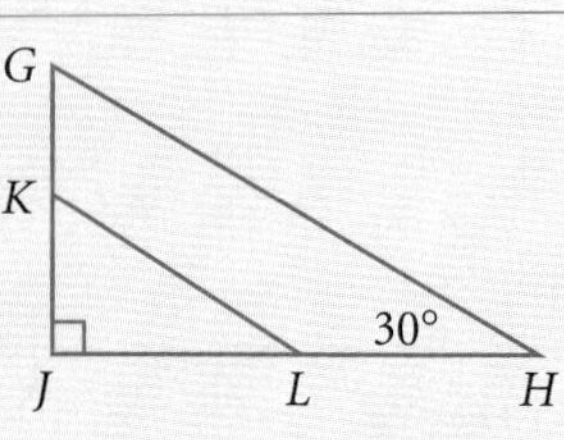

10. Find KL.

11. Find the area of $\triangle JKL$.

12. A sketch that fills a 4″ × 6″ rectangular region is to be enlarged to fit onto an $8\frac{1}{2}$″ × 11″ piece of paper. A scale factor of 1.7 is used.

a. What are the length and width of the enlarged image?

b. The enlarging machine does not print within a $\frac{1}{4}$-in. margin around the edges of the paper. Can the entire image be printed?

13. Sketch a right triangle, $\triangle ABC$, with a right angle at B. Label the hypotenuse and the legs adjacent and opposite to $\angle A$. Then write each of the three trigonometric ratios of $\angle A$ as a formula involving the lengths of its adjacent leg, its opposite leg, and the hypotenuse.

14. Find the area of rhombus $WXYZ$ in the figure below.

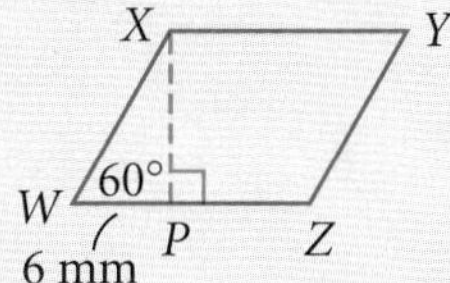

15. Well-known artists, such as Leonardo da Vinci and the French impressionist George Seurat, used golden rectangles in their paintings. The canvas $ABCD$ is a golden rectangle. Each of the smaller rectangles is also a golden rectangle. Choose one of the smaller rectangles, and give a paragraph proof that it is a golden rectangle; that is, prove that its sides are in the same ratio as $\frac{AB}{BC}$.

Fine Arts

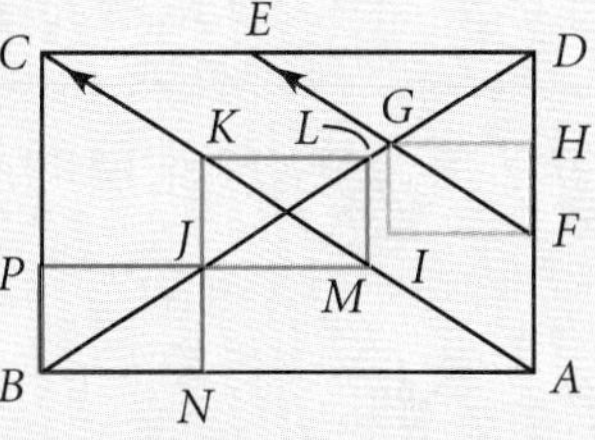

16. A swimmer starts out due north across a lake at 40 m/min, but encounters a 22 m/min current running from east to west. Find the swimmer's actual speed in the water and the angle between the actual direction and the intended direction.

Science

17. At a point 50 ft in front of you, a helium balloon is released and floats straight upward. When the balloon's angle of elevation from the ground is 13°, how far above the ground is the balloon? Draw a sketch to illustrate your solution.

PERFORMANCE TASK

Carefully draw a right triangle and the altitude to its hypotenuse. You will notice that the altitude divides the triangle into two smaller triangles. Use a protractor to measure all of the angles in your figure. Record your data. Repeat the process for two more right triangles. On the basis of your observations, make a conjecture about the relationship among a right triangle and the two triangles created by the altitude to its hypotenuse. Then write a deductive argument to justify your conjecture.

Chapter 8

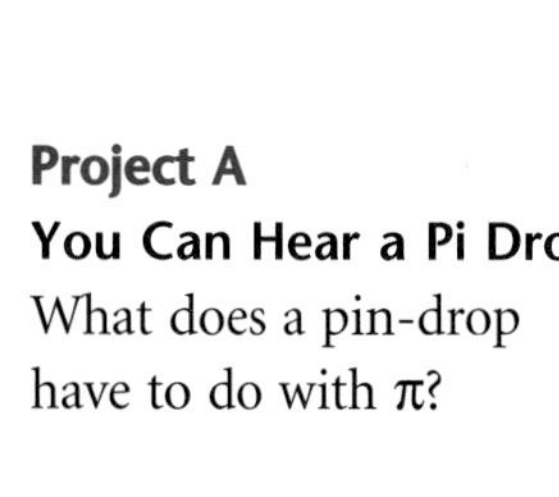

Project A
You Can Hear a Pi Drop
What does a pin-drop have to do with π?

Project B
A Piece of the Pie
What is a market share? When is a circle graph the best visual display of data?

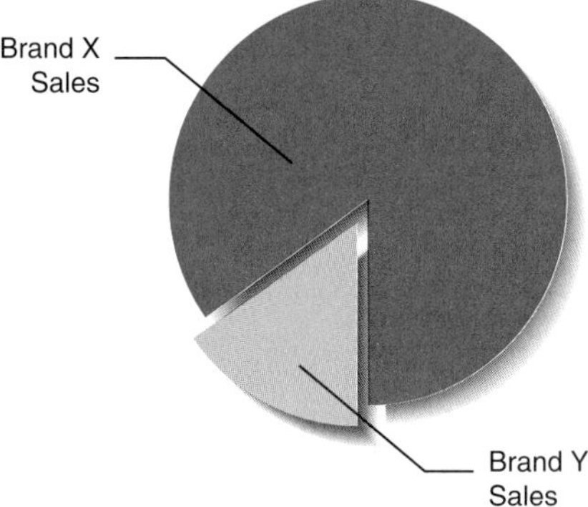

Project C
Round and Round
Where do circles occur in nature? How do they happen?

STEVE GÁNDOLA

I liked math in high school because I did well in it, but I didn't expect to use it.

Today I use math to analyze data and to see how something impacts our business–for example, to see how competition, technology, or industry affects our market share. I use a system of equations to figure it out.

Steve Gándola
Market Analyst
Camera Division
Eastman Kodak Company
Rochester, NY

Chapter 8 Circles and Spheres

GETTING READY

8-1 Circles, Circumference, and Area

In 8-1 you will learn about circles. You will use the following skills from previous courses and chapters.

Find the area of each regular polygon. [6-3]

1.

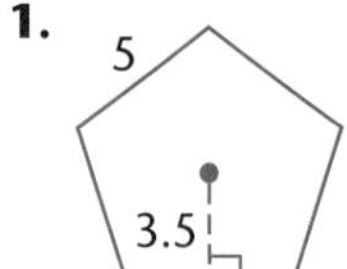

2.

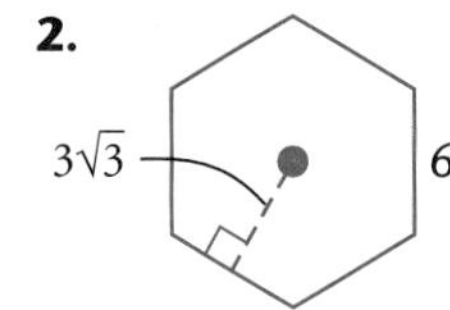

3.

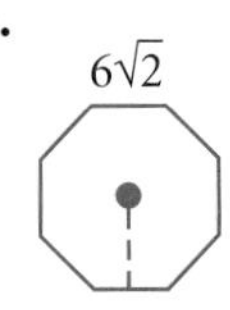

4. $7\frac{1}{2}$

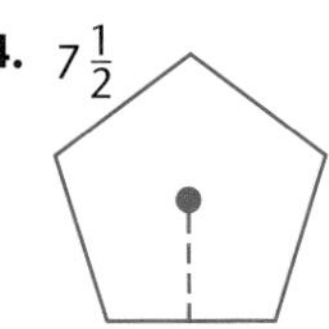

Calculate each number as an exact decimal. [Previous course]

5. 10.01^2 **6.** 1000^2 **7.** $-(0.99^2)$ **8.** $(-0.01)^2$

8-2 Angles, Arcs, and Chords

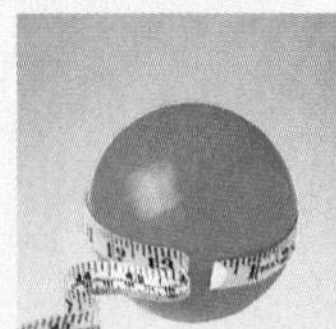

In 8-2 you will investigate angles, arcs, and chords. You will use the following skills from previous chapters.

Find the missing lengths. [4-3]

9. If $AD = 7$ and $AB = 10$, find DC, BC, and BD.

10. If $AB = 18$ and $BD = 9\sqrt{3}$, find DC, BC, and AC.

11. If $AC = 12\sqrt{2}$ and $AB = 14$, find DC, BC, and BD.

12. If $AB = x + 20$, $BD = x + 10$, and $BC = x^2$, find AB, BD, BC, and AC.

8-3 The Inscribed Angle Theorem

In 8-3 you will investigate theorems based on properties of inscribed angles. You will need the following skills from previous courses and chapters.

Find the measure of each angle if $m\angle ABC = x^2 + 4°$ and $m\angle ACB = 7x + 12°$. [4-3]

13. $m\angle ABC$ **14.** $m\angle BAC$ **15.** $m\angle CDA$ **16.** $m\angle BAD$

Solve for *x*. [Previous course]

17. $3x + 2x = 360$

18. $10x + 180 + 2x = 540$

19. $720 \div 2 = 72x$

20. $x + 0.5x = 360$

21. $\frac{3x}{4} = 360$

22. $9x = 1080$

8-1 Circles, Circumference, and Area

Years ago, phonograph records played at a speed of 78 rpm (revolutions per minute). As hi-fi (high-fidelity) recording processes improved, the speed of rotation of the record player slowed to $33\frac{1}{3}$ rpm. Both 78 rpm and $33\frac{1}{3}$ rpm records were recorded by an analog process that transferred sound vibrations to the grooves in the record.

The record is now almost extinct because of the advent of the compact disk (CD). The disk is 12.5 cm in diameter, but the track in which information is coded is thinner than a hair, and has a length of several miles! The CD rotates at a speed of 200 rpm.

A CD is recorded digitally. Digital recording preserves sound information electronically. It is more accurate than analog recording and it is free of the "hiss" that always enters the analog recording process. Although some people still keep their records, the cleaner sound of the CD is making the "LP" record an antique.

?

1. CDs are just one type of circular item. Name three other examples of circular objects, and give reasons why a circle is a suitable shape for each.
2. Why do you think circles, rather than other geometric figures, are used in manufacturing CDs?
3. How is a circle different from a regular polygon? How is it similar to a regular polygon?

8-1 PART A Inscribed and Circumscribed Figures

← CONNECT → ***You've already worked with circles. Now you will look at the mathematical definition of a circle and investigate some polygons that fit perfectly inside and outside circles.***

You may have drawn a circle by using a pencil tied to a piece of string. Tightly holding one point on the string and moving the pencil makes a circle.

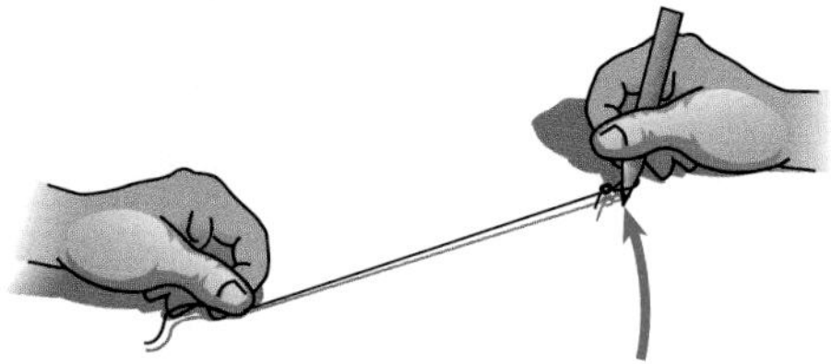

Although this may appear to be an informal way to construct a circle, it is based on the mathematical definition of a circle.

DEFINITION

A **circle** is the locus of points in a plane equidistant from a given point. That point is the **center** of the circle.

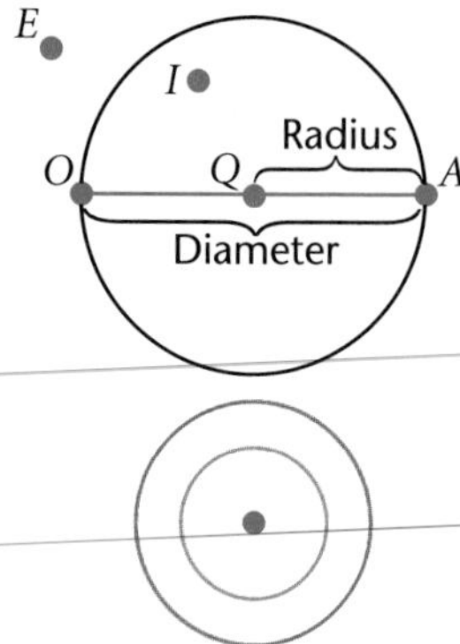

We name a circle by its center. The circle shown is ⊙Q. A **radius** of the circle is a segment from the center to any point on the circle. A **diameter** is a segment that contains the center of the circle and has endpoints on the circle. We also use the words *radius* and *diameter* to refer to the lengths of those segments. Point E is in the **exterior** of ⊙Q and point I is in the **interior.**

Two coplanar circles with the same center are **concentric** circles.

Concentric circles

1. What is the relationship between the diameter of a circle and its radius?

TRY IT

a. Name a radius of $\odot T$.
b. Name a diameter of $\odot T$.
c. Describe the locations of points X and Z.
d. If the diameter of $\odot T$ is 4 cm, what is the radius?

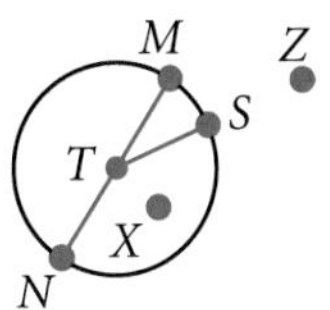

When you draw a polygon that fits perfectly inside a circle, it is **inscribed** in the circle. At the same time, the circle is **circumscribed** around the polygon.

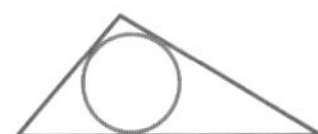

The triangle is circumscribed around the circle. Each of its sides touches the circle at exactly one point.

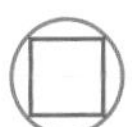

The square is inscribed in the circle. All of its vertices are on the circle.

In the following Explore, you will investigate ways to inscribe regular polygons inside a circle.

EXPLORE: POLYGONS INSIDE, CIRCLES OUTSIDE

MATERIALS

Compass
Straightedge

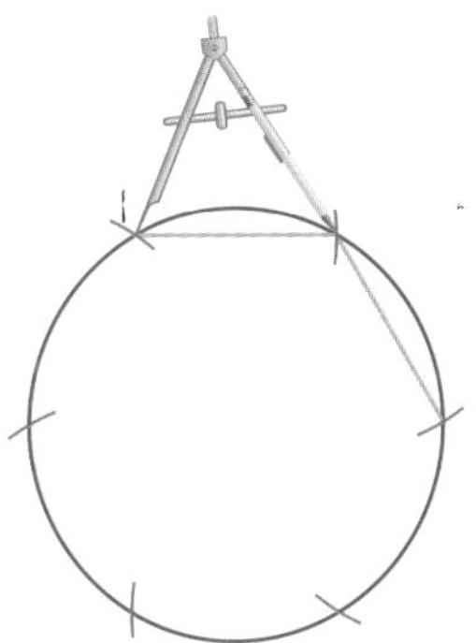

Use your compass to draw one circle on each of four sheets of paper. All four circles should have the same radius.

1. Inscribe a regular hexagon inside one of your circles, using a compass and straightedge. (Hint: Refer to Exercise 25 on page 446.)
2. Develop methods for inscribing an equilateral triangle, a square, and a regular 12-gon in your three remaining circles. Your figures do not have to be constructions; you may choose to use paper-folding or other techniques. Explain how each of your methods works, and compare your ideas with those of your classmates. (Hint: You may want to use the construction in Step 1 as a starting point for some of your work.)
3. Among your four figures, which polygon's area is closest to the area of the circle? Which polygon's perimeter is closest to the circumference (perimeter) of the circle?

REFLECT

1. Explain how you can use a compass and straightedge to circumscribe a circle around a given regular hexagon.
2. Suppose an equilateral triangle, a regular hexagon, and a regular octagon are inscribed in the same circle. Which of the polygons has the largest area? perimeter? Why?

Exercises

CORE

Getting Started Use the circle at the right for each of the following.

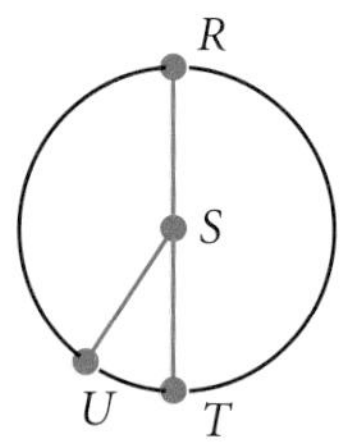

1. Name the circle.
2. Name three radii of the circle.
3. Name a diameter of the circle.
4. If the radius of the circle is 3 cm, what is its diameter?
5. If the diameter of the circle is 16.4 in., what is its radius?
6. How does the pencil-and-string method for drawing a circle work? What does the string represent? How is this method similar to using a compass to make a circle?
7. What do you think is true about congruent circles? Write a definition of congruent circles.

Sketch each of the following.

8. $\odot C$ with diameter $\overline{AB}$ and radii $\overline{CD}$ and $\overline{CE}$
9. a circle inscribed in a square
10. a circle circumscribed around a pentagon

Write the word or phrase that correctly completes each statement.

11. If the vertices of a polygon are on a circle, then the polygon is ___ the circle.
12. The radius of a circle is always half of its ___.
13. Trees add a ring to their cross sections for every year of their lives. If the trunk of a 20-year-old redwood tree has a diameter of 8 in., find the average width of each ring.

Science

14. A record album with a diameter of twelve inches has a label with a diameter of four inches. Find the width of the exposed vinyl on the record.

15. Using the regular-hexagon construction as a guide, construct 30°, 60°, and 120° angles, using only a compass and straightedge.

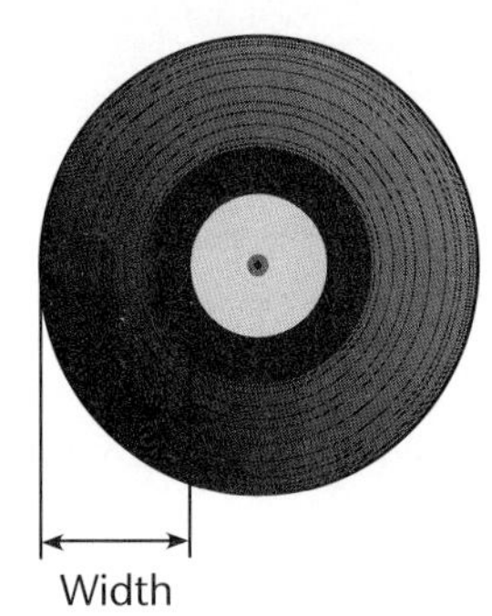

A regular hexagon is inscribed in ⊙*M* as shown. Find each of the following.

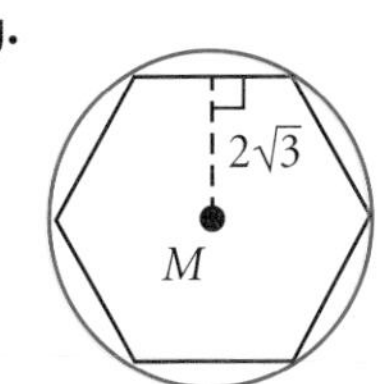

16. the radius of the circumscribed circle

17. the length of each side of the hexagon

18. the area of the hexagon to the nearest tenth

The circle shown has radius 3, and its center is at the origin. Recall that the equation for this circle is $x^2 + y^2 = 9$.

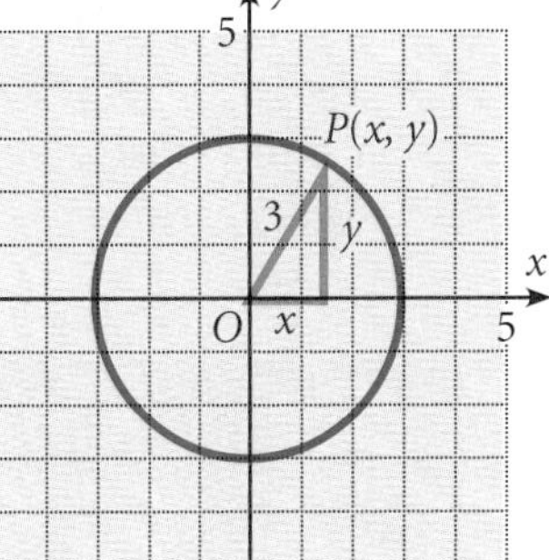

19. Give an equation for the circle with center at the origin and radius 4.

20. Give an equation for the circle with center at the origin and radius $\frac{7}{3}$.

LOOK AHEAD

21. Follow the steps below to find the perimeter of a regular 20-gon with radius 0.5 in.
    a. Draw a radius and an apothem to make a right triangle. Find the measure of the angle shown. (Hint: There are two such angles for each of the 20 sides of the polygon.)
    b. Use trigonometry to find the length of a half-side of the polygon. Use this result to find the perimeter of the 20-gon.

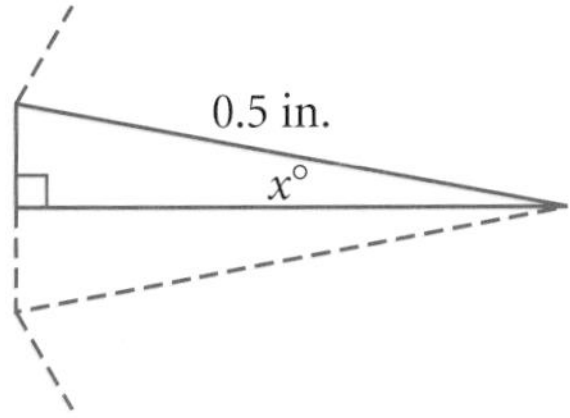

MORE PRACTICE

Sketch each of the following.

22. ⊙L with diameter $\overline{HJ}$ and radii $\overline{LK}$ and $\overline{LM}$

23. a square inscribed in a circle

24. a circle circumscribed around a triangle

25. One way to construct a hexagon is to rotate an equilateral triangle around one vertex five times. How many degrees are in each rotation? Why?

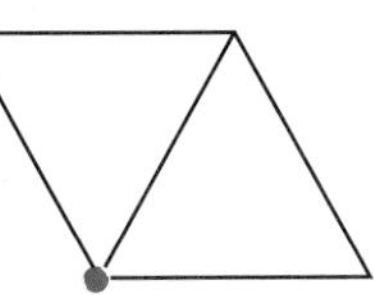

MORE MATH REASONING

26. Sketch an angle, $\angle A$, and construct its angle bisector, $\overrightarrow{AB}$. Then justify this construction. (Hint: Add lines to form triangles in your construction, and use what you know about radii of a circle.)

27. Suppose a circle with radius 3 has its center at (1, 2) as shown at the right.

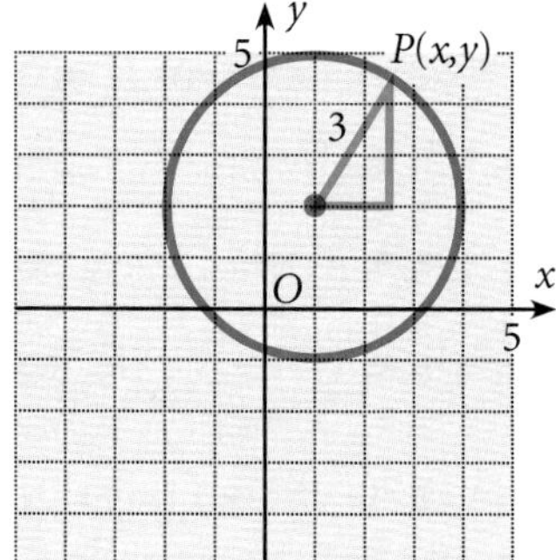

a. Use the distance formula to write an equation that says that the distance from (1, 2) to any point (x, y) on the circle is equal to 3.

b. Square both sides of the equation. This is the equation for your circle. Where does the radius of the circle appear in this equation? Where do the coordinates of the center appear?

c. Write the general equation for a circle whose radius is r and whose center is at (h, k).

8-1 PART B Circles and Tangent Lines

← CONNECT → ***Each of the sides of a polygon that is circumscribed around a circle touches the circle at exactly one point. Now you will discover some of the properties of lines that intersect circles in this way.***

A line in the plane of a circle can intersect the circle in no points, in two points, or in exactly one point. Lines that intersect circles have special names.

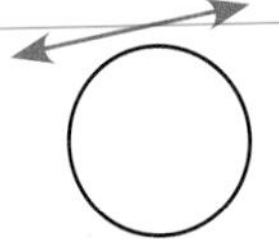

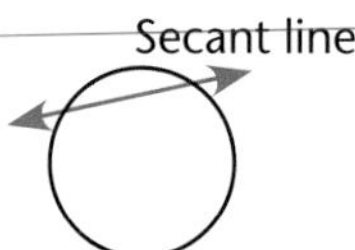

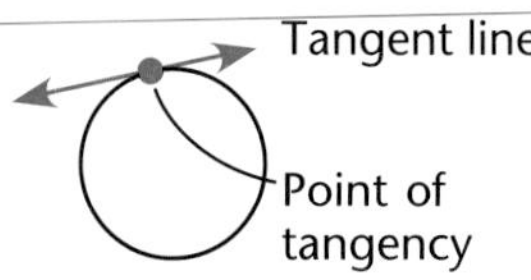

1. **Is it possible for a line that is *not* in the plane of a circle to intersect the circle in two points? one point? Justify your answers.**

EXPLORE: OFF ON A TANGENT

MATERIALS

Compass
Ruler
Protractor

1. Carefully trace or copy the square and regular hexagon shown. Then use a compass to inscribe a circle inside each. How did you find the center of each polygon? How did you find the radius of the circle?

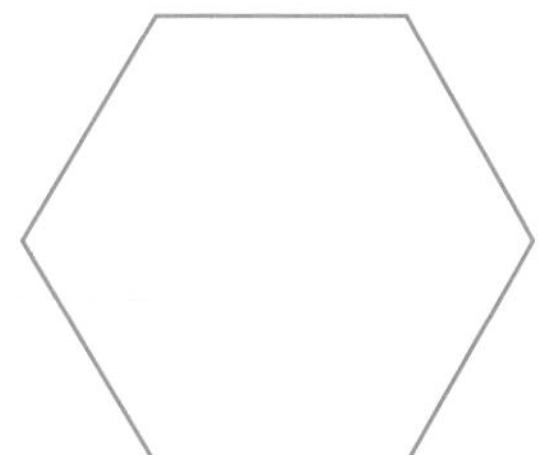

2. The sides of your regular polygons are tangent to the circle. Draw the radius of the circle to each point of tangency. Then measure each angle that the radius makes with the tangent. What conjecture can you make?

3. Investigate the converse of your conjecture. If your investigation leads to additional conjectures, be sure to record these.

4. Draw a circle, and add two tangent lines to your drawing. Extend the lines until they intersect. Then measure the lengths of the two **tangent segments** (from the point of tangency to the point of intersection). Repeat the process, and use your results to make a conjecture.

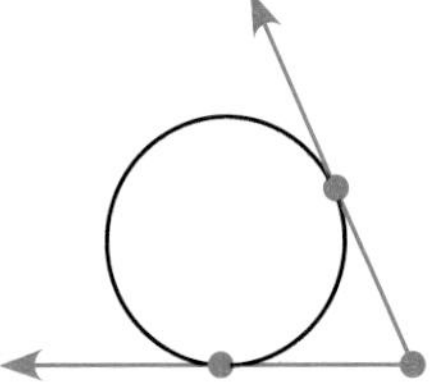

You will see that your conjectures from the Explore are useful in solving problems related to circles.

TRY IT

In the figure at the right, $\overleftrightarrow{AB}$ is tangent to $\odot C$ at B.

a. What is $m\angle CBA$?

b. Find AC.

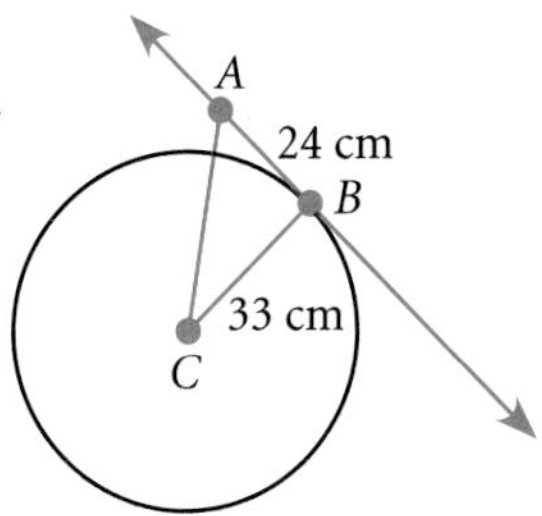

Much of the terminology that we apply to circles in two dimensions is also used to describe spheres in three dimensions.

A **sphere** is the locus of points in space a given distance from a point called the **center** of the sphere. The **radius** of the sphere is a segment from the center to a point on the sphere; the *distance* from the center to any point on the sphere is also called the radius.

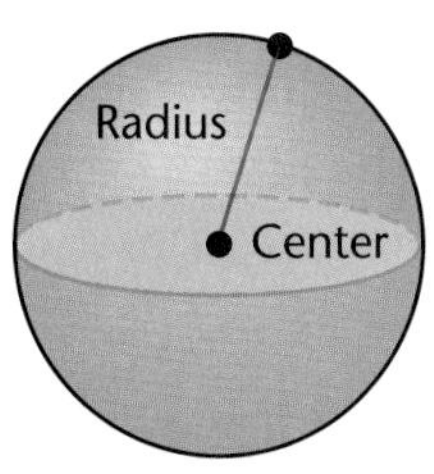

Like tangents to circles, tangents to spheres touch the sphere at exactly one point. A **tangent line** or **tangent plane** contains exactly one point of the sphere. A **great circle** is a circle on the sphere whose center is also the center of the sphere.

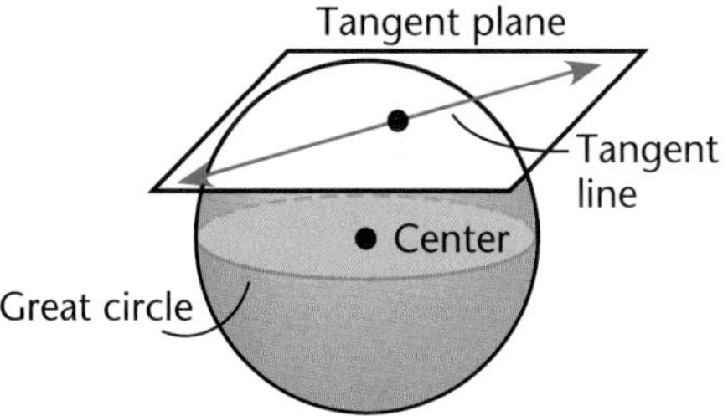

Some of the properties of tangents that you've investigated are summarized below.

THEOREMS ABOUT TANGENTS TO A CIRCLE

If a line is tangent to a circle, then it is perpendicular to a radius at the point of tangency.

If a line coplanar to a circle is perpendicular to a radius of a circle at a point on the circle, then the line is tangent to the circle.

Two tangent segments to a circle from the same exterior point are congruent.

REFLECT

1. Why does the definition of a circle include the words *in a plane*? If these words are left out, what figure does the definition describe?
2. Are any two circles similar? Explain.

Exercises

CORE

Getting Started Use the figure at the right to name each of the following.

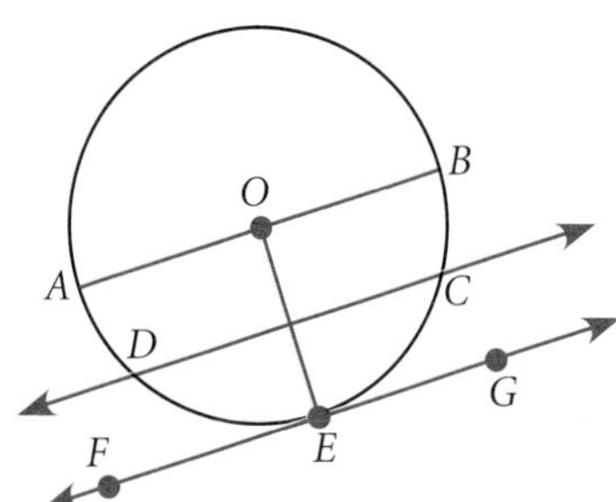

1. a diameter of $\odot O$

2. three radii of $\odot O$

3. a tangent line and its point of tangency

4. a secant line

5. Sketch and label $\odot R$ with radius $\overline{RP}$ and tangent n with its point of tangency at P.

Write the word or phrase that correctly completes each statement.

6. A circle on a sphere whose center is also the center of the sphere is a ___ of the sphere.

7. If a line intersects a circle in two points, then it is a ___ of the circle.

In the figure, $\overleftrightarrow{XY}$ is tangent to $\odot Z$ at Y.

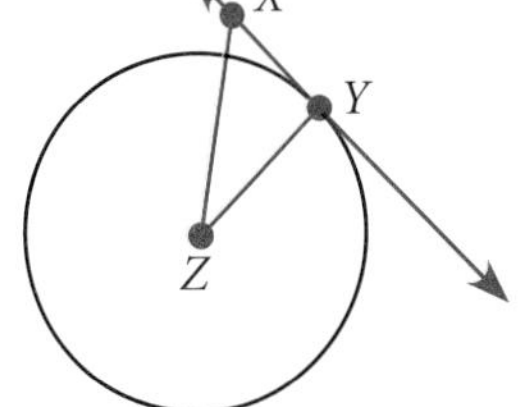

8. What is $m\angle XYZ$?

9. If $XY = 12$ and $YZ = 16$, find XZ.

10. If $XZ = 3.2$ and $XY = 1.4$, find YZ.

11. If $YZ = 7.4$ and $XZ = 9.7$, find XY.

12. The radius of a circle is 7 cm, and the length of a tangent segment from an exterior point A is 12 cm. How far is A from the center of the circle? Explain.

$\odot T$ is inscribed in $\triangle QRS$.

13. Solve for x. **14.** Solve for y.

15. Solve for z. **16.** Find the perimeter of $\triangle QRS$.

17. Prove the following: Two tangent segments to a circle from the same exterior point are congruent.

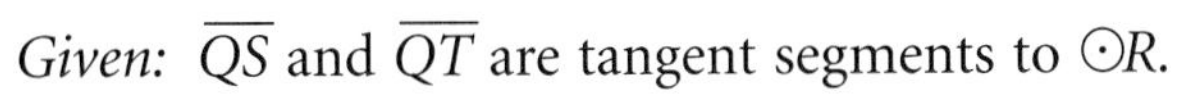

Given: $\overline{QS}$ and $\overline{QT}$ are tangent segments to $\odot R$.

Prove: $\overline{QS} \cong \overline{QT}$

(Hint: Draw $\overline{QR}$, $\overline{RS}$, and $\overline{RT}$.)

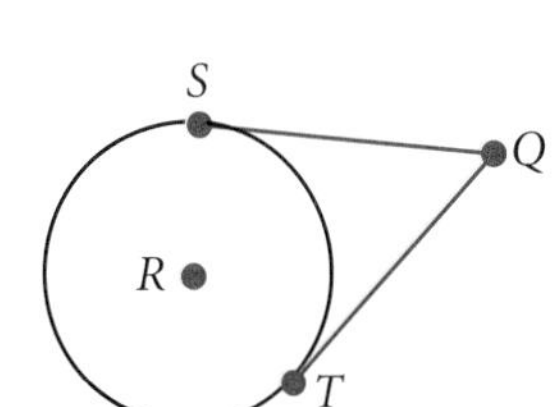

18. Yin Yang In Chinese philosophy, two principles, yin and yang, are often symbolized by a figure like the one shown below. Yin is the feminine principle, and yang is the masculine principle. It is said that the two combine to produce harmony in nature.

A yin-yang symbol can be constructed with a compass and straightedge. Analyze the yin-yang symbol, and describe how it can be made. Use terms like *radius, midpoint, tangent,* and *concentric circles* in your explanation. Then construct your own yin-yang symbol.

19. Suppose a speck of dust on a compact disk flies off the disk while it is spinning. Illustrate the path you think the speck takes. Explain your answer using circle terminology.

Use the figure at the right to name each of the following.

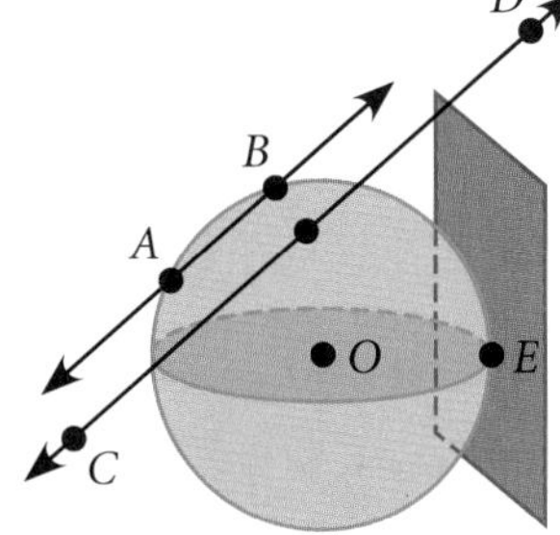

20. the point of tangency for the tangent plane to sphere O

21. a secant line for sphere O

22. a radius of sphere O

23. a line that is tangent to sphere O

LOOK BACK

Find the measure of one interior and one exterior angle of each polygon. [6-3]

24. regular hexagon

25. regular octagon

26. regular decagon

27. Square $HJKL$ undergoes a dilation with scale factor 3 and center H. Give the coordinates of H', J', K', and L', which are the dilation images of H, J, K, and L. [7-2]

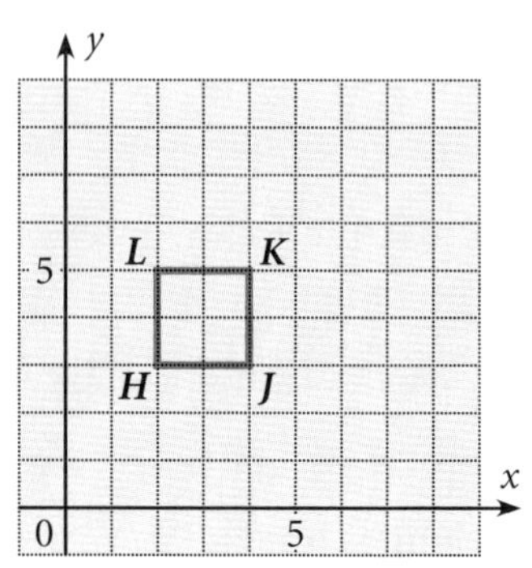

MORE PRACTICE

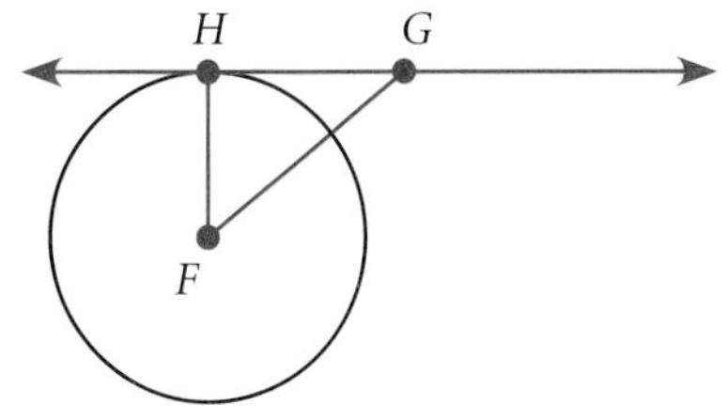

In the figure, $\overleftrightarrow{HG}$ is tangent to ⊙*F* at *H*.

28. If $GH = 12$ and $FH = 5$, find FG.

29. If $FG = 35.3$ and $GH = 26.5$, find FH.

30. If $m\angle F = 60°$ and the radius of ⊙F is 3, find exact values for GH and FG.

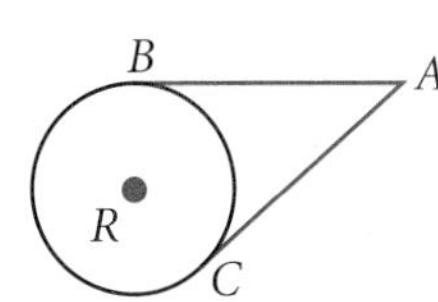

⊙*T* is inscribed in *MNOP*.

31. Solve for a.

32. Solve for b.

33. Solve for c.

34. Find the perimeter of $MNOP$.

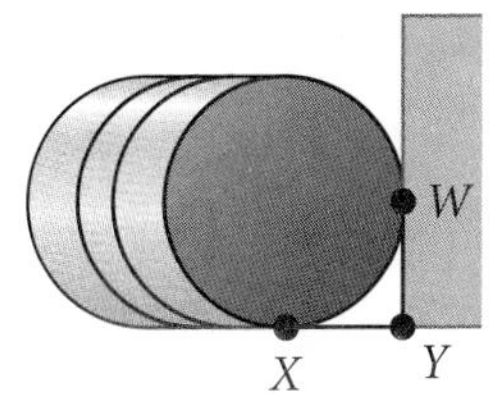

35. *Given:* $\overline{AB}$ and $\overline{AC}$ are tangent to ⊙R at B and C.

Prove: $\angle ABC \cong \angle ACB$

MORE MATH REASONING

36. A large drum of crude oil rolled off a truck and came to rest at edge of a wall. Emergency services officials need to know the diameter of the drum in order to send the proper equipment to reload it. Calculate the diameter of the drum to the nearest tenth of a foot. Assume that $WX = 19$ ft and $\overline{XY} \perp \overline{WY}$.

37. Sun Block During a total eclipse of the sun, the disk of the moon almost exactly covers the disk of the sun at certain locations on the earth (E). The average distance from the earth to the moon (EM) is approximately 237,000 mi. The average distance to the sun (ES) is approximately 93,000,000 mi, and the sun's radius (SR) is about 433,000 mi. Find the approximate radius of the moon, and explain your method.

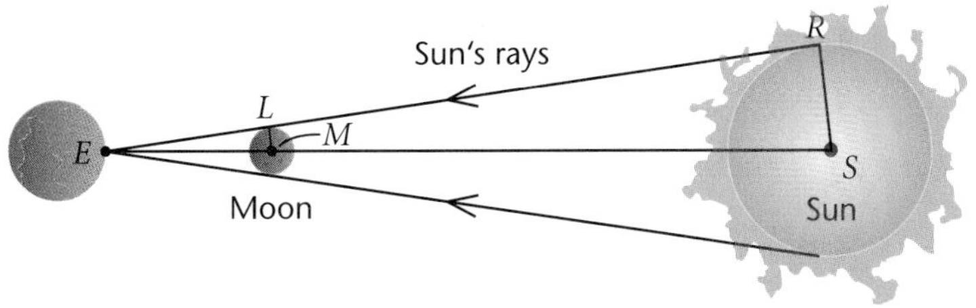

38. Find the equation for the line tangent to the circle $x^2 + y^2 = 25$ at the point (3, 4).

8-1 PART C The Circumference of a Circle

← CONNECT → ***You've calculated the perimeter of many different figures. Now you will discover a formula for the perimeter of a circle.***

As you know, the distance around a polygon is its perimeter. The distance around a circle is its **circumference.** Early in the history of mathematics, people discovered an important fact about the ratio of the circumference to the diameter of any circle.

EXPLORE: EASY AS . . .

MATERIALS

Tape measure
Three circular objects

Use a tape measure to measure the circumference and the diameter of three circular objects. For each object, calculate the ratio of the circumference to the diameter to the nearest tenth. Make a table to organize your results. What pattern do you see? What number do you think is equal to the circumference-to-diameter ratio for any circle?

Now we will look at another way to find the circumference-to-diameter ratio of a circle.

Although it is not always possible to construct inscribed regular n-gons accurately by hand, computers can generate and measure such figures easily.

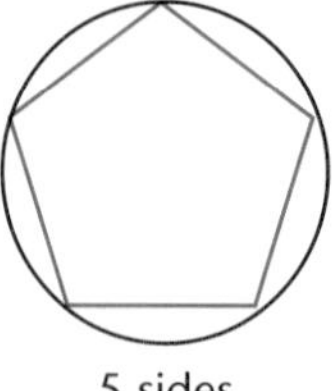

5 sides

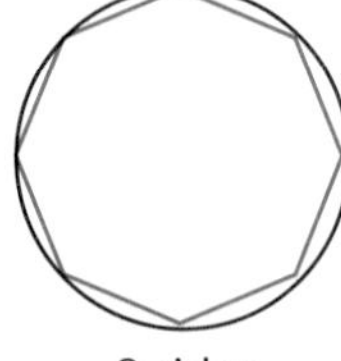

8 sides

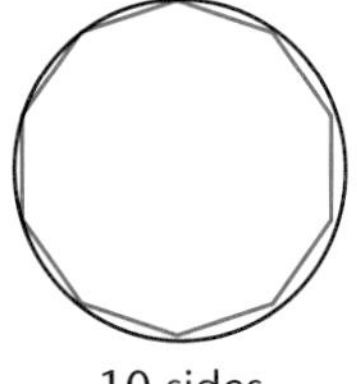

10 sides

1. As the number of sides of the inscribed regular polygon increases, how does the perimeter of the polygon compare to the circumference of the circle?

The table shows what happens as the number of sides of the inscribed regular polygon increases.

Regular Polygons Inscribed in a Circle of Diameter 1						
Number of sides	5	8	10	25	50	100
$\frac{\textbf{Perimeter}}{\textbf{Diameter}}$	2.939	3.061	3.090	3.133	3.140	3.141

Notice that the $\frac{\text{perimeter}}{\text{diameter}}$ ratio seems to approach a particular value as the sides of the inscribed polygons get closer to the circle. This "limiting" value, the ratio of the circumference of a circle to its diameter, is the number π **(pi).**

DEFINITION

The number π is the ratio of the circumference of any circle to its diameter. $\pi = \frac{c}{d}$

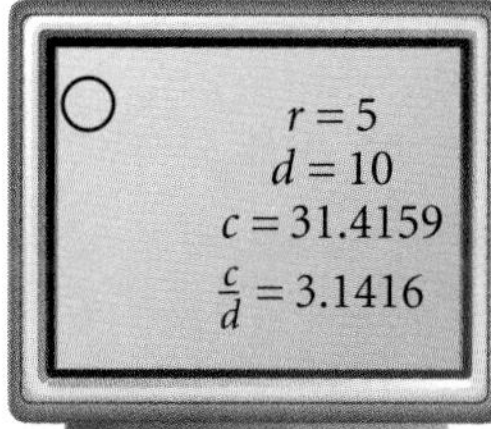

The definition of π leads immediately to two formulas for the circumference of a circle. These formulas are summarized as theorems at the top of page 552.

THEOREMS

The circumference of a circle is the product of π and its diameter, d.

$C = \pi d$

The circumference of a circle is twice the product of π and its radius, r.

$C = 2\pi r$

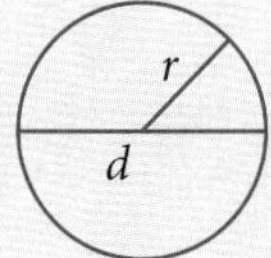

The number π is irrational—it cannot be written as an exact decimal. The first forty-five decimal places of π follow:
$\pi \approx 3.141592653589793238462643383279502884197169399$

Of course, you don't usually need this degree of accuracy. When working with problems involving π that call for an exact answer, leave π in the calculations and the answer. If you need an answer in decimal form, use the π key on your calculator and round your answer as necessary.

EXAMPLE

If the radius of $\odot C$ is 4 cm, what is its circumference to the nearest tenth of a centimeter?

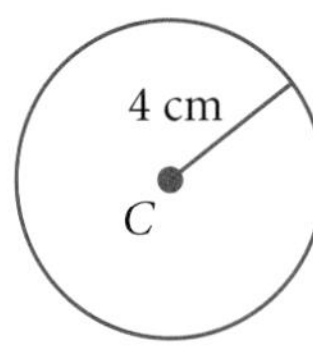

$C = 2\pi r$

$C = 2\pi(4) = 8\pi \approx 25.1$ cm

TRY IT

Round answers to the nearest tenth.

a. What is the circumference of the pan?
b. The circumference of a trash-can lid is 22π in. What is its diameter?

REFLECT

1. Does the ratio of the circumference to the diameter of a circle get larger if the radius of the circle is increased? Explain.
2. In your own words, explain what π is.
3. Suppose you find the perimeter-to-"diameter" ratio for a square, then a regular hexagon, octagon, decagon, 12-gon, etc. What does it mean to say that π is the limiting value for the perimeter-to-diameter ratio of these polygons?

Exercises

CORE

1. Getting Started Find the diameter and circumference of a circle whose radius is 3 in. Give your answers in exact form.

Find the circumference of each circle. Give your answers in exact form and as decimals rounded to the nearest hundredth.

2. a circle with diameter 42 ft

3. a circle with radius 5.7 mm

Find the radius of the circle with each circumference.

4. 24π cm

5. 1.07 in.

6. A rubber belt connects the two flywheels shown. Find the total length of the belt.

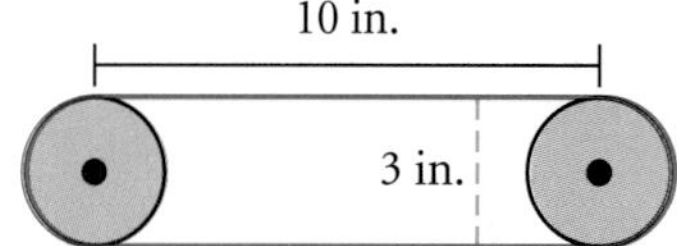

Find the perimeter of each figure.

7.

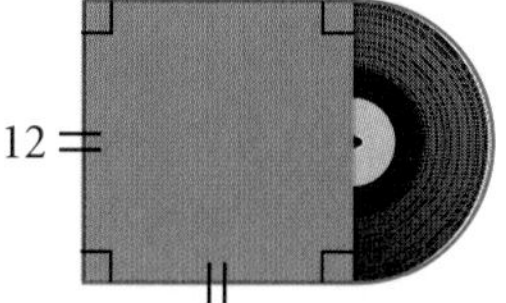

8.

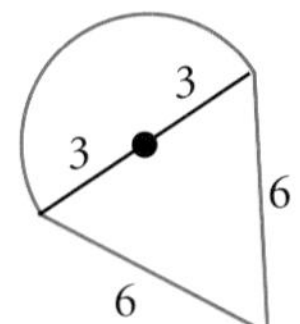

9.

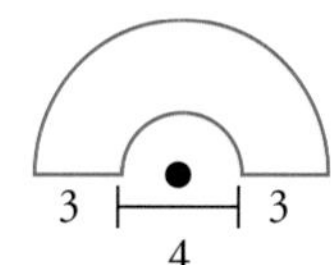

10. If a sphere has radius 22 cm, find the circumference of one of its great circles.

11. This wood spool is about 1.5 in. long and 1 in. in diameter. Draw two different cross sections of the spool that help to show its shape clearly.

12. Fogg Around the World In *Around the World in Eighty Days* by Jules Verne, Phileas Fogg boasts that he can travel around the world in 80 days or less. (Since he was traveling in the late 1800s, he couldn't take an airplane!) What average speed is needed to go around the earth at the equator in 80 days? Use 3960 mi for the radius of the earth, and assume you travel 12 hr each day.

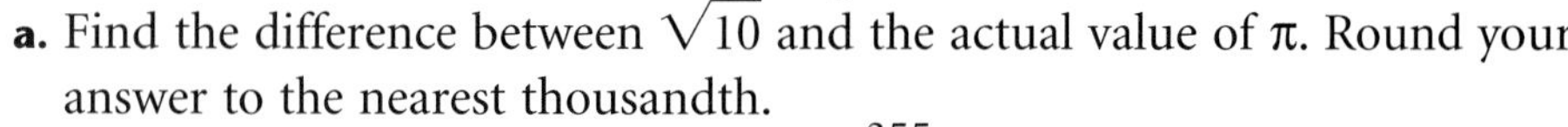

13. Ch'ang Höng (78–139 A.D.), a Chinese astrologer and government minister, used $\sqrt{10}$ as a value for π in his writings.

a. Find the difference between $\sqrt{10}$ and the actual value of π. Round your answer to the nearest thousandth.

b. Tsu Ch'ung-Chih (430–501 A.D.) gave $\frac{355}{113}$ as the "accurate value" for π. Is this approximation closer to the actual value for π than $\sqrt{10}$? Explain.

14. The Inside Track The track shown has semicircular turns. In a race on the track, Manuela got to the inside lane, and Beth was forced to run 1 yd outside of Manuela. In one lap around the track, how much farther does Beth run than Manuela? Why do runners prefer to run on the inside of a track?

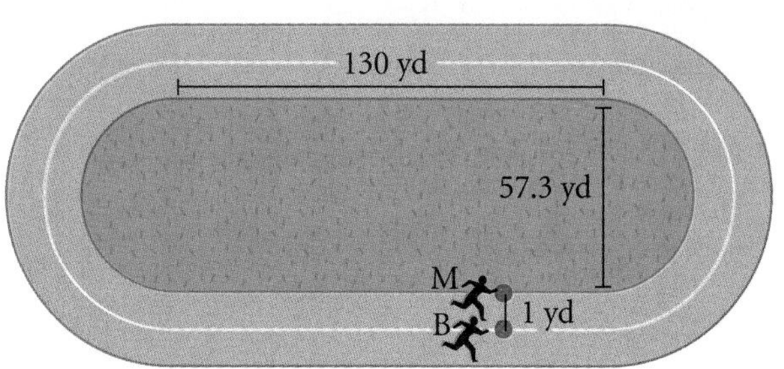

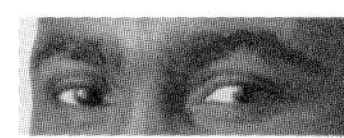

LOOK AHEAD

Evaluate each expression. Round answers to the nearest hundredth.

15. $3x^2$ for $x = 4$

16. $5.24y^2$ for $y = 2.23$

17. $\sqrt{\frac{z}{4.32}}$ for $z = 72.31$

18. Draw a parallelogram.

a. Describe how you can make one cut and move one piece of the parallelogram to form a rectangle.

b. Explain how this rearrangement can be used to justify the area formula for a parallelogram.

19. State the area formula for a regular polygon. Then find the area of a regular hexagon with a radius of five centimeters.

MORE PRACTICE

Find the circumference of each circle. Give your answers in exact form and as decimals rounded to the nearest hundredth.

20. a circle with diameter 31 m

21. a circle with radius 13.8 in.

Find the radius of a circle with each circumference.

22. 15π mm

23. 77.1 yd

Find the perimeter of each shaded figure.

24.

7.6

3

25.

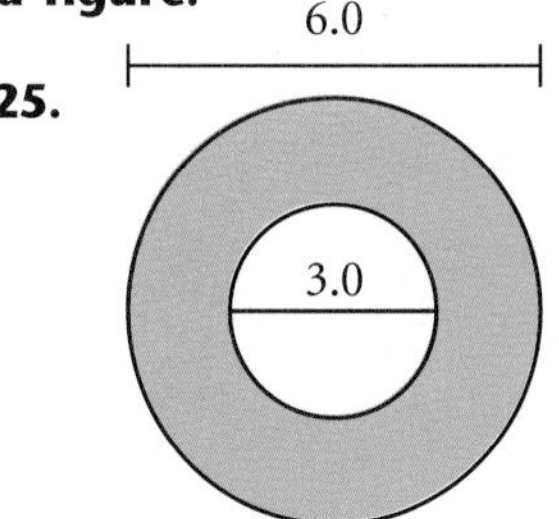

26.

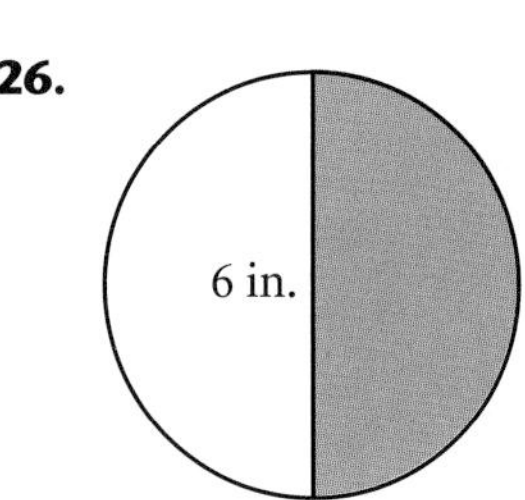

MORE MATH REASONING

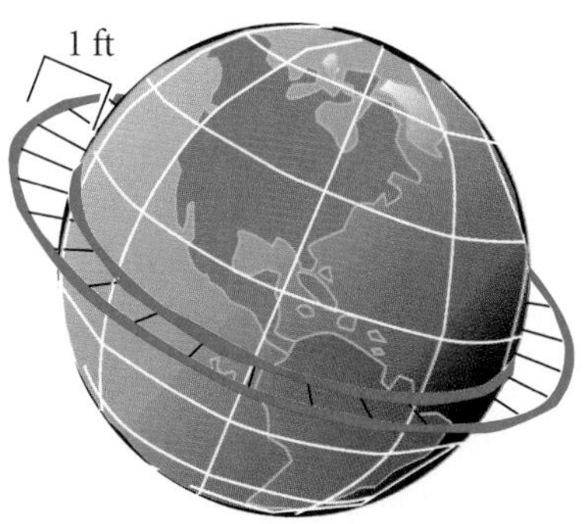

27. Suppose you tightly wrap a ribbon around the earth's equator and then add a second ribbon, supported by one-foot posts, above the first. The ribbons are concentric circles. (Assume that the earth is spherical and that each ribbon forms a circle.)

a. Guess how much longer you think the top ribbon is than the lower ribbon.

b. The radius of the earth at its equator is 20,926,435.2 ft. Find the radius of the top ribbon to the nearest tenth of a foot.

c. Find the circumferences of the top and bottom ribbons. What is the difference?

d. Compare your answer in **27c** to your guess in **27a**. Are you surprised?

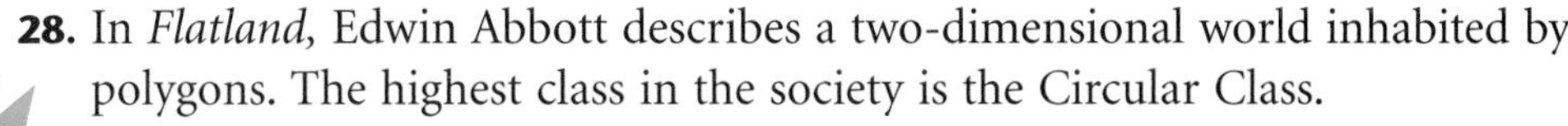

28. In *Flatland,* Edwin Abbott describes a two-dimensional world inhabited by polygons. The highest class in the society is the Circular Class.

"[I]t is known that no Circle is really a Circle, but only a Polygon with a very large number of very small sides. . . . It is always assumed, by courtesy, that the Chief Circle . . . has ten thousand sides."

a. Explain why "no Circle is really a Circle" in Flatland. Why do the inhabitants refer to them as "circles" at all?

b. The perimeter of a Flatland polygon is three feet. Find the approximate radius of the Chief Circle. Explain how you found your answer.

8-1 PART D The Area of a Circle

← CONNECT → ***You know how to calculate the circumference of a circle. Now you will investigate and use the formula for the area of a circle.***

In order to know how much glass is needed for a circular stained-glass window, the artist must calculate the area of a circle. The area formula for a circle may be familiar to you. In the following Explore, you will discover this formula for yourself.

EXPLORE: CUTTING A MEAN CIRCLE

MATERIALS

Compass
Scissors

1. Use your compass to construct a circle with a radius of approximately 3 in. Cut out the circular region. Fold the region in half. Then fold your paper in half three more times.

2. Unfold your circular region, and cut it along the folds to create sixteen wedges. Place the wedges in a row as shown in the lower figure, so that they resemble a parallelogram.

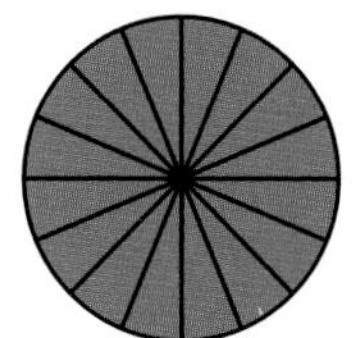

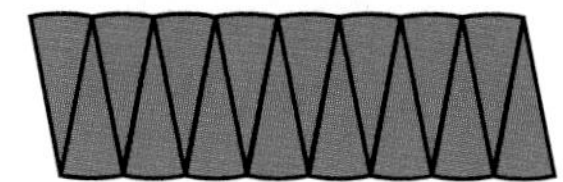

3. What is the area of the "parallelogram" you created? (Hint: Label the base and height of the "parallelogram." The radius of the original circle is r, and the circumference is $2\pi r$. Use this information to find the base and height of the "parallelogram," and then find its area.) How is this related to the area of the circle?

Problem-Solving Tip

See if you can use familiar facts in a new setting.

Now, let's see why the formula for the area of a circle works. Consider a series of inscribed regular polygons.

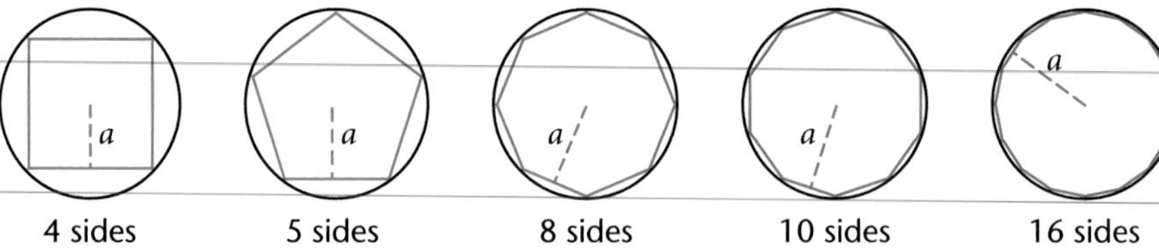

Recall that the formula for the area of a regular polygon is $A = \frac{1}{2}ap$, where a is the length of the apothem, and p is the perimeter of the polygon. As you can see, the greater the number of sides in the regular polygon, the more closely it resembles a circle.

The following calculation shows how we can derive the area formula for a circle.

By substituting the limiting values into the area formula for a regular polygon, you can justify a familiar result.

Area of a polygon $= \frac{1}{2}ap$

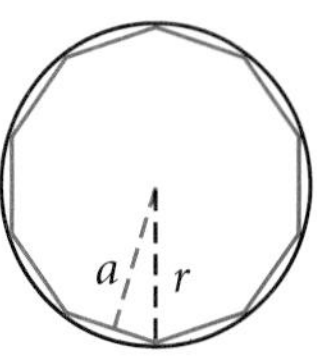

Area of a circle $= \frac{1}{2}rC$ — Substitute the radius for the apothem and the circumference for the perimeter.

Area of a circle $= \frac{1}{2}r(2\pi r)$ — Substitute $2\pi r$ for C.

Area of a circle $= \pi r^2$

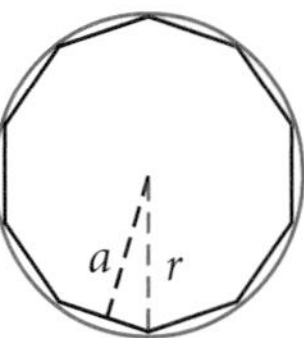

EXAMPLES

Leave answers in exact form.

1. If the radius of $\odot C$ is 3 cm, what is its area?
$A = \pi r^2 = 9\pi \text{ cm}^2$

2. If the area of $\odot C$ is $49\pi \text{ ft}^2$, what is its diameter?
If $A = \pi r^2 = 49\pi$, $r^2 = 49$. Since the radius must be a positive number, $r = 7$ ft and $d = 14$ ft.

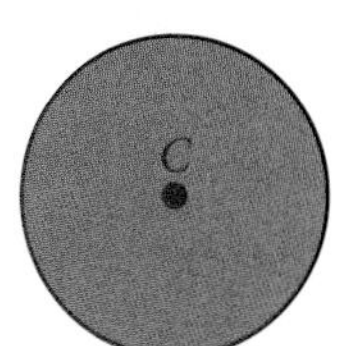

TRY IT

a. The diameter of the Aztec calendar stone shown at the right is 12 feet. This stone, which weighs over 24 tons, may have enabled the Aztecs to calculate the motions of the planets. Find the area and circumference of the face of the calendar stone.

THEOREM

Areas

The area of a circle is the product of π and the square of its radius, r.

$A = \pi r^2$

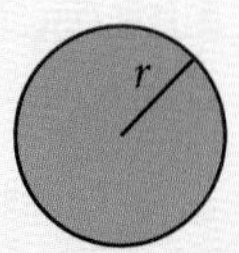

REFLECT

1. Why does rearranging segments of a circle as shown in the preceding Explore give only an *approximate* parallelogram? How can you use this method to get a figure that is closer to a true parallelogram?
2. Do you think a regular polygon with 1000 sides has a perimeter equal to the circumference of its circumscribed circle? Explain.

Exercises

CORE

1. **Getting Started** Find the diameter, circumference, and area of a circle whose radius is 5 cm. Give your answers in exact form.

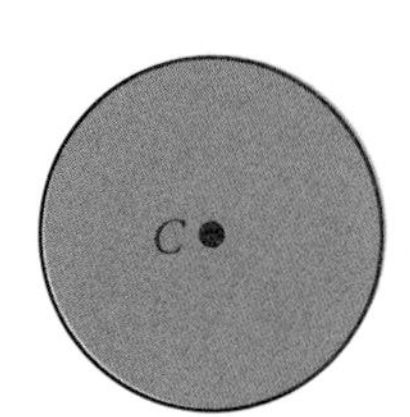

Find each of the following for ⊙C. Give your answers in exact form and as decimals rounded to the nearest hundredth.

2. If its radius is 4 in., find its area.
3. If its area is 25π cm^2, find its diameter.
4. If its diameter is 12.6 mm, find its area.
5. If its circumference is 6π ft, find its area.
6. If its area is 1.75 in.^{2}, find its circumference.
7. Sara Bates, a Cherokee artist, makes circular works of art from natural materials like feathers, berries, and pine cones. Her art uses patterns, repetition, and symbols that recall Cherokee traditions, but her work is a new way of expressing these forms.

Fine Arts

Bates's works are usually from seven to eleven feet in diameter. Find the minimum and maximum areas of these pieces.

8. The radius of the signal of a radio station extends 78 km from the base of the tower. What is the area of the region that the signal can reach?
9. Suppose a square with an area of 100 in.^{2} is inscribed in a circle. Find the circumference and the area of the circle.
10. If the radius of a circle is tripled, what effect does this have on the area of the circle? Explain why your result makes sense.

11. The circumference of a circle is a function of its radius. The area of a circle is also a function of its radius.

a. Graph the function $C = 2\pi r$ on a coordinate plane for r-values from 0 to 4.

b. On the same plane, graph the function $A = \pi r^2$ for r-values from 0 to 4.

c. Compare the shapes of your two graphs. Why does each graph have the shape it does?

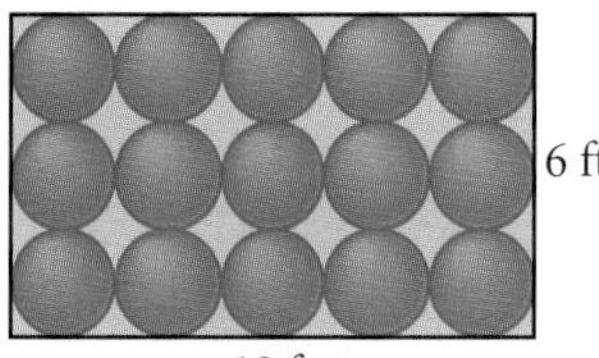

12. Circles of equal radii are packed in a rectangle as shown. If you throw a dart and hit the target, what is the probability that your dart will land inside one of the circles?

13. Suppose you have 240 yd of fencing and want to enclose the greatest possible area with it.

a. Find the area of the largest equilateral triangle, square, and regular hexagon that you can enclose with this amount of fencing.

b. Find the area of the largest circle that you can enclose.

c. Of the four, which figure gives the greatest area for a given perimeter? Do you think this is the best possible figure?

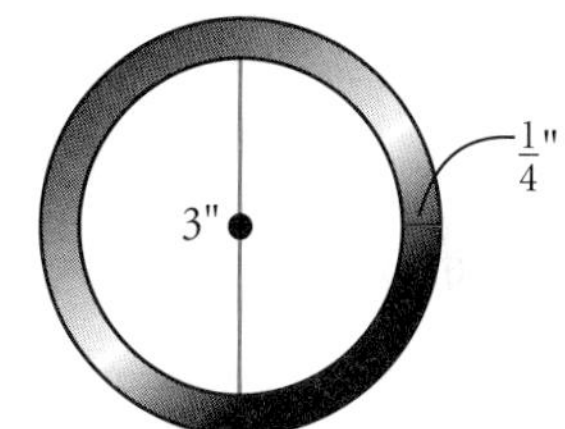

14. The figure at the right represents the cross section of a pipe $\frac{1}{4}$ in. thick, with an inside diameter of 3 in. Find the area of the shaded region.

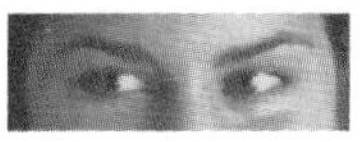

LOOK BACK

15. Prove: If a quadrilateral is a parallelogram, then a diagonal divides it into two congruent triangles. [6-2]

History

16. Asoka (273-232 B.C.), an emperor of the Maruya Empire in India, had sandstone pillars set up throughout the empire. The shadow cast by one of these pillars when the sun's angle of elevation is 61° is 6 m long. How tall is the pillar? [7-3]

MORE PRACTICE

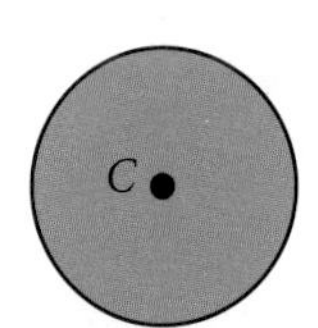

Find each of the following for ⊙C. Give your answers in exact form and as decimals rounded to the nearest hundredth.

17. If its radius is 5 ft, find its area.

18. If its area is 36π in.^{2}, find its radius.

19. If its area is 563 cm^2, find its circumference.

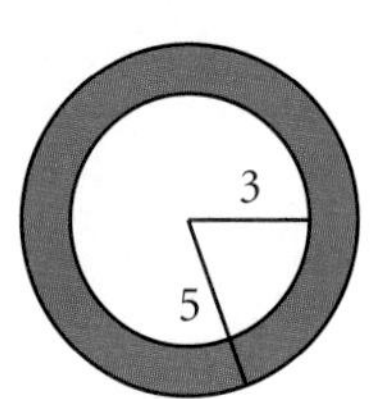

20. Find the area of the *annulus* (the shaded region) shown at the right.

MORE MATH REASONING

History

21. The Yenri Method Seki Kowa, born in 1642 in Edo (now Tokyo), Japan, is credited with developing a calculus native to seventeenth-century Japan. This early form of calculus is known as the *yenri* (circle principle). *Yenri* was a method of finding the area of a circle. Follow the steps to get an idea of how the method works.

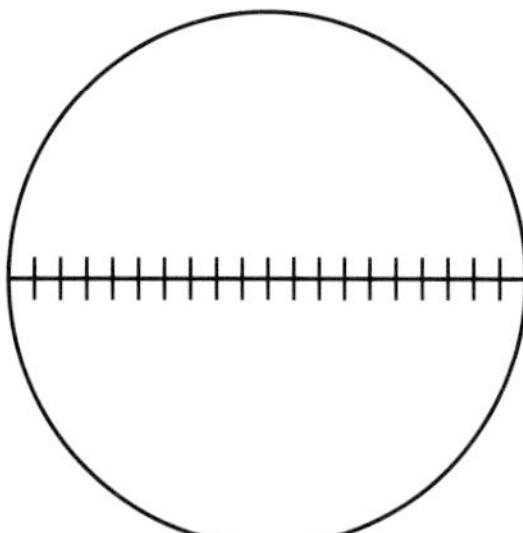

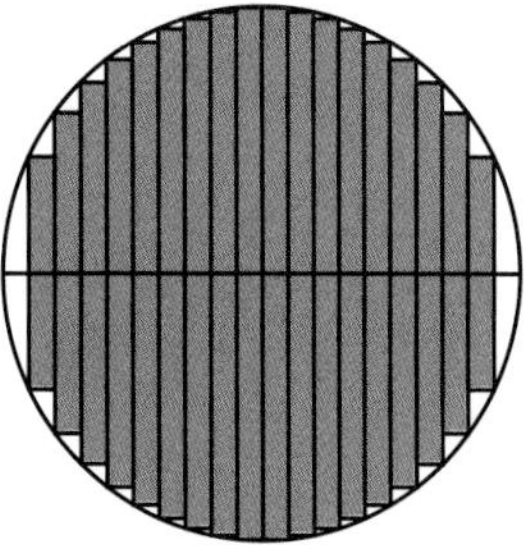

a. Open your compass to 10 cm, and draw a circle on a sheet of paper.

b. Draw a horizontal diameter in your circle. Mark off 1-cm lengths from the center of the circle as shown.

c. Draw vertical segments through each of the points marked off in **21b.** Then draw horizontal segments to form rectangles as shown.

d. Each rectangle has a width of 1 cm. Measure the height of each rectangle. Then find the area of each rectangle, and add all the areas to find the approximate area of the circle.

e. Your result should be a reasonable estimate for the area of the circle. Use the formula $A = \pi r^2$ to calculate the actual area of the circle. Compare the two results.

f. How could you modify this method to get a better estimate of the area of the circle?

8-1 PART E Making Connections

← CONNECT →

Circles are the "shape of choice" for many real-world objects, like utility-hole covers and wheel rims. You've become familiar with some of the terms associated with circles and investigated the formulas for their circumference and area.

Now that you've learned some of the terminology and formulas associated with circles, you can compare some characteristics of $33\frac{1}{3}$, 45, and 78 rpm (revolutions per minute) records and compact disks.

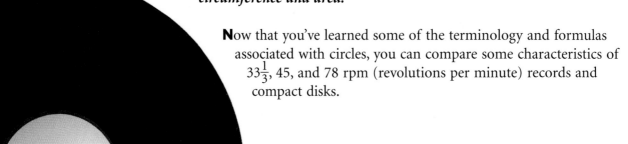

EXPLORE: SOUND CALCULATIONS

The table lists some characteristics of CDs and records.

	78 rpm Record	45 rpm Single	$33\frac{1}{3}$ rpm LP	CD
Diameter	10 in.	7 in.	12 in.	12.5 cm
Speed of Rotation	78 rpm	45 rpm	$33\frac{1}{3}$ rpm	200 rpm

1. Convert the diameter of the compact disk to inches. Then calculate the area of each type of recording. Give your answers in square inches to the nearest hundredth.
2. Aretha Franklin's recording of *Respect* plays for 2 min, 26 sec. How far does a speck of dust on the edge of each type of recording travel during that time? Give answers in inches to the nearest inch. On which type of recording does the speck travel the farthest?

REFLECT

1. The diameters and circumferences of two circles may be very different. Which property of the circles is always the same? Explain.
2. Create an illustrated summary of terms associated with circles.

Self-Assessment

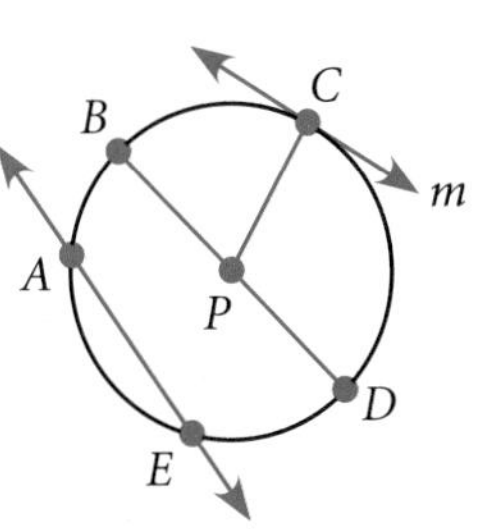

1. Name the circle at the right.
2. Name three radii of the circle.
3. Name a diameter of the circle.
4. Name a secant line.
5. Name a tangent to the circle, and identify the point of tangency.

In the figure at the right, $\overleftrightarrow{HF}$ is tangent to $\odot G$ at F.

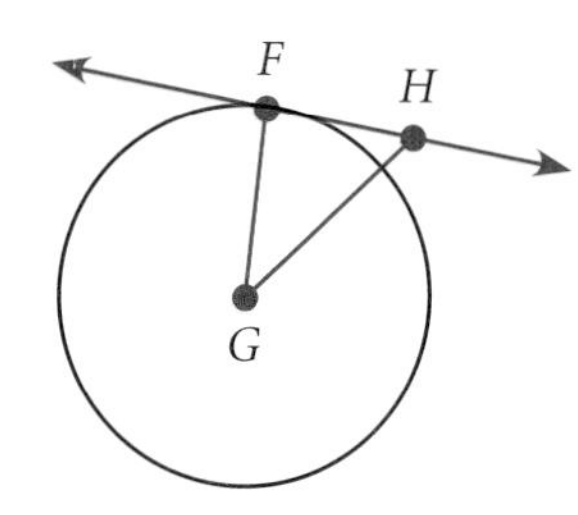

6. What is $m\angle HFG$?

7. If $FG = 4$ and $HG = 5$, find HF.

8. If $HF = 3.7$ and $FG = 5.6$, find HG.

9. If $HF = 14.3$ and $HG = 22.6$, find FG.

10. If the radius of $\odot M$ is 57 in., find its area.

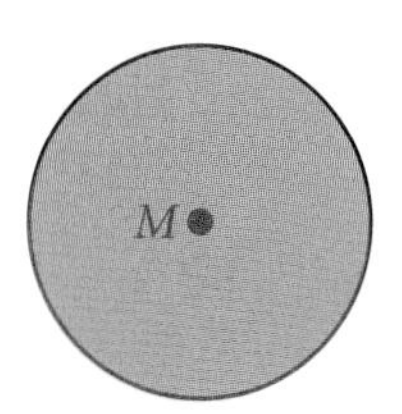

11. If its area is 22.45 cm^2, find its radius.

12. If its area is 121 m^2, find its circumference.

13. A square and a regular hexagon are inscribed in separate circles, each 4 ft in diameter.

a. Make an accurate sketch of each of the figures.

b. Find the probability that a randomly selected point within each circle will be inside the inscribed polygon.

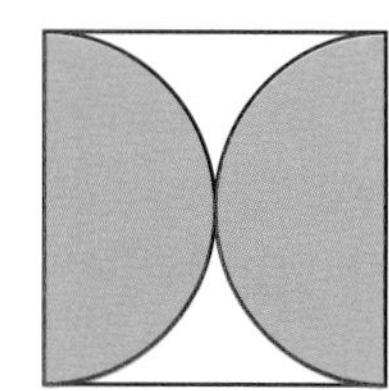

14. Two semicircles are drawn inside a square as shown. What is the probability that a randomly selected point inside the square will lie in a shaded region?

(a) $\frac{\pi}{4}$ (b) $\frac{3}{4}$ (c) $\frac{\pi}{6}$ (d) $\frac{4}{5}$ (e) $\frac{\pi}{2}$

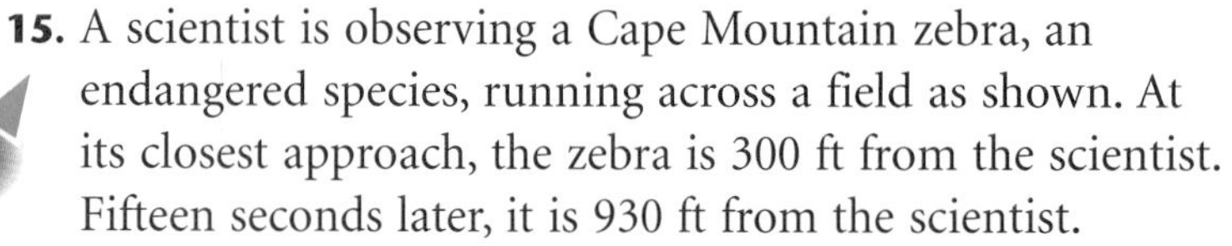

15. A scientist is observing a Cape Mountain zebra, an endangered species, running across a field as shown. At its closest approach, the zebra is 300 ft from the scientist. Fifteen seconds later, it is 930 ft from the scientist.

a. Find the distance CZ and the speed of the zebra in feet per second. [5-3]

b. Find the measure of the angle $\angle CSZ$. [7-3]

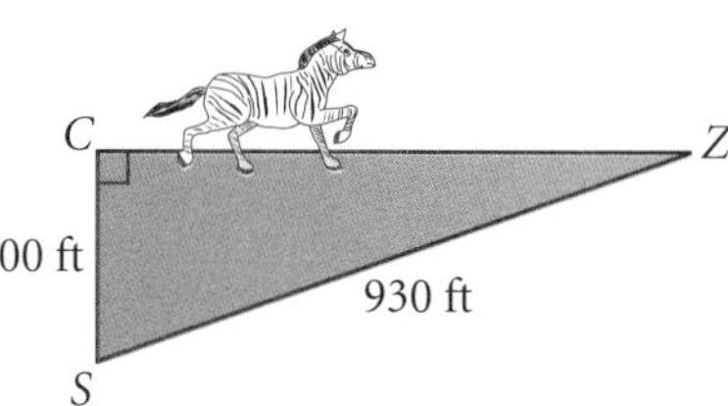

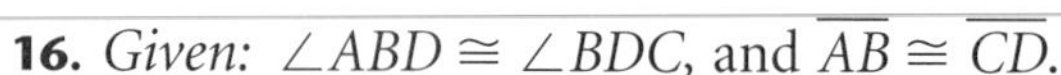

16. *Given:* $\angle ABD \cong \angle BDC$, and $\overline{AB} \cong \overline{CD}$.

Prove: $ABCD$ is a parallelogram. [6-2]

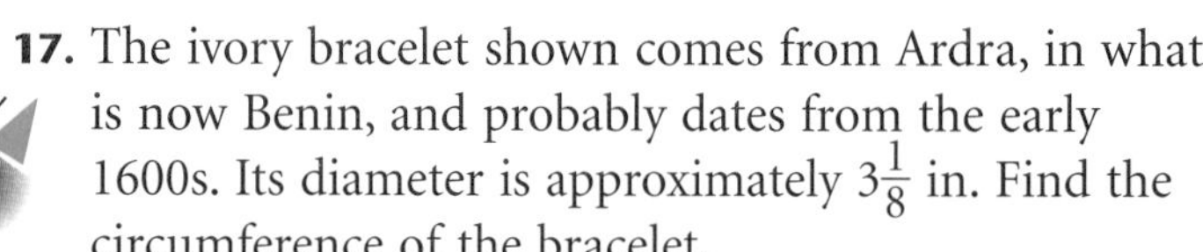

17. The ivory bracelet shown comes from Ardra, in what is now Benin, and probably dates from the early 1600s. Its diameter is approximately $3\frac{1}{8}$ in. Find the circumference of the bracelet.

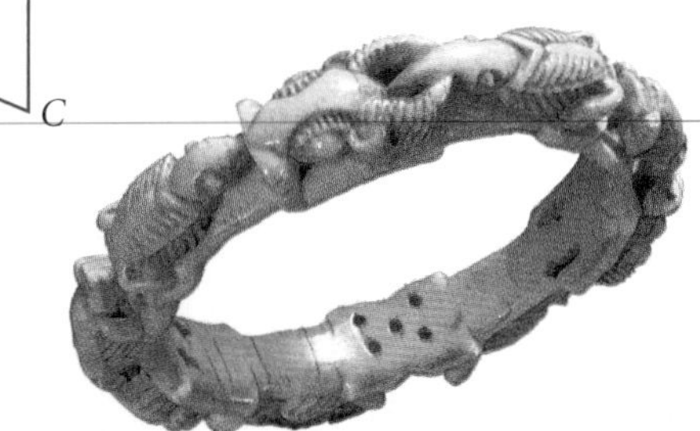

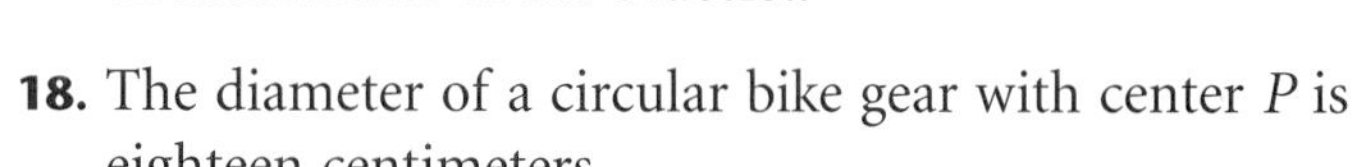

18. The diameter of a circular bike gear with center P is eighteen centimeters.

a. Find the circumference of the gear.

b. If the length of chain $\overline{MN}$ is forty-four centimeters, find the distance PN.

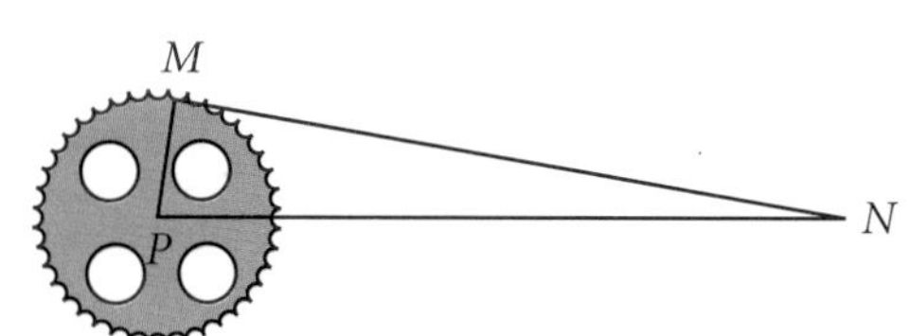

8-2 Angles, Arcs, and Chords

IT'S A BIG WORLD OUT THERE

How do we know how large the earth really is? If calculating the size of the earth seems difficult now, imagine how impossible it must have seemed before anyone had been around the world—or even across the Atlantic Ocean.

Eratosthenes, an ancient geometer, mathematician, geographer, and poet, made one of the earliest calculations of the circumference of the earth. His calculations differ from the present measurement by less than one percent!

Eratosthenes was born in Cyrene (in what is now Libya) around 274 B.C. His nickname, "Beta"(the second letter of the Greek alphabet), may have shown that Eratosthenes was considered the second great thinker of ancient times, after Plato.

In mathematics, Eratosthenes is best known for his prime number "sieve." He started by writing a list of several consecutive whole numbers greater than 1. Next, he went through the list and crossed off all numbers greater than 2 that were multiples of 2:

2, 3, ~~4,~~ 5, ~~6,~~ 7, ~~8,~~ 9, ~~10,~~ 11, ~~12,~~ 13, ~~14,~~ 15, ~~16~~....

Then he found the next number that was not crossed off—in this case, 3—and crossed off all its multiples greater than itself:

2, 3, ~~4,~~ 5, ~~6,~~ 7, ~~8,~~ ~~9,~~ ~~10,~~ 11, ~~12,~~ 13, ~~14,~~ ~~15~~....

The process continued in this way. When it was finished, the numbers that were not crossed off were prime numbers.

?

1. **After crossing off all the multiples of 3 on the list, which multiples would Eratosthenes have crossed off next? Why?**

2. **Explain why the sieve of Eratosthenes works.**

3. **Eratosthenes calculated the circumference of the earth by *indirect measurement*. Explain what you think is meant by this term.**

8-2 PART A Arcs and Central Angles

← CONNECT → ***You already know a great deal about angles in polygons. Now you will work with angles and arcs in circles.***

The circle graph shows the land areas of the continents.

Land Area of Continents

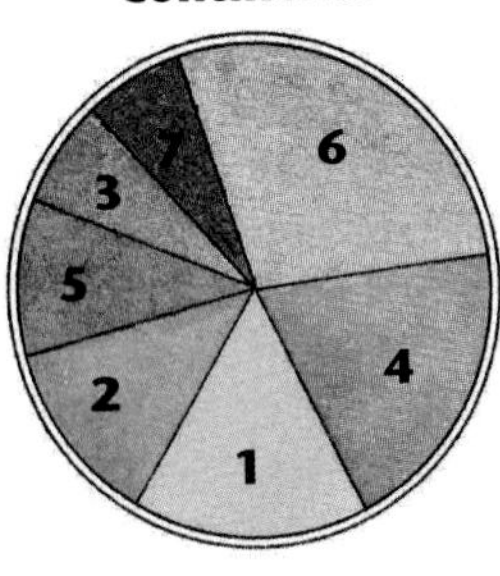

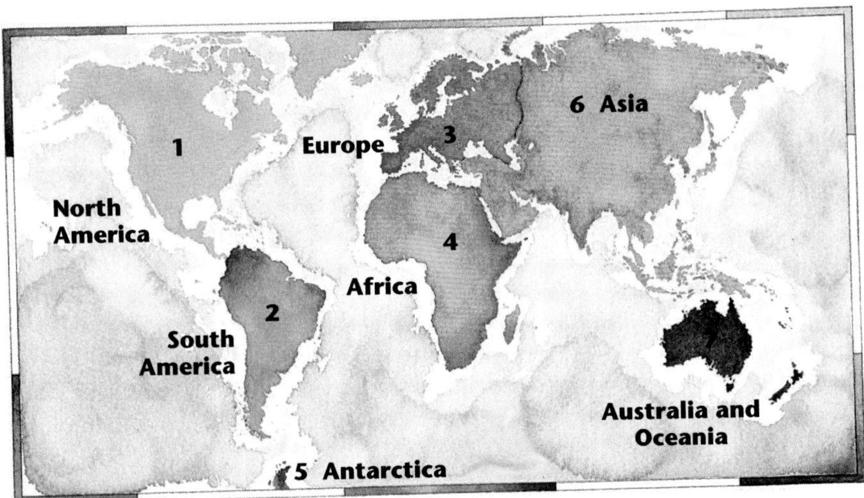

EXPLORE: A SLICE OF DATA

MATERIALS

Compass
Straightedge
Protractor

1. Choose a topic on which to collect data. Use a question from the following list, or use one suggested by your teacher.
   - How many pens and pencils do you have with you right now?
   - How many brothers and sisters do you have?
   - How many hours do you sleep per night?
2. Take a survey. Have each person answer the question, and tally the responses as shown.
3. To make your circle graph, you'll have to find the angle measure of the "pie piece" that represents each response. Calculate and record the angle measure of the pie piece for each response. How did you calculate the angle measures?
4. Make a circle graph showing the frequency of each response. Where did you locate the vertices of the angles in your graph?

The angles in a circle graph and the **arcs** (parts of a circle) they cut off have special names.

When you make a circle graph, the vertices of all of the angles are at the center of the circle. These angles are called **central angles.** Any central angle divides a circle into two arcs.

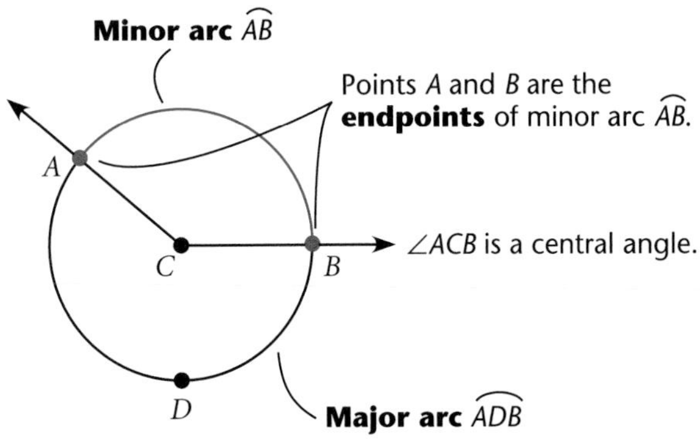

We name a minor arc by its endpoints. Notice that we need to use *three* points to name a major arc. If the endpoints of an arc lie on the diameter of a circle, then the arc is a **semicircle.** Like major arcs, semicircles are named with three letters.

You know that a complete circle has 360°. The measures of the arcs of a circle are based on this idea.

The **measure of a minor arc** is equal to the measure of its central angle. Central angle $\angle WYX$ intercepts minor arc $\widehat{WX}$, so $m\widehat{WX} = m\angle WYX = 80°$.

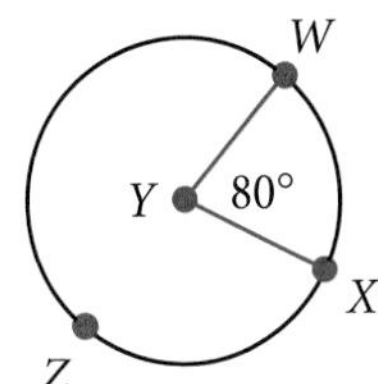

The **measure of a major arc** is 360° minus the measure of its minor arc. $m\widehat{XZW} = 360° - m\widehat{WX} = 280°$.

The **measure of any semicircle** is 180°.

TRY IT

Find each arc measure in $\odot L$.

a. $m\widehat{MN}$

b. $m\widehat{MPN}$

c. $m\widehat{PQN}$

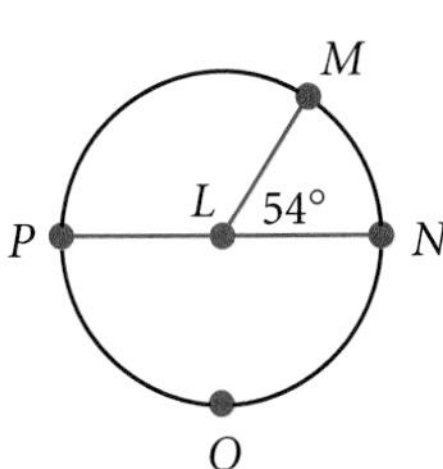

When two arcs are adjacent, you can find the measure of the larger arc they determine simply by adding their measures.

ARC-ADDITION THEOREM

The measure of two adjacent, nonoverlapping arcs is the sum of the measures of the two arcs. That is, if C is on arc $\overset{\frown}{AB}$, then $m\overset{\frown}{AB} = m\overset{\frown}{AC} + m\overset{\frown}{CB}$.

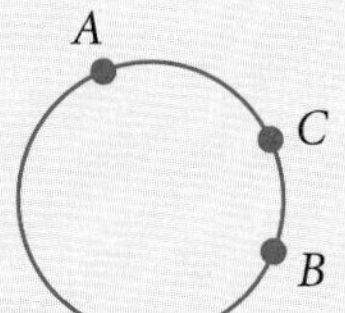

EXAMPLES

Find each arc measure.

1. $m\overset{\frown}{RST}$

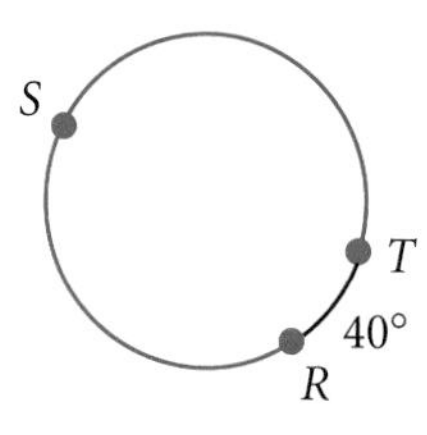

$m\overset{\frown}{RST} = 360° - 40°$
$= 320°$

2. $m\overset{\frown}{DE}$

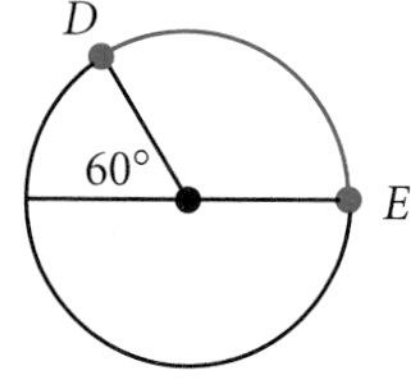

$m\overset{\frown}{DE} = 180° - 60°$
$= 120°$

3. $m\overset{\frown}{HGF}$

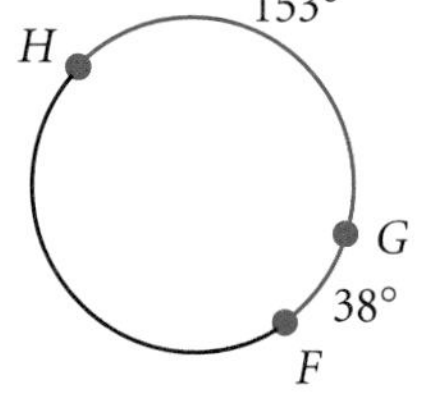

$m\overset{\frown}{HGF} = 153° + 38°$
$= 191°$

Like other geometric figures, arcs of circles can be congruent. Consider the following definition.

DEFINITION

Congruent arcs are arcs in the same circle (or congruent circles) that have the same measure.

REFLECT

1. Explain why the words "in the same circle (or congruent circles)" are needed in the definition of congruent arcs.

2. Explain why the measure of a major arc is equal to 360° minus the measure of its minor arc. Why is the measure of a semicircle 180°?

3. What is the range of possible measures for a minor arc? a major arc? Explain.

Exercises

CORE

Getting Started Use ⊙*D* for each of the following.

1. Name two central angles.

2. Name two minor arcs.

3. Name two major arcs.

4. Name a semicircle.

5. Find $m\widehat{AB}$.

6. Find $m\widehat{ACB}$.

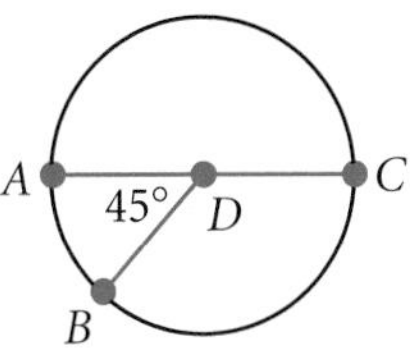

Find each arc measure.

7. $m\widehat{GFH}$

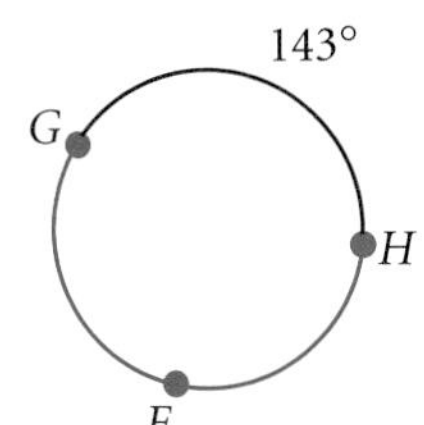

8. $m\widehat{JK}$

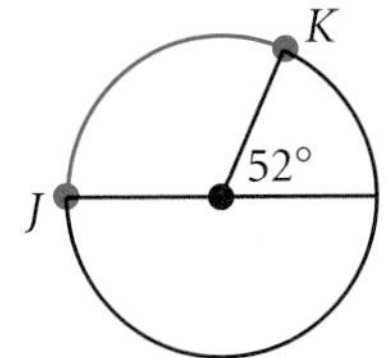

9. $m\widehat{LMN}$

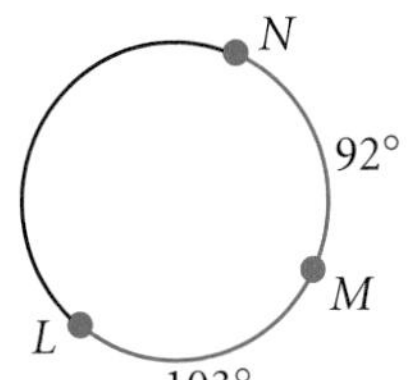

Find each arc measure.

10. $m\widehat{HI}$

11. $m\widehat{KJ}$

12. $m\widehat{HGI}$

13. $m\widehat{KJI}$

14. $m\widehat{GI}$

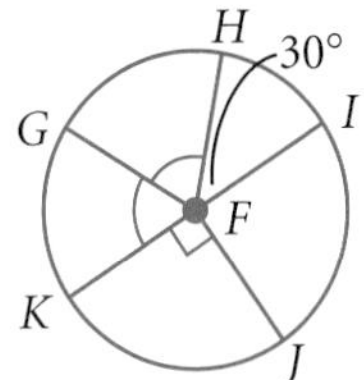

What fractional part of a circle is each of the following arc measures?

15. 90°

16. 270°

17. 120°

What is the arc measure of each of the following fractional parts of a circle?

18. $\frac{1}{6}$

19. $\frac{7}{12}$

20. $\frac{15}{36}$

21. Draw a spinner for a game that has the correct probability for each of the following outcomes. Explain why your spinner works.

• Ahead 1 space	35%
• Pick a card	20%
• Ahead 2 spaces	20%
• Back 1 space	15%
• Lose a turn	10%

22. Find $m\angle PQR$ and $m\angle PRQ$ in the figure at the right. Explain your reasoning.

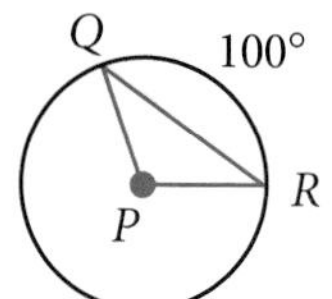

Social Science

23. Draw a circle graph for the given data in the following table. Below your graph, list the measure of the central angle for each data category. (Source: *The 1993 Information Please Almanac.*)

Expenditures of the United States Federal Government in 1992 (in billions of dollars)	
• Social Security and veterans' benefits	321
• Defense	307
• Medicare and health	213
• Interest (on national debt, etc.)	200
• Income security (unemployment, etc.)	196
• Commerce and housing	55
• Other (education, transportation, cost of government, etc.)	151

24. Solve for x in the figure at the right.

25. Prove the Arc-Addition Theorem. (Hint: Use the Angle-Addition Postulate.)

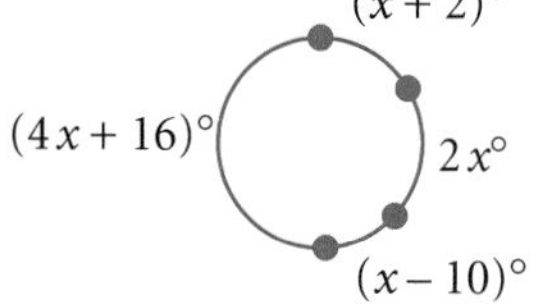

LOOK AHEAD

26. A phone company worker is wrapping telephone cable around a 5-ft-diameter storage spool. To the nearest hundredth of a foot, what is the length of cable needed to go halfway around the spool?

27. **Pi or Pie?** An apple pie was baked in a tin with a nine-inch diameter.
    a. What is the area of the pie?
    b. If the pie is cut into four equal wedge-shaped pieces, what is the area of each?
    c. If the pie is cut into six equal wedges, what is the area of each?
    d. Describe how you calculated your answers to **27b** and **27c.**

MORE PRACTICE

Find each arc measure.

28. $m\widehat{VW}$

29. $m\widehat{UV}$

30. $m\widehat{TYW}$

31. $m\widehat{VWT}$

32. $m\widehat{UW}$

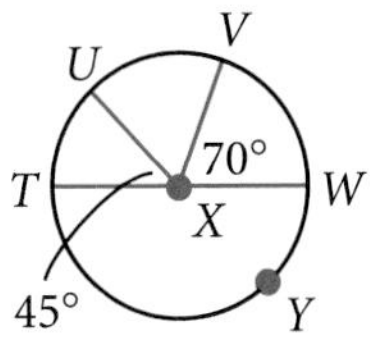

Find each arc measure.

33. $m\widehat{DF}$

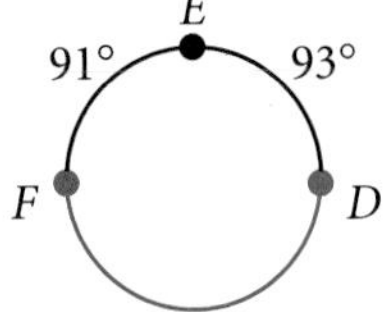

34. $m\widehat{GHI}$

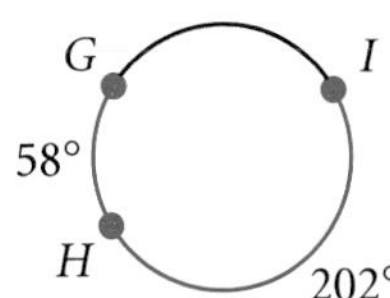

35. $m\widehat{JK}$

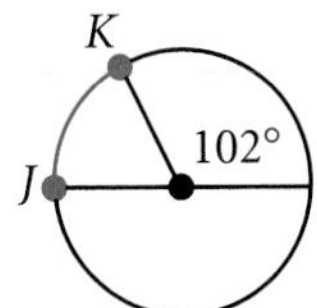

MORE MATH REASONING

Find the measure of the arc of a circle cut off by one side of each regular inscribed polygon.

36.

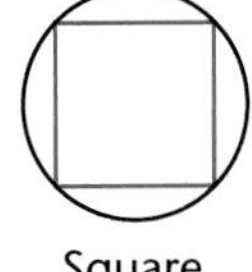

Square

37.

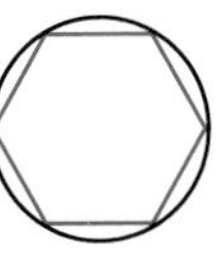

Hexagon

38.

Octagon

39. Sketch a segment $\overline{AB}$, and construct its perpendicular bisector $\overleftrightarrow{CD}$. Then use your knowledge of circles to explain why this construction works.

The *angular velocity* of a rotating object is the measure of the arc it turns through in a given amount of time. Find the angular velocity, in degrees per second, of each object.

40. the second hand on a clock

41. a speck of dust on the outside of a record rotating at 45 rpm

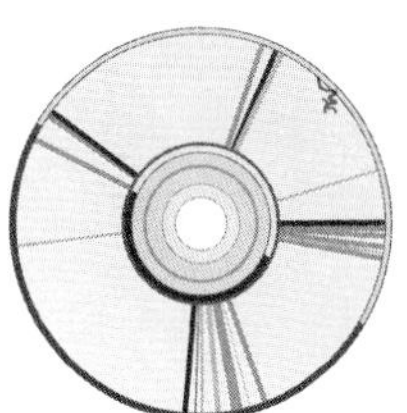

42. a person on the earth's surface

8-2 PART B Arc Length and Sectors

← CONNECT → ***You know how to find the circumference and area of an entire circle. Now you will use proportional thinking to find arc lengths and areas of portions of circles.***

Central angles cut the circumference of a circle into arcs. They also cut the interior of the circle into wedge-shaped regions. You can use proportions to find the **arc lengths** and the areas of these regions.

DEFINITION

A **sector** of a circle is a region formed by two radii and an arc of a circle. *ABC* is a sector of ⊙*B*.

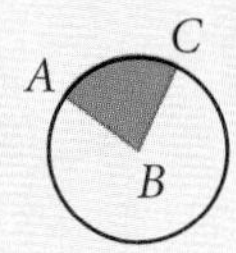

EXAMPLES

In the figure at the right, $\angle JKL$ is a central angle of ⊙*K*.

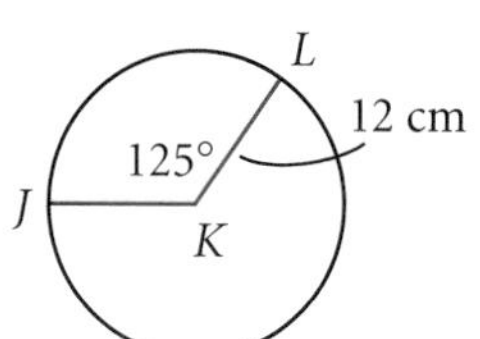

1. Find the arc length of $\widehat{JL}$ to the nearest tenth.

The arc $\widehat{JL}$ covers 125° of the total 360° in ⊙*K*. Thus, 125 is to 360 as the length of $\widehat{JL}$ is to the circumference (total arc length) of the circle.

$$\frac{125}{360} = \frac{\text{length } \widehat{JL}}{\text{circumference } \odot K} = \frac{\text{length } \widehat{JL}}{75.4}$$

The circumference of ⊙*K* is $2(12)\pi \approx 75.4$.

$$360 \times \text{length } \widehat{JL} = 75.4 \times 125 = 9425.0$$

$$\text{length } \widehat{JL} = \frac{9425}{360} \approx 26.2 \text{ cm}$$

2. Find the area of sector *JKL* to the nearest tenth.

The ratio of the area of sector *JKL* to the area of ⊙*K* is equal to the ratio of $m\angle JKL$ to 360°.

$$\frac{\text{area sector } JKL}{\text{area } \odot K} = \frac{\text{area sector } JKL}{452.4} = \frac{125}{360}$$

The area of ⊙*K* is $\pi r^2 = \pi(12)^2 \approx 452.4$.

$$360 \times \text{area sector } JKL = 56{,}550$$

$$\text{area sector } JKL \approx 157.1 \text{ cm}^2$$

1. What is the difference between the length of an arc and the degree measure of an arc?

In the following Explore, you will use proportions to find arc lengths on the earth's surface.

EXPLORE: A TRIP THROUGH AFRICA

MATERIALS

Protractor

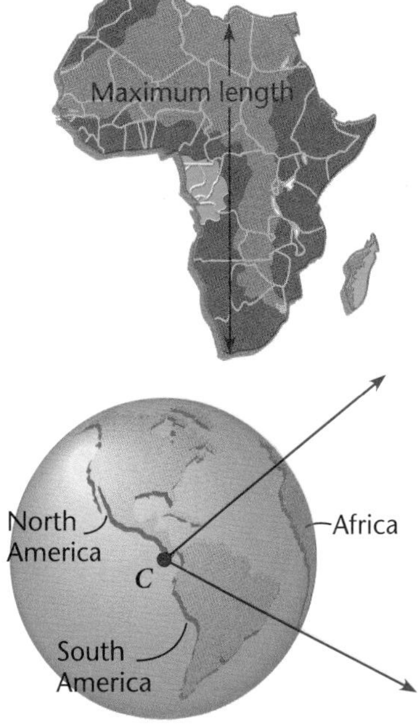

Suppose you want to find the maximum north-south length of the African continent, as shown on the map. The lower figure on the right shows a scale drawing of the earth, including North America, South America, and part of Africa. Point C is the center of the disk representing the earth.

1. The rays on the map go from the center of the circle through the northernmost and southernmost points of Africa on the circumference of the circle. Use a protractor to measure the angle formed.
2. The circumference of the earth is close to 40,000 km. Use this value to find the maximum north-south length of Africa in kilometers.
3. What must be true about the position of Africa in the figure in order to make the calculation work?

TRY IT

In $\odot C$, $m\widehat{AB} = 103°$, and $AC = 20$ in.

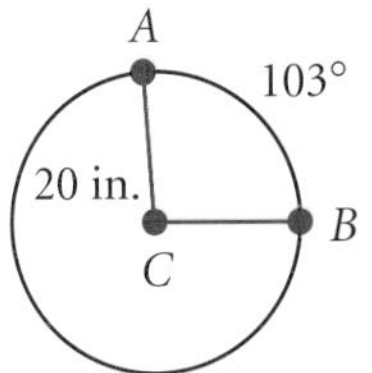

a. Find the area of sector ACB to the nearest tenth.
b. Find the length of arc $\widehat{AB}$ to the nearest tenth.
c. If the circumference of a circle is 21π, what is the length of a 30° arc?

CIRCLE PROPORTIONS

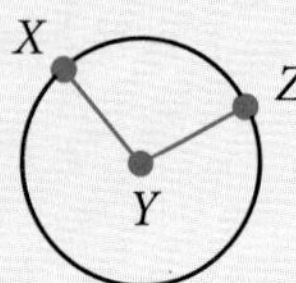

In $\odot Y$, with central angle $\angle XYZ$, all of the following ratios are equal.

$$\frac{m\angle XYZ}{360°} = \frac{m\widehat{XZ}}{360°} = \frac{\text{length of } \widehat{XZ}}{\text{circumference of } \odot Y} = \frac{\text{area of sector } XYZ}{\text{area of } \odot Y}$$

REFLECT

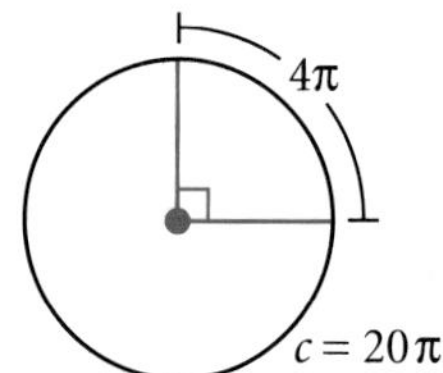

1. Explain why all of the circle ratios shown above are equal.
2. Give a convincing argument explaining why the information shown in the figure at the right cannot be correct.

Exercises

CORE

1. **Getting Started** Suppose a pie has a 10-in. diameter.
   - **a.** Draw a sketch of the pie. Calculate its area and circumference.
   - **b.** Suppose you cut a slice of the pie with a 45° central angle. Modify your sketch to show the sector.
   - **c.** To find the area of the sector represented by this slice, set up a proportion involving 45°, 360°, the area of the sector, and the area of the pie you found in **1a.** Solve the proportion to find the area of the sector. Round your answer to the nearest tenth.
   - **d.** The rim of the sector of pie represents a minor arc of the circle. Set up and solve a proportion to find the length of this 45° arc. Round your answer to the nearest tenth.

Find the length of $\widehat{AB}$ and the area of sector *ACB* for each measure of central angle $\angle ACB$ and radius of $\odot C$. Give answers in exact form.

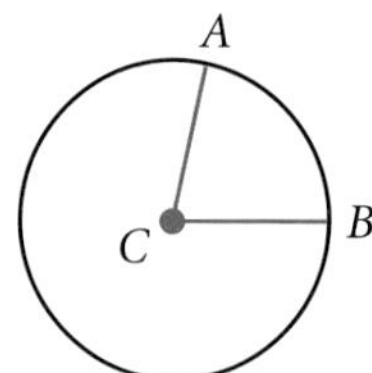

2. $m\angle ACB = 90°$, radius = 10 cm
3. $m\angle ACB = 72°$, radius = 15 in.
4. $m\angle ACB = 55°$, radius = 2.5 ft
5. $m\angle ACB = 55°$, radius = 5 ft

Find the length of each arc in the circle at the right.

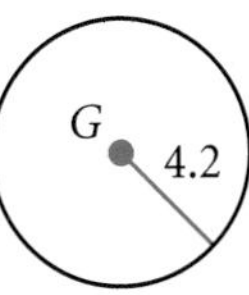

6. a 30° arc

7. a 144° arc

8. a semicircle

9. A **segment** of a circle is the region formed by an arc of the circle and the segment joining its endpoints. Find the area of each shaded segment. (Hint: Can you subtract areas to find the area of the segment?)

a.

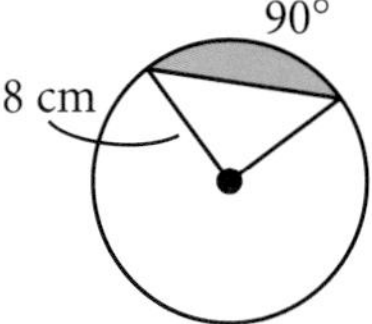

b.

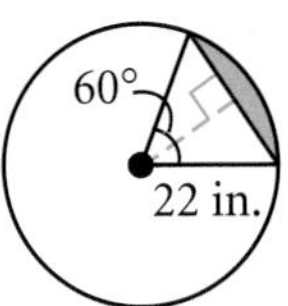

c.

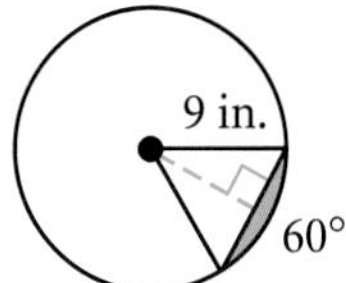

d. Write a brief explanation of your method for finding the area of a segment.

Suppose that contestants on a game show spin a wheel with a radius of 6 ft. It is evenly divided into 24 different sectors.

10. Find the area and arc length of one sector of the wheel.

11. Three of the sectors read "Spin Again."

a. What is the total area of the sectors that read "Spin Again"?

b. What is the probability that a contestant will land on "Spin Again" on any one spin of the wheel?

12. An electric lawn mower with a twenty-meter cord is plugged into an outlet at the corner of the house shown. (Assume the fence is perpendicular to the wall of the house.)

a. What is the total area that can be mowed from this outlet?

b. If the fence was not in the way, what area could be mowed from this outlet?

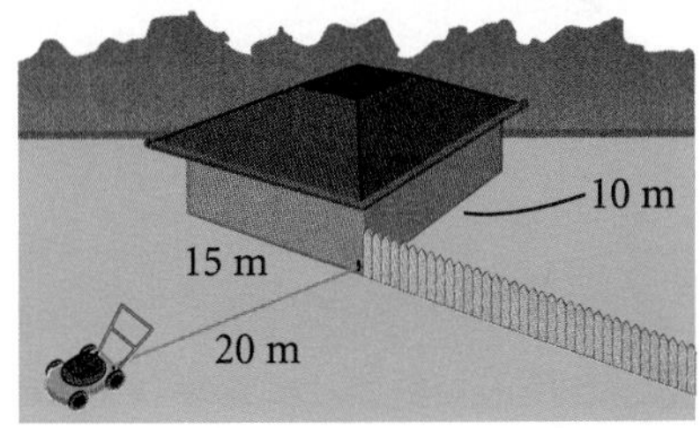

LOOK BACK

13. *Given:* $\triangle ABC$ and $\triangle DEC$ are right triangles.

Prove: $\frac{AC}{DC} = \frac{BC}{EC}$ [7-2]

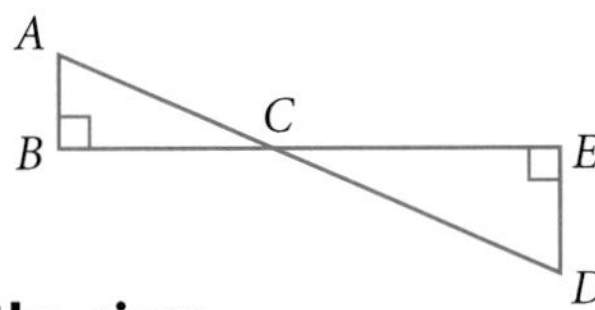

Find the area and the circumference for a circle with each of the given dimensions. Give your answers in exact form and as decimals rounded to the nearest hundredth. [8-1]

14. radius = 3 cm

15. diameter = 16 in.

16. radius = 8.32 ft

MORE PRACTICE

Find the length of $\widehat{RS}$ and the area of sector *RTS* for each measure of central angle $\angle RTS$ and radius of $\odot T$.

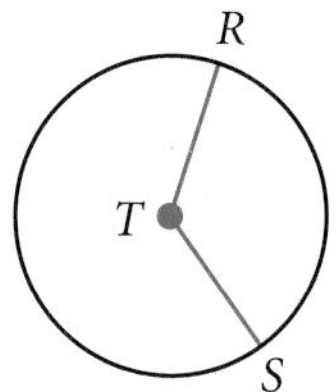

17. $m\angle RTS = 36°$, radius $= 8$ in.

18. $m\angle RTS = 45°$, radius $= 4.8$ m

19. $m\angle RTS = 108°$, radius $= 9.1$ ft

20. Find the area of the shaded segment in the figure at the right.

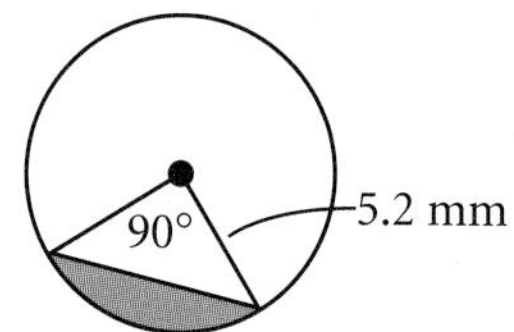

MORE MATH REASONING

21. A 100-m square field is watered by sprinklers at the midpoints of each of its sides. Each sprinkler sprays water in a 50-m radius and covers an 180° arc so that all of its water lands on the field.

a. Draw a sketch to represent this situation.

b. Find the area of the field that is watered by more than one sprinkler.

c. Suppose the watering radius of each of the sprinklers can be adjusted to any radius less than or equal to 50 m. Can you find a way to set these sprinklers so that every location in the field is watered by only one sprinkler? If so, explain your plan. If not, explain why not.

8-2 PART C Radius-Chord Conjectures

← CONNECT → ***You've seen some relationships between radii and tangents. Now you will make conjectures about the relationships between radii and chords.***

As you've seen, secant lines intersect a circle in two points. The photograph at the left shows how the strings of a guitar are similar to secant lines. The segment determined by the points where a secant line intersects a circle has a special name. This is described in the following definition.

DEFINITION

A **chord** is a line segment that joins two points on a circle.

In the figure, $\overline{AB}$ is a chord of $\odot D$.

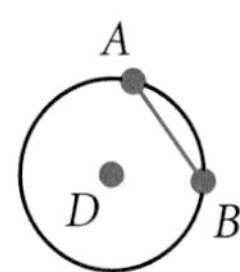

EXPLORE: STRIKING A CHORD

MATERIALS

Compass
Ruler
Scissors
Protractor

1. Use your compass to draw a large circle on a sheet of paper. Mark the center of the circle, and cut the circle out.
2. As shown in the figure, draw two chords anywhere on the circle that do not contain the center. By folding your paper, construct the perpendicular bisector of each chord. Where do the bisectors meet?
3. Add a third chord and its perpendicular bisector to confirm your results from Step 2. Make a conjecture about the perpendicular bisector of a chord.
4. The following two statements are closely related to your conjecture. One of them is true as written, but the other needs some modification. Investigate each statement to see which one needs to be changed. Then rewrite the statement that needs to be changed.
   - If a radius of a circle bisects a chord of the circle, then it is perpendicular to the chord.
   - If a radius of a circle is perpendicular to a chord of the circle, then it bisects the chord.

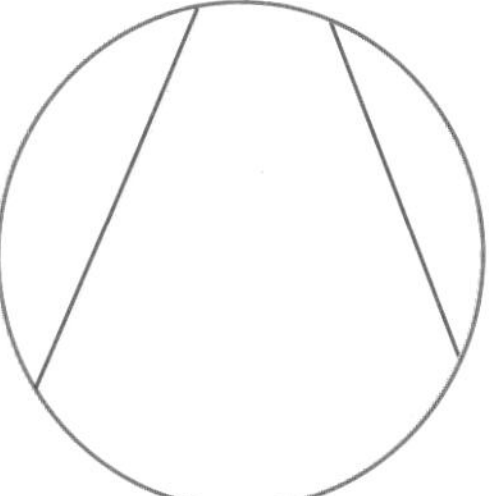

Problem-Solving Tip

Remember to consider special cases.

1. Is there a maximum length for chords in a given circle? Is there a minimum length? Explain.

EXAMPLE

The radius of circle O is 13 mm. The length of chord $\overline{PQ}$ is 10 mm. Find the distance from chord $\overline{PQ}$ to the center of the circle O.

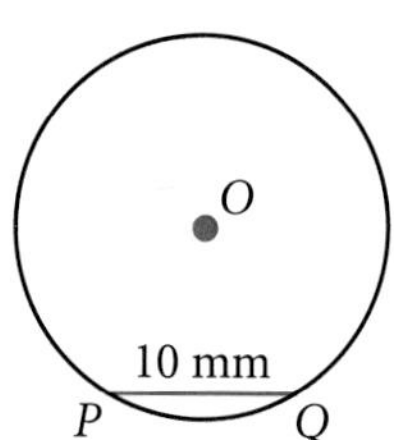

Draw $\overline{OR} \perp \overline{PQ}$. Draw radius $\overline{OP}$ to complete a right triangle.

Since a radius perpendicular to a chord bisects the chord, $PR = \frac{1}{2}PQ = \frac{1}{2}(10) = 5$.

Using the Pythagorean Theorem, $OR^2 + 5^2 = 13^2$.

Therefore, $OR = 12$ mm.

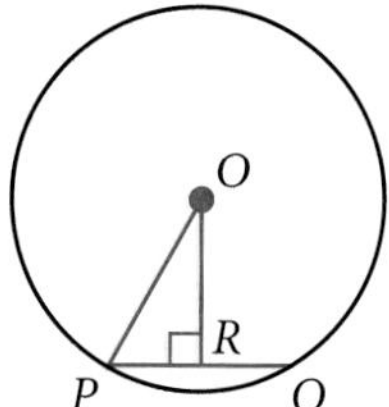

TRY IT

State a conclusion that can be drawn from each figure.

a.

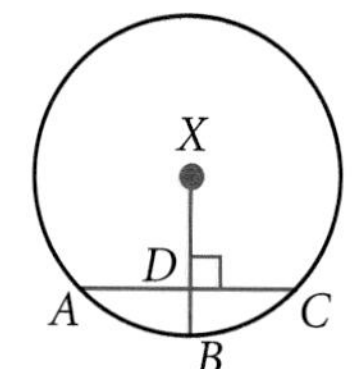

b.

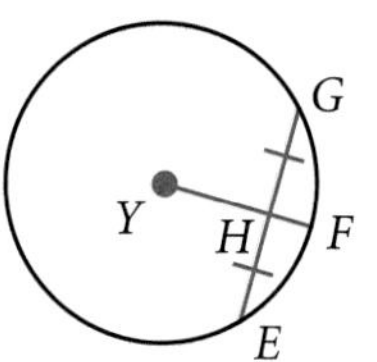

c.

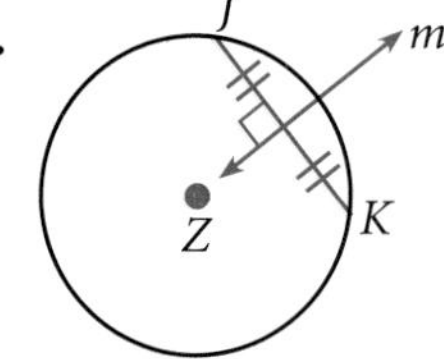

You have investigated the following theorems about chords, their perpendicular bisectors, and radii.

THEOREMS

The perpendicular bisector of a chord contains the center of the circle.

If a radius of a circle bisects a chord of the circle that is not a diameter, then it is perpendicular to the chord.

If a radius of a circle is perpendicular to a chord of the circle, then it bisects the chord.

REFLECT

1. Natasha said that the center of any regular polygon must be the same as the center of its circumscribed circle. Is she right? If she is, give a justification; if not, give a counterexample.

2. Draw a regular hexagon inscribed in a circle. Use your drawing to help you decide whether an apothem of a regular polygon always bisects the side of the polygon it intersects. Explain your conclusion.

Exercises

CORE

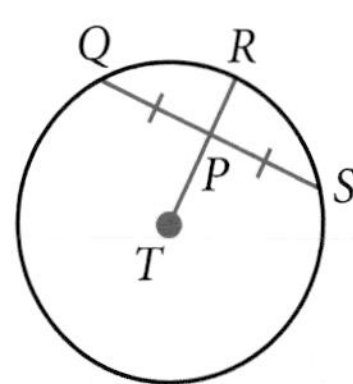

Getting Started Refer to $\odot T$ for Exercises 1–3.

1. If $QS = 14$, what is QP?

2. What is $m\angle TPQ$?

3. What is the relationship between $\overline{TR}$ and $\overline{QS}$?

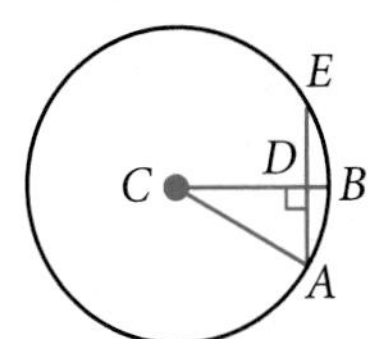

4. $AD = 15$; $AC = 17$. Find the length of chord $\overline{AE}$.

5. $AE = 12$; $AC = 10$. Find the distance of chord $\overline{AE}$ from the center of the circle C.

6. $AE = 24$; $CD = 9$. Find the radius of $\odot C$.

7. From the four terms below, choose the one term that does not belong and explain why.

chord, radius, secant, diameter

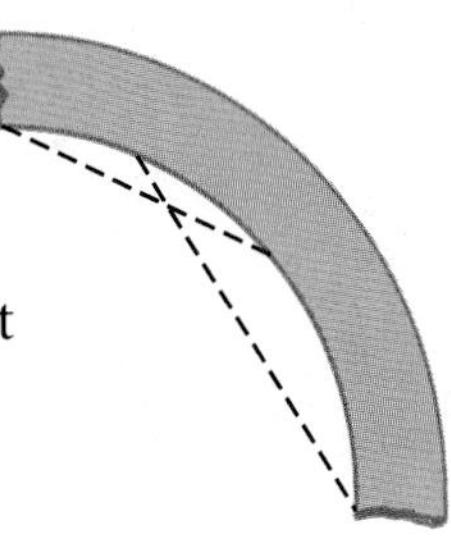

8. A 48-in. chord is 8 in. closer to the center of a circle than a 40-in. chord. Find the radius of the circle.

9. Getting Centered An archaeologist finds a piece of the rim of an ancient wheel. She wants to figure out how big the wheel was. She begins by drawing two chords as shown. Explain what she should do next to find the radius of the wheel.

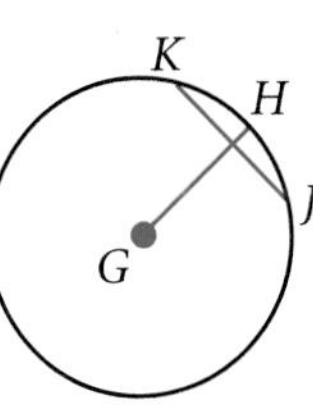

10. In $\odot G$, $\overline{GH}$ bisects $\overline{JK}$. If $GH = 16$ and $JK = 9$, find the distance of $\overline{JK}$ from G.

There is a special relationship between congruent chords and congruent arcs. You will prove this relationship in Exercise 11.

> **THEOREM**
>
> In a circle (or in congruent circles), minor arcs are congruent if and only if they have congruent chords.

11. Prove: In a circle, if two minor arcs are congruent, then their chords are congruent.

Given: Circle O with $\widehat{RS} \cong \widehat{TV}$

Prove: $\overline{RS} \cong \overline{TV}$

(Hint: Draw radii $\overline{OR}$, $\overline{OS}$, $\overline{OT}$, and $\overline{OV}$.)

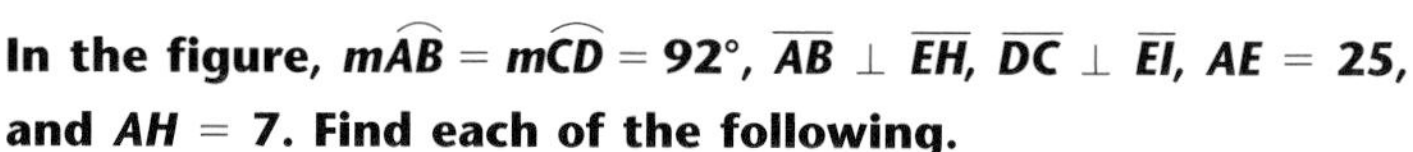

In the figure, $m\widehat{AB} = m\widehat{CD} = 92°$, $\overline{AB} \perp \overline{EH}$, $\overline{DC} \perp \overline{EI}$, $AE = 25$, and $AH = 7$. Find each of the following.

12. AB **13.** DC **14.** EH **15.** EI

16. In the figure at the right, two flywheels are connected with a rubber belt. Line t is tangent to both circles. Line t is a **common external tangent** because it does not cross the line segment joining the centers of $\odot C$ and $\odot D$. Find the length of $\overline{AB}$ if $AC = 10$, $BD = 5$, and $CD = 23$. (Hint: Draw $\overline{CA}$, $\overline{DB}$, and $\overline{CD}$. Then draw a rectangle $ABDX$, where X is a point on $\overline{AC}$. Use the Pythagorean Theorem to find DX.)

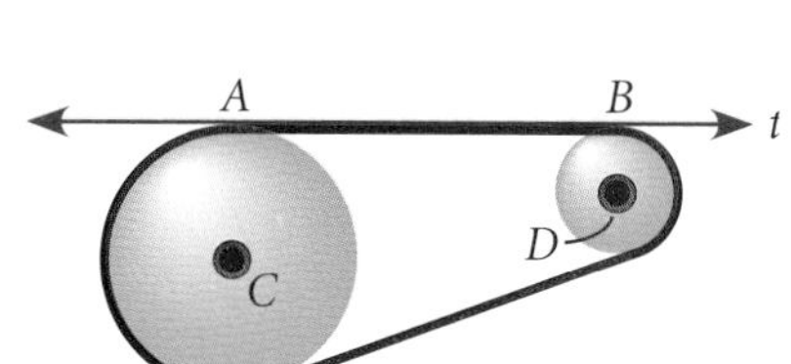

17. Complete the table below to develop formulas for the numbers of chords and arcs determined by n points on a circle. Explain how you developed your formulas.

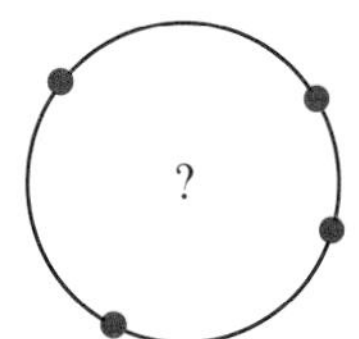

No. of Points	2	3	4	5	...	n
No. of Chords	1	3			...	
No. of Arcs	2	6			...	

LOOK AHEAD

18. Explain the relationship between the measure of a central angle and its intercepted arc.

19. $\angle ABC$ and central angle $\angle AOC$ intercept the same arc. Which angle appears to have a greater measure?

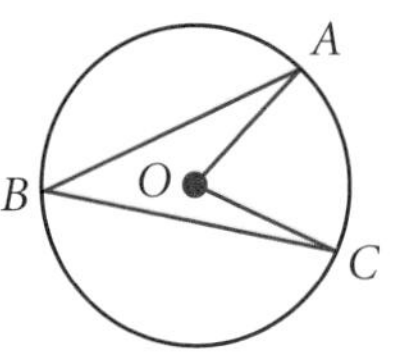

MORE PRACTICE

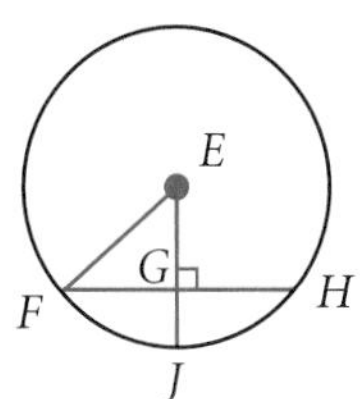

20. $EG = 24$, and $EF = 25$. Find the length of chord $\overline{FH}$.

21. $EG = 15$, and $FH = 20$. Find the radius of $\odot E$.

22. $EF = 2.7$, and $FH = 3.2$. Find the distance of chord $\overline{FH}$ from the center of $\odot E$.

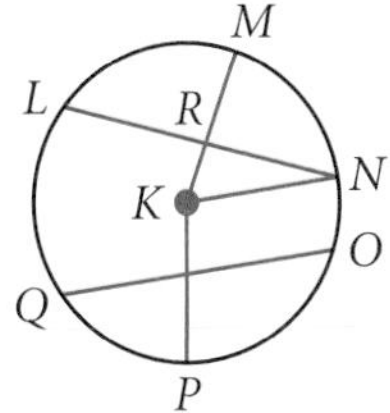

In the figure, $m\widehat{LN} = m\widehat{OQ} = 135°$, $\overline{KM} \perp \overline{LN}$, $\overline{KP} \perp \overline{OQ}$, $KN = 13$, and $NL = 20$. Find each of the following.

23. KM

24. LR

25. RM

26. OQ

MORE MATH REASONING

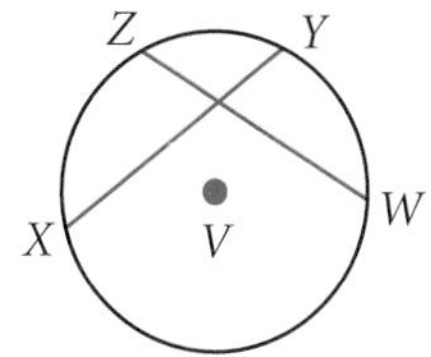

27. Prove: In a circle, congruent chords cut off congruent minor arcs.

Given: Circle V with $\overline{XY} \cong \overline{WZ}$

Prove: $\widehat{XY} \cong \widehat{WZ}$

28. How many lines of symmetry does a circle have? Does any other two-dimensional figure have this property? If so, give an example; if not, explain why the circle is unique in this way.

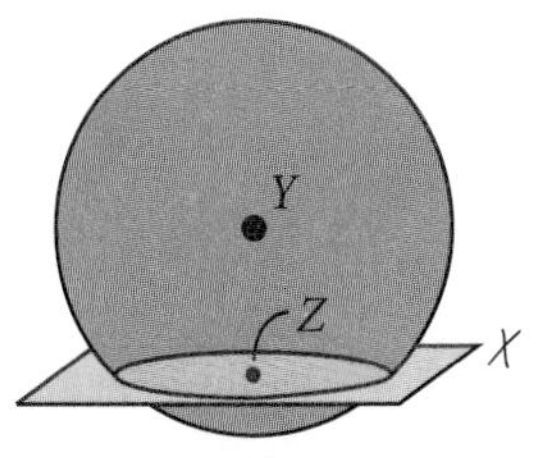

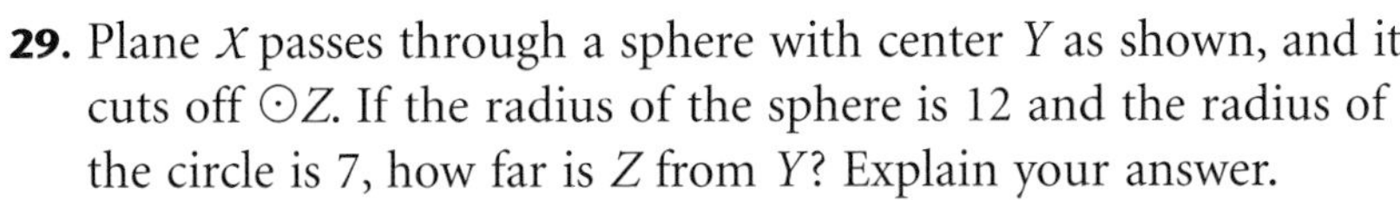

29. Plane X passes through a sphere with center Y as shown, and it cuts off $\odot Z$. If the radius of the sphere is 12 and the radius of the circle is 7, how far is Z from Y? Explain your answer.

30. The photo at the right shows a utility hole cover. The diameter of the cover is four feet. Suppose the cover is slid over the hole so that the center of the cover rests on the edge of the hole. Find the area of the hole that is exposed.

8-2
PART D

Making Connections

← CONNECT → ***Central angles of circles, the regions they determine, and the arcs they intersect allow you to apply proportional thinking to circles. They enabled Eratosthenes to find the circumference of the earth.***

In the following Explore, you will see how Eratosthenes used proportions to calculate the circumference of the earth.

EXPLORE: AROUND THE EARTH WITH ERATOSTHENES

Eratosthenes knew that the sun cast no shadows in Syene, Africa, at noon on June 21. The sun did cast shadows at that time in Alexandria, which is due north of Syene.

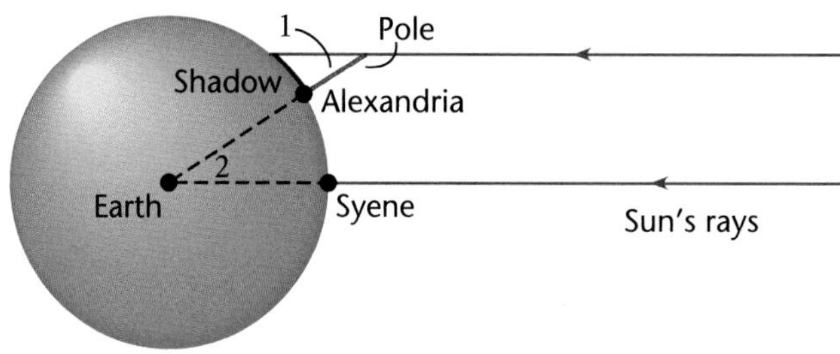

1. Eratosthenes may have used the height of a pole in Alexandria and the length of its shadow at noon on June 21 to calculate $m\angle 1$. Assume that the pole was 16 ft tall and the shadow it cast was 2.02 ft long. Use these measurements to find $m\angle 1$ to the nearest tenth of a degree. Explain your method.

2. Because the sun is so far from the earth, its rays are virtually parallel. What can you conclude about $\angle 1$ and $\angle 2$? Why?

3. When Eratosthenes did his calculations, the main unit used to measure long distances was the *stadium* (plural, *stadia*). Eratosthenes used 5000 stadia for the distance from Syene to Alexandria, an arc on the surface of the earth. Calculate the circumference of the earth in stadia.

4. It is thought that 1 stadium was about $\frac{1}{10}$ of a mile long. Convert your measurement of the circumference of the earth to miles.

5. The actual average value for the circumference of the earth is about 24,874 mi. How close was Eratosthenes's measurement?

REFLECT

1. Sketch a circle and a central angle. Then write three equal ratios involving the measure of a central angle, the length of the minor arc it cuts off, and the area of the sector it determines.
2. In your own words, briefly describe the relationships between chords and radii of a circle.

Self-Assessment

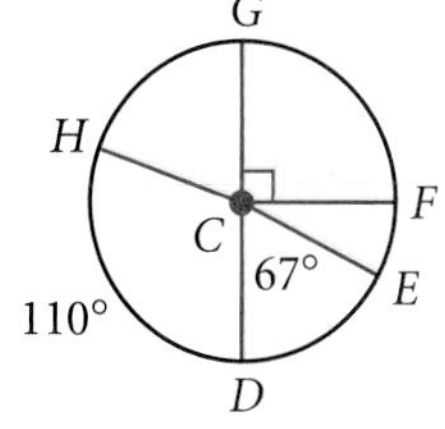

Find each measure.

1. $m\widehat{DE}$ **2.** $m\widehat{EF}$ **3.** $m\angle HCG$ **4.** $m\widehat{HDG}$

5. **Tennis Anyone?** The women's championship at the Wimbledon tennis tournament had the following winners over a twelve-year period. Make a circle graph to illustrate these results.

1981: Chris Evert-Lloyd	1987: Martina Navratilova
1982: Martina Navratilova	1988: Steffi Graf
1983: Martina Navratilova	1989: Steffi Graf
1984: Martina Navratilova	1990: Martina Navratilova
1985: Martina Navratilova	1991: Steffi Graf
1986: Martina Navratilova	1992: Steffi Graf

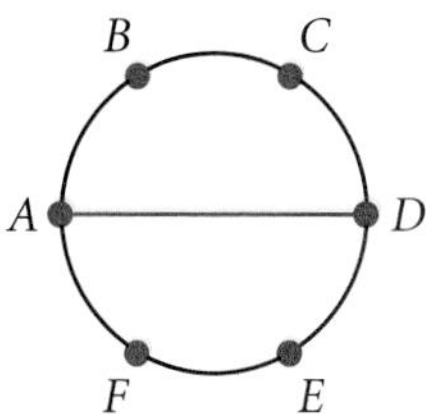

6. In the figure, points A, B, C, D, E, and F divide the circle into six equal arcs. If $AD = 9$, which of the following is the length of $\widehat{AC}$?

(a) 120 (b) 9π (c) $\frac{1}{3}$ (d) 3π (e) $\frac{2}{3}\pi$

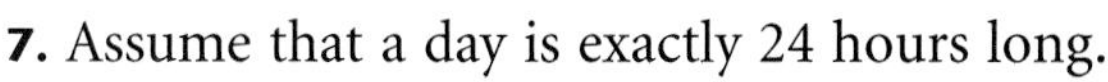

7. Assume that a day is exactly 24 hours long.

a. What is the measure of the arc through which the earth turns in one hour?

b. The circumference of the earth at the equator is about 25,000 mi. Find the distance a point on the earth's equator travels in an hour.

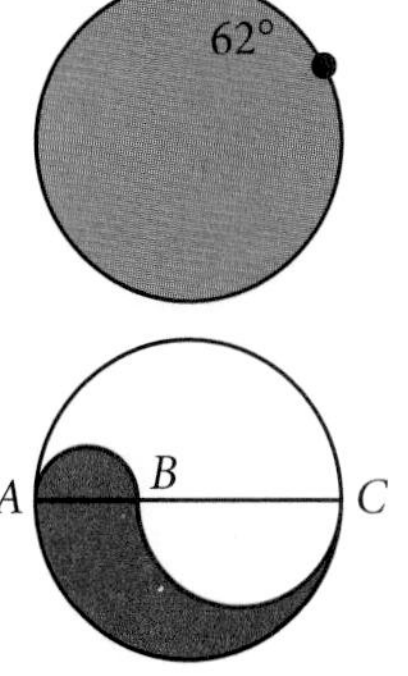

8. Find the area of the shaded circle shown at the right.

9. If $BC = 2AB$, what fraction of the circle is shaded? If the area of the circle is 121π mm^2, what is the area of the shaded portion?

10. Write a similarity statement for the triangles in the figure at the right, and explain how you know they are similar. Then solve for x. [7-2]

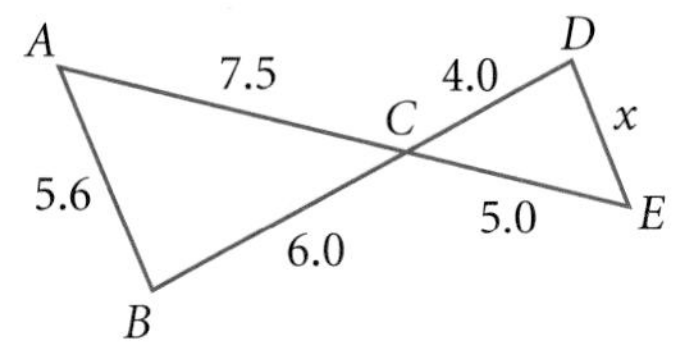

11. **That's Astronomical!** The sun orbits the center of the Milky Way galaxy at a speed of about 8.83×10^9 km/yr. Its orbit is roughly circular, and it takes the sun about 200,000 years to make a complete orbit. [8-1]

Science

a. What is the circumference of the sun's orbit? Express your answer in scientific notation.

b. How far is the sun from the center of the Milky Way galaxy?

c. What is the area of the circular region determined by the sun's orbit?

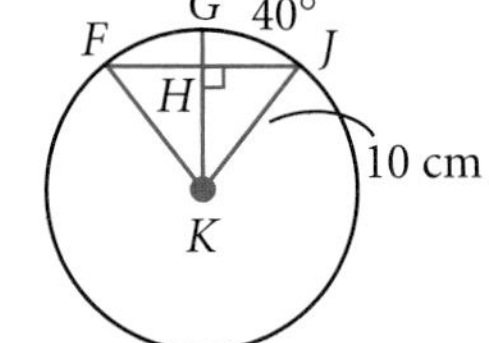

12. Find the area of sector FJK. Write a short paragraph explaining how you solved this problem.

If you know the radius of a circle and the length of a chord, you can calculate the distance from the center of the circle to the chord. Therefore, if two chords of a circle have equal lengths, they should be the same distance from the center.

THEOREM

Two chords of a circle are congruent if and only if they are equidistant from the center.

13. Write a *plan* for proving the following half of the preceding theorem.

Prove: If two chords are equidistant from the center of a circle, then they are congruent.

Given: $ZV = ZY$

Prove: $\overline{WX} \cong \overline{ST}$

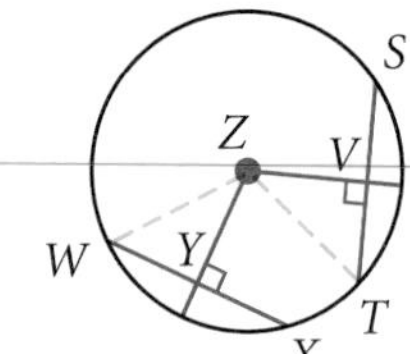

14. **The Grass Is Greener . . .** An automatic sprinkler is set so that it turns through an angle of 220° before returning to its original setting. If the sprinkler sprays water a distance of up to 20 m, find the total area watered by the sprinkler.

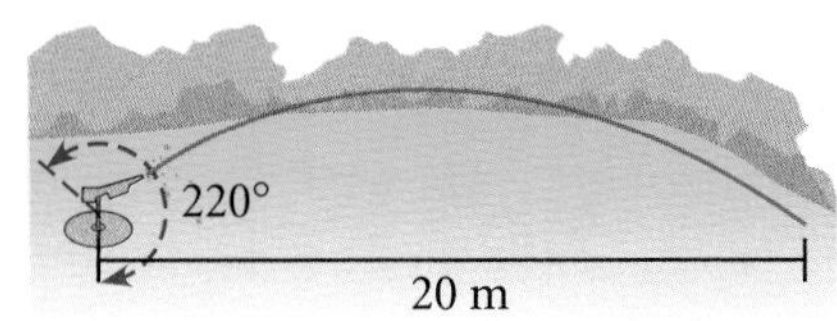

8-3 The Inscribed Angle Theorem

GETTING A KICK OUT OF CIRCLES

What is the world's most popular sport? Football? Baseball? Basketball?

Soccer may in fact be the world's most popular sport. It is the national sport of most European and Latin American countries. Millions of people in more than 140 countries play soccer. In Great Britain and many other countries, soccer is called *football* or ***association football***. The word ***soccer*** actually comes from ***assoc.***, an abbreviation for association.

International soccer competition includes the World Cup Championship, held every four years. In this tournament, 24 nations compete for the world championship. Two years before the championship, nations compete in qualifying rounds to determine which 22 teams will join the host nation and the previous champion in the final rounds.

What do soccer and geometry have in common? A soccer ball is a sphere. Its circumference is 69 cm to 71 cm. The soccer field is a rectangle. It measures from 91 m to 119 m in length, and from 46 m to 91 m in width. Angles and arcs play an important role in determining the best location for scoring a goal in soccer.

?

1. Give some examples of sports situations in which angles or arcs are important.

2. Why do you think a soccer ball is a sphere but a football is not?

8-3 PART A Inscribed Angles

← CONNECT → ***The vertex of a central angle is the center of a circle. Now you will investigate angle-arc relationships when the vertex of an angle is on the circle.***

A polygon that is inscribed in a circle has its vertices on the circle. In the same way, an inscribed angle also has its vertex on a circle.

DEFINITION

An **inscribed angle** is an angle with its vertex on a circle and sides that contain chords of the circle.

In the figure at the right, $\angle BAC$ is an inscribed angle.

You know that the measure of a minor arc is equal to the measure of its central angle. In the following Explore, you'll investigate how the measure of an inscribed angle is related to the measure of its intercepted arc.

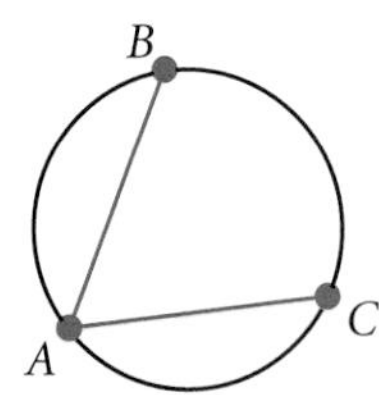

EXPLORE: SIZING UP INSCRIBED ANGLES

MATERIALS

Compass
Straightedge
Protractor
Geometry software (optional)

1. Use geometry software or a compass to construct a circle. As shown below, mark its center, *C*, and two points, *A* and *B*, on the circle. Draw central angle $\angle ACB$. Then place a point *D* on $\odot C$ so that $\overset{\frown}{ADB}$ is a major arc, and draw inscribed angle $\angle ADB$.
2. Measure $\angle ACB$. What other information does this give you?
3. Measure $\angle ADB$. What do you notice? Choose three other locations for point *D* on the circle, and find the measures of $\angle ADB$ and $\overset{\frown}{AB}$ in each case.
4. Make any conjectures you can about the following.
   - The relationship between the measure of an inscribed angle and its intercepted arc.
   - Inscribed angles that intercept the same arc.

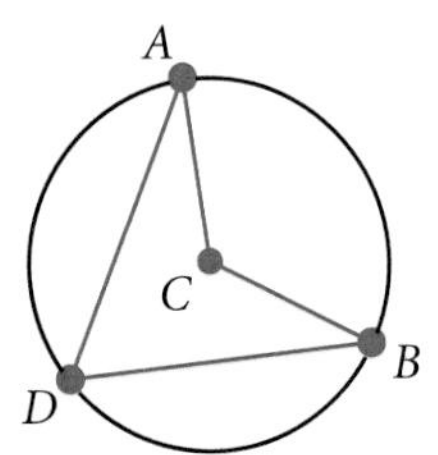

TRY IT

Find the measure of each angle or arc indicated by a variable in the following figures.

a.

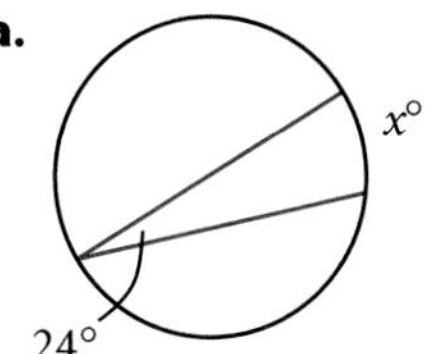

b.

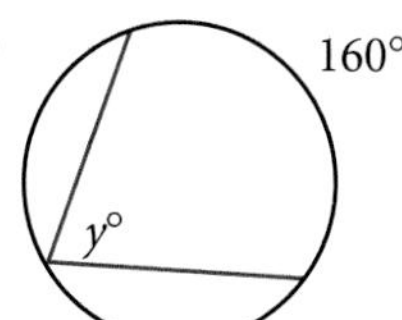

c.

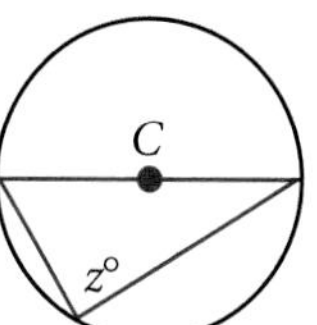

1. What type of inscribed angle intercepts a semicircle? How do you know?

You have investigated three important theorems about inscribed angles and arcs. These include the Inscribed-Angle Theorem and the two related results that are summarized below.

INSCRIBED-ANGLE THEOREM

The measure of an inscribed angle is half the measure of its intercepted arc.

THEOREMS

If two inscribed angles intercept the same arc, then they are congruent.

An inscribed angle that intercepts a semicircle is a right angle.

REFLECT

1. What type of inscribed angle intercepts a minor arc? a major arc? Explain.
2. Suppose you are given a drawing of a circle and its center. How can you make an accurate drawing of a right angle using only a straightedge?

Exercises

CORE

Getting Started Find the measure of each angle or arc indicated by a variable.

1.

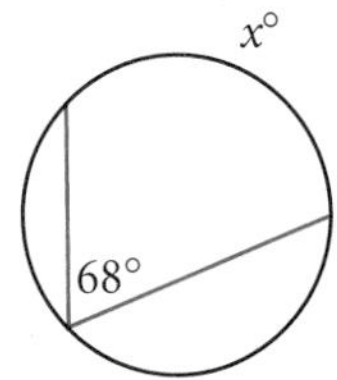

2.

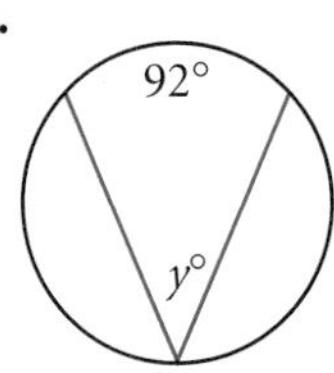

3.

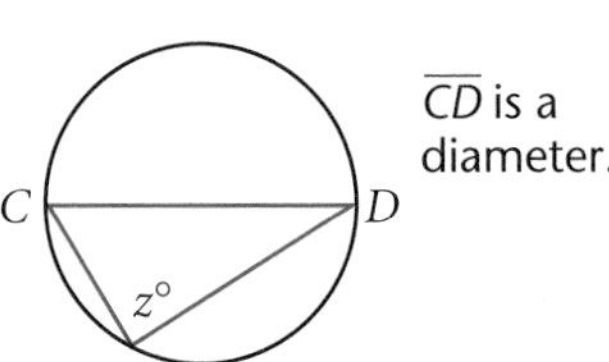

4.

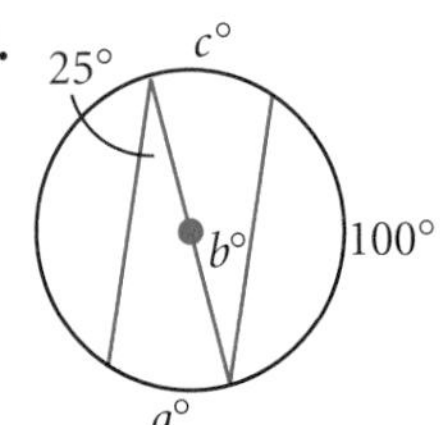

5.

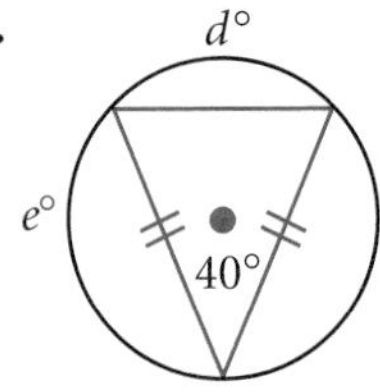

6.

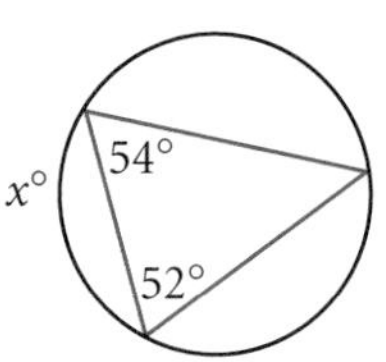

7. Under the Sea A cylindrical underwater tank for viewing marine animals has a window that covers one-fourth of the circumference of its circular cross-section. Find the measure of the viewing angle of a person at the wall of the tank opposite the window. Compare this to the viewing angle of a person at the center of the tank.

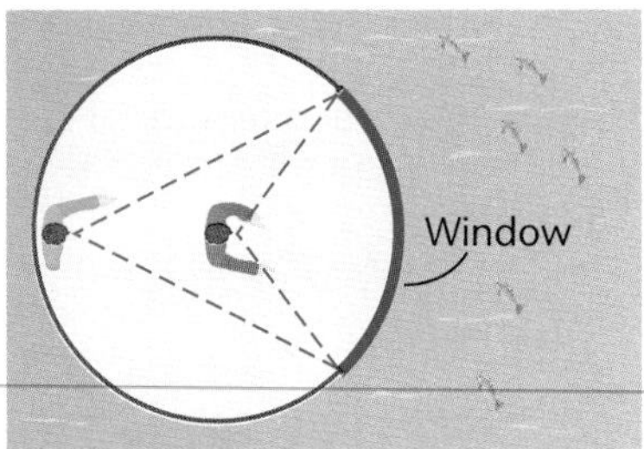

Find each angle or arc measure.

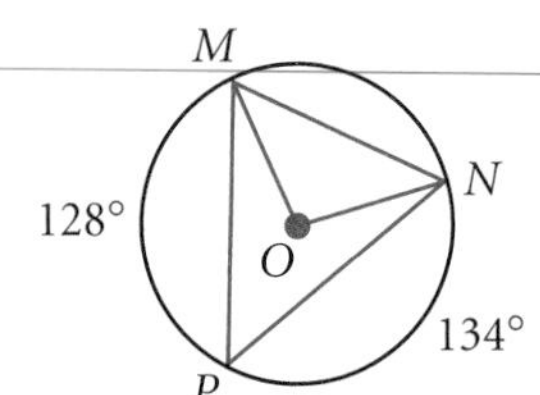

8. $m\widehat{MN}$ 

9. $m\angle NOM$

10. $m\angle MPN$

11. $m\angle MNP$ 

12. $m\angle NMP$

$\overrightarrow{AB}$ bisects $\angle CAD$, $m\widehat{BD} = 95°$, and $m\widehat{AD} = 74°$. Find each measure.

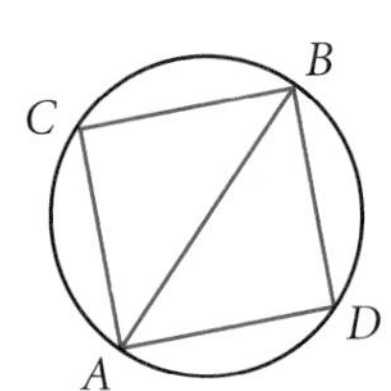

13. $m\angle CAD$

14. $m\angle BCA$

15. $m\angle CAB$

16. $m\angle CBD$

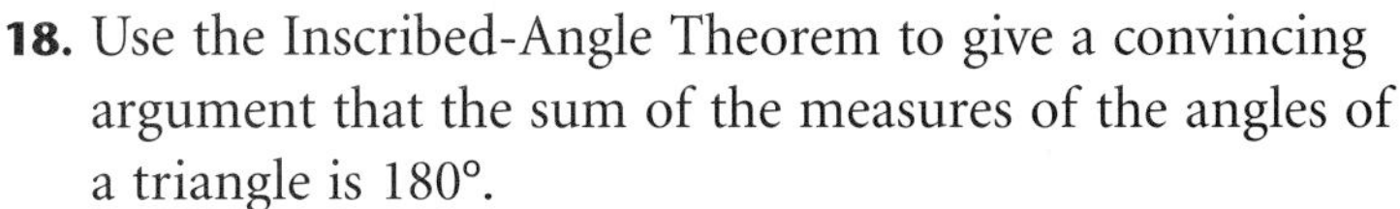

17. Odette cut an opening for a new sink. How can she use a carpenter's square to test whether she has cut a semicircle?

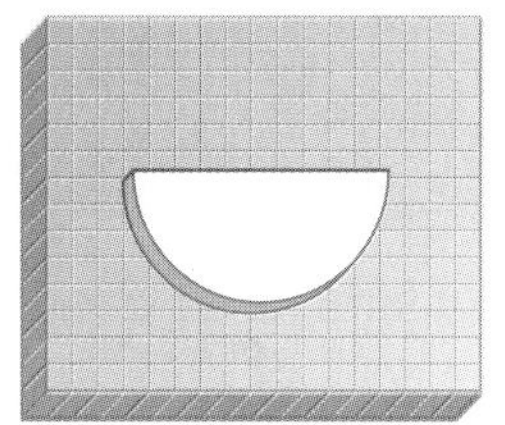

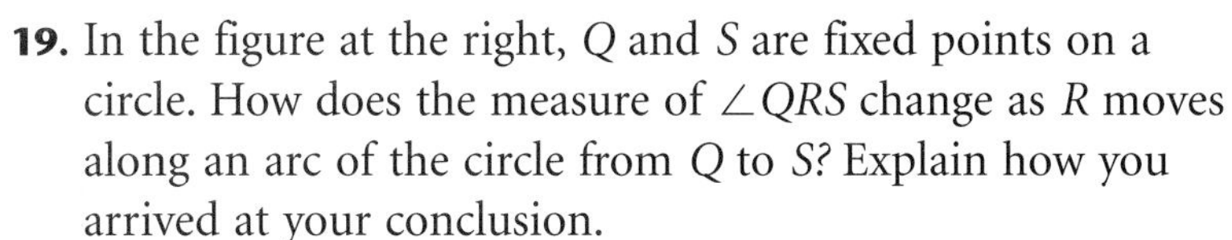

18. Use the Inscribed-Angle Theorem to give a convincing argument that the sum of the measures of the angles of a triangle is 180°.

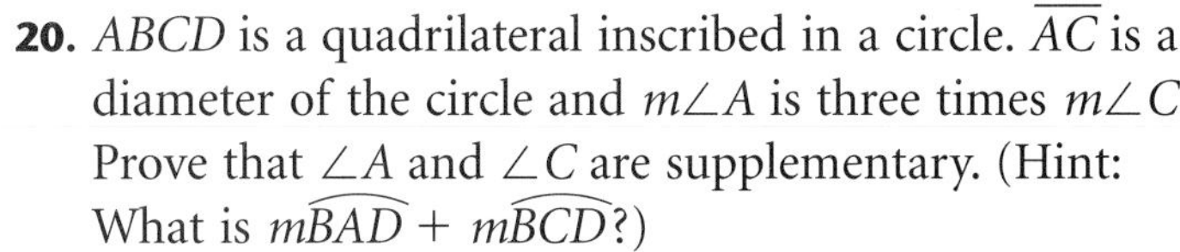

19. In the figure at the right, Q and S are fixed points on a circle. How does the measure of $\angle QRS$ change as R moves along an arc of the circle from Q to S? Explain how you arrived at your conclusion.

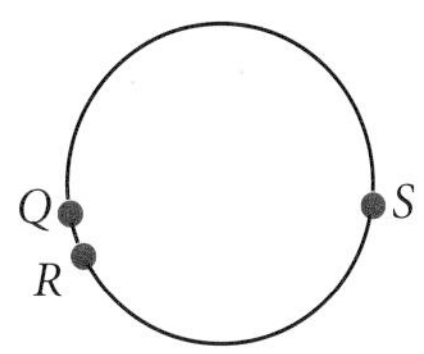

20. $ABCD$ is a quadrilateral inscribed in a circle. $\overline{AC}$ is a diameter of the circle and $m\angle A$ is three times $m\angle C$. Prove that $\angle A$ and $\angle C$ are supplementary. (Hint: What is $m\overset{\frown}{BAD} + m\overset{\frown}{BCD}$?)

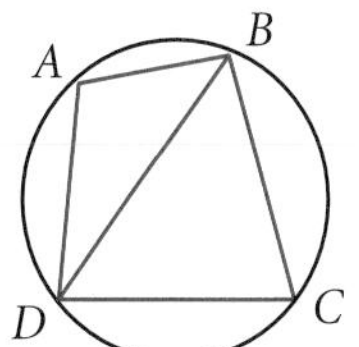

21. Prove: If an angle is inscribed in a semicircle, then it is a right angle.

LOOK BACK

Draw a sketch to illustrate each situation. [8-1]

22. Line m is tangent to $\odot C$ at P, and line n is tangent to $\odot C$ at Q. Lines m and n intersect at R.

23. Line s is tangent to $\odot Z$ at A. $\overleftrightarrow{BC}$ is a secant line that intersects $\odot Z$ at B and C. Line s and $\overleftrightarrow{BC}$ intersect at D.

Find each arc measure. [8-2]

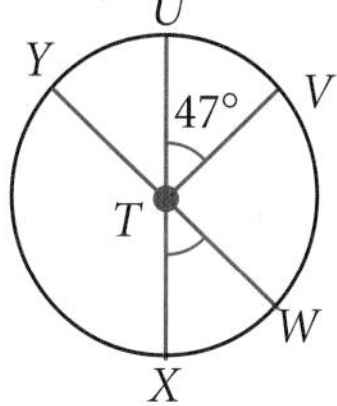

24. $m\overset{\frown}{UV}$ **25.** $m\overset{\frown}{YV}$ **26.** $m\overset{\frown}{UYV}$

27. $m\overset{\frown}{XYU}$ **28.** $m\overset{\frown}{VW}$

MORE PRACTICE

Find each angle or arc measure.

29. $m\overset{\frown}{BC}$

30. $m\angle ADB$

31. $m\angle BDC$

32. $m\angle ADC$

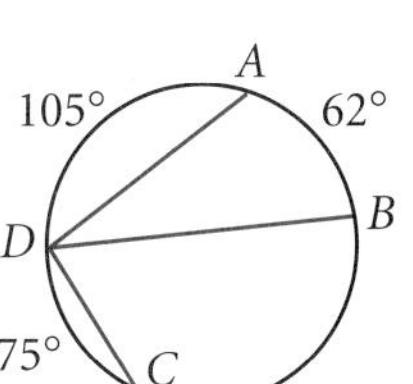

33. $m\overset{\frown}{RS}$

34. $m\overset{\frown}{RU}$

35. $m\angle R$

36. $m\angle S$

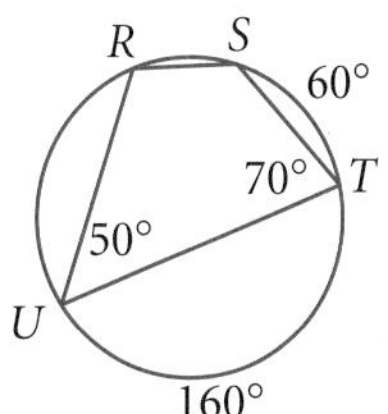

MORE MATH REASONING

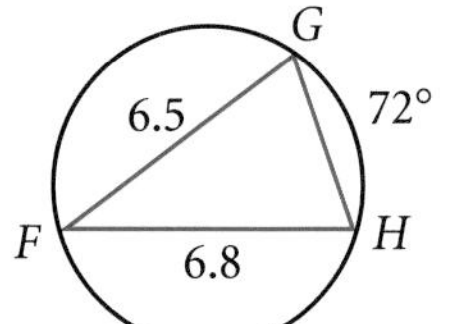

37. $\overline{XY}$ is a diameter of $\odot Z$. Prove that for any point W on $\odot Z$, $WX^2 + WY^2 = XY^2$.

38. $\triangle FGH$ is inscribed in a circle as shown. Find the area of $\triangle FGH$.

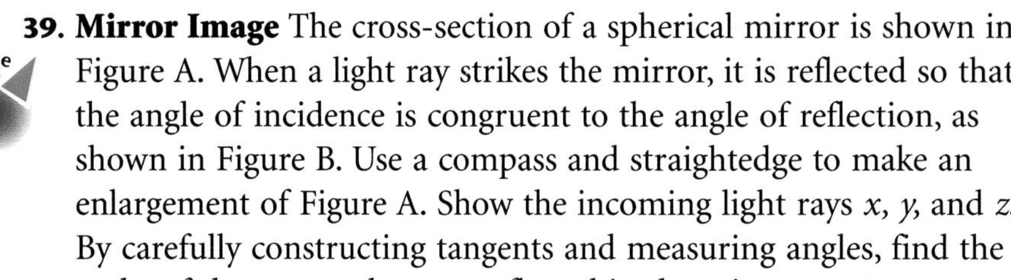

39. Mirror Image The cross-section of a spherical mirror is shown in Figure A. When a light ray strikes the mirror, it is reflected so that the angle of incidence is congruent to the angle of reflection, as shown in Figure B. Use a compass and straightedge to make an enlargement of Figure A. Show the incoming light rays x, y, and z. By carefully constructing tangents and measuring angles, find the paths of the rays as they are reflected in the mirror.

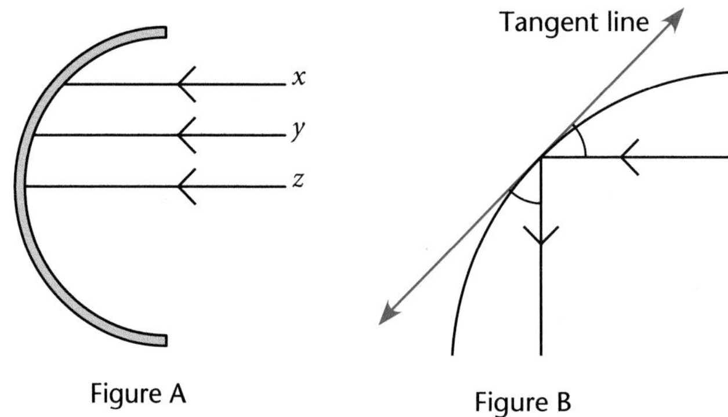

Figure A

Figure B

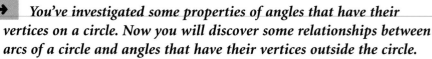

8-3 PART B Angles Formed by Secants and Tangents

← CONNECT → ***You've investigated some properties of angles that have their vertices on a circle. Now you will discover some relationships between arcs of a circle and angles that have their vertices outside the circle.***

The Inscribed-Angle Theorem can be used to discover several other theorems. These theorems include results about tangent-secant angles, which are often seen in the wheels of railroad trains.

You will investigate two theorems related to the Inscribed-Angle Theorem in the following Explore.

EXPLORE: MOVING OUT

MATERIALS

Compass
Straightedge
Protractor
Geometry software (optional)

1. Use geometry software or a compass and straightedge to construct a figure like the one shown below. $\angle AED$ is a **tangent-secant** angle.

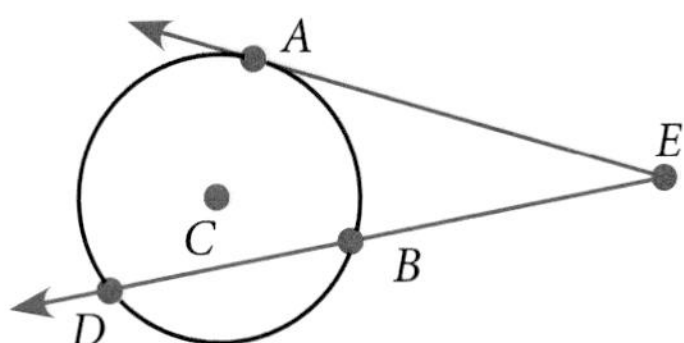

2. Find the measures of the two intercepted arcs. Explain how you did this. Then find the measure of the tangent-secant angle.

3. Repeat Steps 1 and 2 until you think you have found a relationship between the measures of the two intercepted arcs and the measure of the tangent-secant angle. Make a conjecture, and compare your conjecture with your classmates' results.

Problem-Solving Tip

Record your results in a table.

4. Now construct a figure like the one at the right. $\angle FJH$ is a **tangent-tangent** angle.

5. As above, identify a relationship between the measure of a tangent-tangent angle and the measures of the arcs it intercepts. Make a conjecture.

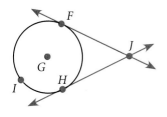

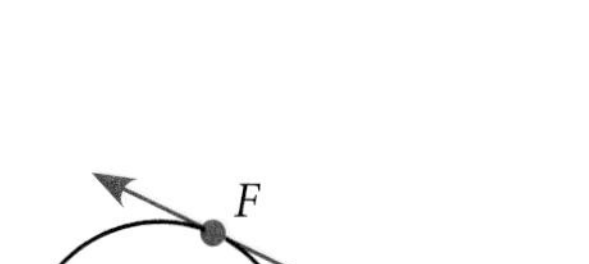

EXAMPLES

1. Find $m\angle VWY$.

The measure of $\angle VWY$ is equal to half the difference of the measures of the arcs it intercepts.

$$m\angle VWY = \frac{1}{2}(m\widehat{VY} - m\widehat{VX})$$

$$m\angle VWY = \frac{1}{2}(146° - 98°) = \frac{1}{2}(48°) = 24°$$

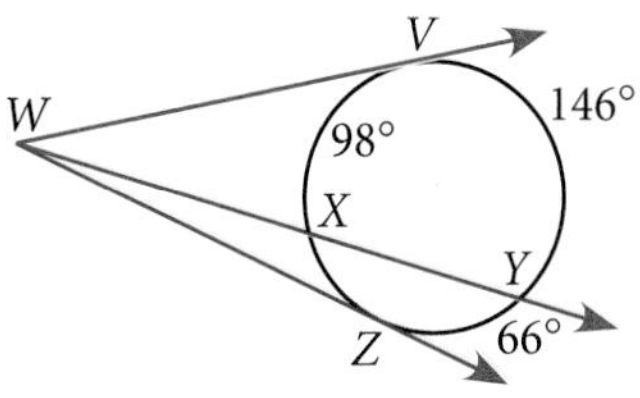

2. Find $m\widehat{XZ}$.

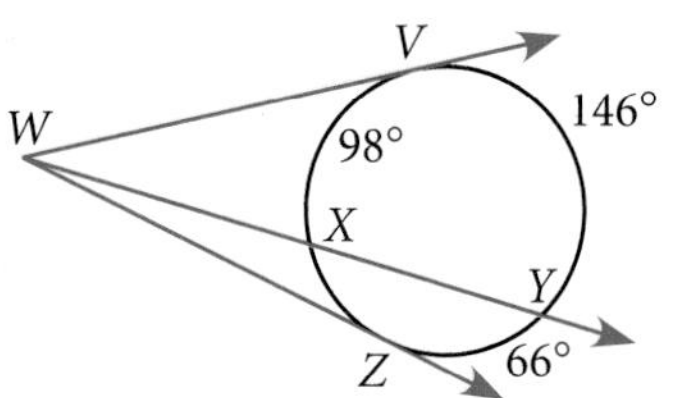

Since a circle has 360°, we can find $m\widehat{XZ}$ by subtraction.

$m\widehat{XZ} = 360° - 66° - 146° - 98° = 50°$

3. Find $m\angle VWZ$.

$m\angle VWZ$ is equal to half the difference of the measures of the arcs it intercepts.

$m\angle VWZ = \frac{1}{2}(m\widehat{VYZ} - m\widehat{VZ})$

$m\angle VWZ = \frac{1}{2}(212° - 148°) = \frac{1}{2}(64°) = 32°$

TRY IT

Find the measure of each angle or arc indicated by a variable.

a.

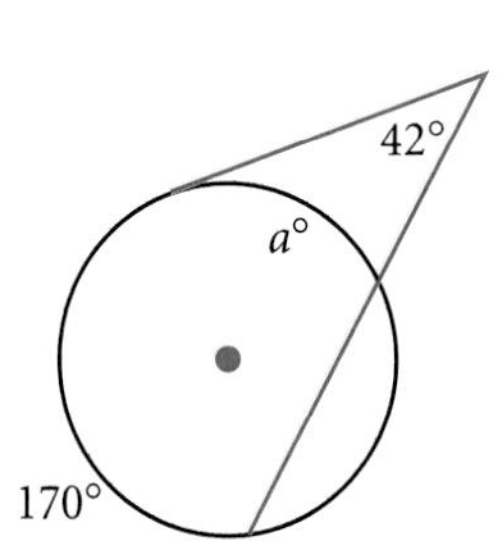

b.

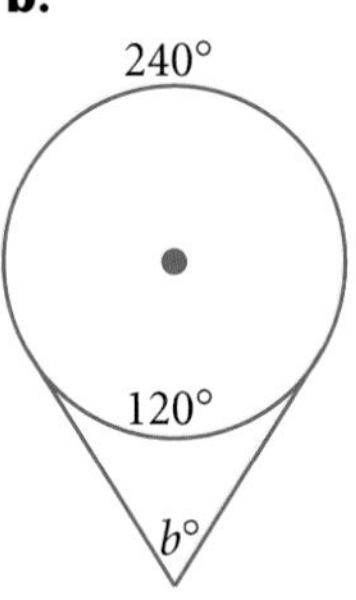

c.

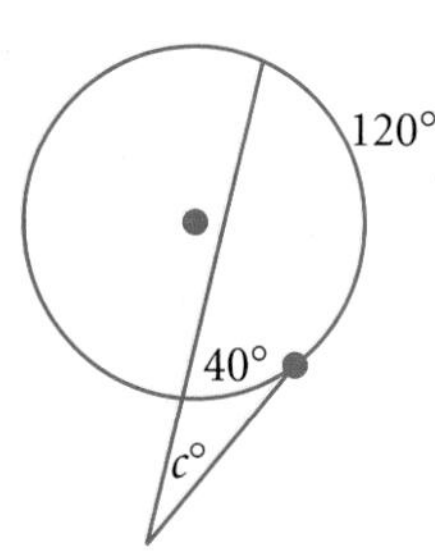

The theorems you've explored are stated below.

TANGENT-SECANT ANGLE THEOREM

The measure of a tangent-secant angle is one-half the difference of the measures of its two intercepted arcs.

$m\angle ADC = \frac{1}{2}(m\widehat{AC} - m\widehat{BC})$

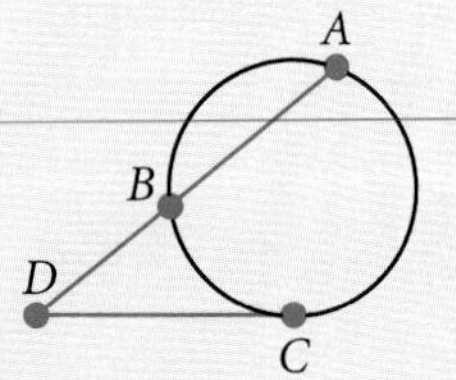

TANGENT-TANGENT ANGLE THEOREM

The measure of a tangent-tangent angle is one-half the difference of the measures of its two intercepted arcs.

$m\angle QTS = \frac{1}{2}(m\widehat{QRS} - m\widehat{QS})$

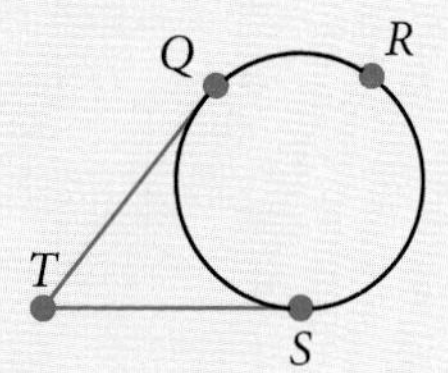

REFLECT

1. Sketch a *secant-secant* angle. How do you think the measure of this angle is related to the measures of the arcs it intercepts?
2. Write one theorem about angle and arc measures that begins, “If an angle intercepts two arcs of a circle and its vertex lies outside the circle . . . ”

Exercises

CORE

1. Getting Started Follow the steps below to find $m\angle A$.

a. What is $m\widehat{BDC}$?

b. What is the difference of $m\widehat{BDC}$ and $m\widehat{BC}$?

c. Take half of the difference you found in **1b.** This is $m\angle A$.

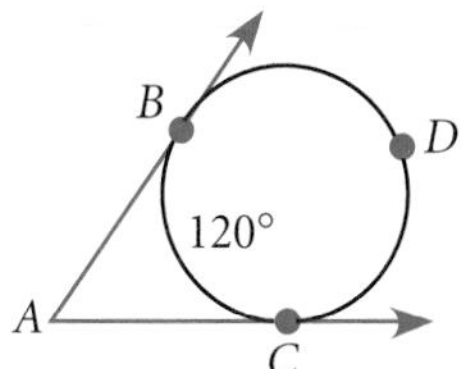

Find the measure of each numbered angle.

2.

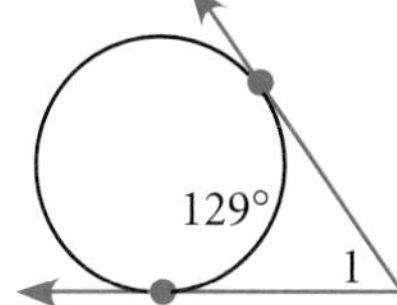

3.

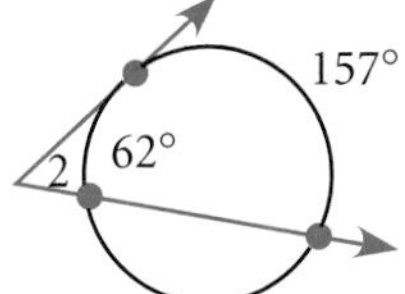

4.

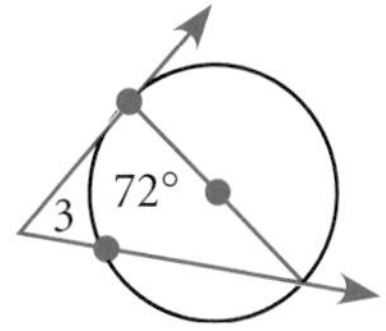

5.

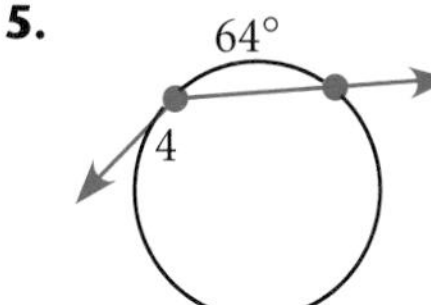

Health

6. Eye See! In a farsighted person, light from nearby objects is focused beyond the retina of the eye, so these objects appear blurred. Assume that the eyeball shown is perfectly round. If $m\angle J = 8°$ and $m\widehat{MN} = 25°$, find $m\widehat{KL}$.

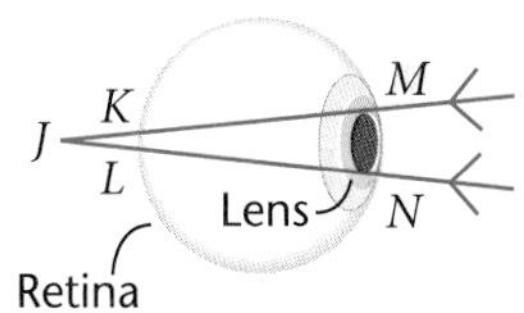

Write the word or phrase that correctly completes each statement.

7. A tangent-tangent angle intersects a circle in ___ points.

8. The measure of a tangent-secant angle is ___ the difference of the measures of its intercepted arcs.

Find the measure of each angle or arc.

9. If $m\widehat{AC} = 152°$, find $m\angle ABC$.

10. If $m\widehat{ADC} = 248°$, find $m\angle ABC$.

11. If $m\angle ABC = 44°$, find $m\widehat{AC}$ and $m\widehat{ADC}$.

12. If $m\widehat{AC} = x°$, find $m\angle ABC$ in terms of x.

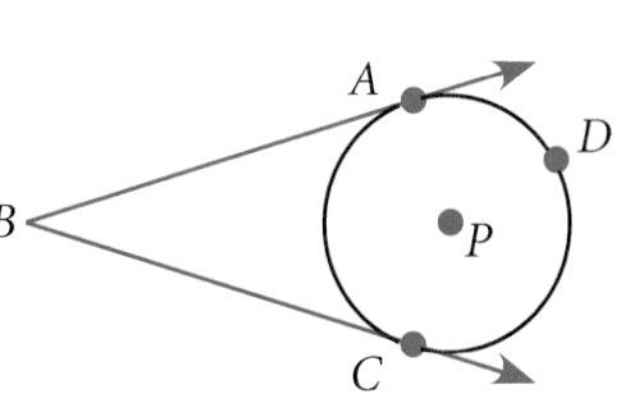

13. In the figure at the right, the area of sector $IJK = 317 \text{ cm}^2$, and the radius of $\odot J = 20$ cm. Find $m\angle IHK$ to the nearest degree.

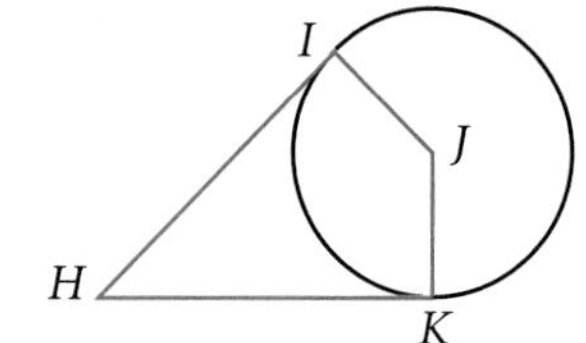

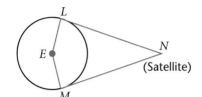

14. According to Harry Garland of Canon Research Center America, NAVSTAR navigational satellites send radio signals that ships at sea can use to find their exact locations. These signals travel in straight lines. The area of the earth that the signal covers is related to the measure of central angle $\angle LEM$.

a. If the length of $\widehat{LM} = 16{,}900$ km and the radius of the earth is approximately 6370 km, find $m\widehat{LM}$.

b. Use your answer to **14a** to find $m\angle N$ and $m\angle LEM$. Explain how you found each angle measure.

There is a theorem for secant-secant angles that follows the same pattern as those for secant-tangent angles and tangent-tangent angles.

SECANT-SECANT ANGLE THEOREM

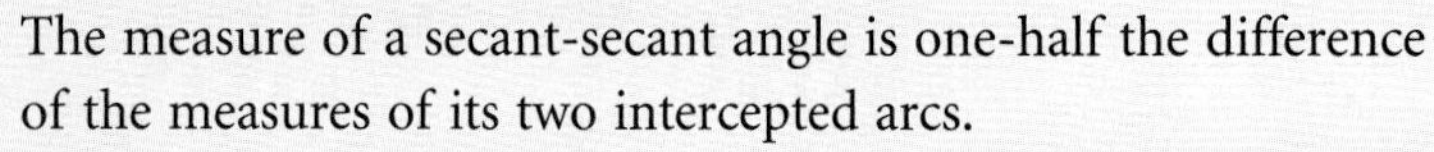

The measure of a secant-secant angle is one-half the difference of the measures of its two intercepted arcs.

$m\angle CAD = \frac{1}{2}(m\widehat{CD} - m\widehat{BE})$

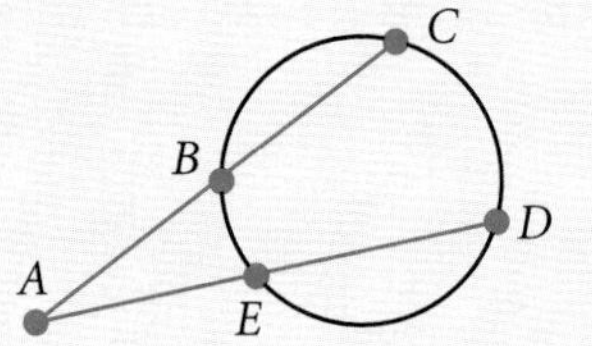

15. Complete the following proof of the Secant-Secant Angle Theorem.

Given: Figure as shown.

Prove: $m\angle CAD = \frac{1}{2}(m\widehat{CD} - m\widehat{BE})$

Proof:

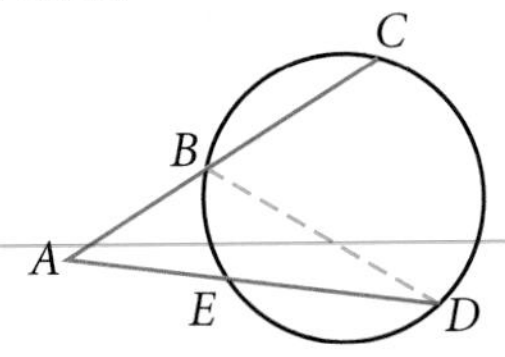

Statements	**Reasons**
1. $m\angle CBD = m\angle CAD + m\angle BDA$	**1.**
2. $m\angle CBD - m\angle BDA = m\angle CAD$	**2.**
3. $m\angle CBD = \frac{1}{2}m\widehat{CD}$, $m\angle BDA = \frac{1}{2}m\widehat{BE}$	**3.**
4. $\frac{1}{2}m\widehat{CD} - \frac{1}{2}m\widehat{BE} = m\angle CAD$	**4.**
5. $m\angle CAD = \frac{1}{2}(m\widehat{CD} - m\widehat{BE})$	**5.** Algebra; Symmetric Property of Equality, Distributive Property

Find the measure of each angle or arc.

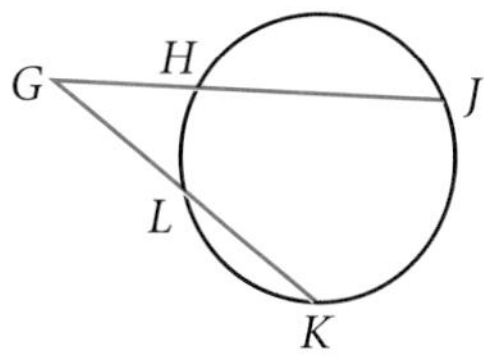

16. If $m\widehat{JK} = 105°$ and $m\widehat{HL} = 41°$, find $m\angle G$.

17. If $m\widehat{JK} = 145°$ and $m\angle G = 38°$, find $m\widehat{HL}$.

18. If $m\angle G = 53°$ and $m\widehat{HL} = 62°$, find $m\widehat{JK}$.

19. If $m\widehat{JK} = (3x - 22)°$ and $m\widehat{HL} = (x - 16)°$, find $m\angle G$ in terms of x.

LOOK AHEAD

Find the area of each figure. Round answers to the nearest tenth.

20.

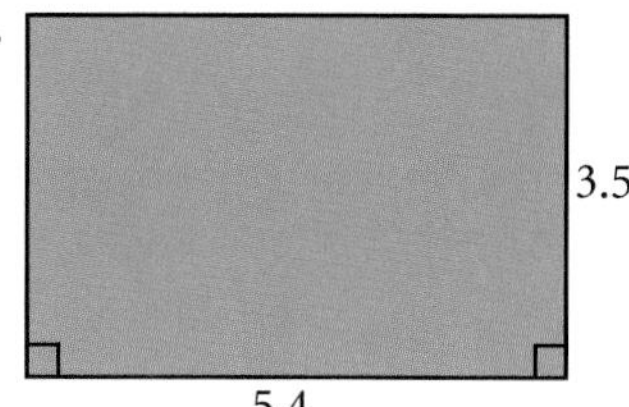

21.

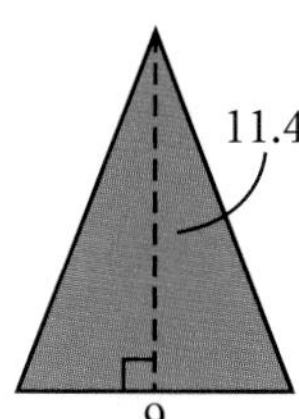

22.

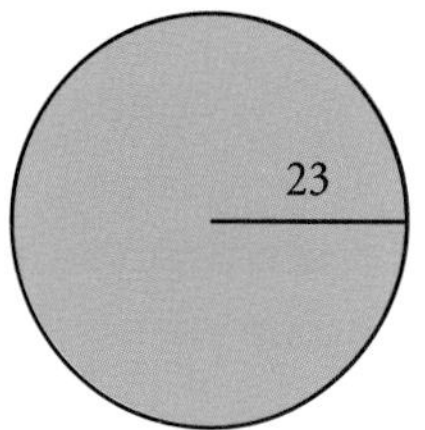

MORE PRACTICE

Find the measure of each numbered angle.

23.

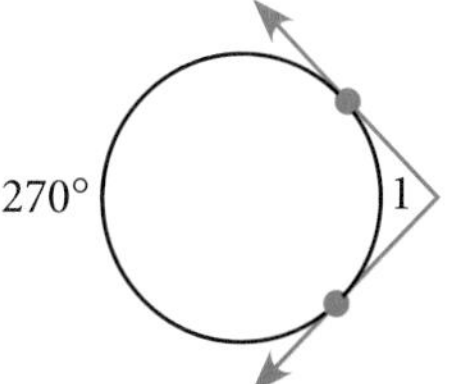

24.

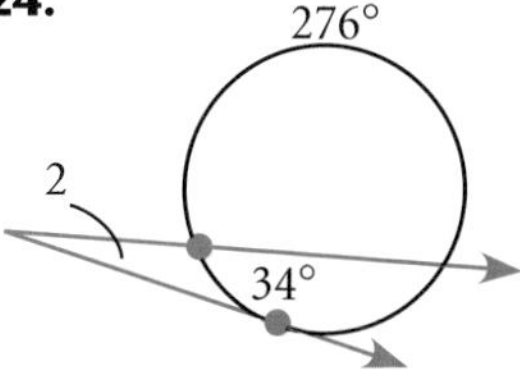

25.

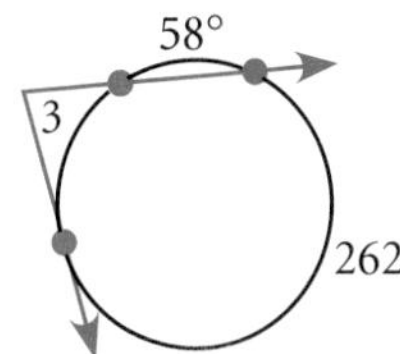

26.

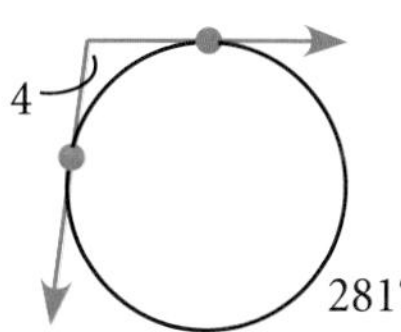

27.

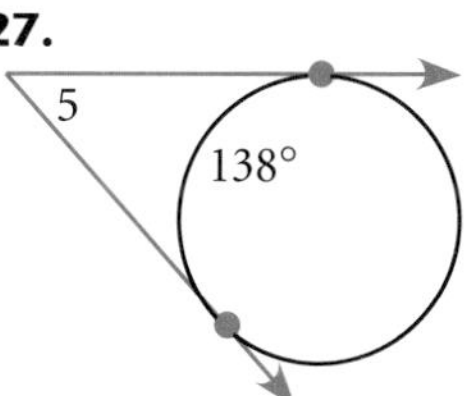

28.

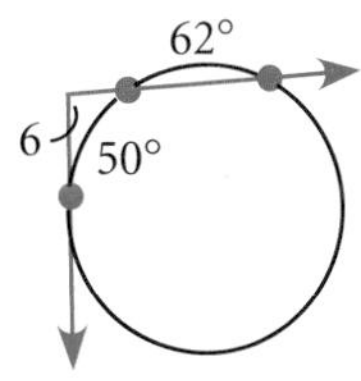

Find the measure of each angle or arc.

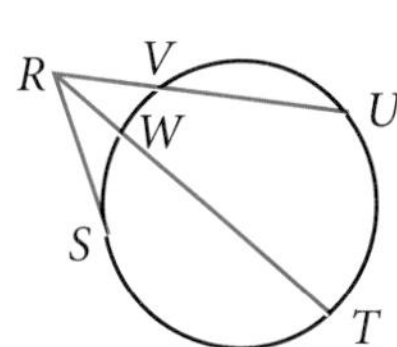

29. If $m\widehat{UT} = 32°$ and $m\widehat{VW} = 27°$, find $m\angle URT$.

30. If $m\angle URS = 77°$ and $m\widehat{VS} = 95°$, find $m\widehat{UTS}$.

31. If $m\angle URS = 68°$, $m\angle TRS = 30°$, $m\widehat{WS} = 41°$, and $m\widehat{UTS} = 255°$, find $m\widehat{VW}$.

MORE MATH REASONING

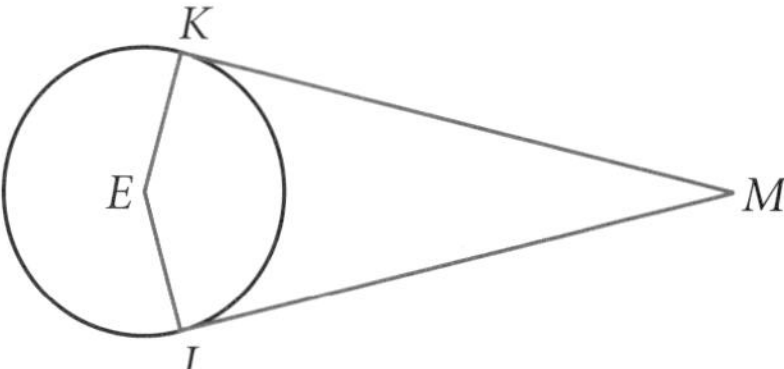

32. Suppose that Mars, M, is rising in your city K at the same time it is setting in city L. The radius of the great circle of the earth shown is 3963.34 miles. The distance from city L to city K is 12,450.58 miles.

a. Find the measure of $\widehat{LK}$. Record your answer to the nearest ten-thousandth. What is $m\angle KEL$? Explain how you found this value.

b. What is true about $\overline{EK}$ and $\overline{KM}$? How do you know this?

c. Draw $\overline{EM}$. What do you think $m\angle KEM$ is? Justify your answer.

d. Use trigonometry to find EM.

e. Why do you think such accuracy was needed in **32a**? (Hint: See what happens if you round your answers in **32a** to the nearest degree.)

33. Soccer goalies know that a player directly in front of the goal is more dangerous than one off to one side, even when the player is the same distance from the goal.

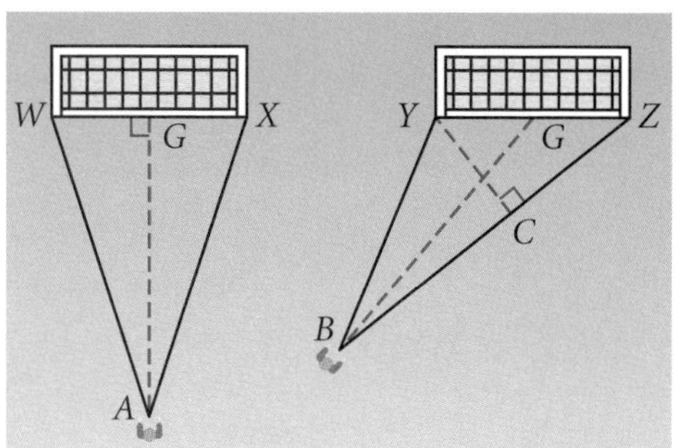

a. Player A is 18 yd from G, the center of the 8-yd-wide goal, so $AG = 18$ yd, and $WX = 8$ yd. Find the measure of the "shooting angle," $\angle WAX$.

b. Player B is also 18 yd from the center of the goal, so $BG = 18$ yd and $YZ = 8$ yd. In this position, $BY = 15$ yd and $YC = 4.22$ yd. Find the measure of shooting angle $\angle YBZ$.

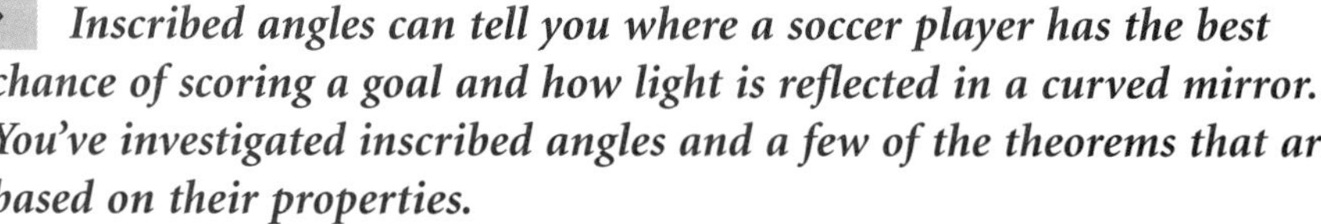

8-3 PART C Making Connections

← CONNECT → ***Inscribed angles can tell you where a soccer player has the best chance of scoring a goal and how light is reflected in a curved mirror. You've investigated inscribed angles and a few of the theorems that are based on their properties.***

When you're trying to score a goal in soccer, you want to have the largest possible angle to shoot for. This is one reason why it's easier to score a goal from the center of the field than from the sidelines. In the following Explore, you will see how inscribed angles affect your chances of scoring a goal in a soccer game.

EXPLORE: GOING FOR THE GOAL

MATERIALS

Straightedge
Scissors
Protractor

As the coach of a soccer team, you know that your next opponent has one very dangerous player. Whenever she gets the ball positioned so that the angle formed by one goal post (A), her position (at the vertex, P) and the other goal post (B) measures 40° or more, she always scores a goal.

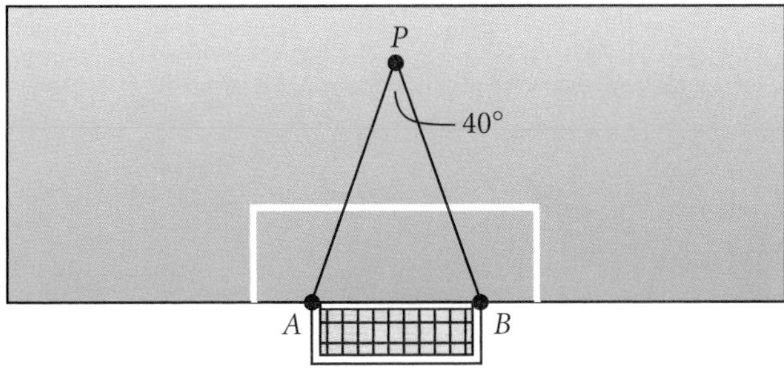

You tell your players never to let this player get the ball to where this angle is 40° or more. They reply that they need a better description of where this "danger area" is.

1. Make a sketch of the part of a soccer field nearest the goal, as shown above.

2. Cut out a large 40° angle. Place it on your sketch as shown. Move it around and mark the locus of points for which the goal posts exactly determine a 40° angle. Describe these points.

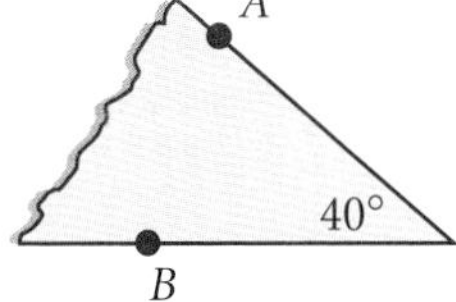

3. Use your answer from Step 2 to help identify all the points where the goal posts determine an angle of 40° or more. Shade this area on your drawing. What does it look like?

4. Suppose the length of $\widehat{AB}$ is 8 yd. Find the radius of the circle. Then prepare an illustration and written description of the "danger area" for your team. Give specific measurements wherever you can.

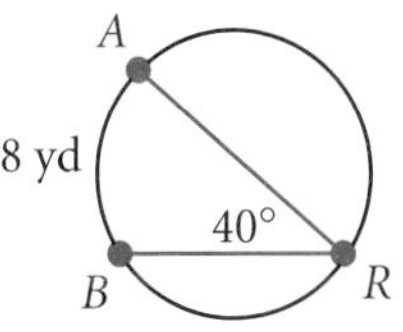

REFLECT

1. Give a short written summary of the relationships between the measures of angles and their intercepted arcs.

2. In your own words, explain why an inscribed angle that intercepts a semicircle must measure 90°.

Self-Assessment

Find the measure of each angle or arc.

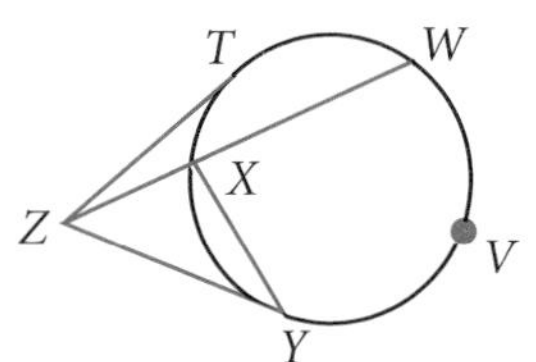

1. If $m\widehat{WVY} = 184°$, find $m\angle WXY$.

2. If $m\angle WXY = 68°$, find $m\widehat{WVY}$.

3. If $m\widehat{TY} = 116°$, find $m\angle TZY$.

4. If $m\widehat{TX} = 32°$ and $m\widehat{XY} = 84°$, find $m\angle TZY$.

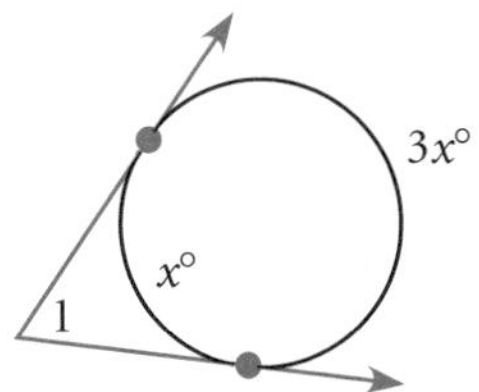

Note: Figure not necessarily drawn to scale.

5. In the figure, $m\angle 1 =$
(a) 45° (b) 60° (c) 90°
(d) 120° (e) 150°

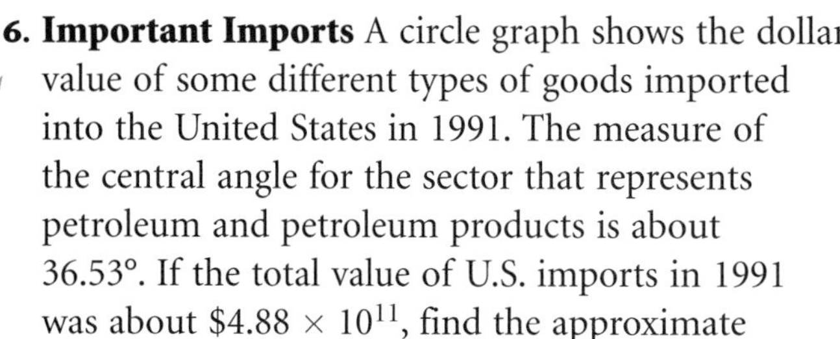

6. Important Imports A circle graph shows the dollar value of some different types of goods imported into the United States in 1991. The measure of the central angle for the sector that represents petroleum and petroleum products is about 36.53°. If the total value of U.S. imports in 1991 was about $\$4.88 \times 10^{11}$, find the approximate dollar value of the petroleum imports. [8-2]

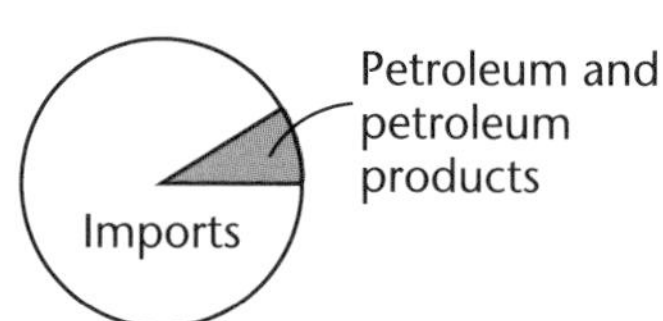

In the figure, $m\widehat{LPN} = 208°$, $m\widehat{PN} = 107°$, and $m\widehat{PNM} = 186°$. Find each measure.

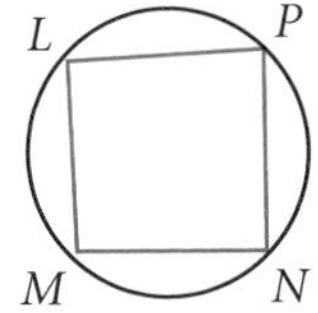

7. $m\angle L$

8. $m\angle M$

9. $m\angle N$

10. $m\angle P$

Industry

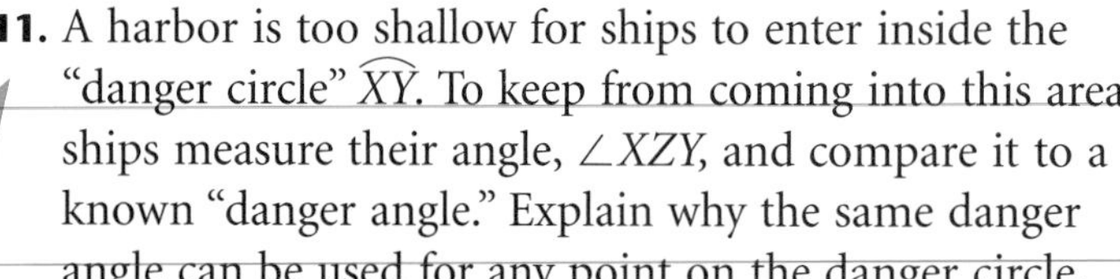

11. A harbor is too shallow for ships to enter inside the "danger circle" $\widehat{XY}$. To keep from coming into this area, ships measure their angle, $\angle XZY$, and compare it to a known "danger angle." Explain why the same danger angle can be used for any point on the danger circle.

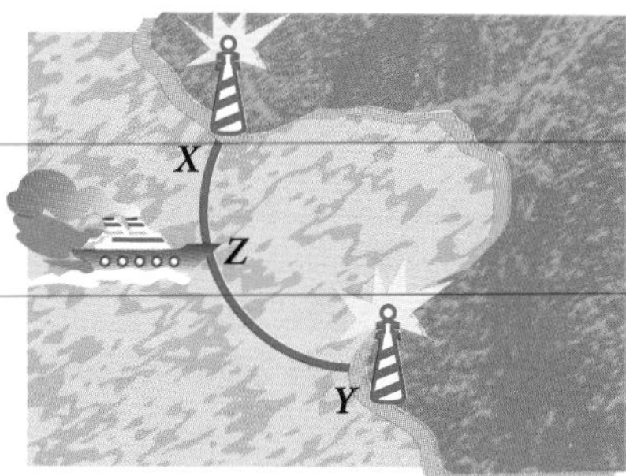

12. A dumbbell weight is stored in a V-shaped rack as shown below right. The radius of the weight is 5 cm, and $UV = 5.6$ cm.

a. Find the distance VT from the tip of the V to the center of the weight.

b. Find $m\angle UVW$, $m\widehat{USW}$, and $m\widehat{UW}$. Explain how you found each of these.

c. If $m\angle UVW$ were 60°, what would VT be?

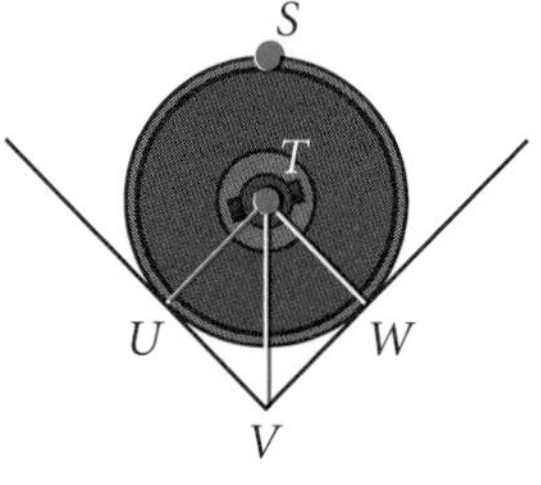

Chapter 8 Review

In Chapter 8, you learned several properties of circles and spheres. You also explored the lines, angles, and regions associated with these figures.

KEY TERMS

- arc [8-2]
- center of a circle [8-1]
- central angle [8-2]
- chord [8-2]
- circle [8-1]
- circumference [8-1]
- circumscribed [8-1]
- concentric [8-1]
- diameter [8-1]
- great circle [8-1]
- inscribed [8-1]
- inscribed angle [8-3]
- major arc [8-2]
- minor arc [8-2]
- pi (π) [8-1]
- radius [8-1]
- secant line [8-1]
- sector [8-2]
- semicircle [8-2]
- sphere [8-1]
- tangent line [8-1]

Determine whether each statement is true or false. If the statement is false, change the underlined word or phrase to make it true.

1. Pi is the ratio of the circumference of a circle to its <u>diameter.</u>

2. The center of a circle is the vertex of <u>an inscribed angle</u> of the circle.

3. A polygon is <u>circumscribed about</u> a circle if each of its vertices lies on the circle.

CONCEPTS AND APPLICATIONS

4. Find the radius and area of a circle with a circumference of 14π. [8-1]

In the figure, $\overleftrightarrow{QZ}$ is tangent to $\odot O$ at Z, $m\widehat{YZ} = 82°$, and $m\widehat{XY} = 70°$. Give an example of each of the following. [8-1, 8-2, 8-3]

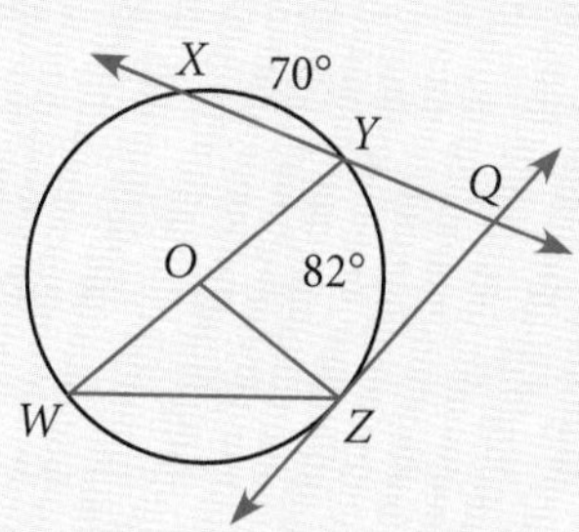

5. an inscribed angle **6.** a secant line **7.** a minor arc

Find each of the following. [8-2, 8-3]

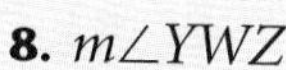

8. $m\angle YWZ$ **9.** $m\angle YOZ$ **10.** $m\widehat{XWZ}$

11. $m\angle OZQ$ **12.** $m\angle Q$

13. A square with a side length of twenty centimeters is inscribed in a circle. What are the circumference and area of the circle? [8-1]

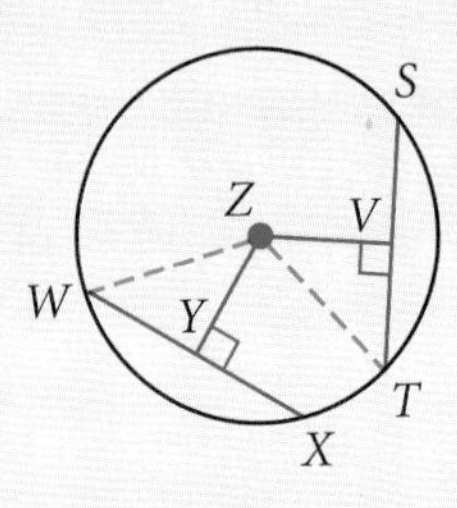

14. Prove: If two chords of a circle (that are not diameters) are congruent, then they are equidistant from its center. [8-2]

Given: $\overline{WX} \cong \overline{ST}$, $\overline{ZY} \perp \overline{WX}$, $\overline{ZV} \perp \overline{ST}$

Prove: $\overline{ZY} \cong \overline{ZV}$

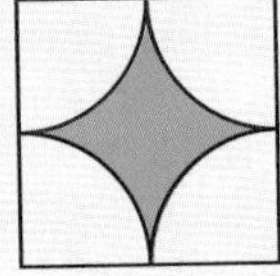

15. Inside a square target of side length 1, four congruent quarter-circles are drawn, tangent to each other and with centers at the vertices of the square. An archer will hit randomly within the square. To the nearest hundredth, what is the probability of hitting the shaded region? [5-1, 8-2]

16. What are the center and radius of the circle with equation $x^2 + y^2 = 13$? [8-1]

Social Science

17. According to the 1040 tax forms for 1993, the $1381-billion budget of the U.S. federal government came from the following sources: personal income taxes, 35%; various other taxes (including social security, etc.), 44%; money borrowed to cover the deficit, 21%. [8-2]

a. Make a circle graph of radius $\frac{1}{2}$ in. to represent these income sources.

b. What is the area of the sector representing borrowed money?

c. To the nearest tenth, give the degree measure and the length of the arc intercepted by the central angle of the sector representing borrowed money.

CONCEPTS AND CONNECTIONS

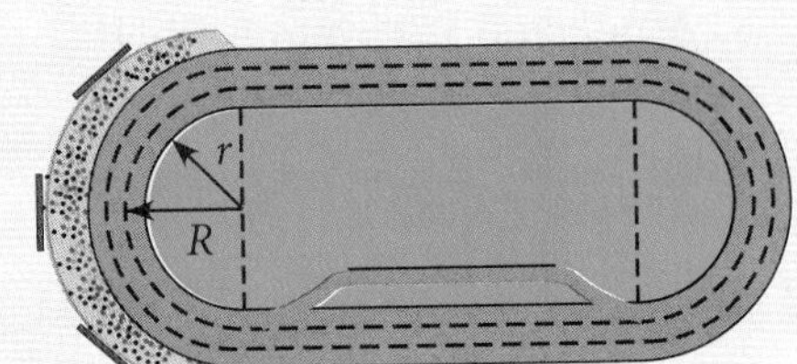

18. Sports In races on an oval track, the leader usually takes the inside lane when going around curves. The oval tracks are actually semicircles connected by straightaways as shown.

a. Assume one runner runs one meter outside the other around the turn. Create a table with columns for radii (r and R), distances around the turn for each runner (d and D), and the difference in distances ($D - d$). Choose values to test various tight tracks (small r) and large tracks. Describe how the radius of the turn affects the difference in distances run.

b. Now develop a general formula for the difference in distances around one turn in terms of r and R.

SELF-EVALUATION

Write a summary of the most important facts from Chapter 8. Include properties and formulas related to angle and arc measurement, length, and area. Provide sketches to communicate your ideas more completely.

Chapter 8 Assessment

TEST

1. The diameter of a circle is 12 m. Find its circumference and area.

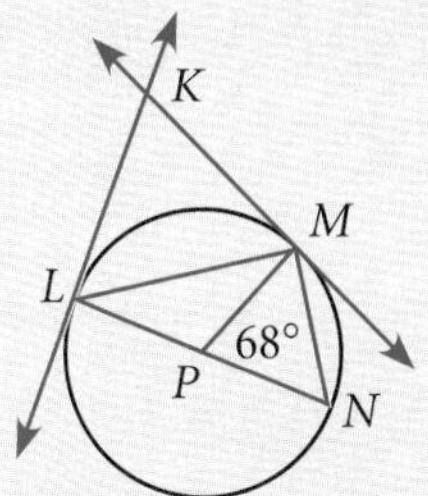

In the figure, $\overleftrightarrow{KM}$ and $\overleftrightarrow{KL}$ are tangent to $\odot P$, whose radius is 20 mm. Give an example of each of the following.

2. a chord **3.** a point of tangency **4.** a radius

Find each of the following.

5. $m\widehat{MN}$ **6.** $m\angle NML$ **7.** $m\angle MNL$

8. $m\angle MKL$ **9.** length of $\widehat{MN}$

10. Give an equation for a circle with its center at the origin and radius 8.

11. A chord of a circle has length 4.2 cm and is 8 cm from the center of the circle. What is the radius of the circle to the nearest hundredth?

12. Write a brief summary of the relationships among a chord, its perpendicular bisector, and the radii of a circle. Include illustrations with your summary.

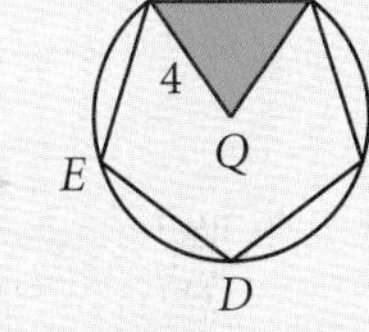

13. Regular pentagon *ABCDE* is inscribed in $\odot Q$ with radius 4.
a. Find the area of sector *AQB* to the nearest hundredth.
b. Use an auxiliary line and trigonometry to find *AB*.

Science

14. The equatorial radius of Jupiter is 44,000 miles—about 11 times that of the earth. However, Jupiter's "day"—the time it takes to rotate once on its axis—is only 10 hr!
a. What is the measure of the arc through which Jupiter turns in 1 hr?
b. Find the distance that a point on Jupiter's equator travels in 1 hr. How does this compare with the earth's rotational speed of about 1000 mi/hr?

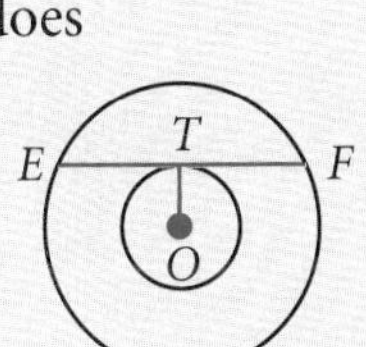

15. The radius of the smaller of two concentric circles is 1.2 m. $\overline{EF}$ is tangent to the smaller circle at *T* and is a chord of the larger circle. If $EF = 3.2$, what is the radius of the larger circle?

PERFORMANCE TASK

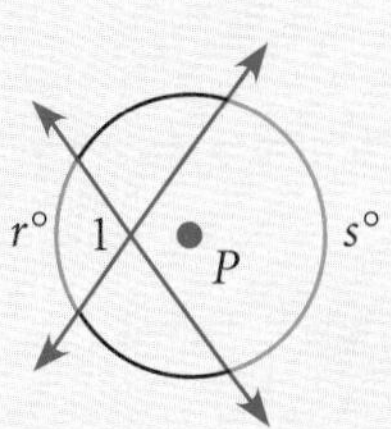

Draw several circles with intersecting secant lines as shown. For each, measure arcs and angles. Then state a conjecture about the relationship between the measure of an angle formed by secants intersecting inside a circle and the measures of the intercepted arcs.

Chapter 9 Surface Area and Volume

Project A
Play Ball!
Did you know that the circumference of the first softball was five inches more than today's standard softball?

Project B
For Here or To Go?
What did take-out restaurants do before the invention of Styrofoam®?

Project C
Shelter the Homeless
Who is Buckminster Fuller, and what is a dome home?

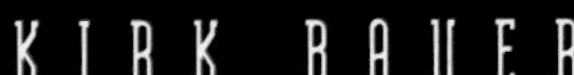

KIRK BAUER

I loved math in high school. I liked the way you could describe the physical world in numbers. I thought I would go into physical science.

I'm proud that I can use sports to help disabled people rebuild and improve their lives. When we hold a competition, we use a system of "handicapping" the participants, in order to "level the playing field." This system enables us to evaluate a blind skier and an amputee in the same event and then award an overall trophy, regardless of the disability. Without math, we could never do this.

Kirk Bauer
Executive Director
National Handicapped Sports
Rockville, MD

Chapter 9 Surface Area and Volume

GETTING READY

9-1 Surface Area

In 9-1 you will calculate the surface area of many three-dimensional objects. You will use the following skills from previous chapters.

Find the area of each triangle. [5-2]

1. $b = 5, h = 7$

2. $b = \frac{8}{3}, h = 3\frac{1}{2}$

3. $b = x + y, h = 3x$

4. $b = 5\sqrt{12}, h = 2\sqrt[3]{27}$

Find the area of each polygon. [6-3]

5. A regular pentagon with $a = 5, p = 30$

6. A regular hexagon with $r = 6$

7. A regular octagon with $a = 4, s = 6$

8. A regular pentagon with $a = 2\sqrt{2}, s = \sqrt{3}$

9-2 Volume

In 9-2 you will see how to measure the volume of familiar solids. You will need the following skills from previous chapters.

Solve for x in each triangle. [5-3]

9. $AB = 4, BC = 5, AC = x$

10. $AB = 5, AC = 12, BC = x$

11. $AC = 8, BC = 10, AB = x$

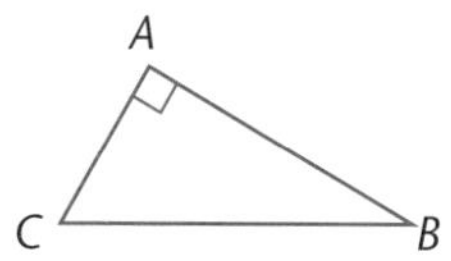

Find the area of each circle. [8-1]

12. $r = 12$

13. $r = 2\pi$

14. $d = 4x$

15. $d = \frac{25}{4}$

9-3 Similar Solids

In 9-3 you will investigate the surface area and volume of similar solids. You will need the following skills from previous courses and chapters.

Given the following similarity ratios of one plane figure to another, what is the ratio of their perimeters? their areas? [7-1]

16. $\frac{4}{3}$

17. $\frac{8}{9}$

18. $\frac{2}{5}$

19. $\frac{x}{y}$

Evaluate each expression. [Previous course]

20. $\left(\frac{4}{7}\right)^3$

21. $\left(\frac{5}{2}\right)^3$

22. $\left(\frac{3}{8}\right)^2$

23. $\sqrt{125}$

24. $\sqrt{\frac{64}{100}}$

9-1 Surface Area

When it's time for breakfast, you probably don't ask yourself, "Should I have the cereal in the rectangular prism or in the cylinder?" But deciding how to package a product requires a great deal of time, creativity, and money. Package designers make trade-offs between how much a package costs, how well it protects its contents, and whether or not the product can be stacked and displayed easily and safely.

Package Engineering, Inc., of Phoenix, Arizona, recently developed corrugated plastic containers. These containers look like cardboard and are as strong as wood, but they are 75% lighter than wood. A small box can support 200 pounds. The containers are recyclable, reusable, and moisture-resistant.

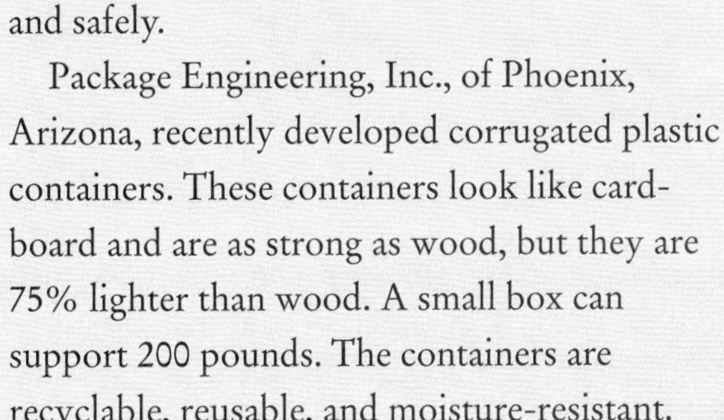

Chesapeake Display & Packaging Co. of North Carolina designed a display for gallon jugs of antifreeze. The display shown below used corrugated trays and partitions that are 35% recycled paper. Using recycled paper saved 475 tons of paperboard in one year. In addition, the materials went through humidity-chamber, compression, impact, and vibration tests that are probably far more severe than actual shipping and warehouse conditions.

1. Products are often packaged in a bag, box, bottle, or can. Name one type of product for which each of these packages is best. Then choose a material (paper, glass, plastic, metal, etc.) for each product's package. Justify your choices.
2. What factors (besides cost, safety, and "stackability") might influence the design of a product's package?

9-1 PART A Surface Area of Prisms

← CONNECT →

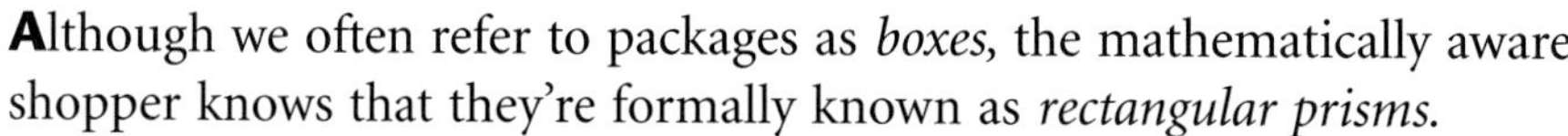

You've studied the areas and perimeters of two-dimensional figures. Now you will use nets to help calculate the surface areas of prisms.

Although we often refer to packages as *boxes,* the mathematically aware shopper knows that they're formally known as *rectangular prisms.*

A **prism** is a polyhedron with two identical polygonal faces, called **bases,** that lie in parallel planes. The other parallelogram-shaped faces are **lateral faces.**

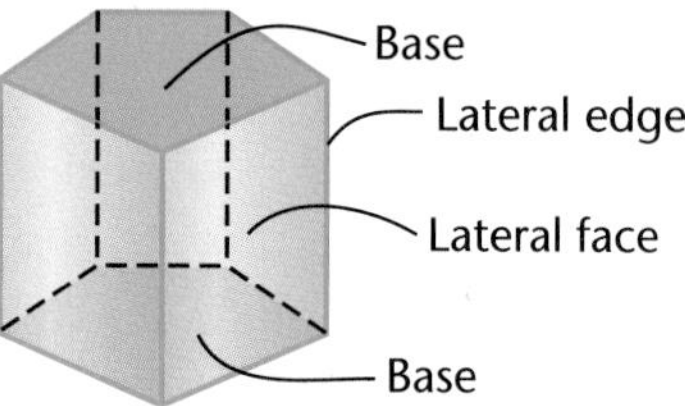

An **altitude** of a prism is a segment perpendicular to both bases whose endpoints are in the planes of the bases. The length of an altitude is the **height** of the prism.

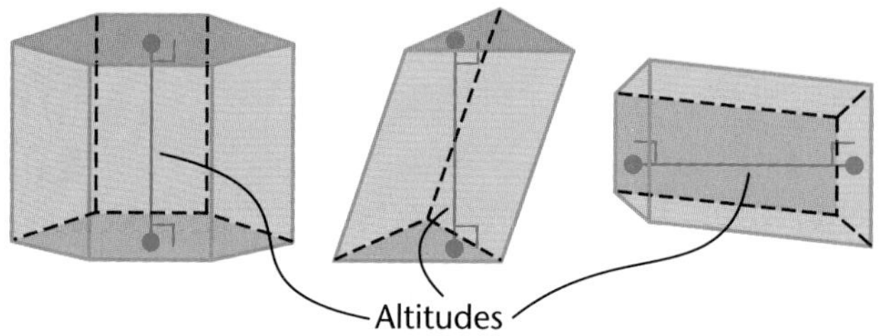

Prisms are classified by their bases. For example, a prism with triangular bases is classified as a triangular prism. If the lateral edges of a prism are perpendicular to its bases, the prism is a **right prism;** if not, it is an **oblique prism.** Unless told otherwise, you may assume that all prisms in this text are right prisms.

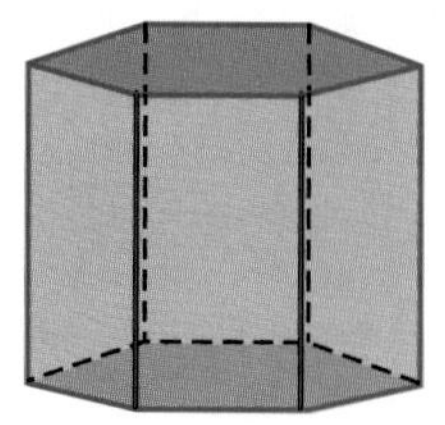

Right hexagonal prism

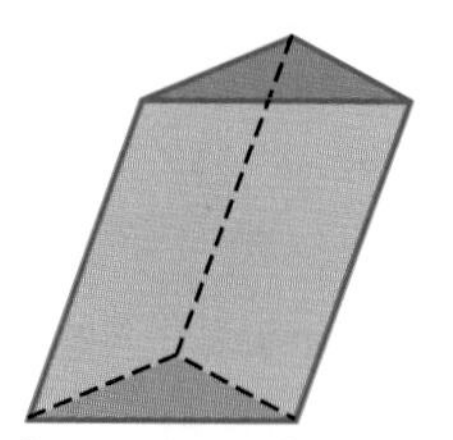

Oblique triangular prism

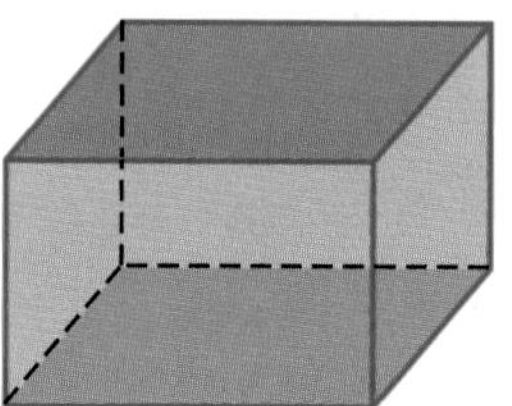

Right rectangular prism

TRY IT

Classify each prism.

a. 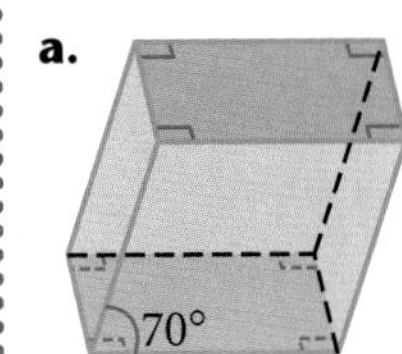

b. 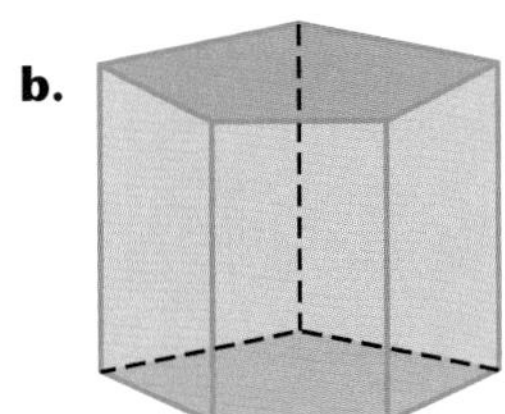

c. 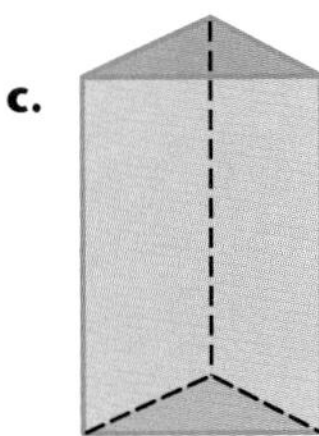

The sum of the areas of the lateral faces of a prism is its **lateral area.** The **surface area** of the prism is the total area of all of its faces, including the bases.

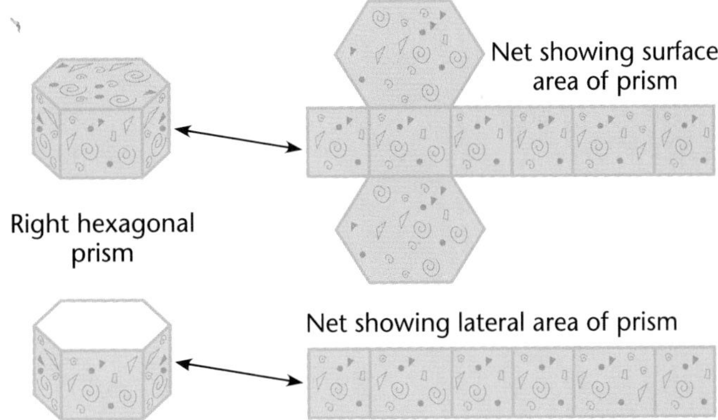

In the following Explore, you will use nets to help discover how to calculate the surface area of a right prism.

EXPLORE: PRISMANIA

1. The photograph shows light refracted through a right triangular prism. Make a sketch of a right triangular prism. Sketch a net for the prism, and describe all of the figures in the net.
2. Suppose you know the height of your prism, h, and the perimeter of its base, p. Use your net to help explain how you can find the lateral area of the prism.
3. Now write a formula for the surface area of any right prism that uses p, the perimeter of the base, h, the height of the prism, and B, the area of one of the bases.

EXAMPLES

1. Find the lateral area of the right prism with right triangular bases shown.

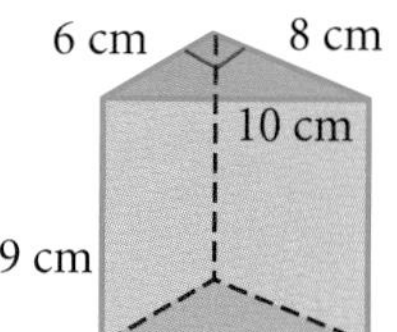

$LA = ph$
$LA = (6 + 8 + 10)(9) = 24(9) = 216 \text{ cm}^2$

2. Find the surface area of the prism.
$SA = LA + 2B = 216 + 2(\frac{1}{2})(8)(6) = 216 + 48 = 264 \text{ cm}^2$

THEOREMS

The lateral area of a right prism is the product of the perimeter of its base and the height of the prism.

$LA = ph$

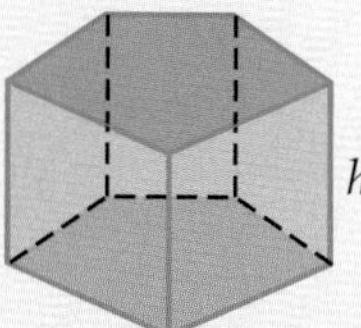

The surface area of a right prism is the sum of its lateral area and the areas of its bases.

$SA = LA + 2B = ph + 2B$

REFLECT

1. Give a formula for the surface area of a cube in terms of its side length, *s*.
2. If a solid prism is cut in half to form two smaller prisms, is the total surface area of the two prisms greater than, less than, or equal to the surface area of the original prism? Why?
3. Give some examples of units that are appropriate for measuring surface area. Explain your choices.

Exercises

CORE

Getting Started **Classify each prism.**

1. 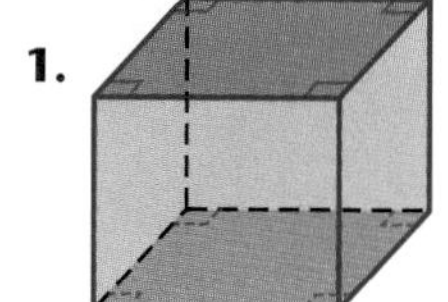

2. 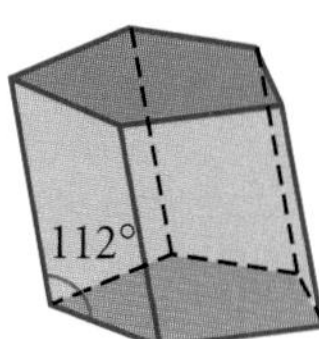

3. 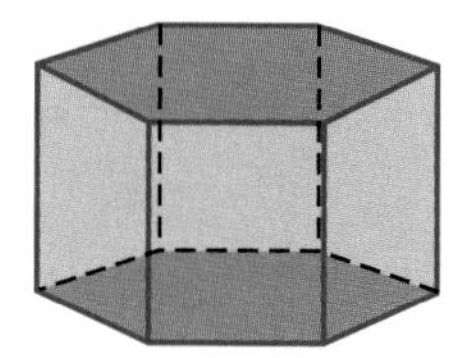

4. 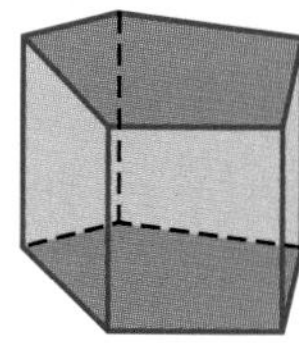

Sketch a net for each prism.

5. 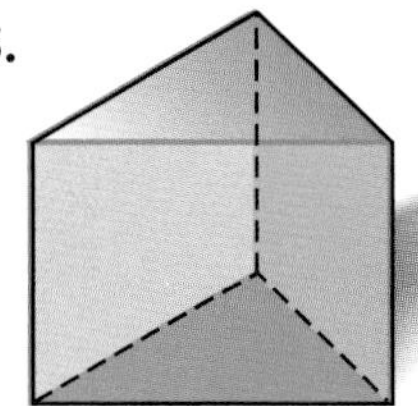

6. 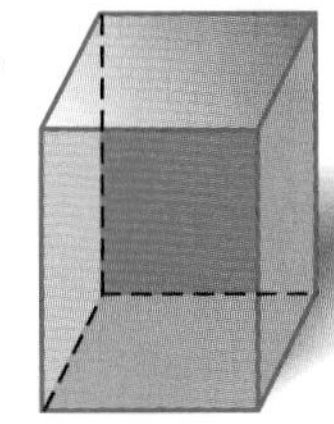

7. 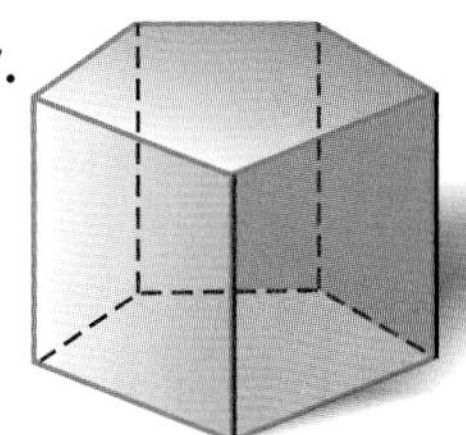

8. 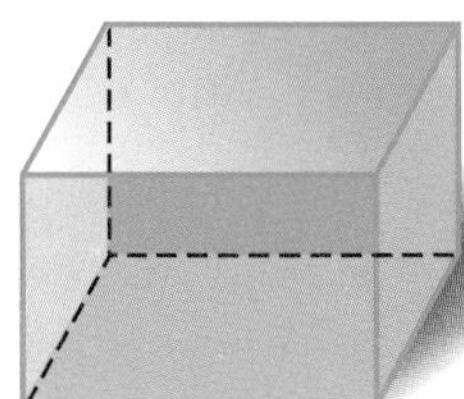

Find the lateral area and surface area of each prism.

9. 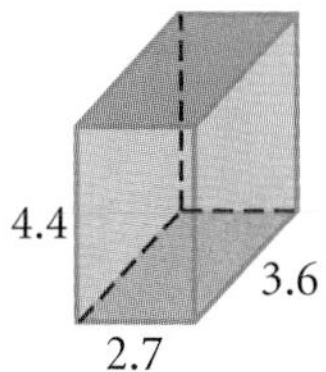

Rectangular prism

10. 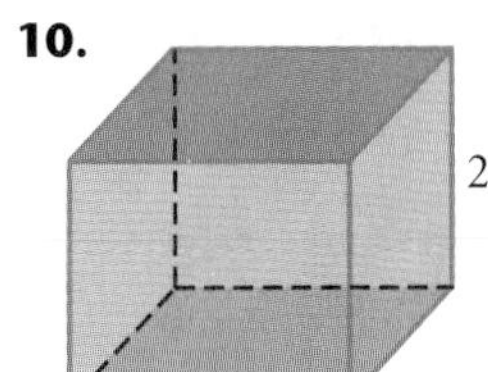

Cube

11. 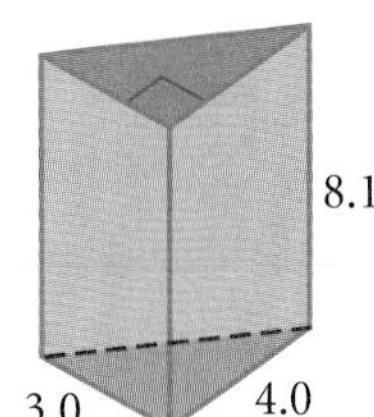

12. 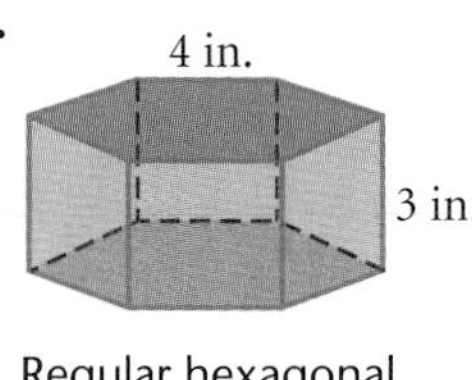

Regular hexagonal prism

Write the word or phrase that correctly completes each statement.

13. A ____ of a prism is a segment whose endpoints are vertices of opposite bases.

14. The length of the altitude of a prism is the ____ of the prism.

15. If the lateral edges of a prism are perpendicular to its bases, then the prism is a ____.

16. Little Red Shed The outside of the shed at the right (including its roof) needs paint. Each gallon of paint costs \$8.99, and a gallon of paint covers 300 ft^2. Assuming that there is no sales tax, how much will it cost to paint the shed? (You must buy the paint in whole gallons.)

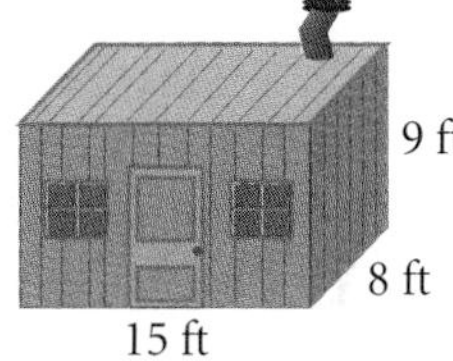

17. What is the difference between the lateral faces of a right prism and the lateral faces of an oblique prism?

18. The box for a videotape is 19 cm tall, 10.5 cm long, and 2.5 cm wide. It is open on one of the long sides, so that the tape can slide in. What is the surface area of the box?

19. In *Gulliver's Travels,* Jonathan Swift describes the land of Lilliput, where people are "not quite six inches high."

The walls of the outer court of the Lilliputian palace are rectangular solids forty feet long, two feet tall, and four inches thick. Find the surface area of one of the walls. (In making your calculations, you may ignore any overlap between the walls and you should include the face in contact with the ground.)

20. The surface area of a cube is a function of one of its side lengths.
   a. Express the surface area of a cube in terms of the length of a side.
   b. Is your answer to **20a** a linear, quadratic, or cubic function? Explain.

21. In a rectangular prism, $h = x$; $w = x - 2$; and $\ell = 2x$.
   a. Find the surface area of the prism in terms of x.
   b. Suppose the surface area of the prism is 112 ft^2. Solve for x.

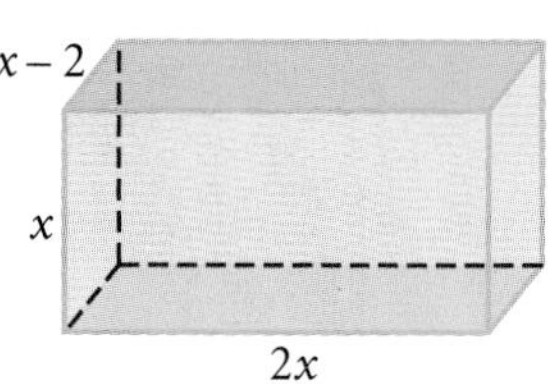

The solid at the right is made of twelve cubes.

22. The edge of each cube measures 1 cm. What is the surface area of the solid?

23. How can you move one block so that the surface area of the solid increases by 2 cm^2?

24. How can you move one block so the surface area decreases by 2 cm^2?

LOOK AHEAD

Solve for *x* in each triangle.

25.

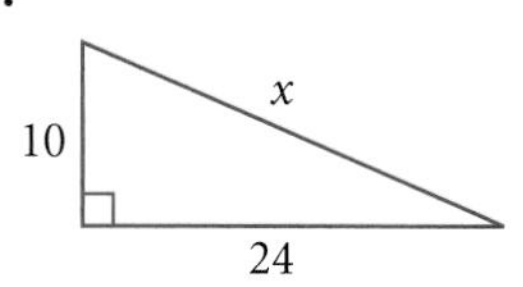

26.

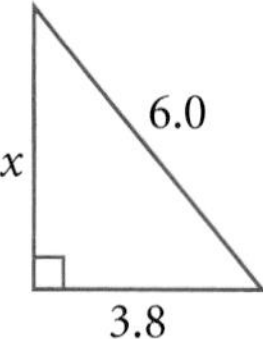

27.

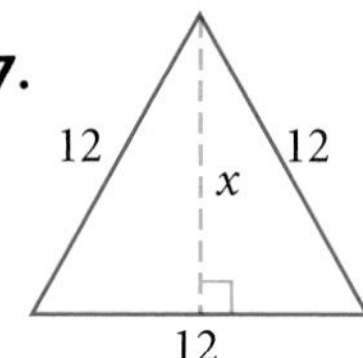

28.

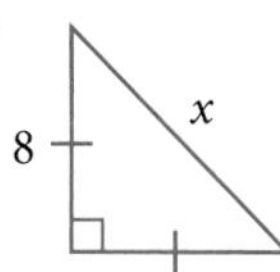

MORE PRACTICE

Sketch a net for each prism.

29.

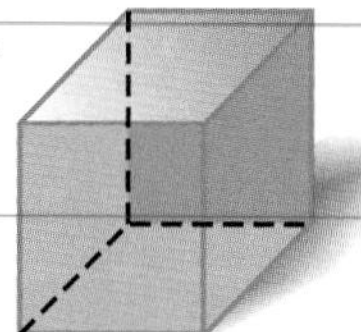

30.

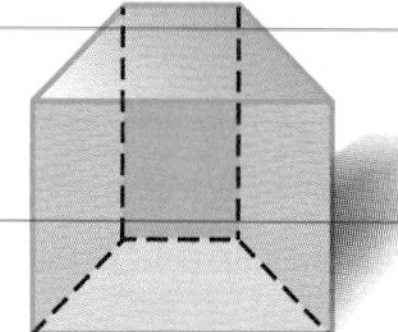

31.

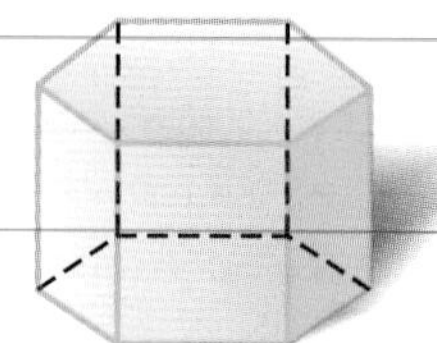

Find the lateral area and surface area of each prism.

32.

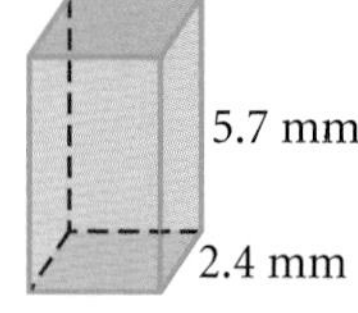

Square prism

33.

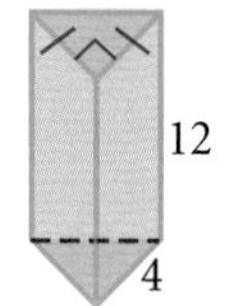

Right isosceles triangular prism

34.

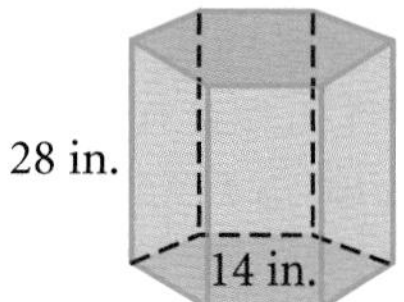

Regular hexagonal prism

The edges of the cubes in each figure measure 1 in. Find the surface area of each solid.

35.

36.

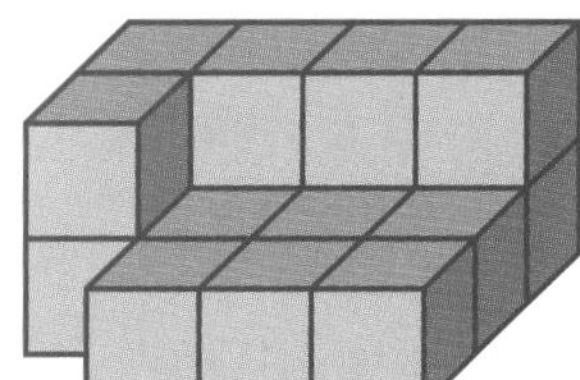

37.

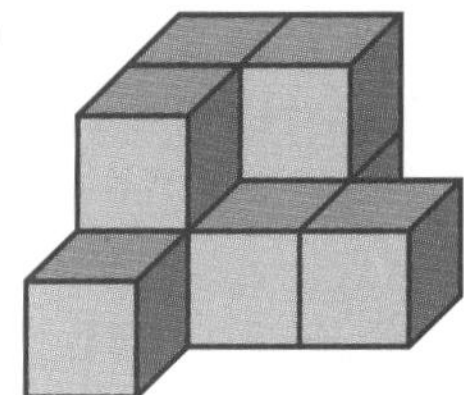

MORE MATH REASONING

38. Chameleocube Crossing The chameleocube is an imaginary animal made up of eight cubes. It can rearrange its cubes any way it wants to as long as at least one face of each cube completely overlaps a face of another cube. One arrangement of the chameleocube is shown at the right.

a. While warming itself in the sun, the chameleocube wants to expose the greatest surface area possible. Describe and sketch a shape for the chameleocube that has the greatest possible surface area. (Hint: There is more than one correct solution!)

b. When frightened, the chameleocube rearranges itself so that the least possible surface area is exposed. Describe and sketch a shape that has the least possible surface area. Explain why this shape is the best.

39. Is the surface area of an oblique prism greater than, equal to, or less than the surface area of a right prism with the same base and the same height? Explain.

Problem-Solving Tip

Make a set of drawings.

40. Not Very Shelf-ish Cruncheteria Cereal (The Cafeteria in a Bowl!) has made a terrible mistake in its packaging! Their boxes—2 in. wide, 6 in. long, and 16 in. tall—are too tall to fit on most people's shelves. Their new marketing director proposes that the width and length of these boxes be increased by 40% while keeping the surface area of the boxes the same. She claims that the new box will fit on a 12-in.-tall shelf. Is she right?

41. Sketch a right rectangular prism that has a surface area of one square meter. Include dimensions in your sketch.

9-1 PART B Surface Area of Pyramids

← CONNECT → ***You've seen how to find the surface area of a right prism. Now you will discover how to calculate the surface area of a pyramid.***

The photograph at the left shows the pyramid of Cheops in Giza, Egypt. A **pyramid** is a polyhedron. The vertices of its polygonal **base** are connected to one other point called the **vertex** of the pyramid. The **height** of the pyramid is the length of its altitude.

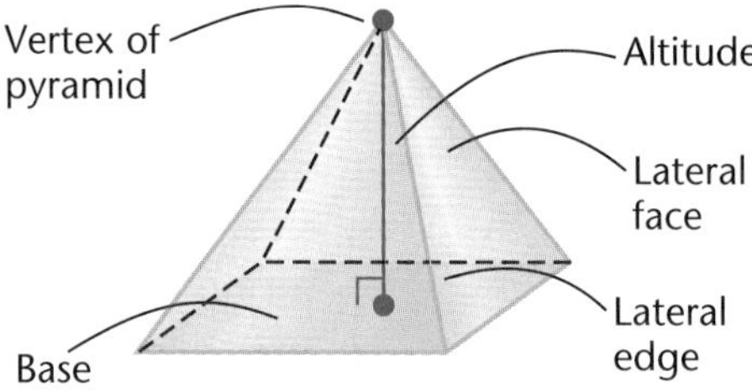

The base of a **regular pyramid** is a regular polygon. All of the lateral edges of a regular pyramid are congruent. Unless told otherwise, you may assume that all pyramids in this text are regular pyramids. The **slant height** of a regular pyramid is the height of any of its lateral faces. Like prisms, pyramids are classified by their bases.

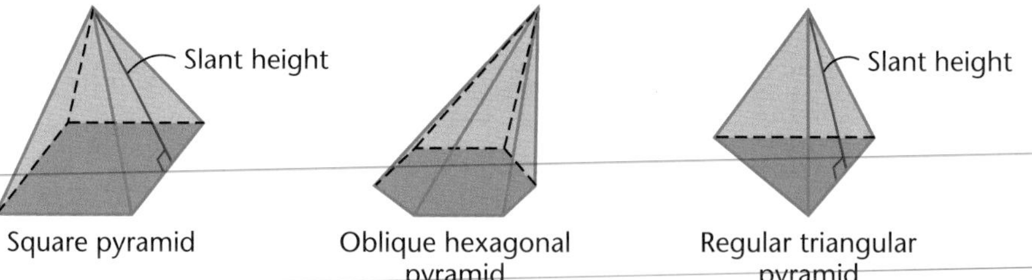

Square pyramid

Oblique hexagonal pyramid

Regular triangular pyramid

1. What do all lateral faces of pyramids have in common?

EXPLORE: NETTING THE WILD PYRAMID

Find formulas for the lateral area and surface area of a regular pyramid with base area B, base perimeter p, and slant height s. Use sketches and nets of pyramids to help you. Compare your results with the formulas your classmates find. When you are confident of your results, explain why your formulas work.

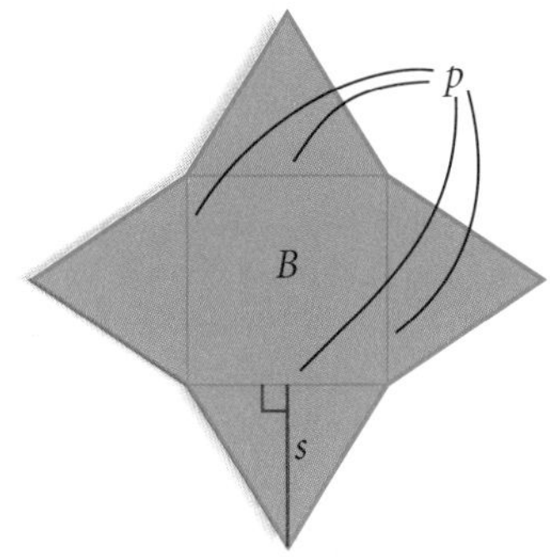

EXAMPLES

1. Find the lateral area of the regular hexagonal pyramid shown.

   $LA = \frac{1}{2}ps = \frac{1}{2}(24)(10) = 120 \text{ cm}^2$

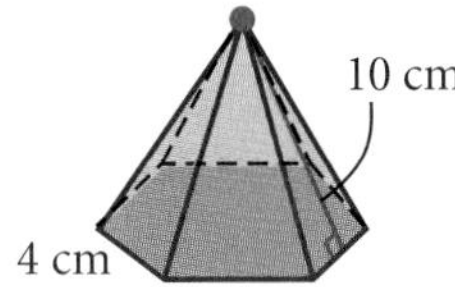

2. Find the surface area of the pyramid.

   To find the surface area, first find the area of the regular hexagonal base.

   Using 30°-60°-90° triangle side-length ratios, the apothem of the hexagon is $2\sqrt{3}$ cm.

   $$SA = LA + B$$
   $$= 120 \text{ cm}^2 + \frac{1}{2}ap = 120 \text{ cm}^2 + \frac{1}{2}(2\sqrt{3})(24)$$
   $$= 120 \text{ cm}^2 + 24\sqrt{3} \text{ cm}^2 \approx 161.6 \text{ cm}^2$$

The results for the lateral area and surface area of a regular pyramid are stated as theorems below.

THEOREMS

The lateral area of a regular pyramid is one-half the product of the perimeter of its base and the slant height of the pyramid. $LA = \frac{1}{2}ps$

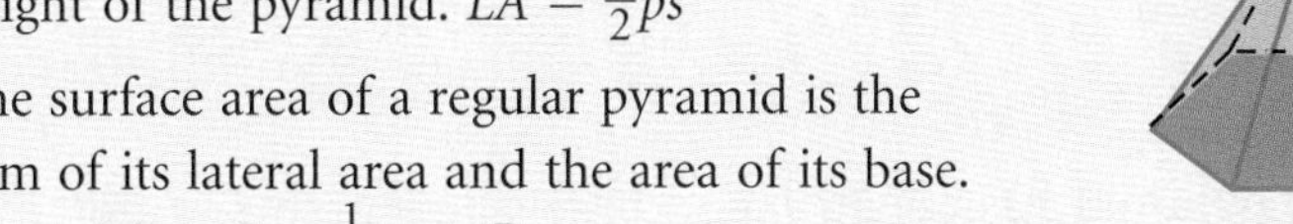

The surface area of a regular pyramid is the sum of its lateral area and the area of its base. $SA = LA + B = \frac{1}{2}ps + B$

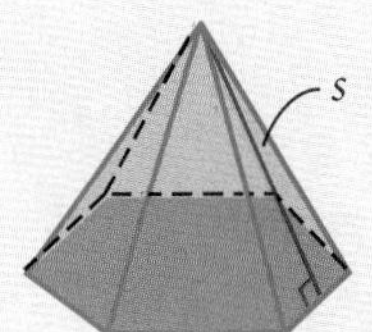

REFLECT

1. Why does the formula for the surface area of a pyramid involve its slant height, rather than the length of its altitude?
2. Can any face of a rectangular prism be considered a base of the prism? Explain. Can any face of a rectangular pyramid be considered its base? Why or why not?

Exercises

CORE

1. **Getting Started** Follow the steps to find the surface area of the square pyramid.
   - **a.** How many lateral faces does the pyramid have? What is the shape of each face?
   - **b.** What is the lateral area of the pyramid?
   - **c.** What figure is the base of the pyramid? What is the area of the base?
   - **d.** What is the surface area of the pyramid?

25 cm
20 cm

Sketch a net for each pyramid.

2.

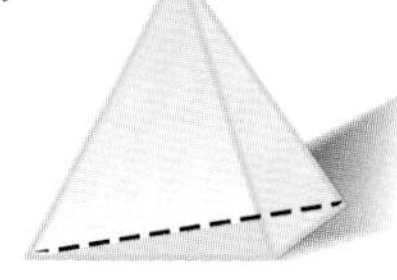

3.

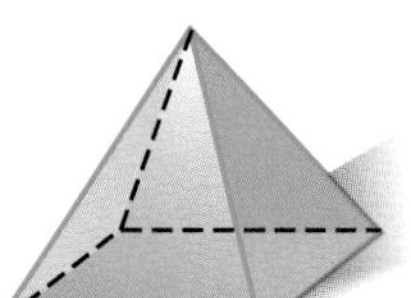

4.

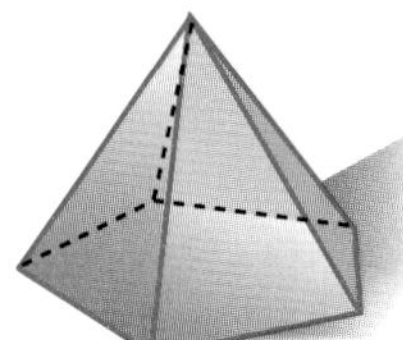

5.

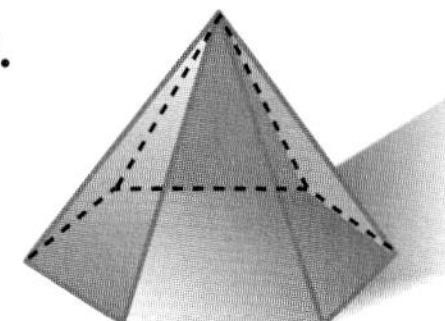

Find the lateral area and surface area of each pyramid.

6.

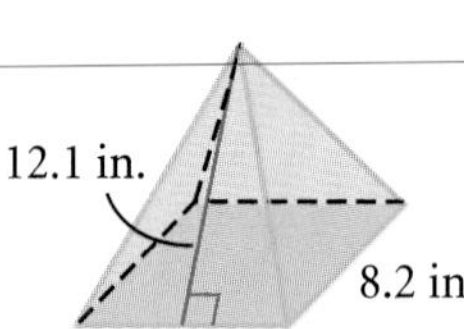

Square pyramid

7.

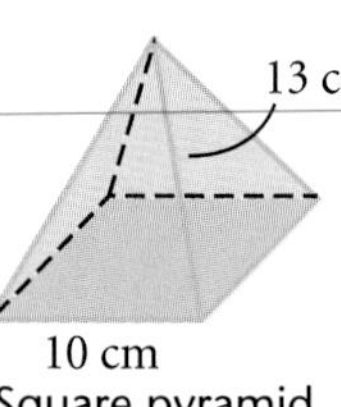

Square pyramid

8.

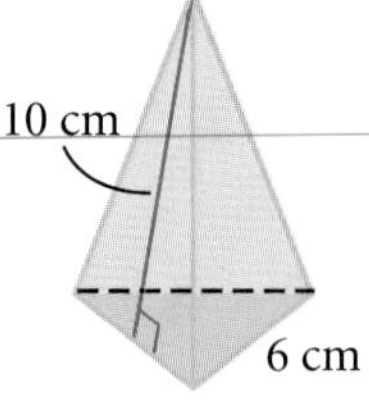

Equilateral triangular pyramid

9.

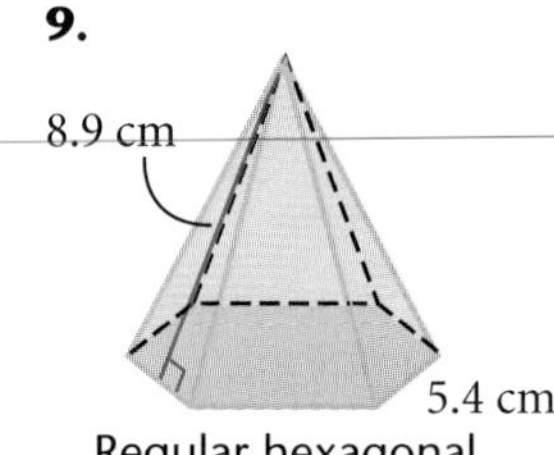

Regular hexagonal pyramid

10. Find the surface area of the square pyramid shown.

11. A square pyramid has height h and base side length ℓ. Find expressions for its slant height and the length of one of its lateral edges in terms of h and ℓ.

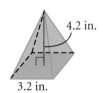

4.2 in.
3.2 in.

12. Time to Find the Area A clock tower in a civic center consists of a square-based prism topped by a square pyramid. Find the lateral area of the clock tower so it can be painted.

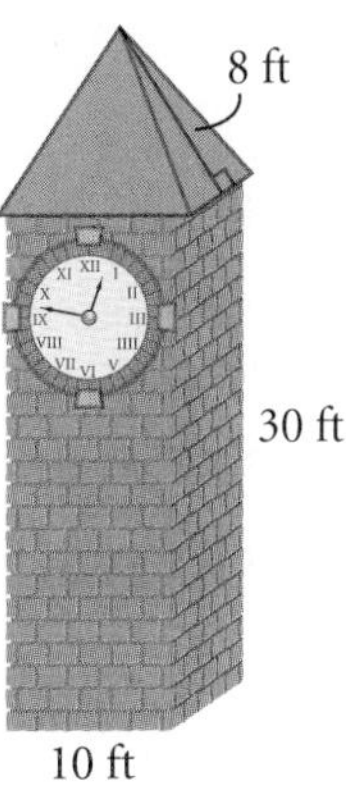

Write the word or phrase that correctly completes each statement.

13. The lateral edges of a pyramid connect the ___ of the pyramid to all of the vertices of the base.

14. The ___ of a pyramid is the distance from the vertex to a side of its base.

15. Goodbye, Mr. Cheops The largest Egyptian pyramid, the Great Pyramid of Cheops (or Khufu), had an original height of about 482 ft. The sides of its square base are 755 ft long. What was its original lateral area?

16. Recall that the regular tetrahedron is one of the five Platonic solids. Find the surface area of a regular tetrahedron with edges six centimeters long. (Hint: What are the measures of the angles of the faces?)

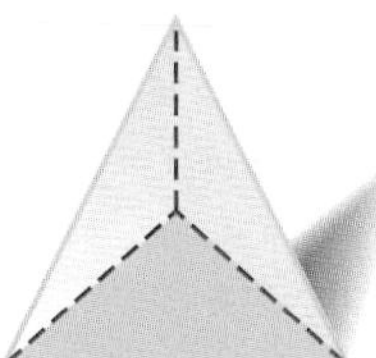

LOOK BACK

17. Solve for x in the figure at the right. Explain your method. [7-2]

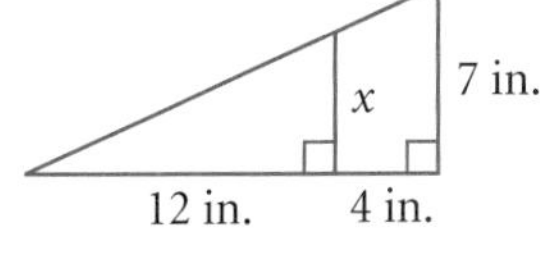

18. Suppose that the packaging for a frozen dinner includes a plate with a 12-in. diameter divided into three sections. [8-2]

a. Find the area of each sector.

b. Find the length of the arc of the plate that each sector determines.

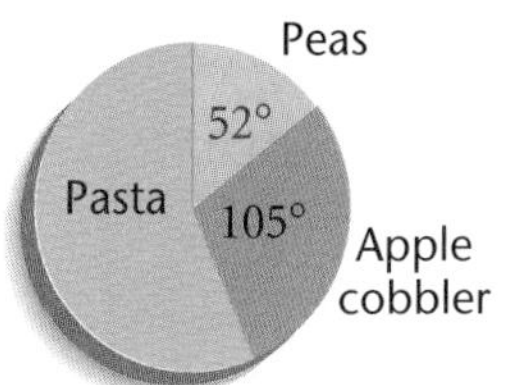

MORE PRACTICE

Sketch a net for each pyramid.

19.

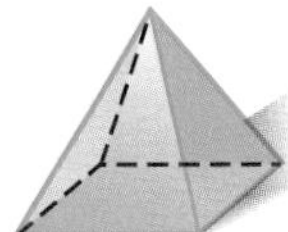

20.

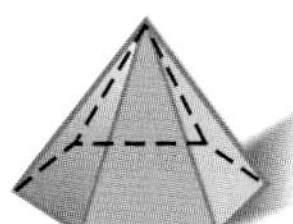

21.

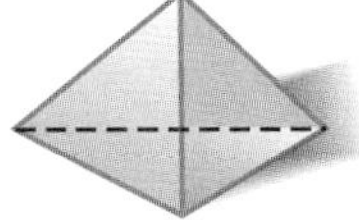

Find the lateral area and surface area of each pyramid.

22.

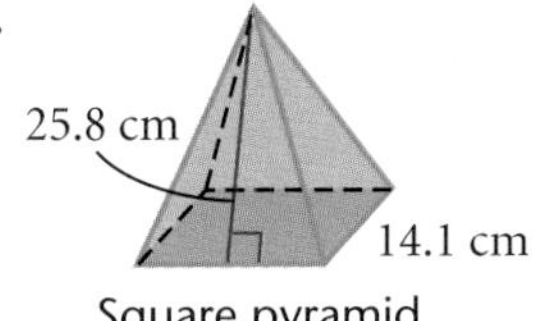

Square pyramid

23.

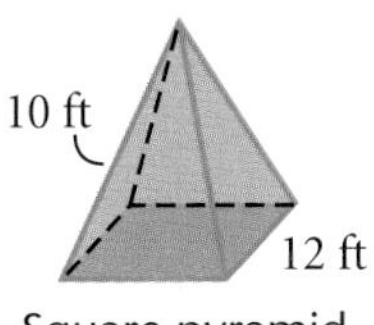

Square pyramid

24.

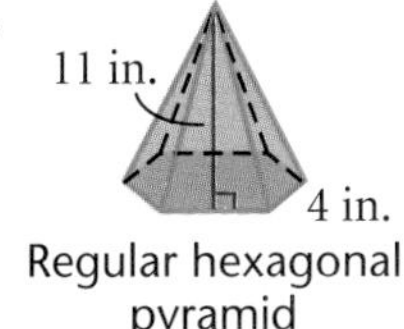

Regular hexagonal pyramid

MORE MATH REASONING

25. A square pyramid is inscribed in a cube with 4-cm sides so that they share a base. Find the surface area of the pyramid and the ratio of its surface area to that of the cube.

26. Sell Those Beans! You work for the Micro Bean Corporation, the world's largest manufacturer of tiny jellybeans. You've decided to try packaging them in regular tetrahedral containers with a small opening at the vertex.

a. If the total surface area of the cardboard used for the container can be no more than 100 $in.^2$, what are the longest possible edge lengths for your container?

b. What are some advantages and disadvantages of a tetrahedral container?

9-1 PART C Surface Area of Cylinders and Cones

← CONNECT → ***You've investigated the surface areas of solids with polygonal bases. Now you will explore the surface areas of solids whose bases are circles.***

Andy Warhol, *CAMPBELL'S SOUP CAN, 1964,* ©1994 The Andy Warhol Foundation for the Visual Arts, Inc.

As shown in the Andy Warhol painting at the left, soup is often packaged in a cylindrical container.

A **cylinder** has two congruent circular bases in parallel planes. The **axis** of a cylinder is the segment that joins the centers of the bases. If the axis is perpendicular to the base, the figure is a **right cylinder.** (Again, assume all cylinders in this text are right cylinders unless otherwise noted.) An **altitude** of a cylinder is a segment that joins the planes of the bases and is perpendicular to them. The **height** of a cylinder is the length of an altitude.

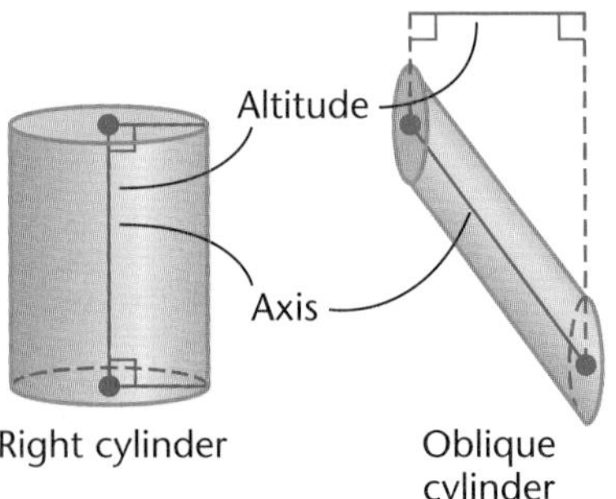

EXPLORE: CYLINDER CUTS

MATERIALS

Can, Scissors

1. Make a single, straight cut, so that you can unroll the label of a can as shown in the photo. What does the lateral surface of a cylinder look like when it is flattened out? How do you calculate the area of this figure?
2. You know the height of the figure you unrolled is equal to the height of the cylinder. How can you determine the length of the figure?
3. Using your result from Step 2, find a formula for the lateral area of a right cylinder. Explain how you found this formula.
4. Suppose that the height of a right cylinder is h, and its bases have radius r. What is the area of each base of the cylinder? Find a formula for the surface area of a right cylinder.

TRY IT

Find the lateral area and surface area of a right cylinder for each set of dimensions. Round answers to the nearest tenth.

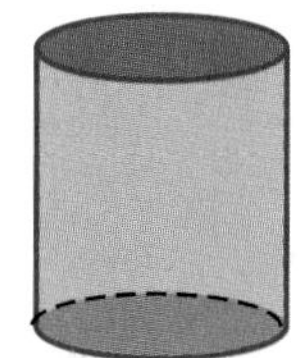

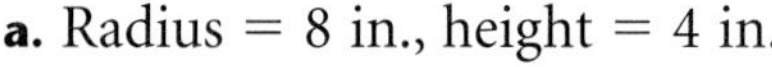

a. Radius = 8 in., height = 4 in.
b. Circumference = 18π cm, height = 14 cm

Like prisms, pyramids have a polygonal base, but instead of having a second base, they come to a point. Cones are related to cylinders in the same way.

A **cone** has a vertex and a circular base. The **axis** of a cone is the segment from the vertex to the center of the base. If the axis is perpendicular to the base, the cone is a **right cone.** All cones in this text are right cones unless otherwise indicated.

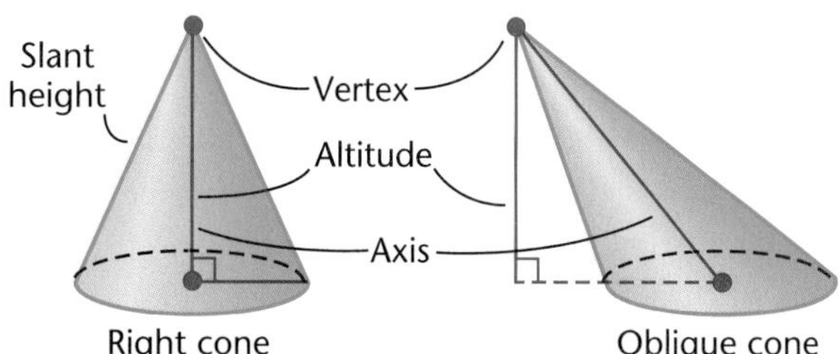

Additional terminology for cones is similar to that for pyramids and is shown in the figure on page 615.

The results for the lateral area and surface area of a right cylinder are presented below as theorems, along with the corresponding formulas for a right cone.

THEOREMS ABOUT CYLINDERS

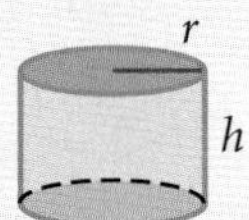

The lateral area of a right cylinder is the product of the circumference of its base and the height of the cylinder. $LA = 2\pi rh$

The surface area of a right cylinder is the sum of its lateral area and the areas of its bases. $SA = LA + 2B = 2\pi rh + 2\pi r^2$

THEOREMS ABOUT CONES

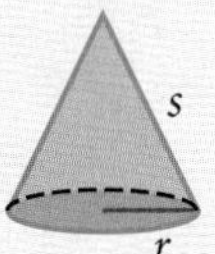

The lateral area of a right cone is one-half the product of the circumference of its base and the slant height of the cone. $LA = \frac{1}{2} \cdot 2\pi rs = \pi rs$

The surface area of a right cone is the sum of its lateral area and the area of its base. $SA = LA + B = \pi rs + \pi r^2$

1. Compare the formulas for the surface areas of a right prism and a right cylinder. Explain the similarities and differences between the two.

EXAMPLES

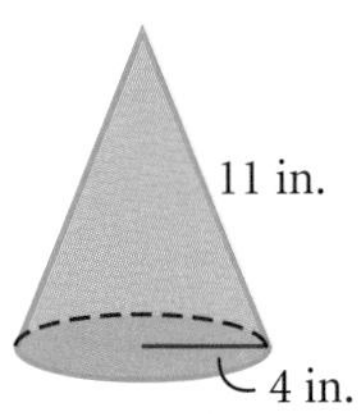

1. Find the lateral area of a right cone whose base radius is 4 in. and slant height is 11 in.

$LA = \pi rs = \pi(4)(11) = 44\pi \text{ in.}^2 \approx 138.2 \text{ in.}^2$

2. Find the surface area of the cone.

$SA = LA + B = LA + \pi r^2 = 44\pi + \pi(4)^2 = 60\pi \text{ in.}^2 \approx 188.5 \text{ in.}^2$

REFLECT

1. Name some products that are packaged in cylindrical containers.
2. Compare the formulas for the surface areas of a regular pyramid and a right cone. Explain the similarities and differences between the two.
3. Sketch a net for a right cylinder. Use the net to justify the formulas for the lateral area and the surface area of a cylinder.

Exercises

CORE

1. **Getting Started** Follow the steps to find the surface area of the cylinder.
   a. What is the shape of the flattened lateral surface of the cylinder?
   b. You are given the height of the lateral surface of the cylinder. To find its width, use the radius of a base to find the circumference of a base. What is the lateral area of the cylinder?
   c. What is the area of one of the circular bases? What is the total area of the bases?
   d. What is the surface area of the cylinder?

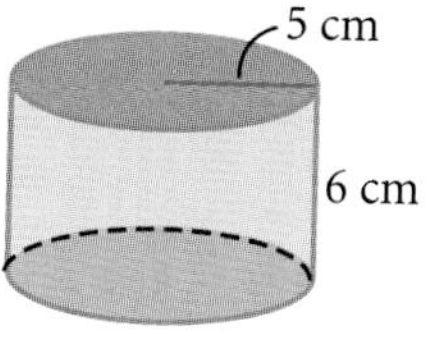

Find the lateral area and surface area of a right cylinder, given each set of dimensions.

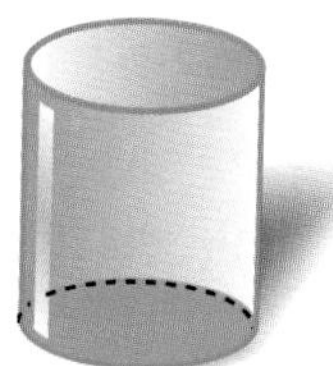

2. Radius = 6 cm, height = 10 cm
3. Base circumference = 8π in., height = 9 in.
4. Radius = 5.5 m, height = 11.4 m

Find the lateral area and surface area of a right cone, given each set of dimensions.

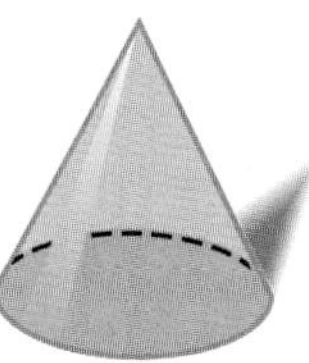

5. Base radius = 3 in., slant height = 8 in.
6. Base circumference = 3π cm, slant height = 5 cm
7. Base radius = 2.4 ft, height = 6.3 ft
8. Base circumference = 22.3 mm, slant height = 8.5 mm

Determine whether each statement is true or false. If the statement is false, change the underlined word or phrase to make it true.

9. The bases of a cylinder are two <u>congruent</u> circles.
10. The <u>height</u> of a right cone is the length of a segment along the surface of the cone from vertex to base.

11. In Hot Water You can make coffee by putting coffee grounds into a conical filter, then putting the filter into a funnel and pouring hot water through the grounds. If the funnel's height is 15 cm and its base radius is 6 cm, what is the surface area of the filter?

12. Suppose that a cylinder has a radius of r units, and that the height of the cylinder is also r units. The lateral area of the cylinder is 98 square units.
   a. Find the radius of the cylinder.
   b. Find the surface area of the cylinder.

13. Eat Your Oatmeal! Suppose that a cylindrical, regular-size box of oatmeal is 9 in. tall and has a radius of 3.5 in. The large box has a height of 11 in. and a radius of 4.5 in. If the boxes are made of cardboard, how much more cardboard does the large box use?

14. An $8\frac{1}{2}'' \times 11''$ sheet of paper can be curled into an open right cylinder in two different ways. Find the height, radius, and lateral area of the two cylinders. If the cylinders are given bases, which has a greater surface area?

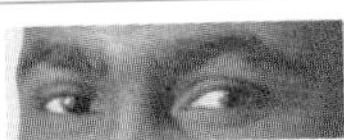

15. A walled, sixteenth-century fortress in Zimbabwe, constructed for the Rozvi monarchs, features a 34-ft-tall conical tower, seen in the center of this photograph. The base of the tower is about 16 ft in diameter. What would the lateral area of the tower be if it were exactly conical?

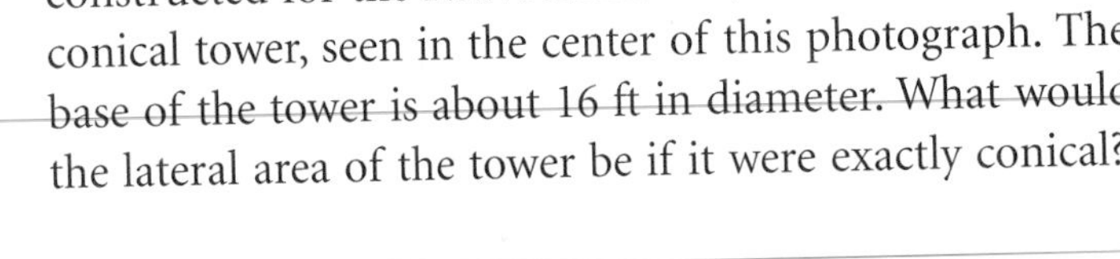

LOOK AHEAD

16. Do you think it is possible for two drink containers with equal surface areas to be completely filled with different amounts of liquid? Explain why or why not.

17. Explain why the area of a rectangle is the product of its length and its width.

MORE PRACTICE

Find the lateral area and surface area of a right cylinder, given each set of dimensions.

18. Radius = 3.7 m, height = 9.2 m

19. Base circumference = 10π ft, height = 15 ft

20. Base circumference = 2.9 ft, height = 7.3 ft

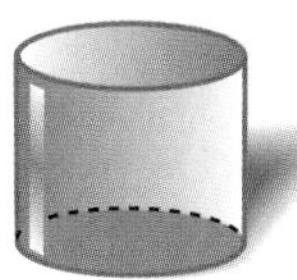

Find the lateral area and surface area of a right cone, given each set of dimensions.

21. Base radius = 6 in., height = 8 in.

22. Base circumference = 8.2 mm, slant height = 15 mm

23. Base radius = 7.2 ft, height = 8.9 ft

24. Base circumference = 4π cm, slant height = 8 cm

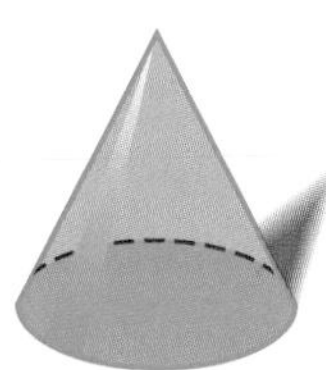

MORE MATH REASONING

25. One of the blocks in a child's building set is a hollow cylinder, as shown in cross section. Find its surface area.

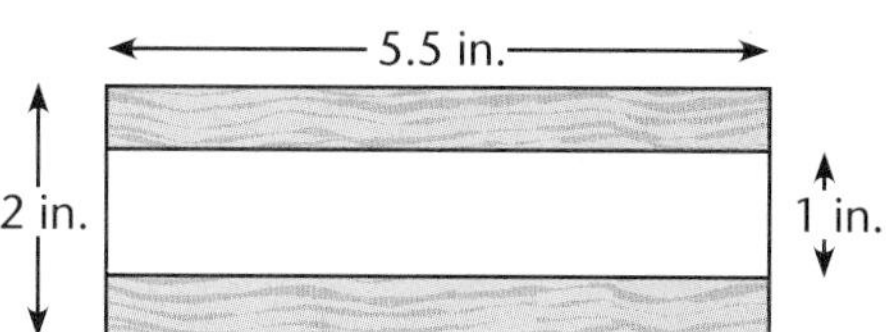

26. Tea for Two A cylindrical aluminum iced tea can is 12.3 cm tall and has a radius of approximately 3.1 cm. A square prism (box) with the same height that holds almost exactly the same amount of liquid has base side lengths of 5.5 cm.

Industry

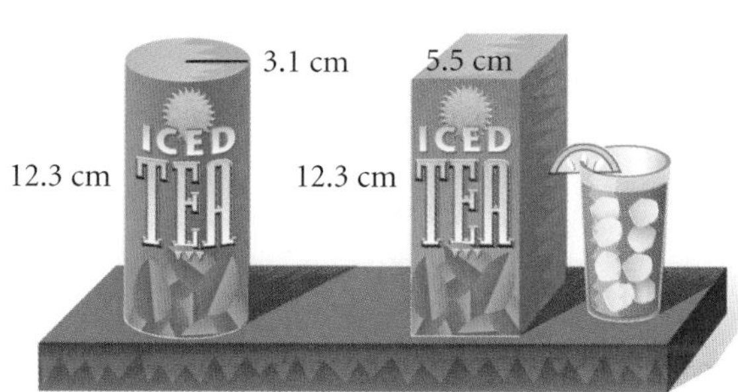

a. Find the total surface area for 24 containers of each type. Identify the container that uses more aluminum, and tell how much more aluminum it uses per 24-container case.

b. Suppose these containers are shipped in cardboard cartons in a 4×6 arrangement. Which uses more cardboard, a carton for cans or a carton for boxes? How much more?

c. Name some other advantages and disadvantages of drink cans and drink boxes. Which container do you think is better for packaging drinks? Why?

9-1 PART D Making Connections

← CONNECT → ***Businesspeople need to know about the surface area of product packaging. Carpenters, map makers, architects, and machinists also work with surface-area measurements. You've discovered how to calculate the surface areas of many three-dimensional objects.***

In the following Explore, you will use your knowledge of surface area to design a new package.

EXPLORE: PACKAGING SELLS!

MATERIALS

Construction paper (optional)
Colored pens or pencils (optional)

You've been selected to design the package for a consumer product.

1. Choose a product that you want to work with. (Possibilities include food, drinks, musical instruments, compact disks, or other products). What are some of the things you will want to take into consideration when packaging this product?
2. The manufacturer has asked for two different designs to choose from. Draw and describe two different package designs for your product. Include the dimensions of your packages, and be sure that the dimensions are reasonable for the product you've chosen.
3. Find the surface area of each of your package designs. Sketch nets of the packages if this helps you in your calculations.
4. What will your packages be made of? Explain why you decided to use these materials.
5. Make sketches of your final designs, showing how the packages will be decorated and displayed. Describe the advantages of each design.

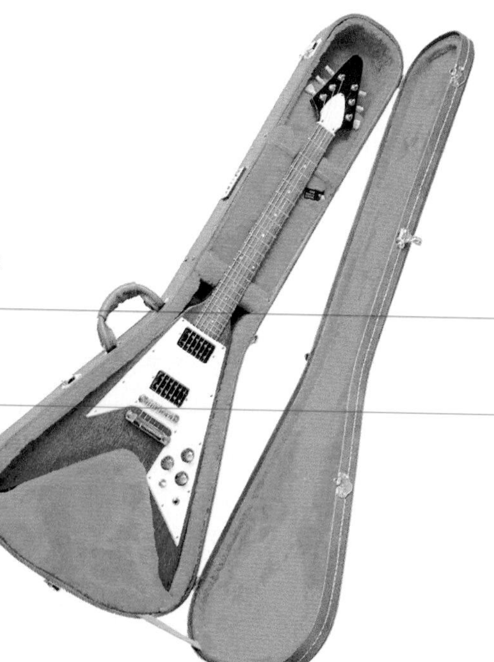

REFLECT

1. Make a table of the lateral area and surface area formulas for right prisms, regular pyramids, right cylinders, and right cones. Summarize and explain the similarities and differences in these formulas as simply as you can.
2. Explain why the pyramid surface area formula you've worked with applies only to regular pyramids, rather than to all pyramids.

Self-Assessment

Find the lateral area and surface area of each of the following.

1.

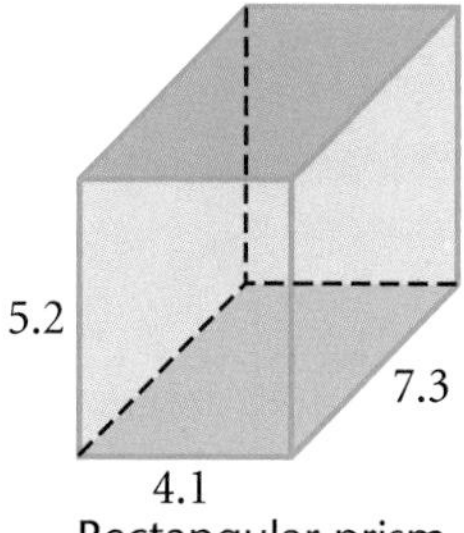

Rectangular prism

2.

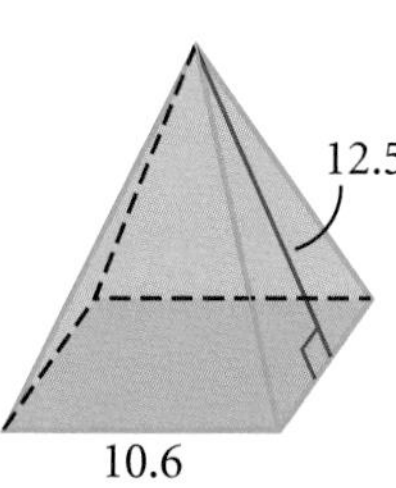

Square pyramid

3.

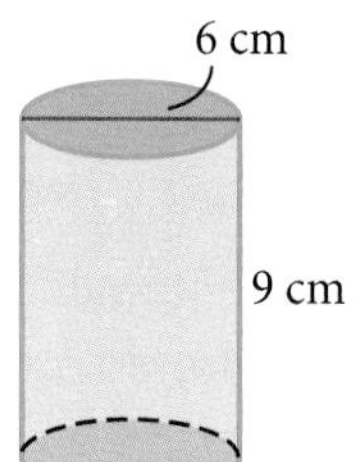

4.

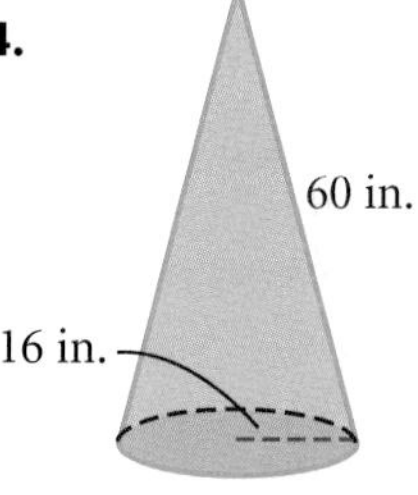

5. Sketch a net for a regular pyramid. Then use your net to justify the formula for the surface area of a regular pyramid.

Health

6. Light-sensitive cell structures, called *cones,* in the retina of the eye enable people to see colors. If a cone has a radius of 0.01 mm and a slant height of 0.05 mm, find the surface area of the cone.

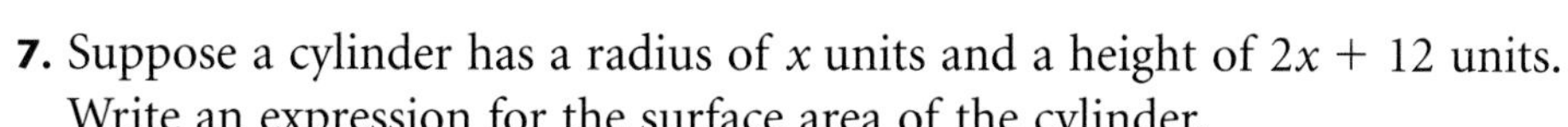

7. Suppose a cylinder has a radius of x units and a height of $2x + 12$ units. Write an expression for the surface area of the cylinder.

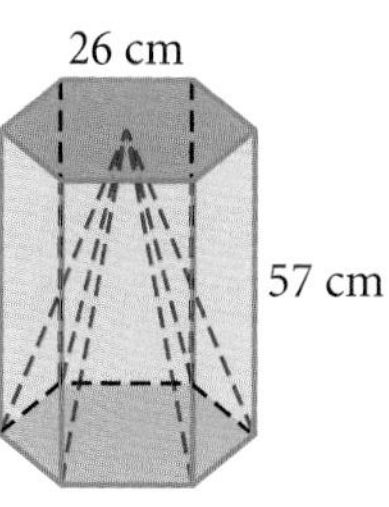

8. A regular pyramid is inscribed in a right hexagonal prism, as shown at the right. Find the surface area of each solid.

9. Suppose cylinder A has twice the radius but half the height of cylinder B. What is true about their lateral areas?
(a) The lateral area of A is twice as large.
(b) The lateral area of B is twice as large.
(c) They are equal.
(d) The lateral area of A is four times as large.
(e) Not enough information is given to solve this problem.

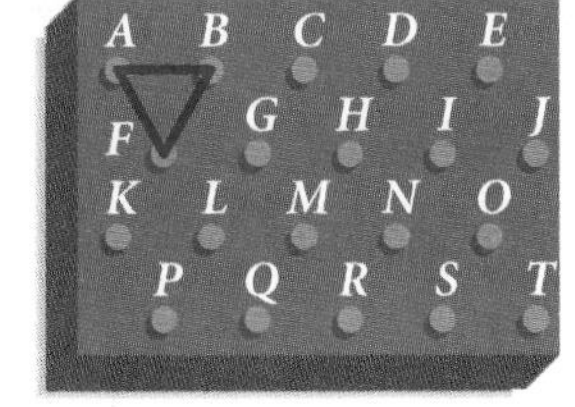

10. a. How many different sizes of triangles similar to $\triangle FBA$ with vertices at grid points are there on the grid at the right? (Do not include triangles on the grid that are congruent to $\triangle FBA$.) [7-2]

b. For each size, name one triangle of that size, and give the similarity ratio of that triangle to $\triangle FBA$.

c. Explain how you know that the triangles you named in **10b** are similar to $\triangle FBA$.

11. A cylindrical package for dried fruit is divided into three equal sectors, as shown.

a. Find the surface area of the cylindrical container.

b. Find the area of each sector of the circular base of the container. [8-2]

c. Find the measure of each arc of the circular base of the container. [8-2]

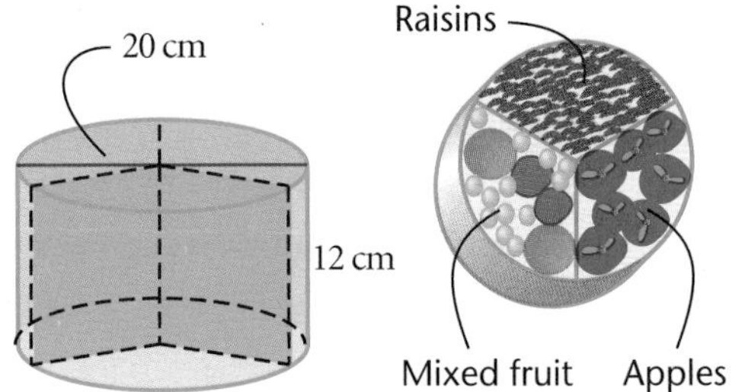

12. Squeeze-A-Mess #1 The container for a brand of children's toothpaste is cylindrical, with a conical tip, as shown. Find the surface area of the container.

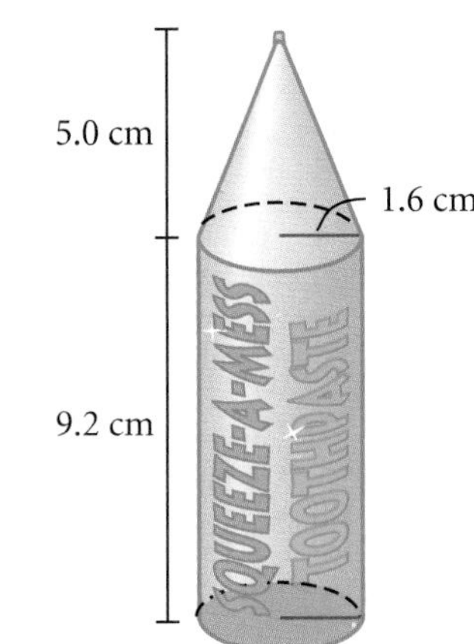

13. A square pyramid has a slant height equal to the length of a side of its base, ℓ. Write an equation that expresses the surface area of the pyramid as a function of ℓ.

Industry

14. A Fluid Design The containers in the following chart all hold approximately the same amount of juice. Find the surface area of each. Then decide which you feel is the best choice for a juice container. Explain how you made your choice, and justify your answer.

Container	**Dimensions**
Cylinder	$h = 10$ cm, $r = 3.5$ cm
Square prism	$\ell = 6.2$ cm, $w = 6.2$ cm, $h = 10$ cm
Square pyramid	sides of base $= 8.5$ cm, $h = 16$ cm
Cone	$h = 16$ cm, $r = 4.8$ cm

15. The definition of the altitude of a prism uses the idea of a segment that is perpendicular to a plane. Give a definition of *segment perpendicular to a plane,* and explain why your definition makes sense.

9-2 Volume

A VOLCANO BLOWS ITS TOP

Although a volcano may be inactive for hundreds of years, it can suddenly reawaken. In *The Eruption and Healing of Mount St. Helens*, Patricia Lauber describes a volcano unleashing its enormous power…

The above photo shows Mount St. Helens, located 95 miles south of Seattle, Washington.

For many years the volcano slept. It was silent and still, big and beautiful. Then the volcano, which was named Mount St. Helens, began to stir. On March 20, 1980, it was shaken by a strong earthquake. The quake was a sign of movement inside St. Helens. It was a sign of a waking volcano that might soon erupt again.

On May 18, 1980, Mount St. Helens erupted. The force of the eruption equaled that of the largest hydrogen bomb ever detonated. Huge trees were uprooted and tossed around like toothpicks. The morning sky turned as black as night. Ash, deadly gas, flying rocks, and heat from the eruption killed about 65 people. Millions of deer, elk, birds, and other wildlife also perished.

When the mountain finally quieted, the eruption had ripped away 1200 ft of mountain-top. The destruction took only minutes. But the process of renewal will take many years.

1. A volcano is an example of a naturally occurring cone. Give examples of other three-dimensional figures in nature.

2. Do you think the surface area of a solid is a good measure of the amount of material it can hold? Explain.

9-2 PART A Volume of Prisms

← CONNECT → *You know how to find the surface area of a prism. Now you will discover how to calculate its volume.*

The **volume** of a solid is the number of cubic units contained in the solid. Volume measures how much a solid can "hold."

A teaspoon holds $\frac{1}{6}$ of a fluid ounce of water. That's about 4930 cubic millimeters (mm^3).

A small glass holds about 8 fluid ounces of water, or 236.6 cubic centimeters (cm^3). It takes 48 teaspoons to fill an 8-ounce glass.

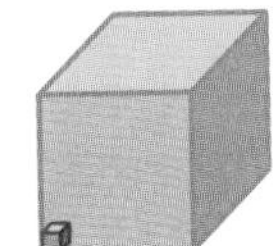

One cubic millimeter

One cubic centimeter has 1000 times the volume of a cubic millimeter.

The volume of a typical refrigerator is about 1.1 cubic meters (m^3). That's 1,100,000 cm^3, the volume of about 4650 8-ounce glasses of water.

Lake Mead (shown on the left), on the Nevada-Arizona border, has a capacity of 35,154,000 m^3. It would take about 148,600,000,000 glasses of water to fill Lake Mead.

The oceans of the world have a total capacity of 317,000,000 cubic miles. That's about 1.32×10^{18} m^3. It would take 37,560,000,000 Lake Meads to fill the world's oceans! Over 97% of the earth's water is contained in its oceans.

WHAT DO YOU THINK?

Maria and Janice needed to convert 2457 cm^3 to m^3. They were asked to explain their reasoning to the class.

Maria thinks . . .

There are 100 cm in 1 m, so there are 100^3 cm^3 in 1 m^3.

Therefore, I need to divide 2457 by 100^3 (or 1,000,000) to see how many cubic meters there are.

$$\frac{2457}{1,000,000} = 0.002457 \text{ m}^3 \text{ or } 2.457 \times 10^{-3} \text{ m}^3$$

Janice thinks . . .

There are 100 cm in every meter. So, I have to multiply 2457 cm^3 by $\frac{1}{100}$ three times to convert it to cubic meters.

$$2457 \times \frac{1}{100} \times \frac{1}{100} \times \frac{1}{100} = 0.002457 \text{ m}^3 \text{ or } 2.457 \times 10^{-3} \text{ m}^3$$

1. If you convert 2457 cm^3 to mm^3, will the resulting value be greater than or less than 2457? Why?

EXPLORE: COUNT UP THE VOLUME

MATERIALS

Cubes (optional)

The photograph below illustrates the volume of a right rectangular prism. One way to find its volume is to count the cubes it holds.

1. Find the volume of the right rectangular prism shown. (Assume the edges of the cubes measure 1 cm.) Explain your method. Then write a formula for finding the volume of a right rectangular prism.

Problem-Solving Tip

You may want to make a model to help in your investigation.

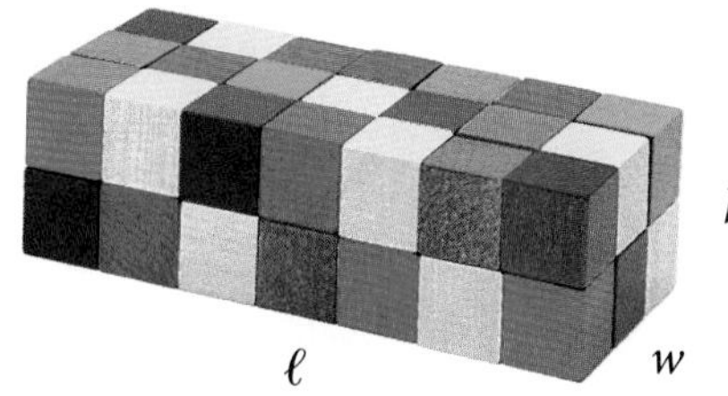

2. The area of the rectangular base of the prism, B, is its length times its width. Using this idea, is there another way to write your volume formula?
3. Does your result apply to the prism at the right? Does it apply to any right prism? Explore this possibility, and then write your conclusion. See if your results agree with those of your classmates.

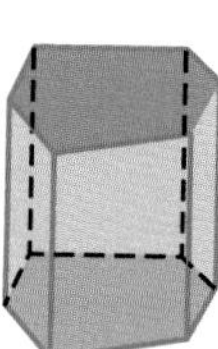

TRY IT

Find the volume of each right prism.

a.

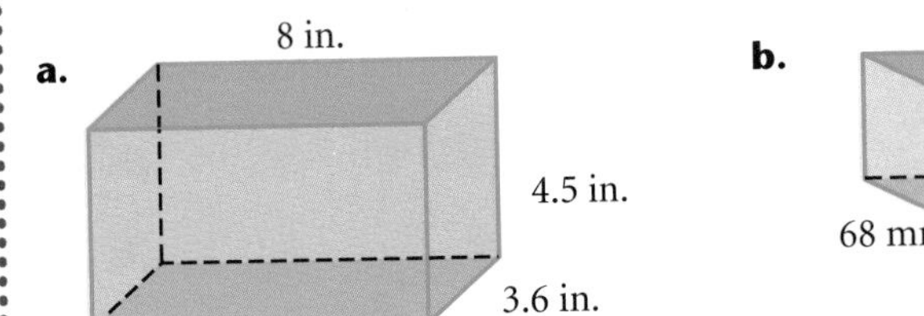

b.

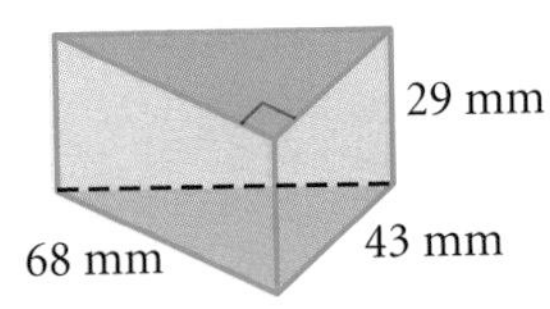

When you found surface areas of prisms, you had to be careful—the formula applied only to right prisms. Let's see whether this is the case for volume as well.

Suppose you have some neatly stacked concert programs several inches high. The stack is a right prism. If you accidentally nudge the stack of programs so that it forms an oblique prism, does the amount of space it takes up change?

No! Unless you add or take away programs, the volume of the stack must stay the same. The area of the base and the height of the stack are also the same as they were before. It seems that the volume of *any* prism is equal to the area of its base times its height.

The sliding stack of programs illustrates a postulate that is useful in deriving volume formulas.

POSTULATE: CAVALIERI'S PRINCIPLE

Suppose M and N are two solids. If every plane that intersects both M and N at the same height cuts off equal cross-sectional areas on each, then the solids have the same volume.

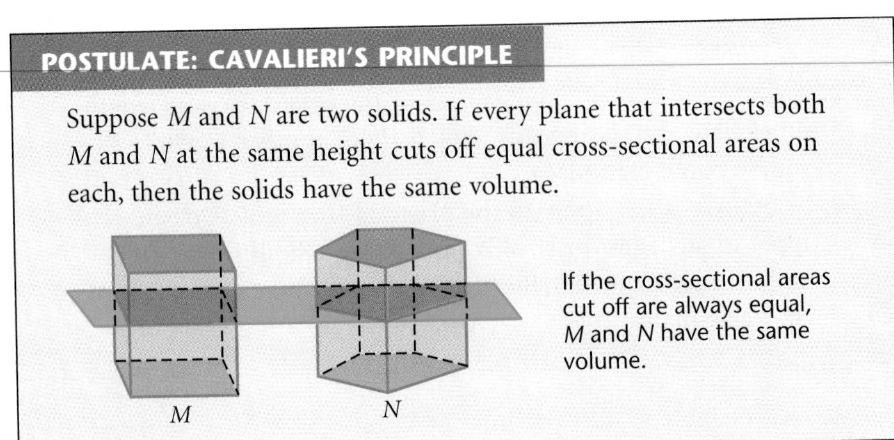

If the cross-sectional areas cut off are always equal, M and N have the same volume.

Cavalieri's principle ensures that if two prisms have the same base area and the same height, then they have the same volume. This is illustrated in the following figures.

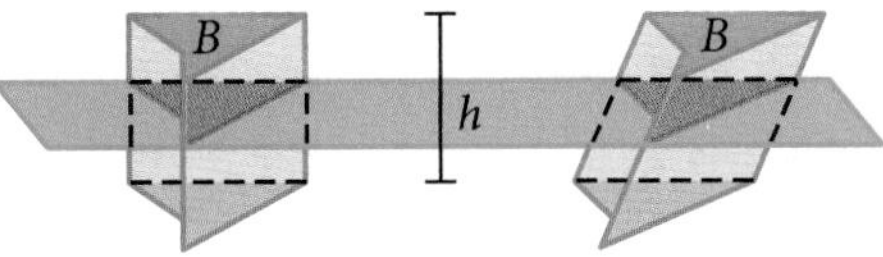

These prisms have congruent bases and equal heights. Their volumes are equal.

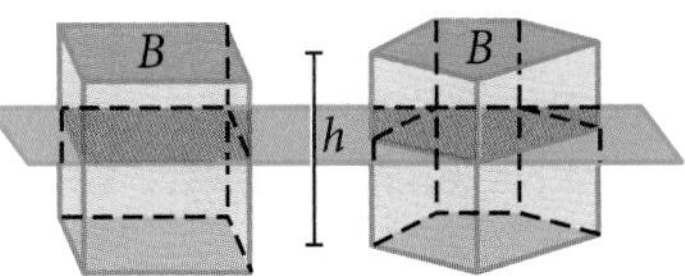

These prisms have bases with the same area and equal heights. Their volumes are also equal.

We can now state as a theorem the specific formula for the volume of a right rectangular prism, as well as a more general formula that applies to any prism.

THEOREMS

The volume of a right rectangular prism is the product of its length, width, and height. $V = \ell wh$

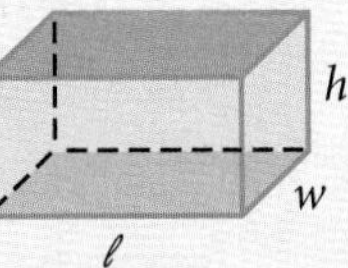

The volume of any prism is the product of the area of its base and its height. $V = Bh$

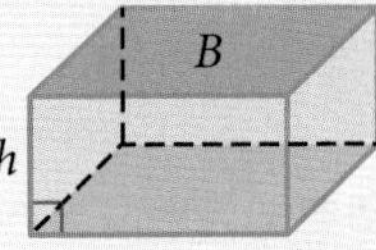

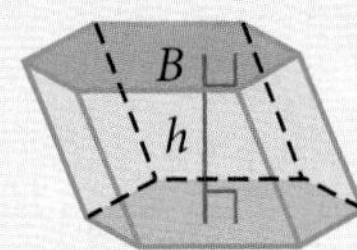

REFLECT

1. If the dimensions of a solid are measured in centimeters, what dimensions are used for its volume? What dimensions are used for its surface area?
2. If you manufacture flour that is packaged in boxes, does the cost of the material for the box depend on its surface area or its volume? Does the cost of the flour itself depend on surface area or volume? Justify your answers.

Exercises

CORE

Getting Started A meter is equivalent to 100 centimeters and to 1000 millimeters. Convert each quantity to the indicated units.

1. 1 cm^2 to m^2

2. 1 m^2 to mm^2

3. 25 cm^2 to mm^2

Complete each statement with the most appropriate unit (m^3, cm^3, or mm^3).

4. The volume of a schoolroom is about 250 ____.

5. The volume of a can of iced tea is 355 ____.

6. The volume of an allergy capsule is about 784 ____.

7. One yard is equal to three feet. How many cubic feet are equal to one cubic yard? Draw a three-dimensional sketch to illustrate your answer.

Convert each quantity to the indicated unit. Explain how you did each conversion.

8. 6 yd^3 to ft^3

9. 22,400 cm^3 to m^3

10. 1728 $in.^3$ to ft^3

Find the volume of each right prism.

11.

40 cm

30 cm

60 cm

Rectangular prism

12.

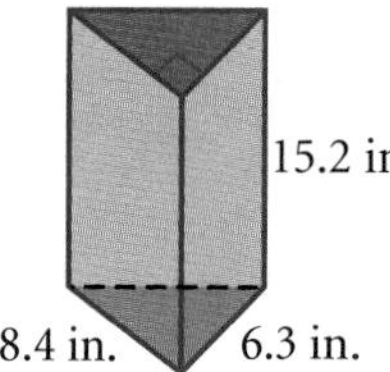

Right triangular prism

13.

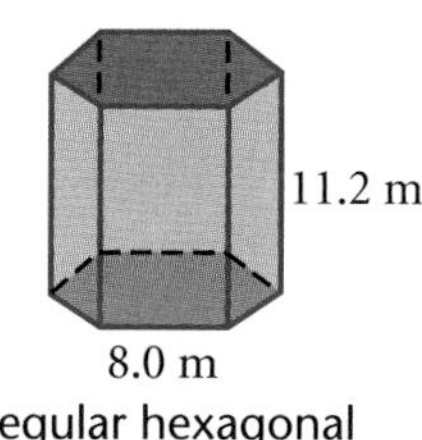

Regular hexagonal prism

14.

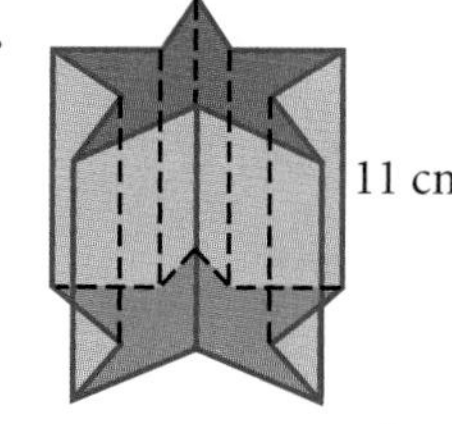

Base area = 50 cm^2

15. Marcia's garden needs watering equivalent to one-third of an inch of rainfall each day. If the garden has the dimensions shown and water costs 1.261¢ per cubic foot, how much will watering the garden in June cost her?

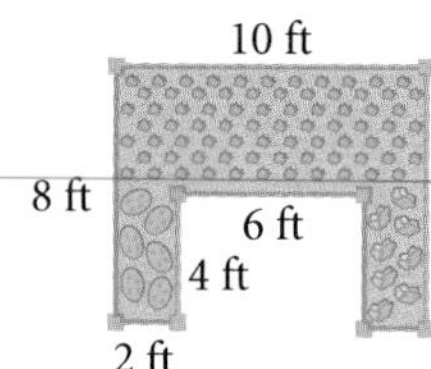

16. Hog Heaven A trough with trapezoidal cross sections has the dimensions shown. How much food will it hold?

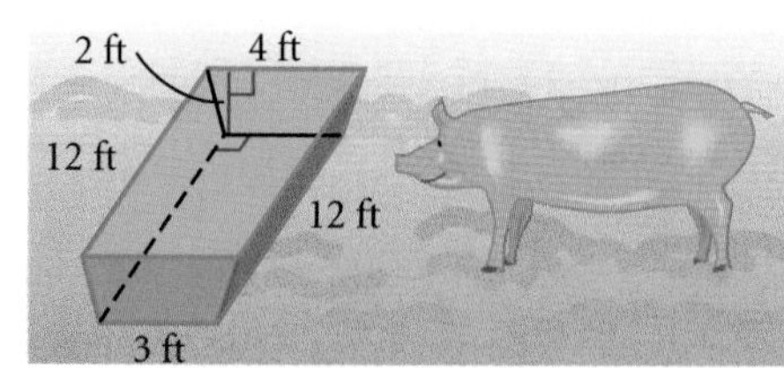

17. A cube has a volume of 27 cm^3. What is the length of one of its diagonals?

Diagonal

18. A cube has edges of length 6 cm. Are its surface area and volume equal? Justify your answer.

LOOK BACK

19. In the figure, $\overline{UY} \parallel \overline{WZ}$ and $\overline{XZ} \parallel \overline{UV}$. Prove $\triangle XYZ \sim \triangle WZV$. [7-2]

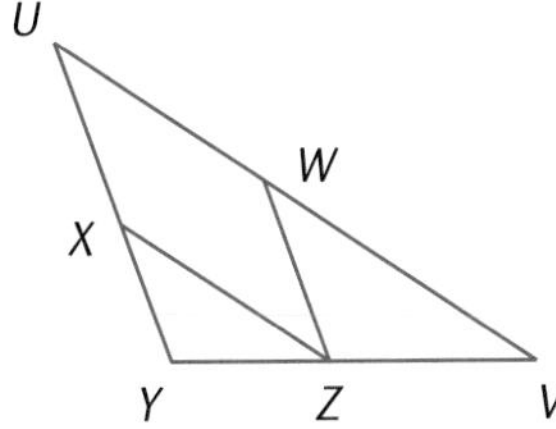

History

20. One of the most famous volcanic eruptions in history, the eruption of Mt. Vesuvius in 79 A.D., destroyed the Roman cities of Pompeii and Herculaneum. From 5 mi (26,400 ft) away in the Adriatic Sea, the angle of elevation to the top of Mt. Vesuvius is about 9°. Find the approximate height of Mt. Vesuvius. [7-3]

Find the surface area of each figure. [9-1]

21.

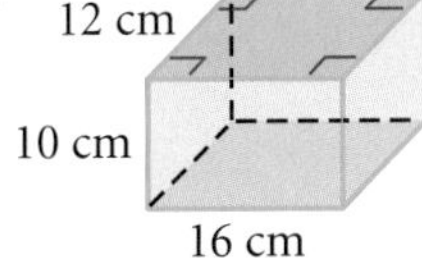

22.

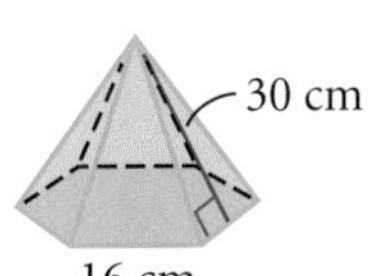

Regular hexagonal pyramid

23.

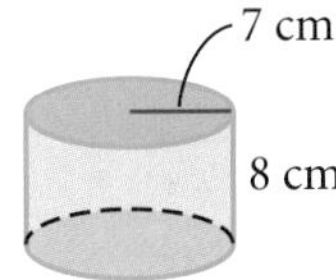

MORE PRACTICE

Convert each quantity to the indicated unit. Explain how you did each conversion.

24. 54 ft^3 to yd^3

25. 700 mm^3 to cm^3

26. 12,000 cm^3 to m^3

Find the volume of each right prism.

27.

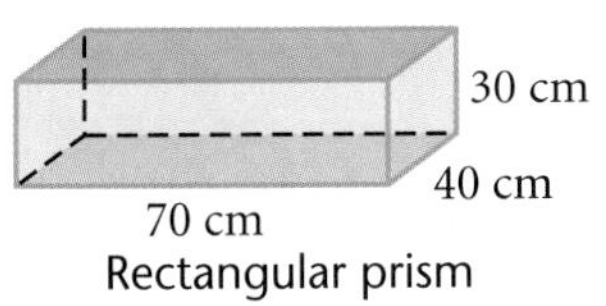

Rectangular prism

28.

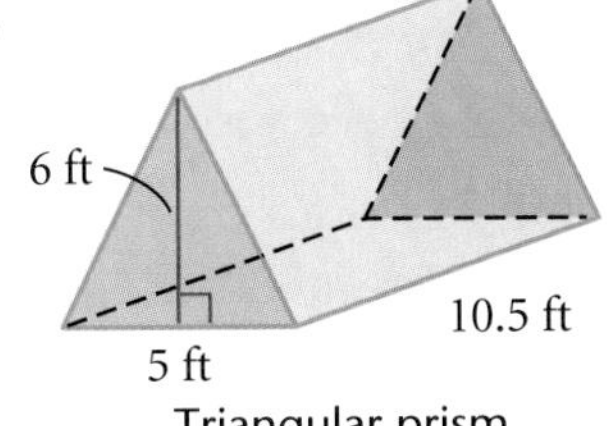

Triangular prism

29.

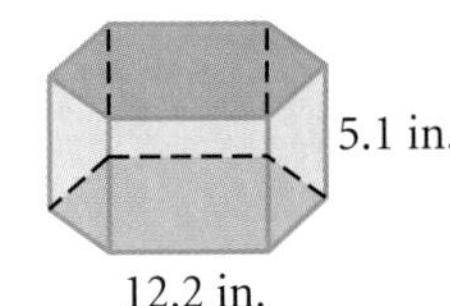

Regular hexagonal prism

MORE MATH REASONING

30. A regular hexagonal prism has a volume of 1300 cm^3. Its height is twice the length of a side of its base. Find the height and the length of a side of the base of the prism.

31. A regular octagonal prism with base side length 6 in. and height 9 in. is inscribed in a rectangular solid as shown at the right. Find the volume of the rectangular solid.

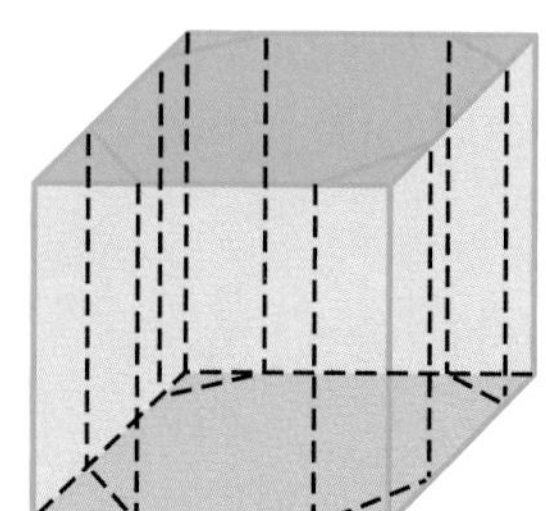

9-2 PART B Volume of Pyramids

← CONNECT → ***You've seen that prisms and pyramids are alike in some ways. Now you will investigate a connection between the formulas for their volumes.***

A pyramid and a prism both have polygonal bases. However, the prism has the same cross-sectional area all along its height, while the pyramid tapers to a point.

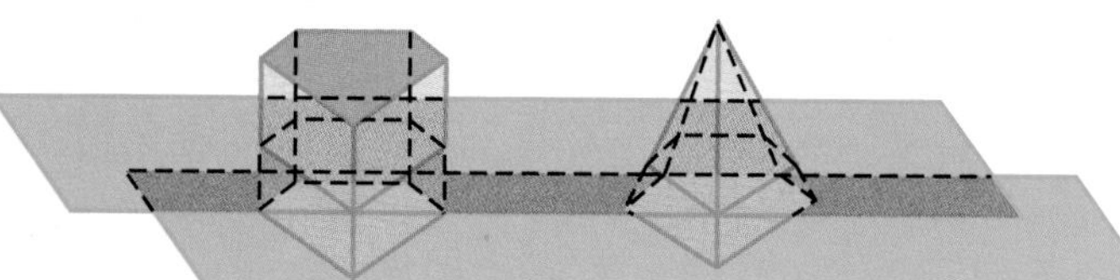

1. If a pyramid and a prism have congruent bases and equal heights, which has a larger volume? Why?

In the following Explore, you will investigate the relationship between the volume of a prism and the volume of a pyramid.

EXPLORE: "IMPRISMING" THE PYRAMID

MATERIALS

Cardboard
Tape
Scissors
Filler material

1. Carefully draw this net for an open prism on cardboard. Cut out the net, and tape it tightly together to form an open prism.

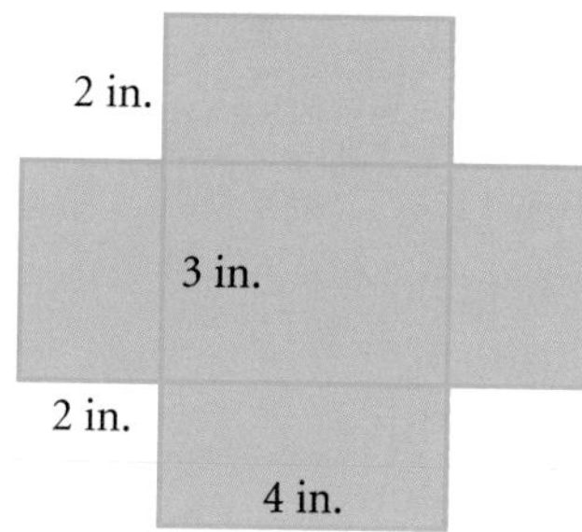

2. Use the dimensions shown to draw two sets of these triangles on cardboard. Then tape them together to form an open pyramid. (When taping the triangles, the two triangles with 4-in. bases should not be taped together.)

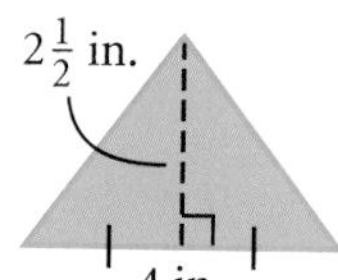

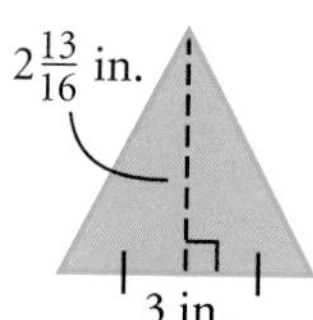

3. Use rice or other material to fill the pyramid. Then pour the contents of the pyramid into the prism. How many times can you fill the prism with the contents of the pyramid? Based on your results, write a formula for the volume of a pyramid with base area B and height h.

TRY IT

Find the volume of each pyramid.

a.

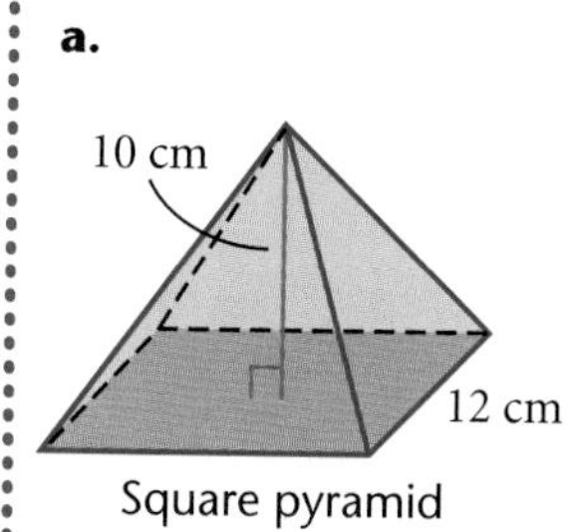

Square pyramid

b.

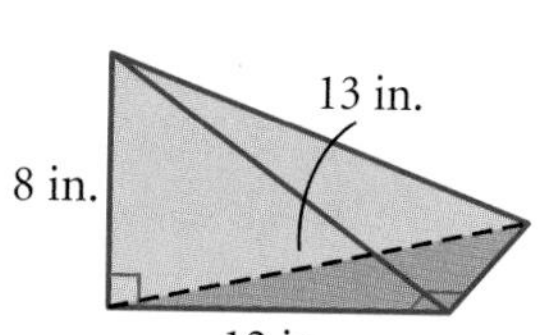

c.

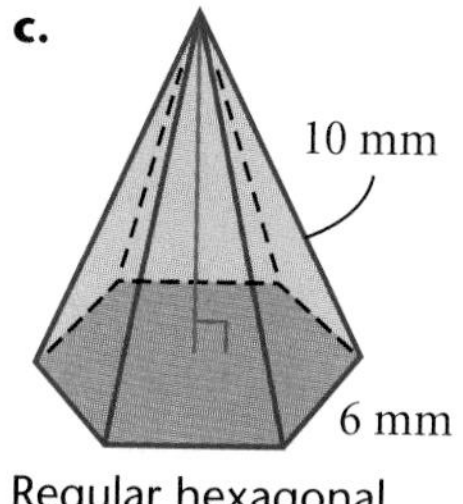

Regular hexagonal pyramid

THEOREM

The volume of a pyramid is one-third the product of its base area and its height. $V = \frac{1}{3}Bh$

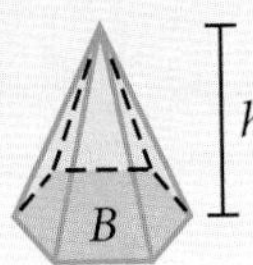

REFLECT

1. Write a volume formula for a rectangular pyramid with base dimensions ℓ and w and height h.
2. The photo at the right shows a structure in Meroe, Sudan, that is a *frustum* of a pyramid. A frustum of a pyramid is created when a pyramid is sliced by a plane parallel to its base. If you know the height and base area of the original pyramid and the height of the frustum and the area of its top base, describe how you can find the volume of the frustum.

Exercises

CORE

1. **Getting Started** Use the square pyramid shown for each of the following.
   a. What is the height of the pyramid?
   b. What is the area of the base of the pyramid?
   c. What is the volume of the pyramid?

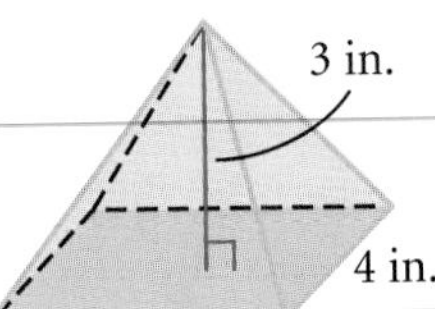

Find the volume of each pyramid.

2.

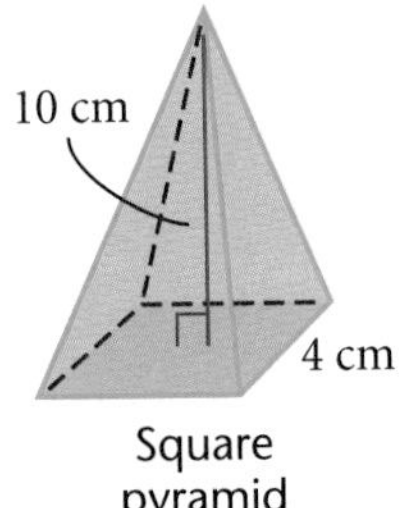

Square pyramid

3.

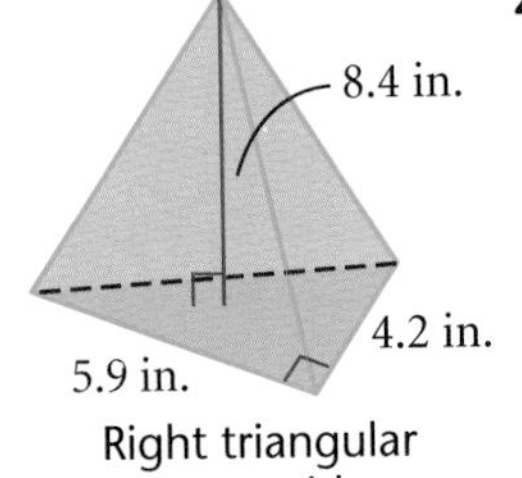

Right triangular pyramid

4.

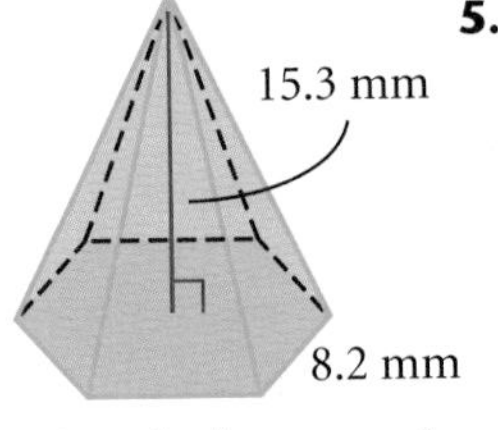

Regular hexagonal pyramid

5.

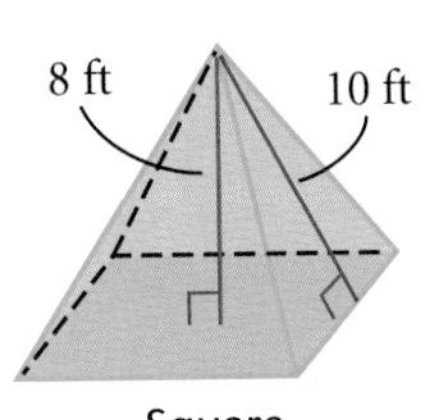

Square pyramid

6. A square prism has a length and width of 10 ft and a height of 15 ft. What is the height of a square pyramid with the same base dimensions and same volume as the prism?

7. **Table Manors** A set of salt and pepper shakers looks like the towers of a castle. The base of each shaker is a square prism with base edges 3.5 cm long and a height of 8 cm. The top is a square pyramid with a height of 1.8 cm. What is the greatest volume of salt that one of the shakers can hold?

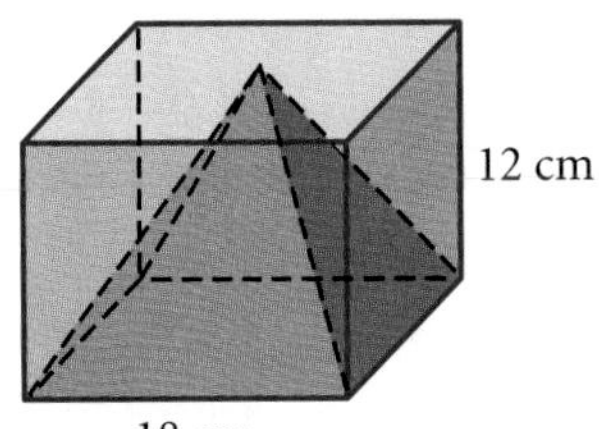

8. A square pyramid is inscribed in the square prism shown. Find the pyramid's volume.

9. The volume of a square pyramid with height *s* and base side length *s* is 9 cubic units. Find *s*.

10. **Pyramid Pencil** A mechanical pencil is in the shape of a regular hexagonal prism topped by a pyramid. Find the volume of the pencil.

11. The numbers 1, 4, 10, … and so on are called *pyramidal numbers.*
    a. Use the figures below to explain why these numbers are called pyramidal numbers.
    b. Find the next two pyramidal numbers.

Top view

Side view

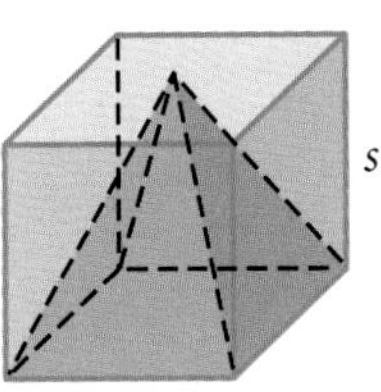

12. A square pyramid is inscribed in a cube, as shown at the right. Prove that the volume of the pyramid is one-third of the volume of the cube.

13. Sketch two different square pyramids that each have a volume of 36 in^3. Include dimensions in your sketches.

14. Write a volume problem about pyramids that has an answer of 100 m^3. Include a complete solution with your problem.

LOOK AHEAD

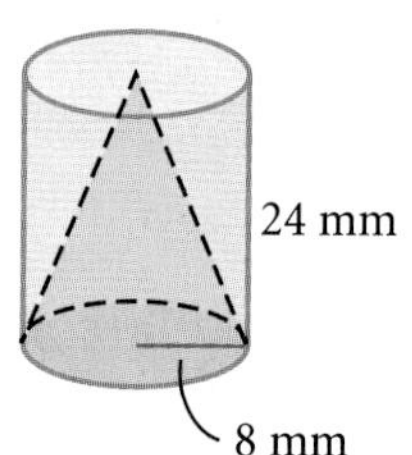

15. The height of a right cone is 24 in., and its slant height is 26 in. Find its radius.

16. A cone is inscribed in a cylinder, as shown at the right. Find its slant height.

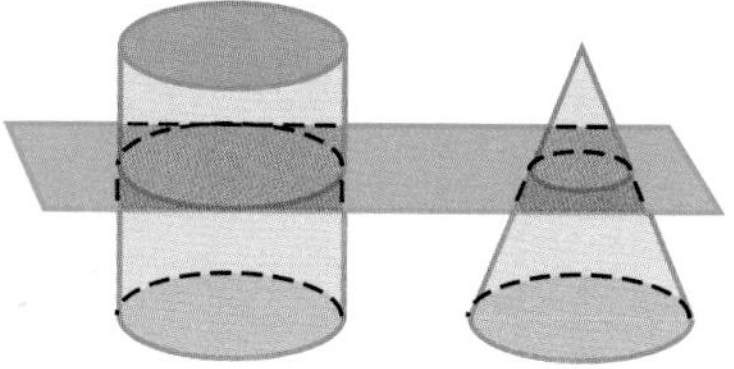

17. A cone and a cylinder have bases in the same plane. They have congruent bases, the same height, and they are cut by a plane parallel to their bases, as shown. What does the cross section of each look like? Which figure has larger cross-sectional areas? Explain.

MORE PRACTICE

Find the volume of each pyramid.

18.

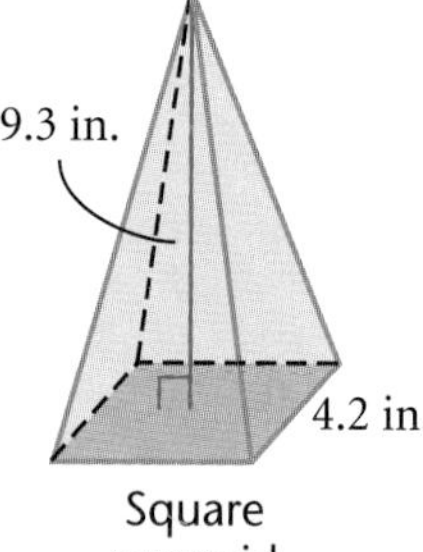

Square pyramid

19.

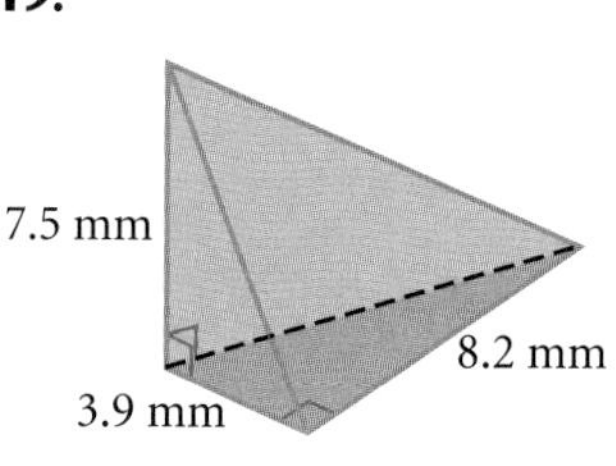

Right triangular pyramid

20.

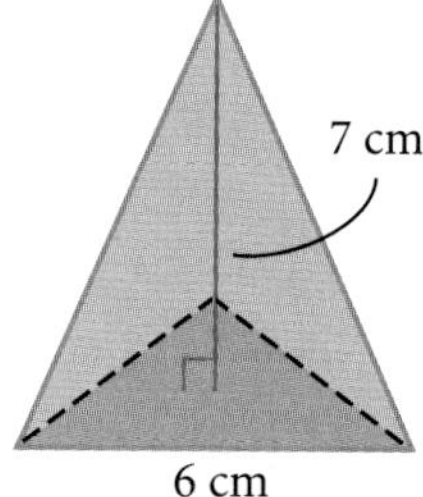

Equilateral triangular pyramid

21. A regular pyramid with a square base 12 cm on a side has a slant height of 20 cm. Find its volume.

22. A regular pyramid with a square base 20 in. on a side has a slant height of 26 in.

a. Find the height of the pyramid.

b. Find the volume of the pyramid.

MORE MATH REASONING

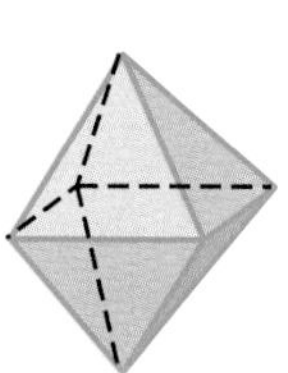

23. Find the volume of a regular octahedron whose edges are 10 cm long.

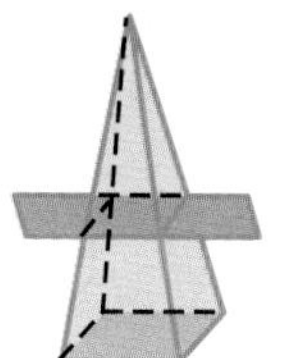

24. A square pyramid has height 30 and base side length 10. A plane parallel to the base cuts the pyramid so that exactly half of its volume is above the plane and half below it. Where does the plane intersect the altitude of the pyramid?

9-2 PART C Volume of Cylinders and Cones

← CONNECT → ***You've already investigated the volumes of prisms and pyramids. Now you will turn your attention to solids with circular bases—cylinders and cones.***

You've seen some similarities and differences among prisms, pyramids, cylinders, and cones.

Write the word that correctly completes each statement. Explain your answers.

1. ***Pyramid*** **is to** ***prism*** **as ___ is to** ***cylinder.***
2. ***Prism*** **is to** ***cylinder*** **as** ***pyramid*** **is to ___.**

In the following Explore, your knowledge about prisms and pyramids will help you investigate the volumes of cylinders and cones.

EXPLORE: FORMULAS THAT MAKE CENTS

MATERIALS

Pennies

1. Take some pennies, and stack them into a cylindrical pile. Call the radius of a penny r. What is the formula for the area of the base of the cylinder?
2. If your stack of pennies has height h, what is the volume of the cylindrical stack? Explain your answer. If you used an idea that you've seen before, include it in your answer. Does this formula work for any cylinder, whether or not it is a right cylinder?
3. What do you think is the formula for the volume of a cone with the same base radius and height as your cylinder? Why? Compare your results with those of your classmates.

EXAMPLE

As part of a science project, Jocelyn used a lathe to help carve a model of a cone-shaped volcano from a wooden cylinder. If the base of the cylinder had a radius of 20 in. and its height was 12 in., find the volume of wood that Jocelyn cut away from the cylinder to make the volcano.

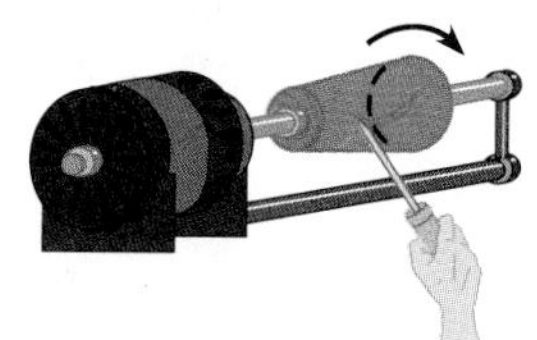

The volume of the wood that is cut away is the difference between the volume of the original cylinder and the volume of the volcano.

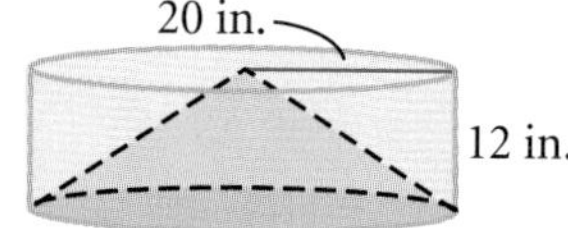

$$V_{\text{cut away}} = V_{\text{cylinder}} - V_{\text{volcano}}$$
$$= \pi r^2 h - \frac{1}{3}\pi r^2 h$$
$$= \pi(20)^2(12) - \frac{1}{3}\pi(20)^2(12)$$
$$= 3200\pi \text{ in.}^3 \approx 10{,}053.1 \text{ in.}^3$$

Jocelyn cut away about 10,053.1 in.^{3} of wood.

The volume formulas you've discovered for cylinders and cones parallel those for prisms and pyramids.

THEOREMS

The volume of a cylinder is the product of its base area and its height. $V = Bh = \pi r^2 h$

The volume of a cone is one-third the product of its base area and its height. $V = \frac{1}{3}Bh = \frac{1}{3}\pi r^2 h$

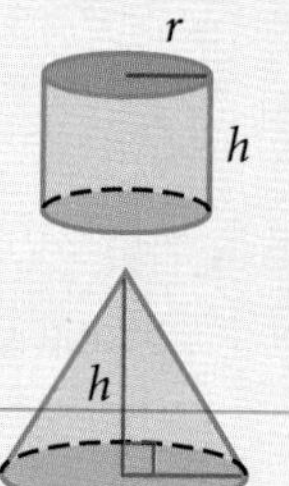

REFLECT

1. Fumiko has a ruler, a cylindrical glass partially full of water, and an irregularly shaped rock. Describe how she can determine the volume of the rock.

2. Describe a method for finding the volume of a frustum of a cone.

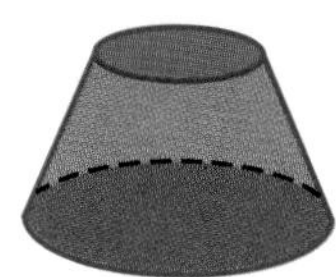

Exercises

CORE

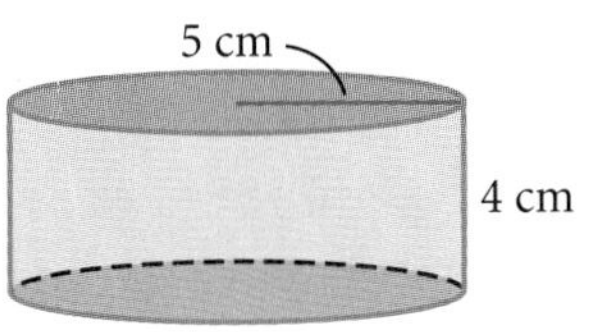

1. **Getting Started** Use the cylinder shown for each of the following.
   a. What is the height of the cylinder?
   b. What is the area of a base of the cylinder to the nearest tenth?
   c. What is the volume of the cylinder to the nearest tenth?

Find the volume of each cylinder and cone.

2. 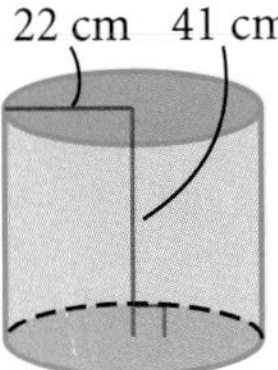

3. 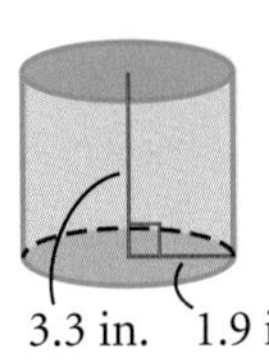

4. 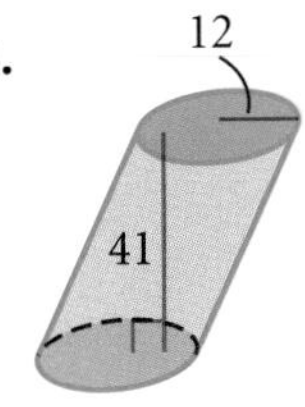

5. 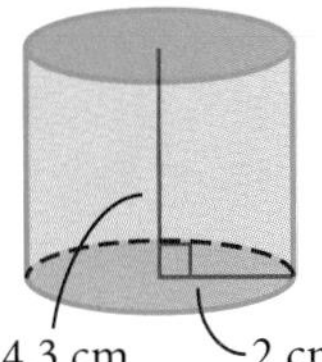

6. 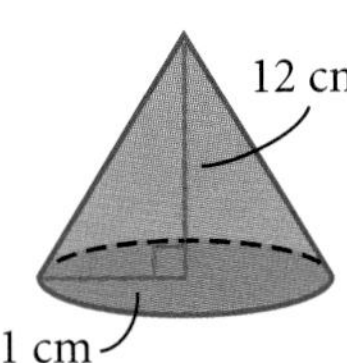

7. 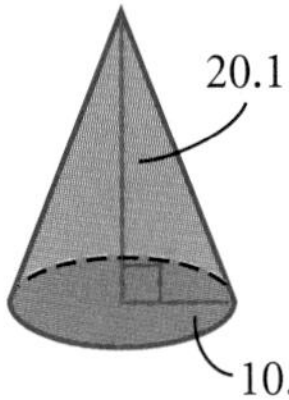

8. 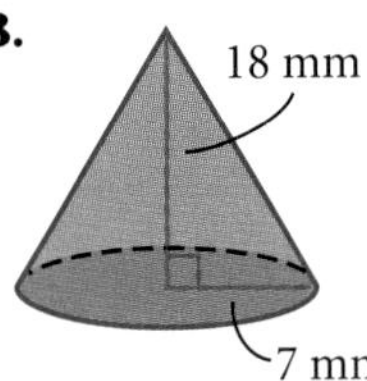

9. 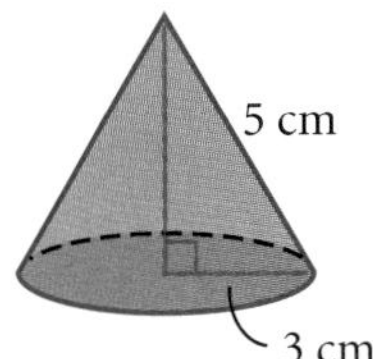

10. **Martian Mountain** The tallest known mountain in the solar system is Olympus Mons on Mars. This extinct volcano is 15 mi high, 336 mi in diameter at the base, and is approximately conical. Find the volume of Olympus Mons.

Science

11. The Bonaventure Hotel in Los Angeles consists of five cylindrical towers. The center tower has 36 floors, and each of the four surrounding towers has 24 floors. Each floor is 10 ft in height. The center tower is 110 ft in diameter, and the outer towers are 85 ft in diameter.
    a. What is the volume of the center tower?
    b. What is the volume of each outer tower?
    c. What is the volume of the entire five-tower structure?

12. a. If the glass at the right is half-full of water, what is the volume of water in the glass?
    b. Suppose you pour the water into a conical container with the same height and radius. To completely fill the cone, what is the minimum height of water needed in the glass?

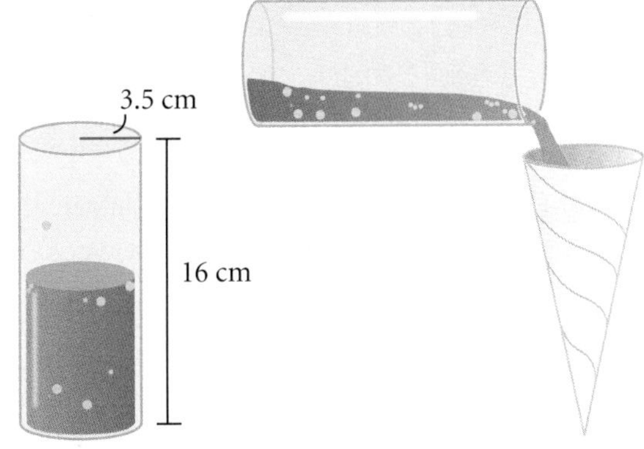

13. The pipes of a pipe organ are metal cylinders. Air forced through the cylinders produces musical notes. The larger the pipe, the lower the note it produces. The largest pipe on one pipe organ has a base diameter of one foot and is thirty feet long. Find the volume of the air inside the pipe.

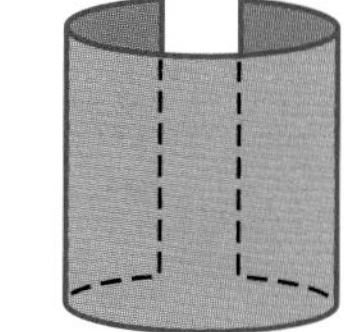

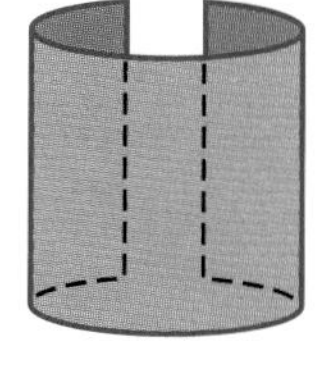

14. Paper Cylinders Any rectangular sheet of paper can be rolled into a right circular cylinder, as shown.

a. You can use an $8\frac{1}{2}'' \times 11''$ sheet of paper to make a right cylinder in two different ways. Use a sheet of paper to model these cylinders. Compare the volumes of the two cylinders.

b. What property of the two cylinders is the same?

15. If you drill a hole through the prism at the right, as shown, does its surface area increase or decrease? What happens to its volume? Are these results the same for any solid, or do they depend on the solid and the size of the hole? Write a brief justification of each of your answers.

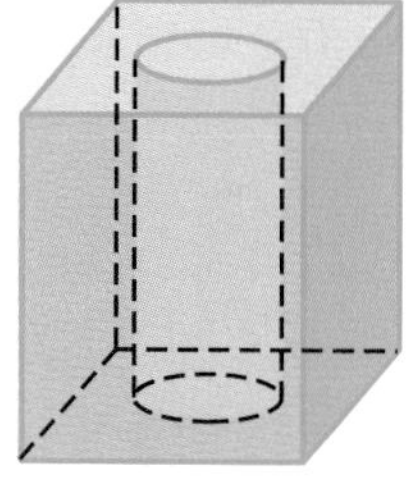

LOOK BACK

16. In your own words, define *sphere.* [8-1]

17. Find the area and circumference of a circle with radius 8 cm. [8-1]

18. Find the radius and area of a circle with circumference 9π in. [8-1]

19. Find the radius and circumference of a circle with area 49π m^2. [8-1]

20. Find the radius of a sphere if the area of one great circle of the sphere is 81π m^2. [8-1]

Find the surface area of each figure. [9-1]

21.

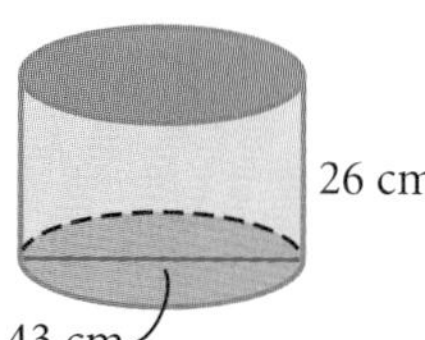

22.

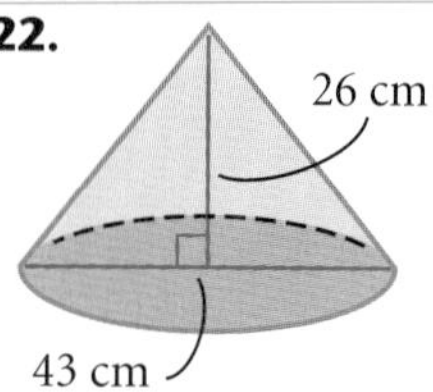

23.

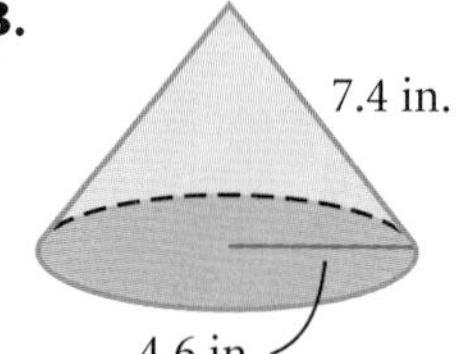

24.

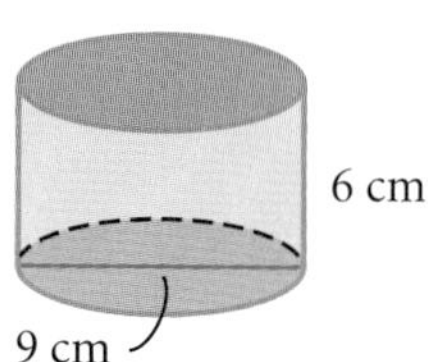

25. In 1943, the first evidence of a volcano appeared in Mexico about 150 mi west of Mexico City. Within a week, the volcano, named Paricutín, was 140 feet tall, and its base had a circumference of $\frac{1}{4}$ mi (1320 ft). Find the surface area of Paricutín one week after its birth. (Paricutín was 7450 ft tall by 1993.) [9-1]

MORE PRACTICE

Find the volume of each cylinder and cone.

26.

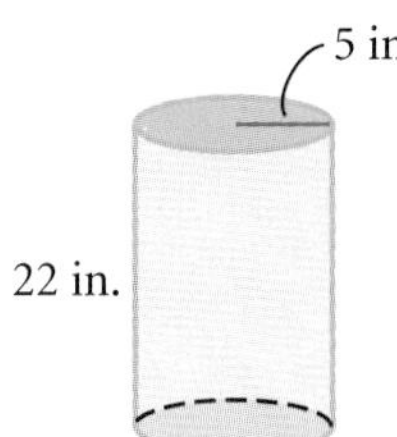

27.

28.

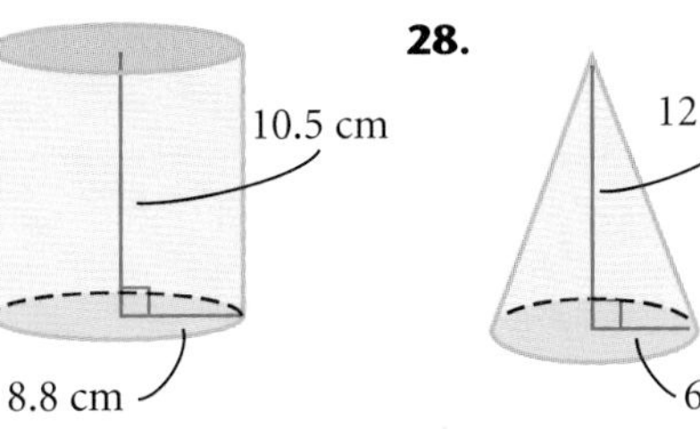

29.

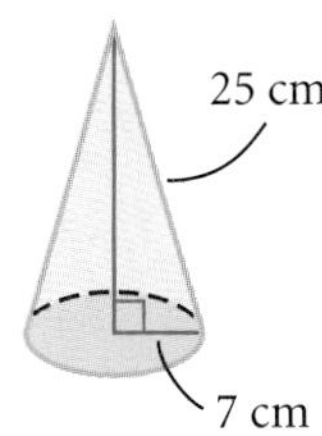

30. A small lead pencil has a cylindrical base and a conical point. Find the volume of the pencil.

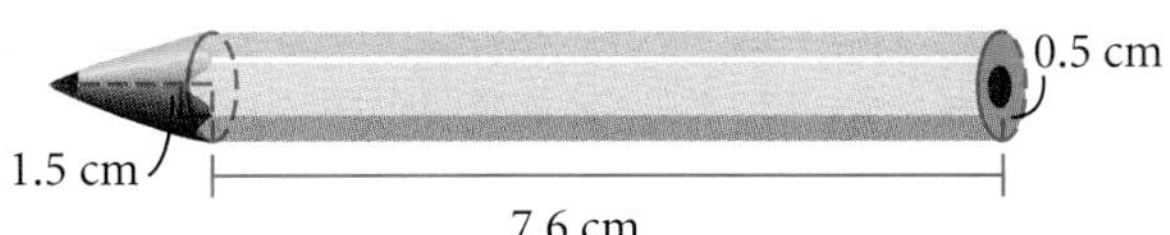

MORE MATH REASONING

31. a. A rubber hose 60 ft long has a $1\frac{1}{2}$-in. outer diameter and a $1\frac{1}{4}$-in. inner diameter. What is the volume of the water the hose can hold? What is the volume of the rubber in the hose?

b. Suppose the hose can fill a 1-ft^3 bucket in 1 min. What is the speed of the water through the hose?

32. The sculpture shown at the right is located in downtown Manhattan. Describe a method for finding the approximate volume of the sculpture.

9-2 PART D Surface Area and Volume of Spheres

← CONNECT → ***You've investigated the surface areas and volumes of prisms, pyramids, cylinders, and cones. Now you will look at the surface area and volume of spheres.***

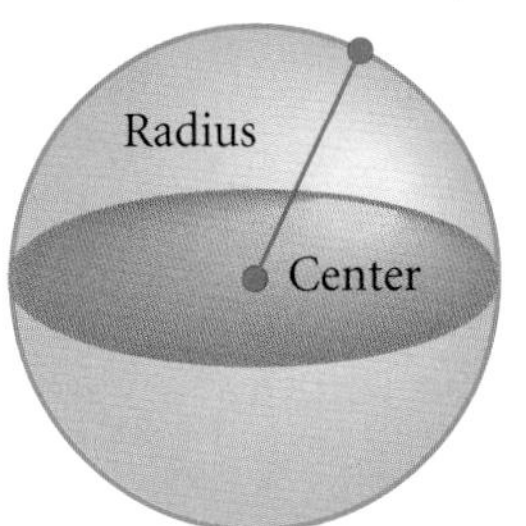

Prisms, pyramids, cylinders, and cones have at least one base. One solid that you've worked with before—the sphere—does not have a base.

You only need to know one measurement to describe a sphere—its radius. Therefore, it shouldn't be too surprising to discover that the surface area and volume of a sphere depend only on its radius.

THEOREM

The surface area of a sphere is 4π times the square of its radius. $SA = 4\pi r^2$

The volume of a sphere is four-thirds the product of π and the cube of its radius. $V = \frac{4}{3}\pi r^3$

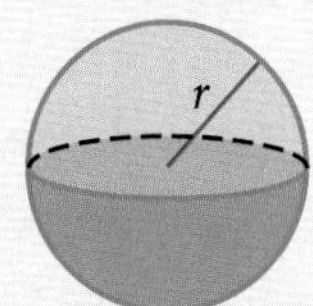

TRY IT

Find the volume and surface area of each sphere.

a. Radius = 5 cm
b. The area of one of its great circles is 4π in.^{2}

In the following Example, you will see how to work back and forth between the surface area and volume formulas.

EXAMPLE

Find the volume of a sphere whose surface area is 36π m^2.

First, find the radius of the sphere.

$$SA = 4\pi r^2 = 36\pi$$

$$r^2 = 9$$

$$r = 3 \text{ m}$$

Now that we know the radius of the sphere, it can be used to find the volume.

$$V = \frac{4}{3}\pi r^3 = \frac{4}{3}\pi(3)^3 = 36\pi \text{ m}^3 \approx 113.1 \text{ m}^3$$

1. Does it make sense to talk about the lateral area of a sphere? If so, what is the formula for the lateral area? If not, why not?

In the following Explore, you will apply the formula for the volume of a sphere to see whether a can is the most efficient container for tennis balls.

EXPLORE: TENNIS, ANYONE?

A cylindrical can of tennis "spheres" contains three balls, as shown. The radius of each ball is about 3.25 cm. Assume they fit snugly in the can.

1. Guess the percentage of empty space (volume) in the can.
2. Find the dimensions of the can. Then calculate the total volume of the three tennis balls and the volume of the can. What percentage of the space in the can is empty? How close is this to your guess?
3. Determine the dimensions of the right rectangular prism (box) that fits the tennis balls best.
4. Calculate the volume of this container and the percentage of wasted space. Compare your results to those from Step 2. Then calculate the surface areas of the prism and the cylinder to determine which container uses more material.
5. What three-dimensional figure do you think is the best for holding three tennis balls stacked on top of one another? Justify your answer.

REFLECT

1. A sphere has radius r. How many circles of radius r are needed to have the same total area as the surface area of the sphere?
2. Find formulas for the surface area and the volume of a hemisphere.

Exercises

CORE

1. **Getting Started** Find the surface area and the volume of a sphere whose radius is 2 in.

Use the given information to find each missing value for the sphere.

2. Radius = 5 cm — Surface area = ___ — Volume = ___
3. Diameter = 8.4 in. — Surface area = ___ — Volume = ___
4. Radius = $8\sqrt{2}$ in. — Surface area = ___ — Volume = ___
5. Surface area = 8π m^2 — Radius = ___ — Volume = ___
6. Volume = 288π mm^3 — Radius = ___ — Surface area = ___

7. The radii of the sun and the planets in the solar system are given below. Assuming all of them are roughly spherical, what percentage of the total volume of the bodies in the solar system is the sun's volume? (We are ignoring the volumes of moons and asteroids.)

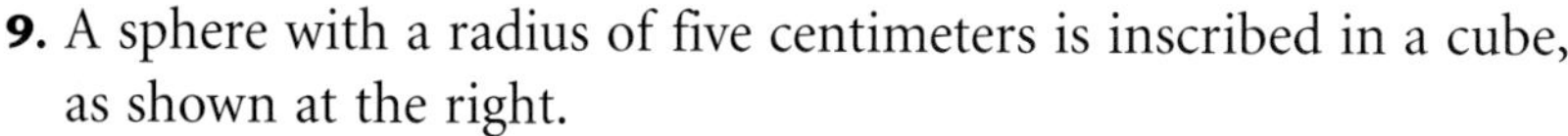

Object	Sun	Mercury	Venus	Earth	Mars
Radius	696,000 km	2440 km	6050 km	6370 km	3400 km
Object	Jupiter	Saturn	Uranus	Neptune	Pluto
Radius	71,400 km	60,300 km	25,900 km	24,800 km	1150 km

8. **Cool Problem #1** An ice cream cone with a height of 5 in. has a radius of 1.25 in. When the cone is filled, a hemisphere of ice cream shows over the top of the cone.

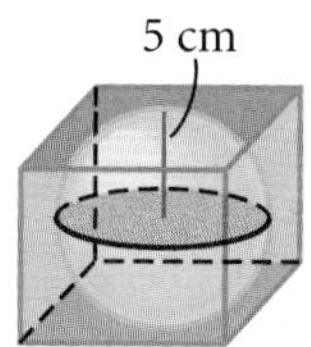

a. What is the total surface area of the cone plus the hemisphere of ice cream?

b. Is more of the ice cream inside the cone or outside it? Explain your answer.

9. A sphere with a radius of five centimeters is inscribed in a cube, as shown at the right.

a. Find the volume of the sphere and the volume of the cube.

b. What is the probability that a randomly selected point inside the cube will also be inside the sphere?

10. Are the formulas for the surface area and volume of a sphere functions? For each formula that is a function, determine whether it is a linear, quadratic, or cubic function, and explain your choice.

11. **Don't Bug Me!** A wood louse (commonly known as a *pill bug*) has a hard shell on the top side of its body. When frightened, it rolls up into a ball, so that only its shell is exposed. If the length of the top of a wood louse's shell is about 1 cm, what are the approximate surface area and volume of the shell? (Hint: What is the relationship between the length of the louse and a great circle of the sphere it rolls into?)

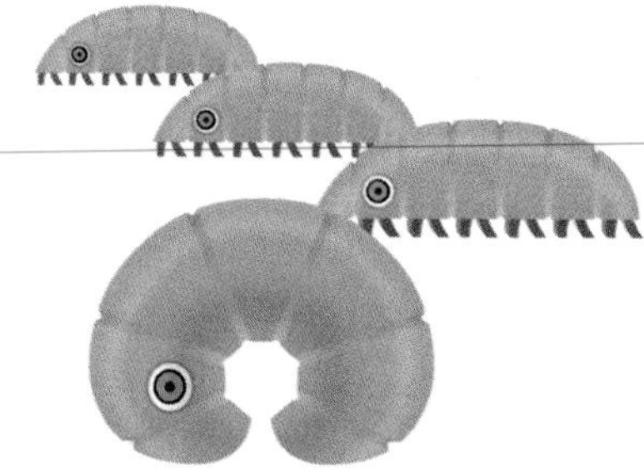

12. It takes 221.7 in.^{2} of black paint to cover a bowling ball. What is the radius of the bowling ball?

13. **The Sky Is Falling!** The average radius of the earth is about 3960 mi. The earth's total land area is about 58,430,000 mi^2. If a satellite falls out of orbit and randomly lands on the earth, what is the probability that it will fall on land?

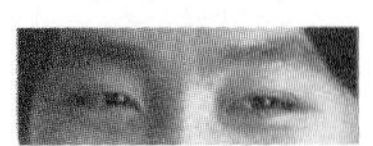

LOOK AHEAD

14. The similarity ratio of one figure to another is $\frac{3}{2}$. What is the ratio of their perimeters? their areas?

Evaluate each expression.

15. $\left(\frac{2}{3}\right)^3$ **16.** $\left(\frac{4}{3}\right)^3$ **17.** $\sqrt[3]{64}$ **18.** $\sqrt[3]{\frac{27}{125}}$

MORE PRACTICE

Use the given information to find each missing value for the sphere.

19. Radius = 5 in. Surface area = ___ Volume = ___

20. Diameter = 0.76 cm Surface area = ___ Volume = ___

21. Surface area = 64π ft^2 Radius = ___ Volume = ___

22. Volume = 36π mm^3 Radius = ___ Surface area = ___

MORE MATH REASONING

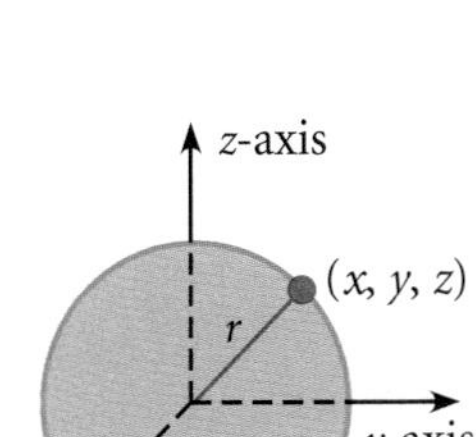

23. A sphere of radius r has its center at the origin of a three-dimensional coordinate system, as shown. A point on the sphere has coordinates (x, y, z). What do you think the equation for the sphere is? Explain why your answer makes sense.

24. Volume of a Sphere A sphere with radius r can be approximated by many tiny pyramids like the one shown.

a. What is the formula for the volume of a pyramid?
The volume of the sphere is approximately the sum of the volumes of the pyramids. If we factor the $\frac{1}{3}h$ out of each individual volume formula, we have the following.

$$V_{\text{sphere}} = \frac{1}{3}h \times (\text{sum of the pyramid base areas})$$

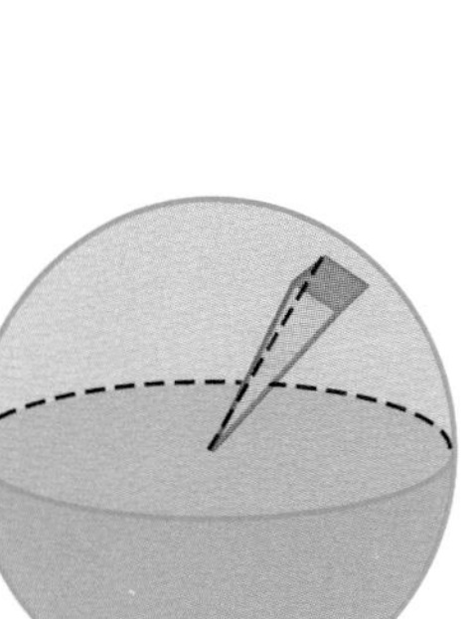

b. In terms of the sphere, what is the height of each pyramid equal to? Substitute this into the above formula.

c. In terms of the sphere, what is the sum of the areas of the bases of the pyramids approximately equal to? What is the formula for this surface area? Replace the sum of the pyramid base areas with this formula.

d. Simplify. What do you find?

9-2 PART E Making Connections

← CONNECT → ***The volume of a three-dimensional figure measures its capacity. When you're deciding which product is the best buy in a grocery store or which cooler to take on a picnic, you're using the idea of volume. You've investigated volume and how to measure it for familiar solids.***

The photographs below show Mount St. Helens before and after its 1980 eruption. You will take a closer look at the volume of this volcano in the Explore.

EXPLORE: MOUNT ST. HELENS AND THE CATERPILLAR

1. Mount St. Helens is approximately conical. Its height on May 17, 1980, the day before its eruption, was 9677 ft. Mount St. Helens is about 30,000 ft in diameter. Find the approximate volume of Mount St. Helens the day before the eruption. Why might your result differ from its actual volume on that day?
2. According to the Caterpillar Tractor Company, the maximum load that their largest dump truck can carry is 240 yd^3. Guess how long it would take this dump truck, carrying a load every five minutes, to haul away the pre-eruption Mount St. Helens.
3. Calculate the answer to Step 2. (Hint: Watch units!) Your answer may seem surprising, considering that the eruption ripped away the top 1200 ft of Mount St. Helens in a matter of minutes!

REFLECT

1. Define *volume* in your own words. What are some similarities and differences between volume and surface area? In your answer, be sure to explain the appropriate units for measuring each.
2. Make a table of the volume formulas for prisms, pyramids, cylinders, cones, and spheres. Summarize these formulas as simply as you can.

Self-Assessment

Find the volume of each of the following.

1.

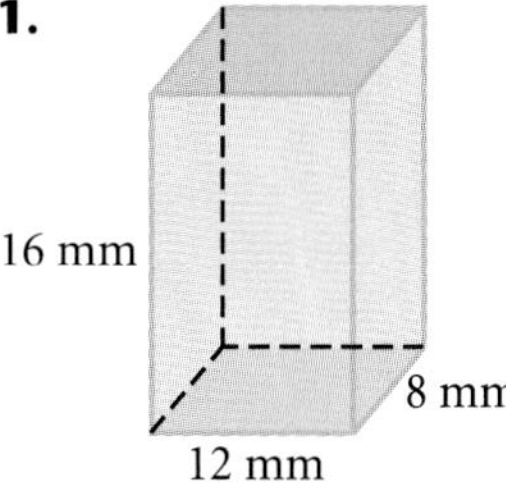

Rectangular prism

2.

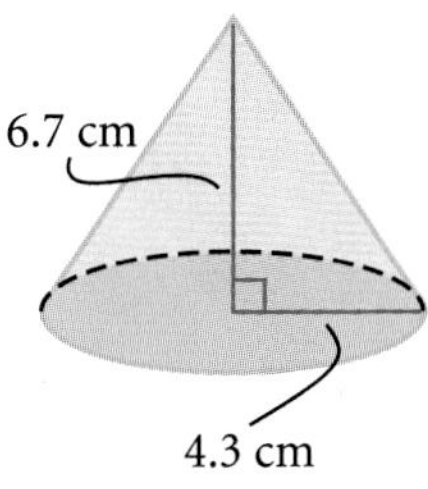

3.

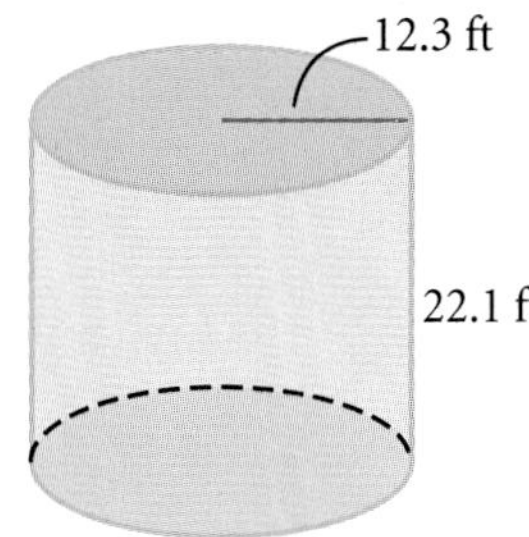

4.

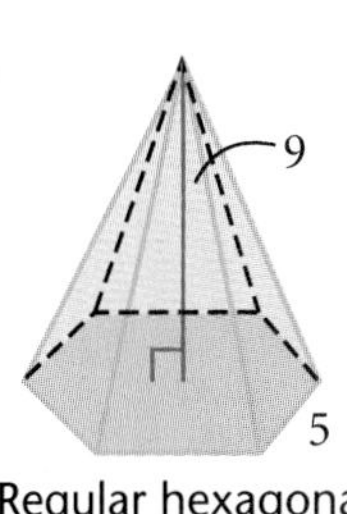

Regular hexagonal pyramid

5. The radius of the earth is approximately 6370 km. The radius of the moon is approximately 1740 km.

a. Find the volume of the earth.

b. Find the volume of the moon.

c. What percentage of the earth's volume is the moon's volume?

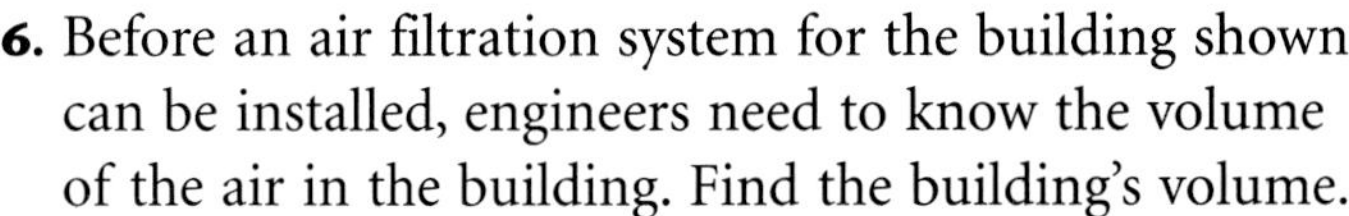

6. Before an air filtration system for the building shown can be installed, engineers need to know the volume of the air in the building. Find the building's volume.

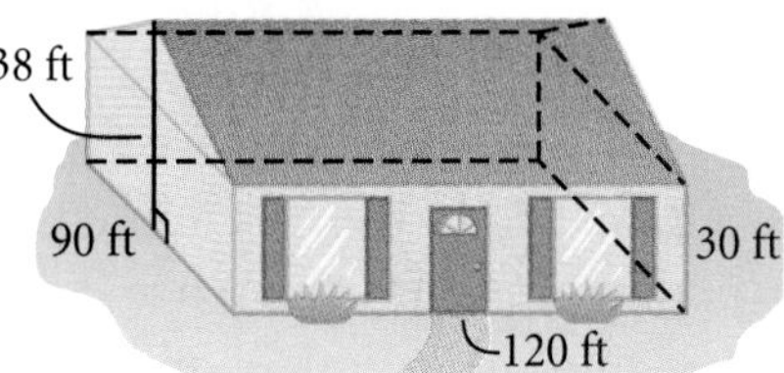

7. The area of the crater of Mauna Loa, a volcano on Hawaii, is 3.7 mi^2. Assuming the crater is perfectly circular, what is its radius? [8-1]

Find the surface area of each figure. [9-1]

8.

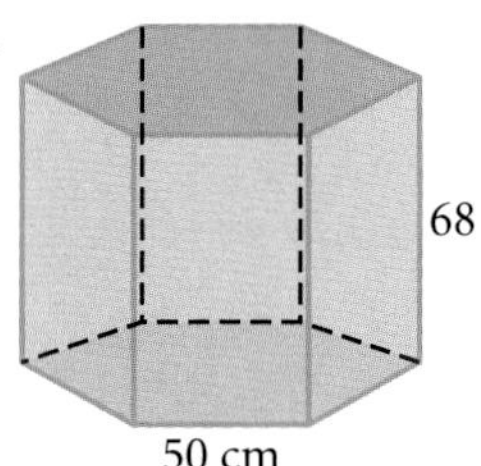

Regular hexagonal prism

9.

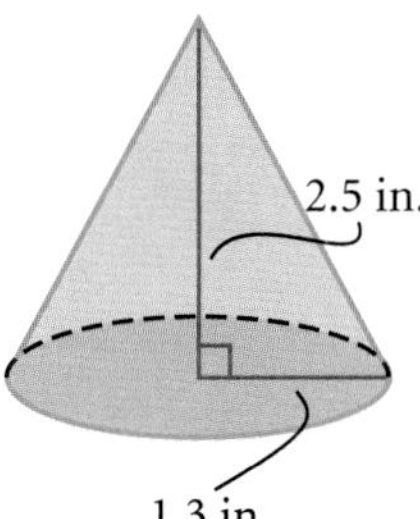

10.

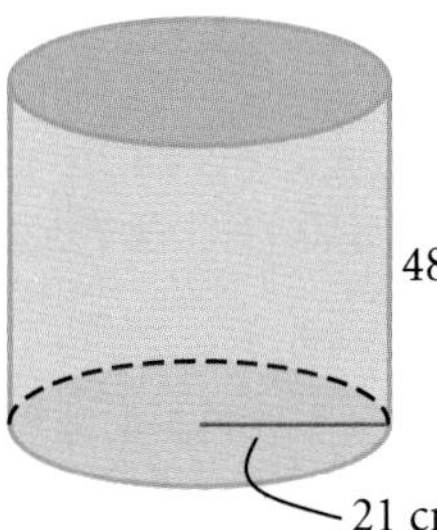

11.

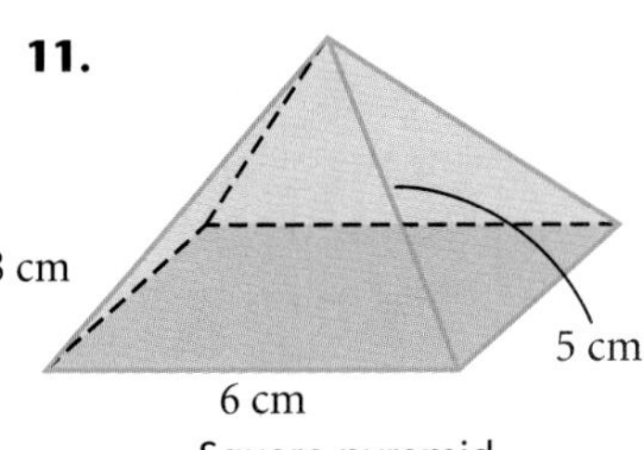

Square pyramid

12. Find the ratio of the volume of sand in the hourglass to the volume of the cylinder holding the hourglass.

(a) $\frac{1}{6}$ (b) $\frac{1}{4}$ (c) $\frac{1}{3}$ (d) $\frac{1}{2}$ (e) $\frac{2}{3}$

13. A cone is inscribed in a square prism with the dimensions shown.

a. Find the volume of each solid.

b. Find the probability that a randomly selected point inside the prism will also be inside the cone.

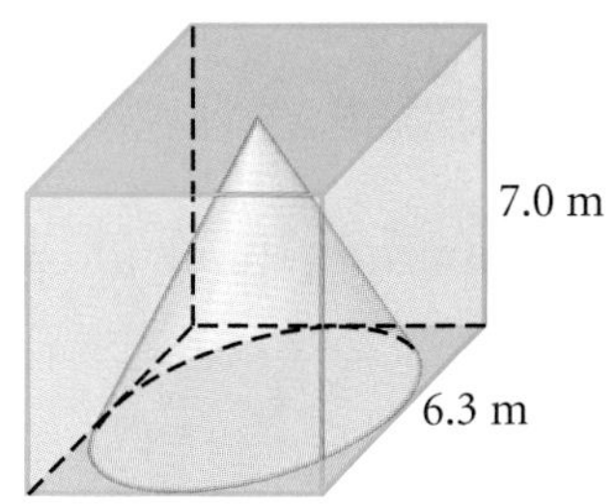

14. A square prism has the same height and volume as the cylinder shown below. To the nearest tenth, what is the length of a side of the prism's base?

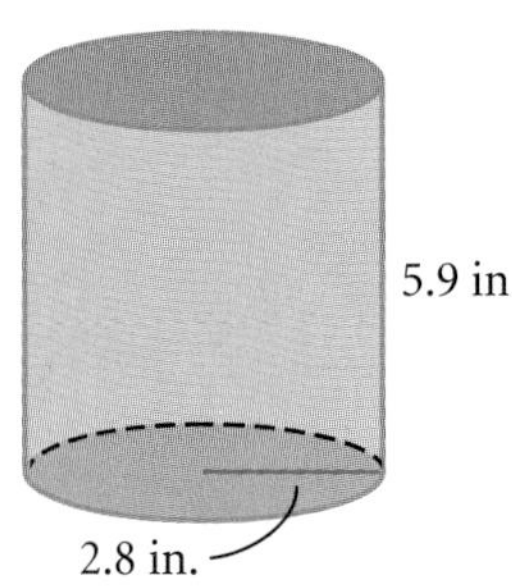

15. A Cool Problem #2 To get some publicity for her new ice cream store, Natalie decided to serve ice cream in square pyramids instead of cones. Her "ice cream pyramids" have the same height and volume as a cone with a radius of 1.25 in. and a height of 5 in.

a. What is the volume of the ice cream pyramid? (Do not include the volume of the ice cream.)

b. What are the base dimensions of the pyramid?

c. What is the difference between the lateral area of the pyramid and that of a 1.25-in.-radius cone?

Industry

16. Squeeze-A-Mess #2 Suppose that the container for a brand of children's toothpaste is cylindrical, with a conical tip and a hemispherical dent in the bottom, as shown. What is the volume of the container? How much volume is lost because the bottom is not flat? Why do you think some containers have indentations like this?

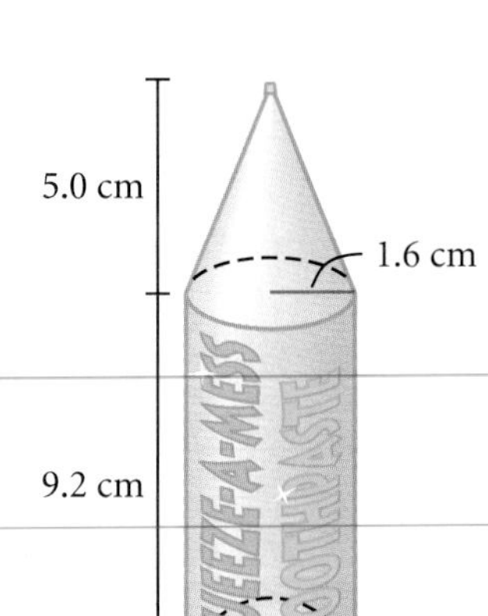

17. A storage tank is a cylinder with a hemisphere on either end. It takes Mike twenty-five minutes to paint one of the hemispheres. How long will it take him to paint the rest of the tank?

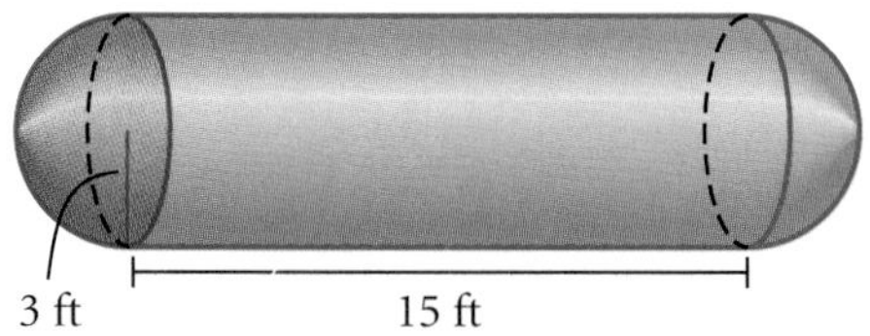

9-3 Similar Solids

why don't **Elephants** have skinny **Legs?**

Why don't animals that weigh several hundred pounds ever look like insects? Although there is a great deal of variation in the way animals look, their appearance and behavior typically relate to their size.

For example, heavy land animals (like the rhinoceros, elephant, or hippopotamus) tend to have stumpy, thick legs. Insects and spiders usually have very long, thin legs in proportion to their bodies.

Although horror movies sometimes show gigantic insects devouring cities, you would probably be just as surprised (and a little frightened) to find an insect the size of a cat. Are there limitations on how large insects can grow? If so, why?

1. **What are some of the problems very large animals face in trying to survive? What difficulties do very small animals face?**
2. **Which animal do you think is more likely to break a leg while running: a rabbit or a race-horse? Why? (Don't base your answer on how fast they run—surprisingly, the domestic rabbit can reach speeds of 35 mi/hr!)**

9-3 PART A Surface Area of Similar Solids

← CONNECT → *You've investigated similarity and surface area as separate topics. Now you will apply the concept of similarity to the surface areas of solids.*

Similar two-dimensional figures have the same shape but not necessarily the same size. If two figures are similar, we know that the lengths of their corresponding sides are proportional, and their corresponding angles are congruent. These properties also apply to similar solids.

The **similarity ratio** of two similar solids is the ratio of the lengths of any two corresponding edges. The radii, heights, and slant heights of the solids are also proportional in the same way.

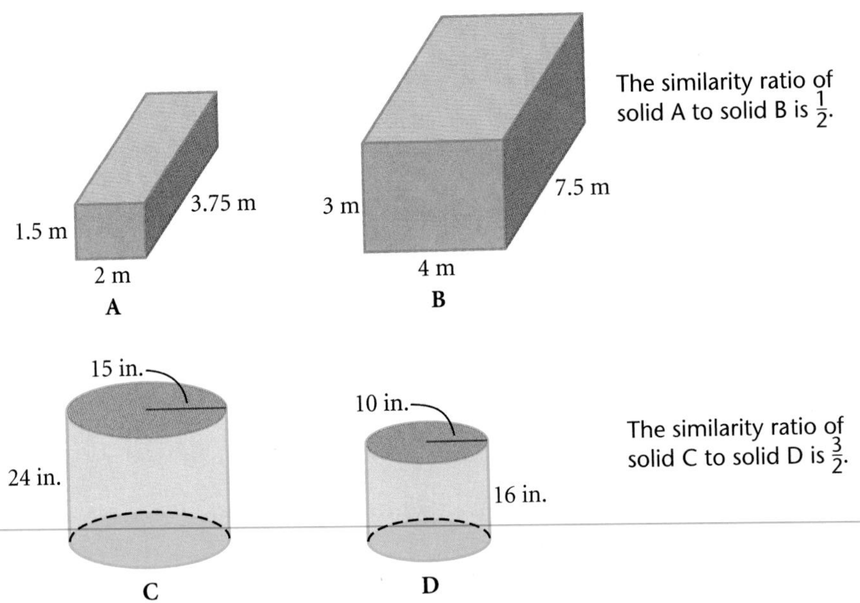

1. What does it mean for two solids to have a similarity ratio of 1?

In the following Explore, you will look for relationships in the surface areas of similar solids. You will also investigate the connection between the cross-sectional area of a solid and its strength.

EXPLORE: A LEG TO STAND ON

1. Sketch a rectangular solid and provide dimensions. Then sketch a second solid similar to the first. What similarity ratio did you use?
2. Find the surface areas of the two solids. (Sketch nets of the solids if this is helpful to you.) What is the ratio of the surface areas of the solids? How is this related to their similarity ratio?
3. In general, the strength of a given material is proportional to its cross-sectional area. This is one reason why thick cylindrical cables, rather than thin wires, are used to support bridges.

   Suppose one animal is 4 times as large as another. (Their similarity ratio is $\frac{4}{1}$.) How many times stronger are the larger animal's legs?

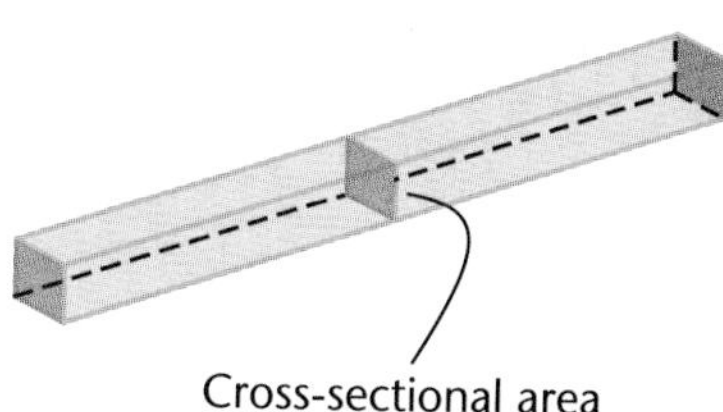

Problem-Solving Tip

You may want to make a mathematical model by choosing a geometric shape and dimensions for the legs of the animals.

In the following Example, you will see another application of similar solids.

EXAMPLE

The surface area of the earth is roughly 13.4 times that of the moon. How many times larger is the earth's radius than the moon's?

The ratio of the surface areas of similar solids is the square of their similarity ratios. Therefore, the similarity ratio is the square root of the surface-area ratio.

Similarity ratio $= \sqrt{13.4} \approx 3.66$

The radius of the earth is about 3.66 times that of the moon.

TRY IT

a. The pyramids shown are similar. Find the similarity ratio of the pyramid on the left to the pyramid on the right. Then find the ratio of their surface areas.

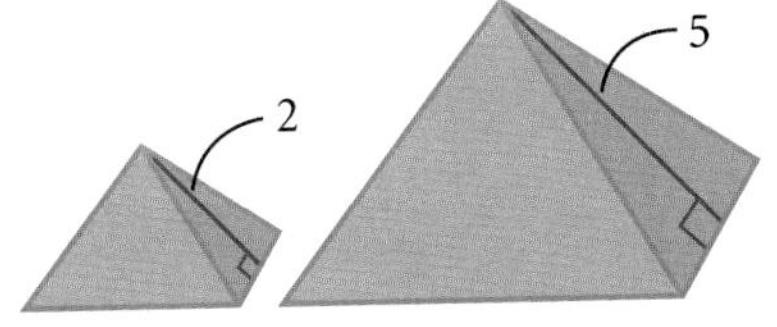

b. A support beam for a ceiling is 6 in. wide and 6 in. high. If you need a second beam with a similar cross section that is 9 times as strong, what should its dimensions be?

The property you explored about the surface areas of similar solids is stated below.

> **THEOREM**
>
> The ratio of the surface areas of two similar solids is the square of their similarity ratio.

REFLECT

Explain why each statement is true, or give a counterexample to show that it is false.

1. Any two cones are similar.
2. Any two cubes are similar.
3. Any two rectangular prisms are similar.
4. Any two spheres are similar.
5. Do you think that the ratio of the lateral areas of two similar solids is also the square of their similarity ratio? Explain why or why not.

Exercises

CORE

Getting Started **State whether or not the figures in each pair appear to be similar.**

1.

2.

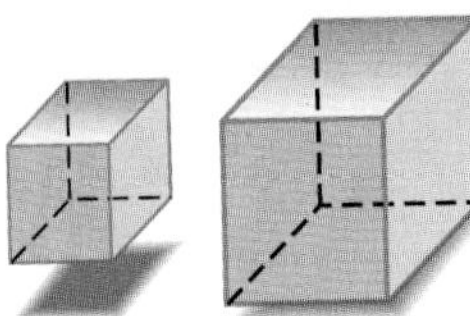

3.

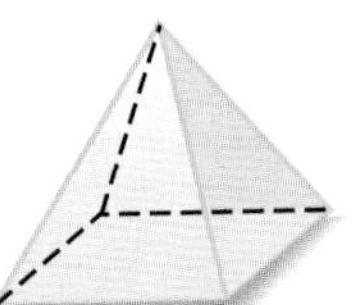

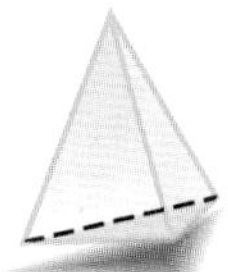

The cones shown at the right are similar.

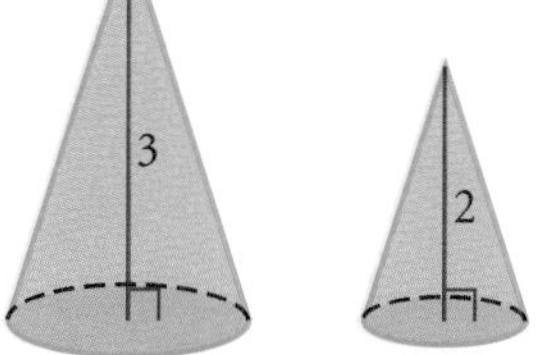

4. Find the similarity ratio of the cone on the left to the cone on the right.

5. Find the ratio of their radii.

6. Find the ratio of their surface areas.

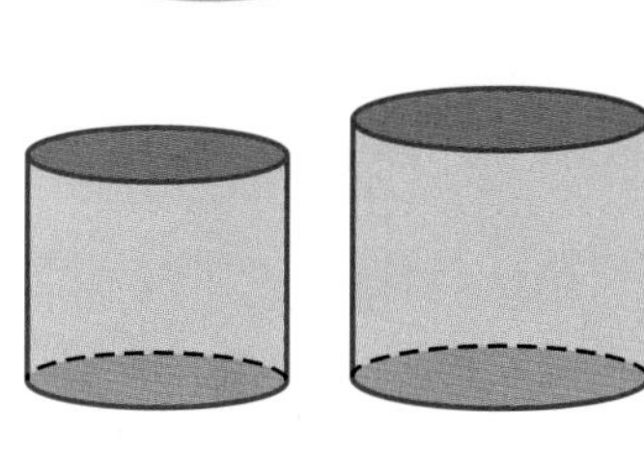

7. The surface areas of the similar cylinders shown have a ratio of $\frac{49}{64}$. What is the similarity ratio of the cylinders?

8. A two-by-four is a board $3\frac{5}{8}$ in. wide and $1\frac{5}{8}$ in. thick. How many times stronger than a two-by-four is a board that is twice as wide and three times as thick?

$1\frac{5}{8}$ in.

$3\frac{5}{8}$ in.

9. According to Lynn Barkley, Collections Manager of the Los Angeles Natural History Museum, the diameter of the tibia (leg bone) of an adult male Asiatic elephant is 75.4 mm. The diameter of the tibia of a California mouse is 1.45 mm. How many times stronger are the elephant's legs?

10. **Udder Destruction** Tara Fye is writing a script for a horror movie. In the movie, a mad scientist enlarges a cow to 100 times its normal size. How much stronger would its legs be than those of a normal cow?

11. Prove: If the radius of sphere A is x and the radius of sphere B is $3x$, then the ratio of the surface area of A to the surface area of B is $\frac{1}{9}$.

12. The ratio of the surface areas of two similar solids is a function of the similarity ratio, k, of the solids. Express the surface-area ratio as a function of k.

LOOK BACK

Two tangent segments intersect a circle as shown. Find each of the following. [8-3]

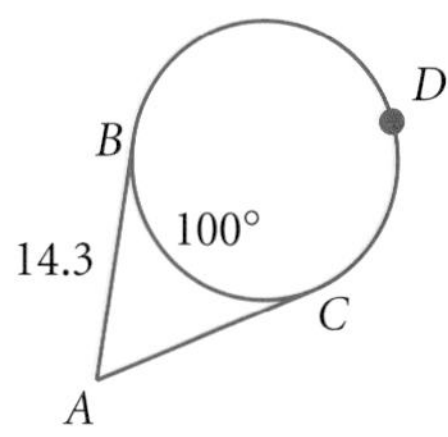

13. $m\widehat{BDC}$ 14. AC 15. $m\angle BAC$

Find the volume of each of the following. [9-2]

16.

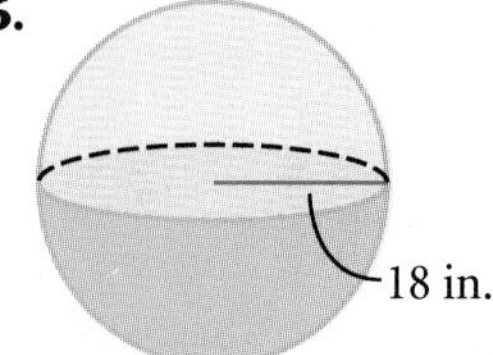

17.

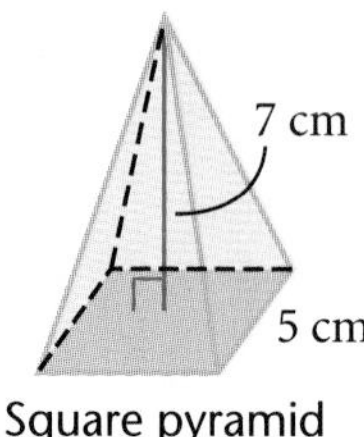

Square pyramid

18.

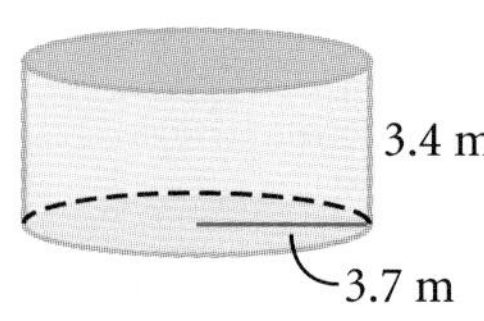

19.

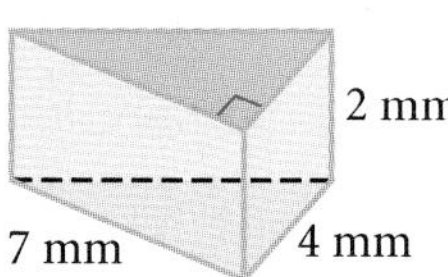

MORE PRACTICE

The cylinders shown at the right are similar. Use these cylinders for Exercises 20–22.

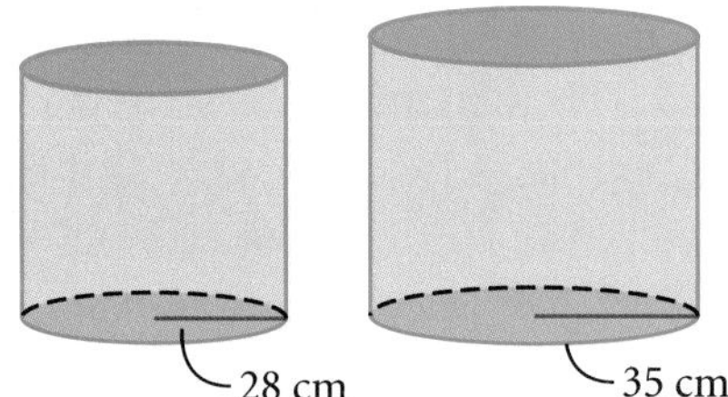

20. Find the similarity ratio of the cylinder on the left to the cylinder on the right.

21. Find the ratio of their heights.

22. Find the ratio of their surface areas.

23. The surface areas of the similar pyramids shown at the right have a ratio of $\frac{25}{36}$. What is the similarity ratio of the pyramids?

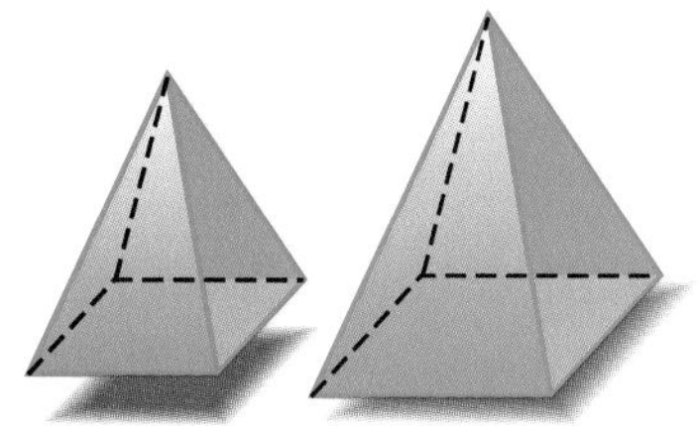

MORE MATH REASONING

24. Some filters contain spherical particles that absorb materials from liquids passed through the filters. The effectiveness of such a filter is proportional to the surface area of the particles. The particles come in two sizes—1 cm in diameter (or 1 particle per cm^3 of filter) and 0.5 cm in diameter (or 8 particles per cm^3). Which size is more effective? How do you know?

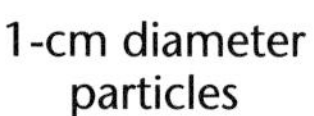

1-cm diameter particles

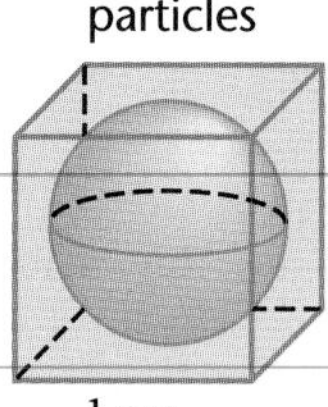

0.5-cm diameter particles

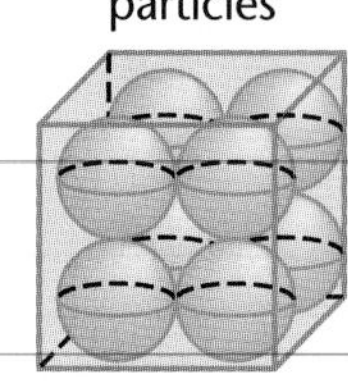

25. Suppose that the cross section of the arm of a person who can curl (lift) a 50-lb dumbbell has a circumference of 13.5 in. Assuming that the strength of an arm is proportional to its cross-sectional area, find the circumference of the arm of someone who can curl a 100-lb dumbbell.

26. Estimate the similarity ratio of the earth to a globe that has a diameter of one foot. Write a brief paragraph explaining how you arrived at your estimate.

9-3 PART B Volume of Similar Solids

← CONNECT → ***You know how the surface areas of similar solids are related to their similarity ratio. Now you will investigate the relationship between the similarity ratio of two similar solids and the volumes of those solids.***

A scale model of an apartment building made out of concrete, brick, and steel would be hard to make and inconvenient to pass around during presentations. But it would be difficult to convince people to move into a real building made out of cardboard and balsa wood! Though the model is similar to the actual building, its weight and strength are quite different from those of the building.

In the following Explore, you will investigate how the volumes of similar solids are related.

EXPLORE: SIMILAR CYLINDERS, SIMILAR ANIMALS

1. Suppose one cylindrical drum has radius r and height h, and another has radius $3r$ and height $3h$. Are the drums similar? Explain why or why not.
2. Find the volume of each drum. What is the ratio of their volumes?
3. Repeat Steps 1 and 2 for spheres of radius r and $2r$. How does the ratio of the volumes of two similar solids relate to their similarity ratio?
4. The weight of an object of a given density is proportional to its volume. Suppose the measurements of one animal are four times the measurements of another, and the two animals are geometrically similar. How many times greater is the weight of the larger animal than the weight of the smaller?

EXAMPLE

Two years ago, José bought a puppy that weighed 2 lb. Since then, it has tripled in length. About how much does the dog weigh now?

The similarity ratio is $\frac{3}{1}$. Therefore, the ratio of the volumes is $\left(\frac{3}{1}\right)^3 = 27$.

Weight is proportional to volume, so the dog now weighs approximately $2 \times 27 = 54$ lb.

TRY IT

a. What is the ratio of the volumes of the two cubes shown?

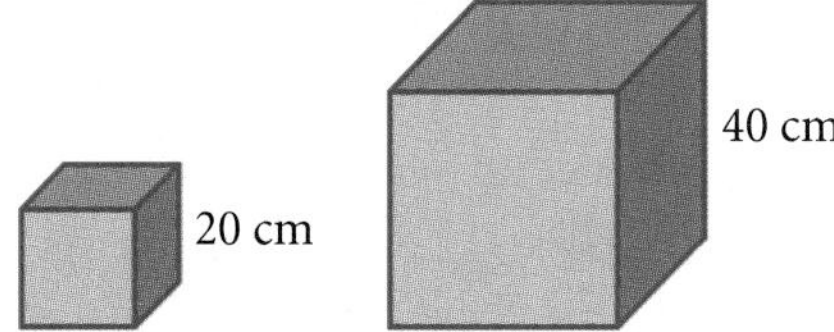

b. The ratio of the volumes of two similar cylinders is $\frac{125}{27}$. What is the ratio of their radii?

c. Suppose that two similar animals have a similarity ratio of $\frac{3}{2}$. The smaller one weighs 100 lb. What does the larger one weigh?

The property you've discovered about the volumes of similar solids is stated below.

> **THEOREM**
>
> The ratio of the volumes of two similar solids is the cube of their similarity ratio.

REFLECT

1. In your own words, explain why the ratio of the volumes of two spheres is the cube of their similarity ratio.

2. Suppose that a small scale model of a car is built out of exactly the same materials as the actual car. Name some properties that will be the same for the model and the actual car and some that will be different. Justify each of your answers.

Exercises

CORE

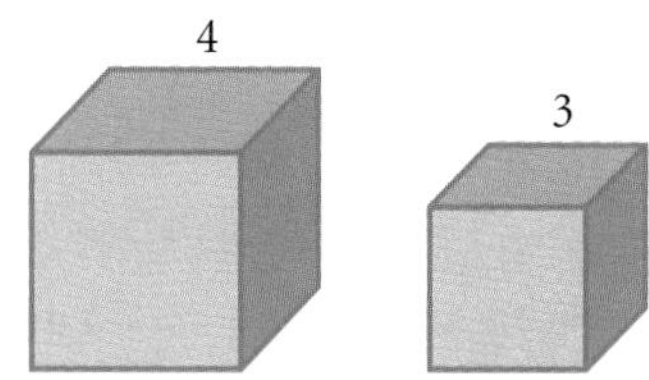

1. **Getting Started** Use the cubes at the right for the following.
   a. Find the similarity ratio of the cube on the left to the cube on the right.
   b. Find the ratio of their surface areas.
   c. Find the ratio of their volumes.

The cylinders shown at the right are similar.

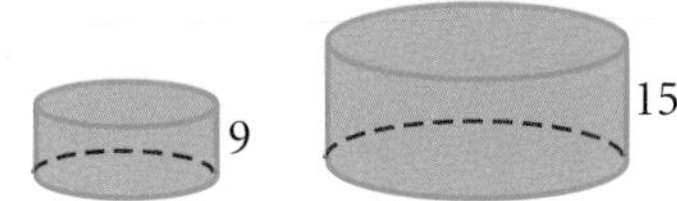

2. Find the similarity ratio of the cylinder on the left to the cylinder on the right.
3. Find the ratio of their radii.
4. Find the ratio of their surface areas.
5. Find the ratio of their volumes.

6. The volumes of the cones shown have a ratio of $\frac{125}{64}$. What is the similarity ratio of the cones? What is the ratio of their surface areas?
7. The surface areas of two spheres are 36π and 324π. What is the ratio of their volumes?

Write the word or phrase that correctly completes each statement.

8. The weight of an object is proportional to its ___.
9. The strength of a beam is proportional to its cross-sectional ___.
10. A 16-in.-long crescent wrench is similar to an 8-in. wrench. How many times heavier is the 16-in. wrench than the 8-in. wrench?

11. **Dairy Disaster** You may recall that Tara Fye's script for *The Cow That Conquered Chicago* features a cow enlarged to 100 times its normal size. How many times more would this cow weigh than a normal cow?

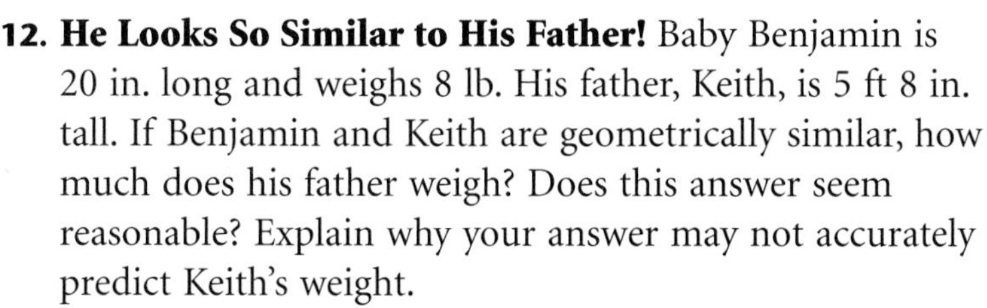

12. **He Looks So Similar to His Father!** Baby Benjamin is 20 in. long and weighs 8 lb. His father, Keith, is 5 ft 8 in. tall. If Benjamin and Keith are geometrically similar, how much does his father weigh? Does this answer seem reasonable? Explain why your answer may not accurately predict Keith's weight.

13. A globe is a scale model of the earth. Suppose that 1 in. on the globe represents 1200 mi on the earth. The circumference of the earth is about 24,900 mi. Find the radius, surface area, and volume of the globe.

LOOK AHEAD

Sketch the image of $\overline{AB}$ for each transformation. Give the coordinates of points A' and B'.

14. a translation with translation vector <1, −3>

15. a clockwise rotation of 90° around the origin

16. a reflection across the x-axis

17. a dilation with center (0, 0) and scale factor 2

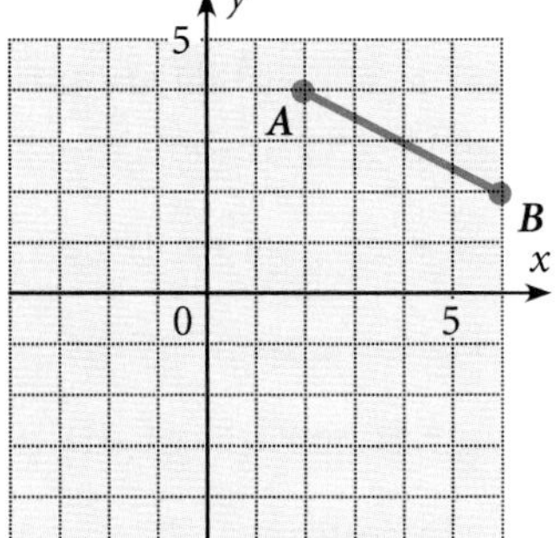

MORE PRACTICE

The square pyramids shown at the right are similar.

18. Find the similarity ratio of the pyramid on the left to the pyramid on the right.

19. Find the ratio of their slant heights.

20. Find the ratio of their surface areas.

21. Find the ratio of their volumes.

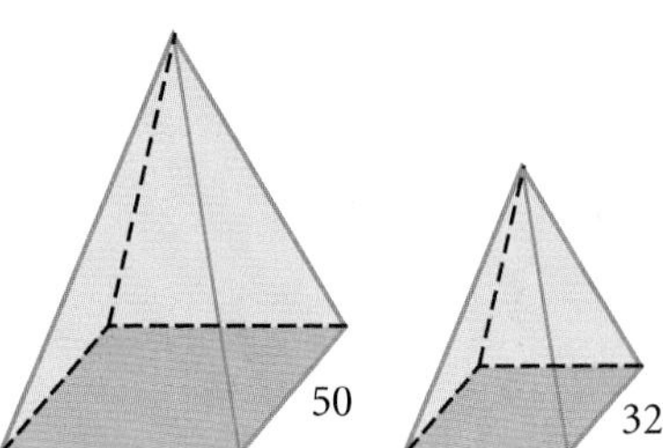

22. The ratio of the surface areas of two similar cylinders is $\frac{81}{25}$. What is the similarity ratio of the cylinders? What is the ratio of their volumes?

MORE MATH REASONING

Science

23. Your heart rate is proportional to the ratio of your surface area (from which body heat escapes) to your blood volume (which keeps your body warm). This is also true for other animals. If a robin is 6.5 in. long and a human's heart beats an average of 70 times per minute, how fast do you think a robin's heart beats? Explain the process you used to find your answer. (Hint: Assume a human is 70 in. long.)

24. My Ant, the Powerlifter You've probably seen tiny insects carrying relatively large objects. For humans, just lifting an item our own weight can be difficult.

Science

a. Model a human by a rectangular solid with a height of 180 cm, a width of 30 cm, and a length of 18 cm. Suppose the density of a human is approximately 1 gram per cubic centimeter (the density of water). What is the weight of this human in grams?

b. Find the length-width cross-sectional area of the rectangular human. If he or she can carry $\frac{1}{15}$ kg for every 1 cm^2 of cross-sectional area, how much should this person be able to carry?

c. Suppose that the similarity ratio of a human to an ant is approximately 150 to 1. Find the following.

   i. the dimensions of the ant
   ii. its weight, if its density is 1 g/cm^3
   iii. its cross-sectional area
   iv. the weight it can carry at $\frac{1}{15}$ kg per cm^2 of cross-sectional area

d. How many ants does it take to carry the same amount a human can carry? What is their combined weight? Which species is more efficient?

e. Explain why small animals can lift and carry more in relation to their size than large animals.

9-3 PART C Making Connections

← CONNECT →

You've investigated the surface areas and volumes of similar solids, and you've seen how you can use similarity to help you understand the way animals look.

The photograph at the right shows an Australian mantis, one of the world's largest insects. In the following Explore, you will see how the volumes and surface areas of similar solids limit the size of insects.

EXPLORE: BIG BUG!

You've just seen a horror movie starring a grasshopper that has been enlarged to 600 times its normal measurements. You're pretty sure that this was done with models and trick photography, but just to make certain, you decide to check things out mathematically.

1. If a "normal" grasshopper is 2 in. long, how long is the enlarged grasshopper in the movie?
2. How many times greater is the cross-sectional area of one leg of the giant grasshopper than the cross-sectional area of one leg of the normal grasshopper? What does this tell you about the strength of the legs of the giant grasshopper?
3. How many times greater is the weight of the giant grasshopper than the weight of the normal grasshopper? Do you think the legs of the giant grasshopper could support its weight? Explain why or why not.
4. Why do many large animals have thick legs? (Hint: Suppose the measurements of the body of one animal are twice as large as the measurements of another. How many times greater is the weight of the larger animal? If the leg measurements of the larger animal were in the same proportion, how many times greater would the strength of the larger animal's legs be than that of the smaller?)

REFLECT

1. Compare the properties of similarity for solids and for plane figures. Describe similarities and differences.
2. Summarize the relationship among the similarity ratio of two solids, the ratio of their surface areas, and the ratio of their volumes.

Self-Assessment

Use the similar cones shown at the right for Exercises 1–4.

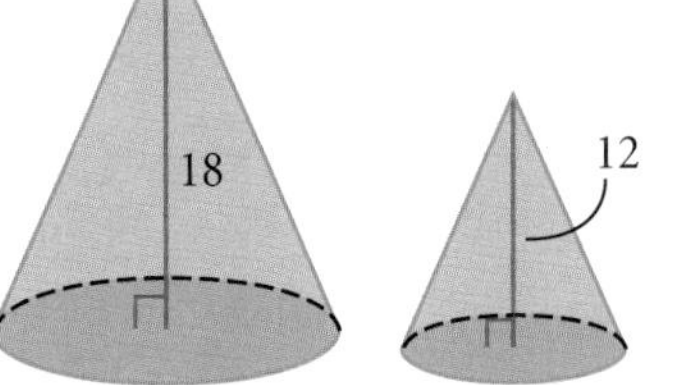

1. Find the similarity ratio of the cone on the left to the cone on the right.

2. Find the ratio of their radii.

3. Find the ratio of their surface areas.

4. Find the ratio of their volumes.

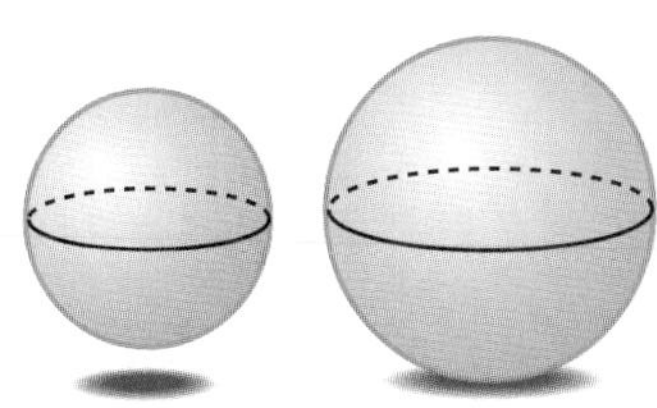

5. The volumes of the spheres shown have a ratio of $\frac{27}{64}$. What is the similarity ratio of the spheres? What is the ratio of their surface areas?

6. Suppose that the corresponding sides of two similar solids have lengths 4 and 9. The ratio of the volume of the smaller solid to the larger is

(a) $\frac{2}{3}$ (b) $\frac{4}{9}$ (c) $\frac{16}{81}$ (d) $\frac{64}{729}$ (e) not here

7. Flakeos come in the two similar box sizes shown. The boxes are filled with equal densities of cereal. If the small box costs \$2.59 and the large box costs \$3.59, which one is a better buy?

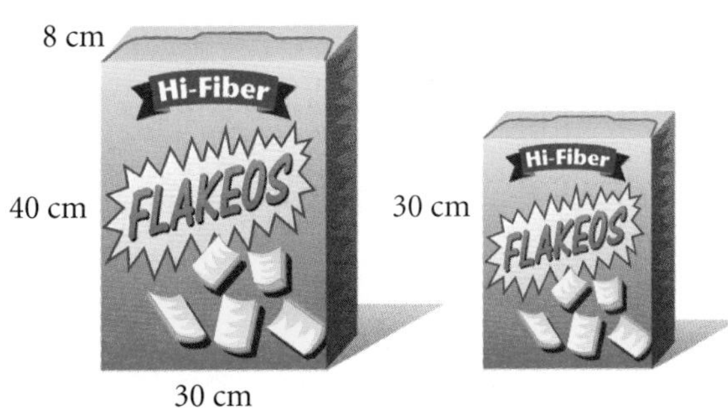

Find the measure of each angle or arc. [8-3]

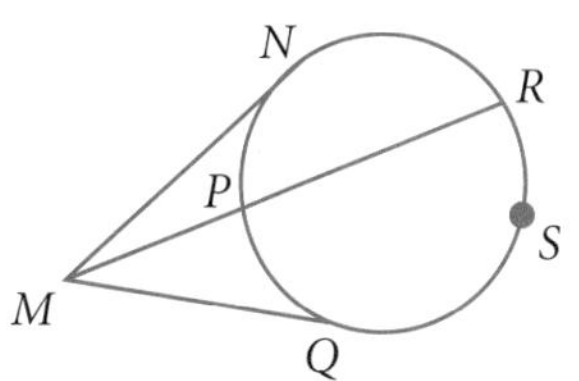

8. If $m\widehat{NSQ} = 286°$, find $m\angle NMQ$.

9. If $m\angle NMQ = 68°$, find $m\widehat{NQ}$.

10. If $m\widehat{QP} = 47°$ and $m\widehat{RQ} = 119°$, find $m\angle PMQ$.

11. In many parts of Africa, homes are built with cylindrical bases and conical roofs. Suppose that the diameter of the base of a home is 15 ft, and its height is 6 ft. The conical roof is 25 ft in diameter, and its height is 4 ft. Find the volume enclosed by the home. [9-2]

12. How Big Should A Leg Be? a. Mammals come in many different shapes and sizes. Make a graph of the measurements given.

Science

Mammal	Weight	Diameter of Tibia (leg bone)
North American moose	600 kg	32.90 mm
Hartman zebra	425 kg	29.70 mm
Black rhinoceros	1035 kg	45.70 mm
Deer	170 kg	20.50 mm
Chimpanzee	60 kg	12.95 mm
Gorilla	200 kg	23.25 mm

Data courtesy of: Kent Yamaguchi, Curator of Education, Santa Ana Zoo, Santa Ana, CA; and Lynn Barkley, Collections Manager of the Los Angeles Natural History Museum.

b. Describe your graph. Does a line seem to fit the points best, or does a smooth curve do a better job? Draw the line or curve that seems to fit your data best.

c. Use your graph to predict the diameters of the tibia of a dog weighing 15 kg and a human weighing 70 kg.

d. What might be some of the sources of inaccuracy in your predictions in **12c**?

13. Why do you think small models of buildings are built of lighter materials than are used in the actual buildings?

14. King Kong was supposed to have been 24 ft tall. Some real gorillas are about 5 ft tall and weigh about 400 pounds.

a. Find the similarity ratio of King Kong to a real gorilla. Round your answer to the nearest whole number.

b. Use your result in **14a** to help find King Kong's weight.

c. How many times stronger would one of King Kong's legs be than the leg of a real gorilla?

d. Do you think a gorilla the size of King Kong could actually exist? Why or why not?

15. A juice company sells a cylindrical 24-oz can of juice that is 15.2 cm tall and 8.0 cm in diameter. They've decided to sell 6-oz cans of juice in cylindrical cans similar to the 24-oz cans. Find the height and radius of the 6-oz can. Explain how you found these values. (Hint: Remember that ounces are a measure of volume.)

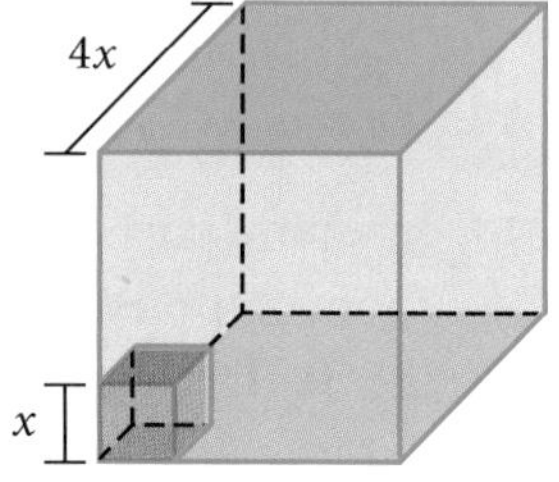

16. What is the probability that a randomly selected point inside the large cube will also be inside the small cube? Explain how your answer is related to the similarity ratio of the two cubes.

Chapter 9 Review

In Chapter 9, you have learned about the properties of volume and surface area for some of the most common solids. By investigating similar solids, you gained insight into the reasons that living things are shaped as they are.

KEY TERMS

altitude [9-1]	lateral face [9-1]	right cylinder [9-1]
base [9-1]	oblique [9-1]	right prism [9-1]
cone [9-1]	prism [9-1]	slant height [9-1]
cylinder [9-1]	pyramid [9-1]	surface area [9-1]
lateral area [9-1]	regular pyramid [9-1]	volume [9-2]
lateral edge [9-1]	right cone [9-1]	

Write the letter of the second pair that best matches the first pair.

1. Pyramid: cone as (a) oblique: right, (b) prism: cylinder, (c) sphere: great circle, (d) cylinder: sphere

2. Oblique: right as (a) vertical: slanted, (b) lateral: regular, (c) cone: cylinder, (d) tilted: upright

CONCEPTS AND APPLICATIONS

Find the surface area and volume of each solid to the nearest tenth. [9-1, 9-2]

3.

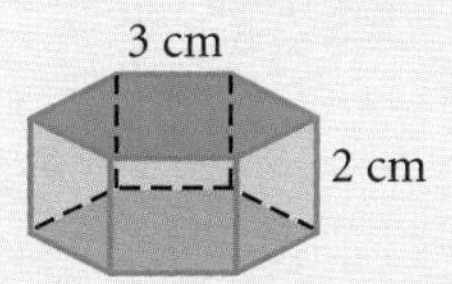

Regular hexagonal prism

4.

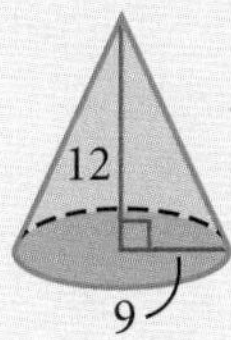

5.

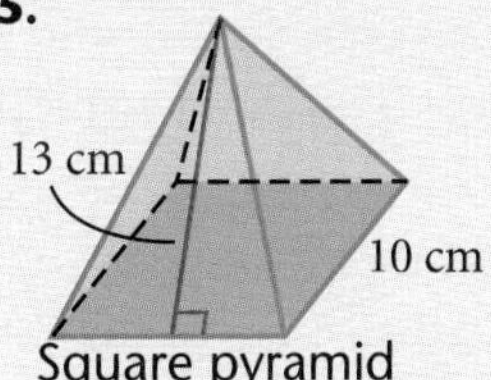

Square pyramid

6.

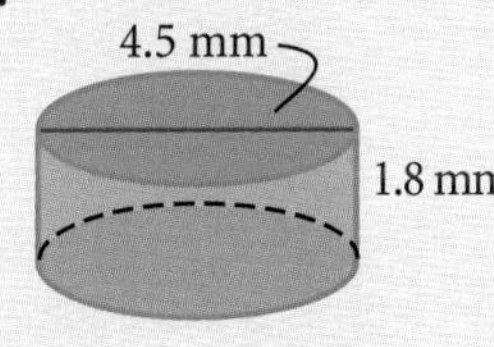

7. The diameter of a ball is $4\frac{1}{2}$ in. Find its surface area and volume. [9-2]

8. The two prisms at the right have the same height. Do they have the same volume? Explain. [9-2]

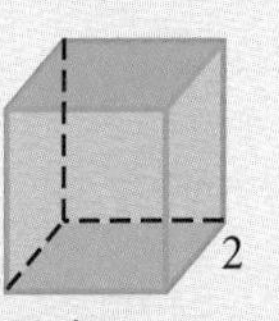

Right square prism

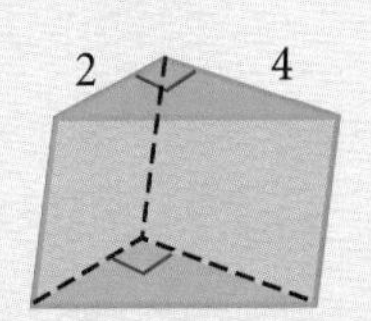

Oblique triangular prism

9. Create a table of formulas for the surface area and volume of a regular triangular prism, a square prism, and a regular hexagonal prism, each with base sides of length *s* and height *h*. [9-1, 9-2]

10. The diameter and height of a cylinder are equal. A cone of the same radius and height is inscribed in the cylinder. What is the volume of the cylinder that is not occupied by the cone? This volume is that of another familiar solid. Describe the solid and give its dimensions. [9-2]

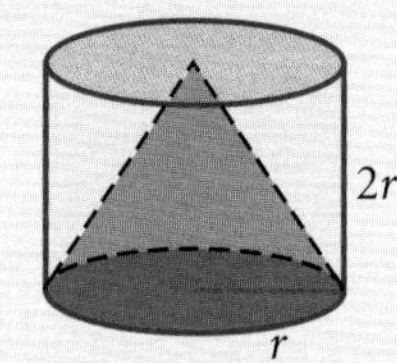

11. In general, the greater an object's surface area in comparison to its volume, the faster it will heat up or cool down. [9-1, 9-2]

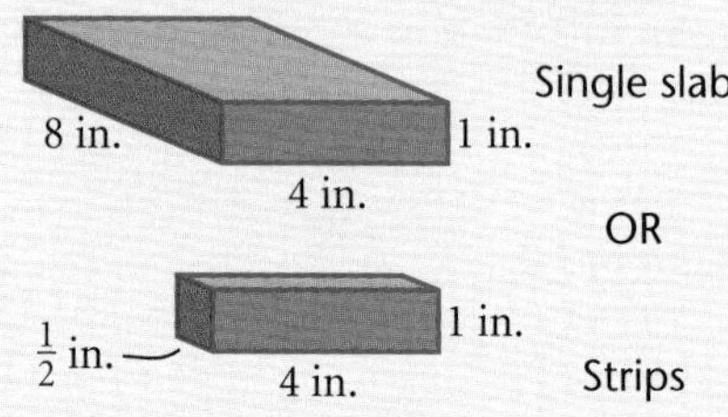

a. Imagine a slice of fish as a rectangular prism. Calculate the surface area and volume of a single slab of fish with the dimensions shown. Find the ratio of surface area to volume.

b. Repeat these calculations for the same slab cut into strips of the size shown.

c. When cooked at the same temperature, which form of the fish will cook more quickly? Which form will hold its heat better during a long meal?

12. A cylindrical petroleum tank has diameter 40 m and height 30 m. How many times more petroleum can a similar tank hold if it is three times as tall? [9-3]

CONCEPTS AND CONNECTIONS

Industry

13. Photography An *enlarger* is used to expose paper to light passing through a negative. The paper is more brightly illuminated when the enlarger's head is lowered because the same amount of light is dispersed over a smaller area. Let L be the total amount of light hitting the paper. Then the intensity of the light is the amount of light per square inch, or $I = \frac{L}{\text{Area of base}}$.

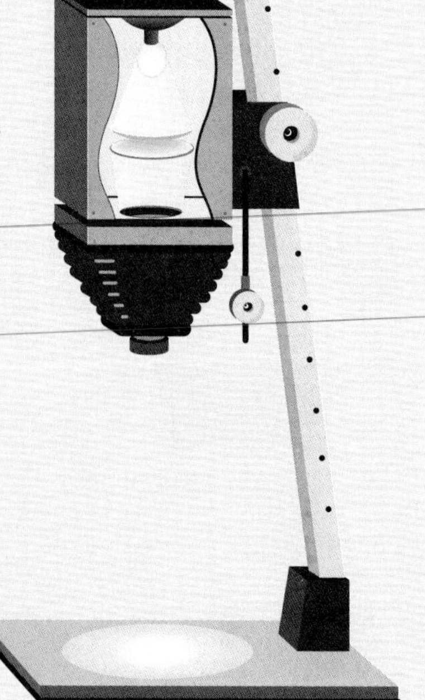

a. Make a table with columns for the height and radius of the cone, the area of the cone's base, and the intensity of light. When the enlarger is 2 in. above the paper, the radius of the cone is 1 in. Fill in a row of the table using this information, leaving entries in terms of L and π.

b. Use similarity to help complete table rows for cone heights of 4 in. and 8 in.

c. Describe how intensity is affected by doubling the height.

SELF-EVALUATION

Write a summary of the most important facts about surface area and volume that you learned from Chapter 9. Describe at least one technique you can use to help learn a concept you found difficult.

Chapter 9 Assessment

TEST

Find the surface area and volume of each solid to the nearest tenth.

1.

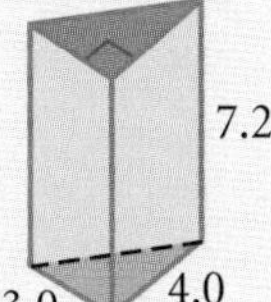

2.

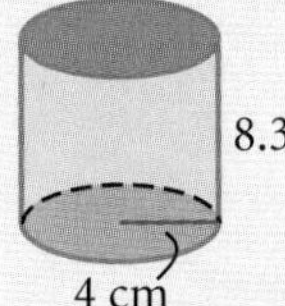

3.

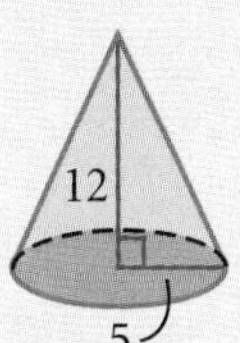

4.

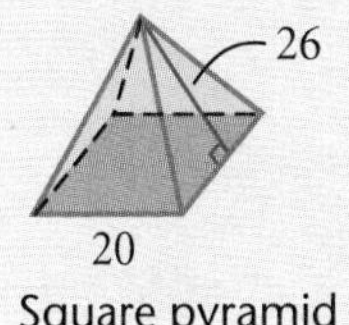

5. The surface area of a sphere is 100π. Find its volume.

6. The similarity ratio between two similar solids is k. Write a summary of the ratios between different pairs of corresponding measures of the solids. Include measures of length, surface area, and volume.

7. If the uniform rainfall over a 2-mi.-square town is 2 in., what is the total volume of rainfall in cubic feet? If all of the rain drains into a small circular lake with a diameter of 0.5 mi, how many feet will the level of the lake rise?

8. The Transamerica Pyramid in San Francisco is approximately a square pyramid. Its base has sides 145 ft long, and the pyramid is 786 ft tall. A 3-ft-tall scale model is built.

a. To the nearest hundredth, what is the side length of the model's base?

b. To the nearest tenth, what is the model's lateral surface area?

9. In the figure at the right, a sphere is inscribed in a cylinder.

a. Find the ratio of the volume of the cylinder to that of the sphere.

b. Find the ratio of the surface area of the cylinder to that of the sphere.

c. Describe what is special about these ratios.

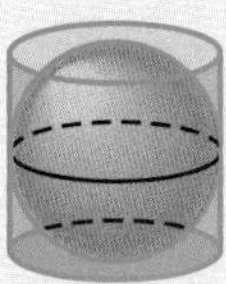

PERFORMANCE TASK

Before it erupted, Mount St. Helens had the approximate shape of a cone with a diameter of 30,000 ft and a height of 9700 ft. After the May 1980 eruption, the volcano lost its top—a cone 1200 ft in height.

One of the World Trade Center towers in New York is a 1350-ft-tall square prism with bases 210 ft on a side. Guess how many World Trade Center towers would make up the same volume as the destroyed top of Mount St. Helens. Then apply properties of similarity to find the approximate volume of the removed volcano top. Also find the volume of the tower and the number of towers that would fit in the volcano top. How good was your guess?

Chapter 10 Transformations and Patterns

Project A
We're Here to Stay
How does a corporate logo give the impression that a company is reliable and stable?

Project B
Grip the Road
How many kinds of tire treads are there? How is tread design matched to road conditions?

Project C
Deck the Walls
How is wallpaper designed? How do interior designers combine motifs on the same wall for unity and variety?

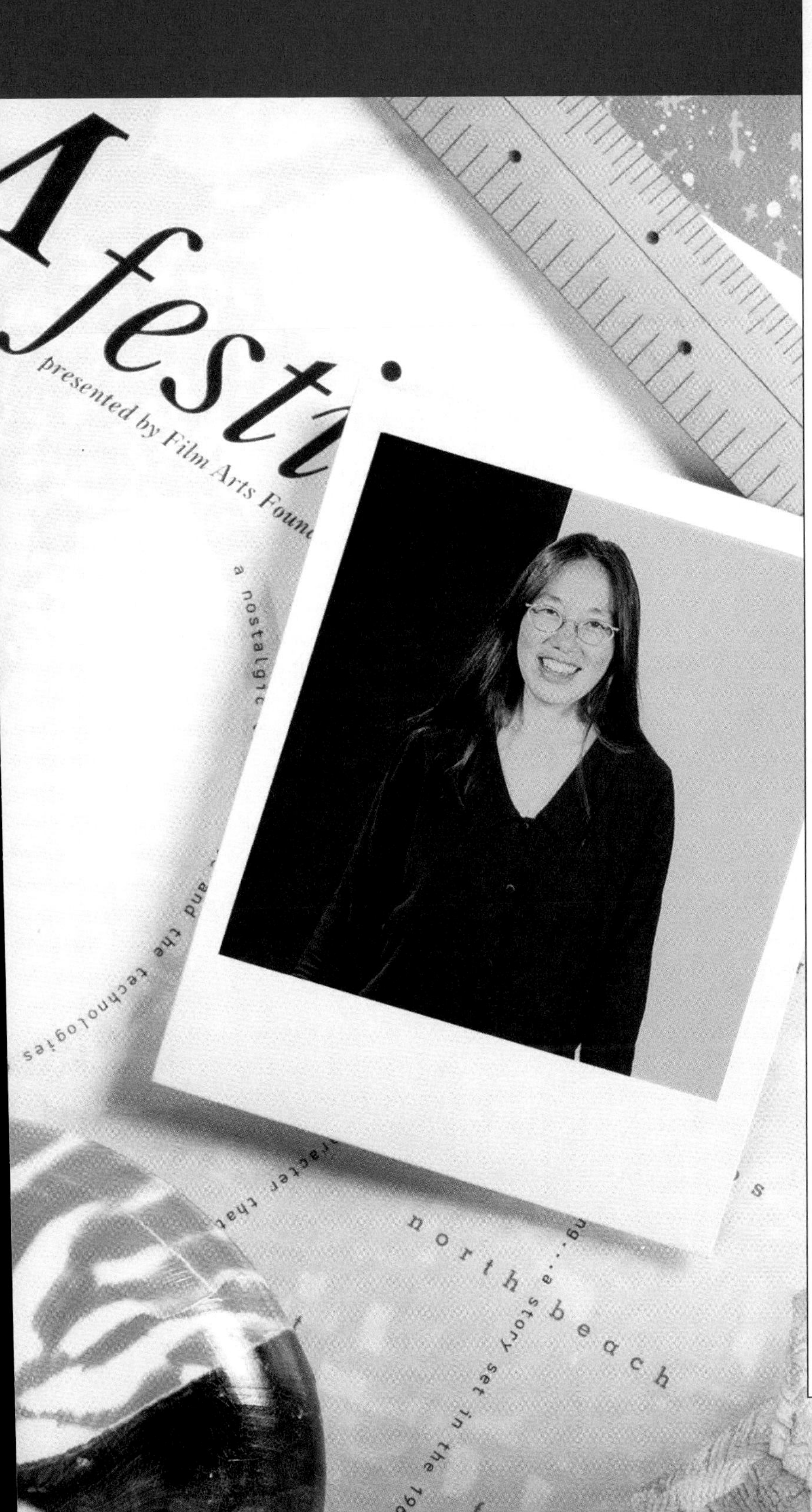

F. TANI HASEGAWA

I never really thought about liking or disliking math in high school. I always liked numbers, and I still find myself counting in my mind as I do things.

Math is a language to me. It can be used to gain an understanding of the world around us, and to show us underlying connections and a certain sense of order. Things like form, pattern, sequence, and rhythm can be expressed mathematically, and are things we live with, create, and find in nature every day. I find beauty in this, and use this in my work to help people visually express ideas and organize information.

F. tani Hasegawa
Designer
OPEN MOUTH
San Francisco, CA

F. tani Hasegawa

Chapter 10 Transformations and Patterns

GETTING READY

10-1 Putting Transformations Together

In 10-1 you will look at combinations of transformations. You will use the following skills from previous courses and chapters.

Graph each equation on a coordinate plane. [Previous course]

1. $y = 2x + 5$ **2.** $y = 3$ **3.** $y = \frac{1}{2}x - 6$ **4.** $x = -2$

5. $y = x^2 + 7$ **6.** $y = (x + 3)^2$ **7.** $y = |x + 2|$ **8.** $y = \sqrt{x + 4}$

Match each figure with the type(s) of symmetry it exhibits: [1-4, 3-2]

a) rotational symmetry **b) vertical line symmetry** **c) horizontal symmetry**

9. **10.**

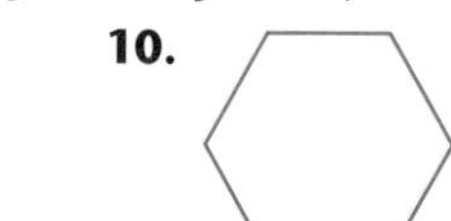

11.

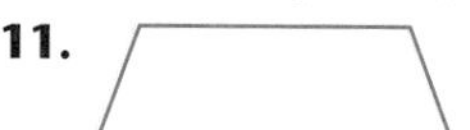

12.

10-2 Classifying Patterns

In 10-2 you will apply your knowledge of transformational geometry and symmetry to frieze and wallpaper patterns. You will use the following skills from previous courses and chapters.

Continue each pattern. [Previous course]

13. Σ ∫ ∫ Σ ∫ ∫ Σ ∫ ∫ Σ ∫ . . . **14.** < > < < > > < < < > > > . . .

15. * - * - * - * - * * - * - * . . . **16.** [[X]] [[X]] [[X]] . . .

Line ℓ is a line of reflection in the figure. What is the reflection image of: [1-4]

17. A?

18. $\overline{EF}$?

19. $\triangle KLM$?

20. J?

21. $\overline{NO}$?

22. R?

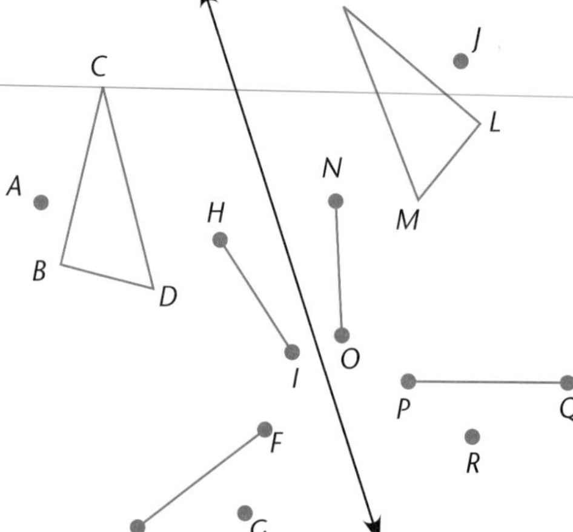

10-1 Putting Transformations Together

Pushing Paper

Mark Thomas is now an engineer for General Motors, but he didn't know much about engineering when his high school guidance counselors suggested it as a career. Now he helps high school students learn all about engineering. Thomas's "paper car" program earned him two national awards including 1993 Black Engineer of the Year for Community Service from *US Black Engineer* magazine.

Thomas developed a 12-week program where students design and build cars made entirely of paper. The cars are 5 ft tall, can be steered, and are designed to run on "push-power" (since real engines give off sparks).

The idea for the program came to Thomas and two colleagues (Vincent and Elliott Lyons) in 1990 while they were getting their master's degrees in mechanical engineering at Stanford University. The three were also teaching engineering at a high school in the San Francisco Bay Area.

Six Detroit area high schools now feature the program. Students attend class twice during the week, and most attend three-hour Saturday sessions. General Motors and two paper companies pay for equipment and supplies, and GM engineers act as instructors.

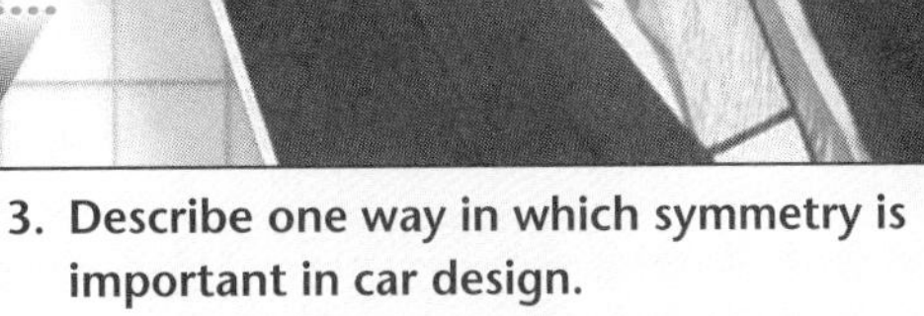

1. **How do you think most students decide on a career to pursue?**
2. **Describe how you might find out more about engineering as a career.**
3. **Describe one way in which symmetry is important in car design.**

10-1 PART A Isometries

← CONNECT → ***You've already studied four transformations: reflections, rotations, translations, and dilations. Now you will review your knowledge of each of these transformations, learn what an isometry is, and see which of the transformations you've studied are isometries.***

A general term for change is *transformation:* for example, from seed to plant, or from caterpillar to butterfly. In geometry, transformations include the reflections, translations, rotations, and dilations that you investigated earlier.

TRY IT

Assume that each image shown in the figures below is created by a single transformation. Determine whether the transformation shown is a reflection, rotation, translation, or dilation. If the transformation is a reflection, identify the line of reflection. If it is a rotation, identify the center and angle of the rotation. If it is a translation, give the translation vector. If it is a dilation, identify the center and scale factor.

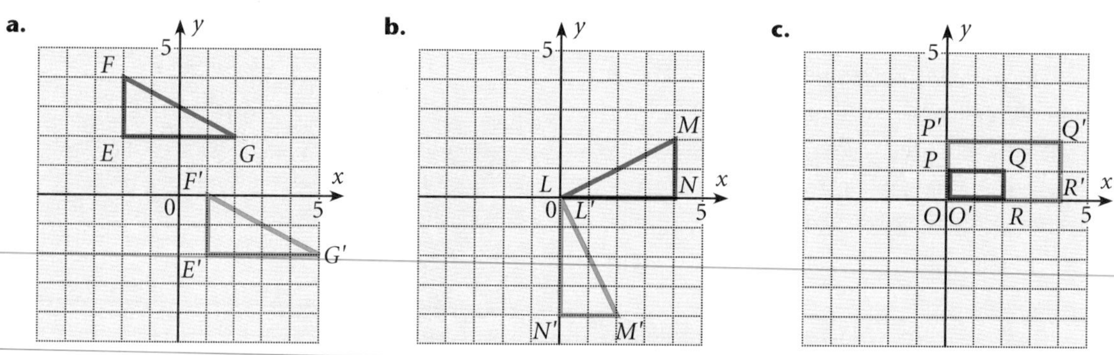

For some transformations, the distance between any two points on the pre-image and the distance between the corresponding points on the image is always the same. (For any points A and B and their images A' and B', $AB = A'B'$.) Transformations that preserve distance have a special name.

DEFINITION

An **isometry** is a transformation that preserves distance.

1. **Isometries can be called *congruence transformations*. Explain why this makes sense.**

In the following Explore, you will review the properties of the four transformations you've studied and discover which of these transformations are isometries.

EXPLORE: ISOMETRY GEOMETRY

MATERIALS

Protractor, Ruler
Geometry software (optional)

1. Use geometry software or a protractor and ruler to investigate the properties of the four transformations. Which preserve distance? angle measure? shape? size? orientation? congruence? (Hint: Start with a simple figure, such as $\triangle ABC$. Then carry out each of the four transformations on the figure.) Prepare a table to show your results.
2. Which of the four transformations are isometries? Explain how you identified the isometries.

THEOREM

Translations, reflections, and rotations are isometries.

REFLECT

1. Suppose you take a paper car, push it 10 ft forward, and then turn it on its top. Is this transformation of the original paper car an isometry? Why or why not?
2. If you take a rubber band and stretch it taut, is this transformation of the original rubber band an isometry? Why or why not?

Exercises

CORE

Getting Started For each pair of figures, identify a single transformation that maps one figure onto the other. State whether the transformation is an isometry.

1.

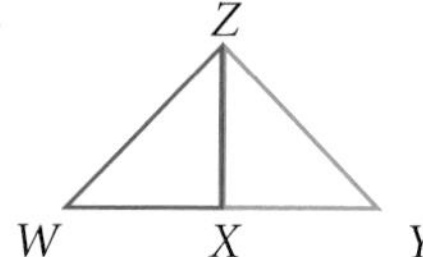

2.

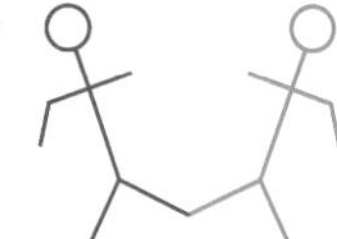

3.

4.

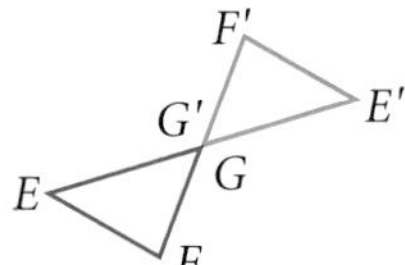

Using the tessellation shown, identify each transformation.

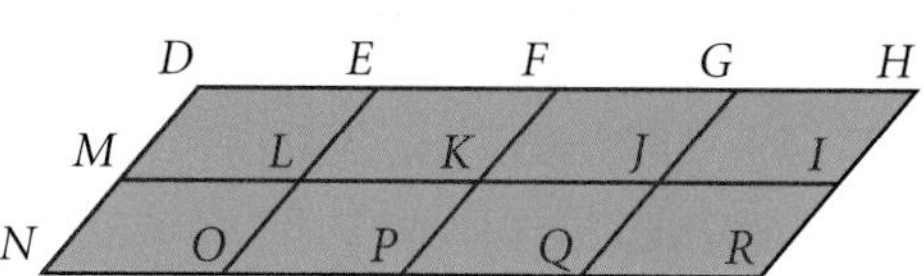

5. Segment $\overline{DE}$ is the image of $\overline{FG}$.

6. Angle $\angle LKP$ is the image of $\angle JKF$.

7. Segment $\overline{ML}$ is the image of $\overline{KL}$.

8. From the four terms below, choose the term that does not belong, and explain why.

rotation, reflection, dilation, translation

Determine whether the transformation shown in each figure below is a reflection, rotation, translation, or dilation. If the transformation is a reflection, identify the line of reflection. If it is a rotation, identify the center and angle of the rotation. If it is a translation, give the translation vector. If it is a dilation, identify the center and scale factor.

9.

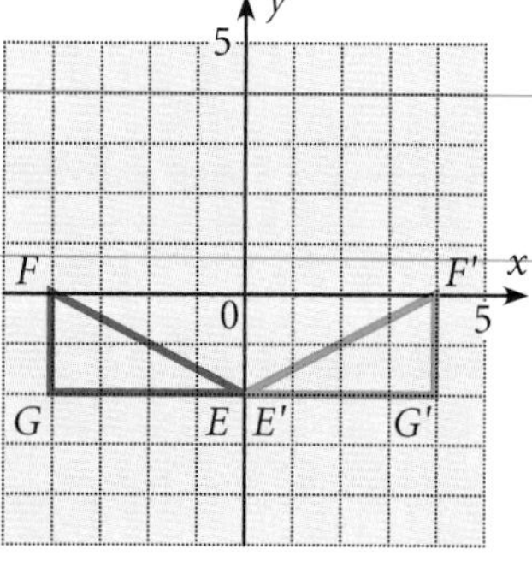

10.

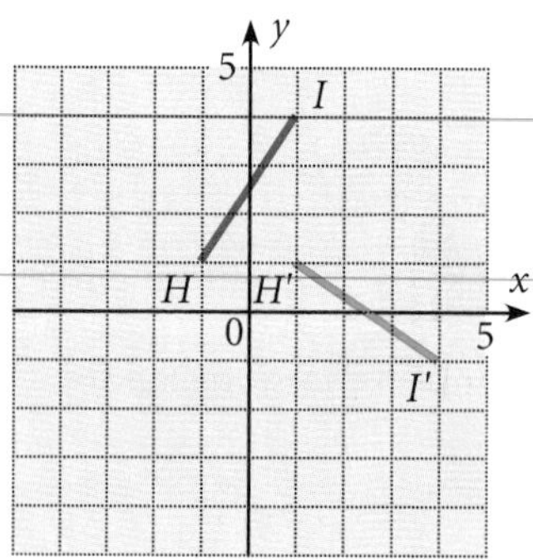

11.

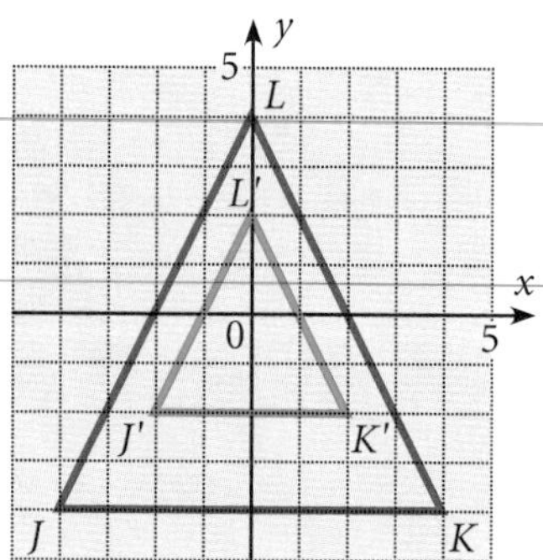

12. A famous psychological test developed by Hermann Rorschach involves looking at an inkblot and describing what you see.

Social Science

a. Sketch a rough copy of the inkblot shown. Show the line of symmetry for the blot.

b. What do you see in this inkblot?

13. **Camping Crisis** Jonah's tent is on fire! He needs to get water from the river and get back to his tent as quickly as he can, so he must find the shortest possible route from his position, J, to the river and then to his tent, T.

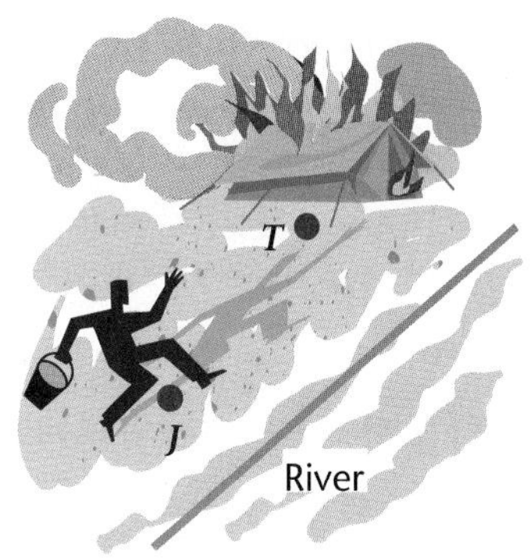

You can find the shortest route from a point to a line to another point by using a reflection. Copy the figure at the right. Reflect T over the line created by the river. Call the image T'. Draw $\overline{JT'}$, and label as P the point where $\overline{JT'}$ intersects the river. The path from J to P to T is the shortest possible path. Why?

14. A dilation is not an isometry. However, one type of dilation does preserve distance. What is the scale factor of a dilation that preserves distance?

15. **Shoreline Shortcut** In a swimming race, contestants begin at A, swim to any point on the shoreline, and finish at B. Copy the figure. Then use a reflection to show where the contestant should touch the shoreline in order to swim the shortest possible route.

LOOK AHEAD

Graph each equation on a coordinate plane.

16. $y = x + 4$

17. $y = x^2 - 2$

18. $y = (x - 1)^2$

19. What is the graph of a quadratic equation called?

20. A single reflection reverses orientation. What happens to the orientation of a figure after it is reflected over two lines? Draw a sketch to illustrate your answer.

MORE PRACTICE

For each pair of figures, identify a single transformation that maps one figure onto the other. State whether the transformation is or is not an isometry.

21.

22.

23.

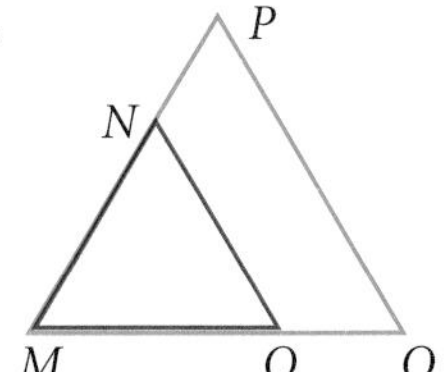

Determine whether the transformation shown in each figure below is a reflection, rotation, translation, or dilation. If the transformation is a reflection, identify the line of reflection. If it is a rotation, identify the center and angle of the rotation. If it is a translation, give the translation vector. If it is a dilation, identify the center and scale factor.

24.

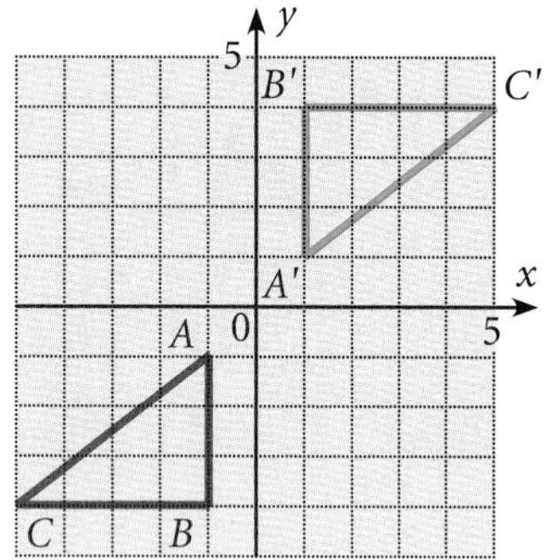

25.

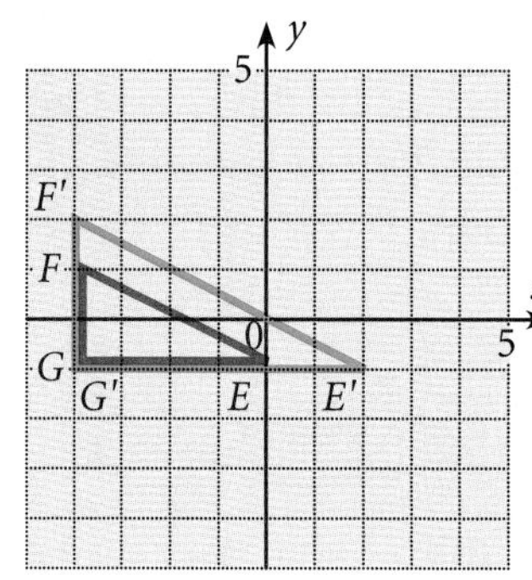

26.

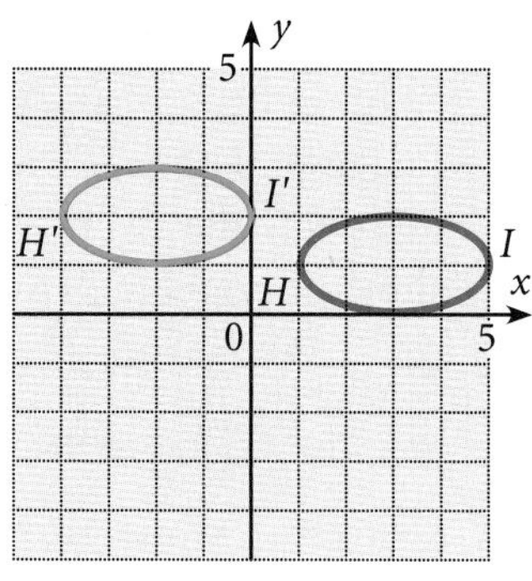

MORE MATH REASONING

27. Mapping the Globe One way to make a flat map of the world is based on wrapping a piece of paper around the equator of a globe to form a cylinder, as shown. C is the center of the earth. Every point P on the globe's surface is projected along ray $\overrightarrow{CP}$ to a point P' on the cylinder.

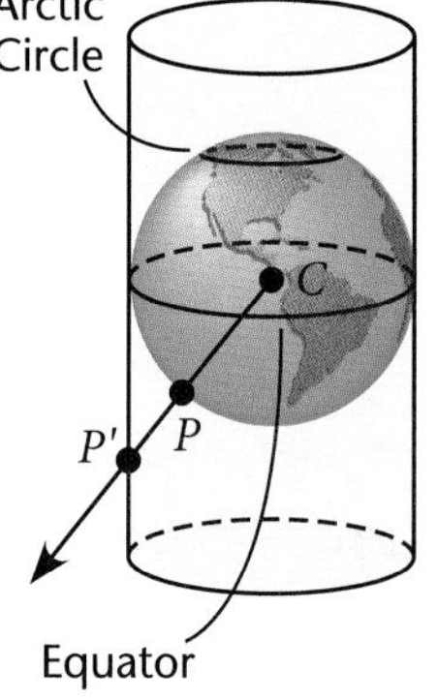

a. Describe the image of the globe's equator.

b. Compare the size of the image of the Arctic Circle to that of the image of the equator.

c. Are there points that have no image? If so, describe them.

d. When the globe is projected onto the cylinder, are distances near the equator distorted more or less than those near the North Pole? Explain.

28. Transformations in Braille In the early 1800s, a fifteen-year-old blind student, Louis Braille, devised an alphabet that used raised dots to represent numbers and letters. Books printed in Braille are read with the fingers.

History

a b c d e f g h i j

k l m n o p q r s t

u v w x y z

Refer to the Braille alphabet on page 672 for the following.

a. Some pairs of letters in the Braille alphabet are reflections of each other. Sketch each pair, and show the line of reflection.

b. Some pairs of letters are rotations of each other. Sketch each pair, and indicate the center of rotation.

c. No pairs of letters are translations of each other. Why?

d. Describe any other patterns that Braille may have used in this alphabet.

10-1 PART B Compositions of Transformations

← CONNECT → ***You've transformed geometric figures, but you have mainly done one transformation at a time. Now you will investigate what happens when a figure undergoes more than one transformation.***

You may be familiar with the idea of a composite photograph—one made by superimposing one or more photographs. Because a computer can make a composite photo look like an actual one, photographs are no longer considered good evidence in court. A popular special effect in movies is called *morphing*. This effect changes one image into another. The photos below show a morphing sequence from the movie *Willow*.

The idea of changing one figure into another using a series of transformations is also important in geometry.

DEFINITION

When two or more transformations are performed on a figure, one after another, the result is the **composition** of the transformations.

COMPOSITIONS OF TRANSFORMATIONS

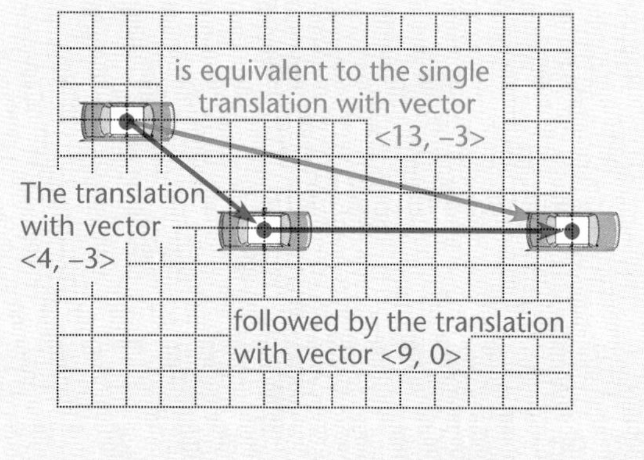

is equivalent to the single translation with vector <13, –3>
The translation with vector <4, –3>
followed by the translation with vector <9, 0>

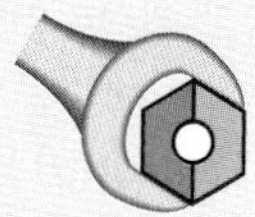

A clockwise rotation of 90°

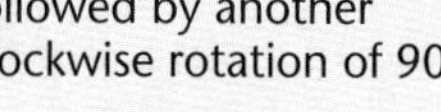

followed by another clockwise rotation of 90°

is equivalent to a single clockwise rotation of 180° around the same center.

In analyzing a composition of transformations, the original figure is considered the pre-image for the composition, and the final figure is the image.

TRY IT

Find a single transformation equivalent to the composition of each pair of transformations.

a. a 75° counterclockwise rotation with center (2, 1) followed by a 38° counterclockwise rotation with center (2, 1)

b. a translation with vector <−2, 7> followed by a translation with vector <9, 3>

We have looked at the compositions of two translations and of two rotations. In the following Explore, you will investigate the composition of two reflections.

EXPLORE: REFLECTING ON COMPOSITIONS

Find a single transformation that is equivalent to the composition of two reflections. In other words, what happens when you reflect a figure over one line, then reflect the image over a second line? Explain how the position of the lines of reflection affects your results. (Hint: Does it matter whether the two lines of reflection intersect?)

MATERIALS

Compass, Ruler

Some compositions of transformations are equivalent to a single transformation. The ones that you have seen are summarized below.

EQUIVALENT TRANSFORMATIONS

These transformations . . .	are equivalent to . . .
Two translations 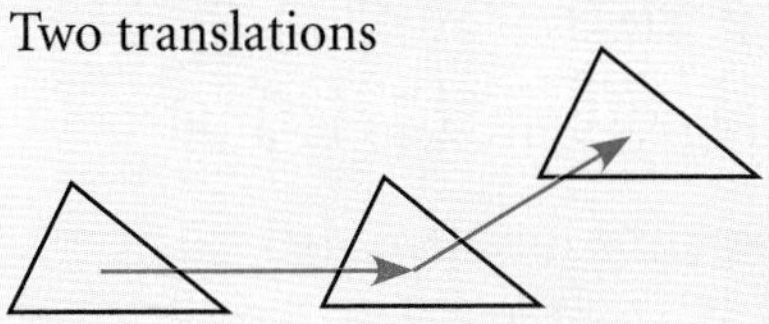	One translation 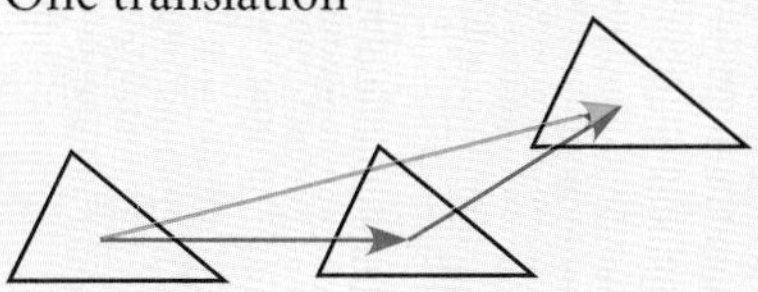
Two rotations (same center) 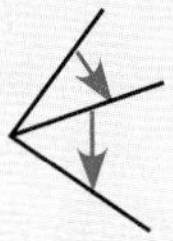	One rotation 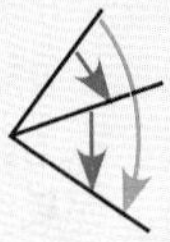
Reflections over two parallel lines 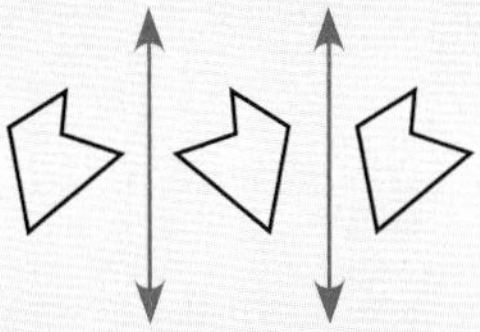	One translation 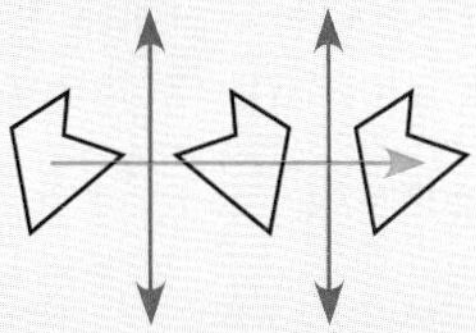
Reflections over two intersecting lines 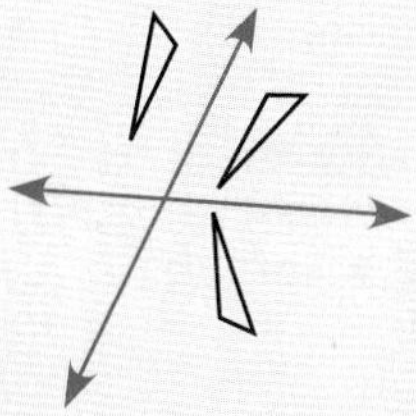	One rotation 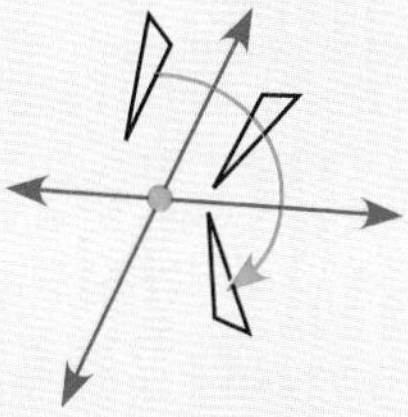

REFLECT

1. Is the composition of two rotations around the same center always equivalent to a single rotation? If so, describe the rotation.
2. Suppose a figure is dilated twice. If the center of the dilations is the same, is their composition equivalent to one of the four basic transformations? If so, which one is it? If not, why not?
3. Reflecting a figure over two intersecting lines is equivalent to a rotation of the figure. Describe the center of the rotation.

Exercises

CORE

Getting Started Complete each statement.

1. Two translations are equivalent to a single ____.
2. Two rotations around the same center are equivalent to a single ____.
3. Two reflections over intersecting lines are equivalent to a single ____.
4. Two reflections over parallel lines are equivalent to a single ____.

Find a single transformation that is equivalent to the composition of each pair of transformations. If this transformation is a reflection, identify the line of reflection. If it is a rotation, identify the center and angle of the rotation. If it is a translation, give the translation vector. If it is a dilation, identify the center and scale factor.

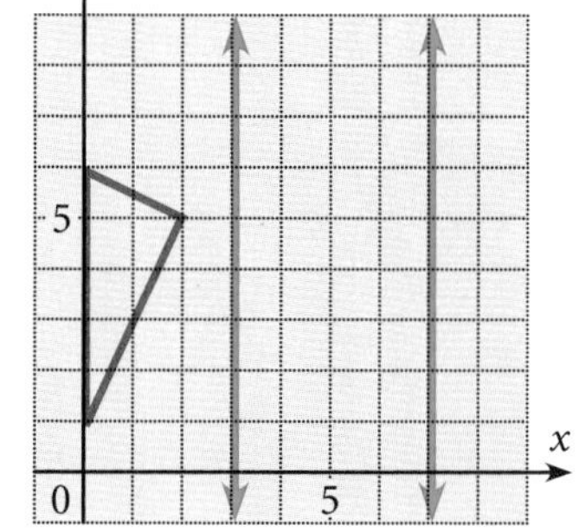

5. a 46° clockwise rotation with center (4, −2) followed by a 71° clockwise rotation with center (4, −2)
6. translation <−4, 3> followed by translation <2, −7>
7. a reflection over the line $x = 3$ followed by a reflection over the line $x = 7$ (Use the figure to help you.)

Complete each statement with *always, sometimes,* or *never.* Explain your answers.

8. The composition of two reflections is ____ equivalent to a translation.
9. The composition of two isometries is ____ an isometry.
10. The composition of two rotations is ____ equivalent to a reflection.

Which of the following compositions of transformations are isometries? Explain your answers.

11. two translations
12. a translation and a dilation
13. two reflections
14. $\triangle BCA$ and $\triangle CDE$ are equilateral. Describe a composition of two or more transformations that maps $\triangle BCA$ onto $\triangle CDE$.

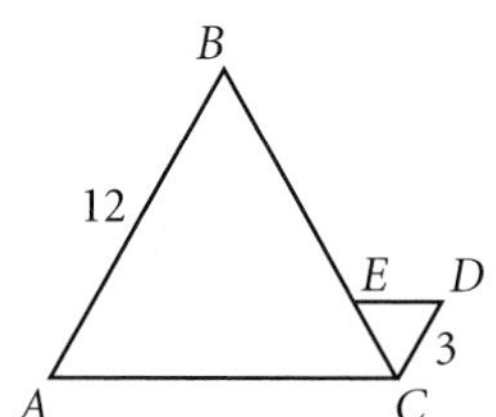

15. Sloppy Copy A malfunctioning copy machine randomly gives copies that are either enlarged by a scale factor of 2 or reduced by a scale factor of $\frac{1}{2}$. If a copy is made, and then a copy is made of that copy, what is the probability that the final copy will be congruent to the original?

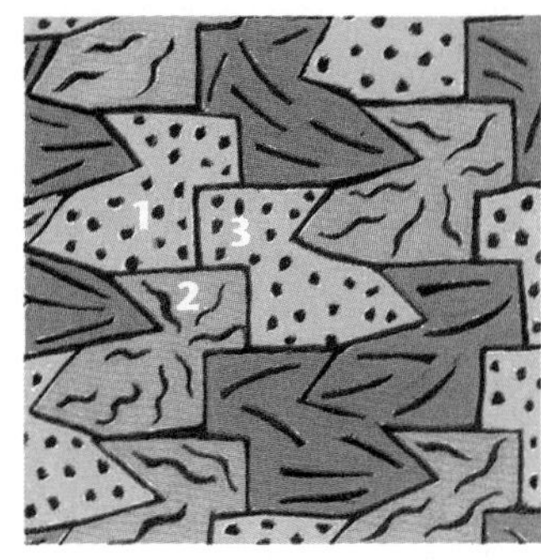

16. Using the tessellation at the right, describe a transformation or composition of transformations that can be used for the following mappings.

a. figure 1 onto figure 2

b. figure 1 onto figure 3

c. figure 2 onto figure 3

***Inverse transformations* are transformations that undo each other. For example, the translation <2, −5> and the translation <−2, 5> are inverse transformations. Find an inverse transformation for each of the following transformations.**

17. translation <−3, 4>

18. a clockwise rotation of 30° around (2, 4)

19. a dilation with scale factor $\frac{3}{2}$ and center at the origin

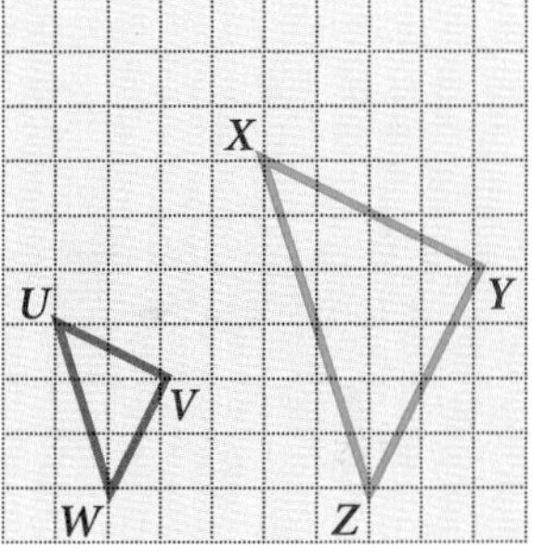

20. The two triangles at the right are similar.

a. Describe a composition of transformations that maps the figure on the left onto the figure on the right.

b. Do you think *any* figure can be mapped onto a similar figure by a series of transformations? Write a brief justification of your answer.

c. A composition of an isometry and a dilation is called a **similarity transformation.** Explain why this term makes sense.

LOOK BACK

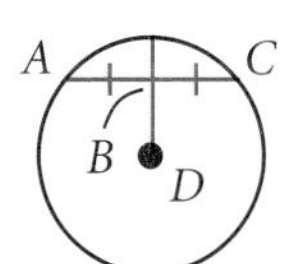

21. $AC = 22$ and $DC = 14$. Find the distance of chord $\overline{AC}$ from the center of the circle, D. [8-2]

22. Box Car A rough design for the body of a car is shown. The design uses two right rectangular prisms.

a. Find the volume of the car body. [9-2]

b. Do you think this design is a good one? If so, explain why. If not, describe some changes you would make, and explain why you would make those changes.

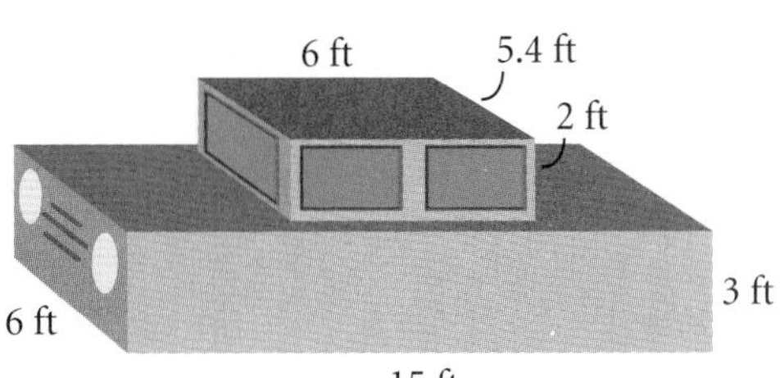

MORE PRACTICE

Find a single transformation that is equivalent to the composition of each pair of transformations. If this transformation is a reflection, identify the line of reflection. If it is a rotation, identify the center and angle of the rotation. If it is a translation, give the translation vector. If it is a dilation, identify the center and scale factor.

23. translation <3, −6> followed by translation <0, 5>

24. a 102° counterclockwise rotation with center (2, −3) followed by a 219° clockwise rotation with center (2, −3)

Which of the following compositions of transformations are isometries? Explain your answers.

25. two rotations

26. a translation and a rotation

27. a dilation and a reflection

MORE MATH REASONING

28. a. The figure at the right shows three vectors. Write a vector-sum equation based on the figure.

b. Are there any similarities between the composition of transformations and vector addition? If so, explain the connection.

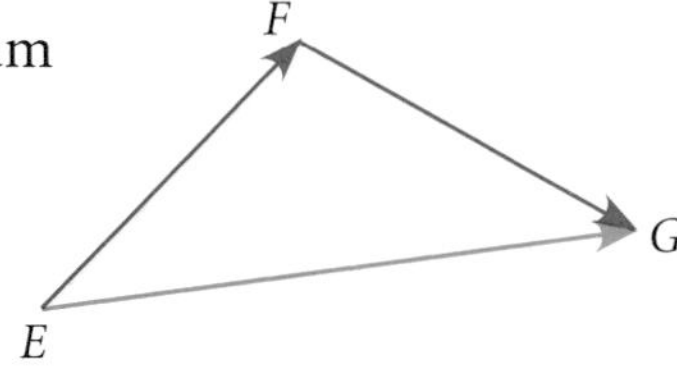

29. Are transformations commutative? In other words, if you perform any two transformations on a figure, do you get the same result regardless of the order of the transformations? Write a brief explanation of the method you used to solve this problem.

30. A line is an axis of symmetry of a cube if a rotation (of less than 360°) of the cube about the line maps the cube to itself. For example, line n is one line of symmetry for the cube shown. How many different lines of symmetry does a cube have?

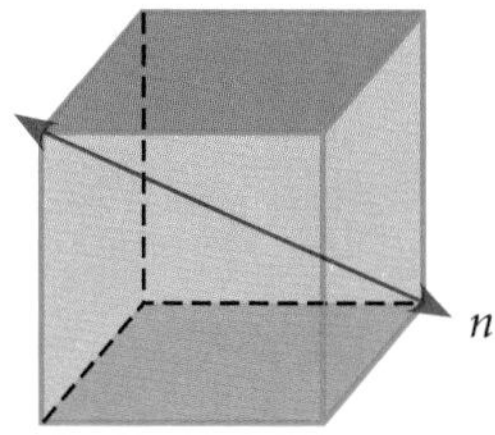

10-1 PART C Transformations of Algebraic Functions

← CONNECT → ***You've already studied functions in algebra. Now you will examine transformations of functions. You will investigate how a change in an equation affects the graph of the equation.***

Although you have usually performed transformations on geometric figures, transformations can also give you insights into the graphs of algebraic functions.

Graphs of whole families of functions are transformations of the graph of a **parent equation.** For example, the graph of any linear equation can be thought of as a transformation or composition of transformations of the parent equation $y = x$.

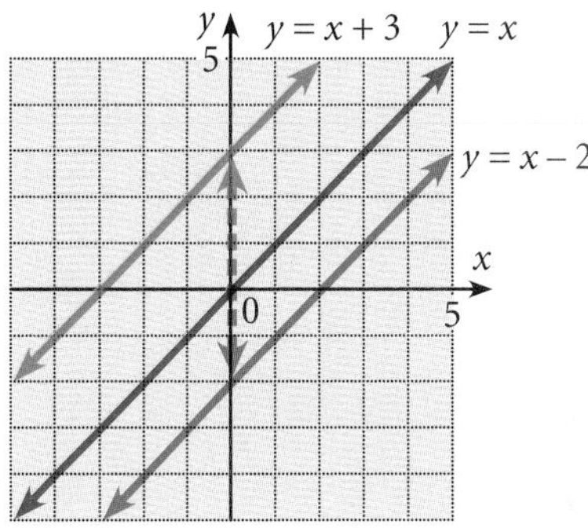

EXPLORE: PARABOLA MOVING CO.

MATERIALS

Graph paper
Graphing utility (optional)

1. On a graphing utility or graph paper, draw an accurate graph of the parent equation $y = x^2$. Then describe the characteristics of the graph. Where is its vertex (turning point)? Does the curve turn upwards (∪) or turn downwards (∩)? Are there any symmetry lines?
2. On the same screen or sheet of paper, graph some other equations of the form $y = x^2 + k$ (where $k \neq 0$), such as $y = x^2 + 2$ and $y = x^2 - 3$. Notice where the vertex of each graph is. Use transformations to compare the graph of $y = x^2 + k$ to the graph of the parent equation $y = x^2$.
3. On a new screen or sheet of paper, graph $y = x^2$ and $y = -x^2$. Use transformations to describe the difference between the graphs. If you need more evidence, graph other pairs of equations, like $y = x^3$ and $y = -x^3$.
4. The graph of the function $y = -x^2 + k$ can be described as a composition of two transformations of the parent equation $y = x^2$. Identify the two transformations. Which one is associated with the negative sign? Which one is associated with the k term?

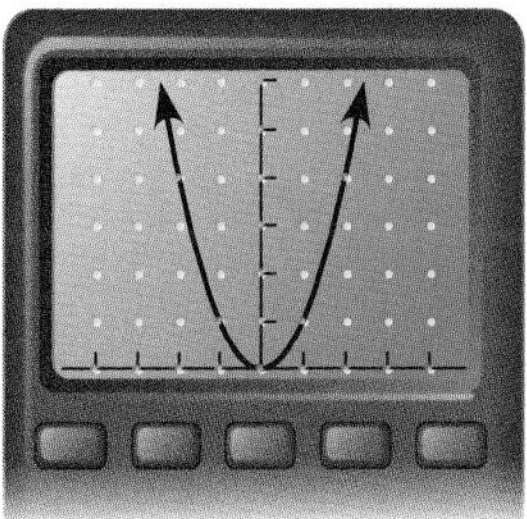

TRY IT

Sketch the graph of $y = x^2$. Starting with this graph as a guide, use transformations to help you sketch the graph of each of the following on the same set of axes.

a. $y = x^2 + 1$ **b.** $y = -x^2 + 1$ **c.** $y = -x^2 - 3$

EXAMPLE

The graph of a parent equation, $y = \Diamond$, is shown at the right. With this graph as a guide, sketch graphs of the equations $y = -\Diamond$ and $y = -\Diamond - 1$.

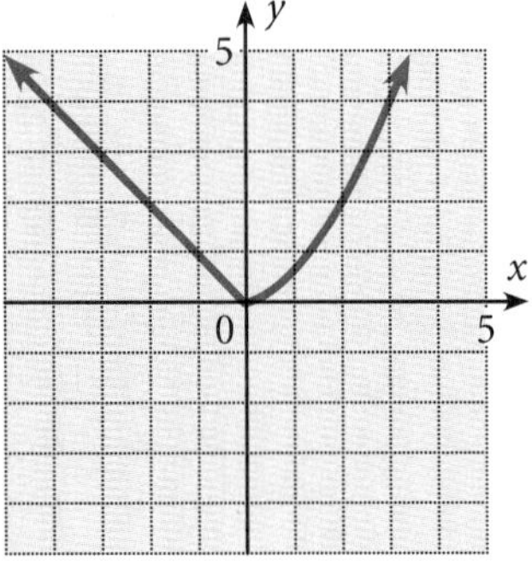

The negative sign in front of the $\Diamond$ in $y = -\Diamond$ tells us that its graph is a reflection of the parent equation over the x-axis. The -1 in the equation $y = -\Diamond - 1$ tells us that the reflected graph is then translated down 1 unit.

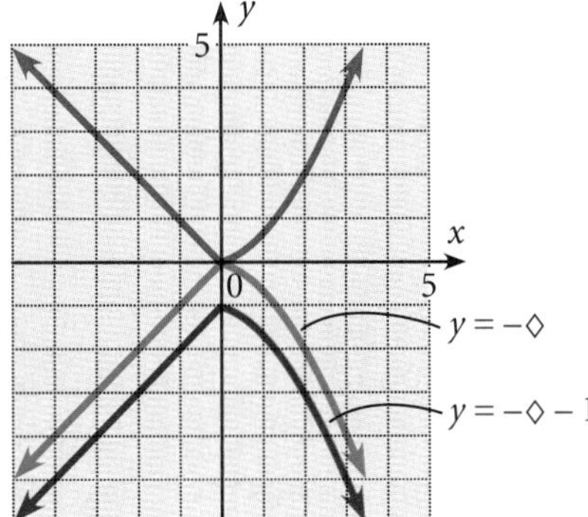

REFLECT

1. What is the vertex of $y = x^2 + k$? How can you tell whether the graph of this equation turns upwards or downwards?

2. Suppose that the point (0, 1) is on the graph of the parent equation $y = \mu$. Give the coordinates of a point on the graph of the equation $y = \mu + 4$.

3. Suppose you are given the graph of $y = \psi$ and need to sketch the graph of $y = -\psi + 2$. Do you get different graphs if you begin by reflecting the graph of $y = \psi$ and then translating the result than if you begin by translating the graph of $y = \psi$ and then reflecting the result? Explain.

Exercises

CORE

1. **Getting Started** Sketch the graph of $y = x$. With this graph as a guide, use transformations to help you sketch the graph of each of the following on the same set of axes. Label each graph.
   a. $y = x + 2$ **b.** $y = x - 3$ **c.** $y = -x + 1$

2. Sketch the graph of $y = x^2$. With this graph as a guide, use transformations to help you sketch the graph of each of the following on the same set of axes. Label each graph.
   a. $y = x^2 + 4$ **b.** $y = -x^2 - 2$ **c.** $y = x^2 - 3$

3. The graph of the parent equation for absolute value functions, $y = |x|$, is shown at the right. Using this graph as a guide, sketch graphs of the following on the same set of axes. Label each graph.

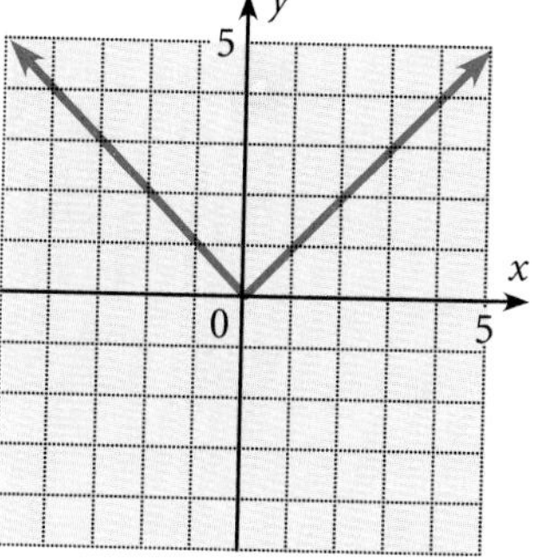

   a. $y = |x| + 3$ **b.** $y = -|x|$
   c. $y = -|x| - 2$
   d. Explain how you used the parent equation to help make your sketches.

Write the word or phrase that correctly completes each statement.

4. The graph of $y = x^2 + 2$ is a ____ of the graph of $y = x^2$.

5. The graph of $y = -x^2$ is a ____ of the graph of $y = x^2$.

Industry

6. **Many Happy Returns** Two students have started their own birthday-card business. They need \$40 for supplies to get started, and they charge \$2 for each hand-drawn card.
   a. Write an equation that expresses their profit, P, in terms of the number of cards they sell, n. Sketch the graph of this equation.
   b. They find that the supplies they need are on sale for 40% off. Write a new equation for their profit.
   c. Sketch the graph of this equation on the same axes. Use transformations to describe the difference between the graphs, and explain why this makes sense.

7. **a.** Draw a graph of each of the following three equations on the same set of axes. Label each graph.
   i. $y = x^2$ **ii.** $y = (x + 2)^2$ **iii.** $y = (x - 3)^2$
   b. Compare the graph of $y = (x + h)^2$ to the graph of $y = x^2$.
   c. Using transformations, make a quick sketch of the graph of each of the following equations on the same set of axes. Label each graph.
   i. $y = (x + 3)^2$ **ii.** $y = (x - 2)^2$ **iii.** $y = (x - 2)^2 + 3$

8. The graph of a parent equation, $y = ¤$, is shown at the right. Using this graph as a guide, sketch graphs of the following on the same set of axes. Label each graph.

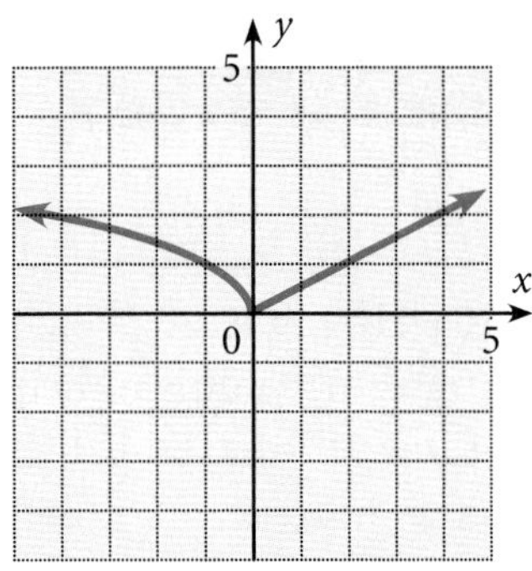

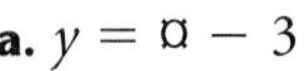

a. $y = ¤ - 3$
b. $y = -¤ + 3$
c. $y = -¤ + 1$

Industry

9. Suppose that a company manufacturing an item discovers that the cost, c, in hundreds of dollars, of producing n items is approximated by the equation $c = \sqrt{n} + 20$.

a. Sketch a graph of this equation.

b. Find the average cost to produce one item for each of the following production levels.

i. $n = 1$ **ii.** $n = 25$ **iii.** $n = 160$

c. Under this model, does the average cost to produce the item increase, decrease, or stay the same as production levels increase? Do you think this is usually true for manufacturing companies?

d. What do you think the number 20 represents in the cost equation $c = \sqrt{n} + 20$?

LOOK AHEAD

Match each letter on the left with the type(s) of symmetry it exhibits on the right.

10. H	(a) rotational symmetry
11. A	(b) vertical line symmetry
12. S	(c) horizontal line symmetry
13. K	

MORE PRACTICE

14. The graph of the parent equation for square-root functions, $y = \sqrt{x}$, is shown at the right. Using this equation as a guide, sketch graphs of the following on the same set of axes. Label each graph.

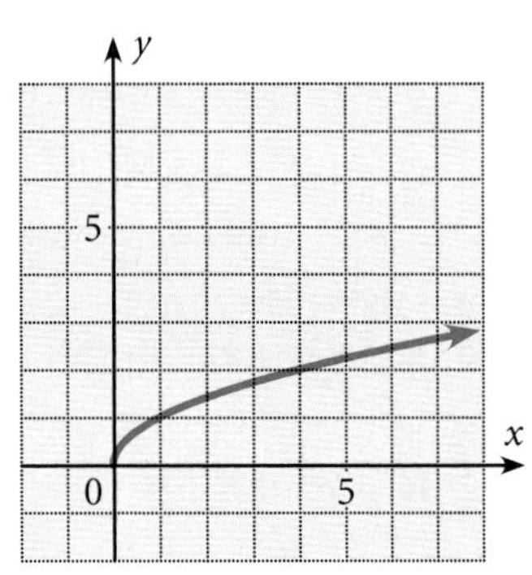

a. $y = \sqrt{x} + 2$ **b.** $y = -\sqrt{x}$
c. $y = -\sqrt{x} - 4$
d. Explain how you used the parent equation to help make your sketches.

15. Sketch the graph of $y = x^2$. With this graph as a guide, use transformations to help you sketch the graph of each of the following on the same set of axes. Label each graph.

a. $y = x^2 + 3$ **b.** $y = x^2 - 2$ **c.** $y = -x^2 - 4$

16. Make a sketch of the graph of each of the following equations on the same set of axes. Label each graph.

a. $y = (x + 1)^2$ **b.** $y = (x - 3)^2$ **c.** $y = (x - 1)^2 + 2$

MORE MATH REASONING

17. **a.** Sketch graphs of each of the following three equations on the same set of axes. Label each graph.

i. $y = x^2$ **ii.** $y = 3x^2$ **iii.** $y = \frac{1}{2}x^2$

b. In your own words, compare the graph of $y = ax^2$ to the graph of $y = x^2$.

c. Make a sketch of the graph of each of the following equations on the same set of axes. Label each graph.

i. $y = 2x^2$ **ii.** $y = 2x^2 + 3$ **iii.** $y = -2x^2 + 3$

d. Describe how the graph of any equation of the form $y = a(x + h)^2 + k$ is related to the graph of $y = x^2$.

18. **Parabolic Profit** Suppose the profit, P, that a small company makes when it manufactures n items is given by $P = -(n - 600)^2 + 250{,}000$. Find the number of items that the company should manufacture so that it makes the maximum possible profit. What is this maximum profit? Describe how you solved the problem.

10-1 PART D Making Connections

← CONNECT →

You've looked at combinations of the four basic transformations. These combinations can help you understand many things, from the graphs of algebraic equations to the mechanisms in a car.

When Mark Thomas's students build their paper cars, they use the same rack-and-pinion steering mechanism found in real automobiles, so that the cars can be steered. The following chart provides an overview of the rack-and-pinion steering system.

RACK-AND-PINION STEERING

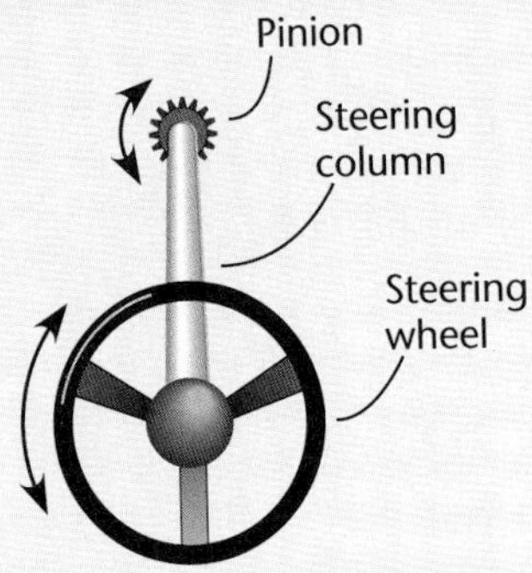

When you turn the steering wheel in a car, the steering column attached to the wheel also turns. The steering column turns a pinion (a small gear), as shown.

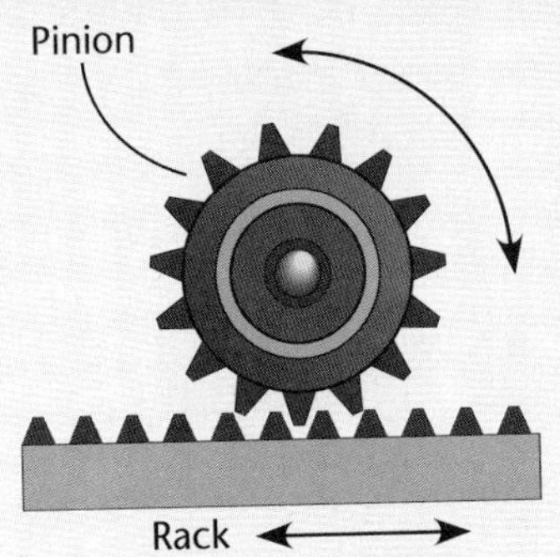

The teeth of the pinion are meshed in the teeth of a rack, as shown above. When the pinion turns, it shifts the rack to the left or right.

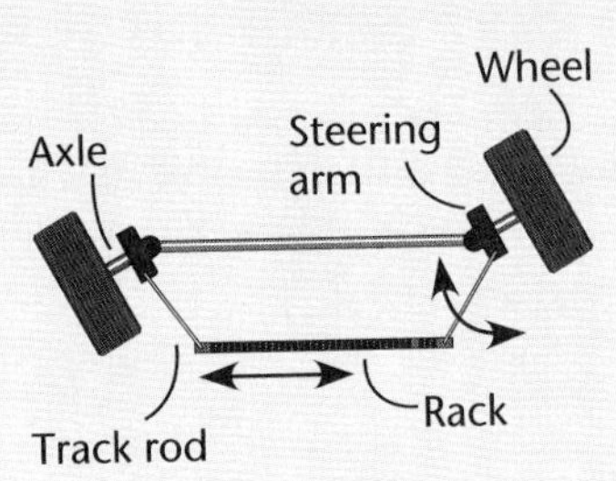

The rack is linked to a track rod, which, in turn, is connected to a steering arm that turns the axles of the front wheels. When the rack moves, the wheels pivot.

In the following Explore, you will see how transformations can be used to understand and describe the rack-and-pinion steering mechanism of a car.

EXPLORE: TURNING THE WHEEL TURNS THE WHEELS

The complete rack-and-pinion steering system is shown at the right.

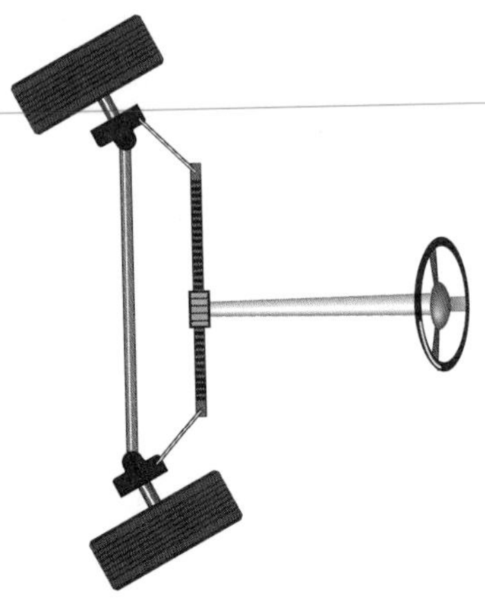

1. Describe all the transformations that occur when a rack-and-pinion steering mechanism is at work. To impress your teacher, explain why turning the steering wheel to the left (counterclockwise) makes the car turn to the left.
2. Describe any of the other movements or mechanisms of a car using the language of transformations. (For example, sliding the front seat backward is a translation.) A mechanically inclined member of your class may be able to explain how movements in the engine make the car go forward.

REFLECT

1. The person at the right is using a pulley to lift a box. Use transformations and the concept of compositions of transformations to explain how a pulley works.
2. Give as many examples as you can of compositions of two transformations that are equivalent to a single transformation.
3. Summarize how changes in equations result in transformations of their graphs. Give examples to illustrate your summary.

Self-Assessment

Find a single transformation equivalent to the composition of each pair of transformations described. Be as specific as you can.

1. a clockwise rotation of $x°$ followed by a clockwise rotation of $y°$ around the same center
2. translation $<a, b>$ followed by translation $<c, d>$
3. a reflection over line m followed by a reflection over line n, which is perpendicular to line m

Which of the following compositions of transformations are isometries? Explain.

4. a translation and a reflection
5. a rotation and a dilation
6. two rotations
7. **More Power to You** Acme Rentals and Begone Cleaners have office buildings located as shown. The power company needs to locate a transformer on a main power line, ℓ, to serve both Acme and Begone. Copy the figure, and show where the power company should locate the transformer to minimize the amount of wire needed. Explain how you found this point.

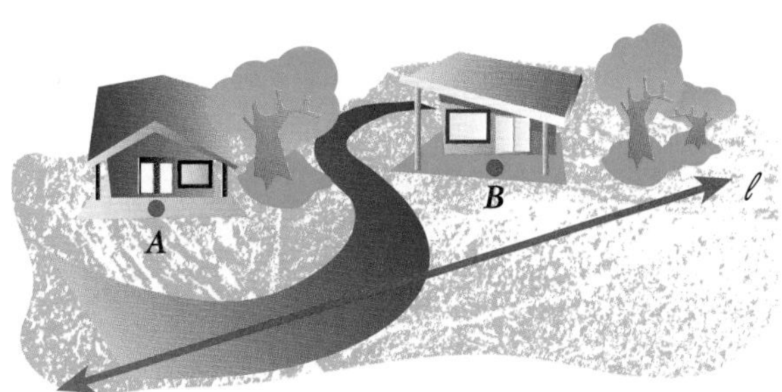

The graph of a function $y = p$ is shown at the right. Using this graph as a guide, make a sketch of the graph of each of the following equations on the same set of axes. Label each graph.

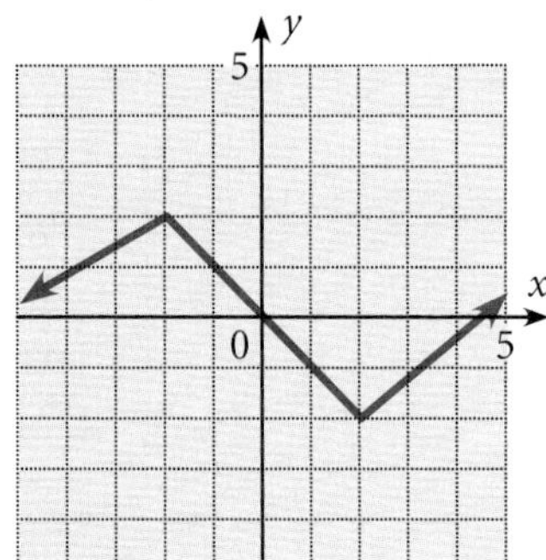

8. $y = p + 2$ **9.** $y = -p$ **10.** $y = -p - 3$

11. Explain how you used transformations to sketch each of your graphs in Exercises 8–10.

12. A car is being tested on a track with semicircular turns. The car is at point A on the turn with center C. How much longer is arc $\widehat{AB}$ than chord $\overline{AB}$? (Hint: Use your knowledge of right triangles to find AB and $m\angle ACB$. Then use proportional thinking to find the length of $\widehat{AB}$.) [8-2]

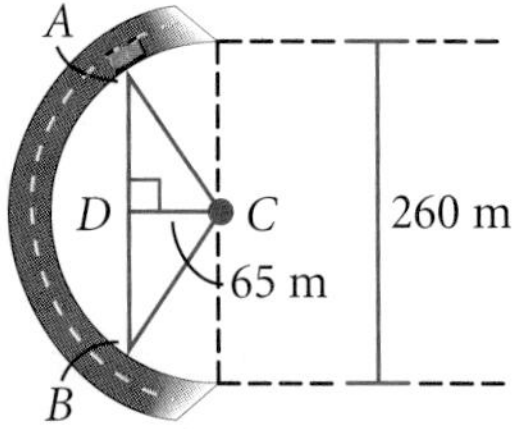

Find the surface area and volume of each figure. Round answers to the nearest tenth. [9-1, 9-2]

13.

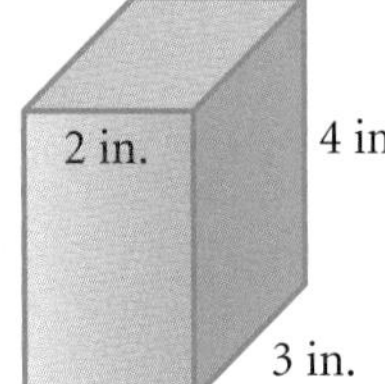

Right rectangular prism

14.

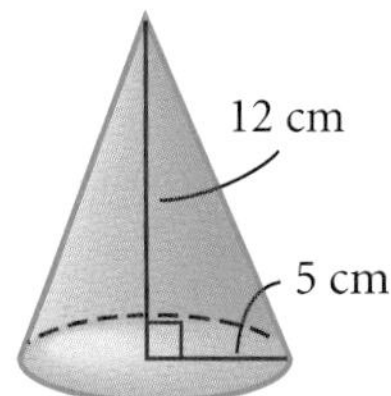

Right cone

15.

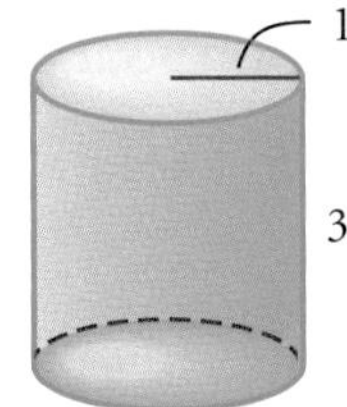

Right cylinder

16.

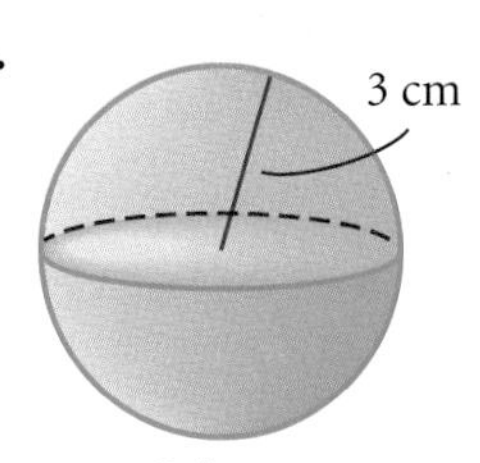

Sphere

17. An equation represents a function if every value you substitute for one of the variables (called the *independent variable*) gives only one value for the other variable (the *dependent variable*).

Are the transformations you've studied functions? In other words, does every point on the pre-image always map onto just one point on the image, or are there times when a pre-image point corresponds to two or more image points? If you think reflections, rotations, translations, and dilations are functions, explain why. If not, explain why not.

18. Rooting for Transformations Suppose you invent a new transformation, called *rootation.* The image of any point (x, y) is the point $(\sqrt{x}, \sqrt{y})$.

a. Are there any points that cannot be rootated? If so, describe them, and tell why they cannot be rootated.

b. Investigate what happens when you perform an infinite number of rootations on a point. Start with the point (81, 16) and rootate it several times. Describe what happens as you continue rootating. Where does the point seem to be going? Will it ever get there? Why or why not?

c. Is rootation an isometry? Explain.

decoration detectives

Do you like solving mysteries? If so, maybe archaeology is the field for you. Archaeologists look at old buildings, tools, and other artifacts to recreate past human behavior. In a way, they are detectives.

As a high school student, Elain-Maryse Solari loved mysteries—not just reading them, but also playing the detective's role. Her love of solving mysteries drew her to archaeology. She majored in anthropology at the University of Arizona in Tucson and received her master's degree in cultural resource management at Sonoma State University in California. She has done archaeological work in Arizona, California, Italy, Wales, and on the Isle of Man.

In Wales, her team explored the remains of a fort from the Iron Age (about 1000 B.C. to 100 A.D.). Unfortunately, acids in the soil had eaten up all the buildings and most of the other archaeological evidence. However, rain falling off the roofs of the ancient structures left rings in the soil. If one ring was below another, the lower ring had to be older. With little evidence other than these rings, the archaeologists were able to determine where structures had been, their size, and the order in which they were built!

Cooper-Hewitt, National Design Museum, Smithsonian Inst./Art Resource, NY

1. **Explain how deductive reasoning plays a role in archaeology.**
2. **Why do you think the archaeologists in Wales concluded that the lower a ring was, the older it was?**

10-2 PART A Frieze Patterns

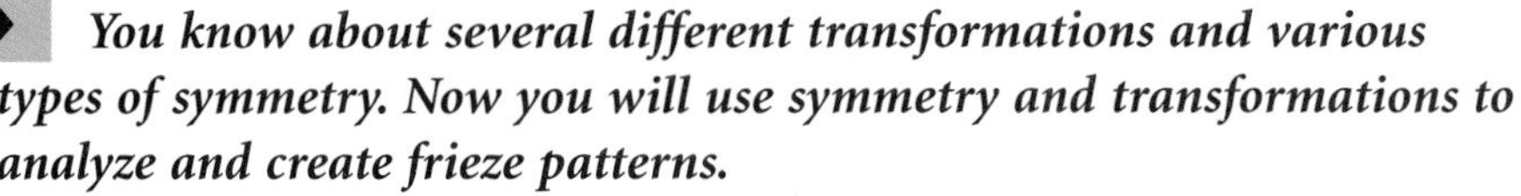

← CONNECT → ***You know about several different transformations and various types of symmetry. Now you will use symmetry and transformations to analyze and create frieze patterns.***

A frieze pattern is a strip design that repeats itself. You can find many everyday examples of frieze patterns in decorative borders on clothing, in the tracks made by tire treads, and in ancient Greek urns.

DEFINITION

A **frieze pattern** is created by repeated translations of a pattern along a line.

All of the frieze patterns that you will work with repeat horizontally. Also, you may assume that all patterns in this chapter continue indefinitely.

Many of these designs have interesting geometric properties, like line symmetry and rotational symmetry. For example, the pattern . . . ΣΣΣΣΣΣ . . . , shown above, has horizontal line symmetry.

Frieze patterns may also feature **glide-reflection symmetry,** which we touched on earlier. The frieze pattern below exhibits glide-reflection symmetry. A pattern has glide-reflection symmetry if it coincides with itself after undergoing a translation and a reflection.

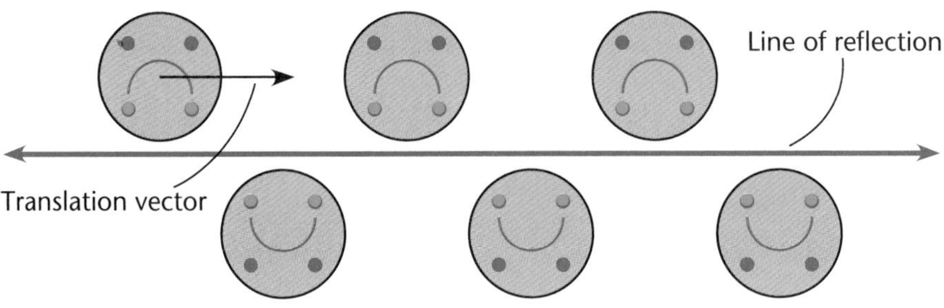

1. How is glide-reflection symmetry related to the idea of a composition of transformations?

EXAMPLE

Does the pattern at the right have glide-reflection symmetry? Why or why not?

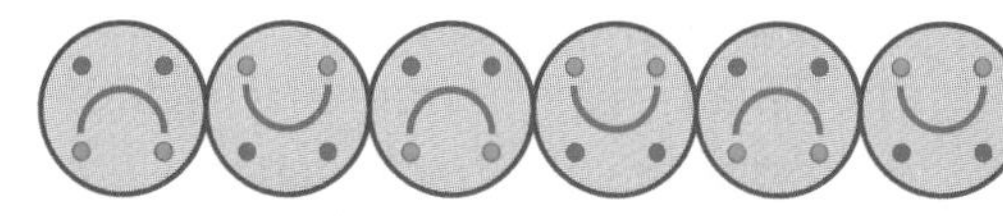

The pattern does have glide-reflection symmetry. The translation vector and the line of reflection are shown.

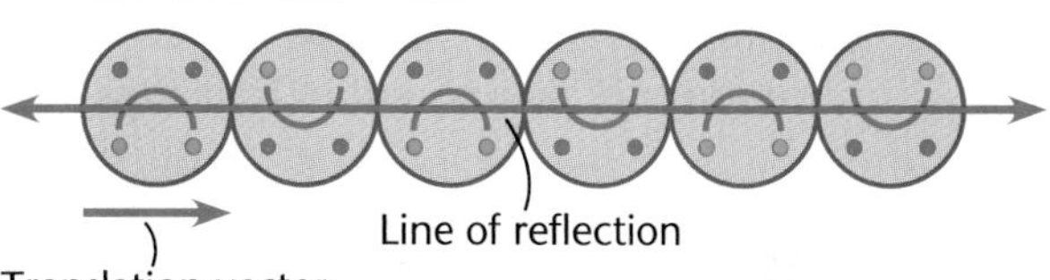

The wave pattern from the border of a second-century B.C. Roman mosaic coincides with itself when translated a certain distance to the right or to the left. When a pattern has this property, we say that it has **translation symmetry.** All frieze patterns exhibit translation symmetry.

TRY IT

Name all of the types of symmetry in each frieze pattern.

a. **b.** **c.**

Because frieze patterns repeat themselves horizontally, there are only a few types of symmetry they can have. In the following Explore, you will sketch examples of different frieze patterns.

EXPLORE: SYMMETRY SEARCH

As you can see in the photo at the right, frieze patterns are important in textile designs. Two frieze patterns are classified as different types if they have different symmetries.

1. Using capital letters, sketch examples of as many different types of frieze patterns as you can. Identify all of the types of symmetry each of your patterns has.
2. Compare your frieze patterns with the ones your classmates designed. While sharing your frieze patterns, list the different types of frieze patterns that you see. How many different types can you identify?

Frieze patterns may have glide-reflection symmetry, half-turn rotational symmetry (point symmetry), and/or line symmetry over vertical or horizontal lines. Due to these limitations, there are essentially only seven different types of frieze patterns! These are summarized in the chart. (Note that redundant symmetries are not listed.)

CLASSIFICATION OF FRIEZE PATTERNS

Type of symmetry (Translation symmetry plus . . .)	Example
No other symmetry	┘┘┘┘┘┘┘┘┘┘
Horizontal line symmetry	]]]]]]]]]]
Point symmetry	↯↯↯↯↯↯
Glide-reflection symmetry	┘┐┘┐┘┐┘┐┘┐┘┐
Vertical line symmetry	∧∧∧∧∧
Vertical line symmetry and glide-reflection symmetry	⊥⊤⊥⊤⊥⊤⊥⊤⊥⊤⊥⊤⊥⊤
Vertical line symmetry and horizontal line symmetry	IIIIIII

REFLECT

1. Briefly explain the difference between translation symmetry and glide-reflection symmetry.
2. Describe some common frieze patterns seen in everyday life.
3. If a frieze pattern is flipped upside down, does its classification change? That is, does it still have the same types of symmetry?

Exercises

CORE

1. **Getting Started** Refer to the frieze pattern at the right for the following.
   a. Does the pattern have horizontal line symmetry?
   b. Does the pattern have vertical line symmetry?
   c. Does the pattern have glide-reflection symmetry?
   d. Does the pattern have point symmetry?

Although any part of a frieze pattern is repeated an infinite number of times, you can always find a minimal piece that can be translated to create the whole pattern. For instance, in . . . TTTTTTTTTT . . . , the piece TTT repeats itself, but a minimal piece that you could translate to make the pattern is a single T.

For each frieze pattern shown, sketch a minimal piece that can be translated to create the pattern.

5. Determine whether the following statement is true or false. If the statement is false, change the underlined phrase to make it true.

   A pattern has glide-reflection symmetry if it coincides with itself after a <u>rotation and a reflection.</u>

Determine whether each pattern has glide-reflection symmetry.

6.

7.

8.

9. **Rubber Band Strand** A *polymer* is a large molecule formed by the repeated bonding of smaller molecules. The figure shown below illustrates a natural rubber polymer strand. Identify and copy a minimal piece for this polymer.

$$\ldots CH_2{-}\underset{}{\overset{CH_3}{\overset{|}{C}}}{=}CH{-}CH_2{-}CH_2{-}\overset{CH_3}{\overset{|}{C}}{=}CH{-}CH_2{-}CH_2{-}\overset{CH_3}{\overset{|}{C}}{=}CH{-}CH_2{-}CH_2{-}\overset{CH_3}{\overset{|}{C}}{=}CH{-}CH_2 \ldots$$

Name all of the types of symmetry in each frieze pattern. The patterns in Exercises 12 and 13 are found on cloth from Mali.

10. MMMMMMMMMMMM

11. 

12. 

13. 

For each of the following, sketch a frieze pattern that has translation symmetry as well as the other type(s) of symmetry listed.

14. Vertical line symmetry

15. Point symmetry

16. Vertical line symmetry and glide-reflection symmetry

17. Sketch and describe a frieze pattern that you've seen in architecture. Describe where you found the pattern.

18. Suppose you choose a frieze pattern at random from the seven different classifications. What is the probability that the pattern will have vertical line symmetry?

19. This border design is from a pair of leggings of the Menominee Indians of Michigan. Sketch each of the different frieze patterns that you see in this design. Then name all of the types of symmetry in each frieze pattern.

LOOK BACK

The surface areas of the similar cones shown have a ratio of $\frac{25}{9}$. [9-3]

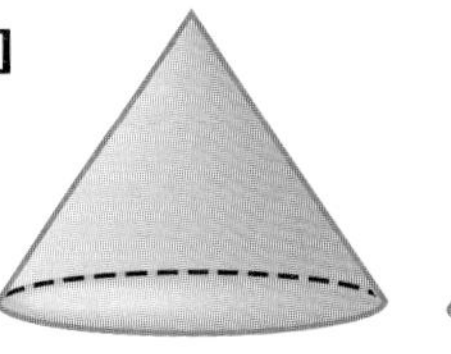
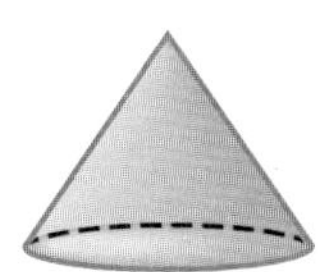

20. What is the similarity ratio of the cones?

21. What is the ratio of the volumes of the cones?

Find a single transformation that is equivalent to the composition of each pair of transformations. If this transformation is a reflection, identify the line of reflection. If it is a rotation, identify the center and angle of the rotation. If it is a translation, give the translation vector. If it is a dilation, identify the center and scale factor. [10-1]

22. translation $<7, 2>$ followed by translation $<-3, 5>$

23. an 82° clockwise rotation with center $(-2, -4)$ followed by a 221° clockwise rotation with center $(-2, -4)$

MORE PRACTICE

For each frieze pattern, sketch a minimal piece that can be translated to create the pattern.

24.

25.

26.

Name all of the types of symmetry in each frieze pattern.

27. AAAAAAAAAAA

28. XXXXXXXXXXX

29.

30.

31. Name all the types of symmetry in the dancette (zigzag) mosaic pattern seen in Islamic architecture (shown at the right).

MORE MATH REASONING

32. Why isn't there a listing in the classification chart for frieze patterns that have both vertical line symmetry and point symmetry?

33. Mass-Produced Pottery The photo at the right shows pottery from the Acoma Pueblo in New Mexico. Suppose you plan to produce thousands of differently sized pottery bowls and pitchers with your trademark frieze pattern (shown below) on each one. The design goes completely around each piece of pottery.

Social Science

TMTMTMTMTMTMTMTMTMTM

You need to design a tool to press this design into the clay. Describe a tool that could be used to do this.

10-2 PART B Wallpaper Patterns

← CONNECT → ***You've already created some frieze patterns and examined their symmetries. Now you will investigate patterns that repeat in more than one direction.***

Frieze patterns repeat forever, but only in a straight line. They're often used for decoration where a wall meets a ceiling. However, to decorate an entire wall, you need more than a pattern that extends horizontally. **Wallpaper patterns** are repeating patterns that cover a plane.

The design at the right is generated by overlapping translations of a regular hexagon. Notice that any row of this design is a frieze pattern. However, the basic pattern repeats itself in several different directions, not just in a horizontal line.

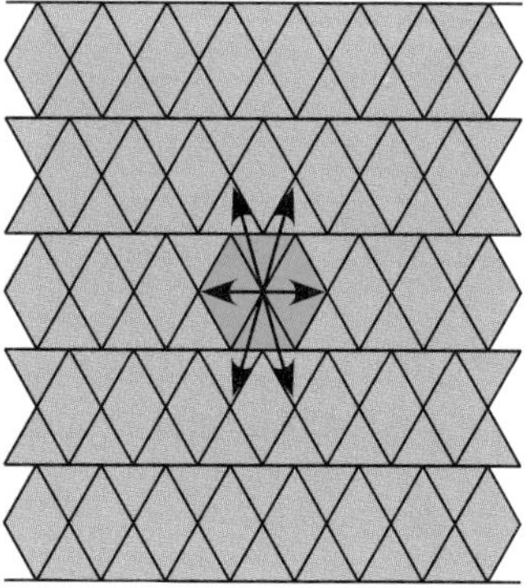

DEFINITION

A **wallpaper pattern** is a plane pattern with translation symmetry along more than one line.

You may assume that all of the wallpaper patterns in this book extend indefinitely.

EXAMPLES

Name all of the types of symmetry in each wallpaper pattern.

1.

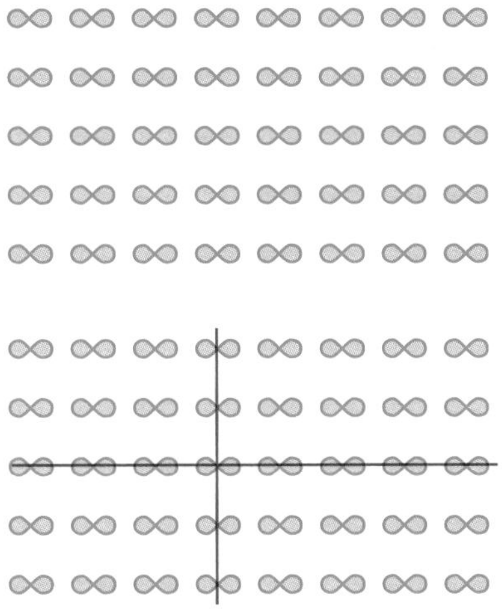

translation symmetry
rotational symmetry: 180°
line symmetry: vertical lines and horizontal lines
glide-reflection symmetry

2.

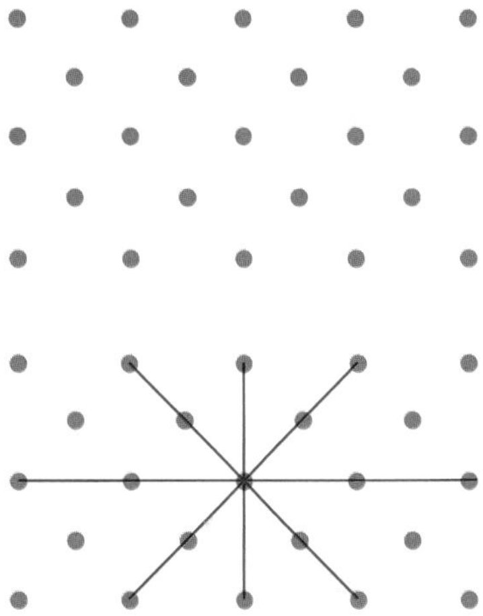

translation symmetry
rotational symmetry: 90°, 180°, and 270°
line symmetry: vertical lines, horizontal lines, lines at 45° and 135° to the horizontal
glide-reflection symmetry

Notice that there are an infinite number of lines of symmetry—we've only shown one of each type. For example, in the design in Example 1, all horizontal lines through the centers of the symbols are lines of symmetry, as are all horizontal lines halfway between the rows of symbols.

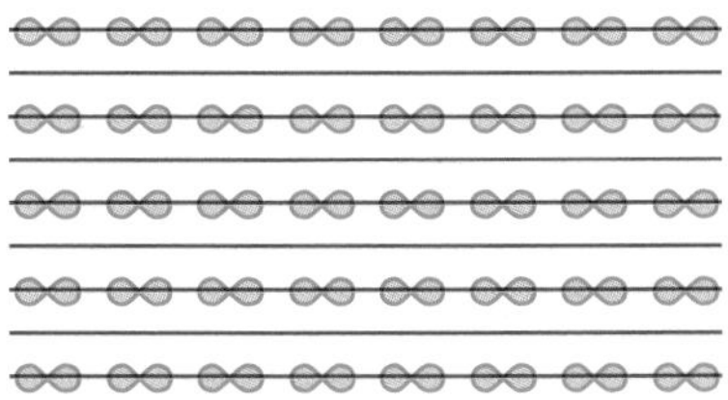

EXPLORE: ON THE WALL

MATERIALS

Protractor
Straightedge

1. Examine each of these African fabric patterns for symmetry by following the steps below.

A

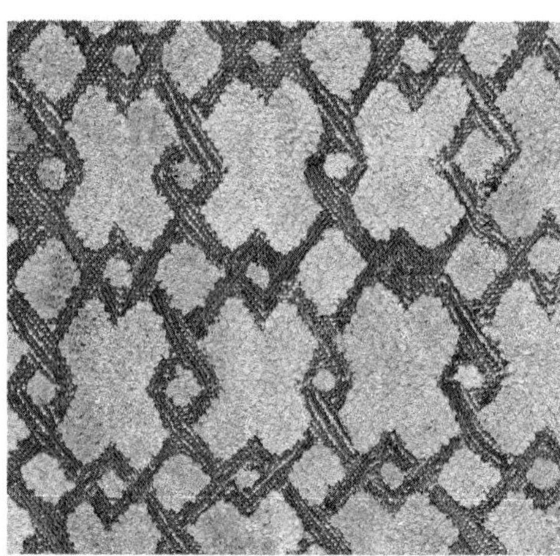

B

a. Determine whether the pattern has glide-reflection symmetry.
b. Examine the design for line symmetry. You may wish to sketch a copy of the design, so that you can test it for line symmetry by folding. Describe all of the different lines of symmetry that you identify.
c. See whether the design has rotational symmetry. Identify one of the centers of rotation, and list the degree measures of all of the clockwise rotations less than 360° that map the design onto itself.

2. Sketch a wallpaper pattern of your own. Describe all of the symmetries of your design. Compare your design to those of your classmates.

It may seem that there should be an infinite number of combinations for the symmetries of wallpaper patterns. However, the fact that they must have translation symmetry limits the possibilities. In fact, there are only seventeen different classifications for wallpaper patterns!

REFLECT

1. Why do you think there are more classifications for wallpaper patterns than there are for frieze patterns?
2. What is the relationship between wallpaper patterns and tessellations of a plane?

Exercises

CORE

1. **Getting Started** Refer to the wallpaper pattern at the right for the following.
   a. Does the wallpaper pattern have glide-reflection symmetry?
   b. Does the wallpaper pattern have line-reflection symmetry? If so, describe the different symmetry lines you identified.
   c. Does the wallpaper pattern have rotational symmetry? If so, list the degree measures of all clockwise rotations less than 360° that map the pattern onto itself.

Name all of the types of symmetry for each wallpaper pattern shown below. All of these patterns are typical *adire* cloth designs made by the Yoruba people of Nigeria.

2. 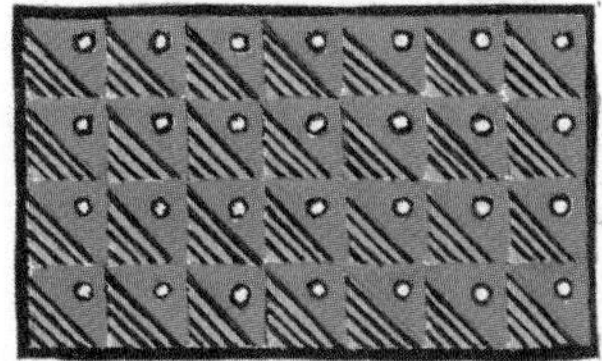

3. 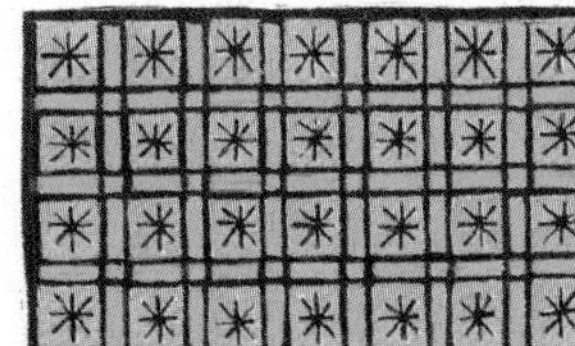

4. 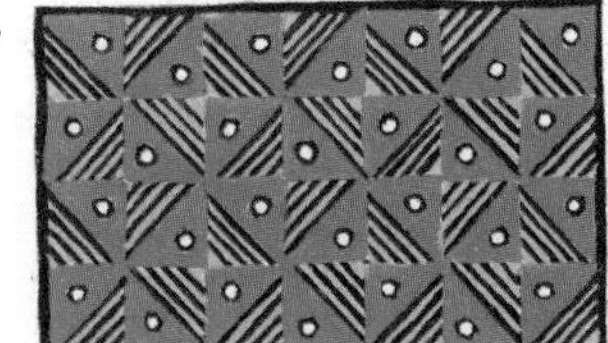

5. Write the letter of the second pair that best matches the first pair.

   Frieze: line as (a) plain: decorated, (b) horizontal: vertical, (c) wallpaper: plane, (d) angle: vertex

Determine whether each statement is true or false. If the statement is false, change the underlined word or phrase to make it true.

6. A wallpaper pattern must have <u>rotational</u> symmetry.
7. A wallpaper pattern is <u>sometimes</u> a tessellation.
8. **Papering the Walls** Suppose you want to wallpaper the interior of the room shown at the right. How many square feet of wallpaper do you need for the job? (Do not include wallpaper for the floor, the door, or the ceiling.)

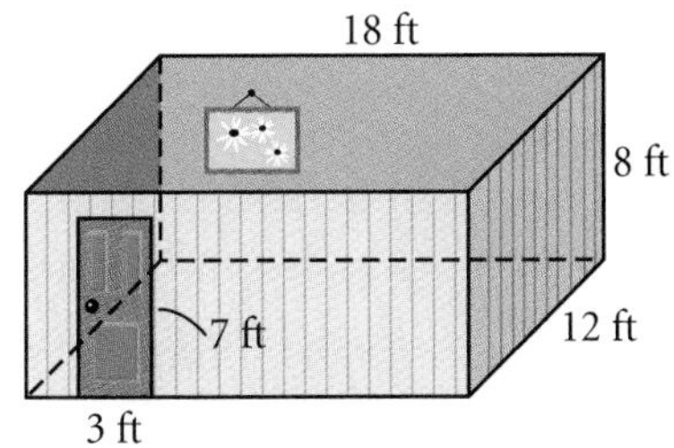

For each of the following, sketch a wallpaper pattern that has translation symmetry as well as the other type(s) of symmetry listed.

9. vertical line symmetry

10. point symmetry

11. rotational symmetry for a 60° clockwise rotation

12. How many different directions are there for translations that map this wallpaper design onto itself?

Problem-Solving Tip

Be sure that you've covered all of the possibilities.

LOOK AHEAD

Find the solution set for each inequality.

13. $x - 6 \geq 10$

14. $3(y + 12) < 30$

15. $7z - 13 \geq 2(z + 8)$

16. If $a + 7 = b$, is $a > b$ or is $b > a$? Explain.

17. Barb's Wire Fence Barb has 8 km of wire fencing, and she wants to enclose a rectangular region of farmland.

a. Assuming each side length must be a whole number, list all of the possible dimensions for the fenced land.

b. Identify the dimensions that give the greatest possible area for the fenced region. What shape is the fenced region with the greatest area?

MORE PRACTICE

Name all of the types of symmetry for each wallpaper pattern.

18.

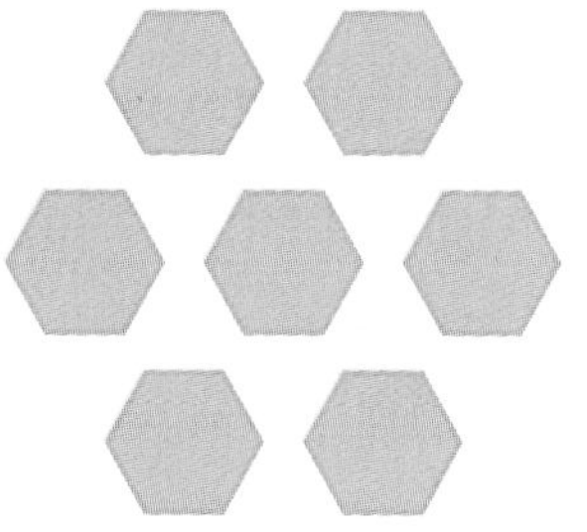

19.

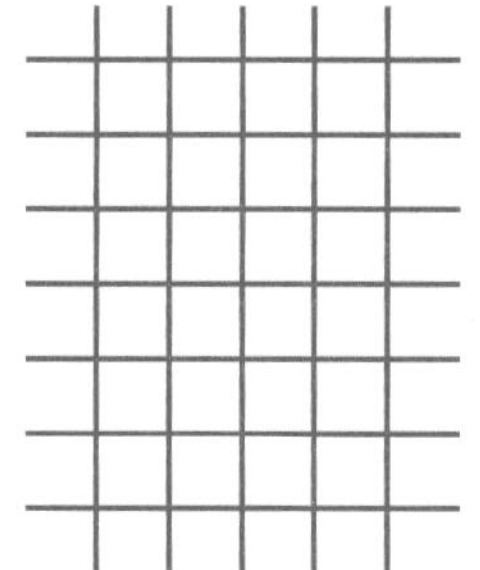

20.

For each of the following, sketch a wallpaper pattern that has translation symmetry as well as the other type of symmetry listed.

21. glide-reflection symmetry

22. horizontal line symmetry

MORE MATH REASONING

23. Wallpaper by Slide Wallpaper patterns are a kind of tessellation. By following these steps, you can make your own translation-based tessellation.

MAKING A TRANSLATION-BASED TESSELLATION

a. Start with a rectangle (or a parallelogram).	**b.** "Nibble" a piece out of the bottom of the rectangle, as shown.	**c.** Translate it to the top of the rectangle.
d. "Nibble" a new shape from the left side of the rectangle, and translate it to the right side of the rectangle.	**e.** Cut out this shape, and use it as your pattern to tessellate the plane.	A helmet? **f.** Now decide what your pattern looks like. Draw in details as you tessellate.

24. A glide reflection can be described as a composition of a translation and a reflection. However, there is another composition of transformations—one that doesn't use a translation—that produces a glide reflection. Describe this other composition of transformations. Make a sketch to illustrate your answer.

Problem-Solving Tip

Eliminate unreasonable possibilities, and then use guess-and-check.

10-2 PART C Making Connections

← CONNECT → ***Studying patterns helps archaeologists to identify and classify ancient artifacts. These patterns are also present in modern design and architecture. You've applied your knowledge of transformational geometry and symmetry to two types of patterns—frieze patterns and wallpaper patterns.***

Archaeologists must be able to identify patterns that are typical of different cultures and time periods. The photograph at the left shows a piece of pottery from San Ildefonso Pueblo in New Mexico. The pottery typically found in this pueblo shows all seven different frieze-pattern classifications. The patterns you will work with in the following Explore are similar to some found on that pottery.

EXPLORE: CLASSIFICATION CLASS

Classify each frieze pattern using the appropriate line, point, and glide-reflection symmetries. If necessary, use the chart on page 690 to remind you of the different types of frieze patterns and their symmetries.

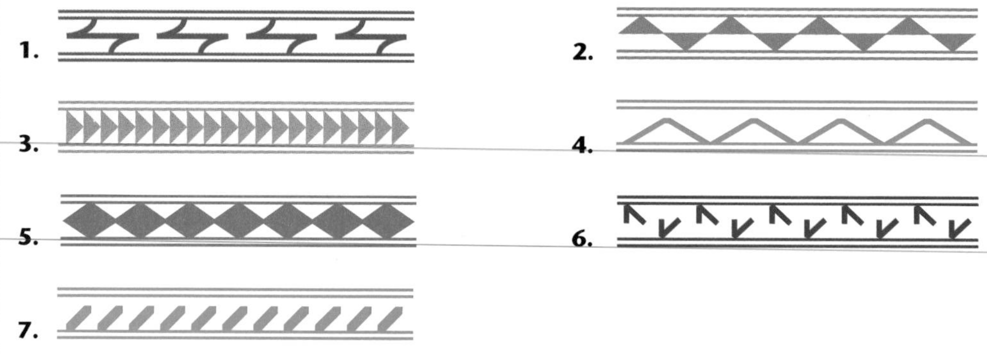

By now you've probably noticed that classification is an important idea in mathematics. In addition to frieze patterns and wallpaper patterns, you've seen how to classify angles, triangles, quadrilaterals, polygons, and transformations.

REFLECT

1. Why do you think frieze patterns and wallpaper patterns are used so often in decorations?
2. Draw the simplest example you can for each of the seven types of frieze patterns. Write a brief explanation of the different types of frieze patterns.
3. Write a short paragraph explaining the similarities and differences between frieze patterns and wallpaper patterns.

Self-Assessment

Name all of the types of symmetry for each frieze pattern or wallpaper pattern.

1. **EEEEEEEEEEEEEEE**

Social Science

2. an embroidery border design from Afghanistan

3. 

4. 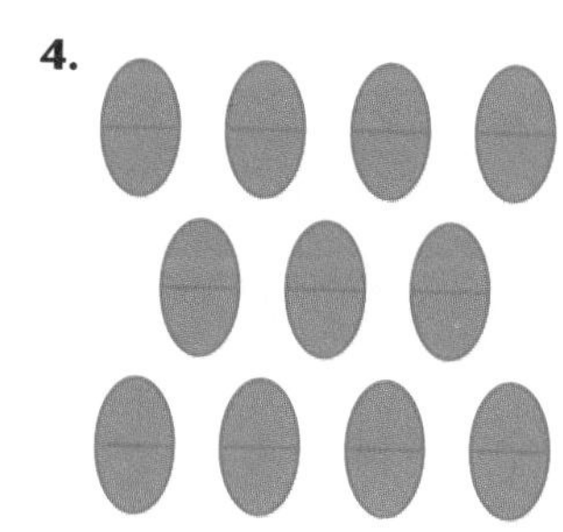

5. 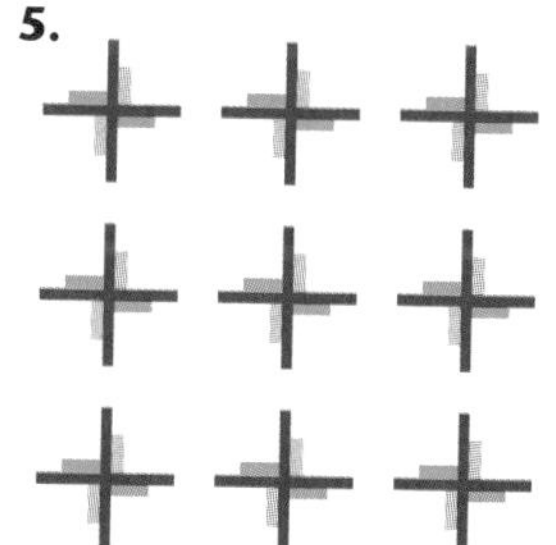

6. 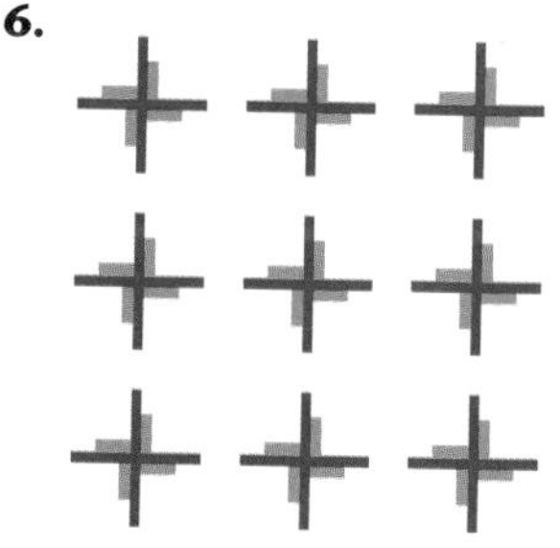

7. **Dig This!** An archaeologist unearths two hemispherical pots. The larger pot has twice the radius of the smaller. [9-3]
   a. What is the ratio of the surface area of the larger pot to the surface area of the smaller pot?
   b. What is the ratio of the volume of the larger pot to the volume of the smaller pot?

8. Compare the graph of $y = x^2$ to the graph of $y = -x^2 + 4$. Use the language of transformations to describe the relationships between the graphs. [10-1]

9. Cristina is an archaeologist. She discovers that all of the pottery of an ancient civilization has the same symmetries as the fragment shown at the right.

At a different site, Cristina finds four more fragments of pottery. Which one might have been made by this civilization?

(a) 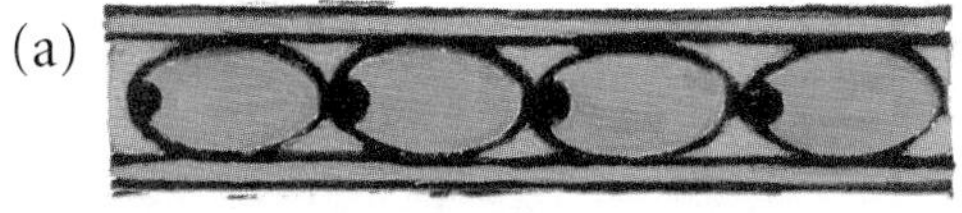

(b) 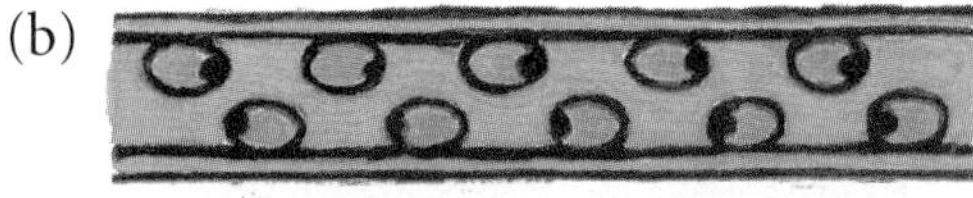

(c) 

(d) 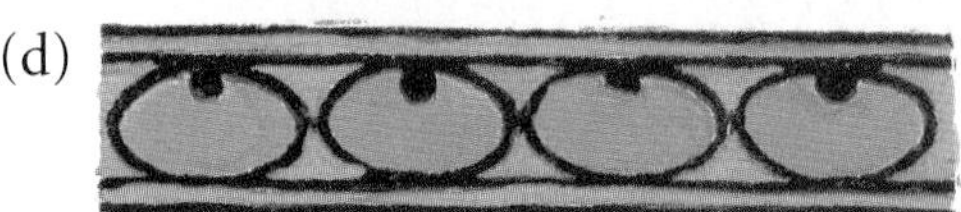

For each of the following, sketch a frieze pattern that has translation symmetry as well as the other type(s) of symmetry listed.

10. vertical line symmetry and horizontal line symmetry

11. glide-reflection symmetry

For each of the following, sketch a wallpaper pattern that has translation symmetry as well as the other type of symmetry listed.

12. vertical line symmetry

13. point symmetry

14. Wave for the Camera! The waves in the photograph were generated by an oscillating wavemaker. Does this wave pattern, as seen in two dimensions, appear to be a wallpaper pattern? If so, identify at least two types of symmetry in the pattern. If not, explain why you feel it is not a wallpaper pattern.

15. Choose the equation that is represented by the graph at the right. [10-1]
(a) $y = x^2 + 4$
(b) $y = -x^2 + 4$
(c) $y = x^2 - 4$
(d) $y = -x^2 - 4$

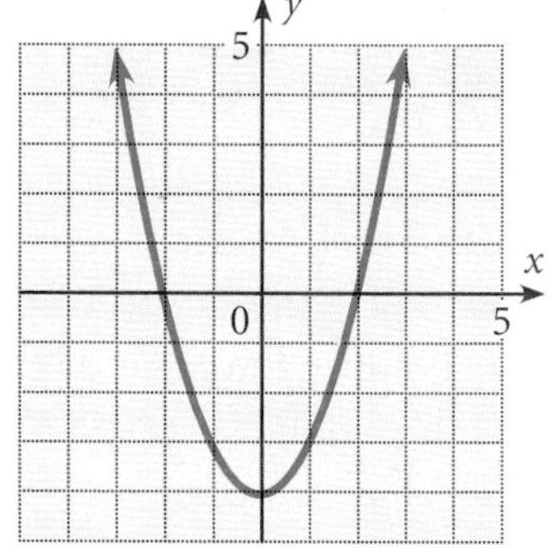

Chapter 10 Review

In Chapter 10, you have looked at applications of transformations. These included their classification and composition. You also learned about the connections of transformations to applications as diverse as algebra, automobiles, and art from all over the world.

KEY TERMS

composition [10-1]
frieze pattern [10-2]
glide-reflection symmetry [10-2]
isometry [10-1]
parent equation [10-1]
translation symmetry [10-2]
wallpaper pattern [10-2]

Write the word or phrase that correctly completes each statement.

1. All frieze patterns have ___ symmetry.

2. A pattern has glide-reflection symmetry if it coincides with itself after undergoing a ___ and a ___.

3. An isometry that changes the orientation of a figure is a ___.

4. Translating a figure and then rotating its image is an example of a ___ of transformations.

CONCEPTS AND APPLICATIONS

Describe a single transformation that is equivalent to the composition of each pair of transformations. Be as specific as you can. [10-1]

5. translation $<2, -10>$ followed by translation $<10, -2>$

6. a reflection over line p followed by a reflection over line q, which is parallel to line p

7. Which of the following transformations are not isometries? [10-1]
(a) translation
(b) reflection
(c) rotation
(d) dilation

8. A sphere is inscribed in a cube so that each face of the cube is tangent to the sphere. If each edge of the cube is 3 cm long, what is the ratio of the surface area of the sphere to that of the cube? [9-1, 9-2]

The parent equation $y = \sqrt{x}$ is graphed at the right. Copy the graph, and then sketch the graph of each function on the same set of axes. Describe how each graph is related to the parent equation. [10-1]

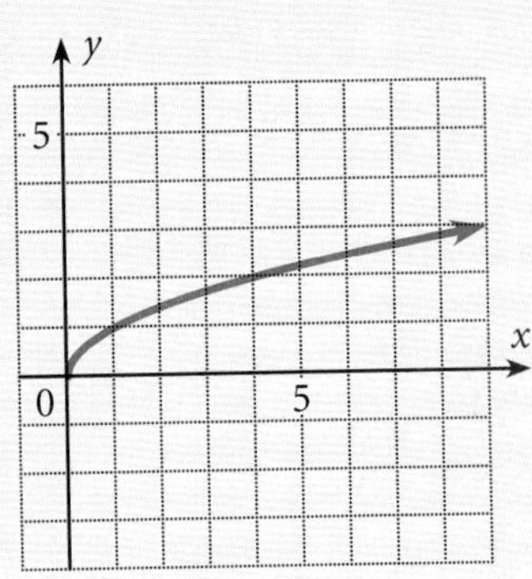

9. $y = -\sqrt{x}$

10. $y = -\sqrt{x} + 5$

11. Draw a frieze pattern with horizontal and vertical line symmetry. [10-2]

12. Write a summary of the seven combinations of symmetry possible in a frieze pattern. [10-2]

The patterns shown are used on clothing of the Menominee people of the Great Lakes region. Describe the different types of symmetry in each pattern. [10-2]

13.

14.

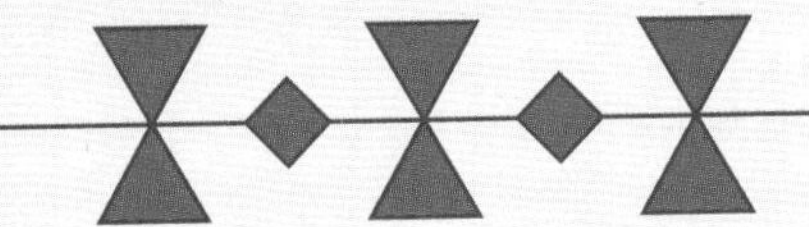

15. List the degree measures of all clockwise rotations less than 360° that map this wallpaper pattern onto itself. [10-2]

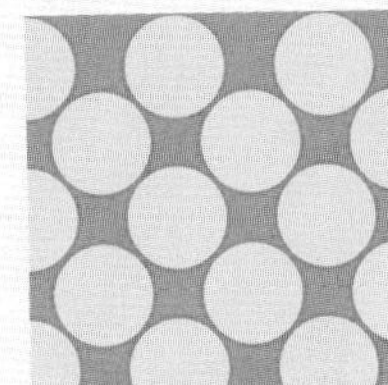

CONCEPTS AND CONNECTIONS

16. Art John T. Biggers' *Third Ward Housing* (1985) shows African-American women in front of rows of "shotgun" houses, common in the south. They were so named because a shotgun could be fired through such a house from front to back without hitting anything. Describe how aspects of the painting are similar to wallpaper and frieze patterns. Explain what Biggers may be trying to communicate by these patterns.

Fine Arts

SELF-EVALUATION

Write a summary of what you have learned about transformations in Chapter 10. Include concepts that relate to isometries, algebraic functions, frieze patterns, and wallpaper patterns. Describe the concepts that you found the most difficult, and discuss your plans to study them.

Chapter 10 Assessment

TEST

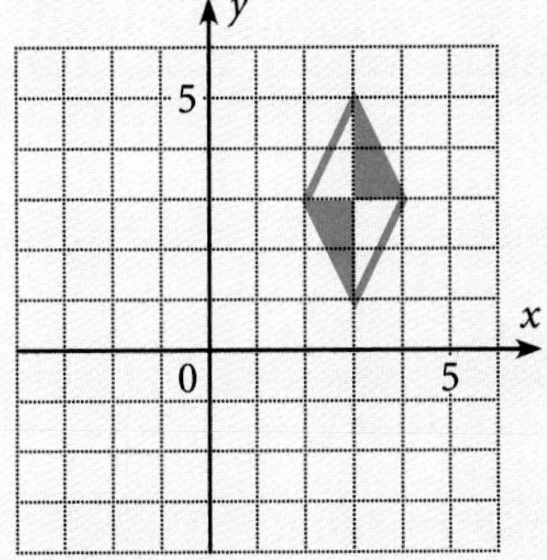

Sketch the image of each transformation of the figure shown. Then describe a single transformation that has the same image as the composition of transformations.

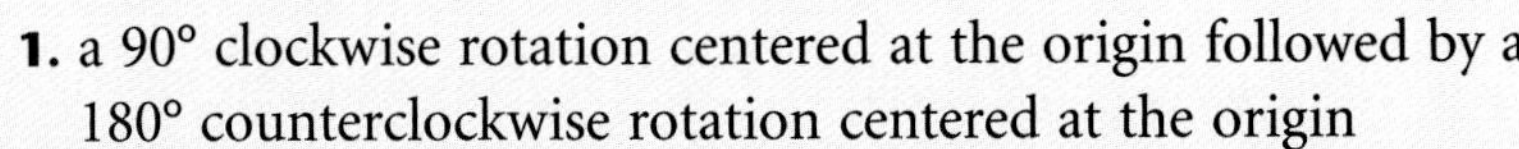

1. a 90° clockwise rotation centered at the origin followed by a 180° counterclockwise rotation centered at the origin

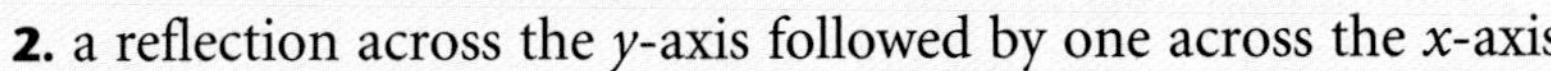

2. a reflection across the y-axis followed by one across the x-axis

3. A poster advertising a concert is reduced to appear on each ticket for the concert. Is this an example of a transformation? an isometry? Explain.

4. What transformation may be applied to the graph of $y = x^2$ to produce the graph of $y = x^2 - 6$. Be as specific as you can.

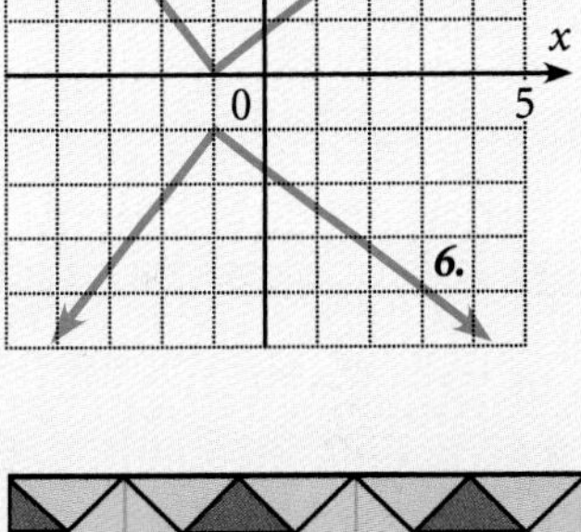

The graph of a parent equation, $y = \beta$, is shown. For each of the other graphs shown in the figure, give the letter of its equation.

5. (a) $y = -\beta - 3$ (b) $y = -\beta + 3$ (c) $y = \beta + 3$ (d) $y = \beta - 3$

6. (a) $y = -\beta + 1$ (b) $y = -\beta - 1$ (c) $y = \beta - 1$ (d) $y = -\beta$

7. Sketch a wallpaper pattern with 60° rotational symmetry.

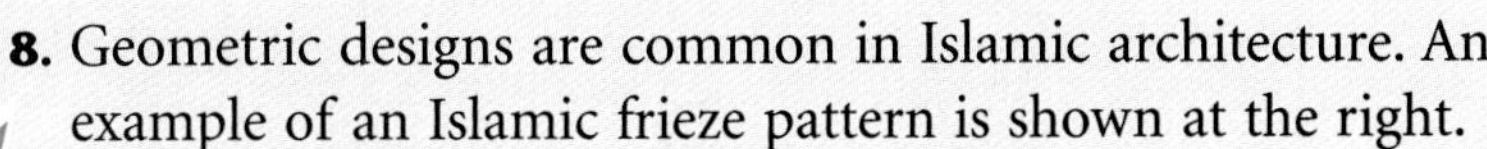

8. Geometric designs are common in Islamic architecture. An example of an Islamic frieze pattern is shown at the right.

a. If the colors are considered part of the pattern, what types of symmetry are present in this frieze pattern?

b. Disregarding colors, what types of symmetry are present?

9. Use the language of transformations to write a brief summary of how the graphs of $y = x^2 + k$, $y = -x^2$, and $y = -x^2 + k$ are related to the graph of the parent equation $y = x^2$.

PERFORMANCE TASK

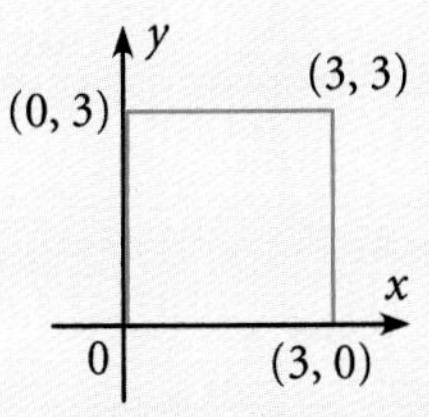

Copy the square. On the same axes, transform the square by mapping each point (x, y) to the point $(x + y, y)$. Repeat the transformation, using some figures of your own. Describe the general effect of such a transformation. Is it an isometry? Does it seem to preserve area? Explain.

Chapter 11 Geometric Inequalities and Optimization

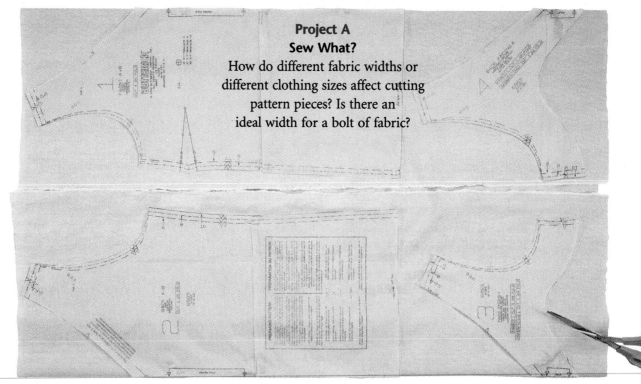

Project A
Sew What?
How do different fabric widths or different clothing sizes affect cutting pattern pieces? Is there an ideal width for a bolt of fabric?

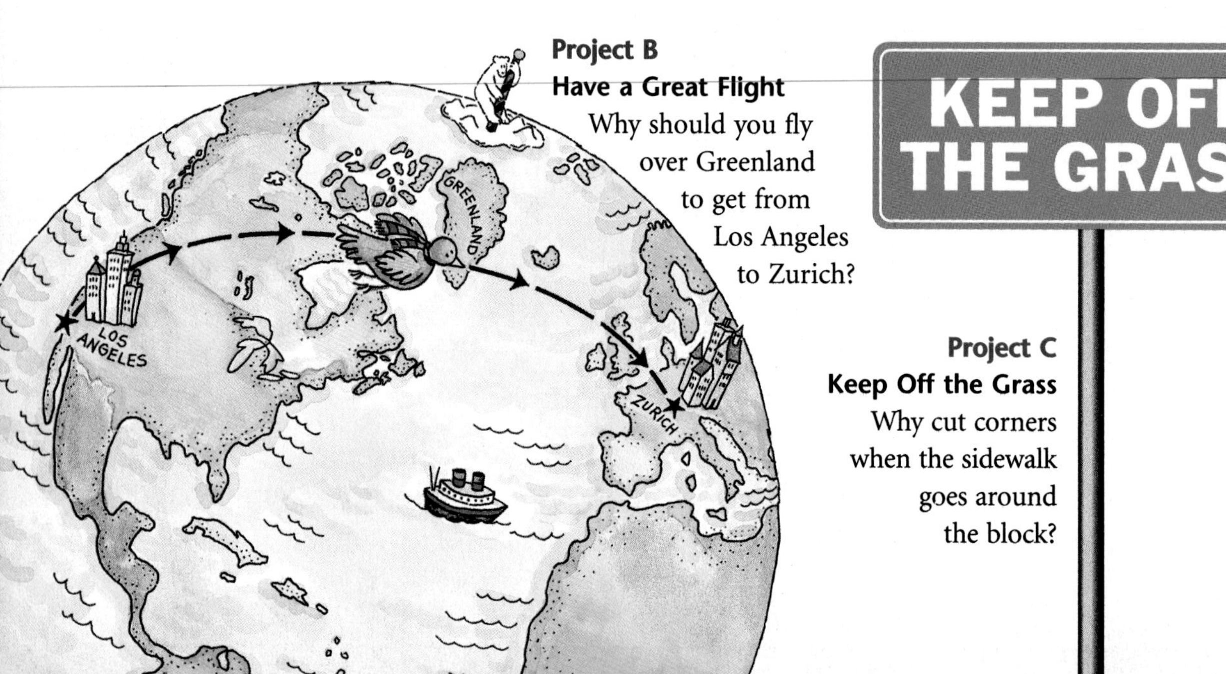

Project B
Have a Great Flight
Why should you fly over Greenland to get from Los Angeles to Zurich?

Project C
Keep Off the Grass
Why cut corners when the sidewalk goes around the block?

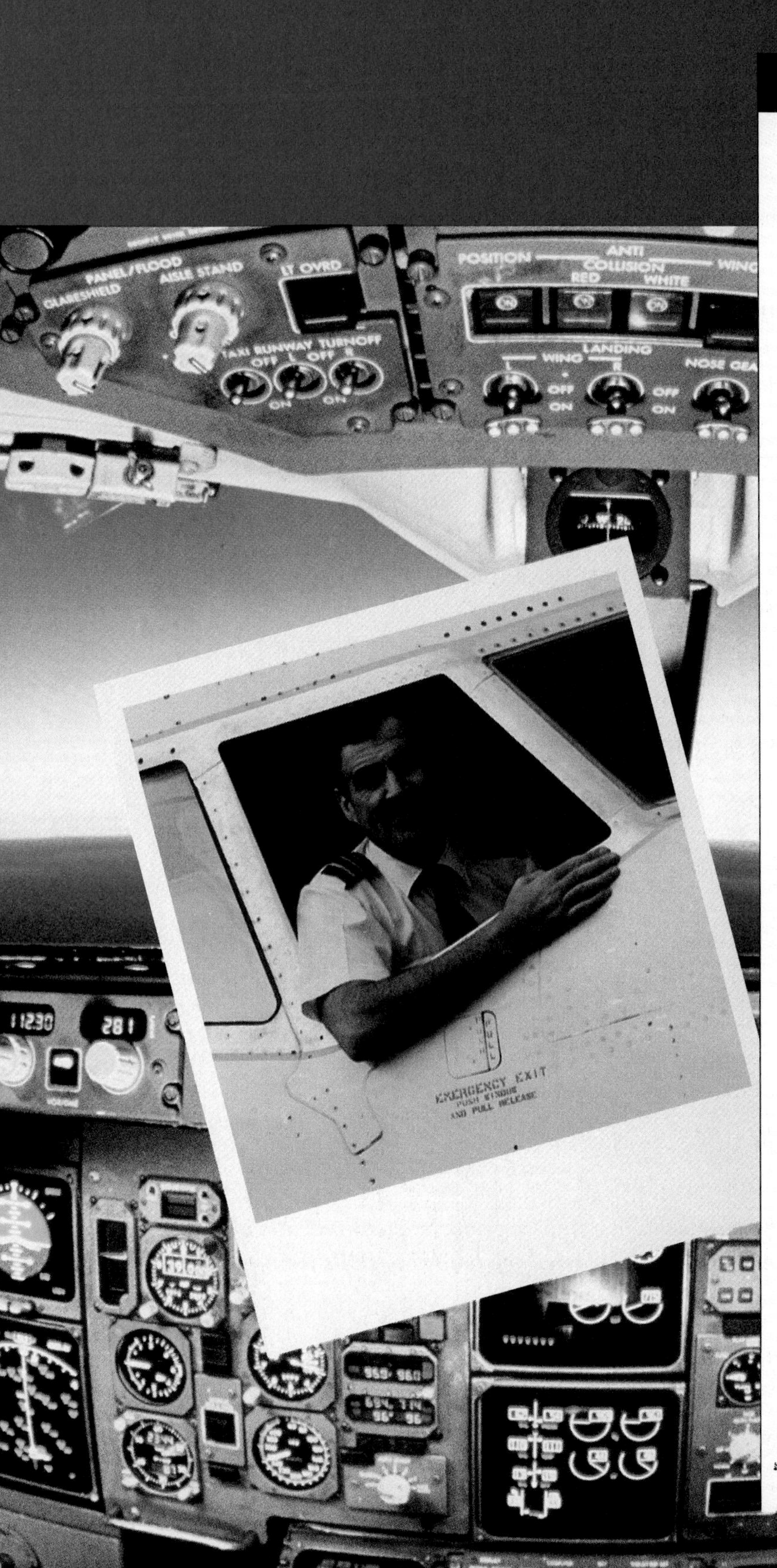

AZZAM BAKKAR

I loved math in high school, although I hated algebra at first. My father wanted me to go into engineering design. My plan was to get into a cockpit.

I've flown military and civilian transports. Math helped me to understand how an airplane functions. I calculate my own fuel economy, too. Math is close to reality.

Azzam Bakkar
Pilot
Continental Airlines
Houston, TX

Chapter 11 Geometric Inequalities and Optimization

GETTING READY

11-1 Indirect Reasoning and Inequalities

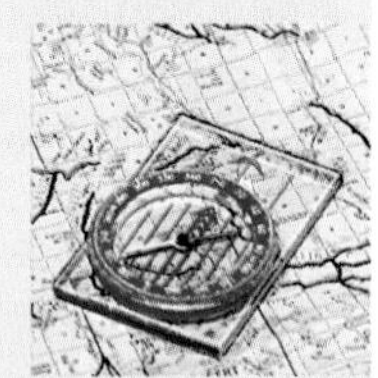

In 11-1 you will investigate shortest paths and explore their connections to inequalities in triangles. You will also look at a new strategy for proofs. You will use the following skills from previous chapters.

Give the inverse for each statement. [2-1]

1. If $|x| > 0$, then $x > 0$.

2. If $x^2 > 0$, then $x > 0$.

3. If $(a + b)^2 = 0$, then $a = -b$.

Write a phrase that means the opposite of the conclusion of each statement. [2-1]

4. If $x + 4 < -12$, then $x < -8$.

5. If $x^2 > x + x$, then $x > 2$.

6. If $a > b$ and $b > c$, then $a > c$.

7. If $-5x > 20$, then $x < -4$.

8. If $15 > -3x$, then $x > -5$.

9. If $AB > BC$, then $m\angle C > m\angle A$.

Which statements contradict each other? [2-1]

10. a. AB is parallel to GH.
b. AB is perpendicular to GH.
c. AB is not parallel to GH.

11. a. $x > 0$
b. $x \leq 0$
c. $x \geq 0$
d. $x \neq 0$

12. a. $x = 2$
b. $x > 1$
c. $x < 3$
d. $x \neq 2$

13. a. In triangle ABC, $\angle A$ is right.
b. In triangle ABC, $\angle A$ is not acute.
c. In triangle ABC, $\angle A$ is obtuse.

11-2 Optimization

In 11-2 you will study ways to optimize geometric and real-world quantities under given conditions. You will need the following skills from previous chapters and courses.

Solve each inequality. [Previous course]

14. $x + 3 > 7x$ **15.** $7x < 28$ **16.** $45 \geq -9x$ **17.** $-12 \leq 4x$

Given the following side lengths, which triangles are right triangles? [5-3]

18. 3, 4, 5 **19.** 8, 17, 15 **20.** 4, 6, 8 **21.** 26, 24, 10

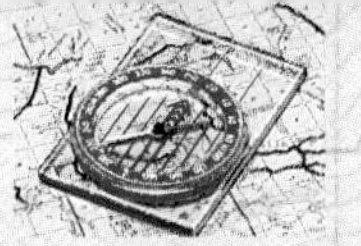

11-1 Indirect Reasoning and Inequalities

Finding Your Way

You may never have heard of orienteering, but the sport is about 60 years old. Orienteering was invented in Scandinavia, and is extremely popular in Norway and Sweden. The goal in orienteering is to get to all of the checkpoints on a cross-country course, in the proper order, before anyone else. Even the best orienteers get lost, but that's half the fun.

The basic equipment of orienteering is a map and a compass. Maps for orienteering competitions are quite complex. These maps feature details not shown on ordinary maps, like boulders, cactuses, and even anthills. Orienteers have to take every obstacle into account when deciding how to get from one checkpoint to another. Although a straight line segment is the shortest path between two points, it is often not the fastest!

Because of the great amount of detail shown, an orienteering map that pictures only a few square miles may take many hundreds of hours to prepare. Yet the competition itself usually takes less than two hours.

?

1. **Describe how driving to visit a friend in another state might be considered a form of orienteering.**

2. **Explain why the shortest path between two points may not be the fastest path between these points.**

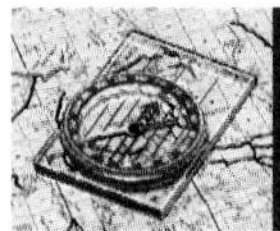

11-1 PART A Indirect Reasoning

← CONNECT → ***The proofs that you've done so far have been direct proofs. In a direct proof, you assume that the hypothesis of a conjecture is true and show that the conclusion must also be true. Now you will investigate another strategy for proof.***

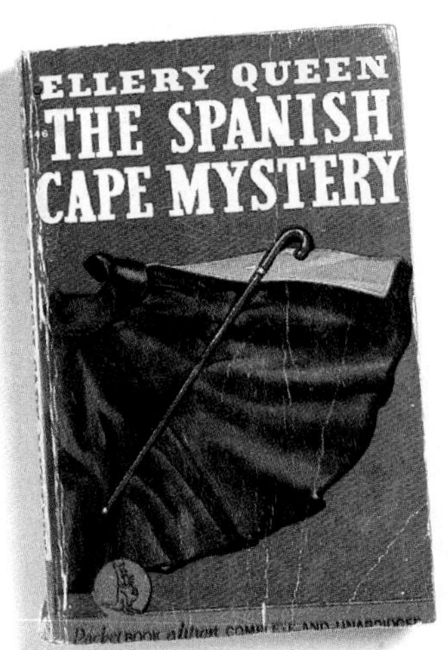

The Ellery Queen mystery series is comprised of about 33 books written from 1929 to 1971.

When using **indirect reasoning,** you show that a statement is true by proving that it cannot be false. In the following passage from *The Greek Coffin Mystery* (1932), detective Ellery Queen uses indirect reasoning to show that a suspect is innocent of murder.

Now, if Mr. Knox had been the murderer, why hadn't he removed the [$1000] bill, as I said a moment ago? . . . You see, his action was so wholly at variance with what he would have done had he been the murderer or the accomplice, that I was compelled to say at that time: "Well, no matter where the guilt lies, it certainly isn't in the direction of James Knox."

To prove that James Knox was *not* guilty, Ellery Queen first assumed that he *was* guilty! He showed that this assumption led to a contradiction.

There are three key steps in an indirect proof.

- Assume that the statement you are trying to prove is false. (If the statement is a conditional, you assume its hypothesis and **negate** its conclusion.)
- Show that this assumption leads to a contradiction of something you know is true.
- Conclude that your assumption was incorrect, so that the statement you originally wanted to prove must be true.

The word *not* is often important when writing the negation of a statement.

Statement	Negation
It is raining.	It is not raining.
The lines are not coplanar.	The lines are coplanar.

1. Give a conditional statement in if-then form. What would you assume in order to begin an indirect proof of your statement?

TRY IT

What would you assume in order to begin an indirect proof of each of the following?

a. If it rains, then I will wash my car. **b.** If $m\angle R = 20°$, then $\overline{ST} \cong \overline{XY}$.

The following Example shows a complete indirect proof.

EXAMPLE

Use an indirect proof to prove the following.

If two lines intersect, then they intersect in only one point.

First, we assume the hypothesis and negate the conclusion of the statement we are trying to prove.

Two lines intersect and they do not intersect in only one point. (That is, they intersect in more than one point.)

In the following proof, we show that this leads to a contradiction.

Proof: Assume that two lines, m and n, both contain D and E. This contradicts the Straight-Line Postulate: "Two points are contained in one and only one line." Therefore, the original statement cannot be false, so the statement "If two lines intersect, then they intersect in only one point" must be true.

D E m n

EXPLORE: NOT FALSE = ?

Use an indirect proof to prove the following.

If a perpendicular segment is drawn from a point not on a line to the line, then it is the shortest such segment.

1. Write the negation of the conclusion of the statement.
2. Assume that this statement is true. In that case, there must be another segment from the point to the line that is shorter than the perpendicular segment. Draw and label a figure showing the line, the point not on the line, the perpendicular segment, and the "shorter" segment.
3. Use the Pythagorean Theorem to show that your assumption leads to a contradiction. What is the contradiction?
4. What do you conclude? Explain how you can justify this conclusion.

Indirect reasoning is an important tool in logic. It is used by mechanics working on automobiles and by physicians in diagnosing diseases. They study the ailments of the engine or patient and list the causes that might produce these ailments. Eliminating possibilities that contradict a known fact can lead them to the actual cause of the problem.

REFLECT

1. Write a short description of indirect reasoning. Why do you think indirect reasoning is called *indirect*?
2. Briefly explain the similarities and differences between direct proof and indirect proof.
3. Paragraph proof is the format most often used to demonstrate an indirect proof. Why do you think this is the case?

Exercises

CORE

Getting Started It's important to be able to recognize contradictions when doing indirect proofs. For each set of statements, identify the two that form a contradiction.

1. (a) $ABCD$ is a rectangle.
   (b) $ABCD$ is a trapezoid.
   (c) $ABCD$ is a quadrilateral.

2. (a) $\overleftrightarrow{AB} \nparallel \overleftrightarrow{CD}$
   (b) $\overleftrightarrow{AB}$ and $\overleftrightarrow{CD}$ are skew lines.
   (c) $\overleftrightarrow{AB} \perp \overleftrightarrow{CD}$

Write the negation of the conclusion of each statement.

3. If it is Monday, then tomorrow is Tuesday.
4. If $3x < 24$, then $x < 8$.
5. If I catch a fish, then I won't throw it back.
6. If $a = b$, then $a + c = b + c$.
7. If $AB = DE$, then $\triangle ABC \cong \triangle DEF$.
8. If $\triangle ABC$ is scalene, then $\angle A \ncong \angle B$.

In Exercises 9–11, write the negation of each statement from a famous author or statesperson.

9. The good of the people is the most important law. [Cicero (106–43 B.C.)]
10. We are not amused. [Queen Victoria (1819–1901)]
11. The report of my death was an exaggeration. [Mark Twain (1835–1910)]
12. If the probability that an event will occur is p, what is the probability that it will not occur?

13. Auto Immobile Mark's car won't start. He knows that there are three likely reasons for this.

(1) His battery is dead. (2) His starter doesn't work. (3) He is out of gas.

When a car's starter needs to be replaced, the car is silent when you try to start it. If the battery is dead, the engine "turns over" slowly, if at all. When Mark tries to start his car, it sounds normal. What do you think is wrong with his car? Explain your reasoning. In your explanation, be sure to discuss any indirect reasoning you may have used.

14. Follow the given steps to prove the following.

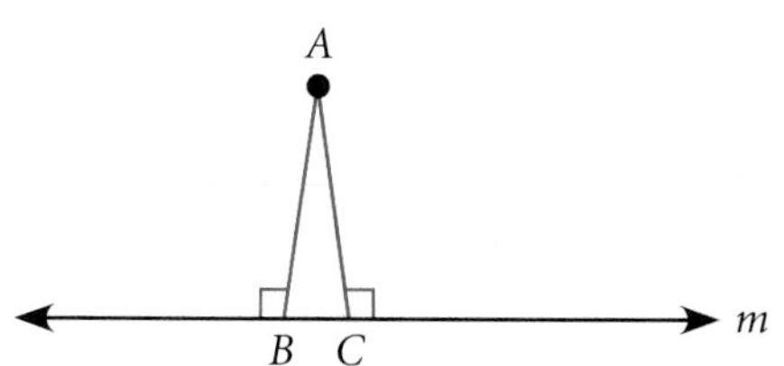

If a point is not on a line, then there is no more than one perpendicular from the point to the line.

a. Write the negation of the conclusion of the statement you are trying to prove.

b. Explain how the figure at the right illustrates this.

c. Explain how assuming that this negation is true leads to a contradiction of a known fact or theorem.

Use an indirect proof to prove each of the following.

15. A right triangle has only one right angle.

16. If $\triangle ABC$ is scalene, then $\angle A \not\cong \angle C$.

17. *Given:* Quadrilateral $PQRS$, $\overline{PQ} \cong \overline{QR}$, and $\overline{PS} \not\cong \overline{RS}$.

Prove: $\overline{QS}$ does not bisect $\angle PQR$.

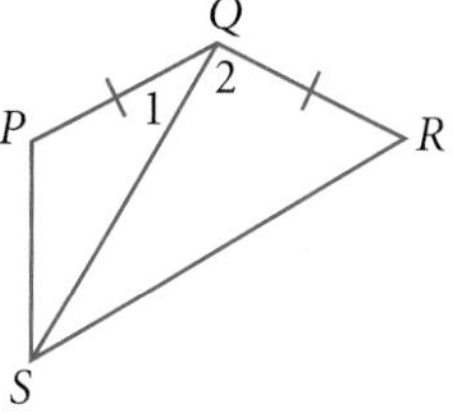

18. Describe a method for finding the minimum distance between two parallel lines. Explain why your method works.

LOOK BACK

Find the sum of the measures of the interior and exterior angles (one at each vertex) for each polygon. Then give the measure of each interior and exterior angle of the polygon. [6-1, 6-3]

19. regular octagon **20.** regular 12-gon **21.** regular 20-gon

$\triangle ABC \sim \triangle EDF$. Find each of the following. [7-2]

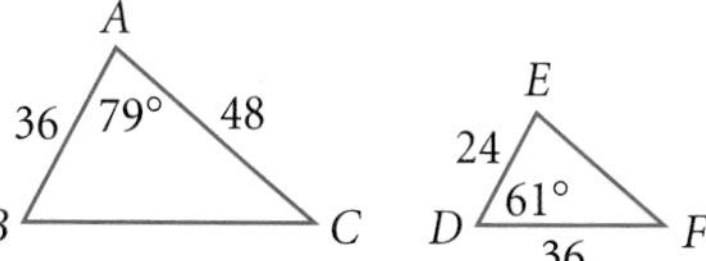

22. $m\angle B$ **23.** BC **24.** $m\angle E$

25. $m\angle C$ **26.** $m\angle F$ **27.** EF

28. Sketch a wallpaper pattern that has translation symmetry and point symmetry. [10-2]

MORE PRACTICE

Write the negation of the conclusion of each statement.

29. If $\overline{PQ} \not\perp \ell$, then $\angle 1$ is not a right angle.

30. If two planes intersect, then they intersect in no more than one line.

31. If ℓ is not parallel to m, then $\angle 1 \not\cong \angle 2$.

MORE MATH REASONING

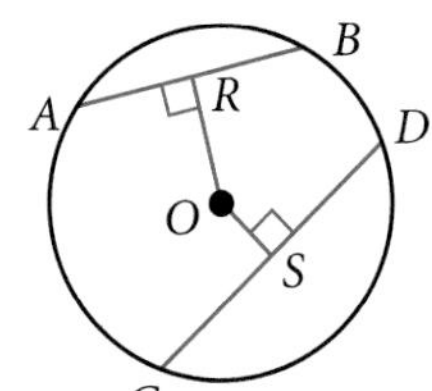

32. Prove: In circle O, if $\overline{AB} \not\cong \overline{CD}$, then $\overline{OR} \not\cong \overline{OS}$.

33. An Indirect Route David rode his motorcycle from Lincoln to Omaha, a 55-mi trip on Interstate 80.

a. If the trip took David 45 minutes, prove that he went faster than the 65 mi/hr speed limit for at least part of the trip.

b. David's friend, Iona, rode with him for the first half of the trip. She claims that David did not go faster than 65 mi/hr while the two rode together. Is Iona telling the truth? Explain.

11-1 PART B Inequalities in a Triangle

← CONNECT → ***You've already explored congruent sides and congruent angles in triangles. Now you will investigate parts of a triangle that are not congruent.***

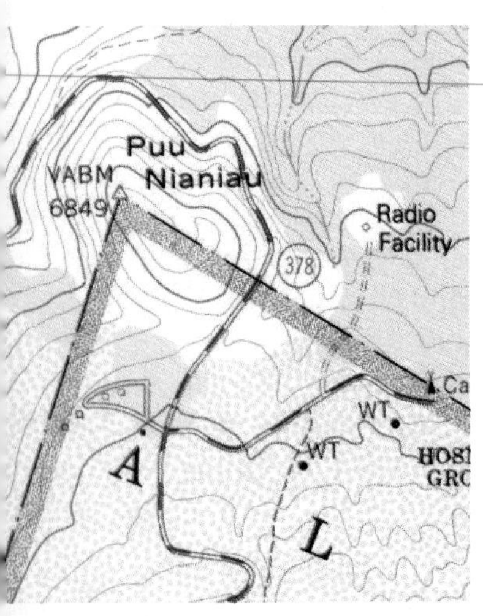

Orienteers can look at a map like the one at the left and visualize their approach to every checkpoint. You can also apply these skills to geometry. If you look at an accurate figure, you may be able to make a good guess at which sides and angles are the largest or smallest. In mathematics, however, you need to make sure that your visual intuition is correct and provide a justification for your ideas.

You will be showing that parts of triangles have unequal measures. To do this, you will need the help of some properties of inequality, which are reviewed on page 715.

PROPERTIES OF INEQUALITY

The following are true for all real numbers a, b, and c.

Trichotomy Law	Exactly one of the following is true: $a < b$, $a = b$, or $a > b$.
Transitive Property	If $a < b$ and $b < c$, then $a < c$.
Addition Property	If $a < b$, then $a + c < b + c$.
Comparison Property	$a > b$ if and only if there is a $c > 0$ such that $a = b + c$.

1. How can you use the Comparison Property to show that the measure of an exterior angle of a triangle is greater than the measure of either of its remote interior angles? (In other words, prove that $m\angle YXZ > m\angle YWX$, and $m\angle YXZ > m\angle WYX$.)

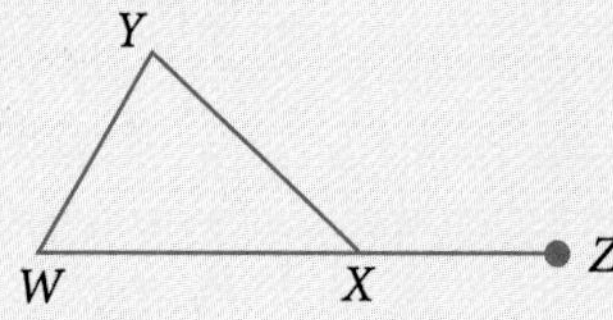

In the following Explore, you will investigate a relationship between the lengths of the sides of a triangle and the measures of its angles.

EXPLORE: THE LITTLEST ANGLE

MATERIALS

Ruler, Protractor
Geometry software (optional)

Draw several scalene triangles. Measure the sides and angles of one of the triangles. Make as many conjectures as you can that involve the longest and shortest sides and the largest and smallest angles. Use your other triangles to check your conjectures. Then discuss your conjectures with classmates.

TRY IT

Name the largest and smallest angles in the triangles in each figure.

a.

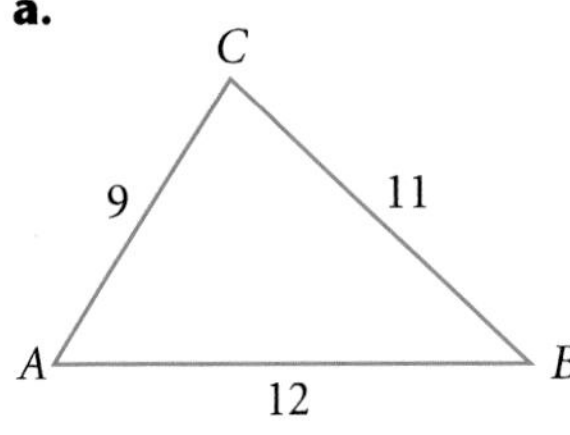

b.

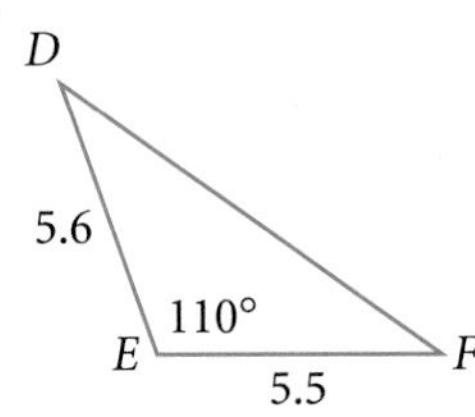

c.

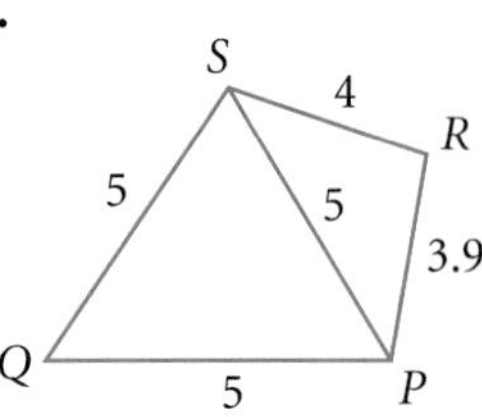

Name the longest and shortest segments in each figure.

d.

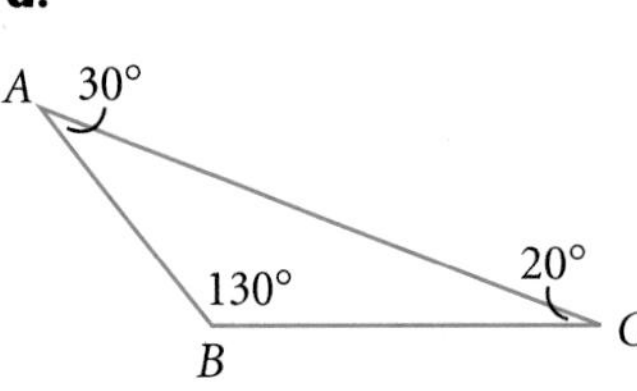

e.

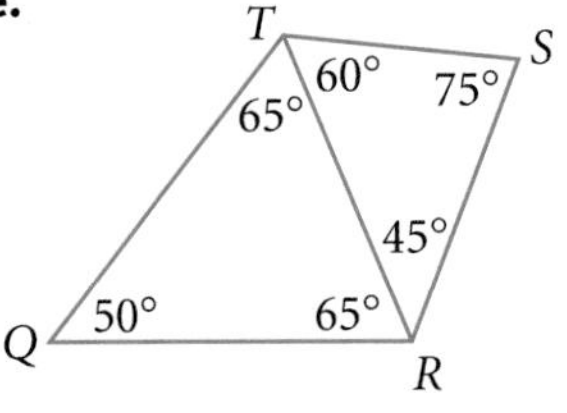

f.

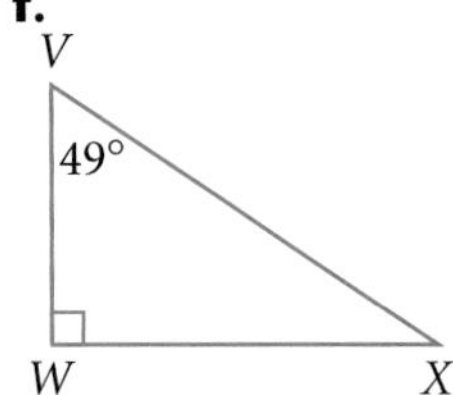

The relationships you've discovered among triangle side lengths and angle measures are summarized below. In Exercise 22, you will use indirect proof to justify one of these theorems.

> **THEOREMS**
>
> If two sides of a triangle have unequal lengths, then the measure of the angle opposite the longer side is greater than the measure of the angle opposite the shorter side.
>
> If two angles of a triangle have unequal measures, then the side opposite the larger angle is longer than the side opposite the smaller angle.

REFLECT

1. Use one of the above theorems to explain why the hypotenuse is the longest side of a right triangle. Then describe another way to justify this fact.
2. How are the two theorems about unequal side lengths and angle measures in triangles related to each other?
3. Is the shortest side of any convex polygon opposite its smallest angle? Explain.

Exercises

CORE

Getting Started Name the largest and smallest angles in each figure.

1.

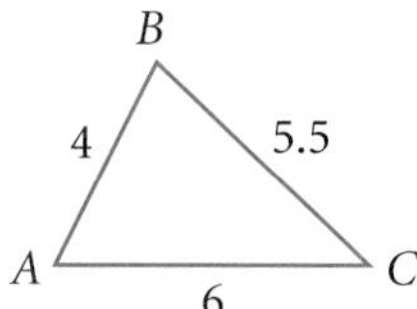

2.

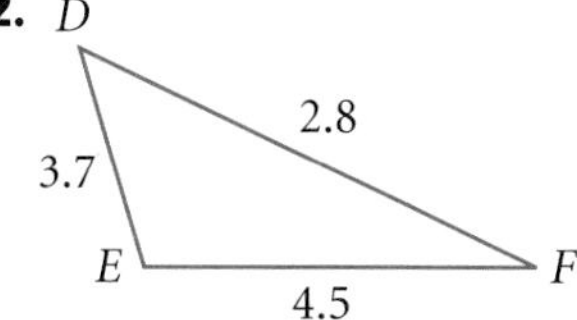

3.

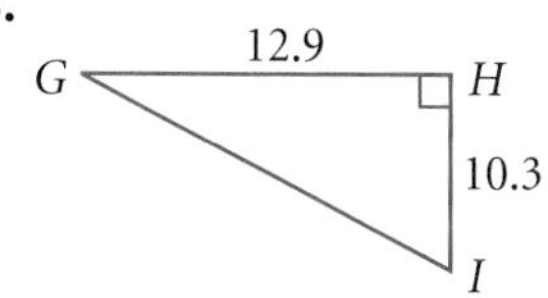

4. Which side of $\triangle QPR$ is the longest? Why?

5. Which side of $\triangle QRS$ is the longest? Why?

6. Which side of $\triangle QPR$ is the shortest?

7. Which side of $\triangle QRS$ is the shortest?

8. Which side of quadrilateral $PQSR$ is the longest?

9. Which side of quadrilateral $PQSR$ is the shortest?

10. List the segments in the figure from shortest to longest.

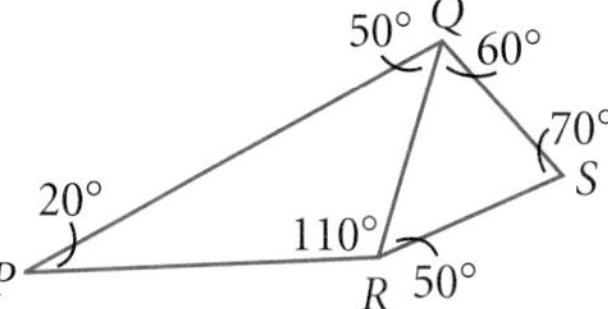

Name the longest and shortest segments in each figure.

11.

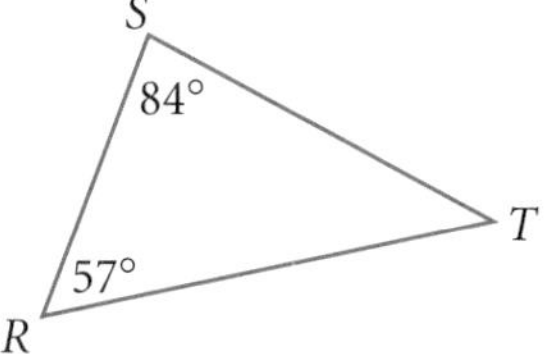

12.

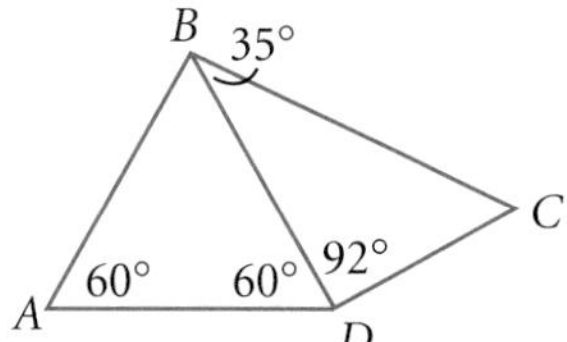

13.

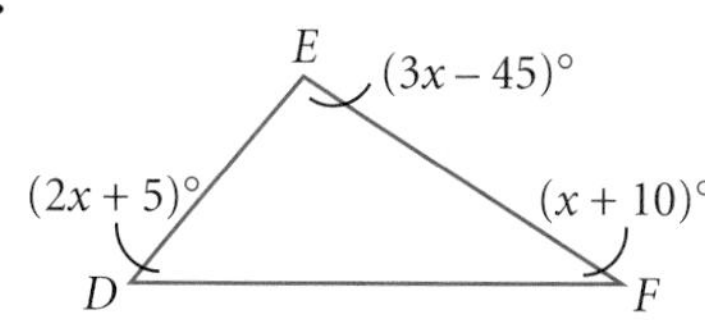

14. The coordinates of the vertices of $\triangle ABC$ are $A(-1, 1)$, $B(2, 2)$, and $C(0, 5)$. List the angles of $\triangle ABC$ from smallest to largest.

15. Ohio Angle On a map, the approximate distance from Akron to Youngstown is 40 miles, the distance from Youngstown to Steubenville is 50 miles, and the distance from Steubenville to Akron is 75 miles. Identify the largest angle of the triangle formed by these three cities, and explain your answer. If you used a sketch to help you, include it with your explanation.

Science

16. Who's Closer? Two participants in an orienteering competition, Alicia and Barika, know each other's location. Alicia, at point A, finds that $m\angle A = 55°$. Barika finds that $m\angle B = 65°$.

a. Who is closer to the checkpoint?

b. Is one participant closer to the checkpoint than to her competitor? If so, which one? How do you know?

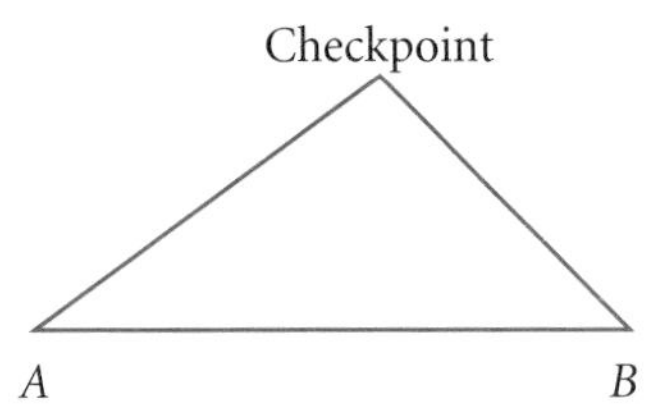

In $\triangle RST$, $RS = 3$, and $RT = 4$. The length of $\overline{ST}$ is chosen randomly from the numbers 2, 3, 4, 5, and 6. Find each of the following.

17. The probability that $\angle R$ is the largest angle in $\triangle RST$

18. The probability that $\angle T$ is the smallest angle in $\triangle RST$

19. The probability that $\triangle RST$ is isosceles

20. The probability that $\triangle RST$ is a right triangle

21. Use an indirect proof to prove the following.

If $\overline{JK}$ is the shortest side of $\triangle JKL$, then $\angle L$ is not an obtuse angle.

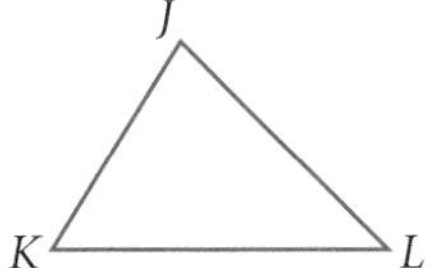

22. Use an indirect proof to prove the following theorem.

If two angles of a triangle have unequal measures, then the side opposite the larger angle is longer than the side opposite the smaller angle.

Given: $m\angle A > m\angle C$

Prove: $BC > AB$

a. Part 1: Assume $BC = AB$.

b. Part 2: Assume $BC < AB$.

c. Why must this proof be done in two parts?

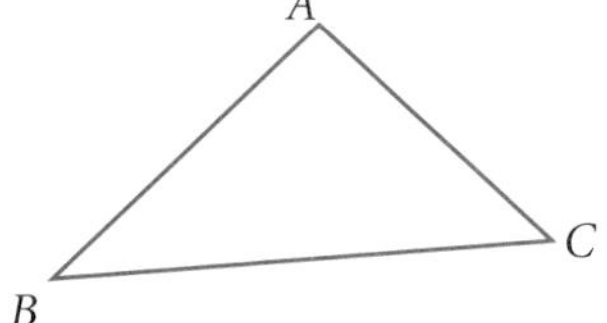

LOOK AHEAD

23. Write a single inequality that combines the two statements $x < y$ and $y < z$.

In the table, the sum of any two numbers in a row must be greater than the third number. Write an inequality that expresses the range of possible values for *c*.

	a	*b*	*c*
24.	3.0	5.0	
25.	10.0	15.0	
26.	1.7	3.3	

MORE PRACTICE

27. Which side of $\triangle WXZ$ is the longest? Why?

28. Which side of $\triangle XYZ$ is the longest? Why?

29. Which side of $\triangle WXZ$ is the shortest?

30. Which side of $\triangle XYZ$ is the shortest?

31. Which side of quadrilateral *WXYZ* is the longest?

32. Which side of quadrilateral *WXYZ* is the shortest?

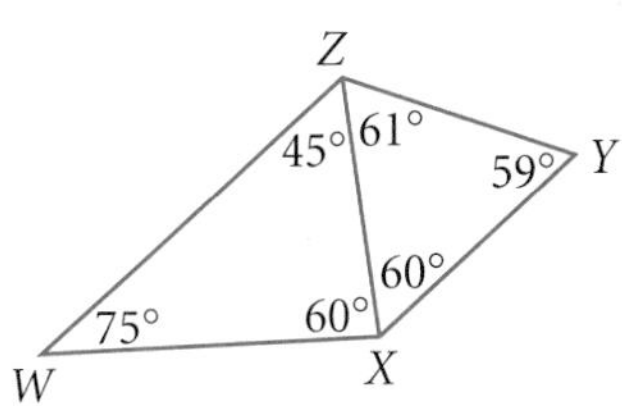

Name the largest and smallest angles in the triangles in each figure.

33.

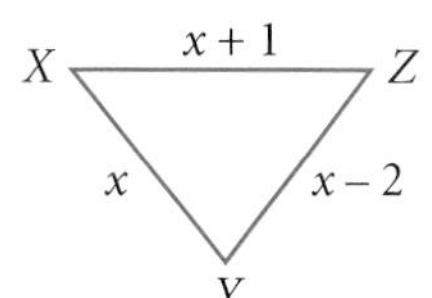

34.

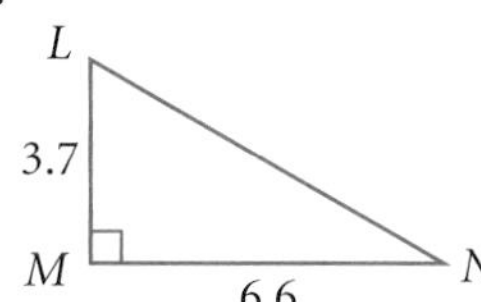

35.

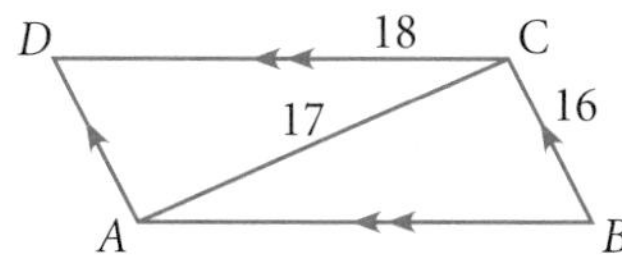

Name the longest and shortest sides in each figure.

36.

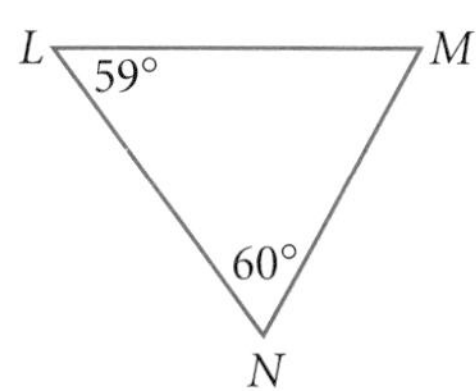

37.

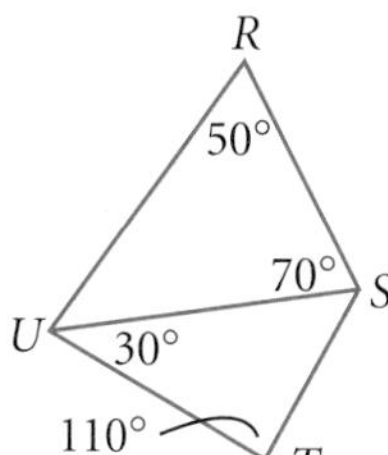

38.

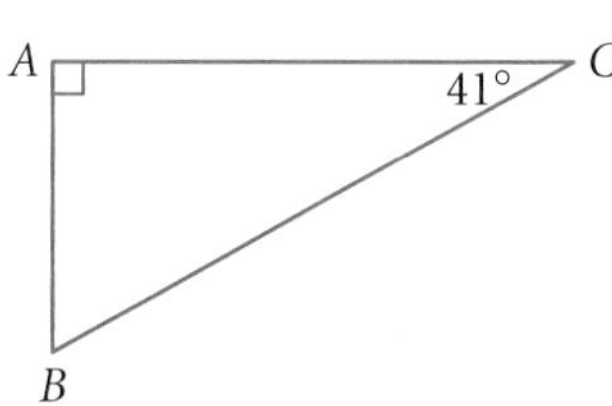

39. The coordinates of the vertices of $\triangle DEF$ are $D(-1, 4)$, $E(2, 0)$, and $F(-3, -1)$. List the angles of $\triangle DEF$ from smallest to largest.

MORE MATH REASONING

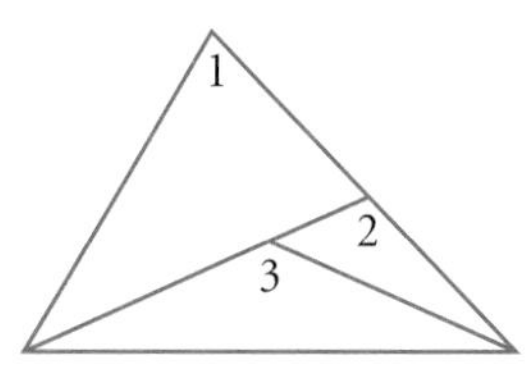

40. Refer to the figure at the right. If $m\angle 1 = 70°$, $m\angle 2 = (2x - 10)°$, and $m\angle 3 = (3x - 40)°$, write an inequality that expresses the range of possible values for x.

41. *Given:* $\triangle ABC$ is isosceles, with legs $\overline{AB}$ and $\overline{AC}$, and R is any point on $\overleftrightarrow{BC}$ that is not on $\overline{BC}$.

Prove: $RA > AB$

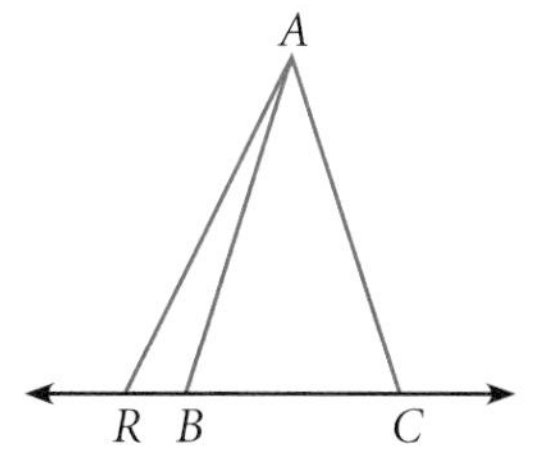

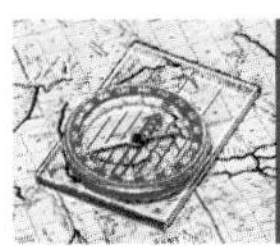

11-1 PART C The Triangle Inequality Theorem

← CONNECT →

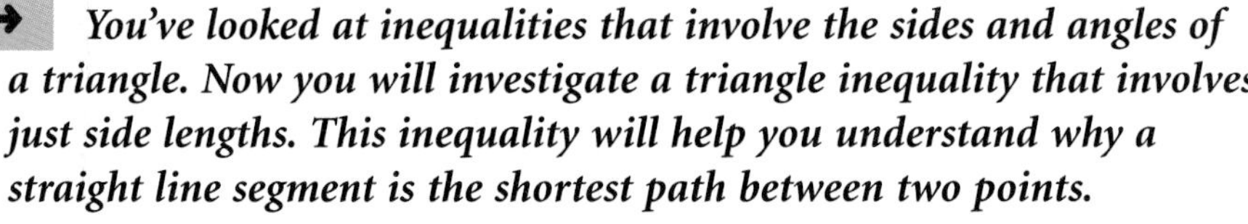

You've looked at inequalities that involve the sides and angles of a triangle. Now you will investigate a triangle inequality that involves just side lengths. This inequality will help you understand why a straight line segment is the shortest path between two points.

Other things being equal, orienteers travel in a straight line from one checkpoint to the next. Why? In the following Explore, you will discover a relationship that governs side lengths in a triangle. This relationship helps you identify the shortest path between two points.

EXPLORE: IS IT A TRIANGLE?

MATERIALS

Scissors
Ruler
Paper

1. Cut out strips of paper 1 cm wide with lengths of 2 cm, 3 cm, 4 cm, 5 cm, 8 cm, and 11 cm. Draw a line segment down the center of each strip, and write down its length, as shown.

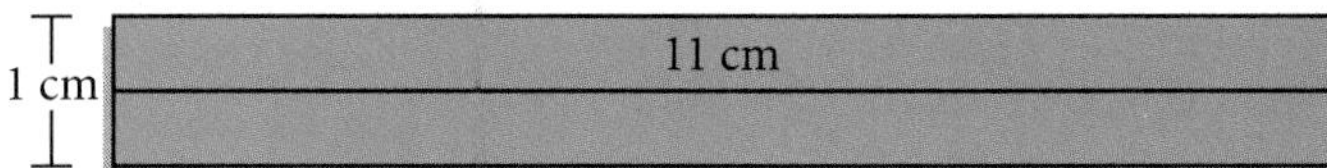

2. Choose three strips at random. See if you can use them to form a triangle like the one shown at the right. Make a table to record the lengths of the three strips and whether or not they form a triangle.

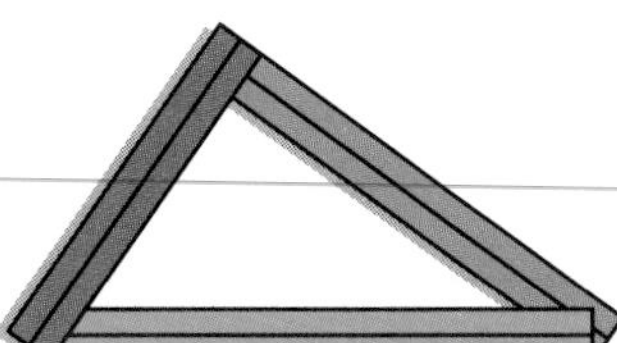

3. Repeat Step 2 until you have several combinations of side lengths that do and do not form triangles. Then write an inequality to describe the relationship among the side lengths of any triangle.

TRY IT

Determine whether each set of numbers could represent the lengths of the sides of a triangle.

a. 4, 7, 10 **b.** 3, 5, 8 **c.** 3, 5, 7.9

EXAMPLE

Two sides of a triangle measure 6 cm and 9 cm. Write an inequality that represents the range of values for the possible lengths of the third side.

Let x represent the length of the unknown side. The sum of the lengths of two sides of a triangle must be greater than the length of the third side.

Therefore: $\quad x + 6 > 9 \quad$ and $\quad 6 + 9 > x$

$x > 3 \quad$ and $\quad 15 > x$

Putting these two inequalities together, we find that $3 < x < 15$. The length of the third side must be greater than 3 cm but less than 15 cm.

The observation you've made about triangle side lengths is stated below.

> **TRIANGLE INEQUALITY THEOREM**
>
> The sum of the lengths of any two sides of a triangle is greater than the length of the third side.

The Triangle Inequality Theorem helps you see why a line segment is the shortest path between two points.

REFLECT

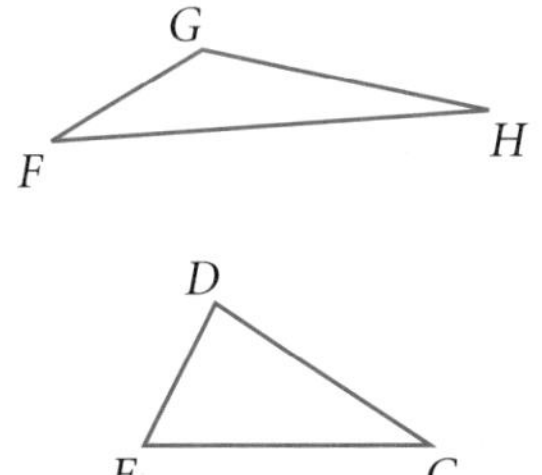

1. Other things being equal, why does an orienteer prefer to travel in a straight line from point F to point H rather than going from F to G to H?
2. Write all the side-length relationships you can for scalene triangle $\triangle CDE$, using the Triangle Inequality Theorem.
3. The two brick sidewalks shown at the right connect buildings A and B. However, people have walked through the grass between the buildings so often that they have worn a path in the grass. Use the Triangle Inequality Theorem to explain why this path is there.

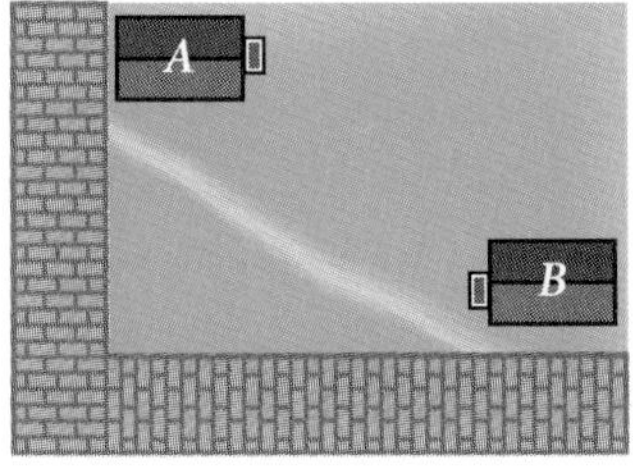

Exercises

CORE

Getting Started Determine whether each set of numbers could represent the lengths of the sides of a triangle.

1. 3, 4, 6 **2.** 10, 12, 22 **3.** 3.2, 5.5, 8.8

The lengths of two sides of a triangle are given. Write an inequality that represents the range of values for the possible lengths of the third side.

4. 3, 5 **5.** $13\frac{1}{2}, 24\frac{4}{5}$ **6.** $n, 3n$

7. Find the shortest route from M to X along the segments shown. (The figure may not be drawn to scale.) Give a value or range of values for the length of this route. Explain how you found the shortest route.

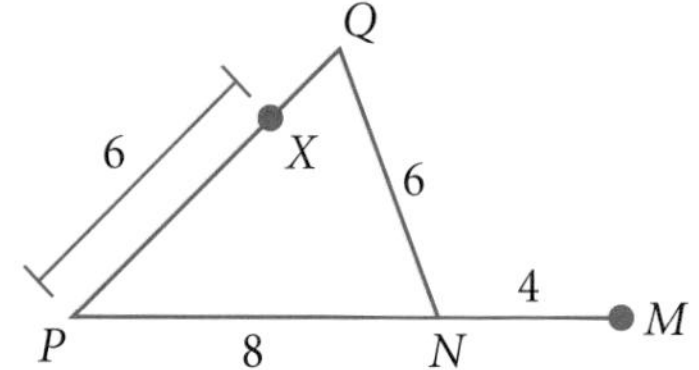

8. Suppose you know that the lengths of all three sides of a triangle are integers and that the lengths of two of its sides are 4 and 7. Give all of the possible lengths for the third side. Explain how you found your answer.

The map shows air travel distances from Minneapolis to four other cities. Use the Triangle Inequality Theorem to find the range of possible distances between the following pairs of cities.

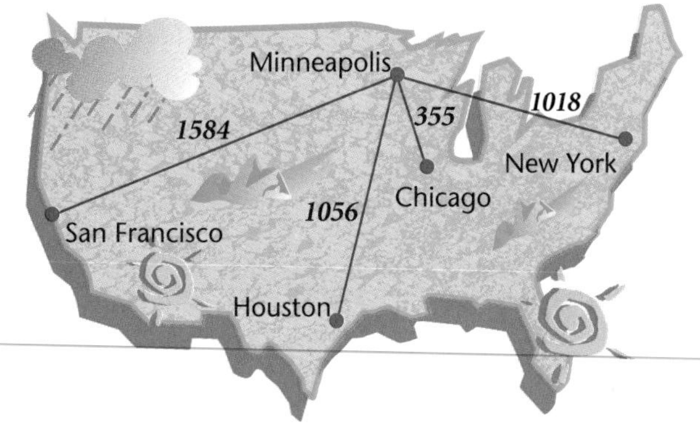

9. Chicago and Houston

10. San Francisco and Chicago

11. New York and San Francisco

12. Use an indirect proof to prove the following.

If $AB + BC = AC$, then A, B, and C are collinear.

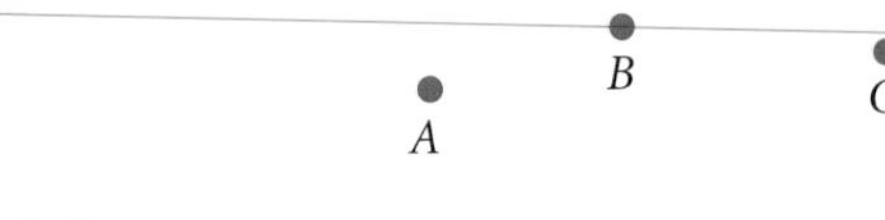

13. Cooking with Geometry When installing a kitchen, it is recommended that the sum of the distances between the sink, stove, and refrigerator should be less than 26 ft and more than 12 ft. Also, no leg of this "kitchen triangle" should be less than 4 ft long or more than 9 ft long.

a. Why do you think these distance recommendations exist?

b. In a kitchen, the sink is 4 ft from the stove, and the stove is 4 ft from the refrigerator. Find the minimum and maximum possible distances from the sink to the refrigerator that meet the preceding recommendations.

14. The Hinge Theorem **a.** Using a ruler, draw $\triangle EFG$ as shown. Measure EF and FG, and then use your protractor to find $m\angle F$.

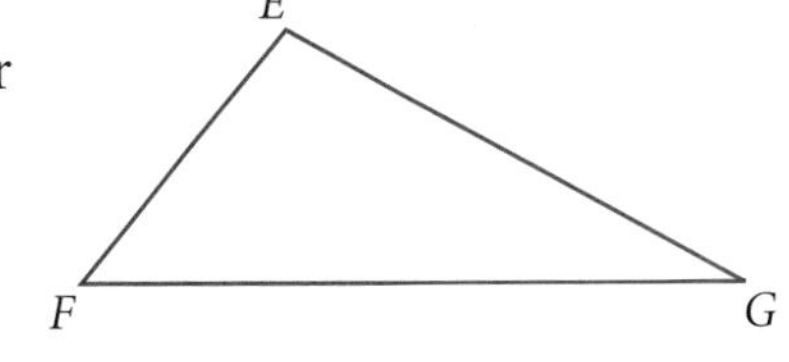

b. Now draw $\angle K$ so that $m\angle K > m\angle F$. Locate points J and L on the sides of $\angle K$ so that $\overline{KJ} \cong \overline{FE}$ and $\overline{KL} \cong \overline{FG}$. Draw $\overline{JL}$ to complete $\triangle JKL$.

c. Measure $\overline{EG}$ and $\overline{JL}$. Which is longer? How does this relate to the relationship between $m\angle F$ and $m\angle K$?

d. The Hinge Theorem begins, "If two sides of one triangle are congruent to two sides of a second triangle and the measure of the included angle of the first triangle is greater than the measure of the included angle of the second triangle, then . . ." Complete the Hinge Theorem.

e. Why do you think this theorem is called the Hinge Theorem?

f. What conclusion can you draw from the figure at the right, using the Hinge Theorem? Justify your conclusion.

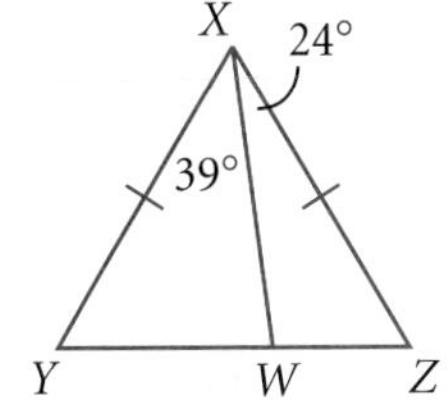

LOOK AHEAD

Solve each formula for the specified variable.

15. $A = \frac{1}{2}bh$, for h

16. $P = 2\ell + 2w$, for w

17. $A = 4\pi r^2$, for r

Rewrite the second equation in each pair so that *y* is in terms of *x* only. (Hint: Use substitution.)

18. $z = 2x$
$y = 3x + 2z$

19. $z = \frac{4}{x}$
$y = 2x^2 + 12xz$

20. $3z + 12x = 6$
$y = 7x^3 + 2z$

MORE PRACTICE

Determine whether each set of numbers could represent the lengths of the sides of a triangle.

21. 2, 7, 8

22. 9, 14, 20

23. $2\frac{1}{2}, 4\frac{1}{3}, 6\frac{2}{3}$

24. 1.5, 9.2, 7.7

25. $\frac{1}{3}, \frac{2}{5}, \frac{1}{4}$

26. 18.5, 5.3, 13.8

The lengths of two sides of a triangle are given. Write an inequality that represents the range of values for the possible lengths of the third side.

27. 10, 15

28. 14, 22

29. n, $2n$

MORE MATH REASONING

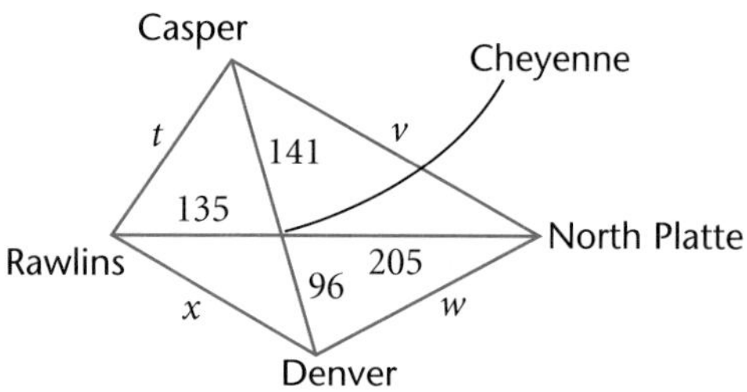

30. The map at the right shows distances between several cities.

Social Science

a. What is the possible range of distances for t? v? w? x?

b. What theorem did you use in **30a**?

c. Each of three travelers drove through all of the cities shown (except Cheyenne) and ended up where they started. Traveler A claimed to have traveled 600 mi, Traveler B 800 mi, and Traveler C 1325 mi. Explain why each of these mileages is possible or impossible.

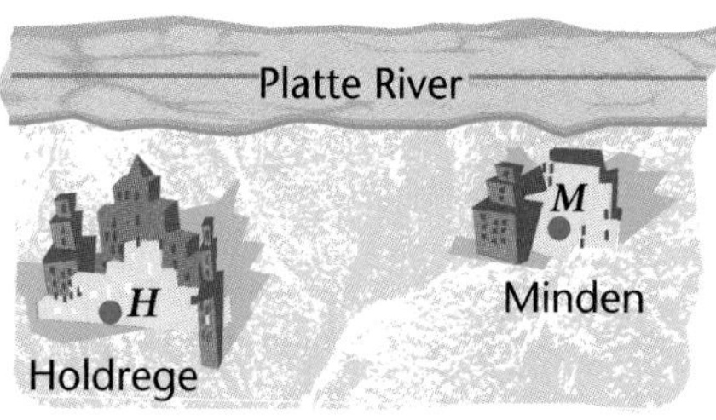

31. Well! A well to supply water to the cities of Holdrege (H) and Minden (M) is to be drilled on the Platte River. The city councils have chosen you to decide where the well should be placed. To minimize costs, you must locate the well so that the distance from Minden to the well to Holdrege is as short as possible.

a. Copy the figure, and find the best location for the well. (Hint: Use a technique from Chapter 10.)

b. Use the Triangle Inequality Theorem and your knowledge of transformations to convince the city councils that you've found the best site. (Hint: Draw any other point, X, on the river, and show that the distance from H to your point to M must be shorter than the distance from H to X to M.)

11-1 PART D Making Connections

← CONNECT → ***Industries that connect locations with wires or cables—like telephone, power, and cable television companies—need to find the shortest paths that join these points. You've investigated shortest paths, explored their connections to inequalities in triangles, and looked at another strategy for proof.***

In the following Explore, you will use geometry to find the shortest path that links two points. As shown on the map at the left, this skill can be important in planning long trips, as well as in orienteering.

EXPLORE: PATH FINDER

Your "geometeering" team is in a competition to find the shortest path from point A to point I. You may only travel along the segments shown in the figure. Beware—the figure is not necessarily drawn accurately!

To win, you must find the shortest path from A to I and justify each decision you make along the way. The first team with the correct path and valid explanations for all of its choices wins the competition. On your mark . . . get set . . . go!

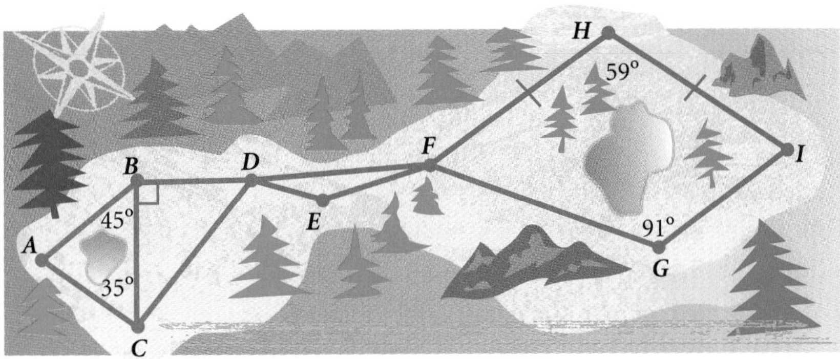

REFLECT

1. In your own words, describe the process of indirect proof.
2. Write a summary of all the inequalities you know relating to triangles. Include drawings with your summary.
3. Is the base of an isosceles triangle always its shortest side? Explain.

Self-Assessment

Write the negation of the conclusion of each statement.

1. If an animal is a horse, then it does not have toes.
2. If $\angle A \cong \angle B$, then $\angle B \cong \angle A$.
3. If I try out for softball, then I might make the team.
4. List the segments in the figure at the right from shortest to longest.

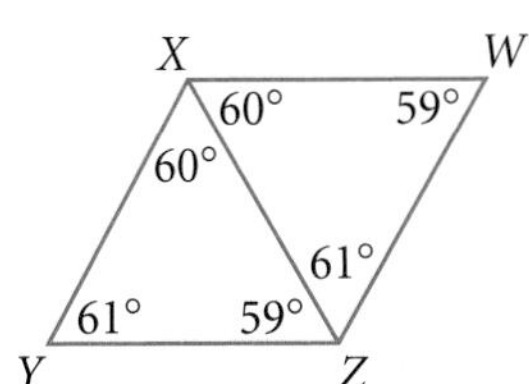

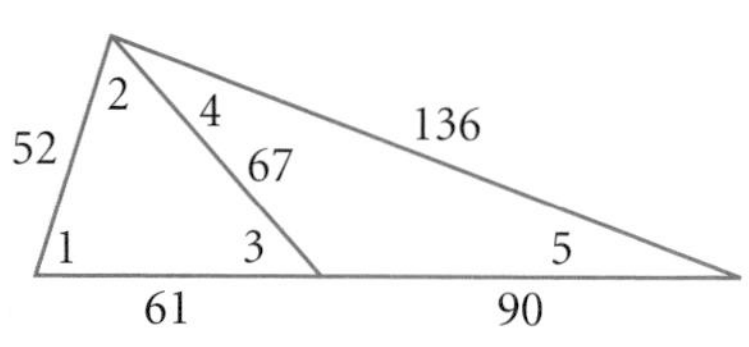

5. List the numbered angles in the figure at the right from smallest to largest.

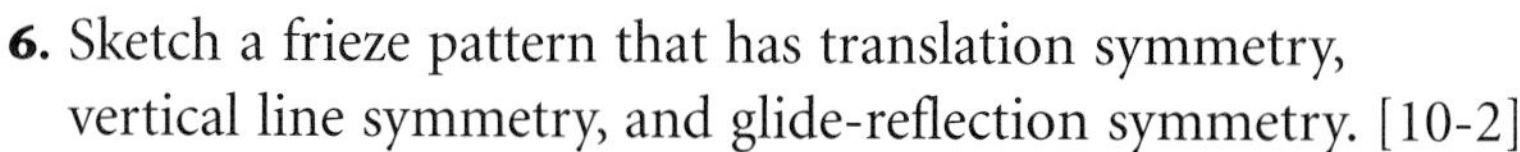

6. Sketch a frieze pattern that has translation symmetry, vertical line symmetry, and glide-reflection symmetry. [10-2]

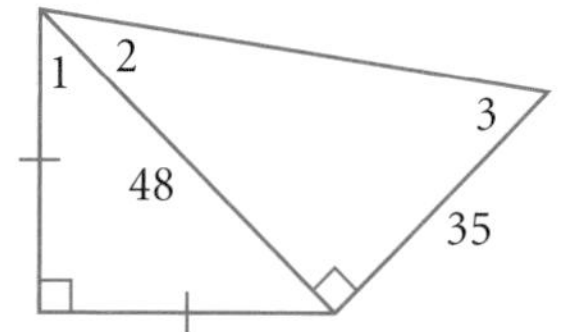

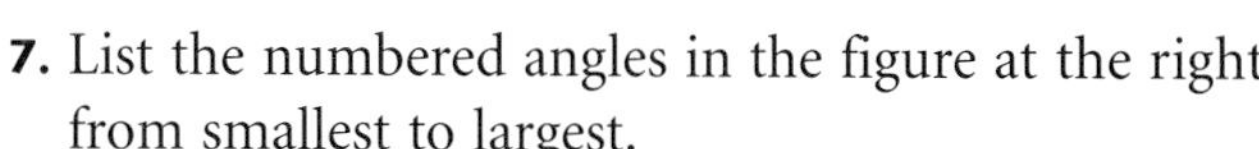

7. List the numbered angles in the figure at the right from smallest to largest.

Find the sum of the measures of the interior and exterior angles (one at each vertex) for each polygon. Then give the measure of each interior and exterior angle. [6-1, 6-3]

8. regular hexagon **9.** regular decagon **10.** regular 15-gon

11. Bogged Down In an orienteering competition, Helena needs to know how far it is across the swamp. Find the distance, and explain how you found it. [7-2]

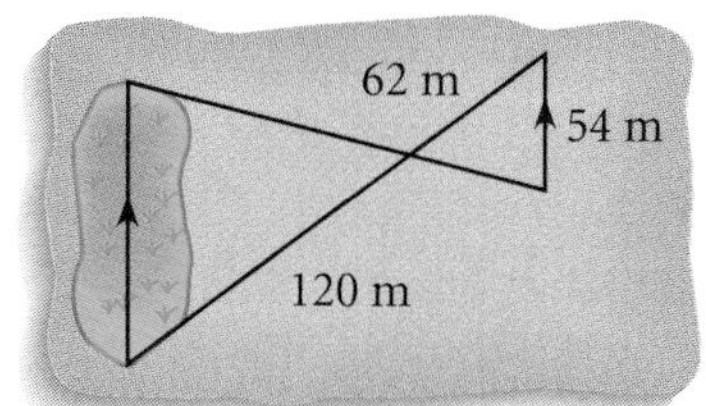

The lengths of two sides of $\triangle EFG$ are given. Choose the number that could represent the length of the third side.

12. $EF = 3$, and $FG = 8$. EG could be
(a) 4 (b) 5 (c) 6 (d) 12

13. $EF = 2x$, and $FG = 4x$. EG could be
(a) $5x$ (b) $6x$ (c) $7x$ (d) $8x$

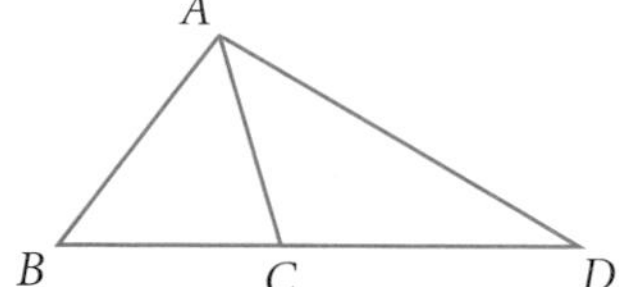

14. Use an indirect proof to prove the following.
If $\triangle ABD$ is scalene and $\overline{AC}$ is a median, then $\overline{AC} \not\perp \overline{BD}$.

15. Marvin is in an orienteering competition, and he has reached Checkpoint 8. There are two ways to reach Checkpoint 9.

He can go directly from Checkpoint 8 to Checkpoint 9, but this route takes him through some swampy ground. He can go at twice the speed if he goes along a dirt path from Checkpoint 8 to point X and then to Checkpoint 9. (The distance from X to Checkpoint 9 is unreadable due to a smudge on the map.)

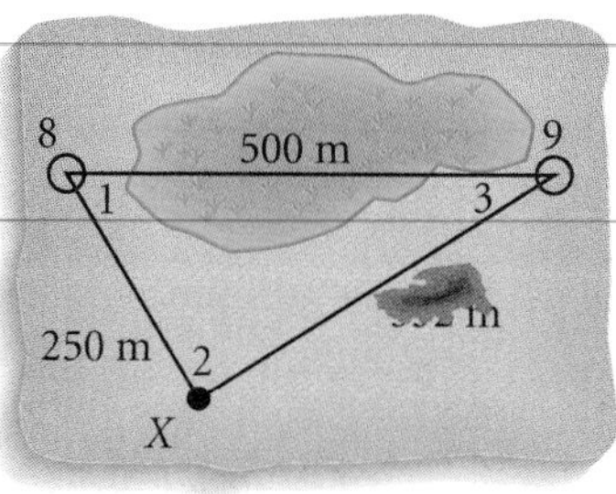

a. Which route should Marvin take? How do you know that this is the faster way for him to get to Checkpoint 9?

b. Which of the numbered angles in the figure is the smallest? Do you know which one is the largest? Explain.

16. Three sticks are chosen randomly from a set of sticks measuring 3, 5, 7, 9, and 11 cm. What is the probability that the three sticks will form a triangle?

a little better all the time

The following passage from *50 Simple Things You Can Do to Save the Earth* shows just how many aluminum cans we use, and dispose of, every year.

Aluminum is the most abundant metal on earth, but it was only discovered in the 1820s. At that time it was worth $1,200 a kilogram, more than gold. According to Worldwatch Institute: "Since its first use as a toy rattle for Napoleon's son, aluminum's use has escalated. The first all-aluminum beverage can appeared in 1963, and today accounts for the largest single use of aluminum.... In 1985 more than 70 billion beverage cans were used, of which almost 66 billion—or 94%—were aluminum."

Aluminum cans, cardboard cartons, and other packaging materials are a major part of the waste disposal problem in the United States. Recycling helps us minimize the amount of trash we generate. However, making containers that use the least possible amount of materials (that is, optimizing the use of the materials) also helps reduce waste and conserve natural resources.

1. Why do you think aluminum was so expensive in the 1820s?
2. Is the best package always the one that makes the most efficient use of materials? Explain.
3. Do you think other countries have as significant a problem with waste disposal as the United States does? Why or why not?

11-2 PART A Optimizing Areas and Perimeters

← CONNECT → ***You've already calculated the perimeters and areas of geometric figures. Now you will find figures that have the greatest area or least perimeter under certain conditions.***

Some problems have only one solution; others have many solutions. For example, there is an infinite number of ways to make a rectangle whose perimeter is 12. When you want to find the best possible solution to a problem, like finding the rectangle of perimeter 12 with the greatest possible area, you are looking for an **optimal solution.**

WHAT DO YOU THINK?

Kimiko and Adam needed to find the dimensions of the rectangle with an area of 1 square unit that has the minimum perimeter.

Kimiko thinks . . .

If I graph the relationship between the side length and the perimeter, I can look for the point that gives the minimum perimeter. Then I can use the coordinates of that point to help find the dimensions of the optimum rectangle.

Length

Area = 1

Width

To make a graph, I need to express the value I want to optimize—in this case, the perimeter—as a function of only one other variable. I'll let w represent the width of the rectangle and let ℓ represent its length. The area of the rectangle is 1, so $\ell w = 1$. Solving for w gives $w = \frac{1}{\ell}$.

The perimeter of a rectangle is $P = 2\ell + 2w$. Substituting $\frac{1}{\ell}$ for w, I have:

$$P = 2\ell + \frac{2}{\ell}$$

$$= 2(\ell + \tfrac{1}{\ell})$$

I can graph this function on a graphing utility. I'll enter the equation to be graphed, using Y and X to represent P and ℓ, respectively.

Y = 2(X + 1/X)

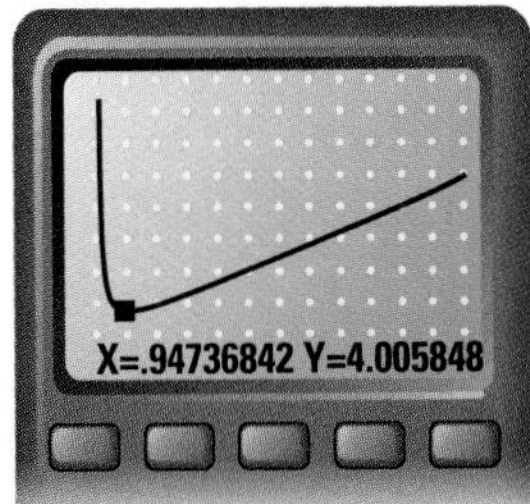

Using an appropriate range gives the graph at the right. I can TRACE to find the point with the least Y-value (perimeter). Reading the X-value for this point tells me that a length of about 0.95 gives a perimeter of about 4.01. If the length is 0.95, the width is $\frac{1}{0.95} \approx 1.05$.

Since I want a more precise answer, I'll ZOOM IN and TRACE again. This gives a perimeter of about 4.00 for a length of about 1.00. If the length is 1, the width is also 1.

Adam thinks . . .

I can make a table of values and look for the dimensions that give the least perimeter. I'll start by choosing a length for the rectangle. Using this length, I can use the area equation $\ell w = 1$ to find the value for the rectangle's width. Using this length and width, I can use $P = 2\ell + 2w$ to calculate the perimeter of the rectangle.

I'll use spreadsheet software to make a table of values. Using the table, I conclude that the 1-square-unit rectangle with the least perimeter is 1 unit long and 1 unit wide.

	A	B	C	D
1	Length	Width	Area	Perimeter
2	10	0.1	1	20.2
3	8	0.125	1	16.25
4	4	0.25	1	8.5
5	2	0.5	1	5
6	1	1	1	4
7	0.5	2	1	5
8	0.3	3.333	1	7.267

1. In the above, what type of rectangle resulted in the minimum perimeter? Why does this answer make sense?

In the following Explore, you will maximize the area of a rectangle that has some limitations on its perimeter.

EXPLORE: HOW OPTIMAL CAN YOU GET?

MATERIALS

Graphing utility (optional)
Spreadsheet software (optional)

You have 400 yd of new fencing with which to enclose a rectangular corral that uses one side of an existing fence. You'd like to build the corral that has the greatest possible area.

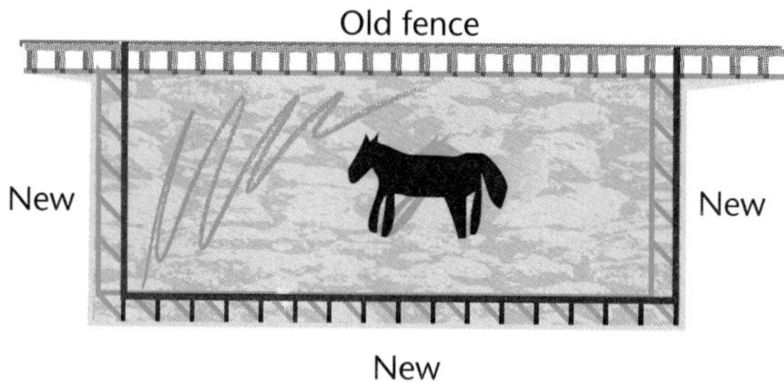

Find the approximate dimensions of the largest corral you can build with 400 yd of fencing. You may use one of the methods shown earlier or come up with one of your own. Give an explanation of your method and your solution.

When you use tables or graphing to solve an optimization problem, you can't be sure that your answer is the best one possible, because a table cannot list all possible values, and a graph has limited accuracy. Many of the methods for finding exact solutions for these problems are topics in calculus.

REFLECT

1. What type of rectangle has the least perimeter for a given area? Is this the same as the rectangle that has the greatest area for a given perimeter? Explain.
2. Suppose we don't restrict ourselves to rectangles. What two-dimensional geometric figure has the greatest area for a given perimeter? Why?
3. Describe some careers or industries in which optimization is important. Give an example of an optimization problem that might occur in each.

Exercises

CORE

1. **Getting Started** Suppose you want to find the approximate dimensions of the rectangle with the smallest perimeter whose area is 12. Use the table to find the approximate dimensions of this rectangle.

Length	Width	Perimeter	Area
3.00	4.00	14.00	12
3.25	3.69	13.88	12
3.50	3.43	13.86	12
3.75	3.20	13.90	12
4.00	3.00	14.00	12

2. Suppose you want to find the dimensions of the rectangle with the greatest area whose perimeter is 20.
   a. Make a conjecture about the shape and dimensions of this rectangle.
   b. Complete the table, and find the dimensions of the rectangle with the maximum area. Does this support your conjecture in **2a**?

Length	Width	Perimeter	Area
1	9	20	
2	8	20	
3	7	20	
4	6	20	
5	5	20	
6	4	20	
7	3	20	
8	2	20	
9	1	20	

   c. Does this table show all of the possibilities for the length and width of the rectangle? Why or why not?

For each graph, estimate the coordinates of the point that has the minimum y-value.

3. 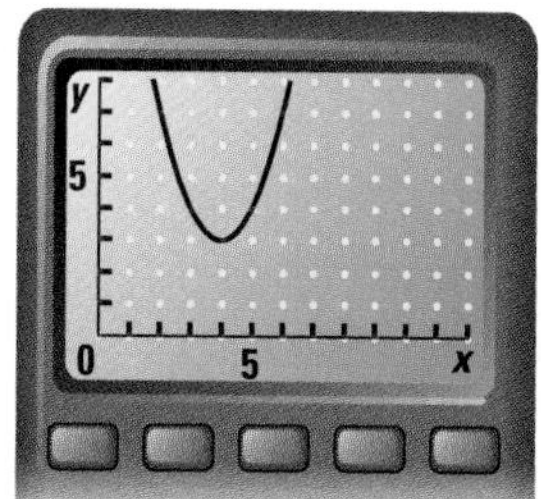

4. 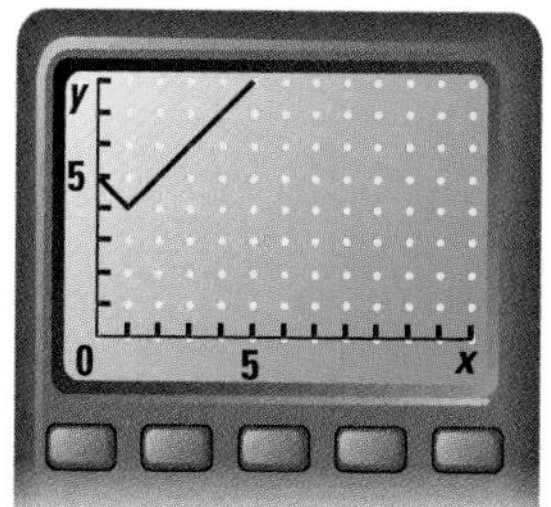

5. 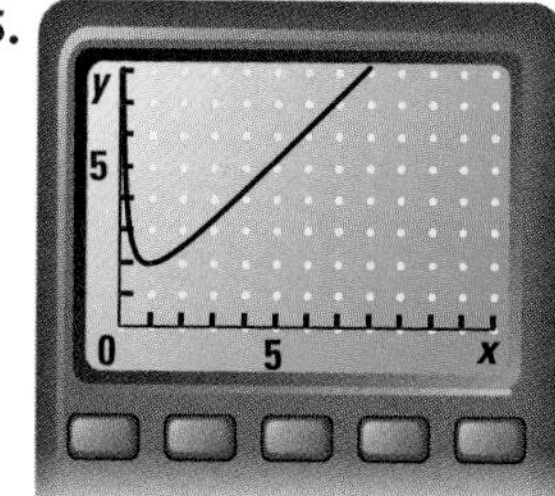

6. **Picket Problem** Consuela has one hundred meters of picket fencing to enclose a rectangular yard. She needs to leave an eight-meter gap in the fence for a driveway. What are the approximate dimensions for the fence that encloses the greatest possible area? (Hint: Make a table.)

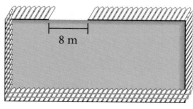

7. **Use the Hypotenuse** A farmer decides to use a diagonal fence to fence off a field at the perpendicular intersection of two county roads. The field must have an area of 4 km^2, and the farmer wants to use the least possible amount of fencing.
   a. Describe where the endpoints of the fence should be. Explain how you found your answer.
   b. You won't see many triangular fields on actual farms. Why?

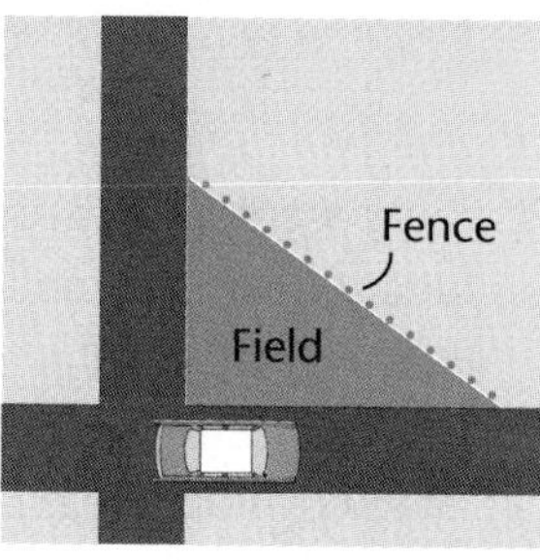

8. What does the data at the right suggest about the triangle with the side lengths shown that has the maximum possible area? Do you think this is true for any values of AB and AC? If so, write a conjecture that summarizes this idea. If not, explain why not.

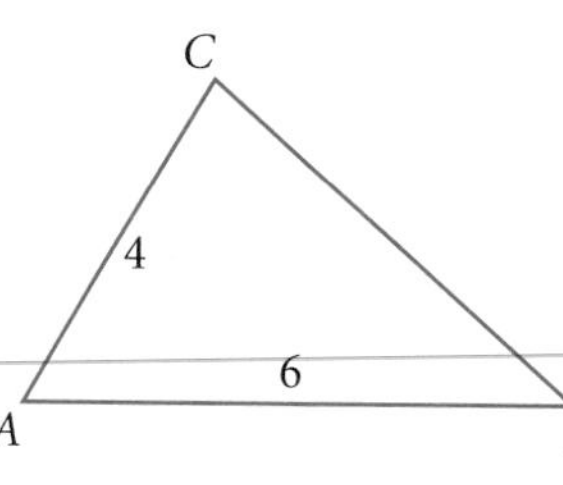

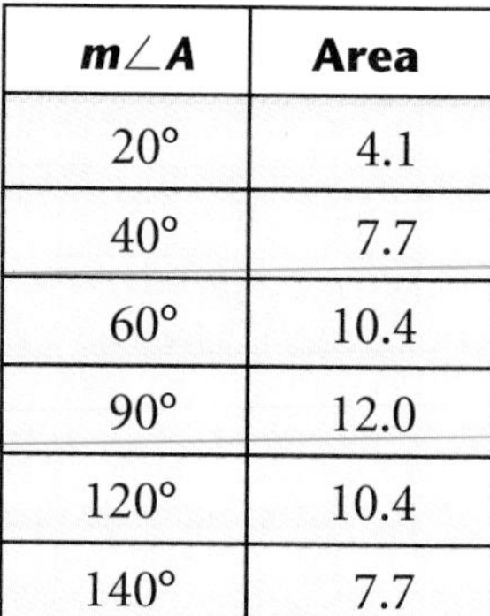

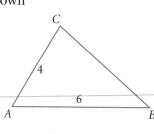

$m\angle A$	Area
20°	4.1
40°	7.7
60°	10.4
90°	12.0
120°	10.4
140°	7.7

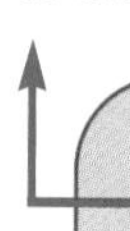

9. **Parabolic Profit** An auto parts company makes a slow-selling, custom-made item. They make all of their year's supply of the item at one time. Suppose that the profit (in dollars) for this item, P, as a function of the number produced, n, is given by $P = -3n^2 + 67n + 700$.

   Find the maximum possible profit for this item and the number of items that the company should produce to achieve this profit.

Problem-Solving Tip

Check that your answer makes sense.

10. Use your knowledge of rectangles to find the dimensions of the rectangle whose area is 36 in.^{2} and whose perimeter is a minimum.

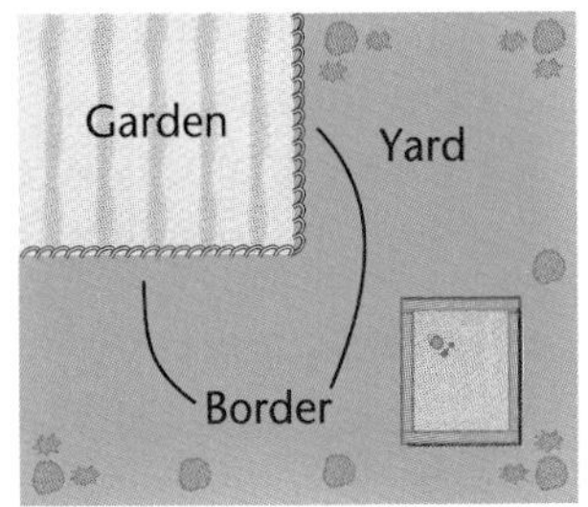

11. Dave's yard is surrounded by a fence. He wants to make a small rectangular garden in a corner of the yard, using a thirty-foot plastic border. Find the dimensions of the largest garden he can make. Explain how you found your answer.

LOOK AHEAD

Find the surface area and the volume of each rectangular prism.

12. length = 4 cm, width = 8 cm, height = 7 cm

13. length = x, width = x, height = h

14. length = $2x$, width = x, height = $3x$

MORE PRACTICE

For each graph, estimate the coordinates of the point that has the maximum *y*-value.

15.

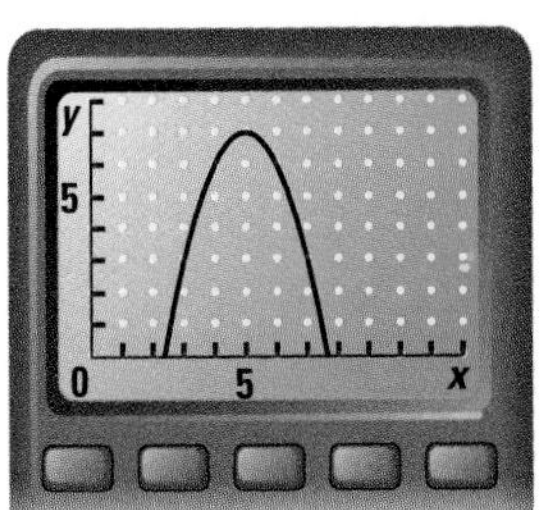

16.

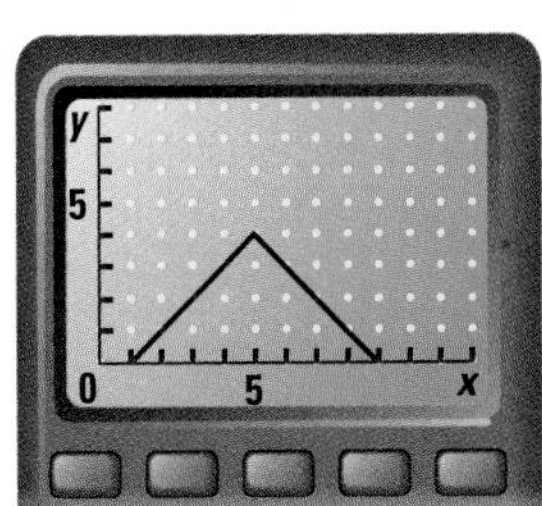

17.

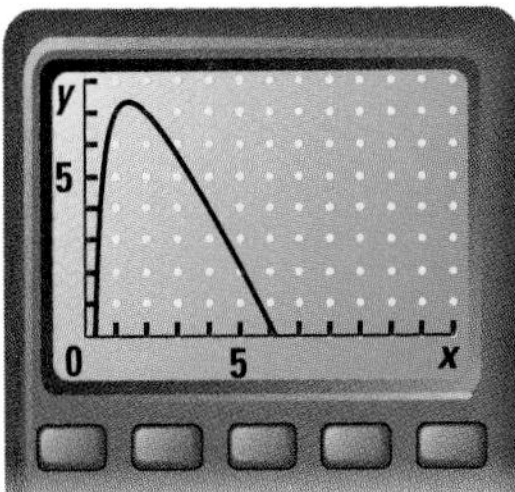

MORE MATH REASONING

18. **Bee Optimal!** The cells in a beehive have regular hexagonal openings.

Science

a. A regular hexagon tessellates a plane. Why is it efficient for bees to use a cell shape that tessellates?

b. An equilateral triangle and a square also tessellate a plane. Of these three shapes, show that the regular hexagon has the maximum area for a given perimeter. Explain the method you used to solve this problem. (Hint: Begin by choosing a convenient value for the perimeter.)

c. Why might bees want to have the largest possible cell area for a given perimeter?

19. A parallelogram has side lengths 3 and 4, as shown. Find the measure of $\angle Z$ that maximizes the area of the parallelogram. Give evidence to support your answer. (Hint: Try trigonometry!)

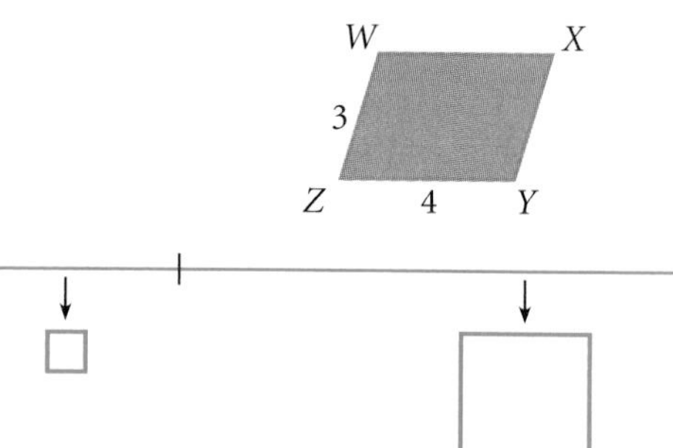

20. **Wire Squares** A piece of wire sixty inches long is to be cut and bent into two squares as shown. How should the wire be cut so that the sum of the areas of the squares is a minimum?

11-2 PART B Optimizing Volumes and Surface Areas

← CONNECT → ***You've looked at maximum areas and minimum perimeters of two-dimensional figures. Now you will apply optimization techniques to three-dimensional figures.***

When you maximize volumes or minimize surface areas, you are working in three dimensions. However, the techniques you will use and the ideas behind them are the same as those for two-dimensional figures.

EXAMPLE

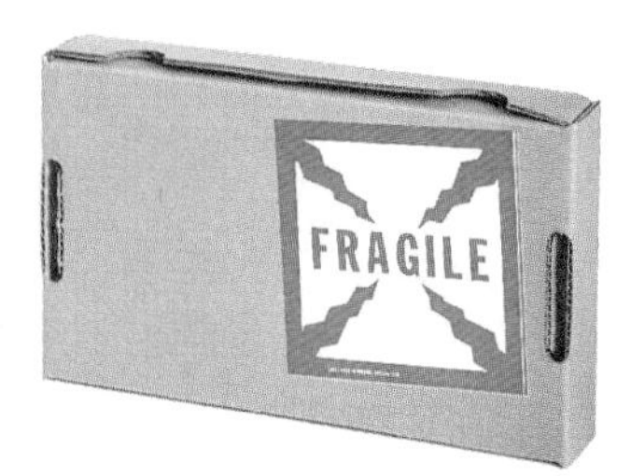

The Peerless Packaging Company wants to manufacture a box whose length is twice its width. The volume of the box must be 9 ft^3. Find the dimensions of the box with the least possible surface area that satisfies these requirements.

Let h represent the height of the box, and let x represent the width of the box. Then the length of the box is $2x$. Since the volume of the rectangular prism is 9, we have $V = \ell wh$, or $9 = 2x(x)(h) = 2x^2h$.

We want to minimize the surface area. For a rectangular solid, the surface area is $2B + ph$. In this case, $SA = 2(2x^2) + 6xh = 4x^2 + 6xh$.

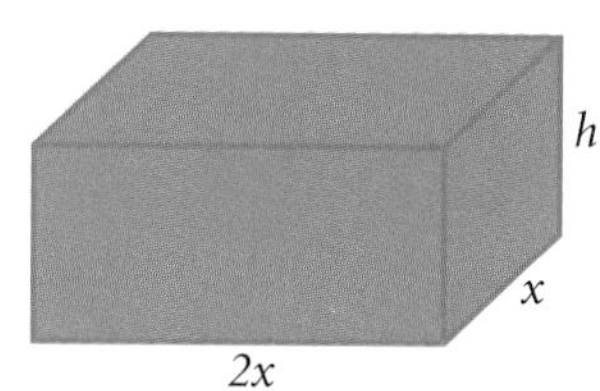

We need to express the surface area in terms of x alone. To do this, we first solve the volume equation, $9 = 2x^2h$, for h. This gives $\frac{9}{2x^2} = h$. Substituting this result into the surface-area equation gives the following:

$$SA = 4x^2 + 6x\left(\frac{9}{2x^2}\right) = 4x^2 + \frac{27}{x}$$

Using a table of values, a spreadsheet (below), or a graphing utility (right), the dimensions we find for the "best" box are 1.5 ft by 3 ft by 2 ft. Notice how we "zoomed in" on our answer in the spreadsheet.

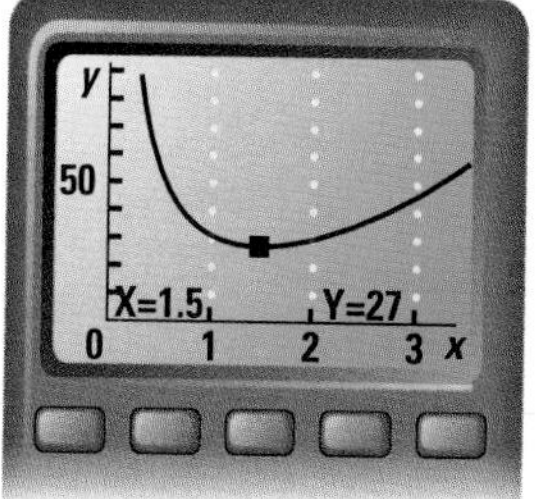

	A	B	C	D
1	x	h	Vol.	$SA = 4x^2 + \frac{27}{x}$
2	1	4.5	9	31.0
3	2	1.125	9	29.5
4	3	0.5	9	45.0
5	4	0.281	9	70.75
6	1.2	3.125	9	28.26
7	1.4	2.296	9	27.12571429
8	1.6	1.758	9	27.115
9	1.8	1.389	9	27.96
10	1.5	2.0	9	27.0

1. **Describe the advantages and disadvantages of using a spreadsheet to solve an optimization problem like the one in the preceding example.**
2. **Describe the advantages and disadvantages of using a graphing utility to solve an optimization problem like the one in the preceding example.**

In the following Explore, you will find the approximate dimensions of the largest box you can make by folding up a sheet of paper.

EXPLORE: THE CHAMPION BOXER

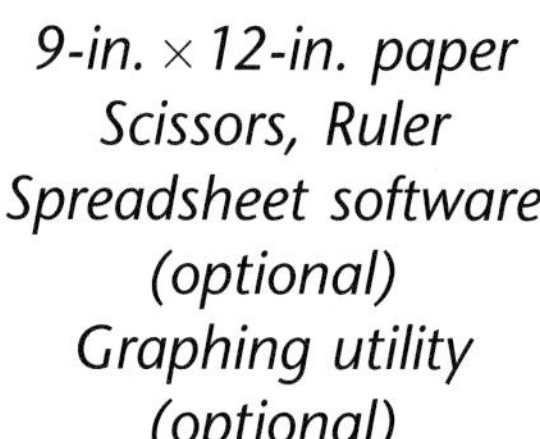

MATERIALS

9-in. × 12-in. paper
Scissors, Ruler
Spreadsheet software (optional)
Graphing utility (optional)

1. Cut out small congruent squares from each corner of a 9-in. × 12-in. piece of paper, as shown. Fold up the sides and ends, as shown by the dashed lines in the figure. Measure the dimensions of your box, and compute its volume. Compare the volume of your box with those made by your classmates. Which dimensions gave the greatest volume?

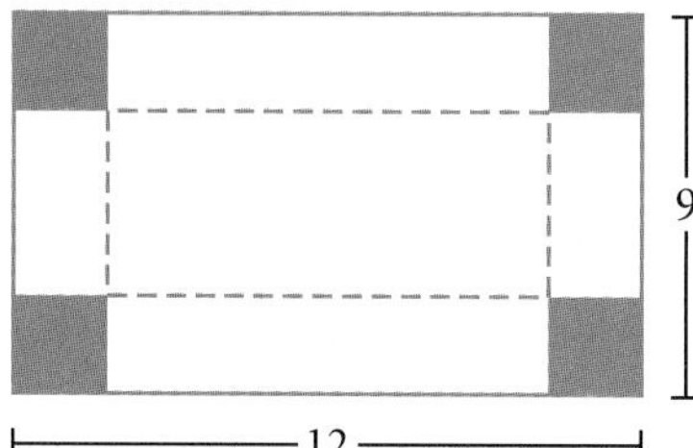

Now use algebra and geometry to confirm or improve your experimental results.

2. Let x represent the side length of the cut-out squares. Express the height, length, and width of the box in terms of x.

3. Write an equation for the volume of the box in terms of x.

4. Find the approximate value of x that maximizes the volume of the box. Give the dimensions and the volume of this optimal box. Compare this box to the one with maximum volume you found in Step 1.

REFLECT

1. Suppose you want to maximize the volume of a solid. You've written an equation for the volume in terms of x and started a table of values, as shown. Can you conclude that the maximum volume of the solid is 20.4? Explain.

x	Volume
1	15.2
2	20.4
3	8.8
4	3.6
5	2.0

2. What are some advantages and disadvantages of finding optimal values by making a table of values? by graphing?

Exercises

CORE

1. **Getting Started** Suppose you want to find the approximate dimensions of the box with the smallest surface area whose height is half its length and whose volume is 32. Use the table to find the approximate dimensions of this box.

Length	Width	Height	Surface Area	Volume
4.00	4.00	2.00	64.00	32
4.50	3.16	2.25	62.92	32
5.00	2.56	2.50	63.40	32
5.50	2.12	2.75	65.16	32

2. Suppose you want to find the dimensions of the box with the greatest volume for which the sum of the length, width, and height is 6.
   - **a.** Make a conjecture about the shape and dimensions of this box.
   - **b.** Complete the table, and find the dimensions of the box with the maximum volume. Does this support your conjecture in **2a**?

Length	Width	Height	Volume
1	1	4	
1	2	3	
1	3	2	
1	4	1	
2	1	3	
2	2	2	
2	3	1	
3	1	2	
3	2	1	
4	1	1	

   - **c.** Explain how the numbers above for length, width, and height were selected. Could some possibilities have been left out without losing any data? Explain.
   - **d.** Does this table show all of the possibilities for the length, width, and height of the box? Why or why not?

For each situation, decide which quantity is to be optimized and whether it should be maximized or minimized.

3. A cardboard carton must have a volume of four cubic feet. You want to use the least possible amount of cardboard to make the carton.

4. You have 144 in.^{2} of wood with which to make a storage box. You want the box to hold as many pennies as possible.

5. You are curling a sheet of metal into a tube with a volume of 2 m^3. You want to use as little metal as possible.

6. A box has a square base and a volume of 64. Make a conjecture about the box with the minimum surface area. Then confirm your conjecture by making a table of values for the length, width, height, volume, and surface area of the box.

7. Suppose you make a box by cutting congruent squares of side length x from each corner of a sheet of paper and then folding up the sides. Find the approximate dimensions of the box with the greatest volume that you can make from a 12-cm $\times$ 18-cm piece of paper. Write a brief explanation of the method you used to solve the problem.

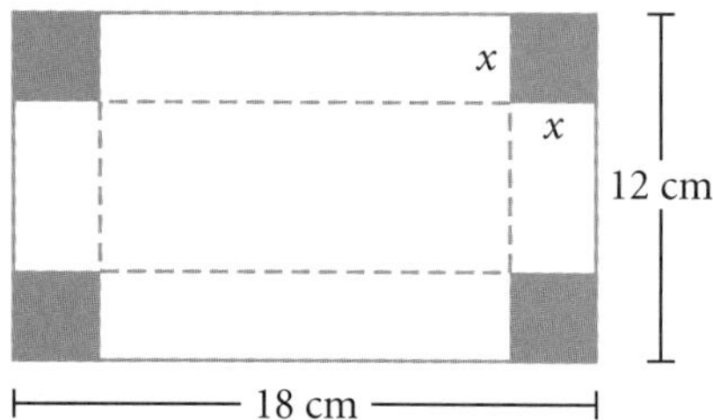

8. You have been asked to design an open box whose length is twice its width and whose volume is 36 in^3. You want to design the box so that it uses the least possible amount of cardboard. Find the approximate dimensions of the box with the least surface area that satisfies these conditions.

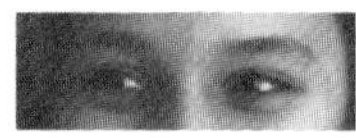

LOOK BACK

9. Find the probability that a point inside the regular hexagon will also be inside the inscribed circle. Express your answer as a decimal rounded to the nearest hundredth. [5-1, 6-3, 8-1]

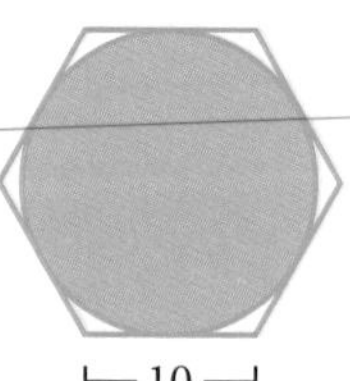

Health

10. **Watery-Eyed and Sneezing** Ralph has had allergic symptoms for almost a year. His allergist, Dr. Rodriguez, believes that he is allergic either to pet hair, house dust, or ragweed pollen (which is at its highest levels in the fall). By talking to Ralph, Dr. Rodriguez discovers the following.
    - Ralph does not own any pets.
    - Ralph's symptoms have not changed with the seasons.

    What do you think Dr. Rodriguez will conclude? Why? If you used indirect reasoning, explain how. [11-1]

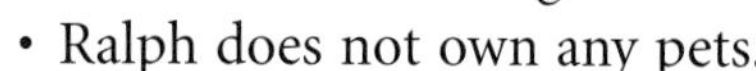

MORE PRACTICE

For each situation in Exercises 11–13, decide which quantity is to be optimized and whether it should be maximized or minimized.

11. You have 120 ft^2 of material with which to build a breeding cage for birds. You want the birds to have the greatest amount of space possible.

12. A juice can must hold forty-six fluid ounces. You want the can to use the least possible amount of aluminum.

13. You have to design a cardboard carton to hold twelve of the juice cans from Exercise 12.

14. Find the dimensions of the box with the greatest volume for which the sum of the length, width, and height is 9.

15. A box has a square base and a volume of 8 cubic units. Make a conjecture about the box with the minimum surface area. Then confirm your conjecture by making a table of values for the length, width, height, volume, and surface area of the box.

MORE MATH REASONING

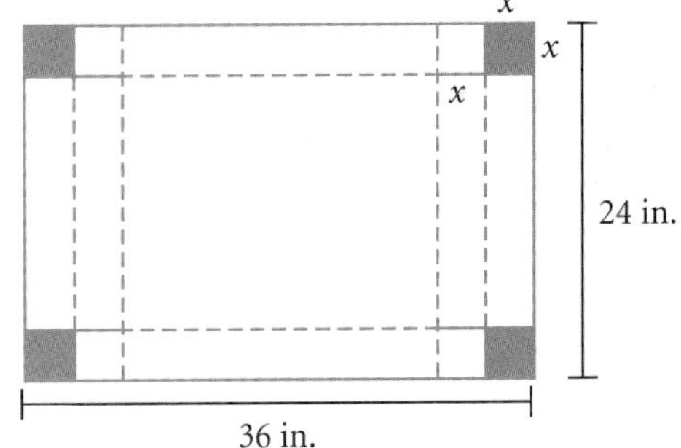

16. Boxed In With the addition of some tabs and slots, the box shown at the right can hold itself together. (Dashed lines indicate folds; solid lines show cuts.)

a. Copy the figure, and add small tabs and slots to the design so that the box can hold itself together.

b. If congruent squares are cut from each corner of a 24-in. × 36-in. piece of cardboard and the sides are folded up to make a box as shown in the figure, find the value of x that gives the box a maximum volume.

17. Yogurt to Go You've been asked by a frozen yogurt company to design a cone for frozen yogurt that uses the least possible amount of material. The interior of the cone should hold 150 cm^3 of frozen yogurt. Find the approximate dimensions for the cone. (Hint: Use the Pythagorean Theorem to express the slant height of the cone in terms of the radius and the height.) Do you think the dimensions you calculated should actually be used for the cone? Explain why or why not.

11-2
PART C

Making Connections

← CONNECT →

Optimization is important in many fields. A package designer is often concerned with using the least amount of material to enclose a given volume. You've studied ways to maximize and minimize geometric and real-world quantities under given conditions.

Most of the cylindrical aluminum drink cans that you see have the same dimensions. Do these dimensions use the least possible amount of aluminum? In the following Explore, you will look for the dimensions of the 12-oz can that uses the minimum amount of material.

EXPLORE: CAN YOU OPTIMIZE IT?

MATERIALS

Graphing utility (optional)
Spreadsheet software (optional)

You've been hired by a drink company to design a 12-fluid-ounce can that uses the least possible amount of aluminum. The can is to be a right cylinder. (Note: 12 fluid oz $\approx$ 21.66 in^3.)

1. Write the formula for the volume of the can in terms of its radius, r, and its height, h. Set this equal to the volume that you know the can must have. Then solve this equation for h.
2. Write the formula for the surface area of the can in terms of r and h. Then eliminate h from this equation by substitution, using your result from Step 1.
3. Use a table of values, spreadsheet software, or a graphing utility to find, to the nearest tenth of an inch, the radius and height of the can that uses the least amount of aluminum. (Hint: The best value for r is between 1 in. and 3 in.)
4. Compare the dimensions of a typical 12-oz can to those you found in Step 3. Are the dimensions of your ideal can different from those of a real can? If so, what reasons might there be for the difference?

REFLECT

1. If both methods are available to you, how might you decide whether to solve an optimization problem by using a table or by graphing?
2. Name some containers for which maximizing the container's volume or minimizing its surface area could be a consideration.
3. Some cans have very different dimensions from those of drink cans. Name some of these types of cans. Why might they be designed differently?

Self-Assessment

For each situation, decide which quantity is to be optimized and whether it should be maximized or minimized.

1. You have eighty feet of fencing with which to enclose a yard. You want the yard to be as large as possible.

2. An air tank must hold 22.4 L of compressed air. The tank should be built from the least possible amount of steel.

For each graph, estimate the coordinates of the point that has the minimum *y*-value.

3.

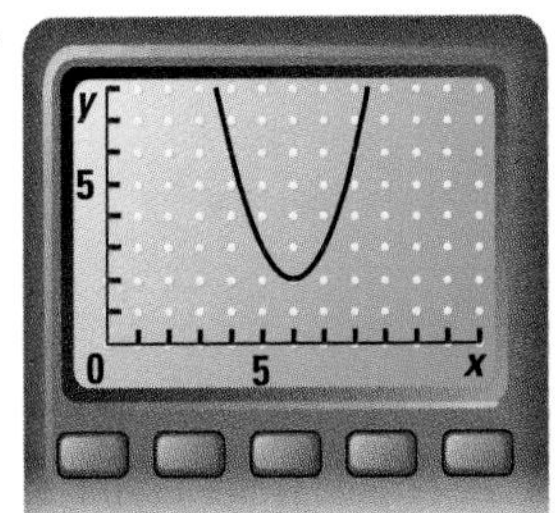

4.

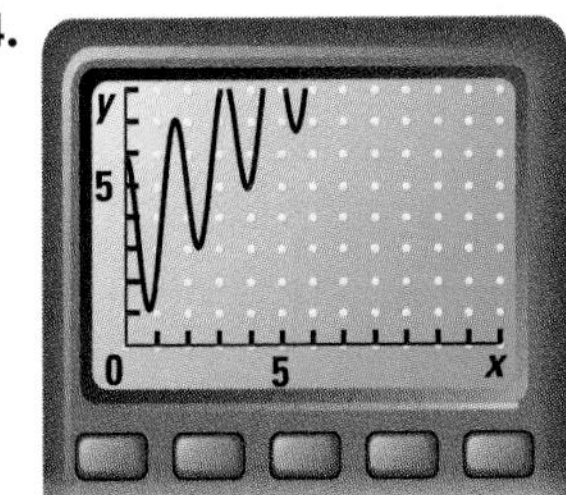

5.

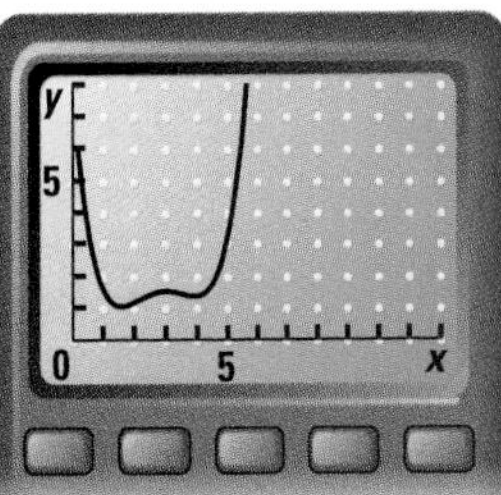

6. Which of the following figures has the greatest area for a given perimeter?
   (a) equilateral triangle (b) square (c) regular hexagon
   (d) regular decagon (e) regular 2000-gon

7. **Fence Me In** The Green Acre Animal Clinic has 500 ft of fence to build an exercise area for small animals. The fence is shown by diagonal lines. What should *x* and *y* be to make the area of the rectangular yard as large as possible?

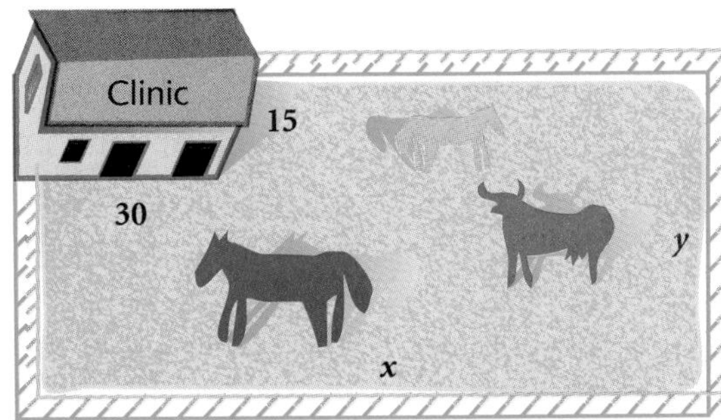

8. Table Talk Use the table to find the approximate dimensions of the box with the greatest volume whose surface area is 112 and whose length is twice its width. Could there be a better answer than the one you identified from the table? If so, explain what you would do next to search for it.

Width	Length	Height	Surface Area	Volume
1	2	18	112	36
2	4	8	112	64
3	6	4.22	112	76
4	8	2	112	64
5	10	0.4	112	20

9. The square shown has a side length of eight units. Find the probability that a point inside the larger circle will also be inside the smaller circle. Express your answer as a decimal rounded to the nearest hundredth. [5-1, 5-3, 8-1]

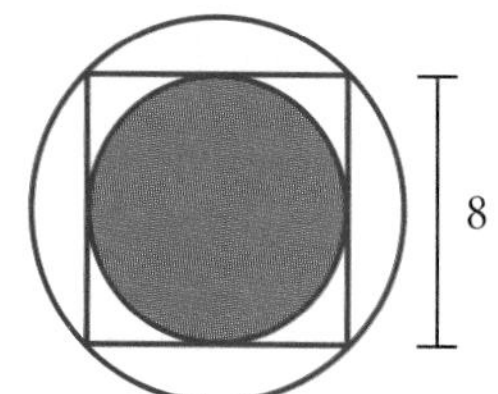

10. Is $\overline{AB} \parallel \overline{CD}$ in the figure at the right? If so, explain why; if not, explain why not. [3-4, 11-1]

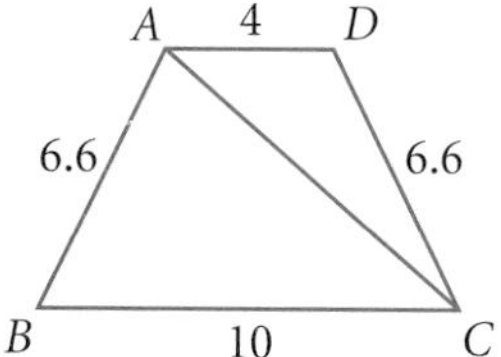

Determine whether each set of numbers could represent the lengths of the sides of a triangle. [11-1]

11. 2, 3, 5 **12.** 84, 32, 101 **13.** 7, 5.2, 2.9

14. You are to design a box whose length is three times its width and whose volume is thirty cubic inches. Find the approximate dimensions of the box with the least surface area that satisfies these conditions.

15. Suppose you make a box by cutting congruent squares of side length x from each corner of a sheet of paper and then folding up the sides. Find the approximate dimensions of the box with the greatest volume that you can make from a 10-in. × 12-in. piece of paper.

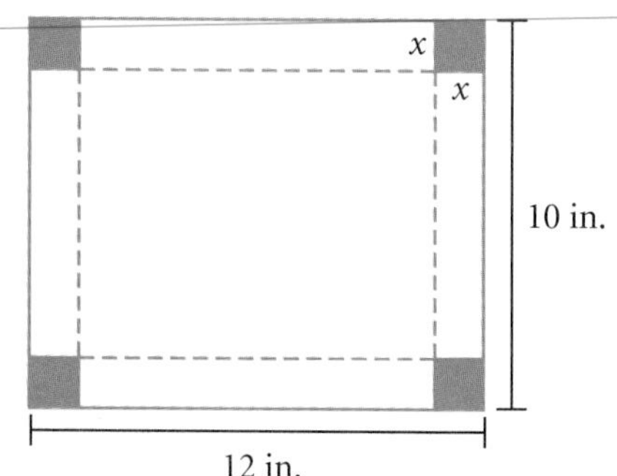

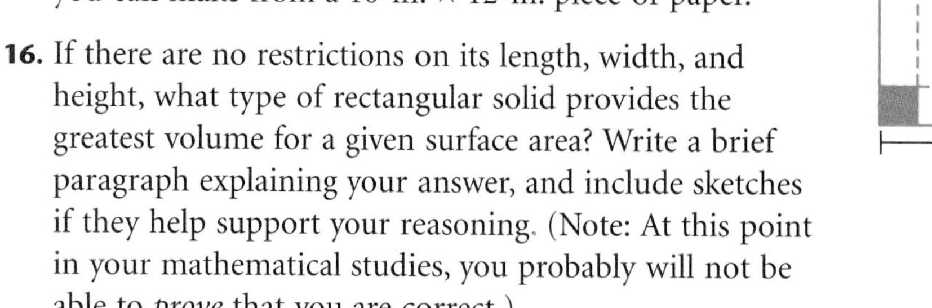

16. If there are no restrictions on its length, width, and height, what type of rectangular solid provides the greatest volume for a given surface area? Write a brief paragraph explaining your answer, and include sketches if they help support your reasoning. (Note: At this point in your mathematical studies, you probably will not be able to *prove* that you are correct.)

Chapter 11 Review

In Chapter 11 you explored indirect reasoning and applied triangle inequalities. You also looked at the solution of optimization problems.

KEY TERMS

indirect reasoning [11-1] negate [11-1] optimal solution [11-2]

Determine whether each statement is true or false. If the statement is false, change the underlined word or phrase to make it true.

1. Indirect reasoning involves making an assumption that leads to a contradiction.

2. The Triangle Inequality Theorem states that the sum of the measures of any two angles of a triangle must be greater than the measure of the third.

3. "If he was at the scene of the crime, then he is a witness" is the negation of "If he is not a witness, then he was not at the scene of the crime."

CONCEPTS AND APPLICATIONS

Write the negation of the conclusion of each statement. [11-1]

4. If humans were meant to fly, they would have wings.

5. If $\angle A$ and $\angle B$ are base angles of an isosceles triangle, then $\angle A \not\cong \angle B$.

6. Consider the statement "The defendant was found guilty." [11-1]

a. Write the negation of the statement.

b. Assume there was a trial and the negation is true. Explain why the negation does not mean that the defendant was found "not guilty." Describe a situation in which the negation is true, but a "not guilty" verdict is not delivered.

7. A circle is circumscribed around a square of side length s. Another circle is inscribed in the square. What is the ratio of the area of the smaller circle to the area of the larger circle? [5-3, 8-1]

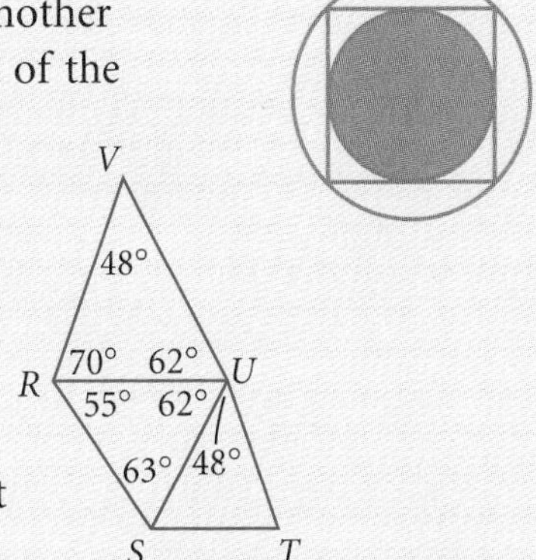

Quadrilateral *RSTU* is a trapezoid. [11-1]

8. Which segment of the figure is the shortest? Why?

9. Which segment of the figure is the longest? Why?

10. Two sides of a triangle have lengths 5 cm and 11.2 cm. What are the possible lengths for the third side? [11-1]

This graph represents a manufacturer's profit per bicycle as a function of the number of bicycles manufactured. [11-2]

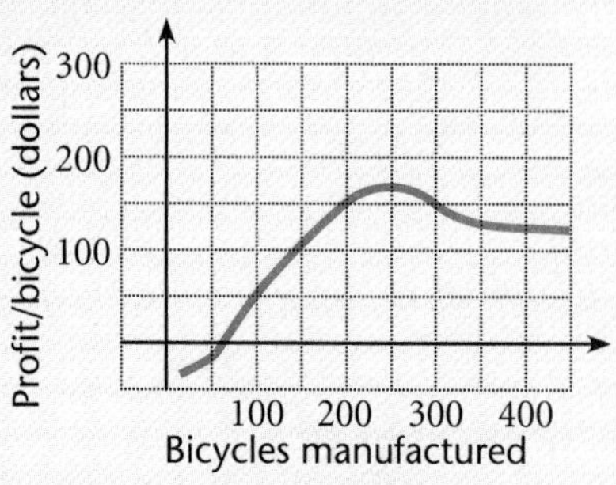

11. What is the maximum profit per bicycle, to the nearest ten dollars?

12. To the nearest ten bicycles, how many bicycles should be manufactured to maximize the profit per bicycle?

13. An open-top cylindrical cup is to have a volume of 100 in^3. Find the radius and height of the cup that minimizes the surface area of the cup. Round answers to the nearest tenth. [11-2]

CONCEPTS AND CONNECTIONS

14. Literature In his book *What Is the Name of This Book?* logician Raymond Smullyan adapts a scene from Shakespeare's *Merchant of Venice,* in which Portia presents her suitor with three small caskets. He will have her hand if he guesses the one containing her portrait. Smullyan adds a twist, giving the gold casket the inscription "The portrait is in this casket," the silver casket "The portrait is not in this casket," and the lead casket "The portrait is not in the gold casket." Portia explains that at most one inscription is true. Use indirect reasoning to determine the suitor's correct choice. Write a convincing argument that your choice is the only possible correct choice.

SELF-EVALUATION

Write a summary of the most important concepts from Chapter 11. Include properties of triangles, techniques of indirect reasoning, and methods of finding optimal solutions. Include areas in which you had difficulty, and describe your plans for reviewing these topics.

Chapter 11 Assessment

TEST

Write the negation of the conclusion of each statement.

1. If an animal is a fish, then it has scales.

2. If $a < b$, then $a + c < b + c$.

3. You are attempting to prove the Exterior-Angle Inequality Theorem by first proving that $m\angle 4 > m\angle 2$. A friend suggests doing an indirect proof by first assuming $m\angle 4 < m\angle 2$. Is your friend's suggestion correct? Why or why not?

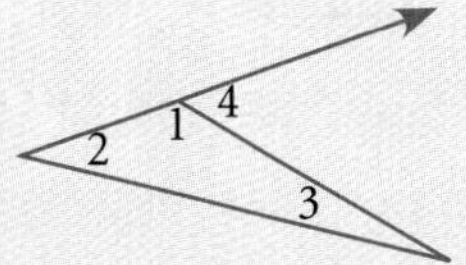

Determine whether each set of numbers could represent the lengths of the sides of a triangle.

4. 10, 13, 23

5. 21, 5, 24

6. $2, \sqrt{3}, 4$

7. In the figure, $\overline{XY} \cong \overline{WY}$. List the numbered angles from smallest to largest. Explain your reasoning.

8. Suppose you need to maximize the area of a rectangle with a given perimeter. Describe a step-by-step process you could use to find the side lengths of this rectangle.

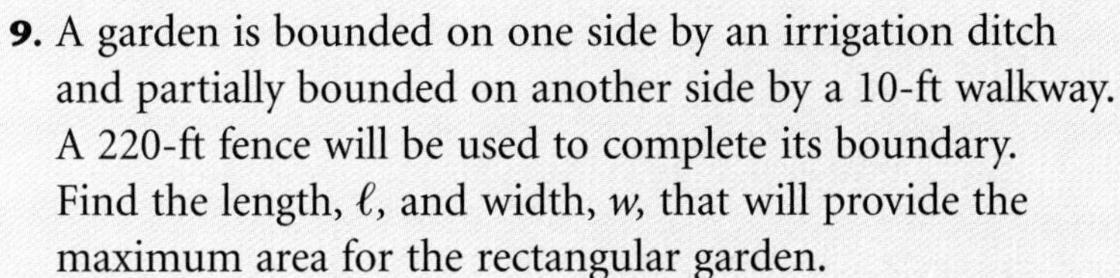

9. A garden is bounded on one side by an irrigation ditch and partially bounded on another side by a 10-ft walkway. A 220-ft fence will be used to complete its boundary. Find the length, ℓ, and width, w, that will provide the maximum area for the rectangular garden.

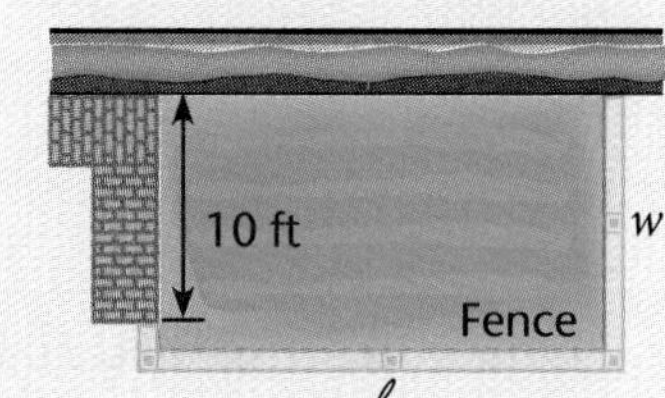

10. An equilateral triangle is inscribed in a circle with a radius of eight meters. What is the area of the triangle?

11. To make a gift box from a 14-in. × 20-in. piece of cardboard, you could make four slits, each of length x, as shown. Then fold up the sides and glue each shaded square to the adjoining side. Find the value of x, to the nearest tenth of an inch, that produces the box with the largest volume.

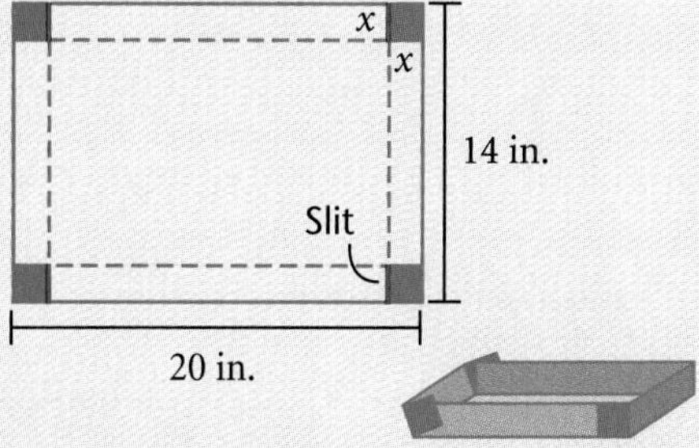

PERFORMANCE TASK

An orienteer must decide whether to travel distance c over the hill shown or take the longer route of distance $a + b$. Make a table with columns for c, r (the speed in mi/hr over the hill), and t (the time over the hill from Checkpoint 1 to Checkpoint 2). Also include columns for a, b, $a + b$, and R (the speed using the longer route). For each row of the table, make up distances for a, b, and c, and choose a speed r (normally between 3 and 5 mi/hr). Calculate t. Then calculate the minimum value for R that makes the longer route the faster route. Vary your choices for a, b, c, and r to complete several rows of the table. Then develop a formula that expresses R in terms of a, b, c, and r.

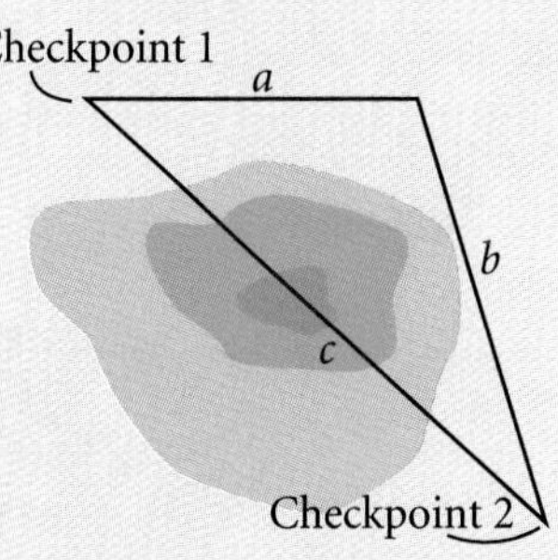

Chapter 12 Astronomy and Geometric Models

6 27 28 29 30 31

Project A
Thirty Days Has September
Is this a leap year? What is the Gregorian calendar, and how did it get started?

Project B
When the Earth Was Flat
How were sunrise and sunset explained before people knew that the earth revolves around the sun?

Project C
Watch It Happen
How far would you travel to see a total eclipse of the sun? How are people affected by events such as eclipses or passing comets?

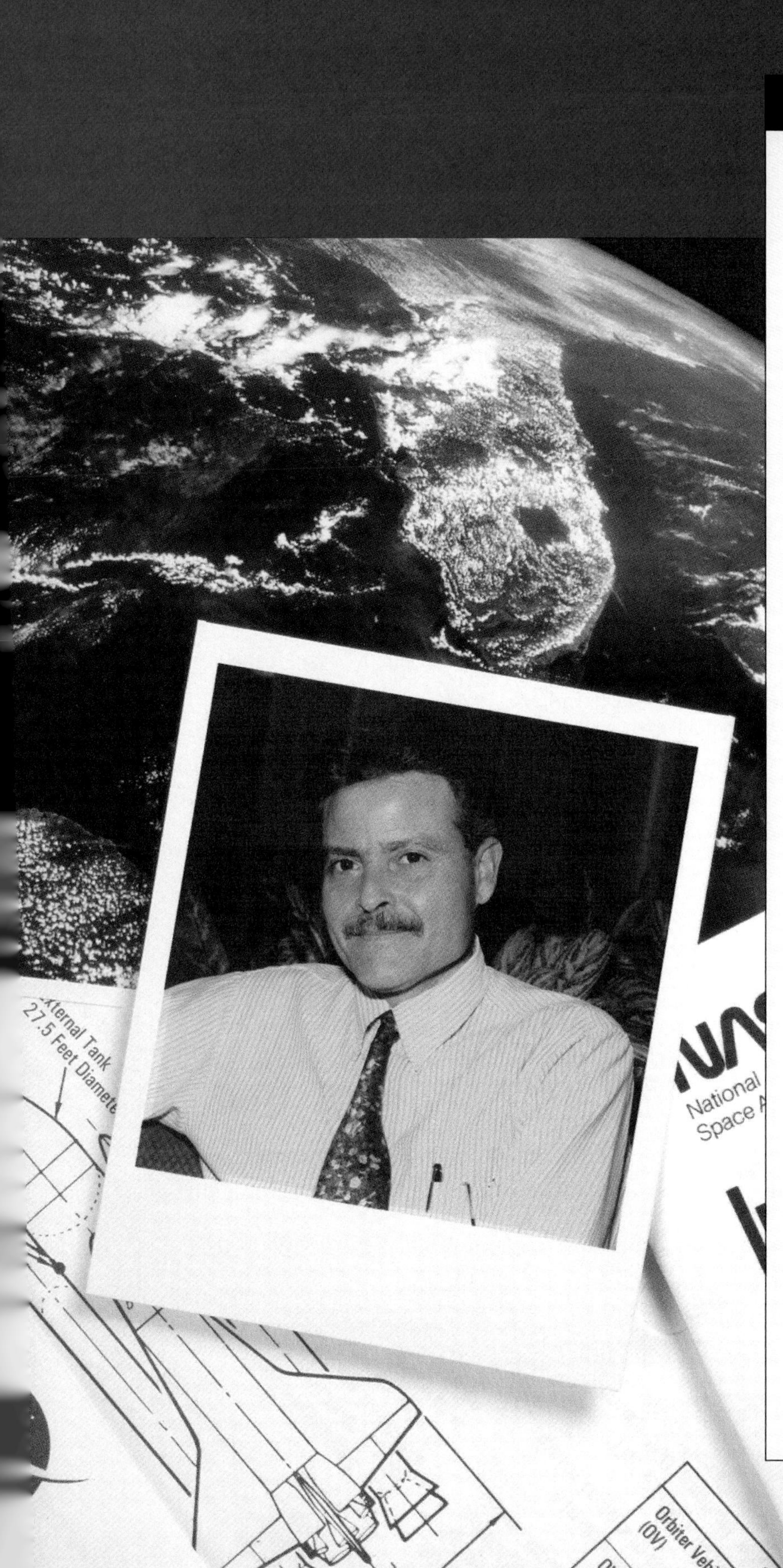

HECTOR DELGADO

I liked math in high school because it was challenging. And I knew I was going to be an engineer. I didn't know what kind of engineer I would be, but I was going to be one.

As an engineer, I use math every day to solve problems related to the space shuttle at the Kennedy Space Center.

Math is a very important tool in our goal to reach for the stars and beyond.

Hector Delgado
Space Shuttle Engineer
National Aeronautics and Space Administration (NASA)
Kennedy Space Center, FL

Chapter 12 Astronomy and Geometric Models

GETTING READY

12-1 Using Geometry to Model the Earth

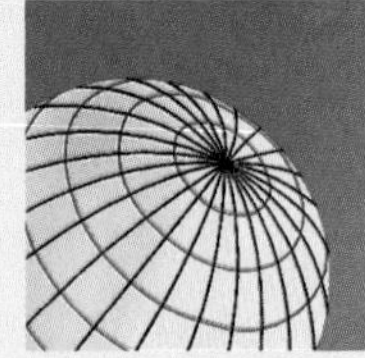

In 12-1 you will investigate ways to measure and model the earth, our solar system, and our galaxy. You will use the following skills from previous chapters.

Which figures are similar? [7-1, 7-2]

1.

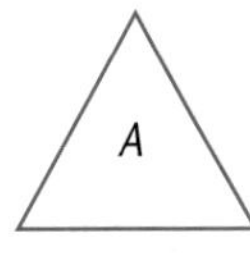

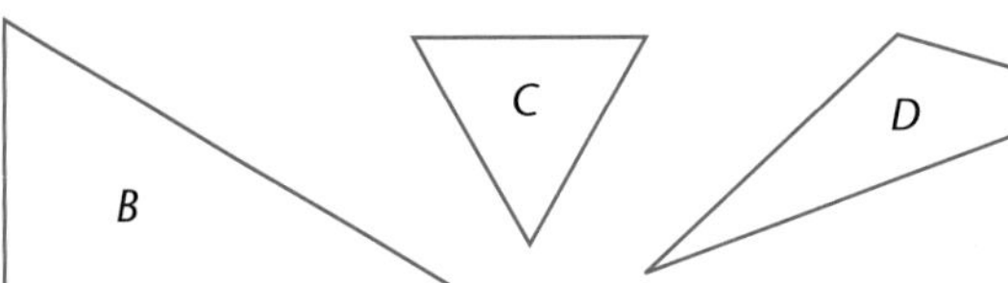

Solve for x. [Previous course]

2. $\frac{360}{24} = \frac{x}{1}$ **3.** $\frac{360}{30} = \frac{30}{x}$ **4.** $\frac{x}{360} = \frac{1}{100}$

Find the missing values for each sphere. [9-2]

5. Radius = 6, Surface Area = ? , Volume = ?

6. Surface Area = 36π, Radius = ? , Volume = ?

7. Volume = 2304π, Radius = ? , Surface Area = ?

12-2 Euclidean and Non-Euclidean Geometries

In 12-2 you will see how a change in the Parallel Postulate affects the properties of some geometric figures. You will need the following concepts from previous chapters.

Identify the missing term in each of these postulates. [2-2]

8. Straight Line Postulate: Two points are contained in one and only one ? .

9. Plane-Intersection Postulate: If two planes intersect, then their intersection is ? .

10. Plane Postulate: Three ? points are contained in one and only one plane.

Tell whether each of the following is a definition, a postulate, or a theorem. [2-2]

11. A term that is built from other terms.

12. A statement proven from other statements.

13. An unproven statement.

14. A deduction.

12-1 Using Geometry to Model the Earth

The Earth and Beyond

Let's take a trip into space. The pictures we'll see on this journey are from Powers of Ten, published by Scientific American. This book shows pictures of the same area taken from various distances, each ten times farther away than the last.

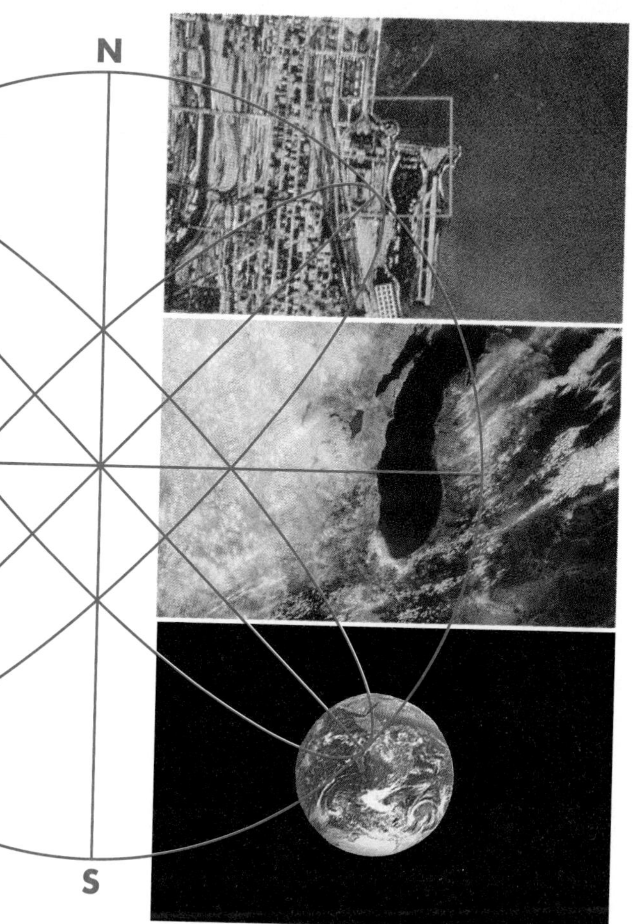

This is downtown Chicago, shown from an altitude of 10 kilometers—about 6 miles. We're a little higher than Mt. Everest, the world's tallest mountain. Over a million people live or work in this region. Soldier Field, the home of the Chicago Bears, and Meigs Field lie inside the square.

Now we're 100 times higher, at an altitude of 1000 kilometers—3 to 4 times higher than the orbit of a space shuttle. We can see all of Lake Michigan and parts of the four states that surround it. Although millions of people live in this area, from this distance we see little evidence of human life.

Now we've zoomed out to an altitude of 100,000 kilometers. This is about one-fourth of the distance from the earth to the moon. The earth and its billions of inhabitants seem isolated in space as they race around the sun at 67,000 mi/hr.

?

1. Suppose you are given photographs of an unfamiliar coastline taken from two different altitudes. Can you tell which was taken from the higher altitude? If so, how?
2. How can you describe Chicago's exact location on the earth's surface?
3. Is it important to know the exact size of the earth? Why? Would this knowledge have been as important thousands of years ago? Why or why not?

12-1 PART A Fractals

← CONNECT → *You know how to identify and draw similar figures. Now you will investigate figures whose parts are similar to the whole figure. Some of these figures can be used to model the earth in fascinating ways.*

Some real-world shapes, like coastlines, mountains, and leaves, may seem too complex to model mathematically. However, in 1982, Benoit Mandelbrot gained worldwide attention by connecting mathematics and nature through **fractal geometry.**

A baseball card of Mike Perez that shows him holding his baseball card suggests a fractal. If you think about this situation, you realize that the card Perez is holding also has a picture of him holding the card. That card also has a picture of Perez, and he's holding a card with his picture, and so on.

A fractal has some of the same characteristics as the "infinite" baseball card. Fractals are patterns that are **self-similar.** When magnified, small parts of a self-similar figure cannot be distinguished from the whole figure. The figure below shows self-similarity.

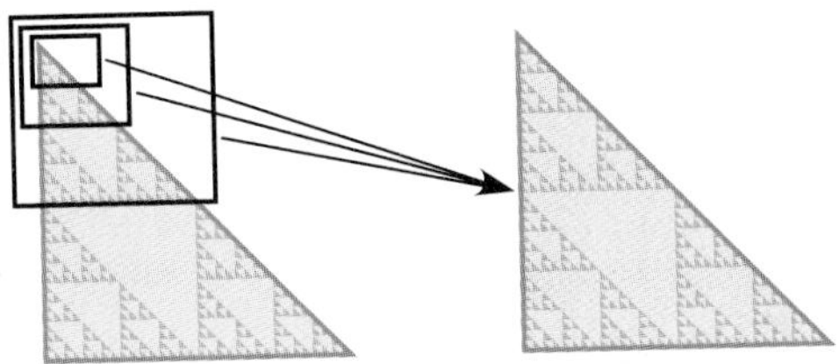

In the following example, we apply a rule that divides a triangle into smaller and smaller triangles. The figure that results is a fractal.

EXAMPLE

Start with a shaded equilateral triangle. Use the following rule.

For each shaded triangle:

a. Connect the midpoints of the sides with line segments.
b. Remove the middle triangle of the four triangles formed.

We can begin to draw this fractal as shown in the series of figures at the top of page 751.

These are the first four stages of the self-similarity pattern.

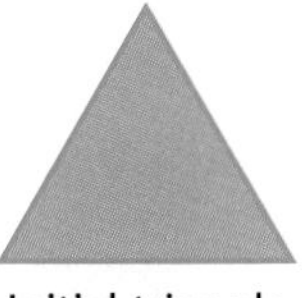
Initial triangle (Stage 0)

Stage 1

Stage 2

Stage 3

Stage 4

The figure created by carrying out this rule an infinite number of times is called a Sierpinski Gasket, after its inventor, mathematician Waclaw Sierpinski.

1. At Step b in creating each stage of the Sierpinski Gasket, what fraction of the remaining area is removed?

In the following Explore, you will investigate several stages of a fractal pattern.

EXPLORE: FRACTAL FIGURES

MATERIALS

Ruler

Initial side (top of triangle)

Stage 1

Stage 2

1. Use the following rule to sketch the first three stages of a fractal pattern. (Hint: Draw with a pencil, so that you can erase.) Start with a large equilateral triangle. Remove the center third of each segment, and replace it with two congruent segments that form an equilateral "bump." Repeat this rule until you have completed three stages of the design. (The figure at the right shows the first two stages of one side of the triangle.)

2. Does this rule eventually form a Sierpinski Gasket? If not, describe your completed pattern.

Computers can be programmed to generate fractals that are much more complex than the ones you have explored. The image at the right is a computer-generated fractal that models a mountain.

REFLECT

1. How is self-similarity related to similarity? How is it different?
2. What is the difference between a fractal found in nature and the mathematical idea of a fractal?
3. Lilia programmed her computer to draw 1000 stages of a pattern for a fractal. If she were to zoom in on a tiny part of this picture, what could she expect to see?

Exercises

CORE

1. **Getting Started** Follow the steps to create a pattern similar to a fractal.
   - **a.** Draw a square. This initial square is Stage 0 of the pattern.
   - **b.** Mark the midpoint of each side of the square. Then connect the midpoints to form a new square. This is Stage 1 of the pattern.
   - **c.** Mark the midpoint of each side of the new square. Connect the midpoints to make Stage 2.
   - **d.** Repeat **1c** two more times to create Stages 3 and 4 of the pattern.

Sketch the next stage of each pattern and describe the rule for the pattern.

2.

Initial square (Stage 0) | Stage 1 | Stage 2

3.

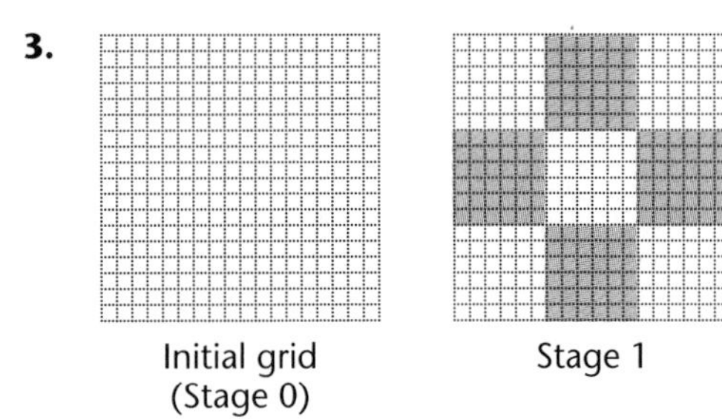

Initial grid (Stage 0) | Stage 1

In Exercises 4 and 5, sketch the second stage of each fractal.

4. Start with an equilateral triangle. Use the following rule.
   a. Divide the sides of each unshaded triangle into three congruent segments.
   b. Connect the dividing points as shown.
   c. Shade the inverted triangles.

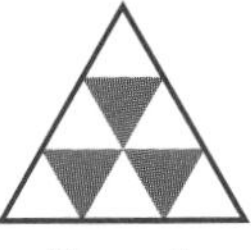
Stage 1

5. Start with a square. Use the following rule.
   a. Divide the sides of each unshaded square into three congruent segments.
   b. Connect the dividing points as shown.
   c. Shade the inner square.

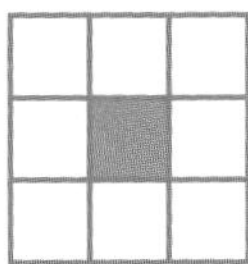
Stage 1

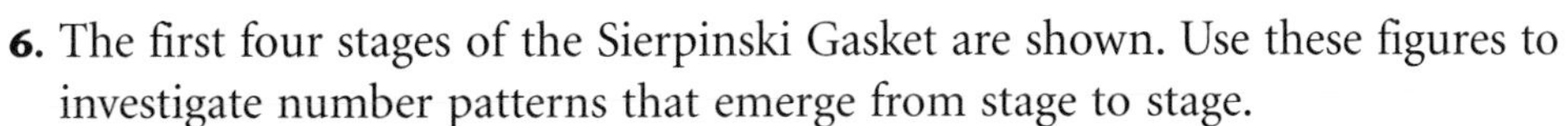

6. The first four stages of the Sierpinski Gasket are shown. Use these figures to investigate number patterns that emerge from stage to stage.

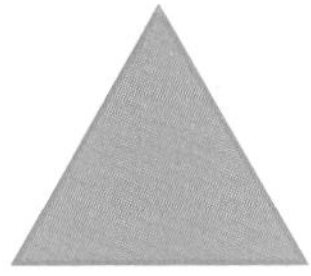
Initial triangle (Stage 0)

Stage 1

Stage 2

Stage 3

Stage 4

   a. Make a table to record the number of shaded triangles for Stages 0–4.
   b. Predict the number of shaded triangles for Stage 5.
   c. Suppose there are t shaded triangles at one stage of the pattern. How many will there be at the next stage?
   d. Write an equation for the number of shaded triangles at Stage n.
   e. Suppose the area of the triangle in Stage 0 is 1. Make a table to record the total shaded area for Stages 0–4. Then predict the total shaded area for Stage 5.
   f. Suppose the shaded area at one stage of the pattern is $\frac{a}{b}$. What will the area be at the next stage?
   g. What happens to the shaded area when you repeat the pattern n times?

7. **Fractals in Pascal's Triangle** The figure at the right shows the beginning of Pascal's Triangle. The number in each hexagon is the sum of the numbers in the two hexagons immediately above it.

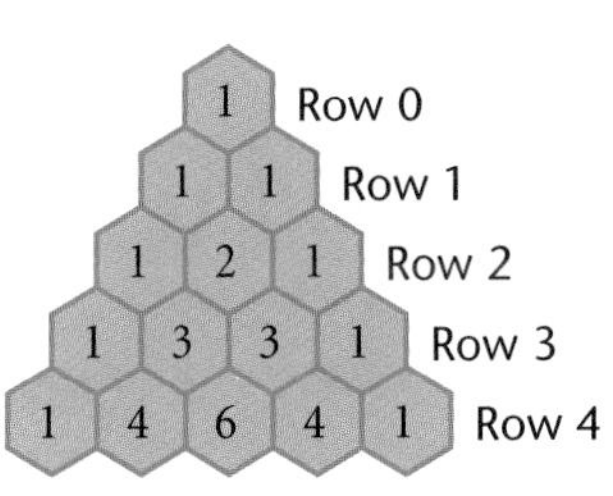

   a. On dot paper, sketch hexagons, and fill in the numbers for Rows 0–7 of Pascal's Triangle.
   b. Shade any hexagons in the first eight rows of Pascal's Triangle that contain an odd number. Look at Rows 0–3 of Pascal's Triangle after shading the odd numbers. How do they compare to Stage 1 of the Sierpinski Gasket?
   c. Now consider Rows 0–7 of Pascal's Triangle after shading the odd numbers. How do they compare to Stage 2 of the Sierpinski Gasket?

8. Create a rule for a fractal design of your own. Sketch the first three stages of the design.

9. Coastlines, mountains, oak trees, and broccoli all have a degree of self-similarity. Identify another example of self-similarity in nature. Explain how your example shows self-similarity.

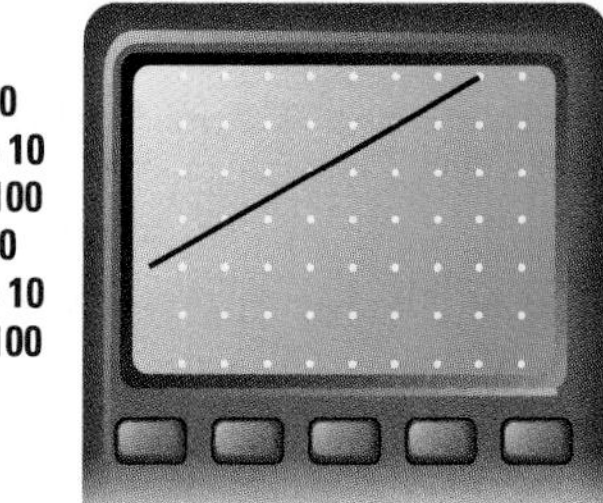

10. Zooming in on the calculator screen shown on top at the right produces the screen shown below it.
   a. If you continue to zoom in on this graph, will it always have the same shape? Explain why or why not.
   b. Do you think this graph shows self-similarity? If so, do all types of graphs have self-similarity? Explain.

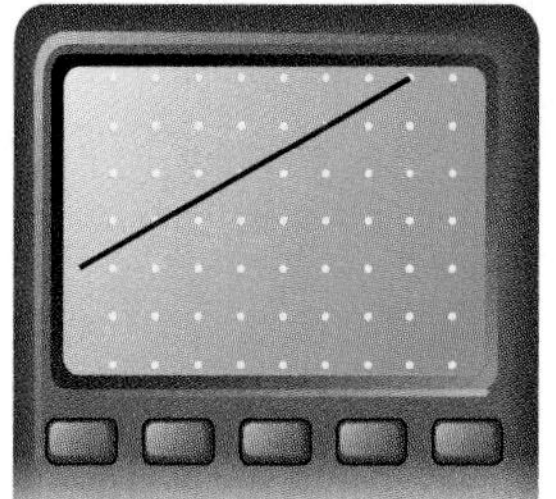

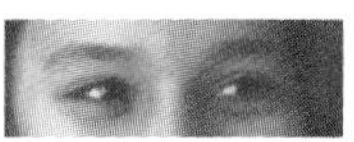

LOOK AHEAD

Find the radius or circumference for each circle described. Round answers to the nearest tenth.

11. $r = 12.4$ in., $C =$ ___ 12. $C = 29.6$ cm, $r =$ ___ 13. $r = 3960$ mi, $C =$ ___

Find each missing value. Round answers to the nearest tenth.

14. $r = 20$, $s = 10$, $m\angle A =$ ___ 15. $r = 20$, $m\angle A = 60°$, $s =$ ___

16. $s = 150$, $m\angle A = 10°$, $r =$ ___

Use trigonometry to find *k* for each $m\angle k$ given. Round answers to the nearest tenth.

17. $m\angle K = 35°$ 18. $m\angle K = 42°$ 19. $m\angle K = 71°$

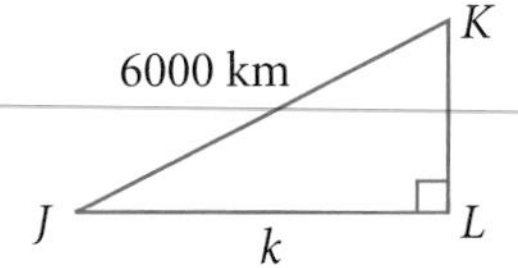

MORE PRACTICE

Sketch the next stage of each pattern, and describe the rule for the pattern.

20.

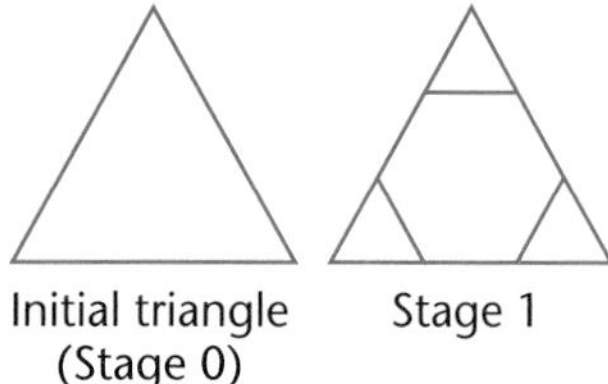

21.

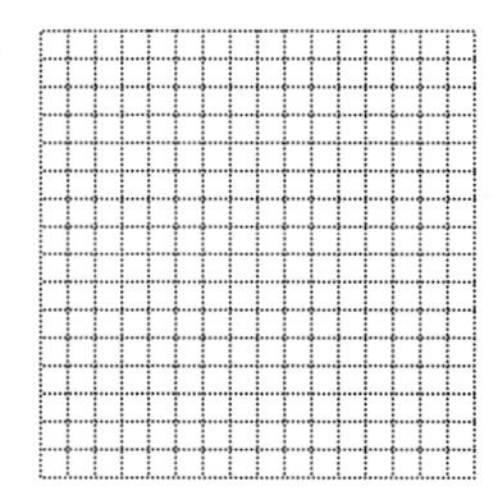

Initial grid
(Stage 0)

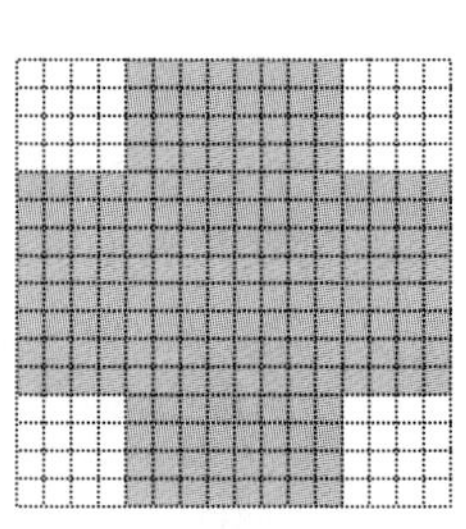

Stage 1

In Exercises 22 and 23, sketch the second stage of each fractal.

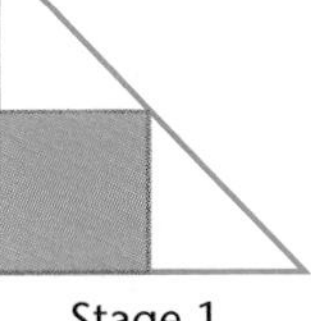
Stage 1

22. Start with an isosceles right triangle. Use the following rule.

a. Find the midpoint of the hypotenuse of each triangle.

b. Make a square in each triangle by drawing perpendicular segments from the midpoint to the legs. Shade the square.

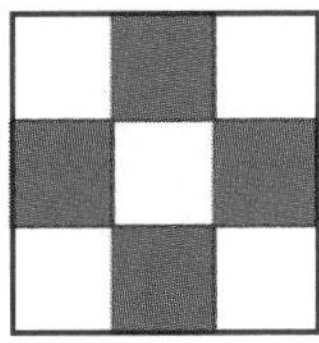
Stage 1

23. Start with a square. Use the following rule.

a. Divide the sides of each unshaded square into three equal parts.

b. Connect the dividing points, as shown at the right.

c. Shade the middle square on each side of these squares, as shown.

MORE MATH REASONING

The Koch Snowflake is formed by starting with an equilateral triangle and adding an equilateral "bump" to each segment at every stage. Stages 0–3 are shown.

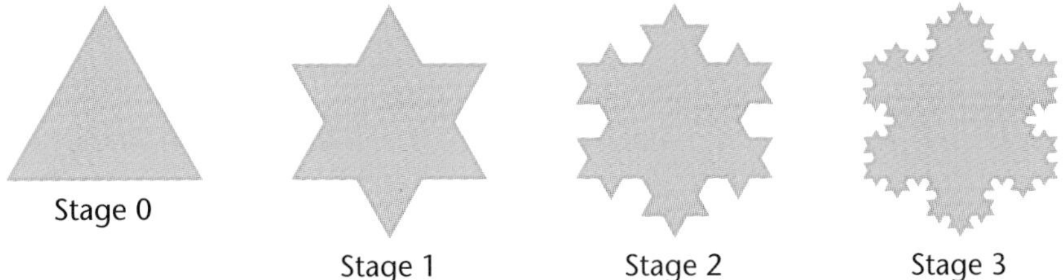
Stage 0 Stage 1 Stage 2 Stage 3

24. Measuring Snowflakes Investigate what happens to the perimeter of the Koch Snowflake as the number of sides increases.

Stage	Number of Segments	Length of Each Segment	Perimeter
0	3	1	$3 \cdot 1 = 3$
1			

a. Complete the table for stages 0–3.

b. Predict the number of segments at Stage 4. Then find the ratio of the number of segments at one stage to the number at the preceding stage.

c. Write an equation in terms of n for the number of segments at Stage n.

d. Assume the length of a side of the original triangle is 1. Predict the length of each segment at Stage 4. Then find the ratio of the length of each segment at one stage to the length of each segment at the preceding stage.

e. Write an equation in terms of n for the length of each segment at Stage n.

f. Predict the perimeter at Stage 4. Then describe the ratio of the perimeters at two consecutive stages.

g. Is the perimeter increasing or decreasing? What will happen to the perimeter of the Koch Snowflake if you repeat the pattern an infinite number of times?

25. Investigate what happens to the area of the Koch Snowflake (described on page 755) as the number of sides increases.

a. Complete the table.

Stage Number	Number of Segments	Number of Triangles Added	Additional Area	Total Area
0	3	0	0	1
1				
2				
3				

b. Predict the number of triangles added at Stage 4. Then find the ratio of the number of new triangles at one stage to the number of new triangles at the preceding stage.

c. Write an equation in terms of n for the number of new triangles at Stage n.

d. Assume the area of the original triangle is 1. Predict the additional area at Stage 4. Then find the ratio of the additional areas at two consecutive stages.

e. Write an equation in terms of n for the additional area at Stage n.

f. Predict the total area at Stage 4. Is it increasing or decreasing as n increases?

g. Does the area of the Koch Snowflake become infinitely large, or does there seem to be a limit on its area? Explain.

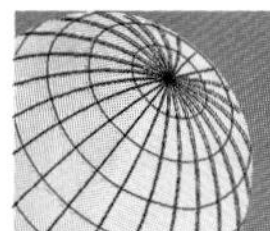

12-1 PART B Longitude and Latitude

← CONNECT → ***You've used maps to model the earth, and you've learned about the properties of spheres. Now you will use a sphere to model the earth and learn how to use latitude and longitude lines.***

When you see mountains or canyons, you may wonder how spherical the earth is. Nevertheless, a model of the earth 8 ft in diameter would be smoother than a polished bowling ball. The highest mountain would be represented by a bump rising only 0.067 in. above the surface, and the difference between the polar and equatorial diameters would not be noticeable. A sphere is, therefore, a good model of the earth.

You know how to use coordinates to locate points on a plane. We also use a coordinate system to locate a point on a sphere. This system is based on two reference lines (like the x- and y-axes).

One of these lines is the **equator.** The equator and the lines parallel to it are called lines of **latitude.** The equator is at 0° latitude, the North Pole is at 90° north latitude (90° N), and the South Pole at 90° S.

The other reference line is the **prime meridian.** This north-south line runs through England, continental Europe, and West Africa. The prime meridian marks 0° **longitude.** Other longitude lines range from 0° to 180°, east or west.

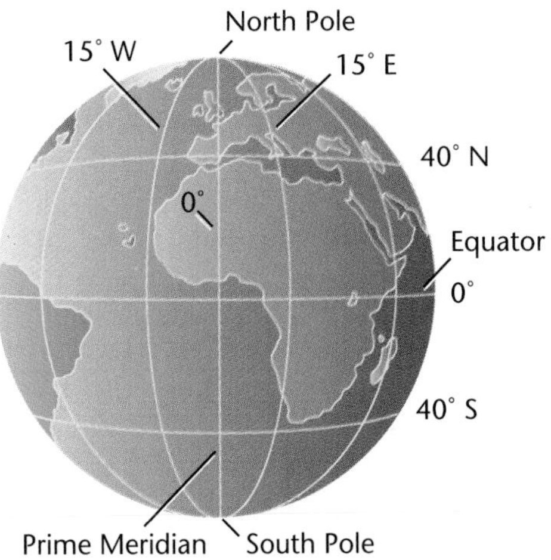

EXAMPLE

Give the approximate latitude and longitude of New York City and Buenos Aires, Argentina.

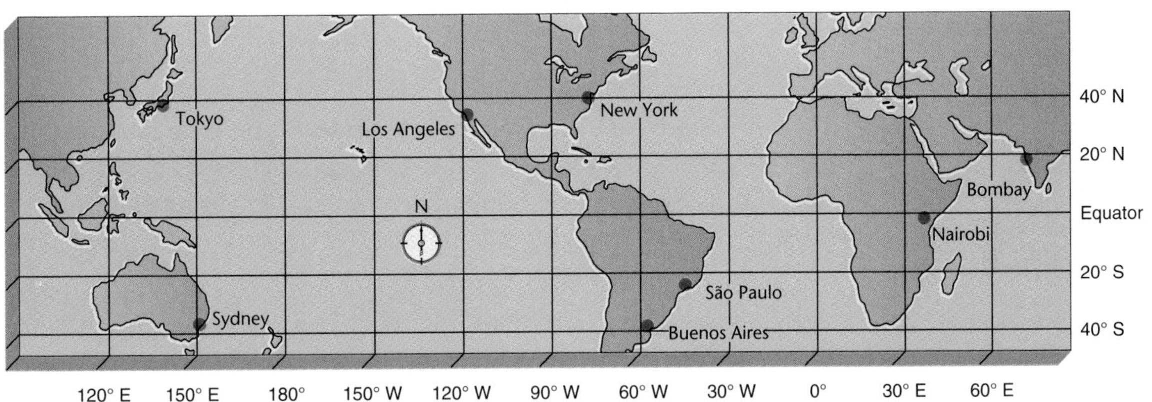

New York City has latitude 41° N and longitude 74° W.

Buenos Aires has latitude 35° S and longitude 58° W.

TRY IT

Give the approximate latitude and longitude of each city.

a. Bombay, India **b.** Tokyo, Japan **c.** São Paulo, Brazil

The average radius of the earth is about 3960 mi, and its average circumference is approximately 24,900 mi. In the following Explore, you will use that information, some proportional thinking, and longitudes and latitudes to measure distances.

EXPLORE: CROSSING THE CONTINENTS

1. The equator passes through South America and Africa. The longitudes of the easternmost and westernmost locations where it touches these continents are given below. Find the width of each continent at the equator. Explain why it is important to use the equator in this situation instead of a different line of latitude.

Continent	Easternmost Longitude	Westernmost Longitude
South America	50° W	80° W
Africa	42° E	9° E

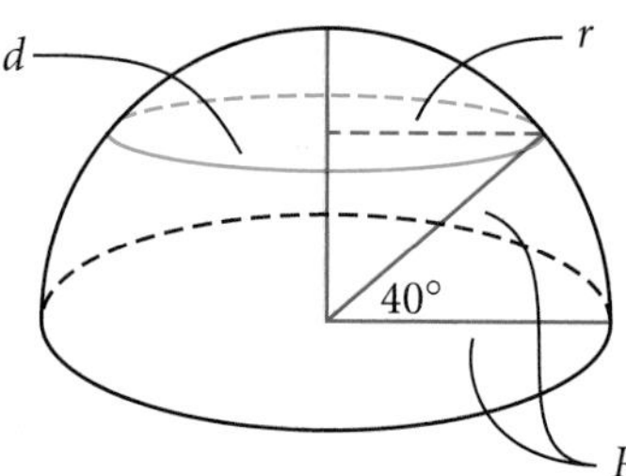

2. To find the widths of continents at other latitudes, we first need to find the length of the latitude line. Calculate the distance, *d*, around the earth at 40° N latitude. Give a detailed explanation of your calculation.
3. At 40° N latitude, Asia extends from 26° E longitude to 128° E longitude. Find the width of Asia at 40° N.

Time zones are based on lines of longitude. If you were looking down at the North Pole, you would see the earth complete one counterclockwise rotation of 360° every 24 hours. Therefore, each 1-hour time zone should correspond to $\frac{360°}{24} = 15°$ of longitude.

1. If the earth rotates 15° in one hour, how long does it take to rotate 1°?

REFLECT

1. Are latitude lines all the same length? are longitude lines? Illustrate your answer.
2. The earth is a three-dimensional object. Why are just two coordinates (longitude and latitude) enough to describe any point on the surface of the earth?

Exercises

CORE

In the Exercises, use 3960 mi for the radius of the earth and 24,900 mi for the circumference of the earth.

Getting Started In Exercises 1–3, use the map at the right to give the approximate latitude and longitude of each city.

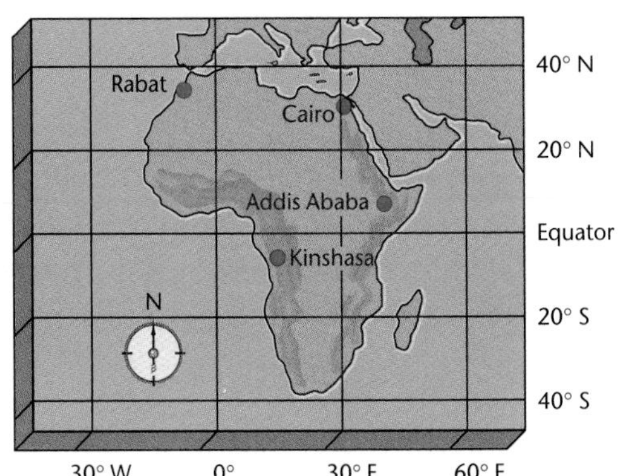

Science

1. Cairo, Egypt
2. Kinshasa, Zaire
3. Addis Ababa, Ethiopia

Science

4. The equator passes through the island of Borneo, in Indonesia. The easternmost location where it touches Borneo is at 117° E longitude, and the westernmost location is at 109° E longitude. Find the width of Borneo at the equator.

The pairs of cities in the following table have approximately the same longitude. Find the distance between each pair of cities.

Science

	Name	Latitude	Name	Latitude
5.	Seattle, WA	47.62° N	Oakland, CA	37.80° N
6.	Santa Fe, NM	35.68° N	Moose Jaw, Saskatchewan	50.62° N
7.	Irkutsk, Russia	52.50° N	Singapore, Singapore	1.23° N
8.	Beijing, China	39.92° N	Perth, Australia	31.95° S

History

9. **Tundra Trek** An expedition led by Robert Peary was the first to reach the North Pole (90° N latitude) in 1909. They traveled by sledge from Ellesmere Island (approximately 83° N latitude) to the pole. The journey from Ellesmere to the North Pole took just over one month. Approximately how far did they travel by sledge?

10. Write the letter of the second pair that best matches the first pair.

    Longitude: latitude as (a) circle: sphere, (b) parallel: perpendicular, (c) x-coordinate: y-coordinate, (d) y-coordinate: x-coordinate

11. Calculate the distance, d, around the earth at 60° N latitude. (Hint: First find the radius, r, of the 60° latitude line.) How does the radius of the 60° latitude line compare to the radius of the earth?

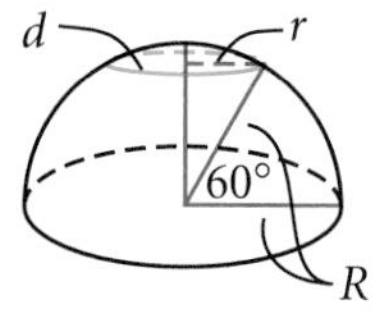

12. At 35° N latitude, the United States extends from 121° W longitude to 77° W longitude. Find the width of the United States at 35° N. Give a brief explanation of the method you used to solve this problem.

Social Science

13. a. How far apart in longitude should the world's time-zone divisions be? Explain.

b. Europe's westernmost point is at 10° W longitude, and its easternmost point is at 65° E longitude. Predict the number of time zones spanned by Europe.

Social Science

14. What to Pack? Alberta is traveling to an unfamiliar city, and she needs to know something about its climate. Will it help her more to know the city's longitude or its latitude? Explain how knowing the longitude or latitude of a city can help her predict its climate. What other information about the city might help Alberta?

LOOK BACK

15. *Given:* $\overline{AB} \parallel \overline{FE}$, $\overline{AB} \cong \overline{FE}$, and $\overline{AC} \cong \overline{ED}$.

Prove: $\triangle ABC \cong \triangle EFD$ [4-2]

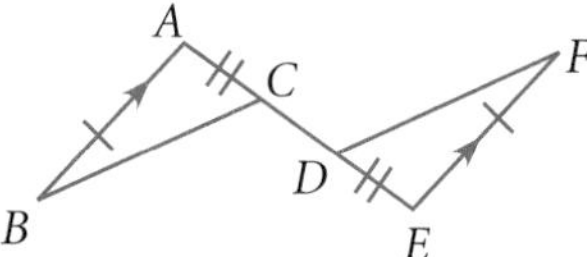

For each graph, estimate the coordinates of the point that has the maximum *y*-value. [11-2]

16.

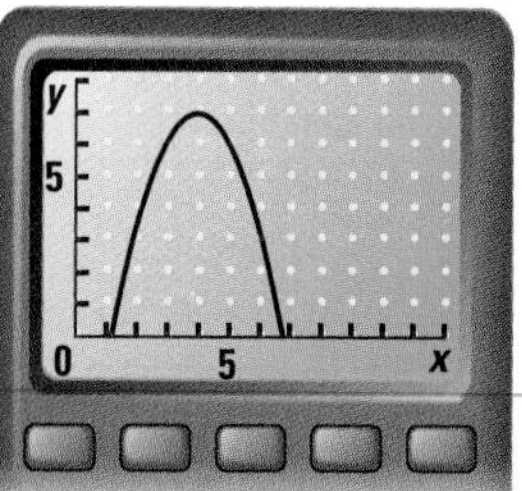

17.

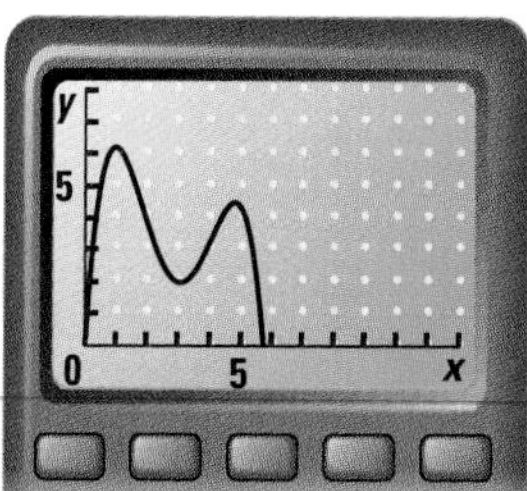

18.

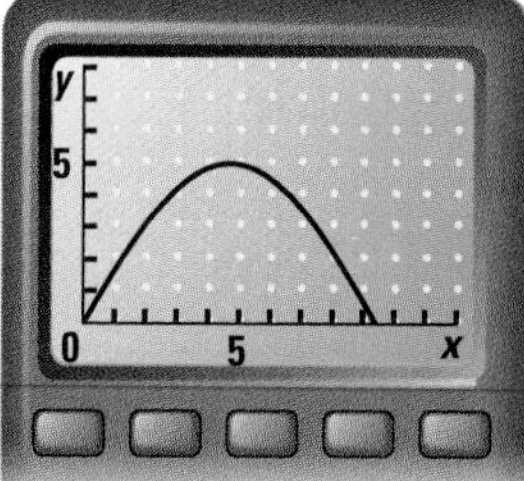

MORE PRACTICE

Give the approximate latitude and longitude of each city.

19. Caracas, Venezuela

20. Bogotá, Colombia

21. Quito, Ecuador

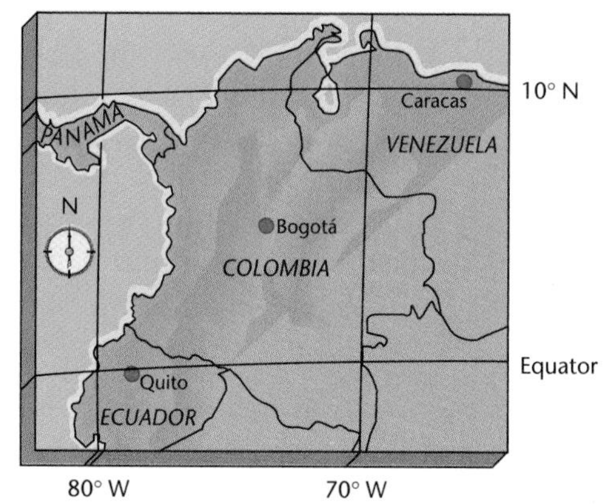

The pairs of cities in the following table have approximately the same longitude. Find the distance between each pair of cities.

	Name	Latitude	Name	Latitude
22.	Cleveland, OH	41.47° N	Columbia, SC	34.00° N
23.	Providence, RI	41.83° N	Quebec, Quebec	46.82° N
24.	Athens, Greece	37.97° N	Hammerfest, Norway	70.63° N
25.	Tokyo, Japan	35.67° N	Adelaide, Australia	34.92° S

26. Calculate the distance, d, around the earth at 45° N latitude. (Hint: First find the radius, r, of the 45° latitude line.) How does the radius of the 45° latitude line compare to the radius of the earth?

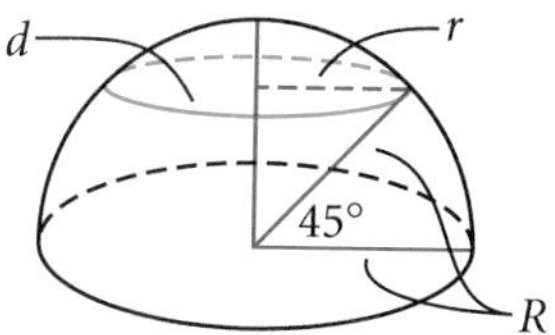

MORE MATH REASONING

27. Suppose Ze-Yuan knows the longitudes of two cities on the equator. Explain how she can use proportions to find the distance between these two cities.

28. Lost at Sea Suppose you're lost at sea and need to find your position. You know that the sun is directly overhead at noon at the equator. At noon, a 30-cm ruler on your boat casts a 24-cm shadow. What is your latitude? Write an explanation of the method you used to solve this problem. If you used a diagram to help solve the problem, include it with your solution, and explain how you used it.

29. Distant Horizons How far can a person see on the earth? Suppose Manuela is at an altitude of h kilometers and is looking at the horizon. The length of the tangent segment t approximates the length of the arc on the earth's surface that she can see.

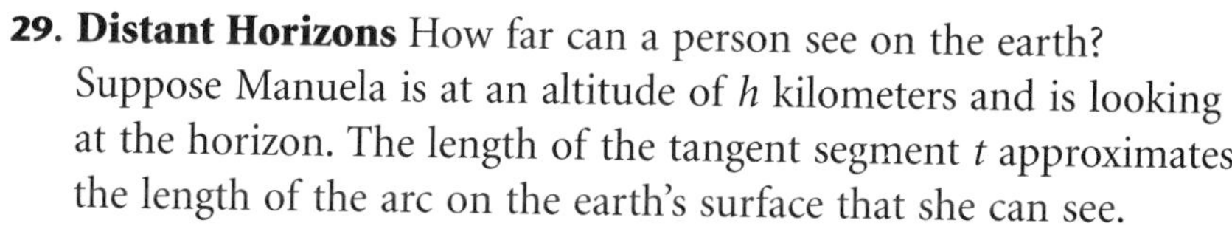

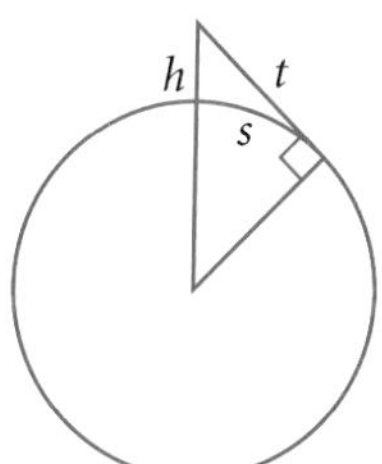

a. Assume the radius of the earth is 6370 km. Derive a formula for t in terms of h.

b. Mt. Everest is approximately 8.85 km tall. Find t for a person standing at the peak of Mt. Everest.

c. Find s, the actual length of the arc on the earth's surface that a person can see from the peak of Mt. Everest. Is t a good approximation for s?

30. The earth makes one complete rotation around its axis each day. Because the distance around the earth at the equator is greater than the distance around the earth at other latitudes, a point on the equator travels farther during one day than points elsewhere on the earth. What does this tell you about the speed at which points on the earth travel?

12-1 PART C Measurement in Astronomy

← CONNECT → ***You've used geometry to measure a variety of objects, including the earth. Now you will apply your knowledge of several concepts to calculate distances and sizes associated with the moon, the planets, and the stars.***

If you need to measure an unknown distance on the earth, you can use a ruler, a tape measure, or the odometer on a car. But how did we know how far away or how large the moon was before anyone had traveled there?

Earthbound humans have been interested in measuring astronomical distances for hundreds of years. You can use your knowledge of geometry to make some of these measurements yourself.

EXAMPLES

1. It takes a radar signal 2.56 sec to make a round trip from the earth to the moon. If radar travels at the speed of light (300,000 km/sec), how far away is the moon?

The round-trip distance is 2.56 sec $\times$ 300,000 km/sec $=$ 768,000 km.

The one-way distance is half of this: 384,000 km.

2. The diameter of the moon covers an arc of about 0.52° in the sky. What is the diameter of the moon?

We can use our knowledge of circles to set up a proportion. The ratio of 0.52° to 360° is approximately equal to the ratio of the moon's diameter to the circumference of its orbit. In Example 1, we found that the radius of the moon's orbit is about 384,000 km. We can use this value to find C, the circumference of the moon's orbit.

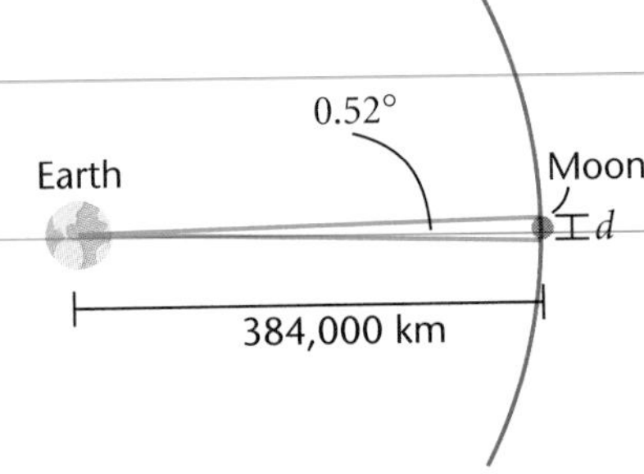

$C = 2\pi(384{,}000 \text{ km}) \approx 2{,}410{,}000$ km

$$\frac{0.52}{360} = \frac{d}{2{,}410{,}000}$$

Solving this proportion shows that d, the diameter of the moon, is approximately 3480 km.

TRY IT

The speed of light is approximately 300,000 km/sec. Find the amount of time it takes light to travel between the following bodies. Give your answers in appropriate units.

a. the earth and Venus (distance at their closest approach: 41,800,000 km)
b. the sun and Jupiter (average distance: 778,300,000 km)

Because distances in space are so large, we need to use some units that measure large distances conveniently.

An **astronomical unit** (A.U.) is the average distance from the earth to the sun—about 150,000,000 km ($\approx$ 93,000,000 mi). This unit is particularly useful for measuring distances within the solar system.

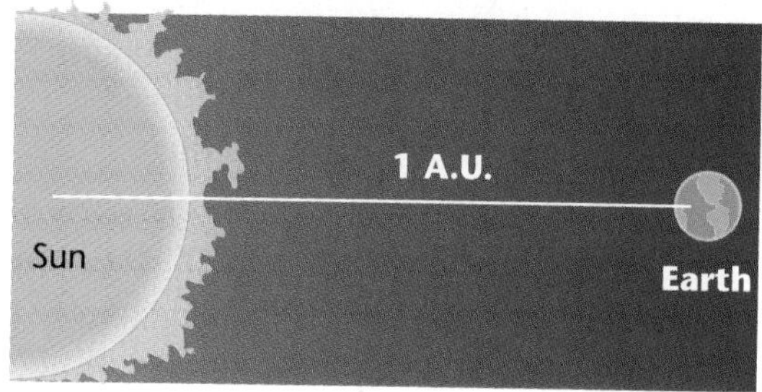

When measuring distances between stars, however, the astronomical unit is still too small to be convenient. Alpha Centauri, the star nearest the sun, is about 270,000 A.U. away! The **light-year** is a more appropriate unit to describe distances between stars and across galaxies. One light-year is the distance light travels (in a vacuum) in one year. Since light travels at a speed of nearly 300,000 km/sec, a light-year is a very large unit, approximately 9.5 trillion kilometers.

CONSIDER

1. **Mars is farther from the sun than the earth is. Is the distance from Mars to the sun less than or greater than 1 A.U.? How do you know?**
2. **Does a light-year measure time or distance? Explain.**

Although all stars (except the sun) are many light-years away, some stars are closer than others. As the earth orbits the sun, we look at the stars from different positions. As this happens, nearer stars appear to shift slightly against a background of more distant stars. This shift is called **parallax.** You can do a simple experiment that illustrates parallax.

Hold your thumb close to your face, and look at it with your left eye closed. Then look at it with your right eye closed.

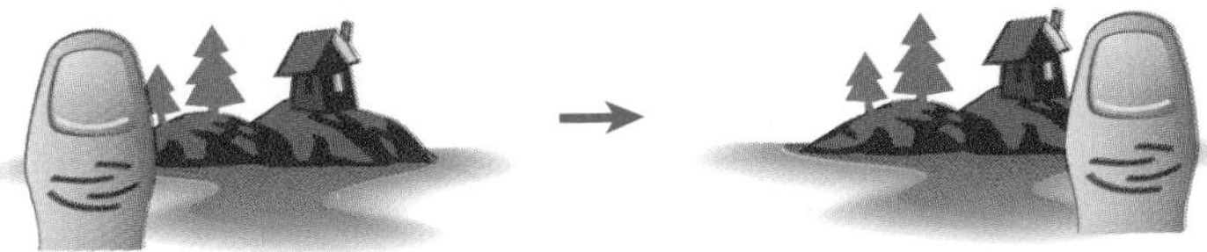

Did your thumb seem to move, while objects beyond it stayed in the same place? When you change your perspective, objects near you seem to move more than distant ones.

EXPLORE: HOW FAR TO THE NEAREST STAR?

When the earth is at position *X* in its orbit, the star nearest the sun, Alpha Centauri (*A*), lines up with a distant star, *D*. Three months later, the earth is at position *Y*. At this time, the measure of $\angle Y$, determined by the lines of sight to star *A* and star *D*, is about $\frac{1}{4800}$ of a degree.

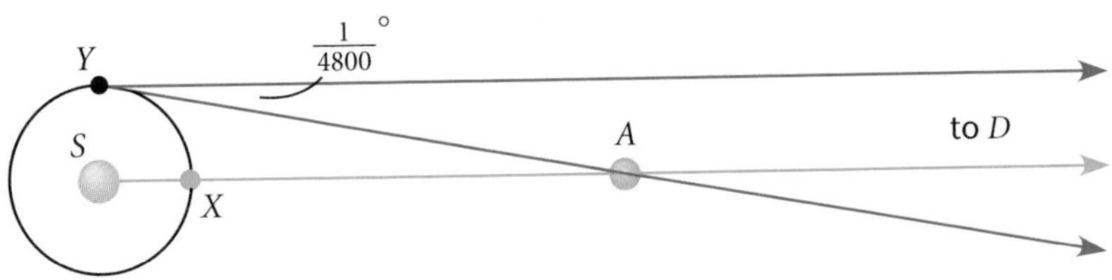

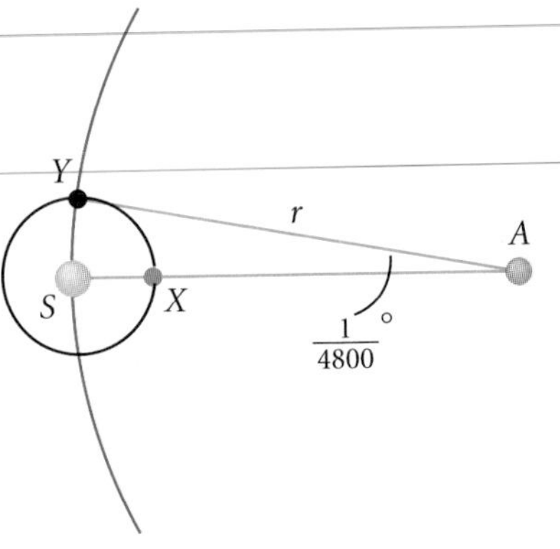

1. Because *D* is so far away, the rays labeled "to *D*" are very nearly parallel. Explain why $m\angle Y \approx m\angle XAY$.
2. To find *r*, the distance to Alpha Centauri, use an imaginary circle whose center is *A* and whose radius is *r*. The ratio of $m\angle XAY$ to 360° is approximately equal to the ratio of *SY* to the circumference of $\odot A$. Set up a proportion involving the measure of the parallax angle ($m\angle XAY$), the distance from the earth to the sun (SY), the distance to the star (r), and 360°. Explain how you set up your proportion.
3. Solve your proportion to find *r* in astronomical units (A.U.). Remember that the distance from the earth to the sun, *SY*, is 1 A.U.
4. There are about 63,200 A.U. in a light-year. Find the distance to Alpha Centauri in light-years.

REFLECT

1. Give some examples of how you've used proportional thinking to measure distances or lengths earlier in this course.
2. In using parallax to calculate the distance from the earth to a star, we assumed that the length of $\overset{\frown}{SY}$ is the same as the length of $\overline{SY}$ (see, for example, the figure on page 764). Is this true? If not, do you think this assumption will lead to a large error in our calculations? Why or why not?

Exercises

CORE

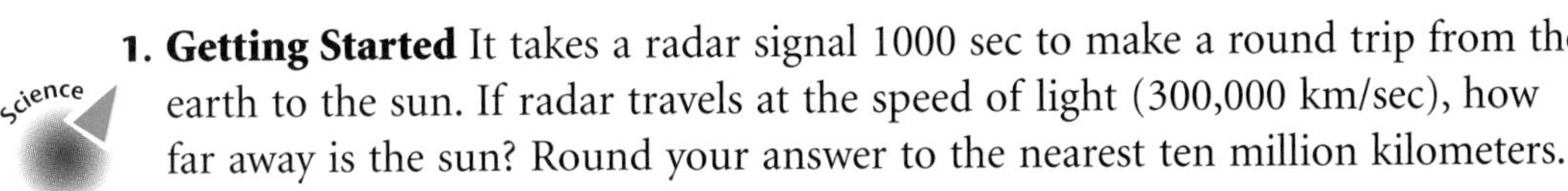

1. **Getting Started** It takes a radar signal 1000 sec to make a round trip from the earth to the sun. If radar travels at the speed of light (300,000 km/sec), how far away is the sun? Round your answer to the nearest ten million kilometers.

The speed of light is approximately 300,000 km/sec. Find the amount of time it takes light to travel between the following bodies. Give your answers in appropriate units.

2. the earth and the moon (average distance: 384,000 km)
3. the earth and Mars (distance at their closest approach: 56,000,000 km)
4. the sun and Saturn (average distance: 1,427,000,000 km)
5. There are approximately 63,200 A.U. in a light-year. If the earth did not move, how many times could a beam of light travel back and forth between the earth and the sun in one year?
6. Recall that the average distance from the earth to the sun is 1 A.U.
   a. Guess the average distance from the sun to Pluto, the most distant known planet, in astronomical units. (This is the average radius of the solar system.)
   b. The average distance from the sun to Pluto is about 5,900,000,000 km. Calculate the average distance from the sun to Pluto in astronomical units. Compare this to your guess in **6a.**
7. From the following group of terms, choose the one that does not belong, and explain why it does not belong.

   light-year, astronomical unit, parallax, mile
8. The speed of light is approximately 186,000 mi/sec (in a vacuum). Using this value, calculate the length, in miles, of a light-year. Briefly explain the method you used to solve this problem.

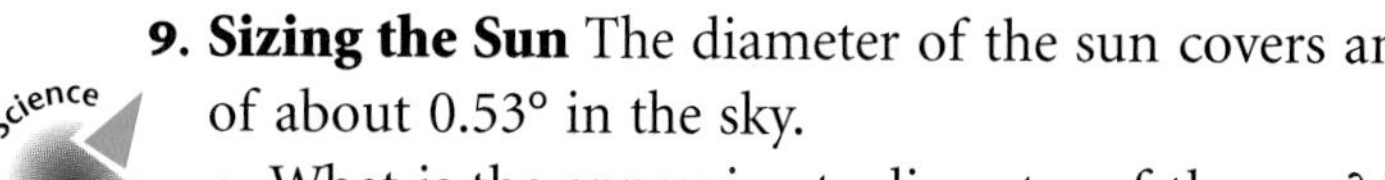

9. Sizing the Sun The diameter of the sun covers an arc of about 0.53° in the sky.

a. What is the approximate diameter of the sun? Round your answer to the nearest ten thousand kilometers. (Hint: You will need to use your answer to Exercise 1.)

b. Compare the measure of the arc covered by the sun to that of the arc covered by the moon, as given in Example 2 on page 762. What do you notice?

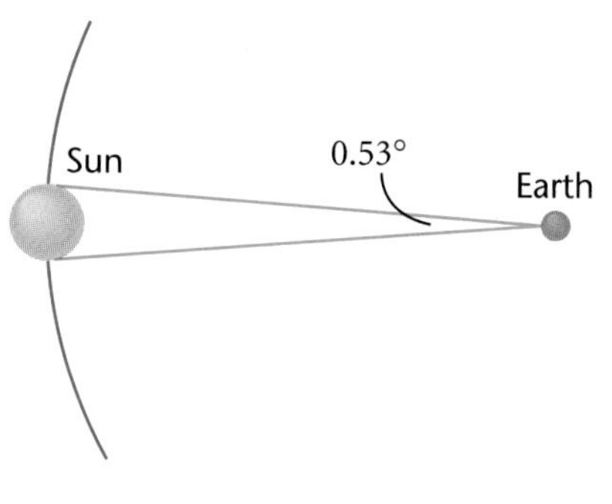

10. Are You Sirius? When the earth is at position X in its orbit, the brightest star, Sirius (I), lines up with a distant star, D. When the earth is at position Y, the measure of the parallax angle, $\angle YIX$, is about $\frac{1}{9720}$ of a degree.

a. Set up and solve a proportion to find r, the approximate distance to Sirius, in astronomical units. (Remember that the distance from the earth to the sun, SY, is 1 A.U.)

b. Find the distance to Sirius in light-years.

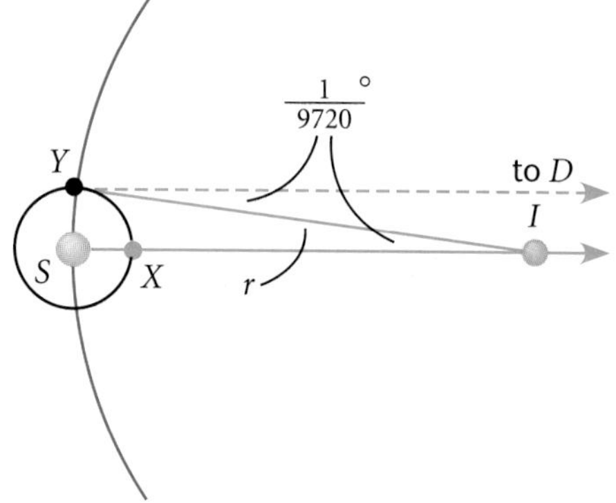

11. a. The parallax angle to the star Altair is about $\frac{1}{18,360}$ of a degree. Find the distance to Altair in light-years.

b. Which is older, the light that has just reached the earth from Altair, or you? Explain your reasoning.

LOOK AHEAD

12. What is a postulate? How is it different from a theorem? Write a brief paragraph that answers these questions.

13. Describe four postulates about points, lines, and planes.

14. State the Parallel Postulate in your own words.

MORE PRACTICE

The speed of light is approximately 300,000 km/sec. Find the amount of time it takes light to travel between the following bodies.

15. the earth and the sun (average distance: 150,000,000 km)

16. the sun and Mercury (average distance: 57,900,000 km)

17. the sun and Neptune (average distance: 4,497,000,000 km)

18. From its moon Callisto, Jupiter covers an arc of about 4.25° in the sky. Callisto is about 1,880,000 km from Jupiter. What is Jupiter's approximate diameter? Round your answer to the nearest ten thousand kilometers.

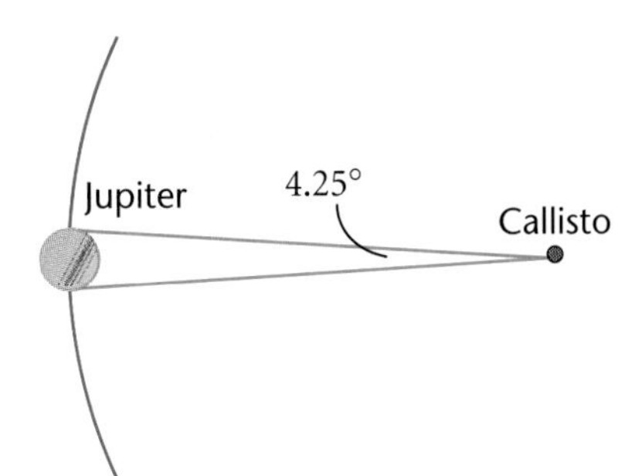

MORE MATH REASONING

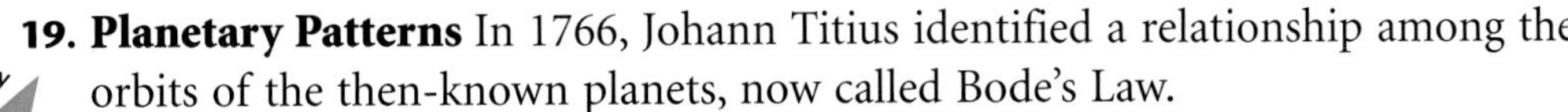

19. Planetary Patterns In 1766, Johann Titius identified a relationship among the orbits of the then-known planets, now called Bode's Law.

a. Describe the number pattern in the first row of the table. Then explain how the numbers in the second and third rows are calculated.

First row	0	3	6	12	24	48	96
Second row	4	7	10	16	28	52	100
Bode numbers	0.4	0.7	1.0	1.6	2.8	5.2	10.0

b. The following table gives the average orbital distances (in A.U.) for the planets known in 1766. How well do these numbers agree with the Bode numbers?

Planet	Mercury	Venus	Earth	Mars	Jupiter	Saturn
Distance	0.39	0.72	1.0	1.5	5.2	9.5

c. Use Bode's Law to predict the distances of the next three planets from the sun.

d. In 1781, the seventh planet from the sun, Uranus, was discovered. Its average distance from the sun is 19.2 A.U. Did this discovery follow Bode's Law?

e. In the late 1700s, astronomers began to search for a planet orbiting the sun between Mars and Jupiter. Why do you think they began this search?

f. In 1801, Ceres, the largest of the asteroids, was discovered orbiting the sun at 2.77 A.U. What should its distance from the sun be according to Bode's Law?

g. Neptune, the eighth planet, was discovered in 1846, and Pluto, the ninth, was found in 1930. Their average orbital distances are 30.1 A.U. and 39.4 A.U., respectively. Do the orbits of these planets seem to follow Bode's Law?

20. Kepler's third law states that the cube of a planet's distance to the sun in astronomical units, d, is equal to the square of the time it takes to go around the sun (its *period*, p) in years. Check whether this law is approximately true for these planets.

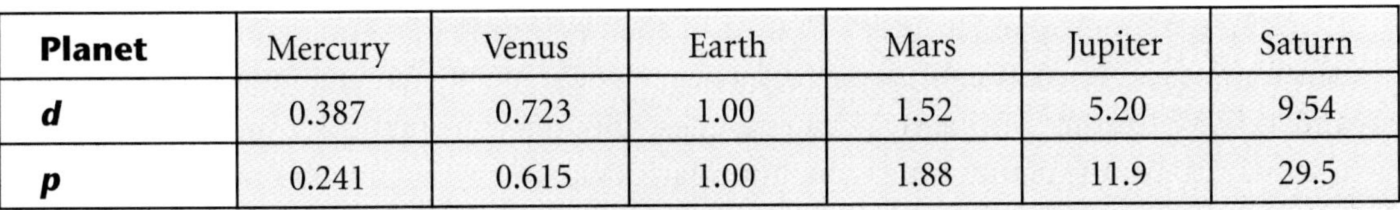

Planet	Mercury	Venus	Earth	Mars	Jupiter	Saturn
d	0.387	0.723	1.00	1.52	5.20	9.54
p	0.241	0.615	1.00	1.88	11.9	29.5

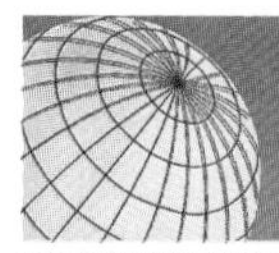

12-1 PART D Making Connections

← CONNECT → ***Geometry has helped people understand the earth for thousands of years. With familiar tools like proportions and new ones like fractals, you've investigated some ways to measure and model the earth, our solar system, and our galaxy.***

The photograph at the left shows a computer-generated fractal. Fractals can be used to model trees, coastlines, and mountains.

The earth itself can be modeled by a sphere, and you have used your knowledge of the angles and arcs of a circle to calculate the distances to stars. In the following Explore, you will use some of these concepts to see how to calculate moonrise times.

EXPLORE: MOONRISE OVER COLUMBUS

What time does the moon rise in your city? This depends on your city's location, the day of the year, and your time zone. For example, moonrise was at 8:56 P.M. near Valencia, Spain (at 0° longitude and 40° N latitude) on January 1, 1994. To calculate the time of moonrise on that day for U.S. cities close to 40° N latitude, you need to make two corrections.

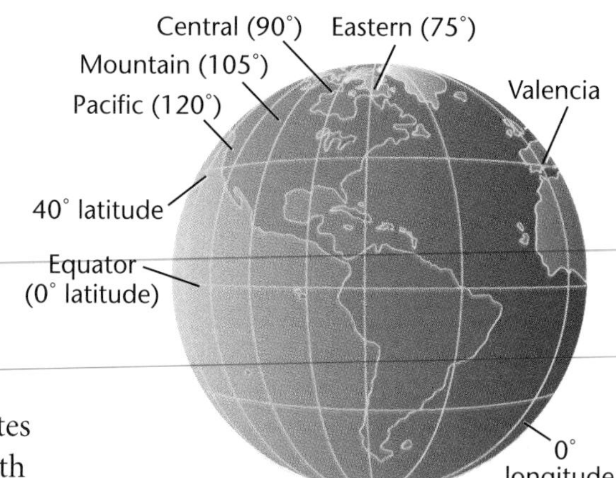

First, because the moon moves, it rises 78 minutes later for every complete 360° rotation of the earth at 40° N. So you need to add a fraction of 78 minutes to the moonrise time in Valencia.

$$\text{Correction for longitude} = \frac{\text{longitude}}{360} \times 78 \text{ min}$$

Second, because the earth turns, you need to correct for how "far along" a city is in a time zone. For every 1° west of the beginning of a time zone, add 4 minutes. Theoretically, time zones begin at 75° W, 90° W, 105° W, and 120° W for the continental United States. (Because of practical considerations, the actual time zone boundaries vary.)

1. Complete the following table.

City	Longitude	$\frac{\text{Longitude}}{360}$	Longitude Time Correction	Local Time Correction	Moonrise 1/1/94
Philadelphia	75.17° W				
Columbus	83.02° W				
Indianapolis	86.17° W	0.239	19 min	45 min	10:00 P.M.

2. What information would you need to be able to calculate the time of moonrise on January 1, 1994, in your city? Do you think you might need to make any modifications to this method for your city? (Hint: What is true about all of the cities in the table?)

REFLECT

1. Describe several examples of how geometry can be used to model the earth and the solar system.
2. A friend who hasn't studied fractal geometry likes fractal designs on T-shirts. She asks you to explain what a fractal is. Write an explanation of fractals for your friend.

Self-Assessment

In the following, use 3960 mi for the radius of the earth and 24,900 mi for the circumference of the earth.

1. Sketch the first three stages for the pattern described below.

   Start with an equilateral triangle. Use the following rule.

   a. Find the midpoint of each side of each triangle.
   b. Connect the midpoints, as shown at the right.

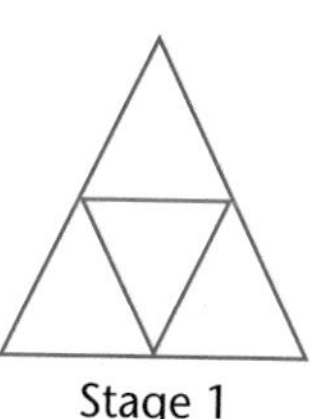

Stage 1

2. Dr. Breen is a scientist who is designing equipment for a future trip to Mars. She determines that each box for soil samples needs to have a 36-in.^{3} volume and that its height should be twice its length. Find the approximate dimensions of the box with the least surface area that satisfies these conditions. [11-2]

Science

3. Light from the sun takes about 760 sec to reach Mars. Find the distance, in kilometers, from the sun to Mars.

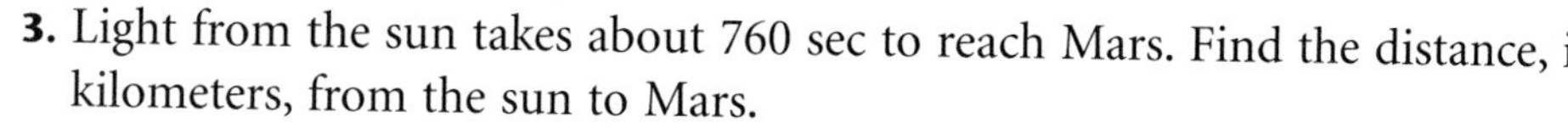

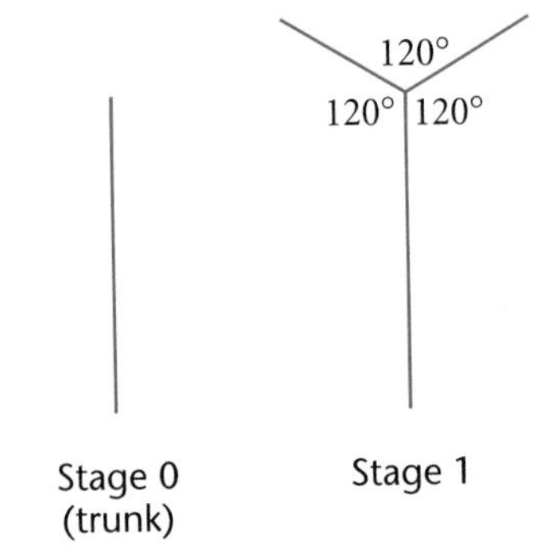

4. The Fractal Tree The following pattern creates a "fractal tree." The trunk is Stage 0. The next stages are made by adding two new branches to each old one, so that all branches make a 120° angle with each other. The new branches are half the length of the old branch.

a. Sketch the first four stages of the fractal tree.

b. Write an equation for the number of new branches at Stage n.

c. The trunk of the fractal tree is 1 unit long. What is the total length of all branches for Stages 0–4? Explain how you found your answer.

d. What is the total length of all branches of the tree at Stage n? As the tree grows through an infinite number of stages, will the total length of its branches grow infinitely, or will there be a limit on the length? Explain your reasoning.

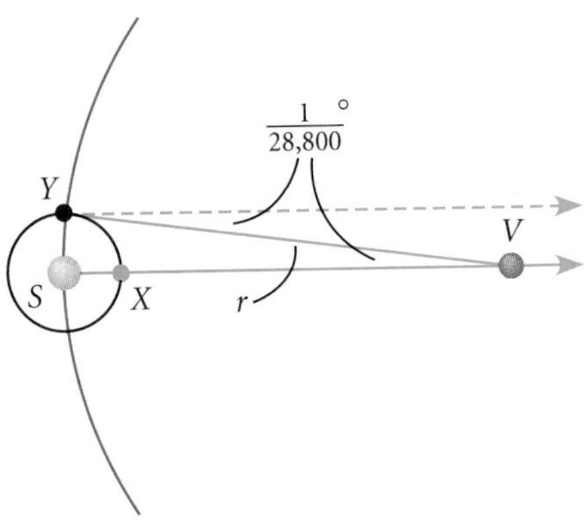

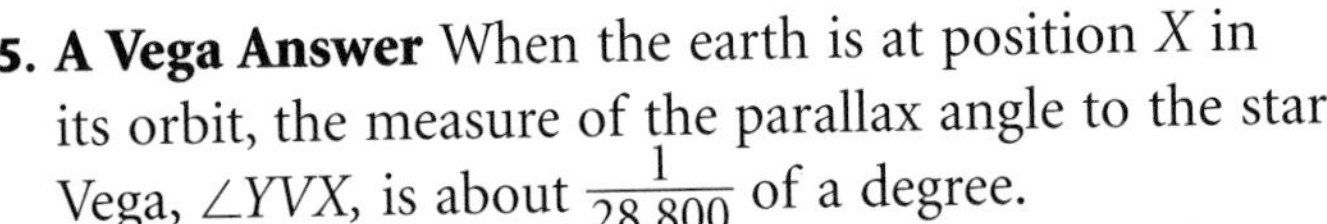

5. A Vega Answer When the earth is at position X in its orbit, the measure of the parallax angle to the star Vega, $\angle YVX$, is about $\frac{1}{28,800}$ of a degree.

a. Set up and solve a proportion to find r, the distance to Vega, in astronomical units. (Remember that the distance from the earth to the sun, SY, is 1 A.U.)

b. Find the distance to Vega in light-years.

6. Latitude lines
(a) meet at the poles. (b) are perpendicular to the equator.
(c) have different lengths. (d) both (a) and (b)
(e) all of the above

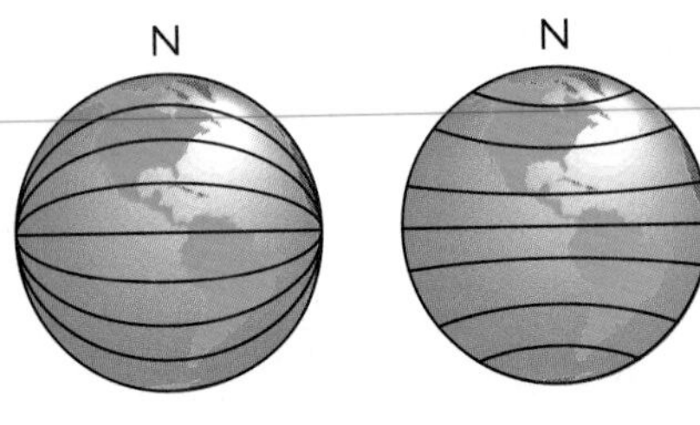
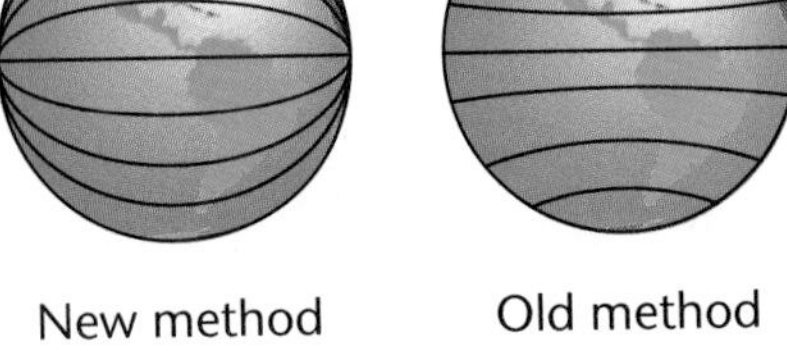

7. Suppose latitude lines were drawn in the same way as longitude lines, as shown at the right.

a. Would this method work? Could you use it to describe the location of any point on the earth's surface? Why or why not?

b. In this method, there are two new landmarks on the earth's surface. Where are they? What would you call them?

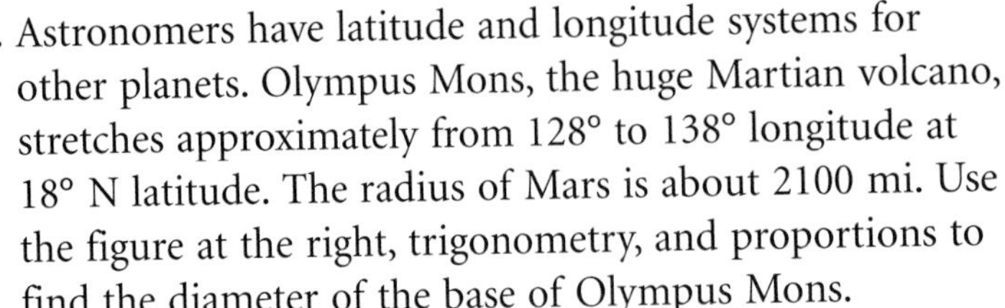

8. Astronomers have latitude and longitude systems for other planets. Olympus Mons, the huge Martian volcano, stretches approximately from 128° to 138° longitude at 18° N latitude. The radius of Mars is about 2100 mi. Use the figure at the right, trigonometry, and proportions to find the diameter of the base of Olympus Mons.

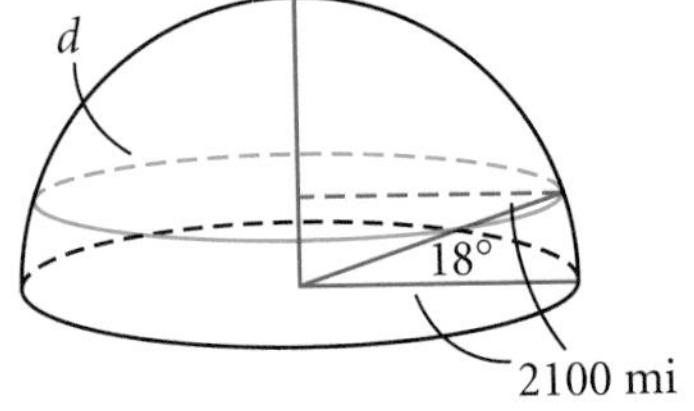

12-2 Euclidean and Non-Euclidean Geometries

THE NATURE OF THE UNIVERSE

A *nebula* is a luminous, fuzzy celestial body. Before the invention of the telescope, only a few nebulae (including the enormous Milky Way and some smaller, fainter objects) were known. Early telescopes showed that the Milky Way was actually made up of individual stars. But what were the other nebulae? Some astronomers and philosophers believed that they were gas clouds within our Milky Way galaxy; others felt that they were other star systems, completely separate from our own.

In 1864, William Huggins found that some nebulae were indeed gas clouds. But in 1922, Edwin Hubble identified individual stars in the Andromeda nebula, and his estimate of the distance to Andromeda showed that it lay far outside the Milky Way. The debate had been resolved in favor of both sides: some of the nebulae were gas clouds within the Milky Way, and some were actually other Galaxies far beyond our own. Ever since, our model of the universe has featured distinct galaxies separated by light-years of empty space.

?

1. **How do you think our model of the universe would be different if all nebulae were gas clouds inside the Milky Way?**
2. **The Milky Way can be seen as a white band stretching across the night sky. In ancient times, it was visible to all observers around the earth; however, there are many people now living who have never seen it. Why? Where do people live who cannot see the Milky Way?**

12-2 PART A Euclidean Geometry

← CONNECT → ***We've used some basic postulates to develop our system of geometry. Now you will review these postulates and discover how theorems depend on our belief that the postulates are true.***

The field of flowers shown at the left is planted in parallel rows for efficient harvesting. As you will see, the decision to plant the flowers in this way can be traced to the system of geometry you've been studying.

Euclid developed this system of geometry around 300 B.C. As a model, it works well when measurements are relatively small, like those used in farms and cities. Some of the postulates you've assumed to be true in Euclid's system follow.

POINTS-EXISTENCE POSTULATE

Space contains at least four non-coplanar points. Every plane contains at least three non-collinear points. Every line contains at least two points.

STRAIGHT-LINE POSTULATE

Two points are contained in one and only one line. (Two points determine a line.)

PLANE POSTULATE

Three non-collinear points are contained in one and only one plane. (Three non-collinear points determine a plane.)

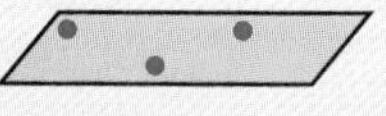

FLAT-PLANE POSTULATE

If two points are in a plane, then the line containing the points is in the same plane.

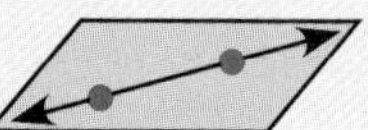

PLANE-INTERSECTION POSTULATE

If two planes intersect, then their intersection is a line.

PARALLEL POSTULATE

Through a given point P not on a line ℓ, exactly one line may be drawn parallel to line ℓ.

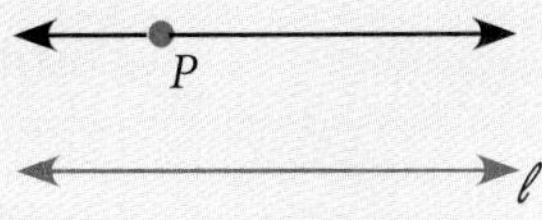

TRY IT

Name the Euclidean postulate illustrated by each statement. (When we refer to a star or planet, assume that we are referring to its center. Therefore, you can think of it as a point.)

a. The earth, the sun, and Jupiter are contained in exactly one plane.
b. There is exactly one straight line that passes through the stars Sirius and Altair.
c. There is only one line through the star Canopus that is parallel to the line that contains Sirius and Altair.

We began our deductive system of geometry with undefined terms, definitions, and postulates. Although you've developed many theorems since then—and used these theorems in proofs—every theorem can be traced back to our undefined terms, definitions, and postulates.

You may be surprised to learn that the proofs of the following theorems depend on the Parallel Postulate.

- The sum of the measures of the angles of a triangle is 180°.
- If a circle has radius r, its circumference is equal to $2\pi r$, and its area is equal to πr^2.
- Parallel lines are everywhere equidistant.

In the following Explore, you will investigate the connection between the first of these theorems and the Parallel Postulate.

EXPLORE: DEPENDING ON PARALLEL

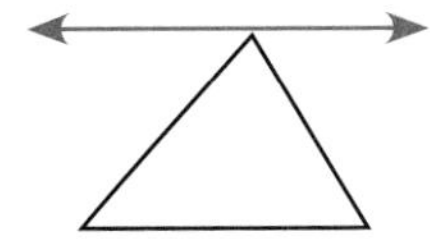

1. Prove that the sum of the measures of the angles of a triangle is 180°. (Hint: Through one of the vertices, draw a line parallel to the opposite side of the triangle.)
2. How does your proof depend on the Parallel Postulate? Discuss your findings with your classmates.

For about 2000 years, mathematicians tried to show that the Parallel Postulate didn't need to be a postulate. However, they found that it was impossible to prove the Parallel Postulate and make it a theorem by using the other Euclidean postulates. As you will soon see, some interesting possibilities arise if we make a different assumption about parallel lines.

REFLECT

1. Euclid believed that his postulates were self-evident truths. Do you think Euclid's Parallel Postulate is *obviously* true? Explain.
2. Mathematicians wanted to prove the Parallel Postulate, so that Euclid's system could be based on fewer unproved assumptions. Why do you think this was important to them?

Exercises

CORE

Getting Started Name the Euclidean postulate illustrated by each statement. (When we refer to a star or planet, assume that we are referring to its center. Therefore, you can think of it as a point.)

1. Only one straight line contains Alpha Centauri and the sun.
2. Pluto, Mercury, and the moon are contained in exactly one plane.
3. There is a line through the star Deneb that is parallel to the line through the stars Castor and Pollux.

You first saw the Parallel Postulate in Chapter 2. You've investigated many postulates, theorems, and definitions since then. Give four examples for each of the following from Chapters 3–12.

4. postulates
5. definitions
6. theorems

Use Euclid's system of geometry to answer each of the following questions.

7. Does a triangle exist that has two right angles? Why or why not?
8. If two coplanar lines are both perpendicular to a third line, are they parallel to each other? Explain.
9. Sketch an angle, and construct its bisector. Explain why this construction works. Which postulates and definitions does this method depend on?

Every theorem in geometry can be traced back to postulates, definitions, and undefined terms. Identify a postulate that is the basis for each theorem.

10. the LL theorem

11. the formula for the area of a square ($A = s^2$)

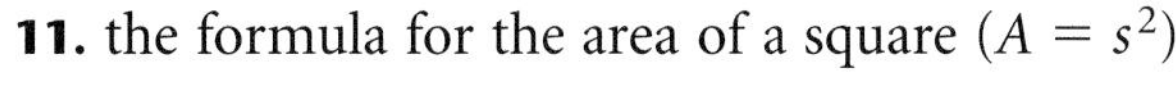

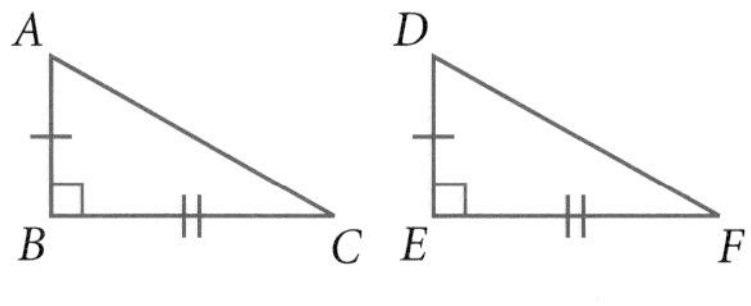

$\triangle ABC \cong \triangle DEF$

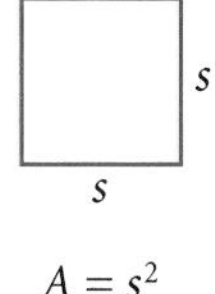

$A = s^2$

12. But It Looks Flat! The idea that the earth's surface is curved became accepted in Greece in about 400 B.C. One observation that supported this idea was that certain stars visible in Egypt could not be seen in Greece. Explain how this observation suggests that the earth's surface is curved.

13. Apollo astronauts traveled to the moon at the rate of 40,000 km/hr. Suppose astronauts travel to the Andromeda Galaxy (shown at the right), which is 2,000,000 light-years away.

a. If the astronauts travel at 40,000 km/hr, how long will it take them to reach the Andromeda Galaxy?

b. At how many times the speed of light would they have to travel to be able to reach Andromeda in your lifetime? Write a brief description of the method you used to solve this problem.

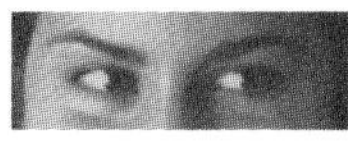

LOOK AHEAD

14. Describe a model you have studied in which you use "parallel lines" that violate the Parallel Postulate. (Hint: You worked with this model earlier in Chapter 12.)

MORE PRACTICE

Name the Euclidean postulate illustrated by each statement. (When we refer to a star or planet, assume that we are referring to its center. Therefore, you can think of it as a point.)

15. The straight line through the sun and the earth is in any plane that contains the sun and the earth.

16. Venus and Mars are contained in exactly one line.

17. There are at least four non-coplanar locations in space.

In Exercises 18 and 19, use Euclid's system of geometry to answer each question.

18. Can two parallel lines intersect? Explain.

19. Is the sum of the measures of the angles in a convex quadrilateral always the same? Why or why not?

20. State the Euclidean postulate illustrated by the figure at the right.

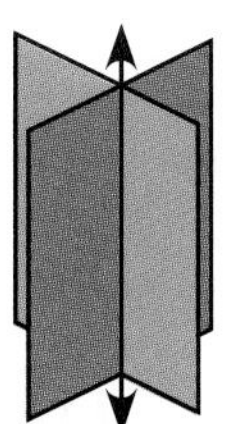

MORE MATH REASONING

21. Paper Clip Geometry Suppose there are five postulates about strings and paper clips.

Postulate A: There is at least one piece of string.

Postulate B: There are exactly three paper clips on every piece of string.

Postulate C: Not all paper clips are on the same string.

Postulate D: There is exactly one string through any two paper clips.

Postulate E: Any two strings have at least one paper clip in common.

a. Make a single sketch that illustrates all of these postulates.

Problem-Solving Tip

You may want to make a model with real objects.

b. Using the above postulates, prove that there are at least five paper clips.

c. What are the minimum numbers of strings and paper clips needed to fulfill all of the conditions of the postulates?

d. How does eliminating Postulate D affect your answer to **21c**? Explain your thinking.

22. Decide which one of the following theorems depends on the Parallel Postulate and which one does not. Justify your choices.

(a) If two parallel lines are cut by a transversal, then the corresponding angles are congruent.

(b) If two angles are congruent and supplementary, then both of the angles are right angles.

12-2 PART B Non-Euclidean Geometry

← CONNECT → ***In indirect proofs, you assumed that a statement was not true and showed that your assumption led to a contradiction. However, assuming that the Parallel Postulate is not true can lead to the creation of a new geometric system in which there are no parallel lines.***

Since the beginning of time, humans have tried to understand planets (such as Jupiter, shown at the left), the solar system, galaxies, and the universe. When we investigate such vast objects, however, we find that Euclid's geometric model has some shortcomings. A **non-Euclidean** system of geometry comes from the work of Bernhard Riemann (1826–1866). Riemann's version of the Parallel Postulate contradicts Euclid's.

RIEMANN'S PARALLEL POSTULATE

Through a given point P not on a line ℓ, there is *no* line parallel to line ℓ.

This statement may seem strange or impossible, but there is a familiar model in which Riemann's postulate makes sense.

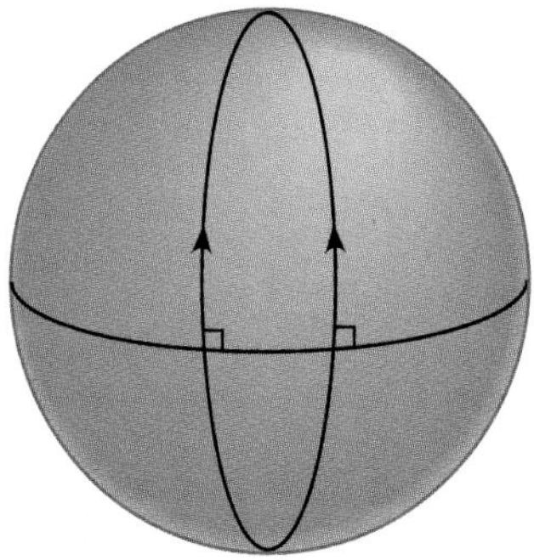

The most familiar examples of Riemannian lines are the longitude lines on a globe. Although they're perpendicular to the equator (and would therefore be parallel in Euclidean geometry), they get closer and closer until they meet at the poles. A sphere illustrates a simple model of Riemannian geometry.

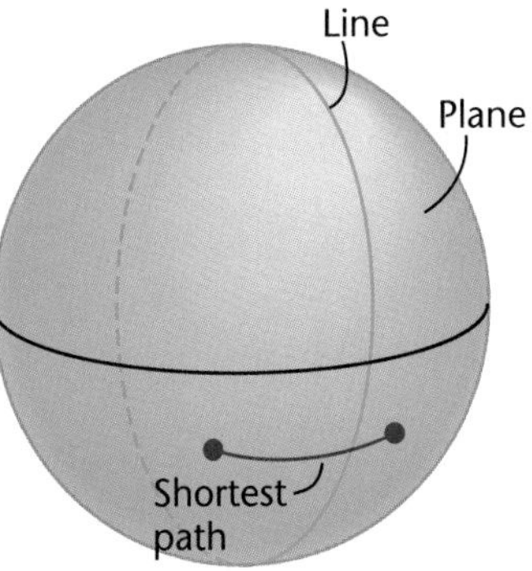

In the model of Riemannian geometry that you will work with, a *plane* is a sphere. In this Riemannian geometry, *lines* are great circles on the plane (sphere). The distance between any two points is the length of the shortest path between them. This path is an arc of a great circle on the sphere, not a straight line segment!

Many of the definitions and properties of Euclidean geometry still apply in the Riemannian system. For example, right angles still measure 90°, and perpendicular lines still form right angles. But some Euclidean properties are not true in Riemannian geometry. In the following Explore, you will investigate how triangles and lines behave in our model of Riemannian geometry.

EXPLORE: INFLATING EUCLID'S IDEAS

MATERIALS

Balloons
Marking pen
Ruler
Protractor

1. Spread a balloon flat on the surface of a table. Carefully draw the largest acute triangle you can on one side of the balloon. Then turn the balloon over, and draw two parallel lines from the top of the balloon to the bottom.
2. Inflate the balloon. What happens to the parallel lines? How is this different from the way parallel lines behave in Euclidean geometry?
3. Measure the angles of the triangle after the balloon has been inflated. How does the sum of the measures of the angles compare to the sum when the balloon was flat? Make a conjecture about the sum of the measures of the angles of a triangle in Riemannian geometry.
4. On a second balloon, draw some geometric figures you'd like to investigate: for example, intersecting lines and other figures. Inflate the balloon, and make any conjectures you can about the properties of these figures in Riemannian geometry. Share your conjectures with your classmates.

In Riemannian geometry, all lines are curved. Albert Einstein (1879–1955) used this idea in the development of his theory of relativity. Einstein said that mass, like that in planets, stars, and galaxies, causes space to curve. (Think of a heavy ball on a sheet of plastic wrap.) Moving objects that are near the ball follow a path in the curved space. This helps explain why planets stay in orbit around stars, and stars stay in orbit around the centers of galaxies.

The following theorems can be proved using Riemann's Parallel Postulate.

- In Riemannian geometry, the sum of the measures of the angles in a triangle is greater than 180°.
- In Riemannian geometry, if a circle has radius r, its circumference is less than $2\pi r$, and its area is less than πr^2.
- In Riemannian geometry, any two coplanar lines intersect.

TRY IT

Answer each question using the properties of Riemannian geometry.

a. If a and b are two coplanar lines, what must be true about them?
b. In $\triangle GHJ$, $m\angle J = 45°$, and $m\angle H = 100°$. What do you know about $m\angle G$?
c. Circle M has radius 2 cm. What do you know about its circumference? its area?

REFLECT

1. Lines drawn on the earth's surface are curved. Explain why they might appear straight for most measurements.
2. Is the shortest distance between two points on the earth's surface really a straight line segment? What does this mean for a pilot trying to determine the shortest flight path from New York to Tokyo?

Exercises

CORE

Getting Started Using our model of Riemannian geometry, name the figure that is equivalent to each of the following Euclidean figures.

1. a line **2.** a plane **3.** a line segment

Answer each question using the properties of Riemannian geometry.

4. In $\triangle XYZ$, $m\angle X = 23°$ and $m\angle Y = 55°$. What do you know about $m\angle Z$?

5. Circle C has an eight-inch radius. What do you know about its circumference? its area?

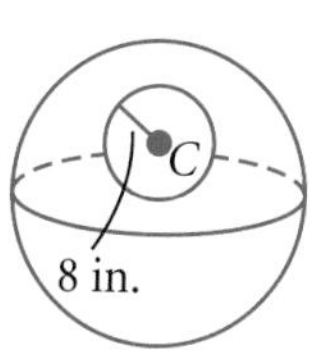

6. If s and t are two coplanar lines, what must be true about them?

Each of the following statements is true in Euclidean geometry. Determine whether each is true for Riemannian geometry. Explain your thinking.

7. A triangle cannot have two right angles.

8. The circumference of a circle with diameter d is πd.

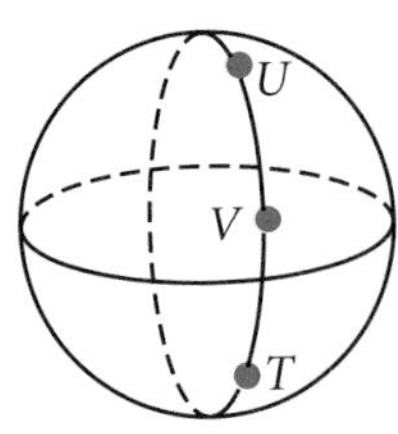

9. In Euclidean geometry, it's easy to tell which of three collinear points is between the other two. Is this true in the Riemannian system? For example, is V between T and U? Why or why not? (Hint: See what happens if the three points aren't all in the same hemisphere.)

10. The Saccheri Quadrilateral Girolamo Saccheri, an Italian priest, tried (and failed) to prove Euclid's Parallel Postulate, using some special quadrilaterals. In fact, he actually developed part of a non-Euclidean geometry.

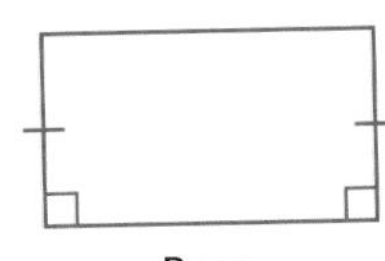

A *Saccheri quadrilateral* has two congruent sides that are both perpendicular to its base. In Euclidean geometry, a Saccheri quadrilateral must be a rectangle.

Make a conjecture about the sum of the measures of the angles of a Saccheri quadrilateral in our model of Riemannian geometry. Support your conjecture with an explanation and an illustration.

Science

11. The Orion Nebula is a gas nebula seen in the constellation Orion. It is within the Milky Way and is about 1500 light-years from the earth. The Andromeda Galaxy, the nearest spiral galaxy to the Milky Way, is about 2×10^6 light-years from the earth.

a. How many times farther away from the earth is the Andromeda Galaxy than the Orion Nebula?

b. As seen from the earth, the Orion Nebula and the Andromeda Galaxy are similar in brightness. How is this possible, given the difference in their distances from us?

LOOK BACK

Science

12. On the 1992 flight of the space shuttle *Endeavour,* Dr. Kathryn C. Thornton became the second American woman to walk in space. Suppose that at the time of the space walk the space shuttle was at an altitude of 200 mi.

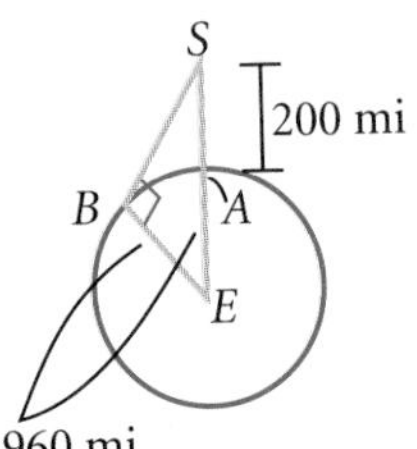

a. When the shuttle was directly above point A, Dr. Thornton could see point B on the horizon. How far was she from point B? [5-3]

b. Use trigonometry to find $m\angle BEA$. [7-3]

c. Suppose a lake is 1100 mi from point A. Could Dr. Thornton see this lake when she was directly over point A? (Hint: Calculate the length of $\widehat{AB}$.) [8-2]

13. Gweru, Zimbabwe (19° S latitude) and Istanbul, Turkey (41° N latitude) have approximately the same longitude. Assuming the earth's radius is 3960 mi, find the distance between Gweru and Istanbul. [12-1]

MORE PRACTICE

Answer each question, using the properties of Riemannian geometry.

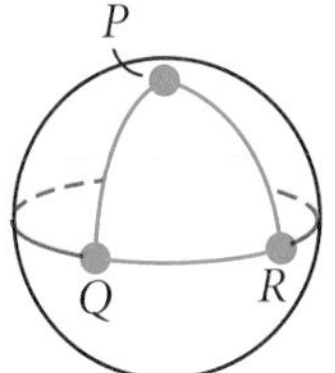

14. If m and n are two coplanar lines, what must be true about them?

15. In $\triangle PQR$, $m\angle P = 80°$, and $m\angle Q = 90°$. What do you know about $m\angle R$?

16. Circle T has radius 4 ft. What do you know about its circumference? its area?

Each of the following statements is true in Euclidean geometry. Determine whether each is true for Riemannian geometry. Support your answers with an explanation or an illustration.

17. The measure of an angle in an equilateral triangle is 60°.

18. If a transversal intersects two coplanar lines so that their alternate interior angles are congruent, then the lines are parallel.

MORE MATH REASONING

19. **a.** The average radius of the earth is 3960 mi. If you always travel the shortest possible path along the earth's surface, what is the greatest possible distance between two points on the earth? What is true about those points? Justify your answer.
    b. Suppose A and B are points on a sphere of radius r. Find the maximum possible shortest-path distance between these points.

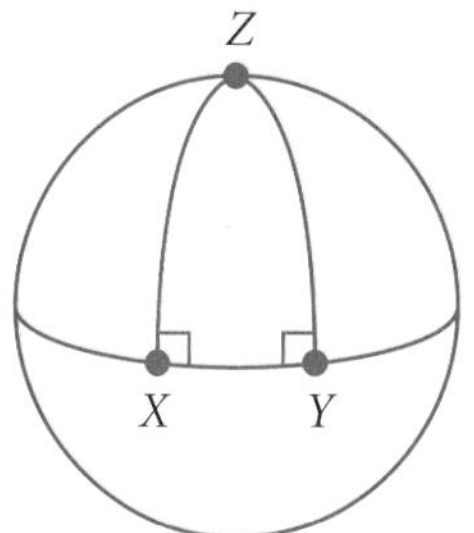

20. **Triangle Angles** We know that the sum of the angle measures of a triangle in our Riemannian model is always greater than 180°. Is there a maximum value this sum can have? If so, find this number. If not, explain why there is no such value. (Hint: Consider a triangle $\triangle XYZ$ whose base $\overline{XY}$ is on the equator of a globe, whose vertex Z is at the North Pole, and whose base angles are right angles. What happens to the vertex angle, $\angle Z$, if you move X and Y farther apart?)

12-2 PART C Making Connections

← CONNECT → *When we developed our geometric system, we started with postulates similar to those proposed by Euclid. You've seen how changing just one postulate—the Parallel Postulate—has allowed mathematicians to develop a completely different system of geometry.*

The study of the universe has close ties to the assumptions of Euclidean and non-Euclidean geometry. Euclid's geometry assumes that planes are flat surfaces. Riemann developed a non-Euclidean geometry in which a plane has curvature.

The following theorems depend on Euclid's Parallel Postulate.

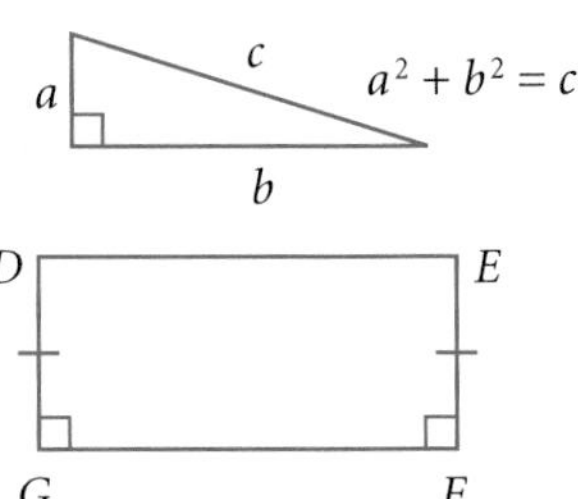

Pythagorean Theorem: In a right triangle, the square of the length of the hypotenuse is equal to the sum of the squares of the lengths of the legs.

If $\angle G$ and $\angle F$ are right angles, and $\overline{DG} \cong \overline{EF}$, then $DEFG$ is a rectangle.

In the following Explore, you will see whether or not these theorems work in curved space.

EXPLORE: IS EUCLID ON THE BALL?

MATERIALS

Graph paper, Scissors
Ball, Tape

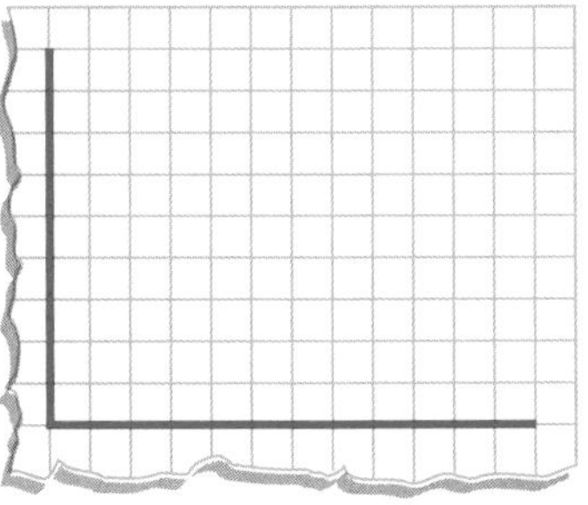

1. Near the bottom of a sheet of graph paper, cut out a long, thin, horizontal strip. You will use this as a ruler later.
2. On the graph paper, draw a right triangle with legs of 9 units and 12 units as shown. According to the Pythagorean Theorem, what should be the length of the hypotenuse? Check by measuring the hypotenuse with your strip of graph paper.

3. On another sheet of graph paper, draw three sides of quadrilateral $DEFG$ so that $\angle G$ and $\angle F$ are right angles, and $\overline{DG} \cong \overline{EF}$. Using a straightedge, draw a dotted line to connect D and E. What type of figure is $DEFG$? What can you say about $\overline{DE}$ and $\overline{GF}$?

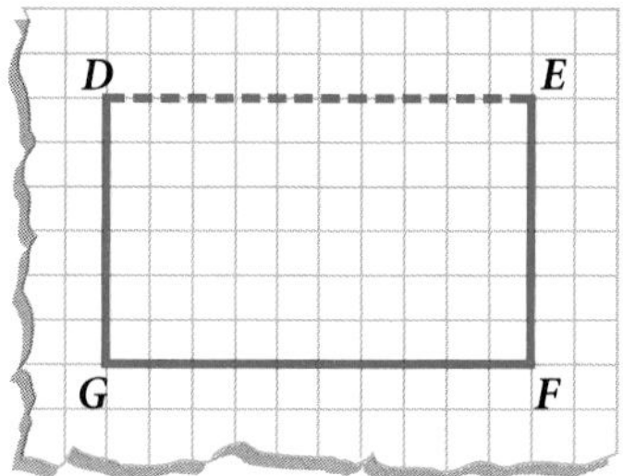

4. Now cut out the legs of the right triangle from Step 2 and the three solid sides of the quadrilateral from Step 3.

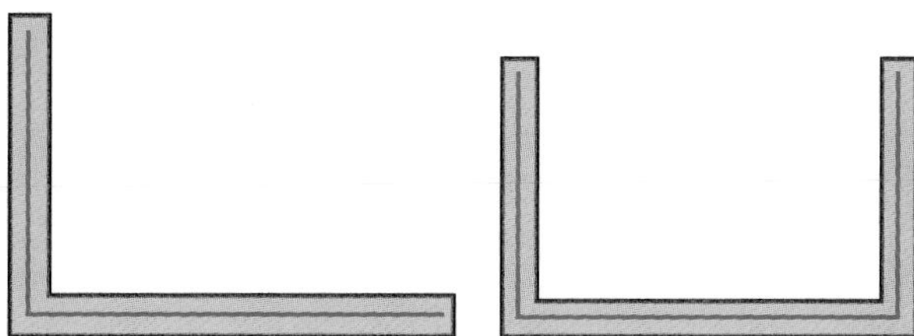

5. Carefully tape the right-angle cutout onto the surface of a beachball or other type of ball. With the strip of graph paper, measure the new hypotenuse. Is it the same length it was on a flat surface, or is it longer or shorter?
6. Tape the three sides of the quadrilateral onto the beachball. With the strip of graph paper, measure the distance across the open side of the quadrilateral. Is it equal to the length of the opposite side? On the ball, is the quadrilateral a rectangle?
7. In general, when is Riemannian geometry a better model than Euclidean geometry?

What is the geometry of the universe? No one knows for sure. Maybe the universe can be described by one of the models that you've examined.

1. Which of the systems of geometry that you've studied do you feel is the best model of the universe? Do you think there may be a different system of geometry that is even better? Why?

As science and technology advance, we need models that explain the universe in greater and greater detail. The geometry that helps us find the height of a tree may not help us measure the size of the universe.

REFLECT

1. Why do you think people from Euclid's time (300 B.C.) to the nineteenth century considered his Parallel Postulate a self-evident truth?

2. Complete the following table to contrast the two systems of geometry you've studied.

Geometry	Parallel Postulate	Description of Planes and Lines	Sum of Angle Measures for a Triangle	Circumference and Area of Circle with Radius r
Euclidean				
Riemannian				

Self-Assessment

Name the Euclidean postulate illustrated by each statement. (When we refer to a star or planet, assume that we are referring to its center. Therefore, you can think of it as a point.)

1. Only one straight line contains Pluto and Mercury.
2. There is a line through the star Rigel that is parallel to the line through the stars Vega and Fomalhaut.
3. The intersection of the plane containing Jupiter, Neptune, and Mars with the plane containing the stars Rigel, Aldebaran, and Antares is a straight line.

Answer each of the following questions, using Euclid's model of the universe. Then answer the same question, using our Riemannian model.

4. Can there be a triangle with two right angles?
5. If two coplanar lines are cut by a transversal so that the corresponding angles are congruent, are the lines parallel?
6. In $\triangle JKL$, $m\angle J = 60°$, and $m\angle K = 60°$. What do you know about $m\angle L$?
7. In our model of Riemannian geometry, which of the following statements is false?
   (a) A sphere is a plane.
   (b) A right angle measures 90°.
   (c) The sum of the measures of the angles in a triangle is 180°.
   (d) There are no parallel lines.
   (e) The shortest path between two points is an arc.

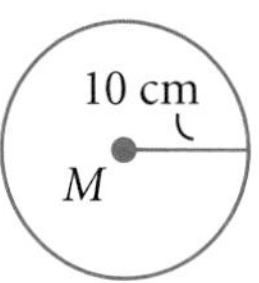

8. Circle M has radius 10 cm. Using a Riemannian model, what do you know about its circumference? its area?

9. The oldest stone monument in the world, the Step Pyramid at Saqqara, Egypt, has a rectangular base 410 ft long and 358 ft wide.

History

a. Find the length of a diagonal of the base of this pyramid, using Euclidean geometry. Express your answer in exact form and as a decimal rounded to the nearest tenth. [5-3]

b. Because the pyramid is on the curved surface of the earth, is the actual length of the diagonal of its base smaller or larger than your exact answer in **9a**? Explain.

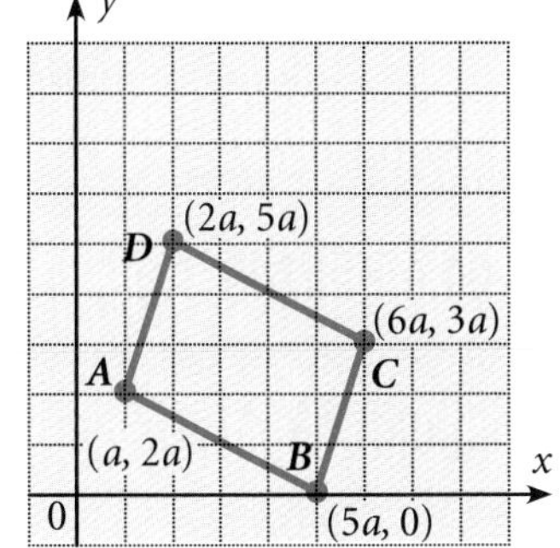

10. Prove that quadrilateral *ABCD* is a parallelogram. [6-2]

11. The Great Wall of Galaxies The so-called Great Wall of galaxies is about 500 million light-years long, 200 million light-years high, and 15 million light-years thick. Assuming that the Great Wall is a rectangular solid (and using a Euclidean model of the universe!), find its volume. [9-2]

Science

12. a. It takes a radar signal 2.2 sec to make a round trip from Neptune to Triton, one of its moons. If radar travels at the speed of light (300,000 km/sec), how far is Triton from Neptune? Round your answer to the nearest ten thousand kilometers. [12-1]

Science

b. The diameter of Triton covers an arc of about 0.47° in the sky of Neptune. What is Triton's approximate diameter? Round your answer to the nearest hundred kilometers.

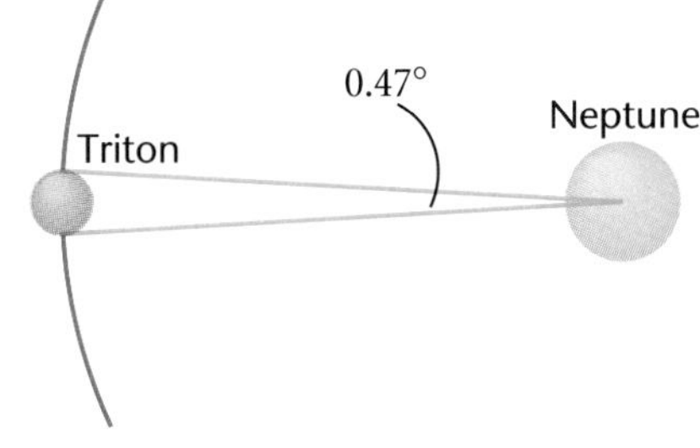

13. The three photographs below "zoom in" on parts of a broccoli plant. Write a brief explanation of how these photographs are related to the idea of a fractal. [12-1]

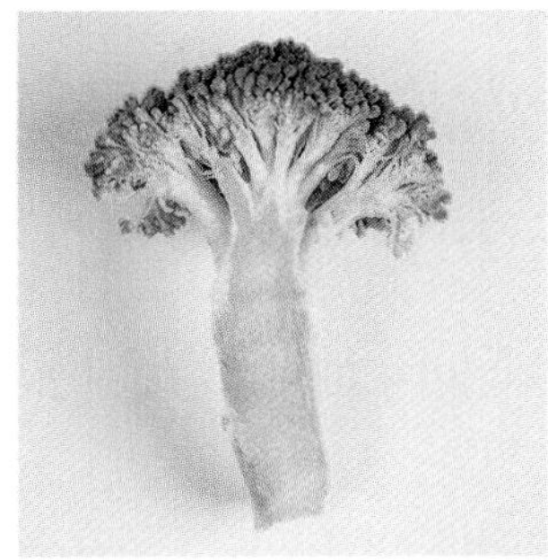

14. How Big Is Forever? Astronomers have argued about whether the universe goes on forever or whether it has a finite size. Does the Euclidean model support either of these conjectures? If Riemannian geometry is a more accurate model of the universe, what does that suggest about the size of the universe? Give a brief written explanation of your answer. (Hint: Consider the difference between a line in Euclidean geometry and a line in Riemannian geometry.)

Chapter 12 Review

In Chapter 12, you learned some indirect techniques that humans have developed to measure the earth and the universe. You were also introduced to fractals, a concept that gives order to what seems to be chaos (and presents us with some fascinating mathematical art on the way).

KEY TERMS

astronomical unit [12-1]	light-year [12-1]	parallax [12-1]
equator [12-1]	longitude [12-1]	prime meridian [12-1]
fractal geometry [12-1]	non-Euclidean [12-2]	self-similar [12-1]
latitude [12-1]		

From each group of terms, choose the term that does not belong, and explain why it does not belong.

1. coastline, broccoli, tomato, Sierpinski Gasket
2. speed of light, astronomical unit, light-year, kilometer

CONCEPTS AND APPLICATIONS

Science

3. The speed of light is about 300,000 km/sec. The mean distance from the sun to Pluto is about 6 billion (6×10^9) km. How long does light take to travel from the sun to Pluto? [12-1]

4. The rule for the fractal shown is to draw and shade an isosceles right triangle with vertices at the midpoints of the sides of each unshaded triangle. [12-1]
   a. Sketch Stages 3 and 4.
   b. Look for a pattern to predict the total number of shaded triangles at Stage 6.

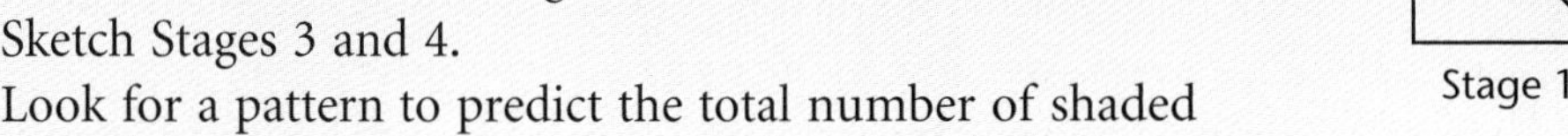

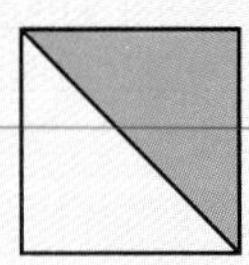

Stage 1

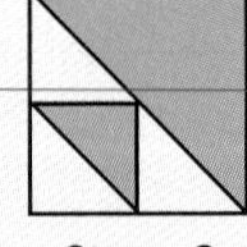

Stage 2

5. Write a summary of how latitude and longitude are measured.

Social Science

6. Manila, Philippines, has latitude 15° N and longitude 120° E. Khartoum, Sudan, also has latitude 15° N and is at longitude 33° E. What is the distance between the two cities? Use 3960 mi for the radius of the earth. [12-1]

7. Describe how to determine the shortest path on the surface of a sphere between two points on the sphere. [12-2]

The lengths of two sides of a triangle are given. Write an inequality that represents the range of values for the possible lengths of the third side. [11-1]

8. 11, 14 **9.** 2, 2 **10.** m, $2m$

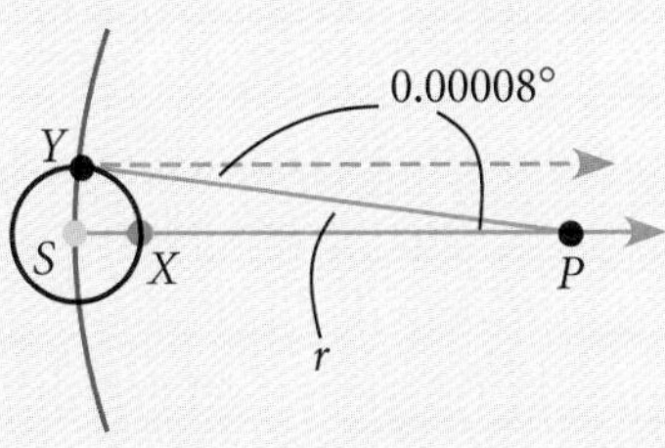

Science

11. The parallax angle to the star Procyon is about 0.00008°. [12-1]

a. Find the distance to Procyon in astronomical units.

b. A light-year is about 63,200 A.U. How many light-years away is Procyon?

Which of the following properties are true in Riemannian geometry? [12-2]

12. Through a point not on a given line, there is no line parallel to the given line.

13. The measure of a right angle is greater than 90°.

14. A triangle may have more than one right angle.

15. Using Riemannian geometry, sketch a situation in which two lines are perpendicular to the same line, but are not parallel to each other. [12-2]

CONCEPTS AND CONNECTIONS

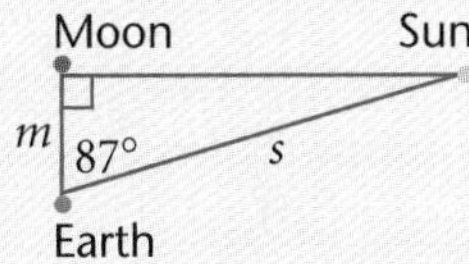

History

16. History of Astronomy Aristarchus of Samos (ca. 260 B.C.) calculated the ratio of the distance from the earth to the moon, m, to the distance from the earth to the sun, s. He observed that when the moon was half-full, the angle between the lines of sight to the sun and the moon was 87°.

a. Why did Aristarchus conclude that the angle at the moon was a right angle?

b. Use a trigonometric ratio to find Aristarchus's value for $\frac{m}{s}$.

c. Calculate the ratio $\frac{m}{s}$, using the actual values $m = 240{,}000$ mi, and $s = 93{,}000{,}000$ mi. Was Aristarchus's result accurate?

d. The correct angle in the figure is actually 89.83°. How would this have affected Aristarchus's result? Describe how small differences in the measure of an angle close to 90° affect trigonometric ratios, and explain why very accurate measurements are needed in astronomy.

SELF-EVALUATION

Write a summary of the most important facts about fractals, longitude and latitude, astronomical measurement, and non-Euclidean geometries that have been introduced in Chapter 12. For each of these topics, describe how they are connected to ideas from earlier chapters.

Chapter 12 Assessment

TEST

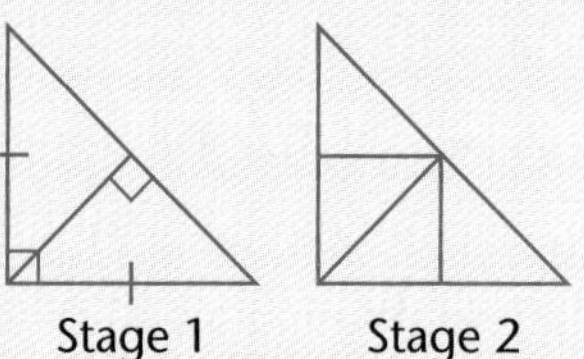

1. Start with an isosceles right triangle. For each stage , draw the altitude to the hypotenuse of all isosceles right triangles.

a. Sketch Stages 3 and 4.

b. How many new segments are drawn in Stage *n*?

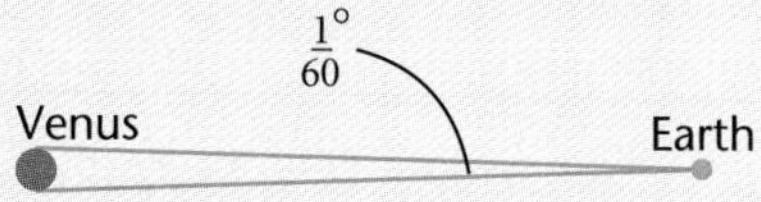

2. At its nearest approach to the earth (about 42 million kilometers), Venus would appear to cover an arc of about $\frac{1}{60}°$ in the sky. What is the approximate diameter of Venus?

3. How long would a transmission traveling at the speed of light (300,000 km/sec) take to reach the earth from Saturn (about 1.5×10^9 km away)?

Determine whether each set of numbers could represent the lengths of the sides of a triangle. Explain your answers.

4. 4, 7, 3

5. 16, 8, 9

6. 4.1, 13.8, 9.5

7. On many world maps, Greenland appears to be as wide as the United States. At about 80° N latitude, Greenland extends from 20° W to 73° W longitude. Find its width at this latitude. (Use 3960 mi for the earth's radius.) Then compare Greenland's width to the approximate 3000-mi width of the United States. Explain why this distortion of Greenland occurs on some maps.

8. Describe the main difference between Euclidean and non-Euclidean geometries.

Which of the following properties are true in Riemannian geometry?

9. No two lines intersect.

10. The sum of the measures of the angles of a triangle is greater than 180°.

PERFORMANCE TASK

Stage 1 after a tail

Stage 2 after a tail

Draw Stage 0 of a fractal, as shown. For Stage 1, draw a segment about 90% as long as the existing segment, about one-third of the way up from the bottom and at a small angle. Flip a coin to determine on which side of the existing segment the new one should be drawn. For a head, draw the segment on the right; for a tail, draw the segment on the left. Flip the coin for each stage, and add a segment to each *end segment,* as shown. Complete and describe Stage 5.

ADDITIONAL LESSONS

PROOF SKILLS AND STRATEGIES

On page 217 you began to organize a formal proof with a five-step process. Step Five in this process is called demonstration. In this step you need to establish a chain of reasoning that leads to the verification of a given statement. This chain of reasoning begins with the given statements and ends with the conclusion. Each statement in the chain must be supported with a reason. The chain of reasoning needs to be planned before the actual proof is written. A good plan identifies the key steps of the proof. The plan can be developed by using various strategies to help identify those key steps. The next few pages are devoted to examining some of those strategies.

A single strategy or a combination of strategies may be necessary to develop a plan for a proof. Skill in planning a proof comes with patient practice, just like developing skills in playing the piano, golf, or tennis.

Read a Diagram

The first step in planning a proof often requires that you study or draw a diagram. Diagrams help us visualize information, see relationships, and keep track of facts. Diagrams may have shortcomings (you need to be aware of those), but they can also be very useful. If agreements about what information can be read from a diagram are established, then they can be very valuable devices for visualizing geometric relationships.

Unless told otherwise, you *may* assume the following:

- Points and lines are coplanar if they look coplanar.
- Points are collinear if they look collinear.
- Two angles are adjacent, vertical, or a linear pair if they appear to be.
- A point is between two other points if it is pictured that way.
- A ray is between two others if it appears to be.
- Two figures intersect when they appear to intersect.

Unless told otherwise, you *may not* assume the following:

- Segments or angles have the same measure even though they appear to be congruent.
- Lines are parallel even though they appear to be parallel.
- Lines are perpendicular even though they appear to be perpendicular.

In general, you can assume position of figures but you cannot assume measure or special conditions (i.e. perpendicular, parallel).

EXAMPLE

1. What information can be read from the figure on the right?

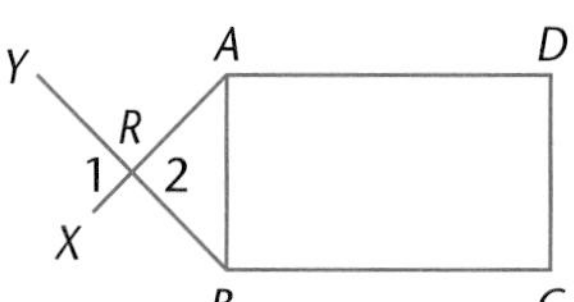

We *can* assume that
$\overline{AX}$ and $\overline{BY}$ intersect at R
$\angle 1$ and $\angle 2$ are vertical angles
$\overline{AB}$ is a side of $\triangle ABR$ and a side of quadrilateral $ABCD$
R is between X and A
R is between Y and B

We *cannot* assume
$\overline{AB} \parallel \overline{CD}$
$\overline{AD} \parallel \overline{BC}$
$\overline{BC} \perp \overline{DC}$, $\overline{BC} \perp \overline{AB}$, $\overline{AD} \perp \overline{DC}$, or $\overline{AD} \perp \overline{AB}$
$ABCD$ is a rectangle

Work Backward

Working backward from what is to be proved is one strategy for planning a proof. In trying to reach a conclusion, we sometimes find that one necessary piece of information is missing. It is a valuable skill to be able to look at what is to be proved and be able to say, "I can prove this if I have this fact," then, "How do I know that this fact is true?" You now need to utilize this information to link statements together in sequential order.

EXAMPLES

2. *Given:* $\overline{AB} \cong \overline{CD}$, $\angle 1 \cong \angle 2$

Prove: $\overline{DA} \cong \overline{BC}$

Plan: Work Backward
$\overline{DA} \cong \overline{BC}$ if these segments are corresponding sides of congruent triangles, namely, $\triangle ABC$ and $\triangle CDA$. These triangles are congruent from the given information and the fact that they share a common side. Thus, $\triangle ABC \cong \triangle CDA$ by SAS.

3. *Given:* $\angle 1 \cong \angle 2$, $\angle 5 \cong \angle 6$

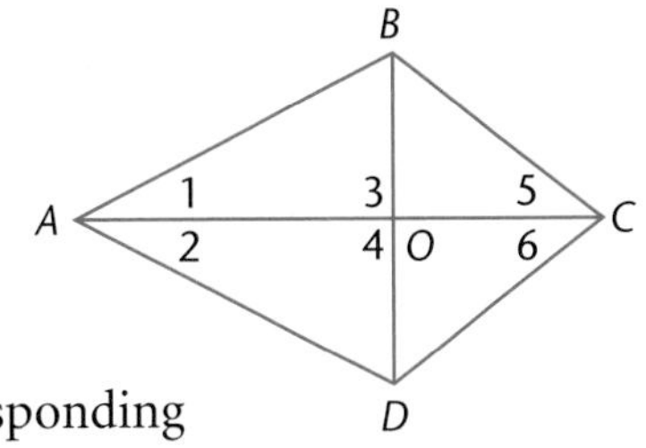

Prove: $\overline{AC} \perp \overline{BD}$

Plan: Work Backward
$\overline{AC} \perp \overline{BD}$ if $\angle 3 \cong \angle 4$.
$\angle 3 \cong \angle 4$ if they are corresponding angles of congruent triangles, $\triangle AOB$ and $\triangle AOD$. To prove $\triangle AOB \cong \triangle AOD$, $\overline{AB}$ must be congruent to $\overline{AD}$. These segments will be congruent if they are corresponding sides of congruent triangles $\triangle ABC$ and $\triangle ACD$. Since $\overline{AC}$ is a common side, $\triangle ABC \cong \triangle ACD$ by ASA.

Work Forward

Another proof skill is to work forward and think of what conclusions follow from the given information. This strategy involves finding a route from *given* to *conclusion,* like a road map from point *A* to point *B*. Which routes lead from *given* toward *conclusion* and which routes lead into *conclusion* from the direction of *given?* To be more specific, in which various directions will the given information lead me, where can I go from here, and will any of the options lead me to the conclusion?

EXAMPLE

4. *Given:* *M* is the midpoint of $\overline{AB}$,
$\triangle ACB$ is isosceles with base $\overline{AB}$,
$\angle 1 \cong \angle 2$

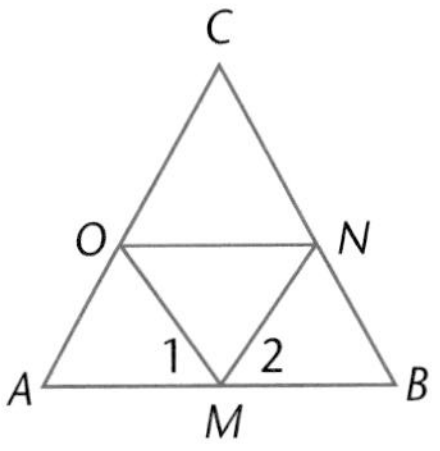

Prove: $\triangle MNO$ is isosceles

Plan: Work Forward
Since *M* is a midpoint, $\overline{AM} \cong \overline{MB}$.
Since $\triangle ABC$ is isosceles, $\angle A \cong \angle B$.
Also, $\angle A$, $\overline{AM}$, and $\angle 1$ are parts of $\triangle AMO$ and $\angle 2$, $\overline{MB}$, and $\angle B$ are parts of $\triangle BMN$. If $\triangle AMO \cong \triangle BMN$, then $\overline{MN} \cong \overline{MO}$ and $\triangle MNO$ is isosceles.

Use an Auxiliary Line

On page 288 the strategy of adding an auxiliary line segment was illustrated. Sometimes it is very difficult to prove a statement from the given set of facts. Introducing an auxiliary point, segment, line, or ray may make a proof much less complicated. A word of caution: You must be able to justify the addition of an auxiliary figure, and you must be careful not to assume too much.

EXAMPLES

5. *Given:* Kite $ABCD$

Prove: $\angle A \cong \angle C$

Plan: Auxiliary line segment
Since there is little given information and two angles need to be established as congruent, it seems as though some triangles need to exist. Draw the auxiliary segment $\overline{BD}$, which we know exists because there is exactly one line joining any two points. By the definition of a kite, $\overline{AB} \cong \overline{BC}$ and $\overline{AD} \cong \overline{CD}$. Therefore, $\triangle ABD \cong \triangle CBD$ by SSS and $\angle A \cong \angle C$ by CPCTC.

6. *Given:* Quadrilateral $ABCD$

Prove: $m\angle A + m\angle B + m\angle C + m\angle D = 360°$

Plan: Auxiliary line segment
The sum of the interior angles of a triangle is 180°. Draw the auxiliary segment $\overline{AC}$, which we know exists because there is exactly one line joining any two points. In $\triangle ABC$ the sum of the interior angles is 180° and in $\triangle ADC$ the sum of the interior angles is 180°. The sum of the angle measures of the quadrilateral is 360°.

Use an Interior Focus

This strategy utilizes the strategies of working forward and working backward. By working forward from a set of given conditions you may be able to establish a pair of triangles as congruent. By working backwards you may need a pair of congruent triangles to establish the conclusion. Focusing on these interior relationships may be the key to completing a proof.

EXAMPLE

7. *Given:* $\angle 1 \cong \angle 2$, $\overline{AX} \cong \overline{AY}$

Prove: $\overline{DC} \cong \overline{BC}$

Plan: Interior Focus

Work Forward: $\angle 1$ and $\overline{AX}$ are parts of $\triangle AXC$. $\angle 2$ and $\overline{AY}$ are parts of $\triangle ACY$. Since they have a common side, $\overline{AC}$, $\triangle ACX \cong \triangle ACY$.

Work Backward: $\overline{DC}$ and $\overline{BC}$ are sides of several triangles. Let's use $\triangle DXC$ and $\triangle BYC$. If these triangles are congruent, then $\overline{DC} \cong \overline{BC}$.

Interior Focus: What information is needed to establish $\triangle DXC \cong \triangle BYC$? Vertical angles $\angle CDX$ and $\angle BCY$ are congruent. $\overline{CY}$ and $\overline{CX}$ are congruent by CPCTC from work forward. By reading the diagram, $\angle AYC$ and $\angle BYC$ are supplementary and $\angle DXC$ and $\angle AXC$ are supplementary. Supplements of congruent angles are congruent. Hence, we have enough information to show $\triangle DXC \cong \triangle BYC$.

The previous example used several of the proof strategies. The following example uses all of the skills and strategies.

EXAMPLE

8. *Given:* $\triangle ABC$ is isosceles with base $\overline{AB}$, $\overline{AC}$ is a diameter of circle O.

Prove: $\widehat{AX}$ bisects $\overline{AB}$

Plan:

Read the Diagram: X is on circle O and $\overline{AB}$.
Side $\overline{AC}$ contains O. Point O is the midpoint of $\overline{AC}$.
Draw Auxiliary Line: Draw $\overline{CX} \perp \overline{AB}$.
Work Forward: $\overline{AC} \cong \overline{BC}$ because $\triangle ABC$ is isosceles.
Work Backward: We will know that $\overline{AX} \cong \overline{BX}$ if the segments are corresponding parts of congruent triangles.
Interior Focus: $\triangle AXC$ and $\triangle BXC$ need to be congruent. $\angle AXC$ is a right angle. Therefore, $\angle BXC$ is a right angle. $\overline{CX}$ is a common side. $\triangle AXC \cong \triangle BXC$ by HL.

REFERENCE CENTER: Additional Lessons

Exercises

1. Prove Example 2.

2. Prove Example 3.

3. Prove Example 4.

4. *Given:* $\overline{CA} \cong \overline{CD}$, $\overline{CE}$ bisects $\angle ACB$.

Prove: $\overline{AE} \cong \overline{DE}$

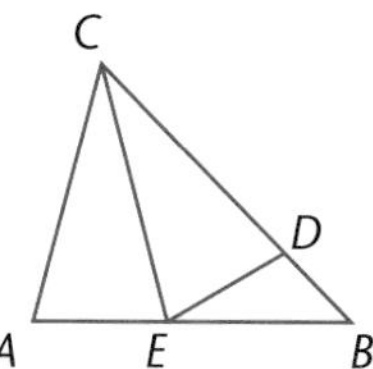

5. Prove Example 5.

6. Prove Example 6.

7. Prove Example 7.

8. *Given:* Parallelogram $ABCD$, $\overline{AF} \cong \overline{CE}$

Prove: $\overline{DF} \cong \overline{BE}$

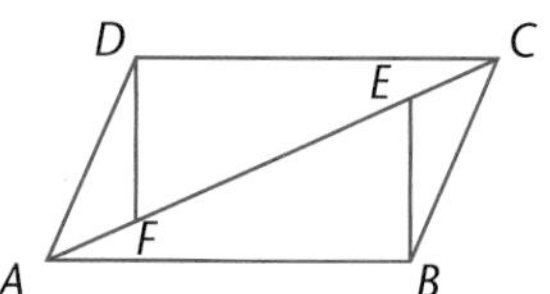

9. *Given:* Trapezoid $ABCD$, $\angle D \cong \angle C$

Prove: $ABCD$ is isosceles.

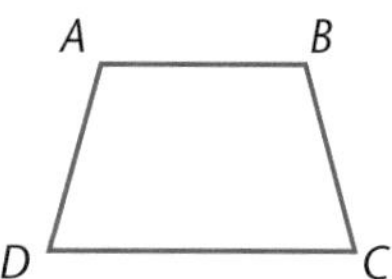

10. *Given:* Lines $l \parallel m \parallel n$, $\overline{AB} \cong \overline{BC}$

Prove: $\overline{RS} \cong \overline{ST}$

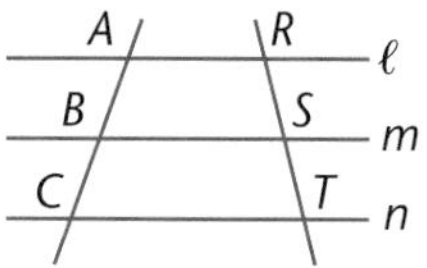

11. *Given:* Trapezoid $ABCD$, E and F are midpoints.

Prove: $\overline{EF} \parallel \overline{AB}$ and $EF = \frac{1}{2}(AB + DC)$

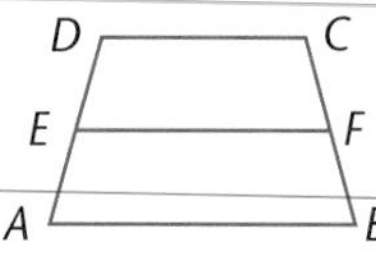

12. *Given:* Trapezoid $ABCD$

Prove: Area $ABCD = \frac{1}{2}(AB + CD)h$

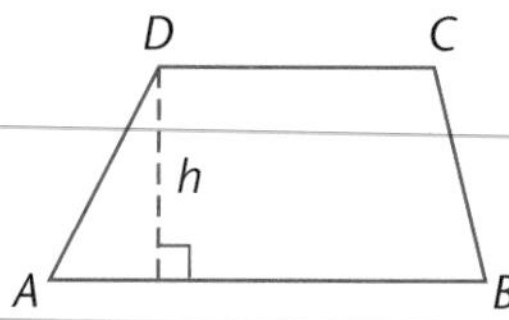

13. *Given:* $\triangle ABC$ is isosceles with base $\overline{AC}$, $\overline{DE}$ and $\overline{EF}$ are midsegments.

Prove: $AFED$ is a rhombus.

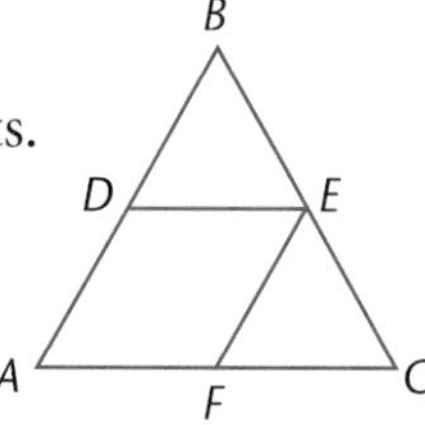

14. *Given:* Circle O, tangent $\overleftrightarrow{AB}$, and chord $\overline{CD}$.

Prove: $m\angle ACD = \left(\frac{1}{2}\right) m\,\widehat{CD}$

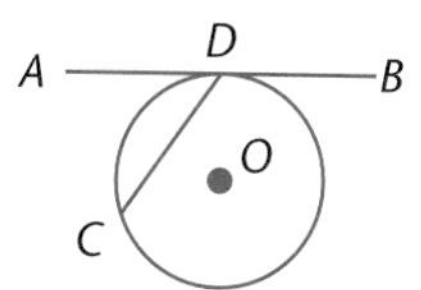

15. *Given:* $\overline{AB} \cong \overline{CD}$, diameter $\overline{XY}$, E lies on $\overline{XY}$, E is intersection of $\overline{AB}$ and $\overline{CD}$.

Prove: $\angle 1 \cong \angle 2$

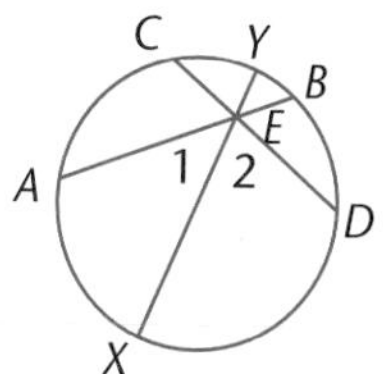

16. Prove Example 8.

17. Prove Example 8 using a different auxiliary line segment.

18. *Given:* Circle O with diameter $\overline{AB}$, $\overleftrightarrow{BC}$ is tangent to circle O.

Prove: $\triangle ABD \sim \triangle BCD$

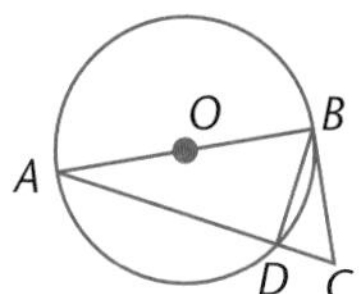

19. *Given:* $\triangle ABC$, $\overline{XS} \perp \overline{BC}$, $\overline{ZR} \perp \overline{AC}$, $\overline{YT} \perp \overline{AB}$

Prove: $\triangle XYZ \sim \triangle ABC$

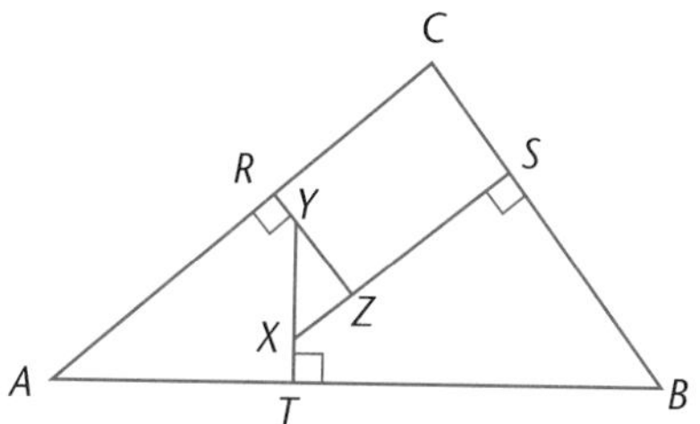

20. *Given:* Circle P, $\overline{AC}$ and $\overline{BC}$ are chords, $\overline{PD} \perp \overline{AC}$, $\overline{PE} \perp \overline{BC}$, $\overline{PD} \cong \overline{PE}$.

Prove: $\angle DBA \cong \angle EAB$

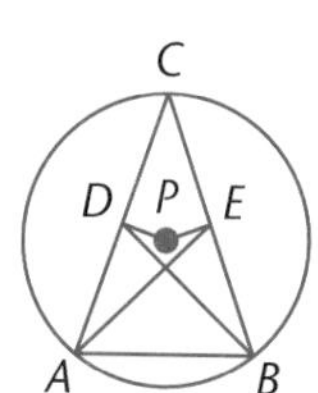

21. *Given:* $\overline{BD} \parallel \overline{CE}$

Prove: $(AB)(CE) = (AC)(BD)$

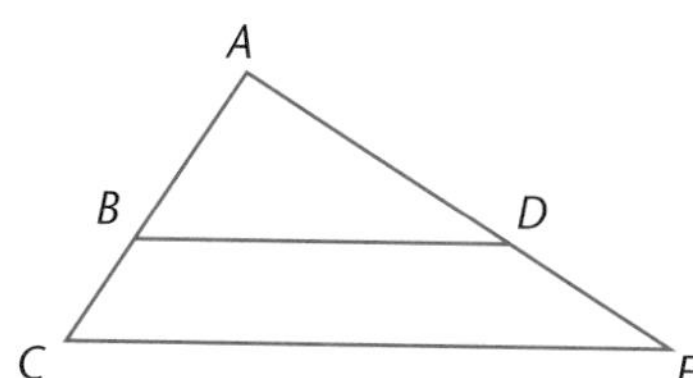

22. *Given:* Parallelogram $YSTW$, $\overline{SX} \perp \overline{YW}$, $\overline{SV} \perp \overline{WT}$

Prove: $(SX)(YW) = (SV)(WT)$

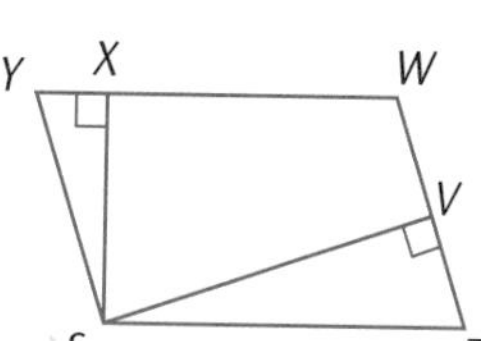

GRAPHING LINEAR EQUATIONS

Equations such as $y = 2x + 3$ are called **linear equations** because their graphs are lines. The coordinates of points on a line can be determined by setting up a T-table.

EXAMPLE

1. Use a T-table to graph $y = 2x + 3$.
Choose -1, 1, and 3 as x-values.

x	Substitute	Result
-1	$y = 2(-1) + 3$	1
1	$y = 2(1) + 3$	5
3	$y = 2(3) + 3$	9

T-table	
x	y
-1	1
1	5
3	9

Graph the points $(-1, 1)$, $(1, 5)$, and $(3, 9)$, then connect them with a line.

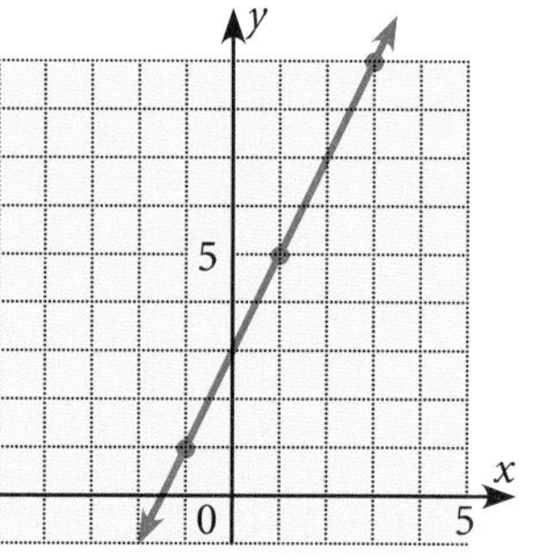

There is a pattern to the coordinates of the points in Example 1. As the x-coordinates increase by 2, the y-coordinates increase by 4. The ratio of these increases is always $\frac{4}{2} = 2$. As you have seen, this number is the **slope** of the line. The slope is the $\frac{\text{rise}}{\text{run}} = \frac{\text{change in } y}{\text{change in } x}$ ratio.

An equation in **slope-intercept form** looks like $\boldsymbol{y = mx + b}$, where m is the slope and b the **y-intercept** of the line. By using the slope and y-intercept, you can graph a line quickly.

EXAMPLE

2. Use the slope and y-intercept to graph $y = \frac{2}{3}x - 1$.
The equation is in slope-intercept form, $y = mx + b$. The slope, m, is $\frac{2}{3}$ and the y-intercept, b, is -1.

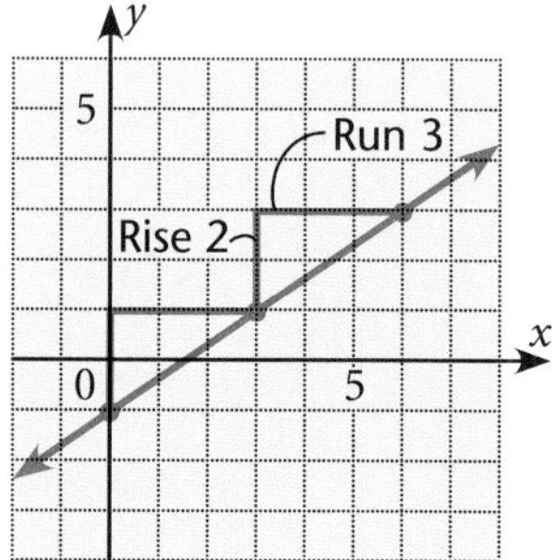

Begin the sketch of the graph at the y-intercept: the point $(0, -1)$ on the y-axis.

Since the slope is $\frac{2}{3}$, rise 2 units and run 3 units to the right.

Do this once more, then connect the points with a line.

The lines in Examples 1 and 2 are *oblique.* Lines can also be vertical or horizontal. The equation of a horizontal line is of the form $y = b$. The slope of a horizontal line is 0, since the line has no rise.

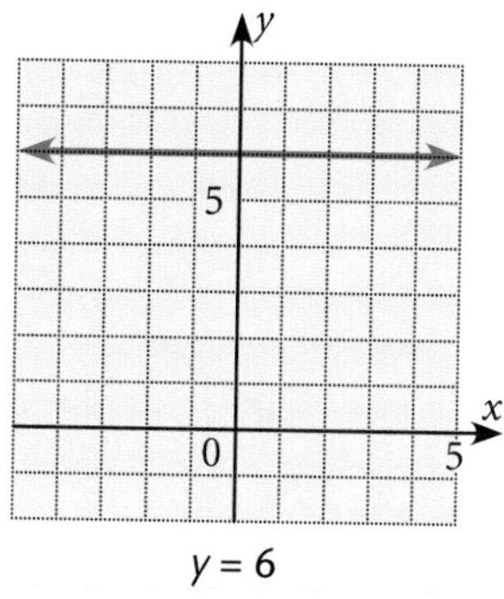

$y = 6$

$x = 3$

The equation of a vertical line is of the form $x = a$. The slope of a vertical line is *undefined,* since its slope is $\frac{\text{rise}}{\text{run}} = \frac{\text{rise}}{0}$, and division by 0 is undefined.

EXAMPLE

3. Graph $y = -1$.
The line is horizontal. All of its points have a y-value of -1.

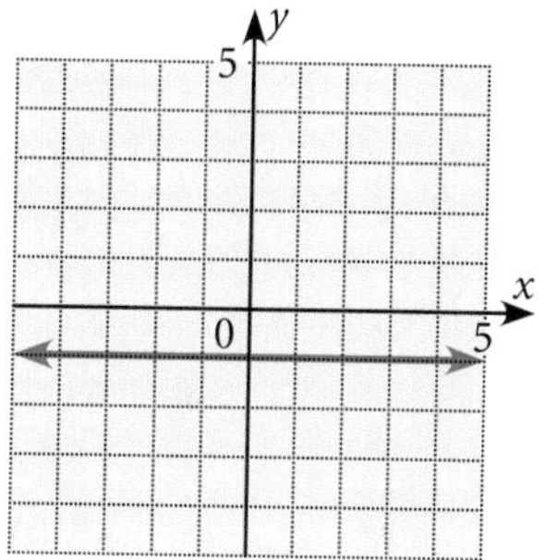

Exercises

1. Is the point $(-2, 3)$ on the line $2x + 3y = 6$? Justify your answer.

Decide whether the following linear equations represent horizontal, vertical, or oblique lines.

2. $y = 3x + 2$ **3.** $x = -4$ **4.** $x + y = 1$ **5.** $y = 1$

Identify the slope and y-intercept of each line.

6. $y = -x + 4$ **7.** $y = \frac{5}{2}x - 1$ **8.** $3x - y = -12$ **9.** $2x + y = 5$

Use a T-table to graph each line.

10. $y = 3x + 3$ **11.** $y = -x + 4$ **12.** $3x - 2y = 12$

Use the slope and y-intercept to graph each line.

13. $y = \frac{3}{2}x - 2$ **14.** $y = 3x - 5$ **15.** $y = -\frac{1}{3}x + 1$

THREE-DIMENSIONAL COORDINATE SYSTEM

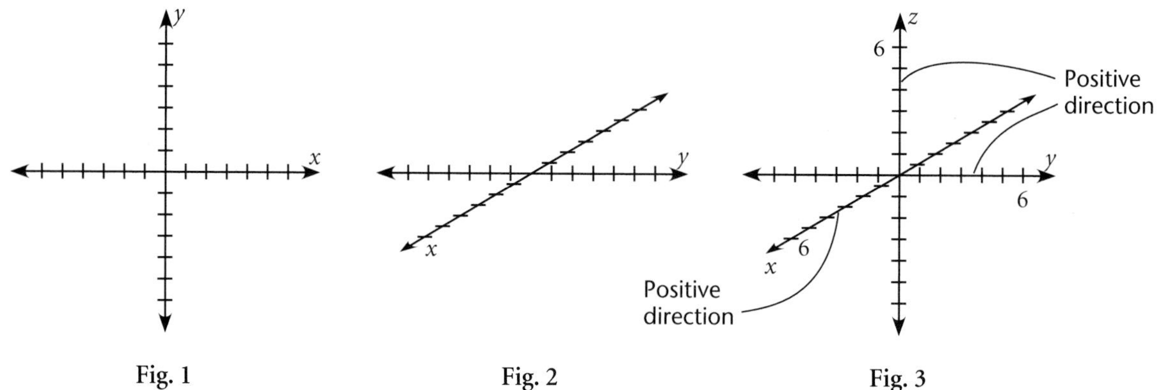

Fig. 1 Fig. 2 Fig. 3

An *xy*-coordinate system allows us to locate points in a two-dimensional plane (Fig. 1). We can use this system as the foundation of a coordinate system for three-dimensional space.

Think of a two-dimensional coordinate system set up on an infinite sheet of paper. Now, in your mind, place the paper flat on an infinite tabletop, so the positive *x*-axis points toward you. In perspective, Fig. 2 is what you see.

To show the third dimension, imagine adding a *z*-axis perpendicular to the table top, going through the origin of the *xy*-coordinate system (Fig. 3). These axes determine the coordinates of all points in space. Each point is represented by an ordered *triple* of numbers (*x*, *y*, *z*).

EXAMPLES

1. Plot the point (2, 3, 4).

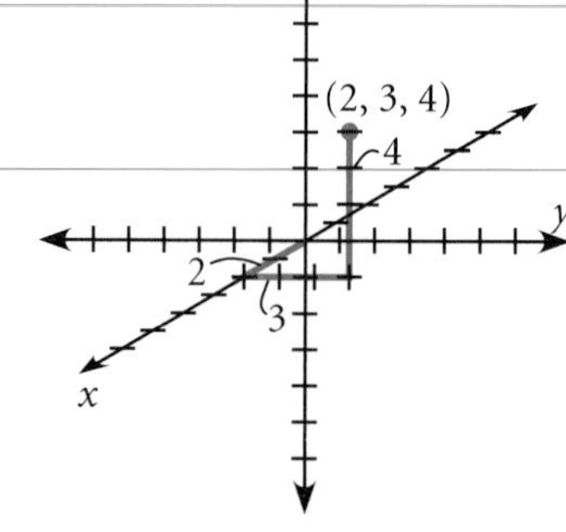

Begin at the origin and move 2 units in the positive direction on the *x*-axis. Then move 3 units in the positive direction on a line parallel to the *y*-axis. Finally, move 4 units in the positive direction on a line parallel to the *z*-axis.

2. State the coordinates of points *P* and *Q*.

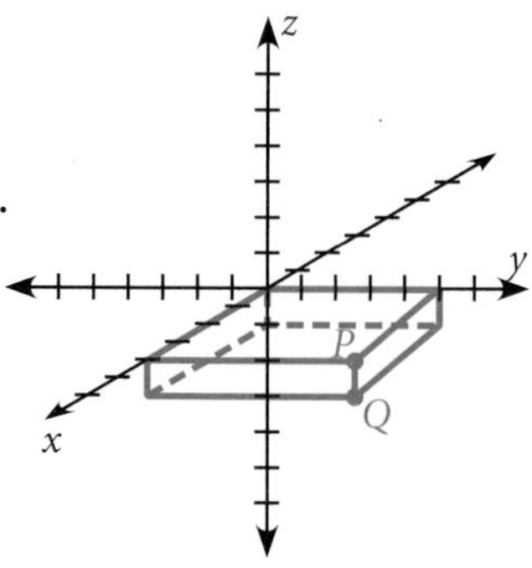

To reach *P*, travel 4 units in the positive *x*-direction, and 5 in the positive *y*-direction. The coordinates of *P* are (4, 5, 0).

To reach *Q*, move 1 unit down (in the negative *z*-direction) from *P*. The coordinates of *Q* are (4, 5, –1).

The distance formula for points on an *xy*-coordinate plane can be adapted to apply to a three-dimensional coordinate system.

DEFINITION

The *distance between two points in space* whose coordinates are (x_1, y_1, z_1) and (x_2, y_2, z_2) is:

$D = \sqrt{(x_1 - x_2)^2 + (y_1 - y_2)^2 + (z_1 - z_2)^2}$.

EXAMPLE

3. Sketch the line segment $\overline{AB}$ with endpoints $A(2, -3, -1)$ and $B(-1, 2, 4)$. Then find AB.

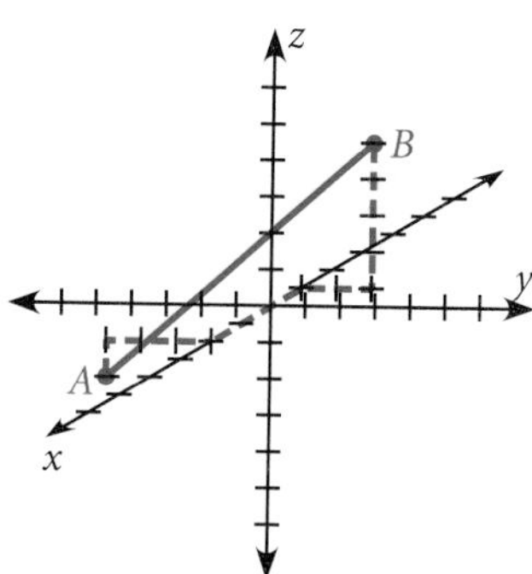

First, locate the points.
Use the distance formula to find the length of the segment.
Let $(2, -3, -1) = (x_1, y_1, z_1)$
and $(-1, 2, 4) = (x_2, y_2, z_2)$.

$AB = \sqrt{(x_1 - x_2)^2 + (y_1 - y_2)^2 + (z_1 - z_2)^2}$ Use the distance formula.

$AB = \sqrt{(2 - (-1))^2 + (-3 - 2)^2 + (-1 - 4)^2}$ Substitute.

$AB = \sqrt{(3)^2 + (-5)^2 + (-5)^2}$ Simplify inside parentheses first.

$AB = \sqrt{59} \approx 7.7$

Exercises

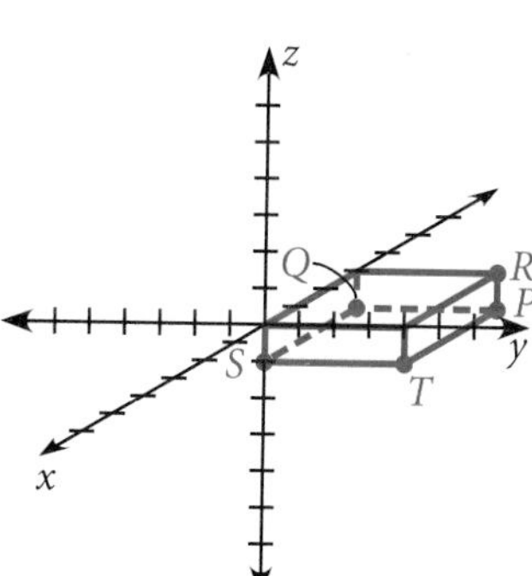

1. Plot the point (3, 5, 2).

2. State the coordinates of *Q*, *R*, *S*, and *T* if *P* has coordinates (−3, 4, −1).

3. Sketch $\overline{YZ}$ with endpoints $Y(0, -5, 3)$ and $Z(4, 0, -4)$.

4. Sketch the triangle with vertices $A(1, 2, 0)$, $B(-5, 0, 4)$, and $C(-3, 4, -2)$.

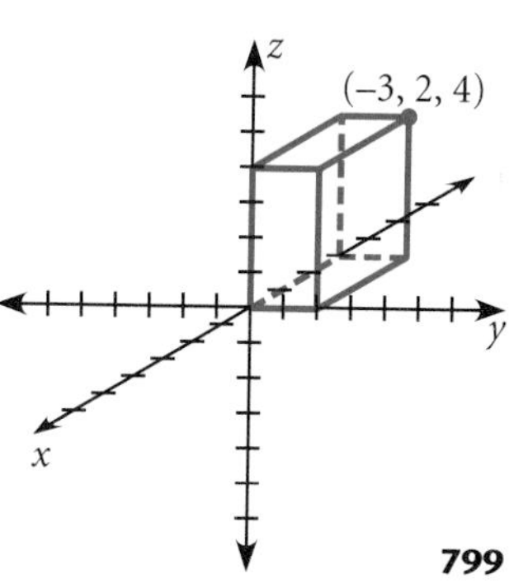

5. $\overline{MN}$ has endpoints $M(4, 1, 5)$ and $N(2, 6, 8)$. Find MN.

6. Find the volume and the surface area of the rectangular solid shown at the right.

7. Sketch a cube in a three-dimensional coordinate system with one vertex at (0, 0, 0). Label the other vertices with their coordinates.

OVERLAPPING TRIANGLES

It is often difficult to understand and interpret complex geometric diagrams, especially if you are trying to identify congruent triangles and corresponding parts.

EXAMPLES

1. Name the eight triangles contained in the figure.

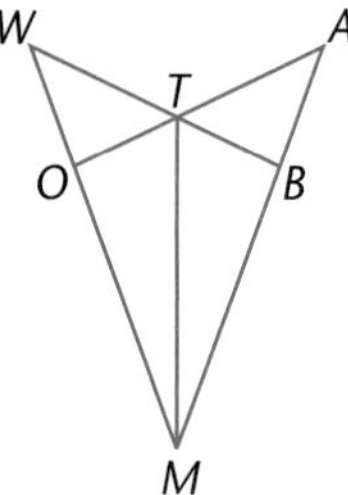

The triangles are $\triangle WOT$, $\triangle ABT$, $\triangle OTM$, $\triangle BTM$, $\triangle WTM$, $\triangle ATM$, $\triangle WBM$, and $\triangle AOM$.

In Example 1, some of the triangles, like $\triangle WMB$ and $\triangle AMO$, overlapped each other. In proofs involving figures like these, the ability to recognize and use overlapping triangles is very important.

2. *Given:* $\angle W \cong \angle A$ and $\angle WMT \cong \angle AMT$

Prove: $\overline{WT} \cong \overline{AT}$

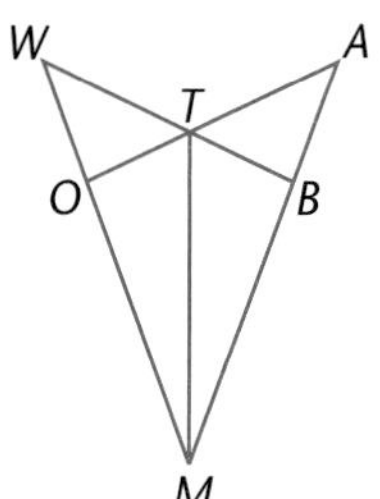

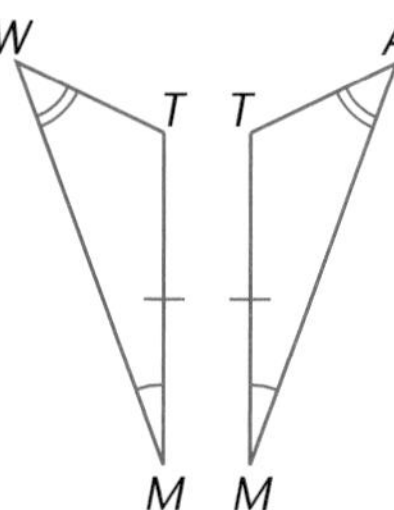

Look for triangles that involve the given pairs of congruent angles and the sides you need to prove congruent.
Six of the eight triangles contain $\angle W$ or $\angle A$ —$\triangle WOT$, $\triangle ABT$, $\triangle WTM$, $\triangle ATM$, $\triangle WBM$, and $\triangle AOM$.

Only two of these, $\triangle WTM$ and $\triangle ATM$, contain $\angle WMT$ and $\angle AMT$.

So, try to prove $\triangle WTM \cong \triangle ATM$ since they contain the given angles and $\overline{WT}$ and $\overline{AT}$ are corresponding parts.

By drawing the triangles separately and marking the congruent parts, you can see that the AAS congruence theorem applies.

Statement	Reason
1. $\angle W \cong \angle A$ $\angle WMT \cong \angle AMT$	**1.** Given
2. $\overline{TM} \cong \overline{TM}$	**2.** Reflexive
3. $\triangle WTM \cong \triangle ATM$	**3.** AAS Theorem
4. $\overline{WT} \cong \overline{AT}$	**4.** CPCTC

Exercises

1. Name all triangles in the figure.
2. Name all pairs of triangles that appear to be congruent.
3. If $\overline{AB} \cong \overline{DC}$, draw the figure to show two different pairs of triangles that might be congruent.

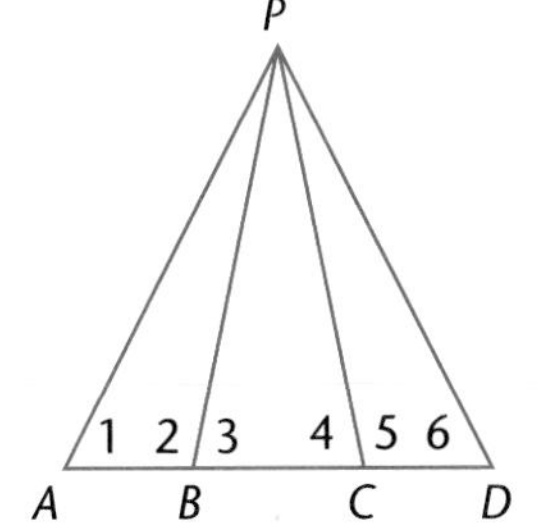

4. Name all pairs of triangles that appear to be congruent.
5. If $\angle 1 \cong \angle 2$, which of the pairs of triangles would you try to prove congruent? What additional information would be needed to prove the triangles congruent?

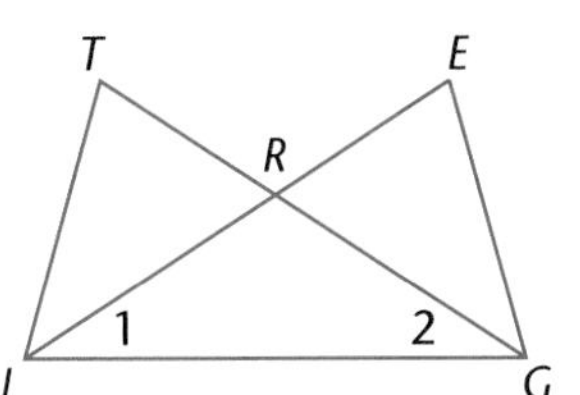

6. *Given:* $\overline{AB} \cong \overline{DB}$, $\overline{AC} \cong \overline{DC}$, $\angle BAC \cong \angle BDC$

   Prove: $\overline{AS} \cong \overline{DS}$

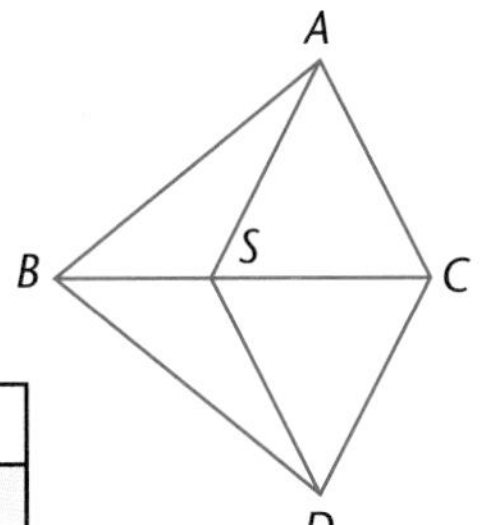

Statement	Reason
1. $\overline{CA} \cong \overline{CD}$, $\overline{CE}$ bisects $\angle ACB$	**1.** Given
2. $\overline{BC} \cong \overline{BC}$	**2.**
3.	**3.** SSS
4. $\angle ABS \cong \angle DBS$	**4.**
5.	**5.** Reflexive
6. $\triangle ABS \cong \triangle DBS$	**6.** SAS
7.	**7.** CPCTC

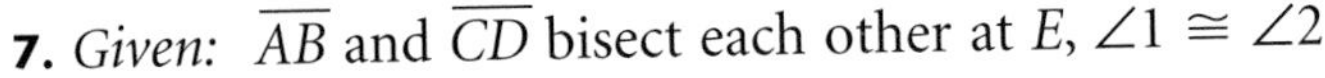

7. *Given:* $\overline{AB}$ and $\overline{CD}$ bisect each other at E, $\angle 1 \cong \angle 2$

Prove: $\overline{DF} \cong \overline{CG}$

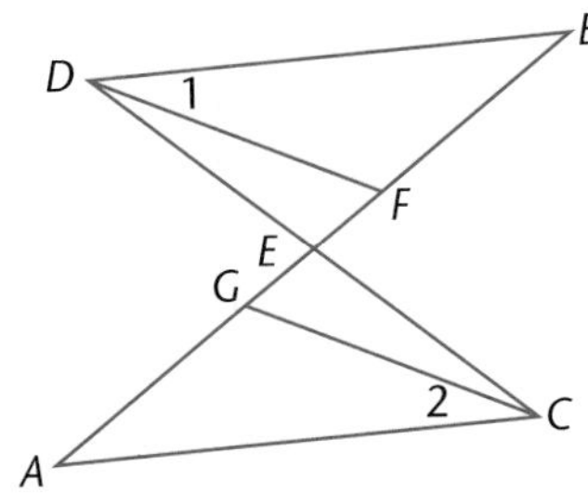

Statement	Reason
1. $\overline{AB}$ and $\overline{CD}$ bisect each other	**1.** Given
2. $\overline{AE} \cong \overline{BD}$, $\overline{DE} \cong \overline{CE}$	**2.** Definition of bisector
3. $\angle DEB \cong \angle CEA$	**3.** Vertical angle
4.	**4.** SAS
5. $\angle DBE \cong \angle CAE$	**5.**
6.	**6.** CPCTC
7. $\triangle ACG \cong \triangle BDF$	**7.**
8. $CG \cong DF$	**8.**

8. *Given:* $\triangle ABC$, D and E are midpoints

Prove: $\overline{DE} \parallel \overline{CB}$ and $DE = \frac{1}{2}CB$

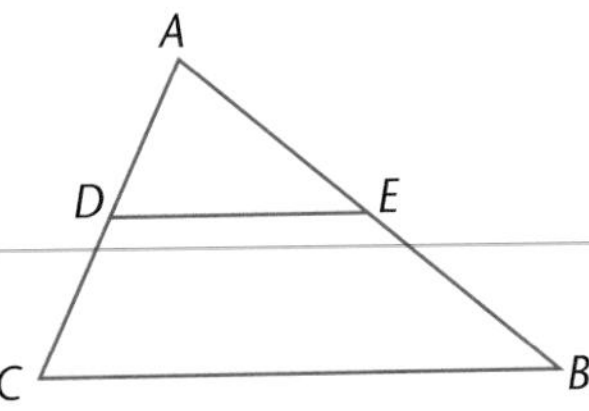

COMPOUND LOCI

On pages 299–303 you saw how to find a locus of points satisfying a given condition. Sometimes more than one condition is imposed upon the locus. In these cases, you need to find the points that satisfy *all* of the conditions. All possible relationships for the loci must be considered.

EXAMPLES

1. Describe the locus of points in a plane equidistant from points A and B and 5 cm from C.

The set of points in a plane equidistant from two points is the perpendicular bisector of the segment joining them. So, the first locus is the perpendicular bisector of $\overline{AB}$. The set of points in a plane 5 cm from point C is a circle.

Possibility 1	Possibility 2	Possibility 3
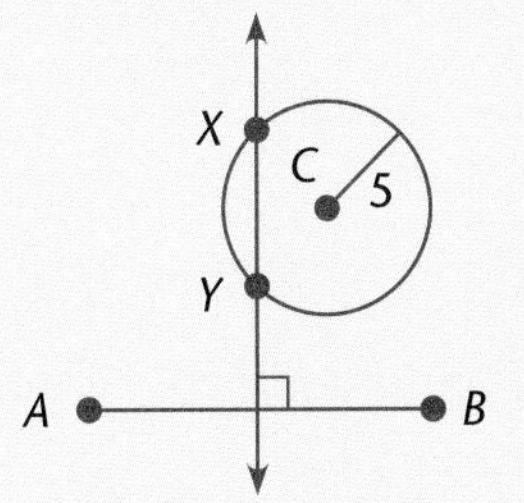	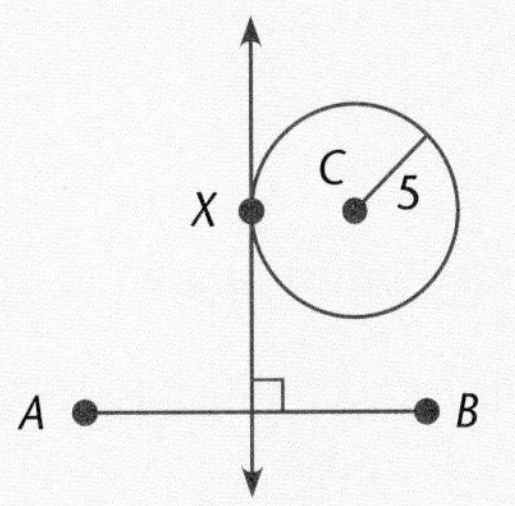	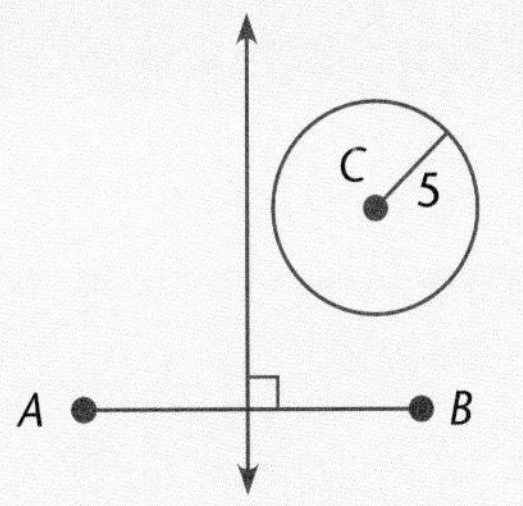
The locus is two points, X and Y, where the circle and perpendicular bisector intersect.	The locus is one point, X, where the perpendicular bisector is tangent to the circle.	There are no points that satisfy all of the conditions.

2. Describe the locus of points in a plane equidistant from three points, P, Q, and R.

The set of points equidistant from any *two* points is the perpendicular bisector of the segment joining them.

P, Q, and R can be joined by three segments. The first locus is the perpendicular bisector of $\overline{PQ}$, the second locus is the perpendicular bisector of $\overline{QR}$, and the third is the perpendicular bisector of $\overline{RP}$.

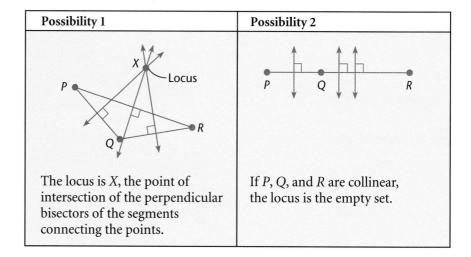

Possibility 1	Possibility 2
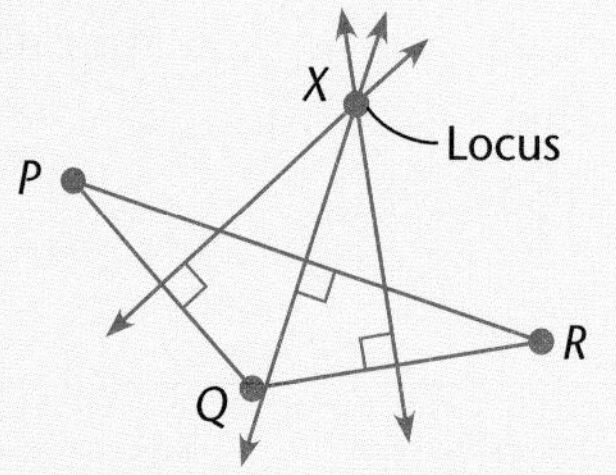 The locus is X, the point of intersection of the perpendicular bisectors of the segments connecting the points.	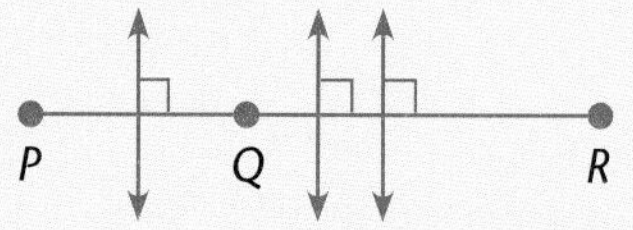 If P, Q, and R are collinear, the locus is the empty set.

Exercises

Assume all figures lie on the same plane.

1. Given two parallel lines m and n and a point P, find the locus of points in the plane equidistant from m and n and 4 cm from point P.

2. Lines p and q intersect. Describe the locus of points equidistant from the two lines and 9 cm from R, the point of intersection of p and q.

3. Point D lies in the interior of $\angle ABC$. Describe the locus of points in the interior of $\angle ABC$ equidistant from the sides of the angle and 2 cm from D.

4. Find the locus of points 2 cm from each of two intersecting lines, g and h.

5. Find the locus of all points equidistant from two points P and Q and equidistant from two intersecting lines, r and s.

6. Find the locus of points equidistant from a line d and a point C.

7. Find the locus of points 5 cm from a segment $\overline{XY}$.

8. Find the locus of points equidistant from the sides of an angle $\angle FGH$ and equidistant from points G and H.

9. Segments $\overline{AB}$ and $\overline{AC}$ are two sides of a triangle. A third segment, $\overline{CD}$, is the altitude from C to $\overline{AB}$. Assume $AC > CD$. How many *different* types of triangles can be constructed? Use loci to help answer this question.

GEOMETRIC MEANS AND RIGHT TRIANGLES

A positive number x is the **geometric mean** of two positive numbers a and b, if $\frac{a}{x} = \frac{x}{b}$. This is equivalent to stating that $x = \sqrt{ab}$.

EXAMPLE

1. Find the geometric mean of 4 and 6.

$\frac{4}{x} = \frac{x}{6} \rightarrow$ $\quad x^2 = 24 \rightarrow$ $\quad x = \sqrt{24} \approx 4.9$

The altitude to the hypotenuse in a right triangle forms two new right triangles. Using the AA Similarity Postulate, you can show that each new triangle is similar to the original triangle.

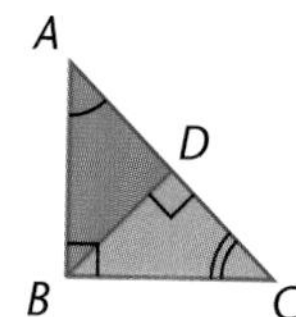

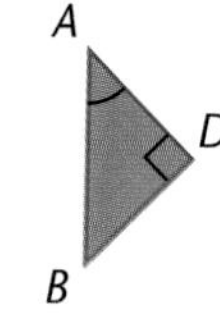

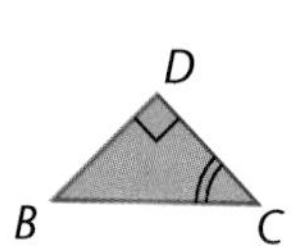

In similar triangles, the lengths of corresponding sides are proportional. For instance, since $\triangle ABD \sim \triangle BCD$, $\frac{DC}{DB} = \frac{DB}{DA}$.

DB is the geometric mean of DC and DA. Notice that, in the original triangle, $\overline{AD}$ and $\overline{DC}$ are the pieces of the hypotenuse created by drawing $\overline{BD}$.

THEOREM

The length of the altitude to the hypotenuse of a right triangle is the geometric mean of the lengths of the two segments on the hypotenuse. Stated as a proportion:

$$\frac{\text{length of one segment of hypotenuse}}{\text{length of altitude}} = \frac{\text{length of altitude}}{\text{length of other segment of hypotenuse}} \rightarrow \frac{x}{h} = \frac{h}{y}$$

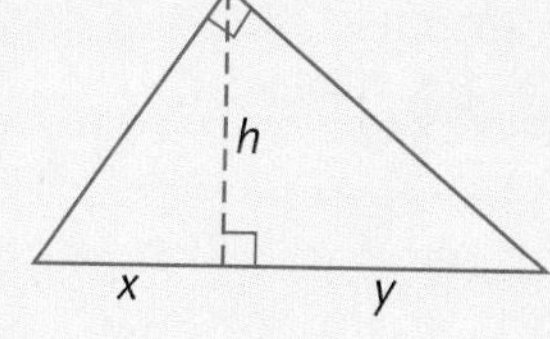

EXAMPLE

2. Find FG, the length of the altitude to hypotenuse $\overline{DE}$.

$\frac{2}{FG} = \frac{FG}{11}$ $\quad$ *FG is the geometric mean of DG and GE*

$22 = FG^2$

$\sqrt{22} = FG \approx 4.7$

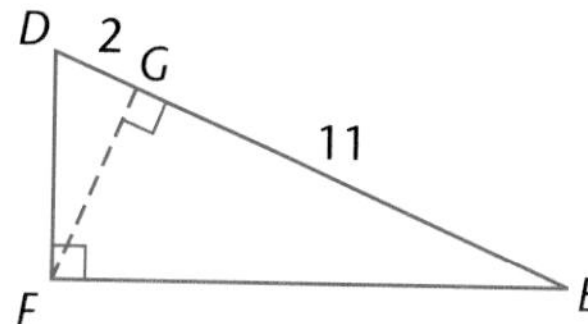

There is a second geometric mean theorem relating side lengths of right triangles. Look at similar right triangles $\triangle ABC$, $\triangle ADC$, and $\triangle BDC$ again.

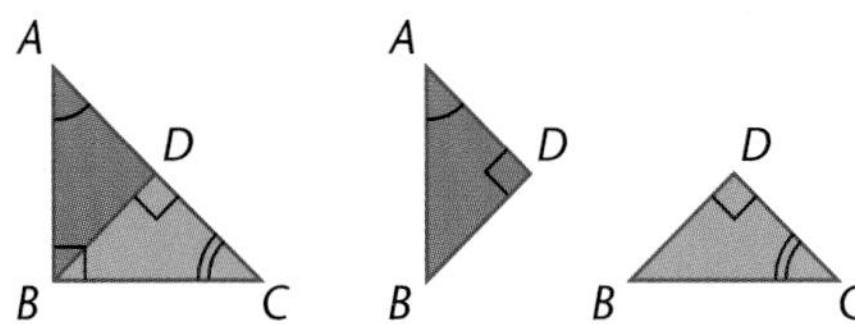

Since $\triangle ABC \sim \triangle ADB$, $\frac{AD}{AB} = \frac{AB}{AC}$. Notice that $\overline{AB}$ is a leg in the original triangle, $\overline{AD}$ is the piece of the hypotenuse closest to it, and $\overline{AC}$ is the whole hypotenuse.

THEOREM

In a right triangle where an altitude is drawn to the hypotenuse, the length of either leg is the geometric mean of the lengths of the piece of the hypotenuse closest to it and the length of the whole hypotenuse. Stated as a proportion:

$$\frac{\text{length of closest segment of hypotenuse}}{\text{length of leg}} = \frac{\text{length of leg}}{\text{length of whole hypotenuse}} \rightarrow \frac{x}{a} = \frac{a}{c}$$

and $\frac{y}{b} = \frac{b}{c}$

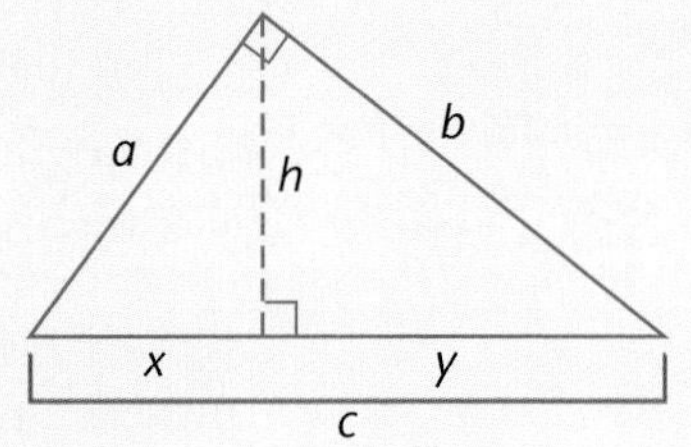

EXAMPLE

3. $\overline{XZ}$ is the altitude to the hypotenuse. $XW = 3$, and $WY = 8$. Find WZ and XZ.

To find WZ, use a geometric mean.

$\frac{WZ}{3} = \frac{3}{8}$ *WX is the geometric mean of WZ and WY.*

$WZ = \frac{9}{8} = 1.125$

XZ can now be found by using the Pythagorean Theorem.

$1.125^2 + XZ^2 = 3^2$

$1.265625 + XZ^2 = 9$

$XZ^2 = 7.734375$

$XZ = \sqrt{7.734375} \approx 2.8$

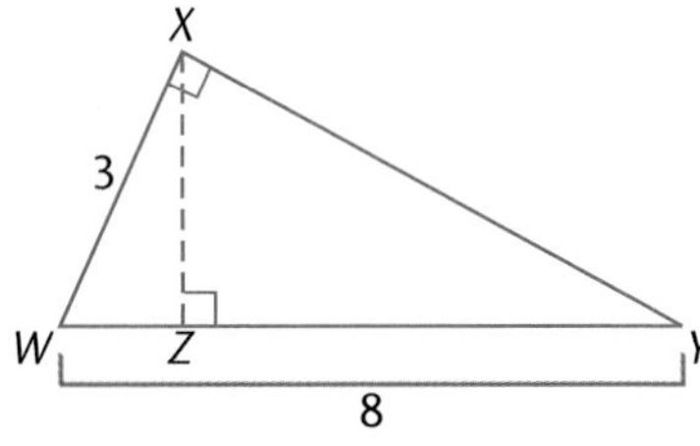

Exercises

1. Name all similar triangles in the figure.

E H F G

Find the geometric mean of each pair of numbers.

2. 6 and 24 **3.** 5 and 10 **4.** 5 and 6 **5.** 18 and 18

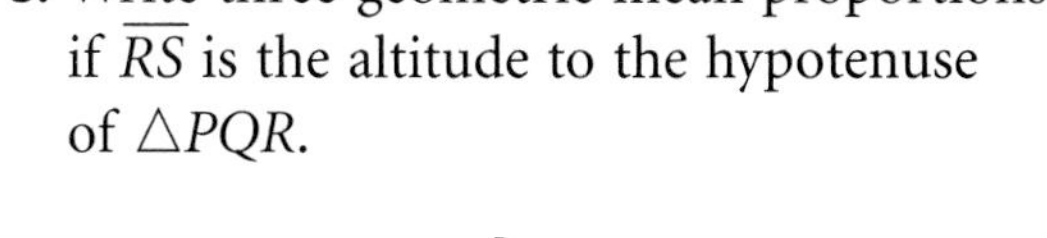

6. Write three geometric mean proportions if $\overline{RS}$ is the altitude to the hypotenuse of $\triangle PQR$.

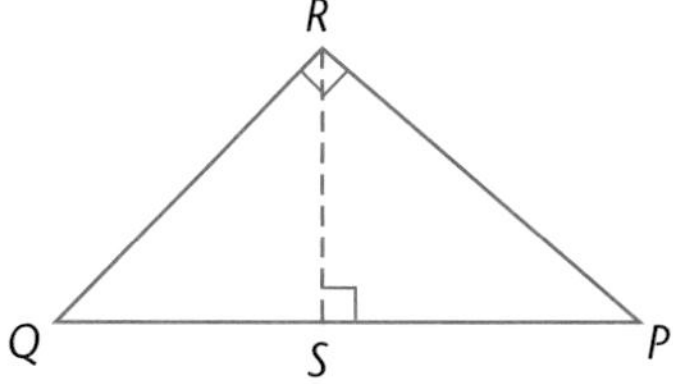

7. *Given:* $\triangle ABC$ is a right triangle with right angle $\angle ABC$. $\overline{BD}$ is the altitude to the hypotenuse of $\triangle ABC$.

Prove: AB is the geometric mean of AC and AD.

(Hint: First prove that $\triangle ABC \sim \triangle ADB$.)

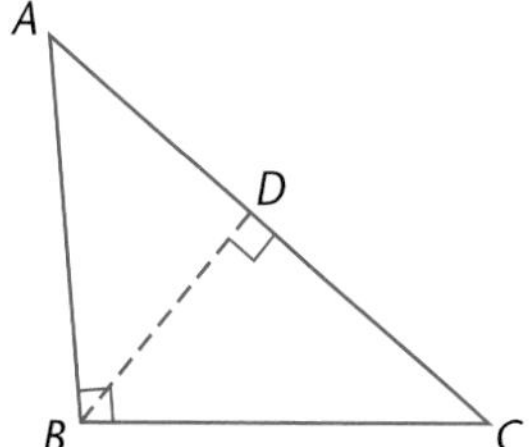

8. $FG = 5$, and EG = 9. Find HG and FH.

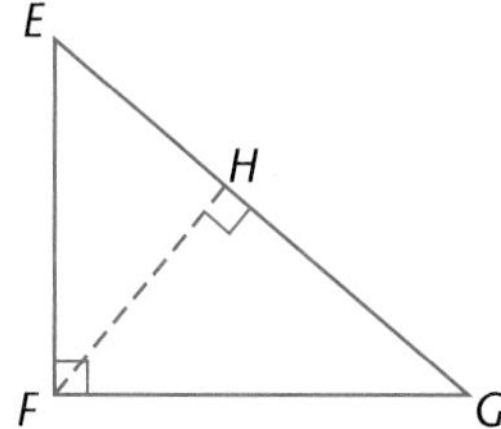

9. $PQ = 16$, and $QS = 6$. Find SP, QR, RP, and RS. Where necessary, round your answers to the nearest tenth.

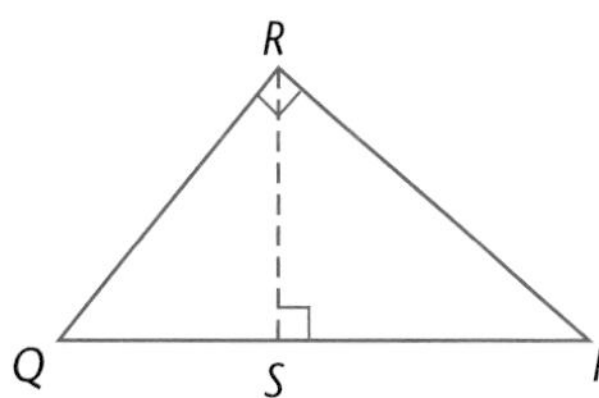

Find each length. Where necessary, round your answers to the nearest tenth.

10. $IJ = 4$, and $JG = 9$. Find JH.

11. $IJ = 6$, and IG = 12. Find IH.

12. $GJ = 9$, and $GH = 10$. Find JI.

13. $IJ = 7$, and $KH = 15$. Find JG.

14. $IH = 5$, and $GH = 12$. Find JG.

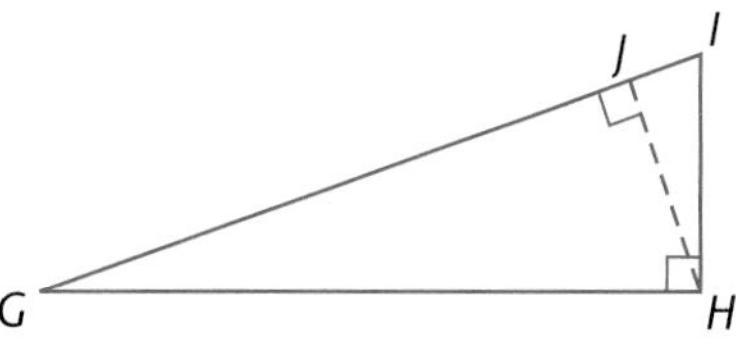

SEGMENTS OF CHORDS, TANGENTS, AND SECANTS

Interesting relationships occur when two intersecting lines intersect a circle. These lines may be:

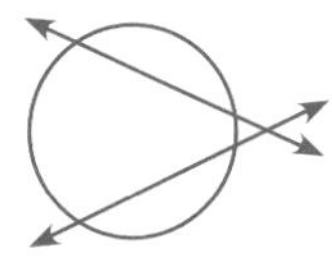

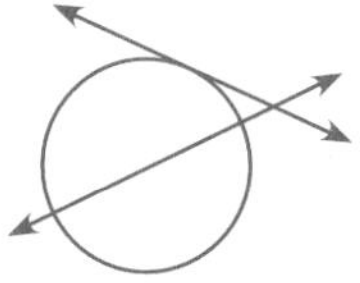

- two secant lines that intersect in the *interior* of the circle,
- two secant lines that intersect in the *exterior* of the circle, or
- a secant line and a tangent line.

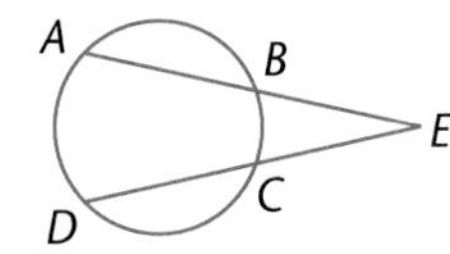

Consider the first type where two secants intersect. Secants $\overleftrightarrow{AB}$ and $\overleftrightarrow{DC}$ determine chords $\overline{AB}$ and $\overline{DC}$, which intersect at point E.

Since inscribed angles $\angle DAE$ and $\angle BCA$ both intersect arc $\widehat{DB}$, they are congruent. Similarly, $\angle ADC \cong \angle CBA$ because they both intersect arc $\widehat{AC}$. So, $\triangle AED \sim \triangle CEB$, by the Angle-Angle Similarity Postulate.

Because the triangles are similar, their side lengths are proportional, and $\frac{AE}{CE} = \frac{DE}{BE}$. Therefore, $AE \times BE = CE \times DE$ — the products of the lengths of the chord segments are equal.

THEOREM

If two chords intersect inside a circle, then the product of the lengths on the segments of one chord is equal to the product of the lengths of the segments on the other.

EXAMPLE

1. Find DE.

$AE \times CE = BE \times DE$ Use the theorem above.

$9 \times 6 = 5 \times DE$

$\frac{54}{5} = 10.8 = DE$

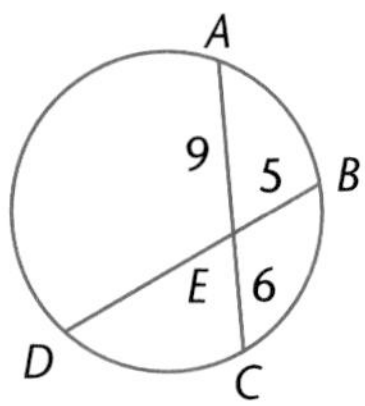

When the intersection point of the secants is in the exterior of the circle, **secant segments** $\overline{FJ}$ and $\overline{IJ}$ are formed. The product of the length of a secant segment and the length of its external part, called the **external secant segment,** is equal to the product of the corresponding lengths in an intersecting secant segment. In the figure, $FJ \times GJ = IJ \times HJ$.

External secant segment, IJ
Secant segment, $\overline{IH}$

> **THEOREM**
>
> If two secants intersect outside a circle, then the product of the lengths of one secant segment and its external secant segment is equal to the product of the corresponding lengths on the other.

EXAMPLE

2. $AE = 12$, $AB = 7$, and $CD = 4$. Find CE and DE.

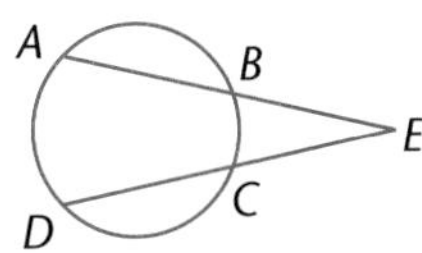

Let x represent CE.
Then $DE = (x + 4)$.

$AE \times BE = DE \times CE$	Use the theorem above.
$12 \times 5 = (x + 4) \times x$	Substitute.
$60 = x^2 + 4x$	Multiply.
$x^2 + 4x - 60 = 0$	Since the equation is quadratic, set one side equal to 0.
$(x + 10)(x - 6) = 0$	Factor.
$x = -10$ or $x = 6$	Set each factor equal to zero and solve.

A length cannot be negative, so $x = CE = 6$.
$DE = CE + 4 = 10$.

When a secant and a tangent intersect outside a circle, the segment from the point of tangency to the point of intersection of the lines is called the **tangent segment.**

In the figure, $CA \times DA = BA^2$. Notice that the product of the secant segment lengths is equal to the *square* of the tangent segments.

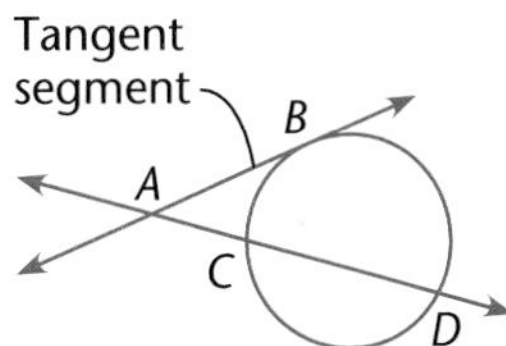

THEOREM

If a secant and a tangent intersect outside a circle, then the product of the lengths of the secant segment and its external secant segment is equal to square of the length of the tangent segment.

EXAMPLE

3. $MN = 12$, and $NP = 6$. Find PQ.

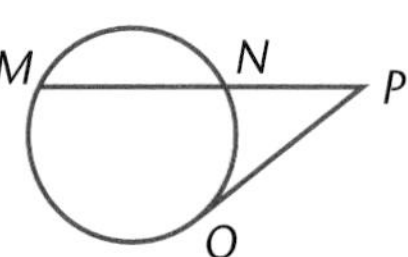

$MP \times NP = PQ^2$ — Use the theorem above.

$108 = PQ^2$ — Notice that $MP = MN + MP$.

$\sqrt{108} = 6\sqrt{3} = PQ \approx 10.39$

Exercises

1. $WP \cdot PY = (\ \ ) \cdot (\ \ )$

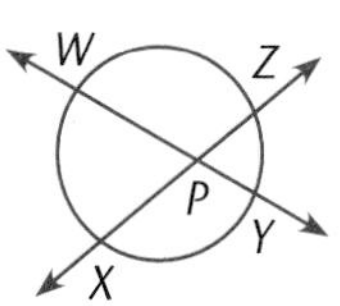

2. $IE \cdot IF = (\ \ ) \cdot (\ \ )$

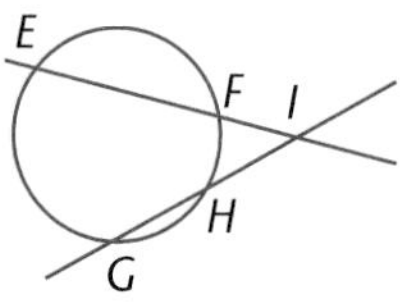

3. $\overleftrightarrow{XF}$ is a tangent. $XG = 4$ and $GH = 6$. Find XF.

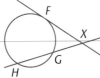

4. $\overleftrightarrow{PA}$ is a tangent and $\overline{PB}$ and $\overline{PC}$ are secants. $PE = 4$, $EB = 18$, and $PD = 5$. Find PC, CD, and PA.

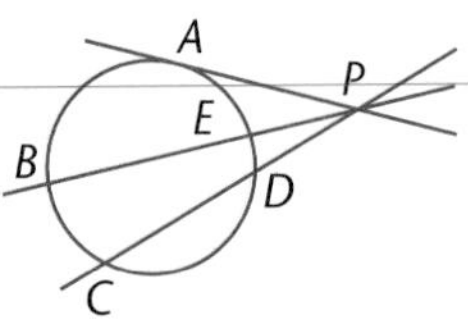

5. *Given:* $\overline{AE}$ is tangent to the circle.

Prove: $(AE)^2 = BE \cdot CE$

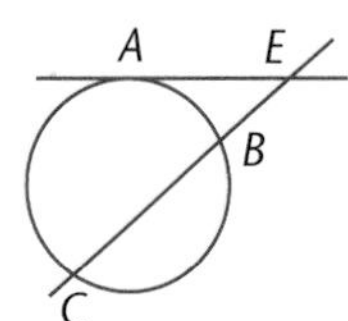

6. $AE = 20$, $EB = 6$, and $CD = 7$. Find CE and DE.

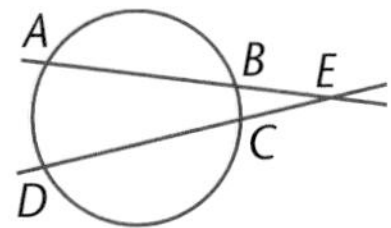

HINGE THEOREM (SAS INEQUALITY THEOREM)

If two triangles have two pairs of corresponding sides and the included angles are congruent, then the triangles must be congruent. By the SAS Congruence Postulate, $\triangle ABC \cong \triangle DEF$.

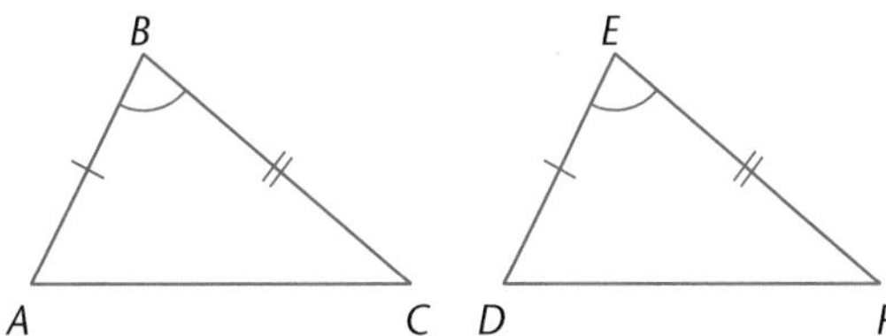

What can you say about triangles where two pairs of sides are congruent but the *included angles* (the angles between the congruent sides) are not?

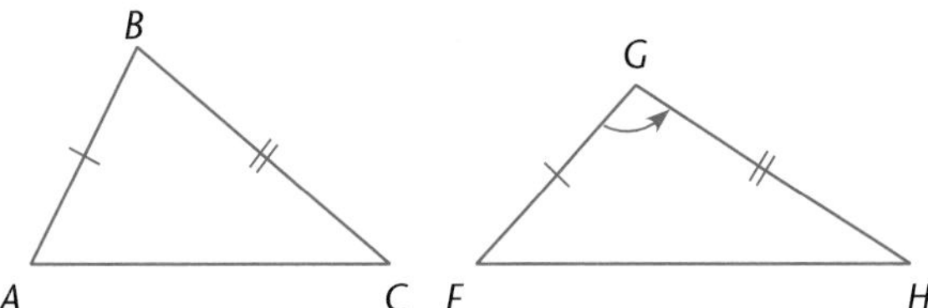

Think of the angle as a hinge. As the size of the angle increases, the hinge opens and the length of the side opposite the angle also increases. In the figure, it is clear that $AC < FH$.

HINGE THEOREM (SAS INEQUALITY THEOREM)

If two sides of one triangle are congruent to two sides of a second triangle and the measure of the included angle of the first triangle is greater than the measure of the included angle of the second triangle, then the length of the side opposite the included angle of the first triangle is greater than the length of the side opposite the included angle of the second triangle.

EXAMPLE

1. If $m\angle P > m\angle X$, write an inequality including QR and YZ.
The triangles have two pairs of congruent sides and $\angle P$ is the larger included angle. Therefore, $QR > YZ$.

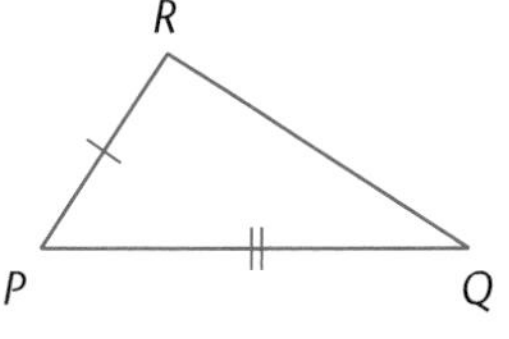

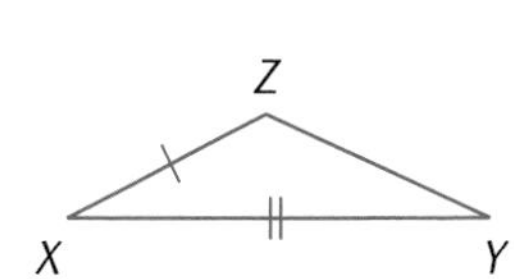

The converse of the Hinge Theorem is also true.

HINGE THEOREM CONVERSE

If two sides of one triangle are congruent to two sides of a second triangle and the length of the third side of the first triangle is greater than the length of the third side of the second triangle, then the measure of the angle opposite the third side of the first triangle is greater than the measure of the angle opposite the third side of the second triangle.

EXAMPLE

2. Write an inequality including $m\angle F$ and $m\angle O$.

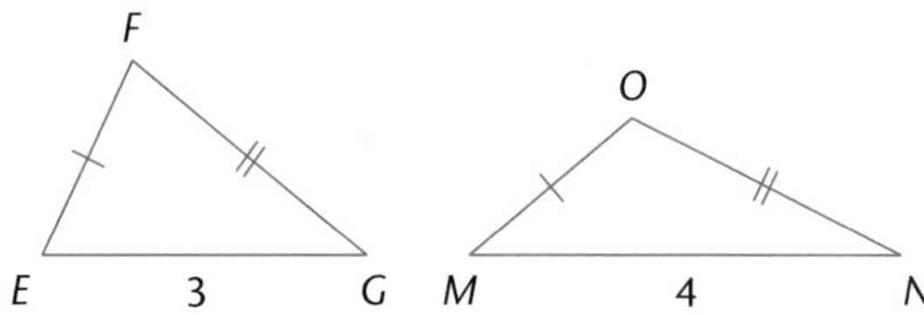

According to the Hinge Theorem Converse, the larger angle is opposite the longer side. Therefore, $m\angle O > m\angle F$.

Exercises

1. Draw $\triangle ABC$ with $AB = 3$, $BC = 4$, and $AC = 6$ and $\triangle DEF$ with $DE = 3$, $EF = 5$, and $DF = 6$. What must be true about $\angle A$ and $\angle D$?

2. *Given:* $GE = EO$. What can be concluded about GM and MO if:

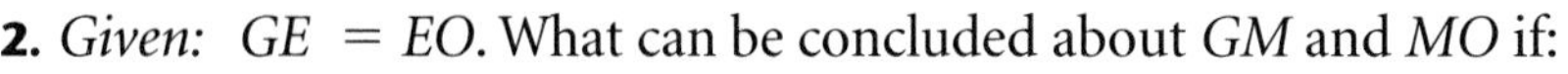

a. $m\angle 1 = 35°$ and $m\angle 2 = 42°$

b. $m\angle 1 = m\angle 2$

c. $m\angle 1 = 40°$ and $m\angle 2 = 36°$

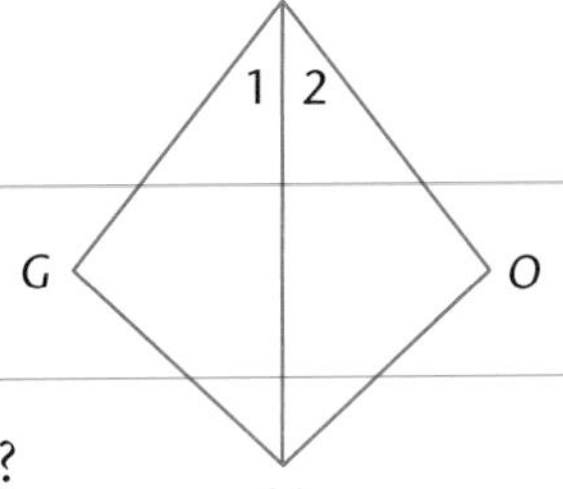

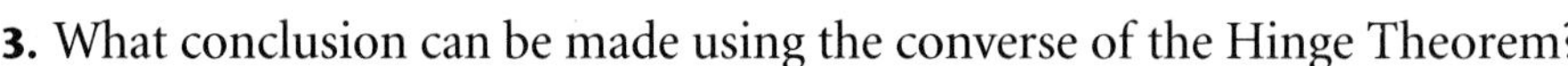

3. What conclusion can be made using the converse of the Hinge Theorem?

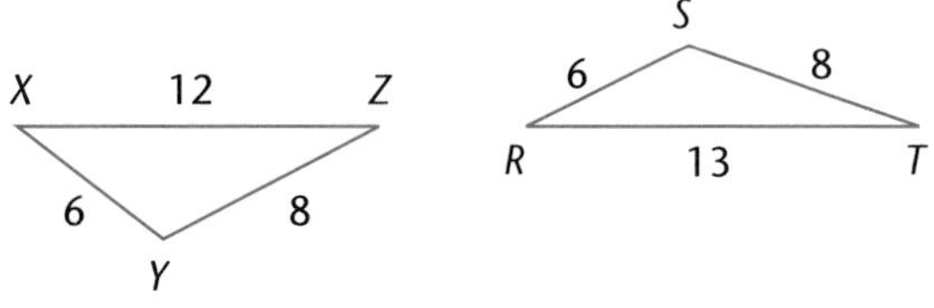

4. *Given:* $AB = BC$, $m\angle ABD < m\angle DBC$

Prove: $AD < DC$

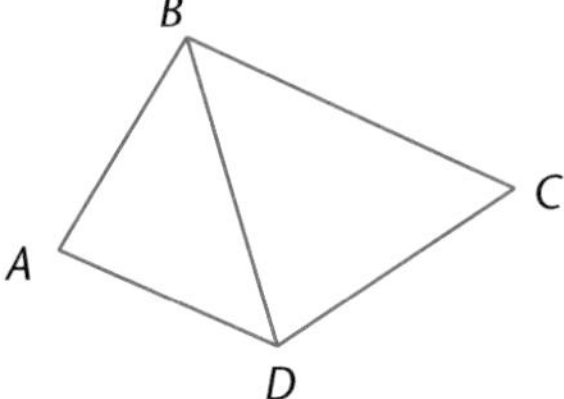

SPIRAL REVIEW

CHAPTER 1 VISUAL THINKING AND MATHEMATICAL MODELS

1-1 USING FAMILIAR MODELS

Use with or after Part 1-1A

Simplify each expression. [Previous course]

1. $5x + 9x - 6x$ **2.** $7r - 4s + 11r + 3s$ **3.** $13x - 8y + 2x - 7y$
4. $5(2 + 3x)$ **5.** $10x - 8(2x - 3)$ **6.** $4y - (6x - 4y) + 2z$
7. $6(x + 2y) - 6(x - 2y)$ **8.** $r(r + 3)$ **9.** $5r + 2r(r - 3)$
10. $2x(x - 4) - 6x$ **11.** $2r(r - 7) - 3r(r + 6)$ **12.** $x(x + y) + x(x - y)$

Use with or after Part 1-1B

Evaluate each expression for $x = 3$ and $y = -1$. [Previous course]

13. $5x - 2y$ **14.** $5y - 2x$ **15.** $6(x + 2y)$
16. $7y(x + 2)$ **17.** $3x(y + 2) - 9xy$ **18.** $x + 2xy - y$
19. $x(x + y) + x(x - y)$ **20.** $x^2 + 2xy + y^2$

Draw a net for the following items. [1-1A]

21. soup can **22.** CD case **23.** shoebox lid **24.** square pyramid

1-2 REASONING AND LOGIC

Use with or after Part 1-2A

Evaluate. [Previous course]

Expression	for $x = 3$	for $x = -2$	for $x = \frac{1}{2}$
1. $6x$			
2. $6x^2$			
3. $(6x)^2$			
4. $-6x^2$			
5. $(-6x)^3$			
6. $-(6x)^3$			

Use with or after Part 1-2B

Solve each equation. [Previous course]

7. $x - 6 = 14$ **8.** $5x = -100$ **9.** $\left(\frac{1}{3}\right)x = 9$
10. $3x - 6 = 15$ **11.** $-2x + 7 = -25$ **12.** $-10 = 7x - 3$
13. $2x - 3 = 4$ **14.** $0.5x + 4 = 12$ **15.** $75 = -3x + 25$

Use with or after Part 1-2C

Find the next member in the sequence and explain the pattern. [1-2A]

16. 1, −2, 4, −8, 16, … **17.** 1, 8, 27, 64, … **18.** 1, 1, 2, 3, 5, 8, 13, …
19. J, F, M, A, M, J, J, … **20.** S, M, T, W, T, … **21.** $\frac{1}{2}, \frac{2}{6}, \frac{4}{18}, \frac{8}{54}, \ldots$

1-3 MEASURING FIGURES

Use with or after Part 1-3A

Evaluate each absolute value. [Previous course]

1. $|10|$ **2.** $|-10|$ **3.** $|3-5|$ **4.** $|5-3|$

5. $|6-(-8)|$ **6.** $|-8-6|$ **7.** $|-9-(-6)|$ **8.** $|-6-(-9)|$

Evaluate each square root. [Previous course]

9. $\sqrt{4}$ **10.** $\sqrt{64}$ **11.** $\sqrt{49}$ **12.** $\sqrt{25}$

13. $\sqrt{36}$ **14.** $\sqrt{16}$ **15.** $\sqrt{81}$ **16.** $\sqrt{100}$

17. $\sqrt{12}$ **18.** $\sqrt{18}$ **19.** $\sqrt{8}$ **20.** $\sqrt{144}$

21. $\sqrt{30}$ **22.** $\sqrt{27}$ **23.** $\sqrt{50}$ **24.** $\sqrt{196}$

Use with or after Part 1-3B

Solve each equation. [Previous course]

25. $2m + 4m = -42$ **26.** $3x + 6 - 7x = 30$

27. $-8(x - 2) = 96$ **28.** $7x - (2x + 6) = 9$

29. $3(x + 2) - 5(x - 1) = -27$ **30.** $5x = 56 - 9x$

31. $1 - 2x = x + 10$ **32.** $12t + 4 = 7t - 16$

33. $2(x - 1) = 4(2x + 7)$ **34.** $4x - (8x - 7) = -5(x + 3)$

Use with or after Part 1-3C

Find the length of segment $\overline{AB}$ for each set of coordinates *a* and *b* on the number line. [1-3A]

a A b B

35. $a = 3, b = 12$ **36.** $a = -5, b = 8$ **37.** $a = 0, b = -11$

38. $a = 15, b = -23$ **39.** $a = -13, b = -15$ **40.** $a = -13, b = 20$

41. $a = -\frac{1}{20}, b = \frac{5}{2}$ **42.** $a = -3.5, b = -7.3$

Find the distance *AB* given the coordinates of points *A* and *B* on the coordinate plane. [1-3A]

43. $A(-6, -1), B(-5, -1)$ **44.** $A(5, 15), B(5, -12)$ **45.** $A(5, 4), B(1, 1)$

46. $A(4, -2), B(11, -2)$ **47.** $A(-1, 1), B(1, -1)$ **48.** $A(0, 0), B(-3, -9)$

1-4 SYMMETRY AND REFLECTIONS

Use with or after Part 1-4A

Draw the figures with the given vertices on a coordinate plane. [1-1B]

1. (1, 1), (3, 1), (1, 3) **2.** (0, 0), (1, 0), (1, 1), (0, 1)

3. (1, −1), (−1, 1), (−1, −1) **4.** (1, 1), (−1, −1), (0, 0)

5. (1, 2), (2, 3), (3, 4) **6.** (−2, −1), (3, −2), (1, 3)

Use with or after Part 1-4B

If $\overline{AB} \cong \overline{CD}$, solve for *x*. [1-3C]

7. $AB = 2x$; $CD = 18$ **8.** $AB = 24$; $CD = 4x$

9. $AB = 4x + 1$; $CD = 25$ **10.** $AB = 6x + 11$; $CD = 15$

11. $AB = 5x + 7$; $CD = 8x + 1$ **12.** $AB = 8x - 7$; $CD = 7x + 3$

13. $AB = 5x + 2(7 - x)$; $CD = 3(2x - 1)$

Use with or after Part 1-4C

For the coordinates listed, determine whether $\overline{AB} \cong \overline{CD}$. [1-3A, C]

	A	*B*	*C*	*D*
14.	$(-1, 2)$	$(3, 5)$	$(2, 2)$	$(-1, -2)$
15.	$(2, -6)$	$(-2, -1)$	$(12, -7)$	$(-9, -1)$
16.	$(-5, -12)$	$(6, 0)$	$(-3, -7)$	$(8, 5)$
17.	$(-4, -10)$	$(8, 2)$	$(9, 5)$	$(-3, -7)$
18.	$(-3, 7)$	$(5, 5)$	$(-1, -12)$	$(-6, -9)$

CHAPTER 2 THE FOUNDATIONS OF GEOMETRY

2-1 THE NEED FOR PRECISE LANGUAGE

Use with or after Part 2-1A

Name two capital letters of the alphabet that have the following types of symmetry. [1-4A]

1. only a vertical line of symmetry **2.** only a horizontal line of symmetry
3. both horizontal and vertical **4.** no line symmetry

Multiply. [Previous course]

5. $6(12x^2)$ **6.** $(2y^2)(4y^3)$ **7.** $3m^2(-m + 10)$
8. $-2x^3(x^5 - x)$ **9.** $(5t + 4)(-3t)$ **10.** $7x(x - 6)$
11. $2x^2(x^2 + 5x - 7)$ **12.** $x(y^2 + 4y + 4)$ **13.** $2a(4a + 5b)$

Use with or after Part 2-1B

How many lines of symmetry does each figure have? Make a sketch of each. [1-4A]

14. rectangle **15.** square **16.** stop sign **17.** circle

Multiply. [Previous course]

18. $(x + 3)(x + 2)$ **19.** $(y - 4)(y + 5)$ **20.** $(m + 7)(m - 8)$
21. $(b - 1)(b + 1)$ **22.** $(2s + 3)(s - 6)$ **23.** $(2x + 5)(3x - 7)$
24. $(2r + 1)(2r - 1)$ **25.** $(2x + 3)^2$ **26.** $(x - 1)(x)(x + 1)$

Use with or after Part 2-1C

27. Plot the given data and draw a trend line through the scatter plot. **[1-1B]**

x	1	2	3	3	5	5	6	7	7	8
y	2	2	4	5	4	7	7	5	8	7

28. For which value of x is y the highest? the lowest?
29. When x is 5, what is the value of y?
30. Use your trend line to estimate y when x is 5.
31. Use your trend line to estimate y when x is 10.
32. Use your trend line to estimate x when y is 10.

2-2 STATING OUR ASSUMPTIONS

Use with or after Part 2-2A

Factor each polynomial. [Previous course]

1. $w^2 - 2w - 15$ **2.** $x^2 + 7x + 10$ **3.** $y^2 - 5y + 4$ **4.** $m^2 + 4m - 21$
5. $m^2 - 2m + 35$ **6.** $x^2 - 8x - 9$ **7.** $c^2 + c - 2$ **8.** $x^2 - 8x - 48$
9. $t^2 + 8t - 33$ **10.** $y^2 - 9y + 14$ **11.** $r^2 + 8r + 16$ **12.** $m^2 - 100$

Use with or after Part 2-2B

Write the following in *if-then* form. Name the hypothesis and the conclusion. [2-1A]

13. A score of 90% on the test will get you an "A."
14. A person who lives in Paris lives in France.
15. A triangle has three sides.

Factor. [Previous course]

16. $2x^2 + 7x + 3$ **17.** $3m^2 + 5m - 2$ **18.** $2y^2 - y - 15$
19. $3a^2 - 2a - 8$ **20.** $4r^2 - 9r + 5$ **21.** $5x^2 + 19x - 4$
22. $4m^2 - 22m + 28$ **23.** $4y^2 + 7y - 2$ **24.** $49x^2 + 14x + 1$

Use with or after Part 2-2C

Write each type of conditional for the statement, "Speeding will get you a ticket." [2-1B]

25. *if-then* form **26.** converse **27.** inverse **28.** contrapositive

Solve. [Previous course]

29. $x^2 - 7x + 12 = 0$ **30.** $x^2 + 2x - 15 = 0$ **31.** $x^2 - 9x + 20 = 0$
32. $2x^2 + x - 10 = 0$ **33.** $2x^2 - 9x + 4 = 0$ **34.** $2x^2 + 9x + 4 = 0$
35. $5x^2 - 20 = 0$ **36.** $3x^2 - 27 = 0$ **37.** $10x^2 - 90 = 0$

Evaluate $\frac{z + w}{2}$ for each of the following values of *z* and *w*. [Previous course]

38. $z = 1, w = 11$ **39.** $z = -1, w = -11$ **40.** $z = 0, w = 50$
41. $z = -12, w = 11$ **42.** $z = 100, w = -236$ **43.** $z = -8, w = 17$
44. $z = 0.5, w = -13.5$ **45.** $z = 499, w = -499$ **46.** $z = 0.01, w = 100$

2-3 DRAWING TECHNIQUES AND PARALLEL LINES

Use with or after Part 2-3A

Calculate the slope of the line that contains the following sets of points. [Previous course]

1. $(4, 1), (-1, -6)$ **2.** $(-1, 6), (2, -7)$ **3.** $(0, -5), (6, 8)$
4. $(-4, 9), (-1, -7)$ **5.** $(-1, 9), (0, 2)$ **6.** $(-9, -5), (-1, -1)$
7. $(1, 5), (5, 0)$ **8.** $(10, 5), (-8, 5)$ **9.** $(a, 0), (0, b)$

Use with or after Part 2-3B

Arrange some or all of the following conditionals in an order that allows you to make the given conclusions. [2-1C]

If A, then B. If W, then Q. If L, then X. If Q, then L. If X, then A.

10. If Q, then X. **11.** If W, then X. **12.** If X, then B. **13.** If W, then B.

Use with or after Part 2-3C

Determine the slope of lines $\overleftrightarrow{AB}$ and $\overleftrightarrow{CD}$ given the coordinates of points *A, B, C,* and *D*. Then graph the two lines on the same set of axes. [Previous course]

14. $A(0, 3), B(4, 11), C(0, -1), D(3, 5)$
15. $A(2, -10), B(-1, -1), C(-4, 14), D(1, -1)$
16. $A(6, -3), B(-10, 5), C(0, -5), D(2, -6)$
17. $A(1, 5), B(-1, -1), C(3, -5), D(-6, -2)$
18. $A(5, 3), B(10, 7), C(8, -5), D(-4, 10)$

CHAPTER 3 ANGLES AND PARALLEL LINES

3-1 ANGLES AND NAVIGATION

Use with or after Part 3-1A

Find the length of segment $\overline{AB}$ for each set of coordinates. [1-3A]

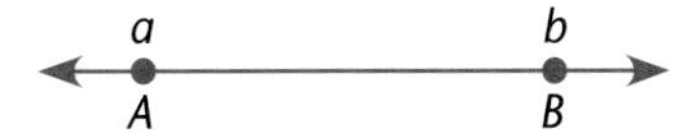

1. $a = 39, b = 11$ **2.** $a = -51, b = 14$
3. $a = 72, b = -44$ **4.** $a = -28, b = -17$ **5.** $a = 41.2, b = -39.4$
6. $a = -\frac{1}{2}, b = \frac{3}{4}$ **7.** $a = 0, b = -7\frac{2}{3}$ **8.** $a = -29.5, b = -13.2$

***R* and *S* are points on the coordinate plane. Find distance *RS* using the given coordinates. [1-3A]**

9. $R(-1, 9), S(7, 3)$ **10.** $R(-9, 7), S(6, -3)$ **11.** $R(7, 13), S(3, 8)$
12. $R(12, -2), S(18, 1)$ **13.** $R(-11, 2), S(2, 11)$ **14.** $R(-8, 2), S(9, -5)$

Use with or after Part 3-1B

***M* is the midpoint of $\overline{JK}$. Find the missing lengths. [2-2A]**

J M K

	JM	*MK*	*JK*
15.	9		
16.		13.8	
17.			17

	JM	*MK*	*JK*
18.			$10\frac{2}{5}$
19.		$3x + 5$	64
20.		$5x + 4$	$11x - 8$

Use with or after Part 3-1C

Given the coordinates of points *A* and *B*, find the coordinates of the midpoint of $\overline{AB}$. [2-2C]

21. $A(8, 7), B(4, 11)$ **22.** $A(-4, 10), B(6, -2)$ **23.** $A(2, -4), B(-2, 10)$
24. $A(6, -4), B(10, 1)$ **25.** $A(1, 12), B(1, -12)$ **26.** $A(4, -2), B(1, -8)$

Complete the table of ordered pairs and graph. [Previous course]

27.

x	1	2	3	4	5
$y = 2x - 3$	?	?	?	?	?

28.

x	1	2	3	4	5
$y = -x + 4$	?	?	?	?	?

Use with or after Part 3-1D

Write an equation of the line that meets the given requirements. [2-3C]

29. Parallel to $y = \frac{1}{2}x + 7$ and through $(0, -1)$

30. Perpendicular to $y = 4x - 7$ and through $(0, 7)$

31. Parallel to $y = 11x - 2$ and through $(0, 5)$

32. Perpendicular to $y = -\frac{3}{4}x$ and through $(0, -2)$

3-2 ROTATIONS

Use with or after Part 3-2A

Name the coordinates of the reflection image for the following points if reflected across the *x*-axis. [1-4B]

1. $(2, 2)$ **2.** $(-2, 2)$ **3.** $(0, 6)$ **4.** $(0, -3)$
5. $(-3, -3)$ **6.** $(4, -2)$ **7.** $(5, -7)$ **8.** $(-4, 8)$

Use with or after Part 3-2B

For the translation <−2, 3>, find the translation image of the following points. [3-1D]

9. $(-1, 1)$ **10.** $(3, 0)$ **11.** $(5, -2)$ **12.** $(-7, -1)$ **13.** $(0, 0)$
14. $(2, -3)$ **15.** $(-2, 3)$ **16.** $(1, -2)$ **17.** $(-4, -3)$ **18.** (x, y)

Name the translation for the given point and its translation image. [3-1D]

19. $P(5, 9), P'(1, 10)$ **20.** $A(-7, 2), A'(2, -7)$
21. $B(5, 0), B'(-7, 4)$ **22.** $X(-3, -5), X'(-6, -10)$
23. $M(5, -2), M'(5, 7)$ **24.** $R(7, -8), R'(-10, -8)$

3-3 PRECISE THINKING WITH ANGLES

Use with or after Part 3-3A

Graph $\triangle ABC$ for $A(1, 4)$, $B(2, -1)$, $C(-4, 6)$. Graph the image $\triangle A'B'C'$ for the given reflection *R* or translation *T*. [1-4C, 3-1D]

1. R across y-axis **2.** R across x-axis **3.** R across line $y = 7$
4. $T\langle -7, -8\rangle$ **5.** $T\langle 4, -6\rangle$ **6.** $T\langle 0, 9\rangle$

Name the bearing that describes each compass direction. [3-1B]

7. east **8.** west **9.** north **10.** south
11. northwest **12.** southeast **13.** northeast **14.** southwest

Use with or after Part 3-3B

Solve for *x* if $\triangle A'B'C'$ is the reflection image of $\triangle ABC$. [1-4C]

15. $AB = 8x$ and $A'B' = 72$ **16.** $m\angle C = 75°$ and $m\angle C' = 5x°$
17. $BC = 3x + 5$ and $B'C' = 40$ **18.** $m\angle B = (2x - 7)°$ and $m\angle B' = 20°$
19. $m\angle A = 70°$ and $m\angle A' = (4x + 10)°$
20. $AB = 5x + 9$ and $A'B' = 8x$
21. $BC = 6x + 7$ and $B'C' = 12x + 3$
22. $CA = x^2$ and $C'A' = 4x - 4$

Use with or after Part 3-3C

Determine the measure of the angle formed by the hands of a clock for each time. [3-1A]

23. 3:00 **24.** 6:00 **25.** 9:00 **26.** 4:00
27. 8:00 **28.** 5:00 **29.** 2:00 **30.** 1:00

Use with or after Part 3-3D

Square *XYZW* is rotated 270° clockwise around *P*. Find each image or pre-image. [3-2A]

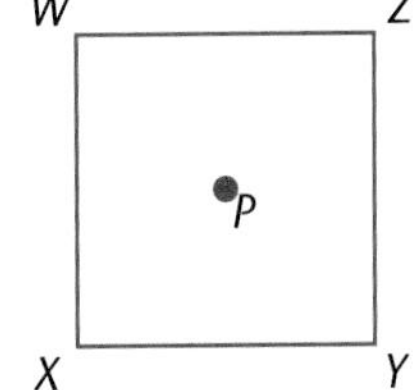

31. image of W **32.** pre-image of W
33. image of Y **34.** pre-image of X
35. image of WZ **36.** pre-image of ZY

3-4 PARALLEL LINES AND TRANSVERSALS

Use with or after Part 3-4A

∠*AGC* is a right angle, *m*∠*EGF* = 10°, *m*∠*DGE* = *m*∠*CGD*, and *m*∠*AGB* = *m*∠*FGE*. Find the measure of each angle. [3-3A]

1. $\angle DGE$ **2.** $\angle CGE$ **3.** $\angle AGB$
4. $\angle BGC$ **5.** $\angle BGE$ **6.** $\angle BGF$

For the figure shown, ∠2 is complementary to ∠3 and *m*∠1 = 130°. [3-3D]

7. $m\angle 1$ **8.** $m\angle 2$
9. $m\angle 3$ **10.** $m\angle 4$
11. $m\angle 5$ **12.** $m\angle 6$
13. $m\angle 7$ **14.** $m\angle 8$

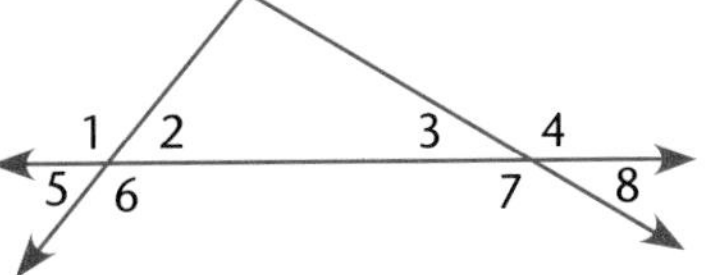

Use with or after Part 3-4B

Solve each system of equations by substitution. [Previous course]

15. $5x + 2y = 10$, $y = 2x + 5$
16. $-2x + -3y = 10$, $y = -2x - 2$
17. $4x - 5y = 3$, $x = y + 1$
18. $4x + 5y = 6$, $x = y - 3$
19. $2x + 4y = 0$, $y = -x + 3$
20. $2x + 7y = -6$, $x = 2y - 3$

Use with or after Part 3-4C

Solve each system of equations using the linear combination method. [Previous course]

21. $3x + 2y = 7$, $x + 3y = 14$
22. $6x + 2y = 2$, $x - y = 7$
23. $2x + 6y = 2$, $3x + 3y = -22$
24. $3x + 2y = 14$, $4x - y = 15$
25. $2x - 5y = -6$, $3x - y = -6$
26. $4x + 5y = 1$, $2x + 3y = 3$
27. $4x + 9y = 0$, $3x + 5y = -3$
28. $2x - 8y = 18$, $3x + 12y = 15$

CHAPTER 4 TRIANGLES

4-1 TESSELLATIONS AND TRIANGLES

Use with or after Part 4-1A

Find the measures of all other angles in the figure. [3-4B]

1. $m\angle 1 = 29°$ **2.** $m\angle 1 = 65°$
3. $m\angle 1 = 5°$ **4.** $m\angle 1 = 179°$
5. $m\angle 8 = 5x$, $m\angle 2 = 2x + 30$

Find $m\angle 4$, $m\angle 5$, and $m\angle 6$ if the angles are in the given ratios. [3-3C]

6. 1:2:3 **7.** 1:2:6
8. 2:3:5 **9.** 3:5:7
10. 1:1:1 **11.** 1:1:2

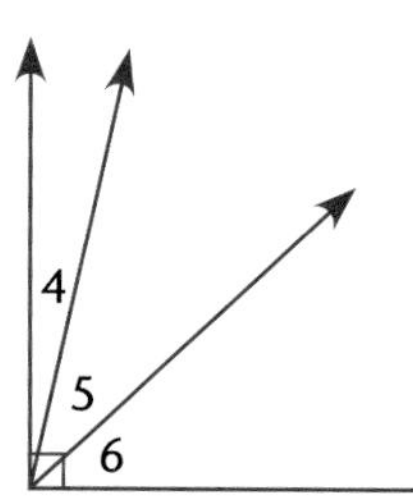

Use with or after Part 4-1B

Use the given information to determine which lines are parallel. Justify your answer with a theorem or postulate. [3-4C]

12. $\angle 1 \cong \angle 5$ **13.** $\angle 8 \cong \angle 9$
14. $m\angle 4 + m\angle 6 = 180$ **15.** $\angle 12 \cong \angle 5$
16. $\angle 4 \cong \angle 9$ **17.** $\angle 2 \cong \angle 7$
18. $m\angle 3 + m\angle 9 = 180$ **19.** $\angle 11 \cong \angle 3$

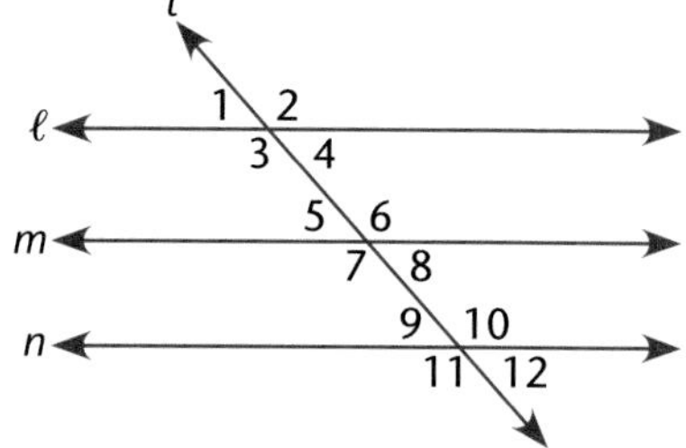

4-2 DEDUCTIVE PROOF WITH TRIANGLES

Use with or after Part 4-2A

Find the measures of the remaining angles given $m\angle 1 = m\angle 3 = 35°$. [4-1A]

1. $m\angle 2$ **2.** $m\angle 5$
3. $m\angle 6$ **4.** $m\angle 7$
5. $m\angle 8$ **6.** $m\angle 2 + m\angle 6 + m\angle 7$

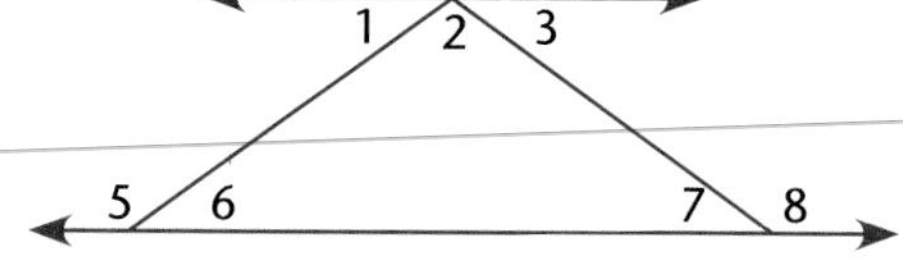

Use with or after Part 4-2B

Complete the table for the triangle shown. [4-1B]

	$m\angle 1$	$m\angle 2$	$m\angle 3$	$m\angle 4$
7.	79°	43°	?	?
8.	?	62°	?	111°
9.	?	15°	18°	?
10.	?	$3x-15$	$6x-5$	160°
11.	?	$14x$	60	?
12.	?	x^2	x	90°

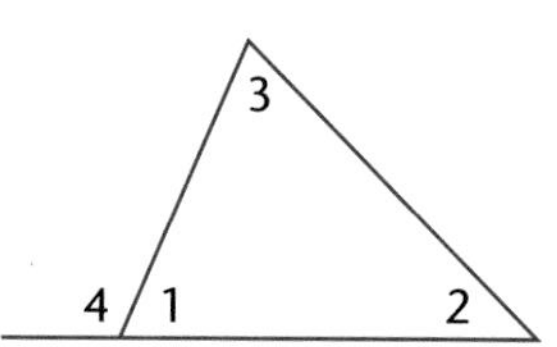

Use with or after Part 4-2C

Complete the table for the triangle shown. [4-1A]

	$m\angle 1$	$m\angle 2$	$m\angle 3$	$m\angle 4$	$m\angle 5$	$m\angle 6$
13.	?	?	110°	?	?	48°
14.	?	30°	90°	?	?	?
15.	?	25°	?	40°	?	?

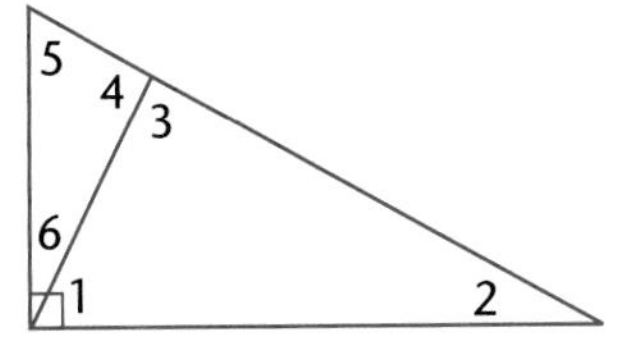

Use with or after Part 4-2D

Write the reasons for each statement. [4-2C]

Given: $\overline{WV}$ and $\overline{YU}$ bisect each other at X. Prove: $\triangle WXU \cong \triangle YXV$.

STATEMENTS	REASONS
$\overline{WV}$ and $\overline{YU}$ bisect each other	**16.** ?
$\overline{WX} \cong \overline{VX}$; $\overline{UX} \cong \overline{YX}$	**17.** ?
$\angle WXU \cong \angle YXV$	**18.** ?
$\triangle WXU \cong \triangle YXV$	**19.** ?

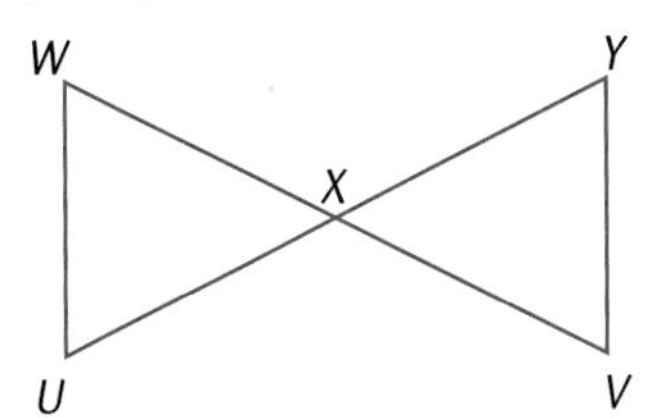

4-3 PROPERTIES OF SPECIAL TRIANGLES

Use with or after Part 4-3A

Give the reason for each statement. Use the figure from exercises 16–19. [4-2C]

Given: $\overline{WU} \parallel \overline{YV}$; $\overline{WU} \cong \overline{YV}$.

Prove: $\triangle WXU \cong \triangle YXV$.

STATEMENTS	REASONS
$\overline{WU} \parallel \overline{YV}$	**1.** ?
$\angle W \cong \angle V$	**2.** ?
$\angle U \cong \angle Y$	**3.** ?
$\overline{WU} \cong \overline{YV}$	**4.** ?
$\triangle WXU \cong \triangle YXV$	**5.** ?

Use with or after Part 4-3B

Give the reason for each statement. [4-2D]

Given: $\overline{AB} \parallel \overline{DE}$; C is midpoint of $\overline{AE}$. Prove: $\overline{BC} \cong \overline{CD}$.

STATEMENTS	REASONS
$\overline{AB} \parallel \overline{DE}$; C is midpoint of $\overline{AE}$	**6.** ?
$\angle 2 \cong \angle 3$	**7.** ?
$\overline{AC} \cong \overline{CE}$	**8.** ?
$\angle ACB \cong \angle ECD$	**9.** ?
$\triangle ACB \cong \triangle ECD$	**10.** ?
$\overline{BC} \cong \overline{CD}$	**11.** ?

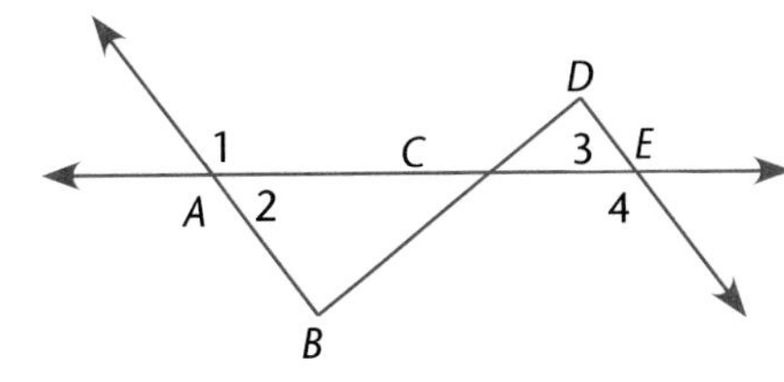

Use with or after Part 4-3C

Give the reason for each statement. [4-3A]

Given: $\angle 1 \cong \angle 4$. Prove: $\triangle RST$ is isosceles.

STATEMENTS	REASONS
$\angle 1 \cong \angle 4$	**12.** ?
$\angle 1$ and $\angle 2$ are supplementary	**13.** ?
$\angle 3$ and $\angle 4$ are supplementary	**14.** ?
$\angle 2 \cong \angle 3$	**15.** ?
$\overline{RT} \cong \overline{ST}$	**16.** ?
$\triangle RST$ is isosceles	**17.** ?

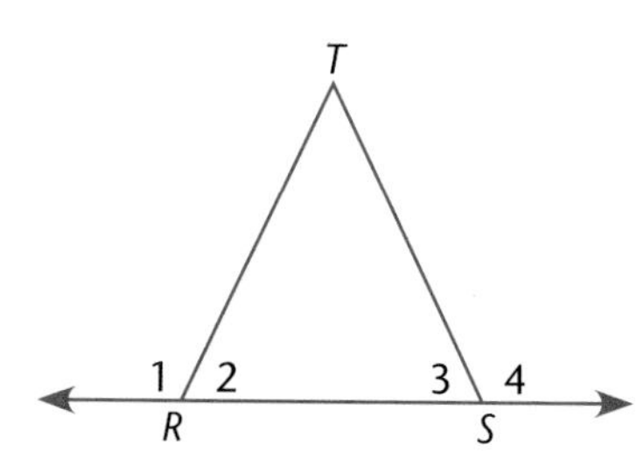

Use with or after Part 4-3D

In the figure above, find the measures of all parts of isosceles $\triangle RST$. [4-3A]

	$\overline{RS}$	$\overline{ST}$	$\overline{RT}$	$\angle R$	$\angle S$	$\angle T$
18.	$2x + 7$	$5x + 9$	$7x - 3$	$4y°$	$(2y + 40)°$	$y°$
19.	$14x - 25$	$12x + 5$	$17x - 35$	$2y°$	$2y°$	$5y°$
20.	$9x$	$4x + 10$	$7x + 4$	$(6y + 30)°$	$12y°$	$7y + 25$
21.	$2x$	$2x + 6$	$3x - 1$	$(8y + 24)°$	$(10y + 12)°$	$6y°$
22.	$6x + 12$	$5x + 7$	$8x + 4$	$5y°$	$5y°$	$(3y + 11)°$

CHAPTER 5 AREA

5-1 UNDERSTANDING AND APPLYING AREA

Use with or after Part 5-1A

Multiply. [Previous course]

1. $(x + 5)(x - 2)$ **2.** $(x - 8)(x + 9)$ **3.** $(2x - 5)(x + 4)$

4. $(x + 2)(2x + 11)$ **5.** $(x + 1)(x + 1)$ **6.** $(3x + 1)(4x - 3)$

7. $(2x + 1)(2x - 1)$ **8.** $(3x + 2)(3x + 2)$ **9.** $(5x + 2)(5x - 2)$

Use with or after Part 5-1B

Solve. [Previous course]

10. $x^2 + 13x + 42 = 0$ **11.** $x^2 - 11x + 18 = 0$ **12.** $x^2 - 6x - 40 = 0$

13. $2x^2 - 3x - 5 = 0$ **14.** $3x^2 + x - 4 = 0$ **15.** $4x^2 - 4x + 1 = 0$

16. $x^2 - 5x = 36$ **17.** $2x^2 = x + 1$ **18.** $2x^2 = 15x + 27$

19. $11x = 10x^2 - 6$ **20.** $3 = 4x^2 + x$ **21.** $4x^2 + 49 = 28x$

Use with or after Part 5-1C

Simplify each square root. [Previous course]

22. $\sqrt{40}$ **23.** $\sqrt{75}$ **24.** $\sqrt{20}$ **25.** $\sqrt{32}$

26. $\sqrt{48}$ **27.** $\sqrt{216}$ **28.** $\sqrt{200}$ **29.** $\sqrt{225}$

Use with or after Part 5-1D

A bag contains 9 red, 7 orange, 10 yellow, 8 green, 3 blue, and 12 brown pieces of candy. Express the probability of choosing one piece of the following colors as a fraction, a decimal, and a percent. [Previous course]

30. red **31.** orange **32.** yellow **33.** blue or green

5-2 DERIVATIONS OF AREA FORMULAS

Use with or after Part 5-2A

Fill in the reasons for each proof. [4-2D, 4-3A, 4-3B]

Given: $\angle 1 \cong \angle 2$; $\overline{AE} \cong \overline{BE}$; $\angle A$ and $\angle B$ are right angles. Prove: $\triangle DAC \cong \triangle CBD$.

STATEMENTS	REASONS
$\angle A$ and $\angle B$ are right angles	**1.** ?
$\triangle AED$ and $\triangle BEC$ are right triangles	**2.** ?
$\angle 1 \cong \angle 2$; $\overline{AE} \cong \overline{BE}$	**3.** ?
$\overline{DE} \cong \overline{CE}$	**4.** ?
$\overline{AC} \cong \overline{BD}$	**5.** ?
$\overline{DC} \cong \overline{CD}$	**6.** ?
$\triangle DAC \cong \triangle CBD$	**7.** ?

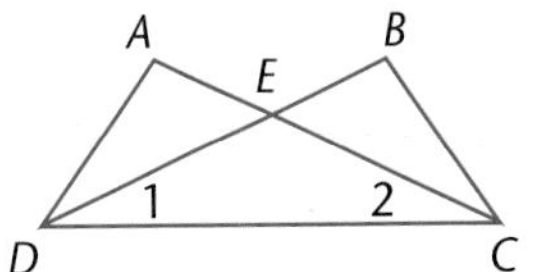

Use with or after Part 5-2B

Find the areas. Assume all units are centimeters. [5-1A]

Triangles	Squares	Rectangles
8. $b = 3\frac{1}{2}, h = 7\frac{1}{2}$	**9.** $s = 8\frac{2}{3}$	**10.** $\ell = 12\frac{3}{5}, w = 7\frac{1}{2}$
11. $b = 11.4, h = 16.2$	**12.** $s = 19.7$	**13.** $\ell = 12.2, w = 8.25$

Use with or after Part 5-2C

Find the areas. Assume all units are centimeters. [5-1A, 5-2B]

Triangles	Parallelograms	Trapezoids
14. $b = 13, h = 9$	**15.** $b = 34, h = 7$	**16.** $b_1 = 12, b_2 = 8, h = 6$
17. $b = 10\frac{1}{2}, h = 12\frac{2}{3}$	**18.** $b = 14\frac{1}{2}, h = 9\frac{1}{2}$	**19.** $b_1 = 9, b_2 = 4, h = 7$

5-3 THE PYTHAGOREAN THEOREM

Use with or after Part 5-3A

Use the given angle measure to find the measures of all other angles. [3-4B]

1. $m\angle a = 55°$ **2.** $m\angle k = 123°$

3. $m\angle n = 175°$ **4.** $m\angle a = x$

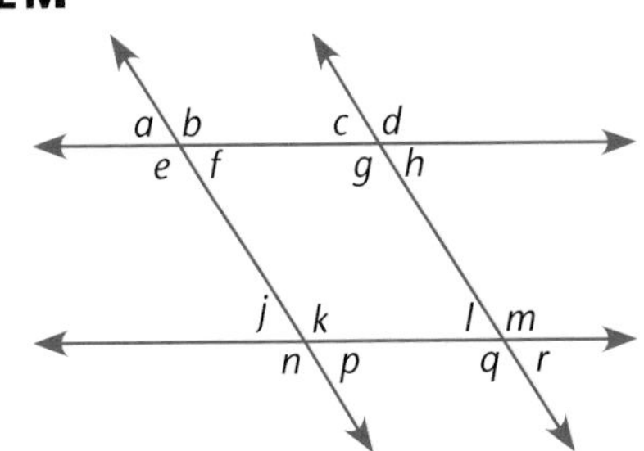

Use with or after Part 5-3B

Multiply. [Previous course]

5. $2 \cdot \sqrt{3}$ **6.** $15 \cdot \sqrt{2}$ **7** $3 \cdot 5\sqrt{2}$ **8.** $4 \cdot 3\sqrt{3}$

9. $\sqrt{2} \cdot \sqrt{3}$ **10.** $\sqrt{6} \cdot \sqrt{5}$ **11.** $\sqrt{2} \cdot \sqrt{18}$ **12.** $4\sqrt{3} \cdot 6\sqrt{2}$

Express each radical in simplest form. [5-3B]

13. $\frac{2}{\sqrt{3}} = \frac{2\sqrt{3}}{\sqrt{3} \cdot \sqrt{3}} = \frac{2\sqrt{3}}{3} = \frac{2}{3}\sqrt{?}$ **14.** $\frac{9}{\sqrt{2}} = \frac{9\sqrt{2}}{\sqrt{2} \cdot \sqrt{2}} = \frac{9\sqrt{2}}{2} = \frac{9}{?}\sqrt{2}$

15. $\frac{10}{\sqrt{2}} = \frac{10\sqrt{2}}{\sqrt{2} \cdot \sqrt{?}} = \frac{10\sqrt{2}}{2} = 5\sqrt{2}$ **16.** $\frac{15}{\sqrt{5}} = \frac{15\sqrt{5}}{\sqrt{5} \cdot \sqrt{5}} = \frac{15\sqrt{5}}{5} = ?\sqrt{5}$

Use with or after Part 5-3C

Find length *AB* for each of the following pairs of points. [1-3A]

17. $A(6, -2), B(-2, 4)$ **18.** $A(4, 5), B(14, 5)$ **19.** $A(4, 7), B(4, -6)$

20. $A(-2, 1), B(4, -8)$ **21.** $A(1, 1), B(-4, 11)$ **22.** $A(1, -2), B(8, 7)$

Use with or after Part 5-3D

Find the missing lengths for the right triangle shown. [5-3A]

23. $a = 3, b = 4, c = ?$ **24.** $a = 6, c = 10, b = ?$

25. $b = 12, c = 15, a = ?$ **26.** $a = 3, b = 6, c = ?$

27. $a = 9, c = 13, b = ?$ **28.** $b = 7, c = 8, a = ?$

29. $a = 5, c = 10, b = ?$ **30.** $b = 3, c = 8, a = ?$

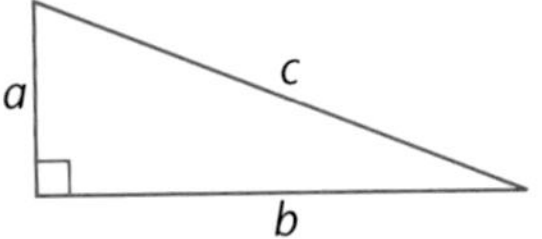

CHAPTER 6 POLYGONS AND POLYHEDRONS

6-1 POLYGONS AND POLYHEDRONS

Use with or after Part 6-1A

Find the missing lengths for the triangles shown. [5-3B]

	f	*g*	*h*
1.	3	?	?
2.	?	?	12
3.	?	11	?
4.	?	?	9

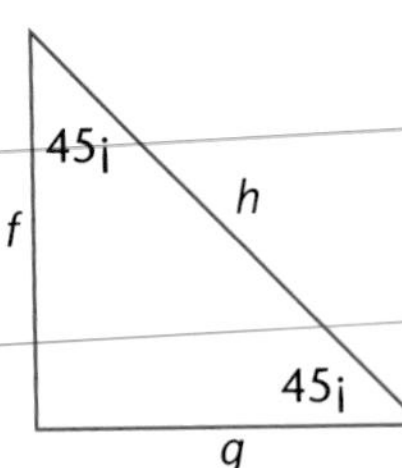

	a	*b*	*c*
5.	5	?	?
6.	?	12	?
7.	?	$\sqrt{3}$	?
8.	?	?	15

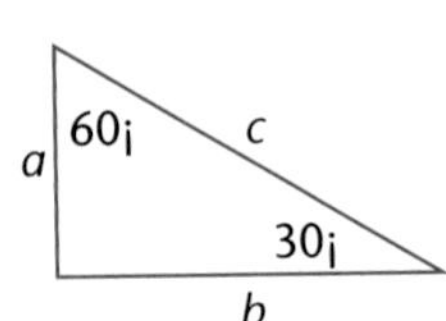

Use with or after Part 6-1B

Complete the table for the four angles of a quadrilateral. [6-1A]

	$m\angle 1$	$m\angle 2$	$m\angle 3$	$m\angle 4$
9.	90°	120°	x°	60°
10.	$2x$°	$(x + 55)$°	$2x$°	80°
11.	$(x + 100)$°	$(x + 50)$°	$(2x + 75)$°	$(x + 50)$°
12.	x^{2}°	$(4x + 40)$°	90°	$(2x + 70)$°
13.	$(2x^2)$°	$8x$°	120°	$6x$°

Use with or after Part 6-1C

Find the area of the figures shown. [5-2A]

14. $AB = 8$ **15.** $AB = 12$

16. $AB = 4$ **17.** $AB = 2\sqrt{3}$

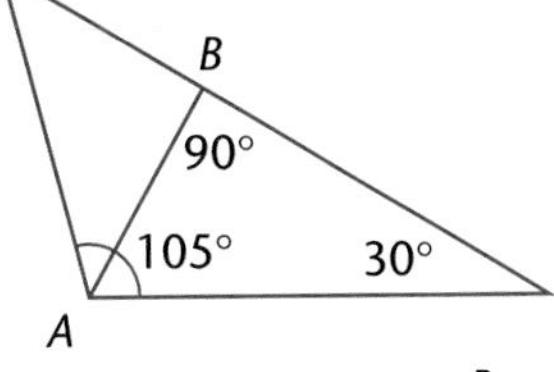

18. $AB = 4$, $BC = 8$ **19.** $AB = 12$, $BC = 4$

20. $AB = 10$, $BC = 8$ **21.** $AB = \sqrt{3}$, $BC = 4\sqrt{3}$

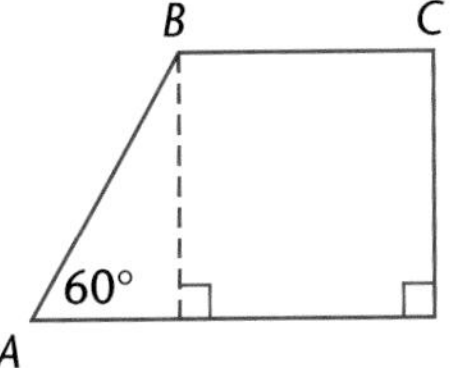

6-2 DEDUCTIVE PROOF WITH QUADRILATERALS

Use with or after Part 6-2A

1. Draw a Venn diagram for the quadrilaterals pictured on page 397. [6-1A]

If a quadrilateral is randomly selected from the set {square, rectangle, parallelogram, rhombus, trapezoid}, find the probability of selecting the following. [6-1A]

2. a parallelogram

3. only one set of opposite sides parallel

4. all sides congruent

5. all right angles

6. no sides parallel

7. no sides congruent

Use with or after Part 6-2B

Write a proof for the following. [4-3A]

8. Given: $\triangle ABC$ with $\overline{CD} \cong \overline{CE}$; $\overline{AE}$ and $\overline{BD}$ bisect each other.
Prove: $\triangle ABC$ is isosceles.

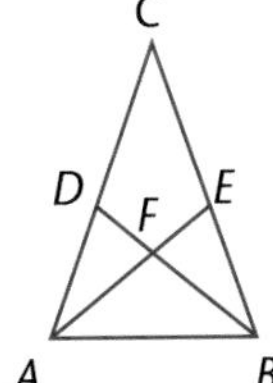

Use with or after Part 6-2C

Find the slope of the line containing the two given points. [Previous course]

9. $A(-5, 8)$, $B(-3, 4)$ **10.** $C(6, 1)$, $D(4, 1)$ **11.** $E(8, -6)$, $F(2, 6)$

12. $J(9, 0)$, $K(9, 5)$ **13.** $L(5, 8)$, $M(7, 9)$ **14.** $P(1, 5)$, $Q(7, 2)$

15. Which of the above lines are perpendicular?

Use with or after Part 6-2D

Find *AB* for each of the following pairs of points. [1-3A]

16. $A(-7, 6), B(-5, 2)$ **17.** $A(4, 3), B(6, -7)$ **18.** $A(5, -8), B(4, 1)$
19. $A(x, y), B(2x, 3y)$ **20.** $A(9x, -y), B(-7x, 2y)$ **21.** $A(6x, -4y), B(7x, 2y)$

Find the coordinates of the midpoint of $\overline{AB}$. [2-2C]

22. $A(8, 6), B(4, 4)$ **23.** $A(-7, 4), B(5, -2)$ **24.** $A(-4, 5), B(-6, 3)$
25. $A(x, y), B(2x, 3y)$ **26.** $A(9x, -4y), B(-8x, 7y)$ **27.** $A(0, 0), B(8x, -8y)$

M is the midpoint of segment $\overline{LN}$. Find the coordinates of N. [2-2C]

28. $L(0, 0), M(1, 1)$ **29.** $L(-1, 1), M(1, 1)$ **30.** $L(5, -8), M(4, 1)$
31. $L(x, y), M(2x, -2y)$ **32.** $L(-x, y), M(x, -y)$ **33.** $L(5x, -8y), M(4x, y)$

6-3 REGULAR POLYGONS AND POLYHEDRONS

Use with or after Part 6-3A

Find the sum of the measures of the interior angles and the sum of the measures of the exterior angles for each polygon. [6-1B]

1. triangle **2.** pentagon **3.** octagon **4.** quadrilateral
5. hexagon **6.** heptagon **7.** decagon **8.** n-gon

Use with or after Part 6-3B

Find the measure of one interior and one exterior angle for each regular polygon. [6-3A]

9. triangle **10.** pentagon **11.** octagon **12.** quadrilateral
13. hexagon **14.** heptagon **15.** decagon **16.** n-gon

CHAPTER 7 SIMILARITY

7-1 SIMILAR FIGURES

Use with or after Part 7-1A

Solve the following proportions. [Previous course]

1. $\frac{x}{12} = \frac{10}{6}$ **2.** $\frac{8}{x} = \frac{2}{9}$ **3.** $\frac{x}{3} = \frac{4}{6}$ **4.** $\frac{3}{5} = \frac{30}{x}$
5. $\frac{4}{x} = \frac{x}{9}$ **6.** $\frac{4}{x} = \frac{x}{(x-1)}$ **7.** $\frac{x}{4} = \frac{5}{(x-1)}$ **8.** $\frac{2}{x} = \frac{(x+4)}{6}$
9. $\frac{x}{3.5} = \frac{8}{7}$ **10.** $\frac{x}{x+1} = \frac{11}{12}$ **11.** $\frac{100}{12.5} = \frac{24}{6x}$ **12.** $\frac{100}{1} = \frac{x}{0.95}$

Use with or after Part 7-1B

Write and graph the equation of a circle with center (0, 0) and the given radius. [5-3C]

13. 5 **14.** 1 **15.** 3.5 **16.** $\sqrt{5}$
17. $\frac{3}{2}$ **18.** $\frac{\sqrt{3}}{2}$ **19.** 0.5 **20** $2\sqrt{6}$

Use a coordinate proof to prove the following. [6-2D]

21. If a quadrilateral is a rectangle, then its diagonals are congruent.

Use with or after Part 7-1C

Fill in the missing information for the rectangles listed in the following table. [5-A]

	Length	Width	Perimeter	Area
22.	11	6		
23.		8		96
24.	$3x$	x	72	
25.	$3x$	$5x$	32	60
26.	x	$x - 2$		35
27.			$2x + 2y$	

Use with or after Part 7-1D

Determine whether the given triangle with sides *a*, *b*, and *c* is acute, right, or obtuse. [5-3D]

28. $a = 11, b = 10, c = 14$

29. $a = 3, b = 9, c = 10$

30. $a = 10, b = 10.5, c = 14.5$

31. $a = 12, b = 13, c = 18$

32. $a = \sqrt{3}, b = \sqrt{5}, c = \sqrt{7}$

33. $a = \sqrt{6}, b = \sqrt{11}, c = \sqrt{17}$

34. $a = 1.5, b = 2, c = 2.5$

35. $a = \frac{\sqrt{7}}{2}, b = \frac{\sqrt{2}}{2}, c = \frac{3}{2}$

36. $a = 2.5, b = 4.5, c = 5$

7-2 PROPERTIES OF SIMILAR FIGURES

Use with or after Part 7-2A

Find *x* in each of the following parallelograms. [6-2A, 6-2C]

1.

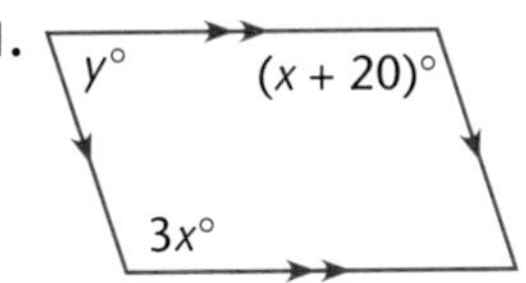

2.

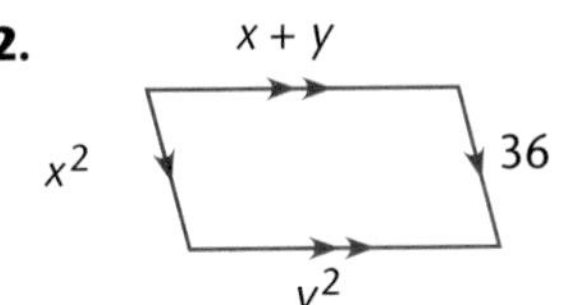

3.

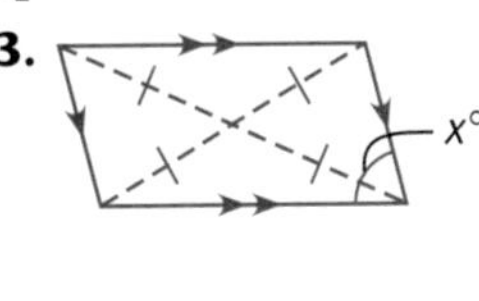

Use with or after Part 7-2B

Determine whether each of the following figures is a parallelogram and state why. [6-2B]

4.

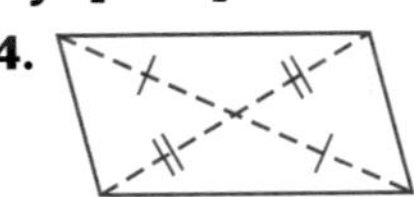

5.

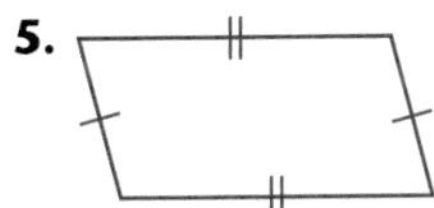

6.

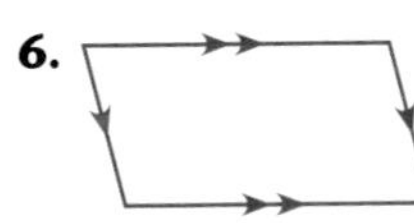

7.

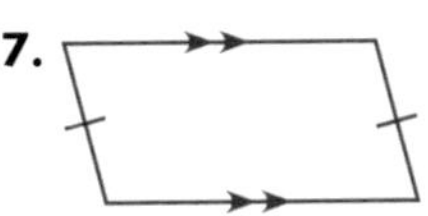

8. $y°$ $x°$ $x°$ $y°$

9. $x°$ $y°$

$x° + y° = 180°$

Use with or after Part 7-2C

Write T or F if the information is true or false for each quadrilateral *ABCD*. [6-2C]

	$\overline{AD} \parallel \overline{BC}$; $\overline{DC} \parallel \overline{AB}$	$\overline{AD} \cong \overline{BC}$; $\overline{DC} \cong \overline{AB}$	$\angle A \cong \angle C$; $\angle B \cong \angle D$	$\overline{AC}$ bisects $\overline{BD}$
10. parallelogram	**a.**	**b.**	**c.**	**d.**
11. rectangle	**a.**	**b.**	**c.**	**d.**
12. rhombus	**a.**	**b.**	**c.**	**d.**
13. square	**a.**	**b.**	**c.**	**d.**

Use with or after Part 7-2D

Explain why each pair of triangles is similar. Then solve. [7-2A]

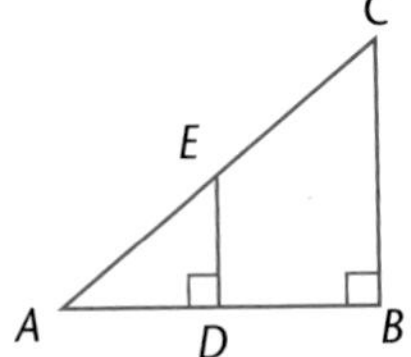

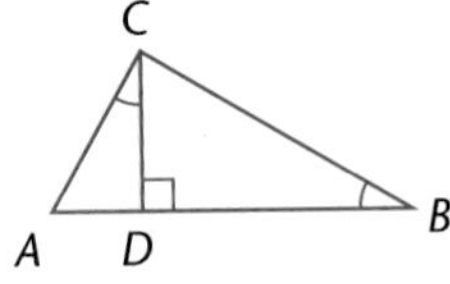

14. $AD = 5$, $DB = 4$, $DE = 6$, find BC. **15.** $AC = 5$, $CD = 4$, $AD = 3$, find BC.

7-3 TRIGONOMETRY

Use with or after Part 7-3A

Given the lengths of the legs of each right triangle, find its hypotenuse. [5-3A]

1. 5 and 12 **2.** 9 and 12 **3.** 7 and 24 **4.** 5 and 5
5. 1 and $\sqrt{3}$ **6.** $\sqrt{3}$ and 2 **7.** 3 and $\sqrt{7}$ **8.** $\sqrt{2}$ and $\sqrt{2}$

Use with or after Part 7-3B

Find the measure of the complement of each angle, in degrees. [3-3C]

9. 45° **10.** 22.5° **11.** 33°
12. $3z°$ **13.** $(90 - x)°$ **14.** $(45 - x)°$

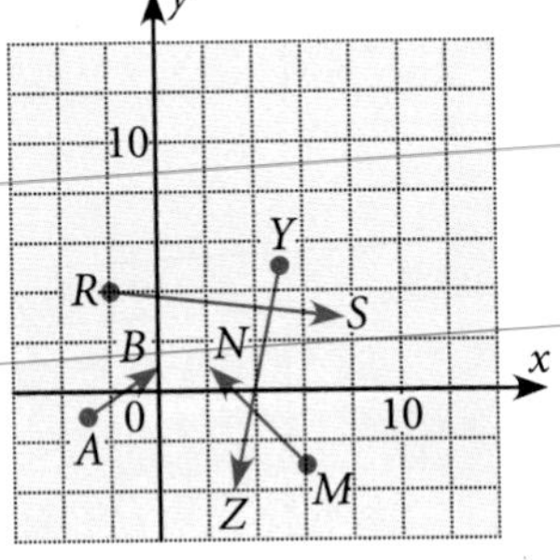

Use with or after Part 7-3C

Determine the length of each of the following vectors. [3-1C]

15. $\overrightarrow{AB}$ **16.** $\overrightarrow{MN}$ **17.** $\overrightarrow{RS}$ **18.** $\overrightarrow{YZ}$

CHAPTER 8 CIRCLES AND SPHERES

8-1 CIRCLES, CIRCUMFERENCE, AND AREA

Use with or after Part 8-1A

Write the equation of a circle with center (0, 0) and point *P* on the circle. [5-3C]

1. $P(3, 4)$ **2.** $P(-7, 2)$ **3.** $P(9, -12)$ **4.** $P(-6, -8)$
5. $P(2, -4)$ **6.** $P(8, -1)$ **7.** $P(-6, 0)$ **8.** $P(1, 1)$

Use with or after Part 8-1B

Given the ratio of similarity *k*, the ratio of perimeters or the ratio of areas, find the remaining ratios. [7-1C]

	k	$P:P'$	$A:A'$
9.	$\frac{2}{3}$	?	?
10.	?	$\frac{3}{5}$	?
11.	?	?	$\frac{9}{16}$
12.	$\frac{5}{1}$	?	?
13.	?	$\frac{2}{7}$	?
14.	?	?	$\frac{5}{9}$

Use with or after Part 8-1C

Find *x* and *y* in each of the following right triangles. [7-3A]

15.
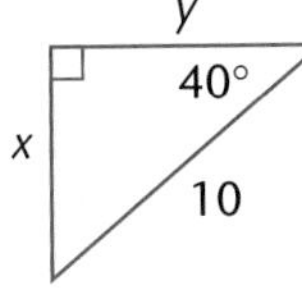

16.
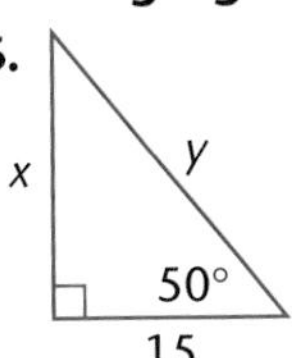

17.
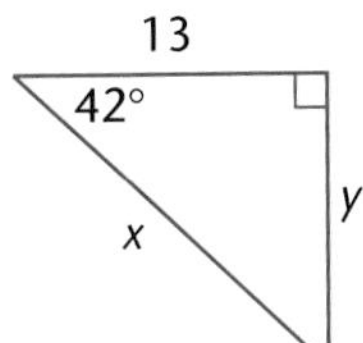

Use with or after Part 8-1D

Find the measure of each acute angle of the following right triangles. [7-3B]

18.
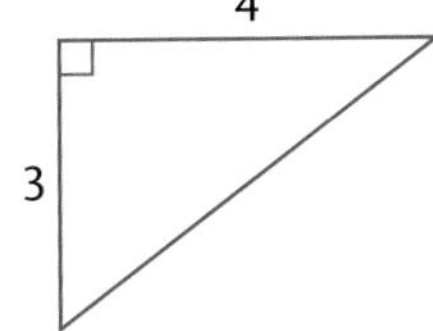

19.
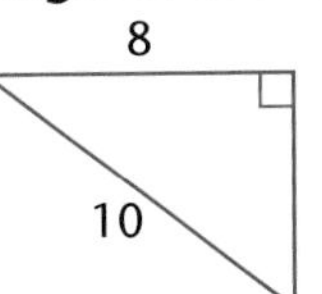

20.
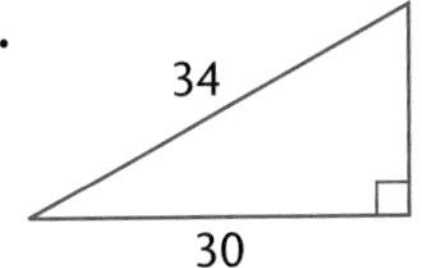

8-2 ANGLES, ARCS, AND CHORDS

Use with or after Part 8-2A

Find the circumferences of circles with the following radii. [8-1C]

1. 12 **2.** 8 **3.** $\frac{2}{3}$ **4.** 4.5
5. 1 **6.** 0.25 **7.** 25 **8.** $\sqrt{3}$

Find the radii of circles with the following circumferences. [8-1C]

9. 18π **10.** 24π **11.** 22 **12.** 13
13. 21 **14.** $\sqrt{3}$ **15.** 50 **16.** x

Use with or after Part 8-2B

Find the areas of circles with the following radii. [8-1D]

17. 12 **18.** 8 **19.** $\frac{2}{3}$ **20.** 4.5
21. 20 **22.** $\sqrt{3}$ **23.** $\sqrt{6}$ **24.** x

Find similar triangles in the figure. Solve for the appropriate variable. [7-2A, 7-2B]

25. $a = 4$, $c = 9$, find b.
26. $b = 3$, $c = 4$, find d.
27. $a = 5$, $c = 7$, find d.
28. $a = 6$, $d = 10$, find e.
29. $b = 8$, $c = 16$, find a.
30. $b = 9$, $c = 12$, find d.

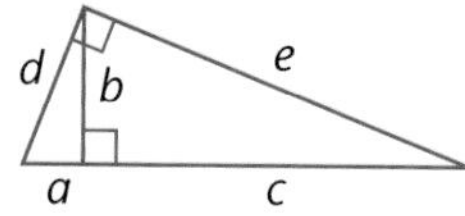

Use with or after Part 8-2C

Find the circumferences and areas of circles with the following radii. [8-1C, 8-1D]

31. 5
32. 12
33. 4.3
34. $\frac{4}{3}$
35. $\sqrt{3}$
36. $2\sqrt{3}$
37. $\frac{\sqrt{3}}{2}$
38. n

Find the circumferences of circles with the following areas. [8-1C, 8-1D]

39. 81π
40. 225π
41. 12π
42. 124π
43. 10π
44. 20
45. 12
46. $x\pi$

8-3 THE INSCRIBED ANGLE THEOREM

Use with or after Part 8-3A

Find the length of arc $\widehat{AB}$ and the area of sector *AOB* for each measure of central angle $\angle AOB$ and radius of circle *O*. [8-2B]

1. $m\angle AOB = 90°$, $r = 15$
2. $m\angle AOB = 55°$, $r = 10$
3. $m\angle AOB = 45°$, $r = 8$
4. $m\angle AOB = 120°$, $r = 13$
5. $m\angle AOB = 30°$, $r = 18$
6. $m\angle AOB = 72°$, $r = 22$

Use with or after Part 8-3B

Find the missing side of the right triangle shown. [5-3A]

7. $a = 9$, $b = 12$, find c.
8. $a = 8$, $c = 17$, find b.
9. $b = 2\sqrt{3}$, $c = 4$, find a.
10. $a = 5$, $c = 5\sqrt{2}$, find b.
11 $b = 3\sqrt{2}$, $c = 6$, find a.
12. $a = 5$, $c = 10$, find b.
13. $a = 4$, $b = 5$, find c.
14. $a = 8$, $c = 14$, find b.
15. $b = 9$, $c = 13$, find a.

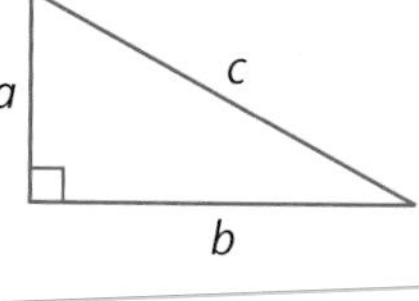

CHAPTER 9 SURFACE AREA AND VOLUME

9-1 SURFACE AREA

Use with or after Part 9-1A

Find the perimeters of the following figures. [5-1A, 6-3A]

1. rectangle with $b = 5$, $h = 12$
2. regular hexagon with $s = 5$
3. regular pentagon with $s = 4$
4. square with $s = 7$
5. triangle with $b = 6$, $h = 4$
6. equilateral triangle with $s = 2$
7. heptagon with $s = 8$
8. decagon with $s = 12$
9. n-gon with $s = a$

Find the areas of the following polygons. [5-2A, 5-2B]

10. triangle with $b = 10$, $h = 15$
11. parallelogram with $b = 11$, $h = 12$
12. square with sides = 10
13. trapezoid with $b_1 = 12$, $b_2 = 7$, $h = 5$
14. triangle with sides = 6, 8, 10
15. triangle with sides 5, 5, $5\sqrt{2}$
16. rhombus with $b = 4$, $h = 3$
17. rectangle with $b = 13$, $h = 7$

Use with or after Part 9-1B

Find the areas of the following polygons. [5-3B, 6-3A]

18. regular hexagon with side = 6
19. regular hexagon with side = 7
20. equilateral triangle with side = 6
21. equilateral triangle with side = 4
22. square with apothem = 4
23. square with radius = 4
24. right isosceles triangle with hypotenuse = $3\sqrt{2}$
25. right isosceles triangle with hypotenuse = 12

Use with or after Part 9-1C

Find the circumference *C* or the area *A* of the following circles. [8-1C, D]

26. $C = 36\pi$, find A.
27. $A = 36\pi$, find C.
28. $C = 20$, find A.
29. $A = 20$, find C.
30. $C = 18\pi$, find A.
31. $A = 18\pi$, find C.
32. $C = x\pi$, find A.
33. $A = x\pi$, find C.

9-2 VOLUME

Use with or after Part 9-2A

Circle *T* is inscribed in $\triangle QRS$. Find each of the following. [8-1A, 8-1B]

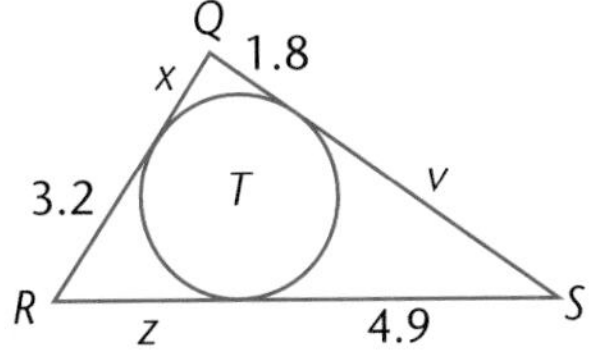

1. x
2. y
3. z
4. perimeter $\triangle QRS$

In the figure, *PT* is tangent to circle *O* at point *T*. [8-1B]

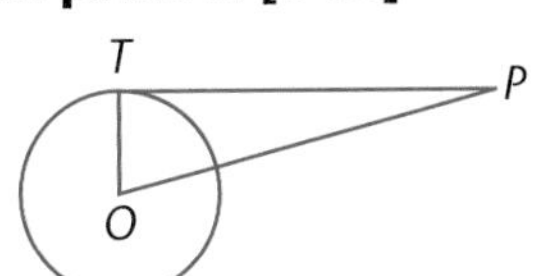

5. $m\angle PTO = ?$
6. $OT = 9$, $TP = 12$, $OP = ?$
7. $OT = 8$, $OP = 16$, $PT = ?$
8. $PT = 6$, $OP = 3\sqrt{13}$, $TO = ?$

Use with or after Part 9-2B

Find each arc measure. [8-2A]

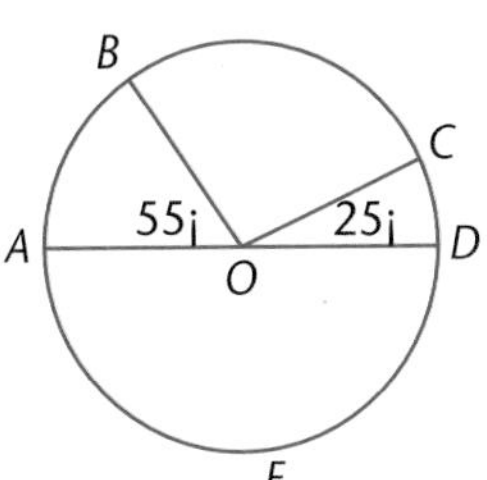

9. $m\widehat{AB}$
10. $m\widehat{CD}$
11. $m\widehat{BC}$
12. $m\widehat{AED}$
13. $m\widehat{ABC}$
14. $m\widehat{BAD}$

Find each arc length. [8-2B]

15. If $OB = 12$, find length $\widehat{AB}$.
16. If $OB = 12$, find length $\widehat{BC}$.
17. If $OB = 12$, find length $\widehat{CD}$.

Use with or after Part 9-2C

Find the area of the segment bounded by arc $\overset{\frown}{QR}$ and segment $\overline{QR}$. [8-2B]

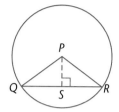

18. $m\angle QPR = 75°$, $PQ = 10$, $QR = 12$

19. $m\angle QPR = 25°$, $QR = 4$, $PS = 9$

20. $m\angle QPR = 60°$, $QR = 18$

21. $m\angle QPR = 120°$, $QR = 24$

22. $m\angle QPR = 90°$, $PS = 3$

23. $m\angle QPR = 90°$, $PQ = 10$

Use with or after Part 9-2D

Find the measure of each angle or arc indicated by a variable. [8-3A]

24.

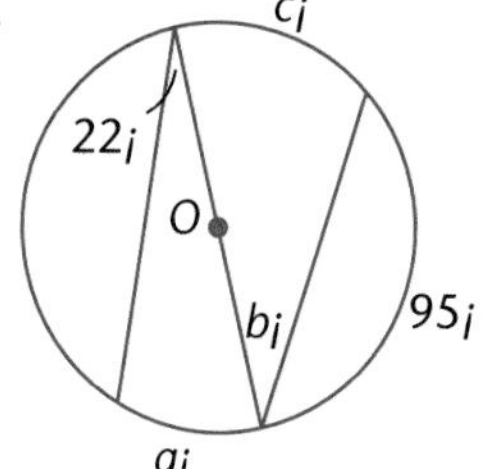

25.

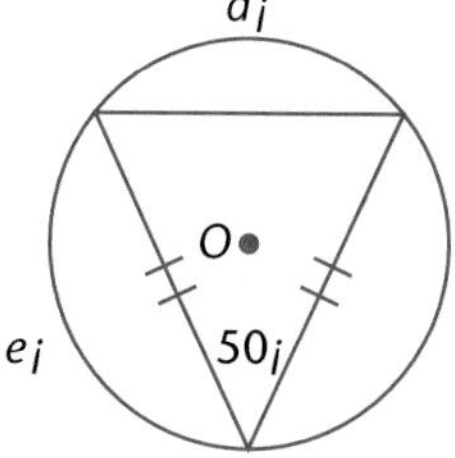

26.

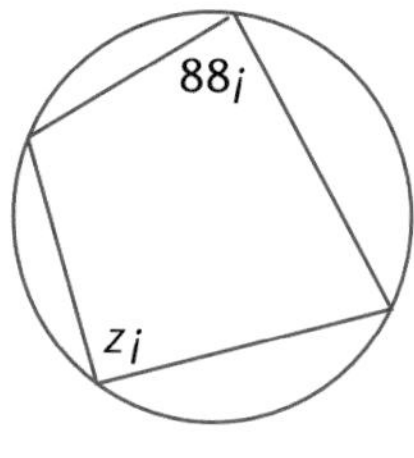

9-3 SIMILAR SOLIDS

Use with or after Part 9-3A

Find the surface area of the following solids. [9-1A, B, C]

1. prism with height 12 and right triangular bases with sides 6, 8, 10

2. prism with height 9 and regular hexagonal bases with side 6

3. pyramid with height 8 and square base with side 4

4. pyramid with height 4 and regular triangular base with side 6

5. cylinder with height 14 and radius 7

6. cone with height 8 and radius 6

7. sphere with radius 10

Use with or after Part 9-3B

Find the volume of the following solids. [9-2A, B, C, D]

8. prism with height 13 and right triangular bases with legs 8 and 12

9. prism with height 9 and regular hexagonal bases with side 6

10. pyramid with height 8 and square base with side 4

11. pyramid with height 15 and regular triangular base with side 4

12. cylinder with height 14 and radius 7

13. cone with height 10 and radius 9

14. sphere with radius 4

CHAPTER 10 TRANSFORMATIONS AND PATTERNS

10-1 PUTTING TRANSFORMATIONS TOGETHER

Use with or after Part 10-1A

The coordinates of $\triangle ABC$ are $A(0, 0)$, $B(6, 2)$ and $C(2, 4)$. All rotations are counter-clockwise. Graph $\triangle ABC$ and its image on the same coordinate axes for each transformation. [3-2B, 7-2C]

1. rotation 90° about (0, 0)

2. rotation 180° about (6, 2)

3. rotation 270° about (0, 0)

4. dilation center (0, 0), scale factor = 2

5. dilation center (0, 2), scale factor = 3

6. dilation center (2, 4), scale factor $= \frac{1}{2}$

Use with or after Part 10-1B

The coordinates of $\triangle ABC$ are $A(0, 0)$, $B(6, 2)$ and $C(2, 4)$. Graph $\triangle ABC$ and its image on the same coordinate axes for each transformation. [1-4B, 3-1D]

7. reflection over y-axis

8. reflection over x-axis

9. reflection over $y = -x$

10. translation <−10, 5>

11. translation <0, −7>

12. translation <8, 0>

Use with or after Part 10-1C

Graph each equation. [Previous course]

13. $y = x^2$

14. $y = x^2 + 1$

15. $y = x^2 - 3$

16. $y = -x^2$

17. $y = -x^2 + 2$

18. $y = -x^2 - 1$

19. $y = 2x^2$

20. $y = 4x^2$

21. $y = \left(\frac{1}{2}\right)x^2$

22. $y = (x - 1)^2$

23. $y = (x + 2)^2$

24. $y = (x + 1)^2 - 2$

10-2 CLASSIFYING PATTERNS

Use with or after Part 10-2A

Name two lowercase letters of the alphabet with the following lines of symmetry. Draw the lines of symmetry in each case. [1-4A]

1. horizontal

2. vertical

3. both horizontal and vertical

4. no line symmetry

Sketch all lines of symmetry for the each of the following regular polygons. [1-4A]

5. equilateral triangle

6. square

7. pentagon

8. hexagon

9. octagon

10. decagon

Use with or after Part 10-2B

For each of the following sets, identify the members that have rotational symmetry using a clockwise angle of rotation greater than 0° and less than 360°. [3-2A]

11. capital letters of the alphabet

12. regular n-gons, $3 \leq n \leq 6$

Determine the area of each quadrilateral, given the coordinates of its vertices. [6-2D]

13. (0, 0), (1, 1), (2, 1), (1, 2)

14. (0, 1), (1, 0), (0, −1), (−1, 0)

15. (−1, 1), (1, 1), (1, −1), (−1, −1)

16. (0, 0), (−2, −2), (−3, 0), (−2, 2)

CHAPTER 11 GEOMETRIC INEQUALITIES AND OPTIMIZATION

11-1 INDIRECT REASONING AND INEQUALITIES

Use with or after Part 11-1A

Solve each inequality. [Previous course]

1. $x + 7 < 4$ **2.** $x - 1 \geq 5$ **3.** $2x + 3 \leq 9$
4. $-x - 7 > 2$ **5.** $4x + 9 < 5$ **6.** $2 - 3x \leq 4$
7. $5 > -3x - 2$ **8.** $7 + 2x \geq 1$ **9.** $6 + 7x \leq 2 - 9x$
10. $-3x + 16 > 19 - 4x$ **11.** $9 - 2x < 5x - 12$ **12.** $4 + 3x \geq 9x - 2$

Use with or after Part 11-1B

Graph each inequality. [Previous course]

13. $y < x + 6$ **14.** $y \geq 2x - 3$ **15.** $y > -x + 2$
16. $y \leq -\left(\frac{1}{2}\right)x - 1$ **17.** $x < 5$ **18.** $y \geq -2$
19. $2x - y \leq 3$ **20.** $2y + x < -4$ **21.** $y > 2x + 2$

Use with or after Part 11-1C

Graph each system of inequalities on the same coordinate axes. [Previous course]

22. $y > x$, $y > -x$
23. $y \leq x + 4$, $y \leq -2x - 2$
24. $y \leq -\left(\frac{1}{2}\right)x + 2$, $y \geq \left(\frac{1}{2}\right)x + 2$
25. $y \geq 4x - 2$, $y \geq -\left(\frac{1}{4}\right)x$
26. $y < 3x - 1$, $y < -3x + 1$
27. $y > -2$, $x < 3$
28. $y \leq x - 3$, $y \geq -2x + 1$
29. $y > \left(\frac{1}{2}\right)x - 1$, $y < \left(\frac{1}{2}\right)x$
30. $y > 3x - 4$, $y < x + 1$

11-2 OPTIMIZATION

Use with or after Part 11-2A

Find all rectangles with the given perimeter *P*, assuming that sides have integer lengths. Then find the area of each rectangle. [5-2A]

1. $P = 12$ **2.** $P = 9$ **3.** $P = 20$ **4.** $P = 48$

Find all rectangles with the given area *A*, assuming that the sides have integer lengths. Then find the perimeter of each rectangle. [5-2A]

5. $A = 8$ **6.** $A = 12$ **7.** $A = 20$ **8.** $A = 48$

Use with or after Part 11-2B

Give all the possible integer-length dimensions of a box with the given volume *V*. Then find the surface area of each box. [9-1A, 9-2A]

9. $V = 12$ **10.** $V = 15$ **11.** $V = 20$ **12.** $V = 16$
13. $V = 27$ **14.** $V = 8$ **15.** $V = 9$ **16.** $V = 1$

CHAPTER 12 ASTRONOMY AND GEOMETRIC MODELS

12-1 USING GEOMETRY TO MODEL THE EARTH

Use with or after Part 12-1A

Each stage of the following figures is made by joining the midpoints of the sides of the previous stage. [5-3B, 7-2D]

1. $BC = 12$, find IJ.

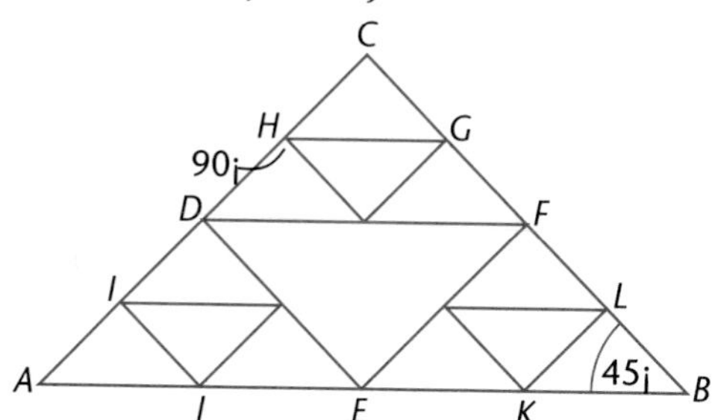

2. $AB = 12$, $CB = 6$, find PM.

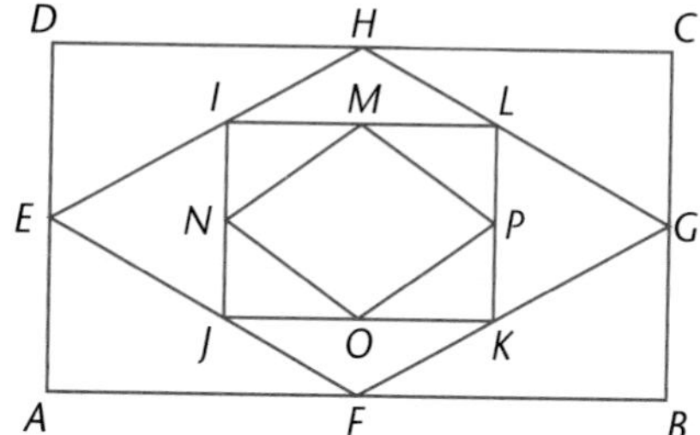

A ski slope is to be built similar to an existing one, but twice as big. Answer the following questions. [7-1C, 9-3A, B]

3. If the original slope is 100 feet high, how tall will the new one be?
4. There is 75 feet of fencing around the base of the original slope. How much fencing is needed for the new slope?
5. If 13,500 pounds of artificial snow covered the original slope, how much snow is needed for the new one?
6. If 50,000 cubic yards of dirt was used to build the original slope, how much dirt will be needed to build the new one?

A baby ant is a third as long as its mother and similar in proportions. [7-1C, 9-3A, B]

7. If the baby is 1 mm long, how long is its mother?
8. If the mother's waist is 0.3 mm, what is the baby's waist?
9. If 0.5 mm^2 of exoskeleton covers the mother's body, how much exoskeleton covers the baby's body?
10. If the baby weighs 2 mg, how much does the mother weigh?

Use with or after Part 12-1B

In the figure at right, *AB* is tangent to circle *O* at *A*. Find the circumference of circle *O*. [8-1A, 8-1B, 8-2A]

11. $OB = 10$, $AB = 8$
12. $m\angle O = 60°$, $OB = 24$
13. $m\angle B = 30°$, $AB = 24$
14. $m\angle O = 45°$, $OB = 18$
15. $OB = 15$, $AB = 12$
16. $m\angle O = 45°$, $AB = 18$
17. $m\angle B = 30°$, $AB = \sqrt{3}$
18. $m\angle O = 45°$, $OB = \sqrt{3}$

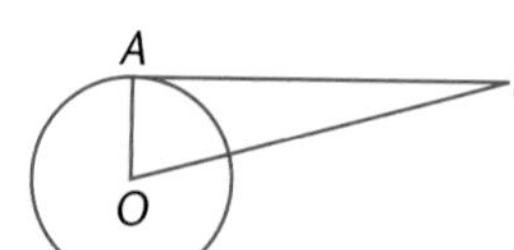

Use with or after Part 12-1C

Find the length of the arc $\widehat{AB}$ given its central angle θ and radius *r*. [8-2B]

19. $\theta = 60°, r = 10$ **20.** $\theta = 45°, r = 15$ **21.** $\theta = 75°, r = 9$
22. $\theta = 90°, r = 12$ **23.** $\theta = 80°, r = 18$ **24.** $\theta = 55°, r = 20$
25. $\theta = 25°, r = 11$ **26.** $\theta = 15°, r = 14$

12-2 EUCLIDEAN AND NON-EUCLIDEAN GEOMETRIES

Use with or after Part 12-2A

Use an indirect proof to prove each of the following. [11-1A]

1. If *ABCD* is a parallelogram, then consecutive angles are supplementary.
2. If *ABCD* is a rectangle, then the diagonals are congruent.
3. If *ABCD* is a rhombus, then the diagonals are perpendicular.
4. If *ABCD* is a parallelogram, then its diagonals bisect each other.

Use with or after Part 12-2B

Determine whether each set of numbers could represent the lengths of the sides of a triangle. [11-1C]

5. 3, 5, 7 **6.** 20, 22, 45 **7.** 15, 17, 30 **8.** 12, 13, 2
9. $5\frac{1}{2}, 9\frac{1}{2}, 15$ **10.** 14, 7, 7 **11.** 4, 5, 6 **12.** 3, 3, 3
13. 6, 12, 7 **14.** 8, 14, 5 **15.** 17, 6, 12 **16.** 3, 5, 1

The lengths of two sides of a triangle are given. Write an inequality that represents the range of values for the possible lengths of the third side. [11-1C]

17. 13, 15 **18.** 8, 11 **19.** 21, 25 **20.** 14, 18
21. 1.5, 1.5 **22.** 45, 64 **23.** 101, 102 **24.** *a*, *b*

25. Determine the perimeter of the smallest square in this figure. $AB = 12$.

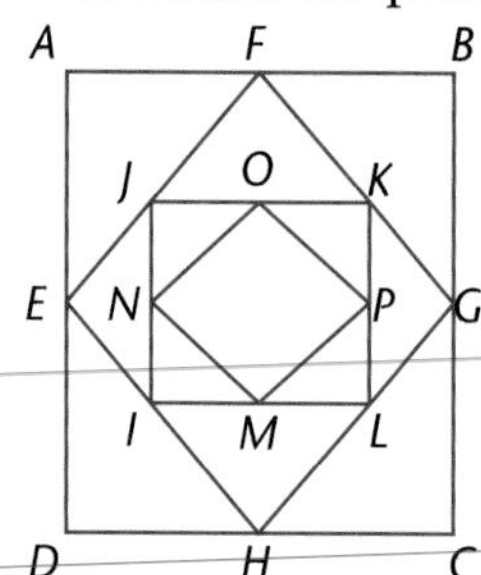

SYMBOLS

$\overleftrightarrow{AB}$	line containing points A and B
$\overline{AB}$	line segment with endpoints A and B
$\overrightarrow{AB}$	ray with endpoint A that contains B
$\overrightarrow{AB}$	vector with origin A and endpoint B
AB	length of $\overline{AB}$; distance between A and B
$\triangle ABC$	triangle with vertices A, B, and C
$\angle ABC$	angle with sides $\overrightarrow{AB}$ and $\overrightarrow{AC}$
$\angle B$	angle with vertex B
$m\angle ABC$	measure of $\angle ABC$
$^\circ$	degree(s)
$\cong$	is congruent to
$\ncong$	is not congruent to
$\perp$	is perpendicular to
$\not\perp$	is not perpendicular to
$\parallel$	is parallel to
$\nparallel$	is not parallel to
$\sim$	is similar to
$\approx$	is approximately equal to
$\leftrightarrow$	corresponds to
$p \rightarrow q$	p implies q
A'	A prime
$<$	is less than
$>$	is greater than
$\leq$	is less than or equal to
$\geq$	is greater than or equal to
$\lvert x \rvert$	absolute value of x
$\sqrt{x}$	square root of x
$\odot$	circle
$\overset{\frown}{AB}$	arc with endpoints A and B
$\overset{\frown}{ACB}$	arc with endpoints A and B and containing C
π	pi (approximately 3.14)
(a, b)	ordered pair with x-coordinate a and y-coordinate b
$<a, b>$	translation of a units horizontally and b units vertically
$\sin A$	sine of $\angle A$
$\cos A$	cosine of $\angle A$
$\tan A$	tangent of $\angle A$

FORMULAS

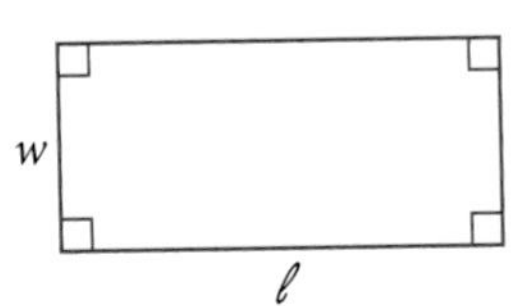 **Rectangle** Area: $A = \ell w$ Perimeter: $p = 2\ell + 2w$	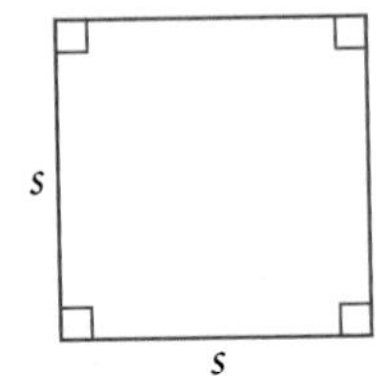 **Square** Area: $A = s^2$ Perimeter: $p = 4s$	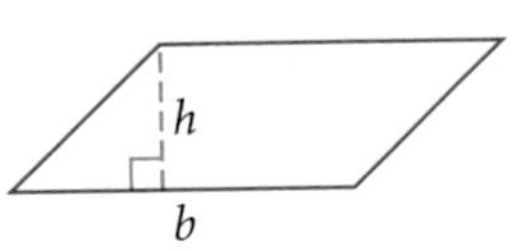 **Parallelogram** Area: $A = bh$
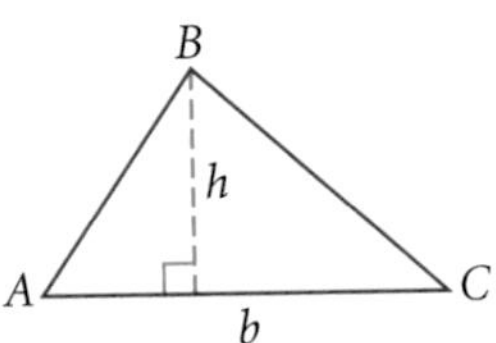 **Triangle** Area: $A = \frac{1}{2}bh$ $m\angle A + m\angle B + m\angle C = 180°$	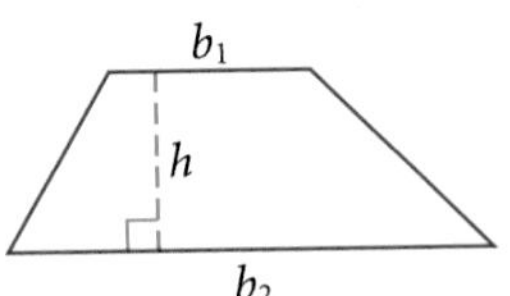 **Trapezoid** Area: $A = \frac{1}{2}h(b_1 + b_2)$	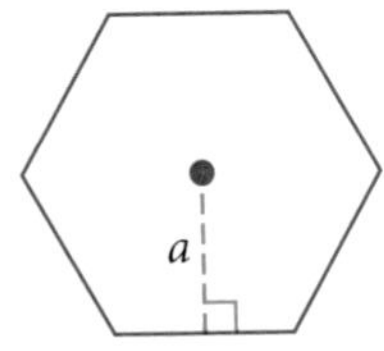 **Regular Polygon** Area: $A = \frac{1}{2}ap$
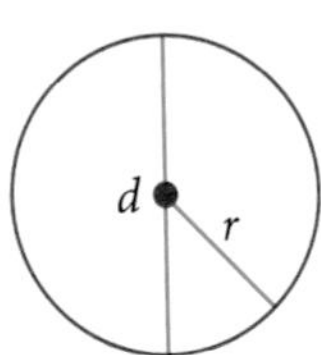 **Circle** Area: $A = \pi r^2$ Circumference: $C = \pi d = 2\pi r$	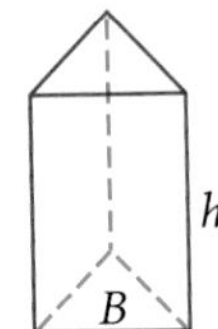 **Right Prism** Volume: $V = Bh$ Lateral Area: $LA = ph$ Surface Area: $SA = ph + 2B$	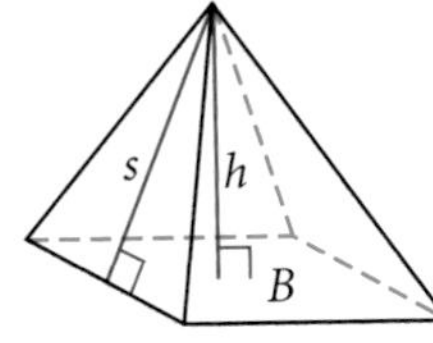 **Regular Pyramid** Volume: $V = \frac{1}{3}Bh$ Lateral Area: $LA = \frac{1}{2}ps$ Surface Area: $SA = \frac{1}{2}ps + B$
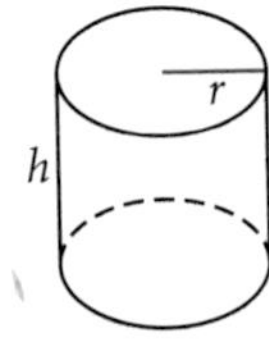 **Right Cylinder** Volume: $V = \pi r^2 h$ Lateral Area: $LA = 2\pi rh$ Surface Area: $SA = 2\pi rh + 2\pi r^2$	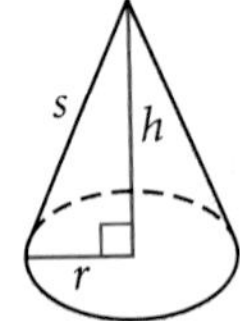 **Right Cone** Volume: $V = \frac{1}{3}\pi r^2 h$ Lateral Area: $LA = \pi rs$ Surface Area: $SA = \pi rs + \pi r^2$	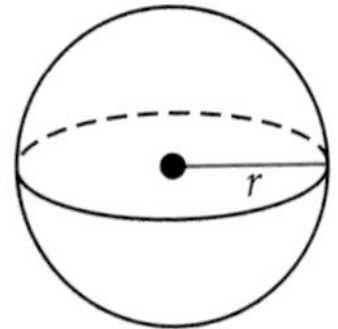 **Sphere** Volume: $V = \frac{4}{3}\pi r^3$ Surface Area: $SA = 4\pi r^2$

POSTULATES AND THEOREMS

POSTULATES

CHAPTER 2

Points-Existence Postulate
Space contains at least four noncoplanar points. Every plane contains at least three noncollinear points. Every line contains at least two points. [p. 116]

Straight-Line Postulate
Two points are contained in one and only one line. (Two points determine a line.) [p. 116]

Plane Postulate
Three noncollinear points are contained in one and only one plane. (Three noncollinear points determine a plane.) [p. 116]

Flat-Plane Postulate
If two points are in a plane, then the line containing the points is in the same plane. [p. 116]

Plane-Intersection Postulate
If two planes intersect, then their intersection is a line. [p. 116]

Ruler Postulate
The points on a line can be paired with the real numbers so that: one of the points has coordinate 0 and another has coordinate 1; for any choice for coordinates 0 and 1 and for each real number x, there is exactly one point on the line with coordinate x; the distance between any two points with coordinates x and y is the absolute value of the difference of their coordinates, $|x - y|$. [p. 120]

Segment-Addition Postulate
Point B is between points A and C if and only if A, B, and C are collinear and $AB + BC = AC$. [p. 121]

Parallel Postulate
Through a given point P not on a line ℓ, exactly one line may be drawn parallel to line ℓ. [p. 143]

CHAPTER 3

Protractor Postulate
Given any line $\overleftrightarrow{AB}$ in a plane with point O between A and B; $\overrightarrow{OA}$, $\overrightarrow{OB}$, and all the rays from point O on one side of line $\overleftrightarrow{AB}$ can be matched one-to-one with the real numbers from 0 through 180 so that: ray $\overrightarrow{OA}$ is matched with 0; ray $\overrightarrow{OB}$ is matched with 180; if ray $\overrightarrow{OR}$ is matched with r and $\overrightarrow{OS}$ is matched with s, then $m\angle ROS = |r - s| = |s - r|$. [p. 192]

Angle-Addition Postulate
If F is in the interior of $\angle EHG$, then $m\angle EHF + m\angle FHG = m\angle EHG$. [p. 194]

Linear-Pair Postulate
The angles in a linear pair are supplementary. [p. 203]

If parallel lines are cut by a transversal, then the alternate interior angles are congruent. [p. 222]

If two lines are cut by a transversal so that a pair of alternate interior angles are congruent, then the lines are parallel. [p. 228]

CHAPTER 4

Side-Side-Side Congruence Postulate (SSS)
If each of the three sides of one triangle are congruent to the sides of another triangle, then the two triangles are congruent. [p. 262]

Side-Angle-Side Congruence Postulate (SAS)
If two sides and the included angle of one triangle are congruent to two sides and the included angle of another triangle, then the two triangles are congruent. [p. 262]

Angle-Side-Angle Congruence Postulate (ASA)

If two angles and the included side of one triangle are congruent to two angles and the included side of another triangle, then the two triangles are congruent. [p. 262]

Side-Angle-Angle Congruence Postulate (SAA)

If two angles and a side opposite one of them in one triangle are congruent to the corresponding parts of another triangle, then the two triangles are congruent. [p. 262]

CHAPTER 5

Area Postulates

For every polygonal region, there is a positive number called the area of the region.

If two polygonal regions are congruent, then they have equal areas. [p. 323]

Area-Addition Postulate

The area of a polygonal region is the sum of the areas of all of its nonoverlapping parts. [p. 323]

The area of a rectangle is the product of its length ℓ and width w. $A = \ell w$ [p. 348]

CHAPTER 7

Angle-Angle (AA) Similarity Postulate

If two angles of one triangle are congruent to two angles of another triangle, then the triangles are similar. [p. 487]

CHAPTER 9

Cavalieri's Principle

Suppose M and N are two solids. If every plane that intersects both M and N at the same height cuts off equal cross-sectional areas on each, then the solids have the same volume. [p. 626]

CHAPTER 12

Riemann's Parallel Postulate

Through a given point P not on a line ℓ, there is *no* line parallel to line ℓ. [p. 777]

THEOREMS AND IMPORTANT RESULTS

CHAPTER 1

The distance between two points on a number line with coordinates *a* and *b* is the absolute value of the difference of their coordinates. [p. 41]

The Distance Formula

The distance between two points on a coordinate plane, whose coordinates are (x_1, y_1) and (x_2, y_2), is $D = \sqrt{(x_1 - x_2)^2 + (y_1 - y_2)^2}$. [p. 41]

The shortest segment from a point not on a line to the line is the perpendicular segment. [p. 48]

Reflections preserve any property of a figure having to do with size. This includes lengths of sides, measures of angles, area, and perimeter. Reflections reverse the orientation of a figure. [p. 74]

CHAPTER 2

If M is the midpoint of $\overline{AB}$, then $AM = \frac{1}{2}AB$. [p. 122]

Midpoint Formula

On a coordinate plane, the midpoint of the segment with endpoints (x_1, y_2) and (x_2, y_2) has coordinates $\left(\frac{x_1, + x_2}{2}, \frac{y_1 + y_2}{2}\right)$. [p. 124]

CHAPTER 3

For vector sums, the following is true: $\overrightarrow{XY} + \overrightarrow{YZ} = \overrightarrow{XZ}$. [p. 167]

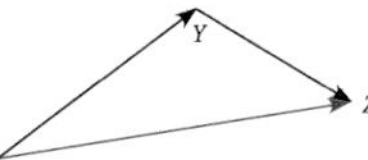

Translations change only the location of a figure. Translations preserve any property that has to do with the size of a figure, including: the lengths of its sides, the measures of its angles, and the area and perimeter of the figure. Translations also preserve the orientation of the figure. [p. 173]

Rotations preserve any property that has to do with the size of a figure, including: the lengths of its sides, the measures of its angles, and the area and perimeter of the figure. Rotations also preserve the orientation of the figure. [p. 186]

Supplements of congruent angles (or of the same angle) are congruent. [p. 204]

Complements of congruent angles (or of the same angle) are congruent. [p. 204]

All right angles are congruent. [p. 205]

Vertical angles are congruent. [p. 209]

Two perpendicular lines form four right angles. [p. 209]

If parallel lines are cut by a transversal, then the corresponding angles are congruent. [p. 222]

If parallel lines are cut by a transversal, then the alternate exterior angles are congruent. [p. 222]

If parallel lines are cut by a transversal, then the same-side interior angles are supplementary. [p. 222]

If two lines are cut by a transversal so that a pair of corresponding angles are congruent, then the lines are parallel. [p. 228]

If two lines are cut by a transversal so that a pair of alternate exterior angles are congruent, then the lines are parallel. [p. 228]

If two lines are cut by a transversal so that a pair of same-side interior angles are supplementary, then the lines are parallel. [p. 228]

CHAPTER 4

Triangle Angle-Sum Theorem

The sum of the measures of the angles of a triangle is 180°. [p. 245]

Exterior Angle Theorem

The measure of an exterior angle of a triangle is equal to the sum of the measures of its remote interior angles. [p. 249]

Exterior Angle Inequality Theorem

The measure of an exterior angle of a triangle is greater than the measure of either of its remote interior angles. [p. 249]

Each angle of an equilateral triangle measures 60°. [p. 249]

The acute angles of a right triangle are complementary. [p. 249]

Properties of Congruence

- Reflexive Property $\overline{AB} \cong \overline{AB}$
- Symmetric Property If $\angle 1 \cong \angle 2$, then $\angle 2 \cong \angle 1$.
- Transitive Property If $\overline{WX} \cong \overline{XY}$ and $\overline{XY} \cong \overline{YZ}$, then $\overline{WX} \cong \overline{YZ}$. [p. 276]

Isosceles Triangle Theorem

If two sides of a triangle are congruent, then the angles opposite those sides are congruent. [p. 287]

Converse of the Isosceles Triangle Theorem

If two angles of a triangle are congruent, then the sides opposite those angles are congruent. [p. 287]

Unique Bisector Theorems

Every segment has a unique midpoint.

Every angle has a unique ray that bisects it. [p. 287]

Leg-Leg Congruence Theorem (LL)

If the legs of a right triangle are congruent to the legs of another right triangle, then the two triangles are congruent. [p. 292]

Hypotenuse-Acute Angle Congruence Theorem (HA)

If the hypotenuse and an acute angle of one right triangle are congruent to the hypotenuse and an acute angle of another right triangle, then the two triangles are congruent. [p. 293]

Leg-Acute Angle Congruence Theorem (LA)

If one leg and one acute angle of a right triangle are congruent to the corresponding leg and acute angle of another right triangle, then the two triangles are congruent. [p. 293]

Hypotenuse-Leg Congruence Theorem (HL)

If the hypotenuse and a leg of one right triangle are congruent to the hypotenuse and a leg of another right triangle, then the two triangles are congruent. [p. 294]

A point is on the perpendicular bisector of a segment if and only if it is equidistant from the endpoints of the segment. [p. 301]

A point is on the angle bisector of an angle if and only if it is equidistant from the sides of the angle. [p. 301]

The centroid of a triangle is two-thirds the distance from each vertex to the midpoint of the opposite side. [p. 307]

CHAPTER 5

The Quadratic Formula

The solutions to the equation $ax^2 + bx + c = 0$ (where $a \neq 0$) are given by $x = \frac{-b \pm \sqrt{b^2 - 4ac}}{2a}$. [p. 333]

The area of a square is the square of its side length s. $A = s^2$ [p. 348]

The area of a triangle is half the product of its base length b and corresponding height h. $A = \frac{1}{2}bh$ [p. 348]

The area of a parallelogram is the product of its base length b and height h. $A = bh$ [p. 348]

The area of a trapezoid is the product of half the sum of the bases, b_1 and b_2, and the height, h. $A = \frac{b_1 + b_2}{2}h$ [p. 354]

Heron's Formula

The area of any triangle with side lengths a, b, and c, is $A = \sqrt{s(s-a)(s-b)(s-c)}$ where s is the semiperimeter (half the perimeter) of the triangle. [p. 355]

Pythagorean Theorem

In a right triangle, the square of the length of the hypotenuse is equal to the sum of the squares of the lengths of the legs. [p. 366]

45°-45°-90° Triangle Theorem

In a 45°-45°-90° triangle, the hypotenuse is $\sqrt{2}$ times as long as either leg. The ratios of the side lengths can be written ℓ-ℓ-$\ell\sqrt{2}$. [p. 372]

30°-60°-90° Triangle Theorem

In a 30°-60°-90° triangle, the hypotenuse is twice as long as the shorter leg (the leg opposite the 30° angle), and the longer leg (opposite the 60° angle) is

$\sqrt{3}$ times as long as the shorter leg. The ratios of the side lengths can be written ℓ-$\ell\sqrt{3}$-2ℓ. [p. 373]

Equation of a Circle

The circle with radius r and center (0, 0) has the equation $x^2 + y^2 = r^2$. [p. 377]

Converse of the Pythagorean Theorem

If the sum of the squares of the lengths of two sides of a triangle equals the square of the length of the third side, then the triangle is a right triangle and the longest side is the hypotenuse. [p. 381]

Pythagorean Inequality Theorems

If the sum of the squares of the lengths of the shorter two sides of a triangle is greater than the square of the length of the longest side, then the triangle is acute.

If the sum of the squares of the lengths of the shorter two sides of a triangle is less than the square of the length of the longest side, then the triangle is obtuse. [p. 382]

CHAPTER 6

Angle-Sum Theorem for Quadrilaterals

The sum of the measures of the interior angles of a convex quadrilateral is 360°. [p. 399]

Angle-Sum Theorem for Polygons

The sum of the measures of the interior angles of a convex polygon with n sides is given by $S = (n - 2)180°$. [p. 405]

Exterior Angle Theorem for Polygons

The sum of the measures of the exterior angles of a convex polygon (one at each vertex) is 360°. [p. 405]

Euler's Formula

For any polyhedron, the relationship between the number of faces (F), vertices (V), and edges (E) is $F + V - E = 2$. [p. 411]

The opposite angles of a parallelogram are congruent. [p. 420]

The opposite sides of a parallelogram are congruent. [p. 420]

The consecutive angles of a parallelogram are supplementary. [p. 420]

The diagonals of a parallelogram bisect each other. [p. 420]

If both pairs of opposite angles of a quadrilateral are congruent, then the quadrilateral is a parallelogram. [p. 425]

If both pairs of opposite sides of a quadrilateral are congruent, then the quadrilateral is a parallelogram. [p. 425]

If the consecutive angles of a quadrilateral are supplementary, then the quadrilateral is a parallelogram. [p. 425]

If the diagonals of a quadrilateral bisect each other, then the quadrilateral is a parallelogram. [p. 425]

Theorems About Diagonals of Special Parallelograms

A parallelogram is a rhombus if and only if its diagonals are perpendicular.

A parallelogram is a rectangle if and only if its diagonals are congruent.

A parallelogram is a square if and only if its diagonals are both perpendicular and congruent. [p. 429]

Theorems About Regular Polygons

The area of a regular polygon is one-half the product of its perimeter and its apothem. $A = \frac{1}{2}ap$

Each angle of a regular n-gon measures $\frac{(n-2)180°}{n}$.

Each exterior angle of a regular n-gon measures $\frac{360°}{n}$. [p. 444]

CHAPTER 7

The ratio of the perimeters of two similar polygons is equal to their similarity ratio. [p. 475]

The ratio of the areas of two similar polygons is equal to the square of their similarity ratio. [p. 475]

The Golden Ratio

In a golden rectangle, the ratio of the length ℓ to the width w is the golden ratio $\frac{1+\sqrt{5}}{2}$ ($\approx$1.618). [p. 480]

SAS Similarity Theorem

If an angle of one triangle is congruent to an angle of another triangle and the lengths of the sides that include the angles are proportional, then the triangles are similar. [p. 492]

SSS Similarity Theorem

If the lengths of three sides of one triangle are proportional to the lengths of three sides of another triangle, then the triangles are similar. [p. 494]

Dilations change the size of a figure (unless $k = 1$). Dilations preserve: the measures of the angles in a figure, the orientation of a figure, the shape of a figure. [p. 498]

Midsegment Theorem for Triangles

A segment whose endpoints are the midpoints of two sides of a triangle is parallel to the third side and half its length. [p. 502]

Side-Splitting Theorem

If a line parallel to a side of a triangle intersects the other two sides, then it divides those sides proportionally. [p. 506]

CHAPTER 8

Theorems About Tangents to a Circle

If a line is tangent to a circle, then it is perpendicular to a radius at the point of tangency.

If a line coplanar to a circle is perpendicular to a radius of a circle at a point on the circle, then the line is tangent to the circle.

Two tangent segments to a circle from the same exterior point are congruent. [p. 546]

The circumference of a circle is the product of π and its diameter, d. $C = \pi d$ [p. 552]

The circumference of a circle is twice the product of π and its radius, r. $C = 2\pi r$ [p. 552]

The area of a circle is the product of π and the square of its radius, r. $A = \pi r^2$ [p. 557]

Circle Proportions

In $\odot Y$, with central angle $\angle XYZ$, all of the following ratios are equal. $\frac{m\angle XYZ}{360°} = \frac{m\widehat{XZ}}{360°} = \frac{\text{length of } \widehat{XZ}}{\text{circumference of } \odot Y} = \frac{\text{area of sector } XYZ}{\text{area of } \odot Y}$ [p. 572]

The perpendicular bisector of a chord contains the center of the circle. [p. 576]

If a radius of a circle bisects a chord of the circle that is not a diameter, then it is perpendicular to the chord. [p. 576]

If a radius of a circle is perpendicular to a chord of the circle, then it bisects the chord. [p. 576]

In a circle (or in congruent circles), minor arcs are congruent if and only if they have congruent chords. [p. 577]

Two chords of a circle are congruent if and only if they are equidistant from the center. [p. 582]

Inscribed Angle Theorem

The measure of an inscribed angle is half the measure of its intercepted arc. [p. 585]

If two inscribed angles intercept the same arc, then they are congruent. [p. 585]

An inscribed angle that intercepts a semicircle is a right angle. [p. 585]

Tangent-Secant Angle Theorem

The measure of a tangent-secant angle is one-half the difference of the measures of its two intercepted arcs. [p. 590]

Tangent-Tangent Angle Theorem

The measure of a tangent-tangent angle is one-half the difference of the measures of its two intercepted arcs. [p. 590]

Secant-Secant Angle Theorem

The measure of a secant-secant angle is one-half the difference of the measures of its two intercepted arcs. [p. 592]

CHAPTER 9

The lateral area of a right prism is the product of the perimeter of its base and the height of the prism. $LA = ph$ [p. 606]

The surface area of a right prism is the sum of its lateral area and the areas of its bases. $SA = LA + 2B = ph + 2B$ [p. 606]

The lateral area of a regular pyramid is one-half the product of the perimeter of its base and the slant height of the pyramid. $LA = \frac{1}{2}ps$ [p. 611]

The surface area of a regular pyramid is the sum of its lateral area and the area of its base. $SA = LA + B = \frac{1}{2}ps + B$ [p. 611]

Theorems About Cylinders

The lateral area of a right cylinder is the product of the circumference of its base and the height of the cylinder. $LA = 2\pi rh$

The surface area of a right cylinder is the sum of its lateral area and the areas of its bases. $SA = LA + 2B = 2\pi rh + 2\pi r^2$ [p. 616]

Theorems About Cones

The lateral area of a right cone is one-half the product of the circumference of its base and the slant height of the cone. $LA = \frac{1}{2}2\pi rs = \pi rs$

The surface area of a right cone is the sum of its lateral area and the area of its base. $SA = LA + B = \pi rs + \pi r^2$ [p. 616]

The volume of a right rectangular prism is the product of its length, width, and height. $V = \ell wh$ [p. 627]

The volume of any prism is the product of the area of its base and its height. $V = Bh$ [p. 627]

The volume of a pyramid is one-third the product of its base area and its height. $V = \frac{1}{3}Bh$ [p. 632]

The volume of a cylinder is the product of its base area and its height. $V = Bh = \pi r^2 h$ [p. 636]

The volume of a cone is one-third the product of its base area and its height. $V = \frac{1}{3}Bh = \frac{1}{3}\pi r^2 h$ [p. 636]

The surface area of a sphere is 4π times the square of its radius. $SA = 4\pi r^2$ [p. 640]

The volume of a sphere is four-thirds the product of π and the cube of its radius. $V = \frac{4}{3}\pi r^3$ [p. 640]

The ratio of the surface areas of two similar solids is the square of their similarity ratio. [p. 650]

The ratio of the volumes of two similar solids is the cube of their similarity ratio. [p. 654]

CHAPTER 10

Translations, reflections, and rotations are isometries. [p. 669]

CHAPTER 11

If two sides of a triangle have unequal lengths, then the measure of the angle opposite the longer side is greater than the measure of the angle opposite the shorter side. [p. 716]

If two angles of a triangle have unequal measures, then the side opposite the larger angle is longer than the side opposite the smaller angle. [p. 716]

Triangle Inequality Theorem

The sum of the lengths of any two sides of a triangle is greater than the length of the third side. [p. 721]

CHAPTER 12

In Riemannian geometry, the sum of the measures of the angles in a triangle is greater than 180°. [p. 779]

In Riemannian geometry, if a circle has radius r, its circumference is less than $2\pi r$ and its area is less than πr^2. [p. 779]

In Riemannian geometry, any two coplanar lines intersect. [p. 779]

GLOSSARY

acute angle

An angle whose measure is less than 90°. [p. 156]

acute triangle

A triangle with three acute angles. [p. 244]

adjacent interior angle

∠1 is the adjacent interior angle to exterior ∠4. [p. 248]

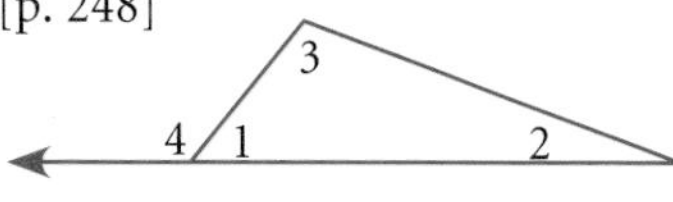

alternate exterior angles

When a transversal t cuts lines p and q as shown, the pairs of alternate exterior angles are: ∠1 and ∠7, ∠2 and ∠8. [p. 216]

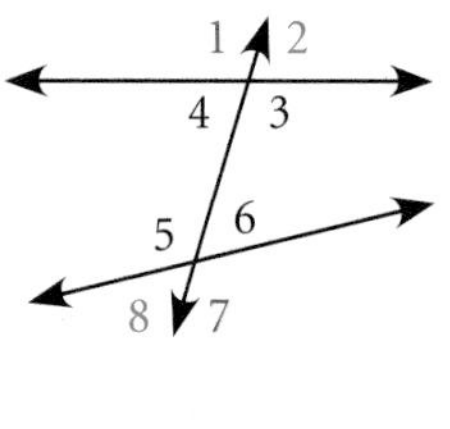

alternate interior angles

When a transversal t cuts lines p and q as shown, the pairs of alternate interior angles are: ∠4 and ∠6, ∠3 and ∠5. [p. 216]

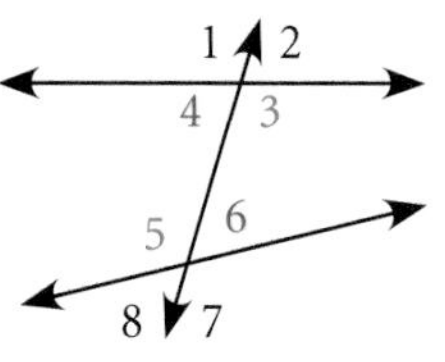

altitude

In a triangle: the perpendicular segment from a vertex to the line containing the opposite side; in a prism or cylinder: a segment (joining the planes of the bases) that is perpendicular to them; in a pyramid or cone: the perpendicular segment from the vertex to the base. [pp. 305, 604, 610, 614, 615]

angle

Two rays (that are not collinear) with a common endpoint. [p. 45]

angle bisector

$\overrightarrow{LM}$ is the angle bisector of $\angle NLP$ if and only if M is in the interior of $\angle NLP$ and $\angle NLM \cong \angle MLP$. [p. 208]

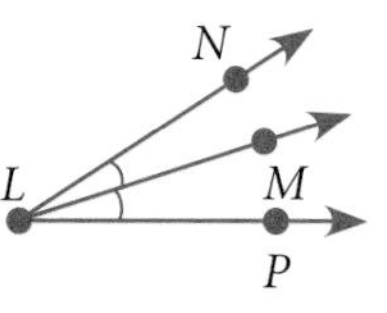

angle of depression

The angle formed by a horizontal line and a line of sight downward from horizontal. The vertex is the eye of the viewer. [p. 518]

angle of elevation

The angle formed by a horizontal line and a line of sight upward from horizontal. The vertex is the eye of the viewer. [p. 518]

angle of rotation

The measure, in degrees, of how far a point, other than the center of rotation, is turned by a rotation. [p. 180]

apothem of a regular polygon

The perpendicular segment (or length of the segment) from the center of the polygon to a side. [p. 442]

arc

Two points and a continuous part of a circle between the points. [p. 565]

area

The number of square units contained in a plane region. [p. 322]

auxiliary line

A line (or part of a line) added to a figure. [p. 288]

axis of a cone

The segment from the vertex to the center of the base. [p. 615]

axis of a cylinder

The segment that joins the centers of the bases. [p. 614]

base angle
In an isosceles triangle, an angle formed by the base and another side. [p. 244]

base of an isosceles triangle
The side opposite the vertex angle. [p. 244]

bases of a prism
Two congruent polygonal faces that lie in parallel planes, whose corresponding vertices are connected by the lateral edges of the prism. [p. 604]

bases of a trapezoid
The parallel sides of the trapezoid. [p. 352]

bearing
Direction given as a three-digit number, representing the number of degrees in a clockwise rotation from due north. [p. 161]

biconditional
A statement that combines a conditional and its converse, when both are true, by using the connector phrase "if and only if." [p. 110]

binomial
A polynomial with two terms. [p. 326]

bisect
Cut into two congruent halves. [p. 68]

center of a circle
The point equidistant from all points of the circle. [p. 540]

center of a regular polygon
The point of intersection of the perpendicular bisectors of the sides. [p. 442]

center of dilation
The unique point which is mapped to itself by a dilation with a nonzero scale factor. [p. 497]

center of rotation
The point about which a rotation turns a set of points. [p. 180]

central angle
An angle whose vertex is the center of a circle is a central angle of the circle. [p. 565]

centroid
Center of balance (or center of gravity). In a triangle, the point of concurrency of the medians. [p. 306]

chord
A line segment that joins two points on a circle. [p. 575]

circle
The locus of points in a plane that are equidistant from a given point. [p. 540]

circumference
The distance around a circle. [p. 189]

circumscribed circle
A circle on which every vertex of a polygon lies. [p. 541]

circumscribed polygon
A polygon whose sides are each tangent to another figure. [p. 541]

collinear
On the same line. [p. 21]

complementary angles
A pair of angles whose measures add up to 90°. [p. 201]

composition of transformations
Two or more transformations performed on a figure, one after another. [p. 673]

concave polygon
A polygon in which a diagonal (excluding the endpoints) lies in the exterior of the polygon. [p. 398]

concentric circles
Two coplanar circles with the same center. [p. 540]

conclusion
The *then* part of a conditional statement. [p. 88]

concurrent lines
Three or more coplanar lines that intersect in the same point. [p. 306]

conditional statement

A statement that can be written in if-then form. [p. 88]

cone

A space figure with a vertex and a circular base. [p. 615]

congruence correspondence

A way of pairing the vertices of two geometric figures so that all pairs of corresponding parts are congruent. [p. 257]

congruent

Having the same shape and size. [p. 52]

congruent angles

Angles with the same measure. [p. 52]

congruent arcs

Arcs in the same circle (or in congruent circles) that have the same measure. [p. 566]

conjecture

A conclusion based on observation. [p. 22]

contrapositive

The resulting statement when the hypothesis and conclusion of a conditional are both negated, then interchanged. [p. 94]

converse

The resulting statement when the hypothesis and conclusion of a conditional are interchanged. [p. 94]

convex polygon

A polygon in which each diagonal (except its endpoints) is in the interior of the polygon. [p. 402]

coordinate plane

The plane determined by two axes, typically the x-axis and the y-axis. [p. 11]

coplanar points

Points that lie in the same plane. [p. 109]

correspondence

A way of pairing the vertices of two geometric figures. [p. 257]

corresponding angles

When a transversal t cuts lines p and q as shown, the pairs of corresponding angles are: $\angle 1$ and $\angle 5$, $\angle 2$ and $\angle 6$, $\angle 3$ and $\angle 7$, $\angle 4$ and $\angle 8$. [p. 216]

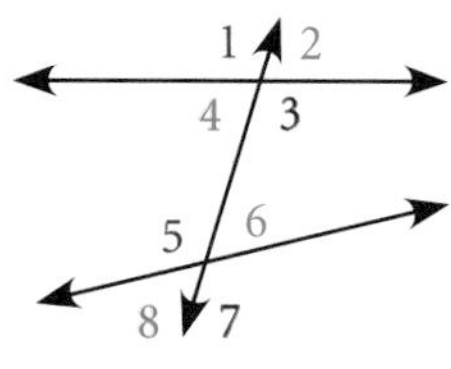

cosine of $\angle A$

For acute $\angle A$ in a right triangle, the ratio of the length of the adjacent leg to the length of the hypotenuse. [p. 512]

counterexample

An example that shows a statement to be false. [p. 25]

cross section

The figure formed by the intersection of a solid and a plane. [p. 400]

cube

A hexahedron with square faces. [p. 8]

cylinder

A space figure having congruent circular bases in a pair of parallel planes. [p. 614]

deductive reasoning

A process where conclusions are drawn from given information by using rules of logic. [p. 31]

degree

A unit used to measure the size of an angle. [p. 46]

diagonal of a polygon

A line segment whose endpoints are any two nonconsecutive vertices of the polygon. [p. 402]

diameter of a circle

A segment, or the length of a segment, that contains the center of the circle and has endpoints on the circle. [p. 540]

dilation

A transformation of a plane that, for a scale factor $k > 0$, maps one point C, the center of dilation, to itself and maps every other point P to a point P' on $\overrightarrow{CP}$ so that $CP' = k(CP)$. [p. 497]

direction of a vector

The degrees of counterclockwise rotation from horizontal of the vector about its origin. [p. 166]

distance from a point to a line

The length of the perpendicular segment from the point to the line. [p. 68]

edge of a polyhedron

A segment that is the intersection of two faces of the polyhedron. [p. 410]

endpoint of a vector

Point B is the endpoint of $\overrightarrow{AB}$. [p. 165]

equal vectors

Vectors with the same direction and length. [p. 166]

equiangular triangle

A triangle whose angles all have the same measure. [p. 244]

equidistant

Having the same distance from a common object. [p. 68]

equilateral triangle

A triangle with three congruent sides. [p. 243]

exterior angle

An angle that forms a linear pair with an interior angle of a polygon. $\angle 4$ is an exterior angle. [p. 247]

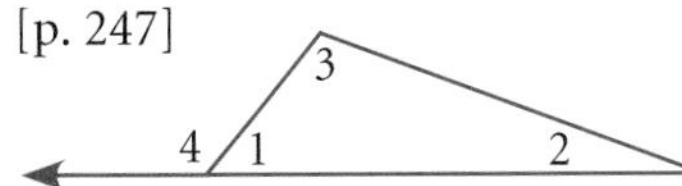

face of a polyhedron

One of the polygons that forms the polyhedron. [p. 410]

fractal

A pattern that is self-similar. [p. 750]

frieze pattern

Repeated translations of a pattern along a line. [p. 688]

function

A relationship between two quantities where the value of one quantity is uniquely determined by the value of the other quantity. [p. 679]

geometric mean

x is the geometric mean between a and b if $\frac{a}{x} = \frac{x}{b}$ and a, b, and x are positive. [p. 489]

geometric probability

The probability of an event as determined by comparing the areas (or perimeters, angle measures, etc.) of the successful regions to the total area of the figure. [p. 338]

glide reflection

A pattern defined by repeating a translation followed by a reflection. [p. 174]

glide-reflection symmetry

The property that a figure coincides with itself after undergoing a translation and a reflection. [p. 688]

golden ratio

The ratio, $\frac{1 + \sqrt{5}}{2}$ (≈ 1.618), of the length to the width of a golden rectangle. [p. 480]

golden rectangle

Rectangle $ACDF$ is a golden rectangle if and only if, when $ABEF$ is a square, rectangle $CDEB$ is similar to rectangle $ACDF$. [p. 478]

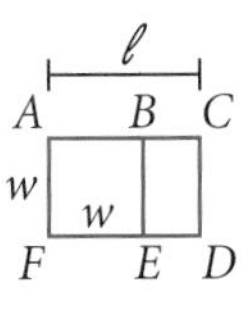

great circle

A circle on a sphere whose center is the center of the sphere. [p. 546]

height

The length of an altitude. [p. 604]

hexagon

A polygon with six sides. [p. 403]

hexahedron
A polyhedron with six faces. [p. 410]

hypotenuse
The side of a right triangle that is opposite the right angle. [p. 244]

hypothesis
The *if* part of a conditional statement. [p. 88]

image
The figure resulting from a transformation. [p. 67]

indirect reasoning
Proving that a statement is true by proving that it cannot be false. [p. 710]

inductive reasoning
Making a conjecture by looking at examples and recognizing a pattern. [p. 22]

inscribed angle
An angle with its vertex on a circle and sides that contain chords of the circle. [p. 584]

inscribed circle
A circle that is tangent to every side of a polygon is inscribed in the polygon. [p. 541]

inscribed polygon
A polygon whose vertices all lie on another figure, the figure in which the polygon is inscribed. [p. 541]

intersection
The set of points that two geometric figures have in common. [p. 20]

inverse
The resulting statement when the hypothesis and conclusion of a conditional are both negated. [p. 94]

isometry
A transformation that preserves distance. [p. 668]

isosceles trapezoid
A trapezoid with congruent legs. [p. 421]

isosceles triangle
A triangle with at least two congruent sides. [p. 243]

kite
A quadrilateral with two distinct pairs of adjacent, congruent sides. [p. 355]

lateral area
The sum of the areas of the lateral faces. [p. 605]

lateral edge
A segment joining the vertex of a pyramid or prism and any vertex of its base. [pp. 604, 610]

lateral face
For a prism: one of the parallelogram-shaped faces that connect the bases; for a pyramid: a triangular face whose vertices are the vertex of the pyramid and any two consecutive vertices of its base. [pp. 604, 610]

legs of a right triangle
The sides that form the right angle. [p. 244]

legs of a trapezoid
The nonparallel sides of the trapezoid. [p. 352]

legs of an isosceles triangle
A pair of congruent sides. [p. 244]

length of a segment
The distance between the coordinates of its endpoints on a number line. [p. 40]

length of a vector
Distance between the origin and endpoint of the vector. [p. 166]

line of reflection
The line over which a pre-image is reflected to produce its image. [p. 67]

line of symmetry
A line that divides a figure into two mirror-image halves. [p. 62]

line segment

A part of a line consisting of two endpoints and all the points between these points. [p. 20]

line symmetry

The property that a line separates a figure into two mirror-image halves. [p. 62]

linear pair

Two angles, $\angle ABD$ and $\angle DBC$, form a linear pair if and only if A, B, and C are collinear and D is not on $\overleftrightarrow{AC}$. [p. 202]

locus

The set of all the points that satisfy a given condition. [p. 299]

major arc

An arc whose measure is greater than 180°. [p. 565]

mathematical model

A representation of something in the real world, using geometry, algebra, or other mathematical tools. [p. 7]

median of a triangle

A segment whose endpoints are a vertex and the midpoint of the opposite side. [p. 305]

midpoint

Point M is the midpoint of $\overline{AB}$ if and only if it divides $\overline{AB}$ into two congruent segments, $\overline{AM}$ and $\overline{MB}$. [p. 110]

midsegment of a trapezoid

The segment that joins the midpoints of the legs. [p. 438]

midsegment of a triangle

A segment whose endpoints are the midpoints of two of its sides. [p. 501]

minor arc

An arc whose measure is less than 180°. [p. 565]

monomial

A polynomial with one term. [p. 326]

net

A pattern that can be cut out and folded up into a three-dimensional figure. [p. 7]

non-Euclidean geometry

A geometry in which the Parallel Postulate is not true. [p. 777]

oblique

A prism, pyramid, cylinder, or cone that is not a right prism, pyramid, cylinder, or cone. [pp. 604, 610, 614, 615]

obtuse angle

An angle whose measure is greater than 90° and less than 180°. [p. 156]

obtuse triangle

A triangle with one obtuse angle. [p. 244]

octagon

A polygon with eight sides. [p. 403]

opposite rays

If point M is between X and Y on line $\overleftrightarrow{XY}$, the rays $\overrightarrow{MX}$ and $\overrightarrow{MY}$ are opposite rays. [p. 157]

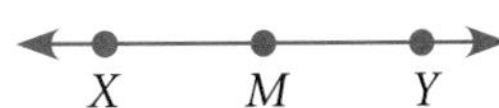

opposite vectors

Vectors with the same length and opposite directions. [p. 169]

ordered pair

A pair of numbers denoting the location of a point on the coordinate plane. [p. 11]

origin

The point of intersection of the axes of the coordinate plane, having coordinates (0, 0). [p. 11]

origin of a vector

Point A is the origin of $\overrightarrow{AB}$. [p. 165]

orthogonal or orthographic view
A view of the top, front, back, left side, or right side of an object. [p. 135]

parallel lines
Coplanar lines that do not intersect. [p. 141]

parallelogram
A quadrilateral with two pairs of parallel sides. [p. 346]

pentagon
A polygon with five sides. [p. 403]

perimeter
The distance around a figure. [p. 323]

perpendicular bisector
A line, segment, or ray that is perpendicular to a segment and divides that segment into two congruent segments. [p. 68]

perpendicular lines
Two lines that intersect at right angles. [p. 47]

pi (π)
The ratio of the circumference of a circle to its diameter. [p. 551]

Platonic solid
Any one of the five known convex regular polyhedrons. [p. 448]

point of concurrency
The point of intersection of concurrent lines. [p. 306]

point symmetry
The property that a figure will coincide with itself after some rotation of 180°. [p. 181]

polygon
A plane figure whose sides are three or more coplanar segments that intersect only at their endpoints (the vertices). Consecutive sides cannot be collinear, and no more than two sides can meet at any one vertex. [p. 402]

polygonal region
A polygon and its interior. [p. 322]

polyhedron
A solid whose faces are polygons. [p. 410]

polynomial
An algebraic expression with more than one term. [p. 326]

postulate
A statement that is assumed to be true without proof. [p. 33]

pre-image
The figure to which a transformation is applied, producing its image. [p. 67]

prism
A polyhedron with two congruent faces that lie in parallel planes, whose other faces are parallelograms formed by joining corresponding vertices of the bases. [p. 604]

proportion
An equation stating that two ratios are equal. [p. 468]

pyramid
A polyhedron formed by lateral edges connecting each vertex of a polygonal base with a point, the vertex, not in the plane of the base. [p. 610]

Pythagorean triple
Any set of three integers a, b, and c that satisfy $a^2 + b^2 = c^2$. [p. 367]

quadratic equation
An equation that can be put into the form $ax^2 + bx + c = 0$, where a, b, and c are real numbers and $a \neq 0$. [p. 332]

quadrilateral
A polygon with four sides. [p. 346]

radius of a circle
A segment, or the length of a segment, from the center to any point on the circle. [p. 540]

radius of a regular polygon
The segment, or length of the segment, from a vertex to the center of the polygon. [p. 442]

radius of a sphere
A segment, or the length of a segment, from the center to any point on the sphere. [p. 546]

ray
A part of a line consisting of one point, and all the points on one side of the line from that point. [p. 45]

rectangle
A quadrilateral with four right angles. [p. 346]

rectangular prism
A prism with rectangular bases. [p. 604]

reflection
A transformation of a figure by flipping the figure over a line. [p. 67]

regular polygon
A polygon that is equilateral and equiangular. [p. 442]

regular polyhedron
A polyhedron with congruent edges and faces, faces that are regular polygons, and an equal number of edges meeting at each vertex. [p. 448]

regular pyramid
A pyramid whose base is a regular polygon and whose lateral edges are congruent. [p. 610]

remote interior angle
$\angle 2$ and $\angle 3$ are remote interior angles to exterior $\angle 4$. [p. 248]

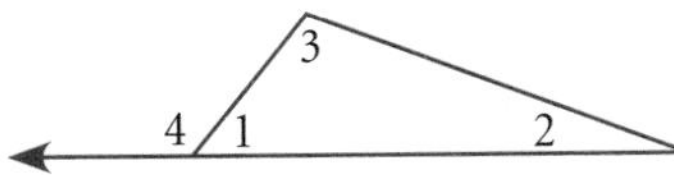

rhombus
A quadrilateral with four congruent sides. [p. 352]

right angle
An angle that measures 90°. [p. 47]

right prism, cylinder, or cone
A prism whose lateral edges are perpendicular to its bases. A cylinder or cone whose axis is perpendicular to its base(s). [pp. 604, 614, 615]

right triangle
A triangle with one right angle. [p. 244]

rotation
A transformation that turns a set of points about one point, the center of rotation. [p. 180]

rotational symmetry
The property that a figure can be rotated onto itself with an angle of rotation between 0° and 360°. [p. 181]

same-side interior angles
When a transversal t cuts lines p and q as shown, the pairs of same-side interior angles are: $\angle 3$ and $\angle 6$, $\angle 4$ and $\angle 5$. [p. 216]

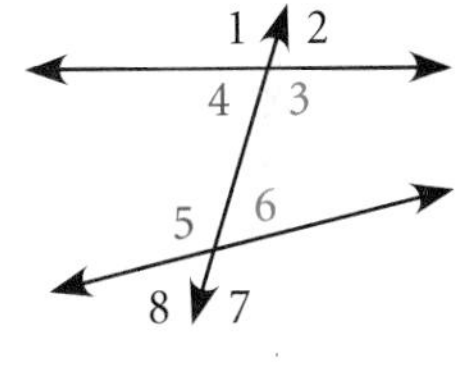

scale factor
A factor by which a figure is enlarged or reduced. [p. 462]

scalene triangle
A triangle with no two congruent sides. [p. 243]

scatter plot
A graph showing a set of points based on paired data. [p. 12]

secant line
A line that intersects a circle or sphere in two points. [p. 544]

secant-secant angle
If each side of an angle is a secant ray to a circle, then the angle is a secant-secant angle of the circle. [p. 592]

sector
A region bounded by two radii and their intercepted arc on a circle. [p. 570]

segment of a circle
The region bounded by an arc of the circle and the segment joining its endpoints. [p. 573]

self-similar
The property that a figure looks the same when viewed at any level of magnification. [p. 750]

sides of an angle
The two rays that form the angle. [p. 45]

similar
The property that figures have the same shape but not necessarily the same size. [p. 462]

similarity correspondence
A way of pairing the vertices of two geometric figures so that all pairs of corresponding angles are congruent and all pairs of corresponding lengths are proportional. [p. 464]

similarity ratio
The ratio of the lengths of two corresponding sides of similar figures. [p. 463]

sine of $\angle A$
For acute $\angle A$ in a right triangle, the ratio of the length of the opposite leg to the length of the hypotenuse. [p. 512]

skew lines
Noncoplanar lines. [p. 142]

slant height of a cone
The length of any segment from the vertex to the circle bounding the base. [p. 615]

slant height of a regular pyramid
The height of any lateral face. [p. 610]

slope
The ratio of the change in value of the vertical coordinates to the corresponding change in the horizontal coordinates, as measured from one point of a line to another.

space
The set of all points. [p. 116]

sphere
The locus of points in space a given distance from a point, the center of the sphere. [p. 546]

square
A quadrilateral with four right angles and four congruent sides. [p. 346]

supplementary angles
A pair of angles whose measures add up to 180°. [p. 201]

surface area of a prism
The total area of all of its faces, including the bases. [p. 605]

symmetry
The property that a figure coincides with itself after some transformation. [p. 62]

tangent line
A line that intersects a circle or sphere at exactly one point is tangent to the circle or sphere. [p. 544, 546]

tangent of $\angle A$
For acute $\angle A$ in a right triangle, the ratio of the length of the opposite leg to the length of the adjacent leg. [p. 512]

tangent plane
A plane that contains exactly one point of a sphere is tangent to the sphere. [p. 546]

tangent-secant angle
If one side of an angle is tangent to a circle and its other side is a secant ray of the circle, then the angle is a tangent-secant angle of the circle. [p. 589]

tangent-tangent angle
If each side of an angle is tangent to a circle, then the angle is a tangent-tangent angle of the circle. [p. 589]

tessellation
A repeating pattern of figures that completely covers a plane region without gaps or overlaps. [p. 242]

tetrahedron
A polyhedron with four faces. [p. 410]

translation
A transformation that moves all the points in a plane a fixed distance in a given direction. [p. 171]

translation symmetry
The property that a figure coincides with itself after a translation. [p. 689]

translation vector
A vector whose direction is that of a given translation and whose length is the distance of the translation. [p. 171]

transversal
A line that intersects two coplanar lines in two different points. [p. 216]

trapezoid
A quadrilateral with exactly one pair of parallel sides. [p. 352]

triangle
A figure formed by three line segments that connect three noncollinear points. [p. 242]

trigonometry
The study of the relationship between angle measures and side lengths of right triangles. [p. 512]

trinomial
A polynomial with three terms. [p. 326]

vector
Vector $\overrightarrow{AB}$ is a model of the straight-line path from point A to point B. [p. 165]

B Endpoint
A Origin
Vector $\overrightarrow{AB}$ or $\vec{AB}$

vector sum
If a set of vectors is shown as a sequence where the origin of each vector (except the initial one) coincides with the endpoint of the previous vector, then their sum is the vector with origin at the origin of the initial vector and endpoint at the endpoint of the last vector. [p. 167]

vertex of a polygon
A point at which two sides intersect. [p. 402]

vertex of a polyhedron
A point which is the intersection of three or more faces of the polyhedron. [p. 410]

vertex of a pyramid
The point, not in the plane of the base, which is a vertex of each of the lateral faces. [p. 610]

vertex of an angle
The common endpoint of the rays forming the angle. [p. 45]

vertex of an isosceles triangle
The angle included by two congruent sides. [p. 244]

vertical angles
Two angles whose sides form two pairs of opposite rays. [p. 207]

volume
The number of cubic units contained in a solid. [p. 624]

wallpaper pattern
A plane pattern with translation symmetry along more than one line. [p. 694]

***x*-axis**
Typically the horizontal axis on a coordinate plane. [p. 11]

***x*-coordinate**
The first number of an ordered pair denoting a point on the coordinate plane, denoting the distance left or right from the vertical axis.

***y*-axis**
Typically the vertical axis on a coordinate plane. [p. 11]

***y*-coordinate**
The second number of an ordered pair denoting a point on the coordinate plane, denoting the distance up or down from the horizontal axis.

SELECTED ANSWERS

CHAPTER 1

1-1 Part A Exercises

1. a. 4 triangles, 1 square
b. Square
c. Triangles

3. 8 vertices, 12 edges, 6 faces
5. a. 6, 5, 4 **b.** 7
c. Possible answer:

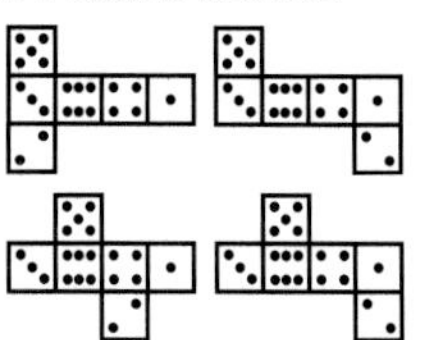

d. $\frac{1}{6}$
7. Cylinder

9.

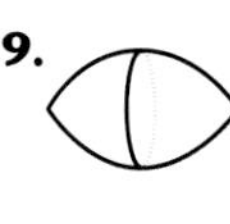

12. a. Basketball court
b. Tomato
15.

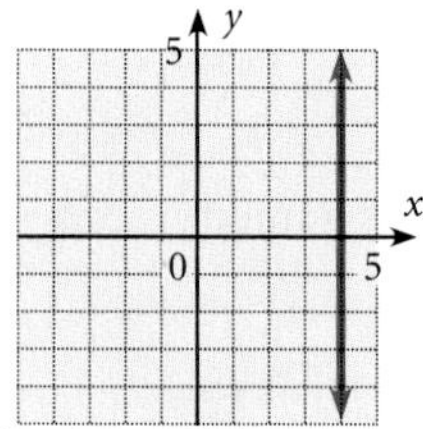

The line is parallel to the *y*-axis and each point on the line has *x*-coordinate equal to 4.
17.

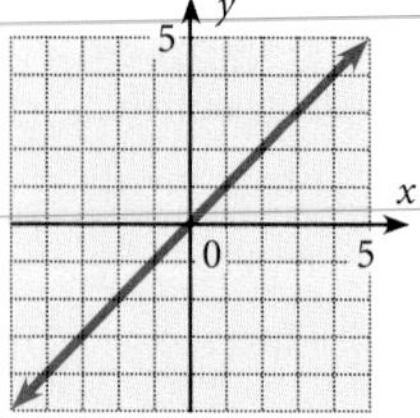

The line splits the angle between the *x*-axis and *y*-axis.
19. Possible answer:

21.

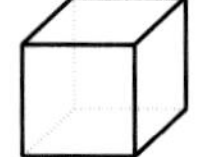

23.

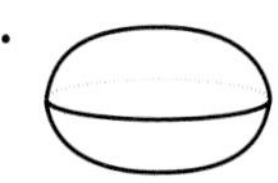

25. 1; 6; 12; 8; 0; 0; 0

1-1 Part B Try It

a–d.

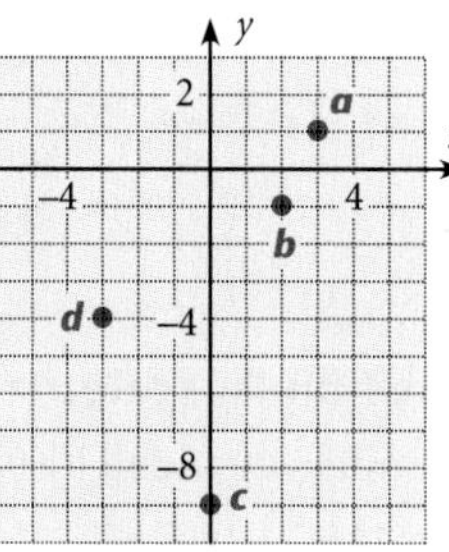

e. Topeka **f.** I: Boston, MA; II: Seattle, WA; III: Phoenix, AZ; IV: Little Rock, AK **g.** *x*-axis: San Jose; *y*-axis: Omaha **h.** (1) $(-9, 6)$, (2) $(8, 1)$, (3) $\left(\frac{5}{2}, -2\right)$

1-1 Part B Exercises

1–7.

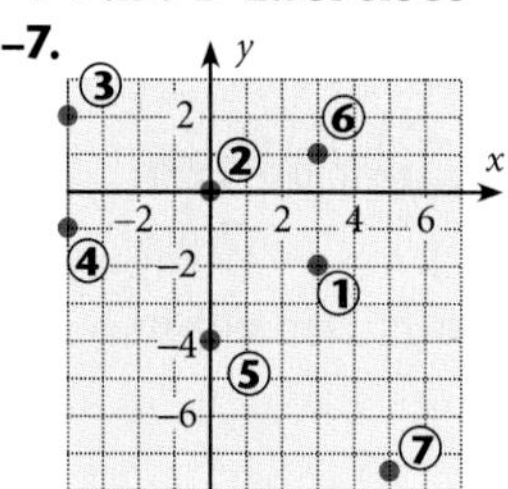

9. (2, 3) **11.** $(-4, -2)$
13.

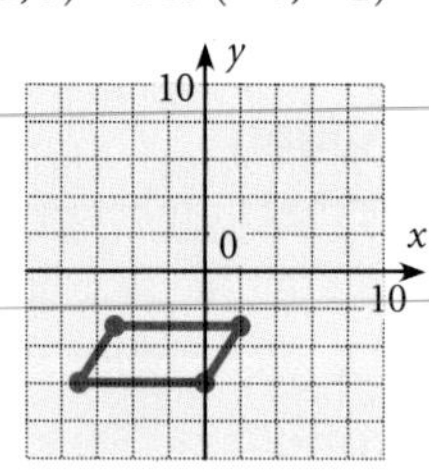

15. Scatter plot **19.** $3y$
21. $3r^2 - 14r$ **23.** 26
25. -216

26–33.

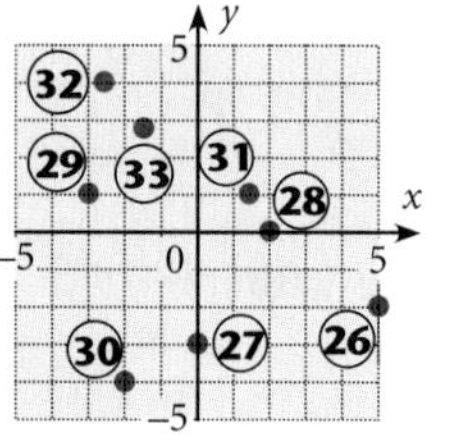

35. $(-2, -1)$ **37.** (2, 0)
39. $(0, -3)$
40–41.

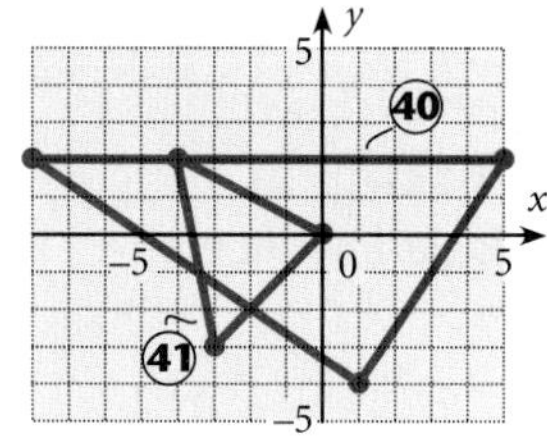

43. a. *C* **b.** *P*

1-1 Part C Self-Assessment

2. a, b, e, f
3.

4. a. An object similar to a tuning fork **b.** The left side shows 3 prongs, the right side 2. **5.** $11x$ **6.** $20 - 21z$
7. -23 **8.** 49 **9.** (c)
10. approximately 1.6.
11. Possible answer: Models can be tested under controlled conditions, modeling does not place astronauts at risk, and it is easier to change a model than to modify a spacecraft. **12. a.** Approximately 45 inches and 64 inches, respectively. **b.** About 82 inches (nearly 7 feet tall).
13. It appears that length and wins are negatively related (longer named cities have fewer wins). This result is probably just an interesting coincidence.

1-2 Part A Try It

a–b. Possible answer:

X M Y
N

c. $\overline{XM}$, $\overline{MY}$, $\overline{XY}$

1-2 Part A Exercises

1. a-d.

Triangles	1	2	3	4
Perimeter	3	4	5	6

e. $p = n + 2$ **f.** 102 **3.** $\frac{31}{32}$

5. Lines: $\overleftrightarrow{AB}$, (or $\overleftrightarrow{AC}$, $\overleftrightarrow{AD}$, $\overleftrightarrow{BC}$, $\overleftrightarrow{BD}$, or $\overleftrightarrow{CD}$), and $\overleftrightarrow{EC}$ (or $\overleftrightarrow{EF}$ or $\overleftrightarrow{CF}$); points: *A*, *B*, *C*, *D*, *E*, *F*; segments: $\overline{AB}$, $\overline{AC}$, $\overline{AD}$, $\overline{BC}$, $\overline{BD}$, $\overline{CD}$, $\overline{EC}$, $\overline{EF}$, and $\overline{CF}$
6. *ABC*; *A*, *B*, *D*; *A*, *C*, *D*; *B*, *C*, *D*; *E*, *C*, *F* **9.** Segment
11.

Tiers high	Triangles
2	4
3	9
4	16
5	25
10	100
n	n^2

15. F; Not books which have had their pages cut out
17. F; A robin is a bird, and this bird is a robin.
19. F; A robin is not a bluejay.
21. 243; 3^n where n = term number **23.** 25; Sequence is a, a^2, $(a + 1)$, $(a + 1)^2$, etc.
25. *G*, *I*, *J* **27.** Yes; two points determine a line.
29.

Month	Total pairs
1	1
2	1
3	2
4	3
5	5
6	8
7	13
8	21
9	34
10	55
11	89
12	144

The total number of pairs for each month past the second is the sum of the numbers of pairs for the previous two months.

1-2 Part B Try It

a. Ostrich
b. Parallelogram

1-2 Part B Exercises

1. Possible answer: Roosters are birds but, being male, they don't lay eggs.
3. Possible answer: Let $a = b = 1$
5. True if he buys a newspaper and eats lunch; False if he doesn't buy a newspaper, or doesn't eat lunch, or both
7. **9.**

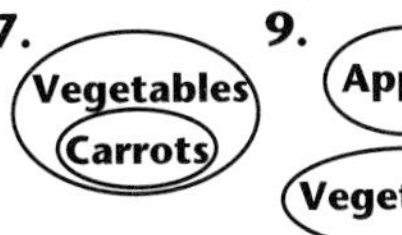

11. F; Line segment
15. $x = 4$
17–19.

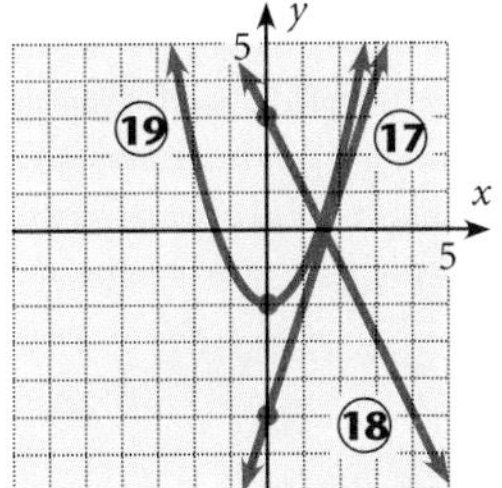

21. Equilateral triangle
23. Possible answer: Kay Bailey Hutchison (R–TX)
25. True if homework done and bedroom cleaned; False if homework not done, or bedroom not cleaned, or both.
27. Some joggers swim (or some swimmers jog). **29.** All squares are quadrilaterals.
31. a.

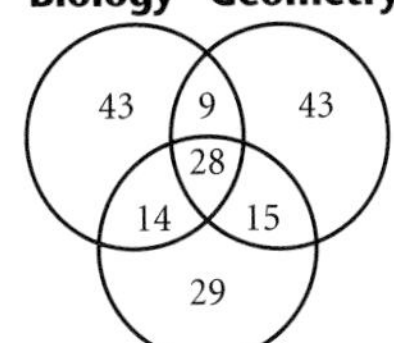

43 will take geometry only
b. $\frac{28}{181}$

1-2 Part C Try It

a. Iguanas have scales.
b. I am not a fish.

1-2 Part C Exercises

1. Fluffy has fur.
2. Chao-Yee does not live in Wyoming. **3.** Kai drew a four-sided figure. **6.** Fill in row 2, column 3, then cell (3, 3), then (1, 1), then the rest in any order to get

5	0	1
7	3	9
8	6	4

8. The statement is true; some snakes are reptiles. However, it is also true that *all* snakes are reptiles.
9. $3x - 2(25 - 3x) = 40$; $3x - 50 + 6x = 40$, Distributive Property; $9x = 90$, added 50 to both sides and combined like terms; $x = 10$, divided both sides by 9. Deductive
13. -1 **15.** -5
17.

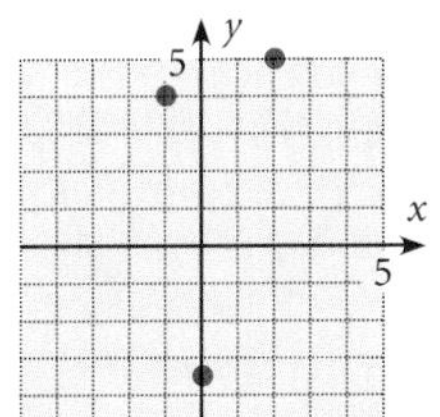

19. Tamika does not live in San Diego. **21.** Every square is a parallelogram.
23. a. Valid **b.** Valid

1-2 Part D Self Assessment

1. Deductive **2.** Inductive
3. Inductive **4.** Deductive
5. 26; $5n + 1$ **6.** 35
7. 125; n^3 **8.** $x = 3$
9. $y = \frac{5}{3}$

10–11.

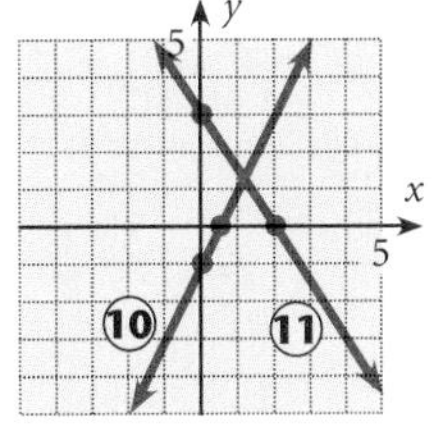

12. Possible answer:
13. (d)
14. a. 2^{n-1}
b. Conjecture: $2^{6-1} = 2^5 = 32$; not valid; works for $n \leq 5$ but not $n = 6$ because for $n = 6$, number of regions = 30 or 31

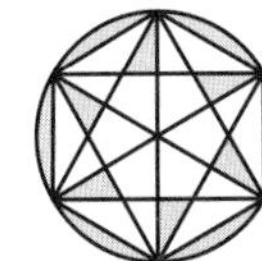

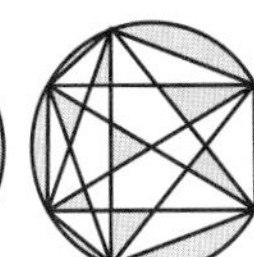

15. $\frac{n(n+1)}{2}$ Inductive, by observing that the nth step added n small squares. Other reasoning is possible.
16. The nth arrival shakes hands with n people - Alice and the $(n - 1)$ who arrived earlier. Therefore, the answer is: $\frac{n(n+1)}{2} = \frac{10(11)}{2} = 55$

1-3 Part A Try It

a. $XY = 2.7$; $XZ = 4$; $YZ = 6.7$ **b.** $RS = 5.1$; $ST = 7.1$; $TR = 6$

1-3 Part A Exercises

1. a. $(x_1, y_1) = (-3, 4)$; $(x_2, y_2) = (6, -4)$ **b.** $x_2 - x_1 = 6 - (-3) = 9$; $9^2 = 81$
c. $y_2 - y_1 = -4 - 4 = -8$; $(-8)^2 = 64$ **d.** $81 + 64 = 145$ **e.** $\sqrt{145} \approx 12.0$
3. 9 **5.** 6 **7.** 7 **9.** 4.1
11. $LM = 6.3$; $MN = 6.3$; $NL = 5.7$; Perimeter = 18.3
14. 10 in. **15. a.** 72 points
b. 1.5 picas **17.** Points: *R*, *S*, *T*, *U*, *V* **18.** *T*, *S*, *R* and *S*, *U*, *V* **19.** $\overleftrightarrow{TS}$, $\overleftrightarrow{TR}$, $\overleftrightarrow{SR}$, ℓ

21. $\frac{1}{16}$; $\left(-\frac{1}{2}\right)^n$, $n \geq 0$
23. 15 **25.** 4.92 **27.** 5
29. 2.1 **31.** 0.76

1-3 Part B Try It

a. $\overrightarrow{MN}$, $\overrightarrow{MO}$, $\overrightarrow{MP}$ **b.** 90°
c. 45° **d.** 137°

1-3 Part B Exercises

1. $\angle BCD$, $\angle DCB$, $\angle C$, $\angle 1$
3. $\angle DBA$, $\angle DBC$, $\angle ABC$, 3 unique angles **5.** 148°
7. Possible answer:

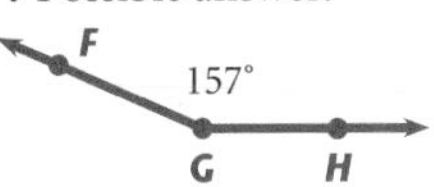

9. Possible answer:

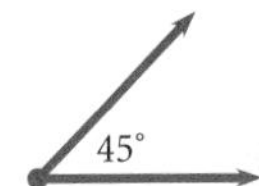

11. Possible answer:

15. 30° **17.** 130° **19.** 90°
21. Possible Answer: 63°
25. 11 **27.** $\overrightarrow{UR}$, $\overrightarrow{US}$, $\overrightarrow{UT}$, $\overrightarrow{UV}$, $\overrightarrow{VU}$ (or $\overrightarrow{VS}$), and $\overrightarrow{SU}$ (or $\overrightarrow{SV}$) **29.** 139°
31. Possible answer:

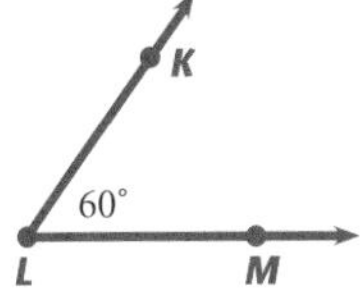

33. Possible answer:

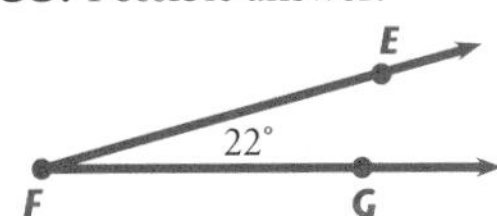

35. The shortest distance from a point not on a line to the line is the perpendicular segment; the shortest distance from a point not on a line to the line is the perpendicular segment.

1-3 Part C Try It

a. Possible answer:

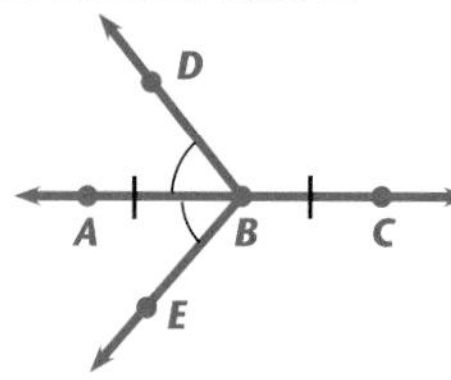

1-3 Part C Exercises

1. *B* and *E*, *A* and *C*, *D* and *F* **2.** Yes, since both have length 2. **9.** 4 **10.** $m\angle ABC = \frac{1}{2}m\angle CBD$ **11.** $x = 8$; $RS = 41$; $MN = 41$ **13.** (c) **19.** Slope $= -3$, intercept $= 1$ **21.** 2 **23.** Undefined (vertical line)

25.

27.

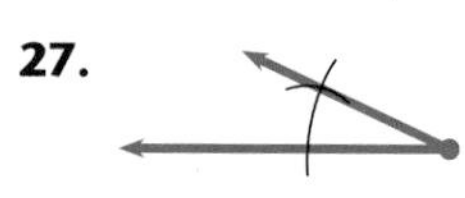

29. $x = 23$; $m\angle DEF = 133°$; $m\angle RST = 133°$

31. Possible answer: Compass may have opened wider while constructing $\angle PQR$, your measurements of $\angle MNO$ and $\angle PQR$ may not be precise, etc.

1-3 Part D Self Assessment

1. No **2.** No **3.** Yes **4.** No, the segment is the same whether it is called $\overline{AB}$ or $\overline{BA}$; Yes, the first letter is the endpoint of the ray; No, the points are any two locations on the line; Yes, the center letter denotes the vertex. **5.** Segments are congruent, lengths are equal. **6.** The notation $\angle PQR$ names the angle, not its size. **7.** $0° <$ angle size $< 180°$. **8.** "Congruent angles" requires the angle measures, not the lengths of their sides, to be the same. **9. a.** 72 **b.** 60° **c.** 51.4° **d.** 45° **e.** 40° **f.** 36° **g.** 2 slices of the 5-slice 144° vs. 120°

10.

11.

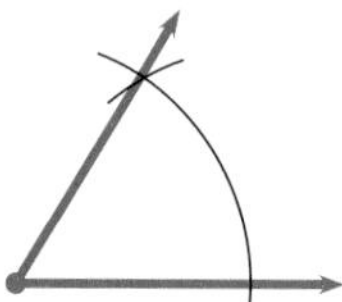

12. $m\angle 1 = m\angle 4 = m\angle 5 = m\angle 8 = 60°$, and $m\angle 2 = m\angle 3 = m\angle 6 = m\angle 7 = 120°$ **13.** (e) **14.** 16; $a_n = (n - 1)^2$ **15.** 63; To get the second number, add two to the first. Subsequent numbers are found by adding 4, 8, 16, … (doubling each time). **16. a.** Approximately 20°, 35°, 55° **b.** approximately 0.36, 0.70, and 1.43 **c.** As slope increases, so does angle measure **d.** Possible answers: Lower pitch means lower profile, less wind resistance; Higher pitch reduces snow buildup; Lower pitch means less attic space to store hot air **18.** Possible answer: Construct a congruent angle, then, using one of the sides of the angle as a base, construct a second congruent angle; Observe that the common side bisects the large angle.

1-4 Part A Try It

a.

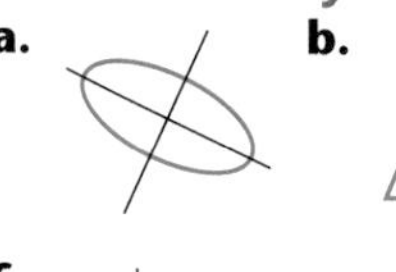

b.

c.

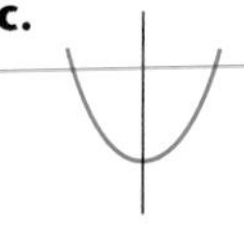

1-4 Part A Exercises

1. One line

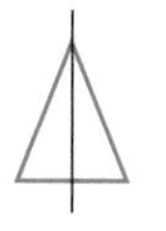

3. No lines **5.** Yes; No

7. No; No **9.**

11. 3

13. 4

15. Line of symmetry (or an axis of symmetry) **17.** Square **20.** Possible answers: WOW, TUT, AVA (name); AHIMOTUVWXY **21.** Possible answers: BOX, BED, HEX; BCDEHIKOX **23.** $\frac{4}{6} = \frac{2}{3}$ **25.** Possible answer: The object and its reflected image form a symmetric pair.

27. **29.**

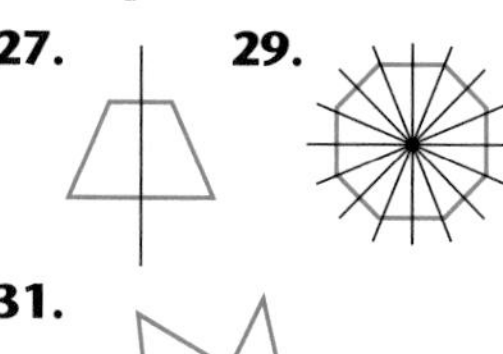

31.

33. a. 6 **37.** If a polygon is divided by a symmetry axis, each side consists of line segments that have congruent segments on the other side.

1-4 Part B Exercises

1.

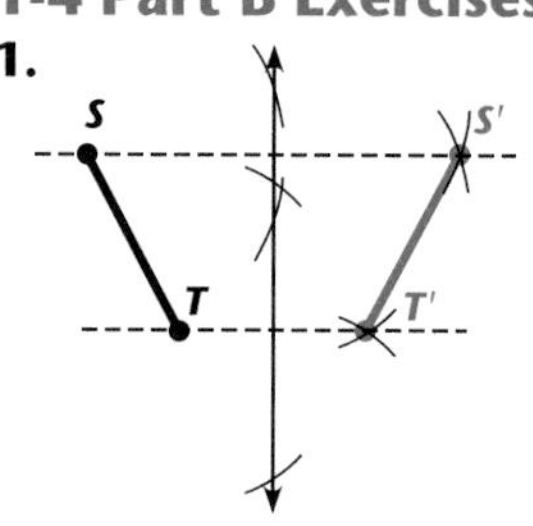

3. *P* **4.** *Q* **5.** $\overline{LK}$ **7.** 90°; In order for *m* to be the line of reflection, it must be a perpendicular bisector of $\overline{XX'}$. **9.** F; Reflection **11. a.** $(2, -3)$ **b.** $(-2, 3)$ **c.** $(a, -b)$ **d.** $(-a, b)$ **12.** One is vertical, one horizontal; The top and bottom halves are reflections of each other, as are the left and right halves.

15.

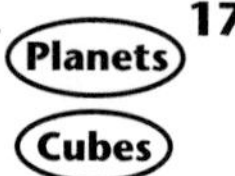

17. Turtles Reptiles

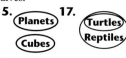

19. 13

21. Possible answer:

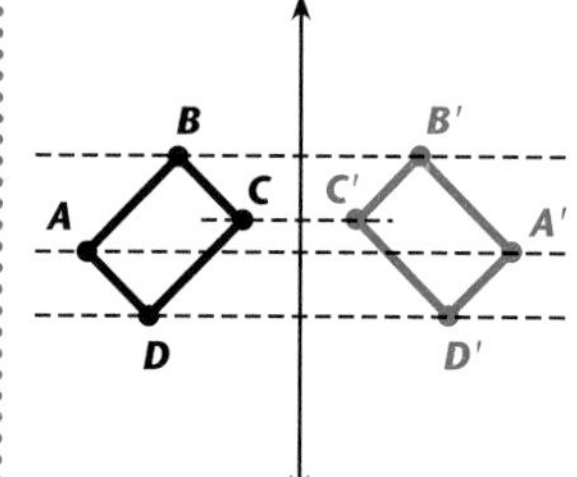

23. *Z* **25.** Triangle *RTS*

27. a.

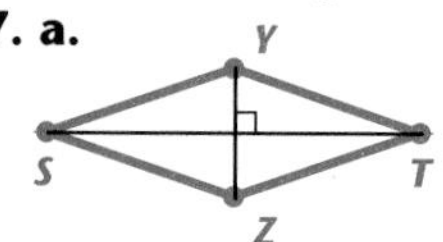

The four segments are congruent.

b.

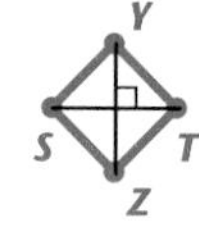

The four segments are congruent and perpendicular. **c.** Possible answer: Connecting the endpoints of the bisectors forms an equilateral parallelogram (rhombus). If the bisectors are congruent, the parallelogram is a square.

1-4 Part C Try It

a. $M'P' = 8$ also **b.** $m\angle PMN = 75°$ also **c.** As you move from M' to P', you are going counterclockwise **d.** Perimeter of triangle *MNP* is 20 **e.** Area of triangle $M'N'P'$ is 24

1-4 Part C Exercises

1. Possible answer:

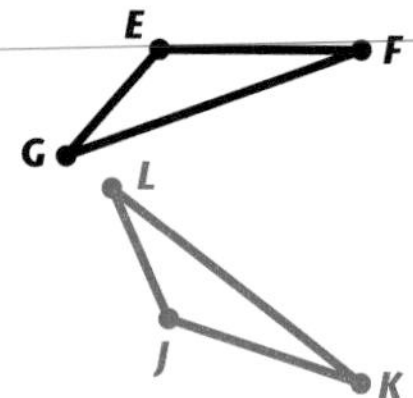

3. 90° **4.** 6 **7.** Possible answer: A segment from a point to its reflection image is perpendicular to the line of reflection. **9.** Possible answer: Reflection preserves the size of a figure.

12. 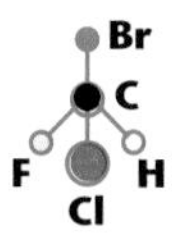

13. If a person lives in San Francisco, then he or she lives in California. **15.** If Kendrick is 16, then he can get a driver's license. **17.** 7.6 **19.** 6 **21.** Always; Possible answer: Reflection preserves size. **23.** Never; Reflection always reverses the orientation.

1-4 Part D Self Assessment

1. *P* **2.** $\overleftrightarrow{BC}$ **3.** $\overline{PQ}$ **4.** *B* **5.** 12 **6.** Yes, the line bisecting the angle

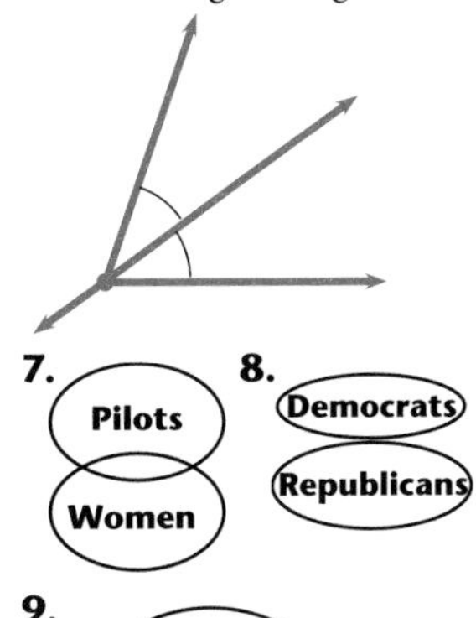

7. Pilots, Women **8.** Democrats, Republicans

9. Things with 2 endpoints, Segments

10. 10 **11.** 4.7 **12.** Reflection preserves congruence but reverses orientation. Possible answer:

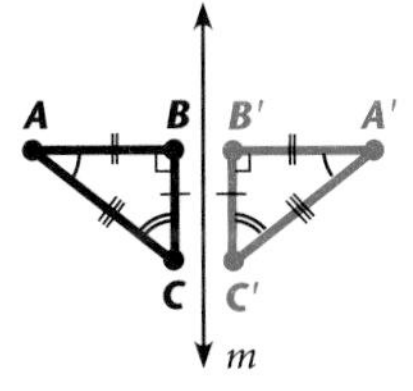

The sides, angles, perimeter and area of both triangles have the same measures as their counterparts; the orientations are reversed.

13. a. Yes **b.** Yes **14.** (e) **15.** Crossbar of F; Loop of Q; Crossbar of N **16. a.** Possible answer: "is not equal to," "is in the same class as" **b.** Possible answer: is "greater than," "is less than" **17.** (2, 1), (2, 5) **18.** (4, 5), (9, 5)

Chapter 1 Review

1. Inductive **2.** Vertex **3.** Image **4.** Right angles (90°) **5.**

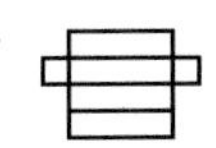

6. $A(1, 40)$, $B(1, 70)$, $C(2, 60)$, $D(2, 90)$, $E(4, 80)$, $F(4, 97)$, $G(5, 100)$, $H(6, 80)$ **7.** *H*; No **8.** About 76 points **9.** $x = -4$ **10. a.** 25 **b.** $4n - 3$ **11.** Possible answer: Deductive reasoning proceeds from the premises to the conclusion by logical steps; Solving an algebra problem, reasoning from "all triangles have 3 sides" and "John drew a triangle" to "John's figure has 3 sides." **12.** Luis is not a freshman. **13.** Marie did not draw a triangle. **14.** 9.4 **15.** 8.1 **16.** $\angle RTS$, $\angle STR$, $\angle T$, $\angle 2$ **17.**

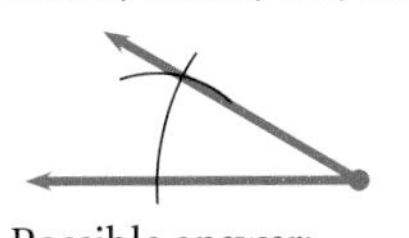

18. Possible answer:

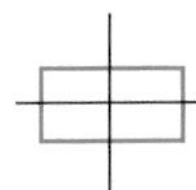

19. *K* **20.** $\overline{MN}$ **21.** Triangle *ABC*

CHAPTER 2

2-1 Part A Try It

a. If you talk on the telephone more than one hour per night, then your grade will drop one letter. **b.** If you use recycled paper, then you will help save our forests. **c.** If a whole number has three or more factors, then it is not a prime number.

2-1 Part A Exercises

1. Hypothesis: you want to stay healthy; Conclusion: you should eat fruits, grains, and vegetables **3.** If it rains, then I won't go swimming. **5.** If medicine is cherry-flavored, then children will love to take it. **7.** If an integer is divisible by 4, then it is also divisible by 2. **9.** If a student is a geometry student, then he or she is a math student. **11.** T **13.** T **17.** 1.875×10^3 **19.** 6.023×10^{23} **21.** 0.0000014 **23.**

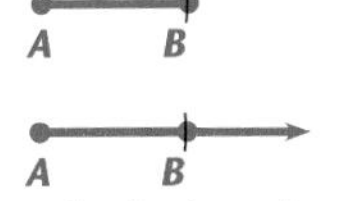

25. Hypothesis: A student enrolls in Algebra II; Conclusion: He will learn about logarithms **27.** If a mosquito bites you, then you will get a bump on your arm. **31.** T **33.** F **35. a.** Your wish is my command. **b.** I am the greatest. **c.** I am the greatest. **d.** Only when the "if" part is true

2-1 Part B Try It

a. Inverse: If you are not fifteen, then you are not a teenager; Converse: If you are a teenager, then you are fifteen; Contrapositive: If you are not a teenager, then you are not fifteen.

2-1 Part B Exercises

1. Inverse: If you don't live in Kyoto, then you don't live in Japan; Converse: If you live in Japan, then you live in Kyoto; Contrapositive: If you don't live in Japan then you don't live in Kyoto. **2.** Original: F. Inverse: If $x^2 \neq 4$, then $x \neq 2$. T. Converse: If $x = 2$, then $x^2 = 4$. T. Contrapositive: If $x \neq 2$, then $x^2 \neq 4$. F **3.** Original: T. Inverse: If two angles are not right angles, then they are not congruent. F. Converse: If two angles are congruent, then they are right angles. F. Contrapositive: If two angles are not congruent, then they are not (both) right angles. T **5.** Original: T. Inverse: If you are not an elephant, then you know how to fly. F. Converse: If you don't know how to fly, then you are an elephant. F. Contrapositive: If you know how to fly, then you are not an elephant. T **7.** T **11.** If $x > 3$, then $x > 7$. **13.** If x is negative, then $-x$ is positive. **17.** Original: T. Converse: If two angles have the same measure, then they are congruent; T. Two angles are congruent if and only if they have the same measure. **19.** 135° **21.** $m\angle A = 180° - m\angle B$ **23.** Original: F; Inverse: If $t^2 \leq 0$, then $t \leq 0$. T; Converse: If $t > 0$, then $t^2 > 0$. T; Contrapositive: If $t \leq 0$, then $t^2 \leq 0$. F **25.** Original: (presumed) T. Inverse: If you are over four feet tall, then you are riding the RocketCoaster. F. Converse: If you are not riding the RocketCoaster, then you are not over four feet tall. F. Contrapositive: If you are riding the RocketCoaster, then you are over four feet tall. T.

2-1 Part C Try It

a. If I clean my room, then I'll be able to go to the store. **b.** Fran will make the honor roll.

2-1 Part C Exercises

1. $\overline{EG} \cong \overline{HF}$ **3.** Washington state had 11 electoral votes in 1992. **5.** Not possible: The chain rule requires the conclusion of one statement to be the hypothesis of the other. **7.** If someone is a baseball player, then he or she wears spikes on natural-grass fields. Ken Griffey Jr. wears spikes on natural-grass fields. **9.** If a number is rational, then it can be written as a fraction. If a number is π, then it can be written as the fraction $\frac{\pi}{1}$. Not possible. **11.** Law of Detachment **13.** If *X*, then *R*. If *R*, then *M*. If *M*, then *Y*. If *Y* then *A*. If *A* then *B*. **15.** $(x - 3)^2$ **17.** $(c - 3)(3c + 5)$ **19.** Harvey

21. A rectangle is a quadrilateral. **23.** If you reflect a segment across a line, then the segment and its reflected image are congruent.
25. a. Carlos and Diane

2-1 Part D Self-Assessment

1. If a figure is a square, then it is a quadrilateral. Hypothesis: The figure is a square; Conclusion: The figure is a quadrilateral. **2.** If you want to be happy, then you should buy Frumworts. Hypothesis: You want to be happy; Conclusion: You should buy Frumworts. **3.** If you drive too fast, then you waste gasoline. Hypothesis: You drive too fast; Conclusion: You waste gasoline. **4. a.** Converse: If my book bag is not heavy, then I don't have a lot of homework. Inverse: If I have a lot of homework, then my book bag will be heavy. Contrapositive: If my book bag is heavy, then I have a lot of homework. **b.** Converse and inverse: F; The student might be carrying only a math book but have 500 problems to do. Contrapositive and original: F; The student might be carrying something besides homework materials in the bag.
5.

Illinois residents
Chicago residents
Dias family

6. A true conditional (the promise) does not necessarily mean a true inverse, and so Detachment using the inverse won't work. **7.** 3.27×10^2
8. 3.042×10^{-3}
9. 1.86282×10^5 **10.** Fumiko found the real, sausage pizza under the sink.
11. (b), (d), (e) **12. a.** Yes
b. *Given:* A conditional statement and the negation of its conclusion. *Infer:* The negation of the hypothesis.

2-2 Part A Exercises

1. a. If a set of points is collinear, then the points lie on the same line. **b.** If a set of points lie on the same line, then the points are collinear.
c. A set of points is collinear if and only if the points lie on the same line. **3.** The converse of a conditional statement is formed if and only if the hypothesis and the conclusion of the conditional statement are interchanged. **4.** If an angle is a right angle, then it measures 90°; If an angle measures 90°, then it is a right angle. **5.** If M is the midpoint of $\overline{AB}$, then it divides $\overline{AB}$ into two congruent segments, $\overline{AM}$ and $\overline{MB}$; If a point M divides $\overline{AB}$ into two congruent segments $\overline{AM}$ and $\overline{MB}$, then it is the midpoint of $\overline{AB}$. **7.** If a segment, ray or line, intersects the other segment perpendicularly, and bisects the other segment; A segment, ray or line is a perpendicular bisector if and only if it intersects a segment at right angles and bisects the segment.
9. 6; 12 **11.** 2.5; 2.5
15. F **17.** Two endpoints, part of line, ray, or segment; Part of a line (ray or another segment) is a line segment if and only if it consists of two endpoints and all the points between them. **19.** 15; 30
21. $\frac{9}{10}$; $\frac{9}{10}$ **23.** T **25.** N can be either (0.5, −1.5) or (0.5, −8.5)

2-2 Part B Try It

a. Commutative Property of Addition **b.** Addition Property of Equality
c. Straight-Line Postulate
d. Flat-Plane Postulate
e. Points-Existence Postulate, Flat-Plane Postulate

2-2 Part B Exercises

1. Flat-Plane Postulate
3. F **5.** T; Straight-Line Postulate **7.** F
9. Symmetric Property of Equality **11.** Distributive Property **13.** Addition Property of Equality
15. Plane Postulate
19. Original: F. Converse: If a number is evenly divisible by nine, it is evenly divisible by three. T. Inverse: If a number is not evenly divisible by three, then it is not evenly divisible by nine. T. Contrapositive: If a number is not evenly divisible by nine, then it is not evenly divisible by three. F **21.** Plane Postulate **23.** F; Let F and G be in the line of intersection of 2 planes. **24.** F; Three points may be collinear
25. F **27.** 20; No

2-2 Part C Try It

a. 1.5; 4.5

2-2 Part C Exercises

1. 4 **3.** $1\frac{1}{8}$ **5.** 19.9 **7.** (a)
9. a. (3) **b.** (4) **c.** (5)
d. (6) **11.** 11 **13.** 11
15. 9 **17.** 1.65 **19.** Yes
21. (2, 3) **23.** $\left(\frac{1}{2}, -\frac{3}{2}\right)$

2-2 Part D Self-Assessment

1. F; Three *noncollinear* points determine three lines;

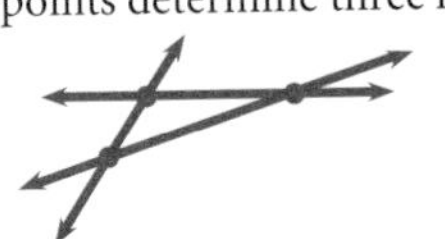

2. F; Two lines ℓ and m intersect at point E. **3.** F; The lines must be coplanar. **4.** T; Plane-Intersection Postulate **5.** Flat-Plane Postulate
6. Flat-Plane and Plane-Intersection Postulates together
7. $LK + KM = LM$; Segment- Addition Postulate
8. P and Q intersect in a line; Plane-Intersection Postulate
9. S is the midpoint of $\overline{RT}$; Definition of Midpoint **10.** (d) **11.** Possible answer: If you are fifteen, then you are a teenager. **12.** Possible answer: If $a > b$, then $b > a$.
13. The result is an inscribed square with half the area **14.** Midpoint between jobs is $\left(\frac{-3+2}{2}, \frac{2-5}{2}\right) = \left(-\frac{1}{2}, -\frac{3}{2}\right)$.
15. No; Postulates cannot be proven.

2-3 Part A Try It

a.

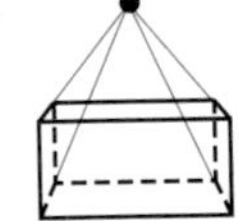

2-3 Part A Exercises

1. One; Directly in line with the reflecting pool **3.** Horizon line
5.

7.

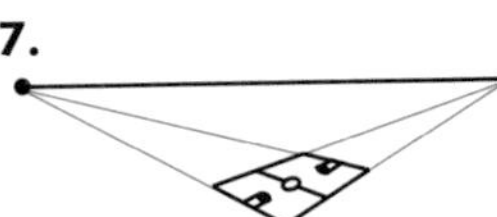

11. $\overline{XY}$ **13.** 56° **15.** T; Flat-Plane Postulate **17.** T; Plane Postulate

2-3 Part B Try It

a. Front and Back   Left and Right

2-3 Part B Exercises

1. Orthographic; Shows only one side of the shuttle.
5. Orthographic **7.** (a) **9.** (c)
11. Possible answers:
a. $\overleftrightarrow{GL}$ and $\overleftrightarrow{LK}$ **b.** $\overleftrightarrow{GL}$ and $\overleftrightarrow{NK}$,
c. $\overleftrightarrow{JN}$ and $\overleftrightarrow{LM}$ **d.** (b) **15.** (c)

2-3 Part C Try It

a. $\overleftrightarrow{FG}, \overleftrightarrow{HC}, \overleftrightarrow{ED}$ **b.** $\overleftrightarrow{AB}, \overleftrightarrow{HC}, \overleftrightarrow{BG}, \overleftrightarrow{CD}$

2-3 Part C Exercises

1. $\overleftrightarrow{BF}, \overleftrightarrow{DH}, \overleftrightarrow{AG}$ **3.** Plane with E, F, G, H **5.** Intersecting
7. Parallel **9.** (d) **14. a.** 40% **b.** 20% **15.** Possible answer: $y = -3x$ **17.** Possible answer: $y = -\frac{4}{3}x$
26. If two lines are noncoplanar, then they are skew. If two lines are skew, then they are noncoplanar.

28. If point B is between points A and C, then $AB + BC = AC$. If $AB + BC = AC$, then point B is between A and C. **30.** Plane with W, X, Y, Z **32.** Not possible; If $p \parallel n$ and $n \parallel m$, then p must be parallel to m **34.** Possible answer: $y = \frac{3}{7}x$ **38. a.** B: (2, 5, 0), C: (2, 5, 3), D: (2, 0, 3), F: (0, 5, 3), H: (0, 0, 0) **b.** Possible answer: $\overline{AH} \parallel \overline{BE}$, $\overline{HE} \parallel \overline{AB}$, $\overline{AD} \parallel \overline{BC}$

2-3 Part D Self-Assessment

1. F **2.** T **3.** F **4.** T **5.** Orthographic **6.** Possible answers: $y = \frac{3}{2}x$, $y = \frac{3}{2}x + 1$, $y = \frac{3}{2}x + 2$ **7.** $y = -\frac{2}{3}x + 5$ **8.** (a) **a.** 120° **b.** 120° (reflection preserves angle measure) **10.** T **11.** F **12.** T **14.** T **15.** F **16.** T **17.** F; Horizontal and vertical lines

Chapter 2 Review

1. Conditional **2.** Postulate **3.** Parallel **4.** Possible answer: If you are a teenager, then you are fifteen. **5.** Original: F. Inverse: If a number is not divisible by 4, then it is not divisible by 16. T. Converse: If a number is divisible by 16, then it is divisible by 4. T. Contrapositive: If a number is not divisible by 16, then it is not divisible by 4. F **6.** F **7.** T **8.** $(x + 6)(x - 2)$ **9.** $(1, -1)$ **10.** $y = 5x + 6$

CHAPTER 3

3-1 Part A Try It

a. $\overrightarrow{EA}$ and $\overrightarrow{ED}$ **b.** Acute: $\angle AEB$, $\angle BEC$; Right: $\angle AEC$, $\angle CED$; Obtuse: $\angle BED$

3-1 Part A Exercises

1. $\overrightarrow{KJ}, \overrightarrow{KL}$ **3.** $\overrightarrow{KM}, \overrightarrow{KN}$ **5.** J, L **7.** Obtuse; 120° **9.** Acute; 50° **11.** Acute **13.** Possible answer:

A B C D

15. a. 2; $\angle BJD$ and $\angle DJL$ **b.** Number of possible angles: 10 Probability: $\frac{2}{10} = 0.2$ **17.** $m\angle DBC = 35°$ **19.** Possible answer: Whales **21.** F **23.** Possible answer: $\overrightarrow{YT}, \overrightarrow{YW}$ **25.** Possible answer: $\overrightarrow{YT}, \overrightarrow{YV}$ **27.** U **29.** Acute: $\angle TYU$, $\angle UYV$, $\angle WYX$; Right: $\angle VYW$, $\angle TYV$; Obtuse: $\angle XYT$, $\angle UYW$, $\angle VYX$ **31.**

rays	angles
1	3 = 1 + 2
2	6 = 1 + 2 + 3
3	10 = 1 + 2 + 3 + 4
4	15 = 1 + 2 + 3 + 4 + 5
10	66 = 1 + 2 + 3 + ... + 10 + 11

3-1 Part B Try It

a. i. 000 **ii.** 055 **iii.** 120 **b.** ≈ 235

3-1 Part B Exercises

1. b. 125° **c.** 235 **3.** ≈ 055 **5.** ≈ 025 **7.** South **9.** Southwest **11.** A, B, E, F, I, J, M, N **13.** East **15.** South **17.** Fly 500 miles at bearing 053. **19.** 306 **21.** ≈ 118 **23.** 158 **25.** No.

3-1 Part C Try It

a. Length: 2.7 cm, Direction: 138°

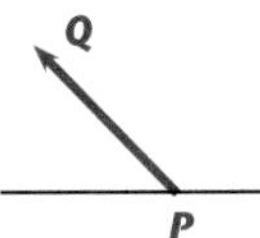

3-1 Part C Exercises

1. $\overrightarrow{CD}$, 33 mm at 126° **2.** $\overrightarrow{QR}$, 28 mm at 72° **3.** $\overrightarrow{XY}$, 52 mm at 354° **5.** 2.7 cm at 247° **7.** $\overrightarrow{JK} + \overrightarrow{KL} = \overrightarrow{JL}$ **9.** (b) **10.** Lengths: $\overrightarrow{OH} = 2\sqrt{5}$, $\overrightarrow{OG} = 4$, $\overrightarrow{OF} = 5$, $\overrightarrow{OI} = \sqrt{29}$; Directions: $\overrightarrow{OH} \approx 153°$, $\overrightarrow{OG} = 90°$, $\overrightarrow{OF} \approx 53°$, $\overrightarrow{OI} \approx 292°$ **12.** $\overrightarrow{AC}$ **17.** $\overrightarrow{RS}$: 2.3 cm at 82° **19.** $\overrightarrow{WV}$: 4.2 cm at 198° **21.** 3 cm at 57° **23. a.** $\overrightarrow{LN}$ **b.** No **25. a.** Same length **b.** $\overrightarrow{XY}$ at 58°, $\overrightarrow{X'Y'}$ at 122° **c.** The lengths of the pre-image and image vectors are the same. If the pre-image makes an angle of measurement a with the horizontal (x-axis) in the counterclockwise direction; then the image makes an angle of measurement a with the x-axis in the opposite direction.

3-1 Part D Try It

a. <1, 4>; $C' = (0, 8)$

3-1 Part D Exercises

1. (c) **3.** (d) **5.** Reflection **7.** F **9.** G **11.** <−1, −7>; P': (3, −2) **13.** $F' = (4, 0)$ **15.** $H' = (-2, 6)$ **17.** (6, 1) **19.** The segment with endpoints (0, 6) and (4, 2) **25.** 180°, 360°, 90° **27.** $\overline{PQ}$ **29.** <2, 5>; H': (−1, 5) **31.** U': (1, −3) **33.** W': (−4, 2) **35.** $(x - 3, y - 2)$ **37.** R': $(c + (t - a), d + (u - b))$

3-1 Part E Self-Assessment

1. Always **2.** Always **3.** Never **4.** Sometimes **5.** Never **6.** Always **7. a.** 0° < measure < 180° **b.** 000 ≤ bearing < 360 **8.** (d) **9.** T **10.** T **11.** F **12.** It is an angle, it measures less than 90°. Angle A is an acute angle if and only if $m\angle A < 90°$. **13.** Reflections and translations both preserve shape, but reflections change orientation. The figure shown is a reflection because orientation is reversed. **14.** <10, 5>

3-2 Part A Try It

a. 180° **b.** No rotational symmetry **c.** 90°, 180°, 270° **d.** 180° **e.** 90°, 180°, 270°

3-2 Part A Exercises

1. F **3.** $\overline{GH}$ **5. a.** 180° **b.** 180° **7.** V **9.** F; Rotational **13.** Yes **15. a.** Six of diamonds does, others do not **b.** $\frac{1}{4}$ **19.** $\overline{IJ}$ **21.** Triangle HIJ **23.** C **27.** Yes; Any number of degrees (either way) **31. a.** 90°, 180°, 270°

3-2 Part B Try It

a. $\overline{CB}$ **b.** S **c.** UT **d.** $\angle CBA$ **e.** SV

3-2 Part B Exercises

1.

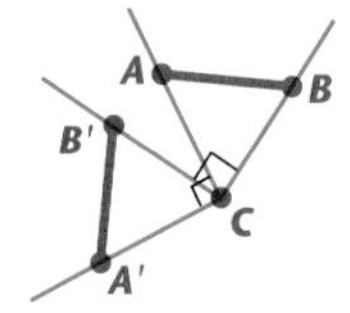

3. O **5.** $\angle PMN$ **7.** $C'(4, 0)$, $D'(4, -3)$ **8.** $C''(0, -4)$, $D''(-3, -4)$ **9.** $C'''(-4, 0)$, $D'''(-4, 3)$ **11. a.** Clockwise from middle of clock face. **b. i.** 1 hour = 60 min **ii.** 15 min **iii.** 30 min **iv.** 6 min **c. i.** 180° **ii.** 270° **iii.** 6° **17.** Q **19.** (1, 3) **21.** (−1, −3) **23.** A parallelogram with a crossbar; Yes

3-2 Part C Self-Assessment

2. (b) **3.** Any non-equilateral triangle lacks rotational symmetry. **4.** T **5.** R **6.** $\overline{ST}$ **7.** $\angle QRS$ **10.** (−2, 0) **11.** (−1, −4) **12.** (4, −3) **13.** (1, −3) **14.** Twice

3-3 Part A Try It

a. i. 45° **ii.** 10° **iii.** 80° **iv.** 95°; Protractor Postulate **b.** $m\angle PRN = 87°$ **c.** $m\angle BAD = 77°$; $m\angle DAC = 60°$

3-3 Part A Exercises

1. 15° **3.** 110° **5.** 30° **7.** $m\angle BCE - m\angle BCD = m\angle DCE$; 43° **9.** $m\angle BCD + m\angle DCE = m\angle BCE$; $m\angle BCD = 39°$ and $m\angle DCE = 37°$ **11.** 70° **13.** 70° **15.** 160° **17.** 39° **19.** 55°; Angle-Addition Postulate **27.** If a figure is a quadrilateral, then it has four sides. **29.** Yes; 90°, 180°, 270° **31.** Yes; 180° **33.** 80° **35.** 160° **37.** 80° **39.** $m\angle BCD + m\angle DCE = m\angle BCE$; $m\angle BCD = 60°$ and $m\angle DCE = 2°$ **41.** They are all possible except the last.

3-3 Part B Try It

a. Possible answer:

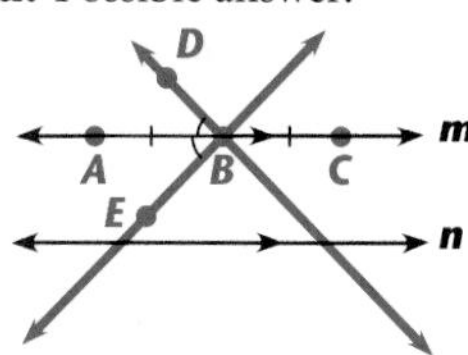

3-3 Part B Exercises

1. Yes **2.** No **3.** Yes **7.** Yes **9.** Yes **11.** No **13.**

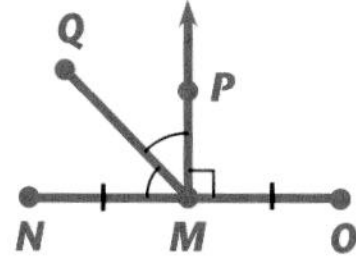

15. $m\angle FGH = 55°$; $m\angle PQR = 145°$ **17.** No **19.** No **21.** Possible answer: Assume $\overline{WZ} \cong \overline{ZY}$; Z is midpoint of $\overline{WY}$; W, Z, Y are collinear; Cannot assume: $\overline{WX} \cong \overline{XY}$; $\overline{ZX} \perp \overline{WY}$; $m\angle W = m\angle Y$ **23.** 25 possible angle combinations, 5 of which make the angle congruent: $\frac{5}{25} = \frac{1}{5}$

3-3 Part C Try It

a. $\angle MTR$ and $\angle MTN$, $\angle RTS$ and $\angle NTP$, $\angle MTS$ and $\angle MTP$ **b.** 69° **c.** 159° **d.** 90°

3-3 Part C Exercises

1. $\angle BEC$ and $\angle CED$ **3.** $\angle AEB$ and $\angle BED$ or $\angle AEC$ and $\angle CED$ **5.** Complement: 78.3°; Supplement: 168.3° **7.** $m\angle NRP = 49°$; $m\angle NRO = 139°$ **9.** $m\angle MRN = 12°$; $m\angle NRP = 78°$ **11.** 30° **13.** F; Right **15.** 142° **17.** 35° **21.** If an artist used geometric forms to represent real objects, then he/she was a cubist. If an artist was a cubist, he/she was not a realist. If an artist used geometric forms to represent real objects, then he/she was not a realist. **23.** U **25.** Complement: 70°; Supplement: 160° **27.** Complement: 34.5°; Supplement: 124.5° **29.** $m\angle 1 = 15°$, $m\angle 2 = 30°$, $m\angle 3 = 45°$ **30. a.** Given information. **b.** Definition of right angle. **c.** Angle-Addition Postulate **d.** Substitution **e.** Definition of complementary.

3-3 Part D Try It

a. $m\angle 1 = 46°$; $m\angle 2 = 134°$; $m\angle 3 = 46°$

3-3 Part D Exercises

1. $m\angle 2 = 148°$; $m\angle 3 = 32°$; $m\angle 4 = 148°$ **3.** $m\angle 2 = 55°$; $m\angle 3 = 125°$; $m\angle 4 = 55°$ **5.** $m\angle 5 = 141° = m\angle 11$; $m\angle 6 = 39° = m\angle 12$; $m\angle 7 = 51° = m\angle 9$; $m\angle 8 = m\angle 10 = 129°$ **7.** 29° **9.** 151° **11.** 82° **13.** $m\angle JKL = m\angle MKN = 156°$ **15.** Definition of complementary **17.** Vertex **18.** If two angles are vertical angles, then they are congruent. **20.** 25° **25.** 48° **27.** 90° **29.** $m\angle JKL = m\angle MKN = 72°$ **31.** Bisect a right angle in a linear pair

3-3 Part E Self-Assessment

1. Complement: 25°; Supplement: 115° **2.** Complement: $(90 - x)°$; Supplement: $(180 - x)°$ **3.** Complement: $(70 + x)°$; Supplement: $(160 + x)°$ **4.** 58° **5.** 32° **6.** 148° **7.** 122° **8.** Possible answer: $\angle LBM$ and $\angle MBC$ **9.** $\angle IMB$ and $\angle BMD$ **10.** $\angle BMD$ and $\angle IME$ **11.** $\angle KBL$ and $\angle LBM$ **12. b.** $m\angle TBU = 140°$; $m\angle RBS = 140°$; $m\angle SBT = 40°$ **13.** Can assume: Things that look straight are; Points of intersection are shown accurately; Points shown on a line are collinear; Unless otherwise indicated, all points are coplanar; Relative positions of points are accurate. Cannot assume: Exact measurement and relative sizes of figures; That lines are parallel or perpendicular; That angles (or segments) are congruent. **14.** (e) **15. a.** Yes; 120°, 240° **b.** No **c.** Yes; 90°, 180°, 270° **16.** The supplement is 90° larger than the complement; x + complement = 90° so complement = $(90 - x)°$; x + supplement = 180° so supplement = $(180 - x)°$; supplement − complement = $(180 - x)° - (90 - x)° = 90°$ **17.** 120°

3-4 Part A Try It

a. r **b.** $\angle 2$ and $\angle 3$; $\angle 6$ and $\angle 7$ **c.** $\angle 4$ and $\angle 8$; $\angle 5$ and $\angle 1$ **d.** $\angle 4$ and $\angle 2$; $\angle 5$ and $\angle 7$; $\angle 3$ and $\angle 1$; $\angle 6$ and $\angle 8$ **e.** $\angle 3$ and $\angle 7$; $\angle 2$ and $\angle 6$

3-4 Part A Exercises

1. $\angle 3$ and $\angle 7$; $\angle 2$ and $\angle 6$ **3.** $\angle 2$ and $\angle 3$; $\angle 7$ and $\angle 6$ **5.** $\angle 4$ and $\angle 6$; $\angle 3$ and $\angle 5$; $\angle 2$ and $\angle 8$; $\angle 1$ and $\angle 7$ **9.** Transversal; A line not an angle **11.** *Rewrite*: Leave as is; *Draw*: A M B *State: Given*: M is the midpoint of $\overline{AB}$; *Prove*: $AM = \frac{1}{2}AB$ **13.** $\angle 2$ and $\angle 3$ **15.** Possible answer: If you are an elephant, then you know how to fly. **17.** Complement: 2°; Supplement: 92° **19.** $\angle 5$ and $\angle 3$; $\angle 4$ and $\angle 6$ **21.** $\angle 3$ and $\angle 6$; $\angle 4$ and $\angle 5$ **23.** $\angle 1$ and $\angle 3$; $\angle 2$ and $\angle 4$; $\angle 6$ and $\angle 8$; $\angle 5$ and $\angle 7$ **27.** $\overleftrightarrow{AB}$ and $\overleftrightarrow{HG}$; $\overleftrightarrow{BC}$ and $\overleftrightarrow{EH}$; $\overleftrightarrow{BF}$ and $\overleftrightarrow{DH}$; $\overleftrightarrow{BE}$ and $\overleftrightarrow{CH}$; $\overleftrightarrow{BD}$ and $\overleftrightarrow{FH}$; $\overleftrightarrow{BG}$ and $\overleftrightarrow{AH}$

3-4 Part B Try It

a. $m\angle 1 = m\angle 3 = m\angle 5 = m\angle 7 = 72°$; $m\angle 2 = m\angle 4 = m\angle 6 = m\angle 8 = 108°$

3-4 Part B Exercises

1. $m\angle 1 = m\angle 3 = m\angle 5 = m\angle 7 = 41°$; $m\angle 2 = m\angle 4 = m\angle 6 = m\angle 8 = 139°$ **2.** $m\angle 1 = m\angle 3 = m\angle 5 = m\angle 7 = 105°$; $m\angle 2 = m\angle 4 = m\angle 6 = m\angle 8 = 75°$ **7.** 76° **11.** If the trenches are parallel and the pipeline crossing the street is a transversal, then the two angles are same-side interior angles, and Damaso's angle should measure 180° − 120° = 60°. **12. a.** iv **b.** iii **c.** i **13.** Inverse: If two angles are not supplementary to the same angle, then they are not congruent. Converse: If two angles are congruent, then they are supplementary to the same angle. Contrapositive: If two angles are not congruent, then they are not supplementary to the same angle. **15.** $m\angle 1, 3, 5, 7 = 160°$; $m\angle 2, 4, 6, 8 = 20°$ **17.** $m\angle 1, 3, 5, 7 = 82.5°$; $m\angle 2, 4, 6, 8 = 97.5°$ **21. a.** No; Definition says parallel lines are coplanar lines that do not intersect. **b.** Yes; Coplanarity and non-intersection are both symmetric. **c.** Yes; If m and n have no common point(s) and if n and p have no common point(s), then m and p have no common points.

3-4 Part C Try It

a. $a \parallel b$ by Congruent Alternate Interior Angles; $b \parallel c$ by Congruent Corresponding Angles; $a \parallel c$ by Congruent Alternate Interior Angles. **b.** Possible answer: Make $\angle 1 \cong \angle 2$, $\angle 1 \cong \angle 4$, or $m\angle 1 + m\angle 3 = 180°$

3-4 Part C Exercises

1. Corresponding angles are congruent **3.** Same-side interior angles are supplementary **5.** $a \parallel b$; Alternate Interior Angles Postulate **7.** $a \parallel c$; Alternate Interior Angles Postulate **9.** $a \parallel b$; Alternate Exterior Angles Theorem **11.** $x = 68$ **15.** *State: Given*: Transversal t cuts ℓ and m such that the corresponding angles 1 and 2 are congruent; *Prove*: $\ell \parallel m$

17. If an angle is acute, then it measures less than 90°. If an angle measures less than 90°, then it is acute. **21.** $c \parallel d$ by Alternate Exterior Angles **23.** $y = 0$; $x = 118$ **25.** $x = 3$; $y = -20$ **27. a.** Definition of linear pair **b.** Linear-Pair Postulate **c.** Supplementary angles **d.** Congruent **e.** Congruent

3-4 Part D Self-Assessment

1. T **2.** F; If $r \parallel s$, then $\angle 2 \cong \angle 5$ **3.** T **4.** F; $m\angle 3 = 156°$ **5.** $\overleftrightarrow{AB} \parallel \overleftrightarrow{CD}$ **6.** Possibly none **7.** Possibly none **8.** $\overleftrightarrow{AC} \parallel \overleftrightarrow{BD}$ **9.** $\overleftrightarrow{AC} \parallel \overleftrightarrow{BD}$ **10.** $x = 9$ **11.** $\angle VXW \cong \angle YXZ$ and $\angle VXY \cong \angle WXZ$ because they are vertical angles. **12.** $\angle YXV$ and $\angle VXW$, $\angle YXZ$ and $\angle ZXW$, $\angle VXW$ and $\angle WXZ$, $\angle VXY$ and $\angle YXZ$ because they are linear pairs **13.** (a) **14.** $\angle 1 \cong \angle 3$, each of measure 45° (Corresponding angles of parallel air lines); $m\angle 2 = m\angle 4 = 122°$ (Corresponding angles of parallel water lines); $m\angle 5 = m\angle 6$ (Corresponding angles of parallel water lines); $m\angle 7 = m\angle 8$ (Corresponding angles of parallel air lines); If water surface $\parallel$ dotted line, then $m\angle 7 = m\angle 8 = 180° - m\angle 1 = 135°$. If water surface and bottom are parallel, then $m\angle 5 = m\angle 6 = 180° - m\angle 2$, or 58°.

Chapter 3 Review

1. T **2.** F; Obtuse **3.** T **4.** F; Supplementary **5.** T **6.** $\overrightarrow{AD}$, $\overrightarrow{AB}$ **7.** Possible answer: $\angle DAE$, $\angle EAB$, $\angle CAB$ **8.** E **9.** No; The distance from P to the lake and to the mountain. **10.** $\overrightarrow{AB}$: Length $= \sqrt{6^2 + 2^2} = \sqrt{40}$; Direction $\approx 18°$; $\overrightarrow{CD}$: Length $= \sqrt{(-6)^2 + (-4)^2} = \sqrt{52}$; Direction $\approx 214°$; $\overrightarrow{EF}$: Length $= \sqrt{2^2 + (-4)^2} = \sqrt{20}$; Direction $\approx 297°$ **11.** Yes; 90°, 180°, 270° **12.** Yes; 180° **13.** No **14.** $m\angle AOD - m\angle BOC = m\angle AOB + m\angle COD$; $130° - 40° = 90°$; Since $\angle AOB \cong \angle COD$, each has measure 45° **15.** $m\angle AOD = m\angle AOB + m\angle BOC + m\angle COD$; $5x° = (x + 10)° + 40° + 2x° = (3x + 50)°$, so $x = 25$; $m\angle AOB = (x + 10)° = 35°$; $m\angle COD = 2x° = 50°$. **16.** $m\angle 1 = 60°$; $m\angle 2 = 30°$; $m\angle 3 = 30°$; $m\angle 4 = 85°$ **17.**

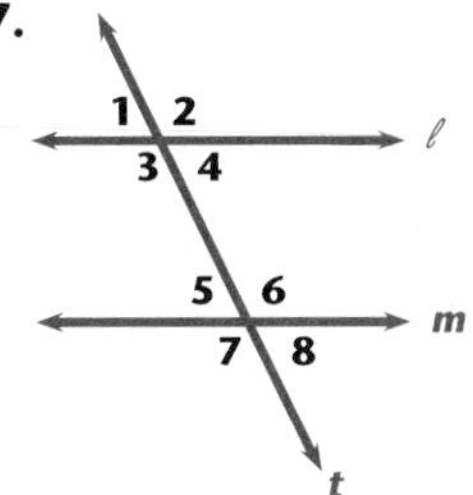

Show for example that $\angle 3 \cong \angle 6$, $\angle 1 \cong \angle 8$ or $\angle 1 \cong \angle 5$, or that $m\angle 3 + m\angle 5 = 180°$. **18.** F **19.** T **20.** $a \parallel b$ **21.** $a \parallel b$ **22.** No parallel lines

CHAPTER 4

4-1 Part A Try It

a. 82° **b.**

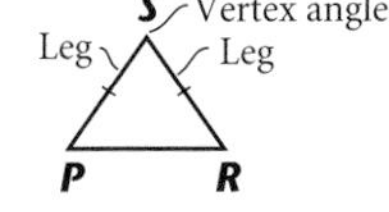

Vertex $\angle S$, legs $\overline{SP}$ and $\overline{SR}$.

c.

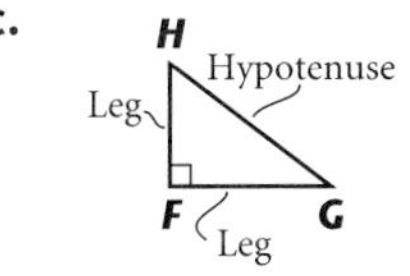

Hypotenuse $\overline{HG}$, Legs $\overline{FH}$ and $\overline{FG}$.

4-1 Part A Exercises

1. Isosceles, right **3.** Equilateral, equiangular **5.** $\triangle MNL$, $\triangle MLN$, $\triangle NML$, $\triangle NLM$, $\triangle LMN$, $\triangle LNM$ **7.** No **9. a.** B, C, D, E, V, W, X, Y **b.** $G, H, I, J, L, Q, R, S, T$ **c.** H, L, M, N, O, R **d.** $\frac{3}{4}$ **11.** 68° **13.** 58° **15.** $m\angle A = 53°$, $m\angle B = 24°$, $m\angle C = 103°$ **17.** $m\angle 1 = 90° - m\angle 2$ **19.** 35° **21.** 60° **23.** Yes **25.** Scalene **27.** 108° **29.** 65° **31. a.** Right, isosceles **b.** 12

4-1 Part B Try It

a. $\angle 1$, $\angle 2$, $\angle 3$ **b.** $\angle 4$, $\angle 5$
c.

$m\angle 1$	$m\angle 2$	$m\angle 3$	$m\angle 4$
83°	40°	57°	97°
32°	84°	64°	148°
55°	71°	54°	125°

4-1 Part B Exercises

1. $\angle 3$, $\angle 4$ **3.** $\angle 2$, $\angle 3$
4–7.

$m\angle 5$	$m\angle 6$	$m\angle 7$	$m\angle 8$
104°	76°	33°	71°
108°	72°	8°	100°
137°	43°	68°	69°
156°	$x°$	$(2x+31)°$	$(4x-19)°$

9. F **11.** 30° **13.** 72° **15.** 110° **17.** *Rewrite*: If an angle is an exterior angle of a triangle, then its measure is equal to the sum of the measures of its remote interior angles.
Draw:

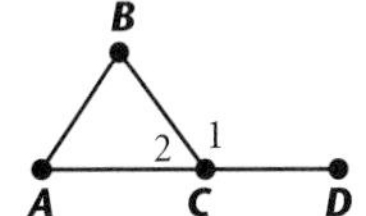

State: *Given*: $\angle 1$ is an exterior angle. *Prove*: $m\angle 1 = m\angle A + m\angle B$ **19.** 45° **25.** By properties of parallel lines, $m\angle 1 = m\angle 5$ and $m\angle 2 = m\angle 4$. Therefore, since $m\angle 3 + m\angle 4 + m\angle 5 = 180°$ (by the Angle-Addition and Linear-Pair Postulates), $m\angle 3 + m\angle 2 + m\angle 1 = 180°$ by substitution.

4-1 Part C Self-Assessment

1. Yes **2.** No **3.** Yes **4.** Always **5.** Sometimes **6.** Never **7.** Sometimes **8.** (c) **9.** *Rewrite*: If a triangle is a right triangle, then its acute angles are complementary. *State*: *Given*: $\triangle ABC$ is a right triangle, $\angle A$ is a right angle. *Prove*: $m\angle B + m\angle C = 90°$
Draw:

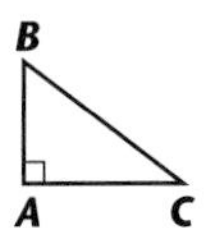

10. The mean is 65.8; The median is 71; The mode is 71. **11.** A triangle cannot have those angle measures. Solving gives $x = 30$, but this would give the $(2x - 70)°$ angle a negative measure. **12.** $m\angle 1 + m\angle 3 = 120°$ by the Exterior Angle Theorem **13.** Possible answer: $m\angle 2 = 60°$ by the Linear-Pair Postulate **14.** Not possible **15.** No **16.** In the picture, $\angle 1$, $\angle 2$, and $\angle 3$ form a straight line at the tessellation vertex. Therefore $m\angle 1 + m\angle 2 + m\angle 3 = 180°$. Also in the picture at the tessellation vertex, $\angle 1$ and $\angle 2$ form the exterior angle of $\angle 3$, $\angle 3$ and $\angle 1$ form the exterior angle of $\angle 2$, and $\angle 2$ and $\angle 3$ form the exterior angle of $\angle 1$.

4-2 Part A Try It

a. $\triangle MNO \cong \triangle TUS$

4-2 Part A Exercises

1. $\triangle DEF \cong \triangle XZY$ **5.** $m\angle L$ **7.** $\overline{RS}$ **9.** 80° **11.** 65° **13.** 6 **15.** 3 **17.** Two **18.** $R(-2, 3)$, $S(-6, 3)$, $T(-8, 7)$ **24.** 112° **26.** 90° **28.** $\overline{RT}$ **30.** $m\angle CBA$ **36.** $\frac{1}{6}$

4-2 Part B Try It

a. $\triangle ABC$ may be congruent to $\triangle OMN$. More information is needed. **b.** $\triangle DEF \cong \triangle RQP$; SAA Postulate

4-2 Part B Exercises

1. $\overline{MN}$ **3.** $\overline{MP}$ **5.** $\triangle ABC \cong \triangle FDE$; SSS Postulate **7.** $\triangle PQR \cong \triangle KJH$; SAS Postulate **9.** $\triangle URS \cong \triangle STU$; SSS Postulate **11.** Yes; SAA Postulate **13.** Yes; SAA Postulate

15.

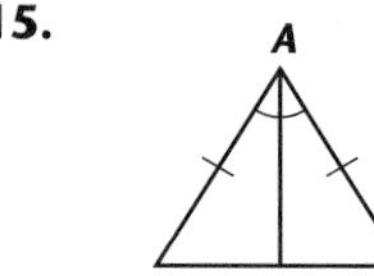

Given: $\overline{CA} \cong \overline{AB}$, D *is on* $\overline{BC}$, $\angle CAD \cong \angle DAB$ *Prove:* D is the midpoint of $\overline{BC}$
19. Vertical angles are congruent **21.** $\triangle ABC \cong \triangle DEF$; SAS Postulate
23. $\triangle ABC \cong \triangle DEC$; SAA Postulate **25.** $\triangle ABC$ may not be congruent to $\triangle DEC$.

4-2 Part C Try It

a. 1. (b), 2. (d), 3. (e), 4. (b), 5. (c)

4-2 Part C Exercises

1. Possible answer: $\overline{GH} \parallel \overline{JI}$, $\angle GHJ \cong \angle IJH$, $\angle HIJ$ is a right angle, $m\angle HGJ + m\angle GJI = 180°$, $\angle GHI$ is a right angle. **4. a.** 1. (c), 2. (b), 3. (b), 4. (a), 5. (d)
5. Reason 1: Given.
Reason 3: Given.
Statement 4: $\angle PQS \cong \angle RSQ$.
Statement 5: $\triangle PQS \cong \triangle RSQ$.
9. $A, B, C, E, F, G, I, J, K, M, N, O$ **11.** 109° **13.** 123°
15. Reason 1: Given.
Reason 2: Given.
Reason 3: Given.
Reason 4. SSS Postulate.
19. a. Possible answer: X bisects $\overline{VY}$ and $\overline{WZ}$. **b.** Possible answer: Show that $\overline{WX} \cong \overline{ZX}$, $\overline{YX} \cong \overline{VX}$ and $\angle WXV \cong \angle ZXY$ to show that $\triangle WXV \cong \triangle ZXY$ by SAS Postulate.

4-2 Part D Try It

a. *Given:* $\overline{ST} \cong \overline{UT}$, and $\angle VTS \cong \angle VTU$ because they are right angles. $\overline{VT} \cong \overline{VT}$ by the Reflexive Property. Now use the SAS Postulate.
b. $\overline{SV}$ and $\overline{UV}$, $\angle VST$ and $\angle VUT$, $\angle SVT$ and $\angle UVT$

4-2 Part D Exercises

1. a. $\triangle ABC \cong \triangle RST$
b. SSS Postulate **c.** Use CPCTC **3.** F; Symmetric

5. Possible Answer:

Statements	Reasons
1. e	**1.** Given
2. b	**2.** Given
3. c	**3.** Reflexive property
4. a	**4.** SSS
5. d	**5.** CPCTC

7.

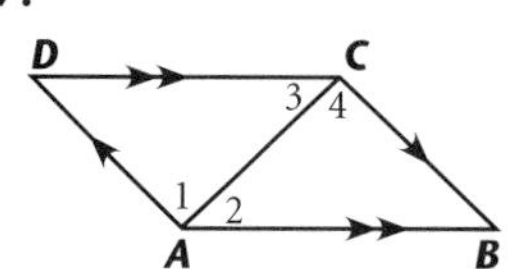

a. $\angle 2$ **b.** $\angle 1$ **c.** If two parallel lines are cut by a transversal, the alternate interior angles are congruent. **d.** Reflexive Property **e.** $\triangle CBA$
f. The ASA Postulate
g. CPCTC **8.** The triangles are congruent by the SAS Postulate. The fences are congruent by CPCTC, so they are the same length. **11.** $\angle N = 96°$; $\overline{OP} \cong \overline{OM}$ and $\overline{OQ} \cong \overline{ON}$ by the definition of *bisect.* $\angle MON \cong \angle POQ$ because vertical angles are congruent. $\triangle MON \cong \triangle POQ$ by the SAS Postulate. $\angle N \cong \angle Q$ by CPCTC. Therefore $x + 48 = 2x$. Solving the equation gives $x = 48$. Then $m\angle N = (x + 48)° = 96°$ **13.** $\angle ADC$
15. $\overline{AD}, \overline{DB}$ **17.** 62 cm
19. 21.1 in. **21. a.** The Reflexive Property **b.** Given information **c.** Given information **d.** *ABC* **e.** *CDA*
f. The SAA Postulate
g. CPCTC

4-2 Part E Self-Assessment

1. Always **2.** Never **3.** Never **4.** Always **5.** (c)
6. ASA Postulate **7.** SAA Postulate **8.** SAS Postulate
9. $NS = 2.8$ mi, $NT = 2$ mi; $\triangle NST \cong \triangle MTS$ by ASA
10. Possible answer: Prove triangles congruent, then any corresponding sides or angles are also congruent. **11.** 110
12. 210 **13.** 240; they differ by 180°. **14.** 48°

15. 6° **16.** 3° **17. a.** Definition of midpoint **b.** Vertical angles are congruent.
c. Given information **d.** SAA
18. 9 **19.** 26 **20. a.** Reason 1: Given. Reason 2: If two parallel lines are cut by a transversal, the alternate interior angles are congruent.
Statement 3: $\angle S \cong \angle U$.
Statement 4: $\overline{RT} \cong \overline{RT}$.
Statement 5: $\triangle URT \cong \triangle STR$.
Reason 5: SAA Postulate.
Statement 6: $\overline{RS} \cong \overline{TU}$.
Reason 6: CPCTC. **b.** Possible answer: Since it is given that $\overline{RU} \parallel \overline{ST}$, $\angle URT \cong \angle STR$ because if two parallel lines are cut by a transversal, the alternate interior angles are congruent. We are given $\angle S \cong \angle U$. $\overline{RT} \cong \overline{RT}$ by the Reflexive Property. So $\triangle URT \cong \triangle STR$ by the SAA Postulate. Therefore, $\overline{RS} \cong \overline{TU}$ by CPCTC.
22. Reason 1: Given.
Reason 2: Definition of *bisect.*
Reason 3: Vertical angles are congruent. Reason 4: SAS Postulate. Reason 5: CPCTC.
Reason 6: If alternate interior angles are congruent, the lines are parallel.

4-3 Part A Try It

a. $\angle A \cong \angle C$ **b.** 62

4-3 Part A Exercises

1. $\overline{FG}$ and $\overline{GH}$ have the same length. **3.** Definition of an *isosceles triangle* **5.** 25°
7. 19 **9. a.** $\overline{CD}, \overline{CE}$
b. Converse of the Isosceles Triangle Theorem **11.** $RS = 17$, $RT = ST = 16$

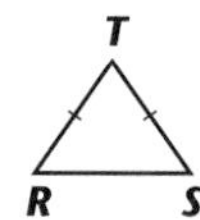

13. *Given:* $\angle 2 \cong \angle 4$ *Prove:* $\triangle XYZ$ is isosceles. *Proof:* 1. (b), Given; 2. (e), Vertical angles are congruent; 3. (a), Transitive Property; 4. (d), Isosceles Triangle Theorem Converse; 5. (c), Definition of *isosceles.* **15.** $\triangle DEF$ is equilateral **17.** SAS Postulate

19. ASA Postulate **21.** 80°
23. 45° **27.** Yes

4-3 Part B Exercises

1. HL Theorem **3.** HA Theorem **5.** $\overline{WX} \cong \overline{ZY}$ or $\overline{ZX} \cong \overline{WY}$ **7.** $\overline{WX} \cong \overline{ZY}$ and $\angle ZWX \cong \angle WZY$, or $\overline{ZX} \cong \overline{WY}$ and $\angle WZX \cong \angle ZWY$ (both). $\overline{WX} \cong \overline{ZY}$ and $\angle WZX \cong \angle ZWY$ or $\overline{ZX} \cong \overline{WY}$ and $\angle ZWX \cong \angle WZY$ (LA only).
9. Reason 1: Given.
Reason 2: Definition of a right triangle.
Statement 3: $\overline{AB} \cong \overline{CD}$.
Statement 4: $\overline{AC} \cong \overline{AC}$.
Reason 4: Reflexive Property.
Reason 5: HL Theorem.
11. a. Possible answer: $\triangle ABH \cong \triangle CBH$, $\triangle ADE \cong \triangle HDE$, $\triangle HFG \cong \triangle CFG$
b. HL Theorem, LL Theorem, LL Theorem, respectively.
15. Reason 1: Given.
Statement 2: $\angle YXZ \cong \angle WXV$.
Reason 3: Given.
Reason 4: If two parallel lines are cut by a transversal, the alternate interior angles are congruent.
Statement 5: $\triangle XVW \cong \triangle XZY$.
Reason 5: SAA Postulate
17. HL Theorem
19. Statement 1: $\angle EDF$ and $\angle CFD$ are right angles.
Reason 1: Given.
Reason 2: Definition of a right triangle.
Reason 3: Given.
Statement 4: $\overline{FD} \cong \overline{FD}$.
Reason 5: HL Theorem.
Statement 6: $\overline{DE} \cong \overline{FC}$.
Reason 6: CPCTC
21. Possible answer: So that we do not conclude that the triangles below are congruent.

4-3 Part C Try It

a. The sphere with radius 2 in. and center at point C.

4-3 Part C Exercises

1. a–c. Possible answer:

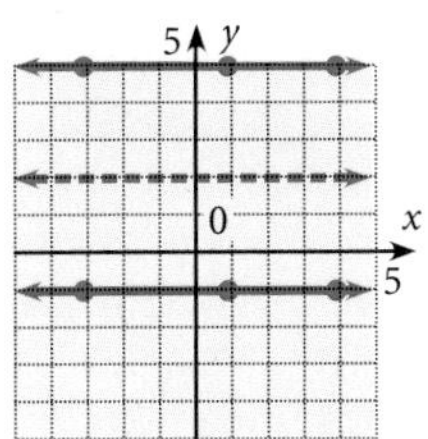

d. $y = 5, y = -1$ **3.** Two lines parallel to m, each 8 cm away. **5.** 2 **7.** The angle bisector **9.** It is the line with slope 1 passing through the origin.

11.

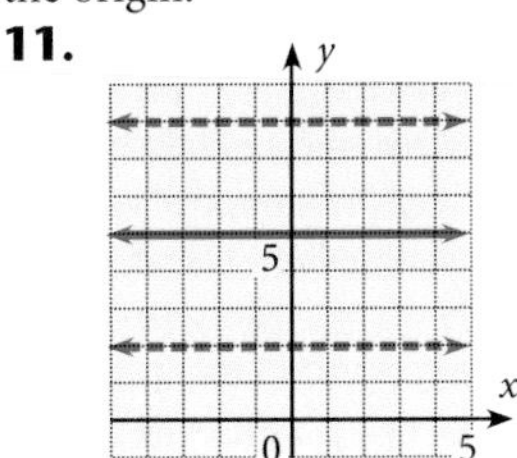

13.

Powerline
Watt
Substation
Millie

Draw the line segment from Millie to Watt. Draw the perpendicular bisector of that line segment until it intersects with the power line. This is where the substation should be: It lies on the perpendicular bisector, so it is equidistant from the two cities.

15. $\overrightarrow{TU}$ **17.** $\overleftrightarrow{VZ} \perp \overleftrightarrow{WY}$

21. Sphere with radius 3 in. and center at point K.

23. 10 **25.** 20

4-3 Part D Try It

a.

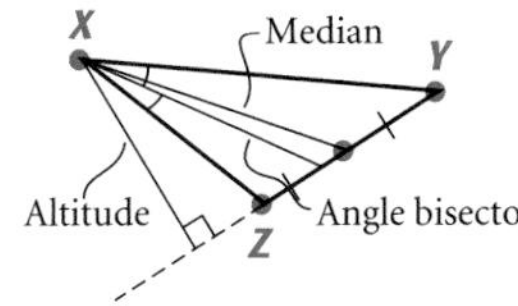

b.

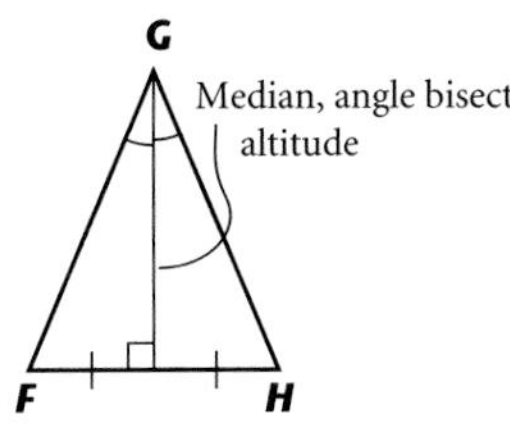

4-3 Part D Exercises

1. $\overline{CG}$ **3.** $\overline{AB}$ **7.** 24 **9. a.** 3 **b.** 6 **c.** 12 **d.** 18 **11.** Since it lies on all three perpendicular bisectors, the point of concurrency is equidistant from any pair of vertices and is therefore equidistant from all vertices.

12. a. Given **b.** Definition of median **c.** $\overline{AD} \cong \overline{DC}$ **d.** Given **e.** Reflexive Property **f.** $\triangle ABD \cong \triangle CBD$ **g.** CPCTC **15.** $m\angle 1$, $m\angle 3$, $m\angle 5$, $m\angle 7$, $m\angle 9$, $m\angle 11$, $m\angle 13$, $m\angle 15 = 58°$; $m\angle 2$, $m\angle 4$, $m\angle 6$, $m\angle 8$, $m\angle 10$, $m\angle 12$, $m\angle 14 = 122°$ **17.** $\overline{HJ}$ **19.** $\overline{LK}$ **21.** 16 **23.** An equilateral triangle; Then the earlier results for isosceles triangles apply three times, with each of the angles in turn taken as the vertex.

4-3 Part E Self-Assessment

1. HL Theorem **2.** HL Theorem **3.** HA Theorem **4.** LA Theorem **5.** 128° **6.** (a) **7.** Line parallel to ℓ and m, halfway between ℓ and m. **8.** The perpendicular bisector of the line segment $\overline{PQ}$. **9.** The angle bisector of $\angle RPQ$. **10.** C **11.** $\overline{JK}$ **12.** $\triangle ONJ$

13. Reason 1: Given.
Statement 2: $\angle 1 \cong \angle 2$.
Statement 3: $\overline{BD} \cong \overline{BD}$.
Reason 4: SAS Postulate.
Reason 5: CPCTC.
Statement 6: $\angle DAC \cong \angle DCA$.
Reason 6: Isosceles Triangle Theorem. **14. a.** Given information **b.** Definition of right triangles **c.** Reflexive Property **d.** $\overline{XW} \cong \overline{ZW}$ **e.** $\triangle WYX \cong \triangle WYZ$ **f.** CPCTC **g.** Y is the midpoint of $\overline{XZ}$ **15. a.** LL **b.** LA **c.** None **d.** HA or LA **16.** Draw the line segment from the post office to the park. Draw the perpendicular bisector of the line segment until it intersects the bike path. This is where the rest shelter should be built.

Chapter 4 Review

1. Hypotenuse **2.** Medians **3.** Isosceles **4.** Locus **5.** 89° **6.** 8° **7.** 102°, 26°, 52° **8.** 242 **9.** $\triangle MNP \cong \triangle RQP$; ASA Postulate **10.** $\triangle UVX \cong \triangle WVX$; SAS Postulate

12. Reason 1: Given.
Reason 2: Linear-Pair Postulate.
Reason 3: Supplements of congruent angles are congruent.
Statement 4: $\overline{DB} \cong \overline{DB}$.
Reason 5: Definition of *perpendicular.*
Reason 6: Right angles are congruent.
Statement 7: $\triangle ABD \cong \triangle CBD$.
Reason 7: SAA Postulate.

13. Draw the line segment from Carterville to Ely. Draw the perpendicular bisector. Any point on the bisector is equidistant from Carterville and Ely. Draw the angle bisector of the angle formed at the intersection of Highway 381 and Interstate 50. Any point on this bisector is equidistant from the two highways. Therefore the point of intersection of the two bisectors is where the water tower is to be built.

14. $BN = 6.5$, $BQ = 8$

15. It is not possible to create a tesselation with any two triangles.

CHAPTER 5

5-1 Part A Try It

a. Perimeter = 80; Area = 400 **b.** Perimeter = 154; Area = 1176 **c.** Perimeter = 92; Area = 288

5-1 Part A Exercises

1. 24 **3.** Perimeter = 34; Area = 60 **5.** Perimeter = 52; Area = 120 **7.** 47 square units **9.** 53 square units **11.** The units are different; A perimeter could be represented by 100 cm, whereas an area could be represented by 100 cm^2.

13. Rectangle = $2l + 2w$; Square = $4s$ **15.** Area = 49 **19.** Binomial **21.** Trinomial **23.** 50.41 m^2 **24.** 864 in.^{2} or 6 ft^2 **25.** 20.35 cm^2 **27.** 24 **29. a.** Blue triangles: 1, 3, 6, 10, 15, ... add 2, add 3, add 4, add 5, ... white triangles: 0, 1, 3, 6, 10, ... add 1, add 2, add 3, add 4, ... **b.** 21:15, 28:21, 36:28 **c.** $\frac{n(n+1)}{2}$ **d.** The limit is 1.

5-1 Part B Try It

a. $x^2 + 6x + 8$

	x	4
x	x^2	x x x x
2	x x	1 1 1 1 1 1 1 1

b. $(x + 5)(x + 2)$

	x	5
x	x^2	x x x x x
2	x x	1 1 1 1 1 1 1 1 1 1

5-1 Part B Exercises

1. a–c.

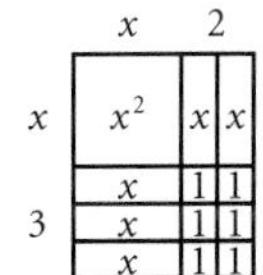

3. x 1 1 1 1 1 1 1

5.

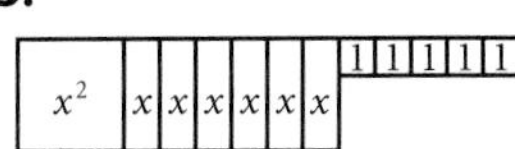

7. $x^2 + 4x + 3$ **9.** $6x^2 + 10x$ **11.** $(x + 3)(x + 5)$ **14.** $x + 2$ **17.** This pair of angles does not help to determine if a and c are parallel.

19. $a \parallel c$ because same-side interior angles are supplementary. **21.** $a \parallel b$ because alternate exterior angles are congruent. **23.** $\triangle IEF \cong \triangle HGF$; SAA Postulate **29.** $3x^2 + 5x + 2$ **31.** $(x + 3)(x + 1)$ **33.** $(x + 5)(2x + 1)$ **35.** 3, 6, 10: Add 3, add 4; The sum is a perfect square. $\frac{(n)(n+1)}{2} + \frac{(n-1)(n)}{2} = n^2$.

5-1 Part C Try It

a. $x \approx -4.32, x \approx 2.32$

5-1 Part C Exercises

1. a. $x^2 + 4x - 7 = 0$ **b.** $a = 1, b = 4, c = -7$ $x = \frac{-4 \pm \sqrt{(4)^2 - 4(1)(-7)}}{2(1)}$ **c.** $x = \frac{-4 \pm 2\sqrt{11}}{2}$ **d.** $x = -2 \pm \sqrt{11}$ **e.** $x \approx -5.32, x \approx 1.32$ **3.** $x = 4, x = -1$ **5.** $x \approx 1.85, x \approx -0.18$ **7.** $x = -1 \pm \sqrt{6}$ **9.** Length = 97 feet; width = 79 feet **11. a.** Length = $2w - 6$ **b.** Area = $(2w - 6)w$ **c.** Width = 50; length = 94 **13. a.** $\frac{3}{8}$ **b.** $\frac{1}{4}$ **c.** $\frac{3}{8}$ **d.** $\frac{5}{8}$ **15.** $\frac{2}{3}$; 0.67, 67% **17.** $\frac{2}{5}$; 0.4, 40% **19.** $x \approx 0.21, x \approx 3.12$ **21.** $x \approx -1.95, x \approx 1.95$ **23. a.** The maximum price is \$30 and the minimum price is \$6.25.

5-1 Part D Try It

a. $\frac{1}{3}$ **b.** ≈ 0.37 **c.** 0.3125 **d.** $\frac{1}{12} \approx 0.83$

5-1 Part D Exercises

1. $\frac{3}{8}$ **3.** $\frac{1}{4}$ **5.** 0.25 **7.** 0.17 **11.** Michigan ≈ 0.68; Indiana ≈ 0.03; Illinois ≈ 0.04; Wisconsin ≈ 0.25 **13.** Complement = 6°; Supplement = 96° **15.** Complement = $41\frac{1}{3}°$; Supplement = $131\frac{1}{3}°$ **17.** 0.28 **19. a.** $\frac{1}{8}$ **b.** $\frac{1}{8}$ **c.** $\frac{1}{2}$

5-1 Part E Self-Assessment

1. 64 **2.** 6.75 **3.** 8.4 **4.** 120 **5.** 76 **6.** 19.8 **8.** 50.8

9. $x^2 + 5x + 6$ **10.** $(x + 2)(x + 4)$ **11.** $x \approx -3.56, x \approx 0.56$ **12.** Reason 1: Given. Reason 2: Given. Reason 3: $\overline{RT} \cong \overline{RT}$. Reason 4: $\triangle RUT \cong \triangle TSR$; SSS. Postulate 5: CPCTC. Reason 6. $\overline{RS} \parallel \overline{TU}$; Alternate Interior Angles. **13.** $m\angle 2, 4, 6, 8 = 85°$; 95° **14.** $m\angle 2, 4, 6, 8 = 131°$; $m\angle 3, 5, 7 = 49°$ **15.** $m\angle 2, 4, 6, 8 = 80.8°$; $m\angle 3, 5, 7 = 99.2°$ **16.** (d) **17. a.** No; The 1990 bar is wider, as well as taller, than the 1980 bar. **b.** The bars should be the same width so that their areas are proportional. **18. a.** 0.16 **b.** 0.06 **19.** $\frac{9x}{x^2 + 9x + 20}$ The total area is $x^2 + 9x + 20$, and the winning area is $9x$.

5-2 Part A Try It

a. 49 **b.** 35.26 **c.** 24.6 in.^{2}

5-2 Part A Exercises

1. 11.04 in.^{2} **3.** 5.4 ft^2 **5.** 166.25 **7.** 2.88 m^2 **9.** 1.7 cm **11.** Possible answer: Quadrilateral does not belong because it is a type of figure, whereas the others are types of quadrilaterals. **13.** 3 (2.7 rounded up) **15.** 0.6 **17.** 0.5 **21.** $(x + 5)(x + 2)$ **23.** 34.04 cm^2 **25.** 3000 ft^2 **27.** ≈ 5.54 cm **29.** 11.5 in.

5-2 Part B Try It

a. Trapezoid **b.** Rhombus, parallelogram **c.** Rectangle, parallelogram **d.** Trapezoid **e.** Square, rectangle, rhombus, parallelogram **f.** 47.5 cm^2 **g.** 37.125 **h.** 30

5-2 Part B Exercises

1. 28 **3.** 319.2 **5.** 55 in.^{2} **7.** 7 units **9.** Rhombus **11.** Possible answer: $\triangle DEC$ and $\triangle BEA$ have equal areas, as do $\triangle ADE$ and $\triangle CBE$. For each pair, construct the altitudes and use SAS to show congruence of triangles. Use CPCTC to show congruence of the altitudes and of the corresponding bases. **13. a.** 0.91 mi^2 **15. a.** Each side length is equal to two radii. **b.** 9.0×10^{-14} mm^2 **17.** 420 **19.** 9.94 **21.** 67.5 m^2 **23.** 9.5 m **25.** Short base = 4; Long base = 8; Height = 11

5-2 Part C Exercises

1. a–d.

$x = 0$	$y = 0$
$x = 1$	$y = \frac{1}{2}$
$x = 2$	$y = 2$
$x = 3$	$y = 4.5$
$x = 4$	$y = 8$

b–c.

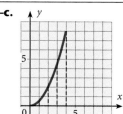

e. First area = 0.25; Second area = 1.25; Third area = 3.25; Fourth area = 6.25 **f.** 11 **3. a.** Approximate area = 36.5 **b.** 0.34 **5.** 19 **7. a.** 8 **b.** 32 **c.** 16 **d.** 48 **9.** $x \approx -0.65, x \approx 4.65$ **11.** 5.625 **13.** Area = 90.

5-2 Part D Self-Assessment

1. 38.08 cm^2 **2.** 2440 ft^2 **3.** 22.04 in.^{2} **4.** 13.1 **5.** $RC = 2$ cm; $\overline{MR}$ is a median. C is two-thirds the length of $\overline{MR}$ away from M on $\overline{MR}$. Therefore $RC = \frac{1}{2}MC$.

6. $NS = 9$ cm; $\overline{NS}$ is a median. C is two-thirds the length of $\overline{NS}$ away from N on $\overline{NS}$. Therefore $NS = \frac{3}{2}$NC.

7.

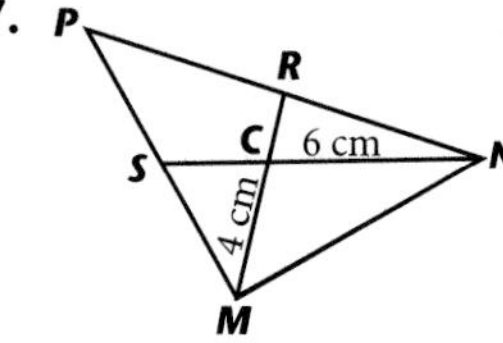

8. 9409 m^2 **9.** Width: 276 miles; Length: 376 miles; Solve the equation $(w)(w + 100) = 103{,}730$. **10.** (d) **11.** Possible answer: Use LL for two right triangles where the diagonals are the hypotenuses. Use CPCTC to show that diagonals are congruent. **12.** Bags of fertilizer = 30; Bags of seed = 5 **13.** ≈ 50 **14.** Area = 20 **15.** Area = 50 **16.** The perimeter will get smaller until C is directly above the midpoint of A and B, after which it will increase again. The area will remain constant, since neither the base nor the height will be changing. **17.** 0.16

5-3 Part A Try It

a. 10; Pythagorean triple = 6, 8, 10 **b.** 24; Pythagorean triple = 7, 24, 25 **c.** 5; Pythagorean triple = 5, 12, 13

5-3 Part A Exercises

1. a. 2, 4 **b.** 20 **c.** $2\sqrt{5}$ **d.** 4.47 **3.** 12 **5.** $2\sqrt{14}$, 7.48 **7.** 20 **9.** $\sqrt{5}$ **13.** 37 miles **14.** 13.90″ **15.** 14.8 ft **16.** Pythagorean triple **19.** $2\sqrt{5}$, 4.47 **21.** 4.24 **23.** $2\sqrt{10} \approx 6.32$ **25.** $2\sqrt{34}$, 11.66 **27.** 10 **29.** $\sqrt{5}$

5-3 Part B Try It

a. $y = 4\sqrt{3} \approx 6.93, z = 8$ **b.** $x = 10, y = 10\sqrt{3} \approx 17.32$ **c.** $x = 5, z = 10$ **d.** $x \approx 2.77, z \approx 5.54$

5-3 Part B Exercises

1. $PM = 6, PN = 6\sqrt{2}$ **3.** $b = 3, c = 3\sqrt{2} \approx 4.24$ **5.** $a = 4.6, c = 6.51$ **7.** $g = 7\sqrt{3} \approx 12.12, h = 14$ **9.** $f = 4, h = 8$ **11.** By the 45°- 45°-90° Theorem, $90\sqrt{2} \approx 127.28$ ft **13.** 389.71 **15.** $10\sqrt{2}$ **17.** $44\sqrt{3}$

18. 12.1 cm **23.** 10.05 **25.** 7.00 **27.** $f = 11, g = 11$ **29.** $a = 7, b = 7\sqrt{3} \approx 12.12$, $c = 14$ **31.** $a = \frac{7}{3}\sqrt{3} \approx 4.04, c = \frac{14}{3}\sqrt{3} \approx 8.08$
33. $\left(\frac{\sqrt{3}}{2}, \frac{1}{2}\right)$ **35.** $\left(-\frac{\sqrt{2}}{2}, \frac{\sqrt{2}}{2}\right)$

5-3 Part C Try It

a. $\sqrt{409}$ **b.** $5\sqrt{17}$ **c.** 3 **d.** 11 **e.** $\sqrt{21}$

5-3 Part C Exercises

1. 21 **3.** 5.66 **5.** $(d - c)\sqrt{2}$ **9.** $x^2 + y^2 = 100$ **13.** $x^2 + y^2 = (9.3 \times 10^7)^2 \approx 8.65 \times 10^{15}$ **15. a.** Given information **b.** Reflexive Property **c.** Given information **d.** Definition of median **e.** Definition of midpoint **f.** SSS Postulate **g.** CPCTC **h.** Definition of angle bisector **17.** 0.44 **19.** 14.45 **21.** $x^2 + y^2 = 49$ **23.** $x^2 + y^2 = 4$ **25.** $y \approx \pm 7.84 \times 10^7$ mi

5-3 Part D Try It

a. Yes **b.** No; Obtuse **c.** No; Acute

5-3 Part D Exercises

1. a. 41 **b.** 49 **c.** Obtuse **3.** Acute **5.** Right **7.** Right **9.** $3\sqrt{3} < x < 3\sqrt{5}$ **11.** The pole will be vertical when 25 feet of cable is extended. **21.** Right **23.** Obtuse **25.** Obtuse **27.** Yes, since one can always multiply the numbers of the triple by a constant to obtain a new triple. **29.** 4, 9, 16; $2^2, 3^2, 4^2$

5-3 Part E Self-Assessment

1. $c = 10$ cm **2.** $c < 10$ cm **3.** $c > 10$ cm **4.** (b) **5.** 0.205 **6.** 0.261 **7.** $\sqrt{300^2 + 225^2} = 375$ cm **8.** $x^2 + y^2 = 100$ **9.** 34.6 ft **10. a.** Two points determine a line **b.** Reflexive Property **c.** Given **d.** Given **e.** $\triangle ABC \cong \triangle CDA$ **f.** CPCTC **11.** $1, \sqrt{2}, 2, \sqrt{5}, 2\sqrt{2}, 3, \sqrt{10}, \sqrt{13}, 3\sqrt{2}$
12. a. $\sqrt{7}$ **b.** 0.23

Chapter 5 Review

1. F; Non-overlapping **2.** F; Quadratic equation **3.** T **4.** F; Rectangle **5.** 23 **6.** 48 **7.** 10 m² **8.** $8\frac{1}{2}$ in. **9.** ≈ 17.07 cm **10.** 288 m **11.** $x^2 + 8x + 15$ **12.** $(x + 10)(x + 2)$ **13. a.** 6.25 ft² **b.** 0.16 **14. a.** $4x^2 + 18x + 20$ in. **b.** 0.9 in. **15.** $AQ = 14, BN = 30$ **16.** Possible answer: Show that $\triangle JNK \cong \triangle LNM$ and $\triangle JNM \cong \triangle LNK$, using the SAS Postulate. Use CPCTC to show alternate interior angles congruent, so the sides are parallel. **17.** 17.04
18. $4\sqrt{2}$
19. 32.0 in. **20.** Applying the Pythagorean Theorem to points on a coordinate plane gives the distance formula. Using the distance formula to find all points in a plane a given distance from the center point gives the equation for a circle. **21.** Possible answer: The farmer will prefer a plan that maximizes the area.

CHAPTER 6

6-1 Part A Try It

a. Possible answers: *DCBA*, *BADC*, *CDAB* **b.** $\overline{DB}, \overline{AC}$ **c.** Rectangle **d.** Possible answer: All rectangles are parallelograms. All rectangles are quadrilaterals. Some rectangles are squares.

6-1 Part A Exercises

1. Possible answer: *ZYXW*, *XYZW*, *WZYX* **7.** T
9. $m\angle 1 = 90°$; $m\angle 2 = 90°$; $m\angle 3 = 105°$; $m\angle 4 = 75°$. The sum of the measures should be 360°. **11.** $\frac{4}{5}$
13. $x = 45$; $m\angle E = 100°$; $m\angle F = 135°$; $m\angle G = 45°$; $m\angle H = 80°$ **15.** $m\angle L = 52\frac{5}{7}°$; $m\angle K = 88\frac{3}{7}°$; $m\angle J = 113\frac{3}{7}°$; $m\angle M = 105\frac{3}{7}°$
Possible answers:
19. **21.**

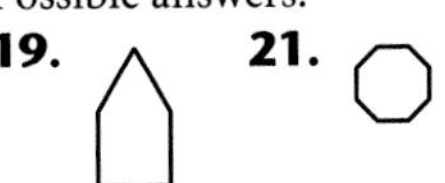

23.

25. Rectangle **27.** Parallelogram **29.** $m\angle C = m\angle A = 60°$; $m\angle ADC = m\angle CBA = 120°$ **31.** $m\angle TXR = 85°$; $m\angle R = 75°$; $m\angle STX = 65°$; $m\angle S = 135°$ **33. a.** 0 **b.** $\frac{4}{25}$ **c.** $\frac{16}{25}$

6-1 Part B Try It

a. Possible answer: *ABCDEF* **b.** Hexagon **c.** 3 **d.** Convex

6-1 Part B Exercises

1. (a) Octagon; (b) Pentagon; (c) Not a polygon; (d) Quadrilateral **3.** Possible answer: *ABCDEF*, *DCBAFE*, *FEDCBA*; Hexagon **5.** Possible answer: Octopus–sea animal with 8 arms; Quadriceps–4 muscles in the upper leg; Quadraphonic–four way sound in stereo. **7.** 8
11. 2160° interior, 360° exterior 540° (a pentagon)
13. 540° (a pentagon)
15. 12 **17.** Triangles, rectangles **19. a.** 720°; Use the Angle-Sum Theorem for $n = 6$. **b.** 120° **21.** 40
23. 55; $\frac{n(n+1)}{2}$ **25.** All; (a) Quadrilateral; (b) Hexagon; (c) Hexagon
27. Possible answer:

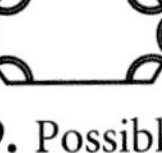

29. Possible answer:

31. Sum of interior angles = 1260°; Sum of exterior angles = 180° **33.** Sum of the interior angles = $(2x - 4)$ 180°; Sum of exterior angles = 360° **35.** 9 **37.** Octagon

6-1 Part C Try It

a. *RST* **b.** *LMTRQ* **c.** 7 faces; 10 vertices; 15 edges

6-1 Part C Exercises

1. *FABE*, *FED*, *EBCD*, *ACDF*, *ABC* **3.** $F = 5, V = 6, E = 9$ **5.** Face 1 is a triangle; Face 2 is an octagon

7. $\overline{PN}, \overline{NM}, \overline{MU}, \overline{UT}, \overline{TS}, \overline{SR}, \overline{RQ}, \overline{QP}$ **9.** 4; Possible answer: You cannot enclose space with three polygons.
11. T **17.** Quadrilateral
19. $F = 12, V = 10, E = 20$; $12 + 10 - 20 = 2$ **21.** $m\angle C = 64°$; $m\angle B = m\angle D = 116°$ **23.** *HGFE*, *ABCD*, *AHGB*, *GFCB*, *FEDC*, *HEDA* **25.** $F = 6, V = 8, E = 12$; $6 + 8 - 12 = 2$
27. Rectangle
29. Possible answer:

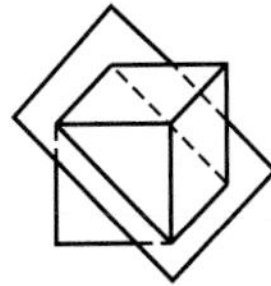

6-1 Part D Self-Assessment

1. $x = 38°$; $m\angle W = 66°$; $m\angle Z = 119°$; $m\angle Y = 38°$; $m\angle X = 137°$ **2.** Sum of interior angles = 1080°; Sum of exterior angles = 360°
3. Sum of interior angles = 2340°; Sum of exterior angles = 360° **4.** 12 pentagons; 12 triangles; 24 quadrilaterals; one 12-gon
5.

Type	Sum of Interior Angles
Pentagon	540°
Triangle	180°
Quadrilateral	360°
12-gon	1800°

6. (c) **7.** 33.64 **8.** 360
9. 600 **10.** Yes; Consider the triangles formed by the poles, their shadows and the rays of the sun. The triangles are congruent by ASA or LA. The poles are the same height by CPCTC. **11.** 3 new faces, 1 new vertex, 4 new edges **12.** $F = 9, V = 9, E = 16$; $9 + 9 - 16 = 2$
13. Nonahedron
14. Possible answer:

15. Possible answer:

16. Not possible

6-2 Part A Try It

a. 135° **b.** 45° **c.** 45° **d.** 7 **e.** 15 **f.** 5.5 **g.** 10.5

6-2 Part A Exercise

1. a. $\overline{AB} \parallel \overline{DC}, \overline{AD} \parallel \overline{BC}$
b. $\overline{AB} \cong \overline{DC}, \overline{AD} \cong \overline{BC}$
c. $\angle D \cong \angle B, \angle A \cong \angle C$
d. $\angle A$ and $\angle D$; $\angle A$ and $\angle B$; $\angle B$ and $\angle C$; $\angle C$ and $\angle D$
3. The opposite angles of a parallelogram are congruent.
5. The diagonals of a parallelogram bisect each other.
7. 10 **9.** 78° **11.** $m\angle WXY = 44°$ **13.** (9, 2), (−1, 2), (1, −2)
17. Possible answer:

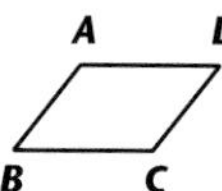

Given: ABCD a parallelogram *Prove:* Angle pairs $\angle A$ and $\angle B$, $\angle B$ and $\angle C$, $\angle C$ and $\angle D$, and $\angle D$ and $\angle A$ are supplementary. Statement 1: ABCD is a parallelogram. Reason 1: Given. Statement 2: $\overline{AD} \parallel \overline{BC}$. Reason 2: Definition of a *parallelogram.* Statement 3: $\angle A$ and $\angle B$ are supplementary, $\angle C$ and $\angle D$ are supplementary. Reason 3: If parallel lines are cut by a transversal, then same-side interior angles are supplementary. Use similar proof to show that other consecutive angles are supplementary.
21. $\triangle EFG \cong \triangle IHG$; SAS Postulate **23.** $4\sqrt{3}$ in.
25. 152° **27.** 42° **29.** The computer is listing triangles where $\overline{BD}$ and $\overline{EC}$ are corresponding parts. It will check to see whether these triangles can be proved congruent.

6-2 Part B Try It

a. Parallelogram; Opposite sides are congruent. **b.** Parallelogram; Diagonals bisect each other. **c.** Parallelogram; Consecutive angles are supplementary. **d.** May not be a parallelogram; The congruent sides may not be parallel.

6-2 Part B Exercises

1. Parallelogram; Both pairs of opposite angles are congruent. **3.** May not be a parallelogram; The conditions for a parallelogram may not be satisfied. **5.** May not be a parallelogram; The conditions for a parallelogram may not be satisfied. **7.** Parallelogram; Both pairs of opposite sides are parallel.
9. Consecutive angles are supplementary. **11.** $x = 7$ and $y = 8$. **13.** $\frac{3}{22}$
17. Possible answer:

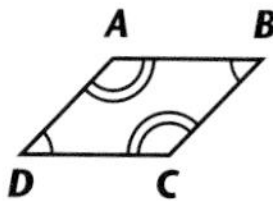

Given: $\angle A \cong \angle C$ and $\angle D \cong \angle B$ *Prove:* ABCD is a parallelogram. *Proof:* $\angle A \cong \angle C$ and $\angle D \cong \angle B$ is given. $m\angle A = m\angle C$ and $m\angle D = m\angle B$ by definition of *congruent.* $m\angle A + m\angle B + m\angle C + m\angle D = 360°$ by the Angle-Sum Theorem for Quadrilaterals. $2(m\angle A) + 2(m\angle B) = 2(m\angle B) + 2(m\angle C) = 360°$ by substituting $m\angle A = m\angle C$ and $m\angle D = m\angle B$. Dividing by two, $m\angle A + m\angle B = m\angle B + m\angle C = 180°$. Therefore the pairs $\angle A$ and $\angle B$, and $\angle B$ and $\angle C$ are supplementary by definition. $\overline{AB} \parallel \overline{CD}$ and $\overline{AD} \parallel \overline{BC}$ since same side interior angles are supplementary. ABCD is a parallelogram by definition.
19. $3\sqrt{33} \approx 17.23$ **21.** 23.55
23. Sum of interior angles = 2520°; Sum of exterior angles = 360° **25.** Parallelogram; Both pairs of opposite sides are congruent.
27. Parallelogram; The diagonals bisect each other.
29. Possible answer:

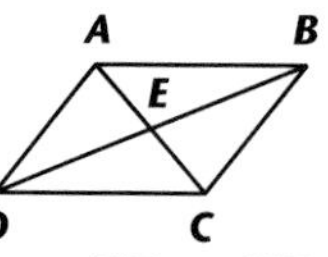

Given: $\overline{AC}$ and $\overline{BD}$ bisect each other. *Prove:* ABCD is a parallelogram. *Proof:* $\overline{AC}$ and $\overline{DB}$ bisect each other by the given information. Let E be the point of intersection. $\overline{AE} \cong \overline{EC}$ and $\overline{DE} \cong \overline{EB}$ by definition of *bisect.* $\angle AEB \cong \angle CED$ and $\angle AED \cong \angle CEB$ because vertical angles are congruent. $\triangle AEB \cong \triangle CED$ and $\triangle AED \cong \triangle CEB$ by the SAS Postulate. Then $\angle BAE \cong \angle DCE$ and $\angle DAE \cong \angle BCE$ by CPCTC. $\overline{AB} \parallel \overline{DC}$ and $\overline{AD} \parallel \overline{BC}$ because alternate interior angles are congruent. Therefore, ABCD is a parallelogram by definition.

6-2 Part C Try It

a. Parallelogram **b.** Rhombus **c.** Rectangle **d.** Square

6-2 Part C Exercises

1. Parallelogram **3.** Rhombus **5.** Parallelogram, rectangle, rhombus, square
7. Parallelogram, rectangle, rhombus, square
9. Rectangle, square
11. Rectangle, square
13. $3x = 15$ because diagonals bisect each other. So $x = 5$. $y - 5 = 15$ because diagonals are congruent and bisect each other. So $y = 20$. **15.** $(2x - 6)° + (2x - 6)° = 90°$ because diagonals of squares bisect angles and angles of squares are right angles. Solve for x to get $(4x - 12)° = 90°$ or $x = 25.5$.
17.

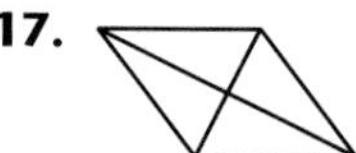

19. a. Rectangle; Diagonals are congruent. **b.** Rhombus; Diagonals are perpendicular but not congruent. **c.** Square; Diagonals are perpendicular and congruent.
23.

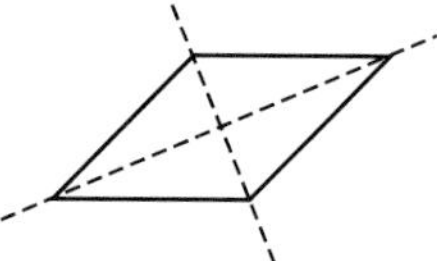

25. Reflect the triangle in one leg. Then reflect the result in the other leg. Reflect once more in the first leg. The four hypotenuses form a rhombus.
27. Possible answer:

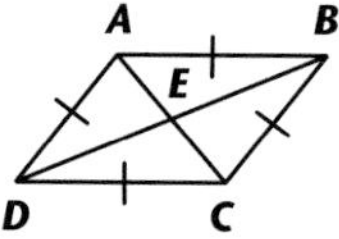

Given: ABCD is a rhombus. *Prove:* $\overline{AC} \perp \overline{DB}$. *Proof:* ABCD is a rhombus by the given information. $\overline{AD} \cong \overline{AB}$ by definition of a *rhombus.* $\overline{AC}$ bisects $\overline{DB}$ because diagonals of a parallelogram bisect each other. $\overline{DE} \cong \overline{EB}$ by definition of *bisect.* $\overline{AE} \cong \overline{AE}$ by the Reflexive Property. $\triangle AEB \cong \triangle AED$ by the SSS Postulate. $\angle AEB \cong \angle AED$ by CPCTC. $m\angle AEB + m\angle AED = 180°$ by the Linear-Pair Postulate. $m\angle AEB = m\angle AED$ by definition of *congruent.* $2(m\angle AEB) = 180°$ by substituting. Divide by 2 to get $m\angle AEB = 90°$. $\angle AEB$ is a right angle by definition of *right angle.* $\overline{AC} \perp \overline{DB}$ by definition of *perpendicular.*
29. 1, 1, −1 **31.** Yes; The slopes are negative reciprocals of each other. **33.** The diagonals are congruent and bisect each other. **35.** The diagonals are congruent, perpendicular, and bisect each other. **37.** $x = 20$; $y = 70$
42. Possible answer: Place two congruent ropes across each other so that they bisect. When the measurements between the adjacent rope ends are equal, mark corners for a square foundation.

6-2 Part D Exercises

1. (c, b); $(c + a, 0)$ **3.** $(a + c, b)$ **5.** Slope of $\overline{HJ} = \frac{b}{a}$, slope of $\overline{GF} = \frac{b}{a}$, slope of $\overline{JF} = 0$, slope of $\overline{HG} = 0$. So $\overline{HJ} \parallel \overline{GF}$ and $\overline{JF} \parallel \overline{HG}$.
7. a. Rectangle; Possible answer: The diagonals are congruent and the opposite sides are congruent. **b.** Possible answer: The distance from (0, 0) to (200, 120) is $\sqrt{(200)^2 + (-120)^2} = 40\sqrt{34}$. The distance from (0, 120) to (200, 0) is $\sqrt{(200)^2 + (120)^2} = 40\sqrt{34}$. The distance from (0, 0) to (0, 120) is 120. The distance from (200, 0) to (200, 120) is 120. The distance from (0, 0) to (200, 0) is 200. The distance from (0, 120) to (200, 120) is 200.
9. Possible answer:

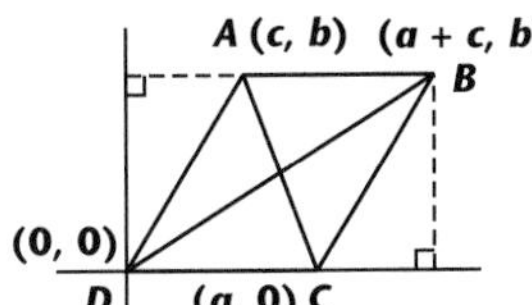

The midpoint of $\overline{DB}$ is $\frac{0 + (a + c)}{2}, \frac{0 + b}{2} = \left(\frac{a + c}{2}, \frac{b}{2}\right)$. The midpoint of $\overline{AC}$ is $\frac{(a + c)}{2}, \frac{0 + b}{2} = \left(\frac{a + c}{2}, \frac{b}{2}\right)$. The midpoints are identical, so $\overline{AC}$ bisects $\overline{DB}$ and $\overline{DB}$ bisects $\overline{AC}$ by definition of *bisect.* **11.** Acute **13.** Obtuse **17.** $F = 5, V = 6, E = 9; 5 + 6 - 9 = 2$.
19. $F(2a, 2b)$ **21.** Possible answer: S is the midpoint of $\overline{LM}$ so its coordinates are $\left(\frac{a}{2}, \frac{b}{2}\right)$. T is the midpoint of $\overline{PN}$ so its coordinates are $\left(\frac{c + d}{2}, \frac{b}{2}\right)$. The slope of $\overline{ST}$ is $\frac{\frac{b}{2} - \frac{b}{2}}{\frac{c + d}{2} - \frac{a}{2}} = 0$. The slope of $\overline{LP}$ is $\frac{0 - 0}{d - 0} = 0$ and the slope of $\overline{MN}$ is $\frac{b - b}{c - a} = 0$. Therefore, $\overline{ST} \parallel \overline{LP}$ and $\overline{ST} \parallel \overline{MN}$. $ST = \frac{c + d - a}{2}$. $MN = c - a$ and $LP = d$. The average of MN and LP is $\frac{MN + LP}{2} = \frac{c + d - a}{2}$. Therefore $ST = \frac{MN + LP}{2}$.
23. a. A is the computer. It asks questions or makes restatements only. **b.** Possible answer: It asks questions using key words from the previous response.

6-2 Part E Self-Assessment

1. Sometimes; When the rectangle is a square.
2. Always; The diagonals of a parallelogram bisect each other and a rhombus is a parallelogram. **3.** Never; When the diagonals bisect each other the figure is a parallelogram, and a trapezoid is never a parallelogram.
4. Rhombus, square **5.** Rectangle, square **6.** Square **7.** (c) **8.** 115° **9.** 3 **10.** 28° **11.** 10 **12.** 30.0 ft **13.** 90° **14.** 120° **15.** 144° **16.** $\overline{AB}$ is always parallel to the ground and $\overline{DC}$ is always parallel to $\overline{AB}$. $ABCD$ is a parallelogram since $AB = CD$ and $AD = BC$. **17.**

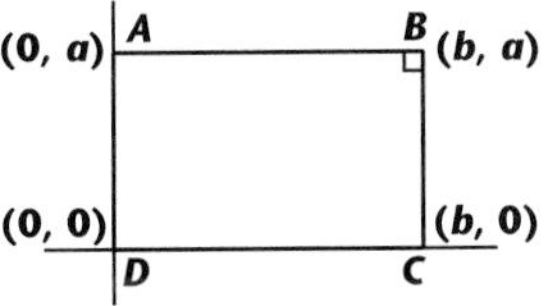

$DB = \sqrt{a^2 + b^2}$. $AC = \sqrt{(0 - b)^2 + a^2} = \sqrt{a^2 + b^2}$. So $DB = AC$. Therefore, $\overline{AC} \cong \overline{DB}$ by definition of *congruent.* **18.** Possible answer: The advantage of a coordinate proof is that you are able to do calculations using the coordinates. A disadvantage is that the coordinate method may involve calculations using the coordinates. Segments can be shown to be parallel, perpendicular, or congruent using coordinate methods.

6-3 Part A Try It

a. Equilateral **b.** Regular **c.** Equiangular **d.** 1086 cm²

6-3 Part A Exercises

1. Regular **3.** Equiangular **5.** Interior angle = 135°; Exterior angle = 45° **7.** Interior angle = 120°; Exterior angle = 60° **11.** Center **13.** Radius **15.** 1545 cm² **17.** 64 m² **19.** 696 in.² **21.** $a = 6\sqrt{3}$; $r = 12$; Area $= 216\sqrt{3} \approx 374.1$
26. The diagonals are perpendicular, congruent, and bisect each other.
29. $x = \frac{-7 \pm \sqrt{37}}{2} \approx -0.46$ or -6.54
31. $x = \frac{2 \pm \sqrt{34}}{3} \approx -1.28$ or 2.61 **33.** Interior angle = 150°; Exterior angle = 30° **35.** 17.6 ft² **37.** $a = 8$; $r = 8\sqrt{2}$; Area = 256 **39.** $a = \frac{8}{3}\sqrt{3}$; $r = \frac{16}{3}\sqrt{3}$; Area $= 64\sqrt{3} \approx 110.9$ **41. a.** 186 in.² **b.** 714 in.² **c.** 4 times greater

6-3 Part B Try It

a. Regular icosahedron
b. Regular hexahedron (cube)
c. Regular tetrahedron

6-3 Part B Exercises

1. Tetrahedron **3.** Hexahedron **5.** Icosahedron
7. Regular dodecahedron
11. Regular hexahedron
13. a. Cube **b.** $F = 6$, $V = 8$, $E = 12$; $6 + 8 - 12 = 2$ **15.** 324° **16.** Possible answers: $\overrightarrow{BC} = \overrightarrow{AD}$; $\overrightarrow{BH} = \overrightarrow{AE}$; $\overrightarrow{AC} = \overrightarrow{FH}$ **19.** $z = \frac{40}{3}$ **21.** $\frac{7}{2}$ **23.** Regular tetrahedron **25.** 180° **27.** Use a regular tetrahedron and put each number on a side.

6-3 Part C Self-Assessment

1. The faces of regular polyhedrons are regular polygons. **2. a.** 120° **b.** 60° **c.** $a = \frac{5}{2}$ mm; $r = \frac{5}{3}\sqrt{3}$ mm; $A = \frac{25}{2}\sqrt{3} \approx 21.65$ mm² **d.** ≈ 4.62 cells **3.** (b)
4.

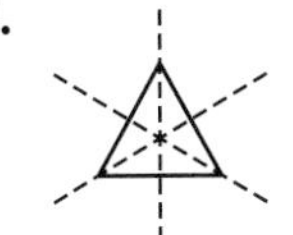

5.

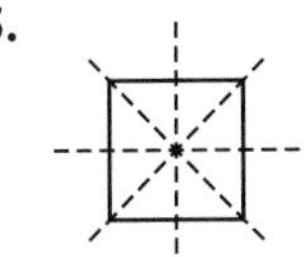

6.

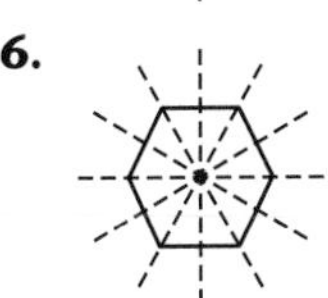

7. n **8.** Possible answer:

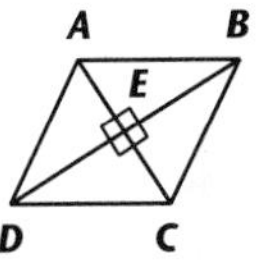

Given: $ABCD$ is a parallelogram, $\overline{AC} \perp \overline{DB}$. *Prove:* $ABCD$ is a rhombus. *Proof:* $ABCD$ is a parallelogram by the given information. $\overline{BD}$ bisects $\overline{AC}$ because diagonals of a parallelogram bisect each other. $\overline{AE} \cong \overline{EC}$ by the definition of *bisect.* $\overline{EB} \cong \overline{EB}$ by the Reflexive Property. $\overline{AC} \perp \overline{DB}$ is given. $\angle AEB$ and $\angle CEB$ are right angles by definition of *perpendicular.* $\triangle AEB \cong \triangle CEB$ by LL. $\overline{AB} \cong \overline{BC}$ by CPCTC. $\overline{AB} \cong \overline{DC}$ and $\overline{AD} \cong \overline{BC}$ because opposite sides of a parallelogram are congruent. $\overline{AB} \cong \overline{DC} \cong \overline{BC} \cong \overline{AD}$ by the Transitive Property. $ABCD$ is a rhombus by definition. **9.** Rectangle; $\overline{AH} \cong \overline{BG}$ and $\overline{AB} \cong \overline{HG}$ so it is a parallelogram. $AG = BH$ so it is a rectangle. It is not a square because $AB \neq AH$.
10. Let x be the width, then $x(x + 48) = 41{,}040$. So $x^2 + 48x - 41{,}040 = 0$. Solve for x to get $x = 180$ (or $x = -228$). 180 ft wide and 228 ft long **11. a.** 36° **b.** 60°

12. Regular tetrahedron; Regular octahedron; Regular icosahedron **13.** From left to right: cut off vertices of a regular tetrahedron, octahedron, icosahedron, and dodecahedron. **14.** Regular octahedron

Chapter 6 Review

1. Apothem; The other terms are all classifications of polygons and polyhedrons. **2.** Center; The other terms all refer to distances/segments. **3.** Interior, 540°; Exterior, 360° **4.** Possible answer:

5. Octagon **6.** 8; Octahedron **7.** Parallelogram; The diagonals bisect each other. **8.** May not be a parallelogram; The congruent sides may not be parallel. **9.** Parallelogram; Both pairs of opposite sides are parallel. **10.** M is at $\left(\frac{b+d}{2}, \frac{c+e}{2}\right)$. N is at $\left(\frac{a+d}{2}, \frac{e}{2}\right)$. O is at $\left(\frac{a}{2}, 0\right)$. P is at $\left(\frac{b}{2}, \frac{c}{2}\right)$. Slope of $\overline{MN}$ is $\frac{\frac{e}{2} - \frac{(c+e)}{2}}{\frac{(a+d)}{2} - \frac{(b+d)}{2}} = \frac{-\frac{c}{2}}{\frac{(a-b)}{2}} = \frac{c}{b-a}$. Slope of $\overline{NO}$ is $\frac{0 - \frac{e}{2}}{\frac{a}{2} - \frac{(a+d)}{2}} = \frac{-\frac{e}{2}}{-\frac{d}{2}} = \frac{e}{d}$. Slope of $\overline{OP}$ is $\frac{\frac{c}{2} - 0}{\frac{b}{2} - \frac{a}{2}} = \frac{\frac{c}{2}}{\frac{(b-a)}{2}} = \frac{c}{b-a}$. Slope of $\overline{PM}$ is $\frac{c}{b-a}$. $\frac{\frac{(c+e)}{2} - \frac{c}{2}}{\frac{(b+d)}{2} - \frac{b}{2}} = \frac{\frac{e}{2}}{\frac{d}{2}} = \frac{e}{d}$. So $\overline{MN} \parallel \overline{OP}$ and $\overline{NO} \parallel \overline{PM}$. Therefore, $MNOP$ is a parallelogram by definition. **11.** 144° **12.** Put 1, 2, 3, and 4 on two faces each and 5 on the four remaining faces. **13.** $a = \sqrt{3}$ in.; $r = 2\sqrt{3}$ in.; Area $= 9\sqrt{3} \approx 15.6$ in.^{2} **14.** $h = 2\sqrt{21}$ cm, area $= 34\sqrt{21} \approx 155.8$ cm^2 **15.** Possible answer: The sum of the interior angles of a convex polygon is given by the formula $(n - 2)180°$ where n is the number of sides. The sum of the exterior angles is always 360°.

CHAPTER 7

7-1 Part A Try It

a. Similar; $\frac{1}{2}$ **b.** Similar; $\frac{3}{1}$ **c.** Not similar **d.** Similar; $\frac{1}{3}$

7-1 Part A Exercises

1. 2 **5.** 22.5 in. × 30 in. **7.** F; The length and width of the sides can be changed independently and the second figure can still be a rectangle. **9.** T; All angles are 60° (therefore congruent) and all the sides, being equal in length, must be the same multiple of the original triangle's sides. **10.** Smallest: 2.6 cm × 3.9 cm Largest: 5.6 cm × 8.4 cm **13.** A to $B = \frac{3}{2}$; B to $A = \frac{2}{3}$ **15.** Similar; $\frac{2}{3}$ **19.** 9 **21.** $2\frac{2}{5}$ **25.** Similar; Similarity ratio $= \frac{2}{1}$ **27.** 8 cm × 12 cm **29.** 11 in. × about 14.67 in.

7-1 Part B Try It

a. $\triangle EFG \sim \triangle JIH$; $\angle E \cong \angle J$, $\angle F \cong \angle I$, $\angle G \cong \angle H$; $\frac{EF}{JI} = \frac{FG}{IH} = \frac{GE}{HJ} = \frac{1}{2}$ **b.** $QRST \sim YXWV$; $\angle T \cong \angle V$, $\angle Q \cong \angle Y$, $\angle R \cong \angle X$, $\angle S \cong \angle W$; $\frac{QR}{YX} = \frac{RS}{XW} = \frac{ST}{WV} = \frac{TQ}{VY} = 3$ **c.** $m\angle E = 67°$, $m\angle G = 107°$, $m\angle N = 43°$ **d.** $x = 14$, $y = 15$, $z = 25$ **e.** $\frac{5}{2}$

7-1 Part B Exercises

1. $\angle A \cong \angle E$, $\angle B \cong \angle F$, $\angle C \cong \angle G$, $\angle D \cong \angle H$ $\frac{AB}{EF} = \frac{BC}{FG} = \frac{CD}{GH} = \frac{DA}{HE}$ **3.** 49° **5.** 15 **7.** $\frac{2}{3}$ **11.** 11.57 **13.** $\frac{DF}{AC} = \frac{3}{7}$ **14.** T: (18, 7); U: (18, 19); V: (2, 19) **15.** T: (6, 7); U: (6, 10); V: (2, 10) **17.** 1599 miles **19.** Building will be 31 m × 52.8 m **21.** $a = 155.56$; $c = 155.56$ **23.** $d = 3023.58$; $e = 6047.17$ **25.** Interior angle = 140°; Exterior angle = 40° **27.** $\angle M \cong \angle P$, $\angle N \cong \angle Q$, $\angle O \cong \angle R$; $\frac{OM}{RP} = \frac{MN}{PQ} = \frac{NO}{QR}$ **29.** 100° **31.** 12 **33.** $\frac{4}{3}$ **34.** Yes; Compare a right isosceles triangle and an equilateral triangle.

7-1 Part C Try It

a. 6 cm^2 **b.** 20 cm

7-1 Part C Exercises

1. a. $\frac{5}{4}, \frac{5}{4}$ **b.** $\left(\frac{5}{4}\right)^2 = \frac{25}{16}$ **3.** Area ratio $= \frac{64}{169}$; Perimeter ratio $= \frac{8}{13}$ **4.** $\frac{3}{2}$ **5.** $\frac{3}{2}$ **7.** $\frac{5}{4}$ **8.** Multiply by $\sqrt{2}$ **10.** Yes; $\frac{\text{Area}_1}{\text{Area}_2} = \text{ratio}^2$; ratio = 1 here, so that the sides are not only proportional, but congruent. Since the figures are similar, the corresponding angles are also congruent, so the figures are congruent. **15.** Yes; Corresponding angles are congruent (here, 90° each); We are given $\frac{l_1}{w_1} = \frac{l_2}{w_2}$, but this can be rewritten as $\frac{l_1}{l_2} = \frac{w_1}{w_2}$; i.e., corresponding sides are in the same proportion. **17.** Area ratio $= \frac{9}{25}$; Perimeter ratio $= \frac{3}{5}$ **19.** $\frac{4}{3}$ **21. a.** 0.20 **b.** 0.79; 4 times part (a).

7-1 Part D Try It

a. 40.5 **b.** 6.2

7-1 Part D Exercises

1. (b) **3.** 0.618 **5.** 161.80 **6.** 0.618; 1.618 − 0.618 = 1 **8.** Golden rectangle; Golden ratio **11.** 19.425 **12.** 3564.5 **13.** 7.5 in.^{2} **15.** $x = 30$; $y = 6$; Opposite sides are congruent. **17.** 1.618 **19.** 18.54 **21.** Cut a strip 8.5 − 6.798 = 1.702 in. wide (and 11 in. long) off along the 11 in. side.

7-1 Part E Self-Assessment

1. Always true **2.** Sometimes true **3.** Always true **4.** Interior angle = 120°; Exterior angle 60° **5.** Interior angle = 150°; Exterior angle 30° **6.** Interior angle= 157.5°; Exterior angle 22.5° **7.** 5 m by 4 m **8.** 2.9 cm by 1.1 cm **9.** 100 cm; 75 cm **10.** 78.125 ft **11.** 90° **12.** 56° **13.** 60 **14.** $\frac{3}{5}$ **15.** $\frac{5}{3}$ **16.** $x = 5$; $y = 4$; $z = 6$; $w = 65$ **17.** $x = 5.83$; $y = 5.14$; $z = 4.17$; $w = 55$ **18.** (d) **19. a.** 11.12 feet **b.** $\frac{\text{Area of Tremendo}}{\text{Area of Comfy}} = 4 = 2^2$. Screen is 2(18) by 2(11.12), or 36 × 22.24 feet

7-2 Part A Try It

a. $\angle ABE \cong \angle CBD$ since they are vertical angles. $\angle A \cong \angle C$ because they are alternate interior angles ($\overline{AE}$ and $\overline{DC}$ are parallel). By the two congruent angle conjecture $\triangle ABE \sim \triangle CBD$. **b.** $\angle ZVY \cong \angle W$ since both are right angles; $\angle Z$ is used in both $\triangle VZY$ and $\triangle WZX$; By the two congruent angles conjecture $\triangle ZVY \sim \triangle ZWX$.

7-2 Part A Exercises

1. 30° **3.** 60° **5.** Not similar; $\angle N = 70°$, so there is no second pair of congruent angles. **7.** Given $\angle WXZ \cong \angle ZXY$ and $\angle WZX \cong \angle XYZ$, $\triangle XWZ \sim \triangle XZY$ by AA; $x = 7.5$; $y = 4.5$ **9.** 37.5 feet **11.** $\angle VXW \cong \angle YXZ$ because they are vertical angles; $\angle W \cong \angle Y$ because they are alternate interior angles of two parallel lines; Thus, by AA, $\triangle VXW \sim \triangle ZXY$. Since the triangles are similar, the corresponding sides are proportional, so $\frac{VW}{YZ} = \frac{WX}{XY}$. **13. a.** $\frac{9}{12} = \frac{12}{16}$, so 12 is the geometric mean of 9 and 16.

b. $\frac{16}{20} = \frac{20}{25}$, so 20 is the geometric mean of 16 and 25. $\frac{9}{15} = \frac{15}{25}$, so 15 is the geometric mean of 9 and 25. **15.** 16 **17.** 128° **19.** $\frac{2}{3}$ **21.** $\frac{4}{9}$ **23.** From the given information, $\angle T \cong \angle Q$. $\angle U \cong \angle R$ because right angles are congruent. By AA, $\triangle TUV \sim \triangle QRS$. **25.** Based on given information, $\triangle FHG \sim \triangle JHI$ by AA; $x = 4$; $y = 10$ **27. a.** Assume $\overline{XY} \parallel \overline{AB}$, so $\angle X \cong \angle B$ and $\angle Y \cong \angle A$ (alternate interior angles); By AA, the triangles are similar. **b.** 3.5 m **c.** 2.5 m

7-2 Part B Try It

a. $\frac{7.8}{5.2} = \frac{8.1}{5.4} = 1.5$; Two pairs of corresponding sides are proportional, and the angles between them are given as congruent, so by SAS; $\triangle JHI \sim \triangle EDF$; $x = 4.8$. **b.** $\frac{TR}{RQ} = \frac{SR}{PR} = \frac{3.2}{9.6} = \frac{1}{3}$. The interior (to the triangles) angles formed by $\overline{TQ}$ intersecting $\overline{PS}$ are congruent because they are vertical angles. Thus, by SAS, $\triangle PRQ \sim \triangle SRT$; $x = 8.4$.

7-2 Part B Exercise

1. $\triangle ABC \sim \triangle DEF$ by SAS **2.** $\triangle GHK \sim \triangle GIJ$ by AA **3.** $\triangle KML \sim \triangle PMN$ by SAS **5.** $\triangle FGH \sim \triangle JKH$ by SAS; $x = 124$; $y = 33$ **9.** $x = 60$; SSS **11.** $x = 6$; SAS **13.** If two triangles are equilateral, all angles measure 60° and are congruent. The triangles are similar by AA. **17.** Extend two line segments along $\overline{RS}$ and $\overline{RT}$. Place the compass point at S and mark segment $\overline{SV}$ such that $\overline{RS} \cong \overline{SV}$; Similarly use the compass to create $\overline{TW} \cong \overline{RT}$. $\frac{RV}{RS} = \frac{RW}{RT} = 2$. Both triangles share $\angle R$, so SAS assures similarity of $\triangle RST$ and $\triangle RVW$. **19.** $\triangle GHI \sim \triangle LKJ$; Similarity by SAS; $x = 3.6$; $y = 75.5$ **21.** Possible answer: $x = 15$; SAS

23.

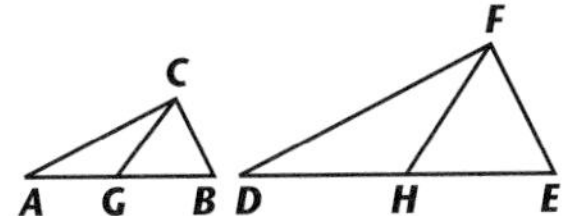

Possible answer: $\triangle ABC \sim \triangle DEF$ and $\overline{CG}$ and $\overline{FH}$ are medians. Show that $\triangle AGC \sim \triangle DHF$ by SAS. Therefore $\frac{AC}{DF} = \frac{GC}{HF}$.

7-2 Part C Try It

a. $IJKL$; C **b.** $\frac{3}{2}$ **c.** $\frac{1}{2}$

7-2 Part C Exercises

1. a. 7 cm **b.** 135° **3.** $k = \frac{1}{3}$ **5.** Scale factor **6.** Similar **9.** Enlargement; $k = 2$; Center of dilation is found by drawing lines through corresponding vertices and observing where lines intersect. **11.** $A' = \left(\frac{3}{2}, 0\right)$, $B' = \left(\frac{7}{2}, 2\right)$, $C' = \left(-\frac{3}{2}, 1\right)$ **13. a.** $\frac{1}{2}$ in. = 60 ft = 60(12) in. = 720 in., so $k = \frac{1}{2(720)} = \frac{1}{1440}$. **c.** Figures and their dilated images are similar, and the ratio of the areas of two similar polygons is (similarity ratio)^2, so $\frac{\text{Area actual}}{\text{Area plan}} = (1440)^2$ **15.** They bisect each other. **17.** They bisect each other and are congruent. **19.** 10 ft × 7 ft **21.** Enlargement; $k = 4$; Center of dilation is one square to the left of the left leg (at the base) of the smaller "A". **23.** $A' = (6, 6)$, $B' = (18, 12)$, $C' = (-3, -9)$ **27.** Dilations preserve the measures of angles in a figure. Hence, a triangle will be similar to its image by AA.

7-2 Part D Try It

a. 8.5 **b.** 57 **c.** 12.4

7-2 Part D Exercises

1. $SW = 50$, $WU = 30$, $US = 40$ **3.** $AC = 20$, $BC = 10$, $BE = 9$ **5.** $m\angle A = 54.5°$; $BE = 8.5$ **9. a.** 16 mm **b.** 8 mm; 20 mm from the horizon measured along the tracks

11. Possible answer: $\overline{EF} \parallel \overline{CB}$ since a midsegment is parallel to the third side. Let G be the point where $\overline{AD}$ intersects $\overline{EF}$. $\angle AFE \cong \angle ABD$ because corresponding angles are congruent. $\angle DAB \cong \angle DAB$ by the Reflexive Property. $\triangle GAF \sim \triangle DAB$ by AA. $\frac{AF}{AB} = \frac{1}{2}$ because $\overline{EF}$ is the midsegment. $\frac{AG}{AD} = \frac{1}{2}$ by the definition of *similar*. $AG = \frac{1}{2}AD$, so $\overline{EF}$ bisects $\overline{AD}$. **13.** Yes; By AA **15.** $GH = 6$, $HJ = 6$, $JK = 18$ **17.** $JK = 14$, $m\angle J = 138°$
19. Reason 1: Given.
Reason 2: Corresponding angles of two parallel lines are congruent.
Reason 3: AA
Reason 4: Corresponding sides of similar triangles are proportional.
Reason 5: Segment Addition Postulate.
Reason 6: Substitution (into Step 4). **21.** 21 **23.** $31\frac{1}{5}$

7-2 Part E Self-Assessment

1. Possible answer: $x = 2\frac{10}{11}$ or 5.5; SAS **2.** $x = 6.66$; SSS **3.** $x = 39$; AA **4.** $\triangle AEB \sim \triangle ADC$; Similar by AA; $x = 3.75$; $y = 9$ **5.** $\triangle HFG \sim \triangle HJI$ by SAS; $x = 53°$; $y = 3.33$ **6.** $\triangle LMK \sim \triangle QPN$ by SSS; $x = 53$; $y = 37$ **7.** 4,629.9 ft **8.** $ST = \frac{1}{2}SV$ and $SU = \frac{1}{2}SW$ since $\overline{TU}$ is the midsegment; So $\frac{ST}{SV} = \frac{SU}{SW} = \frac{1}{2}$. $\angle S \cong \angle S$ by the Reflexive Property. $\triangle STU \sim \triangle SVW$ by SAS. **9.** Area $\triangle ABC = \frac{1}{16}$ area $\triangle XYZ$ **10.** Diagonals bisect each other and are of the same length; $x = 9$, $y = -4$. **11.** Diagonals bisect at right angles; $x = 132$, $y = 14$ **12.** Opposite sides of a rectangle are congruent; $x = 5$, $y = 3$. **13. a.** $\frac{b}{2}$ (half as much); Twice the acreage means twice the crop.

b. If cost per foot of fence is constant, it should cost $\sqrt{2}f$.
15.

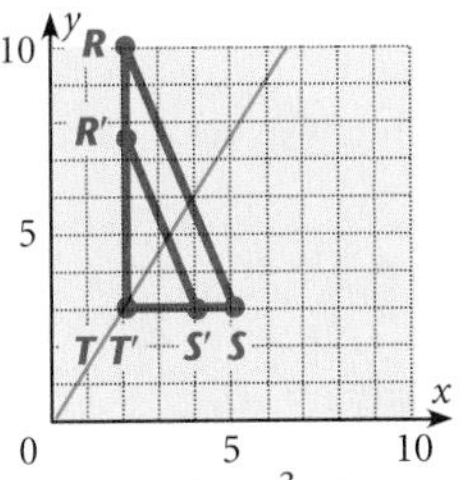

Perimeter ratio = $\frac{3}{2}$; Area ratio = $\frac{9}{4}$ **16.** (a) **17.** Possible answer: Images under dilation are similar to the pre-image **18.** $(k(x - a) + a, k(y - b) + b)$ **19.** Possible answer: Create a scissors-like or pliers-like device where the astronauts can close the handles to pick up/measure the object on the ground by using the distance between the handles to measure the size of the object via similar triangles.

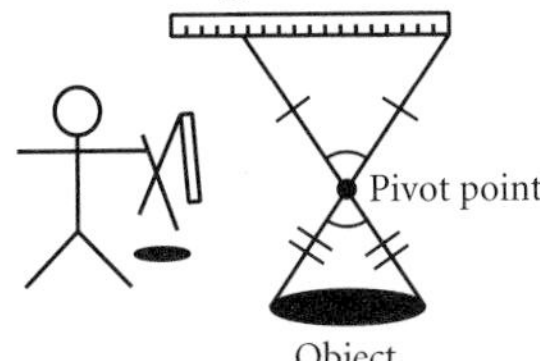

7-3 Part A Try It

a. $\frac{5}{13}$ **b.** $\frac{12}{13}$ **c.** $\frac{12}{13}$ **d.** $\frac{12}{5}$

7-3 Part A Exercises

1. a. $m\angle A = 34°$ **b.** $\tan A = \frac{a}{6}$ **c.** $\tan 34° = \frac{a}{6}$; $6 \tan 34° = a$ **d.** $a \approx 4.05$ **3.** $\frac{15}{17} = 0.88$ **5.** $\frac{15}{17} = 0.88$ **7.** $\frac{15}{8} = 1.88$ **9.** Sine **11.** $\sin 72° \approx 0.95$, $\cos 72° \approx 0.31$, $\tan 72° \approx 3.08$ **13.** $x \approx 3.18$, $y \approx 6.24$ **15.** $x \approx 25.26$, $y \approx 28.88$ **17.** 250.47 m; 52.08 m **20.** 15.66 feet **23.** The tangent can be greater than 1. **27.** $\frac{24}{7} \approx 3.43$ **29.** $\sin 18° = 0.31$, $\cos 18° = 0.95$, $\tan 18° = 0.32$

31. $\sin 89° = 1.00$, $\cos 89° = 0.02$, $\tan 89° = 57.29$
33. $x = 27.64$, $y = 26.14$
35. 61.57 m **37. a.** $x = 1$
b. $x = 1$ **c.** $x = 1$
d. For any angle A, $(\sin A)^2 + (\cos A)^2 = 1$

7-3 Part B Try It

a. 34° **b.** 49° **c.** $m\angle 1 = 49°$, $m\angle 2 = 41°$

7-3 Part B Exercises

1. a. 18° **b.** $\tan A = \frac{h}{d}$
3. 42° **5.** 52° **7.** 28°
9. 61° **13.** about 40 ft
15. $\overrightarrow{ST}$: 4 cm, 44°; $\overrightarrow{UV}$: 4.5 cm, 17°, $\overrightarrow{WX}$: 4.7 cm, 199°
17. 2° **19.** 62° **21.** 63°
23. a. 18° **b.** about 800 ft
c. No

7-3 Part C Exercises

1. Due north at 205 mph
3. a–b.

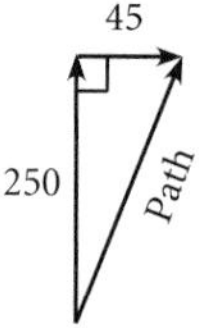

c. 254.02 mph
5. Length = 7.28; $m\angle\mathbf{1} = 16°$

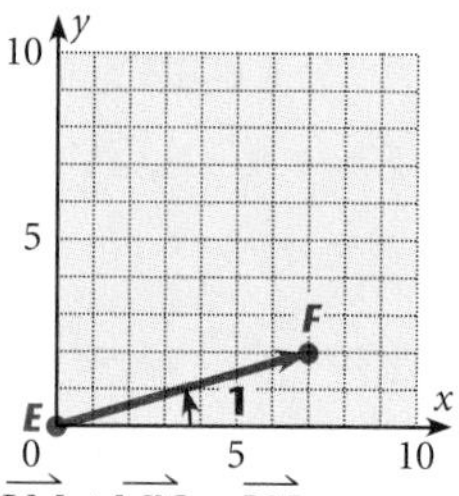

7. $\overrightarrow{LM} + \overrightarrow{MN} = \overrightarrow{LN}$

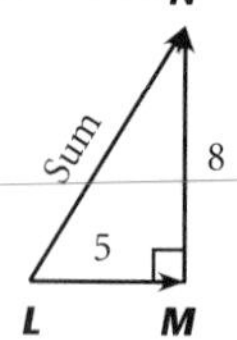

10. $s = 22.83$ mph, $m\angle A = 29°$ **11. a.** Faster
b. Slower **c.** Faster
d. Faster **13.** 166.28 in.^{2}
15. $m\angle VXY = 38°$, $XY = 68.8$

17. Length = 6.32, $m\angle\mathbf{1} = 72°$

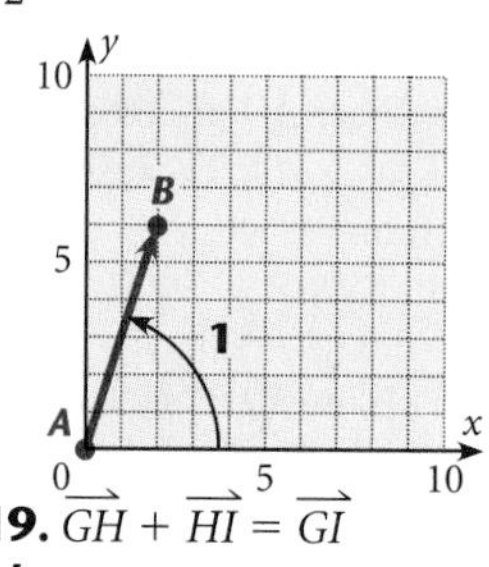

19. $\overrightarrow{GH} + \overrightarrow{HI} = \overrightarrow{GI}$

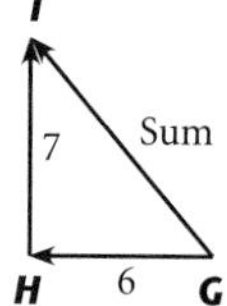

21. $s = 354.40$ mph, $m\angle\mathbf{1} = 74°$

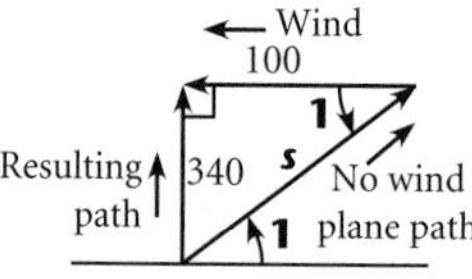

7-3 Part D Self-Assessment

1. $\frac{24}{25} = 0.96$ **2.** $\frac{7}{25} = 0.28$
3. $\frac{24}{7} \approx 3.43$ **4.** $\frac{7}{25} = 0.28$
5. $\frac{24}{25} = 0.96$ **6.** $\frac{7}{24} \approx 0.29$
7. $x = 7.14$ **8.** $x = 39$
9. $x = 28.79$ **10.** 1,117 ft
11. 20.78 cm^2 **12.** 32 cm^2
13. 41.57 cm^2 **14.** $x = 53$; AA **15.** $x = 3.6$; SAS
16. $x = 29$; AA **17.** (a)
18. $\tan \angle 1 = \frac{622}{260} = 2.39$; $m\angle 1 = 67°$

622
1
260

19. 17 m
20. 156.6 mph; $m\angle 1 = 17°$

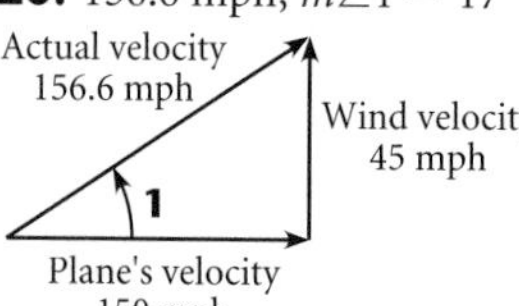

21. Sometimes; $\tan A = \frac{\text{opposite}}{\text{adjacent}}$; If opposite side is shorter than adjacent side, $\tan A < 1$; If opposite side is longer than adjacent side, then $\tan A > 1$.
22. Never; The closer you are, the greater the angle you must look up; As you near the flagpole, you must look nearly straight up; i.e., the angle approaches 90°. **23.** Always; If the acute angle has the known side adjacent, use $\cos A = \frac{\text{known side}}{\text{hypotenuse}}$; If the known side is opposite, $\sin A = \frac{\text{known side}}{\text{hypotenuse}}$; Solve for hypotenuse.

Chapter 7 Review

1. Dilation **2.** The midpoints of two sides **3.** Depression **4.** Greater **5.** T; An equilateral triangle has all angles = 60° and so it is equiangular too; By AA, two such triangles are similar.
6. F; Similarity also requires that the third sides be in proportion, or that the angles between the equal sides be congruent. **7.** $\frac{6}{8} = \frac{3}{4}$
8. 34° **9.** 10 cm **10.** 12.6 cm^2 **11.** $x = 16$, or $x = 9$; SAS **12. a.** $\frac{5}{8}$ in. **b.** 24 ft × 30 ft **13.** Possible answer:

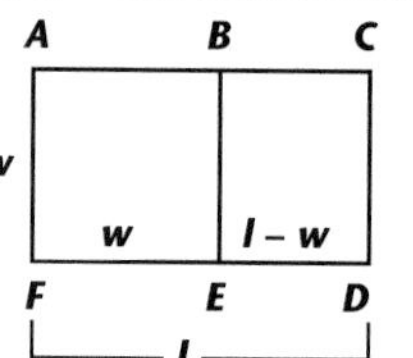

Rectangle *ACDF* is a golden rectangle if square *ABEF* with sides of length *w* makes rectangle *CDEB* similar to rectangle *ACDF*. That is, if you divide a golden rectangle into a square and a smaller rectangle, the smaller rectangle is also a golden rectangle. All golden rectangles are similar. The ratio of length to width, $\frac{l}{w}$, is a constant called the golden ratio, and $\frac{l}{w} = \frac{1 + \sqrt{5}}{2} \approx 1.618$.

14. $\frac{\text{area }\triangle RUV}{\text{area }\triangle RST} = \left(\frac{UV}{ST}\right)^2 = \left(\frac{1}{2}\right)^2 = \frac{1}{4}$ since triangles are similar by AA. area $\triangle RUV = \left(\frac{1}{4}\right)$ area $\triangle RST = \frac{1}{4}$(area $\triangle RUV$ + area $UVTS$) $= \frac{1}{4}$ area $\triangle RUV + \frac{1}{4}$ area $UVTS$; $\frac{3}{4}$ area $\triangle RUV = \frac{1}{4}$ area $UVTS$;
$\frac{\text{area }\triangle RUV}{\text{area }UVTS} = \frac{\frac{1}{4}}{\frac{3}{4}} = \frac{1}{3}$

15. a. 4.5 **b.** $C' = (4, 6)$
16. $\frac{24}{25} = 0.96$ **17.** $\frac{7}{25} = 0.28$ **18.** $\frac{24}{7} \approx 3.43$
19. $x = 23.66$ **20.** $x = 56$
21. $x = 5.54$ **22.** $P = 89.57$, $A = 249.42$
23. a. 180.26 feet **b.** 18

CHAPTER 8

8-1 Part A Try It

a. Possible answer: $\overline{TS}$
b. $\overline{NM}$ **c.** X, interior; Z, exterior **d.** 2 cm

8-1 Part A Exercises

1. ⊙S **3.** $\overline{RT}$ **5.** 8.2 in.
9.

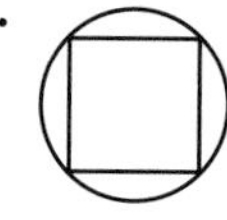

11. Inscribed in **12.** Diameter **13.** 0.2 in. **16.** 4
17. 4 **19.** $x^2 + y^2 = 16$
21. a. 9° **b.** ≈ 3.13 in.
23.

25. $\frac{360}{6} = 60°$; It takes six rotations to go around 360°.
27. a. $\sqrt{(x-1)^2 + (y-2)^2} = 3$ **b.** $(x - 1)^2 + (y - 2)^2 = 9$; 9 is the square of the radius; 1 and 2 are the center's *x*- and *y*-coordinates.
c. $(x - h)^2 + (y - k)^2 = r^2$

8-1 Part B Try It

a. 90° **b.** $AC \approx 40.80$

8-1 Part B Exercises

1. $\overline{AB}$ **3.** $\overleftrightarrow{FG}$; E
5.

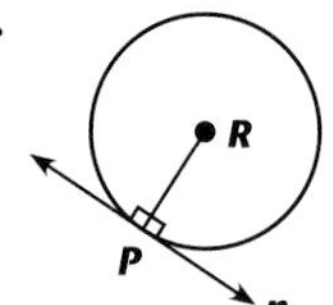

7. Secant **9.** 20 **11.** 6.27 **13.** 2.8 **15.** 3.7 **17.** $\overline{RS} \cong \overline{RT}$; Definition of a *circle.* $\angle S$ and $\angle T$ are right angles; Radii are perpendicular to tangents at points of tangency. $\overline{RQ} \cong \overline{RQ}$; Reflexive Property. $\triangle SRQ \cong \triangle TRQ$; HL theorem. $\overline{QS} \cong \overline{QT}$; CPCTC. **20.** E **21.** $\overleftrightarrow{AB}$ **23.** $\overleftrightarrow{DC}$ **25.** Interior: 135°; Exterior: 45° **27.** $H'(2, 3)$, $L'(2, 9)$, $J'(8, 3)$, $K'(8, 9)$ **29.** 23.32 **31.** $a = 18$ **33.** $c = 13$ **35.** Possible answer: Draw segments $\overline{RB}$, $\overline{RC}$, and $\overline{BC}$. Since $RB = RC$, $\triangle RBC$ is isosceles and $\angle RBC \cong \angle RCB$. Since $\angle RBA$ and $\angle RCA$ are right angles, $\angle ABC$ is complementary to $\angle RBC$ and $\angle ACB$ is complementary to $\angle RCB$. Complements of congruent angles are congruent, so $\angle ABC \cong \angle ACB$. **37.** $LM \approx 1100$ mi; $\triangle ERS \sim \triangle ELM$ by AA so $\frac{LM}{RS} = \frac{EM}{ES}$. Solve for LM.

8-1 Part C Try It

a. 25.1 in. **b.** 22.0 in.

8-1 Part C Exercises

1. 6 in.; 6π in. **3.** 11.4π mm; 35.81 mm **5.** 0.17 in. **7.** 54.85 **9.** 27.99 **13. a.** 0.021 **b.** Yes; It differs from π by only about 0.00000027. **15.** 48 **17.** 4.09 **19.** $\frac{1}{2}ap$; 64.95 cm² **21.** 27.6π in.; 86.71 in. **23.** $r = 12.27$ yd **25.** $9\pi \approx 28.27$ **28. a.** All sides are straight lines; For an n-gon with a large number of sides, the shape approximates a circle. **b.** $r \approx 0.48$ ft; $\frac{\text{Perimeter}}{2\pi}$ gives the radius.

8-1 Part D Try It

a. $A = 36\pi \approx 113.10$ ft²; $C = 12\pi \approx 37.70$ ft

8-1 Part D Exercises

1. $d = 10$ cm; $C = 10\pi$ cm; $A = 25\pi$ cm² **3.** 10 cm **5.** 9π ft²; 28.27 ft² **7.** 38.48 ft²; 95.03 ft² **9.** $C = 10\pi\sqrt{2} \approx 44.43$ in.; $A = 50\pi \approx 157.08$ in.² **13. a.** Triangle: 2,771.28 yd²; Square: 3,600 yd²; Hexagon: 4,156.92 yd² **b.** 4583.66 yd² **c.** The circle. This is the best possible figure. **14.** 2.55 in.² **15.**

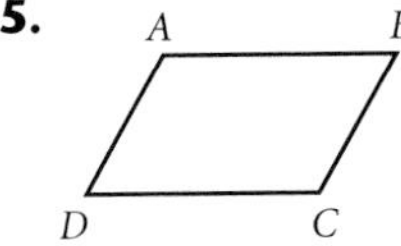

Draw $\overline{AC}$, two points determine a line. $\overline{AB} \cong \overline{DC}$: Opposite sides are congruent. $\overline{AD} \cong \overline{BC}$: Opposite sides are congruent. $\overline{AC} \cong \overline{AC}$: Reflexive Property. $\triangle CAB \cong \triangle ACD$: SSS **17.** 25π ft²; 78.54 ft² **19.** $2\sqrt{563\pi}$ cm; 84.11 cm **21. d.** About 290 cm² **e.** 314.16 cm² **f.** Make narrower rectangles

8-1 Part E Self-Assessment

1. $\odot P$ **2.** $\overline{BP}$, $\overline{PD}$, $\overline{PC}$ **3.** $\overline{BD}$ **4.** $\overleftrightarrow{AE}$ **5.** m; C **6.** 90° **7.** 3 **8.** 6.71 **9.** 17.50 **10.** $3249\pi \approx 10207.03$ in.² **11.** $r = 2.67$ cm **12.** 38.99 m **13. b.** Square: 63.66%; Hexagon: 82.70% **14.** (a) **15. a.** 880.28 ft; 58.69 ft/sec **b.** 71° **16.** $\angle ABD \cong \angle BDC$: Given. $\overline{AB} \cong \overline{CD}$: Given. $\overline{DB} \cong \overline{DB}$: Reflexive Property. $\triangle ABD \cong \triangle CDB$: SAS. $\angle ADB \cong \angle CBD$: CPCTC: $\overline{AD} \parallel \overline{BC}$: Lines parallel if alternate interior angles are congruent. $\overline{AB} \parallel \overline{CD}$: Lines parallel if alternate interior angles are congruent. $ABCD$ is a parallelogram: Definition of a *parallelogram.* **17.** 9.82 in. **18. a.** $18\pi \approx 56.55$cm **b.** 44.91 cm

8-2 Part A Try It

a. 54° **b.** 306° **c.** 180°

8-2 Part A Exercises

1. Possible answer: $\angle ADB$, $\angle BDC$ **3.** $\widehat{BAC}$, $\widehat{ACB}$ **5.** 45° **7.** 217° **9.** 195° **11.** 90° **13.** 180° **15.** $\frac{1}{4}$ **17.** $\frac{1}{3}$ **19.** 210° **22.** $\triangle PQR$ is isosceles, so $\angle PQR \cong \angle PRQ$; $m\angle QPR = 100°$; Sum of ∠'s in $\triangle PQR = 180° = 100° + 2x$; $m\angle PQR = m\angle PRQ = 40°$ **24.** $x = 44$ **27. a.** 63.63 in.² **b.** 15.90 in.² **c.** 10.60 in.² **d.** $\frac{1}{4}$ or $\frac{1}{6}$ of the pie means $\frac{1}{4}$ or $\frac{1}{6}$ of the area. **29.** 65° **31.** 250° **33.** 176° **35.** 78° **37.** 60° **40.** 6°/sec **41.** 270°/sec

8-2 Part B Try It

a. 359.5 in.² **b.** 36.0 in. **c.** $\frac{21}{12}\pi = \frac{7}{4}\pi$

8-2 Part B Exercises

1. a. $A = 25\pi \approx 78.54$ in.²; $C = 10\pi \approx 31.42$ in. **b.**

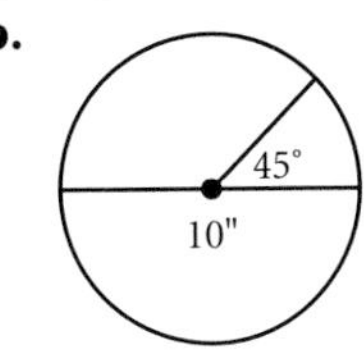

c. 9.8 in.² **d.** 3.9 in. **3.** $L = 6\pi$ in.; $A = 45\pi$ in.² **5.** $L = \frac{110\pi}{72}$ ft; $A = \frac{275\pi}{72}$ ft² **7.** $3.36\pi \approx 10.561$ **10.** $A = 1.5\pi \approx 4.71$ ft²; $L = 0.5\pi \approx 1.57$ ft **11. a.** $4.5\pi \approx 14.14$ ft² **b.** 12.5% **13.** $\angle ACB \cong \angle ECD$: Vertical angles are congruent. $\angle B \cong \angle E$: Right angles are congruent. $\triangle ACB \sim \triangle DCE$: AA. $\frac{AC}{DC} = \frac{BC}{EC}$: Definition of *similar.* **15.** $A = 64\pi$ in.²; 201.06 in.²; $C = 16\pi$ in.; 50.27 in. **17.** $L = 1.6\pi \approx 5.03$ in.; $A = 6.4\pi \approx 20.11$ in.² **19.** $L = 5.46\pi \approx 17.15$ ft; $A = 24.843\ \pi \approx 78.05$ ft² **21. b.** 5707.96 m² **c.** No; One cannot tile a square region with circular sectors without either gaps or overlap.

8-2 Part C Try It

a. $\overline{AD} \cong \overline{DC}$ **b.** $\overline{YF} \perp \overline{EG}$ **c.** m contains Z

8-2 Part C Exercises

1. 7 **3.** $\overline{TR}$ is a perpendicular bisector of $\overline{QS}$. **5.** 8 **7.** Secant; It alone extends beyond the boundary of a circle. **10.** 15.35 **11.**

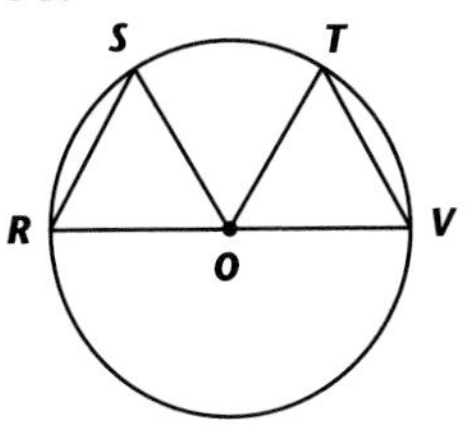

$\widehat{RS} \cong \widehat{TV}$: Given. $m\widehat{RS} = m\widehat{TV}$: Definition of *congruent arcs.* $m\widehat{RS} = m\angle ROS$; $m\widehat{TV} = m\angle TOV$: Definition of *measure of a minor arc.* $m\angle ROS = m\angle TOV$: Substitution. $m\angle ROS \cong m\angle TOV$: Definition of *congruent angles.* $\overline{OS} \cong \overline{OR} \cong \overline{OT} \cong \overline{OV}$: Definition of *circle.* $\triangle OSR \cong \triangle OTV$: SAS. $\overline{RS} \cong \overline{TV}$: CPCTC. **12.** 14 **13.** 14 **15.** 24 **19.** $\angle AOC$ **21.** 18.03 **23.** 13 **25.** 4.69 **27.** Draw $\overline{XV}$, $\overline{VY}$, $\overline{ZV}$, and $\overline{VW}$. $\triangle XVY \cong \triangle ZVW$ by SSS, and $\angle XVY \cong \angle WVZ$ by CPCTC. Since their central angles are congruent, $\widehat{XY} \cong \widehat{WZ}$. **29.** $YZ = 9.75$

8-2 Part D Self-Assessment

1. 67° **2.** 23° **3.** 70° **4.** 290° **5.**

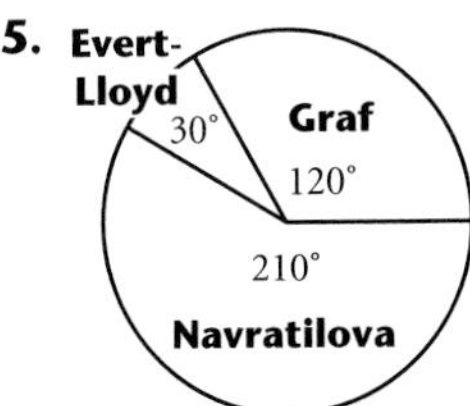

6. (d) **7. a.** 15° **b.** 1041.67 mi **8.** 1298.54² cm² **9.** $\frac{1}{3}$; 126.71 mm² **10.** $\triangle ACB \sim \triangle ECD$. Since $\frac{6.0}{4.0} = \frac{7.5}{5.0} = 1.5$, the triangles are similar by SAS. $x = \frac{5.6}{1.5} \approx 3.73$. **11. a.** $C = 1.766 \times 10^{15}$ km **b.** $r = 2.81 \times 10^{14}$ **c.** $A = 2.48 \times 10^{29}$ km²

12. 69.81 cm^2; The total area of the circle is $100\pi \text{ cm}^2$. Since $m\angle FKJ = 80°$, the sector FKJ fills $\frac{80}{360}$ of the total area. **13.** Show that $\triangle ZWY \cong \triangle ZTV$ by HL. Then $\overline{WY} \cong \overline{VT}$ by CPCTC. Use $WY = \frac{1}{2}WX$ and $VT = \frac{1}{2}ST$, to show that $\overline{WX} = \overline{ST}$. **14.** 767.94 m^2

8-3 Part A Try It

a. 48° **b.** 80° **c.** 90°

8-3 Part A Exercises

1. 136° **3.** 90° **5.** $d = 80$; $e = 140$ **7.** 90° at center; 45° at wall **9.** 98° **11.** 64° **13.** 95° **15.** 47.5° **19.** Angle remains same since intercepted arc doesn't change. **20.** $m\angle A = 135°$; $m\angle B = m\angle D = 90°$; $m\angle C = 45°$ **21.** The measure of an inscribed angle is half the measure of its intercepted arc. For a semicircle the arc measures 180°, so the angle measures 90°.

23.

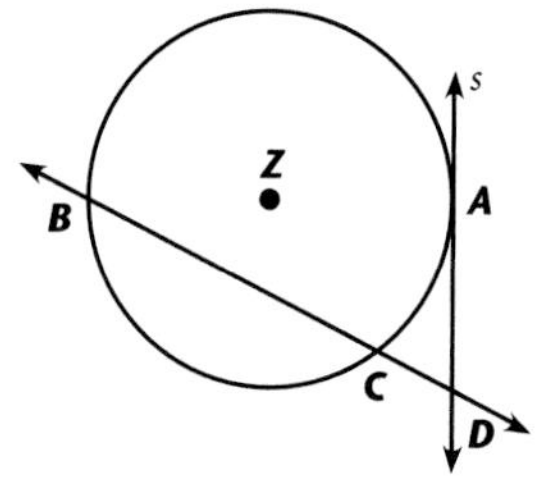

25. 94° **27.** 180° **29.** 118° **31.** 59° **33.** 40° **35.** 110° **38.** 12.99

8-3 Part B Try It

a. $a = 86$ **b.** $b = 60$ **c.** $c = 40$

8-3 Part B Exercises

1. a. 240° **b.** 120° **c.** 60° **3.** 47.5° **5.** 148° **7.** Two **9.** 28° **11.** $m\widehat{ADC} = 224°$; $m\widehat{AC} = 136°$ **13.** 89° **15.** Reason 1: Exterior Angle Theorem.
Reason 2: Algebra; Addition Property of Equality.
Reason 3: Inscribed-Angle Theorem.
Reason 4. Substitution.
17. 69° **19.** $(x - 3)°$ **21.** 51.3 **23.** 90° **25.** 111°

27. 42° **29.** 2.5° **31.** 78° **33. a.** 25° **b.** 16°

8-3 Part C Self-Assessment

1. 92° **2.** 136° **3.** 64° **4.** 64° **5.** (c) **6.** $\$4.95 \times 10^{10}$ **7.** 93° **8.** 104° **9.** 87° **10.** 76° **11.** The danger angle is always $180° - \frac{m\widehat{XY}}{2}$ **12. a.** 7.51 cm **b.** Using trigonometry, $m\angle UVW = 84°$; $m\widehat{UW} = 180° - 84° = 96°$; $m\widehat{USW} = 360° - 96° = 264°$. **c.** 10 cm

Chapter 8 Review

1. T **2.** F; A central angle **3.** F; Inscribed in **4.** 7; $49\pi \approx 153.94$ **5.** $\angle YWZ$ **6.** Possible answer: $\overleftrightarrow{XY}$ **7.** Possible answer: $\widehat{XY}$ **8.** 41° **9.** 82° **10.** 208° **11.** 90° **12.** 63° **13.** $20\pi\sqrt{2}$ cm ≈ 88.86 cm; $200\pi \approx 628.32 \text{ cm}^2$ **14.** Since the perpendicular from the center to a chord bisects it, $WY = \frac{1}{2}WX = \frac{1}{2}TS = TV$, and $\overline{WY} \cong \overline{TV}$. $\overline{WZ} \cong \overline{TZ}$ because radii are congruent. Then $\triangle WZY \cong \triangle TZV$ by HL for right triangles, and $\overline{ZY} \cong \overline{ZV}$ by CPCTC. Therefore, $ZY = ZV$ by definition of congruent segments. **15.** Probability = 0.21 **16.** Center: (0, 0); Radius: $\sqrt{13}$ **17. a.**

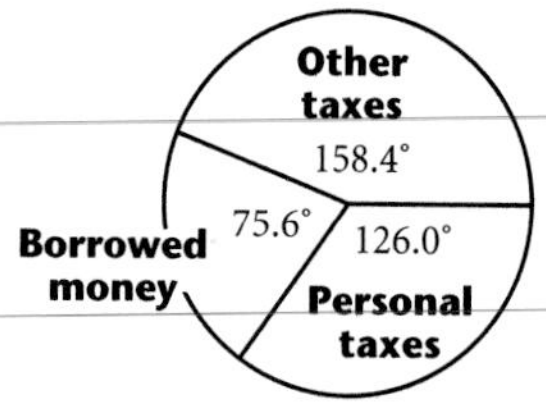

b. 0.16 in.^2 **c.** 75.6°; 0.7 in. **18. b.** $\pi(R - r) = D - d$

CHAPTER 9

9-1 Part A Try It

a. Oblique rectangular
b. Right pentagonal
c. Right triangular

9-1 Part A Exercises

1. Right rectangular
3. Right hexagonal
5.

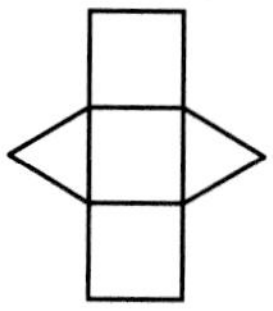

7.

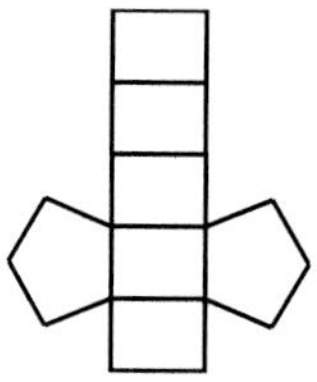

9. $LA = 55.44$; $SA = 74.88$ **11.** $LA = 97.2$; $SA = 109.2$ **13.** Lateral edge **15.** Right prism **17.** In the right prism the faces are rectangles. In the oblique prism the faces are parallelograms. **19.** 188 ft² **21. a.** $SA = 10x^2 - 12x$ **b.** $x = 4$ ft **23.** Possible answer: Move one of the top blocks on the left away from the block it is touching to expose two new faces. **25.** $x = 26$ **27.** $x = 6\sqrt{3} \approx 10.4$
29.

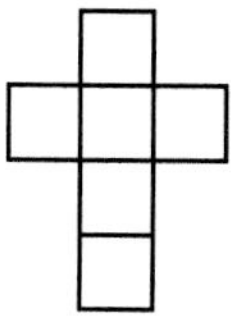

31.

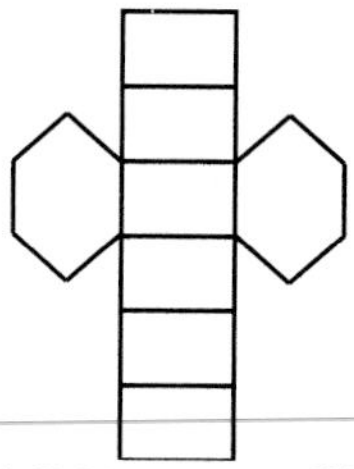

33. 163.88; 179.88 **35.** 36 in.² **37.** 32 in.² **39.** Greater; The lateral area is larger. **41.** Possible answer:

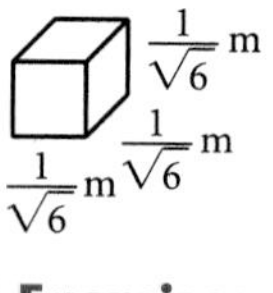

9-1 Part B Exercises

1. a. 4; Triangle **b.** 1000 cm² **c.** Square; 400 cm² **d.** 1400 cm²
3.

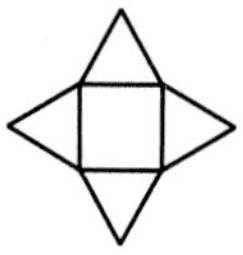

5.

7. 240 cm²; 340 cm²
9. 144.18 cm²; 219.94 cm²
11. $s = \sqrt{\frac{l^2}{4} + h^2}$;
Lateral edge $= L = \sqrt{\frac{l^2}{2} + h^2}$
13. Vertex **15.** 924,473.1 ft² **17.** $x = 5.25$ in.; Use similar triangles
19.

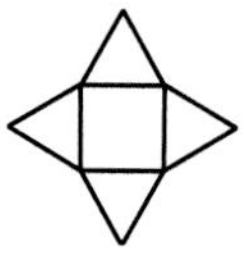

21.

23. 192 ft², 336 ft²
25. 51.78 cm²; 0.54

9-1 Part C Try It

a. $LA = 201.1 \text{ in.}^2$; $SA = 603.2 \text{ in.}^2$ **b.** $LA = 791.7 \text{ cm}^2$; $SA = 1300.6 \text{ cm}^2$

9-1 Part C Exercises

1. a. Rectangle/parallelogram **b.** $60\pi \approx 188.5 \text{ cm}^2$ **c.** $25\pi \text{ cm}^2$; $50\pi \approx 157.1 \text{ cm}^2$ **d.** $110\pi \approx 345.6 \text{ cm}^2$ **3.** $72\pi \approx 226.2 \text{ in.}^2$; $104\pi \approx 326.7 \text{ in.}^2$ **5.** $24\pi \approx 75.4 \text{ in.}^2$; $33\pi \approx 103.7 \text{ in.}^2$ **7.** 50.8 ft²; 68.9 ft² **9.** T **11.** 304.52 cm² **13.** $52\pi \approx 163.4 \text{ in.}^2$ more **15.** ≈ 877.8 ft² **17.** Possible answer: If you divide the rectangle into squares, it has l rows of w squares each. **19.** $150\pi \approx 471.2 \text{ ft}^2$; $200\pi \approx 628.3 \text{ ft}^2$ **21.** $60\pi \approx 188.5 \text{ in.}^2$; $96\pi \approx 301.6 \text{ in.}^2$ **23.** 258.94 ft²; 421.80 ft² **25.** $39\pi \approx 122.5 \text{ in.}^2$

9-1 Part D Self-Assessment

1. 118.56; 178.42 **2.** 265; 377.36 **3.** $54\pi \approx 169.6 \text{ cm}^2$; $72\pi \approx 226.2 \text{ cm}^2$ **4.** $960\pi \approx 3015.9 \text{ in.}^2$; $1216\pi \approx 3820.2 \text{ in.}^2$

5.

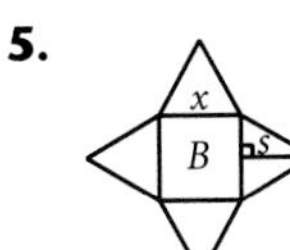

The surface area is the area of the base (B) plus the areas of the triangles. For a base with n sides, the total area of the triangles would be $n\left(\frac{1}{2}xs\right)$. The perimeter is nx, so the total area of the pyramid is $\frac{1}{2}ps + B$. **6.** $(6 \times 10^{-4})\pi \approx 1.9 \times 10^{-3}$ mm^2 **7.** $6\pi x^2 + 24\pi x$ **8.** 12,404.6 cm^2; 6536.6 cm^2 **9.** (c) **10. a.** 4 **b.** Possible answer: $\triangle AGK$, $\sqrt{3}$; $\triangle ACL$, 2; $\triangle AHP$, $\sqrt{7}$; $\triangle ADQ$, 3. **c.** They all are equilateral, like $\triangle FBA$.
11. a. $440\pi \approx 1382.3$ cm^2 **b.** $33\frac{1}{3}\pi \approx 104.7$ cm^2 **c.** 120° **12.** About 126.9 cm^2
13. $SA = 3\ell^2$
14. Cylinder: 296.9 cm^2; Square prism: 324.9 cm^2; Square pyramid: 353.7 cm^2; Cone: 324.3 cm^2. Possible answer: The cylinder, because it uses the least aluminum.
15. A segment perpendicular to a plane is perpendicular to every line in the plane that contains the point of intersection of the segment and the plane.

9-2 Part A Try It

a. 129.6 in.^{3} **b.** 42,398 mm^3

9-2 Part A Exercises

1. 10^{-4} m^2 **3.** 2500 mm^2
5. cm^3
7. 27 ft^3

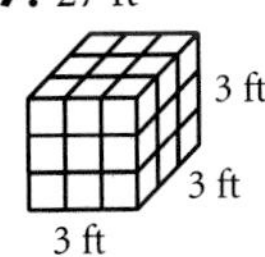

9. 2.24×10^{-2} m^3 **11.** 72,000 cm^3 **13.** $1075.2\sqrt{3}$ m$^3 \approx 1862.3$ **15.** \$0.59
17. $3\sqrt{3} \approx 5.2$ cm **21.** 944 cm^2 **23.** $210\pi \approx 659.7$ cm^2 **25.** 0.7 cm^3 **27.** 84,000 cm^3 **29.** $1{,}138.626\sqrt{3} \approx 1972.2$ in.^{3}
31. 1888.41 in.^{3}

9-2 Part B Try It

a. 480 cm^3 **b.** 80 in.^{3}
c. $144\sqrt{3}$ mm^3

9-2 Part B Exercises

1. a. 3 in. **b.** 16 in.^{2}
c. 16 in.^{3} **2.** $53\frac{1}{3}$ cm^3
3. 34.69 in.^{3} **5.** 384 ft^3 **7.** 105.35 cm^3 **9.** 3 units
13. Possible answer:

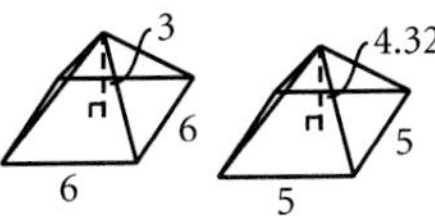

15. 10 in. **17.** Each cross-section is a circle. The cylinder has the larger cross-sectional areas since its side does not taper. **19.** 39.98 mm^3
21. $96\sqrt{91} \approx 915.78$ cm^3
23. $\frac{1000\sqrt{2}}{3} \approx 471.4$ cm^3

9-2 Part C Exercises

1. a. 4 cm **b.** 78.5 cm^2
c. 314.2 cm^3 **3.** $11.913\pi \approx 37.4$ in.^{3} **5.** $17.2\pi \approx 54.0$ cm^3 **7.** $710.803\pi \approx 2233.1$
9. $12\pi \approx 37.7$ cm^3
11. a. $1{,}089{,}000\pi \approx 3{,}420{,}000$ ft^3 **b.** $433{,}500\pi \approx 1{,}360{,}000$ ft^3
c. $2{,}823{,}000\pi \approx 8{,}870{,}000$ ft^3
13. $7.5\pi \approx 23.6$ ft^3
17. $64\pi \approx 201.1$ cm^2; $16\pi \approx 50.3$ cm **19.** 7 m; $14\pi \approx 44.0$ m **21.** $2042.5\pi \approx 6416.7$ cm^2 **23.** $55.2\pi \approx 173.4$ in.^{2} **25.** About 167,000 ft^2 **27.** $813.12\pi \approx 2554.5$ cm^3 **29.** $392\pi \approx 1231.5$ cm^3 **31. a.** About 884 in.^{3}; About 389 in.^{3}
b. 117 ft/min

9-2 Part D Try It

a. $V = 166\frac{2}{3}\pi \approx 523.6$ cm^3; $SA = 100\pi \approx 314.2$ cm^2
b. $V = 10\frac{2}{3}\pi \approx 33.5$ in.^{3}; $SA = 16\pi \approx 50.3$ in.^{2}

9-2 Part D Exercises

1. $V = 10\frac{2}{3}\pi \approx 33.5$ in.^{3}; $SA = 16\pi \approx 50.3$ in.^{2} **3.** $70.56\pi \approx 221.7$ in.^{2}; $98.784\pi \approx 310.3$ in.^{3} **5.** $\sqrt{2} \approx 1.4$ m; $\frac{8\sqrt{2}}{3}\pi \approx 11.8$ m^3 **7.** 99.82%
9. a. $V_{cube} = 1000$ cm^3 $V_{sphere} = 166\frac{2}{3}\pi \approx 523.6$ cm^3
b. 52.36% **11.** About 0.32 cm^2; About 0.017 cm^3
13. 29.65% **15.** $\frac{8}{27}$ **17.** 4
19. $100\pi \approx 314.2$ in.^{2}; $166\frac{2}{3}\pi \approx 523.6$ in.^{3} **21.** 4 ft, $85\frac{1}{3}\pi \approx 268.1$ ft^3
23. $x^2 + y^2 + z^2 = r^2$. This is the square of the distance formula for a point that is r units away from the origin.

9-2 Part E Self-Assessment

1. 1536 mm^3 **2.** 129.73 cm^3 **3.** $3343.509\pi \approx 10503.9$ ft^3 **4.** $112.5\sqrt{3} \approx 194.9$ **5. a.** 1.08×10^{12} km^3 **b.** 2.21×10^{10} km^3
c. $\approx 2.04\%$ **6.** 367,200 ft^3
7. 1.09 mi **8.** 33,390.4 cm^2
9. 16.8 in.^{2} **10.** $2898\pi \approx 9104.4$ cm^2 **11.** 84 cm^2
12. (a) **13. a.** $V_{prism} = 277.83$ m^3; $V_{cone} \approx 72.74$ m^3
b. 26.18% **14.** 5.0 in.
15. a. 8.18 in.^{3} **b.** 2.216 in. × 2.216 in. **c.** 2.45 in.^{2}
16. 78.8 cm^3; 8.6 cm^3 is lost; Possible answer: They have indentations to save money on product. **17.** 150 min.

9-3 Part A Try It

a. $\frac{2}{5}$; $\frac{4}{25}$ **b.** 18 in. × 18 in.

9-3 Part A Exercises

1. Not similar **3.** Not similar **5.** $\frac{3}{2}$ **7.** $\frac{7}{8}$
10. 10,000 times as strong
13. 260° **15.** 80°
17. $58\frac{1}{3}$ cm^3 **19.** 28 mm^3
21. $\frac{4}{5}$ **23.** $\frac{5}{6}$ **25.** $13.5\sqrt{2} \approx 19.1$ in.

9-3 Part B Try It

a. $\frac{1}{8}$ **b.** $\frac{5}{3}$ **c.** 337.5 lb

9-3 Part B Exercises

1. a. $\frac{4}{3}$ **b.** $\frac{16}{9}$ **c.** $\frac{64}{27}$
3. $\frac{3}{5}$ **5.** $\frac{27}{125}$ **7.** $\frac{1}{27}$
9. Area **11.** 10^6 times as heavy **13.** 3.30 in.; 137 in.^{2}; 151 in.^{3}

15. $A'(4, -2)$; $B'(2, -6)$

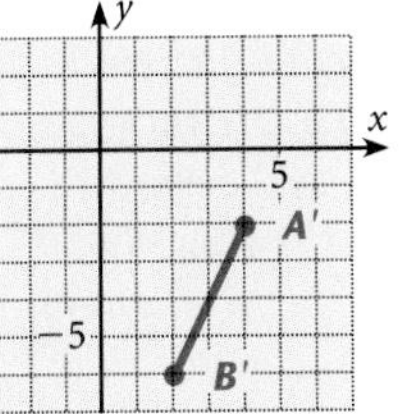

17. $A'(4, 8)$; $B'(12, 4)$

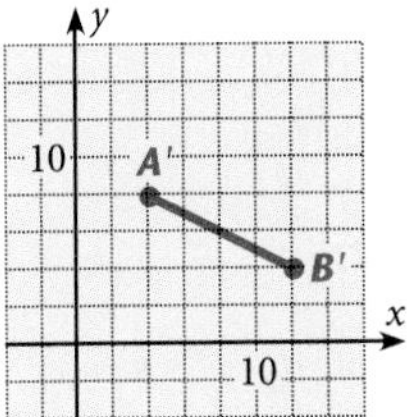

19. $\frac{25}{16}$ **21.** $\frac{15625}{4096}$ **23.** ≈ 754 beats/min.

9-3 Part C Self-Assessment

1. $\frac{3}{2}$ **2.** $\frac{3}{2}$ **3.** $\frac{9}{4}$ **4.** $\frac{27}{8}$
5. $\frac{3}{4}$; $\frac{9}{16}$ **6.** (d) **7.** The larger box **8.** 106° **9.** 112° **10.** 36° **11.** $545\frac{5}{6}\pi \approx 1714.8$ ft^3
12. a–b. Possible answer:

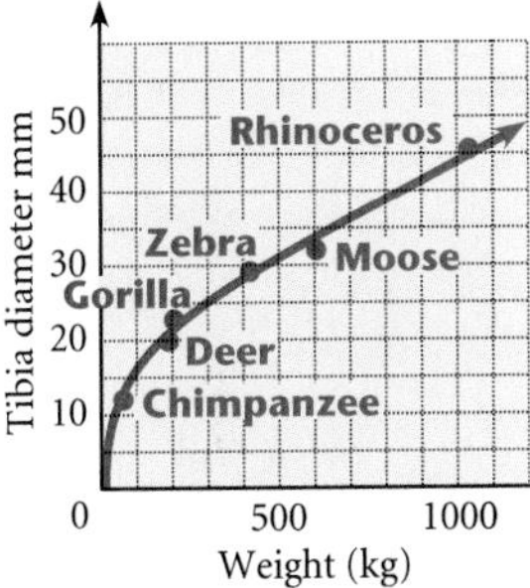

c. ≈ 3 mm for a dog; ≈ 13.5 mm for a human **d.** Possible answer: Differences between dogs and humans and other animals, including number of legs. **13.** Possible answer: Because of the relation between the mass and the strength of building components, light, cheap materials which would not be suitable for the actual buildings can be used in models.
14. a. 5 **b.** 50,000 lb
c. Each leg would be 25 times as strong.

d. Possible answer: No; It is unlikely that its legs would be able to carry the increased weight. **15.** Height ≈ 9.6 cm; Radius ≈ 2.5 cm; The new volume is $\frac{1}{4}$ the old, so multiply old dimensions by $\frac{1}{\sqrt[3]{4}}$. **16.** $\frac{1}{64}$; The answer is the ratio of the volumes of the two cubes, which is the cube of their similarity ratio.

Chapter 9 Review

1. (b) **2.** (d) **3.** 82.8 cm^2; 46.8 cm^3 **4.** SA = 678.6; V = 1017.9 **5.** 360 cm^2; 400 cm^3 **6.** 57.3 mm^2; 28.6 mm^3 **7.** $20.25\pi \approx 63.6$ in.^{2}; $15.1875\pi \approx 47.7$ in.^{3} **8.** Yes; They also have the same base area. **9.** Regular triangular prism: surface area $= 3sh + \frac{S^2}{2}\sqrt{3}$, volume $= \frac{s^2h}{4}\sqrt{3}$; Square prism: surface area $= 4sh + 2s^2$, volume $= s^2h$; Regular hexagonal prism: surface area $= 6sh + 3s^2\sqrt{3}$, volume $= \frac{3s^2h}{2}\sqrt{3}$ **10.** $\frac{4}{3}\pi r^3$; This is the volume of a sphere of radius r. **11. a.** 2.75 **b.** 6.5 **c.** The strips of fish will cook more quickly; The single slab of fish will hold its heat better. The ratio of surface area to volume makes the difference. **12.** It will hold 27 times as much petroleum.
13. c. Each time the height is doubled the intensity is multiplied by $\frac{1}{4}$.

CHAPTER 10

10-1 Part A Try It

a. Translation, vector <3, −4> **b.** Rotation, center (0, 0), 90° clockwise
c. Dilation, center (0, 0), scale factor 2

10-1 Part A Exercises

1. Reflection; Isometry
3. Dilation; Not an isometry
5. Translation **7.** Rotation or reflection **9.** Reflection, y-axis **11.** Dilation, center (0, 0), scale factor $\frac{1}{2}$ **14.** 1
17.

19. A parabola **21.** Reflection; Isometry **23.** Dilation; Not an isometry
25. Dilation, center (−4, −1), scale factor $1\frac{1}{2}$ **27. a.** The equator is its own image.
b. They are the same size.
c. Yes; The North and South poles

10-1 Part B Try It

a. 113° counterclockwise rotation with center (2, 1)
b. Translation with vector <7, 10>

10-1 Part B Exercises

1. Translation **3.** Rotation
5. 117° clockwise rotation with center at (4, −2)
7. Translation with vector <8, 0> **9.** Always; The distance is preserved by each isometry, hence the composition is an isometry.
11. Isometry; The composition of two isometries is always an isometry. **13.** Isometry; The composition of two isometries is always an isometry. **15.** $\frac{1}{2}$ **17.** translation <3, −4> **19.** A dilation with scale factor $\frac{2}{3}$ and center at the origin **21.** $5\sqrt{3} \approx 8.7$ **23.** Translation <3, −1> **25.** Isometry; The composition of two isometries is always an isometry.
27. Not an isometry; The dilation does not preserve distance. **29.** No. **30.** 13

10-1 Part C Try It

a–c.

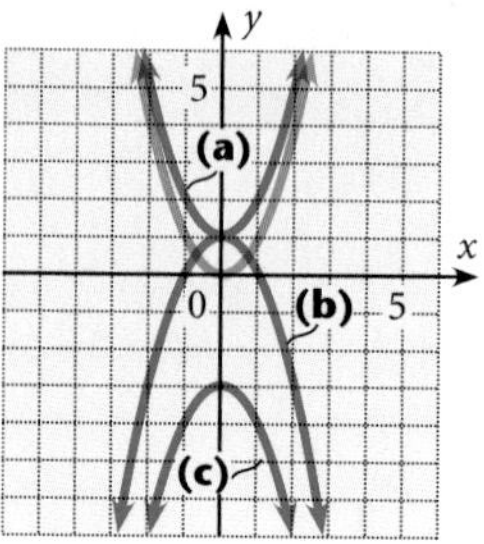

10-1 Part C Exercises

1. a–c.

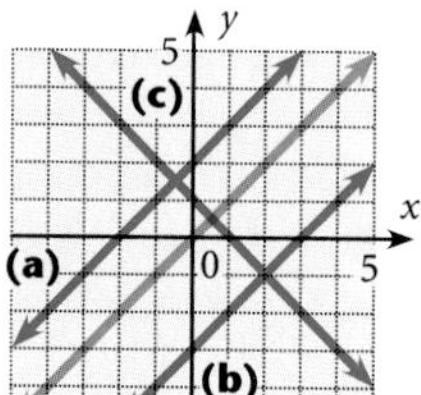

3. a–c.

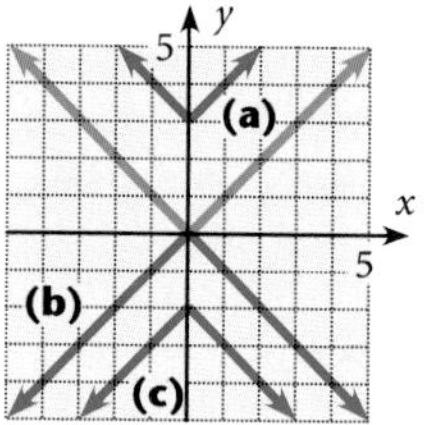

d. Possible answer: The graph of (a) is the graph of $y = |x|$ translated by <0, 3>. The graph of (b) is a reflection of the graph of $y = |x|$ across the x-axis. The graph of (c) is a reflection of the graph of $y = |x|$ across the x-axis followed by the translation <0, −2>. **4.** Translation **5.** Reflection
6. a–c.

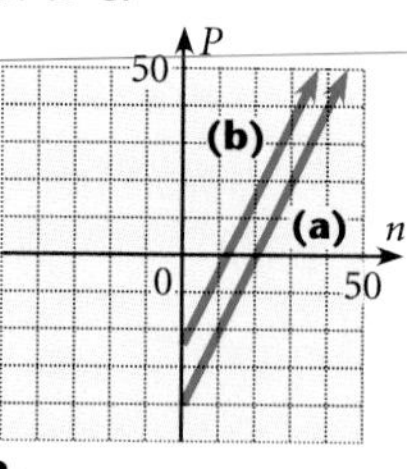

a.
$P = 2n - 40$
b. $P = 2n - 24$ **11.** b;
13. c

15. a–c.

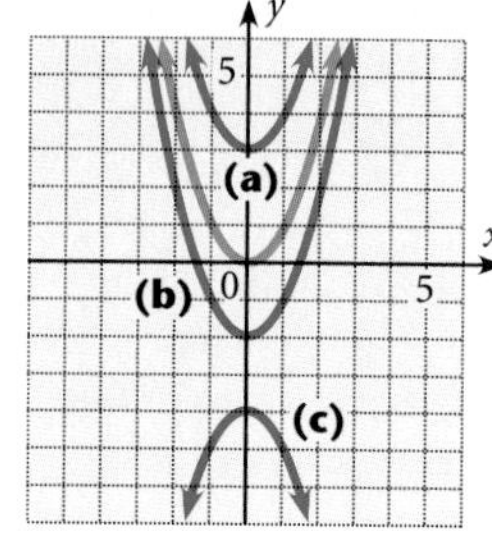

18. $n = 600$, $P = 250{,}000$.

10-1 Part D Self-Assessment

1. Clockwise rotation of $(x + y)°$ around the same center.
2. Translation <$a + c$, $b + d$> **3.** A 180° rotation around the intersection point of the two lines **4.** Isometry; The composition of two isometries is always an isometry. **5.** Not an isometry; Dilation does not preserve distance. **6.** Isometry; The composition of two isometries is always an isometry.
7.

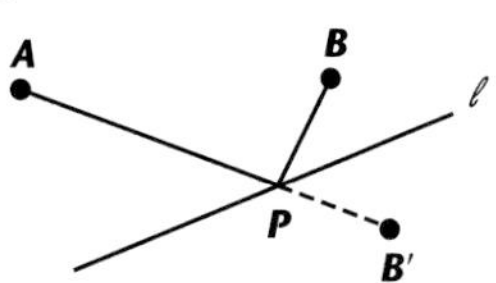

Find B' by reflecting B over ℓ. Locate transformer at P, point of intersection of $\overline{AB'}$ and ℓ.

8–10.

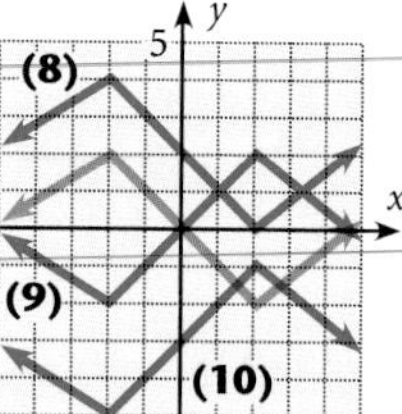

11. The graph of (8) was a translation <0, 2>. The graph of (9) was a reflection across the x-axis. The graph of (10) was a reflection across the x-axis followed by a translation <0, −3>. **12.** ≈ 47.1 m
13. 52 in.^{2}; 24 in.^{3}
14. 282.7 cm^2; 314.2 cm^3
15. 58.8 ft^2; 34.6 ft^3
16. 113.1 cm^2; 113.1 cm^3

17. All are functions because every point on the pre-image maps onto only one point on the image. **18. a.** Points with negative coordinates; Square roots of negative numbers are not defined for real numbers. **b.** (81, 16) $\rightarrow$ (9, 4) $\rightarrow$ (3, 2) $\rightarrow$ (1.7, 1.4); The point seems to be going to (1, 1). No. As you continue to rotate, the coordinates will approach closer to 1, but never reach it. **c.** No, distance isn't preserved.

10-2 Part A Try It

a. Translation, glide reflection, horizontal line, vertical line, point **b.** Translation, vertical line **c.** Translation

10-2 Part A Exercises

1. a. No **b.** No **c.** No **d.** No **3.** Possible answer:

5. F; Translation and a reflection **7.** No

9. Possible answer:

$$\begin{array}{c} CH_3 \\ | \\ CH_2 - C = CH - CH_2 - \end{array}$$

11. Translation, point

13. Translation, vertical line, horizontal line, glide reflection, point

15. Possible answer:

18. $\frac{3}{7}$ **21.** $\frac{125}{27}$ **23.** 303° clockwise rotation with center (−2, −4)

25. Possible answer:

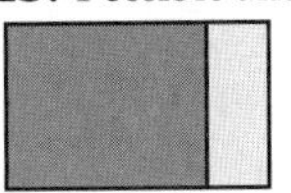

27. Translation, vertical line

29. Translation, vertical line, horizontal line, point, glide reflection **31.** Translation, vertical line **33.** Possible answer: The tool could be a "wheel" with a raised TM frieze pattern for its tread.

10-2 Part B Exercises

1. a. Yes **b.** Yes; Horizontal, vertical, and lines at 45° and 135° to the horizontal **c.** Yes; 90°, 180°, 270° **3.** Translation; Horizontal line, vertical line, lines at 45° and 135° to the horizontal; Rotation: 90°, 180°, 270°; glide reflection **5.** (c) **6.** F; Translation **7.** T **8.** 459 ft^2 **13.** $x \geq 16$ **15.** $z \geq \frac{29}{5}$ **17. a.** 1 km × 3 km and 2 km × 2 km **b.** 2 km × 2 km gives 4 km^2, which is the greatest possible area. The fenced region is a square. **19.** Translation; Rotational: 90°, 180°, 270°; Line: vertical, horizontal, lines at 45° and 135° to the horizontal; Glide reflection **20.** Translation, Rotational: 90°, 180°, 270°, Line: vertical, horizontal, lines at 45° and 135° to the horizontal; Glide reflection

21. Possible answer:

△▽△▽△
▽△▽△▽

24. Reflection and rotation.

10-2 Part C Self-Assessment

1. Translation; horizontal line; glide reflection **2.** Translation; vertical and horizontal line; point; glide reflection

3. Translation **4.** Translation; Rotational: 180°; Line: vertical, horizontal; Glide reflection **5.** Translation; Rotational: 180°

6. Translation; Rotational, 90°, 180°, 270°; Line: horizontal and vertical; glide reflection **7. a.** 4 **b.** 8

8. The graph of $y = -x^2 + 4$ is the graph of $y = x^2$ reflected across the x-axis and translated by <0, 4>. **9.** (c)

10. Possible answer:

IIII

11. Possible answer:

12. Possible answer:

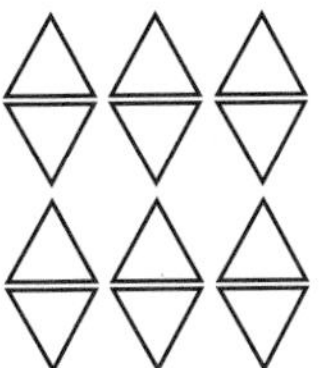

13. Possible answer:

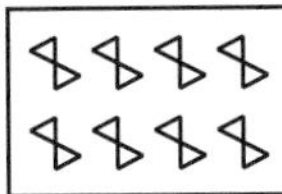

15. (c)

Chapter 10 Review

1. Translation **2.** Translation, reflection (or reflection, rotation) **3.** Reflection **4.** Composition

5. Translation <12, −12>

6. Translation **7.** (d) **8.** $\frac{\pi}{6}$

9–10.

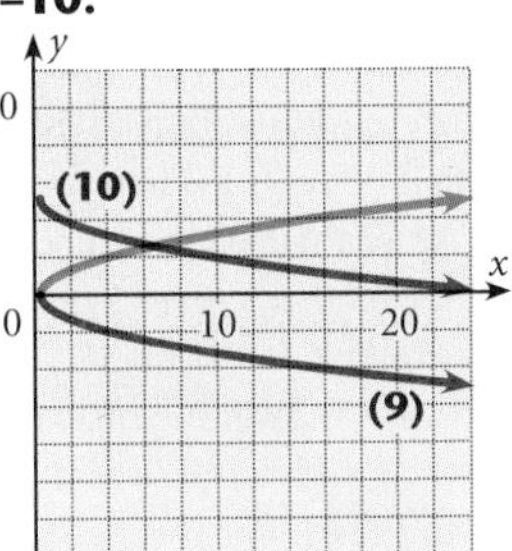

12. Translation; translation, horizontal line; translation, vertical line; translation, horizontal and vertical line; translation, point; translation, vertical line, and glide reflection; translation, glide reflection

13. Translation, vertical line

14. Translation, vertical line, horizontal line, glide reflection, point **15.** 90°, 180°, 270°

CHAPTER 11

11-1 Part A Try It

a. It rains and I do not wash my car. **b.** $m\angle R = 20°$, and $\overline{ST} \ncong \overline{XY}$.

11-1 Part A Exercises

1. (a), (b) **3.** Tomorrow is not Tuesday. **5.** I will throw it back. **6.** $a + c \neq b + c$ **7.** $\triangle ABC \ncong \triangle DEF$ **8.** $\angle A \cong \angle B$ **9.** The good of the people is not the most important law.

11. The report of my death wasn't an exaggeration. **12.** $1 - p$ **15.** Possible answer: Suppose there are two right angles. Then the sum of the measures of the angles in the triangle is greater than 180°, which contradicts the Triangle Angle-Sum Theorem.

19. Interior: 135°; Sum: 1080° Exterior: 45°; Sum: 360°

21. Interior: 162°; Sum = 3240°; Exterior: 18°; Sum = 360° **23.** 54 **25.** 40°

27. 32 **29.** $\angle 1$ is a right angle. **31.** $\angle 1 \cong \angle 2$.

33. a. Suppose he went at most 65 mph. Then his trip took at least $\frac{55}{65}$ hours or $50\frac{10}{13}$ minutes, which contradicts the given information.

b. Iona may be telling the truth, since David could have driven at 65 or less while Iona was with him, and driven faster for the rest of the trip.

11-1 Part B Try It

a. Largest: $\angle C$; Smallest: $\angle B$

b. Largest: $\angle E$; Smallest: $\angle D$

c. Largest: $\angle R$; Smallest: $\angle RSP$ **d.** Longest: $\overline{AC}$; Shortest: $\overline{AB}$ **e.** Longest: $\overline{QT}$ or $\overline{QR}$; Shortest: $\overline{TS}$

f. Longest: $\overline{VX}$; Shortest: $\overline{WV}$

11-1 Part B Exercises

1. Largest: $\angle B$; Smallest: $\angle C$

3. Largest: $\angle H$; Smallest: $\angle G$

5. $\overline{QR}$; $\overline{QR}$ is opposite the largest angle in $\triangle QRS$. **7.** $\overline{QS}$; $\overline{QS}$ is opposite the smallest angle in $\triangle QRS$. **9.** $\overline{QS}$

11. Longest: $\overline{RT}$; Shortest: $\overline{RS}$ **13.** Longest: $\overline{EF}$; Shortest: $\overline{DE}$ **17.** $\frac{2}{5}$ **19.** $\frac{2}{5}$

21. Possible answer: Suppose $\overline{JK}$ is the shortest side of $\triangle JKL$, and $\angle L$ is obtuse. Then $m\angle L > 90°$, and since the angle measures must sum to 180°, $m\angle L > m\angle K$ and $m\angle L > m\angle J$. Thus $JK > JL$ and $JK > KL$; $\overline{JK}$ is the longest side, which contradicts the given fact that $\overline{JK}$ is the shortest side. Therefore, $\angle L$ is not obtuse. **23.** $x < y < z$ **25.** $5 < c < 25$

27. $\overline{ZX}$; $\overline{ZX}$ is opposite the largest angle in $\triangle WXZ$. **29.** $\overline{WX}$; $\overline{WX}$ is opposite the smallest angle in $\triangle WXZ$. **31.** $\overline{XY}$ **33.** Largest: $\angle Y$; Smallest: $\angle X$ **35.** Largest: $\angle DAC$ and $\angle ACB$; Smallest: $\angle CAB$ and $\angle ACD$ **37.** Longest: $\overline{UR}$; Shortest: $\overline{ST}$ **39.** $\angle F, \angle D, \angle E$ **40.** $70 < 2x - 10 < 3x - 40 < 180$, so $40 < x < 73\frac{1}{3}$

11-1 Part C Try It

a. Yes **b.** No **c.** Yes

11-1 Part C Exercises

1. Yes **3.** No **5.** $11\frac{3}{10} < x < 38\frac{3}{10}$ **7.** The shortest route is M to N to Q to X and the length of the shortest route is between 10 and 18. **9.** Between 701 and 1411 **11.** Between 566 and 2602 **15.** $h = \frac{2A}{b}$ **17.** $r = \pm\frac{1}{2}\sqrt{\frac{A}{\pi}}$ **19.** $y = 2x^2 + 48$ **21.** Yes **23.** Yes **25.** Yes **27.** $5 < y < 25$ **29.** $n < y < 3n$ **31. a.**

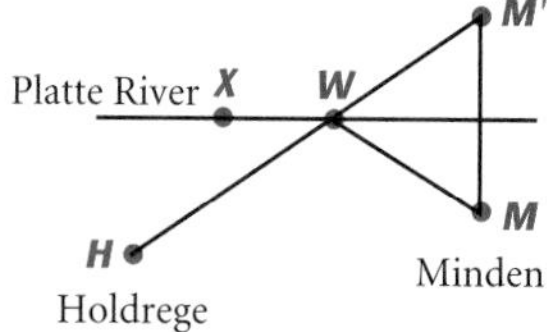

11-1 Part D Self-Assessment

1. The animal does have toes. **2.** $\angle B \not\cong \angle A$ **3.** I cannot make the team. **4.** $\overline{XY}, \overline{YZ}, \overline{XZ}, \overline{WZ}, \overline{XW}$ **5.** $\angle 5, \angle 4, \angle 3, \angle 2, \angle 1$ **6.** Possible answer:

7. $\angle 2, \angle 1, \angle 3$ **8.** Interior: 120°; Sum: 720° Exterior: 60°; Sum: 360° **9.** Interior: 144°; Sum: 1440° Exterior: 36°; Sum: 360° **10.** Interior: 156°; Sum: 2340° Exterior: 24°; Sum: 360° **11.** $x \approx 104.5$ m. **12.** (c) **13.** (a)

14. Possible answer: Assume $\triangle ABD$ is scalene, $\overline{AC}$ is a median, and suppose $\overline{AC} \perp \overline{BD}$. $\overline{BC} \cong \overline{DC}$ by definition of *median*. $\angle ACB$ and $\angle ACD$ are right angles by definition of perpendicular. $\triangle ACB$ and $\triangle ACD$ are right triangles by definition. $\overline{AC} \cong \overline{AC}$ by the Reflexive Property. $\triangle ACB \cong \triangle ACD$ by the LL Theorem. $\overline{AB} \cong \overline{AD}$ by CPCTC, which contradicts the assumption that $\triangle ABD$ is scalene. Therefore, $\overline{AC}$ is not perpendicular to $\overline{BD}$. **15. a.** Possible answer: Marvin should travel by way of point X, since that route has to be less than twice as long as the other (X to 9 is less than 750 m). **b.** By the Triangle Inequality Theorem, $d + 250 \text{ m} > 500$ m, so $d > 250$ m. Therefore $\angle 3$ is the smallest, because it is opposite the shortest side. It cannot be determined which is the largest, since d may be greater or less than 500 m.; **16.** $\frac{7}{10}$

11-2 Part A Exercises

1. 3.50×3.43 **3.** (4, 3) **5.** (1, 2) **9.** $1074; 11 items. **10.** A square of side 6 in. **13.** $SA = 2x^2 + 4xh$; $V = x^2h$ **15.** (5, 7) **17.** (1.3, 7.3) **19.** $m\angle Z = 90°$; The height of the parallelogram is $3 \sin(m\angle Z)$, so the area is $12 \sin(m\angle Z)$. Since the maximum of the sine is when the angle is 90°, $m\angle Z = 90°$.

11-2 Part B Exercises

1. $4.50 \times 3.16 \times 2.25$ **3.** Minimize surface area of carton **5.** Minimize surface area of tube **8.** 6 in. × 3 in. × 2 in. **9.** 0.91 **11.** Maximize volume of cage **13.** Minimize surface area of carton **15.** The box is a $2 \times 2 \times 2$ cube.

17. $r \approx 4.66$ cm, $h \approx 6.60$ cm; No, the radius is too big for its height so the cone is hard to hold.

11-2 Part C Self-Assessment

1. Maximize the area of the yard. **2.** Minimize the surface area of the tank. **3.** (6, 2) **4.** $\left(\frac{2}{3}, 1\right)$ **5.** (1.4, 1) **6.** (e) **7.** $x = 136.25$ ft; $y = 136.25$ ft **8.** Approximate dimensions are $3 \times 6 \times 4.22$; Yes; Possible answer: Check decimal width values between 2 and 4. **9.** 0.50 **10.** No; Possible answer: Suppose $\overline{AB} \parallel \overline{CD}$ then $\angle BAC \cong \angle DCA$ because they are alternate interior angles of parallel lines. $\overline{AC} \cong \overline{AC}$ and $\overline{AB} \cong \overline{CD}$, so $\triangle BAC \cong \triangle DCA$ by the SAS Postulate. Therefore, $\overline{AD} \cong \overline{BC}$ by CPCTC, which contradicts $AD = 4$ and $BC = 10$. Therefore, $\overline{AB}$ is not parallel to $\overline{CD}$. **11.** No **12.** Yes **13.** Yes **14.** 1.88 in. × 5.65 in. × 2.82 in. **15.** 8.38 in. × 6.38 in. × 1.81 in. **16.** A cube

Chapter 11 Review

1. T **2.** F; Sides **3.** F; Contrapositive **4.** Humans do not have wings. **5.** $\angle A \not\cong \angle B$ **6. a.** The defendant was not found guilty. **b.** The negation implies that the verdict was not "guilty." Possible answer: There was a hung jury, so the case had to be retried. **7.** $\frac{1}{2}$ **8.** Use the angle measures of the triangles and the theorem of opposite sides. In $\triangle RUV$, $RU < RV < VU$. In $\triangle RSU$, $SU < RS < RU$. In $\triangle STU$, $ST < TU < SU$. Therefore the shortest side is $\overline{ST}$. **9.** The longest side is $\overline{VU}$. See exercise **8.** **10.** Between 6.2 cm and 16.2 cm. **11.** $170 **12.** 250 **13.** $r = h \approx 3.2$ in. **14.** The portrait must be in the silver casket.

CHAPTER 12

12-1 Part A Exercises

2.

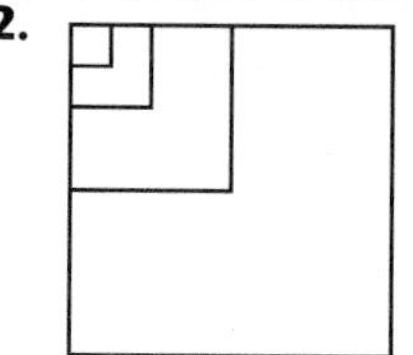

Stage 3

Draw a square in the upper left corner whose side length is half that of the previous square.

3.

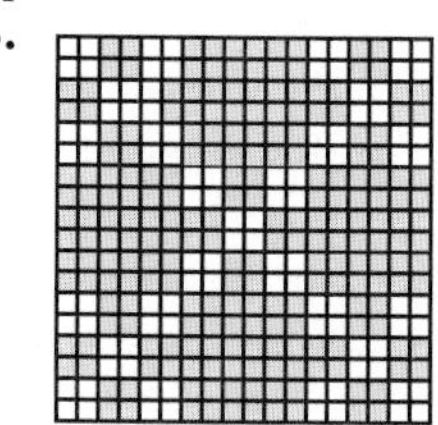

Stage 2

Divide each unshaded square into nine congruent smaller squares and shade the middle squares along the sides of each square just divided.

5.

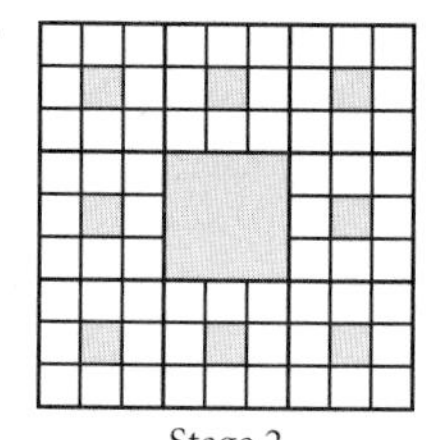

Stage 2

7. a–b.

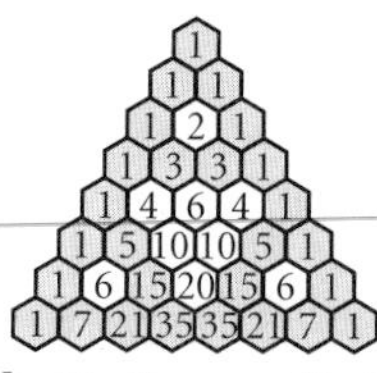

b. Similar **c.** Similar **9.** Possible answer: A fern. Each branch is similar in shape and structure to the original plant. **11.** 77.9 in. **13.** 24881.4 mi **15.** 20.9 **17.** 3441.5 km **19.** 5673.1 km **21.**

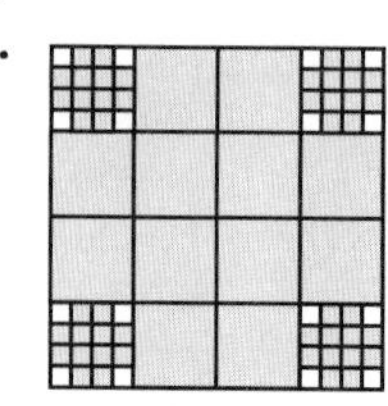

Stage 2

23. 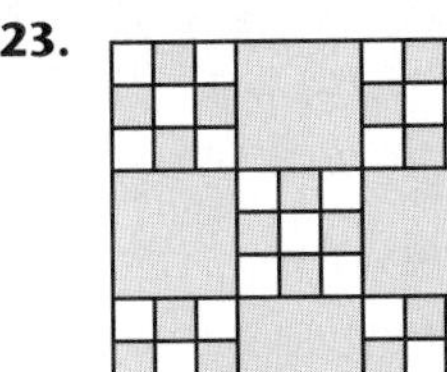

Stage 2

25. b. 192; 4:1 **c.** $N = 3 \cdot 4^{n-1}$ **d.** $\frac{64}{2187}$; $\frac{4}{9}$ **e.** $A = \frac{1}{3}\left(\frac{4}{9}\right)^{n-1}$ **f.** $1\frac{1261}{2187}$; Increasing **g.** There seems to be a limit; The additional area at each stage is $\frac{4}{9}$ smaller than the area added at the preceding stage.

12-1 Part B Try It

a. 18° N, 73° E **b.** 35° N, 140° E **c.** 22° S, 45° W

12-1 Part B Exercises

1. 30° N, 31° E **3.** 7° N, 40° E **5.** About 679 mi **7.** About 3546 mi **9.** About 484 mi **11.** About 12,441 mi; Half the earth's radius **13. a.** 15°; The earth makes a full rotation every 24 hours, so there should be 24 time zones. Therefore, $\frac{360°}{24} = 15°$ per time zone. **b.** 5-6 time zones **15.** Statement 1: $\overline{AB} \parallel \overline{FE}$, $\overline{AB} \cong \overline{FE}$ $\overline{AC} \cong \overline{ED}$.
Reason 1: Given.
Statement 2: $\angle A \cong \angle E$.
Reason 2: Alternate interior angles of parallel lines cut by a transversal are congruent.
Statement 3: $\triangle ABC \cong \triangle EFD$.
Reason 3: SAS Postulate.
17. (1, 6) **19.** 10° N, 67° W **21.** 1° S, 78° W **23.** About 345 mi **25.** About 4882 mi **26.** 17,594 mi; It is $\frac{\sqrt{2}}{2}$ times the radius of the earth
27. Use the following proportion: $\frac{\text{difference in longitudes}}{360°} = \frac{\text{distance}}{24,900}$
29. a. $t = \sqrt{h^2 + 12,740h}$
b. $t \approx 335.9$ km
c. $s \approx 335.6$ km; Yes

12-1 Part C Try It

a. $139\frac{1}{3}$ sec **b.** 43 min, $14\frac{1}{3}$ sec

12-1 Part C Exercises

1. 150,000,000 km **3.** 3 min, $6\frac{2}{3}$ sec **5.** 31,600 **7.** Parallax; It is not a measure of distance. **11. a.** 16.6 light-years **b.** The light is older than any student less than 16.6 years old.
13. Possible answers: One and only one straight line can be drawn through two given points. Three noncollinear points are contained in one and only one plane. If two lines intersect, then their intersection is a point. If two planes intersect, then their intersection is a line **15.** 8 min, 20 sec **17.** 4 hr, 9 min, 50 sec **20.** Kepler's third law, $d^3 = p^2$, is approximately true for the given planets.

12-1 Part D Self-Assessment

1.

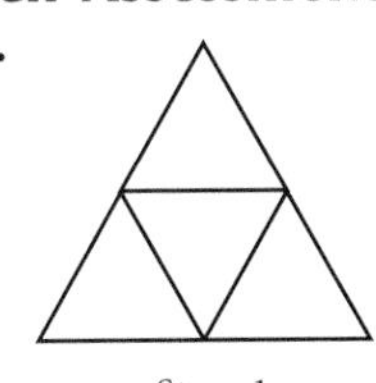

Stage 1

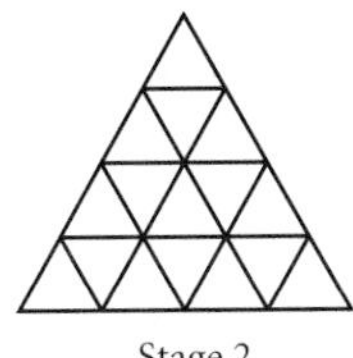

Stage 2

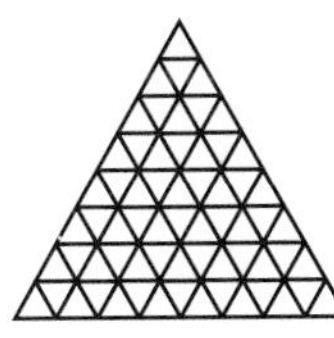

Stage 3

2. 2.4 in. × 3.2 in. × 4.8 in. **3.** 228,000,000 km **b.** $B = 2^n$ **c.** 1 unit; 2 units; 3 units; 4 units; 5 units **d.** $n + 1$ units. Total length of branches will grow infinitely since each stage adds 1 unit to the total length.

5. a. About 1,650,000 AU **b.** 26.1 light years **6.** (c) **7. a.** Yes **b.** At opposite points on the equator; West Pole and East Pole **8.** About 349 miles

12-2 Part A Try It

a. Plane Postulate
b. Straight-Line Postulate
c. Parallel Postulate

12-2 Part A Exercises

1. Straight-Line Postulate
3. Parallel Postulate
5. Possible answers: Acute angles—angles that measure less than 90°. Circle—the locus of points in a plane equidistant from a given point. Right Triangle—a triangle that contains a 90° angle. Rhombus—a quadrilateral with four congruent sides. **7.** No; The two right angles would each measure 90°, and the measure of the third angle would be greater than zero, so the sum of the angle measures would exceed 180°. **11.** Area formula for a rectangle **13. a.** 5.4×10^{10} years **b.** To reach Andromeda in 70 years, the astronauts would need to travel at $\frac{2,000,000}{70} \approx 28,600$ times the speed of light.
15. Flat-Plane Postulate
17. Points-Existence Postulate **19.** Yes, the measure is always 360°. **22.** (a). The conclusion depends on parallel lines.

12-2 Part B Try It

a. They must intersect
b. $m\angle G > 35°$ **c.** Circumference < 4π cm; Area < 4π cm²

12-2 Part B Exercise

1. A great circle on the plane (sphere) **3.** An arc of a great circle **5.** Circumference < 16π in.; Area < 64π in. **6.** They intersect **7.** F; Triangles have more than 180°. **11. a.** About 1333 times

b. Andromeda has a far greater actual (absolute) brightness
13. ≈ 4147 mi **15.** $m\angle R > 10°$ **17.** F; Triangles have more than 180°.
19. a. $3960\pi \approx 12,440$ miles. The two points would be endpoints of a diameter of the earth, since the largest distance between two points on the earth is $\frac{1}{2}$ its circumference. **b.** πr

12-2 Part C Self-Assessment

1. Straight-Line Postulate
2. Parallel Postulate **3.** Plane- Intersection Postulate
4. No; Yes **5.** Yes; No **6.** $m\angle L = 60°$; $m\angle L > 60°$ **7.** (c) **8.** Circumference < 20π cm; Area < 100π cm²
9. a. $2\sqrt{74,066}$ ft; 544.3 ft. **b.** Smaller; For a right triangle in Riemannian space, $a^2 + b^2 > c^2$
10. Statement 1: $ABCD$ is a quadrilateral.
Reason 1: Given.
Statement 2: $DA = a\sqrt{10}$, $BC = a\sqrt{10}$.
Reason 2: Distance Formula.
Statement 3: $DC = 2a\sqrt{5}$, $AB = 2a\sqrt{5}$.
Reason 3: Distance Formula.
Statement 4: $ABCD$ is a parallelogram.
Reason 4: If both pairs of opposite sides of a quadrilateral are congruent then the figure is a parallelogram.
11. 1.5×10^{24} cubic light years **12. a.** 330,000 km **b.** About 2700 km **13.** Each part of a broccoli plant is similar to the whole. **14.** The Euclidean model supports an infinite universe. The Riemannian model suggests a finite universe since all lines are circles.

Chapter 12 Review

1. Tomato; Not example of a fractal **2.** Speed of light; Does not represent a distance

3. 5 hours, 33 minutes, 20 seconds

4. a.

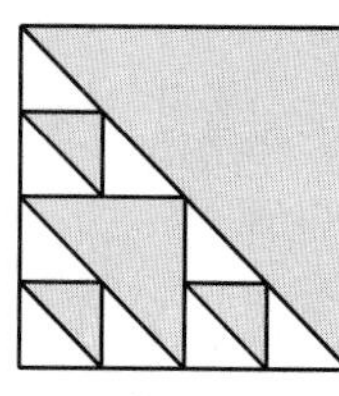

Stage 3

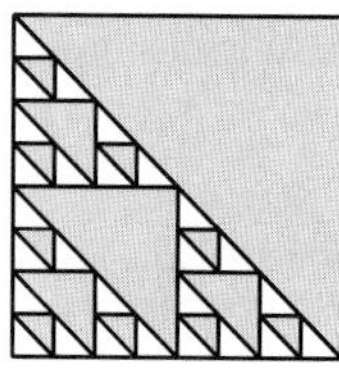

Stage 4

b. 122 **5.** The reference line known as the equator and lines parallel to it are called lines of latitude. The equator is at 0°. The North Pole is at 90° North latitude (90° N) and the South Pole at 90° S. Lines connecting the poles are called lines of longitude. The reference line known as the prime meridian runs north-south through England, Continental Europe, and West Africa. The prime meridian marks 0° longitude. Other longitude lines range from 0° to 180° east or west.

6. About 5808 miles **7.** Determine the length of the arc of the great circle on which the two points lie. **8.** $3 < s < 25$ **9.** $0 < s < 4$ **10.** $m < s < 3m$ **11. a.** About 716,000 AU **b.** 11.3 light years **12.** T **13.** F **14.** T **15.**

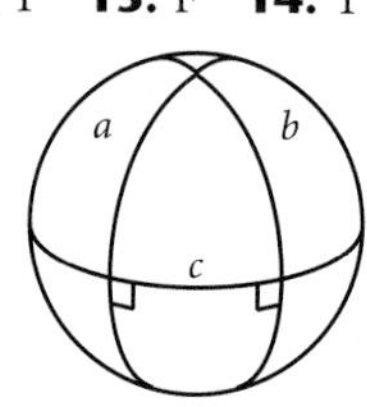

$a \perp c$, $b \perp c$. However, a is not parallel to b. **16. a.** The moon was exactly half full, so the sunlight was coming exactly "from the side."

b. 0.052 **c.** 0.0026; No **d.** This would make his calculation more accurate. Using 89.93°, he would have found $\frac{m}{s} \approx 0.0030$. For angles near 90°, a very small difference in the angle results in a large difference in the cosine.

CREDITS

PHOTOGRAPHS

Front Cover **Top** Art Resource **Bottom** Jerry Jacka Photography/Courtesy: Museum of Northern Arizona, Flagstaff

Spine **Top** Art Resource **Bottom** Jerry Jacka Photography/Courtesy: Museum of Northern Arizona, Flagstaff

Back Cover **BL** Jerry Jacka Photography/Courtesy: Museum of Northern Arizona, Flagstaff **BCL** Art Resource **TCR** Jerry Jacka Photography **TR** Jon Feingersh/Tom Stack & Assoc. **BCR** Cheryl Fenton* **BR** Antonio M. Rosario/The Image Bank **TCL** Giraudon/Art Resource **TL** Thomas Kitchin/Tom Stack & Assoc.

Front Matter **FM 4–5** Jerry Jacka Photography **FM 5B** Brownie Harris/The Stock Market **FM 5T** Jerry Jacka Photography **FM 6B** Gary Gay/The Image Bank **FM 6T** Greg Vaughn/Tom Stack & Associates **FM 7B** Baron Wolman **FM 7T** Kunio Owaki/The Stock Market **FM 8BR** John Ibbotson/Allstock **FM 8BL** Pat O'Hara/DRK Photo **FM 8T** Cheryl Fenton* **FM 9** GHP Studio* **FM 10BL** Norman Owen Tomalin/Bruce Coleman Inc. **FM 10BR** Cheryl Fenton* **FM 10C** GHP Studio* **FM 10T** Stan Osolinski/Tony Stone Images **FM 11L** Cheryl Fenton* **FM 11R** Cheryl Fenton* **FM 12B** NASA **FM 12T** Greg Vaughn/Tom Stack & Associates

Getting Started **i** Ken Karp* **ii** Ken Karp * **iii** Ken Karp*

Chapter 1 **2BC** Frans Lanting/Photo Researchers **2BR** Kjell B. Sandved/Bruce Coleman Inc. **2TR** Roland Birke/OKAPIA/Photo Researchers **6B** ©1960 M. C. Escher Foundation–Baarn–Holland. All Rights Reserved **8BL** Will and Deni McIntyre/AllStock **8TR** NASA **17** Brownie Harris/The Stock Market **22** Flip Nicklin/Minden Pictures **33** Don Mason/The Stock Market **49** Joseph Sohm/Chromosohm/AllStock **51** NASA **56** Ken Kay/Fundamental Photographs **58** Jim Zuckerman/Westlight **60C** Peter Timmermans/AllStock **60L** Kathleen Campbell/AllStock **60R** Bud Freund/Westlight **61** Jerry Jacka Photography **62** Barry Herem/AllStock **65** Dow-Hedren/Westlight **66C** Scott Camazine/Photo Researchers **66L** Science Source/Photo Researchers **66R** Science Source/Photo Researchers **67** Jerry Jacka Photography **71** Jerry Jacka Photography **73T** Larry Lee/Woodfin Camp & Assoc. **77** Jerry Jacka Photography

Chapter 2 **84BR** Laura Riley/Bruce Coleman Inc. **84L** Gordon Langsbury/Bruce Coleman Inc. **84TL** Drawing by Richter, ©1965, 1993 The New Yorker Magazine, Inc. **87** National Museum of American History/Smithsonian Institution **88** National Museum of American History/Smithsonian Institution **89T** National Museum of American History/Smithsonian Institution **96** Dave Bartruff/Stock, Boston **99** Frida Kahlo, *Self Portrait with Monkey,* 1945. Fundacion Dolores Olmedo, Mexico City, Mexico. Schalkwijk/Art Resource, NY **102** Dept. of Clinical Radiology, Salisbury District Hospital/Science Photo Library/Photo Researchers **108** Lisa Quinones/Black Star **114** The Bettmann Archive **118** Greg Vaughn/Tom Stack & Assoc. **129L** Metropolitan Museum of Art, Purchase, Mrs. Charles Wrightsman Gift, 1988 (1988.162) **129R** The Art Institute of Chicago, All Rights Reserved **130** Harald Sund **133L** David Ball/AllStock **133R** Gustave Caillebotte, French, 1848–1894, *Paris Street; Rainy Day,* oil on canvas, 1877, Charles H. and Mary F. S. Worcester Collection, 1964.336. Photograph ©1994, The Art Institute of Chicago. All Rights Reserved. **138** NASA **144** CityFlash Map ©1994 by Rand McNally **146** Don & Pat Valenti/DRK Photo **147** J. McGuire/Washington Stock Photo **148** Drawing by Julia Morgan/Courtesy of The College of Environmental Design, UC Berkeley

Chapter 3 **152L** Metropolitan Museum of Art **156** Michael Holford **160** G. Robert Bishop/AllStock **165** Bruce Berman/The Stock Market **169** Chip Carroon/AllStock **171** Robert Frerck/Odyssey/Chicago **177** Richard Hurley/Courtesy of the John Carter Brown Library at Brown University **180** Mitchell Layton/duomo **182L** Manfred Kage/Peter Arnold, Inc. **182R** Manfred Kage/Peter Arnold, Inc. **191** Bill Ross/Westlight **200** Richard Megna/Fundamental Photographs **203** Momatiuk/Eastcott/Woodfin Camp & Assoc. **210B** P. Rondeau/Allsport USA **216** Gary Gay/The Image Bank **232** Richard Megna/Fundamental Photographs

Chapter 4 **241B** Jean Claude Lejeune/Stock, Boston **241T** M. P. L. Fogden/Bruce Coleman Inc. **242** Peter Aaron **247** Harald Sund **249** Kunio Owaki/The Stock Market **260** Michael Townsend/AllStock **274** James Randklev/AllStock **286** Tim Davis/David Madison Photography **308** Egyptian Museum, Cairo, Egypt

Chapter 5 **318B** Tate Gallery/Art Resource **318BCR** Tate Gallery/Art Resource **319**(background) Baron Wolman **322** Baron Wolman **342** Charles Krebs/AllStock **345B** Lee Boltin Photography **345C** Greg Vaughn/Tom Stack & Assoc. **345T** Werner Forman Archive/Art Resource **346** Cary Wolinsky/Stock, Boston **350T** Jerry Jacka Photography **351** Ford Kristo/DRK Photo **352** Deni McIntyre/AllStock **362** David Hiser/Photographers/Aspen **363** Will & Deni McIntyre/Photo Researchers **365** Columbia University **366** Yale Babylonian Collection **378** Bob Daemmrich/Stock, Boston **380** Michael Holford **385** George A. Plimpton Collection, Columbia University, Rare Book and Manuscript Library

Chapter 6 **395L** Ezra Stoller/Esto Photographic **395R** Armen Kachaturian/The Gamma Liaison Network **396** Pat O'Hara/DRK Photo **398** Greg Vaughn/Tom Stack & Assoc. **400** Greg Probst/AllStock **402** Larry Ulrich/DRK Photo **406** Phil A. Harrington/Peter Arnold, Inc. **407** Jim Harrison/Stock, Boston **409** Catherine Karnow/Woodfin Camp & Assoc. **415** David R. Frazier Photolibrary/Photo Researchers **438** UPI/Bettmann Newsphotos **441** Jeff Foott/Bruce Coleman Inc. **441**(background) M. Antman/The Image Works **442** John Ibbotson/AllStock **449** Paul Silverman/Fundamental Photographs **450** Omikron/Science Source/Photo Researchers **452** John Cancalosi/DRK Photo **454** David L. Brown/Tom Stack & Assoc.

Chapter 7 **458B** America Hurrah Antiques, NYC **458TL** Drawing by Julia Morgan/Courtesy of The College of Environmental Design, University of California, Berkeley **461** © 1994 Turner Entertainment Co. **465** Charles Falco/Science Source/Photo Researchers **469** Kevin Morris/AllStock **473** The Kobal Collection **479C** The Metropolitan Museum of Art, Bequest of Stephen C. Clark, 1960 (61.101.17) **479L** Thomas R. Taylor/Photo Researchers **479R** G. Anderson/The Stock Market **481** Dallas Museum of Art, Foundation for the Arts Collection, gift of the James H. and Lillian Clark Foundation **483** The Kobal Collection; ©Turner Entertainment Co. **485** Shimizu Corp. **511R** Library of Congress **512** Woodcut from *Ryff's Practical Mathematics*/The Bettmann Archive **519** NASA **521** Luis Villota/The Stock Market **522** Vanessa Vick/Photo Researchers

Chapter 8 **542** Runk-Schoenberger/Grant Heilman Photography **548** Alain Evrard/Robert Harding Picture Library **553** GHP Studio* **555** Eric Neurath/Stock, Boston **557** Robert Frerck/Tony Stone Images **558** Courtesy of Sara Bates **559** Stan Osolinski/Tony Stone Images **562** Bernd Kegler/Ulmer Museum **563** NASA **574** Chris Sorensen/The Stock Market **586** Brian Parker/Tom Stack & Assoc. **588** Grant Heilman/Grant Heilman Photography **594** Frank Rossotto/The Stock Market

Chapter 9 **600B** AP/Wide World Photos **603** Courtesy Chesapeake Display & Packaging Co. **605** David Parker/SPL/Photo Researchers **610** Will & Deni McIntyre/AllStock **614** *Campbell's Soup, 1962* ©1994 The Andy Warhol Foundation for the Visual Arts, Inc. **618** Rob Cousins/Robert Harding Picture Library **623**(background) Wide World Photos **623**(inset) Jeffrey Hutcherson/DRK Photo **624T** Jeff Gnass/The Stock Market **629** Eric Carle/Bruce Coleman Inc. **632** F. Jackson/Bruce Coleman Inc. **639** Norman Owen Tomalin/Bruce Coleman Inc. **644B** David Weintraub/Photo Researchers **644T** Steve Marts/AllStock **647L** Leonard Lee Rue

III/Stock, Boston **647R** Stephen P. Parker/Photo Researchers **648** Renee Lynn/AllStock **649** Michael George/Bruce Coleman Inc. **653B** Bob Daemmrich/Stock, Boston **657B** M. P. Kahl/DRK Photo **657T** J. P. Varin/Jacana/Photo Researchers

Chapter 10 **673** Lucasfilm Ltd. **674** Richard Megna/ Fundamental Photographs **687C** Thomas Ives/The Stock Market **687L** Tom Bean/DRK Photo **687R** Cooper-Hewitt Museum **688** Michael Holford **689** Michael Holford from the Verulamium Museum **690** D. Cavagnaro/DRK Photo **694** Jerry Jacka Photography/Courtesy Gallery 10, Scottsdale, Arizona. **700** Jerry Jacka Photography **701** Norman Owen Tomalin/Bruce Coleman Inc. **702** Naval Research Laboratory, Stennis Space Center **704** John T. Biggers' *Third Ward Housing.* Photo by Earlie Hudnall.

Chapter 11 **707**(background) Joe Towers/The Stock Market **709**(inset) Renee Lynn/Photo Researchers **720** C. Yarbrough **727B** Greg Vaughn/Tom Stack & Assoc.

Chapter 12 **746** Giraudon/Art Resource **749** From *Powers of Ten* by Eames and Morrison, ©1982 by Scientific American Library. Used with permission of W. H. Freeman and Co. **752** Antonio M. Rosario/The Image Bank **756** NASA **768** Larry Keenan/The Image Bank **771** Anglo-Australian Observatory **772** Greg Vaughn/Tom Stack & Assoc. **775** Hale Observatories **777** NASA **778B** Tony Craddock/SPL/Photo Researchers

Cheryl Fenton:* viiiTR, xi, xiiT, 2TL, 3(background), 5, 8BC, 8BR, 8TC, 8TL, 9, 10L, 10R, 46, 84TR, 85(background), 95, 153(background), 179, 184, 187, 192, 193, 194, 196, 210T, 238, 239(background), 259, 270, 304, 318T, 319(frame), 341, 370, 392BL, 392R, 393(background), 393(frame), 423, 428, 446, 448, 458TR, 459(background), 468, 528, 536, 537(background), 539B, 550, 570, 579, 600C, 600T, 604, 609, 615, 625B, 641, 653T, 656, 664B, 665(background), 667, 692L, 692R, 696, 706, 709(background), 710, 727T, 734, 740, 747(background), 771, 778T, 785. **Elliott Smith:*** 27 **Geoffrey Nilsen Photography:*** 19BL, 19BR, 19T, 39, 107, 392TL, 413 **GHP Studio:*** ixBR, ixBL, xC, 59, 128, 337, 355, 404, 474, 476B, 476T, 513, 539T, 560, 561L, 561R, 626L, 626R, 635L, 635R **Janice Sheldon:*** 226 **Ken Karp:*** 32, 222, 223, 268, 434, 470, 503, 511L, 583, 620, 624B, 625T, 664T, 669, 715, 728, 729, Look Ahead/Look Back icons **Renee Lynn:*** 6T, 212, 264, 292, 310, 350C, 357 **Tim Davis:*** 21, 43, 73B, 78, 89B, 89C, 92, 104, 115, 131, 135, 137, 152T, 167, 205, 207, 227, 248, 306, 318BCL, 318TC, 324, 364, 418, 514, 564, 568, 601(background)

*Photographed expressly for Addison-Wesley Publishing Co., Inc.

ILLUSTRATIONS

Sherry Bringham: 215b–215r, 218a, 219b, 221b, 224b, 224c, 231a, 232f **Susan Detrich:** 706b **Steve Donatelli/Vivid Entity:** 321b, 461c **Terry Guyer:** 238a, 318a, **Joe Heiner Studio:** 5a, 19a, 39a, 61a, 87a, 107a, 129a, 155a, 179a, 191a, 215a, 241a, 255a, 285a, 321a, 345a, 365a, 395a, 417a, 441a, 461a, 485a, 511a, 539a, 563a, 583a, 603a, 623a, 647a, 667a, 687a, 709a, 727a, 749a, 771a. All icons within section part heads by Joe Heiner Studio. **Kent Leech:** 152a **Maryland Cartographics:** 5d1, 5d2 **Helene Moore:** 16a, 81a, 83a **Chris Peterson:** 39c, 191d, 238c, 417b **Precision Graphics:** All blackline/full-color technical artwork throughout *AWSM Geometry*; all artwork produced electronically. **Mike Reagan:** 29c, 94a, 96a, 155b, 155c, 155d, 177b, 255b, 360b, 365b, 564a, 746b **George Retseck:** 285b, 285c, 285d **Mary Rich:** 677a, 688b, 689c, 691a,b,c,d, 692a,b,c, 697a,b,c,d, 702a,b,c,d,e **Bill Rieser:** 156a, 161a, 161b, 164c, 214a, 224d, 224e, 281a, 281b, 282b, 283a, 304a, 313c, 315d, 336c, 355c, 368g, 369a, 374g, 375c, 413a, 440d, 451a, 451b, 491a, 494f, 596e, 607a,bc,d, 608g,h,i, 612b,c,d,e, 613e,f,g, 617b, 617c, 619a, 619b, 650b,c,d, 652f, 655c, 658a, 659b, 671a, 671b, 685b, 717h, 722b, 724b, 725a, 741c. All Construction and If/Then icons and suitcases by Bill Rieser. **Rob Schuster:** 486a, 518a, 518b, 519a, 524d, 525a, 529e, 530a, 618a, 618b, 619d, 633a, 642d, 645e, 645k, 651d, 655d, 659c **Joe VanDerBos Illustration:** 2d, 5c, 129b, 191c, 563c, 603b **Tom Ward:** 9d, 25a, 79b, 119b, 126a, 126c, 127a, 134a, 157a, 162a, 163a, 163b, 166c, 189a, 189b, 201b, 292a, 303a, 303b, 311a, 316d, 462c, 540a, 554a, 555a, 764a. Base illustration for all calculator and computer screens by Tom Ward. **Jody Wenger:** 474c, 484a, 573e **Nick Wilton/Jennie Oppenheimer:** 22a, 26a, 28a, 29a, 35a, 40a, 58b, 91a, 93a, 97a, 183c, 190c, 195f, 212b, 237d, 256a, 290a, 300a, 334a, 335a, 431d, 445d

TEXT AND ART

CHAPTER 1 1-2 Part D: p. 36, Explore table data from *The 1993 Information Please Almanac.* Opener 1-3: p. 39, UPS Next Day Air label used with permission of United Parcel Service. Opener 1-4: p. 61, from Anthony Berlant, *Walk in Beauty: The Navajo and Their Blankets* (Boston, MA: Little, Brown and Co., 1977); ©1977 by Anthony Berlant and Mary Hunt Kahlenberg; reprinted by permission of Little, Brown and Company. 1-4 Part D: p. 79, alphabet ©1989 by Scott Kim.

CHAPTER 2 Opener 2-1: p. 87, "Truth in Advertising" from Charles Goodrum and Helen W. Dalrymple, *Advertising in America: The First 200 Years* (NY: Harry N. Abrams, 1990).

CHAPTER 3 Opener 3-1: p. 155, from Alan Villiers, "Magellan: First Voyage Around the World," *National Geographic,* June 1976, National Geographic Society; ©1976 National Geographic Society. Opener 3-2: p. 179, text and art from David Macaulay, *The Way Things Work* (NY: Houghton Mifflin, 1988); compilation ©1988 by Dorling Kindersley Ltd.; text: ©1988 by David Macaulay and Neil Ardley; art: ©1988 by David Macaulay; reprinted by permission of Houghton Mifflin Co.; all rights reserved. Opener 3-3: p. 191, excerpted from Paul Doherty, "Hot Times in the City," *Exploratorium Quarterly,* Vol. 16, No. 1, Spring 1992, with permission of The Exploratorium, 3601 Lyon St., San Francisco, CA 94123. Opener 3-4: p. 215, adapted from Ken Brown, *Calligraphy,* Ken Brown Studio of Calligraphic Art, 1977.

CHAPTER 4 Opener 4-3: p. 285, art from *The 1994 Bridgestone Bicycle Catalogue,* illustrated by George Retseck.

CHAPTER 6 Opener 6-2: p. 417, text and art from Daniel Crevier, *AI: The Tumultuous History of the Search for Artificial Intelligence* (NY: Basic Books, div. of HarperCollins, 1993); ©1993 by Daniel Crevier; reprinted by permission of the publisher. 6-2 Part D: p. 438, Exercise 23: text from Joseph Weizenbaum, *Computer Power and Human Reason* (NY: W. H. Freeman, 1976); ©1976 by W. H. Freeman and Co.; reprinted with permission. 6-3 Part C: p. 454, Exercise 14: art from Grace Chisholm Young, *First Book of Geometry,* 1905.

CHAPTER 7 Opener 7-1: p. 461, excerpts from Marcel Delgado, "King Kong and Me," and Fay Wray, "How Fay Met Kong, or The Scream That Shook The World," ©1969 The New York Times Co., from *The Girl in the Hairy Paw,* Ronald Gottesman and Harold Geduld, eds. (NY: Avon Books, a div. of The Hearst Corp., 1976); ©Ronald Gottesman and Harry M. Geduld. Opener 7-2: p. 485, *San Francisco Chronicle* masthead and text from Bill Workman, "Plans for World's Tallest Building Unveiled at Stanford," *San Francisco Chronicle,* April 14, 1993; ©1993 *San Francisco Chronicle;* reprinted by permission.

CHAPTER 9 Opener 9-2: p. 623, from Patricia Lauber, *The Eruption and Healing of Mount St. Helens* (NY: Bradbury Press, 1986); ©1986 by Patricia Lauber.

CHAPTER 11 11-1 Part A: p. 710, from Ellery Queen, *The Greek Coffin Mystery* (Philadelphia: J. B. Lippincott, 1932); ©1932 by Ellery Queen. Opener 11-2: p. 727, text from Worldwatch Institute as cited in *50 Simple Things You Can Do To Save The Earth* (Berkeley, CA: Earthworks Press, 1989). Photos 73a, 207b, 248c, 324a, 364c, 418a, 669a: from *The Geometer's Sketchpad®;* ©1991 by Key Curriculum Press.

CHAPTER 12 12-1 Part A: p. 750, The Major League Baseball Club insignias depicted in this publication are reproduced with the permission of Major League Baseball Properties and are exclusive property of the respective Major League Clubs and may not be reproduced without their written consent.

INDEX

A

Absolute value, distance on a number line and, 40–41
Acute angle, 156
Acute triangle, 244
Addition Property, 114, 715
Adjacent angles, 248
Advertising in America, 87
AI: The Tumultuous History of the Search for Artificial Intelligence, 417
Algebra
area under a curve, 357–361
coordinates in three dimensions, 146, 798–799
equation for a circle, 376–379
equations, graphs, and geometric figures, 327–329
geometric proofs and, 433–438
graphing linear equations, 11–18, 141–146, 796–797
parallel lines and, 141–146
perpendicular lines and, 141–146
properties used in, 114
proportions, similar polygons and, 468–471
optimizing algebraic functions, 728–742
quadratic formula, area and, 332–334
theorems and, 122, 123
transformations of functions and, 679–683
trigonometric ratios and, 512–517
Algebraic models, 4, 11–16
Alice in Puzzleland, 30–31
Alice in Wonderland, 19, 25, 26, 30
Alternate exterior angles, 216
Alternate interior angles, 216
Altitude (See also Height)
of a cone, 615
of a cylinder, 614
of a prism, 604
of a triangle, 305
Angle(s)
acute, 156
adjacent, 248
alternate exterior, 216
alternate interior, 216
Angle-Addition Postulate, 194
bearings and, 161–165
bisector, 207–211, 304
central, 564–565
classification by measure, 156
classification of triangles by, 244
complementary, 201–202
congruent, 52
construction of congruent, 54
corresponding, 216, 257
definition of, 45
of depression, 518–523
of elevation, 518–523
exterior, 156, 247
Exterior Angle Inequality Theorem, 249
Exterior Angle Theorem, 249
of incidence, 212
inscribed, 584–588
interior, 156
linear pair of, 202
measuring, 45–51
naming, 46
obtuse, 156
pairs of, 201–206
postulates pertaining to, 192–196
of reflection, 212
remote interior, 248
right, 47, 109, 156
of rotation, 180
same-side interior, 216
sides of, 45, 156
supplementary, 201–202
tangent-secant, 589
tangent-tangent, 589
transversals and, 216–226
vertex of, 45, 156
vertical, 207–211
Angle-Addition Postulate, 194
Angle-Angle (AA) Similarity Postulate, 487
Angle bisector, 207–211, 304
construction of, 208
definition of, 208
theorem pertaining to, 287, 301
Angle-Side-Angle (ASA) Congruence Postulate, 262
Angle-Sum Theorem
for Polygons, 405
for Quadrilaterals, 399
for Triangles, 245
Angular velocity, 569
Apothem, of a regular polygon, 442
Applications
advertising, 88, 89, 91, 92, 97, 104
aeronautics, 119, 138, 160, 161, 524, 525, 526, 530, 531, 535
agriculture, 318, 319, 350, 364, 369, 477, 510, 574, 628, 698, 732, 772
anatomy, 102, 591
animal studies, 2, 15, 22, 25, 102, 103, 394, 441, 445, 452, 453, 562, 586, 602, 642, 647, 651, 657, 660, 733
archaeology, 380, 385, 400, 436, 469, 521, 577, 666, 687, 700, 701, 702
architecture, 4, 60, 75, 82, 129, 134, 135, 137, 147, 148, 241, 242, 252, 270, 304, 316, 320, 387, 395, 407, 409, 413, 415, 441, 452, 454, 458, 459, 472, 479, 485, 486, 507, 508, 511, 516, 517, 521, 522, 530, 532, 533, 600, 610, 613, 618, 620, 637, 659, 693, 705, 785
art, 4, 61, 84, 99, 129, 130, 133, 171, 174, 178, 184, 206, 240, 241, 259, 260, 316, 318, 326, 334, 445, 468, 478, 479, 481, 482, 505, 535, 555, 558, 562, 639, 688, 689, 692, 693, 696, 697, 701, 704
astronomy, 51, 296, 378, 511, 549, 557, 582, 599, 637, 642, 761–767, 768, 770, 771, 773, 774, 775, 777, 778, 784, 785, 786, 787, 788
biology, 2, 22, 84, 102, 103, 153, 182, 394, 396, 542, 642, 651
business, 3, 39, 58, 85, 93, 259, 264, 331, 337, 466, 467, 468, 596, 602, 603, 619, 620, 646, 664, 677, 681, 682, 683, 685, 694, 744
chemistry, 76, 214, 355, 392, 406, 413, 449, 450, 652, 692
communication, 39, 592
construction, 4, 60, 85, 118, 138, 195, 201, 205, 224, 227, 238, 241, 246, 250, 252, 263, 270, 274, 279, 282, 297, 300, 303, 308, 325, 331, 336, 349, 350, 357, 383, 386, 387, 390, 394, 421, 431, 432, 438, 445, 446, 447, 476, 485, 504, 514, 515, 521, 579, 587, 602, 607, 613, 620, 636, 646, 655, 659, 722, 738, 739
consumer, 58, 59, 87, 93, 264, 337, 468, 474, 475, 476, 484, 522, 568, 596, 602, 603, 604, 607, 609, 619, 620, 622, 628, 646, 659, 660, 734
design, 58, 75, 134, 135, 147, 148, 171, 184, 213, 224, 238, 240, 241, 309, 331, 334, 374, 394, 400, 407, 426, 438, 441, 445, 456, 457, 482, 484, 485, 499, 511, 603, 609, 618, 620, 622, 633, 659, 664, 667, 677, 694, 696, 722, 732, 734, 738, 739, 742
earth science, 51, 66, 157, 402, 416, 485, 529, 530, 549, 623, 629, 644, 645, 756–761
economics, 36, 83, 101, 251, 337, 344, 482
engineering, 85, 129, 135, 154, 189, 190, 201, 251, 255, 270, 282, 285, 331, 345, 459, 562, 603, 639, 645, 667
entertainment, 179, 189, 321, 461, 467, 468, 473, 543, 548, 560, 561, 573, 651, 655, 660
finance, 337, 345, 568, 596, 598, 682, 683
fitness, 313, 316, 426, 596, 652
geography, 5, 12, 94, 96, 152, 155, 157, 235, 360, 363, 365, 436, 469, 521, 523, 529, 533, 562, 563, 580, 629, 645, 714, 723, 757, 759, 781, 786, 788

geology, 51, 402, 406, 413, 644
government, 84, 101, 102, 108, 112, 114, 127, 345, 471, 568, 598
home economics, 188, 210, 662, 706, 722
law, 98, 108, 127, 392, 393, 523, 743
map making, 5, 16–17, 602, 672, 788
medicine, 102, 152, 153, 591, 738
meteorology, 191, 255, 535, 623, 760
multicultural, 22, 32, 61, 62, 71, 77, 99, 115, 129, 152, 171, 172, 184, 215, 218, 241, 255, 260, 285, 316, 335, 345, 350, 351, 362, 363, 365, 366, 368, 380, 383, 385, 395, 400, 411, 413, 442, 454, 469, 478, 485, 494, 500, 511, 512, 516, 517, 521, 529, 533, 548, 553, 557, 558, 559, 563, 583, 659, 692, 693, 697, 700, 701, 704, 705, 709
music, 539, 561, 638
navigation, 152, 154, 155, 156, 157, 160, 161, 169, 176–177, 235, 252, 283, 292, 315, 592, 596, 706
philosophy, 548
photography, 662, 702
physics, 56, 189, 229, 232, 374, 440, 485, 525, 526, 527, 548, 553, 562, 569, 578, 605, 664, 683–684, 685
population, 34, 36–37, 350, 471
psychology, 670
publishing, 43, 467, 468
recreation, 336, 338, 340, 341, 342, 344, 375, 378, 440, 446, 451, 456, 457, 509, 517, 526, 535, 596, 714, 718, 720, 726, 745
space exploration, 18, 138, 510, 775, 780, 785, 788
sports, 4, 18, 27, 43, 50, 102, 180, 210, 214, 237, 286, 335, 340, 374, 389, 391, 489, 493, 526, 527, 535, 554, 581, 583, 594, 595, 598, 642, 671, 709, 750
surveying, 118, 238, 246, 279, 290, 320, 355, 383, 516, 521, 528
technology, 417, 422, 438, 497, 513, 539, 729, 732, 735, 752, 762
travel, 119, 126, 254, 522, 524, 525, 526, 530, 553, 571, 714, 722, 724, 759, 760, 779, 781, 785, 786

Arc(s)
Addition Theorem, 566
of a circle, 565
congruent, 566
inscribed angles and, 585
length of, 570
major, 565
minor, 565
of a sector, 570
semicircle, 585
theorem pertaining to chords and, 577

Arc-Addition Theorem, 566
Archimedean solids, 454
Area (*See also* Lateral area; Surface area)
Area-Addition Postulate, 323
Aztec measurement of, 345
of a circle, 555–560
of irregular polygons, 323
optimizing, 728–734
of a parallelogram, 347–348
polynomials and, 327–332
postulates pertaining to, 323, 348
probability and, 337–341
quadratic formula and, 332–334
of a rectangle, 322, 346–348
of a regular polygon, 443–444, 556
of a rhombus, 353
of a sector, 570–574
of similar polygons, 473–477
of a square, 322, 346–348
theorems pertaining to, 348, 354
of a trapezoid, 353–354
of a triangle, 322, 347–348, 354
under a curve, 357–361

Area-Addition Postulate, 323
Aristarchus of Samos, 787
Around the World in Eighty Days, 553
Artificial Intelligence (AI), 417
Ascending and Descending, 6
Asoka, 559
Associative Property, 114
Assumption(s)
geometric figures and, 197–201
without proof, 107

Astronomical unit (A.U.), 763
Astronomy
astronomical unit, 763
geometric models and, 748–788
light-year, 763
measurement in, 762–767
parallax, 763–765

Auxiliary line, 288
Axis (Axes)
of a cone, 615
of a coordinate system, 11, 146
of a cylinder, 614
of symmetry, 62, 678

B

Banneker, Benjamin, 511, 516, 528
Base(s)
of a cylinder, 614
of a prism, 604
of a pyramid, 610
of a trapezoid, 352
of a triangle, 244, 286

Base angles, 244, 286
Bearings, 161–165
Betweenness, of points, 121
Bhaskara, 366–367
Biconditional statement, 97, 110
Bisect, definition of, 68
Bisector(s) (*See also* Perpendicular bisector)
angle, 207–211, 304
construction of angle, 208
definition of angle, 208
perpendicular, 300, 305
of a segment, 68, 300
theorem pertaining to angle, 301
theorem pertaining to perpendicular, 301
Unique Bisector Theorems, 287

Blake, William, 65
Bode's Law, 767
Bonaparte, Napoleon, 255, 281, 290
Braille, Louis, 672
Brunelleschi, 129

C

Calculus (*See* Underpinnings of calculus)
Calligraphy, 215
Career(s), 4, 6, 17, 18, 22, 32, 58, 59, 60, 75, 82, 84, 102, 118, 129, 134, 135, 160, 205, 213, 246, 263, 326, 331, 357, 374, 395, 407, 413, 421, 432, 460, 461, 482, 504, 514, 516, 521, 577, 620, 645, 664, 667, 687, 700, 702, 712, 740, 769, 780
Career profiles
administrator, 3
archaeologist, 687
deputy district attorney, 393
designer, 665
designer and computer drafter, 459
engineer, 667
executive director, 601
horticulturist, 319
managing director, 485
market analyst, 537
museum collections manager, 651
physical therapist, 153
pilot, 707
space engineer, 747
structural engineer, 85, 485
surveyor, 239

Carroll, Lewis, 19, 34, 35
Cavalieri's Principle, 626
Center
of balance, 306
of a circle, 540
of dilation, 496, 497
of gravity, 306
of a regular polygon, 442
of rotation, 180
of a sphere, 546, 639

Central angle, 564–565
Centroid, 306
theorem pertaining to, 307

Chain rule, 100
Ch'ang Höng, 553
Chord(s)
of a circle, 574–579
congruent theorem, 582

definition of, 575
perpendicular bisector of, 576
theorems pertaining to, 576, 808–810
theorem pertaining to arcs and, 577
***Chōupeï*,** 368
Cicero, 215
Circle(s)
Arc-Addition Theorem for, 566
arc of, 565
area of, 555–560
center of, 540
chord of, 574–579, 582
circumference of, 189, 550, 552
circumscribed, 541
concentric, 540
construction of, 540
definition of, 540
diameter of, 540
equal ratios in, 572
equation of, 377
exterior of, 540
great, 546
inscribed, 541
interior of, 540
length of an arc of, 570
locus of points on, 376
major arc of, 565
minor arc of, 565
radius of, 540, 574–579
sector of, 570–574
segment of, 573
Circle graph, 564
Circumcenter, 317
Circumference, 189, 550–555
theorems pertaining to, 552
Circumscribed figures, 541
Classification
of angles, 156
of frieze patterns, 690
of polygons, 403
of polyhedrons, 410
of prisms, 604
of quadrilaterals, 397
of triangles, 243, 244
of wallpaper patterns, 696
Collinear points, 21, 772
betweenness and, 121
Collinear rays, 156
Common tangents, 578
Commutative Properties, 114
Comparison Property, 715
Complementary angles, 201–202
Congruent Complements Theorem and, 204
in a right triangle, 249
Compositions of transformations, 673–678
definition of, 673
Compound loci, 301, 803–804, 851
***Computer Power and Human Reason*,** 438
Concave figures
polygon, 403
quadrilateral, 398
regular polyhedron, 449
Concentric circles, 540
Conclusion
of a conditional statement, 88
law of detachment and, 100
Concurrency, point of, 306
Concurrent lines, 306
Conditional statements, 88–93
contrapositive, 94
converse of, 94
if-then, 88
inverse, 94
Law of Detachment and, 100
related, 94–98
Cone
altitude of, 615
axis of, 615
correspondence and, 256–260
definition of, 615
formula for lateral area of, 616
formula for surface area of, 616
formula for volume of, 636
oblique, 615
surface area of, 614–619
vertex of, 615
volume of, 635–639
Congruence, 52–57 (*See also* Congruent angles; Congruent triangles)
correspondence and, 256–260
definition of, 52
isometries and, 669
right triangle, 292–294
in similar figures, 464, 468
symbol for, 52
triangle, 256–266
Congruence correspondence, 257
Congruence transformation, 669
Congruent angles, 52, 203–204
construction of, 54
in similar figures, 464, 468
Congruent arcs, 566
Congruent chords, 582
Congruent Complements Theorem, 204
Congruent segments
construction of, 53
in similar figures, 464, 468
Congruent Supplements Theorem, 204
Congruent triangles
Angle-Angle (AA) Similarity Postulate for, 487
Angle-Side-Angle (ASA) Congruence Postulate for, 262
definition of, 258
Hypotenuse-Acute-Angle (HA) Congruence for, 293
Hypotenuse-Leg (HL) Congruence, 294
Leg-Acute-Angle (LA) Congruence, 293
Leg-Leg (LL) Congruence, 293
Side-Angle-Angle (SAA) Congruence Postulate for, 262
Side-Angle-Side (SAS) Congruence Postulate for, 262
Side-Side-Side (SSS) Congruence Postulate for, 262
Side-Side-Side (SSS) Similarity Theorem and, 494
Conjecture(s), 21, 33
about radius and chord of a circle, 574–579
definition of, 22
Connections
angles and navigation, 176
area applications, 342
area formulas, 362
circles and spheres, 560, 580
classifying patterns, 700
drawing techniques, 146
earth models, 768
Euclidean and non-Euclidean geometry, 782
inequalities, 724
lines and angles, 212, 231
mathematical models, 16
measuring objects, 58
optimization, 740
polygons and polyhedrons, 414, 452
precise language, 104
proof with quadrilaterals, 438
Pythagorean Theorem, 385
reasoning and logic, 36
regular polygons and polyhedrons, 452
rotations, 189
similar figures, 482, 507
stating assumptions, 126
surface area and volume, 620, 644, 657
symmetry and reflections, 77
tessellations and triangles, 252
transformations, 683
triangle properties, 310
triangles and proofs, 281
trigonometry, 528
visual thinking, 16, 36, 58
Construction
angle bisector, 208
of a circle, 540
congruent angles, 54
congruent segments, 53
of a cube, 130–131
definition of, 53
midpoint of a segment, 122
perpendicular bisector, 69
perpendicular to a line, 69
Contrapositive statement, 94
Converse(s)
of the Isosceles Triangle Theorem, 287
parallel lines and, 226–230
proving, 291
of the Pythagorean Theorem, 380–384

Converse statement, 94
Convex figures
polygon, 402, 403, 404
quadrilateral, 398, 399
regular polyhedron, 448
Coordinate(s)
of a point, 11–12
of a three-dimensional figure, 146, 798–799
Coordinate geometry, 433
Coordinate plane, 11–12
distance between points on, 41
Coordinate proofs, 433–438
Coordinate system
for locating points on a sphere, 756–757
map making and, 16–17
origin of, 11
quadrants of, 11
three-dimensional, 146
x-axis, 11
y-axis, 11
z-axis, 146
Coplanar lines, 141
and transversals, 216
Coplanar points, 109
Corollary, 249
Correspondence, 257
symbol for, 257
Corresponding angles, 216
of congruent triangles, 257
formed by transversals, 216
of similar figures, 464, 468
Corresponding edges, of similar solids, 648
Corresponding sides
of congruent triangles, 257
of similar figures, 464, 468
Cosine ratio, 512–513
Counterexample, 25–30
definition of, 25
Cross section, 400
Cube
axis of symmetry of, 678
edges of, 9
faces of, 9
perspective drawing of, 130, 131
polycube, 140
surface area of, 606
vector description of, 170
vertices of, 9
volume and, 624
Cubic units, volume and, 624
Cylinder
altitude of, 614
axis of, 614
definition of, 614
formula for lateral area of, 616
formula for surface area of, 616
formula for volume of, 636
height of, 614
oblique, 614
perspective drawing of, 132
right, 614
surface area of, 614–619
volume of, 635–639

D

Data
collecting, 12–18, 564–565
interpreting, 12–18
organizing, 12–18
presenting, 12–18, 36–37, 564–565, 568
da Vinci, Leonardo, 129, 535
Decagon, 403
Declaration of Independence, 107
Deductive proof (*See also* Proof)
deductive reasoning, 30–35, 119–126
deductive system, 119–126
five-step process for, 217
with areas, 352–356
with quadrilaterals, 417–440
with similar figures, 486–495
with triangles, 255–284
Deductive reasoning, 30–35, 119–126
definition of, 31
Defined terms, 33, 108–113
Definition(s)
biconditional statements and, 110
critical attributes and, 109
statement of, 110
undefined terms and, 108
Degree measure
of an angle, 46
of an arc, 565–566
Delgado, Marcel, 461
Deltahedron, 454
Dependent variable, 686
Depression, angle of, 518–523
De Re & Praxi Geometrica, 533
Detachment, Law of, 100
Diagonal
of a cube, 629
of a polygon, 402
of a quadrilateral, 396, 398
of special parallelograms, 429
of a square, 435
Diagram (*See also* Drawings)
Venn, 26, 90–91, 95, 112
Diameter of a circle, 540
Dilation, 496–501
center of, 496, 497
creating a, 496
definition of, 497
isometry and, 668–673
scale factor of, 497
and similarity, 496, 503
Dilation image, 496
Direction of rotation, 180, 181
Direction of a vector, 166, 523–525
Discrete mathematics
classification, 156, 243, 244, 397, 403, 410, 604, 690, 696
congruence, 52–57, 256–266, 293–294
deductive reasoning, 30–35, 119–126
indirect reasoning, 710–714
inductive reasoning, 20–25
similarity, 458–507
transformations, 67–77, 171–176, 180–188, 496–501
Venn diagrams, 26, 90, 95, 112
Distance
between two points, 41, 120
Pythagorean Theorem and, 376–377
Distance formula, 41, 376–377
Distributive Property, 114
Dodecahedron, 410, 449
Drawings
isometric, 135–140
orthographic, 135–140
perspective, 130–135

E

Earth
Goode's projection of, 5
measurement of, 756–761
Mercator projection of, 5
models of, 5, 757
Edge
of a cube, 9
of a polyhedron, 410, 411
of a prism, 604
of a regular polyhedron, 448
Einstein, Albert, 778
Elements, The, 32, 115
Elevation, angle of, 518–523
Endpoint
of an arc, 565
of a line segment, 20
of a ray, 45
of a vector, 165
Enlargement, 462
Equality, properties of, 114
Equation(s) (*See also* Formula)
of a circle, 377
functions and, 679–686
linear, 142–143, 679
parent, 679
quadratic, 332, 679–680
Equator, 757
Equiangular figure
polygon, 442
triangle, 244
Equidistant, definition of, 68
Equilateral polygon, 442
Equilateral triangle, 243, 244
theorem pertaining to, 249
Equivalent transformations, 675
Eratosthenes, 563, 580
sieve of, 563
Eruption and Healing of Mount St. Helens, The, 623
Escher, M. C., 6, 171
Euclid, 32, 115, 126, 143, 772, 774
Euclidean geometry, 32, 115, 126, 143, 772–776

Euler, Leonhard, 238, 411
Euler line, 310
Euler's Formula, 411
Explore, 7, 13, 17, 21, 27, 31, 36, 41, 48, 58, 63, 68, 73, 78, 89, 95, 99, 104, 110, 115, 121, 127, 131, 137, 142, 147, 157, 161, 167, 172, 177, 181, 185, 189, 193, 197, 203, 207, 212, 218, 221, 227, 231, 243, 248, 253, 256, 261, 269, 275, 281, 286, 294, 300, 306, 311, 324, 329, 334, 339, 342, 347, 353, 358, 362, 367, 371, 376, 380, 385, 398, 404, 411, 415, 418, 423, 428, 435, 439, 443, 448, 452, 463, 469, 474, 479, 483, 486, 491, 496, 502, 507, 514, 519, 525, 528, 541, 545, 550, 556, 561, 564, 571, 575, 580, 584, 589, 595, 605, 611, 615, 620, 625, 631, 635, 641, 644, 649, 653, 658, 669, 674, 679, 684, 690, 696, 700, 711, 715, 720, 725, 730, 736, 740, 751, 758, 764, 768, 773, 778, 782
Exterior, of a circle, 540
Exterior angle(s), 156
alternate, 216
formed by transversals, 216
of a polygon, 404–405
of a triangle, 247–249
Exterior Angle Inequality Theorem, 249
Exterior Angle Theorem, 249
Exterior Angle Theorem for Polygons, 405
External tangent, 578

F

Face
of a cube, 9
lateral, 604
of a polyhedron, 410, 411
of a prism, 604
of a regular polyhedron, 448
Fibonacci, Leonardo, 25
Fibonacci sequence, 25, 481
50 Simple Things You Can Do to Save the Earth, 727
Fine, Oronce, 533
Fine arts, 6, 61, 62, 71, 77, 79, 99, 129, 133, 148, 171, 184, 206, 215, 218, 219, 221, 224, 231, 259, 260, 316, 380, 395, 406, 409, 414, 461, 468, 473, 478, 481, 482, 484, 535, 539, 555, 557, 558, 559, 561, 562, 638, 639, 688, 689, 692, 693, 696, 697, 700, 701, 704, 705
First Book of Geometry, 454
Flatland, 555
Flat-Plane Postulate, 116, 772
Force, modeling with vectors, 523–525
Formula
angle-sum for polygons, 405
area of a circle, 557
area of a rectangle, 322
area of a rhombus, 353
area of a square, 322
area of a trapezoid, 354
area of a triangle, 322
circumference of a circle, 552
distance, 41, 376–377
Euler's, 411–414
Heron's, 355
Kepler's third law, 767
lateral area of a pyramid, 611
lateral area of a right cone, 616
lateral area of a right cylinder, 616
lateral area of a right prism, 606
quadratic, 333
surface area of a pyramid, 611
surface area of a right cone, 616
surface area of a right cylinder, 616
surface area of a right prism, 606
surface area of a sphere, 640
volume of a cone, 636
volume of a cylinder, 636
volume of a prism, 627
volume of a pyramid, 632
volume of a right rectangular prism, 627
volume of a sphere, 640
45°-45°-90° Triangle Theorem, 272
Fractal geometry, 750
Fractals, 750–756, 768
Koch Snowflake, 755
Pascal's Triangle and, 753
Sierpinski Gasket, 751, 753
Frame geometry, 285
Franklin, Aretha, 561
Franklin, Benjamin, 196
Frieze patterns, 688–694
classification of, 690
definition of, 688
glide-reflection symmetry and, 688
translation symmetry and, 689
Frustum, 457
of a pyramid, 457, 632
of a cone, 636
Fuller, Buckminster, 600
Function(s) (*See also* Formulas)
algebra and, 332–334, 468–471
equations and, 686
graphs of families, 679
optimal solutions and, 728–730, 732
transformations of algebraic, 679–682
trigonometry and, 512–527
volume and surface area of a sphere as, 642, 643

G

Garfield, James A., 370
Gauss, Karl F., 24
Geometric figures, assumptions about, 197–201
Geometric mean, 489, 805–807
Geometric models, 4, 6–11
Geometric probability, 338
Geometry
coordinate, 433–438
definition of, 6
Euclidean, 32, 115, 126, 143, 772–776
fractal, 750
non-Euclidean, 777–781
Riemannian, 777–779
Glide-reflection translations, 174–175
frieze patterns and, 688
symmetry and, 688, 690
wallpaper patterns and, 694–699
Golden ratio, 478, 480
Golden rectangle, 478–482
definition of, 478
Goode, J. P., 5
Goode's projection, 5
Graph
of an ordered pair, 11
circle, 564
of a function, 679–683, 728–730
linear, 679
quadratic, 679
scatter plot, 12–16, 18
Great circle, 546
Riemannian geometry and, 777
Greek Coffin Mystery, The, 710
Gulliver's Travels, 607
Gutenberg, Johann, 215

H

Half-turn, rotation, 181
Health, 152, 591, 621, 656, 738
Height (*See also* Altitude)
of a cylinder, 614
of a parallelogram, 348
of a prism, 604
of a pyramid, 610
slant, 610
of a trapezoid, 353
of a triangle, 348
Heptagon, 403
interior angle sum of, 405
Heron's Formula, 355
Hexagon, 403
Hexahedron, 410
Hinge Theorem, 723, 811–812
History, 24, 25, 32, 53, 61, 62, 84, 107, 114, 115, 126, 129, 143, 152, 155, 162, 176–177, 215, 241, 255, 281, 290, 308, 310, 321, 335, 350, 351, 355, 362, 363, 365, 366, 368, 370, 378, 380, 383, 385, 400, 411, 413, 436, 454, 494, 500, 511, 516, 521, 533, 539, 553, 559, 560, 562, 563, 580, 613, 618, 623, 629, 638, 672, 687, 712, 727, 759, 767, 771, 772, 775, 785, 787
Hypotenuse, 244, 512

Hypotenuse-Acute-Angle (HA) Congruence Theorem, 293
Hypotenuse-Leg (HL) Congruence Theorem, 294
Hypothesis
deductive proof and, 218
of a conditional statement, 88

I

Icosahedron, 410, 448, 449
If-then statement, 88
Image
dilation, 496
reflection, 67
rotation, 180
transformation, 67, 674
translation, 171
Incidence, angle of, 212
Independent variable, 686
Indirect proof, 710–714
Indirect reasoning, 710–714
Inductive reasoning, 20–25
definition of, 22
and patterns, 21–22
Industry, 43, 58, 61, 135, 146, 189, 297, 309, 337, 394, 407, 485, 539, 560, 561, 592, 596, 603, 614, 619, 620, 622, 644, 646, 652, 662, 667, 681, 682, 683, 685, 694, 708, 722, 724, 732, 734, 744
Inequality
properties of, 715
related to the Pythagorean Theorem, 382
theorems pertaining to triangles, 716, 721
in triangles, 714–724
Inscribed angle, 584–588, 594
Inscribed-Angle Theorem, 585
Inscribed figures, 541
Interior, of a circle, 540
Interior angle(s), 156
alternate, 216
Angle-Sum Theorem for Polygons, 405
formed by transversals, 216
of a polygon, 405
Intersection
of lines at right angles, 47
planes and, 116, 400, 772
point of, 20
of two lines, 20
Inverse statement, 94
Inverse transformation, 677
Isometric drawing, 135–140
Isometry, 668–673
definition of, 668
Isosceles right triangle, 370–371
Isosceles trapezoid, 421
Isosceles triangle, 243, 286–292
theorems pertaining to, 287
Isosceles Triangle Theorem, 287
Converse of, 287

J

Jefferson, Thomas, 84

K

Kahlo, Frida, 99
Kepler's third law, 767
Kim, Scott, 79
***King Kong*,** 461, 473, 482, 483
Kite, 355, 432, 438, 517
Koch Snowflake, 361, 755

L

Lateral area
formula for a pyramid, 611
formula for right cone, 616
formula for right cylinder, 616
formula for a right prism, 606
of a prism, 605–606
Lateral edge, 604
Lateral face, 604
Latitude, 756–761
Lauber, Patricia, 623
Law of Detachment, 100
Leg-Acute-Angle (LA) Congruence Theorem, 293
Leg-Leg (LL) Congruence Theorem, 293
Leg(s)
of a trapezoid, 352
of a triangle, 244, 286
Length
of an arc, 570
Aztec measurement of, 345
definition of, 40
of a segment, 40–44
of a vector, 166
Light-year, 763
Line(s) (*See also* Line segment; Parallel lines; Perpendicular lines)
auxiliary, 288
collinear points on, 21, 772
concurrent, 306
constructing a perpendicular to, 69
description of, 20, 108
Euler, 310
horizon, 130
intersection of, 20
as intersection of planes, 772
linear equations, and functions, 11–18, 141–146, 796–797
naming, 20
noncoplanar, 142
parallel, 141–146
parallel to a plane, 141
perpendicular, 47, 209
planes and, 141–146
of reflection, 67, 688
Riemannian geometry and, 777, 778
secant, 544
skew, 142
slope of, 142
Straight-Line Postulate, 772
of symmetry, 62
tangent, 544–549
transversal, 216
y-intercept and, 142
Line segment(s)
congruent, 52
construction of congruent, 53
definition of, 20
endpoints of, 20
intersection of, 20
measuring, 40–44
midpoint construction, 122
midpoint of, 110
naming, 20
perpendicular bisector of, 300
Line symmetry, 62
frieze patterns and, 688–694
wallpaper patterns and, 694–699
Linear equations
families of, 679
form of, 141–146
graphing, 11–18, 141–146, 796–797
Linear pair of angles, 202, 203
Linear-Pair Postulate, 203
Literature, 19, 25, 31, 34, 35, 38, 65, 128, 155, 179, 196, 349, 417, 438, 533, 553, 555, 607, 623, 710, 712, 744
Locus, 299–304, 803–804
compound, 301, 803–804
definition of, 299
Logic
biconditional statement, 97, 110
Chain Rule, 100
conditional statements, 88–98
conjecture, 21, 22
contrapositive statement, 94
converse statement, 94
corollary, 249
counterexample, 25–30
deductive reasoning, 30–35, 119–126
defined terms and, 33, 86, 108–113
Euclid's self-evident truths, 115
if-then statement, 88
indirect reasoning, 710–714
inverse statement, 94
language of, 19, 25–30
Law of Detachment, 100
logical statements, 26
postulates, 86, 114–119
rules of, 99–104
theories and, 22
undefined terms and, 33, 108–113
Venn diagrams and, 26
Logical statements, 26
Longitude, 756–761

M

Macaulay, David, 179
Magellan, Ferdinand, 155, 176–177
Major arc, 565
Mandelbrot, Benoit, 750

Mapping
composition transformations and, 673–678
dilation and, 496–501
glide-reflection and, 174–175
isometries and, 668–669
morphing and, 673
reflection and, 67–77
rotation and, 180–188
translation and, 171–176
Mathematical models, 7–8, 16 (*See also* Models)
Mathematical structure
Euclidean and non-Euclidean geometries, 771–785
foundations of geometry, 107–128
geometric models, 746–770
logic and language, 87–106
patterns, 687–702
transformations, 667–686
Mean, geometric, 489
Measure
of an arc, 565
angle, 45–51, 46
of an inscribed angle, 585
classifying angles by, 156
of a secant-secant angle, 592
of segment length, 40–44
of a semicircle, 565
of a tangent-secant angle, 590
of a tangent-tangent angle, 590
volume and, 624
Measurement
angle, 156
in astronomy, 762–767
Earth, 756–761
reflection and, 68
Median, 305
Mercator projection, 5
Merchant of Venice, 744
Michelangelo, 129
Midpoint
definition of, 110
formula, 124
on a coordinate plane, 124
on a number line, 122
of a segment, 287
Midpoint Theorem, 122
Midsegment
of a trapezoid, 438
of a triangle, 501–507
Midsegment Theorem for Triangles, 502
Minor arc, 565
Models
algebraic, 4, 11–16
curved space and, 777–778
fractals as, 750–756, 768
geometric, 4, 6–11
maps and globes as, 5
mathematical, 4, 7–8, 16
sphere representing earth, 756
of the universe, 783
vectors as, 523–525
Mondrian, Piet, 481
Morphing, 673
Multiplication Property, 114

N

***n*-gon,** 403, 404
angle measure, 444
Napoleon's Conjecture, 290
NAVSTAR navigational satellites, 592
Negation, 710
Net(s), 7, 58
surface area of a prism and, 605
surface area of a pyramid and, 611
Nonagon, 403
Non-collinear points, 772
Nonconvex polygons, 403
Noncoplanar lines, 142
Noncoplanar points, 109, 772
Non-Euclidean geometry, 777–781
Number
absolute value, 40–41
properties of, 114
pyramidal, 633
Number line
distance between points on, 41
length of a segment on, 40–41

O

Obelisk, 413
Oblique figures
cone, 615
cylinder, 614
prism, 604
pyramid, 610
Obtuse angle, 156
Obtuse triangle, 244
Octagon, 403
Octahedron, 410
Opposite rays, 157
Optical illusions, 6, 9, 18
Optimal solution, 728
Optimizing
area, 728–734
perimeter, 728–734
surface area, 734–739
volume, 734–739
Ordered pair, 11
Orientation of a reflected figure, 74
Origin
on a coordinate plane, 11
of a vector, 165
Orthographic drawing, 135–140
Overlapping triangles, 800–802

P

Parabola, transformations and, 679–680
Paragraph proof, 267
Parallax, 763–764
Parallel, symbol for, 141
Parallel lines, 141–146
definition of, 141
postulates pertaining to, 222, 228
proof of, 226–230
slopes of, 141–146
theorems pertaining to, 222, 228
transversals and, 221–230
Parallelogram
area of, 347–348
conditions for, 425
definition of, 346, 396
proofs with special, 427–432
properties of, 418–422
relationship to other quadrilaterals, 397
theorems about diagonals of, 429
Parallel Postulate, 143, 773
Parent equation, 679
Pascal's Triangle, fractals and, 753
Patterns
fractal, 750–756
frieze, 688–694
inductive reasoning and, 21–22
wallpaper, 694–699
Peary, Robert, 759
Pei, Ieoh Ming, 395, 407, 409, 414, 415
Pentagon, 403
Pentahedron, 410
Performance Tasks, 83, 151, 236, 317, 391, 457, 535, 599, 663, 705, 745, 788
Perimeter
definition of, 323
optimizing, 728–734
of a polygon, 323
of similar polygons, 473–477
Perpendicular bisector
of a chord, 576
construction of, 69
and reflection, 70
of a segment, 68, 300
of a side of a triangle, 305
theorem pertaining to, 301
Perpendicular lines
construction of, 69
definition of, 47
diagonals of a square, 435
and right angles, 47, 209, 211
slopes of, 141–146
symbol for, 47
theorem pertaining to, 209
Perpendicular segments, 120
Perspective, definition of, 129
Perspective drawing, 84, 130–135
Physiology of Common Life, The, 128
Pi, 552, 553
definition of, 551
Pick's Theorem, 351
Plane(s)
description of, 108
intersection of, 772
intersection of a solid and, 400
naming, 108

parallel, 141
parallel lines and, 141–146
postulates pertaining to, 116, 772
Riemannian geometry and, 777
tangent, 546
Plane-Intersection Postulate, 116, 772
Plane Postulate, 116, 772
Plato, 394, 448, 452
Platonic solids, 448–449
truncated, 454
Plimpton 322, 365, 385
Point(s)
betweenness of, 121
collinear, 21, 772
of concurrency, 306
coplanar, 109
description of, 20, 108
distance between, 41, 120
of intersection, 20
naming, 20
non-collinear, 772
noncoplanar, 109
of a perpendicular bisector, 301
rotation about, 180
vanishing, 130
Points-Existence Postulate, 116, 772
Point symmetry, 181, 182
frieze patterns and, 690–694
Polygon (*See also* Regular polygons; specific polygons)
Angle-Sum Theorem for, 405
area of, 322–323, 443–444, 556
area and perimeter of similar, 473–477
circumscribed, 541
classification of, 403
convex, 402, 403, 404
decagon, 403
definition of, 322, 402
diagonal of, 402
Exterior Angle Theorem for, 405
as faces of polyhedrons, 410
heptagon, 403
hexagon, 403
inscribed, 541
naming, 403
n-gon, 403, 404
nonagon, 403
nonconvex, 403
octagon, 403
parallelogram, 346
pentagon, 403
perimeter of, 323
properties of, 402–409
quadrilateral, 346, 403
rectangle, 322, 346
regular, 442–447
rhombus, 352
similar, 464, 468–477
square, 322, 346
theorems pertaining to area of, 348
trapezoid, 352
triangle, 322, 403
Polygonal region, 322
Polyhedron (See also specific polyhedrons)
Archimedean solids and, 454
classification of, 410
convex regular, 448
definition of, 410
dodecahedron, 410
edge of, 410, 411, 449
Euler's Formula and, 411
face of, 410, 411, 449
hexahedron, 410
icosahedron, 410
naming, 410
octahedron, 410
pentahedron, 410
prism, 604–609
properties of, 409–414
pyramid, 610–614
regular, 448–451
tetrahedron, 410
vertices of, 410, 411, 449
Polynomials, area and, 327–329
Poor Richard's Almanack, 196
Postulate(s), 86, 114–119
about angles, 192–196
about transversals and parallel lines, 222, 228
Angle-Addition, 194
Angle-Angle (AA) Similarity, 487
Angle-Side-Angle (ASA) Congruence, 262
Area, 323
Area-Addition, 323
area of a rectangle, 348
Cavalieri's Principle, 626
definition of, 33
Flat-Plane, 116, 772
Linear-Pair, 203
Parallel, 143, 773
Plane, 116, 772
Plane-Intersection, 116, 772
Points-Existence, 116, 722
Protractor, 192
Riemann's Parallel, 777
Ruler, 120
Segment-Addition, 121
Side-Angle-Angle (SAA) Congruence, 262
Side-Angle-Side (SAS) Congruence, 262
Side-Side-Side (SSS) Congruence, 262
Straight-Line, 116, 772
table of, 791–792
Powers of Ten, 749
Power theorems, 808–810
Pre-image
dilation, 496
reflection, 68
rotation, 180
transformation, 67, 674
translation, 171
Prime meridian, 757
Prime numbers, sieve of Eratosthenes and, 563
Prism(s)
altitude of, 604
bases of, 604
Cavalieri's Principle and, 626
classification of, 604
definition of, 604
formula for the volume of, 627
formula for volume of right rectangular, 627
height of, 604
lateral area of, 605
lateral edge of, 604
surface area of, 604–609
volume of, 624–630
Probability, 9, 30, 38, 44, 65, 79, 138, 144, 159, 164, 183, 201, 246, 260, 272, 337–344, 350, 360, 364, 379, 387, 389, 391, 400, 402, 426, 457, 471, 477, 559, 562, 567, 573, 598, 642, 646, 660, 692, 726, 738, 742
area and, 337–344
definition of geometric, 338
Problem Solving
Problem solving is fundamental to the presentation of mathematics in this book and is found throughout.
Problem-Solving Strategies
Draw a Diagram, 38, 312, 609
Eliminate Unreasonable Possibilities, 699
Graph a Function, 728–729, 732, 736
Guess, Check, and Revise, 349, 418, 443, 472, 520
Look for a Pattern, 21, 50, 71, 121, 142, 160, 371, 381, 698
Make a Generalization, 95, 214, 556
Make a Model, 136, 625, 649, 776
Make a Table, 23, 50, 160, 248, 371, 589, 729, 736
Simplify the Problem, 44
Use Logical Reasoning, 230, 575
Work Backwards, 275
Write an Equation, 194, 205, 334
Write an Expression, 34, 214
Problem-Solving Tip, 21, 23, 34, 38, 44, 50, 71, 95, 121, 136, 142, 160, 194, 205, 214, 230, 248, 275, 312, 334, 349, 371, 381, 418, 443, 472, 520, 556, 575, 589, 609, 625, 649, 698, 699, 732, 776
Proof
conditional statements, 88–98, 217–221
coordinate, 433–438
deductive reasoning, 30–35, 119–126
five-step process for deductive, 217
flow-proof format, 124, 206, 267

"if-then" statement 88–93, 217–221
indirect, 710–714
inductive reasoning, 20–25
organizing, 266–274
overlapping triangles, 800–802
paragraph form for, 230, 267–268
plan for, 211, 352–356
skills and strategies, 789–795
two-column format for, 267
using diagrams, 217–221
Properties
addition, 114, 715
associative, 114
commutative, 114
comparison, 715
distributive, 114
of equality, 114
of inequality, 715
multiplication, 114
of a parallelogram, 418–422
of reflection, 73–77
reflexive, 114, 276
of rotations, 186
symmetric, 114, 276
transitive, 114, 276, 715
of translated figures, 173
vector addition, 167
Proportion
arc length and, 570–572
astronomy measurements and, 762–767
enlargement and, 462
geometric mean and, 489
golden rectangle and, 478–482
reduction and, 462
sector area and, 570–572
similar figures and, 462–465, 486–494
Proportional thinking, 462–465, 478–482, 486–494, 570–572, 580–582, 762–767
Protractor, angle measure and, 46
Protractor Postulate, 192
Pyramid
base of, 610
definition of, 610
formula for lateral area of, 611
frustum of, 457
height of, 610
slant height of, 610
square, 11
surface area of, 610–614
volume of, 630–634
Pyramidal numbers, 633
Pythagorean Theorem, 320, 366–370
Converse of, 380, 381
curved space and, 782
distance formula and, 376
inequalities related to, 382
Pythagorean triple, 367

Q

Quadrant of a coordinate system, 11
Quadratic equation, 332, 679–680
Quadratic formula, area and, 332–334
Quadrilateral(s) (*See also* specific quadrilaterals)
Angle-Sum Theorem for, 399
classification of, 352
concave, 398
conditions for a parallelogram, 425
convex, 398, 399
coordinate proofs and, 433–438
definition of, 346
diagonal of, 396, 398
kite, 355
naming, 396
parallelogram, 346, 396, 397, 418–422
properties of, 396–402
rectangle, 346, 396, 397
relationships among, 397
rhombus, 352, 396
Saccheri, 780
square, 346, 396, 429
trapezoid, 352, 396

R

Radius
of a circle, 540, 574–579
of a regular polygon, 442, 443
of a sphere, 546, 639
Raphael, 129
Ratio(s)
golden, 478, 480
similarity, 463
trigonometric, 512–517
Ray(s), 156–160
as angle bisector, 208
collinear, 156
definition of, 45
endpoint of, 45
naming, 45
opposite, 157
vertical angles and, 207
Reasoning (*See also* Logic)
deductive, 119–126
indirect, 710–714
inductive, 20–25
Rectangle
area formula for, 322, 348
definition of, 346, 396
diagonals of, 429
golden, 478–482
relationship to other quadrilaterals, 397
Reduction, 462
Reflection(s), 67–72
angle of, 212
composition and, 673–678
describing, 68
glide-reflection symmetry and, 688
image over a line, 70
isometry and, 668–673
line of, 67, 688
measurement and, 68
orientation of, 74
perpendicular bisector and, 70
properties of, 73–77
size and, 74
translation and, 174–175
Reflexive Property, 114, 276
Regular polygon, 442–447
angle measure, 444
apothem of, 442
area of, 443–444
center of, 442
radius of, 442
theorems about, 444
Regular polyhedron, 448–451, 610
concave, 449
convex, 448
Remote interior angle, 248
Respect, 561
Rhombus
area of, 353
definition of, 352, 396
diagonals of, 429
relationship to other quadrilaterals, 397
Riemann, Bernhard, 777
Riemannian geometry, 777–779
Saccheri quadrilateral and, 780
Riemann's Parallel Postulate, 777
Right angle(s)
congruence theorem, 205
critical attributes of, 109
definition of, 47
inscribed angles and, 585
measure of, 156
perpendicular lines and, 47, 209, 211
Right cone, 615
Right cylinder, 614
Right prism, 604
Right rectangular prism, formula for volume of, 627
Right triangle(s), 244, 292–298
Babylonian mathematics and, 365
geometric mean, 805–807
Hypotenuse-Acute-Angle (HA) Congruence Theorem, 293
Hypotenuse-Leg (HL) Congruence Theorem, 294
isosceles, 370–371
Leg-Acute-Angle (LA) Congruence Theorem, 293
Leg-Leg (LL) Congruence Theorem, 293
Pythagorean Theorem and, 366–370
theorem pertaining to, 249
trigonometric ratios and, 512–517
Rorschach, Hermann, 670
Rosette, 181
Rotational symmetry, 180–184

definition of, 181
wallpaper patterns and, 694–699
Rotation(s), 179, 180–188
angle of, 180
center of, 180
composition and, 673–678
definition of, 180
half-turn, 181
isometry and, 668–673
properties of, 186
wallpaper patterns and, 694–699
Ruler Postulate, 120

S

Saccheri quadrilateral, 780
Same-side interior angles, 216
Scale, map, 469
Scale factor, 462
Scalene triangle, 243–244
Scatter plot, 3–18
Science, 15, 18, 22, 51, 56, 66, 76, 102, 103, 138, 159, 179, 182, 189, 190, 191, 200, 205, 212, 214, 220, 229, 232, 255, 285, 296, 309, 336, 355, 361, 374, 378, 406, 413, 416, 417, 441, 445, 449, 450, 452, 453, 485, 488, 490, 507–508, 510, 511, 519, 523, 524, 525, 526, 527, 528, 529, 530, 535, 539, 542, 548, 549, 562, 563, 569, 578, 580, 582, 588, 594, 599, 603, 605, 623, 637, 638, 642, 644, 647, 651, 656, 657, 660, 667, 684, 685, 687, 692, 727, 733, 749, 761–767, 768, 769, 770, 771, 773, 774, 775, 777, 778, 780, 784, 785, 786, 787, 788
Secant, 544, 588–594
theorems pertaining to, 588–594
Secant-Secant Angle Theorem, 592
Sector, 570
area of, 570–574
Segment(s) (*See also* Lines; Line segments)
of a circle, 573
perpendicular, 120
tangent, 545
Segment-Addition Postulate, 121
Self-similar patterns, 750–756
Semicircle
inscribed angles and, 585
measure of, 565
Seurat, Georges, 318, 479, 535
Side(s)
of an angle, 45, 156
classifying triangles by, 243
corresponding, 257
of a triangle, 242
Side-Angle-Angle (SAA) Congruence Postulate, 262
Side-Angle-Side (SAS) Congruence Postulate, 262
Side-Angle-Side (SAS) Similarity, 491–492
Side-Angle-Side (SAS) Similarity Theorem, 492
Side-Side-Side (SSS) Congruence Postulate, 262
Side-Side-Side (SSS) Similarity Theorem, 494
Side-Splitting Theorem, 506
Sierpinski, Waclaw, 751
Sierpinski Gasket, 751
Similar figures, 462–468
area and perimeter of, 473–477
definition of, 464
polygons, 468–477
self-similar, 750
solids, 648–657
surface area of, 648–652
theorems pertaining to, 475
triangles, 486–495
volumes of, 653–657
Similarity
Angle-Angle (AA) Similarity Postulate, 487
congruence, 464, 468
dilation, 496–501, 503
Side-Angle-Side (SAS) Similarity Theorem, 492
Side-Side-Side (SSS) Similarity Theorem, 494
symbol for, 468
Similarity correspondence, 468
Similarity ratio, 463
for area and perimeter of similar polygons, 475
for similar solids, 648
for the surface areas of similar solids, 650
for the volumes of similar solids, 654
Similarity transformation, 677
Similar solids
surface area of, 648–652
volume of, 653–657
Sine ratio, 512–513
Skew lines, 142
Slant height, 610
Slope
of a line, 141–146, 796–797
of parallel lines, 141–146
of perpendicular lines, 141–146
Social sciences, 10, 34, 36–37, 83, 96, 107, 144, 235, 251, 254, 340, 344, 345, 360, 363, 469, 471, 472, 509, 517, 529, 548, 568, 596, 598, 659, 670, 692, 693, 694, 697, 701, 704, 705, 709, 717, 722, 724, 749, 759, 760, 761, 781, 786, 788
Solid figure(s)
Archimedean, 454
Cavalieri's Principle and, 626
cones, 614–619, 635–639
cross section of, 400
cylinders, 614–619, 635–639
lateral area of, 605, 606, 611
as mathematical models, 8
nets for, 7
Platonic, 448–449
prisms, 604–609, 624–630
pyramids, 610–614, 630–634
regular polyhedron, 448–451
similar, 648–657
spheres, 546, 639–643
surface area of similar, 648–652
volume of, 624
volume of similar, 653–657
Space
curved, 777–781
definition of, 116
Points-Existence Postulate and, 772
Sphere
center of, 546, 639
definition of, 546
formula for the surface area of, 640
formula for the volume of, 640
great circle of, 546
as model of the earth, 756–757
radius of, 546, 639
Riemann's Parallel Postulate and, 777
surface area of, 639–643
volume of, 639–643
Square
area of, 322
definition of, 322, 346, 396
diagonals of, 429
formula for area of, 322, 348
relationship to other quadrilaterals, 397
Statement(s)
biconditional, 97
Chain Rule and, 100
conditional, 88–93
contrapositive, 94
converse, 94
hypothesis, 88, 218
if-then, 88
inverse, 94
justification for, 266
Law of Detachment and, 100
logical, 26
negation of, 710
related conditional, 94–98
Statistics, 34, 36, 188, 249, 251, 254, 255, 380, 398, 409, 449, 471, 477, 496, 565, 568, 581, 596, 598, 660, 729, 731, 732, 735, 736, 737, 738, 740, 742, 753, 755, 756, 767
circle graphs in, 564–568
Straightedge, definition of, 53
Straight-Line Postulate, 116, 772
Strategies for proof, 789–795
Sumario Compendioso, 335
Supplementary angles, 201–203
Congruent Supplements Theorem, 204
Surface area
of a cone, 615–619
of a cylinder, 614–619
formula for a pyramid, 611
formula for right cone, 616

formula for right cylinder, 616
formula for a right prism, 606
optimizing, 734–739
of a prism, 604–609
of a pyramid, 610–614
of similar solids, 648–652
of a sphere, 640–643
Swift, Jonathan, 607
Symbolic Logic, 35
Symbol(s)
for angle, 46
for congruence, 52
for correspondence, 257
for degree, 46
for "is similar to," 468
for line, 20
for line segment, 20
for parallel, 141
for perpendicular, 47
table of, 789
for triangle, 242
Symmetric property, 114, 276
Symmetry, 62–66
axis of, 62, 678
definition of, 62
frieze patterns and, 688–694
glide-reflection, 688
line, 62
point, 181, 182
rotational, 180–184
translation, 689
and wallpaper patterns, 694–699

T

Tables
Formulas, 790
Postulates and Theorems, 791–797
Symbols, 789
Tangent(s)
angles formed by, 589, 590
to a circle, 546
common external, 578
line, 544–549
plane, 546
ratio, 512–513
segment, 545, 808–810
theorems pertaining to, 544–549, 588–594, 808–810
to a sphere, 546
Tangent-secant angle, 589
theorem, 590
Tangent-tangent angle, 589
theorem, 590
Technology
calculator, 513, 519
geometry software, 181, 185, 207, 221, 248, 311, 324, 380, 398, 404, 418, 423, 439, 486, 491, 496, 502, 584, 669, 715
graphing utility, 142, 497, 679, 730, 736, 740
spreadsheet software, 730, 736, 740
Terms, undefined, 33, 108–113
Tessellation, 242, 247, 253, 414–415
definition of, 241
translation-based, 699
Tessellation vertex, 253
Tetrahedron, 410
definition of, 10–11
Thales, 494
Theorem(s)
angle bisector, 301
Angle-Sum for Triangles, 245
Angle-Sum for Polygons, 405
Angle-Sum for Quadrilaterals, 399
Arc-Addition, 566
arcs and chords of a circle, 577
area of a circle, 557
area and perimeter of similar polygons, 475
area of polygons, 348
centroid of a triangle, 307
chords, 808–810
circumference of a circle, 552
congruent chords, 582
Congruent Complements, 204
Congruent Supplements, 204
Converse of the Isosceles Triangle, 287
corollary of, 249
definition of, 33
diagonals of special parallelograms, 429
Exterior Angle, 249
Exterior Angle Inequality, 249
Exterior Angle for Polygons, 405
Geometric mean, 805–807
Hinge, 723, 811–812
Hypotenuse-Acute Angle (HA) Congruence, 293
Hypotenuse-Leg (HL) Congruence, 294
Inscribed-Angle, 538, 585
isometries, 669
Isosceles Triangle, 287
lateral and surface area of a pyramid, 611
lateral and surface area of a right cone, 616
lateral and surface area of a right cylinder, 616
lateral and surface area of a right prism, 606
Leg-Acute-Angle (LA) Congruence, 293
Leg-Leg (LL) Congruence, 293
midpoint of a segment, 122
Midsegment for Triangles, 502
perpendicular bisector, 301
Pick's, 351
power, 808–810
Pythagorean, 366–367, 782
Pythagorean inequality, 382
radius and chord, 576
ratio of surface area of two similar solids, 650
ratio of the volumes of similar solids, 654
Right Angle Congruence, 205
Secant-Secant Angle, 592
Secants, 808–810
shortest segment from a point to a line, 48
Side-Splitting, 506
Side-Angle-Side (SAS) Similarity, 491–492
Side-Side-Side (SSS) Similarity, 494
table of, 791–797
tangents to a circle, 546, 808–810
Tangent-Secant Angle, 590
Tangent-Tangent Angle, 590
transversals and parallel lines, 222, 228
45°-45°-90° Triangle, 372
30°-60°-90° Triangle, 373
Triangle Inequality, 716, 721
Unique Bisector, 287
volume of a cone, 636
volume of a cylinder, 636
volume of a pyramid, 632
Theory, 22
Three-dimensional figures
coordinates of, 146, 798–799
isometric drawings of, 135–140
as mathematical models, 8
nets for, 7
optimizing volume and surface area of, 734–739
orthographic views of, 135–140
perspective drawings of, 130–135
Through the Looking-Glass, 34
Titius, Johann, 767
Transformation(s)
of algebraic functions, 679–683
compositions of, 673–678
congruence, 669
definition of, 67
dilation, 496–501
equivalent, 675
glide-reflection, 174–175
inverse, 677
isometry and, 668–673
reflection, 67–77
rotation, 180–188
similarity, 677
translation, 171–176
wallpaper patterns and, 694–699
Transitive property, 114, 225, 276, 715
Translation(s), 171–176
composition and, 673–678
definition, 171
glide-reflection symmetry and, 688
isometry and, 668–673
wallpaper patterns and, 694–699
Translation-based tessellation, 699
Translation symmetry, 689
wallpaper patterns and, 694–699
Translation vector, 171

Transversal, 216–226
angles formed by, 216
definition of, 216
parallel lines and, 221–230
postulate pertaining to, 222, 228
theorems pertaining to, 222, 228
Trapezoid
area of, 353–354
definition of, 352, 396
isosceles, 421
method for estimating area under a curve, 358–359
midsegment of, 438
relationship to other quadrilaterals, 397
Triangle(s)
acute, 244
adjacent interior angle of, 248
altitude of, 305
Angle-Angle (AA) Similarity Postulate for, 487
Angle-Side-Angle (ASA) Congruence Postulate for, 262
Angle-Sum Theorem, 245
area of, 322, 348–351
base angles of, 244
base of, 244, 286
circumcenter of, 317
classification by angles, 244
classification by sides, 243
congruence and, 256–266
Converse of the Isosceles Triangle Theorem, 287
corresponding parts of congruent, 275
definition of, 242
equiangular, 244
equilateral, 243, 244
Exterior Angle Inequality Theorem, 249
Exterior Angle Theorem, 249
exterior angles of, 247
formula for area, 322, 348
45°-45°-90° Triangle Theorem, 372
Heron's Formula for area of, 355
Hinge Theorem, 723
Hypotenuse-Acute-Angle (HA) Congruence, 293
Hypotenuse-Leg (HL) Congruence, 294
hypotenuse of, 244
inequalities in, 714–724
inequality theorems for, 716
isosceles, 243, 286–292
isosceles right, 370–371
Isosceles Triangle Theorem, 287
Leg-Acute-Angle (LA) Congruence, 293
Leg-Leg (LL) Congruence, 293
legs of, 244, 286
median of, 305
midsegments of, 501–507
Midsegment Theorem for, 502
naming, 242
obtuse, 244
overlapping, 259, 260, 264, 516, 629
perpendicular bisector of a side of, 305
remote interior angle of, 248
right, 244, 292–298
scalene, 243
Side-Angle-Angle (SAA) Congruence Postulate for, 262
Side-Angle-Side (SAS) Congruence Postulate for, 262
Side-Angle-Side (SAS) Similarity Theorem for, 492
Side-Side-Side (SSS) Congruence Postulate for, 262
Side-Side-Side (SSS) Similarity Theorem for, 494
sides of, 242
Side-Splitting Theorem for, 506
similar, 486–495
sum of the angle measures of, 245
30°-60°-90° Triangle Theorem, 373
Triangle Inequality Theorem, 721
trigonometric ratios and, 512–517
vertex angle of, 244, 286
vertex of, 242, 244, 286
Triangle Inequality Theorem, 721
30°-60°-90° Triangle Theorem, 373
Trichotomy Law, 715
Trigonometric ratios, 512–517
Trigonometry
angles of elevation and depression and, 518–523
definition of, 512
vectors and, 523–527
Tsu Ch'ung-Chih, 553
Two-column proof, 267

U

Undefined terms, 33, 108–113
Underpinnings of calculus
area under a curve, 357–361
graphs of functions, 332, 679–680
optimization, 728–730
Yenri, 560
Unique Bisector Theorems, 287
United Parcel Service (UPS), 39

V

Vanishing point, 130
Variable
dependent, 686
independent, 686
Vector(s), 165–170
addition, 167
definition of, 165
equal, 166
opposite, 169
translations and, 171
trigonometry and, 523–527
Velocity
angular, 569
modeling with vectors, 523–525
Venn diagram
biconditional statements and, 112
conditional statements and, 90
contrapositive statements and, 95–96
converse statements and, 95–96
inverse statements and, 95–96
logical statements and, 26
Verne, Jules, 553
Vertex (Vertices)
of an angle, 45, 156
of a cone, 615
of a cube, 9
of a polyhedron, 410, 411
of a pyramid, 610
of a regular polyhedron, 448
tessellation, 253
of a triangle, 242, 244
Vertex angle, 244, 286
Vertical angles, 207–211
definition of, 207
theorems pertaining to, 209
Visual thinking
figure measurement and, 39–60
logic and, 19–38
transformations and, 61–79
using models, 5–18
Volume
of a cone, 635–639
of a cylinder, 635–639
definition of, 624
optimizing, 734–739
of a prism, 624–630
of a pyramid, 630–634
of similar solids, 653–657
of a sphere, 639–643

W

Wallpaper patterns, 694–699
classification of, 696
definition of, 695
Way Things Work, The, 179, 189
Weizenbaum, Joseph, 438
What Do YOU Think, 32, 222, 268, 434, 470, 503, 624–625, 728–729
What Is the Name of This Book?, 744
Wordsworth, William, 349

X Y Z

***x*-axis,** 11
***y*-axis,** 11
***y*-intercept,** 142
Yenri, 560
***z*-axis,** 146